To:

CB/Marketing Professors

at

Univ. of Strathclyde

with best compliments of

B an Mittal

www.NISU.edu/~mittal

CONSUMER BEHAVIOR

How Humans Think, Feel, And Act In The Marketplace

Banwari Mittal

+

Morris B. Holbrook

Sharon Beatty

Priya Raghubir

Arch G. Woodside

OPEN MENTIS

CONSUMER BEHAVIOR

How Humans Think, Feel, And Act In The Marketplace

Banwari Mittal

+

Morris B. Holbrook

Sharon Beatty

Priya Raghubir

Arch G. Woodside

OPEN MENTIS

CONSUMER BEHAVIOR

How Humans Think, Feel, And Act In The Marketplace

Banwari Mittal+
Morris B. Holbrook,
Sharon Beatty, Priya Raghubir,
and
Arch G. Woodside

1st ed.

Cover Design: Banwari Mittal with Martha Rowe and Aanal Mehta
Illustration Art: Aanal Mehta
Graphics: Banwari Mittal and Aanal Mehta
Interior Design: Banwari Mittal and Aanal Mehta
Composition: Banwari Mittal, Jesse armstrong, Aanal Mehta
Copy Edit: Dr. Roxanne Kent-Drury, Maria Nicole Taneglio,
                 and Liz Young

Library of Congress Control Number: 2006939584

ISBN-13: 978-0-9791336-0-2
ISBN-10   0-9791336-0-2

OPEN MENTIS

MY CB BOOK

CONSUMER BEHAVIOR
How Humans Think, Feel, And
Act In The Marketplace

Morris B. Holbrook

Sharon Beatty

Banwari Mittal +

Priya Raghubir

Arch G. Woodside

OPEN MENTIS

To the Concept of a Benevolent God

who wills us all to ill-will no one

and

To the Idea of an unprejudiced respect
for creative works of knowledge

Calling Gracious Understanding

This book has more than its share of gaps. Unbeknownst to us, a table with misaligned columns, an exhibit misplaced, a figure mislabled, a credit footnote missing, a typo survived, an unedited sentence, and so on. Substantively, press deadline compelled us to forego some content that needed **more time for development**. Some 5000+ authoring hours later, the book is still a work far from perfect, limited by time, resources, and, plainly, author capabilities (referring only to myself, BM). Gracious readers, choosing the book with a mind calm and curious, will find the work, with all its flaws, rewarding, **this we are told.**

To The Professor...

Teaching Comes Second

or four years as I wrote this book, I was paranoid about one thing: that I would end up not including someone's pet topics. Then the answer hit me: if I miss, students will still get them—from you, and much better. Relieved, I focused instead on making sure I included everything else. I can't say I succeeded.

As a teacher myself, I have gone through the cycle, sorting through all the reasons to adopt a book (or not). There have been different reasons at different times: a book that includes the latest academic theory-in-the-making; a book with some level of opaqueness so I would have a role; one set in the new cognitive, information processing framework; one with a post-modernist flavor; a book with cases; one that blends theory with practice. Now I will plead guilty: given my goal of making this a comprehensive textbook to serve the needs of our discipline, and following the wisdom of all our other textbook authors, I have ended up with a little bit of all of the above.

But I have strived to make all topics accessible to the student, so I named and renamed some concepts, and redrew a few flowcharts, and "decoded" many theories in student-speak. The resulting transparency now frees you from having to explain the basics and instead use the book as a launch pad for your own creative structuring of a hands-on learning experience for your students.

Guiding my writing throughout has been a singular goal, indeed an obsession: students should read it not because they have to, but because they want to. In this goal too, I have good company—all other CB textbooks do it, admirably well. I do it a little differently.

I made a choice: Teaching comes second; engaging the student comes first. A textbook can be good, very good. But can it also create excitement in the student about the subject itself? I wanted to absolutely, positively enthrall the student.

Toward that lofty goal, not fully met, here is my modest contribution, and I offer it for your consideration. And for a different kind of learning experience for your students.

Sincerely,

-bm

To The Student...

MTV or This Book?

I won't promise that you will enjoy the book over partying, or your favorite TV show, or people watching, or fantasizing about yourself.

Or wait a minute—this last one, we come pretty close. Maybe not fantasizing, but at least thinking about yourself—the book is all about that. It is a book about you. About why you enjoy the TV shows that you do, about your constant search in the store for a perfect match for your persona, about your enchantment with the world of goods.

You spend 80% of your waking hours being a consumer. Now enjoy a few hours reading about it. An impressive body of knowledge it is. But I didn't invent it; I just made it easy and fascinating. So you may relate every concept to your personal life. And at least a few times when you are idling, you may pick up this book instead of watching MTV. Yep, once you get into it, it is sneakily enticing.

Oh, and did I mention this whole fun thing will count as 3 (or 4 or 5) credits!

I wish you well, my friends!

Dr. B.

To The Marketing Executive...

Happy Plotting....

This is not your usual professional reading. And given your busy work life, a 750-page book is the last thing you want to read. Fair enough.

But if your work entails, in one way or another, influencing your consumers, do you want to spend a whole lifetime trying to do it without knowing why it works or how you can make it work better?

You can read it one chapter a week. In 25 weeks, you will have put under your belt a comprehensive body of knowledge—a master template to guide your thinking about consumers.

I wrote it to be easy enough for college students, but also practical enough for the "Tell-me-something-I-can-use-on-Monday-morning" Marketing Executive.

I know, I know, when you graduated, you said, happily, a goodbye to textbooks. I will let you in on a secret: this is popular nonfiction in the guise of a textbook. I have "translated" a lot of things that were textbookish. Now it is a knowledge book that could genuinely compete with your other weekend reading. And something to bring to work on Monday. If your work on Monday will require thinking about consumers, that is.

Happy Plotting!

Ban Mittal, Ph.D.

Acknowledgments

1. To Ayn Rand, for bringing out the nonconformist in me.

2. To Jag Sheth, who introduced me to the wonderful world of book writing.

3. To authors of all CB textbooks— Henry Assael, Eric Arnould , Roger Best, Roger Blackwell, Margaret Craig-Lees, Jim Engle, Del Hawkins, Wayne Hoyer, Leslie Kanuk, Jay Lindquist, Debbie MacInnis, Paul Miniard, John Mowen, Jerry Olsen, J. Paul Peter, Linda Price, Leon Schiffman, Joseph Sirgy, Michael Solomon, Aron O'cass, David Bednall, Robert Widing, among others, who blazed the path I now follow. It is to their works I owe my fascination with the idea of writing a CB textbook.

4. To all CB Scholars and researchers—from Aron Ahuvia to George Zinkhan and everyone in between, whose labors and insights have produced the body of knowledge this book ventures to paraphrase and explain. I am a mere messenger—the utility as well as the joy of the book is entirely due to their contributions to our discipline's literature.

5. To the Honorable Dr. A.P.J. Abdul Kalam, Dr. J.K. Satia, Dr. Jerry Zaltman, Dr. C.W. Park, and Dr. Jagdish N. Sheth, (in chronological order), of whose mentorship I once had the occasion to partake but was too dumb to fully value.

6. To Arch Woodside, Morris Holbrook, Sharon Beatty, and Priya Raghubir, who so graciously accepted my invitation to be a part of this book.

7. To CB educators at various schools (University of Washington, University of Iowa, Colorado State University, University of New Hampshire, San Diego State University, Ball State University, University of Memphis, Washington State University, University of Central Florida, among others), whose professional reviews of the manuscript improved it exponentially, and whose enthusiasm for its distinctions sustained my resolve to bring it to fruition.

8. To Arch Woodside, who has been a friend and guide all these years, through my faults and all. Without his moral support, this book wouldn't have seen the light of the day.

9. To Michael Carrell and Matt Shank, who patiently endured my less-than-full presence in the college hallways and gave full support to what turned out to be a marathon project.

10. To my wonderful support team: copy editing (Dr. Roxanne Kent-Drury, Maria Nicole Taneglio, and Liz Young), graphic Art (Beth Fortnere, Martha Rowe, and Aanal Mehta), book design and composition (Aanal Mehta and Jesse Armstrong), and general content advice—from a reader's point-of-view (Ishi Puri and Brian Russo).

11. To professional colleagues who contributed to the book's Resource materials: Dr Charlene Bebko, Dr. Dipayan Biswas, Dr. Michael Coolsen, Dr. Mary Dato-Conway, Dr. Alan Dick, , Dr Laura A. Flurry, Dr. Ron Lennon, , Dr. Kenneth B. Lord, Dr. Elena Millan, Dr. Lars Perner, Dr.Denver D'Rozario, Dr. Doris Shaw, Dr. Ron Taylor, Dr,. Mary Wolfinbarger. Their contribution will go a long way in enhancing the book's utility for instructional ends.

12. To professional colleagues everywhere, who, over the years (and despite my hibernation), have supported my modest academic—knowledge building and knowledge disseminating—writings, always with a conscientious eye for the intrinsic *content*. It is to their collective goodwill that I owe the desire and drive to offer this book.

13. To friends and family, who, over the last five years, would have liked to see more of me (as well as those, less).

14. For all defects and shortcomings, covert or overt, I alone am to blame, For any and all such merit in the content as you, dear reader, may discern, I am deeply indebted to the 100 per cent support—beyond self interest and above prejudice—of these wonderful individuals.

BRIEF CONTENTS

CONTENTS

BRIEF CONTENTS

CONTENTS

PART I — WELCOME TO THE FASCINATING WORLD OF CONSUMERS

CHAPTER 1 — INTRODUCTION

PART II — INSIDE THE CONSUMER'S MIND

CHAPTER 2 — MOTIVATIONS, EMOTIONS, AND INVOLVEMENT

CHAPTER 3 CONSUMER PERCEPTIONS IN THE MARKETPLACE

PART III — CONSUMERS' ENVIRONMENT

CHAPTER 9 — CONSUMERS' CULTURE

CHAPTER 14 — BUYING FOR MORE THAN ONE

FAMILY, ORGANIZATIONS, AND AFFINITY GROUP BUYING BEHAVIOR

PART V — CONSUMERS' DIVERSITY

CHAPTER 15 — GENDER AND AGE IN CONSUMER BEHAVIOR

CHAPTER 16
ETHNIC AND RELIGIOUS IDENTITY IN CONSUMER BEHAVIOR

CHAPTER 17
INCOME, SOCIAL CLASS, AND GEODEMOGRAPHICS

PART VI — CONSUMER BEHAVIOR IN THE NEW MILLENNIUM

CHAPTER 18 — CONSUMER RELATIONSHIPS WITH BRANDS

LOYALTY, ROMANCE, AND BRAND TRIBES

Who Moved My Topic?

The book is organized in Eight Parts. Part I is the introductory chapter (Chapter 1) that welcomes you, the reader, into the world of consumers. It shows various visions of the consumer, defines consumer behavior, explains on what social science disciplines the field of consumer behavior draws, clarifies who should read/study it and why, and illuminates its necessity and benefits to organizations as well as consumers such as yourselves.

Part II takes us inside the mind of the consumer. Here, in seven chapters, we cover the topics of motivation, consumer perceptions, consumer learning, consumer psychographics, and consumer attitudes. In Chapter 2, we study various motivations of consumers as well as the role emotions play in consumer experiences. In Chapter 3, we describe the psychology of consumer perception and how these perceptions bias and distort the reality of market offerings. In Chapter 4, we examine four models of consumer learning—models that range from the mindless and automated to the deliberate and effortful. We also describe factors that impede or promote the most significant consumer learning—adoption of new product innovations.

In Chapter 5, we peek into consumers' values, personalities, and lifestyles, and describe psychographics, a method of measuring these. In values, we learn about LOV, a list of nine values that capture all consumers' life priorities. We then explain useful concepts of consumer personality, self-concept, and identity and ways of measuring these. Here we explain how consumers construct self-identity and the roles possessions play in it. In Chapter 6, we discuss how values, personalities, and self-concepts come together to form consumers' lifestyles, and how lifestyles are measured as a set of activities, interest, and opinions (AIO) and discuss how, by using such measures, consumers can be profiled in terms of their psychographics.

In the next two chapters, we discuss the topic of *attitude*. Chapter 7 explains what exactly are attitudes and how consumers come to acquire them. We discuss how attitudes encompass both our thoughts and our feelings and how they in turn produce our behaviors. In a battle of the heart and mind, we explain who wins and why. In Chapter 8, we describe various models of attitude change and the differing persuasive power of diverse message appeals such as humor, fear, sex, and emotion.

In Appendix 1, we describe various methods of doing research into our consumers' behavior. We include both qualitative and quantitative methods, thus covering methods to capture consumers' "inside the mind" processes of all types—conscious and unconscious, well formed and nebulous. If you are a student reader, you may want to read this appendix twice: once before you begin Section II, so you will understand how the concepts of Chapters 2 through 8 might be measured, and again after finishing Section II, so you will understand what it is that these research methods measure. This is a familiar chicken-and-egg problem—so don't worry if your first reading leaves you with a few puzzles; your second reading—after Section II—should close the gaps, at which point you should be ready to actually conduct some consumer research projects.

Part III dwells on the external environment of the consumer. In Chapter 9, we describe culture—the "software" that runs the "computer" of our collective lives. Here, we discuss the values society as a whole holds dear, and we discuss the rituals, customs, and myths, and their role in meaning transfer—how we convey, in words and actions, and in our product choices, who we are and what we *mean*. We describe selective cultures of the world so we can broaden our horizons in preparation for reaching the global consumer worldwide. From society as a whole (the topic of Chapter 9), we move, in Chapter 10, to smaller groups and their effect on consumers. We describe *reference groups*—the groups we hold as guide to our own behaviors, and we discuss three types of influences they exercise. We then discuss opinion leaders and *influentials*, people who influence other consumers. We also recognize a new breed of influentials—*e-fluentials*, consumers who spread their word, and influence, through word-of-*mouse*. We also describe the new marketing "twin" phenomenon: buzz marketing and viral marketing, and illustrate how savvy marketers are employing these techniques to spread their brand stories.

Part IV takes us into the consumers' decision and choice processes. In the first of the four chapters in this section, Chapter 11, we describe how consumers make decisions in the marketplace. Here we discuss stimuli that make consumers realize that they need a product. We discuss how consumers search product information and factors that influence how much information to search. Finally, we describe mental calculations and shortcuts consumers use to combine all the product information to make their choice.

In the next chapter, Chapter 12, we describe what happens after the consumer has made a choice. We describe consumer satisfaction—ranging from total absence of it (or even dissatisfaction) to total delight. Here we recognize that consumers approach products, both during the selection stage and during the post-choice consumption experience, either as small or as big matters in life. Accordingly, we discuss these experiences both for high involvement "big" decisions and for low involvement, "don't care much," "small" decision situations.

In Chapter 13, we focus more directly on the act of buying itself. Here, we focus on factors that determine how consumers choose their stores, and once in the store, how they give in to their impulsive urges, or alternatively, how they resist them. We also discuss various motivations for going shopping and how marketers must respond to consumers with different shopping motives.

In the concluding chapter of this section, Chapter 14, we recognize that consumers often make decisions in groups or on behalf of groups. Three such group decision situations are recognized: family buying, organizations, and affinity groups. We explain the additional group processes that modify the individual decision steps described in Chapter 11. Here, we identify how various roles in the buying decision process get shared, how conflicts arise, and how they are resolved.

Now that we have understood the consumers' mental makeup (Part II), their environment (Part III), and how these consumers (equipped with a mental makeup and wrapped in their surrounding environment) face the marketplace and make decisions about products (Part IV), it is time now to recognize that all consumers are not alike. In Part V, we identify and profile various segments of consumers worldwide. In Chapter 15, we profile gender differences (both stereotypical and emerging) and age groups, from the ultra-fickle Gen 'Y' to the so-called "seniors," who are anything but vegetating. Next, in Chapter 16, we recognize the major race and ethnic groups on Planet Earth, and we discuss how marketers must understand and respond to these individuals' ethnic group identities and share and support their ethnic pride.

Next, in Chapter 17, we move to two other major differences among consumers: socioeconomic status (SES) and habitat. Money, power, knowledge—for one reason or another, humans create class distinctions among themselves no matter how egalitarian the proclaimed society. These class distinctions, captured in *SES*, create profound differences both in resources and in tastes, and we examine these for their effects on consumer behavior. Habitat, or "hood" in the language of rap music, is a telltale sign of our lives as consumers, in large part because we choose our hoods according to the types of consumers we are. We describe these hoods as *geodemographic* clusters, separating the markedly different consumptions of the "bohemian mix" consumers of Greenwich, New York, and the "grain belt" consumers of Kansas farming communities, and the like.

In the last section, Part VI, titled, The Consumer Experience—New and Old, we begin with an explanation of consumer loyalty, commitment, and romance with the brands. In Chapter 18, we explore factors that influence consumer loyalty to and fascination with brands; here we also examine how brands have become the new fulcrum of community building, giving us consumption communities and brand tribes. In Chapter 19, we examine consumer behavior in cyberspace. Although we recognized some aspects of cyberspace in various chapters, in this chapter, we take a closer look at consumers who visit the e-marketplace both for browsing and fun and for shopping.

Next, in Chapter 20, we bring, under one roof, three interested parties together—marketers, public policy advocates, and consumers themselves. We outline some unfair practices in which some marketers sometimes engage. We then catalog how public policy protects the consumer from unfair marketer practices as well from their own harmful consumption. Finally, we describe both consumer ethics (actually, the lack thereof) and the self-destructive behaviors of some consumers that a variety of social "minders" (writers, moralists, professors, political leaders, social reformers, and thoughtful consumers themselves) have made it their mission to rectify and mold.

Finally, in the last chapter of the book, Chapter 21, titled Consumer Experience in the New Millennium, we take an excursion into some esoteric realms of consumption—from consumption of authenticity to sports fanaticism to virtual identity consumption. We also gaze forward and sight and profile eight trends in consumer behavior—from revenge of the boomers to market based social relations management. Finally, we map an action agenda for marketers and illustrate how an understanding of consumer behavior should guide their very approach to all marketing activities. In doing so, we recognize that, barring some aberrational strains, most consumer behavior is wholesome. The goals of both marketing and consumers themselves are the same: to satisfy consumer need. And by facilitating this goal, the study of consumer behavior helps us achieve the pinnacle goal of consumers, indeed of humans—*a state of happiness.*

Forward, Backward, Read the Book Any Which Way

Designed as a cornucopia, this book lets you take what you like and then come back for more. It can be read in any order. Each chapter stands on its own and does not require knowledge of the preceding chapters. You can read Part III before Part II; or read Part IV, or V first, if you like. And each of the four readings in the Special Topics section can be read first, last, or in the middle.

For the classroom setting, the book is not a "must cover all" mandate. Of the 21 chapters, covering any 15 or 18 or whatever will still give the value you desire. Within a chapter, sections and topics can be skipped without diminishing the value of other topics. Level 2.0 topics, present in some chapters, may be included or not, with seamless results. Special Topics are dessert, optional by design, but always immensely rewarding. The book is ready to be used without any further adaptations, or it can be used as a platform on which you custom-craft a course to your tastes.

The book offers a repertoire of CB knowledge. In a semester-long course, you will cover most of it, and pave the way for the student to read the rest of it later, read all of it again, and re-read it selectively outside of the "read and test" framework. In the school of life, we are students forever, and the book is designed to serve as a resource beyond the classroom, for the life-long student in us, to keep and savor for years to come.

Request to Reviewers

Reviewers may excerpt up to 5 nonconsecutive pages* and copy the jacket and front and back end matter without seeking further permission.

They are requested, however, to not reveal the tidbits or their location in the book, such as, for example, that there is a bizarre story of a cyber-age event in a New York shoe store in Chapter 2; or a chuckle-inducing example of … (shhhh..!) in the cognitive learning section of Chapter 4 on page …. (shhhh…!); or in Chapter…, there is … (Shhh!)– well, you get the idea!

Thank you and your professional courtesy is greatly appreciated.

Invitation to Copy

OPEN | MENTIS

Welcome to the Fascinating World of Consumers

CHAPTER 1

- Dear Diary—Here Is My Consumer Behavior
- Visions of the Consumer— From Shopper to Reveler
- Exchange, Value, Resources— The Holy Trinity of Market and Consumption
- Marketing Creates a Need!—A Profession Under Delusion
- Seeing The Future First— Marketing's Not-So-Obvious Mission

Phoebe. Phoebe and Rachel—two friends, two roommates. Phoebe is excited to see in their living room a new coffee table Rachel bought that day—an antique apothecary table from Pottery Barn. The problem is that Phoebe hates Pottery Barn because she doesn't like anything that is mass-produced. So Rachel lies about the source of the table, telling Phoebe that she bought the table from the flea market. Phoebe gets all wrapped up, examining the table and taking pleasure in visualizing how, in the drawers of that table, they must have kept all the stuff to make their potions. She is very happy, having something with a history behind it.

One day Rachel and Phoebe are taking a walk when they arrive in front of a Pottery Barn store, and, peeking through the glass door, Phoebe spots an identical table in the store. Afraid the lie she (Rachel) told Phoebe is about to be exposed, Rachel tries to pull Phoebe away, but Phoebe is drawn in by the look of the entire living room display in the store, which, she notices, looks exactly identical to her (and Rachel's) own apartment. She realizes now that, indeed, Rachel had bought not only the table, but also all the other items from this store—items about which, too, Rachel had made up stories of their unique historic origins.

All the items except a lamp, that is. The lamp is there in the store but not in their apartment. While Rachel is begging Phoebe not to be mad at discovering the truth about the source of the stuff in their apartment, Phoebe is actually now contemplating buying that lamp. She takes Rachel inside the store and buys that lamp. Hate Pottery Barn? No, Phoebe actually loves it!

INTRODUCTION

Phoebe. Phoebe Buffay. One of the six most famous *Friends* in TV land, who share their everyday life with one another, and, vicariously, with millions of viewers around the world. A life filled with the usual quota of travails and jubilations of coming to grips with mature adulthood. Of working at a job, a career, a credo. Of falling in love and then falling out of it. Of finding a date and a mate. Of choosing things, buying stuff, admiring it, connecting to it. Of constructing an inner world, only half grounded in the reality of the stuff we buy and use and live our lives with and through; the other half existing only as figments of our imaginations. Show Phoebe a "thing"—like this coffee table, tell her it is an antique, and she has transported herself to an extra-terrestrial experience of the mind. An experience where she is "unique," and proving it is all her "one of a kind" stuff. Tell her instead that it was really mass-marketed ware from Pottery Barn, and she is back on *terra firma*, questioning if it is worthy of her real-self, her cherished identity (no matter that Pottery Barn is actually a store many consider chic). But *terra firma* has, by definition, its own solid footing, and it reminds her that this stuff is real—take it or leave it. She will take it, of course, that coffee table and a few more things—like that lamp out there.

Phoebe. Each one of us has a little bit of Phoebe in us. That is our nature, as humans and as consumers. Male or female, young or old, rich or poor, we are all consumers in the Pottery Barn that the marketplace is. We love it. We hate it. But we can't live without it. From it we pick things, to build the mosaic we call living. It is a hassle. It is fun. But above all, it is an experience.

Welcome to the fascinating world of consumers. In this book, we are going to describe, dissect, and discourse about consumer behavior—human behavior in the world of products. We will study how we think, feel, and act in the marketplace—how we come to see the products the way we see them, how we make our choices from the mind-boggling array of goods, how we buy them and then weave them into the tapestry of our lives. How we consume them to sustain and energize our bodies, feed our minds, and construct our egos and our identities. This is the study of consumer behavior.

WE ARE CONSUMERS—24-7!

We are all consumers. This much must come as no surprise to you. But what you may have not realized is how much of your waking day you spend being a consumer—and we count not just when you are consuming or you are buying something, but rather, as we will explain later, you are a consumer anytime you are even thinking about acquiring and/or consuming anything. To be sure, we also live at least part of our lives not being consumers—like when we are conversing with a friend (without using a phone or any other product), reflecting on our futures or for that matter the future of mankind. But most of the rest of the day is filled with plotting and enacting consumption. Write a daily journal for a week if you like and see for yourself. A group of consumers did just that, at our request. We reproduce one of them (see box: The Diary of a Consumer). This journal was quite representative of all we received in one respect; they all showed the same thing—We are consumers 24-7!

Steve Boyd, a Washington, D.C. resident, doing Yoga—Is he being a *consumer*?

Dear Diary—Here is My Consumer Behavior
by Ellen Tibbs

Monday, 10 July 2006

- This morning on the way to work I bought a Sugar Free Red Bull and Special K blueberry breakfast bar. On the way out I spotted the newest issue of *Cosmopolitan*, grabbed it, got back in line and made my second purchase of the day.
- I ran out of laundry detergent so I went to Kroger to pick some up. ..
- I was walking to my car earlier and saw a woman with a new Coach purse. I am getting sick of the one I am carrying now. Once I save up some money I might treat myself and buy one!
- My friend just called and said she had an extra ticket to go to the Journey concert in two weeks. I really want to go so I told her I would meet up with her later to pay for the ticket.

Tuesday, 11 July 2006

- I got my hair colored and highlighted at the salon, Madalyn San Tangelo this morning.
- My friend Lindsay and I wanted to eat sushi so I placed a carry out order at AOI, a Japanese cuisine restaurant at Newport on the Levee. We both ordered California Rolls, rice and we split an appetizer.
- Lindsay and I are planning to see Pirates of the *Caribbean* with some friends tonight. We don't know if we want to go to see it at the Levee because it costs to park and is kind of a hassle. The other movie theatre we could see it at would be Wilder. We will probably go there because it is close, has free parking and is never crowded.
- I was online today and bought and downloaded music from iTunes. I have a gift certificate for music downloads and bought some songs by James Blunt and Jack Johnson. I also checked out some iPods online because I am thinking of upgrading. I currently have the Mini, but I think I might want a Nano.

Wednesday, 12 July 2006

- I bought gas today at UDF on my way to work. ….I went inside, grabbed a Sugar Free Red Bull (my morning fix) and prepaid for my gas.
- For lunch, I was craving barbeque so I called Hoggy's, a new restaurant near my office and requested they fax a menu. I decided on the pulled pork lunch with a sweet potato and a sweet tea.
- I love my car, but I want a new one. I saw a new dark gray/silver Scion today and want it badly. I called my mom and talked to her about trading my car in for a new car. She said she would have to think about it because she is buying a car for my younger brother.
- I looked online for a desk for my room. I have a computer and printer, but no work station. I usually sit at my kitchen table or on the floor to do homework and it's getting really annoying. I looked at Pottery Barn, Bova and a couple of random sites, but didn't see anything I liked.

Saturday, 15 July 2006

- I bought a Free Mango at Panera Bread ….
- I went shopping today at Kenwood Mall for something to wear tonight. I went to a couple of stores, but didn't find anything. I went into Forever 21 and was excited when I found a white skirt and black camisole. I was even more excited when I found great accessories to match.
- I bought a birthday card and gift bag at Hallmark. It is my friend Brittney's 21st birthday and we are going out tonight. I also need to stop at a liquor store before meeting up so I can buy a mini bottle of Patron to give to her as a present.
- We met at Brio on the Levee for appetizers and cocktails. ..

Sunday, 16 July 2006

- I had a headache this morning and was out of Advil so I went to Walgreen's. I bought water and a bottle of Advil gel caplets. In line I grabbed a new tube of Burt's Beeswax and bought that too.
- I had to buy gas again today. I feel like I filled up! I hate buying gas. It is so expensive and is a pain in the butt. The only thing worse than buying it is to know you will have to buy it again in three days!
- I work at J B Fin's on the Levee, so I went shopping on my break. I went to Hollister and PacSun. I didn't find anything I liked. However, I did buy a new belly button ring from the outside vendor.

Ellen Tibbs is a college senior majoring in Business Administration.

CONSUMERS ARE FASCINATING

As consumers, we are fascinating. Consider a conversation we recently had with a consumer, Jackie, 30. We will let that interview speak for itself, and you decide whether you agree that conusmers are indeed fascinating.

VISIONS OF THE CONSUMER

When we think of consumers such as Jackie, several images come to mind. They are the browsers in the department store, shoppers in the mall, patrons enjoying a meal in a restaurant, visitors standing in long lines at Disneyland, youngsters flocking to video arcades, and old ladies rushing to grab the door-buster sale items. These and many other visions of the consumer can be aptly grouped into the following five categories:

1. Consumer as a Problem-Solver
2. Consumer as an Economic Creature
3. Consumer as a Computer
4. Consumer as a Shopper
5. Consumer as a Reveler

Consumer as a Problem Solver In this vision, consumers are searching for solutions to the needs of daily life, looking for a product or service that will meet that need in the best possible way. Once they find the "solution product," they can relax and move on with their lives. The following self-report from a consumer illustrates this[1]:

> After I purchased my new pants recently, I spent most of my free time thinking about the shoes I already have, which ones would go with the new outfit that was also forming in my mind. Finally, I decided that I didn't have any shoes to go with my new pants. I formed an idea in my mind about the type of shoes that would be a perfect match for my new pants. On Tuesday, I started my search at Payless Shoe Source, but didn't have any luck. I continued my search at Dillard's and JC Penny's but once again I just didn't see what I was looking for. I became very discouraged. I decided that later that evening, my final store to shop would be Shoe Carnival. As soon as I walked in I saw them, the perfect pair of shoes. They were a little pricey at $38.99 but with a 10% sale, I bought them. I was very excited and relieved that I had found the shoes I was looking for.
> —Angie, 22

Consumer as an Economic Creature Consumers are also planners and managers of personal finances; they want to use their money wisely. As such they seek to buy products at the best prices available. This does not mean that they always go for the lowest price (although often they do), but always that they want to maximize their utility. As one consumer stated:

> My fiancée and I always cut coupons before we go grocery shopping. It always saves us at least $20 per trip. We both agree that Kroger and Thriftway are too expensive for our large bi-monthly shopping trips. We prefer to go to Meijer and likely save another $40 just by going there. Once at Meijer, we aren't too picky about the brands we buy. We can often be seen calculating the per unit price based on the Meijer brand versus the name brand with coupon. On most everything, the lower per-unit cost always wins. Oddly enough ketchup is the one item that I purchase based on the brand name. I grew up with Heinz Ketchup and I still prefer it to generic. Other than that, I would rather save money and buy the generic version of canned vegetables, macaroni & cheese, chips, soda, etc.
> —Christopher, 23.

Consumer as a Computer We also see consumers reading package labels, asking salespersons questions, checking-off items on a shopping list, pondering information in

"I Obey My Thirst!"

A Consumer Interview

We intercepted Jackie Cooper, a 30-year old African-American male, walking with a shopping bag in hand, in the Downtown Mall, Cincinnati. Our interviewer was Pamela Ryckman, a junior marketing student, who conducted the interview as part of her class project.

Q. Excuse me sir, would you mind answering a few questions for my class project?

A. Sure, you can ask me anything.

Q. Great, thank you. (Pointing at the shopping bag) What did you buy today?

A. I just bought this new fly Fubu jersey. It is uh, blue and yellow, double zero on the back. It's phat.[1]

Q. How do you buy your clothing?

A. You know, whatever looks good. Stay away from stripes though.

Q. Why?

A. Oh, it could make you look bulky, you know.

Q. What kind of clothes do you buy?

A. Well, I have a lot of Nike. My favorite is Fubu, you know. I also got Sean-John. That is the only kind of stuff I buy.

Q. Why do you like these brands? What do you look for when you buy clothes?

A. Its gotta be comfortable. I have to be able to move in it, or play ball in it, and still go to the clubs … comfortable but still nice.

Q. Do you go on spending sprees?

A. Nah, I try to keep my platinum bill on the D.L.[2]

Q. Are you happy with the way you buy clothes?

A. Yeah, I got my own system. Hasn't failed me yet.

Q. Do you like shopping for clothes?

A. Clothes shopping? Yes, I like it. I love it. You know, I gotta keep my threads on top of the game.

Q. Is choosing clothes a problem for you?

A. Nah, I usually just try whatever catches my eye and I just buy it. I go in, do my business, and then I'm out. … I am like flash … you know flashin' in, flashin' out. Bling blingin'!

Q. What role does clothing play in your life?

A. See, I look at clothing like it's a part of me. It's like people be lookin' at my clothes. It is like they're seein' into my soul. You know what I mean? That's why I dress the way I dress.

Q. Do you pay attention to clothes advertising?

A. Nah, I just buy what I like; I will not bow to any sponsor. I buy what I want! I'm like Sprite—I obey my thirst. That is the way it is.

INTERVIEWER: Ok. Thank you for your time.

1. Pretty hot and tempting.
2. Down Low

Jackie Cooper is a makeup artist and works at a beauty salon in Cincinnati, USA.

their heads, looking at an ad, making sense of instructions on how to use a product—in other words, sorting out all the information about products and the marketplace. Indeed, our brains act like human computers. This vision can be seen in the following self-report from a couple:

> We were in the market for a house. We began by searching the MLS site on the Internet. We searched listings by price, by location, by school district, and by features. Then we found a realtor and let him do the searching. He showed us several houses on the computer within our price range. One house seemed to have all the features but was on a street with no sidewalks, and sidewalks were important to us because we have children. Another house had everything

but the deck was small; a third house had a large deck but the kitchen was small. We tried to figure how much it would cost to make the deck bigger, and we thought that expanding the kitchen would be very cumbersome. We kept turning in our heads the three houses we liked and their various features, and finally, taking everything into account, we settled on the one with the small deck.   —Jenny, 23, and Paul, 24

Consumer as a Shopper This is the familiar image of consumers, coming out of a store, loaded with shopping bags in both hands. Inside the store, they are totally taken in by vast merchandise, enchanted by all that is on display, theirs to have if they like, but to enjoy the sight anyway. Stores and marketplaces are the proverbial Alice's Wonderland for the consumer as a shopper. As one of our research respondents put it:

> I shop all the time. Days, evenings, weekdays, weekends. Whenever I can get out. I shop at department stores and just as much at boutique shops. And I shop online—my favorite site is Alloy.com. I shop for sales and I shop for rare merchandise. If I am getting bored I will go to the mall. In fact if I don't go shopping for 2 or 3 days at a stretch, I begin to feel depressed. I buy very carefully, after full deliberation, but I browse a lot and I window-shop a lot. Mall is a place I couldn't live without. You could say I was born to shop.
>
> Christy, 22

Consumer as a Reveler Finally, we all have visions of consumers just having a good time—at a restaurant, a rock concert, a beach resort on Spring Break—enjoying life with all the wonderful things the marketplace has to offer. Below are two excerpts from consumer interviews.

> I am really big into smelling good. I spend hundreds of dollars on top name cologne. I feel that appearance and smell at first are what make the man what he is. I can be running to the grocery store and I put on cologne. —Chad, 22.
>
> I love attending a live concert. Rap, country, rock, gospel, alternative—I love them all. My favorite band is Dave Mathews—I have got all 14 of their CDs and two live concert DVDs!   —Joe , 23.

We obtained a photo of a group of consumers. When it comes to consumers as revelers, a picture does speak a thousand words!

(Photo: Courtesy of Spark ar Word Press)

All of these visions are true. They exist not only in different consumers, but also sometimes in the same consumer. Thus, we are economic creatures sometimes, watching every penny; at other times, we just want to experience, just want to be revelers, with money as no object. Sometimes, we are assessing a product and soaking up all the information, with our internal computers' drives whirring. A consumer is indeed multi-faceted. And our study will cover all these facets.

Now, we are ready to begin our formal study consumer behavior.

WHAT IS CONSUMER BEHAVIOR?

We define **consumer behavior** as the **mental** and **physical activities** undertaken by consumers to acquire and consume products so as to fulfill their needs and wants.

Our definition of *consumer behavior* has several elements worth noting. Let us discuss these one by one.

Mental and Physical Activities First, consumer behavior includes both mental and physical activities. **Mental activities** are acts of the mind, and they relate to what we think, feel, and know about products. **Physical activities** are, in contrast, acts of the human body, and they relate to what we physically do to acquire and consume products.

When you are contemplating buying a product, even dreaming about it, you are engaging in a mental activity. You are also engaging in a mental activity when you are mulling over a product's benefits and risks; making sense of an advertisement; trying to remember the price of a product in the store you previously visited; trying to recall what you read in Food and Wine magazine about the wines that go well with the pasta you are planning to cook tonight; or just wondering if a three-buttoned suit jacket will be good to wear to a forthcoming job interview or if instead you should stick to the more conservative two-buttoned jacket.

Physical activities include visiting stores, clipping coupons, talking to salespeople, surfing the Internet, test-driving a car, placing an item in the shopping cart, abandoning a shopping cart, and saving empty cartons for later recycling. Physical activities entailed in actual consumption are also included—such as preparation to consume (e.g., setting the table, soaking off grease from pizzas and fries, etc.), consumption situations (e.g., choosing take out or dining in, using cell phone while driving), consumption rituals (e.g., a makeup regimen), or routine trivial behaviors (e.g., TV channel flipping). Indeed, it is by observing consumer inconveniences and improvisations during product use that marketers often conceive new products and tailor their communications. Some activities are hybrids—both physical and mental—such as reading *Consumer Reports,* or reading product labels.

Photo: Steve Boyd doing Yoga on the rooftop of his Washington, D.C. apartment complex

Is this person consuming at this moment?

Yes, the clothes, for starters. Besides, whereas yoga practitioners are expected to shut their minds off all extraneous thoughts, few are able to. For all we know, this person might be thinking, "I should after all buy a proper Yoga mat." Or, for that matter, he might be contemplating which movie he should see later that evening, *Borat* or *A Mighty Heart*.

Remember, evaluating impending purchases, or contemplating future consumptions is also consumer behavior.

Whether in action currently unfolding or in thoughts laced with objects of desire, we are, at any given moment, more likely than not, *being* a consumer. Indeed, then, we *are* consumers 24/7!

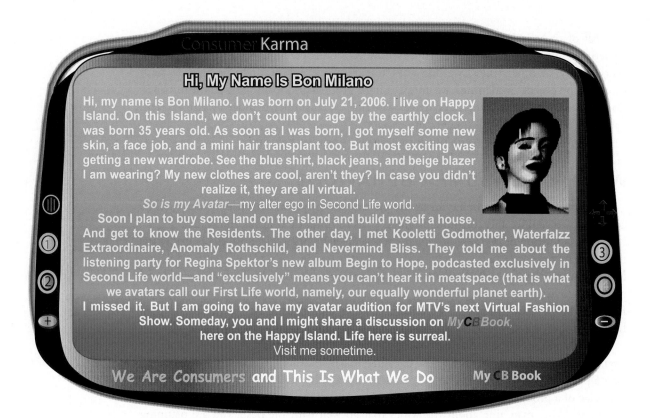

It should be noted that mental and physical activities we study under consumer behavior are not limited to the specific act of buying and using the product. Rather they include activities that the consumer undertakes in preparation for and prior to the actual buying act, and they include activities that continue long after the product is actually consumed or used. When a consumer hears a friend praising a product and makes a mental note to try it sometime in the future, this preparatory activity is part of consumer behavior. Likewise, a few months after using the product, if the consumer suddenly recalls the experience of using that product and chuckles about it, enjoying the memory of past consumption, then that post-use mental activity is also consumer behavior.

Product Second, we use the term *product* broadly, to refer to any physical or nonphysical product or service that offers some benefit to the consumer, including a place, a person, or an idea offered for exchange. Thus, not only are the physical products we buy included, such as a car, a shirt, a golf club, etc., but also services such as a fitness club, college education, wireless phone service, TV programs, and a "breakup letter service"—more on that later. Also included are places such as vacation destinations, outlet malls, or video arcades. And persons such as political candidates or candidates for the student council of your college seeking your votes are included. And, finally, ideas are included such as the idea of opposing a tax levy for a new stadium, donating blood, vegetarianism, or buying virtual ice cream (!) (read about it in Chapter 19). The important point here is that casting your vote for a candidate is just as good an example of consumer behavior as is buying a brand of toothpaste; so is visiting a museum, choosing a college, donating to the Tsunami Relief Fund, reading Malcolm Gladwell's 2005 best seller, *Blink*, or displaying a "Save Our Environment" bumper sticker on your new Element.

Consumers Third, our definition includes the word consumers. In general, a consumer is anyone engaged in the acquisition and use of products and services available in the marketplace. Although a few humans on our planet might well be living lives sustained entirely by self-produced products and services (rather than those acquired in the marketplace), most of us acquire the products and services we need and want through marketplace exchange. Each of us, therefore, is a consumer.

The use of the term *consume*r in this text is broader than in practice, where different marketers call them, instead, by different names. For example, retail stores generally refer to their patrons as customers (rather than as consumers); so do utility companies (e.g., electricity or phone service providers), financial companies (e.g., banks), and service companies (e.g., dry cleaners, etc.). Professional service providers refer to them as clients (e.g., lawyers, real estate agents, tax advisors) or by their more context-specific roles (e.g., doctors call them "patients," educators call them "students," fund-raisers call them "donors," etc.). And personal service providers call them either customers or clients (e.g., palm readers and fortune tellers, massage therapists, and boutiques that do the piercing and tattooing of our bodies). Only manufacturers who do not routinely deal with the end-users of a product (e.g., Procter & Gamble, Johnson & Johnson, Kraft, and General Foods, etc.) refer to these household end users as "consumers." In this text, however, we refer to all of these kinds of acquirers and users of products and services as consumers.

Our use of the term consumer also goes beyond its literal meaning—persons who consume. Of course, some products do get consumed, such as food items, but other products do not get "consumed" (i.e., depleted), such as household appliances or other durables. For these products, we are users rather than consumers. Again, we will use the term *consumers* to refer to the users of all products or services, whether these products are consumables or durables.

Correspondingly, we define **consumption** as any and all usage of products whether or not the products are actually "consumed" away; i.e., depleted. Thus, when we look at our digital pictures and we show them to others or email them, we are consuming them. And of course we also count as consumption activities such as TV viewing, visiting art galleries, and being in a chat-room on our PCs.

Needs and Wants Finally, two important words in our definition are *needs* and *wants*. *Needs* and *wants* are perhaps the two words most freely used by consumers—"freely" in the sense that they seldom ponder before uttering these words. They utter these words merely, but unmistakably, to indicate their desire or intent to possess and/or consume something. Philosophers of diverse ilk have ruminated for centuries as to what *need* and *want* mean, and understandably there is no consensus. Consequently, consumer researchers who study consumer needs and wants also vary in their definitions of the terms. Indeed, it would be futile to search for a definition on which everyone would agree. So, here is the definition we will use in this book.

A **need** can be defined as a discomforting human condition. It can be discomforting in a physiological sense or in a psychological sense. Examples of the physiologically discomforting condition are a hungry stomach or a body unprotected against the winter cold; examples of discomforting *psychological* conditions are feeling bored, feeling insecure, or experiencing being looked down upon. As consumers, we seek products or services in the marketplace exchange so as to alleviate these conditions of discomfort. A **want** is a desire for a specific object or product. The consumer who wants a product judges that it would restore his or her condition to a satisfactory state. Thus, the felt discomfort of a hungry stomach is a need; desire for food and for a specific kind of food is a want. Feeling insecure is a need; desire for the latest model of Nike shoes, even when barely within one's means, is a want.

The definitions we use here differ from common speech, where needs are equated with necessities, and wants with luxuries. There are good reasons for this, which we will explore in a later section. For now, just remember that *need* is your felt discomfort, period. And remember also that the discomfort has to be perceived by the person himself or herself. Thus, a need is not someone else's assessment of your condition. I cannot say that your hair looks long, so you need a haircut, or that your clothes look all faded and worn out, so you need a new pair of jeans. Or, that you don't need a PDA (personal digital assistant), a diamond ring, hair coloring, body piercing, or a HUMMER. It is for you to decide if not having these things is discomforting for you, psychologically speaking. Indeed, then, *need* is a very subjective word. It is a very personal feeling.

Bon Milano in SECOND LIFE: A consumer in the the New Age of Digital Life

NEED IS A VERY SUBJECTIVE WORD.

© General Motors Corp., Used with permission.

Need is a very subjective feeling—this important consumer sentiment is elegantly captured in this ad for HUMMER.

EXCHANGE, VALUE, AND RESOURCES

Three Essentials of Consumer Behavior

There are three essential elements in all consumer behavior. Without these, no "consumer behavior" can take place. And they work in unison—inseparably, as three grand enablers of consumer behavior. These are exchange, resources, and value. Let us examine each.

EXCHANGE

Exchange refers to an interchange between two parties where each receives from the other something of more value and gives up something of less value. Within that specific exchange, what is given up is of less value to the giver than it is to the receiver, so that both parties gain more in value than they give up. Thus, when we buy a shirt, we part with our money (say, 20 dollars or 40 rubles or 25 euros or 120 pesos or 80 yen) because at that time that particular shirt is more valuable to us than keeping that money in our pockets; conversely, when we sell that shirt in a garage sale for one dollar, at that time, that shirt's value to us is less than even one dollar.

Although an exchange can also occur between any two consumers, it is customary to call one of the parties the *marketer* and the other party the *consumer*. A **marketer** is an individual or an organization with an organizational goal that offers products and services in exchange for the consumer's money or (occasionally) other resources. When a marketer primarily seeks money and has making money as the principal organizational goal, then that marketer is referred to as a **commercial entity**. When a marketer offers products and services either free of cost or at a nominal charge insufficient to cover costs or make any profit, the marketer is typically a **non-profit** or social organization. Typically, nonprofit or social organizations promote an idea (e.g., smoking cessation) or a person (e.g., a presidential candidate). An important point here is that the study of consumer behavior is just as useful for non-profit and social and community organizations.

RESOURCES

A **resource** is something we own or possess that people value. Since people value those resources, more or less universally, as consumers we can use them to acquire a whole host of products and services. That is, as humans, we value resources ourselves, and, because other humans value them too, we can exchange some of them to satisfy our needs and wants.

Five Resources

There are five types of resources: money, time, skills and knowledge, body and physical energy, and social capital. Of these, money is the most often used resource for marketplace exchanges—when we acquire products and services, we typically pay for them with money. We also use money to acquire the other four resources. We buy time-saving devices to gain more time; we hire a maid so we ourselves don't expend time in housekeeping chores. We buy books and take college courses to gain knowledge, we buy home-improvement books to learn to do handiwork, and we pay for dancing lessons to acquire dancing skills.

To build our bodies and enhance physical energy as a resource, we spend money and join a gym. We spend time doing yoga. And we buy vitamins and nutrition-supplements to get energy. Finally, we spend time and money to build **social capital**—the network of friends and professional connections that can be of help in our hours of need. We buy designer brand clothes that will help us gain acceptance among our peers. We spend time writing thank-you notes and sending gifts to keep the friends we have. And we pay fees to join social clubs and associations to enlarge our social networks.

Sometimes we use other resources so we can pay less in money. We pay, in part, with our time when we choose to take a cheaper airline flight with a stopover instead of a direct flight. Or when we buy a modular furniture system that we have to assemble ourselves, we exchange our time, physical energy, and skills to save money. If we believe that we have the requisite skills, then we choose a low fee discount broker rather than a full service investment advisor, or we buy stocks online. We use our healthy bodies themselves as a resource when we donate blood or pledge to donate some organ. And good looks are themselves "exchanged" to attract a date, companion, and mate.

VALUE

The third essential element in all consumer behavior is value. **Value** is the sum total of net benefits we receive from an activity or an exchange. Indeed, value is the core goal of all exchanges humans undertake.

> *Value, not money, is the basic currency of all human interaction. When we meet someone, we try to quickly assess how long it would be worth our while to be talking to that person. If an incoming phone call shows up on our caller ID, we promptly decide if we would gain anything by taking that call at that time…. It is even more true of marketplace exchanges. The only reason customers are even in the marketplace is that they are looking for something of value.* (ValueSpace, 2001, p. 3-4.)[2]

Value comes from all the benefits, all the desired outcomes that consumers obtain and experience from their use of products. When a cream eradicates our zits, that is a desired outcome to us and hence a value; when a musical play uplifts our moods, that is a desired outcome and hence it is a value; when wearing a particular suit or dress brings us compliments from others, we are receiving value. And when we feel good about ourselves donating to a charity, we are experiencing value. In everything we buy, in everything we consume, in every advertisement to which we pay attention, from every salesperson to whom we lend our ears, in every store we enter, on every Web site we visit, we seek value.

Thus, value comes in multiple forms. Basically, value accrues when some need is satisfied. Because human needs are countless, so also are forms of value. However, they can be categorized into four major types, captured in the acronym USER: (a) utilitarian, (b) social, (c) ego/identity, and (d) recreational.[3]

Utilitarian value is the set of tangible outcomes of a product's usage (or of an activity). It comprises physical consequences of a product and its effects in the physical world around us and within us (i.e., our body). Also called *functional value*, utilitarian value comes from objects when they enable us to manage our lives as biological and physical beings and to manage our external physical environments as well. Examples include filling our bellies with food, energizing our bodies with nutrients, moisturizing our skin with lotions, navigating physical distance by using a Segway™, etc. But don't mistake it for mere basic necessity. A computer that allows us to write and save letters, a personal jet that enables us to reach places at will, and a digital camera phone that lets us shoot pictures anytime anywhere and then email them instantly to our friends—these products yield specific benefits that are also utilitarian.

Social value comes from our ability to manage our social worlds (as opposed to the physical world). This includes maintaining warm and harmonious relations with others, fitting in with peers, and generally projecting a good image to others. Thus, we get social value when we wear brand name clothing with a certain brand image, and we get social value when we buy someone a gift to affirm our relationship. We also receive social value when we donate blood as part of an office drive, as well as when we boycott French imported products just because everyone among our coworkers does.

Ego/identity value comes from our need to construct and nurture our identities or self-concepts, our sense of ego, our ideas of who we are. Thus, we eat vegetarian food because we value the identity of being an animal saver. We gain ego/identity value by recycling because we believe in preserving the environment. We wear Polo and Donna Karen and drive a Jaguar because we think these brands are very urbane and sophisticated, and we also view ourselves as urbane and sophisticated. Or alternatively, we wear, say, American Eagle and drive a Blazer because we want to nurture our self-identities as being very rugged.

Finally, **recreation value** comes from objects and activities when they recreate our moods and regenerate our mental ability—removing our fatigue and boredom, stimulating the senses, and rejuvenating our minds. Also called **hedonic**, recreation value is obtained from wide ranging forms of consumption: from mild mood-lifters like listening

Two consumers.
Two different self-identities.
Expressed through clothes.

Miguel Young, a "watch repair artist" (L), Sean Foley, an eco-design professor, Fedora hat and tie-dye T-shirt—to each his own, courtesy of the marketplace.

(Incidently, no amount of clever marketing can make Miguel trade his fedora hat for the tie-dye T. And Sean will absolutely, positively not do the trade either. They might as well, but not because of marketing.)

to one's favorite music to the extreme exhilaration at watching ones' favorite sports team win the championship game; from a short coffee break to wallowing in hedonism at the Venetian in Las Vegas.

Of course, many products and activities could simultaneously produce multiple values, and two consumers could use the same product to derive two different values. Thus, a consumer could wear Polo or Donna Karen clothing purely to impress others, whereas another person could wear them, not because of what others think of them, but because he or she sees himself or herself that way. To us the clearest distinction between the two values (social and ego/identity) came from a consumer who said he buys name brand shirts and pants to make an impression although he thinks it is foolish to pay so much for them, and that when it comes to underwear, he buys a store brand; in contrast, another consumer bought only designer brand underwear because he thought he "deserved it."

A car is more than transportation. For some consumers, it is an extension of themselves.

Jamie Schworer, a thirty-something consumer, a resident of Clincinnati (U.S.A.) A marketing graduate, she now runs her own Limo Service business. She bought the 2006 Scion tC the moment she saw it.

About her tC, Jamie say, "I love the quick acceleration and the sleek lines of my tC the best. I am proud to be a Scion tC owner. I am even in the local Scion Car Club!"

Jamie Schowerer and her 2006 Scion tC: does the car reflect her or does she reflect the car?

Does Jamie love her tC? Let the pictures speaks for themsleves.

Make no mistake about it: we sometimes choose a product to impress others, but sometimes we choose it purely to play out our sense of identity. Tons of expensive designer brand undergarments and a dozen or more personal grooming gadgets from Sharper Image get chosen, not because of a desire to impress others (these products have low public visibility), but because we believe we are the kind of person who has the personality suited for those brands.

Another point to note is that while a few products are entirely symbolic with no physical utility (e.g., greeting cards), most products have utility as a minimal core. Many products have physical utility and not much more (e.g., hardware products like duct tape), but most products have, surrounding a physical, utilitarian function, some social, ego/ identity, or recreational value. Clothing, cars, colognes, and being seen in a Starbucks Café sipping a $4.50 Café O' latte offer these multiple values, for example.

We will dwell on these more in subsequent chapters in the book, but for now remember the word USER as your code word to think of the four principal values consumers seek in the marketplace and in consumption.

DOES MARKETING CREATE A NEED?

Some people blame marketing for creating consumer needs. They charge that marketing creates a desire for products we don't need. Does it? Let us examine this closely. Mainly, this charge is based on two prevalent views of what a *need* is. First, the charge comes from those who define true needs as only the basic things we require for survival. Consequently, they argue that we only need a basic car, not a fancy car, but marketers create in us a desire for a fancy car, and that we do not need a $150 Nike shoe, but fancy advertising beguiles us into believing that we do.

The second definitional problem is that, in common parlance, a need is confused with a product. This leads to the argument that no one needed a DVD player until DVDs came along, and no one needed hair transplants until hair transplants became available. A discourse on whether or not we needed something is impossible if we use the terms *need* and *product* interchangeably.

In contrast, we have defined *need* as a condition (an unsatisfactory one), not as a product that improves that condition. So the need to be entertained always existed; DVDs provided a solution. And the need to impress peers or express ourselves had always existed; Nike offers, to some consumers, a way to do it. Consider digital camera cell phones. Before they became available, we did not need digital camera cell phones. In fact, we did not even need cell phones. But the need to be able to call our moms or friends from a place with no payphone nearby had always existed. And every once in a while we were in a place and we were looking at something, some product, some transient scene, and then we wished we could capture it in a photo and show it to a friend far away in real time to get his or her opinion. We had always needed, too, the ability to see the caller's face in our tiny cell phone's screen. Since these possibilities were not available, we dreamed about them every once in a while and then pushed the thought away from our active attention. Until one day, science made available the cell phone, and then the cell phone with digital camera and with email capabilities, and we suddenly recognized these products as solutions to our long-dormant needs. But it was science that gave us those products, not marketing. Marketing brought the news and explained their functions and benefits. The same goes for every invention—from Post-it® Digital Notes to hair transplants, science made them available, and, *after* that, marketing brought us the information and offered the invention at a price (sometimes a hefty sum, mind you). And those who saw these products as solutions to their needs—the conditions that were bugging them—bought them immediately, without much persuasion, whereas others waited a while or never bought them (a high intensity marketing effort, not withstanding!).

Speaking of the products science has brought us, smart consumers would have discovered their benefits even in the absence of marketers, and from them, in turn, all consumers would have. Marketers should be flattered to receive this credit, but it is not duly theirs. Consumers who credit marketers with creating in them the need for all those new inventions are merely shifting responsibility, or guilt if you will, from themselves to marketers.

What about products that are not scientific inventions, but mere packaging of image, you might ask. Like designer brands? Here, too, marketing receives more blame (or credit) than it deserves. Imagine a world where only one brand and one type of shoes (in all sizes, of course) was available, and only one brand and one style of clothes, and only one make and style of car. Would you then have been happier? When people got their clothes tailored, they got them customized not only for size but for style as well; when they sewed them themselves, they always gave them little personal touches, to reflect their personalities. This need to differentiate, not to be stamped from a cookie cutter, to show something unique, is also an inherent human need. What marketers do, to consumers' benefit, is simply to make those varieties, those differentiations in product offerings available to humans who had until then improvised those style differentiations. And in countries where these products are not freely available (and thus there is no marketing), many consumers would kill to get them from the gray market if they could!

Somehow, consumers have their ideas of what will make them happy, and they will do anything to get those things, marketing or no marketing. The important question therefore is this: From where do consumers get their ideas? From diverse sources, actually. From the media for one. From seeing what the film stars are driving, and what the rap artists are wearing. And they observe people around them. Who is wearing Seven7 ™ or True Religion jeans, who is driving the Scion, and who is walking with iPod ear buds as a fashion statement? Thus, it is the media, and it is the society as a whole, the culture, the world around us, or the streets we are roaming—these are the sources of our desires. Marketing is a part of this environment, no more, and no less.

Let us look at it another way. Consider how many products are introduced in a typical year, and how many of them become abysmal failures. With all the marketing prowess behind them, marketers just can't convince enough number of consumers to part with their money to buy those products. And then there is the battle of the brands. In clothing, there is Kenneth Cole, and there is Tommy Hilfiger. Open any issue of *GQ* or *Esquire* and you can find advertisements for both. And yet, why do you buy one brand and not the other? There is a very simple reason: each brand makes a certain brand promise, each projects a certain image, each fits a certain consumer's inner self-image, and the consumer buys that which speaks to him or her. To other marketers, consumers vote a "No"—with their wallets and purses. Yes, consumers respond to advertising, to marketing, but only to the brand and only to the marketer that in fact respond first to what is within the consumer already. As one tattoo artist, describing how he helps his clients choose a design, put it: "The tattoo is already within the consumer; all I do is bring it out for the world to see!"

The Tattoo is already inside you!
This consumer, Victor Strunk, used to sixth-sense extra-terrestrial characters protecting him from dangers both from outside and from within, and then got them on his skin.

Gluttony Rampant at Harvey Nichols Stores in London
Does marketing create gluttony in humans?
Actually, gluttony has existed from the beginning of human existence. Indulging in it ocasionally is one of life's little pleasures. Marketing *mirrors* it, to bring consumers happiness.

(Photo: courtesy of Harvey Nichols and ad agency DDB, London)

SEEING THE FUTURE FIRST: MEETING CONSUMERS' LATENT NEEDS

Consider the telephone. It is a miracle. It was invented in 1876. Suddenly, two persons continents apart could talk to each other. Since then, the technology experts in phone companies have upgraded the device over the years, improving sound fidelity and adding such features as pulse tone, and later speed dial, memory, and mute features. But their gaze remained focused on the telephone device. And while they kept in mind the consumer need the device served, that need seems to have been understood in its most obvious form: the need to talk to someone not within hearing range. They did not look deeper; it was assumed, inadvertently, that whenever someone wanted to talk to a distant person, that other person would be available at that location and at that time, and that he or she would want to talk to the caller. Furthermore, it was assumed that the two would speak the same language! After all, it was not until 1971 that the answering machine was invented.[4] And it was not until 1987 that caller ID was first offered to consumers.[5] And finally, technology experts are only now building automatic, built-in translation software. Maybe marketers had to wait until appropriate technologies were invented; maybe they had to wait until mass-manufacturing of these devices became commercially feasible; or maybe they had to wait until government regulatory bodies cleared the way. Regardless, the important point is that there had been no recognition of these consumer communication needs. No one had bothered to look deeper.

Marketing Is All About Satisfying A Consumer Need

One recent evening, Maria Gutierrez, 17, drove 40 miles to a Torrid store in Brea, California, looking for a prom dress. And she found what she was looking for. Torrid sells fashion clothing and accessories for fashionable teens. The store's décor and merchandise is distinguished, a look suffused only in hot pink and black colors. But that is not the main reason why teens like Maria make a pilgrimage to Torrid stores. Torrid, you see, only sells sizes 12 to 26!

Coming up with oversize teen clothing might seem a small "improvement" in a product category. But it is a huge step forward in meeting a hidden consumer need for a considerable number of consumers—teenage girls who wear a plus size clothing. Torrid set up shop in mid-2001. Before that, women like Maria would sometimes wear a man's shirt, and dressing up for a party was like a "fashion hell." Thanks to Torrid, for young women in plus sizes everywhere, now it is a "fashion heaven."

While teens who needed fashionable clothing in plus sizes had no option before Torrid's arrival only five years ago, adult women who wear plus size clothing were more fortunate. Can you name a store that caters to their needs? If you said Lane Bryant, you are right. Today, the most recognizable name in plus size clothing for adult women, Lane Bryant opened its first store on Fifth Avenue in New York City in 1904, dedicated exclusively to plus size clothing for women. The store chain was acquired in 1982 by The Limited, Inc.[6]

By 2001, the chain had grown to 651 stores, when Charming Shoppes acquired it.[7] Today, with over 700 stores nationwide, the new parent is bringing fashion to plus sizes with zeal. In 2005, it featured the famous Seven7™ jeans with special details such as whiskering, rhinestone embellishments, and embroidered pockets. In June that year, the company signed up Kimberley Locke, "American Idol" Finalist and Curb recording artist. Her promotion of the Seven7™ Jean Collection brings a new message to its target segment. As Ms. Locke herself put it: "Being in the public eye gives me the opportunity to show people that women who are just like me, who are curvy, voluptuous, and have full figures,

Plus-size fit and elegant fashion need not be mutually exclusive anymore. Lane Bryant recently offered fashion jeans brand Seven7™ in a limited edition adorned with Swarovski Crystals. Here, bedecked in it is no less than Kimberley Locke, the brand's spokesperson since June 2005, whose latest single release SUPAWOMAN (Just call me SUPAWOMAN, There is nothing that I can't do,… Are you ready for who I am…) is inspiring women everywhere.

can be beautiful, too."[8]

Consider some other products and see if they *create* a new need, or, merely, albeit admirably, *satisfy* a latent need of consumers.

Self-watering flower pot The pot has two chambers; the lower half is filled with water; a wick from the top half, which contains soil, reaches out to the bottom chamber. Would you buy it? If yes, that is becasue the moment you see it, you recognize it as the perfect solution to a latent need—the challenge of taking care of plants while on vacation. If not, then no amount of marketing effort will make you buy it.

Five Finger Shoes A shoe with five fingers. Yes, the shoe fits your foot and toes

individually; provides the same sole support. Liberate your toes. Walk barefoot. Like the idea? Then, you will buy it. If not, no amount of marketing will make you buy it. (Check it out at www.vibramfivefingers.com.)

Ipod My Photo You send in your photo, and, for $19.99, they will put the iPod, complete with the white ear buds on it. Since its inception in early 2001, the company has been doing brisk business. Did it create a need? Or just gave us one more avenue to exercise our whims, our need to be playful, to make our photos cool and then savor them. (Check it out at www.ipodmyphoto.com.)

Hug Shirt It has *wearable electronics*. It enables a person to send you a hug from far away. Here is how it works: It has two high-tech components, embedded in the fabric: (1) *sensors* that will sense the strength of the touch, skin warmth, and the heart beat of the sender at a distance; and (2) *actuators* that will reproduce the same sensations for the wearer. Yes, now you can hug your teacher everyday. (Check it out at www.cutecircuit.com.)

Finger Ring Suppose you are in a group conversation, and the other person's phone rings. Don't you wish it hadn't. Now you can make it happen. Each person in the group wears a special ring. Then, an incoming call on any of your cell phones will send a vibration to each ring, and each ring-wearer will press a button to allow or disallow the phone to ring. Of course, none of the wearer knows whose phone is receiving the call. This is called *social polling*—let your company decide if you can take the call or not.

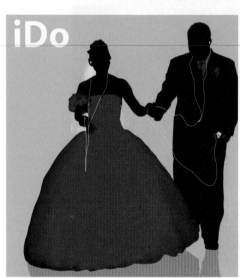

Silent Dating This is a new concept in social networking. You meet up people in a group, but you are not allowed to talk at all. They give you a generous supply of index cards and a pen. Scribble a message on one and slide it over to the other person. And wait for him/her to doodle back. Says one recent, happy, silent-dater: "I haven't had this much fun since passing notes in school." The parties are held in such cities as New York, San Francisco, Washington D.C., and even Beijing. Check out the schedule for the next party at www.quietparty.com.

Now, let us consider briefly what role marketing plays (or will play) for these products. Consider the hug shirt. Okay, "hugging your teacher" was the wrong pitch. How about hugging your spouse, or your children, when you are away from home. If the wearable vest doesn't cost too much, some of us may just buy it. But, and this is an important "but," only if the sensations are realistic; and if we can bring ourselves to believe that the hug we just experienced felt just as if the other person was in "touching proximity." If not, no amount of marketing prowess is going to get you to part with your money. (Unless, realistic or not, you wanted to send hugs to an interesting stranger, but that is another story, and, at any rate, that need too, will have not been created by marketing.) The truth is, many of us can't wait to try it on. At least as a novelty experience, initially, and then, later, also for real emo-interface with a loved one far away.

Will you buy the "social polling" Finger Ring? Yes or No, whatever be your answer, it is *your* answer—the outcome of you determining if it will meet any of your needs. A million dollar ad campaign might make you buy it? No, a million dollar ad campaign will make *you*, at most and if at all, reassess if it will satisfy your need. That is all.

Silent dating, now what can we you say about this cool idea! That other dating scene, with loud music and the noise of a thousand conversations, has been utterly frustrating for any intelligent interaction. Silent Dating is also a fresh breather for the tongue-tied among us. And it is a low risk, reversible, venture (you can always go back to your regular dating venues). More than anything else, it is a new, alluring, sport to play out your spontaneity and your desire for sensation-seeking. (Check out some of the notes someone glided over to you!) Those

Five Finges Shoe
from Vibram

of us, who have this mindset of constant exploration will find it a value; those who do not, will not, marketing or no marketing.

The point is, marketing gets false blame; or, false credit. The irony is that marketers will, when charged, deny that they create a need. In their hearts, though, many believe that they do. After all, all that marketing planning, all that multi-million dollar ad budget, all those positioning games, they couldn't have been in vain. But in all likelihood what they believe is actually false, and that which they deny, knowing they are lying, is actually the truth. Marketing does not *create* a need, period.

Creating Consumer Value: The Supreme Purpose of Business

What is the purpose of marketing? For that matter, what is the basic purpose of business itself? To make money? "Wrong," says Harvard professor Theodore Leavitt, who explains this by an analogy: all humans have to breathe to survive, but breathing is not their *purpose*. Likewise, making money cannot be called the purpose of business.[9] The basic purpose has to relate to why society allows businesses to exist. It is, says Peter F. Drucker, one of the world's leading management gurus, "to create a satisfied customer."[10]

Marketing does not create a need. It creates a satisfied consumer. And in striving to do so, marketing serves a very important role for consumers, and for society. It creates products it hopes will satisfy the latent needs of some segment of consumers; or it commercializes inventions of inventors, adapting them to suit consumer needs and tastes. It brings, too, art, culture, aesthetics, design, and creativity to morph and sculpt a socio-cultural identity for the product—the so called *brand image*, one it hopes will resonate with the target consumer. However, creating that brand image in the marketer's own image will bring all that multi-million dollar effort and all that marketing prowess to naught (see the story of OK Soda in Chapter 7); creating it, instead and as it should, in the target consumer's image (backed by a product that can withstand the burdens imposed by that brand image, and live up to what the brand image promises) will bring admiration (and economic votes, i.e., dollars or Euros or Yen) of its target consumers. (As examples, see any of the brand ads in this book—they, each and every one of them, have been chosen with this criterion in mind). Marketers belabor as well deciding what price will make it a good value for the consumer and still bring the firm fair economic returns on investment. It brings the product to the consumer's doorsteps or to the Web portal on their cell phone screens. And it creates the physical, social, and cultural milieu that makes smooth the acquisition of the product and that invites, enables, and enhances the consumption experience. This is the art of marketing and doing it right is the profession of marketing. This is, in effect, the supreme mission of marketing.

How do you fulfill this mission? How do you create a satisfied customer? How else but by studying consumer needs, by analyzing how the consumer thinks, feels, and acts in the marketplace and how he or she connects products and specific bands to his or her needs. By seeing the "proverbial 'tattoo' that is already within the consumer," so to speak. That is why understanding consumer behavior is of paramount importance to the success of all organizations, commercial or social.

CONSUMER BEHAVIOR AS A FIELD OF STUDY

When we seek to understand consumer behavior, we seek to understand, basically, human behavior, albeit in the world of goods. As an applied field of study, it draws on all four fields of basic social sciences dedicated to the study of human behavior; namely, anthropology, sociology, economics, and psychology. You already know what these fields are, but here is a quick refresher:[11]

Anthropology is the study of humankind in its habitat. It examines humankind's historic development—how people came to live the way they do. It is a study of man in nature—how he survives and adapts and how a culture develops that helps him live and

Self-Parking Cars from Toyota

When it comes to parallel parking a car, even most expert drivers sometimes struggle with the chore, especially on cramped city streets. A fantasy wish runs through our minds: how nice it would be if these cars could park themselves. Well, our fantasy wish might be about to come true. All thanks to the innovative car designers at Toyota Motor Company.

Toyota engineers have invented an automatic car parking system the company calls *Intelligent Parking Assist*, now available on its Prius models in the UK. All you need do is bring the car next to a parking space and press a button on the dash. The car's rear mounted camera and a radar sensor senses and judges whether the space is adequate for the car and then guides the car toward the curb into the parking spot. The system has been available in Japan since 2003 and in the U.K. since 2005. It is soon coming to the U.S. Look for it on a road near you.

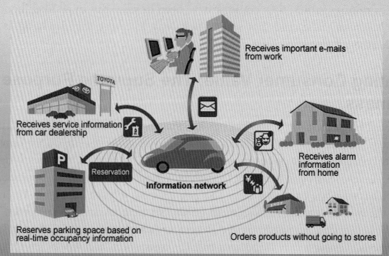

The Intelligent Parking Assist is but one component of a program at Toyota called *Mobility Tomorrow*—Providing mobility that is friendly to people, society, and the environment. One of its works in progress is a collision avoidance and injury reduction system. The roadside sensors mounted on the car will detect approaching vehicles, pedestrians, even a curbside or a roadblock, and warn the driver. In a second application, the system will provide information in real time about traffic conditions ahead and will suggest alternative routes. It will also update information on parking lot availability and make a reservation if desired. A network hookup will send notices for the car's scheduled maintenance, send automatic alerts about an accident or theft, make automatic payments at gas stations, transmit medical records to a preauthorized medical facility, and of course, download your favorite music. The goal of the Mobility Tomorrow program is to enhance your total usability experience. Marketing is a lot of things to a lot of people. But its core purpose is to make a consumer's life more satisfying.

To Keep Romancing the Consumer.

Source: Toyota Motors Corporation Web site.

---

adapt.

Sociology is the study of social systems—groups, organizations, and societies. It examines their structure and how individuals relate to one another in these social groups. It includes the study of social institutions, such as family, church, school, etc., and the part they play in society and in consumers' lives.

Economics is the study of goods—how they are produced, distributed, and consumed. As such it also deals with how societies and individuals allocate their resources on what to produce and what to buy. Economics helps us understand how we spend money, why we save it, and how to gain maximum utility from every transaction.

Psychology is the study of the human mind and mental processes that influence a person's behavior. Here we study how we develop perceptions, how we learn, how we form attitudes, and what motivations drive our behavior.

We apply all these fields in our study of consumers. In fact, as we cover various consumer behavior topics, we will constantly draw on related topics in these source disciplines, define entailed concepts, illustrate these for human behavior in general, and then progress to apply them to the behavior of humans as consumers. Thus, in studying how consumers perceive various marketing stimuli, for example, we will draw on the field of psychology to understand how humans perceive their environments in general, and then apply it to their perceptions of products, brands, and market messages. In seeking to understand how consumers are influenced by peer pressure, we will draw on sociology to understand how groups and reference groups influence us as humans in general, and then apply and extend that understanding to consumer responses to peer pressure in the marketplace. And so on.

Consider our shopper in the mall, Jackie (see the Interview). We find that Jackie has a world-view that is either perfectly normal or perfectly strange—depending on our own world-views. If our cultures and therefore our world-views are different from Jackie's, then we would find it a little strange that he thinks that people can look at his soul through his clothes. He also has a language (dialect, actually) that is not universal English—in his culture, "brotha" does not mean one born of the same parents. An appreciation of these traits in him requires us to draw on anthropology, the study of man and his culture. Of course, his prime goal in buying clothes is to make himself attractive. Here we see the invisible but very real influence of desired significant others on his choice of clothes. Sociology helps us understand which other groups might have influenced his choices as a consumer. And he is worried about not "maxing out" on his credit card, so no matter how much he likes clothes (and other things), he is going to watch his money and make sure he gets good value for it. These are considerations that economics helps us understand.

There are other mental processes going on in Jackie's mind that we will need to understand: how did Jackie come to associate Fubu and Sean John with the kind of image he wants for himself? How is it that he equates his clothes with his soul? And why is it that he claims not to pay attention to advertising and not be influenced by it, even though he declares this accomplishment by using advertising's own slogan, I "obey my own thirst"! Psychology helps us understand these processes of the consumer's mind. Anthropology, sociology, economics, and psychology—all blended into one—that is the study of consumer behavior.

WHO SHOULD STUDY CONSUMER BEHAVIOR?

There are four parties who should be interested in a study of consumer behavior and can benefit from understanding consumer behavior. They are (1) marketers, (2) social organizations, (3) public policy makers, and (d) consumers themselves.

Marketers **Marketers** are the people who connect a business (or organization) to consumers. They present the product and its message to consumers, hoping consumers will find it a source of satisfaction of their needs. And, equally important, they interpret consumer needs and preferences for the benefit of their own organizations so other departments in that firm can design and make products that will satisfy those consumer needs. To play this role effectively, all marketers need to understand consumer psychology and consumer behavior.

Social Organizations The study of consumer behavior is just as useful to organizations whose goal is not to make money but rather to promote public well-being. Indeed, everyone is a marketer. The political parties market candidates, and they should study voter preferences and views. The Red Cross and other agencies seeking volunteers and money are marketers offering "good feelings" in exchange, and they need to understand their

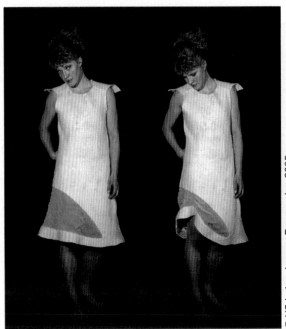

This is *Vilkas*, a kinetic dress. It has a mind of its own. The kinetic hemline rises (over a 30 second interval) about 2 inches to reveal the knee and upper thigh and then falls in a few minutes. And it does so autonomously—on its own. You cannot control it, except by manually pulling it down. States the company's official description: "This initiates a physical conversation between the wearer and the garment, as they fight over control of the body's real estate."
Research Director: Joanna Berzowska;
Model: Hanna Soder; Photos: Shermine Sawalha.

If this has caught your fancy, then it brings you value; otherwise, not. Go ahead, make it a conversation starter. Play your playful self! (Check it out at www.xslabs.net.)

If you think about it, life is about experiences. Products that enable, shape, embellish, and enrich those experiences become endearing to consumers, marketing or no marketing. LIfe as a human and as a consumer alike is an experiential journey. So is, as we wil tell you at the end of this chapter, reading about consumer behavior, especially in this book. Enjoy the journey.

Sending a hug.

The Hug Shirt
from cutecircuit
(used with permission)

donors' psychology. Arts organizations, educational institutions, social and human services agencies, and volunteer social campaign organizers such as Mothers Against Drunk Driving (MADD), all need to understand their consumers—donors, patrons, art aficionados, irresponsible consumers. Even religion is not beyond marketing; an understanding of consumer behavior can help religious organizations reach their goals and serve their clients better.

Public Policy Makers The third party with interest in consumer behavior is public policy makers. They are concerned, as they should be, with protecting the consumer both from marketers' potentially deceptive practices and from consumers' own irrational consumption behaviors. While it behooves marketers always to act in the consumer's interest, sometimes marketers are tempted to engage in opportunistic practices that compromise consumers' interests. To prevent this, lawmakers make laws and various agencies of the government enforce those laws, monitoring business practices. But in order for these agencies to know when a practice is harmful to consumers, it has to know how consumers interpret various marketing programs. For example, the Federal Trade Commission (FTC) recently sued QVC (a cable shopping network) for running infomercials for its dieting and slimming products for women, charging that the ads misled consumers.[12] For this charge to have legs, it would have to be based on an understanding of the psychology of perception and exactly what constitutes consumer deception.

Public policy makers are also concerned with protecting consumers from their own unhealthy behaviors. Thus, the government mandates warnings in all tobacco advertising, for example, but it must study if anyone heeds such warnings, and whether increasing the size of lettering (as it recently required) would help. Thus, a study of consumer behavior is an imperative also for public policy makers concerned with consumer protection.

Consumers Finally, a study of consumer behavior should be of interest (surprise!) to consumers themselves. We spend many of our waking hours and so much of our money contemplating and experiencing consumption (see the Consumer Diary), that under-

Original Sin

Original sin, original consumption.
Here Michael Godard celebrates the **original sin** with his signature olive and martini painting.
Viewing it, buying it, possessing it, displaying it, contemplating it, that is consumption as defined in the book.
(Courtesy: Michael Godard; www.michaelgodard.com)

standing what drives that behavior can be an interesting, even an eye-opening exercise. The good thing about this book and this subject as a field of study is that we can actually relate every topic to our own personal lives. By reading this book, you will understand your motives for buying or not buying something. You will learn the bases of your perceptions and misperceptions about products and brands. You will realize how our brains are imperfect computers but how they still process all product information reasonably well. You will understand, too, how you might be influenced by others and yet continue to believe that your marketplace choices are your own. And, you will recognize how, through consumption, you construct your own identity—connected with some groups but purposely distanced from others.

An Experiential Journey

But don't worry, this is *not* a "preachy" reading. We won't draw your attention to your splurges and shopping sprees, and we won't embarrass you for your stinginess or penny-wise, pound-foolish actions. The book's goal is to describe the consumer phenomenon, not to prescribe it. In fact, we don't really tell you anything about your own behavior at all. You see, when we say "you" will understand your motives, for example, we don't mean that in the book we tell you specifically what *your* motives are. How could we? Rather, what we do is this: we give a litany of possible consumer motives and tell you what sort of behaviors these motives cause and under what circumstances. And we do the same for other topics, such as perceptions, attitudes, and decision-making. Now, that is where the fun begins. You read a topic with all its "whats, hows, and whys" and then apply it to your own personal situation.

We give you a universal template with a collage of mirrors of different shapes and sizes, so to speak, and you find for yourself which mirror reflects you the best. That is where it becomes a learning experience. Or experiential learning. That is why it is a discovery expedition—about yourself and about the world of consumers. Welcome to the expedition!

Enjoying the hug she just received.

The Hug Shirt from cutecircuit (used with permission)

SUMMARY

We began this introductory chapter with a basic fact: we spend most of our waking hours as consumers. We are consumers 24/7! This is because we defined consumer behavior as not just the act of buying and consuming but also as all of the mental and physical activities we undertake when we contemplate and experience products—an ongoing process that begins much before we actually acquire and consume a product, and continues, in our memories, long afterwards.

Taking the viewpoint of consumers 24/7, we portrayed marketplace products as solutions to consumer needs and wants. We then defined *need* as a discomforting condition, whether physiological or psychological, and *want* as a desire for specific solutions to that condition. We next identified three essentials that frame all consumer behavior: exchange, resources, and value. Consumers' marketplace activities are basically an exchange with marketers, where consumers acquire products and part with their money. Money is one of the five resources consumers possess, the other four being time, knowledge, physical energy, and social capital. Sometimes consumers conserve money (i.e., pay less) by supplementing the payment with their time, effort, or skills. And many products are acquired with money so as to build up the other four resources. In all these exchanges, and regardless of whatever resources they invest and expend, what consumers seek first, foremost, and always is value.

We defined value as the set of net benefits consumers receive from an exchange. And we identified four broad categories of value: utilitarian, social, ego, and recreational (i.e., hedonic), captured in the acronym USER. All consumer needs can be grouped into this classification. We then raised a question, "Does marketing create consumer needs?" This charge, often levied against marketing, is based on the mistaken view of consumer needs, we argue. Marketing merely presents products and brings their benefits to consumers' attention, and consumers pick and choose what meets their needs. We point out that many products fail despite great marketing prowess, and the only products that succeed are those that satisfy consumers' needs.

Satisfying a consumer need is the very purpose of business. And in order to do just that, marketers must, we argue, study consumer behavior. The study of consumer behavior is built upon the core disciplines of anthropology, sociology, psychology, and economics. And besides marketers, social organizations and public policy agents too must study it. Lastly, consumers themselves should study it so they may understand their own consumer behavior. This book is directed at all "students" of consumer behavior—and who among us is not a student in the school of life? Our gain from reading the book is twofold—first, we reflect on and understand our own behavior as consumers; and second, we become knowledgeable about how, as marketers, we must fashion our marketing programs so as to appeal to consumers.

KEY TERMS

Anthropology
Consumer
Consumer Behavior
Economic
Ego/Identity Value
Exchange
Hedonic Value

Marketers
Mental activities
Need
Physical activities
Product
Psychology
Recreation Value

Resource
Social Capital
Social Value
Sociology
Utilitarian Value
Value
Want

YOUR TURN

REVIEW+Rewind

1. What is consumer behavior? Isn't it basically people buying products? Why or why not?
2. Who should study consumer behavior and why?
3. How are *needs* and *wants* defined here? Are these definitions different from how we use the words *need* and *wants* in everyday language? Which approach to defining these is better and why?
4. What are the five resources all consumers have?
5. What is the USER model of consumer value?

6. Briefly explain what aspects of consumer behavior are enlightened by various disciplines, such as economics, anthropology, sociology, etc.

THINK+Apply

1. Give an example from your own life in which you exchanged one resource for the other four.
2. Give an example of each exchange value you have sought in recent marketplace exchange.
3. Some accuse marketing of creating consumer needs, making us buy things we did not need. Do you agree

or disagree? Defend your answer.

A Must Do

4. Write a short memo to yourself, evangelizing how this book is going to benefit you personally in your role as (a) a consumer, and (b) a marketing professional (current or future).

PRACTICE✚Experience

1. Write a journal of your own consumer behavior of the past one week, Record one episode each for when you were an economic creature, a problem solver, a computer, a shopper, and (here comes your favorite part) a reveler.

2. Find four advertisements that offer, individually, each of the four values of the USER model, and explain your selections.

3. Interview a consumer (similar to the interview of Jackie in the chapter), and then identify the four values of the USER model in his or her consumer behavior. (Direct your topics so that the interview reveals all four values.)

4. Set up a dialog with a consumer to debate the twin-concepts of *needs* and *wants*. Start by asking what products he or she has bought recently and why. Lead into whether the consumer thinks he or she needed them and then whether he or she thinks marketers created this need. First listen so you understand his or her point of view, and then proceed to argue the point of view laid out in this chapter. Make a note of the consumer's reactions, and then comment on whether your arguments had any effect on his/her initial view.

An Extended Engagement Because this question is fundamental to consumer behavior and marketing, this exercise can become an extended engagement as you read the rest of the book.

Maybe the interview in Question 4 above has caught up with you, and you are now eager to "educate" everyone about this enlightened point of view. Over the next several months, carry on the same dialog with several consumers, and record your experience with their responses. Reflect on and describe why you were successful (in "educating" these consumers) in some cases and not in others. [Remember, for the first half of your conversation, and towards the closing, you are more of a listener, trying to understand the consumer's point of view from the consumer's perspective. If you do this successfully, you will have developed the important skills of listening and be ready to understand consumers firsthand on a variety of topics we will cover in this book.]

In the Marketing Manager's Shoes

Most concepts in the chapter have some lessons for the marketing manager; i.e., they suggest to the marketing manager what to do differently in practice. Indeed, often these applications are implicit in our explanations of the concepts and models in the chapter. Identify at least five specific applications of the chapter's concepts—all of which should be entirely new—different from the examples cited here.

(Photos: Author)

A Photo Quiz

A product can serve more than one need, as captured in the acronym USER. Which needs do the products in this picture serve for this consumer, Giles Hertz?

Discuss the role marketing might have played in Giles' acquisition and consumption experience of these products, especially in relation to the role of other factors or forces in Giles' life.

2002 Suzuki Intruder VS800; helmet by HJC Helmets; jacket by Joe Rockets (Ballistic Series); and cool shades from Serengeti.

Giles Hertz, an attorney, a profesor of entrepreneurship at a U.S. university, and a happy Suzuki Intruder rider.

Consumer Motivation, Emotion, And Involvement

The Fire That Lights Within

- Consumer Motivation—A Fundamental Inner Force
- Needs Vs. Wants
- Inside The Maslow's Hierarchy
- Unconscious Consumption Motives
- Love, Longing, And Lust—A Hundred Faces of Emotion
- Good Mood—Marketers Owe It To You
- Involvement—A Yard Stick For All Our Actions

I Want Nicole Kidman's Nose and Halle Berry's Cheeks!

Beverly Hills, California. The cosmetic surgery capital of the world.

Consumers there, as elsewhere, are increasingly choosing to place their faces under the knife. They want their noses chiseled a bit (or a lot), eyebrows curved a little more, and twin-chins united. They come into the clinics with wish lists. And with photographs of their favorite celebrities. They point out a part of the face in the photograph—that is how they want it for themselves.

Which celebrities have the hottest facial features? According to a recent report, the hottest, most in demand, were these: the eyes of Brad Pitt and Heather Graham; the jawlines of Cate Blanchett and Johnny Depp; the lips of Denise Richards and Benicio Del Toro; and the cheeks of Halle Berry and Dylan McDermott.[1]

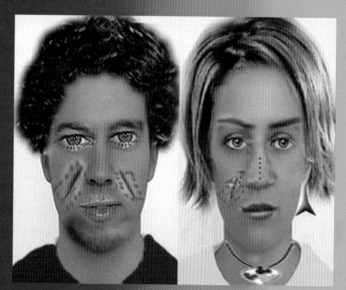

Faces Under The Knife—Pursuing Star Glamour

Julie L. is a 30-year old former NFL cheerleader who now works as a banking professional in North Hollywood. She got a nose job a few years ago; then another one. Still not satisfied, she is now planning a third one. "Especially in a town like Los Angeles, it's all about how you look," she explains.[2]

INTRODUCTION

Meet the new consumer. The consumer with a new face—literally. Achieving it was no cakewalk. This altered face was under the knife for more than four hours. The costs were upward of 10,000 dollars. There was considerable post-surgery pain. The face had to stay in hiding from the public for several weeks. And there was some risk that the face would suffer some permanent nerve damage. But appearance is very important to some consumers. It always has been. Only, until now, they couldn't do much about it. But now medical science has made it feasible. So those of us who can afford it can now have a better face. But more than money, we still need strong motivation.

Motivation is a powerful force in life. Without it, we would simply vegetate; with it, we can accomplish a lot. As consumers, too, we need motivation. It takes money and effort to acquire things—we must have the motivation to want something badly enough that we are willing to devote to it our time and part with our money. There are products we want, and just as surely, there are products we don't want. It all depends on whether or not those products stir our motivations.

---

1. Based in part on a report on ABCNews.com, "Looking like a celebrity: Plastic Surgery at the Frontlines of Glamour,: April 10, 2002; http://abcnews.go.com/Health/print?id=132633 (DoA: October 16, 2005).
2. Ibid. Name (Julie L.) disguised in the present narrative.

But just what is motivation? In this chapter, you are going to find out. We are going to define it, illuminate its true nature, and explain why it has such a strong grip on our lives. We are going to learn some theories of motivation and become familiar with a variety of motivations that instigate our consumption behavior. And, we will also meet two of motivation's siblings: emotions and involvement.

CONSUMER MOTIVATION

The Fundamental Inner Force

Motivation is what moves a person—it is the driving force for all human behavior.

Suppose I met you just yesterday and today I gave you as a gift a copy of a book called *A History of World in 6 Glasses,* by Tom Standage. You would wonder why. What was my motivation? Was it to express my instant liking for you? Or was it to earn an I-owe-you so I could later ask you for a favor? And then why this particular book, you would wonder. Was it to impress you with my elitist literary interests? What, in other words, were my reasons? Reasons for doing something: this is what motivation is. Whenever we want to know someone's motivation, we want to know his or her reasons for doing something.

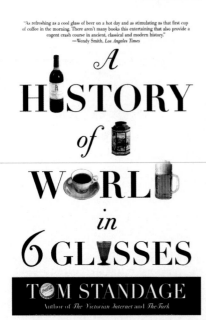

Describing motivation as a "reason for doing something" is fine as far as everyday usage of the term is concerned, but it doesn't tell us much about how we experience it. You might remember, for example, when you wanted to get a copy of *Dead or Alive 4* for Xbox 360 as soon as it was released (which was on December 21, 2005). You just felt driven to do it. "Felt driven"? That is right, motivation is actually a drive you feel; it is the surge of energy that impels you to do something. If you don't do it, or until you do it, you feel very uneasy; you feel a tension, a state of discomfort. This discomfort or tension is what produces the drive to do something. Thus, that drive you feel is a key ingredient in your motivation.

Motivation, then, also means the "drive to do something." That *something* is not random, of course. Rather, it is something that you know will reduce your discomfort. You are driven to attain it. In other words, it is your goal. The thing you want to attain is your "goal object." Goal object is, thus, the second ingredient of motivation.

We are now ready to define *motivation*. **Motivation** is the human drive to attain a goal object. Of course, we need to define drive and goal object also. A **drive** is a force or energy that impels us to act. And a **goal object** is something in the world the acquisition or attainment of which will bring us happiness—by reducing our current discomfort or tension.[3]

Discomfort occurs when you lack something you value—like that Beetle you want so badly. This discomfort is felt as tension, and to overcome it, you feel a certain energy, a desire to do something. Thus, a drive is like a spring, compressed by felt discomfort and therefore under tension and ready to release with force. The greater the pressure (i.e., the discomfort), the greater the released force (i.e., drive). Drive provides the energy to act; goal object provides the direction in which to channel that energy. A person with goal objects but without the drive is just a daydreamer; one with energy but no goal object is akin to a hyperactive child. When energy is expended to attain some goal object, we call that use of energy motivated or **purposive behavior.**[1] (See Figure 2.1.)

Remember, then, to be motivated, you should have both a drive and a goal object. If you don't want to be a daydreamer (like, "It would be so cool to have that Mini!"), then you must have the drive, too. And if you don't want to be an aimless hyperactive, let's-do-something kid in an adult body, then you need some specific goal to channel all that energy. Have both drive and goal, and you will have the motivation—an inner force that will help you achieve your goal—like finally getting that cool green Beetle.

What About Needs and Wants?

Motivation is goal-directed energy. A motivated behavior (i.e., purposive behavior) is goal-driven behavior. Then, what about needs? Isn't it true that our needs drive all of our behaviors? We need food, for example, so we do whatever is required to get food. In the definition of motivation, where does need fit? How are motivation and need related?

In Figure 2.1, notice that the tension or discomfort produces the drive. Thus, tension or discomfort is NOT motivation itself, but rather a precursor to motivation. That tension or discomfort is what *need* is. That is how we defined *need* in the last chapter (review it if you'd like). And, as we explained in the last chapter and as shown in Figure 2.1, that need (i.e., felt discomfort) comes from a felt gap between the current state and the desired state. A need, then, is an instigator of the drive component of motivation. If you don't feel any need, then you will not have any drive.

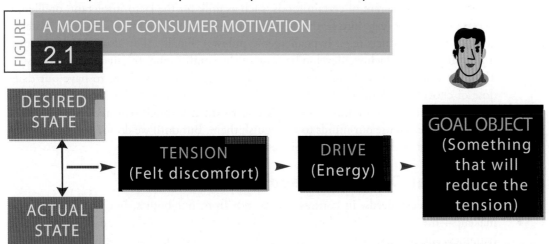

FIGURE 2.1 — A MODEL OF CONSUMER MOTIVATION

Suppose you got a C in a required course last semester. This is not the desired grade for you. You are very concerned about its impact on your grade point average (GPA); you are now feeling discomfort and tension. Consequently, you now feel a strong urge to make up for it this semester, i.e., you are feeling the drive. The goal object is the grade A in your Consumer Behavior course this semester. Thus, given the drive and given the goal object, you have the motivation to read this book closely. And listen to your instructor with rapt attention.

Sometimes, there is only one goal object that can reduce a particular tension. But often the world offers us a range of solutions. To relieve hunger pangs, for example, we must get some food, but what kind of food? The kind of food we feel will satisfy us best becomes our goal object. The desire for a particular goal object is, as defined in Chapter 1, a consumer *want*. Thus, needs and wants are closely related to motivation. Needs provide the drive and the goal object provides the want. Our needs and wants are what make us different consumers.

Well Then, Where Do Needs Come From?

Innate versus Learned Needs

Alright, if needs produce the drive and, in turn, motivation, then where do needs come from? Are we born with them, or do we acquire them? The answer is both. Scholars classify needs into two types: innate and learned. **Innate needs** are needs with which we are born. They are common to all humans, rooted in our survival instincts. Thus, a hungry stomach creates an innate need, and so does a body shivering with cold or burning with heat, exposed to the harsh weather outside. In contrast are **learned needs**, which are acquired in the process of growing up and living. So when you say you feel lonely, dejected, ridiculed, bored, or burned out, you were not born with these needs, and your survival does not depend on overcoming these conditions. Not remedying loneliness or boredom or ridicule or peer rejection would not place our survival in peril, but not remedying them does cause us considerable mental anguish. Respectively, these two types of needs are also called *biogenic* and *psychogenic* needs.

What Our Bodies Need

Biogenic needs are conditions of discomfort stemming from our biology as humans. All bodily discomforts are included in this category, but such needs also go beyond hunger, thirst, and exposure to rough weather. They include tiredness due to working or walking, illness, and loss of motor skills and sensory faculties due to aging (e.g., vision and hearing loss). They also include certain negative conditions pertaining to our bodies, many of which are based in our individual genes, such as oily or dry hair and bad breath. Or our bodies may be intolerant of certain foods, such as milk for the lacto-intolerant, or allergic to certain materials (e.g., bird feathers), which creates the need to find a substitute material and substitute products (e.g., hypoallergenic pillows). Finally, they also include cravings for certain foods, which we develop because of the conditioning of our bodies and tastes. Thus, for example, if we have a so-called "sweet tooth," then we have to have our daily dose of chocolate. Now, this last one is actually a learned need—thus, strictly speaking, not all biogenic needs are innate needs. We learn them through repeated use, and, with strong will, we can use our minds to extinguish them. But until we do so, the conditioned cravings of our bodies do qualify as biogenic needs.

And What Our Mind Needs

Psychogenic needs, in contrast, stem, not from our bodies, but from our mental makeup—the way we think about ourselves and about the world, from how we define happiness and success, to what we consider to be good and bad. Lack of things we consider essential to our happiness and success produces a state of discomfort in our minds and thus creates psychogenic needs. We all want to look cool, and if we come to believe that a Billabong brand of shirt will make us cool, then the discomfort of not having that shirt is a psychogenic need. If we come to believe that adorning our bodies with tattoos will get us the admiration and popularity we seek, then that is a psychogenic need as well.

Then what about a facelift?

Now think back to the facial surgeries we mentioned at the beginning of this chapter. What kind of need do they represent? The correct answer is "psychogenic." Just because what you gain—the goal object—pertains to your body, it is not a bodily or biogenic need. Rather, it is, for these consumers, a psychogenic need. This is because it is, basically, due to their psychological makeup, their way of thinking—both that they are unhappy with their looks and that they covet certain facial features. Just because, to satisfy a need, we do something to our bodies, this does not make it a biogenic need. The need is produced by our views of ourselves as psychological beings, not biological beings; therefore, the perceived need for a facelift is a psychogenic need.

Things We Seek and Things We Avoid

We have defined *motivation* as a goal-directed drive. But this does not mean that goal objects are always desirable. Some goal objects are the ones we want to avoid. The drive we feel to avoid a goal object is also motivation. Consumer psychologists therefore recognize two types of motivations: approach and avoidance.

Approach motivation is the desire to attain a goal object. Approach goal objects (i.e., objects that attract us) are sought or even longed for, such as a Mini Cooper or a new MP3 Player. Being deprived of them creates discomfort and unhappiness.

Avoidance motivation is the desire to protect oneself from an object, such as a bee sting or a stale or unhygienic burger. Technically, approach and avoidance motives are called, respectively, *appetitive* and *aversive*. Of course, one consumer's poison may be another's nectar. Vegetarians love tofu, but avoid meat; most non-vegetarians love meat, and they avoid tofu—some of them may not even know (happily) what it is.

We all want the "approach objects" and we all want to avoid the "avoid objects." Sometimes we are lucky and have to choose between two desirable options—say, out of two toys, we can only have one. That lucky situation is called **approach-approach conflict**. Of course, sometimes we also get totally unlucky and face two options equally undesirable. Got a speeding ticket? Well, you can pay a fine, or you can attend three hours of safe-driving classes (purposely designed, it seems, to bore you!). You are facing what is known as an **avoid-avoid conflict**.

The above two types of conflicts occur when we are faced with two separate options—two equally enjoyable TV shows at the same time, two equally charming dresses, two equally mouth-watering entrees. Or, if we are unlucky, then, two equally tasteless diet foods, two equally overpriced airline tickets, or two equally boring classes (not your CB class!). But there is a third type of conflict, called **approach-avoid conflict**—a conflict we experience when we find an object desirable as well as undesirable. This happens for products

Copy in the ad reads: If you're partial to style, you'll find it here. From sleek curves and contoured handles to the drama of high gloss finishes. After all, when it comes to refrigerators, style does matter.
If you're partial to intellect, you'll find it here. From quick thawing and chilling to the remarkable power of turbo-cooling. After all, when it comes to refrigerators, intellect does matter.
Helping consumers resolve the approach-approach conflict.
(Used with permission of General Electric Co..)

that have both desirable and undesirable features. Unfortunately, products often are a mixed blessing: a part of them is good, but a part of them is undesirable. For example, the taste and sensory pleasure in candies is desirable, but their fat and calorie content is not. Or, the thrill of driving an SUV is desirable, but its low safety rating is undesirable.

As a marketer, your greatest challenge is to minimize the negative aspects of your product while maximizing its desirable properties. Avoidance motives of consumers provide opportunities for marketers just as approach motives do. Blending two usually mutually exclusive attributes in a product (for instance, if we can be allowed to evoke a popular stereotype for the moment, beauty and brains) can bring an unusual value to consumers by banishing their approach-avoid conflict.

A Universal Dictionary of Motivations

Go to the Sharper Image Web site and look at the pictures of various objects. Which ones would you like to buy? Would you be interested in a Saxxy Synthesizer, an electric scooter, wireless boxing robots? A desktop arcade game or a Laser Baseball? If you are, then you have a motivation for each. What motivation is that? You could answer that it is a motivation for a Saxxy Synthesizer, a motivation for an electric scooter, or for a Laser Baseball, and so on. So then how many motivations are there? As many as there are products? If you are a typical consumer, you probably own thousands of things—does it mean you have thousands of motivations? And what can a marketer do with a list of, say, a thousand motivations?[4]

Goal Objects **Galore**

Photos courtesy Sharper Image (www.sharperimage.com)

We therefore need to find a more sensible way of counting and specifying consumer motivations—a way that goes to the core of *why* we need these thousands of products to begin with. There must be, in humans, a core set of needs that make up a short list—short enough to remember and utilize in real-world marketing. The good news is that there is. Psychologists have studied human motives for years and have grouped all of the human motives into a few categories. One of them is psychologist Abraham Maslow, who gave us a short list of five core motives. There are, of course, other lists, but this one has stood the test of time and has become a classic in marketing and consumer behavior. No marketer can ever claim to understand why people buy things without understanding Maslow's theory of human motivation. It is, in other words, "a universal dictionary of motivations"—translating thousands of consumer purchases into five simple need categories.

MASLOW'S HIERARCHY OF NEEDS

Humans Live for Bread and Then More!

The five need categories in Maslow's theory are:

1. Physiological needs
2. Safety and security needs
3. Belonging and love needs
4. Esteem and ego needs
5. Self-actualization needs[5]

Actually, Maslow did more than simply propose this list; he also suggested a pecking order among them—that is, what humans must have first before they seek something else. His theory is called **Maslow's hierarchy of needs**—the order in which humans experience needs. The hierarchy is shown in Figure 2.2 as a pyramid. According to Maslow, the needs at the bottom of the pyramid must be satisfied first; until they are, the higher-level needs remain dormant. But the moment the lower level of needs become satisfied, then, almost inevitably, the next level of needs come to life. Let us look inside this pyramid.

- **Physiological needs** At the bottom of the pyramid are **physiological needs**—i.e., our bodily needs (also called *biogenic needs*). These needs drive us all to seek food, clothing, and shelter. We must satisfy these needs before we worry about anything else. It is a no-brainer—if we are starving, then we must find food before we seek, say, *Halo2*. And we must find clothes before we seek a facelift.

Furthermore, many of the differences in what consumers use and buy are due to physiological (that is, biological) differences; i.e., differences attributble to genetics, race, gender, and age, or some ailments. Examples include soy milk for lactose-intolerant persons (genetics), vision-correcting glasses for weak eyes (due to age or genetics), and custom-made shoes for people with feet of unequal length. For all humans, such needs are paramount. And these must be satisfied before consumers will feel other needs.

FIGURE 2.2

MASLOW'S HIERARCHY OF NEEDS

• **Safety and Security Needs** Closely following physiological needs are **safety and security** needs—the need to be protected from danger. Personal safety is a motive as old as survival itself—early man developed arrows and spears to kill predatory animals that threatened his survival. In modern times, the new weapons are guns and mace, and their purchase and use are on the rise in major urban centers worldwide. Likewise, automobile safety has been a major concern for consumers. Marketers seem to have heard the consumer's voice; they are now placing a renewed emphasis on advanced safety features in new car models—e.g., side air bags and sensor-activated automatic steering correction for lane-straying drivers!

• **Belonging and Love** Next come social motives of **belonging and love**. We are all social creatures, and once our physiological and physical safety concerns are met, our social needs become active. We want to have friends and family, and we want to receive love and affection from others. Without love and affection, our lives feel empty. To satisfy this kind of need, consumers buy products that are well-regarded by others and the use of which will bring them peer approval, affection, and a sense of belonging. The kind of car you choose to drive, the designer logos on the clothes you wear, and whether you get a tattoo or a piercing on your body—each of these is determined, at least in part, by how you think your peers and significant others will look upon your choice. And many products, such as greeting cards, flowers, and other kinds of gifts, are bought specifically to promote relationships with others.

• **Ego and Esteem** Next in the hierarchy are **ego needs**—the need to feel good about ourselves and to have self-esteem. We all work hard to gain success in our individual spheres of activity and to acquire the qualities others consider desirable and virtuous so that we can win our own and others' esteem. We also buy products and services we believe support our self-image. We drive cars, for example, that, beyond impressing others, in our judgment, reflect who we are; we visit stores in which we are treated with respect; and we even buy and give gifts to ourselves because we feel we "deserve them."

• **Self-actualization** Finally, once these physiological, security, social, and esteem needs are satisfied, people begin to explore and extend the bounds of their potential—to become what they are capable of being. This is the need for **self-actualization**—the need to realize one's true potential. To quote Maslow, "musicians must make music, artists must paint, poets must write if they are to be ultimately at peace with themselves. What humans *can* be, they *must* be."[6]

To explain self-actualization, we can do no better than share with you a recent e-mail letter from an ex-student (see Exhibit 2.1). Now, before you ask for a marketing example, let us remind you that a university's efforts to recruit students for a master's program are just as much marketing as selling lemonade is.

Indeed, the self-actualization motive is what drives many adults to go back to school and acquire a new set of skills. And many marketers appeal to consumers' ambitions. (A recent ad from Monster.com poked fun at people who were content with their current mediocre jobs.) Many not-for-profit agencies appeal to the consumer's sense of being a good citizen. The U.S. Army's long-running slogan "Be All You Can Be" and, now, "The Army of One" are calls to a person's need for self-actualization.

In Eastern philosophy, many see their self-actualization as meeting their Creator, becoming what they are supposed to be in a cosmic sense. They spend endless hours meditating and reflecting on the nature of life and its purpose. And in Eastern and Western

---

From: Suzanne V. Buchanan {SMTP:SVBuchanan@yahoo.com}
To: Mittal@NKU.edu
Cc:

Subject: Letter of Recommendation Request
Sent: 1/2/04 1:33 PM   **Importance: Normal**

Friday, January 02, 2004

Dear Dr. ——— -:

I am writing this letter to request a letter of recommendation from you in pursuance of a graduate degree in Middle Eastern Studies, or International Relations with a concentration on the Middle East.

I was very happy with the quality of education I received at NKU and have used many of the skills acquired there in my career. I chose marketing as my first degree to secure a living, and because business comes naturally to me (it runs in the family). Always in my mind was a second degree, one that I would pursue because it fed some thing deeper in me. I started my career as a copywriter for a Greater Cincinnati advertising firm, then moved into recruiting adoptive and foster parents for Butler County, Ohio, and now work for a lobbying association in the greater Washington DC area. Each move was made to satiate my need to serve people in a greater capacity. DC offered more international exposure, the potential to contribute on a larger scale, and graduate schools with the international programs with languages I am interested in.

I am craving the intellectual stimulation, and am ready to move forward at any cost. While I've taken steps towards my direction, like joining the Middle East Institute, taking Farsi lessons for over a year… it's application time now. As you know, one of the three letters most schools require for graduate education should be from the undergraduate institution attended. You, Dr. Mittal, are one of the two professors at NKU who made a difference in my career path.

For me, marketing has become a means of bringing an organization's potential to light. I've evolved into a development specialist whose positions always revolve around strategy and writing… I want to stay in development, but I want to help a region, country, or city. I want to be one of the few who can really comprehend, communicate with, and bring greater understanding between the cultures of the West and Middle East. I have that capacity, and I'm ready to do whatever I can to contribute in this field. This type of international development requires strength, idealism, vision, determination, business acumen, and time; all of which I am willing to give.

I am asking you to be a part of building this future by writing a letter of recommendation for my graduate studies. Thank you for your t ime.
Sincerely,
Suzanne V. Buchanan

Printed with permission. (This story was included after considerable hesitation, hoping readers will accept it for its rare illustrative value. This is the only self-referencing story included in this book—actually, this and six others.)

EXHIBIT   **2.1**   Suzanne's Letter: Self-Actualization At Work

societies alike, religious messages such as "God is within you" are designed to appeal to a believer's need for self-actualization.

How the Hierarchy Works
The Storm Inside the Pyramid

If this pyramid were a five-story building, there would have to be an elevator that only goes upwards and only one floor at a time—or at least that is how the foregoing description of Maslow's hierarchy reads. But that description was for starters, designed to explain the basic pattern. We can now move beyond and look more closely at the hierarchy. Rather than being served by an upward-only elevator stopping at each floor, the pyramid's floors are served by an elevator that can take us to our desired floor nonstop and in either direction. This is to say that the hierarchy Maslow proposes is a broad-brush picture, not a view under a microscope. In fact, within this overall picture hide interesting details. Consumers sometimes jump steps or layers, moving from physiological to ego, or from belonging to self-actualization, and so on. Sometimes, they move back from an upper to a lower floor—such as from self-actualization to ego or love, or from love to the physiological need. How come? It is because a specific need is never satisfied permanently and terminally. We satisfy a need and move on to a higher-level need, but after some time, the old need arises again. Thus, we eat food and are no longer hungry, so we begin to work toward one of our ego needs. But, after about eight hours, we are hungry again, and we must turn our focus back to that physiological need.

Instead of a five-story building with floors connected by an elevator, perhaps a more apt analogy is a submarine in an ocean. The submarine moves relatively effortlessly between top and bottom layers of water, causing many cross currents. These cross currents occur because our needs at any one level of hierarchy recur. They occur, also, because we don't have to satisfy the needs of one level fully before moving on to the next level. Rather, we need to satisfy them only to a good degree. Thus, if we need a place to live, we can rent an apartment in whatever condition it is in and move in. Then we can attend to the task of studying for our classes. After the first test is done, we can attend to making the apartment more livable and buy the essential furniture we need.

The point of the hierarchy is that consumers have to feel at least some modicum of comfort at one level of their needs before they can become concerned about the next level of needs. You can't sell someone a necktie if he is feeling very thirsty. For many consumers, such as those below the poverty line, these needs may remain perpetually less-than-adequately met so that they (these consumers) may never consider upper-level needs. Thus, for perennially poor consumers of some third-world countries, marketers must concentrate on selling food grain and drinkable water and blankets before they can even think of selling them designer clothing and cell phones. At the same time, marketers must not underestimate the possibility of selling cell phones and designer clothing to consumers of the aspiring middle classes in these same countries.

Product Journey up the Pyramid
Or, Why a Chair Comes in So Many Shapes.

There is another fascinating fact about our motivation to acquire things as it relates to Maslow's hierarchy of needs. Consider the three chairs shown here.

What motivates a particular consumer to buy one rather than the other of these three chairs? Their basic function is the same: to satisfy our physiological need to be seated. And that need is well-satisfied by the Hand Chair, for

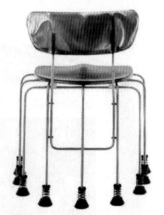

Chairs (from top):
Lips Chair
www.Sexyfurnishings.com

Hand Chair
www.Brightthrift.com

Broadway Chair
(Courtesy:
Bernini SPA)

example, which costs only $90. The other two chairs also satisfy that need; but, in addition, they might meet higher-level needs as well. The Lips Chair would probably appeal to a consumer who thinks that it might be an icebreaker and that friends might hang out at his or her place more often. It will meet, in other words, his or her need for belonging and love. What about the Broadway Chair: who is going to buy it—at $1460? Besides being rich, what else would motivate a person to buy something like this? Most likely, this person is an art connoisseur, or one who believes that others will hold him or her in high esteem, awed by his or her appreciation of the art and beauty of the chair. It will satisfy, in other words, his or her need for esteem.

Recall that we began this quest for coming up with a short list of motivations because counting them as "motives to acquire specific things" would have resulted in a long and unwieldy list of thousands. The short list in Maslow's hierarchy solved that problem. But there is also a bonus benefit. A product is no longer *tied* to a specific need; it can now meet more than one need. A chair must satisfy a physiological need, of course, but, in addition, it can satisfy the need for belonging or esteem needs as well. And this is where the real fun begins, for consumers and marketers alike. Consumers must decide how many and which needs they want a product to satisfy. And marketers must invent new versions of product classes so as to satisfy new combinations of consumers' needs.

A Piece of Maslow's Trivia

Now, we invite you to test your understanding of the five needs in Maslow's theory. Go find an advertisement that addresses each of the five needs, one ad for each need. And then, if you are up to it, go ahead and suggest, for each of the products featured in the ads, how you would modify the message so as to appeal to other needs in Maslow's theory.

Incidently, you might find the Maslow's hierarchy pyramid so cool that you will want to sport it on your clothes; our female mannequin on the cover does!

Consumer Karma

Flash Mobs — The Newest Public Display of Silliness

Flashmobbers
in a New York Shoe store
Courtesy Mike Epstein
satanslaundromat.com

On July 16, 2003, at exactly 7:18 p.m., about 200 strangers entered Otto Tootsi Plohound, a very expensive shoe store on Lafayette Street in Manhattan. They looked at shoes, used their cell phones to call someone, and then they all promptly left at 7:28, disbursing in their separate directions.

Earlier they had all gathered, following instructions received on a Web link, in three nearby bars; at the bars, someone then gave them written instructions (it is only then that they were told about the shoe store being their final staging area): if asked, they were to say they were "on a bus tour from Maryland." And they were to look excited but also bewildered, "as if the shoes were made in outer space."

Gatherings like these are called Flashmobs, linked through specific Internet sites. The term has now made it into the dictionary, where it is defined as "a public gathering of complete strangers, organized via the Internet or mobile phone, who perform a pointless act and then disperse."[1] It all started in Manhattan, and, since then, such "mob events" have occurred in many cities in the USA (e.g., San Francisco, Miami, Minneapolis) and around the world (e.g., Paris, St. Petersburg, and Sydney). Look out, one may be coming soon to your city!

1. Oxford English Dictionary, 2004.

Consumer Karma is Spontaneity and play.   My CB Book

Beyond Maslow—the Psychology of Flashmobs

A few years ago, *Flashmobs* suddenly became the latest craze among some cyber-consumers. (If you haven't heard about them yet, read all about it on Flashmob.com.) Would you ever join the mob? Why or why not? Why do hundreds of consumers join? Can you explain this behavior by using Maslow's scheme of needs?

Chances are, you could not. We could say, of course, that it is to satisfy their need for belonging. That is at best a partial explanation, for the crowds disburse after a mere ten minutes. The Flashmob.com site describes its purpose: *Breathing life and vibrance into the dull corners of modern life.* Perhaps there is something more, like a need for excitement, or a need to shock and surprise bystanders. The problem with Maslow's needs list is that it paints everything with a broad brush, and, as such, it does not pinpoint consumer motivation at this level of detail

There are a number of such consumer behaviors for which Maslow's list does not have a precise answer. Why, for example, do customers walk away when salespersons try hard to sell them something? Why do some people enjoy telling stories to others? Why do people become foster parents, and why do they give to charities? (Note that these, too, are consumer behaviors.) Why do they visit museums? And why do they end-up paying upward of one thousand dollars for a celebrity-worn pair of jeans? Maslow's list gives us answers in broad terms but not precisely. And, it is not designed to—after all how could as few as five motivations cover all the thousands of reasons for human behavior?

Fortunately, other psychologists have proposed more detailed lists. One list popular in marketing is that of psychologist Henry Murray. Murray proposed a list of 12 biogenic and 28 psychogenic needs. See a sampling of those needs in Table 2.1. Review that list and you will realize that Murray helps us define consumer needs at a level more detailed than did Maslow. With a list like this, you now can explain almost any consumer behavior. Looking at that list, what would you say is the motive behind flashmobs? Or such consumer behaviors as impulse buying, being a demanding customer, or playing an opinion leader?

TABLE 2.1 — A Sample of Murray's List of Psychological Needs with Consumer Examples

Need	Definition	Examples
Autonomy	To be independent and free to act according to impulse. be unattached, irresponsible. To defy convention.	Impulse buying; wearing unconventional clothing.
Dominance	To direct the behavior of others.	Aggressively demanding attention in service establishments.
Nuturance	To give sympathy, feed, help, and protect the needy.	Giving to humanitarian causes.
Exhibition	To make an impression. To excite, amaze, fascinate, entertain, shock, intrigue, amuse or entice others.	Wearing high - fashion clothing.
Cognizance	The need to explore, ask questions, to seek knowledge.	Visiting museums; learning about new technology.
Exposition	The need to give information and explain, interpret, lecture.	Playing opinon leaders.

Note. Our descriptions are intuitive, purported to serve Consumer Research needs. For original descriptions, see H.A. Muray. *Explorations in Personality* (New York: Oxford, 1998)

UNCONSCIOUS CONSUMPTION MOTIVES
The Bliss of Not Knowing What Makes Us Buy Things

Suppose we told you that Jane Infosino, one of our neighbors, buys a lot of kitchen appliances; that Mark O'Connor, one of our friends in Denver, Colorado, always wears shoes that are rather heavy; and that Angelica Yoshida, one of our coworkers, always wears white cotton dresses.[8] Why? What do we mean by "why"? Aren't their motivations obvious, you wonder? Jane most likely loves to cook; Mark perhaps does a lot of walking and likes to keep his feet warm in the cold weather of Denver; and Angelica feels that white cotton looks good on her.

These are all good reasons. And, most likely, these are actually the reasons these consumers, Jane, Mark, and Angelica, will give you. But Ernest Dichter disagrees. He believes that Jane Infosino's love of kitchen appliances arises from her desire to gain mastery over her environment; that Mark wears heavy boots to show off his masculinity; and that Angelica's penchant for white cotton is due to a sense of the moral purity she feels in the deep layers of her mind. "Who is Ernest Dichter," you ask, "And could there be anything weirder than these explanations?"

Ernest Dichter was a psychoanalyst trained in Vienna in the early part of the 20th century. A strong believer in Sigmund Freud's ideas about the subconscious in human psyche, he believed that unconscious motives play a significant role in people's consumption decisions. He believed that people suppress a lot of their motives because they are not appreciated by society or that some of these motives seem unwholesome to

TABLE 2.2 — Dichter's List of Subconscious Consumption Motives (A Sample)

Motive	Examples of Consumption Decisions
Mastery over environment	Kitchen appliances, power tools.
Status	Scotch; owning a car in third world economies.
Rewards	Candies, gifts to oneself.
Individuality	Gourmet foods; foreign cars; tattoos.
Social acceptance	Companionship: sharing tea drinking.
Love and affection	Giving children toys.
Security	Full drawer of neatly ironed shirts.
Masculinity	Toy guns; heavy shoes.
Femininity	Decorating (products with heavy tactile component).
Eroticism	Sweets (to lick); gloves (to be removed by women as a form of undressing).
Disalienation (a desire to feel connected)	Listening to and calling in talk shows.
Moral purity/cleanliness	White bread; bathing; cotton fabrics.
Magic-mystery	Belief in UFOs; religious rituals; crystals (having healing power); visiting Elvis Presley museum and buying related products.

Note. Constructed by author based on information in Jeffrey F. Durgee, "Interpreting Dichter's Interpretations: An Analysis of Consumption Symbolism in the Handbook of Consumer Motivations," in Hanne Hartvig-Larsen, David Glen Mick, and Christian Alstead, eds., *Marketing and Semiotics: Selected Papers from the Copenhagen Symposium*(Copenhagen, 1991). The original work by Dichter is documented in Ernest Dichter, *Handbook of Consumer Motivations* (New York: McGraw, 1964).

the motive holders themselves. So we suppress them from our consciousness. But, buried inside the deep layers of our minds, they still influence our behaviors, both in life and in the marketplace. We remain unaware of them, of course—that is why they are called "unconscious motives"—and being unaware serves us just fine. Ignorance here really *is* bliss.

Dichter conducted in-depth interviews with consumers for some 200-plus products. Based on these interviews, he identified a set of subconscious motives/needs that explain why individuals consume certain products. (See Table 2.2.)

Marketers have always looked at Dichter-like claims of unconscious motives with less-than-total belief. But peeping into consumers' unconscious motives has not been entirely fruitless. Consider the following story:

> Back in the Sixties, the Pillsbury Company came out with a new product: quick-baking cake mix. No more need to diligently measure and mix various ingredients; no more need to skillfully monitor the baking process; hours of labor in the kitchen simplified. Homemakers should rush to buy it, right? For some unknown reasons, they were not buying it. When the company researchers asked them why, their typical answer was, "The cake wouldn't taste good." Yet, in blind taste tests, they couldn't tell the difference. Obviously, they had some deep-seated motive against buying quick-baking cake mix, and they wouldn't tell it to us if we asked them directly. In-depth research revealed that the real reason was that this innovative product took away from women their opportunity to practice what they then considered the "art of cake baking."

If you are a total disbeliever in the existence of subconscious motives, ask any grandparents why they buy toys for their grandchildren. They will tell you, invariably, that it is because they love their grandchildren. They are not wrong, but often that is not the whole truth. Few if any will tell you that it is to also satisfy their own need to receive the love and affection of their grandchildren. Or ask people who call in to a radio talk show why they do it. "To express my opinion," will be the answer. Isn't it obvious? Yes, but the obvious answers can be deceptive. Probe deeper and you might discover that it is, at least for some of them, to mitigate their feelings of being alienated from society. The reasons people give may not be wrong. But sometimes they are only half-truths. The other half resides in their unconscious motives.

At any rate, the basic tenet of Dichter's method—digging for consumer motives below the surface—remains valid. In particular, many of the motives on Dichter's list are potentially plausible in particular cases, and a marketer can verify them by unstructured interviews and focus group discussions. For example, some segments of consumers of either gender might see heavy boots or factory-type clothing as masculine, and this can be verified. The industrial giant Caterpillar sells heavy earth-moving machinery, of course, but it also sells its line of shoes, clothing, and other accessories. Many consumers no doubt buy these products for their association with or love of Caterpillar Company, and many buy them for their solid construction and the attractive color motif (black and gold). But it would be worth discovering if some men and women who use these products see them as instruments of masculinity. Since many of these motives are thought to influence consumption decisions unconsciously, the list is most useful for incorporating symbolism into product advertising.

RESEARCHING CONSUMER MOTIVES

Raising Peek-a-boo to an Art Form

You must now be wondering, if many of consumers' motivations are unconscious, how marketers would ever find out about them. Actually, the same question also applies to conscious motives. For example, if you ask consumers why they bought the Lips chair or the Broadway Chair, no one would admit, even if aware of it, that they bought it to win friends or to gain esteem. We like to keep some of our motives private. It is simply not cool to reveal that we are seeking status or affection or love, for example. Thus, there are two reasons why we would not know, by direct questioning, what consumers' real motives for a given purchase might be. First, these motives might be unconscious, and second, consumers might want to keep them private. The question, then, is how to get consumers to reveal them. Fortunately, psychologists have devised a set of procedures to sort of "trick" the consumers' minds into revealing them, unwittingly. We call them "Playing Dr. Motivation."

PLAYING DR. MOTIVATION

UNCOVERING HIDDEN MOTIVES

Motivation Research (MR)

Motivation Research is research directed at discovering the reasons (i.e., motives) for a person's behavior—reasons the consumer is either unaware of or is unwilling to admit in direct questioning. It uses techniques that are disguised and non-structured. The techniques are disguised in that consumers are not able to figure out that you are trying to find out their deep motives. They are non-structured in that the answers are not pre-structured; rather, the consumer is encouraged to say whatever comes to mind.

The general characteristic of these techniques is that the respondent is given a fairly vague and open-ended stimulus and is then asked to interpret that stimulus. Since the stimulus is vague, interpreting it requires that the consumer "project" himself or herself into the stimulus situation. These techniques are therefore called *projection techniques*. From such self-projections from consumers, the researcher is able to infer each consumer's motives for a particular marketplace behavior. These techniques, described below, are all

---

EXHIBIT	2.2	Mason Haire's Projective Technique

MEET CLEVER MR. HAIRE

Since you liked our description of projective techniques, we can't help giving you yet another version—this one by a clever MIT psychologist. His method was so innovative that it has come to be known by his name, Mason Haire. Back in the Sixties, when Maxwell House Coffee introduced instant coffee, homemakers chose to not buy it. When asked, they gave the obvious reason: They did not like its taste. This perfectly innocent answer was not so innocent, for in product development research, consumers had indeed found the test product's taste comparable or better. Obviously, homemakers now had some other reason for not buying the new coffee, a reason they would rather not tell. So to uncover that deeper motive, the company hired our clever Dr. Mason. Here is how he did it.

He made two shopping lists with usual supermarket items, including coffee. The lists were identical except that one included Maxwell House Regular Coffee and the other included Maxwell House Instant Coffee. His research team then intercepted shoppers in supermarkets at random and showed them one or the other of the lists. Consumers were told that the list had been found in a shopping cart, and were asked to imagine and describe the kind of person the owner of the shopping list is.

The findings were revealing. The study respondents who had been shown the list containing regular coffee described the list owner as a very conscientious homemaker and a good

housewife. Those shown thought the list owner was a lazy homemaker and a bad wife!

What is remarkable in the findings of this study is that consumers had no hesitation in saying that the shoppers who used instant coffee were lazy, whereas they never would have admitted that the reason they themselves never bought instant coffee was because of their fear of being perceived as lazy. How did they know what kind of a person the list owner who used instant coffee was? Obviously, by projecting their own motives onto those other consumers!

Although the technique is some fifty years old, it is eminently usable for a variety of products in modern times. For example, suppose that you want to find out whether consumers think that the type of person who reads Time magazine is different from the one who reads Newsweek. Put together two identical collections of magazines except that one includes Time and the other includes Newsweek. Then, show one set to some consumers and the other set to others, and ask each consumer to "guess" the type of person the subscriber is. Or, the image of the users of Visa versus Master Card credit cards by a "lost wallet" procedure: Show consumers a wallet supposedly found on the street. Thus, whenever the purpose is to identify the personality associations people make for the user of a product, these associations can be unearthed by using the Mason Haire technique.

very simple, but they are amazingly effective. Read on.

Third-Person Question Phrasing

Instead of asking "Why don't you buy —— (say, quick baking cake mix)," the question can be phrased as "In your opinion, why do people not buy—?" Consumers would not be hesitant to answer this, and, of course, they are basically projecting their own motives onto other consumers. Their answers, on behalf of others, would reveal to us *their* own motives.

Word Association

Quick, say the word that comes to mind when we say the following words: Blue —— (write your answer in these and following blanks); Angel —-; surfer ——; Europe ——. Your answers might reveal that blue is cool, angel is good-hearted, surfer is sexy, and Europe is exotic. This is word association. For example, the words "instant-baking cake mix" might bring out such associations as "tasteless," "ordinary," "cheap," "lazy," and so on, revealing the reasons consumers might not buy it. Another group of respondents might respond with such words as "convenient," "quick," and "instant gratification," revealing why this group of consumers includes heavy users of instant-baking cake mix.

Sentence Completion

Sentence completion techniques are similar to word association. Here, the consumer is presented with an incomplete sentence and is asked to fill in the blank. For example, an incomplete sentence like, "I drink instant coffee only when I am ..." might elicit such responses as "in a hurry," "in the office," and so on; or, alternatively, such responses as "entertaining at home," or "relaxing." These two sets of responses will reveal two different sets of motives for consuming instant coffee, and, correspondingly, two vastly divergent perceptions about it.

Story Completion

The most common form of story completion is the **thematic apperception test** (TAT), which consists of a series of ambiguous pictures shown to the consumer. The consumer is asked to describe the story of which the picture is a part. To continue with the coffee example, a consumer might be shown someone preparing a cup of instant coffee and asked to describe "the story" surrounding this situation. Someone might say, "the consumer shown in the picture is an office secretary preparing coffee for a high-level executive meeting"; or, another's story might be that the person in the picture is a bored housewife, getting ready to watch daytime TV. These two stories illustrate two very different sets of perceptions, attitudes, and motives for or against the consumption of instant coffee. It is in this story-writing procedure that the "projection," as this set of techniques is called, plays out fully (since the stimulus is quite vague).

A variation of this technique is asking consumers to fill in a blurb in a cartoon, such as the one shown here, designed to find out the "real" reasons why some consumers build their own web pages.

Grocery List 'A'	Grocery List 'B'
- apples	- apples
- oranges	- oranges
- milk	- milk
- peanut butter	- peanut butter
- cookies	- cookies
- cereal	- cereal
- Maxwell House regular coffee	- Maxwell House instant coffee
- bread	- bread
- eggs	- eggs
- cheese	- cheese
- muffins	- muffins
- soup	- soup

DO OUR SHOPPING LISTS REVEAL WHO WE ARE?
(Consumers themselves believe they do.)

EXHIBIT **2.3** TWO SHOPPING LISTS

EXHIBIT 2.4 A Projective Technique to discover motivess

MOTIVATION, ABILITY, OPPORTUNITY: THE MAO MODEL OF ACTION

A lot of consumers have the motivation for a lot of things but end up never achieving many of their goals. Why? Let us consider the following situations. You are motivated to get A's in your courses. But you realize that at least in calculus you will not get an A because math is "just not your thing." Your friend Lisa is good at math, but she works full time and is the mother of a six-month-old, so she simply does not have the time to study. Your friend Immanuel is motivated to become fluent in French and is taking French classes, but he doesn't know anyone with whom he can practice. So, your actions and those of your friends toward achieving their goals are constrained. This reality of human striving is captured in what is called the MAO model. Marketing professors Deborah MacInnis, Christine Moorman, and Bernard Jaworski, who conceptualized the model and gave it the helpful acronym, argue that in order for a consumer to accomplish a goal successfully, three factors must simultaneously be present: motivation or drive to achieve the goal, personal ability to undertake the task required to achieve the goal, and an opportunity to engage in the behavior required to achieve the goal.[9] (See Figure 2.3.)

Much of our consumer behavior is facilitated by the simultaneous presence of the three MAO factors.[10] Thus, we are able to buy the Broadway Chair by Bernini SPA, for example, because we have the motivation (we really believe that buying it is a must for our personality), it is available in the country in which we live (opportunity), and we have got the dough (ability). A consumer who lives in Tavalu, however, may not be able to accomplish his or her goal of buying the chair because it may not be available in that country.

FIGURE 2.3

THE *MAO* MODEL OF CONSUMER GOAL ACHIEVEMENT

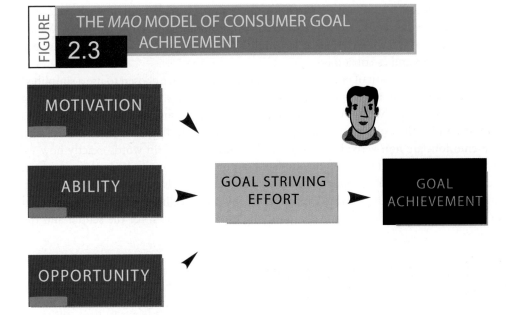

CONSUMER EMOTION

The Inset Copy reads
"Tenderness is a cup of friendship soup made from fun, dreams and laughter. Enjoy these tender moments. Because tomorrow you could wake up with food poisoning."

(www.Diesel.com)

As every teen and twenty-something knows (or at least the trendy or fashionable among them do), Diesel is the name on jeanswear from Europe that is "Oh, so cool." They like its denim, of course, but what they love even more is how the company whispers sweet nothings into their ears. Its advertising captures their world-view, echoes their sentiments, makes them chuckle, and, above all, tugs at their heartstrings. This is the art of emotional selling.

Motivation and emotion are closely related. Similar to needs, emotions are also capable of propelling the person toward relevant goal objects. As consumers, we desire certain goal objects (i.e. products), and, if we are deprived of them, we feel negative emotions. If we attain them, we feel positive emotions. Current negative emotions act as drive, and so do the expectations of positive emotions. Thus, positive emotions serve as approach motivations and negative emotions, as avoidance motivations. Much of the consumption or use of products and services is driven by and immersed in emotions. No wonder, then, that a wide range of products are sold through emotional campaigns, from "Diamonds Are Forever" (in a recent commercial, a young man screams at the top of his lungs, "I love this woman," in a public square before presenting her with an engagement ring) to McDonald's Happy Meal (with a campaign showing cute babies with ear to ear smiles).[11]

What Is Emotion?

As humans, we are creatures of emotion. Emotions lace our lives and guide our everyday actions. We cuddle a baby because we feel affection and love for the little creature. We swear at a rude driver who cuts in front of us because we feel anger and frustration. We feel anxious because we are not prepared for the exam. We are delighted when we ace it. We are ecstatic because Dad bought us the red Mini on our twenty-first birthday. We are overjoyed because someone we met at last night's party sent us flowers. Emotions are our lives—as humans and as consumers.

The technical definition of emotion is complicated, so we have chosen to use a simplified version. **Emotions** can be defined as a sudden surge of feelings. A sudden surge of feeling acts as a strong drive. We are driven to attain the source of that emotion. Gift giving is an apt example. The experience of gift-giving brings us rewarding emotions and feelings. Most emotions are non-verbalizable—we find it difficult to say in words exactly how we feel toward someone, though often our faces communicate our feelings. Just as often, we find it helpful to use products (given as gifts) as symbols of our sentiments. And, sometimes we use greeting cards to capture and convey our feelings. Finding the right card can be an immensely and emotionally gratifying experience, both for the sender and the recipient.[12]

LUST, LOVE, AND LONGING
A Hundred Faces of Emotion

Lust, love, longing. Greed, envy, jealousy. Hatred, contempt, disdain. Pleasure, happiness, joy. Boredom, sadness, depression. Pain, agony, torment. The emotions we experience as humans are numerous (just as our needs are). Once again, psychologists come to the rescue and offer us a manageable list. Psychologist Robert Plutchik has proposed that all human emotions can be summarized into eight types.[13] (See Figure 2.4) Each can vary in intensity as follows.

1. **Fear**—ranging from timidity to terror. A consumer might experience this if, when driving on the expressway, he or she discovers that the car's brakes are not working.
2. **Anger**—ranging from annoyance to rage. A consumer might become angry when a car rental agent says that the car the consumer reserved is not available.
3. **Joy**—ranging from serenity to ecstasy. A consumer might experience joy in an auto dealership when he or she spots a rare model he or she had been looking for.
4. **Sadness**—ranging from pensiveness to grief. A consumer may experience sadness when, calling an airline for a last-minute reservation, he or she is informed that the last seat was just sold.
5. **Acceptance**—ranging from tolerance to adoration. When a consumer goes to a hair salon and the stylist happens to be friendly and highly skilled, the consumer would experience acceptance.
6. **Disgust**—ranging from boredom to loathing. A consumer might feel disgust at finding an insect in his or her soup.
7. **Anticipation**—ranging from mindfulness to vigilance. This is the emotion a consumer experiences while awaiting the announcement of the winning lottery number.
8. **Surprise**—ranging from uncertainty to amazement. A consumer might feel surprise when his or her waiter announces that dessert will be on the house.

MEASURING EMOTIONS

Suppose you are a fragrance marketer and you are creating an advertisement for your brand of cologne. You want to evoke an emotional theme of romance. You create the ad and run the advertising campaign. How would you know the advertisement was successful in evoking the emotion of romance? It would be nice if you could measure the emotions your viewers feel when they see your advertisement, wouldn't it?

Once again, consumer researchers can help.[14] There are two ways, they suggest, of measuring emotions: verbal rating and picture matching. In the verbal rating method, you simply present the names of the eight emotions to consumers and then ask them to circle the emotions they think they experienced when they were watching the ad. (See Table 2.3.) Likewise, as a marketer, you can also measure the emotions consumers experience when using your product—say, a video game, a movie, or a brand of cologne.

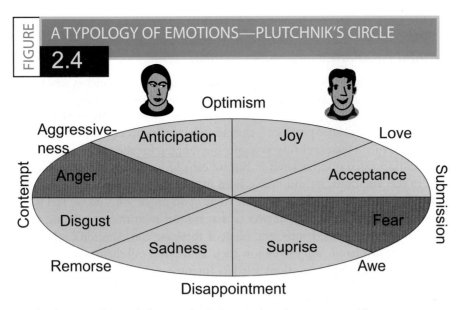

FIGURE	A TYPOLOGY OF EMOTIONS—PLUTCHIK'S CIRCLE
2.4	

This method is simple, and that is good. But it does have one problem: it assumes that consumers recognize their emotions under these labels or that they can verbalize their emotions. Can you verbalize all your emotions? For example, how do you feel when you sit in that Lips Chair we showed you before (flip back to the page if you like)?

You are finding it difficult to name those emotions precisely, are you not? This is normal. The fact is that most of our emotional communication is nonverbal, i.e., we can't put our feelings in words; instead, we show and communicate our emotions through gestures and facial expressions. So why shouldn't we use the same technique to measure emotions? Our second method does just that; it is called (what else?) the **picture matching method**. Ad agencies Foote, Cone, and Belding (FCB) and BBDO use it to test their ads. (They call it *visual image profiling*.) In this method, consumers who have just been shown a test advertisement are shown a set of faces with differing expressions and are asked to mark the face that comes closest to how they themselves felt when they viewed the ad.

This method is very useful for testing commercials. If an advertisement does not produce the desired emotion, you, as a marketer, must modify it until it delivers the desired emotional effect.

TABLE	Measurement of Plutchik's Eight Emotions
2.3	

Plutchik's emotions can be measured by rating the following triads of adjectives, ranging from the mild to the intense. Let's measure your emotions.

Q. How do you feel at the moment? (Please circle all words that apply.)

	Mild ⟵ Moderate ⟶ Intense		
FEAR	threatened	frightened	intimidated
ANGER	hostile	annoyed	irritated.
JOY	happy	cheerful	delighted
SADNESS	gloomy	sad	depressed.
ACCEPTANCE	helped	accepted	trusting
DISGUST	disgusted	offended	unpleasant.
ANTICIPATION	alert	attentive	curious
SUPRISE	puzzled	confused	startled.

Note: Emotions cannot be quantified; accordingly, unlike other measures, this measure does not have numerical values, and at any rate aggregating across the eight emotions would be meaningless. The scale assesses only the presence or absence of an emotion and its intensity.

Source: Adapted from William J. Havlena and Morris Holbrook, "The Varieties of Consumption Experience: Comparing Two Typologies of Emotion in Consumer Behavior," Journal of Consumer Research, 13(3), (December 1986), 394-404. © Journal of Consumer Research, University of Chicago Press.

Almost Emotional

"Moods subtly insinuate themselves in everyday life, influencing what we remember of the past, perceive in the present, and expect from the future."

—Morris Holbrook (2000)[15]

Emotions are quite an experience—they are what make up human life as we know it. The joy of receiving a diamond ring as a gift, the longing for the car of our dreams, the thrill of winning a video game at Level 3. But we can't be on an emotional high all the time. In fact, to feel emotions, we must have been in a state of "no emotion." Only then can we notice the change in our feelings. "But what," you might ask, "do we feel when we are in states of 'no emotion'?" The answer is that we feel such things as being relaxed, bored, tense, anxious, curious, happy, etc. Now, if these are not emotions, what are they? You know them first hand. You even know their name. You call them *moods*.

Moods are simply emotions felt less intensely. They are "almost emotions," if you will. They are also short-lived. They are easy to induce, and they appear and disappear in our consciousness frequently and readily. They are pervasive in that we are always in some kind of mood—a happy mood or a sad mood, an irritated or pleased, amused or bored, a pensive or a "brain-dead" mood. Moods affect our behavior of the moment in general and our responses to the marketing communications to which we might be exposed at the time.[16]

What Happens When You Are in the Mood

What happens when you are in the mood? That depends on whether or not you *know* that you are in the mood.

When You Don't Know You Are in the Mood

We are not always conscious of our moods. For quite some time now, you have been busy reading this chapter. You have been in a relaxed and pleasant and absorbed mood, but you were not saying to yourself, mentally, "I am in a relaxed, pleasant, and absorbed mood." Yet, this mood kept you reading. If you grew tired of reading, you may have perhaps stopped for a while, still without consciously recognizing that you were tired. If you were always aware of your mood, then your mind would not be able to focus on the work you were doing. Thus, moods are not only milder forms of emotions, but sometimes they can be so mild as to not even register on our consciousness (in contrast, we are always aware of our emotions).

In this case, our moods act like a *backdrop* in our consciousness. And, as backdrop, they affect the way we look at our lives and at what is happening now. They work in the background, almost autonomously. The effect of our moods is that we keep on doing whatever we are doing. Thus, if we are in a store and the ambiance and the piped-in music put us in a pleasant mood, we just linger on a bit longer. And buy more—which is very good for the marketer.

And, When You Know You Are in the Mood

Then there are times when we do become conscious of our moods. Whenever this happens, we also become aware of the source of our moods. When the music in the store just puts us in a pleasant mood without our awareness, for example, we may not even be conscious of the music being played; in contrast, if suddenly some tune or lyrics register on our consciousness, then we become aware of the mood and the source, and we, in fact, focus on that source. We pause to listen to the song or the tune. Thus, when we are aware of our moods, we want to approach or stay with its source if the mood is a positive one, and we want to distance ourselves from the source if the mood is negative.

Usually, we become conscious of the mood when the mood intensifies. This type of mood acts as an active driver; in other words, it acts as a motivational force. To illustrate, if the sight of candy or ice cream appeals to us—creates a positive mood—we want to buy and eat that candy or that ice cream. If a dress in the store enchants us, we want to buy that dress. If the smile of the salesperson is beguiling, we want to prolong our conversation.

In addition, the moods of which we become aware can also cause consumer behaviors that don't focus on the source of the mood. Instead, these behaviors may be targeted at other products or consumptions. We received good grades, so we want to buy a cappuccino. We got an email from an old heartthrob, so we want to grab a beer. You are bored reading your calculus book—not this book!—so you switch on your I-Pod.

How Moods Make You ...

Moods make us act in the marketplace, and basically these mood-based acts can be grouped into two categories:

Response to Market Stimuli Mood states have consequences in terms of favorable or unfavorable consumer responses to marketer efforts. Consumer researchers have found that consumers linger longer in positive-mood environments—as when good music is playing in a store, or when a salesperson is not shadowing them as they browse the merchandise. Another effect of mood is evident in how consumers look at advertisements. Consumers tend to recall better those ads that might have created a positive mood. And they feel more positive toward brands whose advertisements create feelings of warmth.[17] Overall, good moods make us respond positively to market stimuli; bad moods make us respond negatively.[18]

Situational Consumption Choices Our moods also affect our consumption experiences. One of the findings of research on this topic is that consumers in negative moods engage in "immediate self-gratification," such as rewarding themselves (eating desserts, drinking, self-gifting, etc.); of course, consumers also engage in these activities when in positive moods ("Dessert? Forget dieting, I deserve it"). Thus, both negative and positive moods (compared to neutral moods) produce self-gratification-oriented consumption. Another mood effect is that the consumption experience itself is more positive when we are in a good mood, and negative when we are in a bad mood. Have you ever wondered why food in a restaurant tastes better when we are with nice company? Nice company produces a nice mood—that is why!

CB *Factoid*

Speaking of motivation, and mood, there is a company that sells stuff to celebrate the state of demotivation. Aptly named Despair, Inc., it strives to boost(!) your despair by "inspirational" thoughts imprinted on mugs, and in posters, books, and videos. One of its posters reads: **Achievement**—*You can do anything you set your mind to when you have vision, determination, and an endless supply of expendable labor.* Another reads: **Adversity**—*That which does not kill me postpones the inevitable.* If the stuff doesn't boost your pessimism, you can call their *Customer Disservice*, whose motto is: *We're not satisfied until you're not satisfied.* Check it out at www. despair.com.

My **CB Book**

Good Mood—Marketers Owe It To You

If moods affect whether or not you buy something or respond positively to market stimuli, it behooves marketers to create the circumstances that create a positive mood in you. Moods are induced in two ways: (a) internal autistic thinking—this happens when you recall some past incident or fantasize about some event; and (b) exposure to external stimuli—you see candy and you feel in the candy eating mood. As a marketer, you can tap into both of these sources; you can arrange marketing stimuli to induce the right mood in the consumer. Here are some marketing stimuli at your command:

- The ambiance of the store
- The demeanor of the salesperson
- The sensory features of the product
- The tone and manner of the advertisement
- The content of the message
- The product packaging or the display of the product itself

What Maslow Missed

Maslow has done us a great service—by capturing all of our core motives. But he did miss one core type—pleasure, enjoyment, recreation, hedonism. Maslow's scheme could not answer such questions as "Why do consumers play solitaire?" or "Why do we go to music concerts?" And, "Why are Club Med and Norwegian Cruise lines doing a thriving business?" Pleasure and recreation are also natural human needs. Consumer researchers call them **hedonic motives**—the consumer need and desire to obtain pleasure. **Hedonic consumption** refers to the use of products/services for the sake of intrinsic enjoyment.[18] The idea of "intrinsic" means that the activity or consumption in itself is enjoyable, regardless of the outcome of the activity. Thus, the game itself is enjoyable regardless of who wins. Theater, music, vacation etc., are enjoyable while we are consuming them even though nothing concrete comes from them. Intrinsic enjoyment comes in one of the following forms.[19]

Michael Godard Captures Consumer Motive for *Hedonism*

Photo Courtesy: Michael Godard

(www.michaelgodard. com)

• **Sensory pleasure**—pleasant sensations of sight, sound, taste, touch, or smell. Examples include taking a bubble bath; luxuriating in a Jacuzzi or sauna; using perfume and colognes; looking at exciting colors in clothing; glancing at strobe lights in a discotheque; choosing home décor; listening to music.

• **Aesthetic pleasure**—reading poetry; visiting an art gallery; taking a course in Greek history.

• **Emotional experience**—watching movies or TV shows; sending gifts; receiving gifts; visiting relatives; long-distance social calling; dating; class reunions.

• **Fun and Play**—videogame arcade; playing sports; dancing; vacationing.

Some activities may be a source of more than one kind of hedonic pleasures.[20]

Do you remember your high school sweetheart? Do you remember the day you first approached her? Or he approached you? Or do you remember how badly you wanted to go to Ibiza on your last spring break? Do you remember that you would have given up almost anything to get a ticket to a U2 concert? Is there anything you yearn for now? The things that you might have yearned for in your life and the things you yearn for

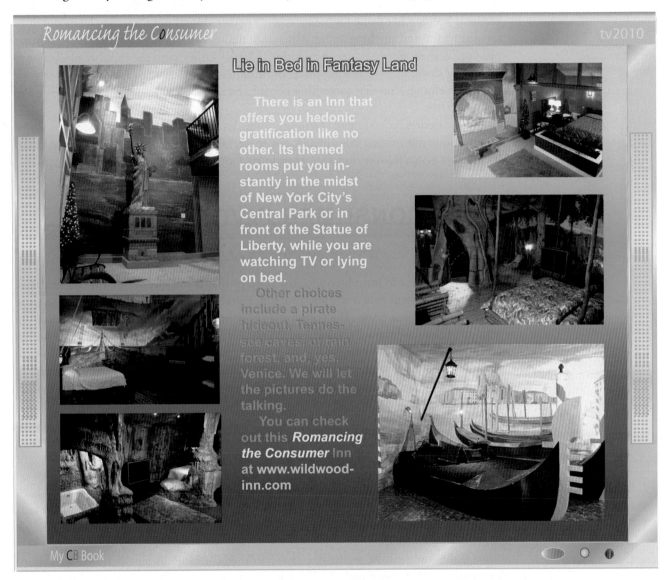

Romancing the Consumer   tv2010

Lie in Bed in Fantasy Land

There is an Inn that offers you hedonic gratification like no other. Its themed rooms put you instantly in the midst of New York City's Central Park or in front of the Statue of Liberty, while you are watching TV or lying on bed.

Other choices include a pirate hideout, Tennessee caves, or rain forest, and, yes, Venice. We will let the pictures do the talking.

You can check out this *Romancing the Consumer* Inn at www.wildwood-inn.com

My CB Book

now—these are called "objects of desire." Desire, you see, is more than a "want," and it is certainly more than a "need." Likewise, it is more than an emotion, and it is certainly more than a mood. It is a motivation, but it is a motivation of the most intense kind. It is an emotion involving a passion attached to an object—a product, a person, a cause, a life goal. Passion that entails fervent longing or yearning. It is a motivation so intense that it can become all-consuming.[21]

Desire works on the pleasure principle. We have desires because we seek pleasure. That is why some think of desire as sinful—as indulgence. Sometimes, we even feel guilty, giving in to our desires. And, desires can, in excess, lead to unhealthy compulsive consumption and obsession. That is the "dark side" of desire. And, if we yearn for something out of our reach, then, that, too, can lead to intense frustrations. Often, though, consumers satisfy desires for unreachable objects by fantasizing about them. **Fantasy consumption** is vicarious consumption; thus, consumers who desire the lifestyle of the "rich and famous" live that lifestyle vicariously by watching TV shows about these lifestyles. A dose of realism often mellows unreachable desires for most people, most of the time. If desires for unreachable goals persist, they can lead to psychotic behavior.

Desire plays a significant role in every human's life. When we desire something, it becomes our life's goal to acquire it, to reach it. Our desires give us goals to live for, to strive toward. Fulfillment of desires is also a source of positive emotion, of satisfaction. Desire is just another name for living; when a person desires nothing, then he or she stops looking forward to anything in life. Absence of desire is lack of hope. Materialistic cultures promote desires; ascetic values curb desires—actually, they curb the number of objects to desire. For desire to serve as a life-force, the number of objects is not relevant; only that we desire something. And that something needs to be reachable. "To desire is to hope; and to hope is to live."[22]

Some desires remain mere yearnings; some desires are fulfilled again and again. Some objects pique our interest continually. For these, we feel deep involvement. About "deep involvement" in a minute, but first let us learn about involvement itself.

CONSUMER INVOLVEMENT

A Yardstick for All of Our Actions

Now we want to introduce you to a concept that is so powerful that it colors all our actions as consumers. And it will absolutely, positively leave its mark on every other concept we will cover in this book. The concept is *involvement*, and it describes our relationship with all of the products we consume or do not consume and all of the activities in which we do or do not want to engage.

Involvement is a general term that can be defined as the degree of interest a consumer finds in a product or service or object or activity. At the most basic level, involvement stems from the *personal relevance* of an object or product or service to a consumer. Paul is not a hunter, so guns are not relevant to him, but he has a cat, so cat foods are relevant. In a very basic sense of involvement, then, Paul is not involved in guns but is involved in cat foods. Perceived relevance, then, identifies a consumer's involvement as a 'yes' or 'no'—involved or not involved—category.

Once we cross the relevance screener, involvement becomes a matter of degree—high or low, corresponding to the *degree* of interest a consumer feels in a product or object. Thus, both table salt and golf clubs are relevant to Paul, but he takes less interest in table salt than in golf clubs.

Of the hundreds of products and services we consume in our lifetimes, we cannot be equally excited about each one. Some we consume casually and take for granted. In these our involvement is low. Others we consume with some interest, pausing to savor their taste, smell their aroma, feel their texture, or hear their sound. Still others—a few in number—we consume with extreme interest. We like them; we enjoy them; we love them. Everyone has a favorite activity, a favorite product, a favorite brand. Some of us are fashion experts; others, car buffs; still others, computer jocks. We are eager to get to know these products—fashions, cars, and videogames—to find out everything there is to know. We get excited whenever the topic comes up. And, of course, we want to be shopping for or using them whenever possible. In these, we have high involvement; and, moreover, in these, we have *enduring* involvement. **Enduring involvement** is the degree of interest a consumer feels in a product or service on *an ongoing basis*.[23] The extreme form of enduring involvement is deep involvment. More on deep involvement in Chapter 18; for now, look at the Mini ad and enjoy the chuckle.

In contrast, there are products or activities in which we become interested only in specific situations, as when buying a product or when consuming something in the presence of an important client or friend. This form of involvement is called **situational involvement**—defined as the degree of interest in a specific situation or on a specific occasion. For example, you are unlikely to take much interest in dishwashers—you use them in your kitchen in a taken-for-granted manner. But the last time you were buying one, you became extremely interested (i.e., involved) in dishwashers—attempting to learn about them, deliberating over various options, and weighing them vis-à-vis your own needs. The involvement that arises at the time of purchase (as different from the consumption situation) has a specific name—**purchase decision involvement**—the degree of concern you experience in making the right choice. The other sub-form of situational involvement is consumption-situation involvement, such as consuming wine at home, unconcerned about the public image of the wine brand, versus consuming wine in company, concerned about the impressions you might make consuming a particular brand of wine. Actually, such anticipated special consumption situations invariably lead to purchase decision involvement.

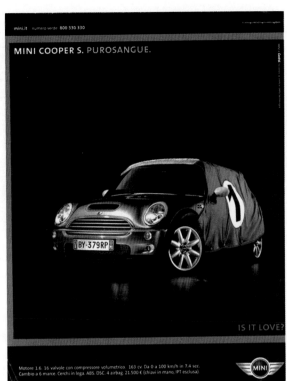

MINI COOPER S. PUROSANGUE.

IS IT LOVE?

(Photo Courtesy: BMW USA)

Deep Involvement in a Brand BMW here resonates the love many consumers feel for their Mini Cooper

The linkage between involvement and motivation should be self-evident. Involvement acts as a "master switch" that turns our motivation on or off. No involvement, no motivation. Low involvement, low motivation. High involvement, high motivation. Enduring involvement, perpetual motivation. Situational involvement: we are motivated when the right situation arises. As black and white as that! This concept, *involvement*, will keep us company throughout this book.

DEEP INVOLVEMENT

Extreme Interest in Things

One special case of enduring involvement is **deep involvement**—defined as a consumer's *extreme interest* in a product or activity on an ongoing basis. Often it borders on product fanaticism. One consumer in Sydney had the brand name 'Apple' tattooed on his forehead. We will have occasion to discuss this particular example further in a later chapter.

The phenomenon of deep involvement is important to study because it is a window on a consumer's key motivations and emotions. People are fanatic about things they deeply care about. They use them for enjoyment, to derive life satisfactions, and even to define their identity for themselves. What are you deeply involved in? Cars? Sports? Art? Gizmos? Cooking? Shoes? If you are, then you know how a significant part of your consumer behavior—contemplating, searching, browsing, buying, collecting, caring, nurturing, and relishing—is dedicated to the object of your deep involvement. You also know first hand, then, how your deep involvement is, for you, a constant source of motivation—perhaps even a reason to live!

You will find a measurement scale of involvement in the Appendix on Research. For now, we must conclude the chapter.

Well, we have completed our excursion. We must now also end this chapter. The fact is, though, that our journey into consumer motivations cannot ever be concluded. Again and again, in the book, we will speak of what motivates consumers. As you buy something tomorrow, or a year from now, you, too, should brood over what your motives were. And see if everything we said about motives holds true for you.

SUMMARY

In this chapter, we explored the three related topics of *motivation, emotion,* and *involvement. Motivation* is goal-directed drive or energy; such energy is provided by felt needs. Various scholars have classified various human needs, and we discussed some of the prominent classifications. Maslow's Hierarchy-of-Needs classification is perhaps the most well-known of these, but we also outlined Murray's social needs system and Dichter's list of subconscious needs (or motives).

Human emotions play a significant role in motivating human behavior. We explained Plutchik's emotional classification system, and, for each emotion in this classification, we identified and illustrated an instance of consumer behavior. We discussed moods as a milder and short-lived form of emotion and outlined some influences of mood on consumer behavior. One specific topic in our discussion of emotions and moods was *hedonic consumption.*

Finally, we discussed consumer involvement as a factor that separates the important from the trivial. It comes in two forms: situational and enduring (the extreme form of the latter is deep involvement). We learned how to measure these, and we understood that, as a master switch of motivation, involvement will color every topic in the rest of the book. How? We look forward to finding out.

KEY TERMS

Motivation
Drive
Goal Object
Purposive Behavior
Approach Motivation
Avoidance Motivation
Maslow's Hierarchy of Needs

Emotions
Primary Emotions
Moods
Hedonic Consumption
Deep Involvement
Involvement
Enduring Involvement
Situational Involvement

REVIEW+Rewind

1. Define and explain the concept of motivation.

2. Explain how the concept of need is related to motivation

3. Explain each need in Maslow's Hierarchy of Needs. Explain any five needs suggested in the Murray's list of needs.

4. List any five of Dichter's motives. How do they differ from Maslow's needs?

5. What is the difference between conscious and unconscious motives?

6. List all methods of researching consumer motives, and explain each briefly.

7. What are emotions, and how are they related to motivation?

8. What are moods and how do they differ from emotions? Give examples of two uses of moods that a marketer can employ.

9. What is involvement? What is the difference between situational and enduring involvement?

10. What is meant by hedonic consumption? List your own hedonic consumptions.

11. Briefly explain the needs for cognition, arousal, and attribution. Give one example of each.

12. Write down scales to measure consumers' (a) enduring and (b) purchase decision involvement.

THINK+Apply

1. Do Maslow's needs always arise in the order of the hierarchy? Explain.

2. Think of one example for each of the motives in Dichter's list, where a consumer's action could be motivated, at least in theory, and at least in part, by that particular motive.

3. With which of these products are you enduringly involved: (a) your car, (b) your MP3 player; (c) your cell phones; (d) any student or professional club; (e) your gym; (e) your brand of cologne; (f) your dishwasher and microwave oven. Explain your answer.

4. Describe a recent consumption (buying or using) activity that caused you to make attributions. List all the attributions that came to mind and then explain the one on which you settled. For this particular set of attributions, what could marketers do to avoid an attribution unfavorable to themselves?

PRACTICE+Experience

1. Find an ad on TV or in magazines that captures each of the needs in Maslow's Hierarchy.

2. Interview five consumers on their reasons for (choose one): (a) joining a health club or gym; (b) joining a sorority or a fraternity or another social club; (c) keeping a Web site or participating in discussion forums. Include a discussion of the sort of activities in which they participate and what sort of activities they enjoy (for a Web site it would relate to what sort of content they maintain on the Web site). List and comment on the possible motives different consumers may have for these activities.

3. Design and conduct a study using the Mason Haire techniques to understand why consumers might (a) download music even when they know it is illegal, and (b) regularly participate in Flash mob events (see www.Flashmob.com).

4. Interview two consumers who might have enduring involvement in some consumption. Document the kinds of activities they engage in to manifest their deep involvement, and understand what kinds of needs it satisfies for them.

5. Interview two consumers on their net surfing behavior —when, why, how often, which sites, and with what feelings, pleasures, and frustrations do they surf the net? Also what role does the Internet occupy in their leisure life (i.e., exclude Internet surfing for work and employer related purposes)? Then, identify and compare these two consumers' (a) motives, where possible, relating them to any of the motives covered in the chapter, and (b) emotions experienced during Web surfing.

In the Marketing Manager's Shoes

Put yourself in a marketing manager's shoes. Most concepts in the chapter have some lessons for the marketing manager; i.e., they suggest what to do differently in practice. Indeed, often these applications are implicit in our explanations of the concepts and models in the chapter. Identify at least five specific applications of the chapter's concepts, all of which should be entirely new— different from the examples cited here.

CONSUMER MOTIVATION, EMOTION, AND INVOLVEMENT

2

Arousal, Cognition, Attribution
Essential Tonics for Your Mind

We are almost done. Except that there are three special motives we need to tell you about. These are: to be engaged, to be informed, and to be a psychic. Their technical names: "need for arousal," "need for cognition," and "need for attribution." Our minds are hardwired for them, in a manner of speaking.

Eager to learn what these are? Well, you are already experiencing the "need for cognition." Cognition simply means thought, information, knowledge. **Need for cognition**— our discomfort with ignorance, our need for information, our need for understanding the world around us, and our need for knowledge are instinctual. Driven by this need, we read newspapers, watch CNN, and eavesdrop on gossip; and, of course, we want to know how much was the regular price of an item now on sale.

Our mind also has a need to be stimulated. Without stimulation, it experiences the discomfort we call "boredom." The **arousal seeking motive** is the drive to maintain our stimulation at an optimal level. This need drives our many consumer behaviors. Hanging out at the mall is just for starters—you can fill in the rest.

Finally, **attribution** is the process of assigning causes— i.e., figuring out why something happened. If your best friend brought you no gift on your birthday, your mind would not rest easy until you figured out why. In the store, the salesperson steers you away from your favorite brand. Keep your mind wondering, or put it to rest by attributing some reason to the salesperson. Attribution, cognition, and arousal keep the mind, respectively, out of wondering, out of ignorance, and into something engaging.

NEED FOR ATTRIBUTION
Why Ask Why?

"Why ask why?" This was a tag line in a beer ad a few years ago, coaxing consumers to choose the advertised brand— without asking why. We don't know how many consumers were driven to choose that brand because of the commercial. But one thing we do know. Viewers would not have stopped asking "why." No one can. We ask hundreds of questions in a single day, many just to ourselves. If someone we met last evening did not call, we ask "why"; if someone did not laugh at the joke we were telling, we wonder why; if our coworker does not compliment us on our new hairdo, we can't wait to find out why? Asking "why"—finding the reason for some event— is a universal human need. As humans we have the inherent motivation to assign cause to all events that we witness and all events that affect our life. The process of assigning causes is called "making attributions." **Attributions** are "inferences that people draw about the causes of events, others' behaviors, and their own behavior."[24] The motivation to assign causes is called **attribution motivation.**

How do we assign causes? Basically, we think up of all the possibilities, and then we accept the one that makes the most sense. If our listener did not laugh at our joke, perhaps she missed the punch line; or, perhaps, she thought the joke had a streak of racism. Our coworker did not compliment us on our hairdo, perhaps because she was just too preoccupied. Or she, in fact, did not like the hairdo and didn't want to say so. If the new friend we met last evening did not call, perhaps he was too busy; or too shy; or perhaps he lost the number; or maybe he is just not interested; or just delaying calling so he doesn't appear "too eager." On and on we go—digging deeper and deeper, like a scientist trying one experiment after another, until we find an explanation that we feel comfortable with.[25]

Attribution Affects Future Behavior That explanation, the specific *cause* we choose for attribution, influences our subsequent action. If the listener perceived our joke to be racist, perhaps we should apologize. If indeed our coworker did not like our hairdo, we should revisit the hair stylist and ask her to restore our previous, usual, hairdo.

Consumer Attribution Behavior This human motivation also shapes our behavior as consumers and our response to what marketers offer us. There are three specific situations where consumer attributions play a significant role: (a) a salesperson's recommendation for purchase; (b) an unsatisfactory product experience; and (c) a product offering that seems "too good to be true." Consider each in turn.

a) Salesperson Recommendation When a salesperson recommends a particular product, we wonder why. We might assume that the salesperson makes more commission on the model, and we may then not follow his or her advice. Alternatively, we might think that perhaps the salesperson genuinely believes the model to be superior. In that case, we would heed his or her advice.

b) Unsatisfactory Product Experience You have bought a used car from a dealer and in six months the transmission fails (the 90-day warranty expired three months ago). Would you buy a used car from that dealer again? That depends on the attribution you make. If you believe that the dealer knew about the defective transmission and did not tell you, then you would never buy from that dealer again. On the other hand, if you make the attribution that the dealer did not know, then, of course, you would consider buying from that dealer again.

c) An Incredible Product Offering When we find a product at a throwaway price, or if the marketer gives away something free, we wonder why. Suppose we find a silk shirt that usually retails for $40 now marked down to $10 in an upscale department store; we would ask why. Perhaps the store just got excess inventory and is trying to get rid of it; or perhaps, alternatively, savvy marketers of silk shirts have discovered that silk is going out of fashion. If we make the former attribution, we would buy that silk shirt; otherwise, we would not.

FIGURE 2.5 A MODEL OF CONSUMER ATTRIBUTIONS

PRODUCT/ SERVICE TRIAL EXPERIENCE → ATTRIBUTIONS → FUTURE BEHAVIOR

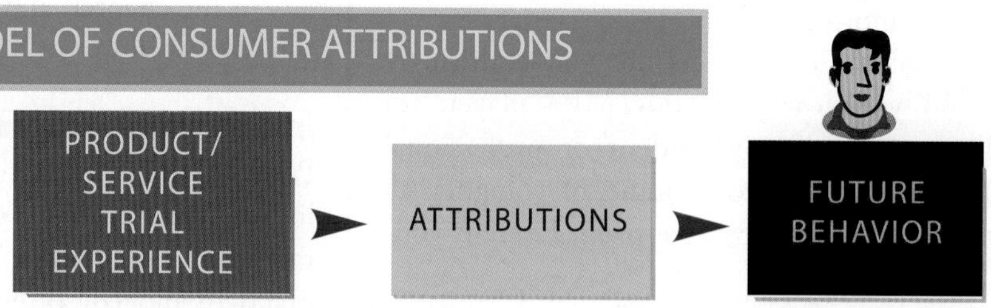

SELF-ACTUALIZATION—A NEW FACET
A Personal Journey

Self-actualization has, actually, two facets we will call Stage and Stream of Episodes. The view you read earlier in this chapter is the stage view—a person reaches the self-actualization stage when he or she conquers lower-level needs. Until we become what we really enjoy being, achieve what we believe is truly meaningful for us, we have not, according to the stage view, experienced self-actualization. In this stage view, self-actualization would have been, as Maslow puts it, "a kind of all-or-none pantheon into which some rare people enter at the age of 60.[1]

Stream of episodes (our term) is a facet Maslow espoused in his later work, *Toward a Psychology of Being*, as what appears to be an expanded (not replacement) view. In this view, we experience self-actualization as an episode, an event, a creative moment in which we feel a sense of personal accomplishment, self-worth, extreme joy. Maslow called these events "peak experiences," and he proposed that one's degree of self-actualization may be indexed by the frequency of such episodes in everyday life. Writes Maslow:

> We may define it as an episode, or a spurt in which the powers of the person come together in a particularly efficient and intensely enjoyable way, and in which he is more integrated and less split, more open for experience, more idiosyncratic, more perfectly expressive or spontaneous, or fully functioning, more creative, more humorous, more ego-transcending, more independent of his lower needs, etc. He becomes in these episodes more truly himself, more perfectly actualizing his potentialities, closer to the core of his Being, more fully human.
>
> …. Not only are these his happiest and most thrilling moments, but they are also moments of greatest maturity, individuation, fulfillment …
>
> Such states or episodes can, in theory, come at any time in life to any person. …. This makes self-actualization a matter of degree and of frequency rather than an all-or-none aff air.[2]

Note that the events of extreme enjoyment are not by themselves episodes of self-actualization. Thus, joys of videogame playing and watching a thriller movie, bungee jumping, reading a Harry Potter book or even a Jane Austen classic are not self-actualization. Nor does consumption that signals our self-concepts (e.g., wearing particular style of clothing or sporting a tattoo—even a tattoo that reflects our deeply-held values) make self-actualization episodes. Rather, self-actualization is a performance (not consumption) episode, in which we perform and create something, and, in creating that thing, we see our true worth, our true self, our individual talent and fulfillment. These creative acts do not have to be master performances or nonmaterial endeavors. Mundane productions count (e.g., cooking, repairing cars, designing a Website, writing a good research paper or a book, teaching a good class), as do material endeavors (e.g., managing a business, learning to play cricket, pumping iron). And of course nonmaterial endeavors count as well (e.g., being a good mom, being a good soldier, being a conscientious gate-keeper—allowing entry to the deserving). What matters is that you are creating something and that creating that thing constitutes for you the meaning of your life, and that you are constantly pursuing, in that domain, perfection. If cooking (or just making soup) is your passion, then you are experiencing a self-actualizing episode every time you cook the best dish you wanted to cook.

We said it is an episode of performance, not consumption. But that production does entail consumption, often if not always. Accordingly, it contains opportunities for marketers. We will leave you to ponder that.

Note also that your self-actualization doesn't have to be of any worth to others or to society. What matters is that it is fulfilling to you. Self-actualization is a deeply and exclusively personal journey. (Disagree? Write: Opinion@mycbbook.com.)

---

1. Abraham H. Maslow, *Toward a Psychology of Being*, 1998 3rd edition, Wiley, p.97.
2. Maslow, 1998, Ibid. 97-98.

Consumer Perceptions

*The only reality
that matters*

CHAPTER 3

PART II   INSIDE THE CONSUMER'S MIND

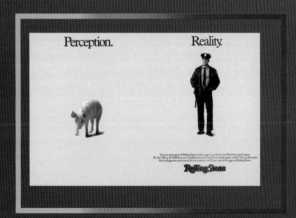

Perception.   Reality.

RollingStone

Do You See What You See?

To show what perception is, we present you a unique picture.

It's of a sculpture of a man dressed in a suit made with some material that has newspaper design printed on it. Next to the man sits a boy. The boy is a real person, who has managed to slide his neck into the space of the arc of the left hand of the sculpture. The boy is holding a newspaper, with the other end of the newspaper slid adroitly between the fingers of the sculpture's right hand. Together, they are reading the newspaper. The boy is obviously happy with this "photo-op."

Did we miss anything? Oh, Yes, the bench on which they are sitting is also wrapped in newspaper print. Now, how would you rate the sculptor—pretty talented, don't you think?

Or should we say,"the mime artist." The man in the newspaper-printed suit is, you see, a live person! Now, you know.

A Sculpture seen recently in Hawaii.
Photo: Courtesy Mike Epstein (www.satanslaundromat.com)

INTRODUCTION

The story of this picture vividly shows a revealing truth about the workings of the human mind: it has a way of seeing things that may or may not be reality. Perception is about how our minds see things. It does not matter what a marketer says a product is or will do. It doesn't even matter in reality what a product is. What matters is how consumers perceive it.

The year was 1985. (That, dear college senior, was just before you were born; so you missed out on all that fuss about a mere mortal soda. But, now, you can read all about it here.) In April of that year, the Coca Cola Company launched "New Coke"—a sweeter concoction than its old product, which the company chose to withdraw from the market completely.

The change was intended to take market share away from rival Pepsi. In blind taste tests, consumers had always rated Pepsi higher than Coke, and it was based on these research findings that the company's product development scientists had concocted a new formula. The result was the New Coke. Just to be sure, prior to the launch of the New Coke, the company had again conducted consumer taste tests, and, in these tests, consumers had consistently rated the new formula not only better than its old Coke but also better than Pepsi.

So it was with great expectations and fanfare that the company launched the new product. Within days, however, there was a groundswell of consumer protest. Whereas a lot of consumers were just angry with the company for taking away something they had been used to drinking for decades, many of them found that the New Coke just did not taste as good. When the blind taste tests were repeated, the results were the same as before but with a twist: consumers pointed to the drink that tasted better, but they thought they had selected the old Coke. When told that the drink they had picked was actually new Coke, they argued that they were probably confused or that the plastic cups must have made the drinks taste different. The fact was, they insisted, the old Coke definitely tasted better. And that is why they said they would not buy the new Coke.

Six weeks later, the company had to bring back the old Coke, under the name Coke Classic. And even two years later, the old Coke continued to outdo the new Coke in sales—about 8 to 1. Such is the power of perceptions. Of things big and small. In our lives as humans and as consumers.

Perception is fundamental to us as humans. It is also the first and inevitable response consumers experience every time they face the marketplace, a marketplace filled with an amazing array of alluring products, all crying out to be noticed, admired, and chosen. That fundamental response, perception, is the topic of this chapter.

We begin this chapter by defining perception, shaping your perception of the word perception itself, if you will. Here, we will introduce you to the 3S model, where each 'S' stands for what happens when you perceive something. If someone were to ask why you perceive something the way you do, you would likely answer, "Because that is the way that thing is." We will explain how that is only half true, and we will tell you about the factors that make up the other half and influence your perceptions. We will then unravel the mystery of perceptual distortion, accounting for biases that distort your perception of reality, everyday.

Since perception influences our way of looking at the world, it affects virtually every instance of consumer behavior in the marketplace. We bring this point home by highlighting the role of perceptions in five domains of consumer behavior: (i) the psychophysics of consumer price perceptions; (ii) country-of-origin effects; (iii) brand image and brand extensions; (iv) perceptual maps and positioning; and (v) sensory marketing. Some of these phrases perhaps sound technical at this time, but after reading the chapter, you will find this understanding of the five domains of consumer perceptions very helpful to you in your role as a (future) marketing manager. Besides, the last topic, and the one that serves as the grand finale to the chapter, sensory marketing, is also our treat to your senses—the visuals and prose we present should, well, delight your senses!

THE PERCEPTION PROCESS

Perception is a basic, fundamental, and inescapable process of the human mind. "Basic" in that anytime we encounter anything—absolutely anything whatsoever—our minds must first perceive it before they can do anything else with it. "'undamental" in that the perception we form of a thing plays a central role in whatever we do with that thing subsequently. "Inescapable" or inevitable in that we can't stop it and we can't control it. Just how do our minds do that? Let us define our terms first.

Perception is the process by which the human mind becomes aware of and interprets a stimulus. The process has three steps, which we call the 3S of perception (see Figure 3.1).

SENSATION

The perception process begins with **sensation**—an event wherein a stimulus comes within the reach of one or more of our five senses: seeing, hearing, smelling, touching, and tasting. A **stimulus** is any object or event in the external environment. When the sensory information from the stimulus reaches the senses, we sense the stimulus; i.e., our minds become aware of the object's presence.

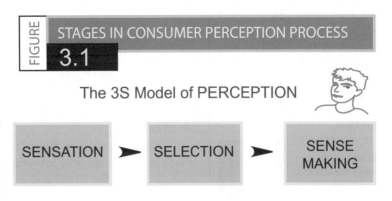

FIGURE 3.1 STAGES IN CONSUMER PERCEPTION PROCESS

The 3S Model of PERCEPTION

SENSATION ➤ SELECTION ➤ SENSE MAKING

Your radio is playing "Come away with me" by Norah Jones in the background as you are reading this book. You are aware of the lyrics (thus, you are sensing them), but suddenly you decide to turn the pages back and look at that newspaper sculpture again, and you get so engrossed in examining it minutely (noticing, for example, that the newspaper is in the Japanese language) that you don't notice when the song finishes and the new song now playing ("Satisfy You" by Puff Daddy) begins. In fact, there is even a commercial break between songs. But you have missed all of the commercials, entirely. You do not even sense them. Thus, for you these stimuli did not even cross the first step in the perception process.

SELECTION

Next, we can either decide to ignore the stimulus or, alternatively, select it to pay attention to its features. **Selection** basically entails paying attention, becoming ready to receive more information about the stimulus.

Now, at this moment, of course, you are paying attention, listening to that Puff Daddy song. Then comes another commercial break. You hear the commercial about some online dating service. You hear it but you are not listening—that is, you are aware of the commercial, but you are not paying attention, instead continuing to read this book. The next commercial from Sylvan Learning comes and goes by. The next commercial is about I-Pod. I-Pod! You suddenly stop reading this book and "focus your ear" to the radio. After all, you have been thinking of buying one. The next commercial is for the 911 Smart Energy Drink. You are into energy drinks, already, consuming about three or four a day, although you have never heard of 911 Smart Energy Drink. So you decide to pay attention to this as well. For you then, these two commercials (I-Pod and 911) have crossed the second step in the perception process.

SENSE-MAKING

The third and final step is **sense-making**—the art of making sense of the stimulus information. That is, we try to judge what the stimulus is and what it means to us. We attempt to interpret the information, be that in the commercial, on the package, from the salesperson, or from our own product trial experience. Most authors refer to this step as "interpretation." But the real nature of the process is sense-making. If we see an abstract painting (such as a cubist artwork by Picasso), we may not be able to interpret it, but as soon as we recognize that it is abstract art or that it is art by Picasso, we have made sense of it, and we say, "Okay," and then move on even if we have not really interpreted what the painting shows.

That I-Pod commercial you heard on the radio was perfectly clear. You understood that you can download the music from your computer and that it works with both Mac and Windows on a PC. You can store some 10,000 songs, enough to last a month's vacation.

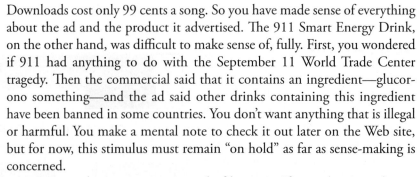

911 ENERGY DRINK

- 911 energy drink was formulated in Geneva, Switzerland by nutritional scientists.
- This energy drink has ±20kj more energy per unit than similar energy drinks.
- This product does not contain glucuronolactone, which is a controversial ingredient, claiming to give one heart pulpitations. Certain other energy drinks have been banned from numerous countries because of this ingredient.

Downloads cost only 99 cents a song. So you have made sense of everything about the ad and the product it advertised. The 911 Smart Energy Drink, on the other hand, was difficult to make sense of, fully. First, you wondered if 911 had anything to do with the September 11 World Trade Center tragedy. Then the commercial said that it contains an ingredient—glucor-ono something—and the ad said other drinks containing this ingredient have been banned in some countries. You don't want anything that is illegal or harmful. You make a mental note to check it out later on the Web site, but for now, this stimulus must remain "on hold" as far as sense-making is concerned.

Sense-making is an innate need of humans. If something puzzles us, if we can't make sense of something, then our minds keep struggling. If a product is sold for $1.00 and there is a rebate for $1.50, for example, it makes no sense to us, and we would not act on it. Our minds do not rest easy if we can't make sense of a movie plot, or if we can't understand the words of a song, or if we can't see the point of an advertisement. Note that these are not failures of interpretations, but failures in sense-making.

Sense making is the most important step in perception. To make sense, we draw on knowledge stored in our memories. Basically, sense-making means recognizing a stimulus as being similar to something already in our knowledge databases. It means placing the stimulus in some category—deciding what it is. We then "file it away" into an appropriate category along with other stimuli or objects already stored in our memories Thus, we see a new car model, look at its style, and put it in the category of family sedan or sports car, as the case maybe. We even stick a mental label on it—like 'stodgy', 'cool', etc.[2]

The Life of a Stimulus—
How It Makes Contact

Sensation, Selection, and *Sense-making* are processes that occur inside the consumer's mind. If you are an advertiser, how do you make this process happen? Writers on advertising describe the process as consisting of three steps: *Exposure, attention*, and *Interpretation*.

These latter three steps are mirror images of the three-step, 3S perception process (see Figure 3.2). For all practical purposes, the three steps can be treated interchangeably as sensation/exposure, selection/attention, and sense-making/interpretation. However, what marketers must manage is the three-step process of exposure, attention, and interpretation.

FIGURE **3.2** CONSUMER PERCEPTION PROCESS
from the Consumer's vs. Marketer's Perspectives

The 3S Model of PERCEPTION

From a Consumer's Perspective: SENSATION ▸ SELECTION ▸ SENSE MAKING

From a Marketer's Perspective: EXPOSURE ▸ ATTENTION ▸ INTERPRETA-TION

The EAI Model of PERCEPTION

©iStockphoto.com/ Angelina Vassileff

That is, marketers must ensure that consumers are exposed to their messages, that the messages hold the consumer's attention, and that the messages are crafted with clarity and contain the desired persuasive content.

EXPOSURE
The Face-off with the Consumer

Exposure means that a stimulus or message comes within the consumer's sensory reach. Exposure determines whether a stimulus even has the opportunity to be sensed by the consumer. If you advertise I-Pod on a country music station, and your target consumers—mostly teenagers— don't listen to country music stations, then the commercial will not gain exposure with your target audience. If you advertise energy drinks in *Vogue* or *Vanity Fair*, for example, then again you would most likely miss your target audience. Thus, proper choice of message delivery media is the most crucial and first step—a wrong choice can cause the first step itself to fail—no face-off with the consumer occurs, and, consequently, no perception is created. Where should the energy drinks be advertised, then? We will let you figure that out.

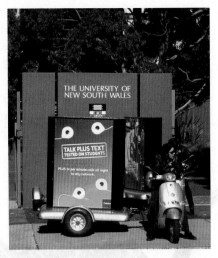

A brand seeking exposure at UNSW, Australia (Spring 2004)

Product Placement
Advertising in Disguise

In the introductory episode of the immensely successful 2004 American television show, *The Apprentice*, which starred real estate business tycoon Donald Trump, a jet was used to transport cast members. The jet was the Marquis Jet, and the Marquis name and logo were vividly visible from the ground. It cost the company nothing except the cost of renting an airport hanger in New York. Within three days after the show aired, the company received hundreds of calls, many from prospective customers. That is the power of exposure. This strategy of embedding a product within media program content is called *product placement*. **Product placement** achieves exposure with the audience because consumers are watching the program by choice.

Consumers often avoid the commercials, sometimes by attending to other tasks and sometimes by switching channels, a process called **zapping**. And when consumers watch prerecorded programs, they fast-forward through the commercials, a process called **zipping**. Now there are devices such as Tivo that automatically record up to three days of programming on all channels, and while playing these back, they automatically skip the commercials! Product placement is the answer to these commercial-avoidance habits of consumers.

Product placement, if done adroitly, works wonders. In the James Bond films, Jaguar XKR is featured; and in the American film that spoofs James Bond, *Austin Powers*, actor Mike Myers endorses Shaguar (Jaguar). In the year 2002, when Austin Powers was playing in theaters, sales of Jaguar rose sharply in America.[1]

An Artist's Rendering (Not claimed to truthfully represent the car used in the motion film)

Breaking Through the Noise

Choosing the right advertising medium can give your product exposure to the consumer. But getting exposure does not mean you will also get the consumer's attention. Or even sensation. For example, if you are in a classroom, all the other students have exposure to you, and you have exposure to them, but this doesn't imply you will have sensed each one of them. At the end of the class period, you will walk out without even having noticed some of them. Exposure yes, sensation no, and attention, definitely not.

Now let us take a marketing example. Suppose you are selling Sweetface brand of clothing, and you launched it with an ad in the February 2007 issue of, say, *Elle*. Lisa, your typical target consumer for this product, is flipping through this magazine. She comes to the page that features your ad, but she flips past it too; she did not notice that it was an ad for a new line of clothing by Jennifer Lopez. It failed to get Lisa's attention. Again, exposure yes, sensation no, and attention, definitely not.

Attention can be defined as allocation of mental processing capacity. When attention is given, the mind focuses on a stimulus, ready and willing to process further information from that stimulus. Getting attention is a major concern for marketers because most consumers face a flood of stimuli. A typical consumer faces more than 3,000 marketplace stimuli in a week.[2] Marketers strive to break through this clutter with stimulus novelty—notice how Coke and Pepsi vending machine displays have changed in recent years.

For a stimulus even to be noticed, it has to make its presence felt to one of our five senses. Thus, it should somehow "catch" our eye, ear, or nose, or leave a taste on our tongue, or feel different on our skin (touch). On one or more of these five sensory characteristics, it should stand apart from the surrounding environment. That is, it should be vivid. **Vividness** refers to a stimulus' brightness and distinctness. Vivid stimuli register themselves on our senses without fail. Vivid sensory characteristics include bright colors, loud noises, strong aromas, strong tastes, or very rough or very silky textures. The key element required for producing the vividness effect is **contrast**—a stimulus' distinct difference from its environment or background. Contrast, along with other strong characteristics, tends to register more intensely on the sensory registers, and accordingly it tends to attract more attention (and thus is perceived more) than do weak sensory characteristics.

Sorry, you missed Lisa' attention for the Sweetface ad. But Lisa did stop to notice when she came to a page featuring Fleuvog shoes. Do you know why? Vividness. The colors (black body frame behind a red shoe) and image are so stunning that they can't be missed even by the peripheral vision of a reader cursorily browsing the magazine. Lisa made a mental note to check it out later. You too can get to know it at Fluevog.com.

Attention
By Choice

Actually, attention comes in two forms: *voluntary* and *involuntary*. **Voluntary attention** is attention given by choice—the consumer chooses to pay attention. **Involuntary attention** is forced on the consumer.[3] It is an intrusion. Now, it is the case that, initially, all advertising must catch involuntary attention; i.e., the attention the advertising catches is of the involuntary sort, at least initially. This is because the consumer seldom proactively seeks an advertisement. Lisa was just turning the pages of Elle; she was not looking for shoes. The Fluevog ad had to intrude upon her attention. It did so by being vivid.

Intrusion is the reason why most consumers find advertising annoying. After all, it interrupts their program viewing. By getting involuntary attention, advertising acts essentially as an uninvited guest. Of course, uninvited does not necessarily mean unwelcome; like a surprise guest to a party who turns out to be likeable, it can become a welcome intrusion. For this to happen, the ad should be relevant to the consumer interest. That is why it is very important that marketers choose their media carefully. Filling print pages and the airwaves with ads that reach non-target consumers will not only waste your media budget, but it will also annoy more of the public.

If consumers find an ad to be relevant, then they will pay voluntary attention. That initially involuntary attention turns into voluntary attention. Because voluntary attention is based on consumer interest, it is also called "high involvement attention." Conversely, involuntary attention is "low involvement attention." Lisa of course decided to pay the Fluevog ad voluntary attention. Consequently, she noticed, to her delight, that inscribed within the body frame is the phrase "Listen to Me!"

The objective of all advertising is, or should be, of course, to elicit high consumer involvement—at least high enough for the consumer to attend to the message. Advertisers seek to accomplish this through meaningful message designs and creative, engaging execution. If consumers decide to devote voluntary attention, then they have "selected" your ad for further intake. Thus, by intruding, you can get involuntary attention and, consequently, consumer sensation for your stimulus, but it still requires consumers' voluntary attention for your stimulus (i.e., message) to advance to the stage called selection.

Surviving in the Attention Economy

All advertising (all marketing stimuli, for that matter) must necessarily first get involuntary attention. But with our lives so over-cluttered with stuff to do and with so many stimuli from so many directions vying for our attention, consumer attention these days has become a scarce commodity. Some have called the present times *the attention economy.*

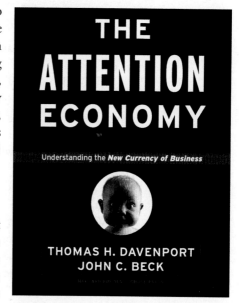

Reprinted by permission of the HBS Press. Jacket design by Mike Fender.
Jacket photo by Andrew Olney/Stone

To survive in this attention-scarce economy, marketers must constantly reinvent new ways to gain exposure and attention. Commercial speech now shows up in strange places—on floor mats in fitness gyms, on TV screens in Wal-Mart, on mini video screens mounted on shopping carts, as place-based ads on cell phone screens, and yes, on the walls of public restrooms—this last one is not a bad idea: it displaces graffiti, and it gets a captive audience. (Of course, it would not be appropriate for all products.) Beyond the ever-expanding media presence, clever message execution also influences consumer attention. Perhaps the cleverest current example of "no fail attention getter" advertising is from Zelnorm®—yes, those exposed tummies used as billboards for marker pen-inscribed words like "Abdominal Pain," "Bloating," and whatever else those tummies might be suffering from.

This particular execution for Zelnorm® has a rare quality worth emulating that all students and practitioners of advertising must note: Anyone can get attention (by doing totally outrageous things, for example—remember the Paris Hilton Car Wash for the Carl's Jr. burger chain?). The creative challenge is to get attention in a manner so that the attention "prop" is also the message.

INTERPRETATION
The Curse of Extreme Creativity

A recent ad from Budweiser depicted some idle young men who phoned each other simply to ask and reply with a one-word slang contraction, "Wasssup." In a later version, one of these young men is sitting at a bar when a more mature customer walks in. The young man habitually asks, "Wasssup?" and the older gentleman unloads his full story. Now, the older man did understand the meaning of the slang, but he didn't know that it was not meant to be taken literally.

Among the viewers too, many older consumers might miss the point of the "wasssup" ad series. And certainly, consumers in foreign

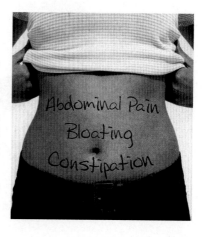

cultures would be at a loss. This exemplifies, simply, a consumer's inability to interpret the ad. In order to make the ad interpretable, an ad creator must understand both the vernacular (slang language) of the target audience as well as its culture.

FACTORS THAT SHAPE PERCEPTION

Or Are Things The Way We See Them?

Now that we know what perception consists of, let us see why we perceive reality the way we do.

If we ask you why you see something the way you say it is, you would most likely answer, "Because that is the way it is." But is it? Sometimes, you would be right, but sometimes not. Try this fun game: the next time you are in a supermarket, facing an aisle full of cereal boxes, try to identify five cereals that you suspect to be relatively healthy, and, likewise, five that you will suspect to be relatively unhealthy. Then read the labels. See for yourself if your initial "suspicions" came true. Or, even if they did, broadly, was the gap between the healthy and unhealthy set in fact as wide as your initial suspicions might have led you to infer?

We have done this exercise with several groups of students, comparing two packages of cereals, Morning Traditions and Cap'n Crunch. Just so we don't spoil your fun of discovering it for yourself, suffice to say that some of us now don't feel as guilty enjoying what we had long abandoned as a juvenile cereal—the delicious "Cap'n."

Now, about your "false" perceptions of those cereal packages: don't blame yourself for those misperceptions. Not entirely anyway. The fact is that there are three factors responsible for all our perceptions.

1. Stimulus characteristics—the properties of the stimulus itself
2. Context—the setting in which the stimulus is encountered
3. Consumer characteristics—consumers' own knowledge, interests, and experiences.

1. STIMULUS CHARACTERISTICS
A Thing Is What It Is

Some of the blame for our misperceptions and credit for correct perceptions should go to the object or stimulus itself. After all, the mind's goal is to capture the "reality" of the stimulus. So, when we perceive something, we can't perceive it to be considerably different

FIGURE **3.3** THREE FACTORS THAT AFFECT PERCEPTION

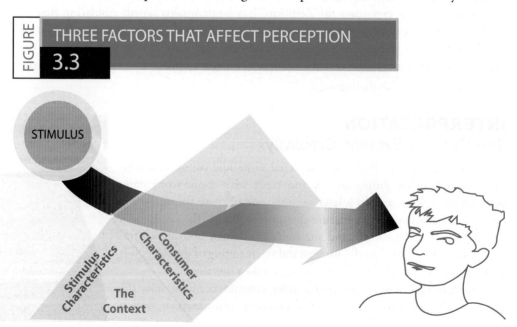

STIMULUS

Stimulus Characteristics

Consumer Characteristics

The Context

from what it is. If we see a car, then that is because the stimulus really happens to be a car. If we perceive a brand of cereal to be healthy, it is because we see that it has whole-wheat flakes, it has nuts, and we do not taste much sugar in it. The reality of the stimulus, i.e., the stimulus characteristics, inevitably determines our perception. Stimulus characteristics themselves can be grouped into two types: *sensory characteristics* and *information content*.

Sensory Characteristics

A characteristic is **sensory** if it stimulates any of the five senses. The sensation step in the perception process depends entirely on the sensory characteristics of the stimulus. Sensory characteristics influence perceptions and consumer response in two ways: through sensory-experience and through cultural symbolism. **Sensory experience** refers to how we feel when a stimulus makes contact with our senses. We are biologically wired to find some sensory characteristics pleasant and likewise some unpleasant. Thus, we find loud, harsh sounds unpleasant and melodic sounds pleasant. We find sweet taste pleasant and bitter taste unpleasant. And so on. Some of these responses develop with conditioning (e.g., we may dislike Indian classical music by such artists as Ravi Shankar or country music by such artists as Garth Brooks simply because we have had no prior exposure to these styles). But eventually they all come to reside in our automated, biological, sense responses.

Cultural symbolism refers to the meaning any characteristic or entity comes to have in a particular culture. Although the term applies to all entities, the focus here is on sensory characteristics.

Color as a Sensory Feature All visual stimuli have three features: color, shape, and texture.[3] Colors have come to have meanings, in part based on how they feel on sight and based, in part, on culture. The meaning of some colors differs across cultures; for example, black is the color of mourning in Britain, but white is the color of mourning in Japan. This meaning applies only to clothing, however, and not to cars—in both countries (and in most other countries in the world) black in cars is considered to signify affluence and gravity.

Most Western cultures share a set of meanings for various colors. Figure 3.4 shows these meanings for seven primary colors along with selected companies that use them.

Marketing Implications of Sense Characteristics

Marketers attempt to influence consumers' perceptions by packaging their products and messages in appropriate colors. Mouthwashes are colored green or blue to connote a

FIGURE 3.4 — MEANING OF COLOR

COLOR	MEANING	USED BY
Pink	feminity, calm	Mary Kay, Barbie, Pepto Bismal
Red		
Orange	movement, construction, energy	Cingular, Easyjet, Home Depot
Yellow	light, future, philosophy	Kodak, National Geographic, The Sim
Green	money, growth, environment	John Deere, Starbucks, British Petroleum
Blue	trust, authority, security	Microsoft, American Express
Purple	royalty, spirituality, New Age	Sun, Yahoo, Barney

Source: The Color Association of the United States (Used with permission)

clean, fresh feeling. One brand, Plax, makes its mouthwash red to distinguish itself from competing brands but also to create the perception that it is medicinal and therefore more effective. Consumers find blue to be the coolest color for display in electronic devices. Most cell phones have adopted it as a popular option. And American Express introduced a blue card targeted at college students and even called it Blue Cash.

Another sensory characteristic is texture, and textures too come to acquire culturally symbolic meanings. Silky textures in clothing, for example, are deemed luxurious in a gender-neutral way in the Eastern cultures but somewhat feminine in Western cultures (where rustic textures are considered masculine). The distressed look in clothing conveyed poverty in most cultures as recently as two decades ago; now, it is "engineered" at great cost in such Jeanswear brands as Seven7™, Rock & Republic, and True Religion and then celebrated by millions of young consumers as the "coolest looking fabric" on our planet!

Information Content

The second characteristic of the stimulus that influences perception is its information content. Information content moves the perceptual process beyond sensation or stimulus selection toward sense-making or interpretation. For example, information about an automobile's engine horsepower, acceleration, and style enables one to categorize (i.e., interpret) it as a performance car or a family sedan.

Of course, sensory characteristics also carry some information. Thus, a color is not merely an attention getter, but is also pleasant or unpleasant, and "hot" or "cold." And a mannequin of Tyra Banks in the display window of Victoria's Secret stores not only draws our attention, but it also conveys the information (at least to some consumers) that this lingerie will make you look sexy.

The important point to remember is that sensory vividness of the stimulus helps us sense it, and informational content helps us interpret it.

Marketing Practice

In the early 1980s, for instance, *Rolling Stone* magazine faced a serious perception problem: Many of its advertisers thought its readers were from the hippie generation of the Woodstock era. Starting with a campaign in 1984 with the theme *Perception versus Reality*, the management met this challenge head on, educating potential advertisers about the changing profile of the magazine's readers and their attitudes. Note that this perception was modified by the information content in the ad (and eventually in the magazine).

Managing perceptions is a moving target. In late 2005, its management sensed that the magazine's perceived target readership was slanted too much toward the young, Gen Y crowd, whereas management wanted the magazine to be seen just as much for a more mature reader. It therefore modified both the content and the look and feel of the magazine. Check out a current issue and a pre-2005 issue and see if you discern any differences.

Of course, the marketplace is full of stimuli that are designed, both by their sensory and information content characteristics, to mold perceptions in the manner marketers desire. Examine a Coca Cola vending machine and see for yourself how different brands from Coca-Cola Company accomplish this. Can you describe what stimulus characteristics are at work here?

2. THE CONTEXT AS A FACTOR
The Company Matters

Look at the Favela chair in the picture. What do you think of it? And how much do you think it costs? Write down your answers before proceeding further. And now let us read about the concept of context.

Context refers to the setting or surrounding in which a stimulus is situated. In interpreting a stimulus, we are always influenced by the context.[4] Say, a restaurant waiter keeps a polite but impersonal demeanor. A waiter with this style could be deemed

Perception.

Reality.

To a new generation of Rolling Stone readers, pigs live on farms. You'll find the cops living in Beverly Hills or on Hill Street, now heralded instead of hated. If you're looking for an 18 to 34 year old market that is taking active part instead of active protest, you'll have a riot in the pages of Rolling Stone.

Rolling Stone

---

unfriendly in a low-to-mid-price, mass-market restaurant such as Applebee's or the T.G.I. Friday's restaurant chain in the United States. The same mannerism in an upscale European restaurant may be perceived, on the other hand, as respectful (i.e., not getting personal).

Consider what happens when we encounter a new product or brand. How we perceive it depends on where we encounter it. For example, if we see a new brand of clothing in a discount store, we would perceive it to be of low quality. On the other hand, if we were to first encounter the same brand in an upscale store, we would think it to be of higher quality. The store serves as a context for the new brand. Indeed all elements of the marketing mix (other than the core product itself) serve as contexts for the core product: the product color and shape, package design, brand name, stores at which it is sold or not sold, the product's price, the salesperson's appearance and personality, the service employee's demeanor, even the production quality of media messages. That is why marketers should craft all marketing mix elements with great care.

Getting back to the Favella chair—what if we were to tell you we found it in an antique store in a run down area amidst cheap furniture? Next, what if instead we tell you we saw it at MoMA director Glenn Lowry's home? Would your perceptions of the chair be different?

Now turn the page and read the actual description about the Favela chair. Go ahead and read it.

Favela chair

What do you think of the Favela chair?
Please, write down before proceeding further (repeat: please take a minute to write down—you will find it very rewarding):

_____

_____

_____

_____

designer: Fernando and Humberto Campana, 2002
manufacturer: Edra, Italy
materials: Brazilian Pinus wood.
Dimensions: 29" high, 26.33" wide, 24" deep.
Price: $2,630.00
www.edra.com

What do you think of the Favela chair, NOW?
(Please, do write down your thoughts about the Favela chair again. And see for yourself how similar or different they are from what you wrote earlier)

_____

_____

_____

_____

Okay, what do you think of this chair now? Write down your thoughts about it again.

When we ask this question, most people show a dramatic difference in how they view the chair before and after reading this description.

Moral of the story: The features describing the chair (e.g., its price, designer, country of manufacture) act as its context.

3. CONSUMER CHARACTERISTICS
The Consumer Still Rules

Finally, consumers' own characteristics influence their perceptions. That is why two consumers may not perceive the same stimulus in a similar fashion. Most Americans love the game of football and find it perfectly normal, but many foreigners who watch the game for the first time are amused that players carry their "foot"-ball in their hands! An 8'x10' room in a European Hotel might look adequate to a Japanese tourist but look awfully small to an American tourist. And a dress that looks too risqué to Kirsten Caroline Dunst may not look exciting enough to Paris Hilton. The consumer characteristics that influence perceptions include: (a) consumer needs and involvement, (b) consumers' sensory and cognitive skills, and (c) consumer familiarity and expertise. (See Figure 3.5.)

Consumer Needs and Involvement Consumer needs give relevance to the stimulus. If you are not hungry, you might ignore or not even notice a roadside restaurant. If you are not into body-piercing, then an ad for body piercing might not even register on your senses, or if it did, you might not pay attention to it. Involvement is, as we discussed in the previous chapter, a state of mind in which a need is felt more intensely or when we are deeply interested in something on an enduring basis. Involvement too affects consumer perceptions. For example, a consumer who is highly involved in car races is likely to notice a product relating to racing cars. Thus, after we have sensed a stimulus, whether or not we select it for further attention depends on our need and involvement in the topic of the stimulus.

Beyond sensation and selection, our interpretations also depend on our needs and involvement. If we are very hungry, for example, then even insipid food might be tasty. If we are bothered because our hair is very flat, and if a new brand of shampoo gave our hair even a little bit of body, then we would rate that shampoo highly. But if our hair had no "flatness" problem, then we might not even notice that brand's quality.

Consumers' Sensory and Cognitive Skills The second consumer characteristic affecting perception is the consumer's sensory and cognitive skills. We differ in the sensitivity of our sensors: some of us have a more developed, keener sense of smell than others. This allows us to smell mild aromas that others cannot and to distinguish between two closely related aromas. Similarly, some of us have more sensitive faculties of hearing, vision, taste, and touch. Correspondingly, our perceptual skills differ. Some of us can perceive depth accurately; some can visualize linear distances or spatial dimensions better (e.g., "Would this table fit into our kitchen?"); and some can remember, while in the store, exactly the visual image of the colors in the bedroom's wall paper design and judge, while in the store, whether a particular drapery color would match.

FIGURE 3.5 — THREE CONSUMER CHARACTERISTICS THAT INFLUECE PERCEPTIONS

Even more importantly, people differ in their cognitive skills. Some of us can manipulate numbers more easily (e.g., "per unit of the product, do these two brands have the same amount of fat?"); some can hold more information in active memory; and others need to write things down as they listen to a product demonstration or a food recipe. Some have a tendency to avoid technical information, while others avidly seek it. These faculties of the mind are called **cognitive skills**—the mental ability to hold and process information. And they obviously influence how consumers interpret and encode a stimulus. A 21-year old college student might find a textbook's prose and examples engaging, whereas a topic scholar (with highly developed cognitive skills) might dismiss it as lacking gravitas.

Consumer Familiarity and Expertise Finally, consumer familiarity with the stimulus category or expertise on the topic influences consumer interpretation. Familiarity affects consumers in two ways. First, familiarity leads to efficiency in organizing information. We are able to recognize and categorize quickly something with which we are familiar. When we see a new product under a familiar brand name (i.e., a brand extension), we quickly know what it is—e.g., that Listerine mint strips are breath fresheners. Second, familiarity is often based on prior repeated experience. Now, this can cut both ways. Familiarity can breed dislike because we get bored as the novelty of a stimulus wears off; or we can feel warmth and comfort in the lap of the familiar and consequently perceive the stimulus more favorably.

Expertise goes beyond familiarity and entails some specialist knowledge. Because of this, expertise helps consumers more accurately categorize and evaluate stimuli. Thus, wine connoisseurs are able to judge wines more accurately than can novice wine consumers. Basically, experience and expertise give consumers a rich, prior stock of knowledge in addition to well-developed feelings and attitudes about things. Such prior knowledge and feelings become expectations—prior beliefs about what something will possess or offer. Expectations influence perceptions in that we often end up seeing what we expect to see.

EXPECTATIONS INFLUENCE PERCEPTION

We drink a soft drink thinking it is our favorite brand Coke, and we find that the drink tastes good, just as Coke should. We see a shirt with a label, Kenneth Cole, and we think it is a high quality, fashionable shirt. We notice that the DVD player is made in China, and we quickly conclude it is a "cheap" import. Again and again, in everyday life, we form these perceptions and quick judgments (sometimes false) because we *expect* things to be like that.

The clearest demonstration of the power of expectations is blind-taste test studies. In beer taste studies, consumers often swear by their favorite brand, proclaiming, for example, that Heineken tastes better than Michelob (or the other way around). But give them a blind taste test, and many can't tell which is which. They need to know the brand name to figure out the taste. Basically, then, their minds (which is where expectations reside) are telling their tongues how something tastes!

PERCEPTUAL BIASES

Or Why We Don't See How Things Are

Since consumer characteristics influence consumer perceptions, these perceptions are seldom objective; rather they are biased or distorted. Some of these distortions occur unintentionally; some occur because we actively control what we want to see or not to see. In either case, to cope with all the mass of stimuli coming at us all the time, our minds employ three selective processes: selective exposure, selective attention, and selective interpretation (see Figure 3.6). These selective processes bias our perceptions.

| FIGURE 3.6 | BIASES IN THE PERCEPTUAL PROCESS |

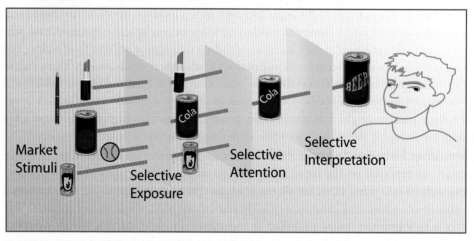

SELECTIVE EXPOSURE
Avoiding Seeing Things

As we said before, as a typical consumer, you face something like 3000 stimuli on an average day. If our minds were to attend to each one of these, we would go insane. Therefore, our minds cope with the barrage of marketing communications and products (and other information in everyday life), by becoming "selective" about its exposure. Consumers look only at a few advertisements, ignoring the rest of them. Want proof? Well, did you notice everyone in class today? Did you notice every billboard on your drive home today? Did you notice every item on the shelf in the supermarket yesterday? You did notice the billboard for The Gap. You did notice the brand of wine with the big sale tag on it. And you did notice that one student whose T-shirt said: Procrastinate Now!

The fact is that we choose what to expose ourselves to. In fact, we even go out of our way to seek exposure to certain things. We buy a newspaper that carries supermarket coupons; we visit Abercrombie & Fitch to see the season's new arrivals; and we search the web for the latest cell phone models. In these and other ways, we choose to expose ourselves selectively to market communications. As consumers, we utilize selective exposure as a tool both to keep out irrelevant information and actively to seek information of personal interest.

SELECTIVE ATTENTION
Avoiding Taking a Note of Things

On Saturday, December 10, 2005, during the writing of this very paragraph, a pop up ad for MotoRazr showed up on my PC. During the ten hours that I had been writing that day, a few other ads had also popped up (apparently defying my cheap—free—pop up blocker, since upgraded), and they were all eye-catching. But I closed them nonetheless, without even noticing what they were for. The MotoRazr ad I noticed with my peripheral vision (as I did the others) and decided to pay further attention. Why? Because I am interested in all new gizmos! So here we are, witnessing the workings of the idea of "selective attention." Even if an advertisement or a product display manages to come face-to-face with a consumer (pop up in his or her face, so to speak), the consumer may still choose to ignore it if it does not relate to his or her interests.

Initially, a person's attention is impelled by the stimulus characteristics of contrast and vividness (i.e., a color advertisement in a black-and-white medium, a loud noise, vibrant colors, a three-dimensional pop-out in a magazine, a special end-of-aisle display in a store, and so on). But subsequent attention depends on the personal interest the stimulus arouses. The stimulus has to "earn" it, so to speak by appealing to consumer interests.

SELECTIVE INTERPRETATION
Avoiding Knowing the Inconvenient Truth

Even if a marketer succeeds in getting the consumer's full attention, it still does not mean the marketer got the consumer to believe in the message. Consumers interpret the content and message of marketing communications selectively. A call by the umpire was unfair if it penalized our favorite team; it was fair if it penalized the opposite team. This sort of selective interpretation is called *perceptual distortion*.

Perceptual distortion refers to information being encoded non-objectively. That is, the consumer sees it as different from reality. This distortion occurs because, as consumers, we see things in a manner that makes those things congruent with and conformable to our prior beliefs.

A recent example comes from the U.S. Secretary of State Colin Powell's 90-minute presentation on February 5, 2003 to the U.N. Security Council, on Iraq's possible link to Al Qaeda, complete with satellite photos and phone conversation recordings. The result of his address: those already supporting the U.S.'s hawkish stand on Iraq found the evidence convincing; those opposed did not. This sort of response happens all the time. Perceptions of Dan Brown's *The Da Vinci Code* are sharply divided among people with prior prejudice for or against the identity of Mary Magdalene and the Holy Grail, as a sampling of reviews on Amazon.com so vividly reveals. Likewise, as professors know only too well, students who come to a course having heard good recommendations about it or about the instructor end up liking the course much more than those who enroll after having heard criticism about it. Such is the power of prior expectations held by the perceiver!

(Pause for a minute and ask if your perceptions of this textbook have been colored by your own prejudices. Actually, it is a vacuous question—the inherent nature of perceptions is that the perceiver believes the reality of the stimulus to be the entire and exclusive determinant of the perceived reality.)

PERCEPTUAL THRESHOLD
Or How Can We Show Up on the Consumer's Radar

Remember what we said about the life of a stimulus? If consumers don't sense it, then its journey toward consumer perception has not even begun. Sensation acts like a gatekeeper—if it fails, then the marketing stimulus is rendered totally inconsequential. It is DOA—dead on arrival!

Of course, not every stimulus gets sensed. Imagine sitting in your classroom. You have been here before—every week this semester. Now take a look around the room. Are the lights today somewhat dimmer than before? No? Are you absolutely sure? What if the university authorities decided to lower the lights just a tad in all the campus buildings. That small decrease in light illumination can save the university a bundle, and you wouldn't even notice it!

Assuming that the university did decide to lower the lights, you didn't notice this change because it was below your **perceptual threshold** (sometimes also called **differential threshold**)—the minimum level or magnitude at which a stimulus begins to be sensed. A related concept is the **just noticeable difference (j.n.d.)**. This refers to the magnitude of change necessary for the change to be noticed. Marketers use this principle to reduce product quantity or size marginally in order to keep the prices constant in the wake of rising costs. Some years ago, a famous candy maker successfully reduced the size of its candy bars by keeping the size change small.

The magnitude of change needed for it to be noticed depends on the base quantity. The larger the base quantity, the larger the magnitude of change needed for the change to be noticed. This is known as **Weber's Law**, named after the German scientist Ernst Weber.[7] For example, a one-half inch reduction in the size of a five-inch candy bar will perhaps not be noticed, but the same reduction in a two-inch long stick of chewing gum is likely to be noticed.[4]

The perceptual threshold depends on two factors. Sensory sensitivity and stimulus change. Not all living organisms have the same sensory powers. Dogs for example, have a much keener sense of smell than do humans. And among humans, the power to sense smells, sights, tastes, sounds, etc., varies from one person to another. Some people have more sensitive noses than others, and some have more developed taste buds than others. Hearing sensitivity also differs. Accordingly, consumers differ in their inherent ability to detect and experience various sensory stimuli. This presents opportunities for marketers to influence consumption. Some drink wine just for its taste, whereas others learn to enjoy its taste as well as its aroma. Explicitly drawing attention to a sensory stimulus property then, can sometimes induce consumers to experience that sensation. The Canadian beer brand Molson, in an ad in early 2006, pioneered this concept—it presented its beer as a fragrance! The copy read:

> "Embrace the fragrance of Molson. Saskatchewen barley, pure Canadian water, aromatic hops. The scent that brings people together. In bars since 1776."

Now, when you consume your beer, at least if it is Molson beer, you won't only be drinking it, but you will be partaking of its aroma as well!

The other factor in crossing the perceptual threshold is the magnitude of change represented by the stimulus. No matter how strong one's sensory organs, they quickly get habituated to a stimulus, which curtails further sensations from it. The intense smell of sulphur is so strong in the air in Rotorua (New Zealand) that, as tourists, some of you might find it difficult to sleep in that city; yet residents live there happily, almost unaware of the pungent smell. What makes you notice any stimulus in the first place is not its absolute intensity, but rather its change—change from the stimulus to which you had been exposed only moments before.

Savvy marketers can put this principle to good use and bring consumers enhanced consumption experiences. Case in point: Febreze® NOTICEables™ by Procter & Gamble. The wall-plug-in air fresheners come in twin fragrance pouches that switch every 45 minutes. When the fragrances alternate, you are sure to notice them and enjoy the fragrant air in the

C.O.N.S.U.M.E.R. K.A.R.M.A.

Dear Diary: This Place Is Heaven... I Mean, It Sucks!

Aug 1. Moved to our new home in Finland. It is so beautiful here. The hills are so picturesque. Can hardly wait to see them covered by snow. God's country. I love it here.

©iStockphoto.com/Galina Barskaya

Oct. 14. Finland is the most beautiful place on Earth. The leaves are turning all different colors. I love the shade of red and orange. Went for a ride through some beautiful hills and spotted some deer.

Dec. 2. It snowed last night. Woke up to find everything blanketed in white. It looks like a postcard. We went outside and cleaned the snow off the steps and shoveled the driveway. Mother Nature is perfect harmony. I Love It Here.

Dec. 12. More snow last night. A winter wonderland. I Love It Here.

Dec. 22 More of that s--- fell last night. I've Got blisters on my hands from shoveling. think the snowplow hides around the corner and waits until I'm done shoveling my driveway.

Dec. 28. More white s--- last night. Been inside since Christmas day except for shoveling out the driveway every time... Can't go anywhere. Got buried in a mountain of white s---.

Jan. 4. Finally got out of the house today. Went to the store to get food...

May 3. Took the car to the garage in town. Would you believe the thing is rotting out from all that salt they keep all over the road.

May 10 Moved to Holland. I can't imagine why anyone in their right mind would ever want to live in that God forsaken country of Finland.

Source: Author of the diary unknown, excerpted from Arch Woodside and Jean-Charles Chebat, "Updating Heider's Balance Theory In Consumer Behavior," *Psychology & Marketing*, where the source was cited as: Koll, Oliver (2000).

©iStockphoto.com/Brandon Clark

My CB Book

Consumer Karma Is Shifting Perceptions

room. You can have the choice of Calypso Breeze & Hawaiian Paradise™, Morning Walk & Cleansing Rain™, Pink Magnolia & Jasmine Breeze™, Vanilla Refresh & Vanilla Bean™, and Clothesline Breeze & Meadow Songs™. (Learn more at www.febreze.com).

Note that the concept of "perceptual threshold" applies only to the threshold for the sensation stage of the perception process, not to the sense-making stage. After a difference has been sensed, whether or not it is deemed meaningful is a separate issue, and that decision occurs in the sense-making stage. Whether a difference is deemed consequential or not depends on the consumer's "sensitivity" to that attribute. Consumers may recognize a price difference of 10 cents between two brands of chewing gum, but at the sense-making stage, they may deem it inconsequential. However, Weber's law may sometimes apply even at this stage. It has been found for example, that a consumer may be willing to travel to another store to save $5 on a $10 item but not on a $200 item.

Earlier, we called a stimulus that failed to achieve sensation DOA—dead on arrival. We were being unfair. The fact is that failing to achieve sensation can sometimes be a good thing. Actually, some stimuli are deliberately kept "sneaky" so that, it is hoped, they fail to be sensed. It is like flying a fighter plane below an enemy's radar sensors. That brand of candy bar reducing its size just a tad is a case in point. In such situations, failing to be sensed is a good thing for marketers.

And it is also the basis of one of marketing's oldest folktales—*subliminal perception*.

SUBLIMINAL PERCEPTION
The Folklore of Sneaky Marketing

Perhaps no other story has been told in marketing more often than this one. In the 1950s, marketing researcher James Vicary conducted a test. In a theater, on the movie screen, the words "Drink Coca Cola" and "Eat popcorn" were flashed for 1/3000 second (below the perceptual threshold level) at five-second intervals. The sales of Coca Cola and popcorn increased during the test period.[5]

As a result of stories like this, people at large sometimes suspect marketers and advertisers of being mysterious con artists, trying to manipulate their minds without their knowledge. And since then, consumer advocacy groups and consumer activists have been trying to find hidden symbols in product package designs or in pictures in advertising. This quest for hidden images in commercial communications, however, has turned up no concrete evidence that such tricks exist or that they work. Marketing researchers who have tried to repeat the Vicary experiment have not been able to replicate his findings.

On trial here is a phenomenon called **subliminal perception**—the perception of a stimulus without being aware of it. **Subliminal stimuli** are defined as stimuli of which one is not conscious. Thus, the stimulus registers on our senses but without our being aware of the registration. For example, if music is playing in a store where we are busy finding what we want, we might not become conscious of it even though it might put us in a happy mood. If someone drew our attention to it, then of course we would know what musical tune it is. But without focusing our attention on it, we have perceived it below the threshold of awareness. This is subliminal perception.

Psychologists have done several experiments to test whether subliminal stimuli work. Typically, the subliminal stimulus is masked by or submerged in a more vivid stimulus on which people are focusing attention. Let us describe one such experiment.[6] A psychology researcher told a group of subjects (that is, people who participate in psychological experiments) that their task was to solve some problems on the computer. Each of them sat at a PC and went through the tasks presented on the computer screen, like solving a puzzle or building a figure. While the steps to these tasks were being presented, some pictures of faces would briefly appear in a corner where they would not interfere with the main task, and these would flash so briefly that they would be below the threshold level of being seen by the human eye. The pictures flashed for half of the subjects were of pleasant faces; the other half were of unpleasant faces.

After some time, a message suddenly appeared: "F 11 Error: failure saving data. You must begin again from the beginning." Secretly, a camera recorded the facial reaction of all subjects. The finding? The subjects whose screens had flashed unpleasant faces were angrier than the other group of subjects![7]

While psychologists still debate if subliminal perception is real, experiments like this one show that it is possible for humans not to be aware of something but to be influenced by it anyway. What then is to be believed about subliminal perception?[8] While the debate continues (and it is not going to be settled anytime soon), here is our summary on this issue:

1. First, research has demonstrated that mere exposure to stimuli can create liking for those stimuli, and that this can happen even without consumers being aware of having seen the stimuli before. This is called **mere exposure effect**.[9]

2. Second, certain stimuli create an instant and automated response in humans. For example, if a commercial contains a soft melody, we might like the advertised brand a little bit more without even being aware of the melody. Making a package more pleasant to look at can have a similar subliminal effect. For example, rounding out the corners of a square label can make the label seem more pleasant (and without consumers noticing the change in the label design).

3. Whether consumers perceive a stimulus subliminally or consciously, it pays to make all elements of marketing stimuli pleasant. It is not necessary for marketers cunningly to embed unwholesome images in advertisements. Pleasant presentations

of all elements of product offerings are all that is needed to create a favorable impression whether or not the phenomenon of subliminal perception actually exists.

PERCEPTUAL ORGANIZATION
Bringing Order to the Chaos of Life

Not only is our world full of stimuli, but each stimulus also generates a multitude of sensations. If our mind took note of all these sensations, it would experience a chaotic state. And it would be perennially overloaded with the work of "seeing" the stimulus. To cope with such an enormous task, and to bring order to its sensing of stimuli, the mind quickly "organizes" the sensations they create in some sensible order. Three principles guide how consumers accomplish this perceptual organization: gestalt, figure and ground, and closure.[6]

Gestalt Look at the zebras in the picture. Done? Ok, now, without looking at it again, answer this question: How many stripes does the standing zebra have? And which of its front legs is positioned forward of the other—left or right? Are the stripes on the side of its belly slanted upward from the left to the right or from right to left? And is the seated zebra's head pointed toward or away from the standing zebra? You didn't notice? But you saw the picture and recognized it as a zebra, right? All of us register and encode stimuli this way—as an overall configuration, without sensing the details. This is called *gestalt perception*, derived from the German word **gestalt,** which means a general, overall image formed in the mind. Humans (and therefore consumers) seldom attend to all the details of a stimulus. Rather they form an overall impression based on a pattern within the stimulus (for zebra, this pattern is a horse-like animal with stripes). It is efficient for consumers to do it this way.

Courtesy: whozoo.org

Marketers need to take note: sometimes consumers are paying only fleeting attention, so they form an overall impression of the brand based on some surface features or overall image in an ad. But even when they pay attention, they don't notice each feature, and often what they notice and retain in memory is merely an overall impression of the advertised product, i.e., a gestalt.

Figure and Ground Now look at the Zebra picture again. Is it really a picture about zebras? Or is it about the outdoor terrain and vegetation in spring? That depends on how you stumbled onto this picture. Were you searching for pictures of animals? Or, alternatively, were you searching for pictures of seasons or landscapes? This is the concept of figure and ground: in any visual, something is the background (ground), and something is the focal object (figure).

Look at the picture of a vase. Is it really a vase or is it, instead, a picture of two human faces? That depends on what you see as ground and what you see as figure. As an advertiser, you would want to make sure that your product and your message remains the figure, rather than becoming the ground. Your message risks becoming part of the ground if you make the ad so humorous, for example, that people remember the joke or the humor, but not your product story or even its brand name.

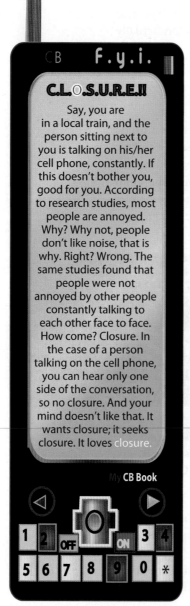

Closure The closure principle suggests that consumers have a natural tendency to complete a partial stimulus, supplying the missing information from memory (assuming of course that they are already familiar with the complete stimulus).[11] If you hear a tune for a song, you automatically begin to hum it; if you read or hear a partial sentence of a familiar jingle, you fill in the rest. Partial information bothers us like an unsolved puzzle, and we make the effort to find the missing information and achieve closure. Utilizing this principle, if marketers omit a letter or two from a familiar brand name or a jingle, then consumers will fill in the blank. In this way, consumers actively participate (rather than seeing the information passively), and this active participation makes the brand name or tagline more memorable. Not too long ago, an ad by a famous brand of Scotch whiskey did just that in its Christmas Holiday advertising. It wrote the headline phrase as _ingle _ells. Can you fill in the blanks to achieve closure (and notice the curious discomfort until you do)?

Actually, consumers need not have been familiar with the brand name or slogan, but only with the words used. If you are preparing a poster, for example, for your campus club, say, the Young Entrepreneur's Club; try to leave out a letter here and there (for example: You g E trepne r's Cl b). The chances are that more viewers will register the poster and your club's name in their minds than if you had spelled it out. That is because sense-making is a powerful, innate need, and achieving closure on an unfinished stimulus helps us meet that need.

MARKETING APPLICATIONS OF PERCEPTION PROCESSES

Marking out a section on "Marketing Applications" is akin to writing a whole chapter on the environment of fish and then marking out a section called "Water." The marketing applications of the perception process have been described throughout the chapter, enmeshed inseparably with the very description of these processes. What we do need to do here, however, is to present some special areas of application—entire topic areas that have developed in marketing simply as an outgrowth of systematic research and practice development by marketers and consumer researchers, anchored in the concepts of perceptions. These are as follows:

1. The psychology of consumer price perceptions
2. Country-of-origin effects
3. Brand image and brand extensions
4. Consumer perceptual maps and positioning
5. Sensory marketing

PSYCHOLOGY OF PRICE PERCEPTION

$9.99 is Good, $10.01 is Too Much!

The psychology of price perception refers to how consumers psychologically perceive prices. Noteworthy aspects of this phenomenon are reference price, assimilation and contrast, and price as a quality cue.

Reference Price A consumer who accidentally walks into a store and discovers a 20 percent-off sale may be delighted, but if the same consumer came in after viewing an advertisement hyping a huge sale, he or she is likely to feel disappointed or even anguished. Why? The concept of reference price explains it. **Reference price** is the price consumers expect to pay.[7] If the actual price is lower than the reference price, it is perceived as a good economic value. The consumer who accidentally walks into the store has the full price as the reference price; in contrast, the consumer who has seen advertisements of "huge savings" has a much lower reference price and is therefore disappointed.[8]

Advertisement or no advertisement, we all have some reference price in mind for a product or service; this is termed the **internal reference price**, the price we believe to be the right price. This differs from the **external reference price**, which is the price the marketer uses to anchor a price advantage (e.g., "compare at___"). Often, consumers' internal reference price comes from knowing the competitors' price. When a price is higher than the consumer's reference price, the marketer may have to "educate" the consumer on the quality superiority that makes the price a good value. One recent advertisement read: "Our competitors' price is lower. That is because it should be!"

Assimilation and Contrast Another important perceptual concept is *assimilation* and *contrast*. **Assimilation** means, simply, that a stimulus is perceived to belong to a category. **Contrast** means that the item is seen as different from the perceptual category. This theory states that consumers have latitudes of acceptance and rejection, so prices (or other information) that fall within the acceptance latitude are assimilated and those that fall outside the zone of acceptance are contrasted and hence rejected. For example, a consumer who is willing to spend up to $10 to purchase a gift might assimilate $9 or $11 but will reject other prices as either too low or too high. Another way this principle works is that consumers have certain cut-off levels for accepting a price, and prices below that level are viewed as acceptable, while those above it are rejected even though the latter may exceed the former merely by 2 cents. Thus, many consumers would perceive a price of $9.99 as falling within the acceptable $10 range, whereas they might perceive a price of $10.01 as unacceptable. That is why marketers adopt the **odd pricing** method—a practice wherein prices are set just below the next round number.

Price as a Quality Cue Consumers often use price as a quality cue—that is, as a basis for making inferences about the quality of the product or service. Such use of price is particularly likely where quality cannot be independently judged.[9] Consumers often assume that a product with a higher price is superior in quality to one with a lower price. Again, this is especially the case when other clues for inferring quality are unavailable.

The use of price as a quality cue can occur for products and services when consumers are seeking psychosocial satisfaction, that is, nonfunctional or non-utilitarian values (see Chapter 1 for a description of these values). For example, for writing pens, a higher price may be valued as a reflection of exclusivity and status. It also may occur for products and services sought primarily for their functional or utilitarian value, especially if consumers cannot judge the quality independently (e.g., judging a higher priced pen to be superior in writing quality).[10]

COUNTRY-OF-ORIGIN EFFECTS
High Fashion Suits from Timbaktoo?

Would you buy a video-cassette recorder (VCR) from Pakistan or Iran? High-fashion suits from Russia, Nigeria, or Timbaktoo? A fine wine made in Mauritius or China? Most probably, your answers to the foregoing questions are "no." What about a VCR from Japan, a fashion suit from Italy, and a fine wine from France? Perhaps, your answers to these questions are "yes." If so, your answers may be driven by "country-of-origin" image.[11]

Country-of-origin effects refer to the bias in consumer perceptions of products and services due to the country in which these products and services are made (or are claimed to be made). Overcoming this bias requires well-conceived informational and educational campaigns. Today, Korean companies face such a bias for their automobiles (e.g., Hyundai) and electronic products (e.g., Goldstar TV). While countries with a poor overall image suffer from this bias, those with a good image benefit from it. A British marketer of electronic products, in fact, exploits the positive image of another country. It assembles its products all over the world but not in Japan; yet it markets them under the brand name Matsui to imply (incorrectly) a Japanese origin.[12]

BRAND IMAGE AND BRAND EXTENSIONS
Listerine Lipstick? You Must Be Kidding!

Brand names influence the perception of products. For new products, brand names act as contexts. They are like pedigrees. Adidas started as a shoe company; now it also sells apparel. Good for Adidas—as the company's good name is going to bring its apparel good consumer perceptions. But if you are a marketer, be careful before you rush to stick your famous brand name on anything. Brand names come to be known, you see, for certain product categories, and brand extensions must remain within the bounds of that category. Brand extensions utilize the principle of assimilation and contrast. Consumers perceive brand extensions to be natural only when those extensions are within the category with which the brand name is associated (assimilation). If the extensions are outside of that product category, then such extensions are seen to be inapt (contrast). Sometimes, such extensions may even create confusion.

Listerine is perceived to be in an oral hygiene product. If the company (most known for mouthwashes) brought out a product extension into, say toothpaste, that would be easily assimilated and accepted by consumers, but if the company wanted to start marketing, say, sunglasses or even makeup products under the brand name Listerine, that would create an anomaly in consumer perceptions of the brand. Consumers would not be able to "organize" this new stimulus, and it would unsettle the brand image even for the company's oral hygiene products. However, a breath mint under the brand name Listerine would be a perfectly natural connection for consumers to perceive—i.e., to categorize and accept,— and indeed this is why Listerine's mint strips are a great success. Now we have a question for you: as a marketer, would you stick the name Listerine on a new brand of lipstick?

HOW BRAND NAMES AFFECT CONSUMER PERCEPTIONS

Brand names clearly affect consumer perceptions of products. In one recent study in the UK, 800 consumers were surveyed about what they thought of the pair of jeans depicted in an advertisement they were shown. The ads (in print) were both for the Levi's brand of jeans, but two versions were created: one showing the brand name on the product and the other without the brand name. In all other aspects, the two versions of the ad were identical. Half the consumers were shown one version and the other half the other version. Each group was asked to rate the pair of jeans on a number of adjective pairs (e.g., stylish/not stylish, expensive/inexpensive). The finding was unmistakable: On an average, consumers who saw the branded jeans ad rated the jeans higher than did the consumers who saw the unbranded jeans version. Even more important, they rated it higher not simply in overall terms but also on most of the attributes. See Figure 3.7. This amply illustrates what consumer psychologists have known all along; namely, that brand names, and the image and reputation those brand names have built, bias consumers' product perceptions.

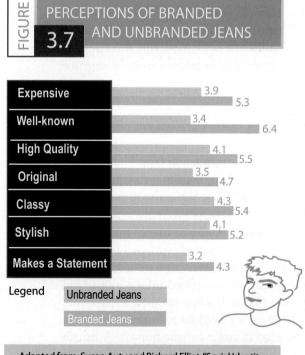

FIGURE 3.7 PERCEPTIONS OF BRANDED AND UNBRANDED JEANS

	Unbranded Jeans	Branded Jeans
Expensive	3.9	5.3
Well-known	3.4	6.4
High Quality	4.1	5.5
Original	3.5	4.7
Classy	4.3	5.4
Stylish	4.1	5.2
Makes a Statement	3.2	4.3

Legend: Unbranded Jeans / Branded Jeans

Adapted from: Susan Auty and Richard Elliot, "Social Identity & the Meaning of Fashion Brands," European Advances in Consumer Research 3, p. 1-10, 1998. Used with permission of the Association for Consumer Research.

PERCEPTUAL MAPS AND POSITIONING
How Marketers Play the Photographer

Which pizza is tastier, Tombstone or DiGiorno®? Which is healthier? And which is the best value for the money? The answers are all a matter of perceptions—how you perceive these pizza brands. And these perceptions are in your mind. There is a map, if you will, in your mind of all these brands of pizza. And likewise, for other products. What marketers do is to capture your mental map on paper, playing *the photographer of the mind*, so to speak. These maps on paper are called *perceptual maps*. **Perceptual maps** are visual depictions of consumer perceptions of alternative brands of a product category in multi-dimensional grids. Dimensions are attributes of the product category—in the pizza example, these are taste, healthiness, price value, etc. Thus, the number of dimensions can be as many as the number of attributes. On paper, we can at best draw three-dimensional pictures, but for convenience we usually draw these maps in two dimensions at a time (along an X axis and a Y axis), covering all attributes with two attributes at a time. As an in-class exercise, two student groups drew their maps as shown in Figure 3.8. Notice how the perceptions of the two groups differ. Note that consumers may never have even tried some of these pizzas—their perceptions are merely impressions. As we know, not all perceptions are based on experience. Indeed, consumers never even try some products because of their unfavorable preconceptions about them. Also note that since the two consumers' perceptions are different, surely both of them cannot be correct, and therefore at least one of them differs from objective reality. It confirms one of our axioms: When it comes to how we see the world, there is no reality, only perceptions. And perceptions, not reality, are what matter. That is why marketers need to take note of consumer perceptions and study these perceptual maps.

Perceptual maps for Pizzas by two consumer groups

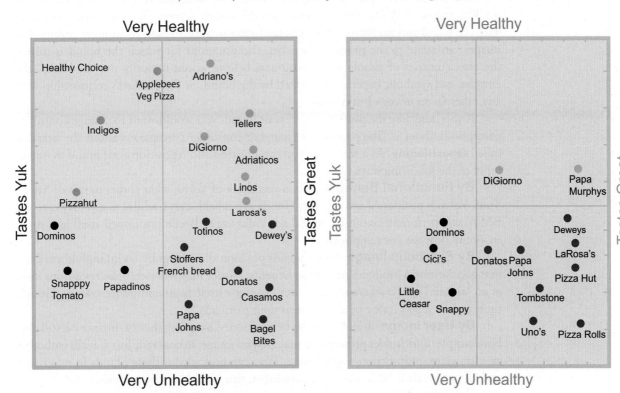

Four Uses of Perceptual Maps

1. **Know who your competitors are** Your competitor is not the company whose brand has the highest market share, nor the company with the brand share closest to yours (in either direction). Rather, your competitor is the company closest to your brand in the consumers' perceptual space; i.e., on the perceptual

maps your consumers draw for you. Thus, positioning maps enable you to see the marketplace and various competitors in it from your customer's point-of-view. And this is a prerequisite to running a successful marketing campaign. It is against these competitors that you have to improve your marketing mix.

2. **Know who your potential new target customers should be** Your potential target market should be the consumers of brands plotted closest to your brand on the map. They are the ones who are likely to have considered your brand and found it acceptable. If in the survey, along with the perceptual maps, you also elicit demographic and media information, then you can target this group of consumers.

3. **Modify the product** Consumers perceive your product as lacking certain features or qualities. This tells you what features you need to improve in your products, so that you can advance your brand on the perceptual map.

4. **Correct the misperceptions** Finally, consider a case of the consumers who have judged your product to be inferior to the products of certain competitors, but who view your product as on par with (if not superior to) these competitors' products when the product is tested and/or analyzed objectively. Obviously, consumers have come to hold misperceptions about your brand. You need to correct these perceptions by communicating the true attributes of your product and by encouraging sampling of your product by these consumers.

POSITIONING AND REPOSITIONING
The Art of Getting Choice Seats

The spot your brand occupies in the consumer's mental map is known as its *positioning*. More formally, **positioning** is defined as consumers' perception of a brand relative to that of other brands in the product category and relative to consumers' goals relevant to the product category. Positioning encompasses the salient features the consumer associates with the brand and the image or images the brand name evokes in consumers' minds. The images can relate to the product's benefits, the situations for which the brand is suited, the characteristics of people who consumers believe would typically use the brand, the emotive and symbolic experiences evoked by the brand, or the product's relationship with any other facets of consumers' lives.

If you don't like the positioning of your brand, you would want to change consumer perceptions about it. The practice of changing consumer perceptions about the brand is called **repositioning**. As a marketer, you can position and reposition your brand in one or more of the following ways.

By Functional Benefits When you think of Volvo, what comes to mind? Safety. Thus, Volvo is positioned as a safe car; Honda as a reliable car; Cadillac as a luxury car; and BMW as a performance car. In an old ad, Volkswagen Beetle positioned itself as a super economy (low gas consumption) car.

By Symbolic Image Some brands position themselves by an intangible attribute that goes beyond a product's utilitarian benefits. Notice how Movado brand positions itself as an "artistic" watch whereas Tag Heuer positions itself as an endurance watch. (Google these brands if you have not already seen their print ads.)

By User Image Brands can also be positioned by giving them a distinct personality. For example, Quicksilver projects a casual, playful image; in contrast, Just Cavalli embodies an ultra glam, pulp-fiction-esque image. (You can find ads for these brands in magazines and images on their Web sites. And remember, this would be "context effect.")

By Usage Situation When a beer advertises itself as "the one beer to have when you are having more than one," it is positioning itself according to a consumption situation.

By Competition Sometimes, brands position themselves by competitive advantage. A classic positioning battle was fought between Hertz and Avis—Hertz had been touting its "largest car fleet, and number 1" position. In response, Avis countered with the "Avis is only Number 2, so we try harder" campaign.

By Values A brand can also position itself according to the larger societal values it stands for. If you know anything about The Body Shop, then you know what stands out the most about it in the consumer mind: no animal testing. Ben and Jerry's is positioned as an environmentally friendly company. Can you think of any other company taking public pride in its values?

By Category Yet another way to position a brand is by carving out a new category. A classic example is Dial soap, which in a campaign several years ago wrapped itself in a prescription Rx label, thus, positioning itself as a germ killer rather than merely a dirt cleaner. And, of course, you remember (perhaps from your "principles of marketing" text) 7Up staking out a new category as an Uncola drink.

REPOSITIONING

Any of the above approaches can also be used for repositioning a brand. Sometimes, the goal of repositioning a product is to move consumers' attitudes toward it to a *different* position. Exemplifying this is an old campaign from Certs (which showed a bunch of cherries and proclaimed that the product contained less sugar than all those cherries). At other times, the goal of repositioning is to broaden the product's current position. An example is Izod's color campaign; Izod did not abandon its 20-something athletic casual clothing appeal; instead, the company just broadened the product's positioning to include a color extravaganza.

One particular challenge brands sometimes face is the burden of the product category itself, or rather how consumers perceive the product category itself. The label consumers give a product category keeps the brand from expanding into broader consumption uses. The chalenege then is to modify consumer perceptions of the product category; to reposition the product category. This, you might recall from your marketing principles textbook, is **primary demand creation**—expanding the demand for the product castegory itself. The hope is, of course, that this will in turn create **secondary demand**—demand for the specific brand that endeavors to create the primary demand. Notice how skillfully Sunkist attempts it in the accompanying ad.

Courtesy: Sunkist Company

Ok, now it is your turn. Find an ad for each positioning approach. Is any one of them also attempting a repositioning? Note this: just because an ad proclaims some feature of the product or brand, it need not score in the positioning game. Rather, that game requires meeting two challenges: (a) the theme and the creativity must not elude the reader (otherwise the ad fails in sense-making and interpretation), and (b) the theme of the ad must make the brand stand out in a field crowded with other brands. Do the ads you collected pass this test and how well?

SENSORY MARKETING

Alluring You Through the Senses

Sensory marketing refers to creating favorable product or brand impressions in the consumer mind by appealing to one or more of the five senses. Through sensory gratification, that is. To do so, the product, packaging, or brand messages are made intensely pleasing to the senses. We will illustrate the ideas of sensory marketing principally by discussing visual appeal since it is feasible to do so on paper. For example, notice the image found on the Web site of an e-tailer named 1stopgourmetshop.com, —the sensory invitation of the steaming hot coffee can't be ignored. Marketing through appeal to the other senses, however, is just as useful, and we also will review these briefly, first, thus saving the more delightful visual tour for the last.

SOUND
The Magic of Melody

Marketers use jingles and music in advertisements to create the appropriate mood. Even the voices of the spokesperson and actors in the ad are chosen to match the brand's desired personality. Products are designed to produce the expected sound. To take one example, consumers do not feel that the car door is securely shut unless it makes a sharp thudding sound when closed. So even though producing doors that close more quietly is feasible, car manufacturers now deliberately design the doors to make a thudding noise. In stores and service facilities alike, marketers play music that consumers would find enjoyable to encourage consumers to linger longer. And now a repertoire of musical ring tones on cell phones is being made available by such companies as zingy.com and tiggypig.com to make the use of cell phones more enjoyable for consumers.

> ### Meet the Taste Scientists
> When It Comes to Taste Buds, Not Every Consumer Is Created Equal.
> Science separates people into two groups, "tasters" and "nontasters," based on their ability to sense a chemical called phenylthiocarbamide. In the late 1970s, Linda Bartoshuk, Ph.D., a taste researcher at Yale University, began to test people for sensitivity to a similar chemical called 6-n-propylthiouracil, or PROP. Her work revealed a subset of tasters, dubbed "supertasters," who were particularly sensitive to PROP's bitter flavor. In comparison to nontasters, supertasters tasted more sweetness in table sugar, more bitterness in foods and beverages such as black coffee, and more sourness in fruits.
> Source: Adapted from Men's Fitness, June 2003, Ethan Quick.

TASTE
Thank Your Taste Buds for It

When companies introduce new foods and beverages, they conduct extensive taste tests, because taste is, by definition, a major factor in the markability of all food and beverage products. Pleasurable taste can increase product consumption. For example, Aqua Vie markets water in seven flavors (Hydrator ™) designed to increase water consumption among consumers. In mid-2003, the company taste-tested a new line of flavored spring water, called Pureplay, specifically targeted to children. As another example, in early 2003, Carbolite Foods, Inc. introduced a new line of candy bars specifically designed for people with diabetes. The bars tasted just like real candy. Consumer taste tests conducted by the company confirmed that people with diabetes who tasted the new bars thought they tasted like "real" candy, with none of the "cardboard taste" usually associated with sugar-free candy bars. And it is because of the pleasures our taste buds seek that International Delight(R) coffee creamers come in 11 flavors (e.g., cinnamon hazelnut, southern butter pecan, etc), and Arizona Iced tea comes in more than 20 flavors (e.g., Asia plum, ginseng, etc.), all to delight consumers with the sensory experience of taste.

THE SENSE OF SMELL
Oh, The Spell of that Hypnotic Fragrance

Who among us, while strolling through the mall, has not been tempted to buy a Cinnabon, or Aunt Annie's pretzel, or a cup of Starbucks cup of Caffe O'Lait? And it didn't matter whether or not we were hungry. The smell coming from mall eateries and coffee shops is simply irresistible. Likewise, we often wander into stores such as The Body Shop, just to smell some new lotions. And if we visit a perfume counter in a department store, we see 30 to 50 feet of counter space dedicated to perfumes and colognes. And each year there are new brands, with manufacturers hoping that consumers will like the olfactory experience of these new fragrances. Magazine pages are filled with strips of perfume or cologne samples.

Smell plays a big role in attracting consumers to stores and products. At the very least, stores should have pleasing aromas.[13] A Phoenix-based company, Digital Tech Frontier, is now marketing a machine called Visual Scentsations. The machine electronically blends and emits aromas that don't stick to clothing or hair. Suppose a store sells bakery products but does not bake on the premises. Using the machine, it can create an authentic baking aroma. The machine can control how far the smell goes and when and where it is released. The company is also selling the machine to airports, public theaters, hospitals, theme parks, and hotels. Who knows, next time you go to a Rainforest restaurant, you might even enjoy the aroma of a rainforest!

THE SENSE OF TOUCH
Touch Me, Touch Me Not

We all know the feeling: we are in a store, we read a sign that says "please do not touch," and we feel as if someone has clipped our wings. We feel that we have been denied one of our basic pleasures while shopping—tactile sensation. Tactile sensation is a significant consumption experience for a number of products. The texture of clothes, bedsheets, and towels; the temperature of food and beverages (which affects not only taste but also touch sensation); the consistency of skin ointments (moisturizing creams, after shave lotions, bath oils, etc.)—these and many other product qualities bring consumers pleasure because they evoke tactile sensation.

Touch is so important to our experience of most of these products that, when not allowed to touch, as consumers we feel almost disabled—rendered helpless in judging and evaluating them. Fortunately, though, tactile surfaces have a rough visual code; that is, through a history of personal experiences of touching and viewing the same surface simultaneously, we learn to recognize the tactile feel of a material by its appearance. That is why we are sometimes content merely to look at the material or look at the picture of the product and evaluate its tactile properties. But often, there is nothing like the real thing and the opportunity to touch it.

This tactile sensory experience (along with the visual treat) is what makes

Experience the Largest Collection of Tactile Experience

In the London's Science Museum, there is a remarkable superstructure, made from some 200 different materials, ranging from lace to slate. It is made by sculptor Thomas Heatherwick who was asked in 1999 to create an object that incorporated the world's largest collection of materials. Understandably, it is also the singular object with the largest number of different kinds of tactile surfaces in the world. Adjacent to the exhibit are swatches of each material that you can touch and feel.

Source: Catherine Slessor, "Materials House by Thomas Heatherwick," Delight, Nov, 1999

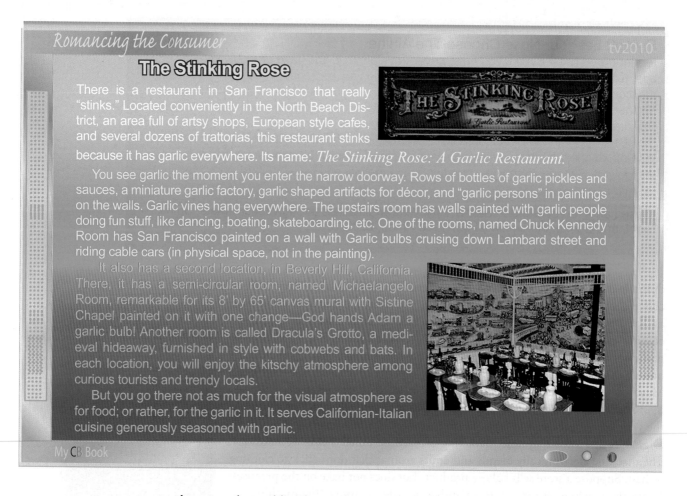

The Stinking Rose

There is a restaurant in San Francisco that really "stinks." Located conveniently in the North Beach District, an area full of artsy shops, European style cafes, and several dozens of trattorias, this restaurant stinks because it has garlic everywhere. Its name: *The Stinking Rose: A Garlic Restaurant.*

You see garlic the moment you enter the narrow doorway. Rows of bottles of garlic pickles and sauces, a miniature garlic factory, garlic shaped artifacts for décor, and "garlic persons" in paintings on the walls. Garlic vines hang everywhere. The upstairs room has walls painted with garlic people doing fun stuff, like dancing, boating, skateboarding, etc. One of the rooms, named Chuck Kennedy Room has San Francisco painted on a wall with Garlic bulbs cruising down Lambard street and riding cable cars (in physical space, not in the painting).

It also has a second location, in Beverly Hill, California. There, it has a semi-circular room, named Michaelangelo Room, remarkable for its 8' by 65' canvas mural with Sistine Chapel painted on it with one change—God hands Adam a garlic bulb! Another room is called Dracula's Grotto, a medieval hideaway, furnished in style with cobwebs and bats. In each location, you will enjoy the kitschy atmosphere among curious tourists and trendy locals.

But you go there not as much for the visual atmosphere as for food; or rather, for the garlic in it. It serves Californian-Italian cuisine generously seasoned with garlic.

My CB Book

---

shopping pleasurable. That is why retail stores display products in places where consumers can touch and feel them. And that is why many e-tailers who started out purely with Internet presences are now opening showcase brick and mortar stores. For example, bluemercury.com started out as an "Internet only" company, but now has two physical locations in Washington D.C., one in Philadelphia; one in Ardmore, Pennsylvania; and one in Princeton, New Jersey. (Curious about what it sells? Well, Google it.)

SIGHT

The Eyes Never Had It So Good!

Finally, there is the sensory experience of sight. This experience works on two levels: visual identity and experiential pleasure. (Actually, all five senses can and do receive stimuli both as identity and as sensory pleasure, but it is easier to illustrate this dual experience of sensation for the sense of sight.)

Visual Identity When we think of any object, brand, product, etc., we visualize it. If we can see it, in our mind's eye, as distinct from other objects, brands, or products, then its visual identity has made an impression on us. Forming this impression means both that we are able to tell it apart from other similar things and that we have certain impressions about it. Brands do it by using brand logos, brand marks, or brand symbols. Thus, most consumers recognize McDonald's by its golden arches, Delta airlines by its the stylized Greek letter delta, and Merrill Lynch by its bull. Companies sometimes change their logos to keep the brand or company's image contemporary. In 2003, petroleum company BP Amoco changed its brand mark from a shield to a multi-layered sunflower. Note that the company still kept the core colors (green ground with yellow figure), but changed the icon. The old shield stood for protection and stability, but that image was not considered relevant anymore. The new figure looks more contemporary, so it certainly creates the perception of a modern company. But beyond that, the company intended the interlocking pattern of sunflower petals (technically called Helio's mark) to symbolize the

From a shield to a vibrant sunburst (named Helios, after the sungod of ancient Greece.)

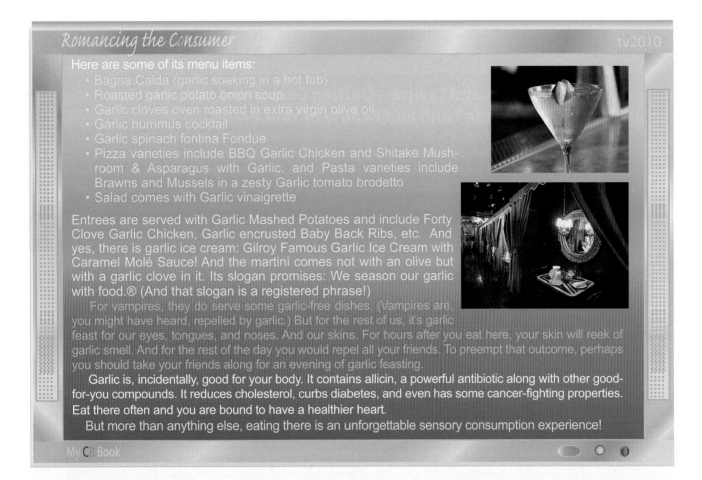

Here are some of its menu items:
- Bagna Calda (garlic soaking in a hot tub)
- Roasted garlic potato onion soup
- Garlic cloves oven roasted in extra virgin olive oil
- Garlic hummus cocktail
- Garlic spinach fontina Fondue
- Pizza varieties include BBQ Garlic Chicken and Shitake Mushroom & Asparagus with Garlic, and Pasta varieties include Brawns and Mussels in a zesty Garlic tomato brodetto
- Salad comes with Garlic vinaigrette

Entrees are served with Garlic Mashed Potatoes and include Forty Clove Garlic Chicken, Garlic encrusted Baby Back Ribs, etc. And yes, there is garlic ice cream: Gilroy Famous Garlic Ice Cream with Caramel Molé Sauce! And the martini comes not with an olive but with a garlic clove in it. Its slogan promises: We season our garlic with food.® (And that slogan is a registered phrase!)

For vampires, they do serve some garlic-free dishes. (Vampires are, you might have heard, repelled by garlic.) But for the rest of us, it's garlic feast for our eyes, tongues, and noses. And our skins. For hours after you eat here, your skin will reek of garlic smell. And for the rest of the day you would repel all your friends. To preempt that outcome, perhaps you should take your friends along for an evening of garlic feasting.

Garlic is, incidentally, good for your body. It contains allicin, a powerful antibiotic along with other good-for-you compounds. It reduces cholesterol, curbs diabetes, and even has some cancer-fighting properties. Eat there often and you are bound to have a healthier heart.

But more than anything else, eating there is an unforgettable sensory consumption experience!

My CB Book

sun, energy, and BP's commitment to environmental leadership.

Visual identity also comes from all other visual aspects of the brand, such as the color and design on the package, color of vehicles and employee uniform in a service company (e.g., UPS's brown), or the look of a store. DHL, a well-known package shipping company in Europe, recently bought US-based Airborne to expand its presence in the United States. With its vivid, yellow colored-images of vehicles and packages, it succeeded in creating a distinct visual identity almost overnight.

Experiential pleasure Beyond the identity, the visual stimuli related to a brand also offer a pleasurable sensory experience (just as stimuli do through other senses). The packaging of Arizona Iced Tea is a treat for the eye (both in the physical brand and in its presence on the company's Web site. And the visual cacophony of colors, shapes, and textures in stores and on merchandise beckon millions of consumers to malls and stores, whether or not they intend to buy anything.[14] Some brands have showcase stores like Niketown and Apple to provide unusual sensory experiences. Some stores even commission renowned architects to design stores and merchandise displays that offer truly unique sensory experiences. Ed Tsuwaki, a well-known Japanese graphic designer, designed unusual swan-necked mannequins that now display clothing in nakEd bunch stores in Tokyo. And fashion retailer DAKS features in its flagship store on Old Bond Street in London a dramatic sculpture group designed by renowned Swedish artist Lars Nilsson.

Attractive cans of Arizona Iced Tea

Milk, Oranges, and Levitra—Getting Consumers to Appreciate the Truth and Beauty of Your Brand

This we have said before, but it bears repeating. More than the product's reality, consumer perceptions of it matter. For a marketer, having a product with desirable qualities is good, even a necessity, but it is not enough. Beyond that, you have to get the consumer to perceive it correctly. And appreciate it. If consumer perceptions fall short of the product's reality, don't blame consumers for it. It is how our minds function. With efficient stimulus coding as our goal, our minds form a perception that sits well with our prior expectations—with our map of the world, so to speak. If we believe, as marketers, that consumer perceptions are currently distorted, then we have the onus, and some "power of product reality" on our side, to mold those perceptions. Savvy marketers have shouldered this responsibility with understanding and grace.

As examples, three marketing communications come to mind—no doubt, there are umpteen others. The famous milk moustache campaign was conceived to battle a typical product image problem—most consumers thought milk was a sissy drink. Is it? Not any more—not after you have seen that now familiar milk moustache on the mouths of celebrities and athletes of every ilk. Milk is now "must have" nourishment for health-conscious adults everywhere. No, it has not exactly become a fashionable drink, but "sissy" it is no more.

As our second example, revist the Sunkist ad you saw earlier. The copy reads: Cookies—well, oranges are round. And moist. And certainly sweet. Okay, maybe you can't call one a cookie, but don't let an orange hear you say that it isn't a snack. Better snacking. Not exactly earth shaking (and it shouldn't be), but if some consumers now began to perceive oranges as snack food, then that is all the ad asks. Advertising should not be a gimmick to "con" consumers into thinking and perceiving what a product factually is not, and this Sunkist ad doesn't act that way. It simply, and gently, nudges consumers' current perceptions with the product's reality.

Our third example comes from a commercial from Superbowl XXXVIII, played in the U.S. on February 1, 2004. The product is Levitra—and endorsing it is no other than well-respected coach Mike Ditka. Bob Dole, before him, had endorsed Viagra, making, in effect, the ailment it treats a non-taboo topic. But a super-performing athlete Bob Dole is not. Levitra makers wanted to make sure the product was not perceived as something meant only for wimpy old men, but that it is perfectly fair game for otherwise potent-bodied, healthy men as well—this is the perception Ditka is supposed to deliver. And he left no doubt in the consumer mind—unlike Bob Dole who spoke of the product but without explicit personal testimony, Ditka proclaimed, "Take the Levitra challenge, like I did."

Will it succeed in creating the perception the company seeks? You decide. But whatever your judgment about any of the above three ads, and about countless others, at least you now know the power of perceptions and how marketers must navigate and shape these through well thought out stimuli design—i.e., all marketing communications.

As you "encounter" exposure from other marketing stimuli in your everyday life, look at them as fodder for consumer perceptions, and judge how well they do (or not) their expected jobs.

In this chapter, we described consumer perception as a three-step process—stimulus sensation/exposure, selection/attention, and sense-making/interpretation. In this perceptual process, we identified the influence of the characteristics of the stimulus or incoming information, the influence of the context, and the role of the consumers' own characteristics. We described how marketers attempt to gain exposure by carefully targeting media audiences and lately through product placement in media events. Once exposed in the right media, the product or advertising message achieves sensation based on the sensory characteristics of the stimulus—the more vivid the stimulus, the greater the likelihood of consumer sensing it. Once sensed, consumers select it for further attention, depending on consumer interest or involvement in the topic presented. And finally, sense-making or interpretation depends on the consumer's prior expectations and the context of the stimulus. For a product, everything serves as context—brand name, package design, price, and the store in which the product is carried. Marketers, therefore, need to fashion these elements of their offerings so that the core products get perceived in the desired fashion.

Next, we described three biases in the perception process: selective exposure, selective attention, and selective interpretation. These processes allow us to escape from (selective exposure) and cope with (selective attention) the barrage of stimuli that constantly face us; they allow us also to complete the task of sense-making (selective interpretation) efficiently. Marketers should be aware of these biases and where necessary design their stimuli to harness these biases in their favor.

In the second half of the chapter, we put these concepts to practical application. Here, we examined five areas of marketing where perceptions influence consumer behavior: (i) the psychophysics of consumer price perceptions, (ii) country-of-origin effects, (iii) brand image and brand extensions, (iv) perceptual maps and positioning, and (v) sensory marketing. Any given price is perceived as good or bad depending on what is known as *reference price*. The country of a product's origin affects consumer perception of a product's quality. Some brand extensions are perceived as natural and are therefore assimilated by consumers; others are perceived as misfits and rejected. Perceptual maps place competing brands in a common space, and these maps then guide the marketer to reposition a brand. Discussion of these practical issues in marketing highlighted the role of perceptual processes in consumer response to marketing programs.

The last application, sensory marketing, concerns how marketers are structuring the entire marketplace environment to appeal to consumers' various senses. In this section, we highlighted the sensory experience of stimuli through each of the five senses: sight, hearing, smell, touch, and taste. Whatever the ultimate benefits and appeal of products, these must first pass through the sensory screens. It behooves marketers, therefore, to design all stimuli with noteworthy sensory experience, with attention to each of the five senses. With the increasing deployment of multi-media technology, both in physical and digital worlds, the potential for sensory marketing is vast. As marketers and students of consumer behavior, becoming aware of consumer perception processes will help you fashion your marketing mix for maximum perceptual advantage.

KEY TERMS

Attention	Perceptual Distortion	Odd Pricing
Perception	Perceptual Threshold	Quality Cue
Sensation	Just Noticeable Difference (j.n.d.)	Country-of-Origin Effects
Sense-making	Weber's Law	Visual Identity
Context effect	Subliminal perception	Sensory Marketing
Stimulus	Gestalt	Positioning
Organization	Closure	Repositioning
Interpretation	Reference Price	Mere Exposure Effect
Expectations	Assimilation and Contrast	

REVIEW+Rewind

1. Describe the three steps in the perception process and illustrate them with an example drawn from your own experience.

2. Define attention and its two forms: voluntary and involuntary. Give an example of each.

3. Perception is affected by three groups of factors—what are these? Illustrate each with an example from your personal experience.

4. Explain perceptual distortion.

5. Explain the concepts of just noticeable difference (j.n.d.) and Weber's law. How can marketers utilize these concepts?

6. What is "mere exposure effect" and its relevance to marketers?

7. Explain the concepts of (a) gestalt, (b) figure and ground, and (c) closure.

8. Explain the concepts of positioning and repositioning. The chapter describes several approaches to repositioning a brand in the consumer mind. Briefly explain each with a current example.

9. What is meant by internal and external reference price? What is its relevance to a company's pricing decisions?

THINK+Apply

1. As a consumer, have you experienced perceptual distortion? Why did these occur in your case?

2. Assess all ads in the book so far in terms of their effectiveness in creating distinct positioning for the advertised brand. Next, find an ad for each method of positioning and repositioning, and comment on their likely effectiveness in creating a distinct "brand perception" in the consumer mind.

3. What advice would you give a company considering a product line extension—should it use family name or new, individual brand names?

4. Assume that you own a clothing company in a country, say, Malaysia. You wonder whether country-of-origin effects will work in your favor or against you in the U.S. and Canada. How will you research this issue? Write a memo "educating the rest of your marketing team," on exactly what effect country-of-origin has on consumers.

PRACTICE+Experience

3. Set up a blind taste test for two brands of cola or power drinks. Have consumers choose between the two brands with their brand names: (a) not revealed, (b) revealed correctly, and (c) revealed falsely (i.e., call each drink by the other's name). Tally, for each condition, the proportion of those who chose the brand they usually and knowingly prefer, versus those who misjudged their brands. Summarize your findings.

4. Get three consumers to draw perceptual maps for

(choose one):

a. Five brands of jeans.

b. Five brands of athletic shoes.

c. Five brands of credit cards.

Then adopt one of the brands as your company's brand, and suggest marketing action to improve its perceptual position, separately, for each of the three consumers.

Visit your local supermarket and browse through the product displays of three categories: beverages, candies and cookies, and men's grooming products. Identify brands that do a good job of (a) establishing a distinct visual identity, and (b) creating pleasurable sensory experience.

3. Visit your local mall and make a list of all stores that utilize one or more of the five sensory stimuli to appeal to consumers. For each selected store, list and describe examples of each of the five sense appeals. Next, choose two stores that might be utilizing some but not all feasible types of the five sense appeals, and suggest how they could bridge this gap.

4. Visit your local mall and make a list of all the stores that utilize one or more of the five sensory stimuli to appeal to consumers. For each selected store, list and describe examples of each of the five sensory appeals. Next, choose two stores that might be utilizing some but not all feasible types of the five sensory appeals, and suggest how they could bridge this gap.

5. Take along a consumer on a cyber tour of www.evian.com. Then interview the consumer about his/her perceptions about this brand. Next, take him/her on a cyber tour of www.dasani.com and interview him/her to understand his/her perceptions of this brand. Repeat this for several other consumers (depending on time allocated to this assignment). Summarize how the two brand perceptions differ, and then exercise your brains (and analyze the two web sites) to figure out what elements of these web sites end up causing these differing perceptions. After a few interviews, you may want to structure consumers' response somewhat. For this purpose, prepare a list of dimensions on which you might want to assess perceptions. And if you really want to add some more fun to the exercise, add www.vitaminwater.com to the mix, thus assessing and comparing consumer perceptions of three brands.

In the Marketing Manager's Shoes

Most concepts in the chapter have some lessons for the marketing manager, i.e., they suggest to the marketing manager what to do differently in practice; indeed, often these applications are implicit in our explanations of the concepts and models in the chapter. Identify at least five specific applications of the chapter's concepts--all of which should be entirely new different from the examples cited here.

CHINESE LAUNDRY

Unless you have missed the scene on women's shoe fashions, you know that the name has nothing to do with laundry. Rather it is the name of a very fashionable brand of women's shoes. Cels Enterprises, Inc. a privately owned women's footwear company headquartered in Los Angeles, launched the brand in 1982, with shoes that ranged from stylish daytime looks to evening collections in dressy metallics and iridescents.

But as time went on, while the shoe kept up with the trends, its visual identity needed an uplift. To the rescue came an innovative firm, Los Angeles based Chase Design Group. Their creativity and brand sense is visible in the new package and logo designs shown here.

Packaging alone doesn't help, of course. Supporting it must be the product's reality the package promises. So, what kind of a shoe is Chinese Laundry? It was featured recently in the final episodes of Emmy Award-nominated reality TV series Project Runway. (Project Runway, now in its 3rd season, is a national design competition in which unknown designers compete for the opportunity to show their collection at the New York Olympus Fashion Week.)

New shoe box

old shoe box

Visual identity builds a brand. It creates an expectation, a perception of the brand. Then it is up to the brand/product to live up to those expectations and help consumers maintain those initial perceptions, or alternatively, let consumers' expectations down. For a brand that will deliver, in actuality, the benefits and value (utilitarian as well as symbolic—e. g. ego/identity supporting, see Chapter 1), **visual identity** can go a long way in helping build the right brand perceptions.

The Consumer
As A
Learner

- Four Models of Consumer Learning
- Consumer Information Processing
- Mnemonics—Helping Consumers Remember
- Adoption of Innovation—The Ultimate Learning Experience
- What Makes An Innovation Hot
- Consumer Nostalgia—Down Memory Lane

In early 2001, Forbes magazine sent its subscribers a curious free gift: a European toy car, resembling Jaguar, with a cat face on it. Okay, it wasn't really a toy car, but it resembled one. In fact, it was better than a toy car. Rather than just look at it, you could actually use it—to surf in Cyberspace.

Called :CueCat, it was a device you could use to scan bar codes. The plan was for each Forbes magazine ad to have a barcode. So, let's say you are reading the magazine, you see an ad for a DVD player, and you want more information on it. All you do is swipe the :CueCat over the barcode, and bingo, the DVD player maker's homepage pops up on your PC screen. (Oh yes, you did have to plug the :CueCat into your PC.) The people who came up with the idea and the device were certain consumers would find it very useful—if they saw an ad in the magazine and wanted more information, they could instantly connect

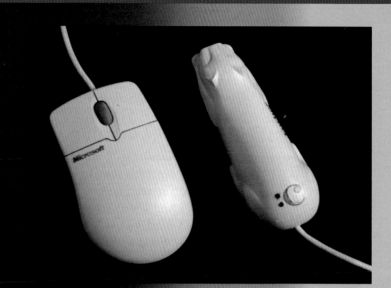

The :CueCat—a device that was intended to scan bar codes and send consumers to the brand's Web site for more information.

to the company's Web site, and then, if they liked, buy the product. The :CueCat would also work on the UPC codes on the product packages themselves, of course. Besides, your mouse could use some company! (It is called :CueCat, remember?)

"In one swipe, it takes you to 20,000 leagues under the sea," said an executive involved in the marketing of the device.[1] While Forbes subscribers (author included) received the cute :CueCat free and home-delivered, anyone could get it at RadioShack.[2] So, now you can hardly wait to go to RadioShack and get your hands on the :CueCat, right? Oh, yeah, right!

INTRODUCTION

The :CueCat was cute all right, but consumers weren't buying it. The company with the :CueCat idea had a vision: One day, all ads in all magazines would carry the :CueCat scannable bar codes. But the idea never took off—and it wasn't just because consumers were not tech-savvy; many were. Consumers just didn't see any advantage to it. After all, if they wanted to go to a company's Web site, all they had to do was Google the company name. Why should they learn this new trick—using the :CueCat? Consumers learn what they want, and don't bother learning what they don't anticipate will be rewarding.

Since marketers are busy teaching consumers all sorts of things about their products, it would help to understand how consumers learn. We are going to explain consumer learning in this chapter, for marketers' benefit and for your benefit as well.

We begin this chapter by defining what it means for consumers to be learners, and we describe four different ways consumers learn. While you are constantly learning, in life and in this book, you should be intrigued by the idea of learning about learning itself. We will tell you about three modes of learning that humans share with other species. Then we will tell you about the fourth mode, unique to humans, and here we will take you deep inside the consumer mind, showing you how it works as a super-efficient computer, serving as a storehouse for a lifetime of information. Of all the things you learn, perhaps the most important to you, at least in your role as a consumer, is learning about new products and deciding what to do about them—adopt them, reject them, or wait a while. Your adoption of new products is especially important to marketers, since millions of dollars or euros or yen are made or lost in their efforts to get you to learn a new consumption or shopping behavior (such as using the :CueCat), to learn a new trick, so to speak. We conclude this chapter, therefore, with advice to marketers about fashioning their products (innovations or otherwise) and their communications so as to mesh with the four modes of consumer learning. Let us begin at the beginning: by defining *learning*.

Consumer Learning Defined

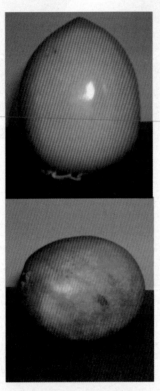

Learning is acquiring a response to a stimulus. Suppose you are in a fruit and vegetable store in an Asian country (or an ethnic store in your own country) and you see persimmons—a fruit you have never seen before. What would you do? And if you saw, say, mangoes—a fruit you tried recently at a friend's home and liked—what would you do? Most likely, you would put the mangoes in your shopping basket and ignore the persimmons. Thus, you would have learned a response to mangoes but not to persimmons. And once you had acquired a response, you would use it automatically in similar future situations.

A learned response can be mental, or it can be behavioral. When we see a shirt with the Kenneth Cole name on it, we conjure an image of well-made, prestigious clothing (a mental response); when we hear Bon Jovi is coming to town, we quickly buy a ticket for his concert (a behavioral response). As humans, we learn because it helps us respond better to our environment. For instance, a child who accidentally puts his hand on a hot light bulb learns never again to touch a hot light bulb. Or, a consumer who gets trapped into buying a substandard product from a mail-order company learns to never again buy anything from that company. In fact, he or she might learn not to buy anything from any mail order firm. Conversely, when consumers wary of the authenticity of sellers on eBay, receive the product just as they expected, they learn to trust eBay sellers. Along the way, as they bid for items a few more times, they even learn the best strategies for bidding, avoiding the mistakes made the first time. With each experience, they learn to adapt their responses better. Thus, the purpose of all human learning is to acquire a potential for future adaptive behavior.

Persimmon (Top) and Mango

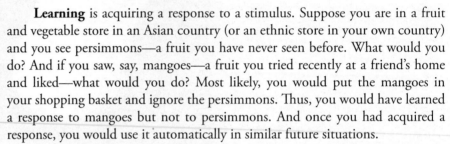

The purpose of all human learning is to acquire a potential for future adaptive behavior.

FOUR MODELS OF CONSUMER LEARNING

Or How the Dog, Pigeon, Monkey, and Computer Get It

There are four mechanisms, or models, of consumer learning. Although you may not know about them, you use all four of them in your everyday life. Consider the following consumer scenarios.

Four Consumer Scenarios

• You give an expensive cologne, Polo, to your friend Miguel on his birthday. But he is not thrilled. He tells you he only uses Curve. "Polo is a little too loud and stuffy... kind of like flaunting your riches," he tells you. "Curve is more subtle and sexy—if you know what I mean," he adds. How can he say that? You are actually wearing Polo yourself, but he has never been able to tell! Where did he learn this notion about Polo anyway?

• Your friend Christèle always flies with Delta Airlines. Once, she opted to take a 6 a.m. flight even though American Airlines had a more convenient 7 a.m. flight. How does Delta get her to show such loyalty?

• Your neighbor's son, David, is in high school; he wears oversized shirts, baggy pants, baseball hats turned backwards, beads, headbands, and earrings. So do his friends. Where did they learn to dress this way?

• You run into your friend Mary Louise at Sydney Harbor and she is excited about a new cell phone she just read about—the Ericsson's soon-to-be-released model 3G K618. "You can make video calls from this. You can take photos of course, but the thing is that you can store up to 700 photos and share them with friends," she tells you. It has Bluetooth™ Streaming, which means you can download full-length music and video clips, and then you can send it to any Bluetooth™-enabled stereo set. And if you happen to see some cool stuff in a store, or a cool scene on the street, you can zoom in on that scene, click the camera button, and then instantly beam that picture to your blog to be seen by your friends. And of course, you can surf the net and receive all your emails as well.

Each of these scenarios represents a distinct model of consumer learning: classical conditioning, instrumental learning, modeling, and cognitive learning. Let us learn more about each.

FIGURE **4.1** FOUR MODEL OF LEARNING

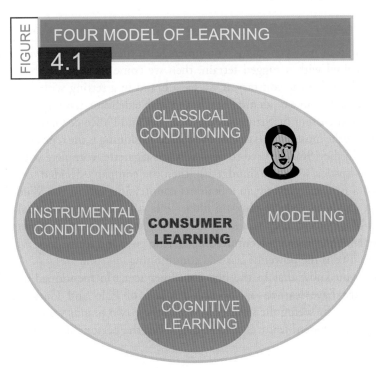

The Most Famous Dog in Psychology

We will talk about consumers in a minute, but first a story about the most famous dog in psychology—known simply as Pavlov's Dog. Ivan Petrovich Pavlov was a Russian psychologist interested in understanding the learning processes of humans and animals. A giant in the field in his time (1849-1936), with a Nobel Prize in physiology, Pavlov studied the human learning process by experimenting on animals. In his experiments, Pavlov harnessed a dog, gave him some meat powder, and observed that the dog salivated. This salivation is an inherited reflex. Next, Pavlov rang a bell just before giving the dog meat powder, and repeated this sequence several times; the dog salivated every time. Then, he merely rang the bell without giving the dog any meat powder. Now, you wouldn't expect the dog to salivate just with the ringing of the bell, would you? Yet in this experiment, the dog did!

This finding was groundbreaking in the study of human learning, but to appreciate it fully, you must first learn a few technical terms. In this experiment, the meat powder is called an unconditioned stimulus, and the bell is called a conditioned stimulus. An **unconditioned stimulus** (UCS) refers to a stimulus to which the consumer already has a pre-existing response. A **conditioned stimulus** (CS) is a stimulus to which the consumer either does not have a response or has a pre-existing response that needs modification, so a new response needs to be conditioned.[3]

In summarizing his findings, Pavlov said he had conditioned the dog to salivate to the bell. In other words, the dog had "learned" the salivating response to the bell. Note that the salivating response to the meat powder itself did not have to be learned, since it already existed as an instinctual response. Rather, the transfer (i.e., conditioning) of this response to the bell, a previously neutral stimulus, is what constitutes "learning."

Because you may have heard this story many times, nothing may seem unusual about it on the surface. But think deeper. The sound of the bell is not inherently appealing to the dog, and the dog had never before salivated on hearing it. However, now the bell successfully elicits that response.

This is **classical conditioning** at work—a process of learning by an extension of a pre-existing response from one stimulus on to another stimulus through exposure to the two stimuli simultaneously.

What Does Pavlov's Dog Have To Do With Marketing?

Believe it or not, as humans, consumers learn the same way. If we see a new product or brand paired with a rugged terrain, then we come to perceive that brand as rugged and masculine. On the contrary, if we see a brand in a setting with soft colors and silky textures, then we come to identify that brand with a delicate, feminine image. Want proof? Just check out current magazine ads for Wrangler and Dolce & Gabanna clothing.

Perhaps the most famous case of classical conditioning is the repositioning of Marlboro cigarettes. In the 1960s, it used to be a woman's cigarette, complete with a filter and pink tip (so the lipstick wouldn't smudge it)! Then the company decided to change its image. It created a fictional cowboy, in a fictional countryside, out in the Wild, Wild West. Of course, it also removed the pink-tip filter. Today, if consumers were asked what type of cigarette Marlboro is, they would invariably say it is a masculine cigarette: and one for the independent, rugged, adventuresome, macho guy (and for women who see themselves that way). This is the power of classical conditioning.

Now you know that in the first consumer scenario mentioned above, your friend Miguel must have learned of the brand image of Polo and Curve through classical conditioning—by seeing the settings in which these two brands were advertised, since the two colognes' inherent features tell nothing about the personality of the two brands.

Classical Conditioning is Everywhere

For classical conditioning to work, what is absolutely essential is constant pairing—your brand should be constantly paired with a desirable setting or with another desirable stimulus. The setting can include any number of things in the ad: color, look and feel of the ad, scenery, music in the jingle or commercial, or even the event being depicted (e.g., two people fighting versus showing affection). Other stimuli in the ad can include other objects or products (e.g., pair your brand of water, say, with a luxury car), soundbites (e.g., lyrics from an Elvis song or the voice of Will & Grace star Megan Mullally), and, of course, specific persons (e.g., pair your brand of toupee with a tycoon or, alternatively, a hard-working athlete).

The magic of such pairings is constantly at work in ads everywhere. Thus, CK perfume is "youthful" because of the teenage models used in the brand's advertising, and Giorgio is "mature" and "richer" because of its Beverly Hills heritage. Coca-Cola uses real life vignettes (with the tag line "Life is Good. Coca-Cola.") to convey its "real-thing" image, while Pepsi uses Britney Spears and Halle Berry to promote its "New Generation" image.[4]

(Courtesy: Stacy Adams)

How do consumers learn which brand of shoes (and clothing) is for whom? Stacy Adams shows its shoes with fashionable clothing with fashionable, urban, trendy, young men; the brand and the wearer add to each other's allure. (allure? See the admiring woman behind.) Here Classical conditioning is at work, superbly, alluringly!

INSTRUMENTAL LEARNING

Or How a Pigeon Learns to Peck

The second learning mechanism takes us to other animals. Psychologist B.F. Skinner experimented with pigeons. He built two doors in a pigeon feed box, one fake and one real. Peck on the fake one and nothing happens; peck on the real one and food grains fall out. After a few trials, the pigeons learned to peck on the right door. This is **instrumental learning** (also called instrumental conditioning or operant conditioning)—a process where one learns behavior because it is rewarding. That is, we learn a response because it is instrumental to obtaining a reward. This is the familiar way we get children to learn good behaviors—"Eat your vegetables and you'll get dessert," we tell them.

Can marketers use this method to help consumers learn? Absolutely. By rewarding the consumer if he or she buys the marketer's brand. Buy my product, and you get a chance to win a prize. Shop at my store, and you get "double your coupon" deal. Use my credit card, and you get some cash back. Fly my airline, and you earn loyalty points good for a free trip—in fact this is how your friend Christèle must have learned to always fly with Delta Airlines.

This reward comes in two forms: extrinsic and intrinsic. An **extrinsic reward** is external to the product; e.g., coupons, sweepstakes, rebates, and loyalty programs such as frequent flyer or frequent hotel stay rewards. Cigna, an insurance company, offers incentives to get its members to engage in pro-health behaviors. In contrast, an **intrinsic reward** is the reward built into the product itself—consumers learn to buy and use a product because they find the product itself rewarding. For example, we learn to use Bed Head shampoo because it renders our hair just the way we want it, and we learn to drink Fruitopia because we savor its taste. We learn to visit the video game arcade Gameworks because we have a good time there, and we learn to buy Twelve Girls Band's new CD *Romantic Energy* because we found their previous releases—*Eastern Energy*, *Journey to Silk Road*, and *Shining Energy*—enchanting. (Check it out at www.twelvegirlsband.com.)

This distinction between intrinsic and extrinsic rewards is important to marketers. If the product is not, in itself, rewarding to the consumer (or not any more rewarding than competitors' products), then, to get the consumer to buy their product, marketers have to resort to extrinsic rewards, such as coupons, rebates, and frequent buyer rewards. However, consumer patronage won through such giveaways is rarely lasting. Rather than luring consumers through constant rebates and promotions, as marketers we should instead make our product itself intrinsically rewarding to the consumer. That way, the consumer buys our product not merely because of a coupon or sale (an extrinsic reward), but because he or she likes our product itself more. That is, as marketers, we have to get the consumer to learn to respond primarily to our product, not to extrinsic rewards. Frequency award programs, and indeed all extrinsic rewards, should serve, at best, as proverbial icing on the cake, but the real lure should be the cake itself.

Please, *instrumentally condition* me...

i am a consumer. instrumentally condition me. and i will learn to buy your products.
instrinsic or extrinsic—which reward is twelvegirlsband offering me?
dare to figure that... or else i will take my money to another marketer who does!

MODELING

Monkey See, Monkey Do

Let's continue with animals. This time, a monkey—actually, a bunch of them. Watch them sometime. One monkey would start scratching his head, or making faces, or swinging from a tree branch, and then all the other monkeys would do the same. This is the third mechanism of learning, called **modeling**—a process whereby learning occurs by observing others.[5]

This "monkey see, monkey do" phenomenon is very much present in humans as well. Children learn much of their social behavior by observing and imitating their elders. We also learn from teachers, celebrities, coworkers, and other role models we admire. Many teenagers adopted the grunge look sported by teen music artist Avril Lavigne or rapper Nelly. You now realize that in the third consumer scenario described above, this is how our neighbor's son, David, must have learned to dress the way he does.

In our day-to-day lives, we observe people we like or aspire to be like, and we learn what they consider good to wear, eat, and do. Thus, clothing with specific designer names becomes popular because influential people wear it. Hairstyles become popular on college campuses based on peer observations. And we choose careers because someone inspires us as a role model. Marketers harness this learning mechanism, for example, when they send product samples to influential and well-respected people, hoping that their followers will adopt the product when they see their leaders and role models using it.

COGNITIVE LEARNING

What an Amazing Supercomputer Our Mind Is!

For this fourth and last method of learning, we move from animals to machines. When people talk about learning, they often are thinking of cognitive learning (rather than the other three forms). **Cognitive learning** refers to learning by acquiring new information from written or oral communication. When we acquire information about something, whether incidentally and passively or deliberately and actively, we learn– cognitively. In reading this book (and in listening to your instructor), you are actually learning cognitively.

Much of our learning about products also happens this way. Before we purchase technical products, we read product brochures, ask salespeople questions, and examine product features. In the fourth consumer scenario, this is how Mary Louise, the friend you met at Sydney Harbor, must have learned about the various features of Ericsson's soon-to-be-released model 3G K618 cell phone. And of course, much of our learning about life or things that are useful to us every day also comes from cognitive learning—by reading informative articles in newspapers, magazines, or on Web sites, and by listening to words of wisdom from sages, consultants, soothsayers, and personal advisors. Read Exhibit 4.1, for example, courtesy of Solis Belt University. (Yes, such a thing really exists!) If you learn anything about belts, then, well, you have just experienced cognitive learning.

Cognitive learning occurs on two levels: rote memorization and problem solving. With **rote memorization**, we rehearse the information until it gets firmly lodged in our long-term memory. Rote memorization can result from active rehearsal (as in trying to memorize the directions to that sushi place in Dallas, Deep Sushi), or from passive, repeated exposure to the information (seeing Deep Sushi ads often). A great deal of advertising aims simply to create a rote memory of the brand name or slogan by repeated presentation. Thus, most consumers around the world have learned by heart such slogans as "Coca-Cola: The Real Thing," and "Pepsi: The Choice of a New Generation." After being exposed to brand names and slogans about a thousand times, consumers end up learning them so well that, at the time of purchase, they remember and look for those brands.

In **problem solving**, we actively process information to reach certain judgments. Suppose you are wondering if you need to buy a T-mobile phone; you look at information about its features, weigh it in your mind, and then say, "Now I understand what T-mobile is and what it will do for me." This is cognitive learning about the T-mobile phone. This

---

Seven Tips For Wearing Belts   EXHIBIT 4.1

The belt you wear, and how you wear it, matters. Make your belt an afterthought at your own risk. Here are seven tips that will keep you looking good in your belt no matter the situation

1 Match your belt to your shoes. As with any fashion advice, there are exceptions to this rule, but belts in general should be the same color as your shoes.

2 Wear a belt that fits your waist. If you're a 36 men's, a 32 inch belt will only emphasize your denial about it.

3 If you're going to own one belt, make it black leather one with a silver buckle. (Go with a regular buckle.) It's the classic look. Canvas, suede, and studded belts work best if you're aiming for more of a casual or street look. A black leather belt is the right choice for dress pants and suits and it works in most casual situations as well.

4 Don't wear a belt with suspenders, unless you're trying to look goofy.

5 If you're going formal, get a dress belts that's an inch and a quarter without braids or special designs. Special designs and braids are for a more casual look.

6 If you're wearing gold jewelry, wear a belt with a gold buckle; if you're wearing silver jewelry, go with a silver buckle. Belts look best when they match your accessories

7 If you've got an elastic waist, cover it with a belt.

Q. Did you learn anything from the above guide? Which model of learning did you just experience?

Source: http://store.soliscompany.com/belts.html
Courtesy: Solis Company.

form of information utilization to form judgments is pervasive in our lives as consumers as we make brand choice decisions.

A variant of this is **insight**—the ability to see the hidden nature of a solution. An example of insight is solving this puzzle: Connect all nine dots with no more than four straight lines and without lifting your pen. You will find the solution somewhere in the book (we don't want to spoil your fun by giving it away right now), but for now we will give you a hint—*think outside the box*. Thinking outside the box is, in fact, a general key to solving all problems that require insight.

The problem solving type of learning obviously requires some mental effort, especially compared to rote memorization. The amount of mental effort depends on how much we want to learn about the product or brand. That depends, in turn, on the level of involvement we feel with the product. Involvement, you will recall, was defined in Chapter 2 as the degree of interest in an object or product. Thus, cognitive learning can be of two types: low involvement learning and high involvement learning.

In **low involvement learning**, the product is relevant but not much is at stake, such as a low priced item of routine use. We want to learn the brand name and possibly learn about its single, most relevant feature, if the information is readily available. So, with a quick glance at a print advertisement, we may learn the brand name Altoids (a mint), and we may also learn about its key feature, namely, that it is a strongly flavored mint. Consumers are unwilling to work hard to read an ad for a low involvement product; that is why these ads should be simple, featuring a visual, and merely a line or two of text if at all.[6]

In **high involvement learning**, the product is very important to us as consumers, and a lot is at stake—such as an expensive purchase of a DVD player or a cell phone, or even a cereal if we are very health conscious. Here, we want to choose the right product and the right brand, and therefore, we want to learn about several of the brand's features and capabilities. So, we read package labels, seek knowledgeable salespersons, search the Web for information, and read or watch the entire advertisement to understand as much information as possible. Let us summarize the four models in terms of what and how we learn (see Table 4.1).

STIMULUS GENERALIZATION AND DISCRIMINATION
The Art of Not Having to Learn All the Time

Consider the child who burned his hand by touching a yellow light bulb; he would never touch a yellow light bulb again, for he has learned that a glowing yellow ball-shaped object is painful to touch. In fact, he would most likely also learn that he shouldn't touch a white, red, or blue light bulb either—or, for that matter, anything that glows, even if it is not hot. This is a good thing; otherwise the poor child would have to learn a new response to each new object and would never have any time to play. Likewise, as consumers, we don't have to learn to respond anew every time we encounter a new stimulus. We quickly and instinctually repeat the response we have made in the past to other *similar stimuli*.

Suppose we are new immigrants from a country where there are no big self-browsing and self-service stores. In fact, there are no stores where you can walk inside the store—instead all the stores are storage rooms with a service window. (Indeed, most stores in many developing countries are set up this way!) Now in our new country, we find superstores where we can wander and browse. We go to one food store and learn that we are not supposed to run around, talk loud, or eat food inside the store; next, we would employ the same behavior in other stores even if these other stores sell different merchandise and have a different ambience, such as a department or jewelry store. This happens because humans learn to see the similarities even when two things are not exactly identical. Psychologists call this process **stimulus generalization**—a process wherein a consumer extends a learned response for one stimulus to other similar stimuli.

However, the child who burned his hand by touching a hot light bulb would not have learned not to touch a hot pan or put his finger in a cup of coffee because he sees these

Think Outside the box: Connect all nine dots with no more than four straight lines and without lifting your pencil or back-tracking.

TABLE 4.1

Four Models of Learning with Marketing Examples

Model	What is Learned	How	Example
CLASSICAL CONDITIONING	Brand Image, in terms of associations NOT necessarily related to inherent features of the brand.	By exposure to the brand along with another stimulus, consumers associate & extend the image of this other stimulus to the brand.	Forming an impression that cologne *Navigator* is for an independent, rugged, determined athletic man (simply because of the mood of the person in the ad)
	Emotional response	If marketers pair an emotional stimulus with the brand, then the consumer begins to feel the same emotion toward the brand.	Tommy Cologne ads show an American flag; the consumer then feels patriotic toward the cologne brand as well.
	Behavioral response	Certain stimuli bring out certain behaviors in humans. Expose consumers to those stimuli along with your brand or place, & consumers will automatically begin to act that way.	Play slow musical melody in the store, and consumers linger longer and buy more.
INSTRUMENTAL CONDITIONING	Brand purchase & use behavior	Because of some incentive we get every time we buy a product (extrinsic reward) Or Because we find the use of the product itself gratifying (intrinsic reward)	Renting movies from Hollywood (instead of another outlet) because of a free bonus movie. Can't wait to visit *Gameworks* when-ever possible because we enjoy it very much.
MODELING	Product or Brand use behavior	By observing people we like.	Buy a four-button jacket suit because you saw your favorite athlete wearing it.
COGNITIVE LEARNING	The intrinsic feature of the product or brand.	By paying attention to product information.	While searching the Internet for hotels in Seattle, you read about W Hotel & learn that it features contemporary urban chic decor, & is wired for Wi-Fi & i-Tunes.
(a) Low Involvement Learning	Brand name, jingles, etc.; at most one or two brand features for a simple and no-risk product.	By repeatedly being exposed to the advertisment; By effortlessly looking at or listening to a simple ad or by simply seeing a a brand package on display	Most consumers have learned "Can you hear me now" tagline for Verizon and know it means that the signal reception is good in all locations.
(b) High Involvement Learning	Consumers learn as much information about a product as there is to learn to solve a problem or make a product choice decision.	By reading the ad carefully or by paying attention to the commercial, or seeking advice from a salesperson or a professional	A consumer considering the Botox procedure to erase facial wrinkles reads its ad entirely, consults a professional & also checks out some information on the Internet.

objects different enough from the glowing bulb. Likewise, the immigrant consumer who has learned the behavioral protocol for a store would be at a loss when visiting a bar for the first time. This is just as well, for otherwise the consumer would have ended up making the wrong response (to his or her social embarrassment). This ability to see two stimuli as different helps consumers to respond to each in an appropriate way. Psychologists call this ability **stimulus discrimination**—a process wherein a consumer perceives two stimuli as different so that the response learned for one stimulus is not repeated for the other. Stimulus generalization is a useful shortcut, but it is a good thing that our minds also know when not to use such shortcuts.

(Courtesy: Stacy Adams)

That Stacy Adams Ad you saw before—look at it again. In addition to the Classical Conditioning method of learning, which other method is at work? Perhaps all three, but at least one more. Can you name it?

Note: Neither advertisers nor consumers need be aware of the specific method. Advertisers strive, simply but importantly, only to create and communicate an image association, and consumers learn it "naturally" by one of the four methods. Naming those methods as this chapter does is consumer researchers' (not consumers') tool of analysis.

A Shortcut for Every Season

Do consumers use this shortcut in all four modes of learning? Yes, they do. In classical conditioning, Pavlov's dog still salivates if the bell is replaced by a device that makes a similar but non-identical sound. Analogously, consumers come to see a brand of chewing gum featured with outdoor winter scenery as refreshing, but also when it is featured with outdoor autumn or spring scenery. Consumers see Michael Jordan with Gatorade and learn to associate Gatorade as a thirst quencher for athletes; if the brand later features Shaquille O'Neil in a new ad campaign, consumers still make the same association. Consumers who learn to buy clothing at the season's end to get a better price (an example of instrumental conditioning) also learn to buy snowplowing equipment at the end of the season and visit tourist spots off season. And in the cognitive learning mode, suppose we learn by reading somewhere that we should not leave audio-cassettes exposed to high sun in midsummer; we then also automatically surmise that, likewise, it is not good to leave videotapes exposed to the sun either (incidentally, this is the "insight" version of cognitive learning.) Thus, stimulus generalization means we get extra mileage out of what we have learned.

Savvy marketers utilize the concepts of stimulus generalization and discrimination to obtain favorable consumer responses. When a product is new but they want it to be seen as being of the same high quality and prestige as the company's other brands, they give the new product the appearance of the familiar brand, by package similarity and the brand name. Thus, new flavors of soup, new varieties of pasta, and new versions of videogames are given a brand family name and are packaged identically to the existing package. Store brands make their products resemble manufacturers' brands, hoping consumers will engage in stimulus generalization. In contrast, when marketers want to attract a new set of consumers, they name the new brand by a different and unique name—for example, Eternity and Obsession colognes (both from Calvin Klein).

CONSUMER INFORMATION PROCESSING MEMORY AND REMEMBERING

Inside the Supercomputer

Whereas the other three models of learning are applicable to non-human creatures as well, only humans have the capacity for cognitive learning because only we have the capability to process information. Of course, our brains, the human supercomputers, are not all created equal. There is this prodigy, Rajan Mahadevan, for example, who once recited from memory some 32,000 digits of pi, a task that took him about four hours. And in the movie Rain Man, Dustin Hoffman memorized all the cards in a deck in less than a second. But let us see what a normal brain can do.

Here is the phone number for London Business School: 44 (0)20 7262 5050; and for the high fashion retailer Louis Vuitton in Sydney, Australia: 61 2 9236 9680; and finally, for The White House: 202-456-1414. Can you memorize these? At least one of them? You are able to memorize the last one, right? This is because it is shorter, but also because it is only seven digits long (not counting the area code). Seven is also the number of digits (more exactly speaking, 'seven plus or minus two') a human can memorize at a time. Seven digits, seven letters, seven names, and so on. Psychologist George Miller has established through research that we are able to memorize seven bits of information, plus or minus two, at a time.[7] When we combine bits of information and treat the combined entity itself as a unit, with a meaning of its own, then that becomes a new single bit of information. This combination of bits into a new unit is called chunking. Thus, 911 is a single bit or chunk that stands for the emergency number to call in the U.S. and 411 is also a single bit, the number to call for information from your local phone company in the U.S. We can memorize seven bits of information, make it into a unit, and then move on to memorizing a new set of seven bits of information. Words we are already familiar with form a unit, no matter how many letters they may have. Thus, President's Delight as a brand name can be memorized quickly because both the words are already familiar.

HOW CONSUMER MEMORY WORKS

Sims Online, Pulp Fiction Bookpurses, and PAL Audio—Good Thing You Remembered at Least Two of Them!

Christmas is only one-week away and you still haven't decided what to buy for your little brother in junior college and your little sister in high school. Luckily, most of the ads you are seeing are for Christmas gifts. In particular, there were three commercials you saw—actually, there were many more, but you don't remember any of the others. Of the three you remember, one was advertising Sims Online, an Internet version of the virtual reality game SimCity, where you take on a persona and build a city in digital space. The Internet version allows you to invite your friends from anywhere to join you. The second ad you remember was advertising Pulp Fiction Bookpurses—fun purses made with vintage pulp-fiction book jackets with titles like Don't Push Me Around and Boy Chaser. The third was advertising a portable radio with a speaker that radiates enough sound to warm a room. It can also be connected to a CD player.

The three commercials seem to be a good answer to your Christmas gift problem. You would buy Sims Online for your brother and the bookpurse for your sis. And, the PAL radio—well, that would be great for you to take on vacations. You make a mental note of these to check them out the next day.

So today, you go to the local software store and buy Sims Online. You will find the PAL radio at a local electronics store. If you don't find it there, then you will check it out on the Internet. But there is a problem with the bookpurse—its actual name is not Pulp Fiction. It is something else but you don't remember. So you don't know where even to start the search. It is a good thing you at least remember the other two. Still, you feel frustrated for not remembering the bookpurse's brand name.

Why didn't you remember it? Don't worry, it is not your fault. This is how a normal brain works, and this is how our memories work. So, just what is memory, and how does it work?

Memory is a place in the human brain where information is processed and stored. It is like a warehouse that holds all we know and all we will ever know over our entire lifetimes. Memory refers to both this storage area and its stored contents. It is divided into three parts: sensory, short term, and long term.

Sensory Memory **Sensory memory** is the ability of our senses to keep information

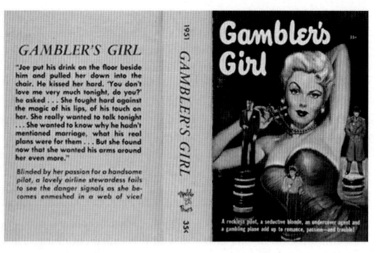

alive briefly. While watching TV ads, for example, only the sounds (voice and music, if any) will register on our auditory senses, and only the visuals will register on our vision senses—only these sensory features of the entire ad, not any meaning or message. These features remain there for less than a second, long enough for us to decide whether we should pay any attention. If we decide to not pay any attention, then they vanish. That is why you do not remember some commercials at all.

Short-term Memory If we decide to pay attention to the sensations, then the information enters our short-term memory. **Short-term memory (STM)** is the part of the brain where information is being held and processed currently. Thus, STM is working memory; that is, we are currently working with it and on it. All new information enters from our senses first into STM. Here, we decide what to do with it: we can decide to memorize it, file it, use it for some imminent decision or action, or discard it altogether.

Long-term Memory Long-term memory (LTM) is the part of the brain where information we do not currently need is stored away. It is stored there in some organized way so that, when needed in the future, it can be accessed. We place it there so our minds are not constantly occupied with the huge amounts of information and knowledge we acquire. It is because of this passive storage that we are not constantly burdened with the consciousness of everything that has happened in our lives and, instead, are free to focus on the matter at hand. In sum, STM is active memory, and LTM is passive memory.

How Short is Short?

Short-term memory has two characteristics: (a) limited capacity, and (b) limited duration. It can only hold very small amounts of information—seven plus or minus two bits, as we mentioned earlier. And it can hold it only for a very short time—just a few seconds. More exactly, STM is basically what we are currently, at this very minute, aware of; it is what is in our consciousness and what our attention is directed toward. For example, right now, you are thinking of Cold Stone Creamery ice cream—we made you think of it. No, you were not thinking of it even a millisecond before you read the word "ice cream" in the preceding sentence, and you will not be thinking of it the second you finish reading the words coffee, Coke, Pepsi, Snapple, Gatorade, Dr Pepper, and Mountain Dew. (Notice how we named seven beverages just to fill your entire STM capacity; of course, if we wanted to leave no chance at all for any of you, we should have named two more.)

Hundreds of Faces and Thousands of Words—All Stored in the Mind

Long-term memory also has two characteristics: (a) unlimited capacity, and (b) efficient organization. LTM is like a huge warehouse, with virtually unlimited capacity. In it, we hold names and faces of hundreds of friends, associates, and public figures; hundreds of events we have experienced in life and just as many more that we read about; words to hundreds of songs, poems, or stories; musical tunes, food tastes, and a spectrum of aromas and colors; and facts about and experiences with literally the thousands of products we consume.

Second, this massive pile of data and information is not just thrown into the storage area. Rather, it is organized systematically, for efficient access when needed. So if a waiter asks you what would you like to drink, you don't think of cereal, a burger, a sandwich, or pasta; instead, you think of coffee, Coke, Pepsi, Snapple, Gatorade, Dr Pepper, or the Dew. Or to make it even more efficient, the fact that you only like to drink Dew with your dinner and Snapple with your lunch is also stored in your LTM. So you think only of Snapple if it is lunchtime and only of Dew if it is dinnertime. Can you imagine what life would have been like if you had to instead think of every object in the world whenever you were called upon to make any choice whatsoever in your daily life? Without the efficient organization of information in LTM, everyday living would be an uphill struggle. Because marketers are interested in ensuring that consumers store and file their brand information in the right place, it behooves them to study this organization of memory and then fashion their product information accordingly. Let us see how STM and LTM communicate with each other.

How Do STM and LTM Talk to Each Other?

Information flows constantly between our two memories. All external information entering LTM must go through STM. And all the information stored in LTM must be brought back into STM to utilize it for a current task. An apt analogy is that of the theater: LTM is the backstage where all the actors and props assemble and wait to be called; STM is the front-stage where actors are currently playing their roles. The process of moving the information from STM to LTM is called encoding, and the process of withdrawing information from LTM to STM is called remembering or retrieval. Let us see how these processes work (see Figure 4.2).

Keeping Information Alive in STM

When we are exposed to new products and services or new information, it is received in the STM (via the sensory memory, of course). If we judge it to be useless, we discard it. If we need it for some immediate task, we keep it alive in the STM. Keeping it alive simply means keeping it in our consciousness, currently. There are two ways to do it: (a) rote rehearsal, and (b) quick coding. Rote rehearsal is repeating the information in our heads, mechanically, that is, without thinking about it. Thus, if the bookpurse ad gave you a number to

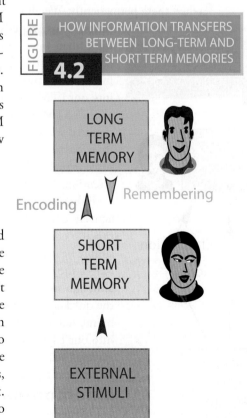

FIGURE 4.2 HOW INFORMATION TRANSFERS BETWEEN LONG-TERM AND SHORT TERM MEMORIES

LONG TERM MEMORY

Encoding / Remembering

SHORT TERM MEMORY

EXTERNAL STIMULI

FIGURE
4.3

QUICK CODING — ROTE REHEARSAL

call (say, 1-800-586-5210), and you were trying to find a piece of paper on which to write it, you might repeat the number in your head.

The second method, "quick coding," is identifying some surface features in the information that help us remember it for the time being. Thus, in the phone number 586-5210, you might notice that there is a '5' at the beginning of both the exchange and individual number codes; and that the second set has 012 (the three lowest sequential numbers) reversed; and in the first set, again reading backwards, add '1' to the common number '5' (thus making '6') and then to this '6' add '2' (remember, the sequence—add '1', and for next digit backwards, add '2'), thus giving us '8'. This is not very helpful but doing it a couple of times might just do, for some consumers. Non-numerical information lends itself to easier "quick coding." The brand name of the audio equipment was PAL and you could 'quick code' it by thinking of the friend (pal) you often vacation with and how he always talks about wanting to buy an audio system. Of course, none of these ideas might work for you; individual consumers have to find their own "tricks" to do the requisite "quick coding."

Transferring Information from STM to LTM

More often, the case is that we expect to use the information at some time in the future (rather than immediately), so we choose to store it in our LTMs. We do this by **encoding**—a process in which we assign it a meaning and then file it in a category of similar things. There are three ways of placing the information in the long-term memory: (1) repetition, (2) mnemonics, and (3) elaboration.

Repetition

We all know numbers, and we all know the alphabet; we know them by heart. We can always recite them without fail at the spur of the moment. They reside in our LTMs, etched there permanently. We all learned them the same way—by repeating them many times. Thus, **repetition**—defined as the incidence of an occurrence more than once, saying something again and again, hearing it often, observing a stimulus, touching it, smelling it, and doing so with the intent to memorize—indeed results in the information being placed into our LTM. This is similar to the rehearsal needed to keep something alive in STM, with two exceptions: First, the rehearsal itself needs to be repeated several times at various intervals (e.g., a day apart, every two to three days, a week later, and so on); and second, because our goal is to place it in LTM, we would be doing the repetition with more focused attention.

Rehearsal is the process of repetition, when the consumer is the one actively doing the repeating. Of course, repetition (but not rehearsal) can also occur without the consumer's intent and effort. Consumers can simply be exposed repeatedly to a stimulus. Such repeated exposure also lodges the stimulus information in LTM even with minimal attention, although some attention is still needed, and the more attention we pay, the quicker the information gets lodged in LTM.[8] This is how so many brand names (e.g., Adidas, PlayStation, Mini Cooper, etc.) got put into our LTM even though we never tried! Marketers are interested in getting their brand names and messages into our LTM, and that is why they repeat their commercials so often.

FIGURE
4.4

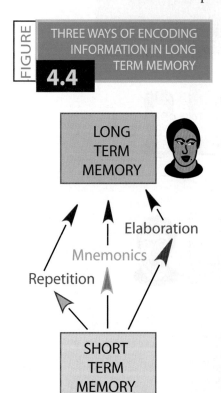

LONG TERM MEMORY

Elaboration

Mnemonics

Repetition

SHORT TERM MEMORY

Mnemonics

Mnemonics are memory devices that help us remember information through some nonsensical associations. Let us illustrate.

Assume you have a second date with someone you met a few days ago. During your first date, you learned that this person prefers Snapple for lunch and Mountain Dew for dinner. It is important for you to remember this information. How would you remember it? Here, mnemonics can help. You see, Dew and dinner both start with the letter "d"; and only Snapple has the letter "l", the first letter of the word "lunch." Got it? There is now a good chance that you would remember it for a while. That is the power of mnemonics!

Faces and names can also be "memorized" with mnemonics. For example, suppose you meet someone named Debra, and she is wearing a very fashionable dress. You could then try to memorize her name by thinking of the always fashionably dressed Debra Messing (star of the TV show Will & Grace). Or if you meet two guys named Bob and Michael, you might notice that Bob's hair is a rough bob cut, and Michael has a hairline resembling the shape of an "M."

As a marketer, can you utilize the power of mnemonics to help your consumers remember your product or message? To stimulate your thinking, we will give three examples. A few years ago, Halls Cough Drops hired comedian Richard Hall, who, in a TV commercial, walked into a room built with the packaged strips of Halls, called the Halls of Medicine. Richard Hall and Halls of Medicine—get it? Recently, Duracell's Coppertop Battery ads showed the product with the copper portion of the battery snapping into position on top of the remaining portion, as the voiceover mentioned the word "coppertop" in the tagline, "Nothing tops the Coppertop." "Coppertop"—get it? Our third example is about J&B—the brand that utilized the "closure principle" in the "–ingle –ells" Christmas print ad (mentioned in Chapter 3). In another print campaign, the company placed the letters J&B at strategic places in consumers' lives; one of these ads showed Hall of Fame baseball player Johnny Bench, and in the background were letters J&B placed on the home plate, and the headline read: "JB at home." "JB at home,"—get it? Now, it is your turn to think of some new mnemonics for your brand, and you are on your own!

Elaboration

The third and last method of placing information in LTM is called *elaboration*. **Elaboration** is the active processing of information in conjunction with other information already in the memory so as to identify meaning in the new information. Thus, whereas rehearsal also involves active processing, only elaboration entails utilization of information already in the memory. And while mnemonics may also include the use of some information already in long-term memory, only in elaboration do we try to link the information in terms of meaning (as opposed to surface or nonsensical features).

Suppose you wanted to commit to LTM the phone number 1-800-586-5210. Given the motivation, you would suddenly realize that '86' is the year you were born and also that in that year the U.S. Declaration of Independence was 210 years old. Now this phone number will be lodged in your LTM (provided you were indeed born in 1986, and provided, of course, that it was your goal to lodge it into your LTM).

In elaborating on it, we try to find any connections the new information may have with our existing knowledge, judge its relevance to ourselves, and assess its future use. Thus, we are not merely accepting information as given but rather scrutinizing it for meaning, and, by active contribution of our own, adding to it. For example, suppose you hear an ad for the Segway Human Transporter—advertised as a revolutionary, high-tech, battery-powered, self-balancing transporter with a top speed of 12.5 mph and a range of up to 15 miles per charge. You chuckle about it and begin thinking:

> Campus parking is a good 10-minutes' walk to the classroom. And the morning traffic is a nightmare, taking a good 20 minutes to drive the 4 miles from home. In that time, with the Segway, I could be in class. I've got 500 bucks in my savings, and if I can get dad to fork over four grand, I can buy this machine. I will save about $400 a year on gas and $200 on parking, so that is cool $600 a year savings. Come to think of it, I will be the first one to use it on campus. Why, I can even imagine myself wearing my favorite gray/black jersey, to match the dual colors of my Segway. Did I say "my Segway" already?!

With elaboration like this, you are likely to have placed the advertised brand information in your LTM, along with images of yourself cruising around campus in your gray/black Segway.

Now, think back to the three commercials you saw; you remembered them because you had visualized a user for each—your siblings and you. And you remembered Sims Online, because you had already heard of SimCity, so you made the mental connection there. You remembered PAL because it stood for Personal Audio Laboratory—the name

To help consumers remembe the brand name is a coveted goal of brand marketers (or should be). With a name like Yellow Tail (a wine from Australia), creatives have a field day. When it comes to devising mnemonics for their brand name, this ad takes the prize.

the company gave the audio device, and because you had already visualized yourself taking it on a vacation with your pal. And the bookpurse was easy to remember because it looked like a book with the jacket image printed on it and the ad said the purse comes with a wallet and dice-ball chain and has a place to hold the cell phone. You even visualized how your sis would use it.

Information Structure This elaboration actually results in knowledge being developed and stored as an **associated network**—a network of various concepts organized and stored in memory. A **concept** is a name or label given to any object or quality of an object, person, situation, or an idea. Examples include mouse, jock, love, hot, cool, clean, culture jam, mojo, etc. These concepts are depicted as nodes interconnected by lines, which represent connections among those objects or qualities.[9] See Figure 4.5.

All knowledge is of two types: *episodic* and *semantic*. **Episodic knowledge** consists of descriptions of events; **semantic knowledge** consists of information about objects and their properties. If we show you a mouse, and tell you, "this is a mouse," that is semantic knowledge. So is your learning that it needs no food and dutifully conveys your wish to your PC. That you received it as a free gift from Microsoft just for being a buzzer on an online Web site that Microsoft sponsors (more on being a buzzer, later, in Chapter 10) is

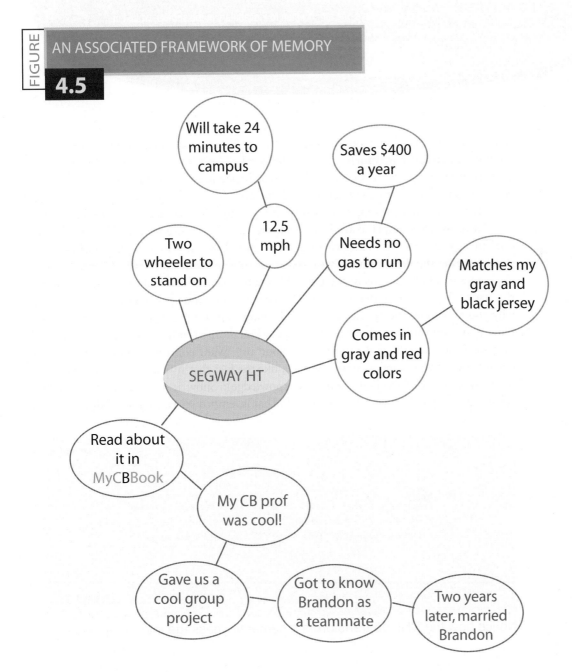

Can I Get A What...What?

Fey and doused, affable and amicable, pliable and neologism. Do you know their meaning? Would you like to? If we told you, would you remember? For how long? Learning new words has always been a challenge for everyone, especially students and test takers. Until now.

Now there is a new method, and those who have tried it, love it. SAT test takers can now sing their way to the test, literally. You see, there is a company called Flocabulary which has composed a large library of lyrics with Hip-Hop style rhymes. So, you listen to these Hip-Hop songs, sing along, and not only will you learn them having fun, but also they will stick in your head longer—all because the lyrics surrounding a word serve as mnemonics.

The company was founded in 2003 by two 20-somethings, Alex Rappaport and Blake Harrison. Rappaport holds a degree in Music from Tufts University, and Harrison has studied at Penn. It is easy to see how their skills and interests would blend to produce Flocabulary. Their mission: to fuse musical styles and seek new ways to bring Hip Hop into the academic world. Together they have compiled more than 1000 words used in SAT tests and have composed them into Hip-Hop rhymes.

Do learners like them? They love them. Says one fan: "I listen to Flocabulary in the shower, while I'm jogging, and first thing when I wake up. ...and your scores soar! – Kimmie

Consumer Karma is Hip Hop   My CB Book

---

episodic knowledge. Correspondingly, the two memories are called *semantic* and *episodic* memories. **Semantic memories** are memories for objects and their properties. **Episodic memories** are memories for events—both that happened in your life (e.g., the first time you met Brandon, whom you later married, in your CB class, while reading this book) and the events you witnessed (e.g., the victory of Pittsburgh Steelers team in Superbowl XL).

Now, which memory comes to you more easily? Right, episodic. That is why you can still narrate every touchdown of the last Superbowl and every episode of Seinfeld. Remembering the definition of *involvement*, or subconscious motives in Dichter's list, or the names of all the nations in the United Nations Security Council, or all the features of the Segway is another matter, for that calls for the more difficult semantic memory. That's why you remember the Spears and K-Fed breakup but not the recipe for mango mousse. Now all this information about the two types of memories is not an idle chore we imposed on you. As a marketer, you can put it to good use. Want consumers to remember some key features of your wireless phone service, like the fact that it works in all the nooks and far away places you frequent (semantic knowledge)? Show it as an obsessive wanderer constantly asking "Can you hear me now?" That is, embed semantic knowledge within an

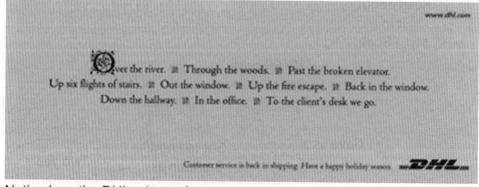

Notice how the DHL ad transforms a semantic message into an episode.

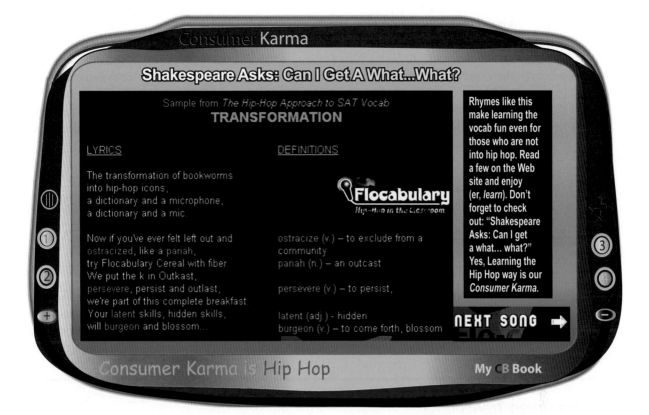

Consumer Karma

Shakespeare Asks: Can I Get A What...What?

Sample from *The Hip-Hop Approach to SAT Vocab*
TRANSFORMATION

LYRICS

The transformation of bookworms
into hip-hop icons,
a dictionary and a microphone,
a dictionary and a mic.

Now if you've ever felt left out and
ostracized, like a pariah,
try Flocabulary Cereal with fiber.
We put the k in Outkast,
persevere, persist and outlast,
we're part of this complete breakfast.
Your latent skills, hidden skills,
will burgeon and blossom...

DEFINITIONS

Flocabulary
Hip-Hop in the Classroom

ostracize (v.) – to exclude from a
community
pariah (n.) – an outcast

persevere (v.) – to persist,

latent (adj.) - hidden
burgeon (v.) – to come forth, blossom

Rhymes like this make learning the vocab fun even for those who are not into hip hop. Read a few on the Web site and enjoy (er, *learn*). Don't forget to check out: "Shakespeare Asks: Can I get a what... what?" Yes, Learning the Hip Hop way is our *Consumer Karma.*

NEXT SONG ➡

Consumer Karma is Hip Hop   My CB Book

episode!

Remembering the Information: Transferring back from LTM to STM

Okay, you have placed this information into LTM; now, how do you retrieve it? There are two mechanisms of retrieving information from LTM to STM: (a) recognition and (b) recall.

Recognition refers to identifying a stimulus as having been encountered before. Thus, it entails being able to access and retrieve the information from LTM based on an external stimulus object that has some resemblance with what is being remembered. It is essentially a feeling of familiarity—the judgment that you have seen the external stimulus object before. In contrast, *recall* involves becoming conscious of some information residing in LTM without the stimulus being present. It is being able to access and retrieve information from LTM without an external stimulus object. Thus, when the consumer standing in front of a vending machine sees the cold drink Fruitopia and remembers having seen the same brand in an ad or at a friend's home, he or she is remembering through recognition. On the other hand, if the consumer enters the store and feels an urge to buy a soft drink and thinks, "Let me buy a Fruitopia," he/she is "recalling" the brand name.

Recall has two forms: unaided and aided. **Unaided recall** involves accessing information without any cue; **aided recall** is accessing information with some clue. So, if we were to ask you what advertisements you saw yesterday while watching *The Real World,* and if you can recall any of the advertisements, then you have recalled those ads unaided. If we then ask, if you saw any ad for an office supply store, and you remember that, yes, you indeed saw an ad for Staples, then this is an aided recall. If you still don't recall, and we then ask if you remember an ad where an old lady in a green sweater talks about giving everybody her green knitwear as Christmas gifts, and then you remember that, yes, you saw that ad for Staples, it is still an aided recall. Thus, recall can require cues of varying degrees. This depends on how strong the memory trace is—i.e., how strong was the impression made when the information was placed in LTM the first time. Strong traces enable unaided recall, and when aid is needed, memories may be activated with merely a hint; weak traces need strong cues.[10]

In the associated network shown here, a recall cue can basically pertain to any one of the nodes or links. When one of these links or nodes is activated, the activation then spreads to other nodes and linkages, bringing them into our consciousness—our STM. Psychologists call this process **spreading activation**—the phenomenon where consciousness of one of the nodes suddenly activates our consciousness of all the other nodes.[11] Thinking of Segway reminds you of MyCBBook. It is like an electric current that quickly flows through the entire circuit.

CONSUMER ADOPTION OF PRODUCT INNOVATIONS

THE ULTIMATE LEARNING EXPERINCE.

Segway™ Human Transporter, N-Gage, and City Lips: Will Consumers Learn to Consume Them?

One of the most challenging problems for marketers is getting consumers to buy new products. In marketers' minds, new products bring new value to consumers. Consumers should be excited about buying them. But about ten new products fail for each one that succeeds. That is a lot of money and effort wasted. And marketers wonder why. From the

Segway Human Transporter

The Segway® Human Transporter (HT) is designed to operate in dense, urban environments as well as indoors, and is the perfect solution for individuals who require portability and maneuverability in tight spaces.

The i180 model is one of the first Segway HTs available with optional Saphion® lithium-ion batteries, which deliver an impressive range of up to 24 miles on a single charge, depending on terrain, riding style and payload.

Equipped with a number of standard features (see inset table), its power assist mode allows you to move it up and down stairs more easily. The control shaft is adjustable to the comfort of the rider and allows the Segway HT to fit in the trunk of many cars. To help prevent theft, each Segway HT comes with its own set of keys, encoded with a unique security identification. The i180 also comes with a mechanical parking stand. And you can get the i180 in three colors combinations: Sport Red, Solar Yellow, and Midnight Blue.

The Segway® HT is so much fun, you may forget how useful and practical it really is. Whether you're running an errand or meeting a friend for lunch, it easily fits into your daily routine. It's smart, simple, and graceful.

Maximum speed:	12.5 mph
Carrying capacity:	260 lbs
Footprint:	19 x 25 in
Weight:	~ 83 lbs
Battery type:	Two lithium-ion or NiMH battery packs
Battery range:	15-24 miles (Li-ion) 8-12 miles (NiMH)
Motors:	Two brushless, DC servomotors
Wheels:	14 in glass-reinforced thermoplastic
Tires:	19 in tubeless, puncture-resistant
Platform height:	8 in
Ground clearance:	3 - 4 in
Display:	Multicolor backlit LCD

consumers' points of view, of course, buying new products means learning whether the new products are really better for their needs. Even more importantly, they have to learn new tastes as well as new habits, like learning to use the :CueCat. To understand what goes into consumer responses to new products (adoption or rejection), from a learning point-of-view, we bring you information about three innovative products introduced recently into the market. Each is a very interesting product, and yet each is also different in terms of how the consumer will assess it as an innovation. Those three fascinating products are the Segway™ Human Transporter, N-Gage cell phone with a game deck, and City Lips Lip Gloss. Read about them on the adjacent pages.

Before we consider how consumers will react to these products, let us learn how consumer researchers define *innovation*. An **innovation** is a product or an idea that is new to the consumer. *Newness* has two dimensions: (1) uniqueness or how different it is from existing products, and (2) age or how long it has existed in the marketplace. Of course, what matters more than the absolute newness is whether the consumer perceives it as unique. Likewise, what matters more than the product's chronological age is when the consumer was first exposed to it. Thus, a product or service that has existed for a long time is still an innovation to a group of people if it was introduced to that subculture or group only recently.[12] Some examples of innovations are computers, televisions, and cellular phones in developing countries; in the United States and Western European countries, examples of innovations are hair transplants, laser keratotomy (an eye surgery operation), male birth control pills, and origami DVD player (www.origami.as).

Of course, uniqueness is also a matter of degree. Some new products and services are only marginally dissimilar from their existing forms, whereas others are substantially dissimilar. Based on the degree to which they are unique, scholars classify innovations as *continuous*, *dynamically continuous*, or *discontinuous*. Consider innovations in vision correction products, and imagine some 50 years ago when eyeglasses were all that existed. With that anchor, the featherweight lenses of the 1990s would be called a *continuous innovation*, contact lenses (first made commercially available in 1973) *dynamically continuous*, and radio keratotomy (or the newer photo keratotomy)—a vision corrective laser-surgery procedure—a *discontinuous* innovation.

N-Gage

Nokia N-Gage™ is a cell-phone + mobile game deck + MP3 music player, with communication and entertainment features. It measures 133h x 69w x 19d (mm) and weighs 135 g. The screen is 176 x 208 pixels, with 12-bit color depth or 4096 colors. The game deck is the first new mobile game deck in years. Cost: $299, plus tax.

Source: Nokia's Web site (date of access: July, 2004). (Used with permission.)

Now then, which of the three products featured here would you consider a discontinuous innovation? The correct answer is Segway™ Human Transporter (HT). N-Gage can be deemed a *dynamically continuous*, and City Lips most likely a *continuous innovation*. Can you argue why or why not?

DESIRABLE CHARACTERISTICS OF INNOVATIONS
Or What Makes An Innovation Hot

Now then, the million-dollar question is: How do consumers learn whether or not an innovation is worthy of their adoption? The answer to this question comes from sociologists who, during the 1960s, studied why some farmers would not adopt new hybrid seed and farming innovations. Sociologists actually turned the question on its head: Instead of asking why people would not adopt innovations, they asked, what is it in innovations that encourages their widespread adoption, or, alternatively, blocks their adoption. That question is more interesting to us as marketers anyway, because the answer permits us to try to build those qualities into our innovations.

We review their answer to this modified question. On the surface, it does not seem to utilize the language and concepts of learning that we covered in this chapter. But learning is certainly involved in consumer adoption of innovations—it has to be, and we would later analyze their answer from the point-of-view of the learning concepts. But first let us understand the original answer to the question: What are the desirable characteristics or attributes of innovations that help their adoption by consumers? They are:[13]

- **Relative advantage** What consumers consider first and foremost is the innovation's **relative advantage**—how much better the innovation is compared to the current product for which it would substitute. For example, the relative advantage of laser eye surgery is that consumers don't have to use eyeglasses or contact lenses anymore.

- **Perceived risk** **Perceived risk** of innovations refers to uncertainty about whether a relative advantage will accrue and whether any unanticipated harm will occur. For example, some consumers might perceive risk in laser surgery or in irradiation of foods. Consumers are less likely to adopt innovations with a high perceived-risk.

- **Complexity** **Complexity** refers to the difficulty in understanding the innovation. Consumers prefer an innovation that is easy to comprehend. The easier it is to figure out, the less complexity it has. For example, many consumers may find the Internet too complex to understand, so they may decide not to adopt it.

- **Communicability** **Communicability** refers to the extent to which an innovation is socially visible or is otherwise easy to communicate about in social groups. For example, taboo topics (such as personal hygiene products) have low communicability. Hairstyles are more visible and are therefore naturally more communicable. The greater the ease with which consumers can communicate about an innovation, the more rapidly and likely they are to adopt it.

- **Compatibility** Consumers want products that are compatible with their behavior and values. **Behavioral compatibility** means consumers won't need to alter their behavioral routines. **Value compatibility** means consistency with consumers' deeply held values. Examples of behavioral incompatibility would be vans that do not fit in the garage, electric cars that may require frequent battery charging, or a medication that adversely interacts with a person's favorite beverage, such as coffee (as do most homeopathic medicines). Examples of value incompatibility are contraceptives for consumers whose religion may prohibit contraception, or, for vegetarian consumers, new food products that use animal derivatives.

- **Trialability** Trialability refers to the extent to which it is possible to try out the innovation on a smaller scale. Trialable innovations are adopted more readily than those not trialable. Contact lenses are trialable, whereas keratotomy is not. Therefore, consumers are likely to adopt keratotomy less rapidly.

When a new product or service is not compatible with consumers' prior conceptions and behaviors, they find it difficult to accept and adopt, even if the new product or service is merely a marginal alteration.

Segway™ Human Transporter, N-Gage, and City Lips—Why Will Consumers Adopt Them?

Okay, let us apply these criteria, one by one, to our three innovations.

Relative Advantage The Segway™ Human Transporter has the relative advantage of making the more expensive car unnecessary for short commutes. It also has the advantage of better maneuvering through busy city traffic. And it provides some exercise. But some consumers may perceive it to be inconvenient during bad weather and find it impractical to store it in their already cluttered and small cubicle. N-Gage has the relative advantage of combining multiple functions into one device (phone, camera, game deck, MP3 player, etc.). City Lips has the relative advantage of making your lips fuller without injections or surgical procedures. If you are shaking your head in disagreement, it brings us to a caveat we wanted to offer anyway. Everyone does not perceive advantages in the same way. Some consumers may not consider these properties as advantageous or may not value them as much. For example, if your commute is 25 miles long, or if you are not at least reasonably fit (can't stand straight due to old age), then Segway™ HT may not have a relative advantage for you. If you do not play videogames and do not listen to music on the go, then N-Gage has no relative advantage for you. And if your lips are already full or you don't consider the appearance of lips important, then City Lips has no relative advantage for you.

Perceived Risk Some consumers might perceive that the Segway™ HT might topple and cause them injury (the device actually has a sophisticated stabilizing gyro mechanism, virtually guaranteeing perfect balance, always). It also may not go with your style, and you might worry that your friends may consider you cheap or weird—a social risk (its users of course consider it, actually, a cool thing to use). N-Gage has no risk except that some might perceive that all the functions may not work as claimed (actually they do). And City Lips could, some might suspect, actually harm your lips (no basis to suspect that).

Complexity None of the three innovations seem too complicated. Maybe some would wonder, how any two-wheeled vehicle such as the Segway balances itself. As for N-Gage, some might ask, isn't combining all those functions one too many? City Lips of course has no complexity whatsoever.

Communicability The three innovations differ sharply on communicability. N-Gage is a personal device, and only a few people would see it while you are using it in public. City Lips is not visible at all; after all you don't want anyone to notice you are using it, do you? The most visible, of course, is the Segway. You cannot use it out of the public eye at all! That is why, once it comes to your city, and a few consumers are seen using it, it has the potential of being adopted quickly by many consumers.

Compatibility N-Gage does not violate any values. For City Lips, we would need to know its ingredients—if it is made with any animal products, for example, some of us may find it violating our values. What about the Segway? Not only does it not violate any values, it in fact echoes and expresses the pro-ecological values of environmentally conscious consumers.

As to behavioral compatibility, the Segway requires a whole new way of conducting life—at least the commute part of life. So this calls for a major change in consumers' behavior. Consumers have to look at that altered behavior as a plus rather than a minus. As for N-gage, inserting a game does entail a multi-step procedure, and therefore some consumers may find it behaviorally inconvenient. Fortunately, at least City Lips calls for no behavioral change—it can be worn over your regular lipstick.

Trialability Trialability is moderate for all three. The Segway is not available widely in physical stores, so it is not easy to take it for a test run. As for N-Gage, although you might be able to inspect it in the store, true trial requires extended use to experience its various features. And finally, City Lips also must be bought to try it.

Summing up, each of the three innovations has some merits and some demerits. They will be adopted by those who see their positive points very favorably and are not that deterred by their negative points. This is how marketers determine target market—which segment is likely to adopt.

Okay, now it is your turn. Read about Oxygen Body Mist (www.oxygenbars.com) and evaluate this product on the desirable attributes of innovations.

An Oxygen dispensing booth
Courtesy: Oasis.com
(Did you spot it on the cover?)

Which Model Do Innovation Adopters Use?

An innovation adoption entails all four models of learning. First and foremost, the consumer has to learn the benefits and relative advantage of the innovation. If they do it by reading about it, then this is cognitive learning. Consumers who are not very skilled in evaluating new product information are not likely to complete the required cognitive learning. Consequently, they are unlikely to adopt the innovation, at least early on. With trialability, consumers basically want to see if the expected utility will materialize. If the trial proves the claimed product benefits, then consumers adopt it with the expectation of getting the reward—the relative advantage. Expectation of the reward is instrumental learning. So also is behavioral or value compatibility—if the innovation is compatible, then it serves instrumental utility.

If you are not a pioneer in adopting the innovation, you look to others for guidance. If others you trust are using the innovation, you assume it must be safe or effective, or sometimes you simply want to be like these others. In all these cases, you are learning the idea of adopting the innovation through modeling—becoming like these others. Finally, marketers often have a choice of how to "position" the new product. By placing the innovation in a proper setting, they create a proper image for the product. N-Gage could have been positioned as a serious gizmo for a more mature consumer, but instead it is being advertised to youth. The Segway can show working class people riding it, or white-collar professionals. And City Lips could be placed in upscale boutiques or in discount drug stores. The image the consumer develops as a result of these positioning props or settings is, as you realize, classical conditioning.

Thus, in adopting any innovation, most consumers have to use all four modes of learning. The next time you buy something completely new, keep a journal of all the methods of learning you employed. Then you will be able to say "I have learned about learning itself!"

CONSUMER NOSTALGIA

Down Memory Lane: Nostalgia and the Pleasures of Consuming the Past

Life is a curious mixture of things. On one hand, we admire all of these innovations—products with space age technology and futuristic designs, but on the other hand, we long for things from eras gone by. This is our way of staying connected to the past. Happy experiences leave memory traces—some of them so strong that we often find ourselves reminiscing about them. Like our prom night. Our 21st birthday. Our vacation on the Greek Island of Corfu. The childhood home in which we grew up. The high school football field on which we played. The car we drove back in the sixties. We reminisce, and we long for those past experiences and for those products from the past. Well, marketers have heard our prayers—they are bringing back those products. And consumers are embracing them with unprecedented fondness. Let us understand just what sort of consumption pleasures such products from the past deliver to consumers.

One cute—and perhaps the smallest—car you see on road these days is the Volkswagen Beetle, fondly called the Bug. (Actually, *Smart*, found in Europe, is the smallest of them all).The first convertible Bug was released in 2003, but its regular (nonconvertible) version first showed up on the road a few years ago, in red, blue, white, black, and of course, its signature "mellow yellow," and it turned heads everywhere. Heads were turning, not because they were seeing something unfamiliar, but rather because they were seeing something old, something they had seen some 30 to 40 years before (or seen them in pictures). And they were enchanted by this revival of the old. The car was actually first made in 1946 and was in vogue until the 1960s or so. Now, Volkswagen had decided to bring it back.

Welcome to the age of retro, or what marketers call the *retro-trend*. Retro products are products that are designed to capture significant stylistic aspects of some old, once popular, but since retired product. What Volkswagen did with the new Beetle, Chrysler did with its PTCruiser and BMW did with the Mini Cooper.

The retro-trend can be seen across a range of products. In children's products, Care Bears—the colorful and cuddly toys from the 80s—are back on store shelves. So are other 80's favorites, such as Strawberry Shortcake, My Little Pony, Teenage Mutant Ninja Turtles, and Masters of the Universe. In clothing, Levi's recently brought back Type 1 Jeans, which mimic the style of the original jeans worn during the California Gold Rush. Coca-Cola recently restyled its packaging to bring back its original trademark, the ribbon design, first developed about 75 years ago. In the music industry, aging boomer Mick Jagger fronts his 40-year-old rock band, the Rolling Stones, on global sold-out concert tours.

Just why are consumers so enchanted with retro products? There is a one-word answer—**Nostalgia**—defined simply as a longing for the things and lifestyles of the past.[14] This nostalgia stems from two motives whose satisfaction provides the enjoyment the consumer is seeking[15]:

1. Reminiscing about the personal past
2. Reexperiencing the lure of a historical era

The first motive, and its related source of satisfaction, is that we have fond memories of our past—where we lived, what we did, with whom we were friends, what we wore, and what we ate. Although for some of us these memories may well be painful, most of our memories are filled with products we then consumed. Remembering these products, and, where possible, re-consuming these products simply gives us the pleasure of familiar experiences. And the familiar is often warm, cozy, and comfortable. Thus, we all like to revisit our alma maters and rejoice at school reunions. By the way, reunions today are a huge business and on the rise. Along the same lines, we enjoy looking through old albums and seeing movies from the times in which we grew up. Participation in these activities takes us back to our personal pasts and allows us to relive these moments from our once-cherished lives.[16]

The second reason is just a fascination with the past—even if one has not personally known that past. That is why one likes to go and see a medieval village, for example. Why so? Sometimes, we are so caught up in the complex life of the current times that when we hear the lore about how idyllic and simple life once was, we develop a fascination with the life of yesteryear. We see an escape, a psychological distancing from the demanding times of the present. This sense of nostalgia is captured by scholars in this observation, "Nostalgia is associated with melancholy and is the alienation of human beings in society as a consequence of their own limitations and finitude."[17] To escape the alienating

Andy Warhol Retro Watch developed by Seiko Instruments Inc. under a license from Andy Warhol Foundation; released: late 2006.(Courtesy: Seiko Instruments USA, Inc.)

The joy of Nostalgia: Rolls-Royce Silver CLoud III 1964

Courtesy: Schowerer Beverly Hills Limousine Service LLC (www.classicrollslimo.biz)

realities of present times, we want to go back, even if only in a small slice of our lives, and in bits and pieces, to that simpler lifestyle of yesteryear.

An example is the imagery that the Fossil Watch Company has created. Fossil has given its brand a personality, an identity that is reminiscent of the 1950s. To cultivate this identity, the company has taken the images, visuals, and artifacts from that era and surrounded the brand with them. These images are everywhere: in its advertising, in the stores, on its brochures, on its special tin box packaging, on its stationery, and even on its Web site. Now "reminiscent" is actually the wrong word: Fossil's core consumers (17- to 24-year olds) were not around during the 50s; therefore, its images could not possibly "remind" them of anything! What, then, do these images mean to them? "What appeals to the 17 to 24 youth," explains Fossil CEO, "is that the images are unique and so different. They look like they are from—not just a different era—but a different planet; the artwork looks surreal, depicting people who are happy (with a little goofy smile). There is certain casual attitude about life in these characters and in these artifacts. And it has just caught the fascination of young people. It has become an aspirational brand. Target consumers think that if they buy this watch, then they belong to a certain group of people, that they are part of some surreal culture, and that they are living a certain experience."[18]

The difference between the two motivations for nostalgia is subtle, and often the same nostalgic product might stimulate both. Read about the Cinema Hotel in Tel Aviv (elsewhere in this chapter—not telling you *exactly where* is our modest effort to make reading the book a bit of a "treasure hunt" fun), and decide for yourself which source of nostalgia it will evoke and gratify for you.

MARKETING WITH NOSTALGIA

Marketers respond to consumer hunger for nostalgia in three ways:

1. Retro fashions and products
2. Memorabilia from the past
3. Nostalgic Lifestyle Islands

Retro Fashions and Products   Retro clothing, retro cars, retro music—we hear these terms every day. What does *retro* really mean for these products? It means, simply, borrowing the product styles from a particular period of history. The late 1996 Beetle shares with its 1946 original only the exterior, egg-shaped signature body style. Everything else is different, not the least of which is that the original had the engine in the back. (Yes, it's true!) The new Beetle has it in the front. Yet the body style alone is enough to make the car a retro product, and it is enough to impart consumers a nostalgic experience.[19]

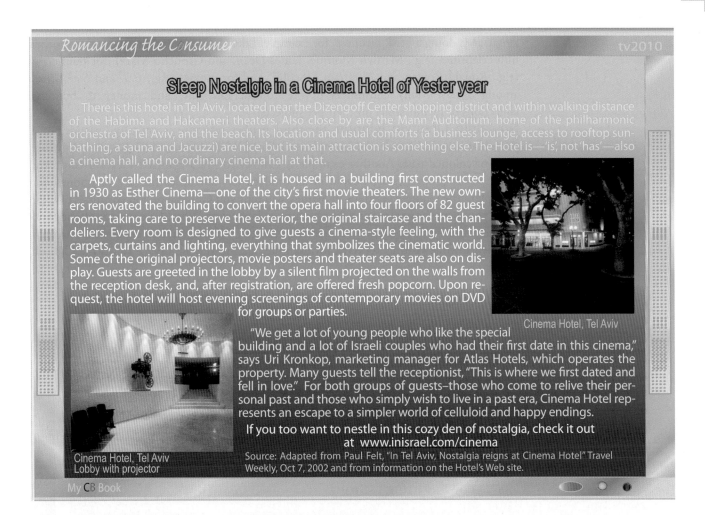

Sleep Nostalgic in a Cinema Hotel of Yester year

There is this hotel in Tel Aviv, located near the Dizengoff Center shopping district and within walking distance of the Habima and Hakcameri theaters. Also close by are the Mann Auditorium, home of the philharmonic orchestra of Tel Aviv, and the beach. Its location and usual comforts (a business lounge, access to rooftop sunbathing, a sauna and Jacuzzi) are nice, but its main attraction is something else. The Hotel is—'is', not 'has'—also a cinema hall, and no ordinary cinema hall at that.

Aptly called the Cinema Hotel, it is housed in a building first constructed in 1930 as Esther Cinema—one of the city's first movie theaters. The new owners renovated the building to convert the opera hall into four floors of 82 guest rooms, taking care to preserve the exterior, the original staircase and the chandeliers. Every room is designed to give guests a cinema-style feeling, with the carpets, curtains and lighting, everything that symbolizes the cinematic world. Some of the original projectors, movie posters and theater seats are also on display. Guests are greeted in the lobby by a silent film projected on the walls from the reception desk, and, after registration, are offered fresh popcorn. Upon request, the hotel will host evening screenings of contemporary movies on DVD for groups or parties.

Cinema Hotel, Tel Aviv

"We get a lot of young people who like the special building and a lot of Israeli couples who had their first date in this cinema," says Uri Kronkop, marketing manager for Atlas Hotels, which operates the property. Many guests tell the receptionist, "This is where we first dated and fell in love." For both groups of guests–those who come to relive their personal past and those who simply wish to live in a past era, Cinema Hotel represents an escape to a simpler world of celluloid and happy endings.

If you too want to nestle in this cozy den of nostalgia, check it out at www.inisrael.com/cinema

Cinema Hotel, Tel Aviv
Lobby with projector

Source: Adapted from Paul Felt, "In Tel Aviv, Nostalgia reigns at Cinema Hotel" Travel Weekly, Oct 7, 2002 and from information on the Hotel's Web site.

My CB Book

Hot Topic has brought back characters and toys from the past; it sells both the actual merchandise and their imprints on t-shirts. Thus, it sells Care Bears and My Little Pony as eye jewelry. Fashion designers scout the globe for historic costume styles, and Target sells retro furniture. And in movies, *Good Morning, Vietnam* (made in 1987) appealed to baby boomers' need for nostalgia; *Dirty Dancing* (also made in 1987) captured a general fascination with the 1960s, using songs from that era, such as "My Girl" and "I Heard it Through the Grapevine."[20]

Memorabilia The marketplace also satisfies consumer need for nostalgic gratification through **memorabilia**—products designed to capture the authenticity of a person, place, or event from a historic period. Thus, Elvis memorabilia is a vast collection of merchandise and images of Elvis and is popular worldwide—one website in the German

language is doing a brisk business, for example. Likewise, memorabilia abounds for other film celebrities (e.g., Marilyn Monroe, James Dean, and Groucho Marx), for politicians (e.g., Ronald Reagan and Abraham Lincoln), and for movies (e.g., *E.T.* and *Star Wars*), among others. Many consumers devote considerable time and money to building collections of memorabilia on their pet subjects.

Nostalgic Lifestyle Islands The third market response is creating "islands" of a particular historic lifestyle. An example is Colonial Williamsburg in Virginia—a showcase town of colonial past. Another example is Club Med, the organized vacation company, where resort properties are devoid of all modern day amenities (no TV or phones, for example). The Chinese Gardens in Sydney will rent you Chinese period costumes to wear while you roam the gardens and take pictures as keepsakes. What these market offerings do for the consumer is to create nostalgic "experiences." If you want to experience one such experience while visiting Tel Aviv, for example, plan to stay in a place called the Cinema Hotel.

tv2010

MyCBBook

*L*earners—that is us. We are constantly learning something. Without learning, our progress as people would stop. Try listing everything you have learned over the past 20 years, or even 10 years. Can you visualize your life today, as a human, if today you knew only as much as you had known 20 (or even 10) years ago? More to the point, without learning about the marketplace over, say, the last ten years, can you visualize your life today even in your role as a consumer—especially if you are now only, say, 21 or even 25 (yes, that means if today you knew only what you knew at age 11 to 15!)? Learning empowers you, in life and in the marketplace.

*F*ortunately, much of that learning comes naturally—by that we mean, without any effort, just by being exposed to stimuli in our world as we go about living everyday life. All learning is, in essence, learning associations. Association between two stimuli (classical conditioning), between an act and a reward (instrumental conditioning), between an act and what that act will make you (role modeling), and between an object and its name e.g., simple brand name awareness (cognitive learning)) or between an object and a property or consequence, e.g., a brand claim (cognitive learning).

*T*hese associations occur in our physical and social worlds, some created by nature, some by society at large, and not an insignificant number of them by marketers. As a marketer, you pair your brand with a celebrity; pair it with certain lifestyle depictions; pair it with an upscale, trendy store; pair it with certain emotions; with certain product benefits; with certain consumer values and aspirations. But you can't "manufacture" them in your image, in isolation with the pairings (i.e., associations) consumers have learned in their world-at-large. You can't put together a pairing of just any two entities you desire to be associated in the consumer mind, and say "Viola! The consumer will have learned (i.e., accepted) that association." Consumers will accept only those pairings (associations) they find intuitively sensible. **As a marketer, LEARN THAT!**

Roman Meal—The Wisdom of Whole Grain

Recently, the company invited consumers to write in maxims that would embody the company's slogan—The Wisdom of Whole Grains ™. The company ran print ads featuring some of the maxims consumers sent in. As the sample of maxims featured here shows, they made for an interesting series of ads. Even more important, the campaigns such as this serve a very useful purpose for the brand.

What does a campaign like this do for the consumer and for the brand.? Why would consumers send in their entries? Would their mindsets about the brand be changed by participating in the campaign? And which concepts covered in the chapter apply?

If it's not pretty, cover it.

– Lisa Price
Brentwood, CA

the wisdom of whole grains

Everything in moderation, and plenty of it.

– Molla Ladd
Dallas, TX

the wisdom of whole grains

If you can't be a good example, be a horrible warning.

– Sharon Gibbons
New York, NY

the wisdom of whole grains

Tell the truth and run.

– Gloria Webber
Union City, NJ

the wisdom of whole grains

(Courtesy: Roman Meal Company)

In this chapter, we discussed the consumer as a learner, describing four models of learning: classical conditioning, instrumental conditioning, modeling, and cognitive learning. Classical conditioning occurs when a preexisting consumer response to a stimulus (product, service, or person) is transferred to another stimulus due to their occurrence together. Instrumental conditioning occurs when consumers learn to engage in a behavior repeatedly because the behavior is rewarding. Modeling occurs by observing other consumers whose behavior we find worth imitating. Finally, cognitive learning occurs when consumers obtain new information.

Marketers take advantage of these learning models by structuring their product communications in a fashion conducive to the learning of desired consumer responses. For example, they use classical conditioning by constantly pairing attractive celebrities or likeable non-celebrities with hitherto neutral brands. Through this pairing, the image of the celebrity rubs onto the product. Marketers also offer frequent buyer rewards as instrumental to consumers learning to patronize those marketers. The modeling method of learning is promoted by giving free product samples to people likely to serve as role models for other consumers. And cognitive learning is utilized by the appropriate design of messages for low-involvement versus high-involvement products.

We then discussed how consumers acquire and process product information and how they remember it. Here we described three types of memories—sensory, short-term and long-term—and examined how information travels between and among them. Understanding the workings of memory and remembering helps marketers create more effective product messages.

Next we discussed how and why consumers learn to adopt or not to adopt a new product innovation. Consumers desire certain characteristics in innovations, namely, relative advantage, low perceived risk, low complexity, easy communicability, behavioral and value compatibility, and trialability. Finally, we discussed the consumer desire for nostalgic consumption, and how marketers are satisfying this consumer need by bringing back retro products like the Volkswagen Beetle and Andy Warhol watch.

KEY TERMS

Learning	Episodic memory	Innovation Adoption
Classical Conditioning	Semantic Memory	Relative Advantage
Chunking	Associative Network	Perceived Risk
Unconditioned Stimulus (UCS)	Rote Memorization	Complexity
Conditioned Stimulus (CS)	Problem Solving	Communicability
Instrumental Conditioning	Stimulus Generalization	Behavioral Compatibility
Modeling	Stimulus Discrimination	Value Compatibility
Cognitive Learning	Innovation	Trialability
Elaboration	Innovators	Nostalgia

YOUR TURN

REVIEW+Rewind

1. Define conditioned and unconditioned stimuli, giving examples of each.
2. Explain extrinsic versus intrinsic rewards, citing examples. What are their relative merits and demerits?
3. In your own words, explain each of the four models of learning. Cite two examples of each, drawing on your own experience as a consumer and recalling instances when you learned via each of the four mechanisms.
4. Compare and contrast high-involvement and low involvement learning.
5. Explain what is meant by rote memorization.
6. Describe what is meant by stimulus generalization and stimulus discrimination. Explain how marketers use these concepts.
7. How short is short-term memory? How long is long-term memory? Explain your answer.
8. Name and briefly describe the three processes by which information is placed into long-term memory.
9. Explain the difference between semantic and episodic memories.
10. What are the three categories of innovations based on their newness? Give an example of each.

11. List any six criteria that an innovation should meet in order to attain consumer acceptance.

12. Explain what is nostalgic marketing. What value do retro products bring to consumers?

THINK+Apply

1. Should marketers try to transform consumers from low involvement to high involvement mode of learning? Why or why not?

2. Given your understanding of how consumers' short and long term memories work, write down three things you would do to make the consumer memory work for your product, assuming your product is (a) a car, (b) yogurt.

3. Evaluate the following products/services in terms of the characteristics of innovation that facilitate their adoption:

   a. Roomba automatic vacuum cleaner (go to www.sharperimage.com and search for Roomba)

   b. Teeth whitening strip (go to www. crestwhitestrips.com)

   c. Clothing fashion such as the recently introduced banded collar shirts. (Visit www. marcobracci.com/banded-collar-shirt.htm; alternatively, type *banded collar shirt* in google. com search engine.)

4. How can you use the concept of modeling in promoting a social cause, say an anti-drug program?

5. Evaluate Super X-ped, a scooter for local sidewalk commute (see picture with link below), using the "desirable characteristics of innovations," commenting on each of your ratings; based on this evaluation, comment on whether this innovation would be adopted fast or slow and by what kind of consumer segments.

   Description of Super X-ped (see picture at link below):

   This is the bad boy of the batch. This is the dream ped that all the pro's use in all those videos' you see. This dude has the ZENOAH G23 ORC engine that everone wants(cause it's fast), the x-ped frame (heavy duty) duel front forks(BOTHY) and that cool grind deck that is a must. Also it comes with billet wheelz an engine gaurd and a stiffened pole handle assy. This sucker does 30mph stock! Add a high performance pipe and this ped easley does 40mph...not for the faint of heart or less experenced. If you have the dough I highly recommend this ped ..but only for the more experenced rider. Once you ride this there is no going back to a slower one. ;-)   Price: $759.00 Delivered.

SOURCE: http://www.rudeboyusa.com/ superx.htm   (Last Accessed, August 27, 2006)

5. Visit two websites: Limited Express (http://www. limited.com/about/exp/ index.jsp) and Dolce & Gabbana Website (http://eng. dolcegabbana.it/main.asp). You will notice that each uses a combination of methods to convey its message and brand story. Can you describe which of the four models of learning each Web site is utilizing? Be specific about what is it you learned and through which method. Also try to memorize a few items you see; comment on how did you memorize them. (Be warned: the second Web site calls for a, well, cosmopolitan mindset!)

PRACTICE+Experience

1. Collect advertisements that illustrate separately how advertisers base their message on one or the other model of consumer learning.

2. Interview 2 or 3 consumers who may have adopted a new product recently. Ask questions to understand how they viewed the new product on innovation characteristics described in this chapter.

3. Assume you have recently accepted a position as marketing director of a local museum. You recall the concepts of instrumental conditioning, and wonder if it can help you develop ideas for getting your member patrons to visit the museum more often. Write a memo for your director, outlining various approaches (utilizing both intrinsic and extrinsic rewards, specifying which is which) to get consumers to visit the museum more often.

4. Interview two consumers and ask them if they remember any commercials they saw the last time they watched TV. Ask them which ones (let them describe the storyline so you may assess how much they remembered). Next, ask them questions that would help you understand what factors help consumers remember or not remember commercials. Write a brief report on what you learned.

In the Marketing Manager's Shoes

Put yourself in a marketing manager's shoes. Most concepts in the chapter have some lessons for the marketing manager, i.e., they suggest what to do differently in practice; indeed, often these applications are implicit in our explanations of the concepts and models in the chapter. Identify at least five specific applications of the chapter's concepts, all of which should be entirely new— different from the examples cited here.

CONSUMER AS A LEARNER

Consumer Values, Personality, And Self-Concepts

The Reality of Our Multiple Selves

- **Values Rule Consumption**
- What Is Your LOV Profile?
- **Freudian Theory—Is Your Id Misbe-havin'?**
- The *Big Five* of Personality
- **Personality or Self-concept—Which Do Consumers Consume?**
- Possessions—Consumers' Extended Selves

Where We Won't Be Going This Summer

Hello, this is Kristoff St. John and this is my daughter Lola. Let me tell you where we won't be going this summer.

Thus opens a TV commercial starring *The Young and the Restless* actor Kristoff St. John and his daughter, Lola. St. John goes on to explain:

You see, in order to perform those stupid tricks, elephants are taken away from their families, they are kept in chains, they are hit with metal bullhooks, shot with electric prods. … Now what kind of life is that?

And then he pleads:

Please don't go to any circus with animal acts. When no one suffers for entertainment, everyone is happy.

The Young and the Restless actor Kristoff St. John with daughter Lola
Photo: Courtesy PeTA, USA

Photo: Courtesy PETA, USA

INTRODUCTION

Cruelty to animals in circuses is an issue very dear to PeTA (People for the Ethical Treatment of Animals) and to hundreds of thousands of consumers who support it.

Around the world, consumer activists petition local governments to ban such circuses. In cities as diverse as Hollywood (Florida), Redmond (Washington), Boulder (Colorado), Buenos Aires (Argentina), Rio De Janeiro (Brazil), Perth (Australia), North Vancouver (Canada), Patra (Greece), and nationwide in India, Singapore, Sweden, Austria, Finland, etc. Elsewhere, activists protest the local media's promotion of "circuses with animal acts" in town; they petition merchants who distribute their leaflets (e.g., recent protests at Cold Stone Creamery, San Diego; Denny's, Burbank; etc.); and celebrities stage live acts depicting animal cruelty.

Don't worry, if you do find yourself in empathy with the campaign, you can still go to circuses that are free of animal acts and are just as much or more enjoyable. The Greatest Show on Earth—the Cirque du Soleil, the New Pickle Family Circus, Cirque Éloize, and others—are exciting and innovative circuses that dazzle audiences without animal acts.

> "The idea that it is funny to see wild animals coerced into acting like clumsy humans, or thrilling to see powerful beasts reduced to cringing cowards by a whip-cracking trainer is primitive and medieval. It stems from the old idea that we are superior to other species and have the right to hold dominion over them."
> —Dr. Desmond Morris, anthropologist, animal behaviorist, author

CONSUMER VALUES

Definition

Is it a good idea to torture animals for the entertainment of humans? For making fur clothing or shoes or other products for human use? For testing products for human use? Should universities have minority quotas for student admissions? Should governments ban all violent video games targeted at children? Or irreverent lyrics by Eminem? Should a fast food burger chain be held responsible if a consumer can show he got heart disease from eating its fattening burgers? And, should motorists be fined for using their cell phones while driving? All these questions call for "value judgments." Your answers will depend on what your values are.

Indian film star Shilpa Shetty dresses up to awaken your VALUES
Courtesy: PeTA India (www.petaindia.com)

Values are desired end-states of life and preferred paths to achieving them. As such, they constitute the purposes and goals for which we believe human life should be lived—ours and others'. They also serve as fundamental rules by which life should be lived. Thus, if we value animal life as much as human life, then saving an animal's life would be a value to us and we would not further our lives by using products made by killing them. If we believe in free individual choice, then we would not favor government regulation of music, video games, movies, and the like. Valuing individual choice could also lead us to not want government regulation of everyday life of individuals; consequently, we would not favor motorists being fined for using cell phones while driving. And, if we believe in individual responsibility, then we would hold the consumer, not fast food burger chains, responsible for his or her own eating behaviors.

Values require us to "take a position" on basic choices we make in the conduct of our lives. As such they undergird and inevitably influence our opinions and choices on all matters, big and small. And, of course, they intimately affect the choices we make as consumers. Indeed, they even influence mundane consumption and everyday activities such as what TV programs a consumer watches. Debra Messing, star of *Will and Grace*, says she is obsessed with watching Court TV because of her obsession with justice and fairness (quoted in *Marie Claire*, December 2002, p. 96).

How many end-states do we value? In other words, how many values are there? Psychologist Milton Rokeach identified 36 values, 18 in each of the two groups, called *terminal* and *instrumental*. **Terminal values** are the goals we seek in life (e.g., freedom, wealth, salvation, etc.), whereas **instrumental values** are the means, paths, or behavioral standards by which we pursue those goals (e.g., honesty, altruism, etc.). Rokeach developed these lists of values for understanding human psychology.[1] Of course, whereas in Rokeach's list values are categorized exclusively in one of the two categories, in practice, some values could be terminal for one person and instrumental for another. For example, some could seek wealth as an end in itself and others as a means. If you want to utilize these lists, simply ask consumers to rank the values in each list and then form segments of consumers with similar rankings. The lists are proprietary and not available for description here, but marketers can obtain them from the copyright holder as footnoted! Knowledge-seeking readers can find it easily with Google search.[2]

What is Your LOV Profile?

Consumer researchers felt a need for identifying values that might be more directly relevant to everyday consumer behavior. For this purpose, consumer researcher Lynn Kahle (along with colleagues Sharon Beatty, Pamela Homer, and Shekhar Misra) developed a List of Values (LOV), consisting of nine terminal values:[3]

1. Self-respect
2. Self-fulfillment
3. Security
4. Sense of belonging
5. Excitement
6. Sense of accomplishment
7. Fun and enjoyment
8. Being well respected
9. Warm relationships with others

This list of values corresponds well to the needs in Maslow's Hierarchy of Needs, except that Maslow includes physiological needs, and LOV adds values of fun and excitement. And Kahle argues that the nine values in LOV relate more closely to our major roles in life, such as marriage, parenting, work, leisure, and so forth, than do the values in the Rokeach value list.

Does LOV explain our consumption behaviors as well? The answer is a definite "yes." In a number of studies, LOV has been found related to consumer activities: for example, people who valued a sense of belonging especially liked group activities. Those who valued fun and enjoyment especially liked skiing, dancing, backpacking, hiking, camping, and drinking. And people who valued a "warm relationship" with others tended to give gifts to others, often for no reason at all.[4]

Beyond these research findings, it makes sense to expect LOV to influence a wide range of consumer behaviors. For example, would you expect shoplifters to value "self-respect" more or less than an average consumer? Who would you expect to enroll in a master's program—someone with a low importance rating on self-fulfillment value or someone with a high rating on it? (And remember, enrolling in a master's program is

> **One Chinese traditional value is "Man-nature orientation"—that man and nature must exist in symbiosis (as opposed to the pursuit of material progress at the cost of preserving nature); in a study of Chinese consumers, those who scored high on this value were found to be more ecologically conscious.**
>
> Source: R. Chan and L. Lau , "Antecedents of Green Purchases: A Survey in China," *J. of Consumer Marketing*, 2000, 17 (4), 338-357.

also a consumer behavior.) Finally, who would you expect to forgo a visit with family for a chance for adventure travel: one who values sense of belonging or one who values excitement? We list several such expected behaviors in Table 5.1 below, with the caveat that these are based not on research but on an intuitive reading of the conceptual meaning of these values. In practice, as a marketer, you should always go beyond available research and build many more intuitive inferences for consumption topics of interest to you, and then you would need to verify them through pragmatic research.

Since consumers differ in their values, LOV can be used to segment consumers. Although any number of segments can be identified in a population, three most sharply distinct values-based segments would be Achievement, Hedonism, and Relationships (it is easy to see which of the nine LOV values would score high for each group).[5] To the Achievement segment, accomplishment and self-fulfillment would be of high value; to the Hedonism segment, enjoying life would be most important; and finally, to the Relationships segment, a sense of belonging and warm social relationships would be of utmost value. Research has found that consumers who value relationships with others are more susceptible to interpersonal influence; consequently, when purchasing products, particularly socially visible products, such as clothing, these consumers place much more emphasis on style and brand image (as opposed to the product's functional features such as durability, reliability, or fit).[6]

TABLE 5.1

Selected Behaviors Produced by LOV

Value (LOV)	Selected Consumer Behaviors
1. **Self Respect**	Shoplifting, changing retail tags. (lack of Self-esteem)
2. Self fulfillment	Enrolling in a part time master's degree course; donating to charities.
3. **Security**	Not running up credit card high
4. Sense of belonging	Taking family vacations; on vacations, visiting with friends & relatives rather than going to new places.
5. Excitement	Adventure travel.
6. **Sense of accomplishment**	Saving for home ownership; self improvement courses; learning professional skills.
7. Fun and enjoyment	Watching sports; vacationing at resorts; leisure activities.
8. **Being well respected**	Avoid edgy and funky clothing; not drink much; shun all deviant consumption.
9. Warm relationships with others*	Personal hospitality and participating in social get-togethers. Gift giving. Heavy use of communication products.

Source: LOV items (but not examples) are from Kahle, Beatty, and Homer, 1986, (See Lynn R. Kahle, Sharon E. Beatty, and Pamela Homer, "Alternative Measurement Approaches to Consumer Values: The List of Values (LOV) and Values and Life Style (VALS)," Journal of Consumer Research 13 (December 1986), pp. 405–409. LOV items are copyright © 1986 by Journal of Consumer Research, Inc. Published by The University of Chicago Press.

Beyond LOV: More Consumer Values

While LOV is an efficient set of values by which to profile consumers, we don't want to leave you with the impression that it exhausts all consumer values. In fact, there are a number of other values—both general as well as consumption specific—that influence consumer behavior. Many of our personal values come from the culture in which we live in, so we will cover them more comprehensively in Chapter 9; even so, we must note at least a few of those values here to illustrate the range of influence values have on consumers. One such value we often learn from our culture is collectivism (versus individualism). In collectivist cultures, people are concerned about the wellbeing of their group and society in general. In individualist cultures, people are focused on their own personal wellbeing even at the expense of their group. Now, these cultural values are not equally assimilated by all members of a society. Thus, in collectivist cultures, some individuals will turn out to be individualists, and vice versa.

Will consumers who value individualism behave differently than those who value collectivism? Yes. A collectivism-valuing consumer will consume in a way that is good for the society as a whole. For instance, if society desires boycotting of foreign goods, then a consumer with a collectivist value will buy only domestic goods; in contrast, an individualist consumer will buy the car that pleases him or her regardless of whether it is domestic or foreign-made. One study in Greece found that consumers who were collectivists were more prone to practice recycling than those who were individualistic.[7]

Another personal value is **materialism**—the extent to which one considers possessing and consuming more and more products as a sign of success. In the above-mentioned recycling study in Greece, materialistic consumers were found to recycle less than an average consumer. As should be self-evident, some consumers' never-ending possession spree is driven and explained by their high materialism

Copy reads: May today bring more potential boyfriends and less potential annoyances. More job opportunities and less "call again in a few months." More future and less saturated fat. A better breakfast starts with no cholesterol, more determination, less sugar, more possibilities.

Brand Silk Soymilk is more than a beverage; it is a "means" as well to consumer goals of being ready for a productive day.

value. Our opening examples allude to a number of other values and the very notable effect they have on our consumption behaviors. To highlight that effect so you are left with no doubt as to how pervasive the influence of values on consumer behavior is, we consider those opening examples worth repeating here:

> If we value an animal's life as much as human life, then saving animal life would be a 'value' to us and we would not further our lives by using products made by killing them. If we believe in free individual choice, then we would not favor government regulation of music or video games or movies, or whatever. Valuing individual choice would also lead us to not want government regulation of everyday life of individuals, and consequently we would not favor motorists being fined for using cell phones while driving. And, if we believe in individual responsibility, then we would hold the consumer, not any fast food chain, responsible for his or her eating behavior.

LINKING PRODUCT ATTRIBUTES TO CONSUMER VALUES

As the foregoing examples show, values can affect the choices consumers make at three levels:

- **Marketplace Activity:** Shoplifting, shopping honesty, shopping constantly, the never-ending quest for possessions, patronizing minority sellers, etc.
- **Choice of Product Category:** Enrolling in personal development courses, purchasing gifts, joining social networking associations, consuming hedonistic products, etc.
- **Preference for Product Attributes:** Seeking travel with adventure versus

connecting and socializing attributes, buying cosmetics that do not use animal testing, valuing symbolic and social prestige attributes of a product, etc.

Note the last point again: values cause consumers to seek different attributes in products. Put another way, consumers prefer different product attributes because of the values consumers possess. Wouldn't it make sense, then, to find out these underlying values behind consumer choice of product attributes? It does, and to accomplish this,

FIGURE 5.1

A MEANS-END CHAIN FOR A HYPOTHETICAL CONSUMER

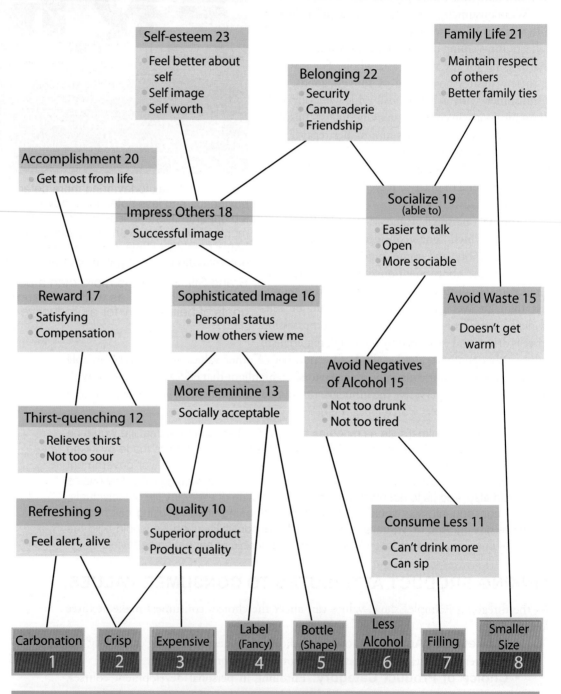

Source: Thomas J. Reynolds and Jonathan Gardner, "Laddering Theory, Method, Analysis, and Interpretation." Reprinted from the *Journal of Advertising Research*, 28 (February/March, 1988), p.19. "© Copyright 1988 The Advertising Research Foundation.

consumer researchers build what they call **means-end-chains**—pathways connecting product attributes to ultimate consumer goals or values. These are simply links between a product's physical features and the consumer's fundamental needs and values. Attributes lead to consequences or benefits, which in turn lead to still other, higher-level benefits. And these higher-level benefits ultimately lead to the fulfillment of values. Marketers draw these links to understand the ultimate purpose for which consumers buy even seemingly mundane products.

To draw these links, consumer researchers use a technique called **laddering**—a procedure to map a consumer's view of how a product's use ultimately fulfills his or her higher level values. To implement the procedure, consumers are asked repeatedly in an iterative sequence: "Why is that feature important to you?" For example: "Why is quick acceleration important to you?" If the answer is, "to maneuver out of traffic situations," we next ask, "And why is that important to you?" And so on.[8] Figure 5.1 shows a *means-end chain* for a hypothetical consumer for a beverage.

CONSUMER PERSONALITY

Our values make us the people we are. A person's persona is one way of summing up that person. A part of personality is genetically given to us, and a part is formed by our social environment. But our personalities are also influenced considerably by our values. If we valued hedonism, for example, then we would develop a happy-go-lucky, pleasure-seeking personality. And if we valued human relationships over self-interest, we would develop a warm, affable personality. Some scholars maintain that our personalities can also influence our values. Thus, values and personality influence each other mutually.

Personality refers to a person's psychological makeup that engenders characteristic responses to the environment in which he or she lives. By *environment, we mean social or physical situations.* By *response, we mean an action or behavior.* All of our actions or behaviors are our responses to environmental stimuli. At a cocktail party, for instance, we see a group of people (environmental stimuli), and we either try talking to them or stand in a corner aloof (response). If we see a lot of new styles of clothes in the store (environmental stimuli), we either rush to buy them, or we deliberate long and hard before making a decision (response). By *characteristic, we mean consistent or typical, natural or spontaneous.* A one-time and hesitant behavior does not count as reflecting personality; rather it is just a random response. Thus, if we notice a consumer splurge on an isolated occasion, we could not say that he or she is a spendthrift. If splurging were his or her typical behavior, and it seemed to come to him or her naturally, only then could we say he or she has the personality of a spendthrift. Likewise, a one-time act of kindness does not make a person kind. Rather, a consistent, repeated pattern of behavior is what truly *reflects* personality.

Notice the word *reflects*. This is because the consistent behavior pattern is not, by itself, personality. Rather, that behavior and the psychological forces (i.e., our psychological makeup) that engender or produce it together make up the personality. Those forces come primarily from our genetics and our values and motives. Some motives are biological or biogenic, that with which we are born; others—psychogenic motives—we learn and acquire based on the rewards and punishments we receive. Values are learned from the environment—from our culture and from our society. We receive these values from society, but we adopt (or reject) them selectively based upon our own personal motives.

Values and motives translate into characteristic behaviors as a continually adapted response to the environment. That is why some words describe all three elements: e.g., "achievement" can be a value as well as a motive, and it leads to an "achiever" behavior pattern (i.e., achiever personality). In practice, however, it is convenient to identify people's personalities simply by their consistent behavioral responses. Everyday descriptions of people (innovative or tradition-bound; dogmatic or open-minded; sociable or aloof;

aggressive or meek; compulsive or calculated; thrifty or indulgent) are actually references to their personalities.[9]

Humans develop personality because it is efficient to build a standard repertoire of responses to one's environment, as opposed to thinking up a new response every time a situation arises. These standard responses, by repeated occurrence, get etched in memory and are involuntarily elicited (i.e., they occur automatically without effort and conscious thought) whenever the situation calls for it. Thus, aggressive consumers get angry when they see that an advertised item is out of stock, or the checkout line too long, or the vending machine out of change. These responses occur instantaneously without deliberation; in fact, to restrain these natural and spontaneous personality responses, conscious thought and control are required.

In psychology literature, two of the dominant theories for explaining the concept of personality are the Freudian theory of personality and the personality trait theory.[10] Every consumer researcher is at least part psychologist. Now it is our chance to know what every psychologist knows.

FREUDIAN THEORY
Is Your Id Misbehavin'?

Recall that, in Chapter 2, we talked about some of our motives being unconscious. Sigmund Freud, the founder of psychoanalysis, was the first to suggest the concept of the unconscious. He argued that human personality is driven by both conscious and unconscious motives. He proposed three divisions of the human psyche: id, superego, and ego. The id is the basic source of inner energy, directed at avoiding pain and obtaining pleasure; it represents unconscious drives and urges. The superego is the moral side of the psyche, and it reflects the ideals of society. It is a person's conscience, trying to keep the id from misbehaving, so to speak. The ego is the conscious mediator between the id and the superego, that is, between the unconscious and impulsive desires of the id and the societal ideals internalized by the superego. The ego helps a person respond to the world in socially acceptable ways. According to Freud, a person's personality is crafted by the interplay of these three forces.[11]

The precise role of these three forces in shaping personality is complex and beyond the scope of our purpose here. Suffice it to say, a broad way to classify people into personality types using Freudian theory is to look at the relative dominance of the id, superego, or ego forces. Persons with a dominant id would be mostly pleasure seeking and self-centered. Persons with a dominant superego would be mostly moralistic and altruistic. Finally, persons with a dominant ego would be mostly practical—and would, in fact, guard their sense of self. In consumer behavior, id dominated persons would seek more hedonistic consumption and be uncontrolling in their desire for buying and consuming. Superego dominated persons would shun anti-social consumption and advocate pro-social consumption (e.g., shun environment-polluting products). Persons with a well-developed ego would show a consumption pattern balanced between the other two types; they would also be more likely to engage in self-growth oriented consumption (e.g., enrolling in skills development courses).

Because many of the id's urges are socially unacceptable, they are suppressed. Subsequently, they find their expression in alternative ways that are more acceptable to society. Behaviors that express themselves in this manner are called *defense mechanisms*.

DEFENSE MECHANISMS

Defense mechanisms are psychological processes we employ to protect our egos. These defense mechanisms make a behavior acceptable to our own sense of right and help us overcome guilt and frustration. When we use them, we either mentally redefine the stimulus (e.g., "That car is not really a luxury car") or redefine our motive for engaging in a particular behavior (e.g., "I didn't buy it because of its luxury features").

You know some of them already. Rationalization, for example. When someone tries to give a rational reason for a seemingly irrational behavior (like why he or she drove 5 miles to save 50 cents on gas), we say they are rationalizing. Other defense mechanisms include projection, aggression, repression, withdrawal, and regression. Read more about them in Table 5.2.

While everyone resorts to these behaviors once in a while, some consumers use them frequently, making these their characteristic behaviors. Some consumers seem to be frequently aggressive; some are constantly blaming others; some always seem withdrawn from their surroundings; and so on. Freud's psychoanalytical theory provides one perspective on why these characteristic behaviors occur.

An important point in Freud's view of personality, and why we study it, is that it explains several consumer behaviors as caused because of certain unconscious motives. Many consumers repeatedly engage in these behaviors

TABLE 5.2	Defense Mechanisms Consumers Employ
Defense Mechanisms come in a variety of forms	
Rationalization	This defense mechanism involves explaining an embarrassing action by a false motive, for which the real motive is supressed from conciousness. For example, a consumer who bought a luxury car to impress others but does not want to admit this motive would rationalize the decision my citing a superior performance feature, even though that feature may have played no role in his or her decision.
Projection	This defense mechanism is at work when we project our own feelings onto others, or blame others for our own shortcomings or attribute personal feelings to others. For example, suppose we break an appliance by wrongful use, we would blame the manufacturer for poor workmanship. Or if we enjoy buying name brand clothes from off-price stores, we would assume that all our co-workers who wear nice clothes must have also been buying them from some off-price stores. Thus, by assuring ourselves that our own motive to buy nice clothes from off-price and irregular merchandise stores is a "normal" behavior in others, we protect our ego from anxiety
Aggression	To become aggressive is to display or inflict pain on someone out of frustration and without justification. For example, a consumer who suspects a certain retailer of price gouging during a market shortage might spoil the merchandise in the store. Or a poor person who is deprieved of basic transportation may slash tires of a luxury car. Now you know why some consumers do this sort of "not cool" things!
Repression	This defense mechanism involves pushing unacceptable thoughts and feelings into unconsciousness. It is one of the most primitive mechanisms. Repression is at work when consumers avoid products that are associated with unattractive situations, and at the same time they deny that association to be the reason for their avoidance. For example, a consumer may avoid products associated with his ex-spouse (or products he consumed in previous marriage). Or children of immigrants, eager to fit into their new enviornment, may avoid their own parental preferences; moreover, they would deny that they are trying to distance themselves from their ethnic origins. They are not lying, mind you, for their motive to distance themselves works subconciously.
Withdrawal	This mechanism is at work when we withdraw from a situation in which are are not successful. Consumers literally withdraw from associations, PTA meetings, health clubs, book clubs, and so on, if they believe that they are not performing well in those settings.
Regression	This mechanism is at work when we revert to childhood behaviors. Attend a very special sales event, and you may very well witness regression. Sometimes adults resort to immature behaviors, pushing and shoving each other, or fighting over limited merchandise. Referring to adults, when we say that they were fighting like children, they infact were. Freud would have said the samething!

Prepared by Author for MyCBBook

for motives not even known to them. When we observe these behaviors, we are puzzled. We need not be puzzled any more: if we see consumers being aggressive in the marketplace, for example, we now know that it is their strong motive to get even (aggression as a defense mechanism). Consumers who believe that a seller is charging an exorbitantly high price, exploiting their helplessness, defend their ego, for example, by vandalizing the seller's merchandise.

And as marketers, too, we can learn something from this. We should never expect consumers to assume the blame for not being able to follow directions, or for inadvertently misusing the product (deliberate misuse and then denial is another matter), or for making mistakes in assessing the product's fit with their needs. Instead consumers would defend their ego by projection—blaming us, the marketers, for all those shortcomings or mishaps. Rather than get defensive ourselves, we should show an understanding of the defense mechanisms consumers are employing. And we should thank Freud for this consumer insight!

TRAIT THEORY
Your Uniqueness Is What Your Personality Is

Whereas Freud's theory seeks to *explain* personality, "trait theory" merely seeks to *describe* it. Unlike the former, it does not deal with the inner, psychological forces; rather, it focuses directly on the "characteristic behavior" portion of the definition. That is, Freud's theory focuses on the "why" of personality; trait theory focuses on the "what."

The trait theory of personality is an approach used to describe a person's personality by means of multitude of characteristics or personality traits. Each trait marks similarities and differences among people. A personality trait is defined as a person's stable and consistent way of responding to the environment in a specific domain.[12] Notice that the definition of a personality trait is virtually identical to the definition of a personality. However, a given personality trait works in a specific domain, whereas a personality is the sum total of all of the personality traits. For example, in the domain of group situations, how a person consistently behaves across group situations will be one of his or her personality traits (e.g., aggressive or friendly). Another domain centers on work and career, and how a person consistently behaves in the workplace will be another trait (e.g., motivated or lazy). A third domain is product acquisition, and, again, how a person consistently behaves in this domain is another trait (e.g., materialistic or frugal). Consistency of response is a hallmark of a trait: persons with a compulsiveness trait consistently and characteristically act compulsively; persons with the personality trait of dogmatism consistently hold on to their beliefs; and variety-seeking persons are constantly changing their preferences.[13]

If personality is the sum total of all the traits, how many traits are there? The answer is, thousands—actually, 4500, to be exact. This magic number is the number of different words people use to describe other people (in the English language), a list painstakingly compiled by psychologist Gordon Allport in the1930s. Of course, no single human being has that large a vocabulary, and the list would be too unwieldy to be of any practical use. Therefore, psychologist Raymond Cattell took Allport's list and (using a statistical technique called factor analysis) reduced it, first to 35, and then finally to 16 fundamental traits that account for a person's behavior.[14] He termed them *source traits*, since, in his view, these were the sources of other *surface traits*, or overt behaviors. These 16 traits are phrased as opposite pairs of adjectives: e.g., reserved/outgoing, conservative/experimenting, etc. (See Table 5.3.) Read the list and circle one adjective in each pair that applies to you. If you have never taken such a ratings test before, this is the first time you will be able to learn your own complete personality profile.

Another set of personality traits is the Edwards Personality Preference Schedule (EPPS), which consists of 15 traits, shown in Table 5.4. More on this in a minute. But first, let us ask ourselves: How do these personality traits influence consumer behavior? Basically, personality manifests itself as action, by definition. Unless we consciously try to restrain ourselves in the marketplace, our personalities are going to produce specific behaviors. Based on Cattell's source traits, if we are outgoing (instead of reserved), then we are going to participate much more in group based consumption activities, and we are more likely to buy products with their public image in mind. In contrast, as reserved consumers, we are probably going to prefer that salespersons keep their distance, leaving us to browse by ourselves. If we are apprehensive, we might feel intimidated in a sophisticated, exclusive restaurant; as self-assured consumers, on the other hand, we are likely to be more certain of our rights in the marketplace and seek to exercise them.

Next, consider Edward's Personality Preference Schedule (EPPS). For some fun, let us set up its applications as a puzzle. In Table 5.5 we have divided the 15 traits into three sets of five, and within each set, we have listed five consumer behaviors, in jumbled order. Your task is to match the traits to the behaviors within that set.

THE BIG FIVE OF PERSONALITY

Although the above two lists are quite useful to characterize a consumer's personality, psychologists were not satisfied with the length of these trait lists. Over the 45-year period from 1945 to 1990, psychologists continued to seek a smaller set that would account for most of Cattell's traits, and other traits as well. The current view has now settled on five factors. This view argues that all of the adjectives people use to describe other people can be encompassed by five broad factors, called **the Big Five** of personality.[15] These are captured

TABLE
5.3

The Sixteen Personality Factors Inventory

16PF® Fifth Edition Primary Factor Scale Descriptors

Factor	Left Meaning	Right Meaning
Warmth	Reserved, impersonal, distant	Warm, outgoing, attentive to others
Reasoning	Concrete	Abstract
Emotional Stability	Reactive, emotionally changeable	Emotionally stable, adaptive, mature
Dominance	Deferential, cooperative, avoids conflict	Dominant, forceful, assertive
Liveliness	Serious, restrained, careful	Lively, animated, spontaneous
Rule-consciousness	Expedient, non-conforming	Rule-conscious, dutiful
Social Boldness	Shy, threat-sensitive, timid	Socially bold, venturesome, thick-skinned
Sensitivity	Utilitarian, objective, unsentimental	Sensitive, aesthetic, sentimental
Vigilance	Trusting, unsuspecting, accepting	Vigilant, suspicious, skeptical, wary
Abstractedness	Grounded, practical, solution-oriented	Abstracted, imaginative, idea-oriented
Privateness	Forthright, genuine, artless	Private, discreet, non-disclosing
Apprehension	Self-assured, unworried, complacent	Apprehensive, self-doubting, Worried
Openness to Change	Traditional, attached to familiar	Open to change, experimenting
Self-reliance	Group-oriented, affiliative	Self-reliant, solitary, Individualistic
Perfectionism	Tolerates disorder, unexacting, flexible	Perfectionistic, organized, self-disciplined
Tension	Relaxed, placid, patient	Tense, high energy, impatient, driven

16PF® Fifth Edition Global Factor Scale Descriptors

Factor	Left Meaning	Right Meaning
Extraversion	Introverted, socially inhibited	Extraverted, socially Participating
Anxiety	Low anxiety, unperturbed	High anxiety, perturbable
Tough-Mindedness	Receptive, open minded, intuitive	Tough-minded, resolute, unempathic
Independence	Accommodating, agreeable, selfless	Independent, persuasive, Wilful
Self-control	Unrestrained, follows urges	Self-controlled, inhibits urges

by the acronym OCEAN[16], which stands for:

- **O**penness Being curious, insightful, imaginative, original, and open to new experiences and diversity.
- **C**onscientiousness Being organized, determined, responsible, and dependable.
- **E**xtraversion Being outgoing, persuasive, and displaying leadership roles
- **A**greeableness Being friendly, sympathetic, warm, kind, and good natured.
- **N**euroticism Being emotionally unstable, nervous, and anxious.[17]

TABLE 5.4

A Summary of Personality Traits Measured by Edward's Personal Preference Schedule

	TRAIT	BEHAVIOR
1.	Achievement :	To do one's best, accomplish tasks of great significance, do things better than others, be successful, be a recognized authority.
2.	Deference :	To get suggestions, to follow instructions, do what is expected, accept leadership of othes, conform to custom, let others make decisions.
3.	Order :	To have work neat and organized, make plans before starting, keep files, have things arranged to run smoothly, have things organized.
4.	Exhibition :	To say clever things, tell amusing jokes and stories, talk about personal achievements, have others notice and comment on one's appearance, be the center of attention.
5.	Autonomy :	To be able to come and go as one pleases, say what one thinks, be independent in making decisions, feel free to do what one wants, avoid conformity, avoid responsibilities and obligations.
6.	Affiliation:	To be loyal to friends, do things for friends, form new friendships, make many friends, form strong attachments, participate in friendly groups.
7	Intraception:	To analyze one's motives and feelings, observe and understand others, analyze the motives of others, predict their acts, put one's self in another's place.
8	Succorance:	To be helped by others, seek encouragement, have others feel sorry when sick, have others be sympathetic about personal problems.
9	Dominance:	To be a leader, argue for one's point of view, make group decisions, settle arguments, persuade and influence others, supervise others
10	Abasement:	To feel guilty when wrong, accept blame, feel need for punishment, feel timid in presence of superiors, feel inferior, feel depressed about inability to handle situations.
11	Nurturance:	To help friends in trouble, treat others with a kindness, forgive others, do small favors, be generous, show affection, receive confidence.
12	Change:	To do new and different things, travel, meet new people, try new things, eat in new places, live in different places, try new fads and fashions.
13	Endurance:	To keep at a job until finished, work hard at a task, keep at a problem until solved, finish one job before starting others, stay up late working to get a job
14	Heterosexuality:	To go out with opposite sex, be in love, kiss, discuss sex, become sexually excited, read books about sex.
15	Aggression:	To tell others what one thinks of them, criticize others publicly, make fun of others, tell others off, get revenge, blame others.

Each of these is actually a *supertrait*, because each contains a number of more specific traits, as described above.

The Big Five theory is relatively new and has not yet been utilized for published research in consumer behavior. But if you solved the Personality Puzzle above, you can easily think of the marketing applications of OCEAN. For starters, Openness can make you adopt new products more readily. Conscientiousness can make you use shopping lists, evaluate product choices more thoroughly, and not take advantage of retailer errors. Agreeableness can make you naturally act like a nice customer in service establishments. Extroversion, perhaps a trait all too familiar, can lead you to engage more in social leisure activities. Finally, neuroticism would likely lead you to engage in escape or compensatory consumption behaviors such as binge eating or gambling. Since it is a collection of *super traits*, overall, OCEAN is much more useful in explaining substantive consumer behaviors (as opposed to explaining specific mundane purchases), such as health promoting behaviors (dieting, exercise); confidence boosting acts, such as appearance altering procedures (e.g.,

TABLE 5.5

A Personality Puzzle

Solve This: For each persoalty trait in the Set, identify a corresponding consumer behavior in the list that follows the Set.

Set 1	Achievement	Deference	Order	Exhibition	Autonomy

a.	Dress attractively; watch comedy-based talk shows such as NBC's Late Night with Conan O'Brian, or CBS's David Letterman show.
b.	Likely to depend on salesperson and friends' advice when making buying decisions.
c.	Likely to resent salesman's hard - selling attempts.
d.	Use shopping lists; buy an organizer, PDA's etc.
e.	Buy products that will enhance relevant skills at work or career or even a hobby.

Set 2	Affiliation	Intraception	Succorance	Dominance	Abasement

a.	Seek out movies and TV shows depicting feelings and deep relationships rather than action dramas or sitcoms.
b.	Buy gifts for others; do more group activities like dining out with friends.
c.	Never take unfair advantage of salesclerk errors.
d.	Principal decision maker for family purchases.
e.	Seek out personal service employees (e.g., hairstylists; nurses, personal accountants, etc.) who would hear consumer's stories with sympathy.

Set 3	Nuturance	Change	Endurance	Sexuality	Agression

a.	Be less tolerant of poor service in stores and service establishments.
b.	More thorough information search for high involvement purchases.
c.	More likely to be early adopters of new products.
d.	Leave more tips in restaurants.
e.	Buy more romantic gifts—flowers, cards, perfumes/colognes, etc.

Prepared by Author for My**CB**Book

We are refraining from publishing the answers here. You can have some more fun, and learning, by discussing the answers with your friends, coworkers, or classmates. The answers are fairly logical, and relatively easy to identify. Even if your answers are different from others, you will have at least learned the central point of the exercise: *Personality Traits do influence consumer behavior!*

liposuction); adoption of hobbies, giving to charities, patronizing the arts, political and social activism, and so on.

MARKETERS' FIVE

To match the Big Five that psychologists have given us, we have culled five personality traits of more direct use to marketers. This is not a standard list, mind you, and different writers may cull different lists. You might add some more traits to the list, but we consider these important and worthy of study.

Innovativeness Have you ever noticed how some people rush out to buy new products as soon as they are introduced? These consumers have the personality trait of **innovativeness**, defined as being predisposed to embrace *new* products, ideas, and behaviors. They are not necessarily seeking instant gratification, mind you, nor are they reckless, impulsive buyers. Rather, these consumers strive to push the boundaries of benefits current products offer, and they are quick to see the merits of innovative products. Want to know if you are innovative? Score yourself on the scale given in Table 5.6.

TABLE 5.6	Measuring Consumer Innovativeness			
Strongly Disagree				**Strongly Agree**
1	2	3	4	5

1.	When new products (relevant to me) come out in the market, I am one of the first ones to buy them.
2.	I am interested in finding out about the latest innovations in products I use.
3.	Often I use products in unusual ways to get more out of them.
4.	It is too risky to buy products as soon as they come out.*
5.	Clothing, music, electronics, food products, or whatever, I usually wait for other people to try out new trends.*

Note: To score yourself, reverse score the items marked *, and then add all item ratings. The higher the score, the more innovative you are, with 15 being the middle point.

Source: Fashioned, in part, after Ronald E. Goldsmith and Charles F. Hofacker, "Measuring Consumer Innovativeness," *Journal of the Academy of Marketing Science,*" 19, 1991, p. 212, which is focused on consumer innovativeness in a product category. More specifically, only the first item in the present scale resembles (but is unidentical with) an item in the cited source. The present scale (which is intuitive and empirically untested) is easy to adapt for specific product categories (e.g., electronics, clothing, appliances, cosmetics, cooking, etc.) by simply inserting the name of the product category instead of the word product or products.

Variety/Novelty Seeker Do you get easily bored with going to the same restaurant, pub, or park? Are you always excited whenever you meet new people? Do you change your wardrobe frequently? Do you have a large collection of perfumes, colognes, neck-ties, shoes, coffee mugs, etc.? Do you have more than one (or two) wrist watches, more than one (or two) pairs of eye glasses, more than one (or two) cell phones, and/or more than one (or two) stress balls (!)? If your answer to these questions is a 'yes,' then you have the personality trait of variety seeking, defined as desiring new and diverse experiences. Variety-seeking consumers embrace change and, innovation or no innovation, want a different "toy" every day, so to speak. Novelty/variety seeking has also been termed sensation seeking, and recent research has found it to be, at least in part, genetically produced.

Hedonism Would you listen to your favorite music 24/7 if you could? Would you go surfing often? Are you much more into sports, television, travel, wine tasting, rock climbing, or bungee jumping than most other people? If you answered "yes," then you have the personality trait of hedonism, defined as seeking maximal pleasure out of life. Underlying this personality trait is the belief that the most important thing in life is to enjoy yourself.[19] Hedonists make pleasure the central theme of life. A whole bunch of industries cater to hedonistic consumers. There is even a business called Club Hedonism and another called Hedonism II, where some consumers take their dream vacations. There is of course a little bit of hedonism in most of us, but it should not overtake our pursuit of more meaningful goals in life, like acquiring useful skills, mastering an art or profession, and making a name for ourselves. Yes, you can watch MTV, but not incessantly, and not at the expense of reading this book!

Vanity The trait *vanity* refers to excessive pride in one's appearance and accomplishments.[20] Consumer researchers who have studied this topic—principally, marketing professors Richard G. Netemeyer, Scot Burton, and Donald R. Lichtenstein, respectively of Louisiana State University, the University of Arkansas, and the University of Colorado—have recognized these two aspects, appearance and accomplishment. Additionally, they argue, however, that a consumer's view of vanity could take two forms: a concern or anxiety and a "positive (generally inflated) view." In effect, then, a consumer could either be dissatisfied with and anxious about his or her appearance; or, when satisfied, he or she could be proud of it and hold an inflated perception. Likewise for accomplishments. Want to know how much "trait vanity" you have? You can score yourself on the scale shown in Table 5.7. Although research on this topic is scanty, this trait has been found to be correlated with materialism, consciousness of one's body in public, clothing concern, consumption of cosmetics, money spent on clothing, and consideration of cosmetic surgery.[21] In popular literature, sheer extravagance is considered vanity.[22] Thus, if a consumer spends, say, $20,000 for a wrist watch, or $2000 for a purse, or $1000 a night for a hotel room, then he or she might be deemed as vain. To the consumer himself or herself, it might simply be a matter of "finer tastes." At any rate, vanity does result in consumption—consumers high in vanity will spend more on higher priced items and on conspicuous consumption.

Uniqueness Seeker Another important trait, and the last one in our list of the *Marketers' Five*, is *uniqueness seeking*. As the name implies, **uniqueness seeking** is a personality trait wherein a person seeks to be unique, different from others. This trait is fueled by one's desire for differentiating oneself from the pack, so to speak. A few satisfy this desire through personal accomplishments—e.g., being a Pulitzer journalist, an Oscar-winning

TABLE 5.7 Measuring Consumer Vanity

Strongly disagree				Strongly Agree
1	2	3	4	5

Physical-Concern Items

1. The way I look is extremely important to me.
2. I am concerned about my physical appearance.
3. I would feel embarrassed if I was around people and did not look my best.

Physical-View Items

1. People notice how attractive I am.
2. People are envious of my good looks.
3. My body is sexually appealing.

Achievement-Concern Items

1. Professional achievements are an obsession with me.
2. I want other to look up to me beacuse of my accomplishments.
3. Achieving greater succes than my peers is important to me

Achievement-View Items

1. In a professional sense, I am a very successful person.
2. My achievements are highly regarded by others.
3. I am an accomplished person.

Note: To score yourself, add all item ratings. The higher the score, the more vain you are, with 36 as the middle point.

Source: : Richard G. Netemeyer, Scot Burton, and Donald R. Lichtenstein. "Trait Aspects Of Vanity: Measurement and Relevance to Consumer Behavior," *Journal of Consumer Research*, 21, March 1995, p. 624. **Copyright © 2001 by Journal of Consumer Research, Inc. Published by The University of Chicago Press (Used with permission.)**

actor, a Nobel scientist, a Hall of Fame ball player, a celebrated artist, a mesmerizing orator, or a revered teacher, for example. For most of us, however, *need for uniqueness* takes the form of visible consumption. If a person looks different in products or objects he or she is donning—clothing, hairstyle, makeup, or body adornments—then he or she is seen by others to be unique, and, in turn, he or she sees him- or herself as different.

Consumer researchers have identified the three forms this trait takes: (a) creative uniqueness; (b) unpopular uniqueness; and (c) avoidance of the commonplace. In creative uniqueness, consumers try to find unique objects, and/or, after purchase, customize the items with some personal touches. Consumers using this approach to uniqueness look for one-of-a-kind items, for antiques, and for items not available in local areas. Unpopular uniqueness takes the form of consumers adopting products that look weird and that go against prevalent tastes. This behavior takes many forms: unusual hairstyles, excessive body piercings, excessive tattoos, grunge clothing, baggy pants, inside-out wearing of shirts, etc. The point is not simply that these products are different; rather, they often are, by prevalent tastes, ugly, weird, unrefined, and "not pretty." The goal of the displaying consumer is indeed to attract attention and shock the "commonplace viewer." Ironically, some of these choices seen initially as weird and ugly become popular (at least among some subgroups) and, with habituation, acceptable and no longer weird to people at large.

The third avenue of satisfying the need for uniqueness is through avoidance of the ordinary. Consumers using this avenue will seek exclusive products; they will also be quick to adopt new trends. However, once the trend becomes popular, they will dump it and move on to another trend. This group differs from the first group in that the first group looks for unique items with the zeal of an explorer and "creates" one's own modifications and embellishments. The third group simply looks for products that are easily available but have not been adopted by masses.

Want to know if you have this trait? Take the survey in Table 5.8 and see for yourself.

TABLE 5.8

Measuring Need For Uniqueness

Strongly disagree				Strongly Agree
1	2	3	4	5

1. I like to look different from an average person.
2. I believe my tastes and preferences are exclusive.
3. I like to stand out in a crowd.
4. Most customs and rules are made to be broken.
5. Clothing, music, electronics, food products, or whatever, I usually wait for other people to try out new trends.*
6. I often look for one - of- a kind products to create my opwn style.
7. I am an accomplished person.

*Reverse-score this item.

Note: To score yourself, add all item ratings. The higher your score, the more uniqueness seeker you are, with 21 as the middle point.

Source: Items are excerpted form a much longer list in Kelly Tepper Tian, William O. Bearden, and Gary L. Hunter, "Consumer Need for Uniqueness: Scale Development and Validation," *Journal of Consumer Research*, 28, June 2001, 50-66. Copyright © 2001 by Journal of Consumer Research, Inc. Published by The University of Chicago Press (Used with permission.)

THE INFLUENCE OF PERSONALITY ON CONSUMER BEHAVIOR

TABLE 5.9

Need For Uniqueness and Consumption

Who is MORE UNIQUE—A Quick QUIZ

In a recent study, researchers compared the uniqueness scores they obtained for selected groups (e.g., tattoo artists) and compared them to their counterparts (non-select groups)" Let's assume they called these groups 'A' and 'B' but won't tell us which is which. Sometimes Group 'A' could be the select group and sometimes it could be the non-select group. The Uniqueness scores of the two groups are listed below. Can you help us figure whether, for each row separately, Group 'A' is the select or the non-select group?

	Group 'A'	Group 'B'
Tattoo and body piercing artists	3.05	2.60
Owners of customized low rider autos	2.99	2.60
Members of medievalist reenactment	2.91	2.60
Student art majors	3.06	2.71
Student purchasers of unusual poster art	2.83	2.71

Incidentally, why the purchasers and nonpurchasers of unusual poster art don't differ significantly on their uniqueness score? And if you were an art major, would you have been more or less unique?

Source: Items are excerpted form a much longer list in Kelly Tepper Tian, William O. Bearden, and Gary L. Hunter, "Consumer Need for Uniqueness: Scale Development and Validation," Journal of Consumer Research, 28, June 2001, 50-66. Copyright © 2001 by Journal of Consumer Research, Inc. Published by The University of Chicago Press (Used with permission.)

The role of personality, just like the role of values, is overarching—affecting all domains of consumer behavior. In a sense, personality is the conduit through which the influences of all other psychological or even biogenic characteristics flow. For example, a person genetically prone to headaches or allergies could bear the discomfort stoically, shunning early medication, or, alternatively, he or she could show hypochondriac tendencies and seek intense medication at the earliest onset of symptoms. (Stoicism and hypochondria are indeed personality traits.) A young person could be staid and be content with "consuming" TV all the time, while a 70-year-old with an active personality could be hiking and skiing. A woman could wear unisex clothes and smoke cigarettes with a macho image, and a man could be a heavier user of cosmetics (men's fragrances, of course) than the average woman!

Indeed, our personalities influence our consumer behaviors intensely. Outgoing persons will participate in out of home and social activities more and therefore will consume products and services relevant to these recreational activities. Similarly, pleasure-seeking individuals will seek hedonistic and experiential products more. People with artistic tastes will frequent performing arts events. Often, achievement-oriented adults seek to improve their skills and aptitudes, so they may register for college courses and buy products and services needed to complete their training. Some consumers are spendthrifts, whereas others are frugal and conservative. Some like to live on credit, while others live within their current cash resources. Even whether or not a consumer is loyal to brands or to stores may depend on personality—some individuals like to stick with the tried and tested, while others like to explore new options.

Yes, you can be oriental *and b*lond. All you need is a high need for uniqueness.

Photo Courtesy: Howard French

Marketers use the concept of personality in brand communications, presenting their brands along with some desired symbolic personality meanings. To accomplish this, they use three related approaches. First, they give a brand the desired personality by showing certain symbolic images in conjunction with the brand—e.g., placing the brand in an outdoor, rugged setting to give it a rugged personality. Second, they carefully choose spokespersons and human models whose known professions, skills, styles, and moods depict the desired personality. And third, they depict the brand in use by typical "target" users whose style, mood, and the "activity of the moment" capture and convey the intended personality image. Indeed, most brands whose primary value to consumers comes from social or ego/identity dimensions of the USER model (described in Chapter 1) differentiate and "position" themselves mainly on brand personality.

S E L F - C O N C E P T

Our Multiple and Extended Selves

Self-concept is the mirror image of personality. Your own face, the face you can touch, is the reality; the face you see in the mirror is its image. Likewise, your personality is who you *are*; self-concept is how you see yourself in your "mind's eye." **Self-concept** can be defined as a person's conception of himself or herself. It is "the sum total of all the thoughts and ideas the person conjures up when he/she thinks of him/herself." Thus, self-concept is

TABLE 5.10

A Scale to Measure Self-Image & Product Image

Instruction: Please rate yourself, as you see yourself, on the following descriptive word pairs, by circling a number in each row closer to the word that describes you. Next rate a specific brand.								
1.	Rugged	1	2	3	4	5	6	7	Delicate
2.	Exciting	1	2	3	4	5	6	7	Calm
3.	Uncomfortable	1	2	3	4	5	6	7	Comfortable
4.	Dominating	1	2	3	4	5	6	7	Submissive
5.	Thrifty	1	2	3	4	5	6	7	Indulgent
6.	Pleasant	1	2	3	4	5	6	7	Unpleasant
7.	Contemporary	1	2	3	4	5	6	7	Uncontemporary
8.	Organized	1	2	3	4	5	6	7	Unorganized
9.	Rational	1	2	3	4	5	6	7	Emotional
10.	Youthful	1	2	3	4	5	6	7	Mature
11.	Formal	1	2	3	4	5	6	7	Informal
12.	Orthodox	1	2	3	4	5	6	7	Liberal
13.	Complex	1	2	3	4	5	6	7	Simple
14.	Colorless	1	2	3	4	5	6	7	Colorful
15.	Modest	1	2	3	4	5	6	7	Vain

Note: To measure product or brand image, the entire scale is repeated with instructions to rate the specified product or brand

Source: Adapted from Naresh K. Malhotra "A Scale to Measure Self-concepts, Person Concepts, & Product Concepts," *Journal of Marketing Research*, Vol. 18 (November 1981), pp. 456-464, scale items on p. 462. Reprinted with permission from the Journal of Marketing Research, published by the American Marketing Association.

your image of yourself, your concept of what kind of a person you are.

Everyone has a self-concept—an image of who he or she is. This self-concept includes both an idea of who a person currently is and who he or she would like to become. These two concepts are respectively called **actual self** and **ideal self.**[23] Often, we also recognize that others don't see us the same way as we see ourselves. The way others see us is called **social self-concept**. Here too, there can be an *actual* social self-concept, and there can be an *ideal* social self-concept—the latter meaning how you would like others to see you. For some, the self-concept pertains to intellectual and/or career accomplishments (e.g., one wants to be a successful writer, engineer, professional athlete, Wall Street financial executive, etc.).[24] For many, the self-concept pertains to the kind of material life they want to live (e.g., rich, famous, etc.).

These self-concepts influence a person's consumption deeply, for people live out their self-concepts in large measure by what they consume. For example, some business students in their senior year begin to think of themselves as well-employed junior executives or business professionals, so they begin to dress to fit the part, retiring their baseball caps, college sweatshirts, t-shirts with beer slogans, and sneakers. According to one report, a few years ago, many Generation Xers, then past their teen years, began to nurture a self-concept of being a "grown up, responsible person," and consequently, they were flocking to tattoo parlors to get their body tattoos removed—the same tattoos that they had sported proudly only a few years earlier.

How do we measure self-concept? For starters, we could simply ask people to describe themselves. For instance, "Tell me how would you describe yourself as a person?" We could then probe further with follow-up questions such as, "Is this how you see yourself now?" or "How do others see you, that is, to them, what kind of a person are you?" and, "What kind of a person would you like to become, in your own eyes? In the eyes of others?"

Consumers choose clothing that reflects their self-image. For consumers who see themselves as "colorful," and "contemporary," Stacy Adams brings just the clothing they can't resist.

(Quiz: From Table 5.7, which other self-concept adjectives would apply to the brand?)

Of course, this approach would require that (a) consumers trust us to share their self-concept (after all a self-concept can be a very private thought), and (b) consumers are articulate enough to put their self-concepts in words. Moreover, this in-depth interview would be time-consuming and costly to implement on a large sample of consumers. So, to measure it more efficiently, we can give consumers a list of words that describe a person—any person—and ask them to check off words that apply to them individually. To implement this approach, marketing researchers have designed a scale of self-concept, shown in Table 5.10. Using this scale, we can ask consumers to rate themselves; furthermore, we can ask them to rate themselves separately in terms of their actual and ideal self-concepts, if we like.

Reflecting your self-concept
Design by lisa lowe for o.r.e
(www.oreoriginals.com)
Courtesy: Rachel Lara, ORE.

One marketing use of the scale is based on the theory of *image congruity*. **Image congruity** theory states that we like to associate ourselves with objects (things, activities, and people) that have an image that is congruent with our own image of ourselves. Thus, if we believe we are contemporary, trendy, innovative, and vain, then we would likely keep friends who are also contemporary, trendy, innovative, and vain. We would avoid activities we see as traditional, old-fashioned, and modest, and we would want to consume only those products and brands (especially if they are conspicuous) that are contemporary and trendy. Being vain, we would want to show off a little, and we would be even more conscious of the right image of things that are conspicuous. In short, our consumption is driven by self-concept-brand image congruence.

This congruence can be assessed by using the self-concept scale. In addition to asking consumers to rate themselves using this scale, we can then ask them also to rate their impressions of a brand, say, Tommy Hilfiger, Rock & Republic, or Stacy Adams. A comparison between self- and brand ratings would reveal which dimensions of a brand's image would need to be modified to bring the brand image closer to our target consumer's own self-image.[25]

Personality or Self-Concept—Which Do Consumers Consume?

At this point, you might wonder, which one explains consumer behavior better—personality or self-concept? Recall again that personality is who you are, whereas self-concept is who you think you are. Now, the latter does incorporate a part of the former—we are aware and accepting of some of our personality traits. For example, if we are optimistic, outgoing, or introverted, then our self-concepts probably includes these. On the other hand, if we are dogmatic, arrogant, selfish, etc., we are probably either unaware or in denial of those traits, and accordingly, our self-concepts would not include these traits. To the extent that selected personality traits are included in our self-concepts, their influence on consumer behavior is shared and overlapping. But what happens when the two don't overlap?

Personality leads to characteristic behaviors, which are, by definition, largely automated. Occasionally we can control them by consciously reigning them in, but mostly they flow naturally (and to us those ways of acting are perfectly normal anyway). Therefore, those of our marketplace behaviors that are our characteristic responses will be better explained by our personalities—marketplace behaviors such as getting angry at sales clerks, rejecting high pressure persuasion, complaining at the slightest dissatisfaction, or, alternatively, feeling timid and avoiding confrontation even in the face of gross inconvenience caused by a marketer, compulsive shopping, compulsive eating, frequent gift giving, being stingy in sharing consumption with others, frequent grooming, and so forth.

In contrast are product and brand choices we make as consumers. Since these are

Dove believes all women have beautiful hair when it's deeply cared for. No matter what length, style, cut, color or texture, you can discover the beauty in your own hair with the deep care in Dove Shampoos and Conditioners. Learn more at www.campaignforrealbeauty.com

Brand Dove builds self-esteem for women

acts of choice (not automated acts), our conscious thoughts about who we are, i.e., our self-concept, rather than our personality, should guide our choices. Accordingly, the kinds of cars we choose to drive, the clothes we choose to wear, the leisure activities we prefer, the food we buy and eat, the beverages we imbibe—for each of these product choices, and as long as we are able to afford them and buy them for reasons beyond pure survival (in the latter case, we would buy the most basic, merely utilitarian/functional version), our choices are based on our self-concepts. Through products, we live our self-concepts. We buy clothing that is rugged or suave, we buy a house that is Victorian or contemporary, we buy a car that is sporty and muscular, or alternatively, luxurious and well-appointed, because we believe that we ourselves are suave or rugged, classic or contemporary, athletic or refined. That is why the self-congruency model described above can be a powerful tool for marketers; using it, we should, as marketers, constantly assess whether our marketing communications are building the kind of brand image that our target consumers would find congruent with their self-concepts.[26]

THE SELF-CONCEPT OF BEING A CONSUMER

The above measurement taps a consumer's self-concept as a person. Consumers have their self-concepts as individuals in general, of course, but they also have a self-concept of themselves in their specific role of being a consumer and a shopper. Illustratively, a consumer could have a self-concept of being a very discerning consumer of specific product categories—such as a wine connoisseur, a music aficionado, an art buff, a sports fan, a collector of fine things, or an anti-materialistic, self-denying consumer (e.g., a Buddhist monk). The consumer could also have a self-concept as a shopper, of what kind

To Each, His Or Her Own Self Concept

I am a 22-year old male who likes the outdoor activities such as freewheeling and boating. I like to enjoy life while at the same time being frugal. I am independent and hate to borrow or rent things. I would rather not finance vehicles and things and wait till I have the money. I have a strong drive for success and am proud of the fact that I have worked for everything I have got.

———0———

I am a fun loving lady who likes to go out with her friends. I am ready to graduate. I am creative—like to do my own things. I love animals, especially kitties. I am hungry all the time. I love food. ———0———

I am a male, 21 years old and am one of those who have no clue what they want in life. I work constantly and make a lot of money and spend that money on things I don't need. For example, I flat out purchased a '04 Mustang only to turn around and buy a second car—a 2003 Ford Mustang Cobra. So basically I have no direction in my life. When I should be thinking of the future, I can only think about what I want to do five minutes from now. My parents say I am stupid, but I'm enjoying life. Is there anything more to life?

———0———

[Excerpted from the author's research files, partially paraphrased and edited from written or verbal protocols.]

I take love very seriously

Nicole Smith, a college senior majoring in Business Administration

I am a strong woman and a woman of color. I have a big heart and I take love very seriously. I am honest and loyal. I believe in God. I am forgiving. I am confident. I am driven. I feel guilty about things others won't think about. I am sensitive and deep thinking. I analyze everything that happens to me. I am passionate. I love to laugh and I love to flirt. I love to make people feel good. I am open-minded. I am not concerned about following the crowd. I care about people's feelings and their rights as individuals. Finally, I am strong and I can't be broken.

Okay, now it is your turn. Write down what is your self-concept. Come on, write it down here. You are not planning to sell this book, are you? All you will get is money for a few beers or a few video rentals or a couple of CDs. What you will forego is the ability to keep the fascinating stories of consumer marketplace; the ability to, one day some 2 months after the course is over or 10 or 20 years from now, pick up this Collectors' Edition book and re-read and re-relate to all the consumer behavior concepts, theories, and practices that so much parallel, and will echo, your own *Consumer Karma*

The call of that Karma, right now, is to write down your honest self-concept, and then revisit and rewrite it every few years, and enjoy the constancy as well as the dynamic shifts in your persona, your identity, your sense of who you are or are trying to become.

of a shopper he or she is, such as thrifty and financially prudent, or as a convenience or personalized service seeker, or as a very time-conscious shopper. Accordingly, consumers could take shopping as a chore, or, as alternatively, as a heroic activity where they have to battle a proliferation of brands all clamoring for their attention, and where they have to triumph by making a wise purchasing decision—becoming "shopping heroes," so to speak!

COMPONENTS OF SELF-CONCEPT

Let us ask, what is included in a person's self concept? Although it can include virtually everything that consumers ever come to own and live with, a systematic list would include the following[27]:

Body For most consumers, their bodies are an integral part of their self images. Of course, the connection they feel between their sense of self and their bodies varies. If you ask a Hindu or a Buddhist monk, for example, and millions of their followers, they would tell you that their bodies have *nothing* to do with who they are.

The soul within, not the body, is the real self. In fact, the very goal of life in Eastern philosophy is to get out of this temporary shell that the body is and meet one's creator. At the other extreme, many consumers (in Eastern and Western cultures alike) are obsessed with their bodies to the extent that the body is the end-all and the be-all of their being. To them, the body—its appearance and shape—defines identity, and sense of self. Consumers around the world spend billions of dollars, euros, and yens on cosmetics and on beauty enhancing services (e.g., hair salons, nail boutiques, tanning booths, fitness clubs, etc.). For many consumers, permanent body adornment with tattoos and piercings is becoming a new source of enjoyment and enhanced living. For those who find their bodies lacking in beauty and shape and who just can't shake their self-concepts off their view of their bodies, new medical techniques such as Botox injections and liposuction are becoming new beacons of hope.

Values and Character
The second component of the self is the set of values a person holds. Earlier in the chapter, we defined *values* as "desired end-states in life and ways to live it." **Character** is the behavior of a person, being tested particularly in the face of tempting opportunities for opposite behaviors (e.g., not pointing out a cashier's mistake when given too much in change). Since we make deliberate choices in adopting certain values and discarding others, and we make sacrifices in living by those values, these choices define us. "I live by those values, because that is the kind of person I am," we tell ourselves. For many consumers, religion is a key source of their values and character, and consequently, it becomes a defining component of their identities. Thus, followers of Jainism value all human life (including insects) and become total vegetarians. Catholics value the life of a human fetus and are, accordingly, pro-lifers and oppose abortions.

Competence and Success
The third component of self is one's perception of one's competence and success. If we view ourselves as competent and successful, then we build positive self-esteem. If we judge ourselves as failures, then we risk suffering from low self-esteem, anxiety, and even depression. How we define success, and likewise competence, varies, of course. To some of us, success is acquiring more money and living a materially comfortable life; to others it might be achieving the ability to put their children through college and raising them to be good citizens. For still others, it might be defined as gaining fame and reputation. This component of the self influences consumption of many competence enhancing products and services, as consumers strive to upgrade their competence and skills, including educational and training programs, and skills classes in such wide-ranging areas as sewing, painting, dancing, music, etc.

Social Roles
Social Roles are a set of behaviors society assigns to individuals based on their positions in social institutions. These institutions include family, workplace, public-service organizations, etc. Thus, society assigns roles to individuals, like a father's role, a mother's role, a supervisor's role, a minister's role, a judge's role, etc. And individuals not only accept these roles, but they take pride in playing them so much that they incorporate these roles into their self-concepts.

Personality Traits
Finally, we also view ourselves in terms of our stable and characteristic

TABLE 5.11	Measure to Test if a Product is a Part of the Extended Self for Consumers*

(Insert product name in the blanks) Strongly Disagree 1 2 3 4 5 Strongly Agree)
1. I feel emotionally attached to my ——————.
2. My —————— holds a special place in my life.
3. My ——————is central to my identity — my sense of who I am.
4. If I lose my —————— I would feel a part of me was missing.
5. I take good care of my ——————.
6. I trust my ——————.

Source. *In part adapted from Kimberly J. Dodson, "Peak Experiences and Mountain Biking: Incorporating the Bikes in the Extended Self," *Advances in Consumer Research*, 1996, Volume 23, eds. Kim P. Corfman and John G. Lynch Jr., Provo, UT: Association for Consumer Research, Pages: 317 - 322. (Used with permission.)

behavioral responses. These, you will recall, are personality traits—the enduring states of our action patterns in everyday life. Thus, we are (and view ourselves as being) patient or temperamental, macho or delicate, stoic or tender, dogmatic or open-minded, outgoing or shy, and so on. Of course, as already mentioned, we do not have to be aware of or acknowledge all of our personality traits. The self-concept includes only those personality traits that the person acknowledges.

THE EXTENDED SELF AND POSSESSIONS

We have all heard the expression, "you can take a boy out of a village, but you can't take the village out of the boy." That is, the village you live in becomes a part of your personality. Indeed, when we try to make sense of people, we don't merely look at the person and their personal characteristics (age, body shape, or temperament) and accomplishments (e.g., education, career, fame); we also want to know what family they come from, what school they attended, what company they work for, what kind of friends they have, what kind of car they drive, and what kind of clothes they wear. We look at others that way and we judge them that way, but what happens when others too look at us that way? We want them to judge us by some of these things but not by others. If we graduated from a big-name school, for example, then, of course, we frequently name-drop our alma mater. If we have a famous dad, we may brandish our pedigree every chance we get. If we are on a typical student's budget and drive an old, dilapidated car, we don't think of that car as reflecting who we are. If we have a genuine Rolex watch, or an authentic Louis Vuitton handbag, then, of course, we want people to take notice.

Thus, it is a fact of life that people judge us by things that are not, strictly speaking, integral parts of ourselves. And we too define ourselves by these things that are outside of our skins, and our minds, and our personalities. This notion of viewing ourselves by things beyond and outside of ourselves is called the extended self. **Extended self** comprises all the external entities and objects that we consider, with pride, as parts of ourselves. By entities, we mean family, school, neighborhood, professional associations, and other institutions; by objects, we mean things we own. Not all the entities with which we have had associations, and not all objects we possess, form parts of our extended selves; only those in which we feel pride. Important entities that become, for most consumers, parts of their extended selves include (a) Ethnic & Cultural Identities, (b) Work Organizations, (c) Family Identities, and (d) Social Networks.

Possessions Important parts of the extended self, for most consumers, are worldly objects, their prize possessions. The things we own define us for two reasons: (1) We spend our lives with them. They virtually surround us, so we begin to see those things which we own as parts of ourselves. And (2) we use things to bring out our inner selves for display so

FIGURE 5.2 POSSESSIONS AND THE EXTENDED SELF

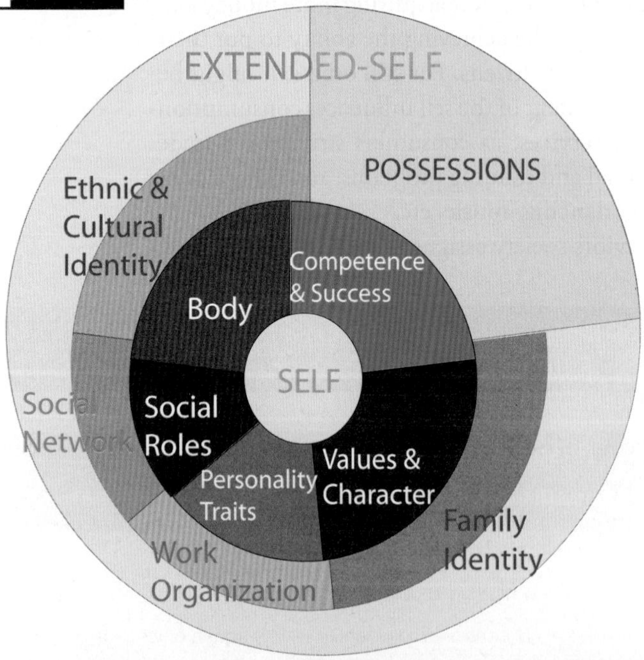

Note: The adjacency of sectors in the internal (core self) circle and sectors in the outer circle (extended self) is incidental to the present depiction. Illustratively, Ethnic and Cultural Identity sector sits adjacent to the Body sector, but they are not necessarily related. That said, the outer sectors *are* placed adjacent to what seemed the closest allies in the inner circle, albeit it is done, in the absence of any current theory, heuristically. It is offered here to stimulate opinion from thoughtful readers.

that others can see us for who we are. Indeed, the products we use and possess are tangible translators of the abstract idea of self-concept. The following three quotes from scholars put it well:

"Our fragile sense of self needs support, and this we get by having and possessing things because, to a large degree, we are what we have." [28]

A man's self is the sum total of all that he can call his, not only his body and his psychic powers, but his clothes and his house, his wife and children, his ancestors and friends, his reputation and works, his lands, and yacht and bank-account. All these things give him the same emotions. If they wax and prosper, he feels triumphant; if they dwindle and die away, he feels cast down—not necessarily in the same degree for each thing, but in much the same way for all. [29]

Clothing, automobile, house are all acquired as "second skin" in which others may see us. [30]

If our clothing, automobiles, and houses serve us as our "second skin," does the hotel we stay in do the same? Embassy Suites employed this concept in a recent ad. An overnight stay in a small hotel the night before a big interview might make a candidate feel small and less important, the ad reminded the reader. A stay in a big comfortable hotel room, on the other hand, just might boost a candidate's self-confidence noticeably before the interview, as any number of business travelers would verify. Yes, good things in life are not merely pleasurable to consume; they are also, at least for some consumers, a source of their enhanced self-concept, an ingredient of their extended selves.

When we **love** some **possessions** and choose them **to reflect us,** they literally become our **second skin.** Here, in this creative eyeful, Francesco Biasia captures this consumer **experience.**
(Courtesy: Francesco Biasia, Italy)

If you are a marketer, then you would like to know whether or not the product you are selling is part of your target consumers' extended self. You can find this out by using a short questionnaire, shown in Table 5.11. Based on this, you can then segment your target markets into those who use the product merely in a taken-for-granted manner, versus those who see the product as part of their extended selves.

ECSTASY NEEDS NO ANIMALS

If Kristoff St. John's call to abandon the circuses with animals has touched a cord in your own personal value system, it doesn't mean you have to forego the thrills of watching a circus altogether. A number of companies offer animal-free circuses. And they are just as world class, the most famous of them being Cirque du Soleil. Read below and see if you can resist making plans to see one soon. Even if a circus has never been on your agenda. One of them could soon be.

7 Fingers The joyous, surrealistic universe of 7 Fingers is filled with the beauty of awe-inspiring aerialists, the startling precision of amazing jugglers, the breathtaking exploits of graceful acrobats, and the wit and humor of seven young international circus performers. (USA. www.les7doigtsdelamain.com)

Circus Luminous A dazzling and original production featuring daring young women on the flying trapeze, innovative choreography, elaborate costumes, and a turn-of-the-century look. (New Mexico. www.wisefoolnm.org)

Cirque du Soleil A blend of music, dance, and stunning athleticism that takes the audience on a metaphorical journey. This circus breaks all the rules, and its art is in a constant state of evolution. Cirque has won more than 100 awards and distinctions from various organizations and institutions for originality in its shows and excellence in management. There are eight Cirque productions that run simultaneously. (Montreal, Canada. www.cirquedusoleil.com)

Contd...

My CB Book

Contd...

Cirque Eloise Combines theatre with acrobatic performances, poetry, and circus thrills. Acrobats, clowns, jugglers, trapeze artists, and musicians team up to create a rich and subtle tango of emotions. (Montreal, Canada. www.cirque-eloise.com)

Cirque San Jose Dancing bears and parading elephants aren't part of the package in Silicon Valley's new resident circus. Cirque San Jose provides performances that are part intimate minstrel circus, part musical, and part surrealistic play. It combines the story-telling traditions of the theatre with the "ooh-aah" thrills of a circus acrobatic performance. (San Jose, California.)

Cloud Seeding Circus Nontraditional glitter and excitement. Starring with the artists are exquisite sculptured objects that manifest as puppets. (Gainesville, Florida. www.cloudseedingcircus.com)

Flying Fruit Fly Circus Performances are a blend of circus, dance, theatre, and live percussion with attitude. Australia's Flying Fruit Fly Circus has established itself as one of the world's premier youth performing arts companies. (Albury, Australia. www.fruitflycircus.com.au)

Imperial Circus of China Considered the best of all Chinese circuses, it has played an important role in cultural exchanges between China and other nations. Its excellent performances have been warmly welcomed and highly appreciated by audiences around the globe. (Orlando, Florida. www.Imperialcircus.com)

Swamp Circus Theatre All-human circus theatre with an environmentally flavored artistic direction, a commitment to arts in the community, and a taste for adventure. Work is characterized by a unique blend of innovative, high-energy circus theatre, live music, and ecological themes. (South Yorkshire, England. www.swampcircus.com)

Source: Information excerpted from Peta.org Web site.

My CB Book

C.O.N.S.U.M.E.R. K.A.R.M.A.

The last Friday of November—that is day-after-Thanksgiving—is the biggest shopping day in North America. Teeming millions of shoppers flood the shopping malls, and cash registers in almost every store ring non-stop. If you visit any of these malls and big sotres, you will be surrounded by shoppers hustling through aisles of merchandise. But outside some of these stores, you might also run into a herd of people just standing by idle and buying, well, NOTHING! They are celebrating the Buy Nothing Day.

Buy Nothing Day (BND) was founded by Vancouver artist Ted Dave in 1991 and subsequently promoted by the Canadian Adbusters magazine. The intent of the event is to raise public consciousness against the culture of excessive consumption.

Protesters in cities around the world—although their numbers are small—gather on streets, sporting posters, and requesting shoppers to NOT buy anything. They also hand out some free-stuff (usually utilitarian items of small monetary value) to emphasize that life can be enjoyed without spending too much. And they encourage buying things that do no harm to our planet (recycled clothing) and that also constitute cultural progress (e.g., arts and theater).

In Japan, there is a new twist on the event's celebration. Organizers there call it the "eco-holiday of the 21st Century." They have invented a mascot, called Zenta Claus, who sits quietly "in the middle of the busiest shopping frenzy, and meditates, reminding people of the value of "things you cannot buy" and to enjoy the day without damaging the earth." Their mission, reflecting the mission of BND world-wide:

> 20% of the world population consume 86% of the world's resources, says a 2001 UNDP report. On BND, lets stop and think. What can we do to make the world more just, peaceful and sustainable? On a personal level, we want to change the way we look at shopping—not a harmless pastime, but an act of choice connecting us to the people who make our stuff and the incinerators that burn it when we throw it out. On a political level, we want to promote alternatives to the global use'n'toss economy: fair trade, family businesses, socially and ecologically sustainable business, true cost economics."

Why meditate on Buy Nothing Day? The organizers explain:

Silence is most underrated in our culture, partly because it doesn't add to the GNP, and it makes your self a little less persistent. Advertising is based on the premise that people want to feel good about themselves, that is, that they will do whatever it takes to prop up their ego. When you meditate and don't identify yourself so strongly with your small self, you will find that you don't need most of the things that advertising tries to sell you.

If you have an interest in making a "Zen" statement about how consumer-oriented societies have gotten out of hand, please plan your own Zenta Claus non-action outside a major department store or shopping mall near you!

We are consumers and this is what we do.

Sources: http://en.wikipedia.org/wiki/Buy_Nothing_Day and http://www.adbusters.org/metas/eco/bnd/ From BND Japan Web site; From BND Japan Web site; http://www.ddh.nl/pipermail/bnd-list/2002/000078.htm

Tommy Girl Grows Up

Ashley Meyer (a 20-something consumer), when asked to describe how clothes define her identity, submitted this photo essay.

(1) My Tommy phase; (2) My Abercrombie phase; (3) Hat phase; (4) Sparkle phase (notice he intense "bling," "Bling" thing on my wrist; (5) Get dressed for a party—my favorite, and (6) My Professional phase (current phase)

Q. Have Clothes played a role in your own evolving identity? What will your photo essay look like?

Romanticism—A Consumer Personality Trait Worth Knowing About

Romanticism Are you driven more by feelings than facts? Do you live a little bit on the edge or always follow the safe path? Would you call yourself intuitive rather than over-analyzer? Would you like your date to be sentimental or more practical?

Do you like heart-warming stories or would you rather read straight-forward news? If your choice is the first option, then you have the personality trait of **romanticism**—defined as being sensitive to feelings. The opposite trait is called **classicism**, the quality of being straightforward and unemotional. As a romanticist, you tend to be intuitive, imaginative, creative, even poetic. As a classicist, on the other hand, you are a no-nonsense rationalist, unmoved by emotional considerations, and preferring the unadorned. As a romanticist, in leisure and work alike, you are likely to prefer somewhat risky and edgy pursuits; as a classicist, you are likely to pursue more proven, or at least more considered paths.[31] While consumer research on this topic is scanty, we can at least infer this much: as marketing communicators targeting classicists, we should use functional appeals, documenting and demonstrating the functional benefits of our offerings; on the other hand, if we were targeting romanticists, we would better deploy symbolic appeals, and let the emotional side of our products show.

LAST WORD

tv2010

MyCBBook

Values, Personality, and our sense of self—these three concepts are so deep, and psychological literature on them so vast, that no single chapter can cover them comprehensively. Necessarily then, we have barely been able to sample a part of the subject matter. There are many important values, not covered here, that consumers around the world have embraced. And human personality traits, related to life in general and in the consumption domain in particular, can add up to thousands in number. *The Big Five* is personality psychologists' bold and innovative tool to rein in this vast inventory of human personality traits. But underneath these *supratraits* lie more specific, "mini" traits, so to speak, and often in consumer behavior, these "mini traits" play a more clearly discernible role.

Traits such as optimism or pessimism, shyness or assertiveness, confidence or hesitation, risk-averse or risk-taking, thoughtfulness or spontaneity, being expressive or reserved, frugal or extravagant—and the list can go on—these traits influence our consumer behaviors day in day out, even more so when they are also incorporated in our self-concepts.

Values, personality, and a sense of the self are three sides of the triangle that a person is, psychologically speaking. To know a person is to know these three things about him or her. These are also the three things that define one as a person. Ponder your own values. Rate yourself on various personality traits **And pen your self-concept**-what it is made up of and what entities and products are embraced in your extended self-concept. Then ponder how it influences your behavior as a consumer. It can be an immensely useful exercise in self-awareness. It will open a window to yourself, so to speak. We hope you will undertake such a self-reflective and introspective exercise.

We began this chapter with a discussion of personal values—what aspects of life are important to us. We understood the importance of values ("the value of values," if you will) in our lives. They are like a compass, we learned, that can and does guide the course of our lives—as humans and as consumers. Along the way, we met LOV, a list of nine values proven useful in consumer research. And we illustrated how values ultimately relate to product attributes. If you have ever wondered, to take one example, what a cell phone's SMS feature has to do with a teenager's life value of success or competence or efficiency, *means-end chains* could explain why.

Next, we shed light on the concept of personality— our consistent ways of responding to the environment. What it is and how we come to acquire it was mostly a mystery to us before reading this chapter, but not any more, thanks to Freud and a group of trait psychologists. The Freudian Theory illuminates the nature of personality as a set of conscious and sub-conscious motives and urges. Trait theory views personality as a set of patterned and consistent behaviors. Defense mechanisms were described as the ego's attempt to manage anxiety and protect the self from being slighted. Many defense mechanisms account for significant occurrences of product use or nonuse. We then described the *Big Five* theory of personality and its role in consumer behavior. We also presented what we call the "Marketers' Five"—our list of five personality traits that affect consumer behavior immensely.

Next, we discussed self-concept (our ideas about the sort of person we are), and we described actual, ideal, and social variations of it. We also discussed how possessions play a role in defining our identities as consumers—our extended selves. Are you obsessed with your body? Then your body plays an important role in your self-concept. What about your character, your friends, and your accomplishments—are these a part of your self-concept as well? They are if you choose to make them. And your possessions? Would you feel a void in your life if one of your possessions were taken away from you? If yes, then that possession is a part of your extended self-concept. Self-concept directs our purchases toward products that are congruent with our self-concepts; that is why it is important to marketers to understand the concept of self-concept.

And let us remind you that this summary is no substitute for reading the chapter. So go back and read on!

KEY TERMS

Values	Projection	Uniqueness Seeker
Terminal Values	Aggression	Actual Self
Instrumental Values	Repression	Ideal Self
List of Values	Withdrawal	Social Self-concept
Materialism	Regression	Image Congruity
Means-End Chain	Trait Theory	Character
Laddering	Innovativeness	Extended Self-concept
Personality	Variety Seeking	Social Roles
Defense Mechanism	Vanity	Romanticism
Rationalization	Hedonism	

YOUR TURN

REVIEW+Rewind

1. What are values and what role do they play in consumer behavior?
2. How do values relate to product attributes?
3. How would you define personality and self-concept? How are the two concepts related?
4. Briefly explain the six defense mechanisms described in the chapter, and illustrate each with an example from your experience.
5. What components make a consumer's self-concept? Explain each concept briefly.
6. Name and briefly explain any five personality traits from Edward Personality Preference Schedule (EPPS).
7. What are the *Big Five of Personality*? Explain each briefly, and cite one marketing application of each.
8. Explain the concept of self-concept brand image congruence. How does it explain a consumer's brand choice?
9. What is meant by *extended self*, and what role does consumption play in this concept?
10. Briefly describe in your own words each of these traits: vanity, sensation-seeking, hedonism, materialism, and uniqueness seeker. What importance do these

REVIEW+Rewind

1. What are values and what role do they play in consumer behavior?
2. How do values relate to product attributes?
3. How would you define personality and self-concept? How are the two concepts related?
4. Briefly explain the six defense mechanisms described in the chapter, and illustrate each with an example from your experience.
5. What components make a consumer's self-concept? Explain each concept briefly.
6. Name and briefly explain any five personality traits from Edward Personality Preference Schedule (EPPS).
7. What are the *Big Five of Personality*? Explain each briefly, and cite one marketing application of each.
8. Explain the concept of self-concept brand image congruence. How does it explain a consumer's brand choice?
9. What is meant by *extended self*, and what role does consumption play in this concept?
10. Briefly describe in your own words each of these traits: vanity, sensation-seeking, hedonism, materialism, and uniqueness seeker. What importance do these traits have in predicting consumer behavior?

THINK+Apply

1. Identify the relative importance of LOV components in your own LOV profile. How does your own LOV profile affect your own consumer behavior?
2. Based on List of Values (LOV), consumers can be placed into one of the three segments. Find three advertisements, one for each segment, that would appeal to only that segment but not others.
3. In your own case, what relative roles do various component of self-concept play, individually, in your self-concept? How does the particular combination of these components affect your consumer behavior?
4. The chapter asks a question: "self-concept or personality: which do consumers consume?" In your own case, name five marketplace behaviors that are influenced more by your personality, and, likewise, name five behaviors that are influenced by self-concept.
5. Assume you are a brand manager for (a) a line of clothing; (b) organized tours abroad, and (c) one-of-a-kind items of home décor. Which of the personality traits mentioned in the chapter would be most relevant to your identification of your target market? Why?

PRACTICE+Experience

1. Interview two consumers and draw means-end chains for their clothing styles—the styles that make their wardrobe. Identify implications of the means-end-chain for clothing behavior of these consumers.
2. Get a sample of consumers to rate themselves on the self-concept scale; then have them rate two brands of jeans; also ask them which of the two brands they would prefer more. Calculate the congruence scores and see whether these congruence scores predict their relative preferences. Why do you think they might not have? Repeat this for two brands of (a) cars and (b) colognes.
3. Find two consumers who you know differ on vanity. Verify that by using the vanity measurement scale. Then interview them to identify how their consumer behaviors are different. Repeat this for the uniqueness trait, and based on your interviews, profile the consumption differences between the high and low uniqueness seeker consumers.
4. Your task is to interview several consumers to find out if there is any possession they consider a part of their extended self-concept and the manner in which that possession became a part of their self-concept. Later you will compare two consumers who named the same product.
   a. First, construct an Interview Guide (your consumers won't understand the terms *self-concept* or *extended self-concept* and you should not use these technical words in interviewing lay consumers).
   b. Specifically explore how consumers' self-concepts play out in their possessions. Describe your findings.
   c. What does this exercise teach you that you could apply if you were a marketing manager of that product?

In the Marketing Manager's Shoes

Put yourself in a marketing manager's shoes. Most concepts in the chapter have some lessons for the marketing manager; i.e., they suggest what to do differently in practice. Indeed, often these applications are implicit in our explanations of the concepts and models in the chapter. Identify at least five specific applications of the chapter's concepts, all of which should be entirely new—different from the examples cited here.

HOW POSSESSIONS BECOME ONE'S EXTENDED SELF

You just read that possessions become part of our extended self-concept. But just how? What psychological or sociological processes occur so that some possessions are incorporated into our extended self-concepts but others are not? There is no research-based, comprehensive answer to that question. Reflect on how this happens in your own life and you are likely to find the following four processes at work[32]:

By Congruence Based Choice Since consumers choose symbolic products based on the congruence between perceived brand personality and their own self-concept, such products are, upon acquisition, ready to be part of consumers' selves. Choosing a sexy or suave pair of jeans for our sexy or suave persona makes that pair of jeans part of our extended-self.

By Resource Investment in Acquisition If we had to invest a lot of resources (money, time, energy) finding and selecting a product, then, to psychologically justify the investment, we tend to view that product as part of our extended selves. For this reason, more expensive purchases, hard to find purchases, and purchases for which we might have been saving for a long time are more likely to become part of our extended selves. Collections are a special case: a collection signifies a special interest. Because a great deal of time, effort, energy (and sometimes money) are invested in acquiring a collection, that collection (more than isolated objects) is more likely to be seen as a part of the self. Many consumers build collections for a lifetime—stamps, baseball cards, sports paraphernalia, coins, vintage wines, dolls, guns, and the like. Many get so emotionally attached to their collections that, if they were to lose them, they would feel bereaved.

By Bonding Through Use When we invest resources (time, money, and effort) in the use of products, we tend to view those products increasingly as part of our extended selves, more than when we had barely acquired them. Thus, the new computer does not really become "my computer" until it is mastered and customized. The teenager who buys a guitar required for his high school music class never really views it as part of his extended self if he does not develop good skills using it. Success in using a product is, thus, another important source of a product becoming the extended self.

With many products, we develop an emotional bond after acquisition and through use.[33] First, this is due to enjoyment of the product. If the product is a recreational product and we have spent a considerable number of hours enjoying it, then we feel attached to it. In fact, many products we enjoy using become objects of our love and affection. We might love our car, for example, with its worn out leather seat that has acquired a permanent form to fit our body. Second, if the product serves us repeatedly in symbolically expressing our inner selves to others, we begin to see that product as our true friend. All of us have a wardrobe where some clothes are more special than others. We all have one shirt, or dress, or suit that makes us feel extra special every time we wear it. Such garments have become part of our extended selves more so than the rest of our clothes.

Memories Products that are associated with some memories (e.g., gifts from loved ones) become parts of our extended selves. This is because memories are a precious part of our lives, our biographies; the objects connected with those memories are like props in the play of life.

For marketers, this concept has significant implications. If consumers did not define their extended self-concepts through products, then there would be no opportunity to position brands with anything other than utilitarian features. It is because consumers use products as props in defining themselves that marketers are able to create a persona for products. The challenge is to find out what type of product persona appeals to which segment of consumers. Marketers can research this by depicting a particular product in an alternative creative ad (i.e., with alternative images), and having consumers make ratings based upon opinion statements, such as: "I see myself in this," or "This is just not me" or "this is just soooo me!" or "I would be proud to own this," or "I will feel great using this."

Consumer Lifestyles
And
Psychographics

The Art of Writing
Consumer Biographies

- Lifestyles—Bohemians, Soccer Moms, and Other Consumer Types
- Psychographics—Your Lifestyle by Numbers
- VALS ™—A Lifestyle Portrait of American Consumers
- You Got Psychographics, Now What?
- Materialism Vs. Voluntary Simplicity—The Yin and Yang of Consumption

Hello, I am Bianca Hutton, the surfer, golfer, fashionista girl from Finland, now "living it up" in the American marketplace.

I am an upbeat, positive girl who likes to smile. I never really get angry or annoyed but feel that people sometimes act in a very disappointing way. I like attention but do not put myself in the spotlight. I aspire to be something great, but I cannot plan my life to the last detail. I live by the motto that everything happens for a reason. I also believe that people need to educate themselves constantly and I try to look for cues in books, in TV series and from work and school experiences. I am compassionate and, in addition to my hobbies (golf, tennis, piano, horse riding, choir, skiing), I volunteer my time for many different causes.

Bianca Hutton, a not-so-ordinary consumer, still discovering her identity

Back home I am strictly the pearls-and-Polo girl. Here in the U.S., on any given day you can find me in as many as four different outfits: casual, student look for the classroom; athletic sweats for the gym; a golfer ensemble in the afternoon; sorority girlwear in the evening; and a preppy business suit look somewhere in between. My wardrobe betrays my inner dilemma—I have not yet determined exactly who I am inside.

My surfer girl outfit unlocks my passion for a carefree lifestyle, and the Bohemian side of me comes through more in conversation. My grown-up look makes me feel determined and motivated, ready to succeed in life and tackle any problem with a level-headed, intelligent approach. I have come to the conclusion that although I can put up a front of being mature and well-rounded, my desire to wear ripped jeans and a t-shirt with a surf brand logo on it means that I am still a child at heart and that I am still discovering who I am and who I want to be.

INTRODUCTION

Bianca, the star of our story above, is in some ways a typical, recently graduated 20-something woman. And yet, in some ways she is unique as well. Like many Americans and Europeans, she juggles school, work, sports, and family and friends. But she juggles as well between her many identities. Her brief autobiography is a window into her personality and her sense of self. It is also a window into her consumption habits (although her present write up is limited to consumption of clothing). Marketers wish they could get every consumer to write such autobiographies. So they do the next best thing—they write them for their consumers. And call them "*psychographics.*"

This chapter deals with consumer psychographics and their role in helping marketers understand the consumer. There are four components of psychographics—values, personality, self-concepts, and lifestyles. Values, personality, and self-concepts (which we covered in the previous chapter) are partly interdependent, and the three in turn influence lifestyles—how consumers choose to live. Psychographics are ways to graph (i.e., measure) consumers' values, personalities, self-concepts, and lifestyles. Let us look closely.

PSYCHOGRAPHICS

Psychographics are characteristics of individuals that describe them in terms of their psychological and behavioral makeup. The word itself means graphing (or measuring) a person in terms of his or her psychological make up. That is, psychographics describe a person in terms of his or her *mental* makeup and the *behaviors* it produces. It comprises the sort of things people do in everyday life and what they think about those things and about matters that fill their world. Some consumers are into hunting and barbecuing; others like fishing and bowling; and still others go to theaters and museums frequently. These behaviors are accompanied by thoughts and feelings—their ideas about what is right or wrong; how they view their present, and what they expect of their future. Consumers also harbor inner desires and motivations about what else they can do with their lives and with their time and money. They hold views about themselves, about who they are and what they want to become. And they construct their everyday living around these self-perceptions, desires, and goals. All these clusters of thoughts and actions make up psychographics.

An important facet of psychographics is lifestyle. So closely related are the two concepts, in fact, that often the two terms are used interchangeably. But there is a significant difference. Curious about it? Let us first understand what "lifestyle" means.

LIFESTYLE

Values, personality, and *self-concept* are abstract ideas. It is in our lifestyles that they materialize and take concrete shape. They form both its engine and its navigator, driving and guiding its flow. **Lifestyle** is simply the way we live—our pattern of living. That pattern of living comprises the activities we undertake, the way we spend our money, and the way we use our time. Consider these two portraits:

Thelma Thelma stays at home, taking care of her two children. She spends her days productively, immersed in running a household. She enjoys cooking and baking, especially baking cakes. She sews her own clothes and dresses modestly. She wears very little makeup. And she spends most of her time at home even on the weekends, entertaining relatives and friends at home.

Candice Candice is a working mom. She likes to go out rather than stay at home and dislikes household chores. She attends parties where there are a lot of people and a lot of music and dancing. She also frequents art galleries, theaters, and museums. And she likes to dress in high fashion and loves to shop in boutiques.[1]

Thelma and Candice live their everyday lives differently. They have different lifestyles, that is.

How do consumers live their lifestyles? How else, but by doing activities that inevitably entail the use of products and services? Thelma obviously eats out less, but she buys more food items from the supermarket than does Candice. Candice, on the other hand, uses baby-sitting services more than Thelma does. Candice also uses drycleaner services more, whereas Thelma buys more laundry detergents. Candice is a frequent visitor to fashion boutiques whereas Thelma sews most of her own and her family's clothing, and buys the rest at a department store. Candice's ideal vacation would be a trip to Europe, whereas Thelma's would be a camping trip with family. When it comes to building a lifestyle, consumers are like artists, producing a piece of art, and they use products to build the beautiful mosaics of their lifestyles. Products are the building blocks of lifestyles. Because commercial products play a major role in consumers' enactment of their lifestyles, lifestyles can explain consumer behavior significantly.

Sean Foley, an eco-conscious professional, happy with his bohemian, artistic persona

Every consumer has a unique lifestyle. Lifestyles differ vividly, for example, between urban and rural consumers. In fact, they differ widely within an urban area itself. To illustrate how lifestyles differ and explain significant consumer behavior, let us view a portrait of two American lifestyle types—both urban, identified through research—called *Bohemian Mix* and *Kids & Cul-de-sacs*.[2]

Bohemian Mix The Bohemian Mix are young residents of urban hodge-podge neighborhoods. The majority (3 out of every 4) are never married or are divorced singles, and they are predominantly students, artists, writers, actors, and the like. They live somewhat adventuresome, funky lives, exercising both their bodies and minds, hanging out at sidewalk cafes, public libraries, bookstores, and health food stores. They participate heavily in discussion groups, social and voluntary organizations, benefit programs, public demonstrations, and protest campaigns on social issues.

Kids & Cul-de-sacs This group defines the typical suburban American family. With young children at home, they are predominantly white or Asian, upper-middle-class professionals, soccer moms, and barbecue dads. A principal weekend activity is a trip to the supermarket for grocery shopping, especially to a warehouse store like Price Club. Their leisure activities are centered around their children: school games, class projects, video rentals, visits to the zoo or local theme park, and fast food or pizzeria restaurants. Their favorite vacation spot is Disneyland.

A Kids and Cul-De-Sac consumer group

Notice how dramatically different these two lifestyles are. Do these lifestyles require different products? Of course, they do. How else would consumers live their lifestyles differently? Consider the product consumption differences between these two lifestyle groups:

Products Consumed by the Bohemian Mix Bohemians shun domestic cars, and they disproportionately buy foreign cars. Since they live on apartment lined city streets, their cars are compact—a Mini Cooper or a Volkswagen Beetle, or, if they can afford it, a used (or, as they call it in Australia, "pre-loved") BMW. They consume healthy foods, and they shun fast food restaurants like McDonald's or Jack in the Box both because they perceive the food to be unhealthy and because they dislike cookie cutter restaurants. You also won't find them hanging out at bars; instead their hangouts are art galleries, coffee shops, and leftist bookstores.

Products Consumed by the Kids & Cul-de-sacs These consumers own multiple vehicles, at least one of which is usually a minivan or SUV, perfect for carting around kids. Their preferences are spread equally between domestic (e.g., Mercury Villager) and import cars (e.g., Toyota Previa). They read such magazines as Golf Digest and Travel & Leisure. On TV, they watch Wall Street Week and news and talk shows. They are not excessively health-conscious. They often barbecue, and they seek out family-style mainstream restaurants.

LIFESTYLE AND MARKETING

Since consumers buy products to build the mosaic of their lifestyles, wouldn't it make sense that products be marketed by the lifestyles to which they belong? A lot of marketers are doing just that. These marketing applications can be divided into three broad categories: (a) selling product constellations, (b) brand alliances, and (c) positioning by lifestyles.[3]

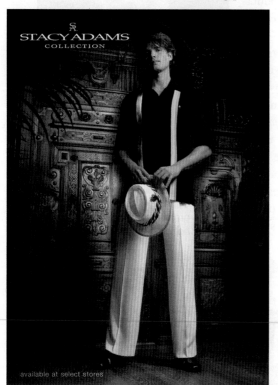

available at select stores

Clothing brands are often positioned by lifestyles. In this ad from Stacy Adams, color, fabric, style, and the model, all come together to depict the mosaic of a fashionable, out-on-the-town lifestyle.

A. Selling Product Constellations Products are, as we said before, the building blocks of lifestyles. However, consumers don't choose their products haphazardly; rather, for each lifestyle, a certain set of products seems to fit together. For example, a surfer's lifestyle requires a surfboard, surfing gear, skin protection products, surfing media content (magazines and videos), a personal music player system, a utility vehicle, and perhaps even picnic-ware. These products form, for the surfer, a **consumption constellation**—defined as a group of products that are consumed together in a typical consumption setting. Rather than having to buy these from different sellers or different areas of a store, it would be nice if the consumer could buy them in a one-stop shopping place. Marketers should therefore sell these products as a constellation to meet a consumer's consumption constellation needs.

Several marketers are doing just that. Only a few years ago, all that the Automobile Association of America (AAA) did at its service outlets was to give you maps and trip guides, and at its travel agency, it booked your tours. (In addition, it dispatched emergency roadside assistance to stranded motorists, of course.) But now, visit an AAA branch office, and you will find merchandise ranging from detailed location guides, luggage, travel accessories, car purchase and repair assistance, and financial services, as well as credit and insurance services. And, should you need it, they will make you a passport picture.

B. Brand Alliances A special case of product constellation is co-branding and brand alliances. You are no doubt familiar with how airlines and hotels award loyalty points that can be redeemed wih vendors of either service. Often other companies run joint promotions that make sense, such as a Broadway Theater ticket plan with an upscale restaurant offering, or a credit card offer from a fraternity with special discounts at stores near college campuses.

If we were to buy tires, our principal concern would be performance—what the tire does for the car and for our driving. But its performance on the road (solid grip, for example) gives us ability, control, and confidence. "Precision control" and "groomed for grip" could very well be metaphors for our living itself. Why, those tires that give our life a style even leave t-r-a-c-k m-a-r-k-s that are fashionable enough to adorn our clothing. Such brand connections are subtle but real, and for reasons of subtleness even more gratifying for us— at least those of us who see having control on the road as part of our self-concept. We are style setters; why shouldn't our tires be?

Style Setter

Miles of style with precision control.

Groomed for grip, wet or dry, with elegant SUV technology.

Make your move on Bridgestone Dueler tires.

GET UP TO A
$100
MAIL-IN REBATE
on a set of four select Bridgestone Dueler tires.*

bridgestonetire.com   1-800-807-9555   tiresafety.com

PASSION for EXCELLENCE

C. Positioning by Lifestyle Often marketers try to "position" their brand by lifestyle. To accomplish this, various elements of the marketing mix can be utilized. Products can be designed to appeal to consumers of specific lifestyles, and distribution outlets can be selected based on the lifestyle of consumers they attract. Moreover, product communication campaigns can depict the purported lifestyle.

Beyond such obvious lifestyle—based brand depictions in advertising, the "positioning by lifestyles" strategy is a much broader (and richer) option. How so? Let us count the ways.

C.1. Lifestyle Specific Media Products

Visit any magazine store, and see how many magazines there are on very specific interests and leisure activities. There are magazines for women (e.g., *Woman's Day, Cosmopolitan, Perth Woman*); for golf fans (e.g., *Golf Digest*), for music lovers (*Spin*), for lovers of the outdoors (*Outdoors, Field & Stream*), for transvestites (U.K. based *Repartee)*, for the techno-literati (*Wired*), and for gadget lovers (*Sync*—this not-for-the-timid magazine was aborted in January 2006). Likewise, Web sites such as iVillage.com, Oxygen.com and DailyCandy.com are devoted to women's interests and feature wide-ranging interest areas (e.g., parenting, romance, cooking, etc.). Although consumers with a mere passing

Clothes for a fashionable lifestyle
Photo courtesy of El Pachuco Zootsuits®/www.elpachuco.com

interest might also occasionally read such magazines or visit such Web sites, for many consumers, their lifestyles revolve around their special interests, and these media products cater to their lifestyle needs. Note that this is product-based lifestyle positioning; that is, the contents of the "products" (i.e., magazines) themselves are tailored to appeal to consumers of specific lifestyles.

C.2. Physical Presence in Consumer Lifestyles

Here, although a product itself may also be fashioned to appeal to specific lifestyle groups, the product's scope is enlarged by placing the product in the contexts of consumers' other lifestyle interests. For example, coffee itself has nothing to do with musical events or listening; however, Nescafe's Australian web site allows you to download selected music freely. And it shows vignettes of "slice of life" situations in which, as part of your lifestyle, the company hopes you will consume Nescafe. The company thus hopes to place its brand in the midst of your life-at-large.

This strategy is also at work when companies sponsor events that appeal to consumers of certain tastes and lifestyles. In 2001, Ford wanted to court Gen Y consumers for its Focus brand. It became the title sponsor of the Area One Music Festival, headlined by alternative music star Moby. The event comprised a tour of 16 cities. At each event, a deconstructed version of the car was specially equipped with a sound system and a DJ stand. Detroit techno star Juan Atkins was one of the other attractions. Earlier, Ford had used a soundtrack by Atkins in its introductory ad campaign. "Techno music is part of the DNA of the brand," says one Ford spokesperson. Of course, that is because that music is also part of the DNA of Gen Y. Ford's goal is "Endless Brand Experience"—integrating the brand into the lifestyles of its young consumers.[4]

C.3. Emotional Positioning by Lifestyle

Another variation on lifestyle positioning is when a product's communication is designed to build an emotional connection between the brand and the consumer's product-related life interests. A good example of this strategy is a campaign launched a few years ago by running shoe maker Saucony. Until 2001, the brand had run mostly product-focused ads. In 2001, it embarked on a lifestyle campaign, which portrayed scenes from a runner's life. For example, one print ad showed a closet with a single pair of dress shoes and one blue suit, with the rest of the closet filled with several running suits and a pile of running shoes. A race number was taped to the door. Tagline: "Saucony Owners: Loyal to the Sport."[5]

C.4. Lifestyle Niche Echoing

In the foregoing two sub-strategies, the product is aimed at the general user of the product category; the marketer just looks for common

YOUR BIG LIFE PROJECT

We all have projects in life. Some are small—like doing the weekly laundry this coming Sunday; others are big—like finally getting that tattoo you have been debating for the past one year. Or, if you are an appearance-anxious boomer, getting that twin-chin united by facial surgery. *Life projects* are significant goals and major events that we strive to bring to fruition. Thus, not all projects in life are *life projects*; only those which will have a major impact on our lives, with which we remain obsessed for considerable time, which currently occupy our minds constantly, whose completion we look forward to, and which entail considerable investment of time, money, and physical energy. Thus, weekend laundry does not qualify, but the twin-chin project certainly does.

Here are some others that would qualify. To graduate; to find a job; to remodel your home; to travel to Asia; to learn how to play guitar; to learn to tango; to learn to speak the French language fluently; to lose 15 pounds of body weight; to read all the books mentioned in this book (e.g., Tom Standage's *A History of World in Six Glasses*); to get an eternal date (sign up on e-harmony.com); to get a spouse; to adopt a child from a third world poor family; to start your own blog; to digitize all your photos.

Each of these projects reflects your lifestyle and entails significant consumption. Each also brings, when completed, immense satisfaction to the person striving toward that goal. These projects have a finite duration: one month, one year, five years. (Their accomplishment might take as little as a week, but, to qualify as a *life project*, the total time of our obsession with them has to be much longer, say, at least a month). Life projects are important to give meaning to life. Without them, life remains dreary and purposeless. Most people have three or four life projects at any stage in their lives.

Now consider this. Over and above these life projects, which have a finite duration and which differ from person to person, there is one overarching and perpetual life project we all have. It begins very early in life and it never ends. It is, and here comes our big proposition, *to build and implement our lifestyles.*

We spend considerable amount of time, money, and energy to choose and constantly flesh out our lifestyles. We go to the marketplace to collect the ingredients that will help us assemble a lifestyle. Then we constantly, day in day out, keep embellishing and adapting it. Every consumer, every one of us, has this BIG LIFE PROJECT. With no exceptions. Yes, even monks have it!

Yes, as marketers we need to know what your current life projects are. Then if we can relate our offerings to your life projects, we will have brought you important and significant value. But even more importantly, we need to study your BIG LIFE PROJECT—your constant endeavor to live your lifestyles. We need to map, in other words, your lifestyles, your psychographics.

ground, from a lifestyle point-of-view (e.g., love of music for the Focus event, love of sport for Saucony shoes). In contrast is a strategy where the entire marketing program (from product design to distribution to advertising) is conceived, from inception, to echo a particular lifestyle niche.

To illustrate this strategy, let us visit the store Hot Topic. If you are looking to meet some teenagers who are into punk or Goth (think Avril Lavigne), there is perhaps no better place, at least as far as a mall goes. The retail store sells clothing to the "definitely not mainstream" youth. A welcome sign here reads: "Come in or you suck." The background music is excruciatingly loud. Of course, it also sells CDs of the same music. On display are such brand names as Morbid Threads and Vamp, and T-shirts display such insulting sentiments as "Wow, you're ugly" and "I know how you feel, I just don't care." Its racks are filled with tons of body jewelry, and it sells licensed gift cards featuring images such as

Moving forward? In a sense, all consumers do—especially when driving a car. But there is a deeper level of "moving forward"—moving ahead in life. Moving forward has been your pursuit, your life project, your sense of who you are. Your car fits into that pursuit—or it should. If it is a car that echoes your moorings, your strivings, then it keeps you moving ahead. O, The Oprah Magazine invites Toyota owners to write a story about how they are "moving forward." With sample inspirational thoughts (" I will become my own role model," reads one) to get you started, the campaign is an invitation to express your self-concept as a "moving forward person." Prizes include life-coaching seminars, which consumers who are engaged in "moving forward" will surely value immensely.

Brands must eventually connect to consumers via their self-concepts and by advancing their strivings. Just the kind of mission that brand Toyota is qualified to pursue. And what better medium of expression than O, the emotive, inspirational, and personally touching magazine for millions of readers.

SpongeBob SquarePants and the rock group Korn. Many of its customers buy the cards not to send to someone, but to keep for themselves![6]

The above examples have amply illustrated a cornucopia of approaches marketers use to appeal to consumer lifestyles. Let us move on.

MEASURING LIFESTYLES

These lifestyle marketing strategies look fascinating, but you can't use them until you know how to measure your target consumers' lifestyles. The question is, how can we measure lifestyles? Intuitively, it is very simple: we can simply observe consumers and see what they are doing all the time. Alternatively, in an open-ended interview, we can just ask consumers a series of questions about what kinds of activities they engage in, how they spend their leisure time, and what their interests are.

From consumer responses to these open-ended questions, and from consumer narratives as they describe themselves, we can prepare a comprehensive psychological profile of the consumer. This would, however, be kind of a qualitative measurement, feasible only for a small group of consumers. In practical marketing, we need to measure and analyze lifestyles for a large number of consumers; therefore, we need a quantifiable measure. Psychographics comes to the rescue.

PSYCHOGRAPHICS

Putting Humpty Dumpty Back Together

Values, personality, self-concept, and lifestyle—these all describe consumers' psychological makeup. Each one looks at it with a different lens, but together they provide a more comprehensive view. This view is woven together by psychographics. *Psychographics* are, as mentioned previously, characteristic profiles of consumers that describe them in terms of their psychological and behavioral makeup. By *makeup*, we mean relatively enduring inventory and arrangement. Thus, psychographics include mental (psychological), permanent entities; e.g., values, self-concepts, even opinions. **Opinions** are our beliefs about things, and they derive from our values. Self-concept is a specific type of opinion— it is our opinion about ourselves. Psychographics also include one's behavioral makeup, that is, relatively enduring behaviors; these are, you would realize, personality traits. And lifestyles are the manifestations of all these mental and behavioral entities in everyday living.

Psychographics accomplish one more thing—they measure these entities *quantitatively*. And we do need a quantitative measure in order to be able to analyze large samples of consumers. For this purpose, consumer researchers have come up with a measure called **AIO inventory**. *AIO* stands for "activities, interests, and opinion," and it comprises a set of statements to which respondents indicate their agreement or disagreement on a numerical scale. A sample of these statements is presented in Table 6.1.

To analyze and interpret data from the measures based on AIO statements, researchers group together people with similar responses. These groups, thought to have relatively similar values, self-concepts, and lifestyles, can then be described in terms of their AIO profiles, called *psychographic profiles*. Conceptually, **psychographics** are, as we already noted, the sum total of values, self-concepts, personalities and lifestyles. The appeal of psychographics in marketing from the outset has been their quantifiability. Like demographics, psychographics are based upon quantitative measurements. These profiles are excellent indicators of how people are thinking and where they are going with their lives, as described below.

VALS™: A PSYCHOGRAPHIC PROFILE OF U.S. CONSUMERS

One of the most used psychographic profiling schemes is called VALS™ (formerly an acronym for Values and Lifestyles). Originally developed by SRI International, VALS is now owned and operated by a spin-off, SRI Consulting Business Intelligence (SRIC-BI). VALS divides consumers into eight groups (see Figure 6.1). This grouping is based on two dimensions: primary motivation and resources.

Primary Motivation According to SRIC-BI, in all behaviors, consumers are driven by three primary motivations: ideals, achievement, and self-expression. Consumers motivated primarily by ideals are driven by their principles and guided by knowledge. Achievement-motivated consumers seek products that reflect and communicate their success. Finally, consumers motivated by self-expression desire to engage in activities that give expression to their inner senses of self, engaging in a variety of social and physical activities.

Resources Resources refer to the full range of psychological, physical, demographic, and material means and capacities people have available to them. Resources encompass education, income, self-confidence, health, physical energy, innovativeness, and leadership. It is a continuum, on the vertical axis, from minimal to abundant. Resources generally increase from adolescence through middle age, but decrease as age advances, as do depression, financial reversal (e.g., layoff), and physical or psychological impairment.

Using the *primary motivation* and *resources* dimensions, the VALS scheme defines eight segments of adult consumers who have different attitudes and exhibit distinct consumption tastes and practices. These segments are *Innovators*, *Thinkers*, *Believers*, *Achievers*, *Strivers*, *Experiencers*, *Makers*, and *Survivors*. A brief profile of these segments is presented in Exhibit 6.1

Want to know what group you belong to? The VALS classification survey enables marketers to identify a consumer's VALS type and is shown in Table 6.2, but to score yourself on it, you must go to the Internet at www.sric-bi.com/VALS/surveynew.shtml.

PSYCHOGRAPHIC SEGMENTATION
Adventures in Dissecting the Consumer

The VALS system is the most well-known but by no means the only system of profiling consumers by their psychographics. For example, U.S. based research company LifeMatrix has identified ten psychographic segments among U.S. consumers, with such names as "tribe wired" and "dynamic duos." See Exhibit 6.2.

Today, in every world region, there is a research enterprise, commercial or non-

TABLE 6.1

AIO STATEMENTS

Sample activities, interests, and opinions defining lifestyle categories

CHILD ORIENTED

When my children are ill in bed I drop almost everything else in order to see to their comfort.
My children are the most important things in my life.
I try to arrange my home for my children's convenience.
I take a lot of time and effort to teach my children good habits.

COMPULSIVE HOUSEKEEPER

I don't like to see children's toys lying about.
I usually keep my house very neat and clean.
I am uncomfortable when my house is not completely clean.
Our days seem to follow a definite routine such as eating meals at a regular time, etc.

SELF-CONFIDENT

I think I have more self-confidence than most people.
I am more independent than most people.
I think I have a lot of personal ability.
I like to be considered a leader.

INFORMATION SEEKER

I often seek out the advice of my friends regarding which brand to buy.
I spend a lot of time talking with my friends about products and brands.

FINANCIAL OPTIMIST

I will probably have more money to spend next year than I have now.
Five years from now the family income will probably be a lot higher than it is now.

PRICE CONSCIOUS

I shop a lot for specials.
I find myself checking the prices in the grocery store even for small items.
I usually watch the advertisements for announcements of sales.
A person can save a lot of money by shopping around for bargains.

FASHION CONSCIOUS

I usually have one or more outfits that are of the very latest style.
When I must choose between the two, I usually dress for fashion, not for comfort.
An important part of my life and activities is dressing smartly.
I often try the latest hairstyles when they change.

HOMEBODY

I would rather spend a quiet evening at home than go out to a party.
I like parties where there is lots of music and talk. (Reverse scored)
I would rather go to a sporting event than a dance.
I am a homebody.

COMMUNITY MINDED

I am an active member of more than one service organization.
I do volunteer work for a hospital or service organization on a fairly regular basis.
I like to work on community projects.
I have personally worked in a political campaign or for a candidate or an issue.

Source: Adapted from William D. Wells and Douglas J. Tigert, "Activities, Interests, & Opinions," *Journal of Advertising Research* 11 (August 1971), p. 35. "© Copyright The Advertising Research Foundation. (Reprinted with permission.)

commercial, that has measured that region's (or for a country in that region) consumer psychographics.

SRIC-BI itself runs a similar research program in Japan. The company also has a U.K. VALS and a VALS Global Framework. Likewise, to understand European consumers as a unit, the ad agency Backer Spielvogel Bates Worldwide runs Global Scan, a program to survey consumers in 17 countries. It measures 250 attitudes (130 specific to one country, and 120 cross-culturally pertinent), and, based on the results, it has identified five global psychographic types: Strivers, Achievers, Pressureds, Adapters, and Traditionals. In a similar vein, the advertising agency DMB&B recently did a 15-country survey and found four European consumers groups: Successful Idealists, Affluent Materialists, Comfortable Belongers, and Disaffected Survivors.[7]

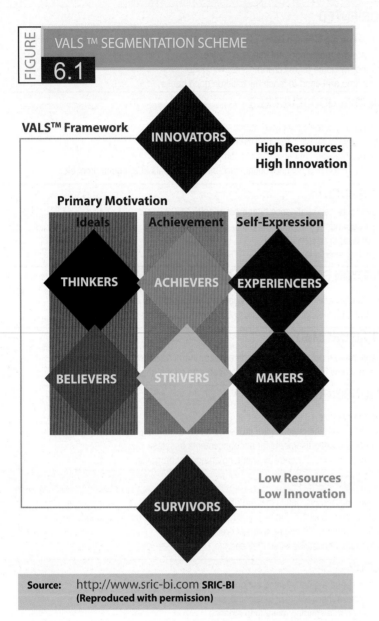

For an illustration and to broaden your perspectives beyond your borders, in Exhibit 6.3 we present the VALS groups for Japan, also prepared by SRIC-BI. Do take the time to study the Japan VALS scheme, for it offers an intriguing insight into the mindset of the Japanese consumer.

Notice anything different between the Japanese and the American VALS™ systems? Or between the Global Scan and the European system mentioned above? The names of many groups are different, as are their descriptions. At first, you might think this is so because these are from different countries, and you would be right, but only partially. In fact, the names (and descriptions) differ even among the psychographic profiles prepared by different research companies within the same country.

Why are these psychographic names of consumers different? The answer is multi-fold. First, note that these segment names are creative labels given by researchers. That is, they are nicknames their creators came up with to capture each segment's characteristics, and as nicknames they are inevitably subjective. Despite differing nicknames, however, some consumer segments are broadly the same type of consumers—they have to be, for, after all, humans are humans, no matter who researches and nicknames them. Just as surely, many lifestyle segments are different, unique to a country and culture—they have to be, for after all cultures across some countries differ greatly, and cultures necessarily and strongly influence, bound, and define lifestyles of their people.

Another reason is that the questions asked in various surveys are not always the same; different researchers ask different questions that try to measure different aspects of consumers' personalities and lifestyles. Some measure only leisure activities, others measure people's beliefs and all activities or lifestyles, and still others measure lifestyles *and* values *and* self-concepts. Thus, different psychographic studies differ because they are different slices of

Look What CB Researchers Found

- **Thinkers (Formerly Fulfilled):** are motivated by ideals. They are mature, satisfied, comfortable , and reflective people who value order, knowledge, and responsibility. They tend to be well educated and actively seek out information in the decision-making process. They are well-informed about world and national events and are alert to opportunities to broaden their knowledge.

  Thinkers have a moderate respect for the status quo institutions of authority and social decorum, but are open to consider new ideas. Although their incomes allow them many choices, Thinkers are conservative, practical consumers; they look for durability, functionality, and value in the products they buy.

- **Achievers:** Motivated by the desire for achievement, they have goal-oriented lifestyles and a deep commitment to career and family. Their social lives reflect this focus and are structured around family, their place of worship, and work. Achievers live conventional lives, are politically conservative, and respect authority and the status quo. They value consensus, predictability, and stability over risk, intimacy, and self-discovery.

  With many wants and needs, Achievers are active in the consumer marketplace. Image is important to Achievers; they favor established, prestige products and services that demonstrate success to their peers. Because of their busy lives, they are often interested in a variety of time-saving devices.

- **Experiencers:** are motivated by self-expression. As young, enthusiastic, and impulsive consumers, Experiencers quickly become enthusiastic about new possibilities but are equally quick to cool. They seek variety and excitement, savoring the new, the offbeat, and the risky. Their energy finds an outlet in exercise, sports, outdoor recreation, and social activities.

  Experiencers are avid consumers and spend a comparatively high proportion of their income on fashion, entertainment, and socializing. Their purchases reflect the emphasis they place on looking good and having "cool" stuff.

- **Believers:** Like Thinkers, are motivated by ideals. They are conservative, conventional people with concrete beliefs based on traditional, established codes: family, religion, community, and the nation. Many Believers express moral codes that are deeply rooted and literally interpreted. They follow established routines, organized in large part around home, family, community, and social or religious organizations to which they belong.

  As consumers, Believers are predictable; they choose familiar products and established brands. They favor American products and are generally loyal customers.

- **Strivers:** are trendy and fun loving. Because they are motivated by achievement, Strivers are concerned about the opinions and approval of others. Money defines success for Strivers, who don't have enough of it to meet their desires. They favor stylish products that emulate the purchases of people with greater material wealth. Many see themselves as having a job rather than a career, and a lack of skills and focus often prevents them from moving ahead.

  Strivers are active consumers because shopping is both a social activity and an opportunity to demonstrate to peers their ability to buy. As consumers, they are as impulsive as their financial circumstance will allow.

- **Makers:** Like Experiencers, Makers are motivated by self-expression. They express themselves and experience the world by working on it-building a house, raising children, fixing a car, or canning vegetables-and have enough skill and energy to carry out their projects successfully. Makers are practical people who have constructive skills and value self-sufficiency. They live within a traditional context of family, practical work, and physical recreation and have little interest in what lies outside that context.

  Makers are suspicious of new ideas and large institutions such as big business. They are respectful of government authority and organized labor, but resentful of government intrusion on individual rights. They are unimpressed by material possessions other than those with a practical or functional purpose. Because they prefer value to luxury, they buy basic products.

- **Innovators (Formerly Actualizers):** are successful, sophisticated, take-charge people with high self-esteem. Because they have such abundant resources, they exhibit all three primary motivations in varying degrees. They are change leaders and are the most receptive to new ideas and technologies. Innovators are very active consumers, and their purchases reflect cultivated tastes for upscale, niche products and services.

  Image is important to Innovators, not as evidence of status or power but as an expression of their taste, independence, and personality. Innovators are among the established and emerging leaders in business and government, yet they continue to seek challenges. Their lives are characterized by variety. Their possessions and recreation reflect a cultivated taste for the finer things in life

- **Survivors (Formerly Strugglers):** live narrowly focused lives. With few resources with which to cope, they often believe that the world is changing too quickly. They are comfortable with the familiar and are primarily concerned with safety and security. Because they must focus on meeting needs rather than fulfilling desires, Survivors do not show a strong primary motivation.

  Survivors are cautious consumers. They represent a very modest market for most products and services. They are loyal to favorite brands, especially if they can purchase them at a discount.

Source: http://www.sric-bi.com **SRIC-BI (Reproduced with permission)**

the same (or similar) pie. But they are all real as views from different angles of a prism.

Psychographics Meets the Real World

Psychographics are a very useful marketing tool today. Before we visit their use in the real world, a brief history is in order. Marketers have always recognized that not all

TABLE
6.2

VALS™ CLASSIFICATION QUESTIONNAIRE

VALS™ Survey

Mostly disagree	Somewhat disagree	Somewhat agree	Mostly agree
○	○	○	○

1. I am often interested in theories.
2. I like outrageous people and things.
3. I like a lot of variety in my life.
4. I love to make things I can use everyday.
5. I follow the latest trends and fashions.
6. Just as the Bible says, the world literally was created in six days.
7. I like being in charge of a group.
8. I like to learn about art, culture, and history.
9. I often crave excitement.
10. I am really interested only in a few things.
11. I would rather make something than buy it.
12. I dress more fashionably than most people.
13. The federal government should encourage prayers in public schools.
14. I have more ability than most people.
15. I consider myself an intellectual.
16. I must admit that I like to show off.
17. I like trying new things.
18. I am very interested in how mechanical things, such as engines, work.
19. I like to dress in the latest fashions.
20. There is too much sex on television today.
21. I like to lead others.
22. I would like to spend a year or more in a foreign country.
23. I like a lot of excitement in my life.
24. I must admit that my interests are somewhat narrow and limited.
25. I like making things of wood, metal, or other such material.
26. I want to be considered fashionable.
27. A woman's life is fulfilled only if she can provide a happy home for her family.
28. I like the challenge of doing something I have never done before.
29. I like to learn about things even if they may never be of any use to me.
30. I like to make things with my hands.
31. I am always looking for a thrill.
32. I like doing things that are new and different.
33. I like to look through hardware or automotive stores.
34. I would like to understand more about how the universe works.
35. I like my life to be pretty much the same from week to week.

Sources: SRIC-BI. (Reproduced with permission.)

consumers are the same. Very early on, they recognized consumer differences in terms of demographics. Accordingly, consumers were differentiated by age, sex, income, family size, etc. Soon marketers realized that demographics told them "who" bought their product, but not "why" they bought it.

To bridge this gap, Motivational Research (MR) was invented. MR is, as we learned in Chapter 2, the practice of identifying some deep-seated consumer motives behind a purchase (or, alternatively, resistance to a purchase). This line of psychoanalytic research gave marketers some comfort, as researchers trained in the Freudian psychology of the unconscious mind solved the mysteries of consumer whims and/or deep, unexplainable consumer resistance to buying specific products (recall that a leading practitioner of this method was Ernst Dichter).

Marketers' love affair with MR was short-lived, however, as MR findings sometimes stretched credulity. More sophisticated analyses applied to demographics could now yield multidimensional profiles. Yet demographics are demographics, and even a multidimensional profile, such as a consumer being "35 years old, married, with 2.5 children, and 1.2 dogs" could not satisfy marketers' thirst for real explanations for consumer behavior. To the rescue came the idea of applying the same quantitative analytical techniques to the measurement of consumer motives. From motives to other aspects of consumers' psychological makeup was then a short leap, and the craft of psychographics, as we know it today, was born.

Today, most psychographic research inventories routinely include demographics as well. That is why many psychographic segment names and descriptions incorporate and are

Lifematrix Lifestyle Segments   EXHIBIT 6.2

1. Tribe Wired: Digital, free-spirited, creative young singles
2. Fun/Atics: Aspirational, fun-seeking, active young people
3. Dynamic Duos: Hard-driving, high-involvement couples
4. Priority Parents: Family values, activities, media strongly dominate
5. Home Soldiers: Home-centric, family-oriented, materially ambitious
6. Renaissance Women: Active, caring, affluent, influential moms
7. Rugged Traditionalists: Traditional male values, love of outdoors
8. Struggling Singles: High aspirations, low economic status
9. Settled Elders: Devout, older, sedentary lifestyles
10. Free Birds: Vital, active altruistic seniors

EXHIBIT 6.2

Japan-VALS™: Change Regions and Life Orientations

Japan-VALS™ was designed to explain and model social change in Japan—not only change in institutions or ideas, but change in consumer markets and media as well.

Japan-VALS divides society into segments on the basis of two key consumer attributes: life orientation and attitudes to social change. **Life orientation** is simply what interests or animates a person the most—life, occupational duties, recreational interests. Japan-VALS identifies four primary life orientations: Traditional Ways, Occupations, Innovation, and Self-Expression. Each orientation provides a life theme around which activities, interests, and personal goals are woven.

Crosscutting the variety of life orientations, **change attitudes** stratify society into distinct layers, like overturned bowls nested one inside another. The change-leading segments are in the outermost layers of society; the change-resisting segments are at the center. Change diffuses from one layer to the next, primarily along the channels around different life orientations.

FIGURE 6.2 — JAPAN VALS SEGMENTATION SCHEME

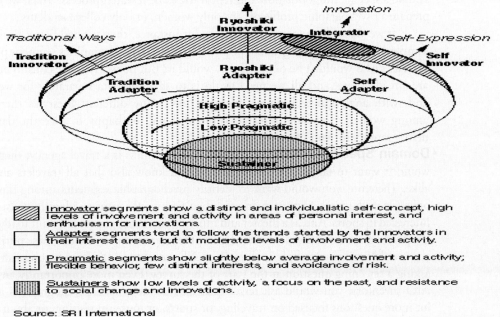

Japan VALS Segmentation System

Innovator segments show a distinct and individualistic self-concept, high levels of involvement and activity in areas of personal interest, and enthusiasm for innovations.

Adapter segments tend to follow the trends started by the Innovators in their interest areas, but at moderate levels of involvement and activity.

Pragmatic segments show slightly below average involvement and activity; flexible behavior, few distinct interests, and avoidance of risk.

Sustainers show low levels of activity, a focus on the past, and resistance to social change and innovations.

Source: SRI International

This design permits Japan-VALS to clarify the processes of social change and innovation diffusion in Japanese society. It also identifies the consumer segments at the core of most consumer markets:

- **Integrators** (4% of population) are highest on the Japan-VALS measure of Innovation. These consumers are active, inquisitive, trend-leading, informed, and affluent. They travel frequently and consume a wide range of media-print and broadcast, niche, and foreign

- **Self Innovators** and **Self Adapters** (7% and 11% of population) score high on Self-Expression. These consumers desire personal experience, fashionable display, social activities, daring ideas, and exciting, graphic entertainment.

- **Ryoshiki Innovators** and **Ryoshiki Adapters** (6% and 10% of population) score highest on Occupations. Education, career achievement, and professional knowledge are their personal focus, but home, family, and social status are their guiding concerns.

- **Tradition Innovators** and **Tradition Adapters** (6% and 10% of population) score highest on the measure of Traditional Ways. These consumers adhere to traditional religions and customs, prefer long-familiar home furnishings and dress, and hold conservative social opinions.

- **High Pragmatics** and **Low Pragmatics** (14% and 17% of population) do not score high on any life-orientation dimension. They are not very active and not well informed; they have few interests and seem flexible or even uncommitted in their lifestyle choices.

- **Sustainers** (15% of population) score lowest on the Innovation and Self-Expression dimensions. Lacking money, youth, and high education, these consumers dislike innovation and are typically oriented to sustaining the past.

Source: SRIC-BI (used with permission.)

informed by demographics as well (e.g., "Renaissance women," or "Accepting Mid-lifers").

Multiple Applications

With this background, we are now ready to put some order into the vast array of lifestyle research options available to marketers eager to use them. (Remember, *lifestyles* is a term marketers use interchangeably with the term *psychographics*.)

- **General Population Lifestyles** A psychographic research project can take a random sample of an entire population (say, of a nation) and identify lifestyle segments of consumers. Many market research companies have already done this for individual countries. Marketing companies can simply buy these standard databases; remember though, that there is much more information within these databases than reported here. For example, most of these research surveys also include questions on consumer use of a wide range of products, and, based on product use indexes, you can choose which psychographic segment to target for your product.

- **Subpopulation Lifestyles** Instead of the general population, we could, of course, sample a specific subpopulation and repeat the same research process. Thus, we could prepare a psychographic profile of, say, only women, or only college students.

    If we are selling women's cosmetics, for instance, then we had better limit our sample to women only. A general, population-based, psychographics segment profile such as VALS wouldn't be of much use, would it? But no worries; the consumer data are already there, and all we need to do is to slice the data separately for women and, with analytical techniques, identify how many different lifestyles there are among women. The same research companies will be happy to slice the data by demographics for you (for a fee, of course).

- **Domain Specific Lifestyles** Suppose your business is a travel agency; then you wouldn't want to target non-travelers. And you know also that all travelers are not alike. Therefore, you would want to identify psychographic segments among travelers only. Or if you were a sports marketer, then you would want to identify consumers interested in sports. And as a theater and museum marketer, you would want to identify the psychographics of those interested in the theater and museums. For these purposes, you would limit your sample to domain specific consumers. You can accomplish it by asking a screening question at the start of the survey. Even more importantly, in your AIO inventory, you would ask fewer questions about general psychographics and a lot more questions focused on traveling, or sports, or museum visiting, or about your domain of interest. From one such research effort came a leisure traveler profile, shown for illustration (see Exhibit 6.4 "Psychographics of Travelers.")

- **Product-Specific Psychographics** A variation of domain specific psychographic study is a survey of the entire population of interest, but with the questions focused on a specific product category. In the previous design (i.e., *domain specific lifestyles*) the domain was a lifestyle activity (e.g., travel or hiking or yoga) of special interest in which not everyone engages. Presently, the focus is on a product category (e.g., cosmetics, organic foods, etc.). The purpose here is to explore how different psychographic groups found in the overall population of interest view their use of the product category. In one such current application, the VALS questionnaire is integrated into a major consumer survey that asks questions about women's cosmetics, for example. The VALS battery can be integrated into any questionnaire designed to investigate a specific product category or service categories from travel to banking to food.

- **Customers' Psychographics** Having been immersed in psychographics for so long in this chapter, you cannot but wonder about the psychographics of your own customers, i.e., the target consumers for the specific products or services or brands you are marketing. You have been in business for many years now, and you have millions of consumers already buying from you. But the lure from competitors is always there, more so these days than in the past. And you don't really know much about your own

Hunkus Maximus: powerfully built species with abundant fur. Only becomes active after sunset, and usually hunts small game in the wetlands around the city center. Does not waste energy on constructing a shelter, as he rarely sleeps in the same place on successive nights. Snarls if he has to stand at the rear of lines, and often ends up fighting rival males. Able to open bottles with teeth.

Mammaus Boyus: quiet, easy-to-care-for species found throughout Oslo. Does not typically travel in herds. Is closely attached to the parents all life long, and rarely leaves the nest until he finds a mate who resembles his mother. Does not provide his own nourishment, but can consume twice his own weight in pizza. Tends to favor watering holes in the campus area, but encounters females in heat only on extremely rare occasions.

Coupleus Permanentus: widespread species which mates for life. The male often sheds his hair and becomes restless around the age of 50. Some abandon the nest to find younger females, but typically return soon thereafter with tail between their legs. The species thrives in outlying suburban areas and surrounding woods. Mushrooms and berries constitute a significant part of the fall diet, but the species will also gather meats and liquid nourishment as far east as the discount outlets in Sweden. Can be observed with a snifter on Saturday nights.

Oldus Snobbus: sociable and convivial species which is primarily active during the day. Prefers level ground, and grazes in the West End and tea-rooms. Sheds the teeth every night, and, like the cow, has four stomachs. One for smoked salmon, one for port wine and two for custard cakes. The species is also common along the coast of Spain where it winters in large colonies.

Blondus Flirtus: long-legged species with protruding chest. Nests in yuppie-rich areas. Attracts males by pushing the chest area forwards and the tail section backwards, while at the same time rapidly blinking the eyes. Is attracted to males with abundant feathers and large nests. Like the magpie, this species is fascinated by shiny objects. Frequently migrates south during the winter, but also thrives in mountainous areas with hotels. Considers itself a delicacy.

A Home For Your Psychographics

Obos, a home-builder in Norway, targets different lifestyles. Although ostensibly the ads are targted simply at different age groups, the real allure of the ads comes from their tongue-in-cheek psychographic profiles typical of those specific age groups..

Copy in the ads in part reads (from top left, clockwise)

Hunkus Maximus. Powerfully built species with abundant fur. Only becomes active after sunset, and usually hunts small game in the wetlands around the city center. Does not waste energy on constructing a shelter, as he rarely sleeps in the same place on successive nights. Snarls if he has to stand at the rear of lines, and often ends up fighting rival males. Able to open bottles with teeth.

Mammaus Boyus. Quiet, easy-to-care-for species found throughout Oslo. Does not typically travel in herds. Is closely attached to the parents all life long, and rarely leaves the nest until he finds a mate who resembles his mother. Does not provide his own nourishment, but can consume twice his own weight in pizza. Tends to favor watering homes in the campus area.

Coupleus Permanentus. Widespread species which mates for life. The male often sheds his hair and becomes restless around the age of 50. Some abandon the nest to find younger females, but typically return soon thereafter with tail between their legs. The species thrives in outlying suburban areas and surrounding woods. Mushrooms and berries constitute a significant part of the fall diet, but the species will also gather meats and liquid nourishment as far east as the discount outlets in Sweden. Can be observed with a snifter on Saturday nights.

Oldus Snobbus. Sociable and convivial species which is primarily active during the day. Prefers level ground, and gazes in the West End and tea-rooms. Sheds the teeth every night, and, like the cow, has four stomachs. One for smoked salmon, one for port wine and two for custard cakes. The species is also common along the coast of Spain where it winters in large colonies.

Blondus Flirtus. Long-legged species with protruding chest. Nests in yuppie-rich areas. Attracts males by pushing the chest area forwards and the tail section backwards, while at the same time rapidly blinking the eyes. Is attracted to males with abundant feathers and large nests. Like the magpie, this species is fascinated by shiny objects.

consumers.

It would be nice if you knew about the psychographics of your present consumers, you chuckle. Well, actually, you can. Just give your current consumers a psychographic survey. Of course, you will have to build your AIO inventory carefully so that it covers, for the most part, only those psychographics that you would intuitively consider relevant to your product domain.

You Got Psychographics, Now What?

Alright, you have completed your research and have collected the psychographic profiles of various consumer groups—for the entire population in a country, for an age or gender group, for a specific domain area, or for your current consumers—whichever seemed relevant to you. Now what? How do you harness this information in your marketing strategy? Here are your options (and opportunities):

1. Choose your target market(s).
2. Create different programs for different segments.

Two marketing professors of Spain (Professors Gonzalez and Bello) recently did a survey of residents of one autonomous community (population size exceeding 100,000) in Spain, obtaining 400 surveys from consumers chosen at random. (Given the limited sampling, the study is illustrative rather than generalizable) The study had more than 100 AIO questions. (see Sample)

The study identified five segments of consumers from the standpoint of their travel habits.

1. Home Loving This group of consumers enjoys quiet and private life, and values family and raising children. Conservative and religious in outlook, they are cautious and take action to protect their future. They visit exhibitions, monuments, and places of natural beauty, and they enjoy wide-ranging reading. In buying products, they prefer name brands, and, as part of their responsibility toward family members, they value quality over price.

Travel Behavior: *Short Trips* Smallest number of short trips. Confined to nearby urban and inland destinations; prefer trips to large cities, where they stay at mid to modest price hotels.

Long trips The segment makes the largest number of long trips (4 days or more), usually domestic, and usually in coastal towns, usually staying with friends and families.

2. Idealistic This group believes in and measures personal success by efforts to create a better world; and it fights against injustice. They like to take up jobs that interest them and then in these jobs they exhibit a strong work ethic, viewing their jobs as contribution toward a better society. They enjoy sports, classical music, concerts, theater, dancing, etc.

They value product quality over price. In addition, they are flexible, and innovative in product adoption.

Their short trips are usually to friends and families, as they like not to spend money on hotels etc. For long trips they like country villages, staying with friend or families or their own vacation homes (owned or rented). The typical journey is with family, lasting over a week.

3. Autonomous Consumers in this group see success mainly as individual freedom and independence. They enjoy life and consider enjoying it a principal goal. Work to them is merely a means to earn a living and aspire to upward social mobility. They are somewhat liberal, politically speaking, and believe that society has not evolved fast enough. They frequent cinemas and nightlife spots, enjoy rock, pop, and disco music.

Largest number of short trips; to city destinations; normally with friends.

For long trips, they spend time in coastal areas; Stay in low-priced accommodations (not with friends)

> **A Sample of AIO Questions Used in the Survey:**
> - Working away from home fulfills me.
> - Society has developed too quickly and has lost all the good aspects of traditions.
> - Working alone is best for me.
> - Prefer to spend the evening at home rather than go out.
> - When people give me gifts, I like them to be something useful.
> - In products, quality is more important than price.
> - To me success means: (Options: having a free, peaceful private life; fighting against injustice; having a lot of fun; rising in society through my job; etc.)
> - Hobbies (Options: Handicrafts; going to cinema; museums and exhibitions; concerts, dances, theater; visiting places of natural beauty; etc.)

4. Hedonists This group sees success in terms of relationships as well as work. Consumers in this group believe they are already fulfilled in relationships and they seek work that is fulfilling rather than managerial. They take life as it comes and enjoy it. They seek products as soon as they are introduced and they score the highest on ecological concerns. On short trips they travel mostly with friends, choose large cities coastal or inland, and patronize high-class hotels.

On long trips, this is the group that selects foreign destinations. Their trips last as long as two to three weeks and they seek medium to high category hotels, apartments and service flats.

5. Conservative This is a home-loving segment, with attention focused on family, on coping with day-to-day problems, and with expectations often not fulfilled. They work to earn a living (rather than as fulfillment) and they aspire to, but seldom achieve, high-level positions purely for utilitarian gains; they are the most materialistic. They are conservative, believe in stricter enforcement of law, are religious and are generally pessimistic about modern society.

They enjoy visits to places of outstanding beauty; they dislike nightlife, modern music, and cinema.

For short trips, which are few, they often travel with friends and families, travel within the region, and stay with friends and family. For long trips, they are attracted to traditional domestic seaside destinations; usually travel with friends and family and also stay with friends or family or in apartments they own or rent.

Note. As is true of all psychographic research, segment names here are arbitrary. Thus, arguably, the segment called Hedonists is not as much hedonistic as the name implies and is most probably outdone on hedonism by Segment #3. More accurate, but no less arbitrary, names for the five segments might be: 1. Family Values and Eclectic Readers, 2. Idealistic and Cultural Leisure, 3. Individualists and Hedonistic, 4. Relationships, Ecology, and Fulfillment Seekers, and 5. Conservative, Home Loving, Unfulfilled, Traditionals. Regardless, it is the detailed psychographic verbal profile (rather than segment names) that is of principal value here.

Source: Ana M. Gonzalez and Laurentino Bello "The Construct 'Lifestyle' in Market Segmentation," The Behavior of Tourist Consumers," *European Journal of Marketing*, Vol. 36, No. ½, 2002, 51-85. (Used with permission.)

3. Court a segment of current consumers.
4. Appeal to lifestyles.

Whether it be a segment of your current customers/consumers or a segment of new consumers, you could use programs that would appeal to consumers' psychographics (rather than use product benefit appeals). This can take the form of advertising themes that are based on psychographics, or it could be an entirely new business concept that resonates with consumers of particular psychographics. We have seen examples of both, in the lifestyle section (and by now we know that lifestyles are psychographics). The ad for Saucony Shoes appeals to conumser psychographics directly. That is, the message verbalizes and depicts a psychographic type. The Hot Topic store, in contrast, is a whole new business concept. To reinforce our understanding of this latter strategy, where the whole business concept is created around a particular psychographic, we take you to a consumer group diametrically opposite to the funky, gothic teenager of Hot Topic: the mature, aesthetic experience seeking consumer of home furnishings and clothing. And the store that captured the heart and mind of this consumer: Anthropologie. Read about it elsewhere in this chapter.

MATERIALISM VERSUS VOLUNTARY SIMPLICITY

The Yin and Yang of Consumption

In this section, we cover an overarching psychographic that captures our consumption style in its entirety (i.e., it covers everything we do as consumers). It is called *materialism*, and its exact opposite is *voluntary simplicity*. Note that these can be viewed as personality traits, and, if and when the corresponding behavior (the behavior engendered by them) engulfs a significant portion of our daily living, as these specific traits usually do, they can also be identified as lifestyles. That is why we discuss them here, at the end of the chapter rather than in specific sections before. Because of their life-engulfing nature and scope, we believe that they warrant inclusion in any chapter on consumer psychographics, and, in fact, in any book on consumer behavior. Of immense gratification to millions of consumers, the former (i.e., materialism) can become a never-fulfilled pursuit for some; the latter, (i.e., voluntary simplicity) an exact antidote, can bring Nirvana to the same consumers. Read on.

MATERIALISM

Materialism is an overarching marker of consumer lifestyle. No matter which VALS group a person belongs to, and no matter what cluster of activities, opinions, and interests define a person, all individuals in their role as consumers can be scored on a single Psychographic factor—*materialism*.

Do you want to own a lot of things, indulge in luxuries, live a very rich and comfortable life, and have a lot of money? Do you consider your possessions an important aspect of your self-identify? If so, then you are what social scientists and consumer researchers call "*materialistic*." The Oxford English Dictionary defines **materialism** as "a devotion to material needs and desires, to the neglect of spiritual matters; a way of life, opinion, or tendency based entirely upon material interests." Consumer researcher Russ Belk defines **materialism** as "the importance a consumer attaches to material possessions."[8]

Based on a review of literature in psychology, sociology, economics, and philosophy, consumer researchers Marsha Richins and Scott Dawson have identified three dimensions of materialism as follows:

1. **Acquisition centrality**—The tendency to place material possessions and their acquisition at the center of one's life.
2. **Acquisition as the pursuit of happiness**—All consumers pursue happiness. However, some pursue it through other things, such as personal skill-based accomplishments or doing good to others, etc. In contrast, materialists pursue

Notice how Samsung ensconces itself in its target consumers' lifestyles.
Courtesy: Samsung Corporatiton

happiness through acquisition of possessions.

3. **Possession-defined success**—This is a tendency to judge one's own and others' success by material possessions.

Table 6.3 presents a scale to measure these three dimensions of materialism.

Researchers Richins and Dawson also suggested several characteristics of materialistic persons. First, materialists value acquisition of possessions more than they value other life goals. They value them more than they value relationships with others, for example. Second, materialistic people are self-centered. Accordingly, they are less likely to be sharing and giving. Materialists also lead a life of material complexity—they rely on technology, they have positive attitudes toward growth, and they lack concern for things in nature. Finally, despite many possessions, materialists tend to be less satisfied with life than others. The lust for goods is insatiable; it always leaves materialists wanting more.

In one study, consumers who scored high on materialism tended to value financial security much more than did an average person. They also placed less value on warm relationships with others and on a sense of accomplishment. Materialists were also likely to spend more buying things than was an average consumer, but they also were less likely to donate money to church organizations or charity and less likely to lend money to friends.[9]

VOLUNTARY SIMPLICITY

The opposite of materialism is simplicity and frugality. Some consumers live a simple and frugal life, of course, because of limited means and resources. But many consumers who are well-off realize that chasing material goods is a never-ending race, that acquiring more actually leaves us less contented, wanting more. Some realize it following some chasing after goods, and some develop that mode of thinking as they grow up as adolescents. When consumers live a simple life, not chasing material goods (and when they do so not because they can't afford but because they don't want to), they are living a life of voluntary simplicity. **Voluntary simplicity** refers to acquiring a belief system that too much consumption is undesirable, and, accordingly, choosing to live a life with fewer products and services.[1]

Voluntary simplicity entails both a belief system and a practice. It is based on the belief that true happiness comes not from materialism but from focusing on and reflecting on life itself—on the nonmaterial aspects of life. And it is practiced through reduced consumption, freeing one's mind of wealth and commercial products, and turning one's attention to inner growth. It also entails cleaning up one's calendar from the clutter of too many appointments and a rushed schedule, and taking the time to "smell the roses," so to speak.

For many, consuming is a process of identity construction. A product confers an identity, prestige, and blissful happiness. However, some who see consumption as a means of overcoming the stress of life actually find that, through consumption, stress is not reduced. In fact, they find that the race to acquire more (and for acquiring the resources to acquire more) creates its own stress. And if their purpose in consumption were to create a self, consumption creates, they realize, a self that is always incomplete and still dissatisfied with its new state or definition. One reaches a point in this self-creation enterprise, looks in the mirror, and wonders, "Is this what I wanted to become?" Then comes a U-turn—dispossession of goods and uncluttering of day-to-day calendars.

Psychologist V. Gecas describes self as comprising three components: self-esteem, self-efficacy, and authentication. **Self-esteem** refers to holding oneself as valued. **Self-efficacy** refers to viewing oneself as effective, in control. Finally, **authentication** refers to realizing that one is what one truly is. One consumer notes his realization of how consumption based self is not authentic:

> " Myths that we tell each other— like don't wear cruddy shoes to an interview— lead us to believe that something external to who we are is going to make us. And I had certainly unconsciously bought into that. ...I had all the stuff that was supposed to make me successful—my car and my clothes, the house in the right neighborhood and belonging to the right health club. All the external framework was excellent, and inside I kind of had this pit eating away at me."

Another consumer said:

> "We had a big house and a housekeeper… and I was driving up and down the freeway to work all the time when I realized, 'This is not me, this is not who I am'"

> (Respondents in a research study by Professor Stephen Zavestoski of Providence College).[11]

The importance of voluntary simplicity is brought home by a practice among some consumers in Japan: they celebrate one day in a year as *Buy Nothing* day. Read about it in Chapter 5.

TABLE 6.3 — A Scale To Measure Materialism

Rate the following statements on a 1-5 scale where 1 = strongly disagree and 5 = strongly agree.

SUCCESS SUBSCALE

I admire people who own expensive homes, cars, and clothes.
Some of the most important achievements in life include acquiring material possessions.
I don't place much emphasis on the amount of material objects that people own as a sign of success.*
The things I own say a lot about how well I'm doing in life.
I like to own things that impress people.
I don't pay much attention to the material objects other people own.*

CENTRALITY SUBSCALE

I usually buy only the things I need.*
I try to keep my life simple as far as possessions are concerned.*
The things I own aren't all that important to me.*
I enjoy spending money on things that aren't practical.
Buying things gives me a lot of pleasure.
I like a lot of luxury in my life.
I put less emphasis on material things than most people do.*

HAPPINESS SUBSCALE

I have all the things I really need to enjoy life.*
My life would be better if I owned certain things I don't have.
I wouldn't be any happier if I owned nicer things.*
I'd be happier if I could afford to buy more things.
It sometimes bothers me quite a bit that I can't afford to buy all the things I'd like.

Note: To score yourself, reverse score the items marked *, and then add up all items. The higher the score, the more materialistic you are, with a score of 45 being the midpoint.

Source: Marsha L. Richins and Scott Dawson, "A Consumer Values Orientation and Its Measurement: Scale Development and Validation," Journal of Consumer Research, 19, 3 (December 1992) pp. 303-17. © Journal of Consumer Research. Publisher: The University of Chicago Press (Used with permission.)

Bobos in Paradise

David Brooks, a NY Times reporter, in his book (*Bobos in Paradise*, Simon and Schuster, 2001) describes a new class of people with a new psychographics. Their psychographics combine the psychographics of two other classes of people, namely bourgeoisie and bohemians. Bourgeoisie were the old aristocracy, who in the pre-1960s and 70s were the elite. Born in cultured, educated, affluent, elite families, youngsters went to Ivy League schools, acquired refined tastes from their etiquette-oriented parents, and held positions of influence. The living room parlor with Victorian decorous furnishings and smooth polished wall surfaces was an invention of this class—the visitors were to be entertained in this formal room. And everything, from dress to table manners to social interactions, had to be prim and proper. Then, in the sixties came the Bohemian class. The hippies, the gypsy, the artsy people who spawned the sexual revolution and the pursuit of care-free rather than materialism-burdened life. You have already read about this class and can read even more in Chapter 17.

In the post 1970 period, the old aristocracy gave way to meritocracy. Anyone who had the requisite aptitude and abilities could get into Ivy Leagues. To advance in life, old family ties were no longer required. This new elite class lacked the training in or the penchant for the refined and formal mannerism of the aristocrat class. Members of this emerging class embraced, instead, many of the values and lifestyle traits of the "more casual than thou" attitude of the bohemian class. And lo, Bobos were born.

Bobos are, according to Brooks, earthy, casual, ecological, and are very concerned about their health. For Bobos, writes Brooks, "it is unfashionable to get sick and die." Being in touch with nature and personal health are very important to them. This is reflected in their clothing, their furnishings, their leisure activities, and even their gadgets. They may never hike Mount Everest, but they have the hiking boots and jackets that would enable them to do so if the opportunity arose. Brooks speaks of those in Silicon Valley who come to work wearing glacier glasses and hiking boots—as if a wall of ice were going to come sliding through the parking lot at any minute.

Bobos have their own code of ethics. A Bobo wouldn't dream of spending $25,000 on something as frivolous as an entertainment system, but they may spend the same amount on a slate shower stall, showing how in touch they are with the rhythms of nature. Anthropologie store was created, according to Brooks, precisely for Bobos.

Bobo's is a term coined by Brooks (by taking the first two letters of the two classes it is an amalgam of) and although the term did not become popular, the Bobo phenomenon is real and Bobos are kicking and thriving.

SUMMARY

Using Bianca's brief autobiographical narrative as a launch pad, we began with an introduction to psychographics as entailing a study of what makes up a consumer—both psychologically and behaviorally. Psychographics include personal values, personality traits, self-concept, and lifestyles. Values, personality, and self-concept—all culminate in lifestyles—the way we live. Here, in the study of lifestyles, we understood a crucial fact of consumers' marketplace behaviors: consumers choose products to build the mosaic that their lifestyle is. A visit to a Hot Topic store, along with a few other marketing campaigns, showed us the magical appeal of lifestyle targeting in the real world.

Psychographics are ways of "graphing the psychological makeup of the consumer" (hence, the name "psychographics"). This is done, we learned, through AIO ("activities, interests, and opinions") statements, and consumer answers to these statements on numerical rating scales enable us to identify segments of consumers that differ on their psychographics. As an example, we reviewed VALS, a values and lifestyle segmentation scheme for North American consumers.

To internationalize our perspective, we also saw the psychographic profiles for two other countries: Japan and New Zealand. We concluded this section with a description of selected applications of psychographic segmentation.

We concluded the chapter with a discussion of two overarching consumer psychographics: materialism and voluntary simplicity. Without these, no chapter on psychographics is complete. They engulf and immerse our entire lives, both in our roles as humans and as consumers, serving us as servants, or, alternatively, controlling us as masters (depending on our perspective on life and on consumption). Read them and decide for yourself what they can do for you!

Anthropolog e—Welcome to Bobo Lifestyles

That is an academic discipline with a French spelling. But we are not speaking here of some college course you take for 3 credits. We speak, instead, of a store-chain that is part museum, part a modern day shopping enclave. Headquartered in Philadephia and with some 85-plus stores in North America, the chain sells women's clothing and home furnishings. But that is just the store demographics. What is fascinating is the store chains's "psychographics."

Enter the store and you are inside a large warehouse-like high ceiling structure with exposed wooden beams. Happily, its largeness is broken down into small islands alongside a meandering pathway, a collection of some 30 or so borderless merchandise display areas, each with an intimacy of its own.

Quirky and artistic decorations abound—on the walls (mixed material curios) and on tabletops (e.g., pebbles, lentils, beads, oversized books.) The tables, on which merchandise is displayed, themselves are rustic, distressed wood you would expect to find in a peasant farmhouse a couple of centuries ago. In fact, most likely, that is where they came from. Hanging on a sparsely populated rack are Jeans—one variety is an inconspicuously branded Level 99 (price $168). Other collections offer eclectic styles and fabrics— from Indian sari material to Moroccan embroidered motifs to vintage Italian. From long classy dresses to flirty midi skirts.

The center of attraction in the particular store we visited (State Street, Chicago, June 2006) is a dining table like no other. It is off–white driftwood, with irregular, rough, broken wood edges, and with 6" diameter tree trunks as its legs. Two gorgeous glass chandeliers hang with jute/hemp ropes. A bench with a mini tiled-look sitting surface and thick wooden branches in natural crisscrossing pattern making the back and arm support. (The table was priced $3800.) Such functional but quirky and definitely unique merchandise is the store's specialty.

True to its name, the store merchandise looks like a collection of some cultural anthropologist. If one were to capture a common thread in the merchandise theme, it will be strung together by such adjectives as: tactile (surfaces that beckon you to touch them), one-of-a-kind, and with a story—you want to know and tell its history; perhaps the happenstance of your discovering and buying it will in itself become a story you will tell your friends.

What kind of customers does the store attract? According to one astute commentator:

> • *The Anthropology customer is affluent but not materialistic. She's focused on building a nest but hankers for exotic travel. . . . She's in tune with trends, but she's a confident individualist when it comes to style. ... She's not "married with two kids"; rather, she's a yoga-practicing filmmaker with an organic garden, a collection of antique musical instruments, and an abiding interest in Chinese culture (plus a husband and two kids).*
> **-- Polly LaBarre, in Fast Company ("Sophisticated Sell," December 2002, p. 93)**

For such chic, part bohemian, part high culture consumers, Anthropologie is indeed an oasis for discovering material goods with nonmaterial stories that resonate one's own identity and psychographics. Anthropologie was one of the first stores in Bobo land (see, below, Consumer Karma: I am a Bobo…), and a visit there will, just like a college course, earn you some credit hours in Bobo lifestyles.

My CB Book

KEY TERMS

Psychographics	Consumption constellation	Self-efficacy	Materialism
Lifestyles	VALS	Authentication	Voluntary Simplicity
AIO inventory	Self-esteem		

And Yes, I have Sinned Boldly At the Krispy Kreme

One of the fun things about reading the book is seeing myself in the book. I am with the Bobos completely in the "more casual than thou thing." I hate to wear ties and dress shoes. I've always been with Linda Ellerbee who said: "If men can run the world, why can't they stop wearing neckties? How intelligent is it to start the day by tying a noose around your neck?" Amen, preach it sister. If I weren't afraid of creating a scandal I would preach in jeans and a t-shirt. Some guys take pride in their tie collection, I take pride in my t-shirt collection.

I don't have any glacier glasses, but I do have the SwissChamp Swiss Army knife ...It's got 50 features... though I have only used a few of them, I am comforted to know that the rest are there should I ever need them. Oh, btw, I also have a cool little pouch to carry it with on my belt. Makes me look rugged and outdoorsy!

I don't have real good hiking boots, but I do have top of the line New Balance cross trainers. These things give my feet and ankles the padding and support I need to run a marathon, play basketball or handle rough terrain. I don't do any of that, but a guy like me needs shoes like this. After all, when I get out of my car to go into the house I ... cross a concrete driveway, walk on some grass, climb a flight of five steps, and walk into a house where the terrain changes rapidly from wood flooring to carpet to linoleum. ... Also, to get from my bedroom to the refrigerator, to the bathroom and to the TV room I have to turn several sharp corners and go up and down flights of six steps, so I need a shoe that [can withstand such punishment].

Oh well, enough silliness for now, the point is that we all have imbibed Bobo values to some degree.

"Everything in the Bobo life is purposeful." Bingo!! For the Bobo, the meritocrat, life is one long graduate school,... even vacations and play are part of the program of self-improvement and self-enrichment. ...

There is such a thing as sin in Bobo-land. In times past, morals were codified by things like the Ten Commandments. In Bobo-land, morals are codified by the CDC and FDA. So, whereas in the past mom and dad may have severely reprimanded their teenage daughter for not wearing enough clothes on the beach, nowadays said teenager daughter can wear dental floss for a bathing suit, but she will get seriously reprimanded for not wearing enough sunscreen.

In the past, smoking pot was socially unacceptable; today eating red meat is socially unacceptable.

I suppose I should qualify that a bit. As an Atkins-era Bobo myself, eating red meat is sanctified and holy, but the Krispy Kreme has replaced the old time brothel as the new den of iniquity. And yes, I have sinned boldly at the Krispy Kreme.

(Author Note. Like David Wayne, author too thinks that it's cool to be a Bobo. Look around and see how very present, though not ubiquitous, they are.]

Source: David Wayne's blog on his blog site
http://jollyblogger.typepad.com/jollyblogger/2004/08/im_a_bobo_hes_a.html

Consumer Karma Is Experiencing the Bobo Land

INSIDE THE CONSUMER'S MIND

MyCBBook

My CB Book

YOUR TURN

REVIEW+Rewind

1. Explain in your own words the concepts of *lifestyles* and *psychographics*.
2. How are psychographics measured? What is an AIO inventory and how is it useful for psychographics?
3. What is the VALS scheme of psychographic segmentation? Name each of its consumer types and explain each briefly.
4. What is meant by "consumption constellations" and why do they exist?
5. Name and briefly explain any four applications of psychographics in marketing.
6. What is meant by "positioning by lifestyles"? In how many ways can a marketer utilize lifestyles to position his/her brand? Explain each briefly.
7. Explain the concepts of materialism and voluntary simplicity? How are they related to the concepts of *lifestyle* and *psychographics?*

THINK+Apply

1. Why should psychographics explain consumer behaviors?
2. Explain the relationship among the following concepts: values, personality traits, self-concepts, lifestyles, and psychographics. Should all psychographic studies measure all these concepts? Why or why not?
3. From the AIO statements (given in the chapter), select only five factors you consider most relevant to differentiating heavy users versus light or nonusers of (choose one) (a) hair styling mousse, (b) wines, (c) videogames. Alternatively, identify AIO statements that would distinguish between consumers whose favorite store for clothes is: (a) Limited Express versus Gap, (b) Pacific Sun versus Hollister.

   Should a marketer construct a separate AIO inventory for each product category? Why or why not? Why can't you use the same AIO inventory for all products?

Lifestyles are the way people live—how they spend their resources (time and money) and what products they consume. No two lifestyles are the same, but by grouping consumers with more or less similar lifestyles, marketers have created hundreds of research-based lifestyle segmentation schemes. We can't cover them all here, and, at any rate, you can't learn them all. The lifestyle segmentation schemes that we did cover, however, must give you ample appreciation of what it takes to create them.

As a marketer armed with this knowledge, you would now need to identify the specific values, personality traits, self-concepts, and lifestyles your target consumers might exhibit. The inventory and examples given here will serve as a useful starting point, and, indeed, you are likely to find many of these applicable for your target consumers as well. Yet the creativity and challenge—and fun—is in identifying and defining the psychological makeup—values, personality/self-concept, and lifestyles—unique to your target consumers.

Self-concept is a powerful thing. It determines the courses of our lives—what we become and what we accomplish. And it determines, even more immediately and in real time, what we consume and the lifestyles we live. The power of that self-concept is visible in the short narrative from Bianca, our chapter opener, and even, more vividly in this brief excerpt from yet another self-narrative:

My name, Fury, implies that I am a fire-spitting diva. The reality is, I'm a nice, respectful, person who rarely gets angry. … I'm black, bald, and confident: I walk with my head held high and my shoulders back. I am 5'8" and wear four-inch heels all the time. I celebrate my femininity by wearing scanty yet classy outfits, like halter with a long blazer pinstripe pants, and of course stilettos. (From Leah Paulos, "Why Men Fear These Women," *Marie Claire*, September 2002, p.188)

Bianca and Fury live the lifestyles and consume the products they do because of who each thinks she is and wants to become. Violate their self-concepts, and they will avoid your products like poison ivy. We speak here not only about the image of the brands and products which need to be, for Bianca, at once trendy and bohemian, and for Fury, at once classy and bold. Indeed, we speak also of how every communiqué from the marketer, every interaction with the firm, has to meet their expectations for respect. Dismiss Bianca as a style-confused Gen 'Y' girl, and she will take her two-country, two-culture consumption enthusiasm to another merchant. Act condescendingly toward Fury, or use advertising that shows women in sexual, submissive roles, and you can forget about ever selling anything to this **fire-spitting diva.**

PRACTICE✚Experience

1. Consider two of your friends who are ostensibly different in their psychographics. Make a prediction in terms of the VALS segment to which each would belong (both primary and secondary segment). Then ask them to take the survey online and submit the survey, and note down their VALS segment as scored by the computer. Then interview them to identify factors that explain why their computer scored VALS profile is different from your predictions.

2. Using the AIO inventory constructed in the earlier section, survey a sample of consumers, say 10 in each group (e.g., Limited Express vs. Gap Shoppers). Calculate mean scores (manually or through a computer) on each AIO statement and then for each factor, and compare and contrast the psychographic profile of consumers who shop at the Limited Express and Gap. Likewise compare and contrast the psychographic profiles of other groups.

3. You are the director of consumer research for a company that markets (choose one): (a) Cirque du Soleil (See information at www.cirquedusoleil.com), (b) Red Bull drink, (c) Camper Shoes, a company that focuses on design simplicity and harmony with nature (see www.camper.com), (d) Anthropologie stores. You want to track lifestyle or psychographic changes your target group might be exhibiting over time. Make a list of psychographic factors most relevant to isolating the target customers for your brand. Then write a questionnaire to measure and track their psychographics.

In the Marketing Manager's Shoes

Put yourself in a marketing manager's shoes. Most concepts in the chapter have some lessons for the marketing manager; i.e., they suggest what to do differently in practice. Indeed, often these applications are implicit in our explanations of the concepts and models in the chapter. Identify at least five specific applications of the chapter's concepts, all of which should be entirely new different from the examples cited here.

Consumer Attitudes: Theory And Concepts

Knowing What to Want And What to Shun

- Attitude—Do You Have It?
- Know-Feel-Do—Which Comes First?
- Know-Feel-Do—How They Make Peace
- Attitude Does What? Four Functions of Attitude
- TORA, TOVA, TOTA—Three Grand Models of Attitude
- Molding Consumer Attitudes—How May I Persuade Thee?

OK—it was the name Coca-Cola Company gave its new citrus-flavored soda concoction, back in Summer 1994, targeted, at young adults.

The taste was a cross between Dr. Pepper, Lemonade, and Coca Cola, and in pre-launch taste tests, young consumers had liked it—saying it was different and it had, well, oomph!

The can was decorated with facial images of apparently young people with no particular expression. A message around the lip of the can read: "OK soda says 'Don't be fooled into thinking there has to be a reason for everything.'" According to one comment, the company wanted to appeal to teenagers and Gen 'Y' consumers—who had a "sense of themselves as sardonic and unsurprizable ('Yeah—it's OK, I s'pose')." It tried to soothe teen angst and anxiety. One brand slogan read: OK-ness is the belief that, no matter what, things are going to be OK.

By Summer 1995, a year after its introduction, the company decided to pull the brand. The teens and youth it targeted just did not see the brand as echoing their emotions. In one of the brand slogans, the company used a rhetorical question: "What is the point of OK? What is the point of anything?" The consumer seemed to have replied. "Nothing. *Nothing* is the point of 'OK,'" they seemed to say—and they didn't want *nothing*!*

INTRODUCTION

The story of OK soda carries an important lesson for all students of marketing. It does not matter what a marketer says a product is or will do. What matters is what consumers come to think of it. The teen and youth of that time period did not think well of OK soda. And based on this opinion, they acted—tossing the brand into the dustbin of history. This fate is meted out to thousands of brands every year.

Before we rush to gloat over our insight as to how OK Soda idea was doomed to fail, let us remember it is hindsight, not foresight. Indeed, OK soda briefly enjoyed a cult following, active even years after it was officially withdrawn. Fans reminisced in newsgroups at alt. fan.ok-soda and held onto unopened and opened soda cans as keepsakes. You can find some unopened cans on eBay even today. There is no telling if the campaign wouldn't have succeeded if continued longer, or in another place and time. A product's success and failure alike depend on consumer attitudes, and this is our point.

*Based on various sources including OK Marketing — A retrospective of the OK marketing campaign by suck.com (February 14, 1996), www.suck.com/daily/96/02/14/ daily.html; en.wikipedia.org/wiki/OK_Soda; www.geocities.com/the_dolce/ok.html. (Last accessed on May 4, 2006.)

At this very moment, thousands of marketers are pitching their products and services to millions of consumers around the world. Standing at consumers' doors, on the telephone, at a business expo, in the mall, on eBay 's auction Website, in TV and radio ads, at upscale boutiques of Florence and Madrid, and from thousands of trailer trucks at flea markets around the world. Are consumers listening to them? How are they reacting to this cacophony of slogans and promises, and to that visual parade of product images? Aside from these marketers of material goods, also soliciting the favorable opinion of consumers are charities, schools, tourist spots, casinos and nightclubs, films, TV shows, sports teams, and even presidential candidates. How do consumers come to form an opinion about these entities? What persuades them to embrace some of theses marketplace offerings—while spurning others? And how can marketers win favorable consumer reactions to their offerings?

This chapter is our answer to these questions. In this chapter, we explain the concept of attitude—the supreme precursor to all of our actions in the marketplace. We take you deep inside the mind of the consumer and witness the dynamic interplay of our thoughts, feelings, and intentions. Here you will also meet TOVA, TORA, and TOTA—no, it is not the name of a new rendition of Depeche Mode's 1981 album or some mountains in Afghanistan; these are, instead, the nicknames of three models of attitude.

We also take a look at the motivational basis of attitudes, explaining the four functions that attitudes serve for us, and through examples we invite you to examine the motivations for some of your own deeply held attitudes—attitudes toward people (stereotypes), and attitudes toward products. Understanding attitudes can help you fashion your market offerings—advertising and all—to be consumer friendly. This chapter is a key, in other words, to getting consumers to have a good attitude toward your product offerings, and, consequently, to throw some dough your way. It is also a key to avoiding the fate of OK Soda. Read on.

ATTITUDE

Do You Have It?

Do you have an attitude? Towards Eminem and his music? Towards the New England football team, the Patriots? Toward the TV show *The Apprentice*? Do you like or dislike them? And which subject do you like the most? And the least? What is your attitude toward this book? What do you think of the Budweiser commercials shown during the recent Superbowl? Do pop up ads on the Internet bother you? Which is your favorite drink—Coke, Pepsi or the Dew? And if OK Cola were introduced today, would you have had a more favorable reaction? All of these questions are designed to elicit your attitude. So, just what is an attitude?

In common parlance, when we refer to your attitude, we simply refer to your 'like' or 'dislike' of something, your opinion about something. If you like something, then your attitude toward it is positive; if you dislike it, then your attitude is negative. However, to understand fully the nature of attitudes, we need to examine a classic definition of attitudes, offered by psychologist Gordon Allport: **Attitudes** are learned predispositions to respond to an object in a consistently favorable or unfavorable way.[1]

This definition has several elements:
- **Attitudes are learned.** That is, no one is born with them. You were not born with an attitude toward Eminem, the Patriots, Coke, or Pepsi, for example, were you? Instead, you learned them during your time here on this earth. And how did you learn them? On the basis of some experience with or information about these things or persons.
- **They are targeted** toward an object **or a class of objects.** If we ask you, what is your attitude or what is your opinion, you will ask, opinion about what or attitude toward what? That "what" is the 'object' in our definition—attitude toward

an object. And that object can be anything—a brand, a product, a company, a class, a movie, a presidential candidate, and even an idea (e.g., the idea of 'freedom of speech'). Thus, we hold different attitudes toward different objects.

- **Attitudes cause response.** That is, they are the reason we respond, or act, in a certain way toward those objects. Thus, we drink Coke and avoid Pepsi (or the other way around) because of our attitudes toward Coke and Pepsi. And our attitudes toward Eminem and his music makes us buy or not buy his albums.

- **The response that attitudes cause is consistent.** Thus, we don't buy Eminem's music today and avoid it tomorrow. And we don't choose Coke today and Pepsi tomorrow (unless our attitudes toward each are equally favorable). Instead, we act toward a given object the same way over a period of time; i.e., consistently.

- **Attitude is a predisposition.** By predisposition, we mean it is our "inclination." Thus, it resides in our mind. We are predisposed to doing something or not doing something. Like we are predisposed (or inclined) to buy Eminem's music and we are predisposed to drink Coke and not drink Pepsi.

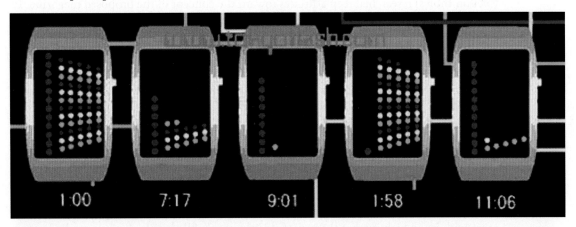

If you have never seen this watch before, then you can't possibly have an attitude toward it. Because no one is born with attitudes.

Now look at it, grasp how time is read on this watch, and then decide if you like or dislike it. You now you have an atttiude, and we mean atttitude *toward the watch.* You just *learned* it. And now you want to get one—that is your *response.* You want it today, and you would want it tomorrow (consistency), unless, of course, you change your atttiude itself (toward the watch). You will buy it as soon as the opportunity arises (predisposition). You can buy it from www.tokyoflash.com.

YOUR ATTITUDE IS WAITING FOR ACTION!!!

Predisposition
Pregnant With Meaning

This word, *predisposition,* is a wonderful word, pregnant with rich meaning. It is the key to the concept of attitude and to understanding the true nature of this concept. No other term can cut it as well. We could say, for example, that an attitude is your opinion about something, and broadly speaking we would be right, but opinion is what you think of something; that is all. It is not quite the same thing as predisposition. We could say attitude is your general evaluation of something—whether you view it as a good thing or a bad thing—and we would be approximately right. But the word *evaluation* does not quite capture it either. Predisposition—it means you have something in your mind—a thought, an opinion, an evaluation, a view, even a feeling—and that you are going to do something about it. You are going to act toward the object of your attitude. Predisposition makes you inclined to act. Thus, an attitude is our mental code to release some action toward something. It is an *action in waiting*.

Action in Waiting

This idea of attitudes as predisposition and predisposition as *action in waiting* is very useful to marketers. Marketers are interested, you see, in predicting consumers' future actions or future behavior. A behavior is something we *do*; an attitude (predisposition) is something we have in our minds. So marketers use consumer attitudes to predict consumers' behaviors. Thus, for example, if marketers knew that you had a positive attitude toward Eminem's music, then they could predict that you would be likely to buy his music CDs. Marketers want to predict consumers' behavior—specifically whether consumers will or will not buy a product, *before* marketers invest the money to make and market the product. For example, in 2003, an entrepreneurial publisher of Bibles conceived an idea about a book that would rewrite the Bible styled like a fashion magazine such as Seventeen and Vogue. But before investing a lot of money in producing the book, the publisher (Nelson Bibles) researched teen attitudes toward the concept of the proposed magazine. In focus group discussions with teenagers, the company found that the number one reason teens don't read the Bible is that it is, as teens put it, "too big and freaky looking." So a fashion magazine format for the Holy Scriptures seemed like a perfect solution. The company published the book in October 2003, titled *Revolve: The Complete New Testament.*[2] If the enthusiasm shown by consumers in their book reviews on Amazon.com is any indication, the book has been a huge success.[3]

Remember, then, the key elements in the definition of attitude:

(i) learned (ii) predisposition, (iii) toward an object (or a class of objects), (iv) to respond or act (toward that object and in a favorable or unfavorable way); (v) consistently.

Review this definition a few times, so you don't think of it as difficult. We want you to have a favorable attitude toward this definition. So that you will be predisposed to do more with it—which is what the rest of this chapter is filled with. Are you ready— oops, we mean, are you *PREDISPOSED*?

MEASURING CONSUMER ATTITUDES

How Do I Know What Consumers Think of My Product?

As a marketer, you might argue that all this conceptual understanding is fine, even great; but what I am interested in is finding out my consumers' attitudes toward my product. You convinced me, you might say, that attitude is a great concept, so I want to utilize it. How do I measure what my customers' attitudes are? Good question.

Because a disposition resides in the consumer's mind, we cannot, of course, directly see it or observe it. But we can ask consumers some questions that could reveal this predisposition. Something very simple like, 'What do you think of Eminem's music?' And they would reveal in their own words, as we all do when asked questions like this, all that is in their minds about Eminem. This 'view of something in their minds' revealed by consumers in their own words is the closest we can come to measuring their predispositions. If we want to do it on a large scale, i.e., for a large number of consumers, and in a way so that the answers from different consumers are comparable, then we should do it using a paper-and-pencil set of questions with numerical rating scales. Such scales are designed to elicit consumers' overall mindset (i.e., predispositions) toward something. Every researcher has his or her own favorite way of phrasing these rating statements. We give below what a majority of consumer researchers would consider an efficient set of measures.

If we wanted to measure consumers' attitude toward Eminem's music, for example, we could use the following set of statements:

I dislike Eminem's music very much	-2 -1 0 +1 +2	I like it very much.
Toward Eminem's music, I feel: unfavorably	-2 -1 0 +1 +2	I feel favorably.
My opinion about Eminem's music is: Negative	-2 -1 0 +1 +2	Positive.

We can average the three items to arrive at the attitude score. Suppose this score comes to −1.67 for consumer Ross, -1.33 for consumer Joey, and +1.33 for consumer Chandler; then, Chandler's attitude toward Eminem's music is favorable, Joey's attitude is unfavorable, and Ross's attitude is even more unfavorable. We can use this measurement method for any product new or old.

Okay, we have given you a way of measuring attitudes. Happy? We mean, happy in your role as marketers? Actually, no. You would now say, "Okay, I now know whether or not consumers have a good attitude toward my product or brand. But what do I do with that knowledge? What, for example, do I do with those who don't have a positive attitude toward my brand? If they don't have a positive attitude, they are not going to buy my brand. How do I get them to have a positive attitude?" Questions such as these get us into how you can change that attitude. To get a handle on that, we need to understand what lies deep beneath consumers' attitudes. We need to cut open the concept, so to speak, and peek inside it to see what factors make up consumer attitudes. We need to look at its composition and the dynamic interplay of its ingredients, its elements. If you peek inside, you will find a model called the ABC model of attitude.

THE ABC MODEL OF ATTITUDE

ABC—these stand for affect, beliefs, and conation.

Psychologists now believe that attitudes are composed of three underlying dimensions: feelings, knowledge, and action intent. That is, when we hold an attitude about an object, typically it is based on some knowledge and beliefs about the object; we feel some positive or negative emotion toward it; and we want to act in a certain way toward it; for example, either embracing it or spurning it. Thus, an attitude is like a three-legged stool, the three legs being thoughts or beliefs (also called *cognitions*), feelings or emotions (technically called *affect*), and action intent (technically called *conation*). These three components comprise the ABC Model of Attitude (see Figure 7.1). Let us look at each component closely.

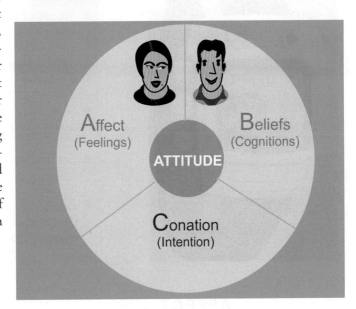

FIGURE 7.1 THE ABC MODEL OF ATTITUDES

BELIEFS
What Do You Know About Me?

Although, sometimes we mindlessly form an attitude toward someone or something, often we base that evaluation on a more detailed appraisal of the person's qualities or brand's features. Remember, we were not born with attitudes, but rather we learn them based on some knowledge or information about the product. This knowledge about a person or product, these appraisals of a person's qualities or a brand's features, are called *beliefs*. More specifically, **beliefs** are expectations about what something is or is not or what something will or will not do. Statements of belief connect an object (person, brand, store, etc.) to an attribute or benefit. Accordingly,

FIGURE
7.2

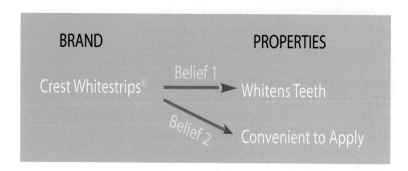

BRAND BELIEFS as a LINK Between a Brand and a PROPERTY the Brand Claims

BRAND   **PROPERTIES**

Crest Whitestrips®

Belief 1 → Whitens Teeth

Belief 2 → Convenient to Apply

a **brand belief** is a thought about a specific property or quality of the brand. (See Figure 7.2.)

Note that just because a product marketer claims a particular quality or feature, it does not mean that consumers will make it part of their brand beliefs. Sometimes, because of distrust of the marketer, personal trial experience, or misperceptions, their brand beliefs could be exactly the opposite of the marketer's claims. Thus, for example, consumer Monica could come to believe that Whitestrips* do in fact whiten the teeth, whereas consumer Rachel could come to believe that the whitening effect would be barely if at all noticeable.

Figure 7.3 shows how beliefs are the basis of consumer attitudes about Wrist Net Dick Tracy FX3200 (you can read more about it on www.Fossil.com).

Now, to the question, What underlies a particular attitude (i.e., an overall predisposition) toward something? The answer is simple: *our beliefs about that something*—and these beliefs form the basis of our attitude. That is, beliefs are the foundations for our attitudes. Beliefs are detailed thoughts; attitude is an overall inclination of the mind.

FIGURE
7.3

COGNITIONS FOR THE DICK TRACY WATCH

Dick Tracy Watch:
Courtesy Fossil Co.

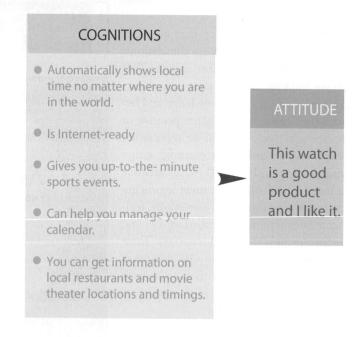

COGNITIONS

- Automatically shows local time no matter where you are in the world.

- Is Internet-ready

- Gives you up-to-the-minute sports events.

- Can help you manage your calendar.

- You can get information on local restaurants and movie theater locations and timings.

ATTITUDE

This watch is a good product and I like it.

AFFECT
Do You Love Me Or Not?

The second component of attitude is *affect* (or feelings). The belief component says in effect, "Tell me the brand features, and its qualities, and I will tell you if I like the brand or not." In reality, we know this not to be entirely true. We know that a dislike for frog or monkey brains as food, for example, has nothing to do with its taste feature. How would we know? We have never eaten these, but we dislike them anyway. Just the vision of these as food gives us the creeps. Thus, thinking (i.e., forming beliefs) is not always necessary for attitude. Rather feelings or emotions can also account for attitudes in some situations. In most situations, of course, we do both: we think and we feel. Thus, we form a positive attitude toward our Harley Davidson, for example, both because we have learned about its attributes and formed corresponding positive beliefs (e.g., it accelerates very fast) and because the thrill of riding it or just the vision of being seen riding it gives us joy. We can measure this feeling component for a Dick Tracy watch as shown in Figure 7.4.

In fact, for many objects, our feelings occur even before we initiate thinking and form beliefs; this is because feelings can and often do arise automatically, whereas thinking (belief formation) takes conscious effort. Feelings arise automatically because we have been conditioned to experience various feelings upon exposure to various attributes of the product. For example, if we see a neon colored shirt, and if we are 35 year old male career professionals, we might feel a repulsion toward it, whereas if we hear a rock and roll musical tune in a commercial, we might instantly feel upbeat. Thus, feelings are a powerful driver of our attitudes. However, consumers' attitudes are explained better when both feelings and beliefs are taken into account.

FIGURE 7.4

AFFECT FOR THE DICK TRACY WATCH

AFFECT

- This watch is so cool.
- I feel thrilled to see it.
- What a joy this product is!

ATTITUDE

This watch is a good product and I like it.

CONATION

So Do You Have Any Intentions of Buying Me?

So we hold certain beliefs about an object—person, product, or brand—and we experience certain feelings about it. What else? Action. We also act toward that object. We see ice cream, and we want to eat it. We see tofu, and we won't put it in our cart. Action often (if not inevitably) follows our thoughts and our feelings.

FIGURE 7.5

CONATIONS FOR THE DICK TRACY WATCH

CONATIONS

- I am likely (unlikely) to buy this watch.
- I intend (do not intend) to wear this watch.

ATTITUDE

This watch is a good product and I like it.

But there is more. Sometimes, action comes as an immediate response to some objects—even before we have had time to think or feel. We see a dollar bill on the street, and we pick it up. We see a cute child, and we kiss or hug him/her. We see a bull running wild, and we run away from it. Quite often then, our attitudes take the form of immediate action rather than an expressed opinion (a belief) or even some focused feelings. Indeed, if we observe someone taking some action or engaging in some behavior, we can infer that person's attitude.

Now note that behavior itself is not the conation component of attitude. Rather, conation means intention; i.e., intention to act in a certain way. Thus, conation is our instruction to the mind that next time the occasion arises, we are going to buy this thing. This conation is what makes attitude an action in waiting. That said, consumer researchers usually treat conation as if it were behavior itself. Conation can be measured as shown in Figure 7.5.

Now we have told you what the three components of attitude are. Our attitudes about any product come from what we know about it, how we feel about it (what emotions and feelings it evokes in us), and whether we have intentions to buy that product. *Think-Feel-and-Do* thus sum up our attitudes.

HIERARCHIES IN ATTITUDE

Or, What Comes First? And What Comes Last?

If you have read this far, you can't help asking, how are the three components—think, feel, and act—interrelated? Do we think first and then act, or do we act first and think afterwards? When we see a person, product, brand, store, or any other object, do we just feel a sudden burst of emotion immediately, and then think about it or act on it? This issue is addressed by the concept of *attitude hierarchy*. **Attitude hierarchy** refers to the sequence in which the three components occur. Scholars have identified three different hierarchies: (a) Learning Hierarchy, (b) Emotional Hierarchy, and (c) Low Involvement Hierarchy. See Figure 7.6.

Learning Hierarchy In the **learning hierarchy,** cognitions come first, affect next, and action last (see Figure 7.6, Panel 'A'). That is, we think first, feel next, and act last. We learn about the brand and form brand beliefs first; these brand beliefs then lead to brand feelings, which in turn lead to brand purchase and use.[4]

Consider an example. Let us say that you need to decide where to go for Spring break: Florida (say, Miami Beach) or Cancun. You find out how far these places are in terms of the travel time, the cost of travel, and the cost of a hotel room. What activities does each site offer? Can you do snorkeling there, or white water rafting, for example? Then, after thinking over all this information, you begin to have pleasant, good feelings toward one of these destinations, and a bad feeling toward the other. Or you feel so-so toward the one (say, Florida), and much more excited toward the other (say, Cancun). Based on these feelings, you then choose Cancun. We call this learning hierarchy a "rational" hierarchy. Your attitude towards a vacation spot is based on a rational way of looking at objects or brands. (By the way, don't think this is not a marketing example; choosing a vacation destination is just as much consumer behavior as buying, say, a refrigerator.)

Emotional Hierarchy "Wait a minute," you might say. "The last time I decided on my Spring break plan—well, what happened was that we were with a bunch of friends watching this show on cable TV, *MTV Spring Break*. It was basically a live scene from Cancun, where lots and lots of college students were having one big party on the beach. And we said, "That is it. That is where we are going." This was the **emotional hierarchy** of attitude. Here you *feel* first, then act, and think last (see Figure 7.6, Panel 'B'). Based on your emotions—attraction or repulsion toward certain brands or persons or things—you embrace or avoid them, buy them, use them. Finally, through experience, you learn more about them.

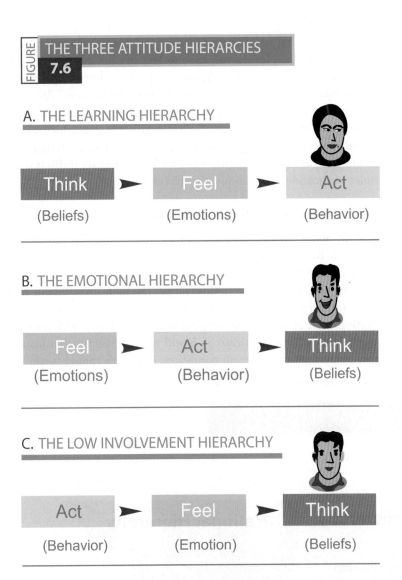

FIGURE 7.6

THE THREE ATTITUDE HIERARCIES

A. THE LEARNING HIERARCHY

| Think | ▶ | Feel | ▶ | Act |
| (Beliefs) | | (Emotions) | | (Behavior) |

B. THE EMOTIONAL HIERARCHY

| Feel | ▶ | Act | ▶ | Think |
| (Emotions) | | (Behavior) | | (Beliefs) |

C. THE LOW INVOLVEMENT HIERARCHY

| Act | ▶ | Feel | ▶ | Think |
| (Behavior) | | (Emotion) | | (Beliefs) |

HOW INVOLVEMENT SHAPES THE HIERARCHY

Now, you might say that some of my friends do choose their vacation spot this way. Me? I just go along wherever my friends are going. I don't even care if I go. Yes, we know there are many consumers like that. That is why consumers are different. And fascinating. One universal truth about consumers is that they differ in their involvement in various activities and likewise in their product choices. Recall that we had defined *involvement* (in Chapter 2) as the degree of interest a consumer takes in a product or activity. When consumers have a stake in a product choice, it is a case of *high involvement*. With low stakes in the choice, involvement is low. Your involvement in the vacation destination choice is low.

The learning and emotional hierarchies described above are high-involvement hierarchies, as both occur when consumers have high stakes in the decisions, such as the choice of a spring break destination for most consumers. In contrast are decisions with low stakes, such as picking up a new variety of bread. With these, consumers don't want to take the time to think or acquire a lot of product knowledge, nor do they feel particularly thrilled about the products. Rather they buy the product casually, with feelings and thoughts to follow with product use.

Low Involvement Hierarchy Suppose that you are in the neighborhood convenience store browsing the cold drinks vending machine and you notice a new kind of energy drink 911. Its white can with red lettering is attractive, and the energy logo is

vibrant and looks inviting. What would you do before you buy it? Do you have to know a whole lot about it? Not really. Nor do you have to feel any notable emotions about it. Instead, what you are likely to do is just put the coin in, push the button, and grab the can. Out of the store, you take the first sip, and you say "Umm! This is good." And you like it. Then you pause to note what flavor it has, and then maybe you even read the ingredients information on the label. Thus, in this case of a low-involvement product selection and consumption, action comes first. Feelings come next, and cognitions or thoughts last. This low-involvement hierarchy is shown in Figure 7.6, Panel 'C'. Now, see if this is true for you as far as your choice of vacation destinations is concerned.

Involvement and Attitude Formation

One clarification about involvement is in order. Involvement is not dichotomous (i.e., just high or low). Rather it is a matter of degree. The low-involvement hierarchy described above occurs at the very low-end of involvement when something is utterly of no consequence to the consumer. In the middle range, the high-involvement hierarchies occur, but with less intensity of thought or feeling. The emotional hierarchy still begins with affect (or feeling), but at the middle range it is likely to begin with a mood rather than deep emotion. And the rational hierarchy is still relevant, except that instead of the extensive thoughts of the high-involvement condition, just a few thoughts will drive feelings. This situation is depicted in Figure 7.7.

FIGURE 7.7 INVOLVEMENT AND ATTITUDE HIERARCHY

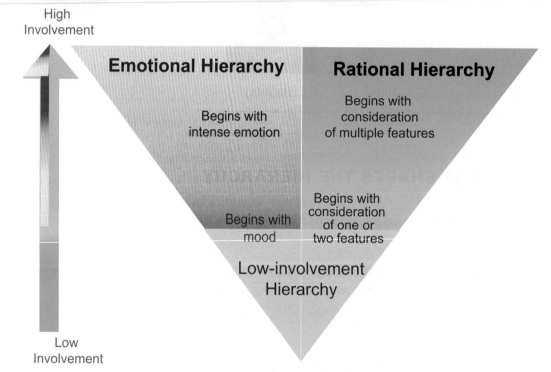

High Involvement

Low Involvement

Emotional Hierarchy

Begins with intense emotion

Begins with mood

Rational Hierarchy

Begins with consideration of multiple features

Begins with consideration of one or two features

Low-involvement Hierarchy

MARKETING IMPLICATION OF ATTITUDE HIERARCHY

These hierarchies have marketing implications. We all know that consumers look at some products as primarily rational purchases and at others as primarily emotional purchases. We want consumers to have a positive attitude toward our products. So how do we go about building it? Here the hierarchies come to our aid. For primarily rational products (like home appliances), we must provide consumers a lot of product knowledge, so they can then base their decisions on rational grounds. We would fail if instead we began to

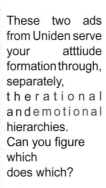

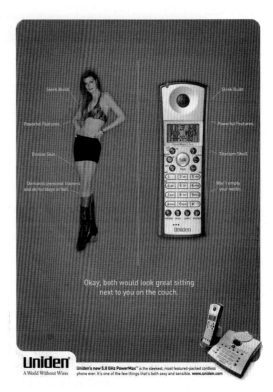

These two ads from Uniden serve your attiude formation through, separately, the rational and emotional hierarchies. Can you figure which does which?

appeal to their emotions. But once they have formed beliefs, then some emotional appeals will help to move them to action.

For emotional products, in contrast, we should first hook consumers emotionally. Talking about product features would only fall on deaf ears. Consider what would happen if we tried to sell someone a product like a diamond as a romantic gift by enumerating its physical and performance features. In this case, though, once consumers are hooked emotionally, our next step should be to make it very convenient to buy (remember, in the emotional hierarchy, feelings are followed immediately by action).

For extremely low involvement products, on the other hand, we don't need to tell consumers much about the brand—as long as we have made the brand name familiar. Our first priority should be to make it very convenient for them to buy it. Marketers stimulate low involvement purchases by using attractive product displays. Consumers see them, and they just reach out for them. In the middle range of involvement, if the product has some performance features that consumers usually worry about, then we should advertise those features—but we should limit our advertisement or sales-story to one or two features and not beat them over their heads with details (remember, consumers are not much motivated to devote mental effort). Or if the product is of an emotional nature but elicits only moderate involvement, then we should try to evoke some mood (not deep emotions). In either case, convenient display and availability is the next most important thing, as consumers will take action soon after giving it a little bit of thought or experiencing a little bit of feeling, as the case maybe.[5]

Consistency Among Think, Feel, and Do

If you could just look inside the consumer's mind where these three components of attitude reside, what kind of relationship would you expect to find? Would they be fighting among themselves, or alternatively, living in harmony. The answer, according to psychologists, is that they wouldn't be fighting, although each would be trying to mold the other in its own image. That is, if there is a favorable thought about a product and an unfavorable feeling, then the thought would be trying to bring the feeling into line with itself; on the other hand, the feeling would be attempting to tell the thought to think of

FIGURE 7.8 | THREE COMPONENTS IN HARMONY

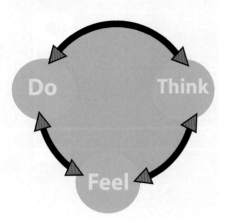

some negative belief about that product. This shouldn't look far fetched to you, as we all know how sometimes our hearts are trying to persuade our thinking minds, and vice versa.

The fact is that although the three components develop in a hierarchical fashion, they always imply one another. That is, no matter which formed first in the consumer's head, after they have stabilized, they exist together. And they exist in harmony. That is, consumers cannot harbor a set of thoughts and beliefs about a brand without bringing into line their feelings about it. Nor can they harbor some feeling about the brand without also bringing brand beliefs into line. Likewise, a consumer cannot have thoughts or feelings and not have corresponding intensions to act. The consumer cannot continue to believe, for example, that Honda is a more reliable car than Ford, but continue to buy Ford time after time. And a consumer cannot feel repulsed and angry every time he or she hears Eminem but still continue to buy his music.

Consumers' thoughts, feelings, and actions have to exist in harmony. For example, suppose that you recently bought a new CD release of Eminem, and after listening to it a few times, you realized that you don't really enjoy this sort of music anymore. In this case, you would have to modify some cognitions (e.g., "his lyrics really are nonsensical"), and, sooner or later, related conation too (e.g., "I won't buy it in the future"). In other words, your thoughts, your feelings, and your actions have to be consistent with one another.

Thus, in contrast to the previously described hierarchical models, Figure 7.8 shows the arrows going in both directions among all three of the components. The hierarchical models show us the sequence in which the components initially got formed. The present figure shows, instead, how the three components shape one another and co-exist in harmony.

FOUR FUNCTIONS OF ATTITUDE

Why Should We Hold Attitudes At All?

So far we have described what attitudes consist of and how they are formed, but not why they are formed and why we hold them. The answer is that they perform some function or serve some purpose for us. The overall function they serve is that they guide our approach/avoidance behavior. If we see an acquaintance across the hallway, we walk toward him or her if our attitude toward him or her is positive; if our attitude is negative, we turn away, pretending not to have noticed. If the next commercial is for our favorite presidential candidate, we stay focused and watch; if it is for a candidate we dislike, we walk away to do other more useful chores. If we see a five-cheese pizza on the menu and Greek salad, we shun the pizza and order salad or the other way around. But beyond this overarching function of approach-avoidance, are there more specific functions that attitudes serve? The answer is "Yes."

Psychologist Daniel Katz called this perspective the **functional theory of attitude**.[6] According to Katz's theory, people hold certain attitudes (or come to acquire those attitudes) because these attitudes serve one or more of the following four functions: utilitarian, value-expressive, ego-defensive, and knowledge. To illustrate these functions, we take you to U.S. Presidential Elections of 2004. We chose this context for two reasons: First, marketing applies, as you know, not only to commercial products and services, but also to arts, public wellbeing projects, voter choices, and myriad other fields, and many of you might just as well be planning to work for such non-traditional "marketing" organizations. Second, a U.S. Presidential election does make one of the best contexts to illustrate this concept, because voter feelings often run high. But don't worry. We will follow this up with examples of consumer attitudes toward everyday commercial products.

Four Functions in Voter Attitude

In the U.S. Presidential Elections of 2004, incumbent president George W. Bush was defending his seat against a respected senator from New England, veteran John Kerry, the nominee from the Democratic Party. Now, as is inevitable, some voters had a favorable attitude toward Mr. Bush and others did not. Why?

Here is how functional theory would explain it. Some voters expected to benefit personally from Mr. Bush's promised tax cut; that is Mr. Bush would bring these voters some utility (personal benefit). In effect, then, their attitude served a **utilitarian function**—offering them a personal benefit.

Other voters may not have cared for the tax relief; rather, what might have been important to them was that they were *pro-lifers* (not *pro-choice*), and Mr. Bush held the same pro-life values. These voters formed a favorable attitude toward Mr. Bush because of the **value-expressive** function. Conversely, pro-choicers had a negative attitude toward President Bush because his pro-life values were opposite to their own pro-choice values.

Still other voters may have liked Mr. Bush simply because, to them, John Kerry was an unknown person, whereas they had known Mr. Bush for the previous four years. And all other things being equal, we feel more comfortable with familiar people. This is the **knowledge** function. As humans, we like familiar things; we dislike uncertainty.

Finally, suppose a candidate had inadvertently slighted a group of voters or even an individual voter. That group or individual voter would then feel his/her ego hurt; in return, the voter would have to dismiss that candidate as being unworthy of his/her vote. That is, the voter would defend his/her ego tit-for-tat, by discrediting that candidate, or by developing a dislike for him or her. This is the **ego-defense** function of attitude.

Four Functions in Market Exchanges

Now to the commercial products scene. Consumer attitudes toward most everyday products are based, actually, on the utilitarian function. We like Vidal Sassoon brand of shampoo, for example, because it leaves our hair looking full. We like Honda cars because they will last a long time. And we may like fur coats because they keep us very warm in cold weather.

Many consumers like recyclable products because they have pro-environmental values. Many like Body Shop shampoos because the company does not use animal testing.

TABLE 7.1 Four Functions of Attitude

FUNCTION	DEFINITION	EXAMPLE
Utilitarian	The attitude object serves some utility.	I like George Bush because he will reduce Taxes. I like Vidal Sassoon because it does wonders for my hair
Value-expressive	The attitude object expresses one's values.	I like George Bush because he is like me, a pro-lifer. I like Body Shop shampoo because the company does not use animal testing, a cause I support.
Knowledge	The attitude object reduces uncertainty; gives us the comfort of knowing.	John Kerry is an unknown quantity to me; therefore I don't feel good about voting for him. I love People magazine because it keeps me informed about all the stars.
Ego-defense	The attitude object helps us protect our ego (self-esteem).	I don't like that candidate because he snubbed me. I don't like French restaurants, period. [Real reason: not being able to pronounce menu items threatens this consumer's self-esteem.]

And many don't like fur coats because they abhor the killing of animals. These are examples of value-expressive reasons for consumer attitudes. (Note that contrary to some early consumer research, value-expressive does not mean expressive of our images or symbolic associations, but expressive of our deeply held values about life. The ability of a product to help us express our identities or self-images is also, in truth, a utilitarian function.)

Next, many consumers like to read *People* magazine, for example, because it keeps them informed about their favorite stars. If we are taking a date to dinner—we had better go to a restaurant we know well so there will be no mishaps. Try a Tofu burger? We had better not—we don't know what it will taste like. Such attitudes are attributable to the knowledge function. The best examples of knowledge function are provided by "knowledge products," such as the Discovery Channel, or an encyclopedia like Encarta (a Microsoft software product), or a Web site full of information.

And now to the ego-defensive function. A consumer might dress nicely and drive a nice car (perhaps beyond his means) so that his neighbors will think he is successful in his career. He will take his date to a steak place rather than to the famous French restaurant in town because he can't pronounce the names of the exotic menu items there. Thus, this consumer's positive attitude toward dressing up nicely and his negative attitude toward French restaurants are both based on the ego-defense function. We might note that all these examples taken from our everyday lives (or from popular culture) are just as much examples of consumers' marketplace behavior as buying, say, a detergent or some candy. Table 7.1 summarizes these four functions with examples.[7]

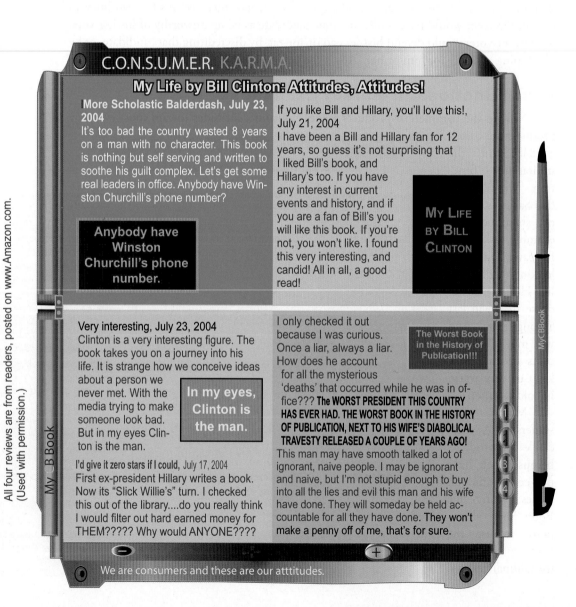

C.O.N.S.U.M.E.R. K.A.R.M.A.

My Life by Bill Clinton: Attitudes, Attitudes!

All four reviews are from readers, posted on www.Amazon.com. (Used with permission.)

More Scholastic Balderdash, July 23, 2004
It's too bad the country wasted 8 years on a man with no character. This book is nothing but self serving and written to soothe his guilt complex. Let's get some real leaders in office. Anybody have Winston Churchill's phone number?

> **Anybody have Winston Churchill's phone number.**

If you like Bill and Hillary, you'll love this!, July 21, 2004
I have been a Bill and Hillary fan for 12 years, so guess it's not surprising that I liked Bill's book, and Hillary's too. If you have any interest in current events and history, and if you are a fan of Bill's you will like this book. If you're not, you won't like. I found this very interesting, and candid! All in all, a good read!

> MY LIFE BY BILL CLINTON

Very interesting, July 23, 2004
Clinton is a very interesting figure. The book takes you on a journey into his life. It is strange how we conceive ideas about a person we never met. With the media trying to make someone look bad. But in my eyes Clinton is the man.

> **In my eyes, Clinton is the man.**

I'd give it zero stars if I could, July 17, 2004
First ex-president Hillary writes a book. Now its "Slick Willie's" turn. I checked this out of the library....do you really think I would filter out hard earned money for THEM????? Why would ANYONE????

I only checked it out because I was curious. Once a liar, always a liar. How does he account for all the mysterious 'deaths' that occurred while he was in office??? **The WORST PRESIDENT THIS COUNTRY HAS EVER HAD. THE WORST BOOK IN THE HISTORY OF PUBLICATION, NEXT TO HIS WIFE'S DIABOLICAL TRAVESTY RELEASED A COUPLE OF YEARS AGO!** This man may have smooth talked a lot of ignorant, naive people. I may be ignorant and naive, but I'm not stupid enough to buy into all the lies and evil this man and his wife have done. They will someday be held accountable for all they have done. **They won't make a penny off of me, that's for sure.**

> The Worst Book in the History of Publication!!!

We are consumers and these are our atttitudes.

Why is it important to know the function of an attitude? Because if we want to change a consumer's attitude toward something, we need to address the function it serves for that consumer. Telling a consumer how good the product's ingredients are (i.e., explaining the product's utilitarian function) would not help if the basic reason the consumer dislikes the product is because of the company's exploitation of child labor or because of its adverse effects on the environment (both relate to the value-expressive function), for example.[8]

MULTIATTRIBUTE MODELS OF ATTITUDE AND BEHAVIOR: TOVA, TORA, TOTA

One of the ideas we described earlier in the chapter was that beliefs are the basis of attitudes, particularly in the learning or rational hierarchy. Consumers learn about product features and <u>form</u> brand beliefs; these brand beliefs then lead to attitudes. You might want to say, okay, I want to be rational, so I want to base my attitude largely on rational beliefs. But not all of my beliefs are equally important to me; for instance, perhaps I don't care about some product features and qualities (which is what beliefs are about), whereas some other features are very useful to me. How do I combine these diverse beliefs to form an attitude?

Fortunately, for us, consumer researchers have already answered this question. The answer lies in multiattribute models. **Multiattribute models of attitude** suggest that overall attitude is based on the component beliefs about the object, weighted by the evaluation of those beliefs. There are three such models: (1) Theory of Value Assessment (TOVA), (2) Theory of Reasoned Action (TORA), and (3) Theory of Trying to Achieve (TOTA)[9]. Of these, TORA is the one most commonly used by marketers, and you will find it useful too. Let us explore it.

THEORY OF REASONED ACTION (TORA)

Martin Fishbein, a well-known scholar and a professor of psychology at the University of Illinois at Urbana-Champaign, proposed this theory. According to **the theory of reasoned action** (TORA),[10] our attitude toward an object is based on the consequences the object has, weighted by the desirability or undesirability of these consequences. (See Figure 7.9.)

Attitude = the extent to which the object will lead to a consequence (or the product will yield a certain benefit or cause certain harm) X the desirability or undesirability of that consequence—calculating this for each consequence and then summing across all relevant consequences

As an example, assume that consumer Nicole rates two Internet service providers, Earthlink and Netzero, as shown in Table 7.2. Using the data from the table, we can compute the consumer's attitude toward each service provider by using Fishbein's formula, as follows:

$A_{EARTHLINK} = 3(3) + 4(2) + 3(-3) + 2(-1) = 6$
$A_{NETZERO} = 5(3) + 4(2) + 3(-3) + 5(-1) = 9$

In this example, Nicole's attitude toward both services is positive, but it is more positive toward Netzero. Other consumers might well have different perceptions about the four attributes, as well as different evaluations (desirability or undesirability) for the attributes; consequently, they will have different attitudes.

FIGURE 7.9 THEORY OF REASONED ACTION (TORA) (The Basic Model)

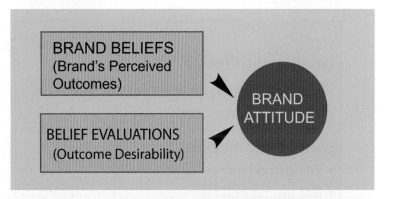

BRAND BELIEFS (Brand's Perceived Outcomes)

BELIEF EVALUATIONS (Outcome Desirability)

BRAND ATTITUDE

Multi-Attribute Model: Brand Attitude is based on Brand Beliefs (about the brand's consequences or outcomes) Weighted by Evaluations of Those Consequences.

TABLE
7.2

EXAMPLES OF CONSUMER ATTITUDES: TWO INTERNET SERVICE PROVIDERS

ATTRIBUTES	EXPECTATIONS about ATTRIBUTES (Unlikely 1 2 3 4 5 Likely)		EVALUATION OF CONSEQUENCES Very Bad Very Good -3 -2 -1 0 +1 +2 +3
	Earthlink	Netzero	
1. The connection will be established successfully every time.	3	5	+3
2. The connection will be established speedily.	4	4	+2
3. The connection will be dropped in the middle of the session.	3	3	-3
4. The price (monthly fee) will be high.	2	5	-1

Note: All attribute ratings are hypothetical and are used here merely for illustration. At any rate, even these hypothetical attribute ratings are examples not of any objective evaluations, but of perceprions of one hypothetical consumer.

Just so you don't think this math work was unnecessary busywork, look at Table 7.2 again. If we told you only what Nicole's brand beliefs about the two Internet services were, you wouldn't know how to figure out Nicole's attitude toward each brand. The multi-attribute model, TORA, helps you figure that out.

And TORA helps you figure out something else. Suppose we know that two of our friends, Colin and Bridget, have the same brand beliefs about tofu. Both believe that tofu is good for health but doesn't taste all that great and is rather cumbersome to cook. Yet, their attitude toward tofu is not the same—Colin's attitude is unfavorable, whereas Bridget's is favorable. Why? Look at Table 7.3. The reason is that Colin and Bridget differ in how desirable or undesirable they consider taste versus healthfulness of food. Now use the multiattribute model and calculate the attitude score and see for yourself how TORA explains why Colin dislikes tofu whereas Bridget likes it. In fact, if we didn't tell you that they do, you would have predicted it. And most marketers want to predict consumer attitudes toward their brands; for enabling this, they should be thankful to TORA.

We are almost done with the Fishbein's multiattribute model, but if you want to get a bit more sophisticated, read about the Fishbein's Extended Model.[11] (See Exhibit 7.1.)

TABLE
7.3

Two Consumers' Attitudes Toward Tofu

	Colin	Bridget
Beliefs about Attributes*		
• Eating tofu will be good for your health.	4	4
• Tofu will not taste good.	5	5
Evaluations of Attributes**		
• Being good for health is...	+2	+3
• Not tasting good is...	-3	-1

* Measured as Unlikely 1 2 3 4 5 Likely

** Measured as Very Undesirable -3 -2 -1 0 +1 +2 +3 Very Desirable

EXHIBIT 7.1   FISHBEIN's EXTENDED MODEL of BEHAVIOR

TORA actually covers more than attitude; it goes on to explain how attitudes then lead to behavior. Fishbein argued that an attitude captures our personal beliefs but that sometimes we are forced to act not entirely in accord with our wishes and our own brand beliefs; rather, and often, the expectations of others also influence our behavior. For example, someone may personally have an unfavorable attitude toward giving donations to an abortion clinic but may end up doing so due to the expectations of his or her co-workers or neighbors. These wishes of others are captured in the concept of **subjective norm**—what others expect us to do (i.e., normative expectations). These normative expectations are formed because of other people's desires and our own motivations to comply with them. These are computed by the same multiattribute weighting; i.e., the expectation of a specific person multiplied by our motivation to comply with that person's wishes (and then totaling this across all such persons who have expectations of us).

The personal attitude and subjective norm are then adjusted according to their relative weight (i.e., how important it is for a consumer to follow his or her own attitude versus the perceived need to comply with the expectations of others) and then summed. This weighted sum then leads to behavioral intention, which in turn, and finally, drives actual behavior. We know this is rather complex to follow at first, so take the time to follow its logic in Figure 7.10.

The distinctive advantage of Fishbein's extended model is that it accounts for social normative pressures as well as one's own internal beliefs about the consequences of a particular behavior—such as buying a specific brand of car. Explain to a teenager all you want about how utterly injurious to health smoking is, or how wearing a seatbelt can save his or her life in an automobile accident; yet if the teenager's peers consider smoking cool or wearing a seat belt "uncool," then your fact-laden pleas are probably going to fall on deaf ears. In many situations, the consumer's own assessments and personal attitudes are in favor of one alternative, but subjective norms temper them in favor of another.[11]

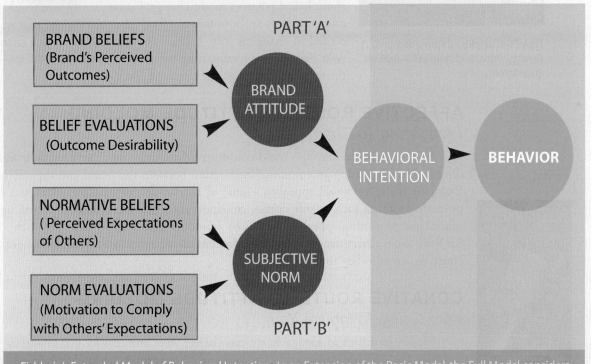

FIGURE 7.10

THEORY OF REASONED ACTION (TORA)
(The Full Model)

Fishbein's Extended Model of Behavioral Intention: In an Extension of the Basic Model, the Full Model considers both personal attitudes and expectations of people we consider our referents (here called *Subjective Norm*).

7   CONSUMER ATTITUDES

How May I Persuade Thee?

As marketers, we are interested not only in understanding and measuring consumers' current attitudes but also in molding and shaping them. If our brand is new, then we want to form, in the consumer's mind, a favorable attitude toward our new brand. If our brand has been in existence and consumers already hold an attitude toward it, and if that attitude is negative or less positive than their attitudes toward competing brands, then as marketers, we would surely want to modify that attitude. How can we accomplish that?

Here, the three-component model comes to our aid. The three-component model says, you remember, that beliefs (or cognitions), feelings, and action all influence one another; furthermore, a consumer tries to maintain them in harmony. Therefore, if we change one component, the other two components will follow suit, and the attitude (which consists of all three components) will be changed. Therefore, it is possible to mold an attitude by first molding or changing any one component. Accordingly, it gives us three choices or three routes by which to achieve this: (1) the cognitive route, (2) the affective route, and (3) the conative route. (See Figure 7.11.)

COGNITIVE ROUTE TO ATTITUDE MOLDING
I Am Going To Convince You

To follow the cognitive route, as a marketer, we provide an association (i.e., Brand 'A' has property 'X') with the product or service; if the consumer accepts that association,

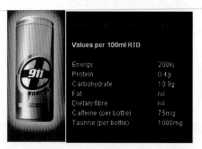

then a brand belief is formed. For example, suppose you knew nothing about soya, a Chinese food crop. Then you read somewhere that soya is a good source of protein, thus acquiring a new belief about soya (cognition formation). Or suppose you had a belief, say, that potatoes are fattening. And then the potato company gave you the facts: potatoes are fattening only if consumed as fries; by themselves, they have only about a hundred calories apiece. Then, your belief about baked potatoes might change. Consequently, you would look more favorably at the potato as a food item. Notice here that we succeeded in changing your attitude about potatoes by first changing your belief about its fattening property (or lack of it). In this case, the marketer has taken the cognitive route.

Read the product information on 911 Energy drink and help your attitude, cognitively.

AFFECTIVE ROUTE TO ATTITUDE MOLDING
I Am Going To Charm You

As marketers, we may also mold consumer attitudes by first changing their feelings directly and by creating an emotional connection between the brand and the consumer. Domestic marketers could appeal to a sense of patriotism, for example. Marketers often promote products such as soft drinks, colognes, and food with mood-inducing upbeat music. Just presenting appealing images of a product creates good feelings—such as the Air Walk shoes advertisement does. These feelings then create more favorable thoughts and create an intent to buy the product.[12]

CONATIVE ROUTE TO ATTITUDE MOLDING
I Am Going To Induce You

Finally, in this third approach, we can change your attitudes by first changing your behavior. For example, suppose you are unaware of a new shampoo (and therefore have no existing attitude toward it), and you receive a free sample and try it. In getting consumers to try it, marketers induce their behavior directly. Upon trial, a consumer may come to like the product—thus developing a favorable attitude.[13] Marketers also induce a con-

sumer to buy a product with special deals and coupons. Once the behavior is induced (e.g., the consumer buys a brand because of coupons), the cognitions and feelings will fall into place. Part of the appeal of this approach is that it may sometimes be easier to get consumers to try a sample than to convince them to think or feel in a new way. "Just try it," marketers often urge, confident that the experience will win the consumer over.

Use All Three Gateways

For some products, all three routes are possible. Suppose you have never donated blood, and thus you have no thoughts or feeling about it—that is, you have no attitude about it. Then, a marketer could tell you the benefits (to you and to others) of donating blood. Or the marketer could appeal to you emotionally by explaining how you could be saving a precious life. And, finally, a marketer can just get you to donate blood as part of a group campaign.

FIGURE 7.11
THREE Routes to Attitude Molding

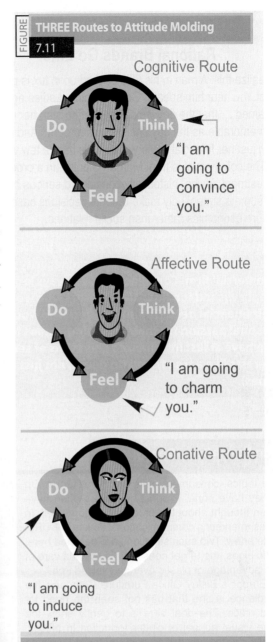

Cognitive Route

"I am going to convince you."

Affective Route

"I am going to charm you."

Conative Route

"I am going to induce you."

Winning your atttiude toward 911 Energy Drink through the *affective route*.

Especially if you look only at the photo and move on.

If you take in the text informaiton as well, then you will have also bolstered your attitude cognitively.

Rational Brands Go Emo!

Visualize this. A man in his 50's decked up in tux is proposing a wedding toast. You hear him speak: "Good evening, Ladies and Gentlemen. ... I have dreamed ... that the day we sent her off to start her own family is every bit as memorable as the day she first joined ours." And then he concludes: "But I am just her financial advisor. Now let's hear a few words from her dad."

The commercial is from Morgan Stanley. In a product category (investment advice) historically considered serious business, where consumers supposedly make rational decisions based on considerations of pure economics rather than social relations. **But come to think of it, nothing entails emotions (fear, hope) and requires comfort, assurance, and trust between exchange parties more than in the handing over of one's future financial security management to a commercial firm. Consumers have always looked to, or at least deeply wished for, financial advisors who would understand their financial needs intimately and who would guide them with personal passion for their wellbeing. Kudos to those marketers who have at last internalized this ethos of serving consumers' interests like a true friend (in deeds, not just in words, one hopes).**

An HSBC Courtesy Cab

(Reprinted with permission from brandchannel.com, Image by Tasha Walters)

Contd...

My CB Book

Attitude Formation—Gently

On some topics, consumers have strong attitudes. On others, they have none. Product non-users often have never even thought about the product category itself. In such cases, marketing communications' task is to FORM an attitude anew. Two such situations are depicted here. For plastic pipes, the target consumer is made aware of a relative advantage of plastic over galvanized iron.

For Europe's Bisley Office Furniture Company, the target audience is one that has not seen the need for organized office. The goal here is to gently show the reader the visual appeal of clutter reduction in offices. The creativity in the ads will produce a chuckle, helping brand atttitude.

The plastic pipe ad works purely via the rational/think/cognitive route. The Bisley ad amuses, and works, at least initially, via the affect/feel route. Both are delightful, and we believe stand up to the communication challenge they faced—namely, helping form consumer attitude where none existed.

Copy reads: Galvanized iron pipes crack due to corrosion. Our plastic pipes don't. (courtesy: Mudra Communications, India, and Reliance Industries, India.

SAVE LOTS OF SPACE
Introducing BISLEY InnerSpace

SAVE SPACE
New: BISLEY InnerSpace

(Courtesy: Bisley Kolle Rebbe)

Contd

Then there was a print campaign Mercedes ran a few years ago. The ad had Marilyn Monroe's face. That is all. No car, no car name, no text. Except a single word headline: Glamour. That and the little beautiful signature mole on Ms. Monroe's face was actually the Mercedes' tri-star logo. In another print ad in the series, a box of expensive chocolate with varied shapes had one chocolate in heart shape—with the tri-star logo on it! The single word copy on the printed page: Love.

Finally, third and last in our narrative is the really heart-warming story of an HSBC taxi seen a few years ago in New York City. HSBC is an Asian bank, which, in an act rare in the industry, decided to run a cab service for HSBC customers. If you have an HSBC bank card, you simply hail this red-and-white checkered cab (if you see it nearby, that is), and ride to your destination—FREE!

But there is more than just the free ride. The driver is dressed in khaki pants, a white button down shirt, and a bright red bow tie. And he is one of the most knowledgeable cabbies you will come across, familiar not only with every street in New York City but also able to talk about a wide range of subjects. He is a happy face person, proud that he is an ambassador of the bank. You will find him swerving the car to avoid a pigeon, stop for pedestrians and wave a smile at them, and never, never cut another car. After all, HSBC cab is recognizable and has HSBC name written on it, and his job is to create awareness and good feelings toward the name HSBC, among riders, fellow cabbies and drivers, and pedestrians alike.

He is one of the select few drivers HSBC recruited based on their skills to drive in and through hectic and maddening traffic of New York City with total calm and an unparalleled ability to connect with the riding customers. The social skills were assessed in a contest held at the Iridium Jazz Club, with celebrities as judges!

And the cab itself? It is a vintage 1981 model with a red and white checkered-design and totally cool looks.

These are all well-established, solid brands, and they have sought, and attained, a respectable consumer brand attitude. Only, now, they are pursuing an emotional basis for that attitude.

My CB Book

SOURCE: The HSBC story based on "Branded Life, Johnnie Morello drives customers to the brand," brandchannel. com, November 3, 2003. (http://www.brandchannel.com)

Motivating
Low Involvement Behavior

What is your attitude toward garbage—we mean toward the idea of placing your garbage in a trash can rather than just drop it anywhere? Most people don't hold any beliefs against it, nor do they have any negative feelings about the idea. On the other hand, they are not strongly motivated to do it either—pitch the trash in trash cans and nowhere else no matter what the effort. Except for some of us with heightened sense of civic ethics and/or aesthetics, for most consumers, it is a *low involvement* matter. They will do so if it is convenient. That is why, in most cities, local governments place trash cans every few blocks. China goes a step further—it does trash cans in style. See a sampling here. Harnessing the *low involvement hierarchy* par excellence. (Photo courtesy of Kathy Fogel)

Motivating
Low Involvement Behavior

CONSUMER STEREOTYPES
They Are Bad but Functional

Stereotypes represent a special case associated with the knowledge function, and their pervasive existence (we all have them) signifies just how extensive and material the role of attitude is. A **stereotype** can be defined as a perception we come to form about a whole category. Based on that stereotype, we then readily characterize a person (or object) without regard to his/her individuality.

Thus, stereotypes are attitudes toward a *category* of objects or persons. We hold them toward a category of people (e.g., Asian Americans) and toward a group of products, such as those made in Hong Kong. They enable consumers to efficiently "order" the world around them—that is, to give some structure to the world, to understand it in terms of what is what. Thus, stereotypes serve the "knowledge" function of attitudes. For decades, consumers have held a stereotype of car salesmen (especially the used car salesmen), for example, as highly unscrupulous, manipulative con artists; some companies such as Saturn and AutoNation are now fighting hard to overcome and change that stereotype through their marketing campaigns.

Did you notice that this chapter is somehow different from the preceding ones? In this whole section, appropriately titled "Inside the mind of the consumer," we have peeked deep inside the psyche of the consumer. This chapter, like those preceding it, also looked at the workings of the consumer mind, but with a crucial difference.

All of the previous chapters dealt with the basic processes of the human mind—perceptions, motivations, learning, and memory.

These are universal processes with which all humans' brains are equipped. The earlier chapters also looked at the psychological make-up of consumers produced by genetics and learning from environment and culture—factors that make each consumer the unique person that he or she is. These chapters were, then, about the consumer as a person, period—not about the marketplace.

In the present chapter, in contrast, and for the first time, we bring that person to the marketplace and see how he or she reacts to specific products and brands. Consumer attitudes are not about the consumer per se; rather they are about his or her reactions to products and brands. They at once enmesh both the consumer and the product or brand. They are a projection by the consumer, of his or her will, his or her desires, onto the products. They are a declaration of his or her liking or disliking of the product.

In a free marketplace, marketers live or die by consumer attitudes. That is why it is important for us to understand how consumer attitudes are formed. Here, we did cover quite some ground, ranging from simple description such as "like/dislike" to complex characterizations such as "predispositions"; from its rational and emotional sides to its complex multi-dimensional structures; and from psychological functions to practical applications in persuasion.

In the game of life, we are all marketers, trying to persuade others to our points of view. Next time you find yourself persuading someone, consider what you have learned about how people form attitudes. Then consider what you can do to shape that attitude in your favor. And in your role as a consumer, remember it is your attitude that the marketer is trying to win. Reflect on how your mind is made up about various brands, and reflect on whether you should revisit some of your brand attitudes.

Most of all, as marketers, never forget that the way to a consumer's wallet is through the consumer's mind. Whether through rational or emotional appeals, you have to win favorable consumer attitudes. Winning consumer attitudes is not a matter of clever advertising or some gimmicky promotion, mind you. And you can't shoot from the hip and hope that your market offerings and your messages will find believers.

Rather, to build positive and enduring consumer attitudes, you will need every bit of knowledge about how attitudes are formed and shaped. For that knowledge, read and reread this chapter, and do so with *involvement*.

Like OK Cola, countless products fail in the marketplace everyday, and for only one reason: they have failed to win a favorable consumer attitude. Must we, as marketers, not know, therefore, what an attitude is and how it is formed? We must. Therefore, we embarked upon an in-depth exploration of the classical definition of attitude—a learned predisposition. Next, we opened up its internal structure and we found, lying underneath, three components: beliefs or cognitions (thoughts), affect (feelings), and conation (action tendency or intent to act). We learned also that as consumers we acquire these three components in a specific sequence, depending on how rational or emotional we are. And we learned also that the three components exist in harmony.

Next, we discussed a functional theory of attitude. Advanced by psychologist Daniel Katz, this theory expounds on the motivational reasons why consumers hold attitudes at all. They hold attitudes, according to Katz, because these attitudes serve one or more of four functions: utilitarian, value-expressive, ego-defense, and knowledge. Often marketers, particularly of more important causes, don't take cognizance of these functions, and, consequently, they fail to address the root cause of attitudes.

Next, we introduced you to TORA—a multiattribute model of attitude structure. While somewhat complex to describe, understanding it is proportionately rewarding. We learned that TORA—theory of reasoned action—proposes that our attitude toward something is based on our component beliefs about the outcomes weighed by our evaluation (i.e., relative desirability) of these outcomes. That sounds sensible and logical, and TORA allows us to analyze consumer attitudes numerically and for a large number of consumers.

Having understood what attitudes are, we turned attention, naturally, to how to mold them. Here, we immediately recalled an inside secret we had learned earlier: no matter where you begin, all three components come into sync, and come to live in harmony. If they live in harmony, then we could, as marketers, set the process in motion by introducing any of the three components. It is true, we learned, that there is a cognitive or belief formation route to attitude formation—tell them about product attributes; and an emotional or feelings route—appeal to their emotions about the product; and a direct action route—induce the consumer to try our product. In time, all three components will converge.

We are now ready to deal with attitudes, ours and those of our consumers. If we apply the lessons of this chapter correctly, we will ensure that our product does not meet the fate of *OK Cola!*

Affect
Attitude
Attitude Hierarchy
Belief
Brand Belief
Conation

Ego-defense Function
Emotional Hierarchy
Fishbein's Extended Model of Behavior
Functional Theory of Attitude
Knowledge Function
Learning Hierarchy

Multiattribute Model of Attitude
Predisposition
Stereotypes
Theory of Reasoned Action
Utilitarian Function
Value-expressive Function

REVIEW✚Rewind

1. Define the concept of consumer attitude? Explain each of its elements.
2. How are attitudes measured?
3. Name and explain the three components of the ABC model of attitude.
4. Define belief and illustrate it with one belief statement about any brand.
5. Describe the statements by which each of the three components is measured.
6. What is meant by the word *hierarchy* in attitudes? How do learning and emotional hierarchies differ, and how do these in turn differ from the low-involvement hierarchy of attitudes? Illustrate each with a consumer example.
7. What is meant by the consistency between the three components?
8. What are the four functions of attitude? Explain each.
9. What is a consumer stereotype? Explain with an example.
10. Describe the TORA model.
11. Describe the extensions in the "Extended Fishbein Model."
12. Name and briefly explain the three modes of changing people's attitudes. Illustrate each by a marketing example.

7   CONSUMER ATTITUDES

203

1. What significance does the concept of attitude have for marketers? Why would you, as a marketer, want to measure consumer attitudes?
2. For each of the three attitude components, give two examples, drawing on your own attitudes toward any products or services.
3. Think of your current attitude toward any product, brand, organization, celebrity, musician, TV shows, courses, books, or whatever. Now identify one of these attitudes that serves, say, the utilitarian function; likewise identify one attitude for each of the other three functions.
4. Write down a complete survey to measure your attitude (all three components of it) toward: (a) your wireless service, and (b) your hair salon.
5. The three components of attitude are supposed to be consistent. Can you name an example from your own life as a consumer in which the three components may not be congruent? Discuss what your experience is with holding this attitude—are you constantly bothered and in struggle about it, or are you hardly bothered by it? How do you cope with this inconsistency?

PRACTICE**+**Experience

1. You want to measure consumers' attitudes toward body-piercing. Write down a questionnaire to measure these, taking into account all of the attitude components. Then administer this survey to two consumers, one with body piercing and the other without. Compare all attitude components. Do their attitudes differ along all components, and if not, how do you explain it?
2. Interview two consumers with significant body piercing and/or tattoos to understand their attitude toward consumption of tattoos and body piercing. Make sure you probe deeply to elicit their deep-rooted motivations for and gratifications from tattoos and body piercing. Identify which of the four functions these consumer attitudes serve for each of these two consumers.
3. Survey three consumers using a questionnaire that measures (a) the three components of attitude, (b) the Theory of Reasoned Action, and (c) the Extended Fishbein Model. Measure these for two competing brands of a high involvement product with which the chosen consumers should be very familiar (e.g., two PDAs or two video game players—show pictures and brief descriptions to them). Then compute the models for each consumer and see if the models work —the brand that is rated higher on components of the model more favorably is also the brand the consumer prefers more. Explain your results.

In the Marketing Manager's Shoes

Put yourself in a marketing manager's shoes. Most concepts in the chapter have some lessons for the marketing manager; i.e., they suggest what to do differently in practice. Indeed, often these applications are implicit in our explanations of the concepts and models in the chapter. Identify at least five specific applications of the chapter's concepts, all of which should be entirely new—different from the examples cited here.

A Photo Essay and a Quiz
Wear Your Bricks in Style

Bricks are bricks. What do you look for when you are buying bricks. That they be strong; be shaped as perfectly rectangular blocks; the color should not fade; and the material should not decay. May be it should come in a choice of colors. It is a pretty drab and dull thing to choose. Right?

Think again. At least a company named Hanson Bricks sees bricks otherwise. In this utterly delightlul set of visuals, the company shows us how bricks are a "fashion statement." Or should be.

Take the time to enjoy the ads, and then we will have a couple of questions for you.

It also covers the most fashionable neighborhoods.

Hanson
The face of brick™

HANSONBRICK.COM
1.877.HANSON8

DISCUSSION QUESTION

Okay, it is time to do some analytical thinking. Who would these ads appeal to more, to a high or a low involvement consumer? Or, alternatively, can these ads transform a low involvement consumer into a high involvement consumer? Or into a different kind of high involvement consumer? (did they do this for you?)

The ads take you on an emotional hierarchy route, don't they? Does it mean the consumer would abandon the rational route?

Will the same approach work for a new brand of bricks? Why or why not?

Finally, what would you suggest as prerequisites for a company or a brand to embrace a similarly adorable message strategy?

THEORY OF VALUE ASSESSMENT (TOVA)

You have already read about TORA; now meet its cousin TOVA. Well-known psychologist Milton Rosenberg proposed this theory, actually called the *value-instrumentality model* (TOVA being our name for it). According to the **theory of value assessment** (TOVA), our attitude toward an object is based on how well it promotes the values in which we believe, weighted by the relative importance to us of those values:

Attitude = the extent to which the object will promote a value X the importance of that value to the consumer—calculating this for each value and then summing across all relevant values.

Take a consumer who is considering patronizing a store owned by a minority person. His response depends on his attitude, and to find his attitude, we need to add together each of the values this behavior satisfies (e.g., patriotism, encouraging the disadvantaged, rewarding the spirit of enterprise, and so on), weighted by the importance of these values to the consumer.

How does TOVA differ from TORA, you might wonder. Here is how. In TOVA, the beliefs are about our deeply held values—thus, it applies to attitudes that serve a value-expressive function. The objects of attitude here are such that they evoke our deeply held values. These objects include fur, animal tested products, products made with inhuman labor, artificial foods, products proscribed by religion, etc. In contrast, in TORA, the consequences are all "value neutral" product benefits or harms. This model applies, therefore, to products where attitudes are based on the utilitarian function—cars, appliances, food products, etc. And one more thing. TOVA works well with value-based consumer segments (e.g., pro-choice versus pro-life voters; pro-environmental voters and their counterparts; and so on). In contrast, TORA works best with benefit segmentation (e.g., health-conscious versus taste craving consumers of food; economy versus status image for a car; etc.).

THEORY OF TRYING TO ACHIEVE. (TOTA)

TORA and TOVA have one more cousin, one with a bit more muscle, if you will. Accordingly, it can handle a bit more complicated situations, and it is called TOTA.[14] The problem is that TORA and TOVA work well when the "reasoned behavior" in question is a one-time action—like buying an SUV instead of a gas-economizing small car, or undergoing laser eye vision surgery, or getting a tattoo. How about dieting, trying to quit smoking, becoming a vegetarian, taking up an exercise program, etc.? These require repeated concerted actions, and there is no guarantee you will succeed. Theory of Trying to Achieve (TOTA) models how a consumer would decide whether or not to try to achieve some goal, such as weight reduction or adopting a healthy eating pattern. This model is shown in simplified form in Figure 7.12, and is illustrated for a consumer trying to lose weight.

As this figure shows, attitude toward trying (ATT) is based on three sub-attitudes: attitude toward success, attitude toward failure, and attitude toward the process itself. We may love the idea of becoming slim or, instead, be merely pleased; e.g., "It will be kind of nice; that is all" (attitude toward success). On the flip side, if we fail, we may feel miserable, or instead we may see the failure as no big deal (attitude toward failure). And finally, we may feel good or bad about the very regimen of exercise and eating (attitude toward process).

Of course, each of these three sub-attitudes are in turn based on their own multi-attribute models—i.e., perceived consequences of succeeding, of failing, and the process, weighted by the desirability of these consequences (not shown in figure). This is illustrated by two consequences of each attitude below. These can be measured by asking the consumer to indicate how likely he or she thinks it is that each consequence will occur and then also how desirable/undesirable each consequence is. Multiplying the two and adding up across all consequences would give us the three attitudes.

Next, the Attitude toward Trying is also affected by two expectations: expectations of success and expectations of failure. If consumers expect to succeed, then they are likely to keep at it; instead, if they expect to fail, then they may not even begin. (Success and failure are not always exactly opposites; a consumer may define success only when he or she loses say 10 lbs but may define failure if no weight were lost at all.) This completes part 'A' of the model (see Figure 7.12).

Part 'B' extends the model from "attitude toward trying" to "intent to try and actual trying." Here, two new factors enter the picture. The first is "social norms toward trying"— i.e., the expectations of our significant others. As we all know, when it comes to trying lifestyle changes, expectations of significant others can sometimes play a big role, even more than our own attitudes. And the second factor is "the recency and frequency of past behavior." The more recently you tried and the more frequently you have tried some difficult change, the more likely are you to try again.

This, then, is the theory of trying. See for yourself how it works for some of your endeavors. For starters, you may want to complete the list of the consequences of trying for weight loss in the above list, and then complete all other components of the model. And then reflect on each component—what can you change so as to help yourself get better at trying?[15]

FIGURE 7.12 A THEORY OF TRYING TO ACHIEVE (TOTA)

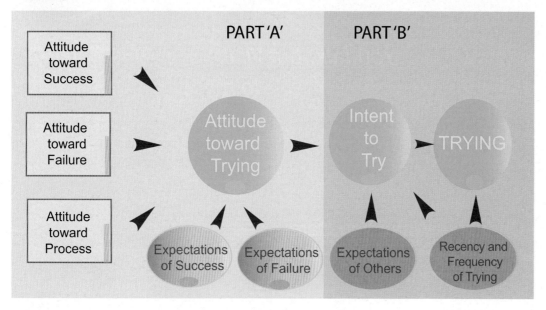

PART 'A'   PART 'B'

Attitude toward Success

Attitude toward Failure

Attitude toward Process

Attitude toward Trying

Intent to Try

TRYING

Expectations of Success

Expectations of Failure

Expectations of Others

Recency and Frequency of Trying

Legend

Internal States   External Constraints and Factors   Consumer Activity/ Behavior to be explained

Consequences of Succeeding, Failing, and the Process in Trying to Lose Weight

Success	Failure	Process
• Get better data	• Increased risk to health	• Working out at gym is boring
• Have to buy new clothes	• Might suffer career opportunity loss	• Have to eat bland food

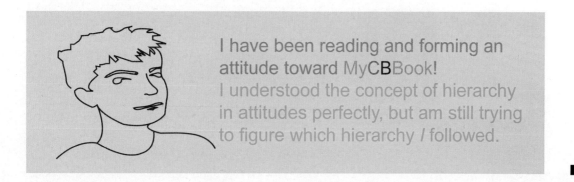

I have been reading and forming an attitude toward MyCBBook!
I understood the concept of hierarchy in attitudes perfectly, but am still trying to figure which hierarchy I followed.

Molding Attitudes:

Consumer Response To Market Communications

You talk, but I'll listen to myself.

- Attitude Change—When You Care Vs. When You Don't
- Heider's Balance Theory
- When Consumers Persuade Themselves—Active Vs. Passive Audiences
- Fear, Humor, Sex, Celebrity—When Do They Work?
- Getting Customers To Like You— Persuation in Interpersonal Selling

Every year from July 7th-14th, Pamplona, Spain is busy with activities surrounding "Encierro," the famous bull-running festival of San Fermin.

On the morning of July 7, hundreds of young men gather at Santo Domingo. Then a herd of bulls is released from their corral, and the young men start running, with the bulls behind them. At first the bulls are far behind, and the runners are running slowly. Then, as the bulls get closer, the runners start running faster, making their way though city streets filled with cheering spectators. In the mile long run, some drop out, some get stampeded, and a few, fueled by a fresh adrenaline rush, make it safely to the finish line. Later that day, there is a bullfight in a big arena where the bulls fight until they get killed.[1]

Photography by Ander Gillenea
Photo Courtesy PeTA, USA

Of immense thrill to thousands of spectators, there is one group that is NOT pleased—People for the Ethical Treatment of Animals (PeTA). To protest against the event, they organize a different kind of run: "Encierro Human," humans only—clothes optional. Started in 2002, members and activists run just two days before the bull run event. In July 2005, almost 600 activists ran the streets, many unclad, with only a poster in hand, much to the delight of an amused crowd of spectators, and chanting "Stop the bloody bullfights!"

These runners are telling the world, says PeTA's campaign coordinator William Rivas-Rivas, "that the torture of bulls will not be tolerated and that caring, daring and baring individuals will be back every year until the bulls are left out of the annual festivities." [2]

INTRODUCTION

Will PeTA and its "Running of the Nudes" campaign succeed in stopping the bullfight? It is difficult to predict—for three reasons. First, the bull run is a sacred ritual, honoring patron saint, San Fermin. Second, it is a big tourist attraction that pulls in a good deal of money for local businesses. And third, it is, well, a time-honored tradition, and a source of thrill to millions of Spaniards all across Spain. So, only time will tell.

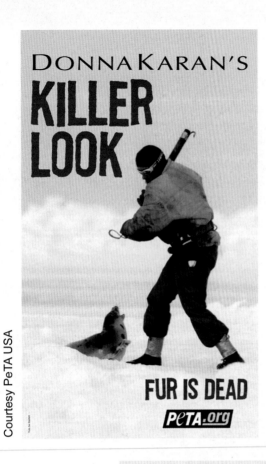

DONNA KARAN'S

KILLER LOOK

FUR IS DEAD

PeTA.org

PeTA has been quite successful, however, with its other campaigns. One of its most famous campaigns has been against fur (since fur is obtained by killing animals). That campaign has garnered the public support of celebrities ranging from Alicia Silverstone, Charlotte Ross, Goran Visnjic, Dennis Rodman, and Charlize Theron, among others. Its posters and print and video ads are graphically moving, such as the one depicting Donna Karan as an animal butcher. Its protest campaigns have resulted in many fashion and youth retailers such as H&M, Forever 21, Gap Inc., Banana Republic, and others pledging not to sell fur clothing. On November 30, 2005, PeTA finally succeeded in eliciting the same pledge from a longtime holdout, J. Crew.[3]

What does it take to change people's attitudes? Look at the PeTA ad featuring Donna Karan; does it alter your attitude toward the use of fur clothing? Why or why not? This question is of great interest to marketers. In this chapter, we are going to describe various theories and methods of changing consumer attitudes.[4] If you suspect that these theories, well, being theories, are dull, then, along the way, we are also going to change your attitude toward these theories themselves. Attitude change, you'll find, is one of the most fascinating topics, and it is also one of the most practical ones—a tool marketers deploy every day. So read on.

ATTITUDE CHANGE

When You Care versus When You Don't

Suppose we want to change your attitude toward using fur—to get you to start using fur if you are not already using it, or to get you to stop using it if you do. You would use fur if you developed a positive attitude toward it; you would stop using it if you developed a negative attitude toward it. How do we develop this new attitude in you? This depends on whether wearing or not wearing fur is a high involvement or a low involvement issue for you.

INVOLVEMENT AND THINK-FEEL GRID FOR ATTITUDE CHANGE

If you think of all the issues in your life that require decisions (e.g., who to vote for, whether or not to attend a PTA meeting, whether or not to wear fur, whether or not to send Lisa flowers, etc.) and all the product and brand choices you have to make (e.g., which cola to drink, which ear to pierce, which movie to see this weekend, etc.), your attitudes toward these issues and objects can be divided into four quadrants on a grid. This grid is formed by two axes (or dimensions): the "involvement axis" and the "think-feel axis."

Is your involvement in the issue high (e.g., should you sign up for the U.S. Army, should you paint your car pink or green, etc.) or is it low (e.g., should you cut through the lawn or take the pathway, should you save the can for later recycling or just toss it in the nearest trash can, etc.)? And, is the issue or the choice of the brand or product a rational (THINK) matter with you (e.g., which cereal is good for my health?), or you get pretty emotional (FEEL) about it (e.g., "Is there a better way to show her my love than to tattoo her name on my arm?")? Cross these two dimensions or axes and we could locate your attitude change problem in one of the four quadrants. This grid was invented by the ad agency Foote, Cone, and Bolding (FCB), so it is aptly called the FCB Grid.[5] See Figure 8.1.

Now, our message will have to be designed differently depending on the quadrant. First, in the two THINK quadrants, our message will have to be rational—this means we will have to tell you what the product does and what concrete benefits it will deliver to you. In the HIGH INVOLVEMENT THINK quadrant, we will present you with as many features and benefits as our product has, giving you the strongest argument we can muster (e.g., "You should join the Army because it will train you in rare and useful skills, you will learn discipline, you will stay fit, earn a good salary, and build a career"). In contrast, in the LOW INVOLVEMENT THINK quadrant, you want to hear a rational argument, but you don't want to exert too much effort in thinking about it. You will want to know quickly one or two good things about that brand. Accordingly, in this quadrant, we will focus only on one or two simple rational brand benefits.

For the "feel" issues or product choices, with high involvement (HIGH INVOLVEMENT FEEL) we will have to make the message emotional. Rather than tout the product's physical or rational benefits, we will have to move you emotionally—whether that emotion is fear, hope, love, guilt, pride, or whatever. "You should join the Army," we might say, "because it will make your nation proud, you will protect innocent civilians against barbarian oppression, and you'll serve an honorable cause."

Lastly, in the fourth quadrant (LOW INVOLVEMENT FEEL), we will present the brand visually to create a positive impression, and/or we will set it up in a good mood setting. Essentially and foremost, the purpose of our ad here is to create a positive mood in the consumer—provide the consumer with a pleasant or humorous thought or image and cause him or her to smile or even chuckle about our brand, thereby creating an affectively charged cloud in the consumer mind.

FIGURE **8.1** THE FCB GRID OF INVOLVEMENT

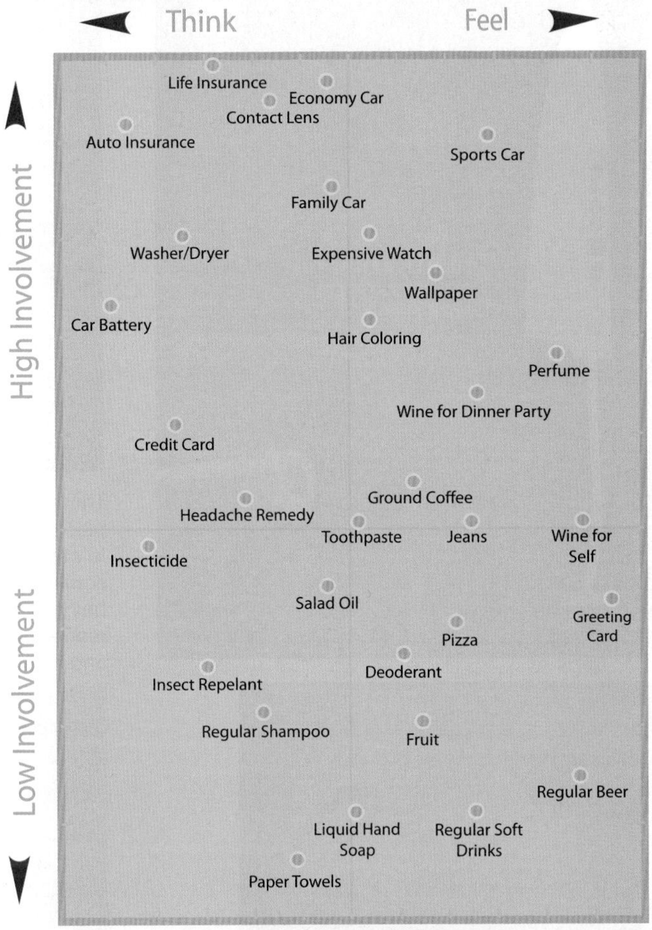

Source: Brian T. Ratchford, "New Insights About The FCB Grid," *Journal of Advertising Research*, 1987, 27, 4, p. 31. ©Copyright The Advertising Research Foundation. (Reprinted with permission.)

Central and Peripheral Routes

A "low involvement ad" should present a brand visually and present only a single *simple* product benefit. But what happens if we present an ad with long copy and many brand details even for a low involvement product? Well, for starters, consumers are not going to read a long ad for a brand of salt or mouthwash, for example. But suppose a mouthwash company did advertise its brand using a long copy. How would different consumers read it?

Questions such as this have always intrigued consumer researchers. Recently, researchers have found a pretty good answer, summed up as the "Central and Peripheral Route to Persuasion."[6]

Through the **central route**, as consumers, we process the message with attention. We center our attention on the message, read the entire text or listen to all the words, think them over, and then choose to accept the message or, alternatively, to dismiss it. If we find

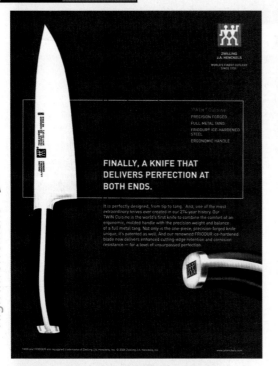

FINALLY, A KNIFE THAT DELIVERS PERFECTION AT BOTH ENDS.

High Involvement ▲

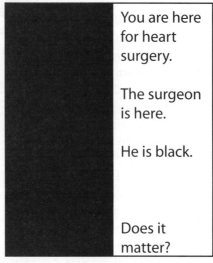

You are here for heart surgery.

The surgeon is here.

He is black.

Does it matter?

The "surgeon is black" ad with this gist was placed in media some years ago. (Source information unavailable.) No claim of actual resemblance with the original ad is being made. The goal in this rough rendering is merely to capture the gist, and it is used here for illustration only.

Low Involvement ▼

Photo courtesy Procter & Gamble

Copy reads: It's like a dust magnet. The Swiffer Duster has fluffy flexible fibers that actually trap and lock dust better than ordinary feather dusters. And its extendable handle reaches virtually everywhere.

Courtesy: VCD, Paddington, NSW, Australia.

It might shock you to see the Swiffer and Diet Coke ads in the low involvement quadrants. Let us clarify. The ads themselves are NOT *low involvement* ads. Rather, it is that dusting is not a highly involving topic, not at the time consumers are seeing the ad anyway; and the Diet Coke consumer may be involved in the brand, even highly involved, but there is not much more he/she cares to know about a soda. The task then is to say something simple and quick (THINK—the swiffer ad), or show a quick-impression visual (FEEL—diet coke). To get attention and catch the fancy of such "low involvement," "I am not concerned about it now," consumer is precisely the challenge low involvement ads typically face. The vibrant colors in the Swiffer ad serve to capture attention, and then the simple "ordinary duster+magnet=Swiffer" message, presented both visually and in text, drives home the brand benefit to the otherwise low involvement consumer.

In the diet coke ad, it is the admirable creativity that will in fact engage the reader, transforming him/her into a more involved consumer. As to the **J.A. Henckels knife** ad (see copy on facing page), it communicates the "high tech" features of this precision perfect knife. The ad will attract mostly "high involvement consumers," but it has to hope also, rightly, that those not currently involved will, should they take the time to read the ad, feel educated that not all knives are the same. As to the **black surgeon** ad, its intended FCB audience is one with strong prior attitude (i.e., prejudice), a condition of high FEEL INVOLVEMENT.

the message believable, then we accept it and are persuaded; if not, then we dismiss the message and are not persuaded.

Through the **peripheral route**, we process the message superficially. We don't pay attention to the exact words, nor do we bother to read or hear the entire message text. Instead, we are impressed (or unimpressed) by some superficial elements of the ad. For example, if the ad is visually pleasing, or there is a character in a TV commercial who is funny or annoying, or even that the ad seems to contain a long list of benefits, then based on these mere peripheral elements, we form a quick impression about the brand. This is attitude change occurring through the peripheral route, a route we choose when we are not involved with the product being advertised.[7]

Back to the mouthwash ad with the long copy—the high involvement consumers are very likely to read the entire ad, and based on their acceptance of the argument, they will most likely be persuaded. Low involvement consumers, on the other hand, may only notice the colorful bottle, and will perhaps infer, without reading the copy, that the ad contains a scientific explanation of how the product works. And if there were a scientific explanation, then, they would figure, the brand must be good. That is their peripheral processing at work!

Elaboration Likelihood Model

Actually, through the central route, consumers do more than merely pay attention to the entire ad content. They elaborate on it. They construct a vision of the product or of themselves using the product. An ad for a new mountain bike makes them visualize how the new drive chain in the bike would give them more thrust for the same amount of footwork, or how they would enjoy it at the next summer camp. This happens, of course, only when consumers have high involvement in the product. Just as the **elaboration likelihood model (ELM)** states: the higher the consumer involvement, the higher the likelihood that the consumer will elaborate on the message.[8]

What is the advantage if consumers "elaborate"? First, the message will get processed fully, so consumers will have noted all the points made in the ad. And, second, since they will have personally and consciously interacted with the message, they will be more likely to remember the message later. Of course, processing with elaboration is a double-edged sword: The message goes through intense scrutiny, and, therefore, if the message is hype (flimsy, hollow, and not credible), then the attitude change happens in the wrong direction, i.e., against the brand.[9]

> ### Ponder This
> Of course, "wrong" means from the marketer's perspective; from the consumer's perspective, an elaborated message always leads to more realistic brand perceptions. In peripheral processing, consumers trade efficiency for accuracy. Some brand perceptions are formed quickly and may be inaccurate; but because the product or brand choice is not very consequential (that is why the consumer used low involvement processing), the slight inaccuracy is not harmful.

Want to see more elaboration in the ELM itself? Follow this description with Figure 8.2. It begins when the consumer is exposed to the message. He or she judges the message topic as either high or low involvement, and based on that judgment he or she decides to pay high (focused) or low (cursory) attention. High attention stimulates central processing and, correspondingly, high elaboration; in contrast, low attention results in peripheral processing and low elaboration, or, in fact, no elaboration at all.

With elaboration, the message is either judged relevant and truthful, and, consequently, positive brand beliefs are formed. Or, alternatively, the message is evaluated as hyped and untruthful, and negative brand beliefs are consequently formed. These beliefs (e.g., "this wine is well made") and associations (e.g., "it is for really cool people") are strong (i.e., the

Zwilling J.A. Henckles ad (facing page) reads: It is perfectly designed, from tip to tang. And, one of the most extraordinary knives ever created in our 274-year history. Our Twin Cuisine is the world's first knife to combine the comfort of an ergonomic, molded handle with the precision weight and balance of a full metal tang. Not only is the one-piece, precision-forged knife unique. It's patented as well. And our renowned Friodur ice-hardened blade now delivers enhanced cutting edge retention and corrosion resistance—for a level of unsurpassed perfection.

FIGURE
8.2

Elaboration Likelihood Model

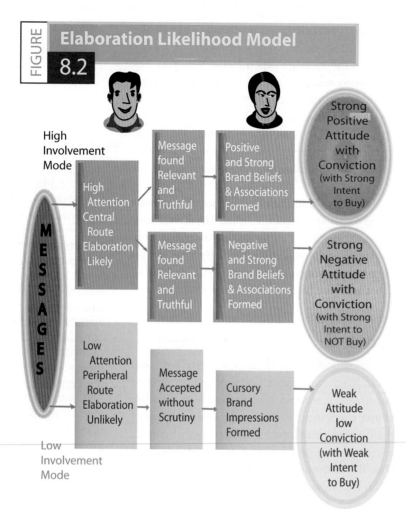

High Involvement Mode

MESSAGES

High Attention Central Route Elaboration Likely

Message found Relevant and Truthful

Positive and Strong Brand Beliefs & Associations Formed

Strong Positive Attitude with Conviction (with Strong Intent to Buy)

Message found Relevant and Truthful

Negative and Strong Brand Beliefs & Associations Formed

Strong Negative Attitude with Conviction (with Strong Intent to NOT Buy)

Low Attention Peripheral Route Elaboration Unlikely

Message Accepted without Scrutiny

Cursory Brand Impressions Formed

Weak Attitude low Conviction (with Weak Intent to Buy)

Low Involvement Mode

consumer is confident about them), well considered as they are. These beliefs and associations are also multiple in number, based either on a multi-claim message or on internal elaboration, and in turn produce attitudes that are well founded in the consumer's mind, attitudes that are more certain, strong, and marked by conviction. In turn, they lead to a strong intent to buy (if the formed attitude is positive), or an equally strong intent not to buy (if the formed attitude is negative).

In the low elaboration, peripheral processing mode, quick impressions are formed pertaining to the brand as a whole (e.g., "here is this new soda") or its single attribute (e.g., "okay, so this soda has fewer calories"); based on a single, quick belief or impression, the resulting attitude is weak (e.g., "I am not sure, but then it doesn't really matter—I mean I don't have to be absolutely sure") and ephemeral (not enduring), with "a take it or leave it" intent (e.g., "Okay, maybe I'll try it sometime").

MOLDING ATTITUDES THROUGH MULTI-ATTRIBUTE MODELS

Learning about the multi-attribute model in the last chapter took some work. You can now put all that hard work to some use. As a marketer, you can deploy that model to change consumer attitudes.[10] You might have noticed that the essence of the multi-attribute model (TORA) is the multiattribute format of the attitude structure (i.e., beliefs weighted by evaluation of belief content). Given this structure, we can change consumer attitudes in three ways[11]:

1. By changing a specific component belief, which can be accomplished by changing the perception of the corresponding attribute level or associated consequence.
2. By changing the importance that the consumer assigns to an attribute or to the evaluation of that consequence.
3. By introducing a new attribute (i.e., evaluation criteria) into the consumer's evaluation process.

Let us consider the example of Earthlink versus Netzero discussed in the previous chapter. To improve consumer attitude toward its brand, Earthlink has the following options:

- The company can improve its connection success rate and communicate this improvement to the consumer.
- Since it already has a superior rating on speed, it can try to emphasize the desirability of high speed, thus raising the speed's evaluation from the current rating of +2 to, say, +3.
- Earthlink can offer some new feature like a spam filter or privacy protection, and then communicate to the consumer the importance of this new feature.

For technological products, this last option is particularly appealing. Since technological products are always evolving (e.g., portals like Earthlink, browsers, cell phones, PDA's, etc.), consumers are always looking for new features, and companies that can bring new features to the market sooner are more likely to win the consumer attitude battle.

Consider the new features Earthlink has introduced within only the last five years: the user now has the ability to check email by phone; to check PC performance and fix errors; to protect against email virus; to block unwanted email; ability to sort emails by date, sender name, and subject; send customized reminders, alerts, sports scores and other information to mobile phones; to automatically forward IMs (Instant Messages) to a mobile phone; get notification when a buddy is online; to send receive emails via a PDA; and so on. These are new attributes for many consumers; these are also the new frontiers of attitude battle in all sorts of gizmos.

In this ad, from India, Levi's flashes its Button Fly feature, hoping the new attribute will further bolster consumer attitudes toward the brand.

Copy reads: Made from the same steel that goes into your car's chassis. Button Flies. (The dog regrets biting, and, in excruciating pain, barks: e o w w w)

Courtesy: J. Walter Thompson, Banglore, India, (Featured in Lürzer's Int'l Archive, Vol. 6, 2005)

> ### Ponder This
> While we call them tools of attitude molding, don't blame modern marketing for it. Note that when we say "you can change an attribute perception," we don't mean that it is possible to change it in thin air. Rather, we mean that IF your product indeed has some attributes to a degree consumers have somehow underestimated, THEN you can attempt to bring their perceptions in line with reality (but not beyond).

HEIDER'S BALANCE THEORY

FIGURE **8.3** HEIDER'S BALANCE THEORY

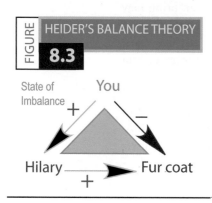

State of Imbalance

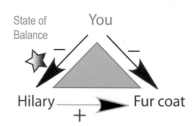

State of Balance

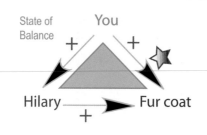

State of Balance

State of Balance

LEGEND

Liking →
Disliking →
What Changed ✦

You love and adore pop princess Hilary Duff. And it is good that she loves animals and, being an animal lover yourself, you are thrilled that she has just come out with a cosmetics line of her own which is kept animal-cruelty free. Made by Townley Cosmetics, it is called "Stuff by Hilary Duff." Now, suppose one day Ms. Duff decides to start promoting fur coats by Donna Karan? This is going to cause you some mental anguish, for sure, but the question is, how are you going to make peace with it? Heider's balance theory can help us answer that question.

Fritz Heider, a social psychologist, proposed a theory in 1946 that explains how we deal with conflict in our attitudes toward any given two entities.[12] In the above example, the two entities are Ms. Duff and fur. **Heider's balance theory** maintains that in any relationship between three entities, a state of imbalance cannot be sustained, and it will be resolved by altering one of the relationships. The third entity here is "you." The relationships among these three entities are imbalanced, which is why you are experiencing a conflict or dissonance. There are three options available to you: a) you start liking fur, b) you start disliking Ms. Duff, or c) you get Ms. Duff to stop liking and promoting fur. Each option represents an attitude change. Either your attitude toward fur will have to change, or your attitude toward Ms. Duff will have to change, or you will have to change Ms. Duff's attitude toward fur.

Achieving any of these options is easier said than done. Which way the change would occur depends upon which current attitude is stronger. If you really like Ms. Duff a lot, then you will have to modify your attitude toward fur. You don't have to start liking it, but you do have to stop disliking it, so that seeing Ms. Duff wear and promote fur doesn't keep you from enjoying her music. But if you cannot stand fur at all, then you must give up watching Ms. Duff on MTV.

Seen any application of this theory lately? Firms always use likeable celebrities to endorse their brands. And good thing, Pepsi doesn't run those commercials with Michael Jackson anymore!

Now, we have a quiz for you. What is your opinion of vegans? Or, about the practice of yoga? Are they cool secrets to living healthy lives, or, alternatively, some utterly senseless remnants of the hippy era? Now, what if we were to show you this headline:

> Avril Lavigne Goes Vegan
> "I'm on a vegan diet, I do yoga every day, I work out, I'm totally spiritual ..."
> (*Calgary Sun*) Source: PeTA Web site (DoA: April 21, 2006)

Now, what is your opinion of being a vegan? Or, the practice of yoga? That depends on your attitude toward Avril Lavigne herself. On this, we will let you work out the Heider's triangle.

ATTRIBUTION THEORY

You have met this theory before—remember the motive for attribution. As humans, we are hardwired to assign causes to events. To whom or to what we assign causes is something we learn, but the basic instinct to assign causes is an innate motive.[13] Marketers need to make sure that consumers don't misattribute a product's failure to the company if in fact the consumers themselves are at fault. We will let you devise ways to ensure that. Note though that preventing a wrong attitude is just as important as changing an attitude.[14]

Marketers can and do also use attribution theory to mold attitudes. Suppose there is a brand of cereal you have never tried and have felt no desire to try. Now suppose there is a $1 coupon (for a $2 box!); would you buy it? Many consumers would. And then what? They use it and don't think much of it; their attitude toward that cereal then remains unimproved. Why? Because, they attribute the reason for their buying and consuming that cereal to the hefty deal they got. Instead, give them a smaller incentive, say a coupon worth only 25 cents; in this case then, they will attribute the cause for choosing and using it to their own preferences. And if the brand of cereal were any good, they would begin to think of it in a positive light.

While there is the possibility that many consumers would not be attracted by a small deal (such as only 25 cents off), is it really worth getting people to buy your product with a huge bribe (i.e., a big coupon)? Do you really want them to attribute the purchase to the external- (coupon) rather than an internal (themselves) factor? Remember, blame or credit, internal, directed-to-self attribution always helps.

SELF-PERCEPTION THEORY

A related theory is *self-perception*, advanced by psychologist Daryl Bem.[15] Bem proposed that we infer our attitudes from our own behavior. If we are screaming (behavior), then we must be angry and annoyed (attitude). In case the "new idea" in this theory has not hit you, recall that the classical theory we covered in the previous chapter was that our attitudes cause our behavior. But Bem's theory says, instead, that sometimes we don't have attitudes of which we are conscious; put differently, we are sometimes not conscious of our attitudes just *prior* to our behavior. If so, our attitudes don't cause our behavior—the behavior erupts as a direct response to some stimulus; or perhaps the attitude operates at a subconscious level. In these cases, says Bem, if we go looking for our attitudes, we end up inferring them by observing our behavior and assigning a logical attitude to it. "If we are using a product," we tell ourselves, "then we must like it. Yes, we do like it. Our attitude toward that product? Well, of course, it is favorable!" Got it?

There are two pragmatic versions of the theory that marketers can use; these are called "foot in the door" and "door in the face." With the **foot in the door** technique, a marketer makes a small request which the consumer cannot (or usually won't) refuse; subsequently, the marketer makes a larger request. A political campaign organization will ask you, for example, to display a small sign in your front yard, or to show up at a short meeting in the neighborhood. If you comply, then, later, you may be asked to put a larger banner in your front yard or to become an active volunteer in the campaign. How is this "foot in the door" technique explained by self-perception theory? Well, consumers figure that because they have put up the small signs in their front yards, then they must actually like the political candidate. This inferred attitude then acts as a precursor to subsequent behavior (and here we fall back on the classical attitude-causes-behavior theory).

With the **door in the face** technique, the marketer makes a large request that is sure to be refused; subsequently, after the consumer declines the first request, the marketer then makes a much smaller request, which is what the marketers wanted of the consumer in the first place. Having refused the larger request, the consumer happily accedes to the smaller request. Ask a resident voter to put a big sign in the front yard, and, when refused, ask if he/she won't at least agree to place a small sign. Now this actually is a combination of self-perception and another theory called the **law of reciprocal concession**.

From the self-perception point of view, the consumer looks at his behavior of having refused and finds it at odds with his usual "nice person" behavior. It brings to salience the consumer's attitude of being a "nice, helpful" person. This attitude then leads the consumer to comply with the more reasonable request. From the "reciprocal concession" perspective, the consumer notices that the requester has made a concession, and the consumer feels that it is now his or her turn to reciprocate.

If you are now wondering how to choose between these two exactly opposite techniques (foot in the door versus door in the face), there is no easy answer. Savvy persuaders develop a knack for knowing which one would work in a particular circumstance.

Sure, political campaigners are marketers too, but if you are looking for an example from conventional business firms, then consider the following. A business gets a consumer to sign up for a basic service plan with an initial low payment (foot in the door), and then convinces the consumer to add on extra services. "They must have bought the service," consumers would figure, "Because they wanted and liked the service." Alternatively you could quote a customer a full price and then offer a reduced price (door in the face).

The next time you find a salesperson playing this persuasion game, try to infer which technique he or she is deploying.[16]

ACTIVE VERSUS PASSIVE AUDIENCE THEORY

Seen any silly commercials lately? Or any that assume that consumers—that's us—are totally stupid, clueless, and gullible? How come such ads even get made? Do their creators believe that they can get away with anything, say whatever they wish to, and that we will believe it? The answer is "yes." These advertisers literally believe that they have total control over the consumer's mind; they truly think that consumers will accept whatever they are told. This is called "passive audience" theory.

According to the **passive audience theory**, consumers' minds sit there, passively, and absorb whatever is thrown at them. Does it really work that way? Only infrequently, and in a very limited way. We might get irritated a bit or pay no mind, and whatever little does happen to stick in our mind might stay there for sometime. Perhaps we will remember the brand name, but our mind is unlikely to accept the brand's message uncritically—unless it is a very low involvement product for us.

Diametrically opposite is the "active audience" theory. The **active audience theory** holds that consumers are actively processing the information in the ad, and that it is they who are persuading themselves. Here is how to prove it: after showing consumers an ad, ask them what they think of the advertised brand. Their answers will contain ideas that were not there in the ad to begin with! Let us repeat, they will tell you totally new "arguments" about the brand—arguments the advertiser didn't even make in the ad. That is proof that rather than passively absorbing the information, consumers are actively debating the ad's message and generating their own arguments—what are known as, cognitive responses.[17] **Cognitive responses** are simply the thoughts generated in the mind upon exposure to a message.

Indeed, to understand why consumers were or were not persuaded by an ad, consumer researchers conduct ad processing research, and it is done like this. Consumers are shown an ad and are then asked to write down everything that came to mind while viewing the ad. Each unit of thought (usually each sentence), called a "cognitive response," is then coded into one of three categories: support arguments (e.g., "Yes, if it is made with no preservatives, then it is healthier"), counter arguments (e.g., "How could such a big car be fuel-efficient?"), and source derogation (e.g., "What does this spokesperson know about gizmos!"). If you also measure their overall attitudes toward the advertised brand, you will find that the following holds:

Attitude toward the advertised brand = f((support arguments – counter arguments) – source derogation)), where 'f' is some coefficient.

Across consumers, then, those for whom "support minus counter minus source derogation arguments" are fewer will be less persuaded than those who generated more positive than negative arguments. This method helps advertisers diagnose, and then change those elements of the ad that might be causing the negative cognitive argument.[18]

You must already be suspecting that such an active processing—generating cognitive arguments—must be occurring only for high involvement topics/consumers. You are right. Low involvement advertising works in a different way.

HOW LOW INVOLVEMENT ADVERTISING WORKS

We do look at commercials like couch potatoes—lazy and passive, mentally speaking, of course, but only when we are not involved in the advertised brand, which is most of the time. In what kinds of products are we uninvolved? Well trivial products like super market items. What about cars, cell phones, refrigerators, or home security? Yes, these are important, but we are not really involved in processing any information about these products either, unless, of course, one of them breaks down and we need to buy it again. It doesn't matter, then, whether the product is a high or low involvement product by itself (meaning whether it is expensive or low cost, among other things); instead, most of the advertising hits us in our low involvement mode—when we are not paying attention. So, what good is this advertising if consumers are not paying attention? Actually, a lot, and precisely *because* consumers are not paying attention. This is an intriguing paradox. Here is how it works:[19]

When we are in low involvement mode, our minds are on strike, so to speak; we do not want to exert our faculty of arguing. We are not paying attention, but a little bit of information gets through and becomes lodged in our minds. When the ad is repeated several times, a lot of information in the ad eventually succeeds in lodging itself in our minds—minds that were passive, and absorbing information unwillingly but also unknowingly, like sponges. When we are highly involved, by contrast, we are alert, and we actively counter-argue; but when we are not involved, we are uninterested. At the same time, and by virtue of our lack of interest, all of our defenses are down! What better opportunity for a commercial message can there be? Now you have it: most advertising doesn't do much on any single occasion because we are not paying attention, but by repeated exposure, that advertising succeeds in making an impression on our minds, sometimes even better than when we are paying attention and scrutinizing the message.

Low Involvement advertising* works by repeated exposure to simple messages. But involvement or no involvement, all ads have to be interesting, perhaps low-involvement ads even more so. DHL here delivers a significant message—that it serves its customers with zeal, dedication, even enjoyment ("We come back for more."). Its challenge, and accomplishment, in these ads is to say it simply, with strong visual brand identification.

*Recall that low involvement is a characterisitc of the target consumer, not of the ad itself; thus by "low involvement advertising," a convenient phrase in use by consumer researchers, we mean advertising directed at consumers who are not much involved in the product at the time.
(Images Courtesy of DHL and its ad agency Ogilvy Mather.)

Attitude Toward the Ad

FIGURE
8.4
ROLE OF ATTITUDE TOWARD THE AD

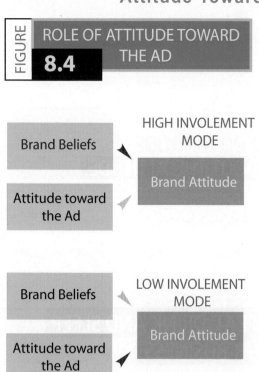

Have you sometimes noticed that an ad is cute, but you still don't think much of the product? Or alternatively, that you find the ad annoying but you buy the product anyway? Does your opinion of the ad itself affect what you think of the product? The answer is, that sometimes it does, and sometimes it does not.

Here is what happens. In the high involvement mode, we pay close attention to the message, and based on that close attention, we form brand beliefs. Based on these brand beliefs, we will buy the product, despite an annoying or unlikeable ad. Or, alternatively, based on these brand beliefs, we will not like the brand and will not buy it, despite a likeable ad. Now then, it is not that the likeability or unlikeability of the ad has not played a role. It has, but it is only one of the factors, and, for high involvement products, it is a relatively less important factor. The more important factor is the message content and resulting brand beliefs. And where brands are otherwise comparable and the consumer loyalty or preference is divided between two brands, the one with a likeable ad might well win.

For the low involvement consumer, on the other hand, brand beliefs are hardly there, and whatever few brand beliefs are there, they may not play a major role. Instead, the ad itself acts as a peripheral element, which then can play a major role in creating brand attitude. And that's why attitude-toward-the- ad itself matters a lot for low involvement products; indeed, that's why low involvement product ads should be likeable, interesting, and entertaining.[20] See Figure 8.4.

This does not mean that high involvement ads can afford to be dull and boring; rather, given a strong message, they might work *despite* the ad being boring. Involvement or not, it still behooves ad creators to try making every ad *engaging*.

This idea of modes of attitude change, based on low involvement versus high involvement, is very important. Be on the lookout to experience some of these modes of changing brand attitudes the next time you are watching TV. When did you pay attention to the brand message, and when did you let the mere look and feel of the commercial make a brand impression on you?

APPEAL TYPES

The Anatomy of an Ad

If an ad itself can contribute to resulting brand attitude, it behooves us to look at the ad messages themselves. Are some message appeals more effective than others, and under what conditions? How do various appeals work or not work on the consumer mind? The main types of appeals are: (a) emotional versus rational, (b) humor, (c) fear, (c) sexual, (d) two-sided versus one-sided, and (e) comparative versus noncomparative appeals.

Emotional versus Rational Appeals

Whereas rational appeals are made to mold our thoughts, emotional appeals are made to mold our feelings. Since, as humans, we experience many emotions, emotional appeals can use one or more of the following emotions:

- Romance: "Buy some chocolate and feel the romance."
- Sympathy: "Please donate to feed the hungry."

- Altruism: An appeal to deeper goodness in us (e.g., "Donate your time for church activities").
- Ego-massaging: "You deserve it, you have earned it."
- Relationships and nostalgia: An appeal to evoke memories of deep connections with specific others (e.g., "Mom, I called you just because I love you" or "This anniversary, make her a bride again; buy her a second diamond.")
- Fantasy and excitement: "Dream on. Buy this car and imagine ____ hitching a ride with you."

Obviously, emotional appeals primarily work best for expressive products, whereas rational appeals are required (and work better) for functional products.[21]

Humor Appeals

Humor works by:
- Aiding exposure: Escape zapping and zipping: (i.e, make consumers not want to avoid the commercial by switching channels (zapping) or by fast-forwarding while watching a prerecorded program (zipping).
- Holding attention: Getting people to listen to or watch the ad (rather than shift their attention to something else);
- Helping memory: Making people remember the ad by the joke.
- Gratification: Adds to the enjoyment people derive from the use of media. It leaves a pleasant feeling by having amused the consumer, and this pleasant feeling rubs off on the brand.[22]
- Multiplier effect: Repeated self-rehearsal. People like to tell jokes and talk about funny commercials; doing so further helps memorizing.

Humor works best when:
- Consumers already have a positive attitude toward the brand. (With initially negative consumer attitudes, humor might work only if it is self-deprecating.)
- The product is light, low in involvement.
- The product is not upscale, and gravitas is not the aspired positioning for the brand.
- The product pokes fun at itself (rather than at other brands or other people).
- The joke and brand message are integrated. For example, in an airline ad, a man comes home with flowers for his wife. He begins to undress (to bare briefs) as he walks toward the interior of the house, only to discover his in-laws waiting. The airline was promoting its cheap fares! (Had this ad been for a company selling flowers, the humor would have stood unconnected with the message.)

Remember, humor can backfire when:
- The ad makes fun of a specific group.
- It is in bad taste, relative to the sophistication or culture of the audience.

Below, we leave you with a few examples of recent ads with humor. Judge for yourself whether and how humor would work in these ads.
- Brand Energizer's Pink Bunny shows up in all the places (e.g., in the shower). Isn't this the

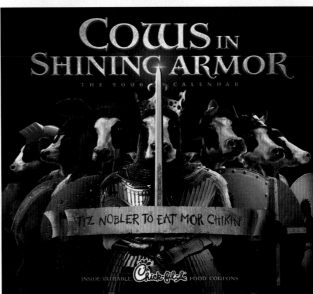

This chuckle-inducing campaign from Chick-Fill-A has endured for years. One of the most outstanding illustrations of the use of humor in advertising, in a manner that amuses and homes in the brand message at the same time. (Image courtesy of Chick-Fill-A Company)

Energizing Bunny?

- Cheaptickets.com: Father and son are standing at the edge of a public swimming pool. The son points out a quarter on the pool deck, and the father lets go of the son (who falls into the pool) just to get the quarter. Tagline: *We like cheap customers!*
- Capital One Credit Card: Shows an unnamed competitor always saying "No" to customer requests. A character, playing a new employee, saying "yes" gets stung with hilarious torture.
- Maker's Mark: On a billboard in Times Square, a liquor bottle sits horizontal and empty; the copy reads: "Disappears Faster than Five Biggest Accounting Firms!" (Remember Enron?)

Fear Appeals

Fear Appeals bring home the severity of the impending consequences, but they can also alienate consumers if the ads do not offer immediate remedial steps that are feasible. The fear induced should not be very strong. And message arguments or sources should be strong enough to discourage counter arguing.[23] Fear works best when:

- Consumers are not sufficiently motivated. It raises the problem's salience; it helps to lift consumers out of apathy and inaction.
- The solution is clear and not too difficult to implement.

Fear may backfire if consumers can't implement the solution or decide they do not want to. Then there is, for them, only one option—to dismiss the threat and disparage the fear-mongering ad.

Most consumers have self-selectivity bias—they dismiss a negative-consequence ad by rationalizing that "it won't happen to me." To counter this tendency, an ad should show not only the risk consequences but also the risk probability as well. A current TV commercial for Zocor (a cholesterol control medication) shows two identical and perfectly normal looking persons going about their chores, when one of them falls down suddenly—due to high cholesterol. The message: "Anyone may be suffering from high cholesterol!"

Sexual Appeals

Sexual appeals come in two forms: (a) sexual suggestiveness and nudity, and (b) sexual themes or romance. They induce emotions through arousal, excitement, even lust. This type of appeal is implemented in one of the following forms:

- Skin is shown.
- Female or male body is shown in suggestive poses.
- **Couples are shown in an intimate embrace, especially in states of partial undress.**
- Sexual innuendo is presented in the text. Two examples from past ads: "Does she or doesn't she?" And "Nooner" (for Houlihan's Restaurants offering quick lunch service).

Sexual appeals work by[24]:

- At the very least, attracting and holding attention.
- Raising the salience of brand-name.

This type of appeal can backfire when:

- Sexual standards of a culture are violated.
- Sexual appeal is unrelated to the message.

Even if it doesn't backfire, a suggestive ad may just not accomplish anything when it doesn't relate to the product's message. In a now famous 2005 commercial for Carl's Jr./Hardee's, Paris Hilton is shown in a revealing bathing suit, striking sexy poses while washing a car and eating a burger. The ad received a lot of publicity, but it did very little for Carl's Jr./ Hardee's sales.

Sexual appeals work best when:

- They are integral to some product benefit; e.g., for colognes, yes, but for hamburgers, no.
- The use of sex is tongue-in-cheek. A European ad (in the1990s) showed a woman eating a brand of ice cream and making orgasmic sounds. Everyone knows that it

is hyperbole; ice cream doesn't actually cause an orgasmic experience, so everyone chuckles.

Note that sexual appeals work differently depending on the gender of the viewer. Generally, males have been found to like sexual appeals more (or object less) than females do, no matter what or who is shown in the sex-centered ad. Also, when a female body is shown in ads, males tend to like it, whereas females tend to dislike it. In some research studies, these same females liked or didn't object to sex appeals when a male body was shown.[25]

Note also that simply showing flesh—even a lot of it—does not naturally make an ad sexual—or at least it does not make the ad sexual in a bad sense. The human body is, after all, a beautiful thing, and it can be shown with class and celebrated, so to speak. Two campaigns come to mind. In a campaign released in 2004 (and still running), a Dove ad shows a lot of skin (with women in underwear). However, because its pretext is to show realistic consumers in many shapes and sizes, the ad is unlikely to produce any lewd thoughts. Instead, it is likely to enhance the perceived relevance of the ad. Another example is a 2005 print ad by Pirelli showing a totally naked statuesque male body ready to sprint off a tire. (see www.Pirelli.com.)

Two-Sided (Versus One-Sided) Appeals

One sided or two sided—that is the question. **Two-sided messages** present both the merits and demerits of a product, brand, or issue. Consequently, they help by raising credibility of the advertising company itself. They also break the initial resistance consumers have toward any advertising in general ("Here comes another self-hyping commercial!"), especially for a consumer with an initially negative view of the brand.

Two-sided messages work best:
- When an issue really does have two sides (e.g., the issue of U.S. troop withdrawal from Iraq, being demanded by many Americans by late 2005).
- When a product does have some less desirable outcomes (e.g., side effects from some drugs).

Research has found that two-sided messages work better when the audience is initially opposed to an issue or has an unfavorable attitude toward the brand. For consumers already in favor of the brand, one-sided messages are more persuasive.[26]

There are two ways of making brand messages two-sided. In one version, you acknowledge the shortcomings of your brand while promoting its merits. In a milder version, you acknowledge "no superiority" of your brand on some less important features and then claim superiority on the more important features.[27]

The negative side acknowledges the brand's past mistakes or inherent shortcomings and, consequently, makes the company look more honest. (The simplest example is, of course, "Yes, we are expensive, but we are worth it.") The negative side also *immunizes* against competitor's potential negative advertising (i.e., by anticipating counter messages).

Use a two-sided message when the negative pertains to a minor attribute and when involvement is high. Don't use two-sided or comparative messages for low involvement consumers—the negative side may stick.

Two-sided messages works best when:
- A negative attribute is already well-known and is acting as a blocker of consumer preference, and you can explain it away.
- The negative attribute is a minor irritant. You present it in the context of other benefits, thus trying to switch consumer evaluation from, say, a lexicographic to a compensatory mode, as discussed in Chapter 11. (It won't work if the negative attribute is a major flaw.)
- You can refute a negative.
- The message shows humility: Acknowledging the brand's weakness can lower audience defenses, putting the audience in a more receptive mood. (This is especially effective when it shows a human weakness, when the weakness is "unavoidable," or

When you call, you get a knowledgeable person within 60 seconds. **We think impatience is a virtue too.**

Call up, and in less than a minute, speak to a knowledgeable live person ready to help you. No holding for hours. No getting the runaround.

It pays to Discover®

Discovercard.com

The Comaprison here is not explicit but implied.
Courtesy of Discover Card Financial Services

when it is not under marketer's control.)

- You can explain that the negative attribute was necessary to get the positive benefits.

Example: "When is a diet pill worth $153? When it works, really works." (TV Commercial for *Leptoprin* seen in November 2005). Also, the same brand uses another two-sided message to the effect: When you need to lose only 5 or 10 pounds, Leptoprin is not for you; use other products. But when you need to lose 20, 30, or even 50 pounds, consider Leptoprin."

[Note: The author implies no endorsement of this product and claims no knowledge of it—beyond having watched the ad.]

Two-sided messages also work because of a phenomenon called *immunization* or *inoculation*. "My opponent will tell you that I have tried marijuana. Let me tell you under what circumstances." This is a hypothetical quote, but you have no doubt heard statements like this from political candidates. By admitting it before hand, they are prepping you, the voter, for the imminent accusation by the opposition party. This is called **inoculation theory**.[28]

"Our competitors can offer you a cheaper price, but ask them whether they use sweat shops" is the kind of inoculation that can save firms some lost customers when competitors come charging with their lower price messages.

Comparative (Versus Non-Comparative) Advertising[29]

In **comparative advertising**, the advertised brand compares itself to competing products or brands. There are two versions of this approach: direct and indirect. In the direct version, the advertiser names a specific competitor; in the indirect version, the brand simply mentions competitors as a group, as in "compare with leading brands." The direct version is bolder, but it also must stand on truth—i.e., the claim of superiority being made must in fact have been proven. Direct comparison advertising works best for utilitarian products with objectively measurable and demonstrable features.[30]

Sometimes a brand compares itself not to other brands but to another product category. For example, a Lifesavers ad once showed a page full of the mints against a cherry, with the one-line copy: "There is more sugar in this cherry than in all these Lifesavers!" Comparative advertising works well for smaller brands; this is because people feel sympathy for an underdog brand. Avis' now famous "We try harder; we are only #2" illustrates this type of advertising.

An extreme form of indirect comparison is "implicit comparison" or comparison by implication only. Here, the competitor is not named at all; however, viewers who have suffered the competition can make the connection. A current Discover Card print ad proclaims: "In less than a minute, you get a knowledgeable live person."

Remember, all tricks are culture specific. In non-combative, cooperative cultures of the East, comparative ads may not go well, especially if they are too brutal. Economic interests do rule supreme everywhere, so if your ad pointed out some real difference that consumers value, then consumers will like it because they will benefit from it. Yet it shouldn't be too harsh or cruel. Do it gently.[31]

SOURCE CREDIBILITY

Consumer persuasion depends not just on the message but also on the source's credibility. A **source** is any person or organization that is conveying the message or stands behind the message. At the most obvious level, the source is the person shown in the ad. Where no person is shown, the source is the company marketing the product. Actually, even when there is a spokesperson, the ultimate source is always the marketer, although some consumers may never consciously think of this ultimate source.

Types of Sources Sources are of following types: (a) stars and celebrities, (b) experts, (c) company spokespersons, (d) actors and ad models, (e) real users, real people who are unidentified, and (f) real people identified by name. Have you ever wondered how advertisers decide what type of source to use? If you were an advertiser, what source would you use? To answer that question, you have to understand something about source characteristics.

Source Characteristics There are three characteristics of sources that affect persuasion: credibility, attractiveness, and similarity. **Source credibility** refers to how credible (believable or trustworthy) the source is judged to be by the target audience. Credibility depends, in turn, on two sub-characteristics: source expertise and source independence. Judgments of **source expertise** are made based upon the profession, education, or personal experience of the source. Thus, a doctor promoting a drug, or a sportsperson promoting a sports shoe, or a computer professor promoting software, will all garner credibility, whereas a claim that "I am not a doctor but play one on TV" will not.[32]

Source independence refers to the separation of the source from the company that would benefit from the message. Independent sources such as *Consumer Reports*, product critics in the media (e.g., restaurant reviews published in newspapers and magazines), and unpaid spokespersons earn their credibility by virtue of their independence. Professionals shown in the ads are often paid by the advertiser, but the public either doesn't know or doesn't dwell on such payments. Some consumers assume, often correctly, that fee or no fee, the professionals have a code of not lying just for the money. It is assumed also that the professionals who claim that they benefit from a product do actually use that product.

The second source characteristic that determines a source's effectiveness is **source attractiveness**—the quality of making an emotional connection with the viewer. Often this quality comes, literally, from the source's physical appearance or talent. Stars and celebrities are, in their very physical persona, attractive, and they inspire a viewer's own pro-message attitude because viewers aspire to be like them. Alicia Keys is featured in an infomercial for *Proactiv* Solution (an acne eradicating cream—a good commercial if you want to see the normally-not-seen acne-spotting face of the music diva). And on the company's Web site (www.proactiv.com), you can watch a video featuring Vanessa Williams!

Using celebrities, however, does have a few drawbacks (in addition to costing the advertiser a lot of money, that is). Consumers often dismiss the product benefits celebrities proclaim as unattainable (e.g., "Paris Hilton is beautiful to begin with, so this makeup product of course works on her. But it won't work on me"). Consumers may also reject the

Flies 21 feet into the air

Makes birds jealous

Kirsten Lawton, Champion Trampolinist

What does she have for breakfast?
Silk.® Why? No cholesterol, 6 grams of soy protein and less saturated fat and sugar.* Plus a great smooth and creamy taste. Silk.® Rise and Shine.®

For Silk Soymilk, Kirsten Lawton, Champion Trampolinist, lends her support. Her profession requires good health, strength, agility, and energy for the "day's work." As an ace trampolinist, she soars high, and so does *source credibility* for this ad. (Image used with permission.)

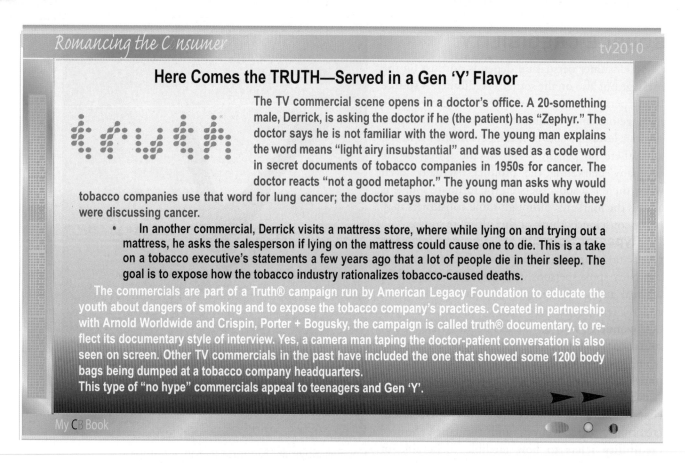

Here Comes the TRUTH—Served in a Gen 'Y' Flavor

The TV commercial scene opens in a doctor's office. A 20-something male, Derrick, is asking the doctor if he (the patient) has "Zephyr." The doctor says he is not familiar with the word. The young man explains the word means "light airy insubstantial" and was used as a code word in secret documents of tobacco companies in 1950s for cancer. The doctor reacts "not a good metaphor." The young man asks why would tobacco companies use that word for lung cancer; the doctor says maybe so no one would know they were discussing cancer.

- In another commercial, Derrick visits a mattress store, where while lying on and trying out a mattress, he asks the salesperson if lying on the mattress could cause one to die. This is a take on a tobacco executive's statements a few years ago that a lot of people die in their sleep. The goal is to expose how the tobacco industry rationalizes tobacco-caused deaths.

The commercials are part of a Truth® campaign run by American Legacy Foundation to educate the youth about dangers of smoking and to expose the tobacco company's practices. Created in partnership with Arnold Worldwide and Crispin, Porter + Bogusky, the campaign is called truth® documentary, to reflect its documentary style of interview. Yes, a camera man taping the doctor-patient conversation is also seen on screen. Other TV commercials in the past have included the one that showed some 1200 body bags being dumped at a tobacco company headquarters.

This type of "no hype" commercials appeal to teenagers and Gen 'Y'.

My CB Book

physical beauty or talent of these stars as unworthy of pursuit, sort of as a defense mechanism. In short, the stars are considered to be too different from the consumer.

Source similarity is the third and last characteristic that influences persuasion. **Source similarity** refers to how similar to themselves consumers see the spokesperson to be. This is the reason ordinary people used as spokespersons may sometimes have a more persuasive effect on the audience than a celebrity would. That is why a lot of advertisers have always used models that look like most of us. Lately, even star-heavy brands such as Nike have resorted to depicting more realistic women in their ads.

Next question: How would you make the ad messages themselves credible? Answer: By one of these means:

1. State the facts. Support the message with scientific facts, statistics, objective numbers, etc.
2. Cite authority (e.g., JD Powers, government studies, etc.)
3. Obtain testimonials from experts, from unpaid real people, and/or from paid real people
4. Corporate reputation. On this last item, remember that no matter which type of spokesperson you visibly use in the ad, ultimately, in the consumer mind, it is your company that is bringing to the consumer that message. Therefore, your company's reputation holds the strongest weight in message credibility.

One potent means of making a message more credible is by avoiding any hype. One recent advertiser went further: "Aleve helps me play, but it does not make me a better player." We will call it preemptive anti-hype. It takes guts, and it takes sincerity.

MATCH UP HYPOTHESIS

You wouldn't use Gwen Stefani to pitch, say, the economic manifesto of the next Republican Party's presidential candidate, would you? Or ask *Freakonomics* coauthor and University of Chicago economics Professor Steven Levitt to pitch a new brand of grunge clothing, would you? No. This obvious conventional wisdom is technically called **match-up hypothesis**—the celebrity chosen for promoting a brand should have an image similar to the brand's image (or desired image). Celebrity sources have, as you know, two different kinds of appeal: expertise and attractiveness. Decide which one you need for your brand and seek that kind of celebrity.[33]

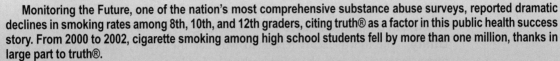

The centerpiece of the campaign is a touring van that shows up around the country, distributing materials to young people who gather up to participate in and further spread the "Truth." You can check its schedule on its Web site www.thetruth.com.

How effective is this campaign? here are the facts:

- Seventy-five percent of all 12 to 17 year-olds in the nation—21 million—can accurately describe one or more of the truth® ads.
- Nearly 90 percent of youths aged 12 to 17—25 million—said the ad they saw was convincing.
- Eighty-five percent—24 million—said the ad gave them good reasons not to smoke.

Monitoring the Future, one of the nation's most comprehensive substance abuse surveys, reported dramatic declines in smoking rates among 8th, 10th, and 12th graders, citing truth® as a factor in this public health success story. From 2000 to 2002, cigarette smoking among high school students fell by more than one million, thanks in large part to truth®.

Shaping consumer attitudes, especially about issues of deep personal consequences and some that go against the populist pulls of peer pressure and "looking cool" dude images of Camel-esque advertising is no easy task. The Truth® Campaign attempts it with amicable success by capturing the youth ethos of "no hype" commercial talk; and by turning peer pressure on its head to form a following around a street-based campaign (the Van tour); and most of all by speaking the target consumers' language.

Based in part on the Truth Campaign's Web site www.thetruth.com

My CB Book

But within each kind, you should match, furthermore, the specific image you desire for the brand; e.g., Gwen Stefani for *Hot Topic* and Brittany Spears for *Bebe,* for example, not the other way round. Or Alan Greenspan for financial investments and CNN's Dr. Sanjay Gupta for stem cell research, for example.

Now, you could of course pair Hollywood star Angelina Jolie and Columbia University economist Jeffery Sachs to film a documentary on the economy of Kenya—this innovative idea was being implemented by MTV in late 2005. How and why this teaming idea satisfies the match-up hypothesis—and satisfy it certainly does—is a question we will leave you to ponder.

GETTING CUSTOMERS TO LIKE YOU

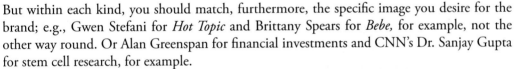

Persuasion in Interpersonal Selling

A special kind of source is a salesperson. A real human communicates with consumers face to face or on the phone. How does persuasion work for the salesperson? No matter how deserving your message, if your audience does not like you, the messenger, they are not going to hear your message. Every salesperson first has to get the customer to like him or her as a person. And in the game of life, everyone is a salesperson. So, here is how to get others to like you.[34]

You could meet a total stranger, and, within five minutes, that person can decide whether he or she likes you or not. How does that happen? Basically there are five factors at work: (1) good looks, (2) common ground, (3) aspirational persona, (4) utility, and (5) being liked in return. Let us briefly discuss each.

Good Looks Let's face it, other things being equal, looks matter. We are perhaps biologically wired to feel pleasant when we look at a person with good looks. This is unfair, but let us note that to look good, one doesn't have to be a beauty queen or a handsome Casanova. Personal grooming and a happy facial expression can make most of us look good. That is why most service establishments have personal grooming prescriptions, and many explicitly advertise "hiring happy faces."

Common Ground The second factor that creates liking between two persons is some "common ground," i.e., the sharing of some characteristic. This can be a common ethnic background, profession, technical background, alma mater ("Oh, you are a Hoosier too!"), interest and hobbies, or favorite sports team. Sometimes, even an indirect similarity of background or interest helps (e.g., "You are from Belgium? My brother lived there once!")

Aspirational Persona If we find out that a person has a quality we admire or to which we aspire to, we immediately begin to look at that person in a favorable way. This is the reason why we like sports personalities and other celebrities; this is also why we like role models in our lives. However, this is also the reason we can develop an instant liking for someone we have just met. If we come to know that the person we are meeting is an accomplished author (perhaps textbooks don't count!), or a champion chess player, or is heavily involved in community work, etc., then we might find that person inspiring; we might find his or her persona to be something we would aspire to. Consequently, he or she would earn our respect, and in turn, our liking.

Utility The fourth factor relates to whether the person can be of some use to us. If two persons move into the neighborhood, we like the one who has a pick-up truck and would be willing to loan it to us. We like a classmate who can teach us how to prepare a multi-media presentation. We like a salesperson who can give us free product samples. Whereas all other factors are psychological/emotional, the prospect of any utilitarian gains is the only rational consideration. Too rational, actually—devoid of valuing a person as a person.

Being Liked Finally, the single most important factor is knowing that the other person likes us. We like people who like us. Period. It doesn't matter if they have nothing else to offer, we like them because they like us. Alternatively, no matter how much talent they have and how useful they might be, if we sense they don't like us, then we won't like them either. And of course, the more we think they like us, the more we like them.[35]

Here is another version of the Levi's ad you saw before, promoting the steel button on its flies.
This is an example of altering the multi-attribute equation in brand's favor, by introducing one new feature into the decision calculus. But there is more. ...

Courtesy: J. Walter Thompson, Banglore, India, (Featured in Lürzer's Int'l Archive, Vol. 6, 2005)

We all want others to see the world our way. That is the crux of attitude change. How we form our attitudes, and once formed how we modify them, is not random. When it comes to our own attitudes, we would vehemently deny that our attitudes are random, arbitrary, and flimsy. Rather, they are, we would claim, based on logic and thought. Why should it be any different when it comes to others' attitudes? Indeed, everyone's attitudes, about products and issues, are based on some systematic processes, at least most of them. So, psychologists who have studied these processes have come up with some underlying theories, and understanding and following these theories is certain to give us more success in persuading others.

Yet it would be presumptuous to believe that as a marketer you have the power to mastermind consumer attitudes. Consumers, most of the time, persuade themselves (remember the "active audience" theory); your job is simply to provide the right information the right way. Yes, sometimes, or even often, they absorb information passively. Sure, sometimes, they let the ad and commercial communication do its trick on their unguarded minds; but that too is their choice—certain matters are simply not important enough to them. It is they who choose, in life and in the marketplace, what messages they allow to soak-in unguarded, what they will accept and with what sort of message validity indicators (remember "source characteristics"?). Once again, if you read these parameters of the consumer mind correctly, then you will be able to fashion your message so that it agrees with their mode of persuading themselves.

Are you frustrated as marketers that sometimes it is just impossible to persuade consumers, knowledge of these theories notwithstanding? Why? Don't the same theories explain why persuasion will NOT occur?

And is it not just as well that marketers can't mold consumer attitudes any which way they like? Wouldn't you as a consumer want to keep personal autonomy and allow marketers to guide your attitudes in a manner that serves, merely but amicably, your own modes and goals of *self-persuasion*? Why should it be any different when the roles are reversed—i.e., when you are the marketer and the target of your communications is the consumer?

That way, both the fur merchant and PeTA have an equal opportunity to lure your mind, er, to serve your agenda of self-persuading yourself—you being the consumer (or the marketer truly resonating with the consumer)!

(Opinion? Write: opinion@my bbook.com.)

Levi's Ad . ...

The multi-attribute model assumes a central route and high involvement processing; but what if the consumer does not care much about button flies? The ad could then work via the peripheral route. The attitude-toward-the-ad could transfer and influence the consumer's brand attitude. If you liked the ad, then you will chuckle about it, and, without being fully conscious of it, find your attitude become more favorable.

   Should the consumer become more engaged in the ad, the possibilities go farther. The message could work, subconsciously (remember Dichter from Chapter 2?), at bringing a new level of the sense of security, or even helping the consumer feel more empowered. Something worth chuckling about.

   Or the ad's creativity could produce a buzz. From any angle you look, the ad is worth a second look, don't you think?

This chapter gave us a repertoire of techniques to mold and change consumer attitudes, many of which are segregated according to low and high involvement. To begin with, the Involvement and Think-Feel Grid showed us how products and consumer concerns can be typed by a low/high involvement level and whether the consumer decision is a rational (thinking) or an emotional (feeling) decision. Persuasive messages then have to be crafted accordingly. Also related to involvement levels, two modes of processing—peripheral and central—were described, and movement from the peripheral to the central mode was captured in the model called the Elaboration Likelihood Model (ELM). The multi-attribute model of attitude of the previous chapter was also shown to offer us three different message options.

Next, we made acquaintance with (a) Heider's balance theory, (b) Attribution Theory, (c) Self-Perception Theory, and (d) Active Versus Passive Audience Theory. Heider's Balance Theory helps us resolve the dilemma we face when a person we love or admire is friendly toward a product or issue we detest. Attribution theory explains attitude change as a process where we as consumers internally answer "why" something happened.

Self-perception Theory works akin to the Attribution Theory's precepts: we infer our attitudes by attributing the cause of our behavior to our own attitudes! Finally, Active Versus Passive Audience Theory portrays consumers as passive recipients versus active thinkers when they are exposed to a message. If in the active mode, they generate their own arguments, called *cognitive responses*, which, rather than the message's original content per se, then determine the resulting attitude.

Attitude Toward The Ad itself was identified as an influencer of Brand Attitude, albeit in less or more intense fashion depending on the level of involvement. Given the role of the ad in brand attitude molding, we looked at various appeal types. We reviewed (a) emotional, (b) humor, (c) fear, (d) sexual, (e) one- versus two-sided, and (f) comparative messages, describing their relative effectiveness. In this context, we also came to understand how source characteristics make ad spokespersons and celebrities effective or ineffective.

We ended the chapter with a short treatise on how attitude-molding works in interpersonal encounters—how you can, in other words, get others to like you!

Central Route
Peripheral Route
Elaboration Likelihood Model
Heider's Balance Theory
Self-perception Theory
Foot-in-the-door
Door-in-the-face

Law of Reciprocal Concessions
Active Audience
Passive Audience
Cognitive Response
Zipping
Zapping
Two-sided messages

Comparative Advertising
Source Credibility
Source Independence
Source Attractiveness
Source Similarity
Match-up Hypothesis

REVIEW+Rewind

1. Draw the Think-Feel and Involvement Grid, and show two products in each quadrant.
2. Explain the concept of central and peripheral routes to persuasion. Explain how these concepts relate to consumer involvement.
3. Explain the elaboration likelihood model and its relationship with consumer involvement.
4. Does attitude toward the ad affect consumer brand attitude? How?
5. List the three options to change consumer attitude, using the multiattribute model of attitude.
6. Describe Heider's balance theory and explain how it is related to consumer attitude change.
7. What is self-perception theory and how is it related to attitude change?

8. Give an example each of "foot-in-the-door" and "door-in-the-face" strategies of attitude change.
9. Describe active versus passive audience theory and its relevance to advertising message creation.
10. Describe the conditions under which each of the following types of ad appeals is likely to work: (a) humor, (b) fear, and (c) sexual appeals.
11. Give an example of a two-sided message and explain why and when it is likely to be more effective than a one-sided message.
12. What makes a source credible? What is the principal advantage of using a celebrity?
13. Explain the concept of *match up hypothesis*. How does it relate to the use of celebrity in ads?

THINK+APPLY

1. Suppose you have developed expertise in (a) Web site design, (b) teaching the game of chess, (c) golf tutoring, or (d) being a DJ at ethnic weddings, and you want to advertise your services. Which of the various attitude change methods would you employ for each of these services and why?

2. 2. As an advertiser, suppose you use a celebrity to endorse your product. In the middle of the ad campaign, a news story develops which questions the celebrity's behavior on two counts: (a) the celebrity is not actually a user of the product, (b) the celebrity faked his/her talent (e.g., a singer caught lip-syncing) or had unethically bolstered his/her performance (e.g., an athlete caught using steroids, etc.). For each of these instances, how would Heider's Balance Theory play out in terms of consumer attitudes toward your brand if your brand is (a) closely related to the celebrity behavior in controversy, and (b) not related to it?

3. Think of two examples each of "foot-in-the-door" and "door-in-the-face" techniques that you yourself can utilize to receive a favor from someone who is (a) a friend, or (b) a stranger.

PRACTICE+EXPERIENCE

1. Next time, you see a commercial for a product new to you, soon after watching it, write down all the thoughts that occurred while you were watching the commercial. Now review these thoughts and flag them as support and counter arguments. How do these thoughts relate to your overall attitude toward the advertised product?

2. Ask a few friends to write down their thoughts for any two commercials they watch during the forthcoming week, and also to rate their overall attitude toward the advertised brand. Ask them to give you only their thoughts (and keep the overall attitude ratings with them). Then score the thoughts (support, counter) and predict their attitudes. Check back with your friends. How good was your prediction, and why or why not?

3. Find an ad that uses comparative advertising and comment on whether it employs direct or indirect comparison, and whether the ad would have been more effective without a comparison.

4. Ask (a) a friend and (b) a total stranger for the favors you thought of in an earlier question. Were you successful? Comment on why or why not.

5. Survey a sample of consumers to assess all three components of attitude toward vegetarianism. In the survey, include at least two vegetarians and three heavy meat eaters with a negative view of vegetarianism. How would you change the latter group's attitude so that they would consider reducing meat consumption, if not eliminating it altogether? Describe alternative approaches. (Note: Separate approaches may be more effective for each of the three anti-vegetarianism consumers.)

6. Visit American Legacy Foundation's Website (www. americanlegacy.org) and review the organization's current campaign. Using everything you know about attitudes and behavior from this chapter, evaluate the campaign in terms of its potential to accomplish its goals.

In the Marketing Manager's Shoes

Put yourself in a marketing manager's shoes. Most concepts in the chapter have some lessons for the marketing manager; i.e., they suggest what to do differently in practice. Indeed, often these applications are implicit in our explanations of the concepts and models in the chapter. Identify at least five specific applications of the chapter's concepts, all of which should be entirely new—different from the examples cited here.

(Courtesy: VCD, Australia)

A Photo Quiz

Was Our tagging of this ad as a *low involvement, feeling ad* (in the FCB grid) an oversimplification? Does it not also reflect a consumer's total immersion in the brand—the consumer is totally wrapped in the brand, enchanted, and experiencing the beverage like an elixir.

In fact, the mere looking at the ad is infectious—we almost feel the mood ourselves!

Consumer Culture

*Our Shared
Code for Living*

Welcome to Snake Alley, Taipei: The Home of the World's Most Bizarre Beverage

September 6, 2004. From the moment we arrived in Taiwan, and even beforehand, there was a constant buzz among the students about DRINKING THE SNAKE BLOOD.

At the logistical pre-port meeting the night before we docked in Keelung, the ship's physician, "Dr. Milt," stood before the student body, and as he always did before a port of call, he rattled off a list of health warnings specific to the destination. Number One on his list that evening was "Whatever you do, please don't drink the blood of snakes." He cited hepatitis and salmonella as possible complications. Only an idiot would want to expose himself to either one. So, naturally, at the first opportunity, several groups of students headed for Snake Alley in Taipei to drink the snake blood. We witnessed it firsthand. But I am getting ahead of myself.

The big attraction at Snake Alley has always been, and probably always will be, the cobras. If you happen to be a cobra in Snake Alley, you are out of luck. First, you are likely to be taunted by your captor in front of a group of squirming bystanders. Then you'll get hit on the head and strung up. The crowd will gasp as your underbelly is slit open with a sharp knife. Your skin will be peeled back and your heart exposed, still beating. Things only get worse. Your heart is ripped out and placed on a table, where it continues to beat. Then your main artery is cut. You bleed out into a glass.

Rachel Barnett, a dance major at San Jose State University (left) and Jennifer Temple, then a junior at Colorado State University, at Snake Alley in 2004.

The bile from your gall bladder is emptied into another glass. Meanwhile, your heart is still beating over on that table. By then you probably don't care anymore. But the audience does. They are anxious to drink your body fluids. Chinese folklore holds that your essence has curative properties, and can act to "strengthen masculinity." Your blood or bile will be mixed with rice wine and served in shot glasses—for a price, of course. The buyer may or may not be Chinese. That night a large number of SAS students, male and female, were scrambling over each other for a chance to chug some snake blood. … That night, lots of the kids drank snake blood.

During the long bus ride back, a student who was, apparently, having second thoughts, asked our faculty biologist, "Surely it's safe to drink the snake blood," otherwise the government wouldn't allow it?"

Hey Dorothy, I have news for you. You're not in Kansas anymore.

Excerpted with permission from Ginnie Saunders (www.ginnie.com)

INTRODUCTION

Do you find this practice of drinking snake blood strange? Why do certain behaviors seem strange to some people and normal to others? It all depends on culture. We will more formally define culture shortly, but for now—so we can begin to talk about it—we can think of culture as a way of life. And by 'way of life' we mean the different things one does in everyday living and the manner in which one does them. In Taiwan, eating snakes, critters, dog parts, etc., is considered normal, whereas in many other countries, this would be unthinkable. And, of course, such differences are not limited to food. Consider some other things people do differently around the world:

- In Asia and the Far East, young boys and girls don't date; they just marry someone their parents arrange. (This time-honored tradition is now changing, especially among the educated, urban families.) In contrast, in much of the West, extensive dating often precedes marriage between two people.
- In the United States, Western Europe, and Australia, most teenagers begin to earn their own money and must support many of their purchases from their own earnings or do without those products. In the Eastern countries, the young are full-time students until graduation from college, with no part-time jobs, and their parents provide for all their needs.
- In Amsterdam and much of the Netherlands, when you visit a restaurant, you are basically assigned a seat, not a table. Thus, if you are a party of three, you can expect to share a table of four with a single person seated at the fourth chair. In much of Western Europe and most of North America, this would be unthinkable.
- The French eat their salad after the main course; Italians eat it before.
- In Europe, people pour their colas in the glass first, and then add only one or two cubes of ice; in the U.S., they first fill the glass with ice and then pour in the cola.

On and on it goes. Everywhere you look, people of different cultures do things differently. And that way of doing things comes naturally to them; it is deeply ingrained. As far as they are concerned, that is the only way it is, and should be, done. This manner of doing things, this "way of life" is going to influence people's behavior as consumers. It does—immensely and pervasively.

This chapter is about that all-pervasive force in our lives. First, we define culture and describe its essential properties. We also open the big treasure box that culture is and examine its diverse contents. It includes values and norms, customs and traditions, arts and crafts, and myths and material goods. We describe the role these entities play in consumers' lives.

We then describe how cultural values differ between and across societies. Culture survives and, where necessary, adapts, because it serves certain useful functions in society; we learn about these functions. Culture is, we find out, the dictionary that translates the meaning of everything we do and everything we consume. We take a close look at this "meaning translation" function of culture.

We end the chapter with an appendix on cultural profiles of selected nations.

CULTURE

The Blueprint for Everyday Living

What is culture? **Culture** can be defined as everything humans learn from and share with members of a society. That "everything" includes both what to do and how to do it. As such, it is an unwritten blueprint on how to conduct everyday living in a society so as to fit into that society. It is the implicit knowledge we acquire simply by living in a social group or community about how things are done in that group in a way that's acceptable to all others. That implicit knowledge tells us what is deemed edible and what is not; what to wear at home and what to wear in public; how to interact with people; and what should be the relationship between men and women, between adults and children, between the preacher and her disciples, and between strangers on the street. It is part of our collective mental conditioning that makes us act properly as if it were our second nature. And because it is collective conditioning, we share it with other members of our nation, region, or group.

Learning and sharing are two essential processes of culture. Our biological behavior and our genetically inherited instincts are not culture, since these are not learned. Likewise, our individual, idiosyncratic behaviors are not culture, since they are not shared. Thus, our biological nature—to feel hunger pangs, to walk with our heads at the top and legs on the ground, to smile when happy, and to seek and eat food when hungry—these are all our biological nature, not culture. But eating with a spoon and fork, or chopsticks, is culture. So are break-dancing, covering our mouths when yawning, and forming a line at the supermarket checkout. If you can think of anything that we learn and do as a member of a society (which means it is shared in that society), then it is culture.

The opposite of culture is 'nature,' both human and physical. Our human nature is what we are born with. And outside our bodies, physical nature exists—distinct from man-made alterations of it. Thus, our human nature is to be utterly selfish, but culture reins in our personal desires (à la Freud's id versus superego). And in the physical world, rivers, oceans, and trees are nature, but dams, bridges, and genetically altered foods are culture (specifically, material culture; see below).

ELEMENTS OF CULTURE
The Rich Contents of the Treasure Box

Culture is, thus, a vast and deep treasure box, with rich contents that include the following elements:

Values Values are a society's ideas as to what in life is worthy of pursuit and how those pursuits should be conducted. Thus, values include desirable ends as well as desirable means to those ends. Democratic and modern societies value liberty, equality, and individual rights, for example. In contrast, in many traditional societies, individual rights are deemed subservient to the rights of the group, tribe, or clan.

Norms Norms are unwritten rules of behavior. They are "do's and don'ts" guides. Norms are more specific than values and dictate acceptable and unacceptable behavior. For example, to lower the window shades while undressing and to be polite to strangers are norms in much of the civilized world.

Rituals Rituals are a set of activities preferred in a fixed sequence and repeated periodically. They can be either (a) utilitarian or (b) symbolic. Utilitarian rituals have demonstrable useful outcomes. Examples include daily baths and afternoon tea (a British ritual). Symbolic rituals have no practical utility but are followed for tradition and have a symbolic meaning in a specific culture. An example is wedding rituals, which differ markedly from one society to another. Table 9.1 lists various rituals.

Customs Customs are ways of doing something. For example, when to wear which clothes is dictated by a custom. It differs from rituals in that a ritual is an event or activity, whereas a custom can be a ritual, but it can also be an act that is not like an event. To wear a black tie to a formal dinner is a custom (i.e., a convention), not a ritual; but for the bride and groom to do the first dance at the wedding reception is a custom and a ritual. Customs also differ from norms in that violation of norms is strongly sanctioned, whereas violation of custom is merely ridiculed.

Myths Myths are stories that express some key values of a society. For example, the story of Santa Claus is a myth in much of the Christian world. It expresses the value that if you live your life as a "good" person, then good things will come to you (e.g., Santa will bring you gifts).

Knowledge, Science, and Technology All knowledge is also culture. Knowledge is fundamentally the basis of beliefs on which we base our actions. Only a century ago, a significant proportion of people, especially in underdeveloped countries,

TABLE 9.1 Various Rituals in Society

RITUAL	EXAMPLES
Exchange rituals	Giving gifts; The practice of dowry in India (now illegal but still practiced covertly by many).
Possession rituals	House warming party; worship ceremony in Asia before starting a business.
Grooming rituals	Bathing; using or not using scents and perfumes.
Divestment rituals	Redecorating a house; exorcising ghosts and spirits.
Religious rituals	Going to church on sundays (Christians); praying five times a day (Muslims).
Rites of passage	Marriage, graduation , birthday, and so on.
Social/Relational ritual	Greeting, empathizing, mentoring, mating, and so on.
Family rituals	Mealtime, bedtime, story-time, and so on.

Prepared by Author for MyCBBook

Photo: Author

unleash your music™

sound systems for iPod® and MP3

Courtesy: Sharper Image

Material Culture: How humans shape materials to serve consumption in cultures worlds apart

believed that sickness and diseases were curses from evil spirits. Based on this belief, they shunned all medication and would instead commission voodoo rites to exorcise the ghost of the evil spirits. The modern age of enlightenment and scientific advances sets us culturally far apart from the societies of yester-year.

Science and technology are also culture since they are learned and shared and reflect a society's belief and practice in attaining mastery over nature. The large-scale adoption of microwave cooking, wireless communications, and body augmentations is as much a part of the culture as is the absence of these same things from such protected societies as the Amish.

Laws Laws are norms with legal sanctions. For example, smoking in a friend's house may violate a norm but is not illegal. In contrast, smoking inside an airplane is now illegal and punishable. A society's laws reflect that society's values. For example, the anti-cloning law recently passed by the U.S. Congress reflects our value about the dignity of human life. Similarly, the anti-dowry law in India passed in 1971 reflects modern Indian society's value of equality of the sexes and the dignity of women.

Arts The arts—music, paintings, literature, etc.—are also culture. They represent a society's appreciation of the aesthetic experience; often the art of an era and of a society also represents its values, obsessions, and life-conditions.

Material Culture Finally, all man-made objects are also part of culture. They represent the degree of affluence and progress of a society in contrast to the life lived entirely in and with nature (such as the life actor Tom Hanks had to live in the U.S.-made movie Castaway). It may at first appear jarring to you, but the fact is that all man-made materials and man-made objects are part of our culture—thus, the chairs, soaps and detergents, wines and beers, our cuisines, cell phones, HDTVs, and supersonic jets—all represent culture, specifically material culture.

Getting Culture—How Do We Learn It?

How do we learn our culture, as children and as adults? Learning one's own culture is called **enculturation**. Learning a new culture is called **acculturation**. Enculturation happens during childhood, mostly, as we are growing and learning the ways of the world. Acculturation happens when we migrate to a new society, or when we spend a considerable part of our lives with persons from other cultures. Immigrants learn the host culture by acculturation even as they retain the culture of their country of birth. As part of this culture, they also learn new consumer behaviors. People who marry people of another culture, or become close friends with people of another culture, or get exposed to other cultures through international travel, acquire and assimilate many practices and consumption behaviors of these "foreign" cultures.

CHARACTERISTICS OF CULTURE

Every concept, every thing has certain characteristics—the essential, defining properties of that thing or concept. Culture also has characteristics—six of them (see Figure 9.1).

First, **culture is learned.** We are not born with it. Accordingly, instinctive behavior, which we possess from birth, is not culture. Thus, the act of crying or laughing is not culture; however, knowing when it is proper to cry or laugh in public is culture since that is something we have to learn. Some cultures, such as the Chinese culture, "condition" people to not express emotions in public, whereas Italians learn to be very expressive of their emotions in public. If we lived in America or Australia, for example, and if we moved to, say, Japan, South Africa, or Egypt, then we would have to learn the local cultural beliefs about food, clothing, and social interaction.

Second, **culture regulates society**. Culture makes everyone behave. It does so by offering norms and standards of behavior and by sanctioning deviations from that behavior. Everyone in a culture knows what rules to live by. Life runs smoothly because, for example, we queue up in supermarkets and at bus stops, we don't toss garbage in our neighbors' yards, we show up on time for meetings, and we don't abuse, slight, or inconvenience strangers on the street or other shoppers in the mall.

FIGURE 9.1 SIX CHARACTERISTICS OF CULTURE

Third, **culture makes living more efficient.** Because culture is shared (by definition), we don't have to learn things anew as we encounter new people and new situations within the same culture. Once you have learned the Egyptian culture, for example, you can use the same etiquette in interacting with all Egyptians. Living in your own culture, you know whether to take a gift and what gift to take when invited to someone's house, so you do it without having to think up a new "solution" for every host.

Fourth, **culture is adaptive.** Culture is a human response to the environment, and as the environment changes, culture is likely to adapt itself to the new environmental demands. For example, when there were no telephones, people would visit their friends' homes without prior appointment; in the modern age of ubiquitous and instant connectivity, such "dropping by" would be frowned upon.

Fifth, **culture is environmental.** It envelops everyone's life alike and always. Like environment, we take culture for granted, acting in sync, without even being aware of its presence, until someone breaks a norm. Strangers in an elevator don't directly face each other; and this is done without thinking, until someone actually deviates from this automated behavior.

And, sixth, **cultures are hierarchical.** Multiple cultures are nested hierarchically. The culture of the larger group constrains and shapes the culture of the smaller groups within it. Imagine that you are a middle-income Hispanic family in the United States. What is the culture in your family? It is actually the culture of the middle class, nested inside the culture of the Hispanics, in turn nested inside the U.S. culture.

The Foundation of Culture

Values are our ideas about what is desirable in life, why life is worth living. As individuals, we have values—and in Chapter 5, we called them *personal values*. We might value freedom more than wealth; or a relaxed life more than fame; or environmental preservation more than technology. Now, we can ask, "Where did these personal values come from?" The answer is, from culture. Our society instills them in us, as part of socialization. Thus, while many values differ across individual consumers, many personal values are present throughout the entire population of that society. The values a society as a whole embraces are called **cultural values**.

Societies differ in many aspects of everyday life—dress, language, food habits, living arrangements, family formation, etc. These are substantial and very visible differences; but even more important are the differences in cultural values. Values are not tangible and therefore not visible, but they influence everything else in that culture. If you want to understand why people in a society act the way they do, you have to know what its values are. As such, values are the foundation of a culture. They are like the hidden, underwater radar system that silently keeps guiding the ship of a society's everyday life.

CORE AMERICAN VALUES[1]

Values are so basic that in fact every citizen must know the values of the society in which he or she lives, and, for contrast, the values of a few other societies different from his or her own. Here is a brief profile of six of the many American core values:

Individualism   North American culture deems individuals responsible for their own success, which is achieved through individual ability. It is considered acceptable that individuals be self-oriented, serving and guarding their personal interests (as opposed to sacrificing for the group or society).

Freedom   Individuals are free to practice any religion, support any political party, play any sport, participate in any peaceful protest, speak their minds, pursue any career, choose any product, live anywhere, travel anywhere, adopt any line of work or employment, and, in general, pursue any dreams they fancy.

Merit, Competitiveness, and Accomplishment   In American culture, individuals are expected to be competitive to gain success; it is a merit-based society where you get what you deserve (not what you need) and personal accomplishments are honored.

Materialism   American culture values material success. As such, it does not look down upon someone pursuing material wealth (in some cultures it might be deemed greed), and a wealthy person is considered successful with or without any nonmaterial accomplishments.

Change and Scientific and Industrial Progress   American culture values change rather than tradition, and it believes in the power of science and technology to bring solutions to problems such as diseases, aging, poverty, resource shortages, etc., and to produce new comforts and opportunities such as space travel, virtual experiences, and anti-aging miracles. It also values industrialization and the efficiency of mass production.

Belief in the Equality of Opportunity   All persons living and breathing on American soil (including those who are visiting America only temporarily) are deemed equal in the eyes of the law of the land. And such equality is not merely protected by law, but indeed valued as a natural human right in the American culture. This equality means, of course, only equality of opportunity, not equality in status, positions, outcomes or entitlements.

East Vs. West

The core American values are representative of cultural values of many Western countries (Canada and Western European countries). Many of the core cultural values of the East differ sharply from those of Western societies. Some Eastern values, in visible contrast to the Western values, include the following:[2]

Collective Identity Individuals are expected to show consideration for the well-being of their family, group, or organization. Individual identity is often known by the group's identity; individual personality is submerged in the group identity.

Inner Harmony Rather than striving for mastery of the external environment, and achieving material success or individual triumph at the cost of bruised competitors, harmony with others, inner peace, and stability are valued. Happiness is sought in spiritual triumph over desires rather than in material acquisitions.

Respect for Tradition While the West is oriented to the future, sometimes even disparaging the past as backward looking, Eastern societies value the past as a source of wisdom and order, and they sustain and practice tradition for continuity and to counterbalance the supposed upheaval and chaos of modernity and radical change.

Respect for Hierarchy In the West, interpersonal relationships are nurtured horizontally—among peers and equals. In the East, hierarchical relationships (e.g., parent-child, teacher-disciple, etc.) are valued just as much and relished as sources of emotional gratification.

Humanism In Western societies, universal laws apply, and every one is treated to the same set of governing rules and regulations. In contrast, in the East, matters are considered in a much more personal manner, taking the individual's circumstances into consideration. Technically called universalism-particularism (more on this later), we refer to it here as 'humanism,' where, favors are expected and routinely granted due to personal relationships. Neutral rationalism is de-emphasized in favor of humanism.

Cross-Cultural Appreciation

Most Westerners are proud of their values, as they should be. But this is no reason to be smug. Other nations have different values, and they too are proud of their values, as they should be. Rather than be smug, as world citizens, we need to be aware and appreciative of other cultures and their values. Every cultural value has a rationale behind it; the need is to see a foreign culture through the eyes of the people of that culture. For starters, then, let us read about cultural values in Russia and their historic backdrop—a society currently under intense political, economic, and cultural transformation, and, in years to come, sure to become (along with China) a fast growing market for world products. Many of its cultural values sharply contrast with those in the U.S. (see Table 9.2).

TABLE 9.2 Selected Russian Cultural Values

Communal Versus Individual Orientation	In sharp contrast to the American core value of individualism, Russia has placed, from earliest times, communal good (the group) above that of the solitary individual. The Russian word sobornost (communal spirit, togetherness) promotes an equal distribution of societal benefits.
Durability	The long-suffering, enduring character of Russia's people—through deprivation, hardship, change, upheaval and innovation—is admirable. Stability of institutions, traditions, habits and attitudes, in the midst of decades of disruption and chaos, speaks to the long-lasting, resolute nature of Russia's institutions and people.
Patience	In conferring with Russians, or settling a business or military matter, tenacity, stamina, and composure merit great attention. Lengthy, tedious ways of doing business, with the expectation that time and a self-possessed "waiting-it-out" will accomplish much, characterize many negotiations with Russian managers.
No Compromise	To settle differences by mutual concession, so commonplace in American ways of life can be seen as a sign of weakness and betrayal by many Russians. In Russian, the word for compromise (kompromiss) possesses a belittling, pejorative connotation. Truth, justice, "speaking one's mind" and unwillingness to compromise often characterize the Russian approach.

Source: Excerpted from http://www.goehner.com/russinfo.htm. Courtesy Duane Goehner.
Note: An unstoppable reading on Russian Culture is Yale Richmond, *Nyet to Da—Understanding the Russians*, Intercultural Press, 3rd ed., 2003.

UNIVERSAL CULTURAL VALUE DIMENSIONS
What Tells Societies Apart

While reading through the lists of core American and Russian values, did you notice that some values are held common and that some are unique? This poses a problem: How do we prepare a coherent and succinct portrait of value differences for all the countries together? Wouldn't it be nice if there were a common template? Luckily for us, a Dutch social scientist named Geert Hofstede asked the same question. And with meticulous research that measured, analyzed, and compared cultural values across some 50 countries, he identified five dimensions on which societies differ.[3] Hofstede is a cultural anthropologist, mind you, not a market researcher, but the field of consumer behavior is rich precisely because it has borrowed from diverse, basic disciplines in the social sciences. If you ever had the opportunity to market to consumers around the globe, these five dimensions (plus one more we will describe below) would prove immensely useful as a template to understand differences as well as similarities among these consumers. To understand these dimensions, answer the quiz question for each dimension below.

Individualism versus Collectivism
The 'Me' Culture Rules

The Quiz Question: In my society, most people will:
   a. Not usually sacrifice personal pleasure for the good of the society at large.
   b. Will usually put the good of society above their personal interests.

If you checked 'a,' your society is individualistic; otherwise, it is collectivistic. **Individualism** versus **collectivism**, one of the most significant cultural value dimensions, concerns whether, in a society, the well-being of an individual is considered more important than the well-being of the group as a whole. Cultures marked with individualism value self-interest over group interest, and they value unlimited personal freedom and survival of the fittest. On the contrary, cultures of collectivism exhibit close ties between individuals , and they value group interest over self-interest, a limited amount of personal freedom, and group protection. Simply put, this cultural value dimension classifies societies as "me" cultures versus "we" cultures.

In general, as already mentioned, western societies are more individualistic, while eastern societies value collectivism. The principal implication of this for marketers is that individualistic appeals (e.g., "stand out from others") so commonly found in U.S. advertising would be unsuitable for collectivist societies of Asia or for Asian and Hispanic consumer groups in america.[4]

Power Distance
No Egalitarians Allowed

The Quiz Question: In my society, most people will:
   a. Always bow to people of higher status and boss people of lower status, even in off-work, social situations.
   b. Expect to be treated with dignity and respect by all no matter what their station in life might be.

If you checked 'a,' your society values large power distance; checking 'b' shows it values small power distance. **Power distance** refers to the extent to which the less powerful members of the society accept the authority of those with greater power. In societies with large power distance, superiors or persons of higher social strata are expected to maintain their distance from subordinates, and members of lower strata are expected to act in a subservient way. Follow the same practice in small power distance societies, and you would likely get in trouble.

The sources of power can be many: money, education, political position, etc. But don't confuse 'power distance' with power difference—it is not about absolute "power" differences among people that matter; rather it is the submissive role the less powerful willingly accept toward those more powerful. For example, there is a great divergence in power in the U.S.

(consider the professor versus the student; the Donald versus the Omarosa—see www. omarosa.com), just as much as say in Bangladesh or Russia; but psychologically, everyone in the U.S. feels equal, and the less resourceful need not kowtow to the more resourceful.

Does this value influence our consumer behavior? Yes, it does. In cultures of small power distance, decision-making is more participative. Thus, if you were selling a product to a specific member of the family in Egypt or Malaysia (countries with large power distance), you would have to appeal to the head of the household (to whom all family members defer). In contrast, in countries like U.S. or Australia, you would have to appeal to the whole family or to the specific member of the family for whom the product is intended. High power distance—appeal to authority; low power distance— appeal to the target consumer directly. Got it?

Uncertainty Avoidance
The Torture of Not Knowing

The Quiz Question: In my society, most people would:
    a. Feel uncomfortable going on a blind date;
    b. Consider blind dating a thrill.

If you checked 'a,' your society values certainty; checking 'b' shows that uncertainty doesn't bother people much. **Uncertainty avoidance** refers to the extent to which people in a society feel threatened by ambiguous situations and want to avoid them. Some societies accept the "unknowability" of the future, while others deem and desire the future to be predictable. The former socialize their members into getting used to a certain degree of uncertainty and living each day as it comes. Other societies value knowing as much as possible and planning for all contingencies. Uncertainty avoidance leads people to not as much take risks and, consequently, to become less entrepreneurial and less innovative.

Northern Europeans generally have lower tolerance for uncertainty than do people in Mediterranean nations. Therefore, consumers in Northern Europe, compared to those in the Mediterranean nations, would be less likely to buy products without first being certain about their benefits, and less likely to try unfamiliar service providers. And you can imagine where you would be able to sell more insurance!

Masculinity Vs Femininity
Why Men Do Cry

The Quiz Question: In my society, most people will:
    a. Desire money, success, and power over harmony and peace of mind.
    b. Embrace harmony and tranquility over money and success.

If you checked 'a,' your society values masculinity; checking 'b' shows femininity is valued. Some societies value such things as money, success, power, and mastery of the environment, and such qualities as assertiveness, etc. (deemed to be 'masculine' traits in humans). As such these are called **masculine cultures**; in contrast, those societies that value such things as harmony, peace of mind, caring for others, and quality of life (deemed to be 'feminine' traits in humans) are called **'feminine' cultures**.

Accordingly, in feminine cultures, consumers tend to reject environmentally unfriendly products and products whose benefits are primarily materialistic in nature. Consumers in masculine cultures, in contrast, seek products that promise material success and adventure rather than tranquility. A new car, for example, may be positioned in masculine cultures as an outdoor adventure car with a high power engine—a 'macho' car, so to speak —whereas in feminine cultures, the more desirable appeal would be the aesthetics of the car and of the peaceful, harmonious experience of riding or driving it.

High Context versus Low Context
Why We Have To Ask What You Mean?

The Quiz Question: Which statement do you better understand?
    a. The professor said there would be no surprise quizzes in this course.
    b. The saleswoman said, "I am no Paris Hilton."

You don't have to answer this one. It is obvious that everyone would understand Statement 'a,' whereas only those familiar with Paris Hilton would understand Statement 'b.' Analogically, in some cultures, people communicate in a manner so that no special knowledge of that culture is required; in other cultures, everyday speech is full of idioms and clever phrasing so that, to understand it, you need to be familiar with that culture.

Cultural anthropologist Edward Hall gave us another cultural dimension—high versus low context.[5] In **high context cultures**, to understand something, you need to know the context. Behind everything, there are layers of meaning not immediately apparent. People in high context cultures use symbols and nonverbal cues in communicating with others. They are much more polite to one another and very indirect in conveying their unpleasant reactions. In **low context cultures**, in contrast, to understand the meaning of something, you don't have to look at the context; the thing in itself is self-explanatory. And people are explicit in their communication. Asian societies are high-context and Western societies are low-context cultures.

If an American consumer doesn't like a product, he or she will simply announce to the salesperson that he or she doesn't like it. A Japanese consumer would say, instead, that he "would think about it." This is because in the Japanese culture, rejecting someone's offer is considered impolite, even in commercial settings. The important point is that interpreting "would think about it" would require familiarity with the context, the Japanese culture. Also, in high context cultures there is greater use of soft-selling. Advertisements emphasize harmony and oneness with nature and use indirect, symbolic messages, avoiding direct comparisons with competitors. Low context cultures use simplicity, directness, and explicitness in communications.

Universalism Vs Particularism[6]
No Absolutes Here!

The Quiz Question: In my society, most people will believe that:
  a. The same rules should apply to all;
  b. Each case needs to be considered on its own merit.

Another cultural anthropologist, Fons Trompenaars, suggested a few new dimensions, one of which has been widely discussed by consumer behavior researchers. It is 'universalism versus particularism.'[7] In the above quiz question, if you checked 'a,' your society values Universalism; checking 'b' shows Particularism. Cultures also differ in whether the rules governing life are considered absolute, to be applied uniformly to all, or, alternatively, they are viewed as flexible, and the circumstances of the specific case are considered more important. Belief in the universal application of the same rule is called universalism. Valuing the individuality of each situation calls for particularism. Westerners go by universalism, applying universal principles and playing by the rules; Easterners, on the other hand, display particularism, going by their feelings on each case. Keep this in mind when you deal with consumers in foreign societies.

Table 9.3 shows selected countries at the opposite ends of these value dimensions.

Different Cultures, Different Norms

Cultures differ not only in values but also in norms. This is natural for those norms that are based on values, but many norms develop simply as a tradition or cultural habit. An awareness of differences in norms for everyday behavior can come in handy whenever you interact with people of different cultures, even within your own town. Again, a sharp contrast is offered between many norms of the East and West. Here is a brief selection.

Offering and Sharing If an Easterner goes out with friends, he or she never buys something to eat or drink for him/herself alone; if two friends go out, each would ask the other person for his/her choices, order for both, share the purchased item, and each would offer (sometimes insist) to pay for both no matter who ordered. "Going Dutch" is a Western norm, and it is entirely second nature for Westerners in group settings to order and consume individually, a practice that would make their Easterner friends uncomfortable

Chivalry In the West, women are treated as equals; many of these women would find it offensive to be patronized or given priority (although a male opening the door for them is appreciated). In contrast, Eastern women expect men to do small chores for them, hold the door, serve them first, carry their bags, etc.

Candid Talk
Westerners are much more open in communications. They believe they are just being honest when they express their opinions and displeasure freely, whereas Easterners are hesitant to be candid because they think they would be hurting your feelings. In normal discussions, Westerners participate with visible energy, often interrupting, eager to fill any silent moment. Easterners, on the other hand, look more quiet and brooding, as if contemplating what is being said, and in fact letting several moments of silence pass before volunteering an opinion.

Informality in Social Relationships
Westerners (especially Americans) become very informal, addressing you by your first name even in the first encounter. They would find it awkward if

TABLE 9.3
Countries at the Opposite Ends of Univeral Cultural Values

Cultural Value	Countries
Individualism/Collectivism	
Individualism	USA, Australia, the United Kingdom, Netherlands, Canada, Italy, Denmark, Sweden, France.
Collectivism	Guatemala, Panama, Venezuela, Indonesia, Pakistan, China, South Korea, Mexico.
Power Distance	
Large Power Distance	Malaysia, the Philippines, Mexico, China, Arab World, India, Brazil, HongKong, France, Thailand.
Small Power Distance	Austria, New Zealand, Sweden, Switzerland, Germany, Great Britain, Australia, Canada, United States.
Uncertainty Avoidance	
High Uncertainty Avoidance	Greece, Portugal, Guatemala, Belgium, Japan, Spain, France.
Low Uncertainty Avoidance	Singapore, Jamaica, Denmark, Hong Kong, Sweden, UK, USA.
Masculinity/Feminity	
Masculinity	Japan, Austria, Venezuela, Switzerland, Italy, Mexico, UK, USA
Feminity	Sweden, Norway, Netherlands, Denmark, Thailand, South Korea
Universalism/Particularism	
Universalism	Germany, Switzerland, Britain. USA
Particularism	Latin America, Japan.
High/Low Context	
High Context	Most Asian Countries (e.g., China, Japan, etc.)
Low Context	Most Western countries (USA, Canada, etc.)

Note: Countries are listed in descending order with the highest scoring countries listed first.

Sources: Adapted from Geert Hofstede (2001), *Culture's Consequences: Comparing Values, Behaviors, Institutions, and Organizations*, Beverly Hills, CA, Sage Publications; Nitish Singh and Arun Pereira, *The Culturally Customized Web Site*, Burlington, MA: Elsevier, 2005.

you tried to maintain a distance. Easterners, on the other hand, retain formalness in addressing and greeting each other for a long time and reserve informality for close friends. Once a close friendship is established, they make strong personal commitments to each other.

With this knowledge of values and norms across cultures, you are now ready to face the world—almost. Actually, though, you also need to learn something about rituals, customs, and myths.

CULTURAL PRACTICES: RITUALS, CUSTOMS, AND MYTHS

The Power of Protocol

If values form the bedrock of culture, cultural practices form its flora and fauna, making our journey through life more enchanting, and, as always, channeling our consumption. Cultural practices are behaviors that are rooted in the traditions and history of a cultural group. We discuss three of these practices: rituals, customs, and myths. Their one essential characteristic is that they are supra-logical—they cannot be explained by logic.

RITUALS

Rituals serve no ostensible function in the present time and make no sense. However, historically, they did have a purpose, and they are all rooted in traditions. Consider the wedding rituals in Western culture—such as lifting the veil and throwing the bouquet. Did these rituals serve any purpose when they began? Read about them in Table 9.4 and find out.

Today of course they serve no utilitarian purpose, but they do serve two non-utilitarian purposes: one is symbolic, giving the wedding a sacred status, an idea we will explore in the next section. The other is hedonic—we enjoy these rituals because they take us away from everyday drudgery. Seeing the bride in a bridal gown is an aesthetic pleasure, and seeing the bride throw her garter for some lucky person to catch is enchanting.

While the wedding ritual itself has a large number of consumption events, which all can cost huge sums of money, there are umpteen other rituals in everyday consumption, as described Table 9.1. Take the grooming ritual, for example. We simply need to examine our dressers and our makeup kits to realize how much of our money and time is happily expended everyday in personal grooming. From shaving creams to shampoos to gels, from foundation creams to mascara to eyelashes, and from bath oils to aromatic soaps to bottled perfumes, the extensive grooming accessories and even more extensive grooming techniques (gleaned from thousands of pages of advice and tips in glamour and lifestyle magazines) are as essential to our living as modern consumers as food and shelter are. If you don't believe culture has anything to do with it and that these are cultural rituals, ponder what men and women did, say, a mere five hundred years ago, or more to the point, how most men and women groom even today in remote rural villages of Africa or Southeast Asia.

Furisode

Customs

Turning to customs, an example is the unique clothing that people of a given culture wear. Consider the Japanese kimono. Not only is the kimono itself a custom, but the custom also dictates what kind of kimono is appropriate, depending on the person's age and marital status, the season or event. Young unmarried women wear a kimono with long sleeves called furisode—a colorful kimono—very vibrant, colorful and rich with patterns and with flowing sleeves that hang almost to the ankles. Older women or those who have married, wear a kimono with short sleeves called tomesode—designs are smaller or solid and the colors are more subdued.[8]

Today, and for most Japanese women, kimonos are reserved for ceremonial occasions such as weddings. Most Japanese wear regular Western style clothing. Why then, you might ask, are we discussing kimonos? Kimono making was once a thriving industry in Japan; today, it is an industry in decline. That is precisely our point—a clear illustration of the power of custom in dictating consumption behavior. A custom can start and sustain a whole industry; its decline and demise (often due to cultural adaptation to emerging circumstances) can banish it.

Tomesode

Dowry, Bride Price, and Other Strange Cultural Practices

While they do not make sense in present times, all cultural practices are functional in their origin, no matter how weird or repulsive they might seem today. Consider the customs of dowry and bride price. In a minute we will tell you why, in the context of present day consumer behavior, we chose to describe these dying practices. But first note their cultural significance: although they are exact opposites, both serve the same function, in two different circumstances. Dowry means the bride's parents had to make a huge payment to the groom before he would agree to marry the woman. Bride price means the groom had to make the payment to the bride's family.

TABLE 9.4

The History of Selected Wedding Traditions

Lifting the Veil	Veils were originally meant to symbolize the virgin bride's innocence and modesty. These days, our society considers the veil a purely romantic custom. But in parts of the Middle East and Asia, the veil is still used to hide the bride's face completely. The first lace veil is said to have been worn by a woman named Nelly Curtis, George Washington's adopted daughter, who married one of his aides. Apparently, the first time the aide ever saw her, she was behind a lace curtain. He was mesmerized by her beauty. Nelly, the story goes, made herself a lace veil for the ceremony in an effort to duplicate the effect.*.
Bridal Showers	were meant to reaffirm the friendships between the bride and her friends, and give her moral support. The idea dates from the 1890's, when a woman held a party for her newly engaged friend. The bride-to-be stood in the middle of the room while a Japanese paper parasol filled with little gifts was turned upside down over the bride's head.
Best Man	When the marriages were by kidnapping, the groom needed the help of a warrior friend, who would help him fight off other men who wanted this woman, and also help hide the bride and groom so as to prevent her family from finding them.
Bridal Party	In the Anglo-Saxon days, grooms got their brides by kidnapping them, with the help of friends—the "bridesmen" or "brideknights." They would make sure the bride got to the church and to the groom's house afterwards. The bride also had women to help her, the "bridesmaids" or "brideswomen."
Tossing the Bridal Bouquet & Garter	This dignified custom began in the thirteen hundreds in France, where the guests used to chase the bride and tear off her garter because they believed it was good luck. To save herself, her leg, and her dress, the bride began removing it voluntarily and tossing it into the eager crowd. Later, the bouquet was added to this toss. The lucky recipient of the bouquet is now believed to be the next woman in the group to get married. The man who catches the garter is supposed to be the next groom.*
Carrying the Bride across the Treshold	This wedding custom originated in Italy-Rome. The bride had to be carried across the threshold because she was (or pretended to be) reluctant to enter the bridal chamber. In those days, it was considered ladylike to be hesitant at this point-or at least look hesitant. (Another legend has it that the bride was carried over the threshold to protect her from any evil spirits lingering there).
The Wedding Ring	is worn on the third finger because the ancient Romans believed that the vein in the third finger ran directly to the heart.
Wedding Cake	The wedding cake was a fertility symbol. Ancient Romans would bake a cake made of wheat or barley and break it over the bride's head as a symbol of her fertility. Later, it became a tradition to pile up several small cakes, one on top of the other, as high as they could, and the bride and groom would kiss over the tower, trying not to knock it down. If they were successful, it meant a lifetime of prosperity.
Tying the shoes to the bumper of the car	The wedding cake was a fertility symbol. Ancient Romans would bake a cake made of wheat or barley and break it over the bride's head as a symbol of her fertility. Later, it became a tradition to pile up several small cakes, one on top of the other, as high as they could, and the bride and groom would kiss over the tower, trying not to knock it down. If they were successful, it meant a lifetime of prosperity.
Bride on the Left	When the groom fought off other warriors wanting his bride, he would hold onto her with his left hand, while fighting them off with his sword in his right hand, which is why the bride stands on the left, and the groom on the right.
The Honeymoon	When the marriages were by "capture" of the bride, the groom disappeared for a while so that the bride's family couldn't rescue her. By the time they were found in hiding, the bride would already be pregnant.
The Best man's Toast	This originated from the French, who placed a piece of bread at the bottom of a glass and then drank "down to the toast."

Excerpted from NATURAL HISTORY OF LOVE, by by Diane Ackerman, copyright ©1995, by Diane Ackerman., p. 268-273. Used by permission of Random House.

Dowry is an ancient custom in Hindu India, intended to compensate the groom's family for having to feed one more person. Although it has been now outlawed, it is still unofficially practiced by many. Today, many parents in India happily give many presents

Products as Cultural Symbols
12 Symbols of Life in African Culture

In African wedding ceremonies, the officiant may administer the twelve symbols of life, each representing the love and strength that brings two families together:

Wine   The mixing of the blood of the two families Wheat   Fertility and the giving of life and land

Pepper   Heated times the families will have

Salt   Healing and preservation of marriage

Bitter Herbs   Growing pains of married life Water   Purity, dissolution of bitterness

Spoon, Pot   Healthy food that builds strong families Broom   Cleanliness of health and wellbeing

Honey   Sweet love between a black man and woman Spear   Protection of the sanctity of home and community

Shield   Honor and pride of the home

Bible or Koran   Symbol of God's truth and power

Source: Adapted form: ttp://www.africanweddingguide.com/history/symbolsoflife.html

to the groom's family (even when the latter do not demand it), because they can afford it and they want to help their daughter and her groom set up a new household (there is no custom of bridal showers in the Indian tradition).

Among Africans, the opposite practice prevails—the practice of bride price, called *Lobola*. It is reported to have had two rationales: (1) to pay the bride's family for taking away a "domestic worker" and (2) to keep fickle-minded suitors away and test the commitment of a serious suitor. If a man was willing and able to assemble a large sum and give it away, then he was really committed to the union. Although many modern African people consider the practice derogatory, many defend it on the ground that the two rationales of the origins of Lobola still apply.[9]

Bridal Showers and Bridal Registries

What has replaced these customs in the modern day? If you guessed the answer from the subheading here, you guessed right—bridal showers and bridal registries are modern day equivalents of dowries and the bride price. They serve the same purpose—helping a new couple set up their household. Today, showers and registries are big business. Every department store and gift shop has a bridal registry set up: go there and ask for it by the bride's name. You will get the bride's wish list, specifying exact size, color, and brand name. Violate this custom—by not contributing to the bride's gift chest, and see how much you endear yourself to the bride. If you really want to be remembered as a favorite contributor, thanks to an enterprising tour marketer, TheBigDay.com, you can now buy the couple their honeymoon trip to a resort island—or you can buy pieces of it. And let us remind you that this practice—of bridal registries—is not universal, and it is therefore a very cultural thing. Indeed, the practice of going on a honeymoon is itself a western cultural concept—now, of course, well permeated into at least the urban population segments everywhere. But none of these socially learned concepts—dating, wedding, honeymooning—none of these would endure if they were not widely shared and accepted in a given society.

Myths   The third cultural practice is myths. **Myths** are tales and stories handed down through history without known origins and with no test of truth. Nobody knows if they happened, but they ring true (albeit sometimes with some stretch of credulity). They amuse us, and they have a kernel of "feel good" after-taste in them—like the victory of good over evil. There are two kinds of mythical stories: (1) superhuman, (2) human. Superhuman stories entail some mythical character performing superhuman feats, or some superpower bestowing an incredible, impossible blessing or curse on someone's human deeds. In contrast, human myths

An African Myth

The Man with the Goat

Once upon a time, looking for employment, a barefoot villager left home with his only prize possession, a goat.

Along the road, hiding in the bushes, was a hungry thief wearing new shoes. Sighting the traveler with a goat, he instantly thought of a trick to steal the goat. He placed his shoes in the middle of the road, each a few hundred yards apart. When the villager arrived near the first shoe, he looked at it but left it untouched and moved on. A few minutes later, when he saw the second shoe, he got so excited that he forgot about the goat and ran back to get the first shoe. However, the thief had by now already retrieved back the first shoe. Feeling sad, when the villager came back to the spot where he had left his goat, he found neither the second shoe nor the goat.

Source: Adapted from http://eev2.liu.edu/e3/stargazer/africa.htm (DoA November 5, 2003).

CONSUMERS' ENVIRONMENT

My Indian Wedding, My American Wedding: Wedding customs differ across cultures. Among other things, they entail different style of clothing. Without apt "consumption"—of clothing and other accoutrements—as guided by culture, some of life's milestone events will just not be the same.

(Photo: Sagar Kakani and Jennifer Wehking, in an Indian wedding ceremony, left, and in an American wedding ceremony, right.)

entail mythical stories of ordinary people doing ordinary things, with good things or bad things coming to them. Such human stories are myths because their historic truth cannot be proved. In myths, the star of the story can be a hero or an anti-hero. The mythical story of the Hindu monkey god Hanumana is of the former kind—superhero and hero; the African mythical story of the goat and the shoe is of the latter type—human and anti-hero.

Now these myths have a "moral" to teach. The Hindu monkey god's feat has two morals: (a) no evil power will succeed over good intentions, and (b) total loyalty and dedication means you should be willing to even 'move mountains.' The African myth of the man with a goat teaches that if you stray from a promise you have made to your family (or a goal you have set yourself) and are tempted by other distractions, you can lose everything.

The Deeper Functions of Ritualistic Cultural Practices

If you found this tour of wedding rituals, honeymoons, and monkey gods amusing, that is because most cultural practices do contain an element of amusement. But there is a deeper side to all this: all ritualistic practices serve deeper, fundamental functions. These functions are: (a) achieving sacredness, (b) value inculcation, and (c) meaning communication (see Figure 9.2).

a. Achieving Sacredness

Precisely because ritual practices cannot be explained logically, they acquire the status of sacredness. Thus, in a Hindu wedding, for example, the bride and groom 'walk' around the fire seven times; in an African wedding the bride and groom sweep together with a broom. Why? Answer: This is how it is done; without it, the wedding <u>has</u> not occurred. As humans, we constructed a concept called 'wedding,' and we wrote a script for it. That is the way it is, and it is not to be questioned. After all, so it may not be taken lightly, a wedding does need to be sacred.

But those rituals do have a meaning, you might argue. Those knowledgeable about these rituals will point out, correctly, that the seven circles in the Hindu wedding accompany the seven vows the groom takes, and the broom jumping signifies a public display of intended cooperation and sharing of responsibilities by the couple. But think again: Couldn't the Hindu groom say his vows another way? And why couldn't the African

Hindu Monkey God Hanumana

Prince Rama (actually, an incarnation of the Hindu God Vishnu) was roaming the forests (in a 13-year long exile engineered by his jealous stepmother), with his wife and brother in tow. One day, something bit the brother, and to save his life, a sage prescribed an herb. The herb was grown on a distant mountain and it had to be brought in before daylight. Hanumana, who had enlisted himself as Rama's disciple and helper, and who was bestowed with the power to fly, was dispatched to fetch the medicinal herb. The herbal plant was to be recognized by the special glow it emitted.

When Hanumana arrived at the mountain, he found all of the bushes glowing. A demon, who would love nothing more than to see Rama's brother die, had, by his magical powers, created a glow in every bush on that mountain. Perplexed, Hanumana uprooted the entire mountain, put it on his palm and flew back the whole distance. The sage identified the medicinal herb and saved young prince Rama's brother's life.

Hindu Monkey God Hanumana

couple take a vow to cooperate and share, instead of doing the broom-sweeping? How about making those vows a document that is signed and notarized? You could do that, but that will make, you see, the whole thing totally "so earthly," removing from it the aura of it being something "heavenly," something sacred. Of course, many Hindu couples are now getting married in a civil court, but that is not a Hindu wedding. And many Christians are getting married in civil courts, but then those are not Christian weddings.

If this topic of sacredness has caught your fascination, and we hope it has, then you should read, in this chapter, *CB BrainDish: The Sacred and The Profane.*

b. Value Inculcation

Cultures also inculcate values—remember 'values' are the bedrock of culture. Many values are inculcated by the indoctrination by our elders—"Johnny, you can't steal your friend's toy"; "Lisa, nice girls don't lie"; or "Tom, you shouldn't bully your classmates." Everyday, we receive value lessons, as direct exhortation and through rewards and sanctions.

But there is another, less painful, way to receive values. In bedtime stories, folktales, and epics, values get passed from generation to generation. These tales and stories are called myths. And you have seen how mythical stories all have a moral, a life lesson.

c. Meaning Communication

Rituals as well as customs have symbolic meanings. Wearing black when in mourning is a custom that conveys that you feel sorrow. It could have been any other somber color, but we settled on black, and now the problem of how to communicate your sorrow and sympathy is solved. Chinese wear white to a mourning, and that is fine too, for in their community, white has come to communicate sorrow. Likewise, if you wear a conservative suit, you communicate that you mean business. Companies that are now making it their custom for employees to wear business casual are communicating that they are innovative and are open to new ideas. Communication of meaning is an important function of culture; let us look at it more closely.

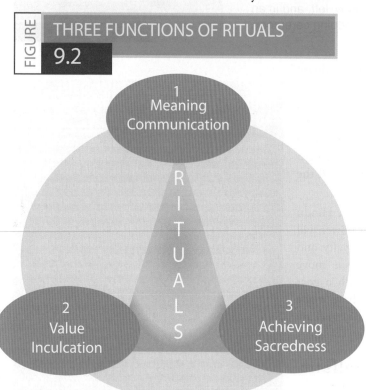

FIGURE 9.2
THREE FUNCTIONS OF RITUALS

RITUALS

1 Meaning Communication

2 Value Inculcation

3 Achieving Sacredness

CULTURE: A WEB OF MEANING

If we were to put our fingers on the single, most significant purpose of culture and indeed its very essence, we would say it is 'meaning.' Meaning is what culture is all about; culture serves as the conduit of all meaning in life. Much of our everyday living depends on social communications—our communication of 'what we mean' with other humans. Culture is like the underground wiring that lights up the whole city; it is our underground cable that conveys meaning to all inhabitants of the society. All these social communications can be grouped into four categories: (a) desires and expectations—what we want and expect from others; (b) values and tastes—what our own values, tastes, and preferences are; (c) identity—what our self-concept and our identity is; and (d) sentiments—perhaps the most important, what our feelings toward others are, and what sort of relationships we desire with them.

We communicate these through language, where we use words to mean more than what they literally do, but even more frequently we communicate these through gestures, actions, public display of our possessions, and consumption of products that have symbolic meanings. We choose the products we believe carry the intended meanings. Put another way, we encode our intent in these products. At the receiving end, our listeners and our audience decode these, inferring our intent. Two people of the same culture understand the figurative meaning of words and gestures they exchange, and they understand the silent language of our actions, our possessions, and our consumption choices. People from two different cultures either don't see the same meaning, or they misread it. Culture is the grand interpreter; it is the dictionary of the silent language.[10] See Figure 9.3.

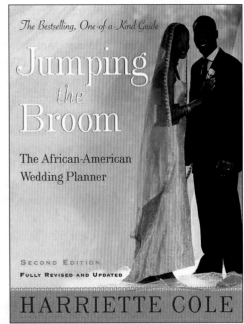

Photo Reprinted by arrangement with Henry Holt and Company, LLC.

MODERN DAY MYTHS AND URBAN LEGENDS

The mythical stories of Hanumana and the man with the goat described above illustrate the role of myths as value conveyors in popular culture. What do they have to do, you might ask, with consumer behavior? But myths are myths, and the modern day consumption myths are no different. Perhaps the most famous of these is the myth of Santa Claus. Believed (or make-believed) by millions of consumers around the world, the moral 'value' lesson of that myth is unmistakable: "Good things will come to you if you act well." And that myth now accompanies an elaborate ritual—the celebration of Christmas as a big holiday when everyone is supposed to give a gift to family and friends. Retail businesses do as much business during the week of Christmas as they do over several months iduring rest of the year!

CB BrainDish

THE SACRED AND THE PROFANE

Sacredness is an intangible entity that is other-worldly. It may be a god, angels, saints, ancestors, superheroes, mystical experiences, and the like. Objects that pertain to these intangible, unearthly entities also become, by association, sacred. Thus, the Bible and Quran are sacred; the temple, the church, the mosque, and the synagogue are sacred. So is the family alter (in the Chinese culture), the river Ganges (in the Hindu culture), and the Olympic torch. In fact, since the sacred is intangible, we use worldly objects to make it tangible, by linking certain objects and activities to the sacred. Four noteworthy properties of sacredness are:[1]

- Sacred things belong to "a different order of reality."
- Sacred things are treated with reverence.
- People interact with the sacred through rituals.
- People feel a deep personal connection with sacred things

We do not question the "reality" of sacred things. They belong to a different order of reality, and we take them on faith. Since they are other-worldly, we also treat them with reverence. We interact with them through rituals, such as the worship ritual, or an annual day of remembrance, i.e., Mexicans celebrate the Day of the Dead to remember all their dead. In these interactions, we feel a special, even spiritual connection with them. That is why the experience of the sacred is a source of great personal satisfaction to many consumers.

The absence of sacred is the mundane—the everyday things and worldly practices like grooming and eating and watching TV. The diametrically opposite is profane—vulgar, sinful, and taboo. Of course what is considered taboo, sinful, and prurient is itself part of cultural norms and is relative to a culture and a time in history. Vivid images of sex acts in ancient stone carvings on the façade of holy temples of Khajuraho in India are testimony to the fact that some ancient civilizations viewed sex differently. In modern times, The Museum of Sex opened in Manhattan, New York, in early 2003.[2]

---

1. .Adapted form Russell W. Belk, Melanie Wallendorf, and John F. Sherry, Jr., "The Sacred and the Profane: The Theodicy of the Odyssey," *Journal of Consumer Research*, 16, June 1989, 1-38.
2. Joel Stein, "Having Sex, Museum Style," TIME, October 21, 2002, p. 92.

A special type of myth is one whose origins are located in our lifetimes. These are called **urban legends**.

As an example, consider the urban legend about Dr Pepper's new can supposedly introduced in late 2001, in the wake of 911, to capitalize on the intense patriotic feelings the 911 event had aroused in Americans. Its substance as well as its *modus operandi* (i.e., how urban legends spread in a population) can be best gleaned from a newsgroup entry on a Web site, as follows:

> For those who have not heard, the bottlers/manufacturers of Dr Pepper and their other products have started a "new" can campaign. They are putting patriotic scenes on them. One is the Empire State Bldg. with the pledge of allegiance...but ... they left off the words..."under God." They felt it might "offend" some. I don't know about you, but as a Christian, I am boycotting their products! They said they didn't "have room" for those words, but yet they had room for "indivisible" on the can!
>
> Please pass this along to others and see if we can get a message out to Dr Pepper ... if having "under God" on cans offends them, then they don't need our money with "in God we trust" on it!   (Source: Courtesy Murray Wells, Urban Legend Blog, ulblog.org)

FIGURE 9.3 MEANING COMMUNICATION WITHIN A CULTURE

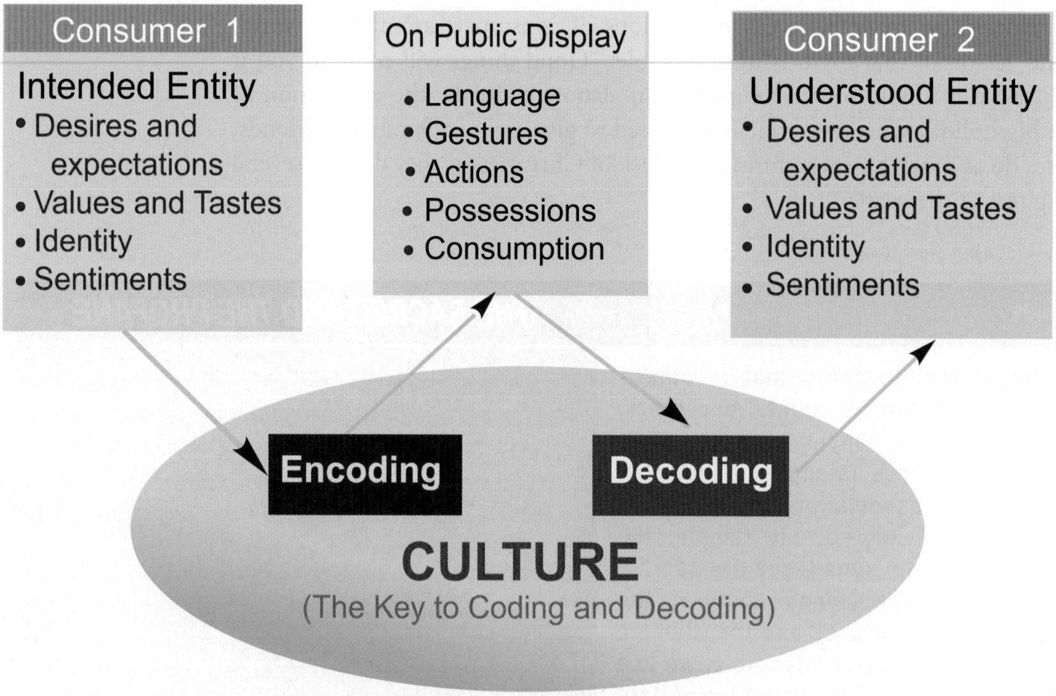

Consumer 1	On Public Display	Consumer 2
Intended Entity • Desires and expectations • Values and Tastes • Identity • Sentiments	• Language • Gestures • Actions • Possessions • Consumption	**Understood Entity** • Desires and expectations • Values and Tastes • Identity • Sentiments

Encoding   Decoding

CULTURE
(The Key to Coding and Decoding)

Does this urban legend serve any purpose? Yes, it does. In the U.S., there had been a move for sometime by some interest groups to delete the words "under God" from the Pledge of Allegince because their use in government business violates, as some argued, the constitutionally guaranteed separation of church and state. In fact, the San Francisco Ninth Circuit Court of Appeals ruled in favor of the argument in June 2002. Later that same month, the U.S. Senate unanimously voted to support the Pledge, rebutting the court's decision. While the urban legend arose and spread before these legal and political decisions, the genesis of the legend and the rush of email activity it generated in the wake of the constitutional debate proves the point—for the supporters of "under God," the legend was a handy tool to oppose the secular forces, and in this case, it was also closely tied to consumption.

We have been citing the marketing and consumer behavior implications of culture throughout, but this is a good place to pull together a more extensive account of how culture and its various elements impact consumer behavior and marketing practice. Let us begin with the most obvious connections and impacts—continuing our tale of rituals, customs, and myths.

Most rituals and customs entail consumption of products and services. Many holidays are customs, and they entail elaborate ritualistic activities. Christmas is perhaps the most celebrated ritual around the world. The Fourteenth of February, celebrated as Valentine's Day in much of the Western world, generates the highest 24-hour floral sales of the year and is second only to Christmas in the number of greeting cards sent. Products such as candy, stuffed animals, wine, perfume, and restaurant meals receive a big boost on this day. Overnight on one February the 13th, Federal Express delivered more than three million pounds of roses! That was enough to fill seven 747 cargo jets—flying from South American to North American florists. By the next morning, there were $331 million worth of flowers in the shops of florists and retailers around the country.[3] Likewise, In Israel, Passover is celebrated by nearly every household. In much of the Muslim world, Ramadan is the period of fasting and prayers (when many businesses and stores actually close down), followed by a bout of festivities and consumption.

In order to even know what products and services are needed, you have to know what a particular ritual or custom in a particular society is. Suppose you set up business to supply products for a Chinese wedding, or you were a wedding planner for a Jewish wedding. You would have to know what each wedding ritual entailed. Secondly, for products and services used in rituals and customs, what we would call the "fidelity of form" matters. A bar soap maker can choose the color and the shape of the soap any which way, or a soup maker can choose any container shape; but the form—the packaging and presentation—of goods intended for use in rituals has to be exactly as specified in the script (written or oral) of the ceremony.

CROSSING CULTURES: MARKETING BLUNDERS

Knowing the so-called script for cultural rituals is a prerequisite for meeting the consumer needs for ritualistic consumption. If you want to serve beer on St. Patrick's Day, as a marketer, you must know how to make the beer green. But an understanding of cultures—all elements of culture—is required, in fact, for all manner of marketing, whether or not related to ritualistic consumption needs. The annals of marketing are filled with stories of cross-cultural marketing blunders committed by unsuspecting marketers just because they forgot to check the local culture. Below is a brief litany of actual blunders, potential traps, and some pointers for future reference.

Lost in Translation Foremost among these blunders are the ones due to an obvious factor: differences in languages. These mistakes come in two forms: (a) the brand name acquires some undesired meaning in a foreign language, and (b) when translated, a message loses its original meaning.

When Colgate introduced a toothpaste in France, under the brand name Cue, it learned that in France, the word 'cue' is sexual slang. Coca Cola's Fresca was Mexican slang for lesbian. Ford's truck model Fiera translated into Spanish as "ugly old woman." Its Caliente model caused amusement in Mexico, where the word is slang for street walker. Also in Spanish, GM's Nova became "It doesn't go"!

Likewise, the copy theme or tag line may be translated inaccurately. In Spanish, Hertz's tagline "puts you in the driving seat" became "Let Hertz make you a chauffeur." GM's "Body by Fisher" became "Corpse by Fisher" in Flemmish. In Chinese, Kentucky Fried Chicken's "Finger-lickin Good" became "Eat your fingers off."

Across cultures, product meanings get lost or distorted because everyday behaviors

Halloween and Holi

Just like the Seven Wonders of The World, there are perhaps a handful of cultural festivities that are at once bizarre and utterly delightful. We bring two of them to you.

The first is Halloween. If you live in North America, on the evening of October 31, you will witness something quite a feast for the eyes. It begins with a relatively timid ritual where children dress up in costumes and go door-to-door, collecting candies. "Trick or treat?" they ask when someone opens a door. Nobody challenges them to show a trick; instead they are given a candy readily. Also, there are haunted houses for children to visit during the surrounding days.

For adults, the fun begins late in the evening. They dress up in costumes ranging form devilish outfits and ugly, scary makeup to fancy dresses and masks, mimicking celebrities and movie characters. One popular albeit clichéd option for a group of friends: Hugh Hefner and playboy girls! People gather at private parties and in pubs and nightclubs, to show and see, and sometimes to win a prize in a costume contest.

The lure of the prize (up to $5000 in some contests) draws wild imagination from many; From total body paint to salt and paper shakers, cereal killer (boxes of cereals pinned on killer costume), ER theater on a patient with body organs sprinting out, adults dressed as babies, as belly dancers, as King Tut, and, yes, even as Gandhi!

Blue Witch: Jessika Flint of Charlottesville (VA) as Lavinia from *Crimson Cult*

At the other end of the globe is a cultural festival called *Holi*. Holi is an Indian festival of fire and color, literally. Actually, a national campfire and paint spraying party! It is celebrated over two days, in late March. On the night before, a bonfire is lit, one in virtually every neighborhood, commemorating the burning of a demon in a Hindu epic. For weeks before that, youngsters collect firewood (tree branches, wood planks, old furniture, whatever). Then on the designated night, everyone gathers around the bonfire, some singing folksongs, some just watching, and some hopping from one neighborhood to another to see other bonfires.

The next morning, everyone comes out in their not-so-new clothes, ready to spray (and be sprayed on) colored water and dry color. On friends and strangers alike. You might be hit with a balloon full of colored water from a total stranger; or a more adventurous group of strangers might hoist you and dunk you in a tub of colored water. Of course, what you really enjoy is rubbing wet or dry paint on the faces of friends, family members, coworkers, and people you love.

Later in the evening, with everyone washed up and donning new or near-new clothes, people visit friends, in a whirling tour, who offer sweet treats. It is a time, some believe, for even old enemies to become friends again. And the color on your faces and bodies? Well, some of it stays on for days. Shows you really had fun (or "fun" was forced on you)!

These cultural rituals are utterly delightful— for revelers and spectators alike!

Holi Photo: Courtesy Sweta Thota

CONSUMERS' ENVIRONMENT

MyCBBook

of people differ in meaning. An American underarm spray ad showed a woman applying the spray to a shaved underarm; the ad backfired in Italy because Italians do not consider a woman respectable if she shaves her armpits.

To avoid such blunders, as a marketer, you should use back-translation, a method where a foreign translation is translated back into the original language by a different person. The back-translated version is then compared with the original version.[11]

Written Script Another aspect of language is how it is written and read. Arabic is read from right to left. So, before and after comparison ads, when translated into Arabic, would be totally absurd if the before and after placement of images is not reversed. Interestingly, this might actually work well if you are advertising a diet and fitness product or service, because, in most Arabic countries, slight heaviness, not thinness, is valued as beauty in women. But if your ad is comparing clothing before and after a wash, you can consider your ad money a total wash out. Also, keep in mind that the Arabic magazines are read from back to front (from an English, Spanish, or any of the European language point-of-view, of course); so be careful in laying out the "next" page.

Colors Various colors don't mean the same thing in different cultures. In Brazil, purple signifies death; in Western Europe and the U.S., it is black; in Hong Kong, Japan, and India, it is white; in Mexico and Taiwan, it is yellow; and in Singapore, it is green. White lilies suggest death in England. In Mexico, yellow flowers symbolize death; but in France, they signify infidelity. The color blue is feminine in Holland, but it is masculine in Sweden.

Wait, there is more to such symbolism than meets the eye. You wouldn't pack gifts in these colors in these countries, but on other products, per se, the colors are used routinely without evoking the death symbolism. In the U.S., for example, where black is used for mourning, the same color is considered trendy and classy in evening dresses and majestic in cars. In India, white clothes are worn for mourning, but that is because death rituals are deemed to be sacred; indeed, in clothing, white is considered a color of "purity" and is accordingly used for all worship ceremonies and in everyday clothing. In Japan, yellow is used widely, but wear a solid yellow suit in Japan and you would be offending your Japanese customers—there, yellow color in clothing is reserved for the royalty.[12] In China, wear a white carnation to a business meeting, and you might as well forget doing any business—there and in other Pacific countries, the white carnation is a symbol of death. The moral of the story: It is a good idea to check with your local culture guide what colors are appropriate for specific uses.[13]

Numbers and other symbols Likewise, numbers have symbolic meanings that differ across cultures. In the U.S. and India, two otherwise vastly different countries, the number 13 is considered unlucky. In Japan, it is the number 4. So, in Japan, you don't want to pack your products in packs of four. As an example of a symbol, an owl is considered bad luck in India, but it signifies wisdom in America. In Korea, a snake symbolizes wisdom; in most other countries, it symbolizes danger.

Standards of Nudity and Taboo Topics Standards in the acceptance of nudity

---

CULTURES THAT SAVE FACE!

One particular cultural value in the Eastern societies is so unique that we "got to" tell you about it. This entails the concept of face found in the Asian cultures, most prominently in China and Japan. Face refers to self-respect, and everyone in these societies is expected to "maintain face." Now, keeping self-respect is important in all societies, but nowhere is "losing face" deemed so disgraceful as in China and Japan (along with a few other Asian nations). Keeping face is every human's right and losing it implies that you have even fallen below being a human. Because it is every human's right (unless he or she does something wrong), others are expected to honor it and not cause anyone to lose face. That means you must not criticize a person, and if you need to call attention to his or her poor performance, you must do so indirectly. Thus, if a waiter brought you a wrong order, for example, you would politely ask for a different order (not a "correction" but a "different" order). If you disagree with someone, you would not say so explicitly (this would mean you are causing him or her to lose face); rather, you would say that you are "not sure." One has to be intensely acculturated to understand both the nuances of behavior necessary to help others keep face and to realize its prowess on peoples' psyche in those cultures.

vary across cultures. In Western Europe and Australia, nudity in public media is accepted much more than in the U.S., which in turn is more accepting than the Eastern countries such as India, China, Thailand, etc., are. It is least accepted in Islamic countries such as Saudi Arabia. A perfume ad for Guerlain (Paris) showed a scantily clad woman strolling on the Champs-Elysees in Paris with Arc de Triumph in the background; in the Arabic version, while the Arc de Triumph was retained in the background (the French association is valued for perfumes in Arabic countries as well), the model had to be fully clad.

Sex and personal hygiene products are discussed freely on American TV. In much of Asia, they are a taboo. So, you couldn't advertise contraceptives, for example, on Chinese, Thai, or Philippine TV until after it was past bedtime for children, and magazine ads for Viagra and Levitra, so common in U.S. and Western magazines, could not be run in these countries.[14]

Product Consumption Differences Product consumption differs across cultures. Wine is a staple beverage in Europe to be consumed with every meal; in the U.S., it is a leisure and celebration drink. Two-wheeler mopeds and horse-driven carriages are still used as the principal means of transportation in some countries, as are water-taxis. Mini skirts or even midis are not worn in Arab countries. Foods obviously differ not only across countries but also across different ethnic groups within the same nation.

For consumption with a cultural twist, consider alcohol consumption in Japan: Japanese culture sanctions it, even in excess! Male employees generally go out to drink after work with their coworkers and bosses. It is considered an insult to coworkers or to one's boss to refuse a drink. Often, people get drunk. But in Japan, getting drunk is not seen as a stigma. In fact, there is implicit support for it—it is seen as an emotional outlet for the Japanese who, under the norm of consensus-based decision-making, otherwise keep their personal feelings bottled up! If you ever get to market your product to consumers of a foreign culture, your number one priority should be to adapt your product to suit the local culture.

VALUE COMPATIBILITY IN MARKETING COMMUNICATIONS

Perhaps the most important marketing implication of cultural differences is the need to ensure that your ad reflects the values of local culture. A recent ad for Kiplinger showed a line up of business executives with one of the executives facing the camera. The headline proclaimed, *Stand out from the crowd.*[15] Would you run that ad in countries like Japan, China, Philippines, or Pakistan—even after you replaced the models with local faces? And why not?

As this litany shows, the nuances in each culture are so many and so subtle that your best bet is to have a local culture guide check all your marketing communications. And don't ever send abroad a salesperson who is highly ethnocentric. Here is why.

CULTURAL ETHNOCENTRISM

Do you believe that your culture is superior to all other cultures? Many people do. This is called *ethnocentrism*—the belief in the superiority of one's own culture over all others. This helps ethnocentric people and nations maintain a degree of self-esteem, as individuals and as a nation. But taken to extremes, it can result in ill will toward other cultures and an unwelcoming attitude toward foreigners. People who travel around the world become more cosmopolitan in their outlook and more appreciative of other cultures. While they retain a healthy respect for their own culture, they acquire an understanding and appreciation of foreign cultures and greater tolerance of their cultural practices.

Do you qualify to visit with your overseas customers? To find out, you need to take a test, shown in Table 9.5. Go ahead, take it. How did you do? If you score high, you are too ethnocentric. You need some exposure to other cultures and to learn to admire their uniqueness.

The consumer behavior most affected by ethnocentrism is buying products of foreign origin. Consumer researchers have called this particular behavior *consumer ethnocentrism*—consumers' proclivity to view the buying of foreign goods as unpatriotic. It is easy to measure by a scale called CETSCALE, shown in Table 9.6. Rate yourself on it too, and see where you stand. Individuals with high "consumer ethnocentrism" are—('least' or 'most', you decide) likely to buy foreign made goods.[16] But don't confuse this score with your *general* ethnocentrism. Your "consumer ethnocentrism" means only that you take pride in buying domestically and helping your nation that way. High *general* ethnocentrism means, on the other hand, that you consider all other cultures inferior to your own, and that most likely you are a chauvinist.

THE SILENT LANGUAGE OF CULTURE
How to Avoid Putting Your Foot in Your Mouth

Even if you score well on the general ethnocentrism scale—scoring well means not being too ethnocentric—you are still not ready to meet your client in a foreign culture. You also need to understand certain invisible and unwritten cultural nuances—what cultural anthropologist Edward Hall calls, "the silent language of business."[17] This silent language can be summarized along six dimensions: formality, friendships, personal space, time, explicitness, and business relationships.

Formality and Protocol As already mentioned, Americans become informal quickly and begin to address even first-time business acquaintances by their first names. In contrast, in England and many other parts of Europe, as well as in Asia, using first names would be rude. In fact, in many Asian and Middle Eastern countries, even close friends continue to address each other with a salutation added to their

CROSS-CULTURAL *FAUX PAS*

Toyota Ads Bite the Dust in CHINA

In Late 2003, Toyota launched an advertising campaign in China for its new brand Prado. Within months, the company had to pull back the campaign and apologize. As the flood of scathing emails sent to the company revealed, the campaign had hit a nerve with many Chinese consumers. The reason: unbeknownst to the company, the campaign was insulting to the Chinese sense of patriotism in a way only someone familiar with Chinese culture and history would reckon.

The campaign showed stone lions saluting and bowing to a Prado Land Cruiser SUV. The ad copy said: "You cannot but respect the Prado." The ads were supposed to reflect the car's imposing presence on the road, according to an agency spokesperson. But to Chinese, it was a surrender of national pride.

For starters, Prado translated into Chinese as badao, which means "overbearing," or "rule by force." Next, the stone lions resembled those flanking the Marco Polo Bridge near Beijing, which is the site of the opening battle in Japan's invasion of China in 1937. Patriotism ranks high among Chinese values (as it does in most other nations), so one can imagine the wrath the campaign would engender. This cross-cultural marketing blunder is a vivid commentary on how an insider understanding of cultural symbolism—symbols in culture—is an absolute prerequisite for sensible marketing in any culture.

Note that on the car company's part, this is an innocent mistake. The company withdrew the ads immediately, and, in good conscience, apologized: "We want to express our sincere apology for the unpleasant feelings they have generated among Chinese readers."

Based on a report in "JAPAN: Toyota recalls 'offensive' sports vehicle ads in China," Asia Media, The Straits Times, Friday, December 5, 2003. People's Daily, Beijing, Friday, December 05, 2003.

TABLE 9.5	A Scale to Measure General Ethnocentrism

Strongly disagree				Strongly Agree
1	2	3	4	5

1. My group's culture is the best.
2. I have no desire to learn other cultures.
3. The world would be better off if all countries adopted the culture of my country or group.
4. I feel that most of the customs and rituals observed by people of other cultures are silly and absurd.
5. I believe that all cultures can learn from one another.

Note: Some items need to be reverse-scored; can you figure which ones? After scoring each item in the correct direction (to align with the direction of item '1'), add the item scores. If your overall score is 20 or higher, you are definitely ethnocentric.

last name. To an Easterner, then, the informality of the American salesperson can be very off-putting.

There is a particular protocol that the Japanese follow when they meet a business counterpart. It is called *meshi*, an exchange of business cards. Each person presents the card to the other—presents, not gives, mind you; that means, the card is handed over with both hands and turned so it is ready to be read by the receiver. Each person then reads the card loudly, in turn, and acknowledges the other. This reading of the card also enables each person to understand the other in terms of hierarchy and status.

Friendships In Western cultures, friendships are formed easily, or rather the word, *friend* is used much more casually. This is a mixed blessing: on the one hand, people are friendly and helpful even to strangers and even in first encounters. But, on the other hand, it dilutes the meaning of the word 'friendship.' In Eastern cultures, the word is reserved for someone for whom you have true affection, and friendships are considered lifelong commitments. A western salesperson might say, "As a friend, I would advise you …," and to a customer from an eastern culture, this would sound very insincere, especially if the salesperson were to then follow up his or her pitch with business-like negotiations and hard selling.

Personal Space Cultures also differ in what is considered personal space. Latin Americans and Saudis stand much closer to each other than do Americans. Watching an American and a Latin American talking while standing can be entertaining. The American is

TABLE 9.6 — CETSCALE: A Scale to Measure Consumer Ethnocentrism

	Rate the following on a 0-10 point scale where 0 means strongly disagree and 10 means strongly agree.
1.	We should always buy products made in our own country rather than imports.
2.	Our country should import only those products that are unavailable here..
3.	Buy products made in our own country; keep our country working.
4.	Purchasing foreign-made products is unpatriotic.
5.	All imports should be curbed, banned, or heavily taxed.
6.	Foreign manufacturers should not be allowed to put their products on our markets.
7.	It may cost me in the long run but I prefer to support and buy domestic products.
8.	We should not buy foreign products because it hurts our nation's industry and puts our own people out of work.
9.	It is always best to purchase products made in our own country.
10.	For me, to buy domestic products rather than imports is a matter of national pride.

Note: 1. Add your ratings across the ten items. Your score would be between 0 to 100; scores above 50 indicate that, as a consumer, you tend to be ethnocentric. The higher the score, the more "consumer ethnocentric" you are. A perfect score of 100 shows you are devoted to always buying the products made in your own country. 2. The original scale is 17-item long, phrased for American consumers. To make it shorter as well as country neutral, we adopted nine items, paraphrased them for generality, and added the tenth item anew. [the remaining 8 items in the original scale are these: (a) American products, first, last, and foremost. (b) it is not right to purchase foreign products. (c) A real American should always buy American-made products. (d) We should purchase products manufactured in America instead of letting other countries get rich off us. (e) There should be very little of trading or purchasing of goods from the countries unless out of necessity. (f) Foreign products should be taxed heavily to reduce their entry into the U.S. (g) We should buy from foreign countries only those products that we cannot obtain within our own country. (h) American consumers who purchase products made in other countries are responsible for putting their fellow Americans out of work. Note that to make it applicable to any country, the context "American" should be modified as we did in the items we adapted.]

Source: Adapted by author from Terence A. Shimp and Subhash Sharma, "Consumer Ethnocentrism: Construction & Validation of the CETSCALE," *Journal of Marketing Research*, 24, August 1987, p. 282.

constantly walking backwards, trying to maintain his or her personal space, while the Latin American tries, constantly, to bridge that gap. Standing far away, Americans can seem aloof and cold to Latin American customers. Not being aware of this cultural difference can also lead to an advertisement that depicts people standing either too close to or too far from one another, depending on your cultural perspective.

Time The sense of time is different across cultures. First, cultures differ in whether life is fast paced or slow paced, and, correspondingly, whether consumers in general are rushed and value time too much or they are relaxed and less concerned about time. Americans, for example, are generally time conscious, and Netherlanders and Japanese are extremely so; in contrast, Mexicans and Latin Americans are more relaxed. Thus, Americans want to accomplish a business deal quickly and move on. Mexican customers, on the other hand, want to take their time and feel that the American, always in a rush, is being rude.

This difference in sense of time implies that the American concept of fast food restaurants would not receive the same enthusiasm in the relaxed paced cultures of Mexico and Latin America, for example. In these and many Eastern countries, McDonald's and other fast food outlets must position themselves, as they in fact do, as sources of "different" food and convenience (as opposed to speed). And salespersons from Western cultures should not expect to complete a sales transaction quickly.

Also, the importance placed on punctuality differs greatly. Much of the Western world and industrialized nations value punctuality; perhaps Japan takes the prize for running its commerce with precision punctuality. In contrast, in many Eastern countries, to be late is the norm rather than an exception. Perhaps India would take the prize for lateness. In Japan, local and interstate trains run on the dot. In India, in contrast, a common joke is that if a train is on time, it is perhaps the previous day's train! If you are a salesman selling to Indian consumers, don't be surprised if the Indian is late by as much as half an hour, or if they keep you waiting for an hour or longer.

Explicitness Americans and most Westerners are very explicit and direct in communication; in contrast, Easterners and especially the Japanese are very polite and indirect. They will never say "no" to your face. Rather, they will say "it will be difficult." If you are a Western salesperson in Japan, you would annoy your customers if you did not understand this subtlety in communication.

The Japanese also like to be contemplative rather than quick-witted or quick-reacting. There is a story of an American sales team trying to sell something to a group of executives in a Japanese firm. At the end of the proposal presentation, the Japanese executives sat silent for some time. The Americans took this to mean that the Japanese were unwilling to buy, so they offered a lower price. Still no response, they made yet another offer, and, then, yet another. All they met with was still more silence; frustrated, they left. They never realized that the Japanese were not conveying resistance at all. Rather, it was their culture to not react to a proposal right away; not to be contemplative and give the proposal serious consideration and evaluation would have, in their minds, constituted disrespect for the proposal. Besides, unlike in America, in Japan, no single person makes a decision unilaterally; they like to build consensus. Incidents like these bring home a powerful lesson: as a marketer, if you are dealing with customers from foreign cultures, you should know cultural rules of implicit and explicit communication in that country or society.

Relationships and Business Cultures also differ in whether they keep business and social relationships apart. Some cultures keep business and personal relationships independent; others will do business only with people they know and can trust. Latin Americans and Middle Easterners, for example, are unwilling to discuss business unless they come to know you and can trust you. Americans, on the other hand, see business as a formal, impersonal transaction, where contractual obligations substitute for personal trust. To Americans, what matters is the reputation of the company with which they do business; to Latin Americans, the identity of the person with whom they are doing business matters. They are not buying from a company; rather, they are buying from a person.

Bhangra Magic for Cross-Cultural Heart Beats

It is Friday evening and you are at New York Sports Club at 91st and 3rd. You are not a member yet but you have come along at the invitation of a friend. Well, you are in for quite a surprise—nothing of this sort you have seen before at any health club, or anywhere else for that matter. There are members playing racquetball, swimming in the pool, "baking" in the sauna, pumping iron, boosting their cardio on treadmills, or just sitting by the juice bar, of course. But leaving all these options behind, you and your friend join an aerobics dance class in progress. The music is strange; the moves are strange; the shrill everyone bursts out with at intervals is strange. Let us follow the moves.

People raise their arms and push them up and down while turning their hands (as if screwing a light bulb); shrug their shoulders, tromp their feet; they raise one leg and hopscotch on the other. They go forward, backward, sideways, in circles. The trick is to do all this all at once, in sync with others, and to the super fast rhythm of a dhol (Indian drum).

At first you hesitate, then you start following the moves, then the moves begin to come to you naturally, then you join the shrill as well, then you are perspiring profusely, and your heart is thumping sky high, beating as fast as it ever has. An hour of moving your body to a never before rhythm and 500 burned calories later, you are ready for the Sauna. But before you leave, you better buy a DVD of the

workout, for you will not find it anywhere else, and you won't be able to resist yearning to sweat it out to its rhythm again.

The music and dance you just experienced is called Bhangra, a festive folk dance from India (specifically, from the Punjab region), originally improvised to celebrate harvest times. And it is standard fair at most festive gatherings of Indians (at least those who come from the Punjab region), at home and abroad. But lately it has permeated into the mainstream music scene. The music remix with lyrics and beat from Bhangra are played in trendy clubs in New York, L.A., Athens, Florence, and Ibiza, among others. And it has been incorporated into the music of such artists as Missy Elliot, Jay-Z, and Jennifer Lopez.

Bringing it to fitness workouts is Sarina Jain, justly referred to as the Jane Fonda of Bhangra, who founded the Masala Dance Fitness Inc. in New York. Jain is the resident fitness guru for British Broadcasting Company's Asia Radio Network and is the producer and choreographer for four Workout CDs/DVDs. If you are wondering how this dance form from the folk culture of an Eastern country has

become a great marketing success (the Workout CDs or DVDs are being used in many fitness clubs in major US cities and the UK), you have to just watch one of those DVDs. Or better yet, catch Ms. Jain herself performing in one of the regular sessions at fitness venues in New York or San Francisco (where her sister, Sheila runs the West Coast branch of the Masala Dance Company—Masala by the way means spice mix). Ms. Jain is a vivacious personality with electrifying energy, and has a degree in marketing to boot. And the two Jain sisters have understood how to blend dhol rhythms with the science of aerobics, and how to serve Eastern culture to enchant the Western consumers' hearts—in this case, literally, by boosting the heart's rhythm.

POSTMODERN GLOBAL CULTURE:
A Myth or Reality?

In this concluding section of the chapter, we ponder a question that has, for some time now, occupied the minds of social scientists (cultural anthropologists, sociologists, economists, and consumer researchers), guardians of public policy, and consumer activist groups. There is a fear, in some quarters, that the Western style consumption and related consumption values of materialism and commercialism are corrupting otherwise sane consumer societies everywhere. Is this true? Scholars disagree. One camp argues:

Today's Global culture has ties to no place or period. It is contextless, a true mélange of components drawn from everywhere and nowhere, realized through the network of global communication systems.[18]

Today, you can be in any corner of the earth, and you will be able to find your favorite brand of clothes, toiletries, luggage, watches, soft drinks, and even fast food. Coke is everywhere, and McDonald's and Kentucky Fried Chicken (KFC) are opening stores in the once forbidden central economies of China and Russia. In every sense of the word today, Gucci and Banana Republic, Timex and Rolex, Levi's and IBM are global brands. The TV series *Survivor*, *Friends*, and *The Apprentice*, or their reruns are being watched worldwide. The Volkswagen Beetle mania is back worldwide, and American-style rap music is being integrated with domestic music in India and other countries. In dress, cuisine, and media viewership, Western capitalism is evident everywhere. Such shared consumption is cited as cause for concern that cultural diversity is on its way to extinction, and that we are headed toward a culturally homogenized world!

Russell W. Belk, a creative consumer researcher and marketing professor at the University of Utah, disagrees, arguing that obliteration of distinct cultures is not a real threat. Belk cites three factors resisting such a threat.[6] First, consumers admit foreign cultural symbols and icons, but they do so keeping the foreignness of these foreign things visible (as opposed to absorbing them seamlessly)—example: Tokyo Disneyland has an American façade. Second, consumers view global culture as hyper-real (i.e., a make-believe reality to be indulged in occasionally), distinct from the local culture, which is real. For example, Bollywood films are now watched on DVD by consumers of many nationalities around the world (check out *Bride and Prejudice*, for example, an Indian film maker's adaptation of Jane Austen's classic, available in movie rental stores like Blockbuster). And third, consumers individualize foreign products and practices before adoption—for example, McDonald's non-beef burgers in Hindu India. This of course is a simplified version of Belk's more sophisticated analysis. Belk also offers a tongue-in-cheek commentary on the threat of globalization. See the box, "The Consumer Revolt Against the Saints of Commerce,"—Belk's narrative in that tale is pure joy, so read on.[19]

Can Starbucks Become a Pub?

One company that has adapted to the Japanese penchant for drinking is Starbucks. Since Starbucks is famous for coffee latte, you wouldn't go there if you were looking for wine or beer, would you? You could, if you lived in Japan. Many Starbucks shops added wine and beer to their menu in late 2003. The Seattle-based, world famous coffee company had opened 503 outlets at the end of 2003 in Japan, the first one opened in 1996 in Tokyo's Ginza district. But to keep up with the Japanese consumers' beverage consumption culture—Japanese drink beer and wine and green tea more often than they drink coffee—the company's Japan subsidiary approved a country-wide policy to sell beer and wine in its stores in Japan. So while the U.S. stores sell only coffee beverages, its stores in Japan sell beer and wine; and green tea Frappuccino. How successful has this cultural adaptation been? In July 2003, when the company opened its new store in the Nagano prefecture, it broke the worldwide first-day sales record.[1]

Another example of cross-cultural adaptation is the way Barbie is sold around the world—the Barbie that consumers buy differs across cultures. For Africa, the company had to make an African version—darker skin and curlier hair. In India, the original blond American Barbie was okay since Indian children value it precisely for its American appearance. In contrast, in Japan, they had to "Japanize" it a bit: shorter and less curvaceous, with less blond hair and brown eyes.

1. http://www.starbucks.co.jp/en/company_history.htm

The Consumer Revolt Against the Saints of Commerce

The year is 2995 A.D. Archaeologist Gucci Toyota Rolex, a recent graduate of Ralph Lauren University (once Karl Marx University) in Budapest, sits in his IBM sensatorium seeking clues that will help him understand the obscure origins of the major world holidays. He believes that some of these holidays, including Coke Day, Elvis Day, Saint Johnny Walker Day, the Day of the Levi's, Sony Feel-Man Day, and the Feast of the Seven-Eleven, may have originated almost a millennium ago in the 20th or 21st century. But the evidence is far from clear. No major catastrophe or war has obliterated the relevant data. In fact, the period since the likely origin of these holidays is now known as the Pax McDonald's, due to the extended period of world peace that was ushered in after McDonald's first entered what were then known as China, the Soviet Union, and Eastern Europe. This signaled the peaceful global conquest by Saint Ronald McDonald, at a time when McDonald's sold only food products and the people of the world spoke a variety of languages. No, there is a lack of data because, at some point after the development of United World Government and Entertainment Incorporated, history simply lacked any tension to make it interesting. There was also convincing evidence that history was a source of discontent and neuroses. So when people learned to stop recording the trivia of daily and yearly events, history stopped as well.

As a result, even the details of Saint Ronald's birth and life are lost in the mists of antiquity, along with the biographies of lesser deities such as Colonel Sanders, the Michelin Man, and Mickey Mouse. Although he accepts the catechism that history is bunk, Gucci hopes that if the roots of current celebrations and their patron saints can be pieced together, this proof of divine inspiration will help stop a strange sociopathology spreading among a growing number of the people of the earth: heretic asceticism! Not only does this barbaric and nihilistic cult refuse to worship Saint Ronald, but they reject all of our major holidays and refuse to consume the associated products and services to which they are constitutionally entitled. Recently they have also begun to boycott such sacred sites as Marlboro Country, Ford Country, Sesame Street, Disney Universe, and even McDonaldland. What is worse, they fail to show any enthusiasm for the games, even when such arch rivals as Nissan and Toyota contest. Obviously, such hereticism is dangerous and threatens not only the economy but our essential values. Gucci has no desire to kindle nostalgia for a long dead past, but by returning to the origins of world holidays, perhaps the nonbelievers can be made to accept the legends celebrated by these holidays and their sacrilegious apathetic behavior can be stopped before it spreads farther.

Source: Russell W. Belk, "Hyperreality and Globalization: Culture in the Age of Ronald McDonald," *Journal of International Consumer Marketing*, 8, no. 3/4, (1995) pp. 23-37. Reproduced with permission.

CONSUMERS' ENVIRONMENT

e-Consumer Behavior. Do universal cultural value dimensions have relevance to Web portals? According to a recent research study, they do. A content analysis of a sample of Japanese Web sites and likewise of U.S. Web sites revealed that the two groups of Web sites did indeed differ on the extent to which they reflected the cultural value dimensions.

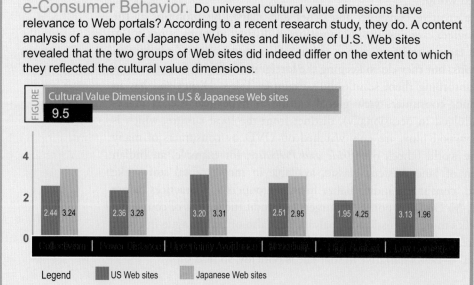

FIGURE 9.5 Cultural Value Dimensions in U.S & Japanese Web sites

	Collectivism	Power Distance	Uncertainty Avoidance	Masculinity	High Context	Low Context
US Web sites	2.44	2.36	3.20	2.51	1.95	3.13
Japanese Web sites	3.24	3.28	3.31	2.95	4.25	1.96

Legend: US Web sites — Japanese Web sites

Scores are mean values on five-point scales: Not depicted at all (1) to prominently depicted (5). Websites were rated by two doctoral students in marketing, who served as judges.

Source: Excerpted and Adapted from Nitish Singh and Hisako Matsuo, "Measuring Cultural Adaptation on the Web: An Exploratory Study of U.S. and Japanese Websites," *Journal of Business Research*, 2002.

Usually, when you think of culture, you think of unique everyday behaviors of people in foreign societies. Thus, the way some men in Saudi Arabia dress (a long flowing coat and a head scarf or cap) is culture to you, and when you see most Chinese eat with chopsticks, that is culture to you—assuming that you live in North America, Mexico, Europe, or Australia. Young adults in Asia marry without dating and that is culture to you. The unique behaviors of your own society don't seem like culture to you, mainly because you don't realize that these are unique behaviors. And non-unique behaviors of any society (such as the daily bath) don't seem culture to you, because you don't realize that a daily bath is a behavior we are not born with but learn as members of society. Similarly, computers, cars, and fast food don't qualify as culture in everyday language because these are just ordinary objects. The fact is, however, that everything humans learn to make and everything humans learn to consume, and if that way of making things and that way of consuming things is shared across people in a society, then all of those things are, by definition, *culture*.

Some think only of fine arts and jazz and symphony as culture and they think of drug culture (of the type shown in the movie *Pulp Fiction*) as *lack* of culture. But if you have understood this chapter, then you know that in the eyes of anthropologists (scientists who study culture), there is no "lack" of culture and no negative culture. Yes, high culture, popular culture, trash culture, counter culture, heroin culture, gay culture, rap culture, 'Bollywood' culture and Hollywood culture, Washington D.C.'s political culture and Vancouver's bohemian culture, Amish culture, and Silicon Valley culture—all are cultures worthy of study and, for marketers, worthy of note. If you want to study any of these cultures, you can simply watch the consumption practices (that include customs, rituals, and everyday activities) of its people. From these overt practices, you can infer the cultural values that necessarily underlie and produce those behaviors. Better still, read cultural accounts by thoughtful writers including essays and works of acclaimed fiction.

One thing we cannot afford to do, however, is to bring an attitude of smugness about our own ways of living. That would make us extreme *ethnocentrics*— a trait that would turn us into modern day cave dwellers, blind to all the rich experiences our culturally diverse world has to offer.

The best way to experience and appreciate culture and its all-pervasive prowess is to get exposure to people of foreign cultures. Travel abroad if you get a chance. But you can find plenty of it within your homeland. Diverse subcultures abound in most countries, the prime example being ethnic subcultures.

So telling are ethnic subcultural differences, in fact, that we were tempted to include them here; or, at the very least, cover them in an immediately following chapter and title that chapter *Subcultures*. We chose instead to hold on to it until all the concepts of consumer behavior (including decision making) will have been covered in a way applicable to consumer behavior *everywhere*. So we cover ethnic groups in a later (and more U.S.-centric) segment of the book where our goal is to describe *differences* among consumers in the U.S.

In the present chapter, we chose to focus only on the universal concepts of culture. In this endeavor, we leave no stone unturned, and neither should you. We excerpt for you cultural profiles of selected countries (Appendix 'A', attached at the end of this chapter). We have tried to make these cultural profiles as fascinating as they come. Even if you decide to do nothing else in life, but especially if you decide to, at least read Appendix 'A,' and later the book from which that Appendix is excerpted.

You will never look at the world the same way again; and for that you will be a better person— a better consumer and a better marketing thinker.

We began this chapter with a definition of culture and a description of its elements—what is included in it. Defining it as the sum of all that we learn and share with others, we argued that it serves as a blueprint for everyday living. Values form its foundation, serving as a source of personal values for us, and serving also as the wellspring for all of its other elements: norms, cultural practices, science and technology, and material objects. Cultural practices include rituals, customs, and myths.

Why does culture exist? It exists because, we argued, it serves certain functions: it regulates society and it makes living more efficient. Along with these two purposes, culture has other properties: it is learned (by definition), it is adaptive (otherwise it will lose its function), it is hierarchical (subcultures are nested within broader cultures), and it is environmental (we are immersed in it and, consequently, are seldom aware of it).

Cultures differ and these differences can be captured in six universal value dimensions. All the countries of the world can be differentiated with this template of six universal values. And we also highlighted the importance of recognizing, beyond the six universal value dimensions, some additional values unique to a culture, illustrating our point with a value contrast between USA and Russia.

Moving on, we described the role of rituals, customs, and myths, both in life per se and for consumption. Rituals, customs, and myths are all value carriers, and often they also serve a function. Ritualistic cultural practices often give sacredness to activities they surround (e.g., wedding rituals), thus making those activities and

events of special value to us as consumers. In all cases, and at the very least, rituals have symbolic value, attaching and conveying meaning to otherwise ordinary consumption. In this context, we presented a model of how culture acts as a meaning communicator.

Following this theoretical treatise, albeit interspersed throughout with practical examples of consumer behavior, we turned explicitly to an extended account of the culture's impact on marketing practices. Here, we illustrated the sources of historical marketing blunders, ranging from naive translation to ill-fitting adaptation of product offerings and disastrous unawareness of cultural symbolism in advertising.

Finally, and to conclude the chapter, we dwelled on a burning issue that has been hotly debated by social scientists and public interest groups alike: Is the spread of Western, materialistic culture corrupting us all; and is such diffusion of culture and consumption homogenizing us, with dilution of cultural heritage and diversity? Are we becoming global consumers, and is it a good thing or a bad thing? Don't think for a moment that this is a mere academic question; its answer will affect all marketers, immensely. If there is an increased resentment, for example, against the so-called *McDonaldization* everywhere, there can be a backlash against marketers who seek to target consumers beyond their borders. The arguments on both sides are rich and thoughtful, and we believe you should read them yourself. On that note, we conclude this chapter.

Culture	Particularism	Myth
Enculturation	High-context culture	Rituals
Acculturation	Low context culture	Sacred
Cultural values	Power distance	National culture
Collectivism	Materialism	Popular culture
Individualism	Voluntary simplicity	Subculture
Universalism	Uncertainty avoidance	Religion

REVIEW✚Rewind

1. How is culture defined in the chapter? What are its characteristics? Discuss why it is important to study culture to understand consumer behavior.

2. Explain in your own words a myth, a custom, a ritual, a norm, and a value, and give a new (not used in the chapter) example of each.

3. What are the universal cultural value dimensions?

Explain each and then name two countries for each end of the cultural value.

4. In face-to-face meetings with foreign customers, why is it important to understand the cultural differences that deal with friendships, time, and personal space?

5. Explain the concept of cultural ethnocentrism? What is its relevance and usefulness to marketers?

6. What functions are served by cultural ritual practices? Illustrate each with a cultural practice with which you are familiar (different from the ones described in the chapter).

7. Draw the model that depicts how culture transfers meaning.

THINK+Apply

1. Review, in your mind, the six universal cultural value dimensions. Suppose you were designing an advertisement for a brand of car for a Western country like Canada, America, or France, and separately for an Eastern country like Saudi Arabia, China, or Japan. How would you make that ad different so it is in harmony with each of the six cultural value dimensions? Now repeat this exercise for a brand of cologne.

PRACTICE+Experience

1. Select two consumers from different national cultures. Interview them to identify how their values and norms differ and how this influences their consumption.

2. Choose any *one* of these countries: (i) Qatar, (ii) Australia, (iii) Portugal, (iv) Malaysia, or (v) Nigeria. Do an Internet search to learn about some prominent cultural values in that country. Next, also research any rituals surrounding (choose one): (a) the birth of a baby; (b) a wedding, (c) a religious festival, or a (d) a non-religious festival. Then identify if any cultural values are reflected in these rituals. Next, identify if any special products and services are used in these rituals.

3. Review the national cultures from the Appendix. You are planning to visit each country as a member of a team of fashion trend spotters working for The New York Times. Assuming that it is better for the team to visit a country where the culture is less dissimilar to your own host country's culture, in which sequence would you advise the team to visit these countries. Also write the team a memo on what cultural adjustments the team members should make in their behaviors when visiting the first country and then again when visiting the second country, and so on.

In the Marketing Manager's Shoes

Put yourself in a marketing manager's shoes. Most concepts in the chapter have some lessons for the marketing manager, i.e., they suggest what to do differently in practice; indeed, often these applications are implicit in our explanations of the concepts and models in the chapter. Identify at least five specific applications of the chapter's concepts, all of which should be entirely new—different from the examples cited here.

Painting by Paul Ruben
Concepts of beauty, as related to body shape (slim versus plump) change through time and across cultures.

A MODEL OF MEANING PRODUCTION AND CONSUMPTION IN A CULTURE

When we consume products, it is their meaning we consume—this we have said already. Also we understood how two people in the same culture communicate meaning. Now we raise our understanding to a higher level. We ask an even more fundamental question: How do products come to acquire meaning in the first place? Who produces this meaning? And what role does culture play in the consumption of meaning. The answer to these questions is captured in the model of meaning production and consumption.

It all begins with culture. Using language, humans in all cultures give some names to objects (e.g., we choose to call them pants or skirts, silk or cotton, etc), persons (e.g., man or woman, jocks or geeks), and qualities (e.g., masculine or feminine, slim or plump, sophisticated or simpleton). Note that the point is not that we choose to call a skirt a skirt or a geek a geek or sophisticated quality sophisticated; rather, the point is that we choose to call some type of person a geek, a garment of a particular shape pants, and a certain quality and characteristic sophisticated. That is, the object, person, and quality exist already; culture and language just give them names. All objects have certain qualities to them, both physical (e.g., slim or plump, long or short) and conceptual; i.e., conceived only in our minds (e.g., ugly or beautiful, useless or effective). Physical qualities are integral with objects. As to conceptual qualities, we assign them, based on their (the objects') tangible sensory features (i.e., how they look, sound, taste, smell, and feel on touching) and based on what they do for us; i.e., their outcomes, their consequences (e.g., fires burn, shampoos cleanse hair, lipsticks make our lips look more beautiful). These qualities and outcomes are seen as desirable or undesirable based on the values and norms of the culture. Thus the fundamental source of meaning is cultural values. Meaning to the properties/qualities comes from cultural values—what a culture and society consider desirable. Sociologists call them cultural categories—the division of the world's objects and qualities into groups with given names; e.g., masculine or feminine, upper class or lower class, intellectual or peasant, nerd or jock, modern or traditional, sophisticated or simpleton. All of these are cultural categories, and culture assigns them meaning.[1]

Take jocks and geeks. Certain objective qualities go with them—by definition. Jocks are into sports, have strong bodies, and are not much into studies or intellectual pursuits; geeks are studious, high in academic achievement, not likely to be in sports and not likely to have muscular bodies. Are they desirable or undesirable? That depends on whom you ask. In western countries, high school students are in awe of jocks, and they ridicule geeks; in eastern cultures, while jocks are not necessarily ridiculed, they sometimes tend to be dismissed as dimwits, and it is, instead, the academically accomplished who are held in high esteem.

Take another example: If a woman wanted to look attractive, should she be slim or plump? That again depends on what culture you are in.

In the U.S., Europe, and Australia, for example, slim women are considered better looking. In India and many other Eastern countries, on the other hand, plump, full-bodied (though not obese) women are deemed more attractive (although this trend is changing among today's youth). Actually, even in Europe, slimness was not always valued; plumpish figures were. Just look at all the classical paintings by European artists, most notably by Peter Paul Rubens whose art even gave a name to women with figures of that genre—Rubenesque (as in the famous Greek bride Nia Vardalos).

One more example: In much of the western world, men don't wear silk (except in ties); in contrast, in such eastern countries as China, India, Thailand, Philippines, and Japan, men's silk shirts are considered more prestigious than shirts of other material. And, whoever decided that men shouldn't wear skirts (they don't—except in Scotland), and women shouldn't wear pants (thought now they do)? Again, culture. Now then, we know that objects, persons, and properties (both physical and conceptual) derive their names and associated meanings from culture at large. The next question is how *specific* products and brand names acquire these meanings.

MARKETER SYSTEM AND FASHION SYSTEM

Products are given meaning by (a) *the marketer system*, and (b) *the fashion system*. The *marketer system* consists of all the agents involved in bringing the product to the market. Principally, these are product makers, product sellers (salespersons and retail stores), and product advertisers. Product makers place the physical qualities in the product (and in its packaging) that have the desired meaning in the broader culture. Sellers (salespersons and retail stores) put in meaning by pricing (price has quality and class connotations in a culture) and by their own characteristics and qualities (e.g., the lifestyle of the salesperson, the atmosphere of the store), which in themselves have specific meanings in a culture.

Finally, advertising (or, more generally speaking, marketing communications) is the most powerful means of associating extraneous qualities with the product. Advertising uses symbols, language, and other objects and people (ordinary people as well as celebrities) chosen from desired cultural categories. A Piplin leather purse ad features a friendly, personable hometown American girl, so that is the meaning transferred to Piplin brand of leather purses. A Dooney & Bourke ad, in contrast, features an avant garde, European girl with an attitude, so that is the image and cultural meaning that comes to be attached to the Dooney & Bourke brand. (Go ahead, google these brands, or browse a current issue of Vanity Fair, Vogue, or Cosmopolitan, and see for yourself.)

The Fashion system refers to a society's collective ideas (or conventional wisdom) about what is in fashion and what is out of it. The agents in this system are what we will call cultural gatekeepers—people who, through their position and reputation, exercise influence and promote certain cultural meanings. There are three types of cultural gatekeepers: (a) designers, (b) the media, and (3) celebrities and other cultural icons. Designers are creative, innovative artists, collecting ideas from eclectic sources, and through their designs they communicate what is fashionable in a culture and for whom. Media include books, movies, TV programs, magazines, newspapers, etc., and all of them promote the cultural meanings of things. They do so first by depicting persons in conjunction with certain objects and qualities in their entertainment programs (e.g., show certain style of furniture in a show about upper class nobility), and second by editorializing certain opinions. Finally, celebrities serve for many as role models, and their images rub on to the products they are seen using in real life.

Consumers As Meaning Producers

The next question is, what role do consumers themselves play in determining the final meaning of products. First, consumers acquire products with certain meaning (as produced by the marketer and fashion systems). Some of these products they adopt and consume "as is." In so doing, they directly embrace the cultural meanings that come with these products. For example, Mercedes comes with the cultural meaning of material achievement, and Mercedes owners happily consume that meaning. Second, in some cases, following the acquisition, consumers modify product meanings by certain augmentation processes, called rituals—and rituals are activities that follow a certain protocol (steps to carry them out) and have symbolic meaning (whether or not they have any tangible effect). Four rituals are relevant here: (a) possession rituals, (b) exchange rituals, (c) grooming rituals, and (d) divestment rituals.

Possession rituals are rituals or sets of activities we perform to transform or modify products obtained from the marketplace. We may wash new clothes, install new software on PCs, wait to get our cars in the right color, repaint and re-decorate a house we just bought, have a religious ceremony (in many Eastern cultures) when first entering a new home, or hold a house-warming party (in many Western cultures). In so doing, we add on to the objects certain qualities that have the cultural meaning we desire. Exchange rituals are bestowed on products we receive as gifts. Gift giving is a highly symbolic ritual, and the gift item we receive acquires meaning from the sentiment of the gift-giver. Grooming rituals are two-fold:

grooming ourselves and grooming the product. In grooming ourselves, we use a variety of products, and although some of their meaning came with them when we bought them in the marketplace, the final and total meaning really comes from how we put together all the grooming products—using the same makeup products we could create for ourselves either a basic, well-groomed look, or alternatively, a look others in that culture would consider sexy. Second, we also groom the product—for example, we could wear a polo shirt casually, or we could get it starched and ironed. We keep our cars clean and shiny or let them accumulate everyday dirt. We customize our PC desktops by getting them the skins we like. These product-grooming rituals give these products (and, by association, us) the meaning we desire. Finally, divestment rituals are activities we perform before discarding or parting with a product. Sometimes, we want to keep the meaning we have invested in a product intact, so, if we have to part with it, we try to identify and give it to someone who will keep that meaning intact (e.g., we transfer a family heirloom or a pet). If we don't want others to share that meaning, then we try to remove what we might have added to the product. All these factors are brought together in Figure 9.4.

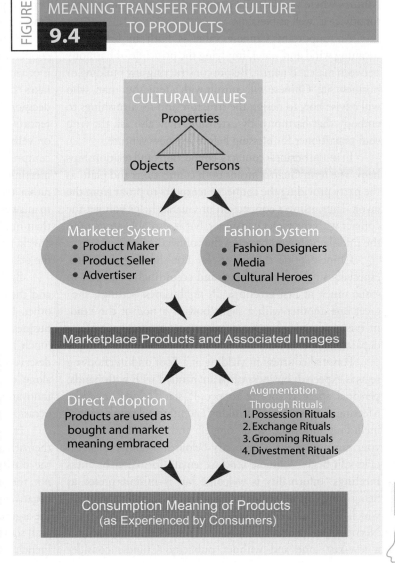

FIGURE 9.4 MEANING TRANSFER FROM CULTURE TO PRODUCTS

CULTURAL VALUES

Properties

Objects   Persons

Marketer System
- Product Maker
- Product Seller
- Advertiser

Fashion System
- Fashion Designers
- Media
- Cultural Heroes

Marketplace Products and Associated Images

Direct Adoption
Products are used as bought and market meaning embraced

Augmentation Through Rituals
1. Possession Rituals
2. Exchange Rituals
3. Grooming Rituals
4. Divestment Rituals

Consumption Meaning of Products
(as Experienced by Consumers)

APPENDIX 'A'
SELECTED CULTURES FROM AROUND THE WORLD

A marketer communicating with consumers around the world needs to develop an awareness, nay appreciation, of the cultures present in various countries. Here is a starter:

China

Historically, Chinese tend to be ethno-centric, considering their country to be the center of the universe, and their race to be superior. The Chinese character for the name China means the central nation!

Chinese welcome foreigners but are cautious about trusting them. Some knowledge of Chinese language and culture is appreciated, but show too much of it, and they are likely to become suspicious that you might be trying to get too close to them!

If you pay a Chinese consumer a compliment, he is unlikely to respond with a "thank you." This shows, not arrogance, but modesty, as Chinese tend to deny or diminish the value of their accomplishment.

Family is very important and its well-being comes before anything else. Senior family members are revered and obeyed. Aging brings dignity and status (unlike in Western cultures where youth is at a premium) and elders are sought for advice as well as blessing.

An important Chinese value is faith in feng shui, meaning wind and water, implying the principle of harmony between man and nature. Before constructing any building or business site, Chinese will consult with a feng shui man, who will advise how to design the structure and its furnishings to embody that harmony. By extension, they also ask the feng shui practitioner for blessing before any new venture.

In initial business contacts, connections and relationships help. The term Guanxi means both connections and graft, as the party providing the connection expects to profit from the favor. Thus, using a connection or Guanxi helps you get the contact with the target consumer, but it also obligates you to the middle man who provides the connection.

Chinese pride themselves for not showing emotions, especially in the first meeting, and accordingly tend not to smile much at first greetings. In nonbusiness settings, they greet one another with a slight bow or a nod of the head; in business settings, a handshake upon greeting as well as departure is common.

Personal courtesy in yielding at a door and in choosing seats is expected; business cards are handed with both hands; personal space is shorter so people stand closer together. Meetings begin with tea drinking and informal conversation, including introduction of oneself and a brief history of your business. Trust is necessary before substantive business talks can begin. Chinese tend to remain formal at business meetings. Informality is welcome but is misinterpreted as being much more than intended by the casual manner in which Westerners display it.

Negotiations proceed slowly and are best conducted at a low-key tone and without publicity. Chinese consider negotiations basically a win-lose proposition and thus attempt to seek as many concessions as possible, sometimes restarting the negotiations just when you thought you had concluded them; or they often delay the progress in the hope that you will make concessions at the last minute to close the deal. Furthermore, they don't like to say "no," so they will say things like "It will be inconvenient." In general, you will hear them say "yes," but this implies not agreement but only that "I am listening." It is important to them that all parties maintain "face."

France

French business organizations are highly centralized, with well-defined formal command and control lines of authority. The planning is centralized, and consequently, there is little commitment to it by those who would implement it. On the surface, at least, there is rigid formality in how managers interact with each other and in adherence to the written rules. Below the surface, however, there is an invigorating subculture of informal networking and tacit flexibility. While rules are seldom broken, they are constantly distorted or ignored. The familiar phrase in French organizations is--*le cas particulier*--"this is a special case!"

French managers are very competitive (as opposed to cooperating in teams). Indeed a manager would be dismayed if others did not compete with her or him. Group consensus takes the back seat to individual initiative. Most of the decision-making oriented communication is via written reports and proposals (rather than by oral presentations or verbal discussions). These are detailed, well structured, comprehensive, clear, and well written. Managers call meetings with a detailed agenda to inform and coordinate rather than to discuss. People come prepared to contribute, to answer objections, and to question others, but never more than mildly. To ask tough questions is considered a personal attack, and this norm for interacting in public keeps in check the otherwise fiercely competitive rivalry.

Business colleagues use last names, at least in public, and they shakes hands no matter how well they know each other. Bosses do not socialize with subordinates after work; business lunch with the boss is rare and formal. Usually, lunch is regarded as "private time," and food is deemed to deserve the main attention. Thus, the working lunch eaten alone or with colleagues or with salespersons is a recent innovation, restricted to some companies and only practiced occasionally.

French people enjoy abstract thought and consider themselves philosophers. The pragmatic matters less than the clarity of logic. They will tolerate the impractical but not the inconsistent. In business dealings, they will react negatively to your idea initially because they want to hear the arguments. Rational arguments supported by facts rather than sentimental pleadings are key to successful negotiations. French managers dislike direct confrontations and prefer to

CONSUMERS' ENVIRONMENT

work around problems.

The French seek novelty and elegance. This shows up in French consumers' quick adoption of gadgets and other innovations, and in their valuing aesthetics in product design and also in the use of language. They prefer wit to a belly-laugh and use humor that is more intelligent and satirical. In business presentations and meetings, humor is rarely used. If you used humor in presentations to business clients in France, you would be regarded as flippant. Similarly, personal remarks should be avoided.

Business begins with establishing a personal relationship. The French want to know you and expect you to show interest in their country. Personal relationships are valued for their own sake. The French believe that there is more to life than work; accordingly, they admire hard work but not workaholism. Work and family are considered separate. Being successful at the job is not considered adequate. Colleagues are expected to be lively and interesting, and well-informed and appreciative of finer things in life.

When you meet people as well as when you take leave of them, you shake hands with everyone, including children. When you praise a French person, you are likely to hear a self-deprecating comment since French are modest in accepting compliments. French are well-informed about other countries and cultures, so it pays to be informed about French history, politics, and culture.

In public, French avoid laughing or speaking loudly, chewing gum, or walking and drinking, or walking and smoking simultaneously.

Germany

Germans are very ambitious, success oriented, and competitive. The outward signals of success are the size of a person's office and the car he or she drives. Work and home are considered separate, and few Germans ever take the work home.

German organizations are hierarchical with strict lines of authority. Planning is top down. Superiors are supposed to govern out of competence and knowledge even though subordinates always take down orders unquestioningly. The organizations are very bureaucratic: everyone's role is well defined and written down. Procedures are well documented, and everyone is supposed to work by the book. Perfectionism both in business and private life is a hallmark of Germans. Obsession with detailed planning is accompanied by low tolerance for uncertainty. Opportunism is seen as a lack of organization and planning.

Decisions are taken conservatively and cautiously, with contingency plans and fall-back options. Decisions are taken by senior management rather than by consensus with those who would be affected. However, anyone with expertise is invited to offer opinion, which is seriously listened to. Subordinates are expected to offer opinion only if well informed. Meetings between managers and subordinates are largely for conveying information rather than for discussions. Compliance rather than consensus is expected. Communication is top down, largely when it is necessary to inform subordinates.

German views on the role of women in society are the most traditional. Progress toward accepting women in top positions in the organizations has been slow.

Germans are very formal and private persons. German society is very normative, and eccentricity of even the mildest form is frowned upon. A German would not hesitate to point out if you do something out of line, even something as trivial as taking off your jacket. Policing each other's behavior is deemed as a social duty.

German businessmen and managers always keep their jackets on unless alone. They address each other formally by their last names, especially in meetings. There is no place for humor in business meetings. Joking is common among close colleagues in private, but among strangers or in formal meetings, it makes people uncomfortable. Colleagues often take lunch together, but lunch hour is not to talk business. After office hours, getting together for drinks is not a regular practice, but when it does happen, it is used as an occasion for camaraderie and having a good time.

In sharp contrast to the excessive formality in public life is the informality in private life. There, friendship and warmth are highly valued. Intimacy is restricted to a few and is highly valued.

Punctuality is very important to Germans. Everyone arrives on time and leaves on time. Working late is neither expected nor rewarded. During the working hours, you work hard, but then that is the end of it.

India

As the largest democracy in the world, India embodies the value of egalitarianism alongside the deeply rooted caste and class system. Persons born in lower castes were discriminated against for centuries, but now it is common for even the lowest classes to command high positions both in politics and civil service. However, labor or menial work, historically the exclusive occupation of lower castes, continues to be considered undignified. Most middle-class and upper-class families will hire household help for dishes, laundry, and cleaning, not necessarily because the homemaker is working but simply because it is the proper thing to do. Until recently, most people who owned cars also retained a chauffeur rather than drive their car themselves (except in big cities and centers of commerce).

In businesses, rank and the respect that comes with it are zealously guarded. Accordingly, subordinates display a subservient behavior, and superiors treat their subordinates in a condescending manner. A Westerner who behaves in a more egalitarian manner toward the subordinates of his or her counterpart at the negotiating table may therefore discomfort both the subordinates and the superior alike. Since physical labor is not respected, superior managers will never do any physical work, including moving their own chair, for example; they wait for the subordinate to do it for them. Clerks and personal assistants disproportionately occupy an office roll, and it is not uncommon for an executive office to have a lower staff person simply waiting outside the closed office door for the call bell to ring. Peons will bring for you whatever you need, including carrying your briefcase. As a seller, you may not usurp this custom by insisting on carrying your own briefcase, or by otherwise treating the peon in an egalitarian fashion. However, many business firms are becoming Westernized, and such customs and rituals may be conspicuously absent in such firms.

Age is revered in India, as in most other parts of Asia (unlike in the West). Family members are respected. Even friendships formed during adult years manifest more respect than informal camaraderie. Except in childhood or adolescent friendships, where informality is common and first names are used, adults refer to each other with respect, adding the Indian equivalent of "Mr." or "Mrs." or "Dr." after the last name of acquaintances, friends, business associates, seniors as well as juniors and subordinates, and of course business consumers. If you are younger than your consumer, even if your rank in your own company is higher, you would be offending if you did not address the consumer with respect.

Indians have a strong belief in destiny or fate and, for this reason, tend to work less hard or work fewer hours, and also tend to be contented with what they have.

Guests and visitors to homes are considered a godsend and are welcomed with a sense of duty and reverence ("A guest/visitor is a god" is a popular adage in India, followed in words as well as deeds). Even if a stranger knocks on the door, he or she will be welcome, invited into the house, and offered at least a glass of water. Friends drop by without announcement, a carryover from the days when virtually no one had phones to make the prior appointment--thus the Indian name for guests is "dateless," meaning those who came without an appointment.

This social practice spills over to business. While business introductions from mutual friends help, "cold" calling or, more generally, a cold letter is quite accepted. Requests for impromptu meetings or showing up without prior appointments is not frowned upon either. Indeed, the executive you are calling upon will make an effort to see you, if at all feasible.

Indians are famous for being late, although in business appointments, this is changing. In part, this practice is the consequence of Indians (as in Latin and Arab cultures) marking time not as much by clock as by events so that the proper beginning time for a subsequent event is whenever the preceding event concludes. If you delight at the prospect of meeting your business consumer without appointment, you should understand why keeping time is generally not in the Indian character.

Indians generally greet one another with a *Namaste*--the word is audibly spoken along with a gesture in which both palms are placed together at the chest level with a slight bow of the head. However, when greeting consumers, a handshake is accepted and appropriate, with these exceptions: when greeting women consumers, a "namaste" is appropriate,

not the handshake (though younger women executives or younger businesswomen would gladly shake hands if offered); when greeting very senior or older executives or business consumers; when greeting government officers; and, definitely, when greeting political cabinet members, even a junior minister in the foreign trade department.

Business cards are given by the caller such as a salesman, rather than by the consumer (but they are willingly offered if you ask for it), and they are given casually (unlike the elaborate protocol that Japanese follow). Generally, small talk begins the business exchange, but it is brief and the consumer is eager for you to come to the point quickly. Touching (such as for putting your arm around the shoulder or for patting) is considered awkward among business exchange parties. During the same meeting, smiles are as common as seriousness in face expressions, reflecting the emotional reaction of the moment, as Indians do not try to hide their emotions or their opinions.

In consumer markets, haggling over price is as common in India as in Latin America and Mexico. Even though fixed price shops and one-price merchandise are becoming prevalent, especially in large cities, the practice of bargaining or seeking some concessions is quite accepted everywhere. Merchandise is being sold in bulk, and such buying options exist along with he ption of buying prepackaged consumer goods. Despite the popularity of manufacturers' brands, both domestic and imported, the reputation of the retailer is crucial in store selection, and retailers influence brand choice, since their advice is often sought and accepted.

Italy

At the middle- or upper-management levels, executives relate to one another on the basis of personal alliances and trust rather than being limited by the formal organization. For an outside supplier, therefore, finding the decision maker becomes an art. In sharp contrast to the German organizational culture, rules and formal procedures are almost always ignored, and flexibility is considered an Italian virtue. Getting things done is what counts.

Planning is generally absent. Businessmen and managers value an entrepreneurial recognition of opportunities rather than strategic plans.

Personal relationships are valued among colleagues. The delegation of responsibility is by trust in the individual rather than by position. Teams work only with a respected leader.

Meetings are small and informal. Often they appear to be social gatherings. Formal presentations are not common. People use meetings as an opportunity to exhibit their status, style, and elegance. Everyone is entitled to offer an opinion, and everyone is expected to be agreeable to the speaker. The worth of the idea depends more on status than on its intrinsic validity. The purpose of the meetings is to sense people's mood regarding a decision rather than to make decisions. Most decisions are taken in informal, behind-the-scene discussions.

Business managers consider it important to demonstrate

intelligence and education. Even the most mundane conversations about business are filled with references to such notable figures as Aristotle, Adam Smith, and John K. Galbraith. Being well educated and familiar with the classics is considered a social necessity.

For business, Italians dress formally. Looking sharp is considered a sign of good taste.

In social interaction, courtesy and good manners are desired. Italians will easily tolerate inefficiency and even incompetence, but not arrogance or rudeness.

Italians are not sticklers for punctuality, but it is considered rude to keep others waiting. While it is considered desirable not to be late for the next appointment, it is also considered rude to break off the current meeting or engagement. Thus, time and being on time are considered tools to organize activities rather than as ends in themselves.

Thus, it is second nature to Italians to be constantly juggling each other's appointment schedules. If you are a salesperson calling on an Italian businessperson, for example, you may be invited into the tail-end of the previous meeting, which may then take a significant amount of time to conclude.

Japan

To Japanese, harmony is more important than honest opinion or truth. Saving face and maintaining dignity are critical in all situations. Individuality is sanctioned, and blending in and being a team player are rewarded. People with higher rank, political position, seniority, or age are respected and obeyed. Japanese corporations are very hierarchical. Japan has been a male-dominated society, and Japanese are unaccustomed to dealing with woman businesspeople, although among younger businesspersons, this is changing.

Decisions are made by consensus. The consensus building process, called *ringi seido,* is very time consuming. Written proposals, called *ringi-sho,* are circulated throughout the departments and then upward, with prolonged discussion and analyses at each level. In business, Japanese are very process oriented, following procedures and rules closely and disfavoring any bending of rules.

Japanese smile generously. They speak softly and dislike aggressive mannerism of Western businesspersons. They stand two to three feet apart, in part to allow body language such as the bow. They will escort you to the door or the elevator and expect you to do the same.

Japanese place great importance on relationships and contacts. Accordingly, cold calling is unwelcome, and a business person must obtain an introduction from third parties, and yet be careful not to ask too much of them, for this will obligate them to those whose favor they are seeking for you. A great deal of time is spent at first meetings just to get acquainted.

Socializing among business colleagues and with clients is important and considered part of a workday, so much so that many will leave the office in the early evening hours to socialize (eat and drink) and then return back to the office in the evening to conclude the workday. Many business deals are, in fact, made in social settings such as over dinner or on a golf course.

Japanese businesses are tied into a web of financial and nonfinancial relationship of cross-ownerships and mutual obligations. These network arrangements, called Keiretsu, have made it difficult for foreign businesses to penetrate, all the more reason why introduction by mutual associates is important.

Presenting business cards is an elaborate protocol. The card is presented with both hands and with words while facing the receiver, who then reads it slowly and carefully to show respect for the giver of the card. It is then placed on the table facing you so you can refer to it from time to time; it is rude to put it in the pocket right away.

To Japanese, bowing is an art form. Junior executives and younger persons bow first and at a steeper angle than do senior executives and older persons, although they do not expect it from foreigners. Handshakes, offered in deference to Western custom, are light.

Gift giving is a conspicuously noticeable part of Japanese social life, and, by extension, of business life as well. The gift selection and its presentation (i.e., packaging) is done with great deliberation and care. Aesthetic presentation is as important as the appropriateness of the gift content. First-time business gifts should be low- or moderate-priced, lest they obligate the receiver more than is in order, and because room is needed for subsequent gifts that need to be more expensive. But more than the price, the reputation and quality of the gift is of paramount importance.

Mexico

If you can learn only one thing about the Mexican culture, it is the manana syndrome. *Manana* is Spanish for "tomorrow," but the cultural meaning of the term goes deeper than its literal meaning. It connotes priorities rather than procrastination.

To Mexicans, family and social obligations come first; business later. The *familia* (Spanish for "family") is a broad term extending to several generations, and horizontally to aunts and uncles, nephews and nieces, grandparents, cousins, and their families. Holidays are grand family reunion days, and old and young alike enjoy being at these gatherings. Teenagers do not view these as social obligations and they do not look bored. They enjoy their elders and respect them and in turn receive much valued affection. If you are invited to their home, remember, they are putting their family, their life, their pride on display for you to admire and respect. Show interest in the family, treat all family members with respect, and never, never ask or expect a Mexican to postpone a family concern to deal with the business at hand more efficiently.

Mexican businesspersons are not aggressive (and so they won't like it in you); they work at a relaxed pace but this should not be mistaken for laziness. Therefore, you must learn to work at a relaxed pace.

Mexicans like flexibility, and, from their vantage point,

they perceive most U.S. and Canadian businessmen to be "set in their ways." In Mexico, deadlines are flexible, as a rule; in all contracts, therefore, you need to allow for inevitable extension of deadlines.

Lunch hours are long, lasting two to four hours, with a multicourse meal over the relaxed atmosphere and conversations about friends and family. A business lunch with a salesperson is the same, without any talk of business. But the Mexican consumer is trying to assess you in this social set up as to your worthiness for his trust and dealing with you; this therefore, from the Mexican's viewpoint, is a *business lunch*!

Along with manana and familia, a third cultural element guides the Mexican cultural life, namely fiesta. Fiesta means fun, enjoyment, pleasure. If you see men drinking and dining with friends, with free-flowing tequilas, with Mariachi bands, colorfully dressed senoritas, and colorful pinatas for children, you are witnessing a fiesta in progress. This zeal for living, for fun and celebration, is what sustains a Mexican's morale and high productivity during work hours. Whatever else you may sell to Mexicans, you can't sell them "stress-release seminars"!

Netherlands

The Dutch have a strong belief in the power of human aspirations and effort; at the same time, however, they believe that the forces of nature have to be respected. Dutch like to innovate but also wish to minimize risks.

The Dutch are predominantly egalitarian; they are frugal, using money wisely. Dutch organizations are generally egalitarian and open, and it is common for people to cut across reporting lines if needed. The hierarchical nature of organization and authority seen in other cultures is anathema to the Dutch. The authority is to be camouflaged rather than exhibited. The boss is deemed to be "one of us," as a collaborator rather than as an authority figure.

Communication in the Netherlands is open and sincere. Nobody attempts to hide things or manipulate information. There is preference for oral communication rather than written. This practice is termed *buurten,* which means "visiting" (i.e., exchanging or communicating information orally).

Dutch businesses have frequent and regular meetings based on a formal agenda. The Dutch are open to and welcoming of new ideas, but will adopt them only after thorough research and clarity. In sharp contrast to Italian practice, ideas are seen separate from the person who offers them and are therefore judged on their own merit. The Dutch therefore tend to be direct in offering comments and ideas, a trait that might be offensive to those from cultures where speech is vague, indirect, and nonconfrontational.

Decisions are made by consensus (not by majority vote), which may take a long time to reach. But since these are based on consensus, the implementation is fast.

Dutch businesses value frugality. Showing off is to be avoided. Offices, clothes, cars, even food--all are kept simple and subdued. Socializing takes place over coffee rather than over meals, so if you are invited to someone's home, it is more likely to be after dinner.

Punctuality is valued, and there is an obsession to use every minute productively. The Dutch look for solid personal relationships and consider it important to honor commitments.

United Kingdom

Meetings are considered very important in the United Kingdom. Most decisions are made in meetings. They are discussed, analyzed, ratified, and implemented in meetings. Meetings take up a good proportion of any given business day, and they are not considered an interruption of work. They are informal in style, and, although participants are not always well prepared, they do not hesitate to make comments and express opinions. Decisions are made by consensus, and all meetings have to have a resolution and a decision; otherwise they are considered a failure.

British are very group oriented. Individual initiatives are frowned on. Individuals always seek group support before implementing any idea or action plan.

The British tend to use first names among colleagues and also among all business contacts, even without a face-to-face meeting. Handshaking is limited to first meetings. The usual greeting is "How do you do?" with the expected response being the same interrogative.

Rank and status distinctions are common; British would generally feel less comfortable without them.

In social dealings, it is important to be "a nice person." One is supposed to be courteous and unassuming, rather than assertive and arrogant. Humility and self-deprecation are valued. Being polite in conversation is a British trademark. Direct confrontation and argument are avoided, and vagueness and hints mark the British conversations. These may mislead a foreign manager into thinking that British managers lack clarity and decisiveness.

Work does extend into private life. It is acceptable to take work home or to work in the office after hours, and sometimes even on the weekends.

It is considered impolite to come on time to social gatherings! Usually, you are expected to arrive 10 to 20 minutes late. This has extended to business life, where everyone is generally 10 minutes late for meetings.

In sharp contrast to German and French business etiquette, humor is expected and desired. Business discussions are filled with levity and witty remarks. British humor can be sarcastic, self-deprecating, sexist, jocular, or racist. Both men and women participate equally in humor, including sexual innuendo. Women are easily found in managerial positions in British businesses, particularly in service industries.

It is common for colleagues and business associates to lunch together. Conversations can be social or shop talk. After-hour socializing at the pub is also common.

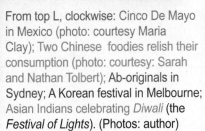

From top L, clockwise: Cinco De Mayo in Mexico (photo: courtesy Maria Clay); Two Chinese foodies relish their consumption (photo: courtesy: Sarah and Nathan Tolbert); Ab-originals in Sydney; A Korean festival in Melbourne; Asian Indians celebrating *Diwali* (the *Festival of Lights*). (Photos: author)

Reference Groups, Opinion Leaders, and e-fluentials

- Reference Groups—Limiting Extreme Individuality
- Referents—Good To, Have To, Love To
- Opinion Leaders—Mono or Poly?
- Influentials and e-fluentials—It Takes Many to Diffuse Innovations
- Word of Mouse
- Buzz Marketing—W-O-M With A Twist

Welcome to the Hash Club—Here You Don't Need To Be What You Have To Be Out There!

Too bad you weren't here on the famous Beale Street (Mission, San Francisco), yesterday, around 6:30 p.m.[1]

For if you were, you'd have witnessed an unusual sight. Suddenly, out of the Beale St. Bar and Grill, some 100 runners poured out, all dressed in red—jump suits, hot pants, mini skirts, full length gowns, robes, togas, and yes, even lingerie—but all red! From there, they jogged their way through the meandering city streets, jaywalk style—crossing streets, parks, bridges, and whatever came their way, all following a lead runner who marked the 9-10 mile long impromptu trail. And then at the finish line (which was in a park), they stopped, only to start a bout of frenzied merry-making– chugging beer, playing games, posing for pictures, mooning the audience, and chugging more beer.

Hashers of SanFrancisco during the Red Dress Run one recent year
Photo: Courtesy Norman Wheatly and Donohue Michael ("Voyeur")

No, they were not members of some fraternity, out for a Mardi Gras bash. They were, instead, grown up adults from all walks of life—single moms and dads, artists and managers, teachers, even judges, and families with children! They were members of San Francisco Hash—the local chapter of a worldwide organization called the Hash House Harriers.

Just what is this organization? It all started some sixty-six years ago, in Kuala Lumpur (Malaysia), when a British officer (chartered accountant, actually) started the prank, basing it on the British game Hares and Hound, and named it after a local pub, nicknamed Hash House for the cheap food it served.

Today there are some 1000 local chapters in 137 countries—you can find them in Sydney (Australia), Mexico, Singapore, Hyderabad (India), Moscow, Copenhagen, and of course, Great Britain. Their favorite sport is to drink and run—the organization bills itself as "a drinking club with a running problem"! Every member has a nickname, and the club officers are called the "mismanagement team." Local club Web sites offer guides for new members—for example, the Biloxi (Mississippi) Chapter's Web page offers what it calls "A virgin's guide to hashing." It also offers this window into the informal network's goals and pursuits:

HASHING is a state of mind...

> ...a friendship of kindred spirits joined together for the sole purpose of reliving their childhood or fraternity days, releasing the tensions of everyday life, and generally, acting the fool amongst others who will not judge you or measure you by anything more than your sense of humor. College professors or students, colonels or privates, managers or assembly line workers, doctors or plumbers... all are gathered together without concern for social status or education. They are gathered for the sport and the camaraderie and take on a new personality, for they are now...."HASHERS"

INTRODUCTION

The curious thing about the Hash groups is that their members are caring, socially integrated inhabitants of their "regular world" communities. They follow all the rules of society-at-large and live life as perfectly "normal" citizens—except when they assemble in one of the Hash group events. The group provides the social support they need to act out their inner child, even if just for a couple of hours every few weeks. In their Hash groups, they break norms (how society expects them to behave), but don't think for a minute that they are, even in these moments of anarchy, completely norm-less. Indeed, the organization has a detailed set of rules of its own, including procedures for running (e.g., "Trails should not go through private property without owners' permission"; "clean up the trash ... you did bring trash bags didn't you?"[2]) The facts of life in the "regular" world as well as in these Hash groups are that every group has some norms, and to remain a group member, one must obey those norms. It is by enforcing these norms that groups influence us, both as humans and as consumers.

Courtesy: Mary Juric

Consumers are social creatures. Friendship groups, such as this one, play an important role in our lives, both as humans and as consumers.

Consumers are social creatures. As such, they live, work, play, and consume in groups of other consumers. These groups influence consumer decisions immensely, as consumers buy and consume products and services that will please the groups to which they belong. The purpose of this three-part chapter is to describe these group influences and the intricate ways in which they both guide and constrain our behavior as consumers. In the first part, we define reference groups and identify three forms of influence they exercise. If you wonder why your wardrobe has come to resemble those of André 3000 or Maya Jupiter, now you will know why. We next discuss variations in consumer susceptibility to interpersonal influence (SIPI)—allowing you to understand why your best friend may not have followed your lead, as far as the wardrobe goes.

In the second part, we describe opinion leaders—a group of people whose opinions matter—who are also known as *influentials*, along with its e-subtype, *e-fluentials*. Highly coveted by marketers, these individuals can make an innovation a market success. In the last and third part, we discuss how innovations spread—how members of this elite reference group carry and diffuse the pro-innovation (and occasionally, anti-innovation) virus. We also discuss word-of-mouth and word-of-*mouse* and their marketing applications: viral marketing and buzz marketing. You cannot be studying consumer behavior in the new millennium and not know what all the 'buzz' on buzz marketing is about. After reading this chapter, you will.

REFERENCE GROUPS

Limiting Extreme Individuality

Reference groups are persons, groups, and institutions one uses as points of reference. These are people one looks to for guidance in establishing one's own values and behaviors.[3] Reference groups influence individual behavior by serving as points of reference, as sources of norms, values, and conduct.

Note that a reference group does not have to be a "group." It can be a person, such as one's parent, or a role model. And of course, it can be a group, like one's fraternity members. It can also be an organization or an institution. **Institutions** are more permanent groups or entities with a pervasive and universal presence in a society, such as schools, religions, and family. Any person, group, or institution that serves as a point of reference is called a **referent**.

Since no one lives in isolation, every consumer has at least one referent—even the Bohemian Mixers (Chapter 17) or Goth girls. Most have several. No one lives totally by himself or herself, for him/herself, and of him/herself.

What is a Group Anyway?

Just what is a group? Let us define the term formally. **Groups** can be defined as two or more persons sharing a common purpose. The essential and defining quality of a group is a common purpose. To pursue this common purpose, group members:

- share some values,
- recognize interdependency,
- assume specific roles,
- communicate mutual expectations and evaluations, and
- are able to provide some reward or punishment, tangible or intangible.

To understand these essential properties, let us take an example. People gathered at an interstate bus station are simply a collection of people. Once on the bus, they assume the roles of passengers and have some expectations of civil behavior from their fellow passengers; yet in a large measure, they are still merely a collection of people. A small crisis, such as a wheel swung into a ditch, can turn this collection of people into a group, with the common purpose of safely extracting the bus from the ditch. The passengers begin to show concern for one another's safety, some assuming leadership roles, others dutifully following, each asking for and offering help and cooperation.

Although a collection of people pursuing common goals during a short-term crisis can be thought of as a group, in general, groups are more enduring. The sharing of an ongoing, enduring existence is in fact what may turn a collection of people into a group. Thus, regular commuters on a metro bus may form friendship groups, and people living on the same street may become a group—a neighborhood group—and regular participants in online chat communities might begin to acquire the characteristics of a group.

Not All Groups Are Alike

Family, work groups, professional organizations, your fellow fraternity brothers or sorority sisters—these are all groups. Certainly, they are not alike and they are not going to influence us equally and in the same manner. They don't. To identify key differences among different types of groups, sociologists have classified them in many ways. Following are the principal classifications.

Primary versus Secondary Groups

Primary groups are groups with whom a person interacts frequently (not necessarily face-to-face) and considers their opinion or norms important to follow. In **secondary groups**, the contact is infrequent, and the norms of the group are considered less binding or obligatory. Examples of primary groups are family, work organization, church groups, etc. Examples of secondary groups are distant relatives, occupational groups like associations of doctors, lawyers, engineers, musicians, theater artists, and so on.

Formal Versus Informal Groups

Groups can be formal or informal. In **formal groups**, membership is granted by a formal admission into the group. There are written rules for admission into the group and written procedures about the conduct of group's business. These groups also have

Courtesy: Vicky Chalmers (posted on Flickr)

The members of the group on the facing page were friends already, here sharing some moments of constructive fun. The group above became a group for the explictt purpose of forming the pyramid. Which of the classifications for groups described here apply to each?

Both groups influence group members as humans and as consumers.

But the former influences, mutually within its memebrs, more than consumption, It influences, in manner loud as well as subtle, their values, interests, and choices, which in turn influence consumption.

norms for group members' conduct and behavior. **Informal groups**, in contrast, have few explicit rules about member behavior. Family is an informal group, whereas the American Marketing Association is a formal group.

Ascribed Versus Choice Groups

Groups can also be classified based on whether or not the person has the freedom to choose the group. A **choice group**, as its name implies, is a group a person voluntarily decides to join. An **ascribed or assigned group** is one in which membership is automatic—you don't have a choice. Examples of ascribed groups (membership by birth) are family, relatives, and tribe. Examples of assigned groups are team members on specific projects, your fellow class members (you have the choice to register or not for a course, but you do not have the freedom to choose your classmates), and a group of prisoners. Strictly speaking, only the family into which you are born is an ascribed group. Membership in all other groups occurs with some degree of choice. Thus, membership in the family you form by marriage and even your religious group (if you abandon your religion of birth and join another) entails some choice.

Associative Versus Dissociative Groups

Groups can be associative or dissociative. Associative groups are those with which we want to associate or to which we want to belong. Contrarily, dissociative groups are those with which we want to dissociate. Generally, consumers want to associate with peers who have similar values and lifestyles, and they want to dissociate with groups (or at least with the lifestyles of these groups) they find unappealing, as is evidenced by the mutual distaste among the so called jocks and geeks.

Membership Versus Symbolic Groups

Groups can also be classified based on whether the membership is real or symbolic. **Membership groups** are those in which an individual claiming to be a member is so recognized by the head or leader and/or key group members, even when the membership is informal. **Symbolic groups**, on the other hand, have no provision or procedure for granting membership. Symbolic group memberships operate on a psychological level; the consumer simply deems himself or herself to be a member of that group (or desires to be a member) and voluntarily and unobtrusively adopts the group's norms and values. Membership groups include the family, YMCA or other community organizations, professional associations, and so on. Symbolic groups include, for example, seniors in high school who begin to view themselves as college students; seniors in college who begin to emulate young professionals in their field, etc.

When a person is not already a member of the group (real or symbolic) but desires and expects to become a member, it is called an **aspirational** group. Most people aspire to be members of some group, and they expect to move up into this group. Since they aspire to be like this group, they emulate and adopt the behavior of its members (and use the same products and brands) even before they reach that membership status.

These dimensions of group membership can be combined to produce a number of group types. In Table 10.1 and 10.2, we give two examples of these combinations.

CONDITIONS FOR REFERENCE GROUP INFLUENCE

Although the influence of reference groups on consumers' choices is pervasive, reference groups do not influence every

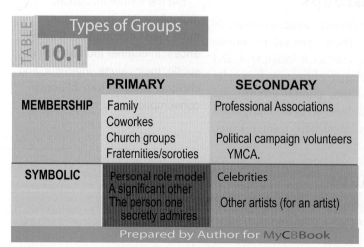

TABLE 10.1 Types of Groups

	PRIMARY	SECONDARY
MEMBERSHIP	Family Coworkes Church groups Fraternities/soroties	Professional Associations Political campaign volunteers YMCA.
SYMBOLIC	Personal role model A significant other The person one secretly admires	Celebrities Other artists (for an artist)

Prepared by Author for MyCBBook

consumer decision for every product or service. When we are buying mulch for our lawns, hiring a carpenter to build a deck in the backyard, or deciding where to go for a quick lunch, we are not thinking of any reference groups we might have. But if we are buying a tree to plant in the front yard, we might worry about our neighbors' opinion on it. Or if we were taking a date out for dinner, we had better think about the kind of restaurant we would go to.

The important question, therefore, is this: when and under what conditions does reference group influence occur? Behavioral scientist Francis S. Bourne gave this answer: Reference group influence occurs the most for products that are conspicuous.[4]

Moreover, Bourne proposed that there are two dimensions of conspicuousness: exclusivity and public visibility. If everyone owns and uses a product or service, then the ownership and use of that product or service has no exclusivity. Accordingly, there will be no basis for being concerned about others' opinions on it. The second dimension, visibility, is critical because a product or service has to be visible and identifiable in order for reference group members to approve or disapprove of it.

Based on Bourne's ideas, consumer researchers have suggested that the reference group influence may occur for the ownership of the product per se, or for the choice of a specific brand, or both. This will depend on whether a product is a luxury or a necessity (since everyone owns a necessity, necessities are not considered exclusive, whereas luxuries are) and whether the product is used in private or in public (private products are not visible while in use, whereas public products are).

Combining the two dimensions yields four combinations (see Table 10.3).[5]

1. Publicly consumed luxuries—In this case, reference groups will influence both whether or not the product will be owned and which brand is purchased.

2. Privately consumed luxuries—Here, reference group influence will be strong for the ownership of the product (because it is a luxury) but weak for the brand

TABLE 10.2 Classification of Groups by Membership Type

TYPES OF MEMBERSHIP	INFORMAL	FORMAL
BY CHOICE	Volunteer groups Community Friendship groups Cultural heroes	School Workplace Fraternities
ASCRIBED OR ASSIGNED	Family	Religion

Prepared by Author for MyCBBook

TABLE 10.3 Private-Public, Luxury-Necessity, Product-Brand Influences

PRODUCT / BRAND	WEAK REFERENCE GROUP INFLUENCE (-)	STRONG REFERENCE GROUP INFLUENCE (+)
	PUBLIC	
Strong reference group influence (+)	*Public necessities* Influence: Weak product and strong brand. Examples: Wristwatch, automobile, man's suit.	*Public luxuries* Influence: Strong product and brand. Examples: Golf clubs, snow skis, sailboat.
Weak reference group influence (-)	*Private necessities* Influence: Weak product and brand. Examples: Mattress, floor lamp, refrigator.	*Private luxuries* Influence: Strong product and weak brand. Examples: TV game, trash compactor, icemaker.
	PRIVATE	

(left side: NECESSITY; right side: LUXURY)

Source: William O. Bearden and Michael J. Etzel, "Reference Group Influence on Product and Brand Purchase Decisions," *Journal of Consumer Research 9* (1982), pp. 183-94. ©Journal of Consumer Research, University of Chicago Press (Used with permission.)

choice (since it will be used in private, out of public visibility).

3. Publicly consumed necessities—In this case, product ownership influence will be absent or weak since everyone owns it anyway, but brand level influence will be strong due to public visibility.

4. Privately consumed necessities—Finally, for products that are necessities and, in addition, are consumed privately, neither product ownership nor the choice of specific brands is likely to be influenced by reference groups.

TYPES OF REFERENCE GROUP INFLUENCE
Good to, Love to, Have to

The next question is this: why do we as consumers accept influence from our reference groups? What power do they possess over us to affect how we spend our money and what we consume? To understand these issues, consider the following three consumer purchases:

- Neil, 26, wanted to buy a suit he could wear in winter as well as in summer. He went to a department store and tried on a few suits. He liked one that was dark gray but the salesman recommended one that was olive as being more appropriate for year around use. So Neil bought the olive colored suit.

- Julia, 19, had been fancying the idea of wearing a low cut pair of jeans, the kind she had seen Christina Aguilera wear. So this past weekend, she finally took out her savings and bought a pair. On Monday she would wear them to the school. (Some schools in US have forbidden such clothing, but, luckily for her, her school has not.)

- Hirosho, 35, got laid off from a dot-com company in the bay area, where he was a product developer. He then took a job as an industrial salesman in the Midwest. His job title was not the only thing that changed for him; now, he could no longer wear his cargo pants and tee-shirts to the office. Instead, he had to wear a white shirt and a tie—something he dreaded. Reluctantly, he bought a couple of each.

All three consumers have been influenced by reference groups—however, that influence is not of the same kind. There are three kinds of reference group influences: informational, normative, and identificational.[6] (See Table 10.4.)

TABLE 10.4	Types of Reference Group Influences for Consumers			
TYPE OF INFLUENCE	**BASIS**	**EXEMPLARS**	**PRODUCTS**
Informational	Expertise	Professional advisors Professional enthusiasts Experienced consumers	Medication Computers Travel destinations
Normative	Material rewards Sanctions	Work groups Familly	Work clothes Alcohol
Identificational	Self-concept enactment	Cultural heroes (e.g., sports athletic celebrity)	Shoe brand

Source: Adapted and modified by the authors based on Robert E. Burnkrant and Alain Cousineau, "Informational and Normative Social Influence in Buyer Behavior," *Journal of Consumer Research* 2 (December 1975), 206-15. ©Journal of Consumer Research, University of Chicago Press (Used with permission.)

Informational **Informational influence** occurs when a consumer is influenced by the product information someone provides. A person's power to exercise this influence on another person comes from his/her expertise. There are four types of "expert" referents: (a) professional advisors, such as doctors, lawyers, tax accountants, stock brokers, and car mechanics; (b) product enthusiasts, such as computer buffs who get excited whenever new software is released; (c) **market mavens**—individuals who are generally knowledgeable about the marketplace happenings and possess information about a range of products, prices, distribution outlets, and even special promotions in effect at the time; and (d) other experienced consumers who have used the product before and can therefore benefit us by directing us to products they have found beneficial or away from products they have found performed poorly.

Much word-of-mouth communication occurs simply because members of the last three groups are inclined to share their views on products. Salespersons also frequently exercise this influence because we naturally expect them to possess product information; besides, often they are the only product experts conveniently available precisely when we need such advice—at the point of purchase. In our three scenarios, Roberto's choice of the suit he bought was influenced by the salesperson, and this influence was informational in nature.

Normative **Normative influence** occurs when a consumer's decision or action is based on his or her desire to conform to the expectations of someone else. The force behind this influence comes from the referent's power to reward or punish the consumer's behavior. There are four types of normative referents:

1. **Parents and Family Members:** Parents and family members exercise influence on youngsters because they have the power to reward or punish them. Children and adolescents may not watch, read, eat, wear, or drive what their parents do not approve. For dependent children, especially, this reward/punishment often comes in the form of money—if parents are not willing to pay for a style of clothing, junior must simply compromise on his preference. Similarly, spouses influence each other's consumption choices simply by showing pleasure or displeasure at the other's choices (showing pleasure or displeasure constitutes bestowing a reward or punishment).

2. **Friends and Peers:** Identifying the power of reward and sanction that friends and peers possess is straightforward. If you want to keep your friends, then you must keep them happy. You must fit in, or you may become an outcast or a target of ridicule.

3. **Regulatory Bodies and Other Public Institutions:** Government and other regulatory bodies simply mandate, under threat of punishment, certain behaviors (which include consumption behaviors). Thus, you must wear a helmet if you want to ride a bicycle; and you must cover your body if you want to roam the streets! Schools mandate dress codes, and religious institutions mandate wide ranging consumption. For example, Sikhs in India must cover their heads with turbans; and Moslems may not eat pork.

4. **Work Organizations:** Employers exercise referent power since they control a resource of great value to us— our wages! You have to follow the company code in personal behavior as well as in what you may choose to consume at work; e.g., the kind of clothing you wear, the kind of car you drive, and even what office decor you choose. In our scenarios, you would recognize Hirosho as the target of precisely this type of reference group influence.

Identificational **Identificational** influence occurs when a consumer emulates the behavior of another person. The force behind this influence is the referent's attractiveness as a role model or as an identity definer. We all have a role model, someone we look up to, someone we admire, someone we aspire to be like. We then emulate his or her tastes, his or her lifestyle, even mannerisms. These referents define for us a self-concept, a personal identity, which we adopt and then enact with the accoutrements that go with that identity. Identificational referents can be classified in three groups:

1. **Personal acquaintances** For many of us, our role models come from among those we know intimately in our everyday life. A parent, a senior in college, the

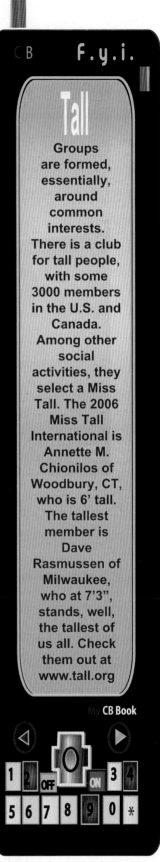

CB   **F.y.i.**

Tall

Groups are formed, essentially, around common interests. There is a club for tall people, with some 3000 members in the U.S. and Canada. Among other social activities, they select a Miss Tall. The 2006 Miss Tall International is Annette M. Chionilos of Woodbury, CT, who is 6' tall. The tallest member is Dave Rasmussen of Milwaukee, who at 7'3", stands, well, the tallest of us all. Check them out at www.tall.org

My **CB Book**

president of our literary club, the coach of our basketball team, the music teacher, or perhaps even the old high-school classmate who always got a prom date—some aspect of their lives touches us, some accomplishment of theirs inspires us, some visible aspect of their lifestyles as consumer intrigues us. To identify with such persons, we acquire the same consumption accoutrements that we see them using.

In an age where most young people look to sports celebrities as role models, here NYC Department of Education presents a more rewarding alternative—a role model that shows a career path rather than merely offer spectator entertainment, and the one that is both more personally fulfilling and societally more needed.
(Courtesy New York City Department of Educaton, The Appleseed Foundation, and The Advertising Council)

2. Cultural heroes Cultural heroes such as sports celebrities and film and music stars inspire millions of consumers around the world. Children and adolescents in their impressionable years are particularly mesmerized by these celebrities, whom they watch for several hours a day, often at some cost to their productive hours.

3. Social archetype groups **Social archetype** groups are categories of persons sharing a lifestyle, such as bohemians, literati, jocks, bookworms, cowboys, etc. Even some consumers outside of these groups find these groups fascinating—some of them anyway. They want to associate with these groups, assimilate their culture, and invariably emulate some consumption choices to gain at least a token identity of the group.

In our three scenarios, Julia's purchase of low cut jeans is an example of identificational influence. Her referent for this choice is the cultural hero Christina Aguilera. Unlike normative referents, this cultural hero can neither punish nor reward Julia; to wit, Miss Aguilera is not going to write Julia a personal letter of commendation for her choice! Instead, what Miss Aguilera does for Julia, and for millions of other teen girls around the world, is to define a self-identity—one of a young, effervescent, fun-loving, trendy teenager.

To help you remember them, we nickname them as 'good to,' 'love to,' and 'have to.' Go, figure which is which.

Identity Adoption versus Identity Distancing

Identificational influence can work in either direction. When we find some group's image appealing, we want to adopt that identity, and, consequently, we want to emulate their behaviors, preferences and tastes, and consumption choices. On the flip side, if we find some group's image unappealing, then we want to distance ourselves from its identity, its image. In the former case, the group serves as an associative identification group; for the latter, it serves as a dissociative identification group. In the 1980s, in America, break dancing, rap music, and hip hop baggy clothing started out as features of urban black teenagers' lifestyle, primarily as symbols of an anti-establishment stance; however, for some reason, suburban white teenagers found these style choices "cool," and these styles quickly became a general youth fashion.

In sharp contrast are motorcycle riders, in their leather jackets, chains, and tattoos. One particular group is known as the Hell's Angels, and most people do not want to be like them. Of course every "extreme" consumer (one whose tastes and behaviors are far from mainstream) inspires identity adoption among some consumers; just as likely, he or she also inspires identity distancing among others. But identity adoption and distancing occurs routinely even with normal consumers as referents. Many adolescents grow up in the image of their same-gender parent, but many also develop their tastes in styles that are diametrically opposed to those of their parents. Consequently they wish to carve out their identities in ways that are sharply distanced from their image of their parents.

Battle of Referents

It would be nice if we could choose our referents; sometimes we can, and sometimes we can't. For example, we can choose Andrè 3000 but not our parents. Many times diverse referents are in conflict—we can please one only by displeasing another. We want to dress up like Andrè 3000, but our parents would rather not see us decked out in that bright, checkered jacket. An expert (e.g., a movie critic) may advise us to go see *Serenity*, but our significant other—our heartthrob—might make us see *In Her Shoes*. Many of our choices are conflicted precisely because different referents pull us in divergent directions. How we resolve such approach-avoidance dilemmas depends, in part, on how gullible we are—i.e., on our susceptibility to influence.

HOW SUSCEPTIBLE ARE CONSUMERS?

Although all of us are influenced by reference groups, we do differ in our ability to follow our own minds. Some of us are pretty independent-minded, not much concerned with pleasing others; on the other hand, some of us are always anxious about other people's opinions. This individual characteristic is called **Susceptibility to Interpersonal Influence** (SIPI), defined as consumer motivation to follow other people's expectations and advice.[7]

This characteristic is not simply a matter of habit or of casually following someone's advice for the sake of expediency. Rather, it is rooted in strong motivations to please and/or emulate others. High SIPI's or "high susceptibles"—persons who have a high level of SIPI—are very uncomfortable at the very idea of what others might think of their actions or market choices; as such they are driven by a desire to avoid disapproval and to win kudos. In contrast, "low SIPI's" or "low susceptibles"—consumers with low levels of SIPI—are relatively less conscious of and anxious about others' views of their consumption practices.[8]

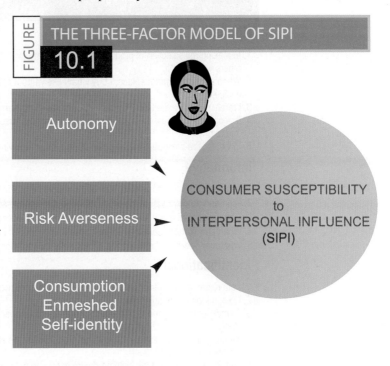

FIGURE 10.1 THE THREE-FACTOR MODEL OF SIPI

Autonomy

Risk Averseness

Consumption Enmeshed Self-identity

CONSUMER SUSCEPTIBILITY to INTERPERSONAL INFLUENCE (SIPI)

What makes consumers more or less susceptible? Three factors: autonomy, risk averseness, and consumption enmeshed self-identity (see Figure 10.1). Lets us explain each:

- **Autonomy** refers to the desire to feel free to do whatever one wants. It comes from a level of confidence in one's own ability and tastes. Autonomy-exhibiting consumers have high self-esteem—i.e., they feel that they are competent. They are also high in self-efficacy—i.e., they are in fact able to control outcomes, or achieve their goals. So they are less susceptible to others' influence.
- **Risk averseness** refers to how much risk people are willing to accept. All consumer decisions, and life choices for that matter, entail certain risks, and risk-averse consumers want to tread cautiously. One way they minimize their perceived risk is by seeking and following others' advice. So they are more susceptible to oth-

ers' influence.

- **Consumption enmeshed self-identity** means the extent to which a person defines his or her identity by consumption. At one extreme are consumers who believe "that you are what you consume"; at the other end are consumers who feel that a person is defined by his or her knowledge and character and goodness of the heart rather than by consumption.

Furthermore, corresponding with the three types of influences, consumers could differ on their susceptibility to the type of influence. Some consumers could be susceptible only on information, others on norm, and still others on identification. Information-based susceptibles are likely to be performance-risk averse, eager to avoid products that might turn out to be 'lemons'. They are also likely to not have much confidence in their own skills and knowledge to judge the product's qualities. Norm-based susceptibles are paranoid about peer disapproval and about fitting in. They would never deviate from a group's expressed wishes, and they would in fact actively seek out advice to ensure that their choices would be approved. Finally, identification-based susceptibles are fascinated

TABLE 10.5 Measuring Consumer Susceptibility to Interpersonal Influences

Please mark your opinion by writing a number in front of each question using the following scale:

Strongly disagree	More disagree than agree	Feel neutral	More agree than disagree	Strongly agree
1	2	3	4	5

Normative

1. In making my selection of products and brands, my over-riding concern is that my friends and significant others would like it.
2. When I am in the marketplace, I buy what I like without bothering about what others would think of my choice.*
3. I rarely purchase the latest fashion styles unless I am sure my friends approve of them.
4. If people would know the make or brand of a product I use, I would purchase only the brand they expect me to buy.
5. In life, for the most part, I do my own thing without worrying about what others might say.*

Informative

1. I often depend on information from other people for making my product selections.
2. I can and do buy most of the products without a salesperson's advice or help.*
3. I am never sure of my selection without asking a few people if they think those products are good.*
4. When people talk about their experiences with products, I listen.
5. Whatever decisions I make in life, I frequently look to information from others on the subject.

Identificational

1. I often identify with other people by purchasing the products and brands they use.
2. I like to look like people I like.
3. To make sure I buy the right product or brand, I often observe what people similar to me are buying and using.
4. Keeping up with Joneses – trying to have or do what the so-called 'successful people' have or do--is not my thing in life.*
5. I am happy with who I am, with no desire to imitate anyone else.*

Note: When giving the survey to someone else, remove the headings and jumble up the questions. Later, sort them back under the three headings. Reverse score the questions marked *, and sum the scores within each heading and also compute a grand total. No national norms exist, so mid-point scores (i.e., 3 for each heading and 9 for the grand total) may be considered as being middle-of-the road. The overall score would range from 3 to 15, and dividing this into three equal intervals, we could say that a score of six or less would make you a low-SIPI, and a score of 12 or more a high-SIPI.

Source. Composed by author, with adaptations and extensions of scales suggested in the literature--for example: William O. Bearden, Richard G, Netemeyer, and Jesse E. Teel, "Susceptibility to Interpersonal Influence," *Journal of Consumer Research*, 1989, March, 473-481; and William O. Bearden and Randall L. Rose, "Attention to Social Comparison Information: An Individual Difference Factor Affecting Consumer Conformity," *Journal of Consumer Research*, 1990, March, 461-471. © *Journal of Consumer Research*. Published by The University of Chicago Press. (Used with permission.)

by certain others (be they remote celebrities or people they personally know in their lives); they are driven to imitate or emulate these others.

Now, could these three bases of susceptibility coexist in the same consumer? While there is no research on this topic, human nature is such that we would say that at least some consumers (but by no means all of them) would score high on all three types of susceptibilities. They are super-susceptibles, you could say. How susceptible are you? To test, we have composed a measurement scale (Table 10.5). Check it out for yourself.

OPINION LEADERS

When we want to influence someone's behavior, basically we can take three routes: First, we can simply go on living our normal lives, let them observe us, and hope that they find our behavior and tastes appealing and that they will therefore emulate us. Second, we could explicitly tell them to "just do it," brandishing our power to reward or punish. Finally, we could tell them what we think of something and hope that they follow our advice. If they do, and if a lot of people like them do, then we become an opinion leader.

Opinion leadership is defined as the giving of information and advice, leading to the acceptance of the advocated position by the recipient of the opinion. This definition has two elements. First, the opinion leader must hold an opinion on a topic and recommend an action pertaining to it (e.g., recommend adoption of a new product); second, the opinion recipient must follow the advice and adopt the recommended course of action.

Opinion leaders have two essential qualities, both necessary for their success: expertise and trustworthiness. **Expertise** is defined as possession of knowledge about a topic, or product—especially knowledge that is not yet common knowledge. Since a person cannot be an expert on everything, opinion leadership is, by necessity, topic-specific. Thus, no one is an opinion leader across the board. Rather, opinion leaders are experts on a single product or service. For example, John may be an expert on DVDs and Steve an expert on fashionable clothing.

Trustworthiness, the second requisite for opinion leadership, refers to the perceived benevolence and dependability of the opinion giver. It is founded on the requirement that the opinion giver has no vested interest in promoting a position. That is why, despite expertise, the salesperson is often not an opinion leader. Some salespersons are exceptions: they make it their business to earn their customers' trust by giving impartial advice. By adopting a consumer's perspective, salespersons can leverage their expertise to help the consumer make a wise decision and in turn help their firm. This is an unmistakable implication marketers should understand about opinion leadership and its role in consumer acceptance of new products and brands and even of existing brands that are previously untried by specific consumers.

Opinion leaders are generally the first wave of adopters of new products. As such they serve as opinion leaders for those who have yet to adopt an innovation. Nonadopters can also be opinion leaders, but only if their nonadoption is due to the innovation being irrelevant to their own personal needs. In such cases, their expertise makes them opinion leaders, not their personal use of the product. For example, physicians and pharmacists are opinion leaders for medicines, even if they have not used the medicine themselves.

Even when opinion leadership is based on personal adoption, another dimension of trustworthiness comes into play: Is the adopter similar to the opinion follower? If not, the opinion receiver may discount the opinion leader's experience as irrelevant or less relevant. This is why true innovators are unlikely opinion leaders. As the very first ones to adopt, innovators take so much risk that they are seen not to represent the mainstream, and they therefore do not generate a degree of comfort among those who perceive them as too dissimilar. Some innovators may even be nondiscriminatory: They adopt everything, whether good or bad, often because they are obsessed with innovation and change for its own sake.

In addition, opinion leaders also have the following personal characteristics:
- High product involvement
- Recognized as leaders
- Socially well integrated
- More exposed to a variety of media sources, especially news and information media programs (rather than merely entertainment oriented media)
- Hold leadership and formal office positions in social, political, and community organizations

IDENTIFYING OPINION LEADERS

Suppose you want to find out who in your community are opinion leaders, say, for new fashion clothing. You could use one of the four methods:
1. Observation
2. Self-Designation
3. Sociometry
4. Key-Informant

To use the **observation method**, we simply go to a community and observe people's patterns of interactions; from these observations, we identify persons who interact with many others and who seem to command respect from others. To identify opinion leaders among students, for example, we would just hang out in the college cafeteria, library, and hallways for a few days and observe who interacts with whom.

In the **self-designation method**, we ask members of a community themselves to answer a few questions that would reveal if they believe people seek their advice on a topic. The self-designation method, then, is simply a survey method we use to measure consumers' opinion sharing activity. One such survey used by sociologists and consumer researchers is shown in Table 10.6. As students, you might want to ask these questions of some of your friends and see if their scores on these questions match your personal view of whether or not they are opinion leaders.

In **sociometry**, a researcher asks the residents of a community or members of a groups who they (each one individually) would consult with or look to for information about the topic or product under consideration. Persons receiving the highest mentions are are noted as being opinion leaders.

In the **key informant method**, instead of asking everyone, we ask prominent people in a community to name a few persons they consider able to influence others' opinion on a given topic. (Of course, the key informants may themselves be opinion leaders, and as such may be named by other key informants.) For our task of promoting a music device on a college campus, we would ask some designated position holders, such as presidents of student organizations, to name a few students they consider influential on the topic.

Identifying Opinion Leaders in Large Populations

Three of the above four methods (the exception is the survey method) work best with small communities. Small communities are relatively isolated, so that the opinion leaders and opinion seekers live in and are confined to a narrow geographical area. And they know each other. Indeed, much of the research and applications of these methods were done in early sociological studies in rural areas such as among farming communities. Before we consider their adaptation for large populations, however, we must note their usefulness for a substantial proportion of the world's consumers. Much of the world's population indeed lives in small communities—more so in underdeveloped and developing countries, but also in industrialized nations. And in these communities, there is need to promote a large array of products (e.g., telephone, ATM machines, savings instruments, solar heating) and, even more importantly, social programs (e.g., vaccines, birth control, personal hygiene, etc.).

Moreover, even in industrialized nations and even in major metropolitan areas, most consumers carve out their own small communities with which they identify and interact frequently. Thus, there are ethnic communities, professional groups, Parent Teacher

TABLE
10.6

A Scale To Measure Opinion Leadership

The product used here, for illustration purposes, is consumer electronics. The survey is adaptable for any product category.

In answering the following survey, please think of conversations you generally have with others about consumer electronic products such as TVs, DVD's, computers, MP3, PDA's, cell phones, etc.

Q1. Compared to other people you know, are you more likely to be asked, less likely to be asked, or about as likely to be asked for your opinion about consumer electronic products?

Strongly disagree	More disagree than agree	Feel neural	More agree than disagree	Strongly agree
1	2	3	4	5

Q2. During the past six months, to how many people have you given an opinion about one or more of these products?

To no one	To very few	To quite a few	To many	To a lot of persons
1	2	3	4	5

Q3. In your discussions with other people you know, if the topic turns to consumer electronic products, are you more likely to give or receive information and opinion?

Much more likely to give	Somewhat more likley to give	About equally to give & receive	Somewhat less likely to receive	Much more likely to receive
1	2	3	4	5

Q4. How likely are you to be used as a source of advice?

Not at all likely	Somewhat likley	Fairly likely	Quite likely	Very likely
1	2	3	4	5

Q5. Thinking back over past one year, would you say you have influenced others' decisions on consumer electronic products-- about buying or not buying and about which brands and makes to buy or not buy

Never	Rarely	Sometimes	Often	Frequently
1	2	3	4	5

Q6. When it comes to making buying decisions on consumer electronic products, do you depend a lot on other people's opinion, or are you able to determine on your own which product and brand and make to buy or not buy?
1. Depend almost entirely on other people's opinion
2. Depend a lot on other people's opinion
3. Balanced use of my own view and other people's advice
4. Largely able to decide on my own with some advice from others
5. Able to make my own mind almost independently.

Computing the score: Reverse code Q 3a and then add up all questions. The score can range from 6 to 30. Since the middle point is 18, following interpretation is suggested:
- 5-11   Not an opinion leader at all
- 12-15   More of an opinion follower than an opinion leader
- 16-20   Opinion exchanger rather than a leader or a follower
- 21-24   Opinion leader rather than a follower
- 25-30   Strong opinion leader

Note: The survey is composed by author based on measures used by various researchers—principally, "Overlap of Opinion Leadership Across Consumer Product Categories". King, Charles W.; Summers, John O.. *Journal of Marketing Research*, Feb70, Vol. 7 Issue 1, p43-50; Fred D. Reynolds and William R. Darden, "Mutually Adaptive Effects of Interpersonal Communication," *Journal of Marketing Research*, 8 (November 1971), pp. 449-454. See also Leisa Reinecke Flynn, Ronald E. Goldsmith, and Jacqueline K. Eastman, "Opinion Leaders and Opinion Seekers: Two New Measurement Scales," *Journal of the Academy of Marketing Science* 24, Spring 1996, 137-47; and Terry L. Childers, "Assessment of Psychometric Properties of an Opinion Leadership Scale," Journal of Marketing Research, 1986 (23), May, 184-88. No population distributional norms exist on the scale scores but you should expect a majority to be, by definition, opinion seeker/follower rather than opinion leader.

Associations (PTAs), book clubs, neighborhood organizations, and umpteen other interest groups (e.g., baseball leagues, nature exploration groups, and Elvis Presley fan clubs). Thus, much of the social life, in populations large and small, is in fact lived in small communities.

At any rate, the methods described above can be adapted for large population groups as follows. Along with identifying who is an opinion leader, if we could also record some personal characteristics (such as age, education, socioeconomic status, occupation, participation in leisure activities, etc.), then we could, through cross-tabulation, identify the demographic characteristics of opinion leaders. In large population groups, then, we need to survey merely a sample rather than the whole population—and this would be true for each method. Based on the findings of the cross-tabulation analysis, we could then project, for the larger population, the characteristics of opinion leaders. This could then help us target our marketing program (advertising, program brochures, free samples, group activities) to those opinion leaders. One car company did just that. The year was 1993. The Chrysler Corporation was planning the launch of its new model, the LH. It identified what it called "thought leaders," described as prominent individuals who might influence others to buy the car. And it gave them the new car for three days to drive.[10] Chrysler was using opinion leaders to target the luxury car segment of consumers.

Opinion Leaders: Mono or Poly?

There is one important question we must ask: Are opinion leaders able to influence their followers only on one specific topic or on multiple topics? In other words, are they monomorphous—single topic influencers, or are they polymorphous—multiple topic influencers?[11] The correct answer is that they are somewhere in between. Most research has found that opinion leaders are indeed, more often than not, monomorphous, with expertise and source of advice on a single topic area. However, that topic is sometimes very focused and at other times somewhat broader. Thus, a topic can be defined narrowly (e.g., fashion clothing), or broadly (e.g., fashion). Now then, among the fashion clothing opinion leaders, some might be opinion leaders merely on casual fashions, while others might also be opinion leaders on work clothing. Some of them could also be advisors on personal appearance fashion as a whole (clothing, cosmetics, hairstyles, and other body-adornments such as tattoos). Still fewer of them might also be advisors on such distantly related fashion topics as interior decoration. But it is unlikely that they would be advisors also on electronics, sports, leisure activities, etc.

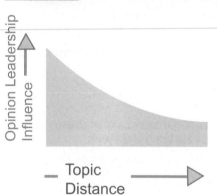

FIGURE 10.2 Topic Distance and Opinion Leadership Inf;uence

Topic distance refers to how far the topic is from the core topic of interest and expertise of the opinion leader. As the topic distance increases, opinion leadership influence fades. See Figure 10.2

Of course, a few opinion leaders do exercise influence in *several* topic areas (though still by no means in all topic areas). And they exercise at least some degree of influence on a large number of people. These opinion leaders are a special category of people. They are called influentials. We discuss this group below.

INFLUENTIALS

Influentials. They are the leading indicators of what Americans will be buying. [They have been]—for more than five decades—from choosing energy-efficient cars in the 1970s to owning computers in the 1980s to adopting IRAs in the 1990s to being the trailblazing users of the Internet and cell phones today. And influentials have led the way in social development as well—from the revival of self-reliance in managing their own healthcare, money, and consumption to mass skepticism about the marketing claims of everything from breakfast food to politicians.
Ed Keller and Jon Berry, Authors of *The Influentials*.[12]

Who are the Influentials in U.S.? First things first. They are equally divided by sex: half of them are males, and half females. But on other demographics, they differ from the population as a whole. As Table 10.7 shows, in age, they are slightly older, and more of them are married. They are also more educated, more likely to be dual income couples, have a higher median income, and hold an executive or a professional job. With their relative prosperity, they are more likely to own a home and multiple-cars, and they are more likely to be financial planners and savers.

In their psychological makeup, Influentials are much more optimistic about their own future, believing in the prospects of achieving a "good life" if not already achieved (83 vs. 71 percent), and have an internal locus of control, believing in their own ability to influence their life chances (82 vs. 63%). Their leading values are protecting the family, honesty, enduring love, stable personal relationships, knowledge and learning, and work that is fulfilling. Power, wealth, status, and looking good are not that important (although they already possess some of these resources). Indeed, materialism is not their obsession, but neither is austerity. Rather, they like to experience and enjoy good things in life (e.g., a vacation home, travel, fine dining, etc.). It is just that, unlike materialists, these "good life" resources are not the end all and be all of their lives.

In terms of their activities and interests, Influentials read more newspapers, books and varied magazine (50-60 percent vs. 30 percent among the general population) but watch less TV. Perhaps the most prominent characteristics of Influentials is that compared to an average adult American, they are much more active in their communities, volunteering in social and charity work, and they are much more interested in news and current events and in civic issues (see Table 10.7).

TABLE 10.7

A Profile of Influentials

	Influentials	General Population
Demographics		
Age (18+)	45.2 years	42.9 years
Married	70%	57%
Attended college	80%	50%
Graduated from college	49%	23%
Dual Income couples	41%	31%
Median income	$55,200	$37,300
Executives & Professionals	34%	15%
Own a home	74%	60%
Own multiple cars	78%	60%
Do Financial planning	71%	50%
Participation in:		
Political group	58	29
College Alumni group	57	29
Interest/hobby group	57	35
Professional group	43	22
Social/volunteer group	47	21
Very interested in:		
News and Current events	76	51
Politics	51	18
Environment	57	35
Other countries & people	43	21

Source: Ed Keller and Jon Berry, THE INFLUENTIALS: One Americann in Ten Tells the Other Nine How to Vote, Where to Eat, adn What to Buy, Free Press, 2003.
Adapted with the permission of The Free Press, a Division of Simon & Schuster Adult Publishing Group. Copyright © 2003 by Roper ASW, LLC. Allrights reserved.

Of course, by definition, Influentials are sought much more for their advice on a variety of issues: health problems (44 vs. 32%), vacation destinations (38 vs. 21), restaurants (54 vs. 21), music (31 vs. 24), and automobiles (33 vs. 17).

Although, there is a great deal of diversity within and among the Influentials themselves, the following portrait (by no means representative) of one Influential illustrates the nature of their persona and their advisory influence.

Sophie Glovier An MBA from Columbia University. Five years ago, she left her executive job at the Young & Rubicam advertising agency. The Princeton, New Jersey mother of three has now become a power volunteer. She organizes the annual major fund drive for Delaware Raritan Greenway (a land preservation group), and she is the founder member of a social group called Hubridas (named after a beloved pub during her college days)—a social group of area residents that gather four times a year for fun and social activities ranging from barn dance to scavenger hunt. She serves on the board of Tech for America, a national organization that places best teachers in poor school districts, and is an ace fund-raiser for many local organizations.

Glovier leads a very focused life, organized with "to do" lists. She reads widely from New York Times to People magazine and Martha Stewart Living. She has a large circle of friends and an even larger network of acquaintances—her address book is crammed with a few hundred names, and there are some 250 names on her Christmas card list. To stay in touch, she uses phone calls, emails, and, most of all, in-person contacts.

Many of these friends have organic milk delivered to their homes from Moo Milk Express. Sophie was the catalyst who got them into things organic.[13]

Kirstie Lou Alley is an apt opinion leader for Jenny Craig.

One of her hobbies: Shopping for smaller sizes every week!

Among her Turn-On's: Helping people and Jenny Craig's Chicken Fet-tuccini. Among her Turn-Off's: Ugly shoes and Small minds.

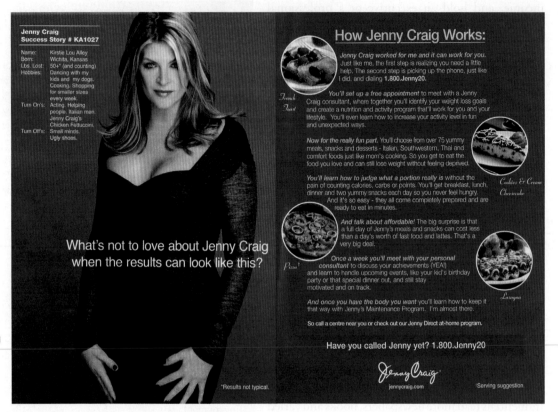

E-FLUENTIALS

A New Breed of Influentials in the Cyber Age

E-fluentials are a subgroup of Influentials—the persons who are net-savvy and who also influence other people both offline and online. Thus, their influence is not limited to word-of-mouth; rather they influence people via word-of-mouse as well. That is, they also exercise their influence in cyberspace.

Who are these e-fluentials? To answer this question, a market research company called Burson-Marsteller collaborated with RoperASW, a research company that polls consumer trends. Based on its research findings, it describes e-fluentials thus:

E-fluentials make waves They project their opinions far beyond the scope of their individual contacts. An e-fluential imparts an experience to 14 individuals on average. The vast majority spreads the word through multiple communication channels. Furthermore, these electronic town criers are as likely to share information on products and services offline as they are to relay their experiences online.

E-fluentials comprise about 10% of the U.S. online population (i.e., about 11.1 million). By definition—since they are opinion leaders, they get asked about twice as often by others for advice on wide ranging topics from healthcare to new technologies. And, also by definition, they express more confidence in sharing their opinions with others. They visit both company Web sites and opinion sites (such as Planetfeedback.com) more than do other online consumers, and they double check the information found on these Web sites. They are online more often than others and they participate in newsgroups, discussion forums, bulletin boards, and listservs (a type of online channel). Most importantly, they believe, much more than do others; in the power of the Internet as an opinion influence channel. See Table 10.8.

TABLE 10.8

What Distinguishes E-fluentials

	E-fluentials	General online consumers
Online Presence		
Go online more than once a day.	74	45
Spend more than two hours a day online.	53	22
Participation in Multiple Online Channels		
Read e-mail from *listservs*.	62	18
Read bulletin board posting.	51	14
Visited online magazines & other Information sites that do not have well-known offline names.	34	11
Tech-Media Involved		
Read Wired magazine.	17	5
Faith in the Power of the Internet		
The Internet is a great way to stay in touch with others.	89	62
The Internet is a terrific medium for allowing me to express my opinions to a broad audience.	65	29

Source: http://www.e-fluentials.com/research/index.html
Reproduced by permission.

N-Gage, Segway, and Optimus—Looking for a Few Influentials

Will you be one of them?

N-Gage, Segway, and Optimus—they are cutting edge products—amazing, cool, and innovative. You have already met N-Gage and Segway in Chapter 4. You may recall briefly that N-Gage is an all-in-one gizmo, combining a video game system, music storage and player device (MP3 style), and a cell phone. Segway is a two wheel urban human transporter that drives at 12 miles per hour and is based on advanced gyro technology so that it automatically keeps you upright even as you lean!

Now meet *Optimus—Optimus wireless keyboard*, to be exact. It is a new keyboard for your computer, but it's not your grandfather's keyboard. The new keyboard has icons on its keys; the keys light up when you strike them; the keys can switch between a dozen languages; and you can rearrange icons like you arrange your desktop. It is not here yet, but a designer shop named Art Lebedev Studio in Moscow is awaiting patent on the technology. Look for it to appear soon. Would you? And, even more importantly, would you be one of the first ones to buy it?

Courtesy: Art Lebedev

Optimus Keyboard

If yes, when will you buy it? As soon as it shows up on store shelves, or much later? That is, will you be one of the first ones to buy, or one of the last ones? Will you be in other words, an opinion leader or a follower? This is not a judgmental question, mind you. Very few people adopt an innovative product at first—after all, they all carry some risks, as we saw in Chapter 4. It is in the nature of innovations that they spread through a population slowly. Of interest to marketers is a study of how innovations spread and what roles opinion leaders and followers play in this process.

OPINION LEADERS AND FOLLOWERS
It Takes Many to Diffuse Innovations

Sociologists and consumer researchers have studied this process, and they call it diffusion. The word diffusion means spreading, and, therefore, diffusion process refers to the spreading of an innovation's acceptance and use through a population. How does an innovation spread through a population? The answer: like an epidemic! A few people get the epidemic at first—maybe only one person gets it, then it spreads to two, then four, then eight, then sixteen, and so on. That is, it spreads exponentially, at first, and then it slows down—only because there are few people left to catch it. Same thing with innovations. A few people adopt it at first, say about 100; then they spread it to 400 (each one to four), who then spread it to 1600, then to 6400, then to 256, 000, then to 1.12 million, then to 4.48 million more, then to 17.96 million more, then to 71 million, and so on—you get the picture. The important point is that, when it comes to people adopting a new idea or innovation, they do it the same way they catch a contagious disease! See Figure 10.3.

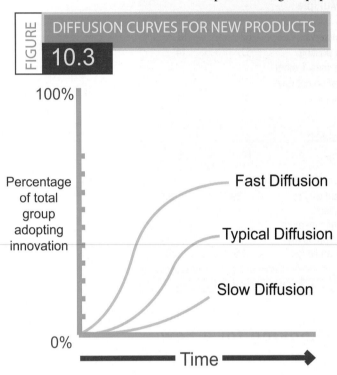

FIGURE 10.3 DIFFUSION CURVES FOR NEW PRODUCTS

What has this got to do with opinion leaders and followers? Well, it does, and in this respect the process differs from the spread of epidemics. Epidemics treat everyone equally, spreading to whoever is exposed. That is because people have no control over catching a disease (once they are exposed); in contrast, when it comes to adopting an innovation, they do it, for the most part, of their own free will. Accordingly, they decide whether to adopt it sooner or, alternatively, later. They choose, in other words, to take the plunge and show leadership, or alternatively, to be cautious and follow others' leads.

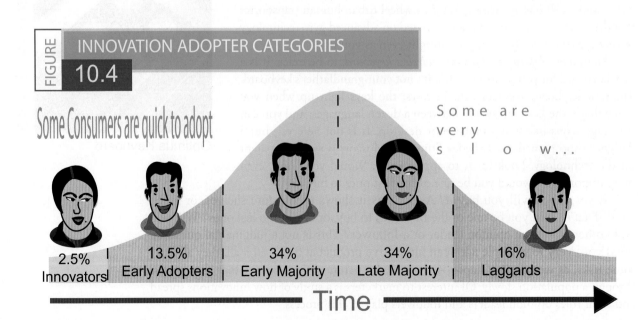

FIGURE 10.4 INNOVATION ADOPTER CATEGORIES

Some Consumers are quick to adopt

Some are very slow...

| 2.5% Innovators! | 13.5% Early Adopters | 34% Early Majority | 34% Late Majority | 16% Laggards |

Time

We can actually plot the adoption timing of these leaders and followers on a graph showing how quickly or how late various consumers in a society adopt innovations. What is the idea, you might ask? Because the products are so different, every graph would look different, wouldn't it? So what can we learn by plotting such graphs? Well, an interesting thing happens here: all the graphs look alike! And this common form is a bell-shaped curve, shown in Figure 10.4.

| TABLE 10.9 | ILLUSTRATIVE MEASURES OF CONSUMER INNOVATIVENESS |

Please rate the following statements in terms of your agreement or disagreement.				
Strongly Disagree				Strongly Agree
1	2	3	4	5
1. I like to take a chance.	1 2 3 4 5
2. I like to try new and different things.	1 2 3 4 5
3. When it comes to taking chances, I would rather be safe than sorry.*	1 2 3 4 5
4. I like to wait until something has been proven before I try it.*	1 2 3 4 5
5. If people quit wasting their time experimenting, we would get more accomplished.*	1 2 3 4 5
6. When I see a new brand on the shelf, I usually pass right by.*	1 2 3 4 5
7. In general, I am the first (last) in my circle of friends to buy a new _____ when it appears.	1 2 3 4 5
8. I like to buy new _____ before others do.	1 2 3 4 5

*These items must be reverse-scored.

Note: 1. In the blank spaces, fill in broad product categories such as fashion clothing, tech gizmos, new products, etc. 2. While there is no normative score standard, a score above the middle point (after summing up all eight items) would indicate innovativeness; i.e., scores above 24 would indicate innovativeness.

Source: Items compiled from several sources, e.g., Clark Leavitt, John Walton (1975), DEVELOPMENT OF A SCALE FOR INNOVATIVENESS, in Advances in Consumer Research Volume 02, eds. Mary Jane Schlinger, : Association for Consumer Research, Pages: 545-554. Ronald E. Goldsmith and Charles F. Hofacker, "Measuring Consumer Innovativeness," *Journal of the Academy of Marketing Science*, 19 (1991), 209-221; Fred D. Reynolds and William R. Darden, "Mutually Adaptive Effects of Interpersonal Communication," *Journal of Marketing Research*, 8 (November 1971), pp. 449-454

Innovators and Laggards, and All the Consumers in Between

Marketers have given these consumer groups some names, depending on how early or late they adopt an innovation. On the bell curve, they are divided into five groups. The first groups of adopters are called *innovators*. The middle three groups that follow are called *early adopters*, *early majority*, and *late majority*, in that order. The last to adopt are called '*laggards*'—an unfair label, actually, so take it sportingly if you are the last one to adopt. The dividing line between groups is drawn based simply on statistical distribution (i.e., one and two standard deviations in either direction from the mean). That is why the groups divide the bell curve so symmetrically.

Innovators The first 2.5% of the population to adopt an innovation are called innovators. Their defining characteristic is that they adopt *independently* of other people.

According to scholarly research in this field, innovators are a different type of people—compared to an average person, they are/have:[14]

- Risk takers
- Variety seekers
- High product interest
- Less well integrated with other members of the society
- More individualistic and independent in thinking

And they come from upper socioeconomic status.

To see how innovative you are, take the survey in Table 10.9.

Early adopters are the first group of consumers who deliberate rather than rush, but are independent in their thinking and are quick to evaluate and reach a decision on an innovation.

Early majority is a large group of consumers (34%) who are very deliberate, and who adopt an innovation if they do not see much risk in it.

Late majority is equally large (34%), but their behavior is exactly the opposite of the early majority—they are very skeptical of anything new, are extremely risk-averse, and resist adopting unless an innovation has been proven useful and safe. Finally,

Laggards are most hesitant to adopt anything new and try to resist or postpone adopting the new product or new behavior.

THE ADOPTION PROCESS
Why Are Imitators Late to the Party?

The adoption of an innovation refers to the consumer acceptance of an innovation for continued use. Some innovations are adopted relatively quickly, while others take a long time before receiving widespread adoption. Two principal factors distinguish innovations from current products and cause most people to be cautious: (1) As new product categories, innovations lack evaluation criteria, so consumers don't know how to appraise them; and (2) their benefits and negative outcomes are unknown or not established by experience. Therefore, consumers engage in a long, deliberative process before adopting the innovation. This adoption process has been characterized by the acronym, AIDA, which signifies a sequence of four stages, or four mental states, that an adopter goes through: awareness, interest, desire, and action. (See Figure 10.5).

The AIDA model suggests that when adopting an innovation, consumers pass through these four mental states in a hierarchical order. First they become aware of the innovation. Then they become interested in it and learn more. If what they learn tells them that it would be of use to them, then they feel a desire for it. Finally, they take the necessary action to acquire it. Awareness, Interest, Desire, and Action–AIDA. Remember it; it applies to all of us, for all innovations.

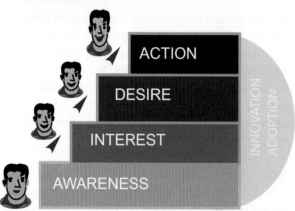

FIGURE 10.5 THE AIDA MODEL : STAGES IN CONSUMER ADOPTION OF INNOVATIONS

Because innovators and early adopters are independent thinkers, they are able to progress through these four steps quickly. Because they are the first groups to adopt, innovators and early adopters are risk takers. Those who adopt later, who, as a group, can be called imitators, are risk avoiders; they wait to see whether the risk takers' experience has been satisfactory.

There you have it—later adopters (imitators) use early adopters as role models and opinion leaders for their adoption. That is why innovation adoption is, just like the spread of an epidemic, a process of group and social influence.

Contrary to the popular view, rejection does not make a person non-innovative. Putting off the trial adoption does. Or, even more strictly, a non-innovative consumer is someone who does not show curiosity to learn more (i.e., to gather more information) after exposure to a new stimulus, or avoids further information and puts off active evaluation of the innovation. That is why we consider 'laggards' a somewhat unfair label for the last group of adopters.

TWO-STEP VERSUS MULTI-STEP FLOW OF COMMUNICATION THEORY

Whom Can Followers Trust—And why advertising does not suffice

Since the advent of the mass media, it has become easy (though not inexpensive) to spread the word about your product to millions of consumers around the world. Just put it on TV or the radio, and the whole world will know who you are and what you are selling. The truth is, that mass media doesn't really reach the masses; it may reach their ears and eyes alright, but it does not reach their minds. Only some people are persuaded by the mass media; you have met them before—opinion leaders. The rest of the masses look to opinion leaders for their news and for their tips on products.

This insight was first advanced by sociologist Paul Lazarsfeld, under the rubric of "the two-step flow of communication theory." *The two-step flow of communication theory* suggests that communication from mass media reaches the masses in two-steps—first from mass media to opinion leaders and then from opinion leaders to the masses.[15]

Is the theory valid today? Yes, in its overall insight, it is. But in its details, it is much more complex, entailing many more flows. Accordingly, it is proper to call the modern version of the theory as a "multi-step flow of communication theory." This theory captures the following multiple flows and processes (see Figure 10.6b):

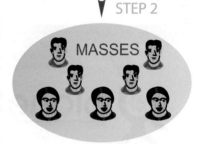

FIGURE 10.6A THE TWO-STEP FLOW MODEL OF COMMUNICATION

1. Mass media does reach the masses, but the masses pay attention mostly to entertainment media; in contrast, the news media reaches opinion leaders who are much more tuned into news and new developments.

2. Even if the masses are exposed to product and event news through mass media, mass media at best only makes them aware. In contrast, opinion leaders seek and receive detailed information about new products and events from media.

3. Opinion leaders are able to make up their minds based on the news and information they receive from mass media; in contrast, the masses do not make up their minds without seeking advice from opinion leaders. For the masses, then, mass media serve the crucial function of bringing awareness so they can seek further information and advice from opinion leaders.

4. Of course, as in the two-step flow, opinion leaders still spread some of the word proactively to the masses.

Thus, this multi-step flow theory does not negate the two-step theory; rather it augments and extends it. And it further bolsters the role of opinion leaders in the persuasion process.

FIGURE 10.6B THE MULTI-STEP FLOW MODEL OF COMMUNICATION

STEP 'A': Mass media reaches masses directly and at least creates awareness, though not conviction.

STEP 'B': Masses then SEEK advice from opinion leaders.

As a marketer, you need to target both groups. Put general brand news in mass media, and put more detailed and technical information in special interest media—remember opinion leaders are interested in specific interest topics!

WORD OF MOUSE: SHARING OPINIONS IN CYBERSPACE

The Internet is a powerful medium—a pervasive, omnipresent channel not only for marketer-initiated messages, but also for consumer-initiated messages. The chatter on the Net is a source both of enjoyment and opinion sharing for a substantial number of consumers. There are four platforms for expressing one's opinion in cyberspace: (a) e-mails, (b) feedback sites, (c) chat rooms and fan sites, and (d) Weblogs.

emails Emails are of course simply the cyber equivalents of old-fashioned letters carried by postal mail. But there are several key differences, three of which are particularly relevant to spreading opinion by word-of-mouse. First, email is easier, faster, and free; second, it reaches many at once; and third, it has viral-ability. Emails take less effort to write–many netizens use shorthand (e.g., all letters lower case, abbreviations such as 'u' for 'you', etc.). Emails also don't cost any postage, and they reach the recipients in a matter of minutes. Because of this spontaneity and immediacy, more consumers are likely to use e-mail to share their opinions on the experiences of the day (with marketplace objects as well as life activities) with their friends and family. Second, email can be sent to many simultaneously. Some consumers maintain address lists on the email server, and rather than pick and choose their recipients, they simply send to the entire list. Later, the recipients use the same e-mail to reply, and they can mail the reply to all recipients if they like by simply using the "Reply All" option, thus setting in motion a forum-like opinion sharing. Finally, emails can be forwarded to others with a simple click of the mouse, and this means the message can spread like a virus.

Feedback sites Many Retailer Websites provide users and consumers the opportunity to post their opinions about a product they bought on that site. Amazon.com, for example,

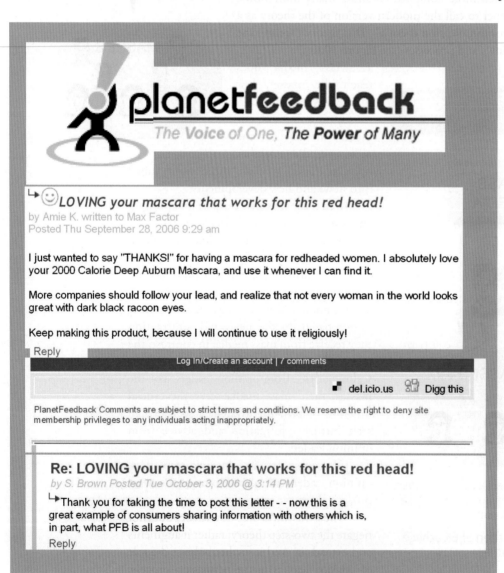

posts reader reviews of the books and music it sells. Then, there are organizations that operate a Website solely for the purpose of offering such opportunities to consumers. Two prominent sites are <u>epinions.com</u> and <u>planetfeedback.com</u>. On Epinions.com consumers post their reviews of products and retailers they have used. The Planetfeedback.com site similarly invites readers to post their views, although here the comments take the form of complaints, compliments, and suggestions. Both sites provide the opportunity for other readers to post their reactions to the original comment.

Exibit 10.1 shows one such posting onplanetfeedback.com.

Chat rooms Chat rooms are Websites with an instant messenger-enabled (IM-enabled) message posting window where a consumer can post messages in real time and others can respond to the messages immediately. The format is conversational, with real-time interactivity. Other related formats are Newsgroups, Message boards, and Lists (technically called Listservs). A consumer registers on these sites and then posts messages; some sites allow unscreened postings, whereas others are screened by a moderator. The Yahoo! site (http://www.yahoo.com), for example, hosts thousands of groups, organized by interest area, where members and fans post messages about their favorite topics, including choice of music, artists, movies, colleges, UFO's , and other consumption objects.

Weblogs The fourth medium for spreading the word in cyberspace, **Weblogs** are journals or logs people keep on their personal Websites. Called *blogs* for short, they are personal accounts of one's everyday activities, mundane and significant. Included in these are consumption experiences—which invariably entail some commentary about products consumed in the episode. Who reads them? There is no research on this, but it is safe to surmise that a group of close friends periodically access them, sometime because the "blogger" invites the visitor by sending out an email. But more important is the fact that some of the bloggers are celebrities with a fan following, and their blog words do carry weight. Visit RuPaul's Weblog, for example (www.Rupaul.com), and you will find an entry on his favorite music and movies. One of his favorite movies is *Monsoon Wedding*, an internationally acclaimed cross-cultural epiphany that the average moviegoer of the world hasn't even heard about; in another of his postings, he shares his latest obsession—Alligator Bread! See Exhibit 10.2 *Excerpts from Rupaul.*

Public blog sites There are also a few public blog sites—cyberspace equivalents of medieval agoras. Maintained by independent organizations, these are Web sites accessible to the public users to blog their musings. One of these sites is www.hiptop.com, and one recent entry logs a blogger's experience with 1-800-Flowers. (see inset).

Are you by now sufficiently amazed at the clever ways in which word-of-mouse finds its way across cyberspace? Wait—there is more. The latest fad is moblogging—blogging using the mobile phone. Say you are at a store and

---

WORD of MOUSE

1-800-FLOWERS
One quick post-Valentine's after-thought: this was the first year I used an online service to buy my wife flowers - in the past I had heard stories of people not receiving their orders on the right day, etc. But after working with 1800flowers.com, I would do it again in a heartbeat. Prices were reasonable and the flower arrangement was gorgeous. I would definitely check them out if you haven't used an e-tailer before.

posted at 07:46am 15 Feb 2003 on hiptop.com

Excerpts from the Weblog of RuPaul

EXHIBIT 10.2

Tuesday, December 17, 2002
FAVORITES OF 2002
MY FAVORITE / MOST PLAYED ALBUMS OF 2002:
1) living proof....cher
2) fever....kylie
3) more than a woman....toni braxton
4) ask a woman who knows....natalie cole
5) faithfully....faith evans
MY FAVORITE MOVIES OF 2002:
1)   sordid lives
2)   monsoon wedding
3)   swept away

Monday, April 29, 2002
ALLIGATOR BREAD
after the t-ball game, we all reconverged over at my sister's house where the conversation quickly turned to my latest obsession...alligator bread from victor benes bakery in gelsons supermarket. the first time i tasted it was at tom's house three weeks ago and it hasn't left my consciousness since. i got everybody so worked up that we had to load up the mini van and drive to marina del ray to get some "gator bread". my whole family was in exstacy after the first bite. yesterday i called michelle visage and asked her if she had "ever tasted alligator bread?" she said "no." "well hold on honey!" i said " i'll be over there in thirty minutes". ...

Excerpted from:
http://www.rupaul.com/2002_04_01_archive.shtml
(Reprinted by permission.)

you see something you like or don't like; you can simply take a picture with your camera-equipped mobile phone, add a text message, and through wireless Internet, and without having to find a laptop or PC, right from the store where you are, you can send off that picture along with your comments to hiptop.com for instant automated posting!

Why blog w-o-m works? Are bloggers opinion leaders? Are they influentials? Why does their word-of-mouse matter? It matters because even if they do not carry any expert power or role model influence, bloggers are perceived to be independent commentators, sharing their opinions for no personal gain. This independence is what makes them trustworthy, in cyberspace and physical world alike. But in cyberspace, because we connect with strangers and never see their faces, trusting total strangers seems to have become second nature for cyber surfers. Actually, they are not opinion leaders, but opinion sharers. And an opinion shared is an opinion influenced, particularly in cyberspace.

WORD of MOUSE

It travels fast. It travels far. And it connects people. Sometimes it is mundane. Occasionally it is *dark*—*a la* the congressman-pager IM exchange. Happily, occasionally, it produces results utterly heartwarming, and it produces them at the speed of the Web.

Shannon Syfrett, 15, a ninth-grader at Central Academy in Macon, Miss., was doing a six-week long science project. Named "How Fast or Far," the goal of the project was to find out how fast and how far does the word of mouse travel. So she started a chain letter asking people simply to write to her and also to pass on the letter to friends and acquaintances. On January 13, 2002, she emailed the letter to 23 people she knew. On January 14, she got over 200 replies; by January 24, the number of replies grew to more than 5000 every day. On February 5, 2002, when she pulled the plug in desperation, she had received 37, 584 emails, one every 2.3 seconds.

And the messages came from all corners of the world. It came from a Lutheran minister in Tempe, AZ who didn't know Shannon and who forwarded it to a friend teaching English in Vietnam; the English teacher replied and forwarded Shannon's letter to a friend in Antarctica. A woman in Ohio forwarded Shannon's letter to her aunt, a missionary in Papa New Guinea, who in turn sent it to an acquaintance running an orphanage in Mongolia. Shannon heard from an engineer in Chernobyl, and she heard from an Air Force sergeant on the Indian Ocean island of Diego Garcia.

And the replies were not simply "auto- replies" or "got it" acknowledgments; most contained personal messages. A woman from Sweden wrote, "It was too cold for the reindeers to go out." A farmer from California wrote about his new dairy with 25,000 cows. And a man from the Arabian Gulf wrote: "Email comes fast but Jesus will travel faster when you ask him into your heart."

Source: Adapted from June Kronholz, "After the Science Fair: Dear World, Please Stop

BUZZ MARKETING

W-O-M with a Twist

If you were sitting around in one of the cafes on Sunset Boulevard in Los Angeles on a Summer evening in 2001, the chances were that an attractive 20-something would pull up outside on his eye-catching Vespa and drop in. He might even have bought you a latte, and if you admired his Vespa, a scooter you had never seen before, he would promptly have scribbled for you the address of the nearby dealer. And as a bonus, he would have whispered a secret in your ear—that is where rap artist Sisqo and Hollywood star Sandra Bullock bought their Vespas! This was classic buzz marketing at work. These seemingly enchanted Vespa riders were actually marketing messengers hired by the European

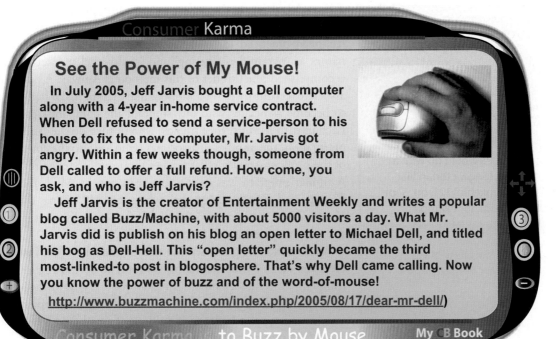

See the Power of My Mouse!

In July 2005, Jeff Jarvis bought a Dell computer along with a 4-year in-home service contract. When Dell refused to send a service-person to his house to fix the new computer, Mr. Jarvis got angry. Within a few weeks though, someone from Dell called to offer a full refund. How come, you ask, and who is Jeff Jarvis?

Jeff Jarvis is the creator of Entertainment Weekly and writes a popular blog called Buzz/Machine, with about 5000 visitors a day. What Mr. Jarvis did is publish on his blog an open letter to Michael Dell, and titled his bog as Dell-Hell. This "open letter" quickly became the third most-linked-to post in blogosphere. That's why Dell came calling. Now you know the power of buzz and of the word-of-mouse!

http://www.buzzmachine.com/index.php/2005/08/17/dear-mr-dell/)

Consumer Karma ... to Buzz by Mouse   My CB Book

motorbike company's US affiliate Piaggio USA to spread the word.

This is buzz marketing in action. **Buzz marketing** refers to the rapid-spreading of product news through word-of-mouth. Perhaps the most colorful description of buzz marketing is penned by a business writer Nancy K. Austin:

> Buzz is busy talk. The CNN of the street. It's hugely influential. Buzz is not merely onomatopoeic; it is big-time, no nonsense force. Once it is on the move, buzz is potent and widespread and lawless, which of course makes it irresistible. Brisk and a little unstable, buzz is a weather system that whirls into, and eventually out of, your life. Buzz is the Tornado Alley of communication.
>
> —Nancy K. Austin, "Buzz: In Search of the Most Elusive Force in All of Marketing," Inc. Magazine, May 1998, 44-50.

The buzz-bees (the carriers of buzz) differ from celebrity influencers in one aspect: they are not celebrities at all. "We weren't looking for celebrities," says Julie Roehm, the then communications manager at Ford Motor Company who managed a buzz campaign for the company's Gen Y model *Focus*. "We were looking for assistants to celebrities, party planners, disk jockeys—people who seemed to influence what was cool." She gave them a *Focus* to drive around for six months and simply be seen driving it.

Peer-to-peer marketing Peer-to-peer marketing is a special case of buzz marketing, where the goal is not just to spread the word but to get the target audiences to act on the word which comes from their peers. If you are a college student, you might have seen in the hallway some fellow students sitting at a table loaded with T-shirts, pens, cookies; you fill out an application for, say, a credit card, and you get one of these prizes. They are just collecting some money for their campus organization, they will tell you—and they are—but they are not unbiased communicators by any standard. Yet, you happily comply, for the sake of friendship, if not the freebies. This is peer-to-peer marketing.

During one recent school year, a small group of student "volunteers" at Brandeis University collected 200 names, complete with personal information—information fellow students would not easily give a business company. The Magma Group, the youth marketing company that sponsored the project, has some 6000 student volunteers in colleges across the nation who at its bidding will get their fellow classmates to fill out surveys for a freebee.[16]

Viral marketing We all know how a virus spreads—from one person, to two, four, eight, sixteen, thirty two, and so on. Only ten more iterations later, it would reach 65,000 people. With still 10 more, it would have reached 66 million people. Similar to the spreading of

Wondering how to put together an ensemble for your MOH appearance at a friend's wedding. Just post your question on topweddingquestions.com

"What color shoes would go with a spaghetti strap, long victorian lilac dress??" asks punkchic1221, on Sept 29, 2005, 7:17 p.m., for example.

"My suggestion is to ....wear a sexy metallic stilleto in a lilac or a shade lighter or darker. The shoes don't have to match the dresses exactly the color of the shoe just has to be in the same tone as the dress so they don't clash. Metallic shoes are super trendy,." Answers very helpful Lori of Modelbride.com, on Sept 30, 2005, 11:13 a.m.

Check out the entire post at http://www.topweddingquestions.com/forum/Wedding_Attire_C3/Bridesmaids_Attire_F8/color_matching_wedding_shoes_P13098

a virus, **Viral marketing** refers to spreading product acceptance from one consumer to another in an exponential fashion. It has been practiced for quite sometime, under such alternative names as 'pyramid marketing' and 'multi-level marketing.' An accomplished practitioner of this method is Amway. A company associate recruits three (or a number like that) of his or her friends to become associates who buy some of the company's product. Each in turn recruits three friends, who in turn do the same. And pretty soon, the number of associates (who are also the consumers of the product Amway sells) reaches thousands, or even millions. A similar program was used a few years ago by MCI under its *Friends and Family Campaign*, where an MCI long distance phone service customer would qualify for some discount if he or she recruited friends and family members.

Viral marketing got a new life with the advent of the Internet. Here the idea of viral marketing is simply to spread the message using the Internet channel. An example of viral diffusion in cyberspace is the dancing baby video clip that showed up as email attachments on the desktops of millions of email users a few years ago. Viral marketing can occur in two ways: (1) voluntary, or (2) incentivized. Voluntary viral marketing occurs when an email recipient finds the content interesting and voluntarily forwards it to friends. In the incentivized viral marketing, the marketer offers an incentive for forwarding a message to a certain number of people. For example, in September 1999, Asimba.com, a health and lifestyle Website ran a "Friends and Fleece" campaign. If an Asimba.com user recommended the site to ten friends, when the tenth friend registered with the site, the recommender got a fleece as a gift. By June 2000, the company had acquired 200,000 new users through the campaign.[17]

Cyber-buzz Cyber-buzz is buzz through the Internet channel. Although all Internet-based viral marketing is technically cyber buzz, it is best to reserve the term to refer to the voluntary forwarding of email. The forwarding of the email voluntarily implies that the content is inherently interesting, a requirement for email to be forwarded to an exponentially increasing number of recipients and to spread at a super-fast speed, which is what a buzz is, by definition. An example is the campaign by VF Corporation, the maker of Lee Dungarees. The company carefully identified 200,000 young web surfers and emailed them a video, with a built-in click-through icon labeled "Send to a friend." The goal was to get the recipient to visit the company's Website to watch a video game and, along the way, hopefully to browse the new merchandise. Within four months of the initial e-mail, 436,000 consumers had visited the company's Web site. See also Recipe for Successful Buzz (Exhibit 10.3).

GROUP INFLUENCE IN THE MARKETPLACE
Now You See It, Now You Don't

Reference groups, or referents, influence a person's consumer behavior in three ways: (1) when we feel indecisive or inadequate to make product choice decisions, we ask referents whose opinions and judgment we trust. (2) Sometimes, people give us advice whether or not we want it. Sometimes this advice conveys factual material such as which product would work better in a utilitarian or functional sense, and this advice we take if we trust their expertise. At other times, their advice is on matters of personal taste, such as what is in fashion or what purchases and consumption they consider undesirable. (3) Finally, referents influence us silently, just by being there, as we consider their implicit preferences and taste in making our own choices. This influence from a distance, so to speak, occurs both for normative factors—we expect to be rebuked if we ignore their taste, and for identification factors—we cherish imitating our heroes' tastes and consumption choices.

Not every marketable product or service lends itself to buzz marketing. Based on a reading of various writings and after pondering past case histories, we suggest the following ingredients of a successful buzz campaign.

1 **Unique product or message** First and foremost, the product has to be unique and interesting enough to become the topic of social conversations wherever people gather. When someone sights the product, it should arouse curiosity so the consumer looks at the product closely and finds and learns something about it worth telling others. And what he or she learns should be interesting enough so that he or she is eager to talk. Uniqueness of the product was a favorable factor both for the Vespa and the PT Cruiser, and, of course, for the dancing baby.

2 **Inherent human interest story** Beyond uniqueness, what helps tremendously is that the product or topic be of inherent human interest (beyond its utilitarian value). Celebrity gossip spreads like a buzz because people find celebrities an interesting part of their world. It is doubtful that one could create a buzz around commodity products and products that are used to do mere chores. Thus, Rumba, the new robotic vacuum cleaner, is less likely to get any buzz; but a product like bow-lingual (a gizmo, available from Sharper Image, that translates "woof" and a dog's emotions, into words) will, well, buzz!

It is the marketers' creative challenge to find ways of building human-interest stories in otherwise mundane products. Cigarettes themselves are a commodity product, at least for non-smokers. But makers of Lucky Strike undertook an innovative public relations campaign few years ago. It hired young people to roam the streets in major cities; they would offer you a beach chair to sit on and a cup of hot coffee to sip if you were forced out of "no smoking" buildings while you wanted to take a puff—and you could be smoking any brand. The gesture is, at least in appearance, so humane and touching that even anti-smoking crusaders would chuckle about it.

3 **Scarcity and mystery** The product should not be in abundant supply. One that is easily available or easily seen will kill a buzz even before it begins. Of course, large-scale mass awareness is its ultimate goal, but in the initial stages of the buzz, the product should be rare, and the story about it should be known only to a select few. Thus, a mass advertising campaign and a buzz could never coexist. The topic information should look like "secret knowledge." Buzz makers want to feel and look like they have an inside scoop, that they are "in the know," and they are doing you a favor by letting you know. In turn, then, you feel privileged to become the new "in the know." And of course you can't wait to show off your being "in the know," so you carefully tell a "chosen few" others about it. This "mystery chatter" is the modus operandi of buzz.

4 **Authenticity** The buzz topic has to be authentic. A buzz maker can't sing rave praise about a product that turns out to lack any umph. In this respect at least, buzz is like all advertising: a false product performance claim kills a product; a false claim that is mass advertised kills it faster. The author of a book titled Purple Cow packaged the book in a milk carton and sent it to a select few (yours truly included), but this would have been all in vain if the book's contents had not vividly demonstrated the success stories of marketing programs that stood out by being truly different, just as the purple cow does from the herd of white and black and brown cows.

5 **Free Agent** The buzz-bees should be free agents, not hired hands. Before the movie Titanic was released, a glowing review of it appeared on a Web site called www.aint-it-cool-news.com; the Website was run by an Austin, Texas based geeky guy named Harry Jay Knowles, who published the site to disseminate the inside scoop on Hollywood happenings. The thing about Knowles was that he was no hired hand; instead he published stories the movie moguls tried hard to keep hush hush. That pre-release review is credited in part for the skyrocketing success of Titanic. Thus, buzz depends on the apparent impartiality of the talker.

6 **Non commercialism** Finally, and related to the principle of Free Agent, the buzz should have the appearance of a social phenomenon rather than commercial advertising. When Lee Jeans Co. emailed its video clips, the recipients could play the video clips without knowing the sponsor's identity; only after a few months did the company reveal that to play the fuller version of the game, the consumer had to get a code from the label of the Lee Jeans in the stores—by which time the company had already created a following among teenagers who found the video clips rather fun (though silly).

These six ingredients are not absolute requirements, individually, but they are highly desirable. If a campaign lacks any one or more of these ingredients, it would be harder to sustain the buzz. And if one of these ingredients is missing or weak, other ingredients have to work that much harder. For example, the more transparent the commercial aspect, the stronger the other drivers of buzz, such as uniqueness, human-interest, scarcity, etc., would have to be. Vespa's commercialism was apparent, but the product and the 'visual personality' of the riders were attractive

Further reading. Seth Godin and Malcolm Gladwell, Unleashing the Ideavirus (Hyperion 2001); Gerry Khermouch and Jeff Green, "Buzz Marketing," Business Week, July 30, 2001, p. 50-56; Nancy K. Austin, "Buzz: In Search of the Most Elusive Force in All of Marketing," Inc. Magazine, May 1998, 44-50; Emanuel Rosen, The Anatomy of Buzz : How to Create Word of Mouth Marketing (Currency 2002).

Home Parties

You have heard about Tupperware parties—a gathering of women at a friend's (or a friend of a friend's) home, "invited" by referral and assembled around a show-and-tell display of the famous brand of plastic containers. The venerable company, which sells only through what are known as home parties, has grown to $1.2 billion sales in 2005.[1]

Other products that have long used this direct selling approach are Avon and Mary Kay. If you visit one such Mary Kay party, you will find that about 8 to 10 women are gathered in the living room of the hostess. Minutes earlier they had partaken a generous supply of beverages and finger food, and now they are ready to see the hostess demonstrate various skin care and makeup products.

This is not, however, simply a hands-off demonstration you find in the stores. Rather, women are asked to remove their current makeup using small pink mirrors and cotton balls. And then follows some couple of hours of product trial experience well blended with product use education and interspersed with occasional refill trips to the beverage bar. They learn about the importance of toner, cleanser, exfoliant, and about how to choose the right lipstick, blush, foundation, eye shadow, etc., for their skin color.

Although some of the women may have come with some initial reluctance, they are now totally relaxed and immersed in this learn-and-experience session. By the end of the meeting, some hostesses end up billing as much as a thousand dollars of merchandise.

Lately, this home party scene has been joined by such diverse brands as Jockey (under its Jockey Person-to-Person program), Body Shop, Pampered Chef (selling kitchen tools), Unique Baby Boutique, and even Lia Sophie (the costume jewelry company that sells stylish products and that counts celebrities among its customers).

For many women, attending such home parties has become a new source of entertainment, filling the void when they have outgrown the bar scene. Some become loyal customers, attending every party with a particular hostess whether or not they buy on every occasion. A woman who had attended some 40 Pampered Chef parties over the past 40 or so weeks had her husband, left behind at home with kids, feel envious: "I was at home with the kids and thinking, there was really nothing like this for guys."[a]

This account of home parties will be incomplete without a mention of two other brands: Passion Parties and Fantasia Home Parties. As you might have guessed, these companies have hostesses display and educate their guests/customers about such products as pheromone-scented lotions, edible lubricants, blindfolds, fluffy handcuffs, and other passion "enhancement" products. In the crowd (required to be 21 or older) there are women ranging from 22 to 60 years old, and from all walks of life, from a homemaker to a waitress to a financial professional. And some are surprised to find all that "knowledge." And amidst giggles, they buy merchandise they might have never thought of buying, at least not from a mall store.[b]

My CB Book

a Reported in Caroline Hsu, "Party Profits," U.S. News and World Report 10/20/2003.

b. Direct Selling Association as reported in "It's not your mother's Tupperware party," Jennifer Youssef, The Detroit News, May 26 2006.)
Note: Some 15 million people in the United States have shopped or sold products from home. Sales from home parties have reached more than $30 billion
Further reading, in addition to those specifically footnoted: "Home parties—more than Tupperware," **Jennifer Weil,** The Journal News, March 26, 2005; Doris Hajewski, "Jockeying for position: Underwear is latest in home-party sales,"The Milwaukee Journal Sentinel, Jan 30, 2006; And "Selling sex like Tupperware: In-home Passion Parties help women discover the joy of sex toys," Katherine Seligman, Chronicle Staff Writer, San Francisco Chronicle, Sunday, April 25, 2004. A reading of these informed our account here.

Discussion Question: Do friends (or friends of friends) assembled at such home parties serve as referents (reference groups) for the consumer? Which sort of reference group influence is at work here, if any? And how does the setting offer a psychologically more comforting setting (than a retail store might) for the typical attendee.

Every consumer has *reference groups*. They are a fact of life. They influence us intensely, materially, constantly. Is it a good thing? Does a consumer need reference groups? And what would life be without them? The answer is that reference groups are of immense use to us. Why? Because alone we can't master all the information about all the products we need to buy. And we can't acquire all the expertise needed to make sense of that information. So we turn to other experts for advice, and we feel grateful, as we should, that they exist.

Of course, we buy many products to satisfy our personal tastes, so reference groups wouldn't matter or shouldn't matter here, right? The fact is that there is no such thing as 100% "personal" taste. All our personal tastes come from people we admire; i.e., *referents* we choose. When we are in the store, we are seldom sure that the item of clothing we are contemplating would suit our personality. So we ask our shopping pal or someone we think shares our tastes.

Okay, we appreciate the informational and identificational influence, but what of the normative influence? We sometimes accept it gladly, but sometimes we resent it; e.g., a dress code. Either way, for the organizations and referents that impose various norms, it most likely serves some function. Show up in faded distressed jeans at a wedding, and you would spoil the look and feel of the event.

If you yearn for extreme individuality, you will no doubt find ways of excusing yourself from attending those events and indeed from the shackles of those normative referents. And you will find, instead, other referents whose norms you will gladly embrace.

For the rest of us—with no particular desire for extreme individuality, it is tempting to believe we make many choices of our own free will, uninfluenced by any referents, whether identificational or normative. Really? Think again. How did you choose your last product or brand that no one influenced, at least ostensibly? By considering the product's features and qualities, right? For example, you wanted a frugal, environment-friendly car; or you were looking for a shirt at Banana Republic, something that would make you look cool, just as you have imagined yourself to be; or you wanted to avoid a particular store because it carries products made in the third world countries under unfair labor practices.

But where did these ideas come from? How did you come to hold dear these ideas, these values, to begin with? Are you sure nobody was the source of influence for these ideas? The fact is that other people who inhabit our personal worlds (family members, friends, coworkers, role models, and cultural heroes) influence our worldview over our lifetime. That influence occurs in small doses, overtly or subtly, but it is as certain as sunrise.

Referents thus influence our consumer behavior in two ways: directly through brand advice or brand endorsement (overt or covert) and indirectly by molding our values and tastes.

Here then is our Last Word on reference group influence.

Reference Groups have a pervasive influence on Consumer Behavior. They influence what we buy and what we consume, of course. But they influence more—our values, our beliefs, our preferences, our tastes. To understand reference groups is to understand how social forces shape our lives as humans and as consumers.

No consumer behavior is untouched by reference groups, no matter how much you think you are "obeying *your own* thirst."

Now you know better!

In this chapter, we reviewed the types of reference groups and explained the nature of their influence. Depending on the frequency of contact, groups can be primary or secondary; and they can also be membership or symbolic, choice or ascribed. Their influence depends on conspicuousness in consumption, and as such it can occur at the product or brand choice level. This influence is of three types: informational, normative, and identificational. We then described a personality trait of consumers, namely SIPI, their susceptibility to interpersonal influence, and identified factors that make a consumer more or less SIPI.

Next, we described opinion leaders, people whose opinions consumers seek and respect. We described their characteristics and explained four methods of identifying them in a community. Next, we discussed influentials, a group of people who influence consumers by word-of-mouth (w-o-m). Among this latter group, we described a subgroup, e-fluentials, who affected opinion in cyberspace as well as outside of it, i.e., by word-of-mouth as well as by word-of-*mouse*. These opinion leaders play a crucial role in influencing consumers at large, especially on the adoption of innovations. Innovation spreads through consumer populations like an epidemic, and we described this diffusion process. Along its path, we identified five groups, from innovators who are the first to adopt an innovation, to early adopters, early majority, late majority, and laggards. The latter groups depend on the former groups for a favorable w-o-m. Finally, we discussed the relatively novel twin approaches to employing w-o-m— buzz marketing and viral marketing.

K E Y T E R M S

Groups
Ascribed groups
Buzz marketing
e-fluentials
Identificational Influence
Institutions
Informational influence
Influentials

Key informant method
Membership Groups
Normative influence
Opinion leaders
Reference Groups
Primary Groups
Secondary Groups
Symbolic Groups

Susceptibility to Interpersonal Influence (SIPI)
Sociometry
Self-designation method
Viral marketing
Weblogs

Y O U R T U R N

REVIEW+Rewind

1. How are groups defined? Name various classifications of groups, and give an example of each.
2. Name and explain the three types of reference group influences with an example of each.
3. Explain what is meant by Susceptibility to Interpersonal Influence (SIPI); name and explain the three factors that make a person high or low on SIPI.
4. Define opinion leadership and name two "essential qualities" of opinion leaders. Also name some personal characteristics of opinion leaders.
5. Write down some questions to measure opinion leadership.
6. Name and briefly explain the four methods of identifying opinion leaders.
7. Name the five groups based on the timing of their adoption of an innovation; briefly describe the characteristics of each group.
8. Explain the AIDA model and its significance in the adoption of a new product by consumers.
9. Explain the theory of two- and multi-step flow of communication theory and its purpose in marketing.
10. What is meant by (a) word-of-mouse, (b) buzz marketing, (c) peer-to-peer marketing, and (d) viral marketing? Give an example of each.

THINK+Apply

1. Explain how normative and identificational types of reference group influences are different. Give two example of each from your own life as a consumer.
2. Name some people who serve as your opinion leaders, and describe to what extent these persons possess the characteristics of an opinion leader. Also identify what kind of influence each of these persons exercises on you as a consumer.
3. Who are influentials and how are they different from opinion leaders? Can you name some influentials and explain for what kinds of consumers and for what

kinds of products they are the influentials?

4. How does the concept of five adopter categories help a marketer of an innovative product? Think of two innovations, and then outline a long-term marketing program to appeal to each of the five innovation adopter groups.

5. What are the requisites of a successful buzz campaign? Assess whether a buzz campaign could be used by the following marketers: (a) a toothbrush that beeps after 2 minutes of use; (b) a shoe polish that would last for one year; and (c) a hair crème that would grow hair at a much slower rate so that the consumer would need a hair cut only once a year, and available only in selected salons on a limited basis; (d) this book (assuming there were an annual convention of all consumer behavior students). Explain your answer.

6. Think of two or three new products or services to be launched next year that would be suitable for creating buzz. Justify how these products are apt candidates for buzz. Next, prepare a plan for creating buzz for one of these products. Your plan should dwell on (a) which groups will be targeted and how you would identify and harness opinion leaders; and (b) which types of influence would be relevant to each buzz agent.

PRACTICE+Experience

1. Select one of the following "products": (a) clothing fashions; (b) electronic devices like computers, cell phones, DVDs, etc.; or (c) art shows. Now for the selected product category, administer a survey to 10 of your friends to measure their opinion leaderships. Before surveying them, write down your perceptions about each friend in terms of whether or not they are opinion leaders. Also talk to them about the topic area and their topic-related conversations with others. Then compare their actual scores with your predictions, and explain possible reasons for a mismatch, if any.

2. Select a group (e.g., class, church group, ball league, etc.) of which you are a member and apply sociometric and key informant methods of identifying opinion leaders. Did the two methods lead to the same persons being identified as opinion leaders in those groups? Why or why not?

3. Locate a Hash Harry Harriets group in your city, and interview some of its members to understand what group norms exist and what kind of reference group influence the members of the group exercise on one another. Specifically identify what sorts of consumptions their membership in this group has influenced.

4. Search blogs on the Internet and identify some that reflect consumption-related word-of-mouse.

f.y.i.

On Buzz

Buzz is busy talk. The CNN of the street. It's hugely influential. Buzz is not merely onomatopoeic; it is big-time, no non-sense force. Once it is on the move, buzz is potent and widespread and lawless, which of course makes it irresistible. Brisk and a little un-stable, buzz is a weather system that whirls into, and eventually out of, your life. Buzz is the Tornado Alley of communication.

—Nancy K. Austin, "Buzz: In Search of the Most Elusive Force in All of Marketing," Inc. Magazine, May 1998, 44-50.

In the Marketing Manager's Shoes

Put yourself in a marketing manager's shoes. Most concepts in the chapter have some lessons for the marketing manager, i.e., they suggest what to do differently in practice; indeed, often these applications are implicit in our explanations of the concepts and models in the chapter. Identify at least five specific applications of the chapter's concepts, all of which should be entirely new—different from the examples cited here.

The Privilege of Choosing
The Hassle of Knowing How To

CHAPTER 11

PART IV

THE CONSUMER AS CHOOSER AND SHOPPER

- Consumer Decision Process—
  Life Comes At You Fast
- The Ignorance Paradox—I Don't
  Know That I Don't Know
- Judgement Models—Beauty Con-
  tests and Brand Battles
- Top Down or Bottom Up—Not The
  Same Product Choice
- Choosing Expressive Products—The
  Art of Buying Diamonds, Colognes,
  and Lingerie

Ok, so I missed the iPod revolution. For three years after the iPod made its much-trumpeted debut, I managed to resist buying one. My portable CD player filled my needs pretty well, or so I thought. But I can resist no more. The sheer stigma of not owning one when all my friends do is killing me.

And while I am at it, I might as well do my friends one up. I am going to buy an iPod with a photo-viewing feature. So I get on the Internet to check out the features and prices. Apple's iPod 5G with a 30 GB drive is available at Best Buy for $299. Its hard drive will store 500 hours of CD quality music, 25,000 still photos, and up to 75 hours of videos. Can you imagine what this can do for me during my next trip from New York to Sydney?!

I wanted to know more so I typed in "MP3 Player with Photo" in Google search, and Zen Micro kept coming up. Creative Zen Micro Photo to be exact. It's a nifty 8 GB, flash based device (unlike the iPod's hard drive). It has a replaceable battery so I won't have to depend on recharging. And it has an FM tuner so I can listen to the radio if I get bored with my stock music. Also it has a voice recorder, a plus over the iPod (which I can use to record Conan O'Brian's opening monologues, my favorite). One thing that bothers me though is that, on the Zen, I can't listen to the music and browse the photos at the same time. So, my trade-off is now between the voice-recording and simultaneous-photo-browse-and-music-listening options. I think I can forego voice recording, so I should go for the iPod. But then the Zen is priced at $249, a full 50 dollars less than the iPod. Is browse-while-listening feature of the iPod worth fifty dollars? Of course, iPod is cute, but, then, have you seen the über-sexy looks of the Zen? I can't ignore that.

Well, I will have to sleep on that one.

INTRODUCTION

Decisions, decisions, decisions. Life is full of them. From choosing a music player to choosing a wedding ring, from choosing a college to choosing a fraternity to join, and from choosing a president for the nation to choosing the flowers to plant in our gardens, as consumers we face a marketplace of choices galore. Some decisions are easy to make, and we make them in a split second. Others are difficult, and we agonize for days and weeks. Our decisions have consequences. We have to live with our choices. And our choices decide the fates of businesses; some flourish because we choose their products, and others vanish because we reject their offerings. Businesses need to understand how consumers make these decisions.

It is one thing to make decisions, but it is quite another to know how we make them. Although all consumers make decisions, not all understand the process. As students of consumer behavior, it is our opportunity—even our mandate—to understand this process. In this chapter, we will unravel the mystery of how our minds work when faced with a marketplace of choices.

We begin this chapter by placing decisions in perspective as a hierarchy of choices. We then describe a multi-step, systematic decision process. We describe each step from the time the consumer first realizes the need for something to the time the best option is identified. In doing so, we identify various sources of information that consumers use, and we explain various decision or judgment models they employ to accept or reject alternatives. With the best option identified, all that remains to be done is for the consumer to make the actual purchase. Sometimes, however, this is easier said than done. In the final section, we reveal how the last step of acquiring the product can sometimes be derailed and, even more importantly, what marketers can do to prevent it. In sum, the chapter will illuminate what goes on in consumers' minds as they make decisions in the marketplace.

CONSUMER DECISION PROCESSES

Think about it: when you are in the marketplace, what decisions are you called upon to make about any product? Yesterday, you bought a *Some of us lamp*, the nouveau art creation of designer Geatano Pesce, introduced into the market in 2005.

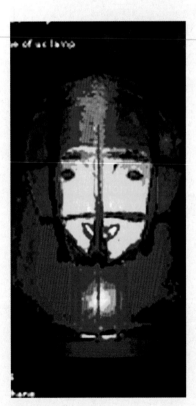

Some of us lamp
by Gaetano Pesce
(Photo Courtesy of Gaetano Pesce)

But it is not like you got up yesterday morning, and said, "Today, I am going to buy a Gaetano Pesce lamp." Instead, a few months ago, you started thinking about buying something spectacular for your living room in time for the New Year's Party at your new apartment on Miami's picturesque Biscayne Avenue. At first, you wondered if you should bother to spend that much money on one more home décor item at all. And then, even if you were so inclined, wouldn't you be better off, you asked yourself, to buy instead a big wall hanging from Morocco that you had seen at a Bal Harbor boutique? For several days thereafter, you debated whether to buy a home décor item at all, and whether it should it be an exotic wall hanging or an awesome designer lamp.

Thus, the first decision to make was whether to purchase the product at all.

You are not alone. All consumers typically face such dilemmas— a series of decisions, namely, whether to purchase the product at all, what (i.e., which brand) to purchase, from where to purchase it, and when to purchase it. Whether to purchase something is the first level of decision that entails weighing alternative uses of money and time resources. Consumers have finite money and time, and they must allocate them judiciously. Alternative demands on money or time may constrain a consumer to postpone or dismiss a purchase altogether. For example, you may abandon the idea of buying any home décor item at all because you must save to buy a state-of-the-art music system instead. Allocating money and time resources entails weighing alternative needs at the level of the product or service category (e.g. an, art curio versus a music system).

Once you do make up your mind to buy a product, you must then decide which brand to buy, when to buy it, and where to buy it. Having decided to buy an MP3, for instance, you must choose between, say, Rio, ZenVision, and iPod. And, if you come to prefer and want an iPod, you could buy it from one of the national chain stores in your city and bring it home today, or you could buy it instead from an online store and wait for delivery by mail. And you must also decide from which online store to buy it. Prices at online stores vary (as they do in bricks and mortar stores)—for example, you could buy an Apple iPod Mini (Blue) 4GB MP3 player for $219 at MSINC, for $239 at Best Options Direct, for $249 at PC Mall, or for $259 at Online Micro. And you have also to weigh risks that might offset a price advantage.

These decisions at various levels of hierarchy can all be called *alternatives*, and the consumer task is to choose from among the available alternatives. Thus, in this section, we will use the term "alternatives" generically to refer to product and service categories, brands, stores, suppliers, and so on,

FIGURE

11.1

CONSUMER DECISION PROCESS

Problem Recognition

Information Search

Alternative Evaluation

Purchase Transaction/ Product Acquisition

Post-Purchase Experience Evaluation

and we will examine consumer choice decisions among alternatives. We will use diverse products to illustrate various elements of the process, so you will see that the process applies to virtually any product you can think of—clothes, food items, electronics, art, entertainment, tattoos, and, of course, MP3 players.

Here then is that decision-making process. It consists of the five steps shown in Figure 11.1.

STEP 1:
PROBLEM RECOGNITION

You are combing your hair, looking in the mirror, as usual. You are about finished, when something about your eyes catches your attention. Under your eyes, some dark rings are beginning to form! In consumer behavior, we would say that you have just "recognized a problem."

The decision process begins when a consumer recognizes a problem to be solved or a need to be satisfied. As a consumer, you notice, for example, that you are hungry and need to get some food, or that the light bulb has blown out and needs replacement, or that the DVD player is skipping again and needs repairing, or that Sally has not called in a while, so you, Harry, had better send her a friendship card.

As this last example shows, a consumer "problem" is not necessarily a physical problem, such as a hungry stomach or dirty laundry or dark circles under the eyes. Rather a **consumer problem** is any state of deprivation. It is a state wherein a consumer feels discomfort or want. In other words, it is a gap between the current state and the desired state. You may recall from Chapter 2 that this gap is also called a "need"—problem recognition and need recognition are, then, one and the same thing. We will call this *The Gap Concept of Consumer Need* (see Figure 11.2).

Correspondingly, **problem recognition** is the consumer's realization of this gap between his/her current

FIGURE

11.2

THE GAP CONCEPT OF CONSUMER NEED

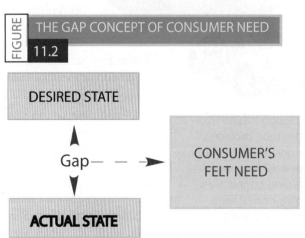

DESIRED STATE

Gap— – →

CONSUMER'S FELT NEED

ACTUAL STATE

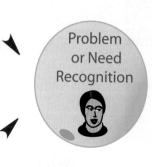

Dissatisfaction with Current State

Problem or Need Recognition

Desire to Take Action to Achieve the Desired State

state and the desired state. It occurs as soon as consumers become dissatisfied with their current state and want to do something to achieve a desired state. (See Figure 11.3.)

What Makes You Recognize a PROBLEM?

Think of all the problems or needs you have recognized as a consumer within this past week. Or reread Ellen's Diary in Chapter 1, and think of all the problems she recognized within a single week. What causes us to recognize these problems? Basically, there are two causes: internal stimuli and external stimuli. **Internal stimuli** are perceived states of discomfort arising from something inside you. This can be a physical condition of your body (e.g., hunger or thinning hair), or it can be a psychological condition, originating in your mind (e.g. boredom, or anxiety about Sally). **External stimuli** are sources of information you see outside—in the marketplace and on the street. Seeing them makes you want them. You smell coffee beans in a mall store, your body begins to crave coffee (a current state of discomfort), and your mind says its is time to have some coffee. You see a Mini Cooper on the road, and you begin to dream of driving it (desired state). And you see a cool person wearing this season's latest hairdo, and you too must have it.

Opportunity Knocking—Ah, The Sweet Smell Of Chocolate

External stimuli come in two forms: "problem stimuli" and "solution stimuli." A **problem-stimulus** is one in which the problem itself is the source of information, such as the sight of dirty laundry or the printer's empty ink cartridge. A **solution stimulus** is the information emanating from a solution itself. Here, exposure to a potential solution arouses the recognition of the need or the problem. This has happened to all of us: we are in the mall, and there is a store making fresh chocolate fudge. We just can't rest easy unless we give in to the sweet smell of chocolate. Likewise, exposure to a new style of dress in a store might make us realize that the dress will come in handy for an upcoming party. Or listening to a pitch about Rejuvex on TV might make us recognize the need for some of the energy supplement. Some consumer researchers have called it, appropriately, **opportunity recognition**[1]—problem recognition aroused by an external, solution stimulus.

Chicago-based Peapod, Inc., provides "stock replenishment service" for groceries, helping consumers solve one of life's many problems. (www.peapod.com)

Marketing communications, product or service samples, window shopping, etc., have their utility precisely because they serve as solution-stimuli for problem-recognition. In other words, they—the solution stimuli—entice us even when we are not feeling any internal deprivation or discomfort to begin with. Opportunity recognition occurs when a consumer is exposed to some external stimulus that promises to improve the current "normal" state. For example, your friend Lisa is at ease with her facial age lines; she has noticed them but has dismissed them as inevitable; and she is not currently bothered by them. Then she sees an ad for Botox, the wrinkle-removal medical treatment, and suddenly she becomes driven to do something about the wrinkles. Botox is the "solution-stimulus," and your friend Lisa was smart enough to have this "opportunity recognition."

Problem recognitions occur in three ways: (1) Through stock depletion; (2) Because of life-stage changes; (3) As a result of developing new tastes. Here is how they happen.

1. Stock Depletion Some "problems" occur simply, and repeatedly, due to stock depletion, such as when we empty a box of cereal. But sometimes consumers are caught unprepared when the stock depletion occurs. Some marketing communications help consumers by reminding them of imminent stock depletion. Remember the "Got Milk?" campaign? Some companies help you by taking care of your repetitive restocking need, such as Chicago's Peopod, which delivers your groceries to your house automatically at pre-specified intervals. Check it out at www.peapod.com.

2. Life Stage Changes New problems arise with new life conditions, such as a growing body, becoming a college student, leaving the parental home, becoming a parent, etc. Embarking on a professional career? Perhaps you will need to find a tattoo parlor to remove all those visible body tattoos!

3. Developing New Tastes Often, we develop new tastes, like tastes for fine arts and theater. We acquire new hobbies (e.g., learning Salsa dancing); we get drawn to Yoga, sushi, and organic food; we become hooked on MP3, SMS, and Bollywood movies (never mind the foreign tongue—subtitles will do, and the dance moves are hilarious); or we are drawn to the idea of plasma TV, or a pair of Diesel jeans, or the idea of a cruise to Alaska. Developing a new taste doesn't necessarily mean acquiring a more mature taste or a taste for the finer things in life. We mean, rather, a desire for anything new, anything not tried before. It includes fantasy realization—suddenly seeing that we can make our fantasies come true; for instance by buying a Mustang or a Mini Cooper. It means embracing new opportunity solutions or accepting new technology.

Unlike the stock depletion and life stage changes, this type of problem is subtle, lurking just behind (or below) our level of consciousness. These problems are brought to our consciousness when we see a solution stimulus—e.g., a new technology, or someone of our own type using a product we never thought of using, or someone telling us how cool some product would be for us. We see cell phones with built-in cameras, and we feel that we need one so that we can digitally capture whatever whenever. Sometimes, marketers make us realize how a product that we never paid attention to has relevance for us—like a Yahoo photo sharing account.

Enough about problem recognition. Except that, for the next week, we strongly advise you to keep a diary, recording all instances of problem recognition, and see how many of each type you experience.

Consumers often remain oblivious to their future needs or problems that are far off their current radar screen. Nationwide helps consumers recognize this problem with its now famous *Life comes at you fast* campaign. Bringing that point home in this creative masterpiece execution is none other than Fabio Lanzoni, the Italian-born American actor and an international fashion icon.

Okay, so you have, as consumers, recognized the need—like you need to do something about your thinning hair. What do you do next? Next, you search for solutions. This stage is called *information search*. Here, you seek out information, first about what alternatives are available in the marketplace and then about various features of these alternatives. On the face of it, the process looks simple and straightforward. But there is more to it. For starters, it takes two forms, depending on how novel for you the problem is, i.e., how familiar you are with the solution product category.

When you are unfamiliar with the product

If you are totally unfamiliar with the solution product for your problem (e.g., thinning hair), then this is how you would most likely proceed: you find out about one alternative, learn a little about it, then come to know of a second alternative, learn a bit about it, then a third, and a fourth, and then you explore these a bit more, learning more about them, going back and forth from one alternative to another. At this stage you might begin to explore yet another, new alternative, or explore the three or four that you have identified. Eventually, there comes a time when you feel that you have explored enough—i.e., you have done enough searching for information.

For your thinning hair, for example, through a search for information, you might have discovered (one by one) some special shampoos, some herbal medicines, and the prescription medicine Propecia. You might explore two or three shampoos, or a couple of herbal medicines closely, and so on.

And when you are familiar

Suppose you want to buy a car. Here, the product category is familiar to you, so the information search focuses on your examining the familiar alternatives in more detail. However, you would rarely perform an information search on all the brands with which you are familiar, much less all the brands in existence. Rather, you would consider only a select subset of brands. In fact, consumer researchers believe that brands are organized in your mind as follows (see Figure 11.4):

- First, there is the **awareness set**—which comprises all the brands of which you are aware as a consumer.
- Next, at the time of decision-making, you remember only a subset of the brands in the awareness set. This subset is called an **evoked set**. The brands you don't remember at the time of the decision are called an **inert set**.
- Of the brands in the evoked set, not all are considered fit for your needs. Those considered unfit are called the inept set and are eliminated right away. The remaining brands are termed the **consideration set**—the brands you, as a consumer, will consider buying.

Try this for yourself. Quickly, what brands of low fat candy come to your mind? Which ones would you consider buying? And what can marketers do to make you think of their candy brand when you think of candy bars?

FIGURE 11.4 AWARENESS, EVOKED, AND CONSIDERATION SETS

AWARENESS SET
(All the brands of which the consumer is aware)

EVOKED SET
(Brands the consumer could recall in memory)

INERT SET
(Brands the consumer could not recall in memory)

CONSIDERATION SET
(Brands considered)

INEPT SET
(Brands NOT considered)

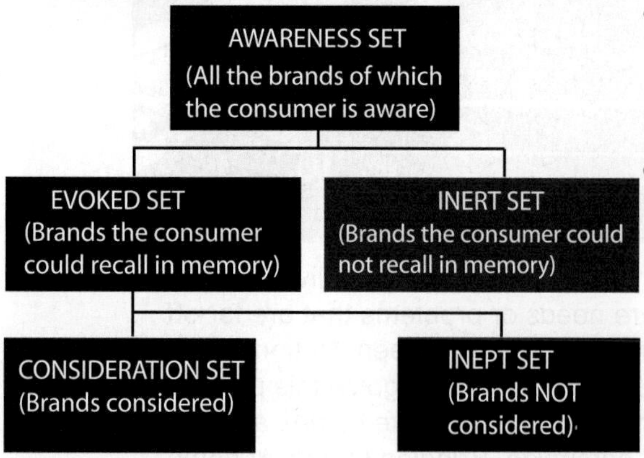

Please Put My Brand into Your Consideration Set

Initially, consumers seek information about the consideration set of brands—which is a subset of evoked sets. New information can bring additional brands into the awareness, evoked, and consideration sets. It should be the minimum objective of all marketing communications to place the advertised brand in its target consumers' consideration set (rather than merely in the "awareness or evoked set"). This is accomplished by highlighting a feature of the brand that its target consumers will find desirable. For example, SmartWater is a brand of bottled water enhanced with electrolytes, so it rehydrates you quickly after, say, a lie-detector test (see www.glaceau.com). By mentioning it, we have placed SmartWater into your awareness set. By mentioning that it is laced with electrolytes, we may have succeeded in placing it into your consideration set as well. Or maybe not. It is for you to decide. If we did, then now you know what it takes for marketers to put their brand into the consumer's consideration set. In essence, marketers have to offer, in advertising and in fact, a brand feature that the consumer will hopefully find valuable.

For net savvy consumers, the concepts of awareness and consideration sets work somewhat differently. If you are a net savvy consumer, and if you wanted to search cell phones, for example, you could go to the RadioShack Web site at www.RadioShack.com and find information on cell phones supported by five wireless service providers: Sprint, Verizon, Alltel, Cingular, and US Cellular. Click on "Sprint" and you will see twelve cell phones; ditto if you click on "Verizon"; and you will see thirteen more if you click the combined link for the other three (some alternatives overlap, but many don't). Given that the list of available alternatives is available on Web sites, consumers do not have to depend on their

Baldness treatment, and Buttocks remodeling, available at Aesthetis Clinic, Paris.

memory (called *internal memory*, as we described in Chapter 4). Instead they can depend on Web sites (which here serve as "external memory") to store all the brand names.

In the Web information environment, therefore, the concept of awareness and evoked sets should give way to what we call the **Recognition set**—the brand names the consumer recognizes as being familiar. The consideration set would be a subset of the recognition set, although occasionally, the consumer might read up on information on a completely new brand and admit it into the consideration set. The consideration set, however, will be a much smaller subset of the recognition set, selected most likely on the basis of brand-name reputation, and often if the product picture looks attractive. On the RadioShack Web site, for example, the consumer would find more than 25 cell phones to view, but it is unlikely that he or she would view more than, say, ten of them. Most consumers would initially view at most five or six before examining two or three in greater detail. Given the help from the "external memory" of the Web, the recognition set would be at least a little larger than the evoked set of the offline information environment, and the consideration set is also likely to be somewhat larger.

Perhaps you realize that it is easy to find information on cell phones; especially if you are net savvy. But information on other products is not as easy to come by. Try finding information, for example, on low-carb foods, on remedies for thinning hair, or on tennis rackets with *liquidmetal* frames. And try finding it in the offline world! Where would you begin? How much time and effort would you be willing to expend? And what would that depend on? Your interest in the product? Your mood? Or what?

Fortunately, consumer researchers have addressed these questions. Let us try to understand them, too, in this order:

- What sources of information do consumers use?
- What search strategies do consumers utilize, and how extensive a search do

consumers undertake?

- What factors determine how extensive an information search consumers will perform?

SOURCES OF INFORMATION

In searching for solutions for your thinning hair, for example, where would you look? You might ask a friend or a pharmacist. You have seen the ad for Propecia in magazines so many times, but you have, in the past, simply turned the page; now, you might actually go through those past issues of magazines to find that ad. And, of course, you could simply go to the Web, and type the keyword "thinning hair" into a search engine. All these are "sources of information." One recent study by the Insurance Research Council (IRC) found that of all consumers who sought car safety information while shopping for cars, 37% asked car salespeople, 29% checked it out in Consumer Reports, 18% sought it from newspaper reports and car magazines, 17% wrote to auto manufacturers, and 15% asked friends.[2]

We may organize these sources into two groups: marketer or nonmarketer. (See Table 11.1.) **Marketer sources** are those associated with the marketer of the product or service. These consist of advertising, salespersons, product/service literature and brochures, and in-store displays. Did we forget any (not counting a telemarketer call)? Yes, the Internet. There is one problem with the Internet, though. If you are looking to send an electronic greeting card, for example, you could go to the Apple's .Mac site at www. apple.com/dotmac/. But only if you knew, to begin with, that Apple offers iCards on its website!

TABLE 11.1 Sources of Information for Consumers	
Marketer Sources	**Non-Marketer Sources**
• Advertising	**PERSONAL SOURCES** • Friends and other acquaintances • Past experience
• Sales Promotion	
• Product/Service brochures	• INDEPENDENT SOURCES Public information (e.g., *Consumer Report*, Better Business Bureau, news reports in media, Government publications such as The Census of Manufacturers)
• Store Displays	• Product or service experts: (e.g., Auto Critic, home appraiser, pharmacist, and so on)
• Company Web Sites	• Internet (bulletin boards, forums, independent portals)

Prepared by Author for MyCBBook

Do You Trust Commercial Speech?

There is another problem with all these marketer sources: can you trust them? That depends, to a degree, on the reputation of the company. In any case, one thing is certain: all marketer sources have a vested interest in providing favorable information; that is why they are also referred to as **advocate sources**—sources that have a vested point-of-view to advocate or promote. As such, consumers view these sources as less than fully credible. Even so, not all marketer sources are equally lacking in credibility.

From the consumer's point of view, advertising would be considered the least credible. Or, at least, most consumers would put their judgment of ad claims on hold, pending further "checking it out." To them, inspection of in-store product displays is the most credible. Product/service brochures generally contain more technical and performance data and are, therefore, particularly useful for high-ticket and technical products and services. As regards salespersons as a source, consumers tend to view them generally with suspicion, but they do consider them a useful source of information. Salespersons, aware of this consumer perception, can improve their effectiveness by (a) becoming knowledgeable about the product or service, and (b) avoiding serving self-interest at the expense of consumer interest. If you are a salesperson (or ever have the opportunity to serve as one), you should be aware of consumer perceptions of salespersons as a source of information. Given the starting disadvantage of a lack of credibility, you should go the extra mile to provide information in a way that appears unbiased and non-self-serving.

Corporate Web sites are a useful source of information for net savvy consumers. If you know, for example, that Propecia is made by Merck, then you can go to that company's Web site at www.merck.com to get information about the drug's efficacy and side effects. "The fact is," says the site, for example, "That 2 years of clinical testing showed that 2 of 3 men regrew some hair (vs. 7% with a sugar pill)." And also that "Only a small number of men had sexual side effects, with each occurring in less than 2% of men."

Don't Forget Your Friends

Now let us look at the other half of the story—the nonmarketer sources. **Nonmarketer sources** are those that are independent of the marketer's control. Since these have no personal interest in providing biased information, they are viewed as nonadvocate sources and are considered more credible. These in turn are of two types: personal sources and independent sources. **Personal Sources** are family members, friends, and other acquaintances with past experience with and/or greater knowledge of the product category. As consumers, you would seek them out, and you would surely value their advice. Furthermore, your own past experience with the product or service is also a credible personal source of information; however, its relevance depends on how much the marketplace has changed (in terms of product or service advances) since your last purchase. If it has been a long time, the marketplace probably has changed a lot, and you had better not rely blindly on your earlier experience.

Independent sources are those not controlled by marketers and also not known to us personally. They in turn fall into three subcategories. First are independent publications and organizations with relevant expertise. For example, Consumer Reports, published in the United States, provides performance data based on product trials by independent judges and based on systematically collected reports of other past users' experiences. And organizations like the Better Business Bureau (BBB) can provide information on suspect practices of specific businesses. Secondly, independent sources include product and service experts such as pharmacists, financial advisors, car mechanics, and art appraisers, and these can be valuable sources of information. Thirdly, various Web sites, run not by product marketers themselves but by independent organizations (e.g., ecolivingcenter. com) or individuals, and Newsgroups and discussion forums are independent sources of information. An example of such forums is hairloss-reversal.com, run by a self-styled web entrepreneur.

We must note that while these sources are "independent" of specific product marketers' influences, many are not objective or unbiased by any means. Some sources (such as some of the online discussion groups) may even be based on ill-informed opinions; you must, therefore, exercise due diligence in paying heed to the information found there.

If You Are Not Knowledgeable

Do you have a tendency to use some of these sources more than others? If you do, one relevant factor is how knowledgeable you are about that product category. In an exploratory study, marketing professor Cheryl Burke Jarvis found that when buying expensive products like electronics, computers, cars, vacations, etc., inexperienced consumers' first source was friends and families followed by a visit to the retail stores and a strong reliance on salespersons. In contrast, experienced and knowledgeable consumers' first source was non-marketer-related independent sources like Consumer Reports, or expert ratings of computers in magazines, etc.; they also consulted with friends, family members, and company Web sites; salespersons were seen as the last resort, for the limited purpose of seeking price and other objective feature information— not recommendations.[3]

What does all this mean to marketers? First, they should exploit all possible channels of information and communication, including the Web. Second, salespeople play an important role, but this role is different for expert consumers versus novices. To cater to experts, you should be highly knowledgeable about the product. Your product knowledge

Blessings of the Information Age

QUESTION: By Anonymous on Sunday, June 16, 2002 - 05:58 pm:

I'm 40 years and I've loss hair problems since the 30 years. I began with Minoxidil 2%, after 5%, Propecia and now Propecia and Minoxidil 5%. Next week I'll go the dermatologist again because my hair loss became worst and worst. My hair started to be thinner and thinner everyday. Now I became depressed. My head seems terrible and I'm horrible. I do'nt desire my old hair never more. I only desire to stop this hair loss because I only have 40! When this will start? I'm terryfied now! How could I work? How could I go to the street?

REPLY: By Tom Hagerty (Admin) on Monday, June 17, 2002 - 09:59 am:

Anonymous;

Since you posted under Female Pattern Baldness, I gather that you are a woman. But why would a woman take Propecia or use 5% Minoxidil? Seeing a good dermatologist seems like an excellent idea. I hope this dermatoligist will spend some time listening to you and not just give you a quick prescription for more Rogaine (minoxidil). The dermatologist should also give you some tests to rule our possible thyroid or low iron problems.

Are you a Spanish speaking person? (I'm Spanish speaking myself.) Hair seems incredibly important among Latin people.

REPLAY: By portuguese on Tuesday, July 02, 2002 - 01:23 pm:

Yes, I'm portuguese. I think hair loss is difficult for all women.

I went to lots of dermatologists. I did a lot of medical exams and I'm OK. I started using good shampoos, after this some special pills, minox 2%, azote in the scalp, Androcour and pill, minox 5%, Propecia, and at last propecia and minox 5%. My hair loss increases a lot during the last months and it appears two nodules (like nuts) in my breast. It's not cancer. Only two big 'nuts' of liquid but I'm afraid. Now I stop having drugs or treatment for hair loss. I'm doing nothing. One day my hair is incredibly bad and on the other day my hair seems calm. When my hairloss seems to stop I'm happy and OK, when my hair loss come again I'm very anxious and depressing.

REPLY: By Rose on Tuesday, July 02, 2002 - 01:48 pm:

Portuguese - I don't think that women should use Propecia. It's a drug only for men and male pattern baldness. There are warnings on the drug that females should not use it.

REPLY: By mwoods on Sunday, July 14, 2002 - 06:18 pm:

I think I can help. Go to http://www.minoxidil.com - there is a solution called Xandrox.....it's by prescription only & your dermatologist would have to fax or mail a copy of your diagnosis. Use the 5% Xandrox DAYTIME formula. It is 5% Minoxidil, 5% Azailic acid with NO propylene glycol- that is what causes your scalp to itch like crazy! I used 2% otc minoxidil & saw no results with it. My derm recommended 5% & I prayed about it.....I said "God, you know I can't use that stuff....my scalp itches like CRAZY with it" & I was talking to another person who told me about Dr. Lee & his 5% solutions without the P.G. & so I had my doctor fax my info- I'm a 28 yr old female with AA, & he recommended Xandrox 5% daytime solution. He says 2% doesn't work very well for most people. After 3-4 wks hair falls out a lot, but my hair was already in the telogen stage, but after it stopped, growth began slowly but surely & my scalp has NEVER itched. Try this, have faith in God- never doubt- things happen for a reason, but I believe we can move mountains in His name! He loves us & wants us to turn to Him. Also, if we agree together in prayer He promises that He'll grant us what we ask (Matt.18:19)- in His time—so don't give up. "Don't fear- just believe" go by faith and not by sight.....& Trust God—forget what people say, doctors say......TRUST GOD! He's always in control!

Source http://www.hairloss-reversible.com/discus/messages/2/10.html?1035255600
(Date of Access: February 12, 2006). Reprinted with permission. from Tom Hagerty.

matters to novices as well, but to them your trustworthiness matters just as much. Finally, don't ever think that whatever you say goes. Consumers rely heavily on non-marketer sources, often to verify the information obtained from marketer sources. Thus, your product's reality (and, based on it, its reputation) speaks louder than your commercial speech. So don't make your commercial speech dishonest. It is worth repeating: consumers rely heavily on non-marketer sources!

SEARCH STRATEGIES
Are You a Simplifier

Okay, you have all these sources of information. What do you want to do next? Search all of them? Only a few of them? Which ones? Let us not go on a wild goose chase.

If you want to save time and effort, you need a "search strategy." What is a search strategy? A **search strategy** is the pattern of information acquisition that consumers utilize to solve their decision problems. We all know that, for everything we buy, we do not search information extensively; also, for any given item we buy, we do not all search the information in the same way or even to the same depth. Information acquisition depends on the search strategy we adopt for a specific purchasing task. Even though as consumers we ourselves may not call them *search strategies*, we do employ some pattern of search.

This pattern can be organized or *ad hoc*, "effortful" or convenience-based, quick or prolonged, and comprehensive or patchy. Correspondingly, we can group the search strategies as (a) systematic and (b) heuristic. What kind of a searcher are you? Well, let us define these two types first.

Systematic Information Search proceeds in an organized pattern, directed at answering specific questions. The questions pertain to problem solving: what features do various product alternatives have, and what are the relative merits and demerits of various brands or alternatives? Consumers carry these questions in their minds, and their search concludes when those questions have been answered. In contrast, heuristics are quick rules of thumb and shortcuts used to make decisions.[4] **Heuristic search** refers to *ad hoc* acquisition of information to reach intuitive judgments.

Systematic	Heuristic
Organized	Ad hoc
Effortful	Convenience based
Prolonged	Quick
Comprehensive	Patchy

Rules of Thumb

Here are some examples of how consumers use heuristics (rules of thumb):

Quick inferences Consumers use partial information to draw broad inferences quickly. Did you think, for example, that if SmartWater is laced with electrolytes, then it must be somehow "high-tech" and hence superior? Most consumers infer from technical sounding terms product superiority even as they may not quite know what that feature means (e.g., Dolby sound, pH balanced, "air-dried," etc.).

Brand name Often consumers use brand names as a guide to making a choice; e.g., "If this new phone is from Nokia, then it must be good." (Incidently, did the name SmartWater by itself made you think that this water must be really smart?)

Past experience Consumers also use past experience to make their choices; e.g., "Last time I flew by JetBlue and everything went well, so I will fly the same airline again."

Recommendation Consumers seek others' judgments and make their choices based on these recommendations; e.g., "My coworker says Echo is a good car, so I will just buy Echo."

We might not see anything odd in the above examples of heuristics. They might look to us perfectly normal and sensible ways to make decisions. Yet, the fact remains that they are easy ways out—if we really wanted not to miss out on the best option, we would really need to search the information fully and on our own, in addition to using these heuristics. But, instead, we often use these shortcuts, thus, saving time and effort. That is the whole point of using heuristics after all—they save time and effort. Do note that although heuristics are not systematic, they are also not irrational. They are rational to their users in terms of the cost-benefit trade-offs. (See Table 11.2. for a comparison of the two search strategies.

Simplifiers Versus Extenders?

The next question is, "Which strategy would you as a consumer employ and when?" This depends on two broad factors: (a) your own cognitive style, and (b) problem complexity. First, consumers differ in their proclivity or zone of comfort in dealing with information; i.e., they differ in their cognitive style. **Cognitive style** refers to consumer mindset about the task of processing information. Some of us are good at acquiring, processing, and evaluating a lot of information; others approach it with trepidation. Thus, when it comes

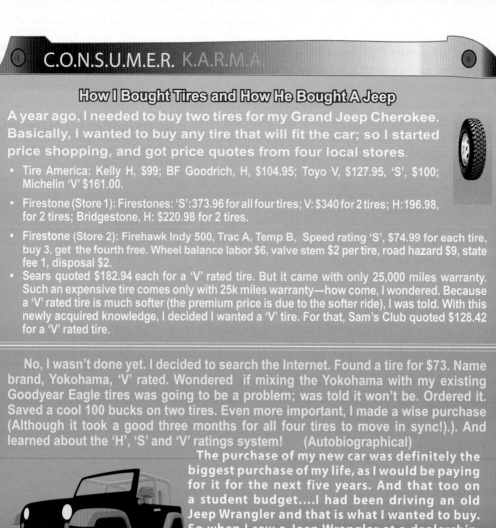

C.O.N.S.U.M.E.R. K.A.R.M.A.

How I Bought Tires and How He Bought A Jeep

A year ago, I needed to buy two tires for my Grand Jeep Cherokee. Basically, I wanted to buy any tire that will fit the car; so I started price shopping, and got price quotes from four local stores.

- Tire America: Kelly H, $99; BF Goodrich, H, $104.95; Toyo V, $127.95, 'S', $100; Michelin 'V' $161.00.

- Firestone (Store 1): Firestones: 'S':373.96 for all four tires; V: $340 for 2 tires; H:196.98, for 2 tires; Bridgestone, H: $220.98 for 2 tires.

- Firestone (Store 2): Firehawk Indy 500, Trac A, Temp B, Speed rating 'S', $74.99 for each tire, buy 3, get the fourth free. Wheel balance labor $6, valve stem $2 per tire, road hazard $9, state fee 1, disposal $2.

- Sears quoted $182.94 each for a 'V' rated tire. But it came with only 25,000 miles warranty. Such an expensive tire comes only with 25k miles warranty—how come, I wondered. Because a 'V' rated tire is much softer (the premium price is due to the softer ride), I was told. With this newly acquired knowledge, I decided I wanted a 'V' tire. For that, Sam's Club quoted $128.42 for a 'V' rated tire.

No, I wasn't done yet. I decided to search the Internet. Found a tire for $73. Name brand, Yokohama, 'V' rated. Wondered if mixing the Yokohama with my existing Goodyear Eagle tires was going to be a problem; was told it won't be. Ordered it. Saved a cool 100 bucks on two tires. Even more important, I made a wise purchase (Although it took a good three months for all four tires to move in sync!).). And learned about the 'H', 'S' and 'V' ratings system! (Autobiographical)

The purchase of my new car was definitely the biggest purchase of my life, as I would be paying for it for the next five years. And that too on a student budget....I had been driving an old Jeep Wrangler and that is what I wanted to buy. So when I saw a Jeep Wrangler at a dealership, I knew that is what I would be buying. And within five minutes, I signed off the purchase documents, accepting whatever price was quoted. (Zac, 22, student; paraphrased for brevity).

Now, dear reader, you have met the ultimate extender and the ultimate simplifier!

©iStockphoto.com/
Brian Sullivan

My BBook

MyCBBook

We are consumers and this is what we do.

---

to processing information, we could be "extenders" versus "simplifiers," undertaking an extensive search task, or, alternatively, looking for simplified and quick answers.

Which type are you? You are an extender if for most decisions you conduct systematic search, seeking information extensively, consulting a variety of sources, taking the requisite time, and deliberating a lot. Alternatively, you are a simplifier if you often adopt the heuristic strategy, drawing quick inferences and relying a lot more on other people's opinions than on your own consideration of information.

Do you sometimes feel overwhelmed with information? Do you feel too much information is coming at you too rapidly—be it from a class lecturer, a computer salesman, a TV commercial, or a Web site? When that happens, you are experiencing what is called an *information overload*—a condition in which the information being presented is too much for you to process as a consumer. Although the sheer volume or complexity or the speed of information is the major cause, your own cognitive style too deserves some of the credit.

The second factor is **problem complexity**—how simple or seemingly difficult the apparent solutions appear at the beginning of the search. This, of course, depends on how new the problem is— if we ran out of cereal this morning, no problem, we have dealt with it before. But if we are losing hair, now that requires some serious searching.

Losing Your Hair is No Routine Matter

On this dimension of problem complexity, all problems can be divided into three groups: routine, extended, and limited. **Routine problems** are those that you, as a consumer, have solved many times in the past. Hence, you will solve them again routinely; i.e., without any new information search effort. **Extended problems** are purchase tasks for purchases never made before, or made long ago, or where risks of wrong choice are high. Finally, **limited problems** are nontrivial, but risks are moderate, and the product or service is not overly complex or technical in terms of its features. We are tempted to give examples, but that would be stating the obvious.

In **routine problem solving**, generally, no new information is considered, and consumers usually solve these problems simply by repeating their previous choices. At the other extreme lies **extended problem solving**, where the information search is extensive and deliberation prolonged. In the middle lies **limited problem solving**—here, the consumer invests some limited amount of time and energy in searching and evaluating alternative solutions.

Here we will mention three problems, one from each category, leaving you to figure out which is which. (1) On your way to class, you felt hungry; (2) you needed to buy an engagement ring; and (3) you needed to buy a tire for your Hummer. Now you are on your own!

FIGURE **11.5** DETERMINANTS OF INFORMATION SEARCH

DETERMINANTS OF SEARCHING

Even for extensive problems, we do not always search for information exhaustively; on the other hand, even for routine problems, sometimes we end up searching for some information. For example, you may have bought greeting cards several times before, but on every one of your sweetheart 's birthdays, you go to the store and spend several minutes, if not hours, making your selection. Why?

On what does this behavior depend? Researchers have found that the extent of information consumers seek depends on five factors: perceived risk, involvement, familiarity and expertise, shopping style, and time pressure. (See Figure 11.5.) It will pay to learn a bit more about each of these, so here we go.

Perceived Risk Perceived risk is the degree of loss (i.e., amount at stake) in the event that a wrong choice is made. It consists of two factors: (a) the degree of uncertainty that a choice may be wrong, and (b) the severity of the consequences of a wrong choice; i.e., what is at stake should a wrong choice occur. Buying a new flavor of coffee with a known brand name has uncertainty about whether you would like the flavor, but the consequences are mild. Buying a suit without trying it on has the similar uncertainty about the suit's fit, but, in this case, and in addition, the consequences of an ill-fitting suit are considerable, especially if you are buying it for an important event. There are five types of risks:

1. **Performance risk** The product or service may not perform well or not as well as some other alternatives. Also included here is the physical safety risk (such as the risk of your SUV rolling over).
2. **Social risk** Reference group members and significant others may not like it.
3. **Psychological risk** The product or service may not reflect oneself.
4. **Financial risk** The alternative may be overpriced; there may exist a lower price.
5. **Obsolescence risk** The alternative may be replaced by newer substitutes.

If you buy a cell phone, for example, you will be concerned that the brand you buy might turn out to be unreliable, the voice quality might be poor, or when dropped it might break. These are all performance risks. If you are considering buying a Mini Cooper (an utterly small European car introduced in the U.S. at the turn of the new century) and are anxious over potential reactions from friends and coworkers, you are experiencing social risk. If you are unsure, yourself, that the Mini would go well with your own self-concept of being, say, a successful brand manager, then you are experiencing psychological risk. We all know what a financial risk is—the product goes on sale the day after we have already bought it, for example. And obsolescence risk is high for fashion fads and technological products—the end of the season clearance at the clothing store seems like a great steal, but maybe the style will become history next year!

The more you perceive the risk, the more extensive will be your information search. Marketers, therefore, attempt to overcome these risks by using various strategies. To overcome performance risks, marketers should and do offer product warranties; to overcome price risks, stores are increasingly offering price guarantees—some even offer to refund 110% of the price difference at a competing area store. Obsolescence risk is overcome by allowing the trade-in of the older model for the new one (as in automobiles), or by offering product upgrades (as in computers). Social and psychological risks are addressed to some extent by liberal return, exchange, or refund policies. If you judge that the product does not fit your style or if significant others dislike your purchase, you may return it to the store without any liability, provided that it is unused. If you have used it, then of course you are on your own. In life as well as in the store, it helps to know your mind and have some confidence in yourself!

Involvement **Involvement** is defined in Chapter 2 as the interest a consumer takes in a product. In buying a greeting card, for example, you would take more interest if you were buying it for a special friend. This involvement means that you are motivated to make as good a choice as possible. Consequently, you would search for more information before making your selection.

Familiarity and Expertise When it comes to buying a product, sometimes we are familiar with the product already. We have used it before, or we have seen the product and seen its advertisements. In that case, obviously, we would not engage in elaborate information search. We would know quickly what to buy. Familiarity and prior experience also imply that the purchase problem is solved in the routine problem-solving mode, as happens with most of the day-to-day purchases of staple items.

The same is not true with expertise, though. *Expertise* is different from *familiarity*. We define **expertise** as the understanding of the attributes of a product or service class. It includes knowledge about an object or a product's composition, properties, and functioning—what it is made of, what capabilities or qualities that composition gives it, and how (and how well) it does whatever job it is supposed to do.

Interestingly, the role of prior expertise is counterintuitive. At first, you would think that consumers with low prior expertise would seek more information to overcome their knowledge deficit—we call this the **deficit hypothesis**. However, it turns out that consumers with prior expertise seek even more information about the impending purchase than do those less knowledgeable.[5] For example, in one recent study of 1,400 car buyers, it was found that the amount of prior experience (i.e., familiarity) was, as expected, correlated negatively with the amount of consumer search effort. However, consumers' general interest in cars correlated positively with their product knowledge (i.e., expertise), and in turn both interest and expertise correlated positively with the amount of search effort.[6]

Ignorance Is Bliss

Although it seems counterintuitive, the fact is that expert consumers seek more information than do novices—even though novices need it more. This occurs because naive consumers do not know what questions to ask; experts do. This explains why sports enthusiasts visit and buy from sports specialty stores, whereas non-enthusiasts buy their sports products from mass merchandisers. This is also why specialty stores have to employ more knowledgeable salespersons than do mass merchandisers. But novices are perfectly happy with their ignorance. You see, experts know what they know; they also know what they don't know. And they want to bridge that gap. In contrast, novices don't know that they don't know. To them, ignorance is bliss. This is what is called the **ignorance paradox**!

Speaking of involvement and greeting cards, a few years ago, a company brought out a greeting cards series called *For When You Are Slightly interested*!

It is *consumer involvement* that drives niche markets.

Indeed, *consumer involvement* is the raison d'être for new niche markets.

Consumer Shopping Style Consumers differ in their shopping styles. Some are avid comparison shoppers who search extensively to get the best value.[7] Others are brand loyal, sticking to known and tried brands, thus finding it unnecessary to search anew for information. Moreover, some find shopping interesting, whereas others find it a boring chore. Naturally, the latter type would search information minimally.

Time Pressure One of the most conspicuous characteristics of the consumer in the new millennium is time pressure. Time has become and is becoming more and more scarce. This is due to many factors: (a) both spouses may work, (b) many consumers are employed in more than one job, (c) many consumers are re-enrolling in school to acquire new skills necessary for a more complex employment market, and (d) new leisure activities are being enabled by technology (e.g., cyber surfing). Some have called the "always on the go" consumer the "harassed decision maker."

Time pressure is making consumers look for more convenient outlets of shopping (e.g., home-shopping networks, catalog shopping, and the Internet). In addition, time-pressed consumers are likely to cut short their information search, comparison-shopping, and decision-making time.[8] Thus, time pressure is the last factor in our list that determines the degree of consumer searching.

Now, then, you have learned the ins and outs of the consumer information search. It is time now to put all that acquired information to use. It is time, that is, to proceed, finally, to evaluating various alternatives about which we now have information. So now we move to the next step.

Alright, you have done enough information search. Now, how do you use all that information to arrive at your choice?

To arrive at your choice, you need two things: evaluation criteria and judgment models. **Evaluation criteria** are standards against which consumers evaluate a product. **Judgment models** (also called "decision models" and "choice rules") are procedures and rules consumers use so as to consider various product attributes to arrive at their product choice. Let us consider each in turn.

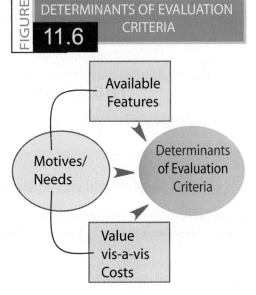

FIGURE 11.6 — DETERMINANTS OF EVALUATION CRITERIA

EVALUATION CRITERIA—
Whose Standards?

As standards to judge various alternatives, evaluation criteria are simply what consumers want in a product. In a cell phone, for example, you would perhaps want long battery life, good sound fidelity, readable large display, a 100-number memory, one touch dialing, and Web readiness. If so, then all of these are your evaluation criteria. Do you want customizable ring tones, also? And voice activated dialing? A built-in speaker? If you do, then these, too, become parts of your evaluation criteria.

Let us ponder a simple question: from where do these criteria come? How did you learn of them? At first, you might think, "The answer is simple: These are the features I want, so these became my criteria." You are right, but only partially. The full answer is this: they come from three sources: Motivation and need, solution feature availability, and perceived value vis-à-vis costs.

In a sense, what features we want are simply our motivations and needs at a greater level of detail. Thus, we not only need food, but we also need hot, nutritious, and tasty food. We not only need a phone to meet the need for communicating anytime anywhere, but we also need to be able to do it conveniently (hence, one touch dialing), and we want to be able to communicate without using our hands (hence, a built-in speaker phone).

Next, if a solution feature is not available in the product (in any of the alternatives), we would not even think of it as required. (We would still seek convenience, but it would not occur to us to translate convenience as hands-free dialing). Note, however, that not all features of a solution alternative become evaluation criteria—only those that meet some need or motive. Thus, motive and available features together make an evaluation criterion.

Finally, if a feature costs money, then we have to assess its value relative to its costs—*value* here being defined as the benefit from that feature. Voice-dial costs $50 extra? Well, we will do without it. Thus, when we enter the marketplace, so to speak (that means when we start the search process), we have an initial and tentative set of criteria in mind; later, we construct more (or drop some of the initial set) as we gather information. (See Figure 11.6.)

JUDGMENT MODELS
Beauty Contests and Brand Battles

First, let us talk about models of a different kind. You might be familiar with beauty contests. Beauty contestants are first scored on different categories: talent, looks, outlook (attitude toward self and world view—remember, contestants are often asked a question or two about some big issue in life), etc. Then the judges add up all the scores. Sitting in the audience, you might wish that they gave more weight to talent; your friend, who is also watching the show, might wish that they based their final choice exclusively on looks. These are all judgment models; your judgment model is different from the event organizers', and, in turn, your friend's judgment model is different from yours. Can you now define judgment models? Very simply, **judgment models** are procedures and rules for taking into account various qualities of an alternative. Their utility? Very simply, again— they guide our choice decisions.

Just so that we can talk about these various judgment models (or "decision rules" or "choice rules"), consumer researchers have given them more specific, technical names. They have divided them into two broad categories: compensatory and noncompensatory.[9] Let us learn about them—so that next time, as you watch Miss Universe contest, you can actually apply them! And of course, you can apply them to the battle of brands.

THE COMPENSATORY MODEL
I Want It ALL

In the **compensatory model**, the consumer arrives at a choice by considering all of the attributes of a product or service (or benefits from a product or service) and by mentally trading off the alternative's perceived weakness on one or more attributes with its perceived strength on other attributes. A consumer may go about making this calculation in two ways. One, he or she might simply add the number of positive attributes and subtract the number of negative attributes each alternative has and then choose the one that has the most positive and fewest negative attributes.

Whereas we sometimes do make decisions based on a simple numerical count of the pluses and the minuses, often we do not consider each plus or minus as equally significant. Some considerations are clearly more important than others, and every minus may not cancel a plus on some other feature. Therefore, we use a truer version of the compensatory model. This, the more systematic approach, is to weigh every product attribute in terms of its relative importance. Let us say, we want to make a choice between wireless service providers Verizon, Cingular, and Sprint. To keep the example simple, let us say there are just three evaluation criteria that we

TABLE 11.3 Applying Compensatory Model to the Choice of a Wireless Service

Evaluation Criteria	Importance	Brand Ratings		
		Verizon	Sprint	Cingular
Reliability	5	8	7	5
Customer-Service	3	6	4	8
Voice quality	2	6	7	4

Total weighted score for:
Verizon = 8x5 + 6x3 + 6x2 = 70
Sprint = 7x5 + 4x3 + 7x2 = 61
Cingular = 5x5 + 8x3 + 4x2 = 57
Therefore, this specific consumer will choose Verizon.

will use: reliability (calls not dropped, calls dialed correctly), voice quality, and customer service. Suppose we could rate each of the three services on these three criteria on a 0 to 10 rating scale (where 0 means very poor and 10 means excellent). Suppose we could also assign an importance rating by dividing 10 points among the three attributes: 5, 3, and 2— reliability is most important to us, so we assign it 5 out of 10 points; customer service is next most important, and we assign it a '3'; and to voice quality we assign a '2' (the importance scores add up to 10). Table 11.3 shows one consumer's ratings (note that these are one consumer's hypothetical ratings and do not reflect the actual quality of these three services). Now all you do is multiply the quality levels with importance weights and add them up for each company. The highest score is 70, for Verizon (see Table 11.3), so using this judgment model, you would choose Verizon.

This model is called *compensatory* because a shortfall on one attribute may be compensated by a good rating on another attribute. In the above hypothetical example, Verizon is actually not as good on customer service as is Cingular and not as good on voice quality as is Sprint (all these being hypothetical statements, of course), but these shortcomings are more than compensated for by its superiority on reliability, which is of the highest importance to our hypothetical consumer.

NONCOMPENSATORY MODELS:
You Either Have It or You Don't

While sometimes we want it all (so we consider all the features or qualities and accordingly use the compensatory model), sometimes we just want one feature or maybe two. Or we want a few features to a certain degree, but we don't necessarily want them all. If there are one or more particular features we want, then the alternative either has it or it doesn't. If the alternative doesn't have that feature (or features), then it is out, no matter what other features it has—those other features won't compensate. We call these judgment procedures *non-compensatory models*, and we will discuss four of them: conjunctive, disjunctive, lexicographic, and elimination by aspects.[10] To help us remember these, let us also give them a phrase:

Conjunctive model	"Must have at least these"
Disjunctive model	"Okay I am flexible; must have either this or that"
Lexicographic model	"I will take the best on the most"
Elimination by aspects	"At least this much on the most"

The Conjunctive Model In the **conjunctive model**, the consumer uses certain minimum cutoffs on all salient attributes. Each alternative is then examined on each attribute, and any alternative that meets the minimum cut-offs on all attributes potentially can be chosen. If an alternative fails to reach the cut-off, even on one attribute, it is dropped from further consideration. If all alternatives fail to reach the cut-off levels, then the consumer may revise his or her minimum cut-off levels or use another decision model. On the other hand, if more than one alternative meet all the minimum cut-off levels, the consumer might resort to another decision model to eliminate further alternatives until only one survives the process. We will illustrate this for the three wireless companies shortly, but let us first define the other three models as well.

The Disjunctive Model The **disjunctive model** entails trade-offs between aspects of choice alternatives. Here, the consumer is willing to trade off one feature for another. For example, a home buyer might say that the house should have either five bedrooms or, if it has only four bedrooms, then it must have a finished basement. Although these trade-offs are also made in the compensatory model, there are important

The headline reads: One of Our Manufacturing Facilities (shows the cow). Copy reads: Lactaid milk is made fresh on the farm with all the refreshing, deicious taste you love and the nutrition you need. But it is lactose free, so it is easy on your stomach. Lactaid® Real Milk from Real Cows.

For consumers whose most impotant criterion is that the milk be natural and real, this Soymilk ad communicates that it is. Helping consumers with their "lexicographic" strategy.

differences. First, the disjunctive model considers the sheer presence or absence of attributes, rather than the degree or amount in which these attributes are present. Second, in the compensatory model, the attributes traded off need not serve the same purpose, whereas in the disjunctive model, they tend to (e.g., a finished basement or an extra bedroom serve the same purpose; namely, more living space).

The Lexicographic Model In the **lexicographic model**, the consumer rank orders product attributes in terms of importance. The consumer examines all alternatives first on the most important criterion and identifies the one with the highest level on that criterion. If more than one alternative remain in the choice set, he or she considers the second most important criterion, examines the remaining alternatives with respect to that criterion, and selects the best. The process continues until only one alternative remains.

Elimination By Aspect The **elimination by aspects** (EBA) model is similar to the lexicographic model, but with one important difference. The consumer rates the attributes in the order of importance and, in addition, defines the minimum required values. He or she then examines all alternatives first on the most important attribute, admitting for further consideration only those that satisfy the minimum cut-off level on this most important attribute. If more than one alternatives meet this requirement, then the consumer goes to the next step, appraising the remaining alternatives on the second most important attribute, and retaining only those that meet the minimum cut-off level on this attribute, and so on.[11]

The Judgment Day—Models in Action

Now let us apply these models to a choice among the three wireless service companies.

For the conjunctive model, let us assume that you require all attributes to be at least average (a value of '5'). Then, Sprint fails on customer service and Cingular is rejected on voice quality; only Verizon meets the cut-off minimum of '5' on all attributes. So Verizon is chosen ("Must have at least these"). To apply the disjunctive model, suppose you are willing to compromise and would accept a brand with either good voice quality or good customer service (good being defined as '7'), and reliability doesn't matter to you. Now, then, Verizon is rejected, but both Sprint and Cingular are acceptable. (Your choice is not made, since you must now choose between the two, but you may do it now by looking at reliability, which is better for Sprint, or by some other criterion.)

Next, applying the lexicographic model, you would simply look at all three services, and, because reliability is most important to you (according to the table above), you would first judge them all on reliability and choose the one with the highest value on this—meaning that you will choose Verizon ("the best on the most"). Suppose that Sprint had also rated '8' on reliability; in that case, you would be left with both Sprint and Verizon, and in the second step you would use customer service as the next criterion—meaning that this time you would choose Verizon (since it rates '6' on customer service versus Sprint's '4').

Finally, to apply EBA, let us keep the same importance ratings, and, in addition, suppose we wanted these attributes to be at least '6'. Note that we don't want all the attributes to be '6', but, if we bother to look at an attribute at all, then it should be '6' or better. Now, Cingular is eliminated in the first step itself (it has less than '6' on reliability). In the second step, we evaluate the remaining two brands on customer service and select Verizon. (Incidently, suppose Verizon rated a '5' on voice quality. It wouldn't matter because our choice was already made.)

Are These Models Sensible?

You are probably thinking to yourself, this can't be real! As far as you know, no consumer uses these models; perhaps they are a figment of the imagination of this textbook writer or of some other scatter-brained professor. Let's assure you, consumers do use them all the time, and so do you. Before we show you how, two clarifications are in order. First, the models are not rules that the consumer "knows" he or she is applying. Rather, the consumer just goes about selecting and rejecting alternatives in some ways, but those ways represent the patterns of these models. Consumers don't have to know them by these names; we consumer researchers have to, so that, when we study consumers' decision processes, we can classify what proportion of our target market uses which models.

Second, consumers don't really assign numbers or do the calculations. Instead, they rate and rank and weigh and select and reject alternatives "qualitatively." They most probably use qualitative labels such as "good," "poor," etc., rather than use numbers. We as researchers assign numbers so that we are able to analyze, using the computer, a large sample of consumers. Thus, consumers use these patterns in a qualitative and therefore somewhat imprecise manner.

Now let us show you how you use these models in your own choices. Remember the beauty contest mentioned earlier. If you want to value all three criteria— looks, talent, and outlook (not necessarily equally)—then you are using a compensatory model. If all three criteria are important to you, and the beauty contestant should at least be, say, average on each, then you are using a conjunctive model. If you say that a contestant should be either very good on looks or very good on talent, then you are using a disjunctive model. And if talent is all you care about, and if you will declare the contestant with the most talent as the winner, then you are using the lexicographic model. You realize that if, out of all contestants, two contestants were equally outstanding on talent, then you might go for looks—whoever of the two has the better looks takes the prize (that is still the lexicographic model, remember!).

Finally, you would be using elimination by aspect (EBA) if you eliminated contestants based on whoever did not get a minimum score on talent (if talent is most important to you), and then the remaining contestants would go to the next test, outlook. Here, some more would be eliminated for not making a minimum score on outlook, and so on. That is elimination by aspect. So, you see, believe it or not, you do use these models—as does every other consumer. All of the time!

Half Empty or Half Full? That Depends on Your F R A M E !

IMPERFECTIONS IN CONSUMER JUDGMENTS

While the foregoing decision models give the appearance of consumers making logical decisions, consumer judgments are seldom perfect. The human mind is not exactly like a computer. It does take in information, but then it does not analyze it precisely. Rather, to save time or mental effort, it interprets that information quickly and intuitively. Consequently, its judgments and interpretations are approximate and often not entirely logical or factual. Let us consider three examples of such imperfections.

Framing Effects on Judgments
The Case of Glass Half-filled or Half-empty

For which would you pay more: a glass of wine that is 2/3rd full, or a glass of the same wine that is 1/3rd empty? You may think this question is silly because you believe that anyone can see that the two options are exactly equal. But think again: Do consumers perceive as equal two food items, one labeled 98% fat free and one at 2% fat? The surprising answer, based on research, is "No." Consumer researchers have found that when consumers are presented with two equal options, one stated in positive terms and the other in negative terms, they invariably tend to prefer the option stated in positive terms. This result is called *framing effect*.

TABLE 11.4	How Framing Affects Consumer Inferences		
	75% lean	75% fat-free	25% fat
Leanness	3.48	3.54	2.50
Greaseless	3.20	3.35	2.49
Taste Good	3.42	3.53	2.58
Quality	3.42	3.33	2.58
Intent to buy	3.01	2.89	2.30

Attribute perceptions measured on 1-5-point scale.

Source: Robert J. Donovan and Geoffrey Jalleh, "Positively versus Negatively Framed Product Attributes: The Influence of Involvement," *Psychology & Marketing*, 16 (7), October 1999, p. 613-630. Used with permission

Framing refers to the context in which information is presented. **Framing-effect** refers to the bias in the interpretation of the information resulting from its framing or context.

A recent research project illustrates this effect. In an experiment, consumers were randomly divided into thee groups. One group was told that a specific meat product was 75% lean; another was told that it was 75% fat-free; and the third was told that it had 25% fat. Consumers were then asked to rate the meat product on leanness, greasiness, quality, and tastiness; they were also asked how likely they would be to buy that meat product. The findings are shown in Table 11.4. Consumers rated the meat labelled 25% fat much more negatively than did those who saw the other two labels. These results are a vivid commentary on how, as consumers, we do not always think rationally. Rather, we interpret the information based on its framing context. Illogical as it may sound, the fact is that as consumers we often think that a glass 3/4 full is better than a glass 1/4 empty!

TOP-DOWN VERSUS BOTTOM-UP CUSTOMIZATION

Top Down
or
Bottom Up?

Imagine that you are out buying a car. You are considering a Ford Taurus, you are told the price of a basic Taurus (say, $18,000), and you are given a list of options with individual prices. You choose options one by one, until you believe you have included all the options you want. This is called **bottom-up customization**—a process wherein consumers build a product starting from the basic version.

Now suppose, instead, that you were given the price of a loaded car with all the options (say, $23,000), and you have the option of deleting the options (with individual prices specified). You delete the options one by one until you feel you have deleted the options you don't want. This is called **top-down customization**—a process wherein consumers build a product starting from the loaded version.

Do you think you would end up with the same car in the two scenarios? The answer is "no"—most of the consumers end up with a more loaded car (with a higher price ticket) in the top down than in the bottom up process. Why does this happen? Researchers have proposed several reasons, two of which are most likely:[12]

- **a. Cognitive Effort** Both adding options and deleting options take cognitive effort—i.e., the consumer has to think over each option and appraise its utility and costs. Suppose consumers want to undertake the effort to process only three options; then starting from a ten-option loaded car, they would settle on a seven-option car. In contrast, starting with a basic car, they would end up with a three-option car.
- **b. Anchoring Effect** The starting price acts as an anchor, as a comparison point, from which they want to judge how much they have moved. Suppose they want to move away by 10%; then from a starting price of $18,000, they end up at $19,800; but with $23,000 as the anchor, they will come down to $20,700, thus ending up with a customized brand $900 more expensive in the top down than in the bottom-up version.

This phenomenon is of great interest to marketers. If they offer a fully loaded model, consumers are likely to end up buying a "more-features" version, but a higher initial price might discourage some consumers at the outset. Thus, marketers must balance these two opposite effects.

CONSUMER GUESSWORK: INFERENCE MAKING

It would be nice if we had all the information we wanted about a product. Often, we don't. So we try to guess at the missing information. That is, we try to make an inference about the missing attribute information. **Inference making** refers to the consumer's act of assuming the missing information to make a judgment about a product. For example, a consumer may reason, "This pair of shoes is twice as expensive, so it must be more durable." In this manner, based on some partial information and some logical expectations, the consumer fills in the missing information.

Partial Information
+
Logical Expectation
= INFERENCE

Just how do consumers fill in the missing information? How do you do it yourself? Scholars have suggested three approaches; read them below and see which one is your favorite:

1. **Interattribute inference** The value of one attribute is inferred based on another attribute. For example, thickness of the fabric in an item of clothing might be used to infer crease-resistance (whether correctly or incorrectly).

2. **Evaluative consistency** The missing attribute is assumed to conform to the overall evaluation of the brand. Thus, if a brand is positively evaluated in overall terms, the brand is assumed to be good on the missing attribute as well, e.g., a VCR's repair record is assumed to be "good" just because consumers judge other attributes to be good.

3. **Negative cue** The consumer may simply treat the missing information as a negative cue and then use one of the two substrategies: avoid altogether the option with the missing information, or assume a low or poor value on this attribute.[13]

Chances are you have used all three of them, but do you favor one of them more than the other two?

SATISFICING

No matter what decision model they use, consumers as decision makers can never consider and appraise all of the alternatives exhaustively. Indeed, consumers *do not* typically make the most optimal choice. As already pointed out, the use of lexicographic or EBA or other noncompensatory models might eliminate a brand from further consideration based on the first attribute even though the brand's other features could have made the brand more attractive in overall terms. Yet consumers are perfectly happy making a choice by using noncompensatory models. This is a concept that Nobel Prize winning psychologist Herbert Simon calls *satisficing*.[14] **Satisficing** refers to a consumer's (or a decision maker's) acceptance of an alternative that he or she finds satisfying, even though there might be a better alternative. Thus, even ardent comparison shoppers finally give up and buy the product or service they find most acceptable from among those they have considered so far, even though they recognize that there might well be a slightly or even substantially better product or service or deal at the next store. This is *satisficing*. If you are a "satisficer" (note: it is "satisficer", not "satisfier"), don't worry; most consumers are, most of the time!

HOW DO CONSUMERS CHOOSE EXPRESSIVE PRODUCTS?
Or the Art of Buying Diamonds, Cologne, and Lingerie

The decision processes we described, especially the decision models (compensatory and noncompensatory), seem to work well for appliances, cars, office products, tools, etc. But surely we won't buy, you would argue, diamonds, cologne, dresses or lingerie this way. In fact, for many of these products, we just fall in love with them at first sight. How do consumers make choices about these "emotional" or symbolic products? The answer is, by using the affective choice mode (ACM), explained below.

To address this issue, consumer researchers have divided products into two categories according to whether they serve, primarily, utilitarian (i.e., functional or performance) needs or, instead (and primarily), social-psychological needs or motives. We would call the former *functional* and the latter *expressive*—we use the latter to express ourselves and our personalities, moods, lifestyles, and tastes. We assess functional products (like appliances, tools, etc.) by assessing their performance feature; processing the information, and using the judgment models we described earlier. We call this the **information processing mode (IPM)**. In this mode, "the consumer is thought to acquire information

How would you choose between these two shirts? Most consumers use ACM for choosing between expressive products like these.

(Shirts available at www.soliscompany.com)

(Photos courtesy of Solis Company)

FIGURE
11.7
THREE FACET OF AFFECTIVE CHOICE MODE (ACM)

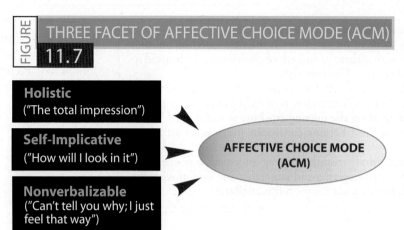

Holistic
("The total impression")

Self-Implicative
("How will I look in it")

Nonverbalizable
("Can't tell you why; I just feel that way")

AFFECTIVE CHOICE MODE
(ACM)

about brand attributes, to form evaluative criteria, to judge the levels of these attributes in various brands, and to combine these attribute-levels for overall brand evaluation."[15]

Emotional Choices

In contrast, expressive products are chosen for their social-psychological values. They are assessed by what is known as the **affective choice mode (ACM)**. In this mode, affect or liking for the brand ensues based, not on attribute information but, on judgments that have three properties: holistic, self-implicative, and nonverbalizable. That is, individual attributes matter less than the overall style, appearance, and total impression (holistic); the product or service is judged in relation to oneself, as in "How will *I* look in this dress?" (self-implicative). Also the decision cannot be verbalized since it was based on nonverbal cues (i.e., picture, appearance) and vicarious emotional experience. See Figure 11.7.

After a brand of clothing has established itself as a high quality brand (from a utilitarian point-of-view), the next layer of consumer value comes from the brand's expressive/emotional appeal. Here, Trigger, an Indian brand of jeans, captures an expressive situation that young men often fancy—the jeans make them irresistible to the opposite sex. This ad from Mudra puts the consumer, unintrusively but surely, in an Affective Choice Mode (ACM). Once transported to ACM, the heart rules!

Photo ad: Courtesy of Mudra Communications Pvt. Ltd., India and
Trigger Apparels Ltd. , India.

The implication of this distinction is two-fold. First, for expressive products and services, you would not seek much feature information, but this would not mean that you don't care and that you are executing a routine problem solving strategy. Actually, the deliberation time may be just as long. Second, marketers of these products should not burden the consumer with a lot of attribute information; instead, they should emphasize the product or service in its entirety (i.e., holistically) and create social/psychological symbolism via nonverbal communication and via association with positive role models or attractive personae.

Having described the ACM process, we must now balance the picture. It is not that, for expressive products, IPM is not used at all; rather, both of the processes are used. IPM is used initially to eliminate some choices using the noncompensatory models. Thus, the consumer may eliminate all dresses that are above a thousand dollars in price and all those that are not pastel in color. But then, when it comes to making the final selection, the ACM process is likely to be the one to determine the consumer's choice.

STEP 4: PURCHASE

Okay, so by now you have rejected many alternatives and have identified the one that meets all your criteria as well as possible. Now comes the moment of truth—you actually part with your cash and get the merchandise. This at first appears to be a straightforward step, but even here consumer behavior is, at times, intriguing. To understand this behavior, let us break down this step into three substeps (as shown in the Figure 11.8). The first substep—choice identification—occurs when the consumer identifies the most preferred alternative, based on the evaluation process just described. In effect, the consumer says, "Ok, this is the one I like and prefer." The next substep is to form a purchase intent—a determination that one should buy that product or service. It is the act of giving self-instruction; e.g., "The next time I am in the market, I am going to buy it." It is to make a mental note, to put it on the "to-do" list, so to speak. The final substep is purchase implementation. This entails arranging the terms of the transaction, seeking and obtaining credit, and, likewise, obtaining the transfer of the title or ownership from the seller, paying for the product or service, and taking possession of the product or service commitment from the seller.

FIGURE 11.8 CONSUMER BEHAVIOR AT THE PURCHASE STEP

Alas, the Journey Is Derailed.

In this overall step (i.e., purchase), after the intent is formed, the consumer now awaits an opportunity to buy the product. The desire to buy the specific alternative is formed, but the actual purchase may have to wait for some time for a number of reasons. The evaluation may have been performed outside the store, and one has to wait until one can go to the store. Or one may have to wait until the required money is available (the consumer begins to save for the purchase). Sometimes, the purchase intention may never be implemented, as, for example, when a consumer almost decides to join a particular weight-reduction program but somehow never actually gets around to doing it. But even if the purchase implementation eventually occurs, the consumer's journey may take a different route. Two factors can potentially "derail the journey": deviation from the identified choice and postponement or delay in implementation.

DEVIATION FROM THE IDENTIFIED CHOICE

The first factor that may derail the consumer purchase implementation is deviation from the identified choice. Several conditions may account for this. First, the preferred brand may be out of stock, thus forcing the consumer to buy a brand different from the one identified. Second, new in-store information may reopen the evaluation process. Third, financing terms may render a purchase infeasible, forcing the consumer either to abandon the purchase altogether or to substitute the purchase with a lower-level model or another brand that is available on preferred terms.

TABLE 11.5

Reasons For Delay in Implementing the Purchase Decision	
Reason	**Mean Importance**
Time Pressure--Too busy to devote the time	3.91
Needed more information	3.43
Couldn't afford at the time	3.19
Not sure if needed the item	2.75
Social and psychological risk if a wrong choice were made	2.70
Felt another product at home would do	2.70
Performance and financial risk if a wrong choice is made	2.65
Expected price reduction or product modification in the near future	2.52
Needed others' consent	2.41
Find shopping unpleasant	2.34

Note: Scores are mean values on a scale 1-5 where 1= this was not a reason and 5=this was very much a reason.

Source. "Reasons for substantial delay in consumer decision making," Greenleaf, Eric A.; Lehmann, Donald R, *Journal of Consumer Research*, Sept 95, Vol. 22 Issue 2, p186-199. © Journal of Consumer Research. Publisher: The University of Chicago Press.

DELAY in IMPLEMENTATION

The second factor is delay in implementation. Causes of delays occur throughout the consumer decision process—from problem recognition through alternative evaluation to purchase. We discuss these here for convenience and because it is the purchase step consumers most often and ultimately delay. One consumer story illustrates delay in implementation. A few years ago, a college student bought a small used car, a Toyota MR2. The car served him well—except when it snowed. His car, lightweight and rear-wheel drive, simply would not pull on the icy road. He decided (i.e., formed a purchase intent) that he would buy a four-wheel drive car (i.e., a 4 x 4) before the next winter. Well, the next winter came, and he struggled through it. A couple of years later, he graduated, got a job, and got a company car (but not a 4 x 4).

A recent consumer study identified the reasons consumers give for delaying their purchase decisions. The study interviewed recent buyers of such products as home appliances, electronics, personal computers, clothing, furniture, sports equipment, and automobiles. These consumers were asked to describe what caused

Romancing the Consumer — tv2010

These Clothes Will Fit Only One Body — Yours!

Intellifit

If you are one of the thousands of consumers constantly challenged to find the right size of clothing, one company has just the right solution for you. The company is Intellifit, and, true to its name, it has found an intelligent way of helping you find a pair of jeans (or other items of clothing for that matter) that will fit you like never before.

All you need to do is walk into a booth in one of the stores that partner with the company. The booth is a circular glass chamber about 8' high and 7' wide. You stand in it, with clothes on, and within only 10 seconds, your body measurements are taken unobtrusively, using a totally safe radio wave. The waves measure every inch of your body by sensing water in the skin. Afterwards, you will get a confidential printout listing the brands and sizes most likely to fit your body. You will also receive a list of retailers—bricks-and-mortar as well as online—which carry those brands and sizes.

Actually, the company goes beyond. Based on aggregate data across consumers, it tells retailers which sizes are likely to be especially sought by consumers. On its Web site, the company lists stores that have signed on to its program. Current listing includes ADASA Hawaii to Western Warehouse. You can also shop by brand. Click on a list of brands, and the Web site will list not only the size that will fit you but also which retailers carry clothes especially for you. Your measurements and profile are stored there, and you can update your information on the Web site by manually entering new measurements or by walking into a booth (installed at one of many retailers listed on the Web site). Check out this must-see Web site at www.intellifit.com.

them to delay the decision to buy these products, and also the factors that subsequently caused them to "close the decision." These factors, along with their importance ratings in this study, are described in Table 11.5. Review this table and see how many apply to your own recent purchasing events. Now, which of those reasons could a marketer have helped you overcome? As you know, one of the techniques marketers use is sales promotions; these are, by definition, limited in duration, thus pushing the consumer to implement the purchase intent now rather than later. Which of the reasons listed in Table 11.5 does this marketing strategy overcome?

STEP 5: POST-PURCHASE EXPERIENCE

Your decision process does not end with the purchase. Rather, the experience of buying and using the product provides information that you as a consumer will use in future decision making. In some cases, you will be pleased with the experience, and you will buy the same product or brand again. In other cases, you will be disappointed, and you may even return or exchange the product. If you are satisfied with your choice, then, in the future, you will simply repeat the choice. If dissatisfied, you will begin your decision-making process again. Of course, you do not have to start at the very beginning (i.e., Step 1, Problem Recognition). Nor, in fact, do you have to search for information from scratch. Rather, you re-open the alternative evaluation process, and you pick up the threads from the previous occasion. Thus, you may remember which brand was your second choice, so you go back to that brand, give it a last-minute check, and buy it. Or you may gather additional information about one or more of the alternatives you had eliminated or not considered in detail the last time and then apply the relevant decision model again to identify a new choice.

To the marketer, nothing should be more important than to ensure that consumers' post-purchase experiences are good, and that consumers are satisfied with their purchases. Only satisfied consumers will become loyal consumers. And loyal consumers are the backbone of a brand or business. We will study these fascinating topics of consumer satisfaction and loyalty further in the next chapter. For now, and before we conclude this chapter, we must address one question that must be bugging you—do consumers always follow these very systematic processes of decision making? You know you don't—not for all decisions anyway. And there are multiple processes described for choosing. So how do choosers choose from among these decision processes themselves? Our answer is summed up in one word—*involvement*.

INVOLVEMENT—THE PERVASIVE ARBITER OF CHOICE PROCESSES

Involvement—you have met this concept before in the book and, indeed, in this chapter. Let us recap what it is. It is very basically, *the importance of a product or issue to us as consumers*. We purchase and consume hundreds of products and services in our lives, but we are not equally involved in all of them. We take some for granted, not even noticing unless something wrong happens. And we purchase them routinely, just repeating the last purchase, or just buying whatever is convenient, cheapest, or most available. For these low involvement products, we have neither the time nor the desire or motivation to follow very deliberative processes. We reserve the more thorough and systematic process for the few highly involving, substantive, significant purchases we make once in a while (such as buying a Hummer or getting a facelift). Involvement helps us choose appropriate processes for each step of the five-step decision model. Let us see how.

Problem Recognition

Problem recognition differs for low- and high-involvement purchases. Low-involvement purchases consist of (a) frequently purchased items (e.g., cereal, milk, pencils, etc.), and (b) first-time purchases of small-ticket items (e.g., a new type of detergent or candy).

Need recognition for such purchases occurs due to (a) stock-outs of frequently consumed products (e.g., out of milk); (b) the incidence of regularly recurring deprivations of the body—internal stimuli—such as feeling hungry; and (c) exposure to external stimuli, such as seeing a low-ticket price on a new product or an ad. Need recognition for frequently consumed products is readily acknowledged. We are out of milk? Okay, noted. Even for new items, low-involvement consumers are able to quickly visualize the value (or lack therefore) of consuming that product. They are unlikely to appraise that need thoroughly.

High-involvement need recognition occurs, in contrast, when a consumer experiences a first-time (not recurring) internal, discomforting condition; e.g., a first-time realization of weakening eyesight, thinning hair, etc. Second, it occurs due to exposure to a new external environment; e.g., making a trip to a foreign country or having to find a dentist in a new city. Third, it occurs when a durable product currently in use becomes defunct and needs replacement, and it entails significant expense; for example, when a washing machine breaks down or our dress shoes are worn out. Finally, high-involvement need recognition also occurs from acquiring a new role (e.g., becoming a mother) or a life-stage change (graduating, entering employment, etc.).

Whether the need recognition occurs from an internal or external stimulus, mere sensation of internal condition (e.g., "It looks like I am losing my hair") or mere exposure to the external or solution stimulus (e.g., "That dress in the store window could come in handy at the next big office party") will not suffice when it is a high involvement decision. Rather, we engage in an in-depth need assessment; we would want to assess the seriousness of the condition and its consequences (e.g., "Am I really losing hair significantly and should I really care about my appearance at this stage in my life?"). Furthermore, need assessment will also include assessment of budget allocation and affordability

Information Search

For most low-involvement choice decisions, the information search is minimal. The moment your mind labels a problem as "low involvement," it goes into sleep mode, so to speak. "Least effort" becomes its self-instruction and operating mode. Most of your low involvement decisions are repeat purchases, so the brand choice is already made—most likely you have a couple of brands you have used, or, alternatively, you have no brand loyalty at all for low involvement products and are quite open to buying whatever brand is available on your next shopping trip or whatever may be on sale. In either case, the search will be short, and whatever search you are going to undertake will most likely remain confined to identifying the least-price source. And the search is likely to be limited in duration, often confined to one search episode (e.g., one visit to one store and a quick scan of items on adjacent shelves).

In contrast, for high-involvement decisions, the information search is prolonged and extensive. Our minds get into high-energy mode. Because the product entails risks, we compare multiple brands and multiple vendors, and we use all the available sources—marketer-, independent-, and personal sources. We read

TABLE 11.6	DECISION PROCESSES FOR LOW Vs. HIGH INVOLVEMENT SITUATIONS	
DECISION STEP	**LOW INVOLVEMENT**	**HIGH INVOLVEMENT**
Need Recognition	• Mostly stock replenishment of frequently consumed products. • Seeing new but small ticket items • Mere exposure to product communications	• First time experienced condition of discomfort • New external environment • A significant/expensive product breakdown • A new role (e.g., becoming a mother) • A life-stage change
Information Search	• Limited • Focused on price and sale • Completed with a single episode of information exposure • Single source considered adequate	• Extensive • Focused on product features as well as price • Carried over several information acquisition episodes • Multiple sources consulted
Evaluation	• Single stage process • Use of non-compensatory model only • Mostly inside the store • Relatively quick communications	• Two stage process • Use of non-compensatory and compensatory models • Outside and inside the store • Long drawn and agonizing

advertisements and product brochures and on-pack product information in depth, and we also examine and compare the product alternatives thoroughly. If the product is enduringly involving, then the information search is ongoing already, but it intensifies when we are considering a purchase in that product category. The search continues for several days and over multiple search episodes. Learning a lot about alternative brands and stores, not effort minimization, becomes the objective of the information search.

Alternative Evaluation

For low involvement purchases, the minimal effort strategy adopted during the information search phase also continues during the alternative evaluation phase. First, since the search phase is short and the search is limited to a single stimulus exposure episode, the evaluative judgment is also concluded in the same episode. The goal is merely to judge whether the product will, in broad terms, fit the purported need.

Much of this evaluation occurs in a store where multiple alternatives are physically available for side-by-side inspection. Evaluative criteria are few (often one or two) and are used in a way that calls for the least cognitive effort. Accordingly, compensatory models of judgment are not used (as they require significant deliberation and effortful weighing of pros and cons). The non-compensatory model most likely to be used is lexicographic, employing one or two features and choosing the alternative that is the best on these features.

For high-involvement products, the evaluation becomes effortful, prolonged, even agonizing. This is when your brain is on full-steam—fully engaged. The consideration set is likely to be large, at least initially, and evaluation criteria are many. Therefore, evaluation typically proceeds in two stages. Consumer researchers Bettman and Park call it a **phased decision strategy**.[16] In the first stage, termed **alternative elimination stage**, consumers narrow down the set of alternatives for closer comparisons. In the second stage, termed **alternative selection stage**, the smaller set of alternatives is further examined. The objective of the first stage is thus to identify all *acceptable* alternatives, whereas the second stage is meant to identify the *best* alternative.

In the alternative elimination phase, the focus is quickly to eliminate the less desirable alternatives and arrive at a shorter list of brands or alternatives. This is done easily by using some non-compensatory model, such as the "elimination by aspect" model, and can be done even before going to the store or without having the alternatives physically available to examine (e.g., eliminate all foreign car brands).

Next, in the second stage (the alternative selection stage), the goal is to identify the final choice. The consumer uses the compensatory model, considering each alternative in its entirety, with simultaneous consideration of all the features, weighing them, pitting one feature's worth against another, mentally compensating for the lack of one feature with the presence or superiority of another feature. If you think that this is a difficult and mind-boggling task, indeed it is; recall, if you will, how agonizing and difficult it was for you to make a very involving, very risky purchase decision the last time you had to make one, like which home you should buy.

Choice and Post-Purchase

Once the choice has been delineated, you might think that the product purchase and post-purchase experience steps ought to be easily implemented, involvement or no involvement. Not so fast—the fact is that involvement influences these last two steps, as well. That influence is, however, so counter-intuitive and multi-layered that it would take a whole chapter to study it. We will do just that, in the next chapter. For now, we should be "satisfied" with how much ground we have covered in our understanding of consumer decision processes and of the greatly helpful arbiter's role that involvement plays in navigating us through those decision processes.

We summarize these decision processes for low and high involvement in Table 11.6. We must clarify, of course, that our foregoing discussion of the entire decision process draws a sharp contrast between low- and high-involvement situations, but that this distinction will be found most clearly only for purchase decisions that fall at the two extreme (low and high) ends of the continuum of involvement. Between the end points, there are many products that dot the entire spectrum of the involvement continuum, and the decision processes for them accordingly fall between these two extremes.

In this chapter, we have given you a grand, panoramic view of consumer decision-making processes. You must be amazed at the workings of your mind—how, standing in the middle of the marketplace, so to speak, your mind sorts out a vast array of products and brands, puts some in memory to be recalled later, labels them as possible candidates for future use or not, considers their various features and expected outcomes, ignores some, contemplates some, weighs them, dismisses some, and embraces others. And this cycle goes on, over and over, as you choose a product today, another tomorrow, yet another the day after, and so on.

Our mind is indeed an amazing machine, a super-efficient computer. It works hard, to help us choose and consume and experience. But it also works smart—it has a self-regulating mechanism, a meta-software program if you will, which tells it when not to work hard. "Simply skip working, it is no big deal," the meta-software sometimes tells it.

You know the feeling: for every task you face, every moment of the day, as a consumer and as a human, your mind is always asking, "How important is this?" That question, you may now realize, is designed to assess your involvement in the product choice at hand.

Involvement is indeed a powerful concept as it directs our minds' energies toward those decision tasks that are of great import to us as consumers. Involvement gives some order to what would have been, otherwise, a chaotic decision process. But that process is still very profound and complex. Our minds learn to execute some of the decision processes as second nature; but for others, called for in high-stakes choice decisions, they do agonize.

If you want to become more aware of these decision processes, keep a journal for a week, recording which decisions your mind agonized over for hours or days, and which ones it made as second nature. Try also to map the specific processes using Table 11.6. If you are like most consumers, then these decision processes will map perfectly. If they don't, are you sure you are not very "involved" even in trivial product choices—like you wanted to buy some M&Ms, but you wanted them all in the colors of your shirt of the day!

SUMMARY

In this chapter, we studied consumer decision making as a five-step process: problem recognition, information search, alternative evaluation, choice, and post-choice. The consumer decision process begins with problem recognition, which occurs due to an internal cue coming from one's unfulfilled needs or from external stimuli evoking these needs or related motives. Once problem recognition occurs, the consumer (a) either relies on prior knowledge and previously learned solutions, or (b) searches for new solutions through new information acquisition and its evaluation and integration. In the information search stage, several determinants come into play, such as perceived risk, involvement, familiarity and expertise, shopping style, and time pressure.

Evaluation of alternatives entails use of compensatory and noncompensatory decision models. The latter include conjunctive, disjunctive, lexicographic, and elimination-by-aspect models. The outcome of these evaluation processes is the identification of a preferred brand and the formation of purchase intent. Such purchase intent is then implemented by the actual act of purchasing. Here we noted that the purchase act does not always occur as planned. Sometimes, substantial delays occur in purchase implementation; and, at other times, the brand actually bought is different from the one planned because of stockouts or new information gained at the time of purchase. In the post-choice phase, the consumer is either satisfied or dissatisfied with the outcome of product use. If satisfied, he or she simply repeats the choice for future purchases; if dissatisfied, he or she revisits the decision process.

The consumer decision process is determined by the consumer's individual characteristics, such as demographics, personality, and motives (all discussed in previous chapters). This chapter focused on the decision process itself—how the individual consumer makes a selection out of an array of product alternatives facing him or her. It gave some further order to those processes by delineating the differences between how these processes unfold for low-involvement versus high-involvement decisions. Understanding this process should help you to be aware of your own future product choice decision-making processes. And understanding these processes is helpful to marketing managers, so that they can determine why some consumers choose their product and others choose a competitor's product. Ultimately, it behooves marketers to structure their offerings and their communications in a fashion that responds to and resonates with consumers' decision-making processes.

KEY TERMS

Consumer Problem
Problem Recognition
Internal Stimuli
External Stimuli
Primary Demand
Secondary (Selective) Demand
Awareness Set
Evoked Set
Consideration Set
Marketer Sources
Advocate Sources
Nonmarketer Sources
Personal Sources

Independent Sources
Search Strategy
Systematic Search
Heuristics
Routine Problem Solving
Extended Problem Solving
Limited Problem Solving
Perceived Risk
Involvement
Ignorance paradox
Compensatory Model
Conjunctive Model

Disjunctive Model
Lexicographic Model
Elimination by Aspects
Satisficing
InformationProcessing Mode (IPM)
Affective Choice Mode (ACM)
Framing
Framing Effect
Information overload
Processing by Brand
Processing by Attributes

YOUR TURN

REVIEW+Rewind

1. Explain in your own words the concepts of *lifestyles* What is problem recognition in consumer behavior? Describe what causes it and when. Describe each type of problem recognition, with two examples. How can marketers utilize this classification?

2. What is meant by 'search strategies'? Explain systematic versus heuristic search strategies.

3. What factors influence the extent of search a consumer would engage in?

4. Explain the following concepts, with examples: (a) judgment models, (b) ignorance paradox; (c) affective choice mode (ACM), (d) satisficing, and (e) solution stimuli.

5. What would you say is the principal difference between compensatory and noncompensatory choice rules? Describe how the following choice rules work: conjunctive, disjunctive, lexicographic, and elimination by aspects.

THINK+Apply

1. Review in your mind the most recent important marketplace decision you made. What sources of information did you use in that decision? Please name each type, and comment on which ones were more useful and why you think so.

2. After a consumer has made a choice, would he or she buy immediately? Why or why not? What can a marketer do to reduce the barriers to consumer acquisition of products immediately after they have made the choice?

3. Reflect on how you might choose each of the following products or services:
   a. Graduate business schools
   b. A restaurant for dinner with your spouse or date on your anniversary
   c. Hotel for a business trip to Eastern Europe
   d. Toothpaste during a business trip to an Asian country where none of your usual brands are available and you don't know any brand names.

   For each, please indicate:
   i. How you will come to know what evaluation criteria to use
   ii. Which choice model you would use and how

4. In explaining the top-down versus bottom-up processing, we used the example of a consumer choosing a car. Can you think of other consumer choice situations where these concepts apply? Explain

your answer. Next, what should a marketer do to benefit from this concept?

(And if you are up to the challenge, comment on whether this would amount to an exploitation of the consumer's ignorance, and whether a consumer well-being agency should explore ways of curbing relevant marketer practices.)

5. You are the marketing director of a hotel company. You discover through research that most guests during the week use a conjunctive model in choosing their hotels; in contrast, most weekend guests use a lexicographic model. First, visualize how these two models will work for a hotel choice. Next, discuss whether your brand messages will be different across the two consumer groups and in what manner.

PRACTICE+Experience

1. Interview two consumers, each on his or her recent purchase of (a) a major appliance and (b) a grocery product never purchased before. The purpose of the interview is to find out how they went about making their brand selections and which decision model they used. Comment on whether the decision process differed for the two consumers, and likewise, for two products. How?

2. Collect two or three advertisements that address various problem-recognition situations; likewise, collect ads that respond to different choice rules.

3. Table 11.6 maps the processes in each of the five decision steps across low and high involvement products. Choose your two recent consumer decisions, one low and the other high involvement. Do the process and steps you took match those described in the table? Explain any discrepancies.

In the Marketing Manager's Shoes

Put yourself in a marketing manager's shoes. Most concepts in the chapter have some lessons for the marketing manager; i.e., they suggest what to do differently in practice. Indeed, often these applications are implicit in our explanations of the concepts and models in the chapter. Identify at least five specific applications of the chapter's concepts, all of which should be entirely new–different from the examples cited here.

DECISION MAKING BY CHINESE CONSUMERS IN MONTREAL   EXHIBIT 11.2

Look What CB Researchers Found

The general process of decision-making varies somewhat from one consumer group to another. An important factor that makes the process different is the cultural background of the consumer. For example, if you observe the buying behavior of immigrants in a country, you will notice differences between immigrants and natives, and also among immigrants from different cultures.

This is illustrated in a study of Chinese consumers in Montreal. In this study, interviews were conducted with recent buyers of electronic equipment (e.g., audio systems, VCRs, televisions, and so on). The study found that the most notable cultural characteristic of this group of consumers was the high value the group placed on thrift and the habit of saving. Correspondingly, buying by debt financing is generally disapproved in this group. Consequently, impulse buying of an expensive purchase was rare among the Chinese. Credit cards are used for convenience, not for credit; most Chinese consumers pay off their entire balances monthly. This is in sharp contrast to North American consumers, who usually finance their major purchases by credit.

This norm of not buying on credit makes every major purchase a three-stage process for Chinese consumers: (1) budgeting for the purchase, (2) accumulating the savings, and (3) implementing the purchase. Information search takes on a different character during these stages. In the budgeting and saving stage, the search is lengthy, broad in scope, and leisurely. The consumer is broadly "scanning the environment" rather than focusing on a specific aspect. The purpose of this search is to become familiar with the product or service category and various brands available in the market, to learn price points, to seek others' general impressions about various brands and features, and to decide on the amount they would like to spend. In the second stage, the search virtually stops, and the consumer focuses on saving the amount needed. Finally, in the third, post-saving stage, which begins after the needed budget amount has been saved, the search is intense, short in duration, and directed at specific information about specific brands and models.

The study also observed some differences in the sources of information Chinese consumers utilized. They distinguished between "factual" and "evaluative" information. They relied on salespersons for the former but not for the latter. Thus, they could ask the salesperson about the product features and other "objective" features, but for judgments about overall product quality, they sought independent sources like Consumer Reports and personal sources like friends and relatives. This general distrust of salespersons also made them rely much more on their own product inspection even for "objective" features. Thus, Chinese consumers tended to search for product information in stores where they could browse without being approached by salespersons.

Because the implementation of the decision process is influenced by cultural background, it is important that marketers study the decision making process for consumers in different countries, and for consumers of different cultural backgrounds within the same country.

Source: Adapted from Kathleen Brewer Doran, "Exploring Cultural Differences in Consumer Decision Making: Chinese Consumers in Montreal," Advances in Consumer Research, Chris Allen and Deborah Rodder John, ed. 21 (1994), pp. 318-22. Reprinted with permission of the Association for Consumer Research.

WHICH JUDGMENT MODEL TO USE WHEN?

An important question we left for this CB Level 2.0 discussion is this: As a consumer, how do you decide which judgment model to use, and when?

Compensatory and noncompensatory models differ in certain aspects. The core difference is that compensatory models take much more effort to apply (you have to weigh all attributes and then sum them up); in comparison, noncompensatory models are easy to apply (e.g., "Choose the contestant who is best looking"). Therefore, the rule for choosing the decision model itself is simple: Use the noncompensatory model if that will suffice; use the compensatory model if you must.

Even within the noncompensatory models, the conjunctive model is the more difficult one—because here, too, you must consider all the attributes (although you do not have to weigh them). The easiest is lexicographic—what is most important to you, and which alternative is the best on that most important criterion (e.g., choosing a date? Choose the richest! Decision problem solved.)

However, noncompensatory models can lead to suboptimal choices. This is because they do not allow the deficiency of one attribute to be made up for by the excess of another. Consequently, an alternative may be eliminated in the first step itself if it is, on that attribute, only marginally inferior to other alternatives, even though on all other attributes it may be substantially superior. In contrast, the compensatory model eliminates the possibility of making such suboptimal choices. However, because it is burdensome to execute, the compensatory model is used sparingly and only for important decisions.[18] Most low-ticket items are likely to be chosen with the help of noncompensatory models.

Thus, a consumer may buy table salt based simply on a single criterion—such as familiarity with the brand, or whether or not it is iodized, or perhaps on price alone. For example, a consumer might consider all brands of salt to be basically the same and say, "Let me buy the one with the lowest price." In this case, the consumer is using a lexicographic model. Another consumer buying an entree might use fat content as the important criterion and then either choose the one with the lowest fat content (thus employing a lexicographic model) or consider all entrees with fat content not exceeding 15% of total calories. Calories per serving might then be used as a second criterion, and, if need be, price as the third.

Brand or Attribute?

In this final topic of this section, we are going to reveal one other very fascinating fact about our judgment models. The compensatory and noncompensatory models differ not just in effort but in how a brand is viewed. You will notice that, in noncompensatory models, we take one attribute at a time (say, fat content for a food item) and examine all the brands against that criterion. In the compensatory model, we take one brand at a time (say, Honda Element), and examine that one brand against all the relevant criteria. Likewise, we then examine the second brand (say, Toyota's Scion xB), and examine that brand, too, against all the criteria. These two strategies are called, respectively, **processing by attribute** (PBA) and **processing by brand** (PBB). Actually, the conjunctive model also entails processing by brand (PBB), but the other three noncompensatory models entail processing by attribute (PBA).

Now you should realize that processing by attribute (PBA) is simpler than processing by brand (PBB)—and this is so for the simple reason that considering all the attributes of a brand is more cumbersome than just considering one attribute at a time. It makes sense, therefore, that we would use PBA for less important decisions and PBB for more important decisions. In the same vein, we would use noncompensatory models for decisions of low importance and compensatory models for high-involvement decisions.

Have you ever wondered why you have no distinct opinion on many of the brands you have had occasion to examine recently? Your laziness, which kept you from using a compensatory model, is the culprit. It's the price you had to pay for using PBA. Next time you love a brand so much as to want to form an opinion about it, use PBB!

Consumer Post-Choice Experience:

Doubt, Satisfaction, Voice, and Loyalty

- Fighting Buyers' Remorse
- Consuming Mindlessly
- Managing Consumer Expectations
  —*Please Stop That Advertising Hype*
- Many Faces of Satisfaction
- Exit, Voice, or Loyalty
- Consumer Involvement—How It Colors
  Post-Choice Experience
- I Complain, I Recycle, I Buy Green
  —Now Model Me

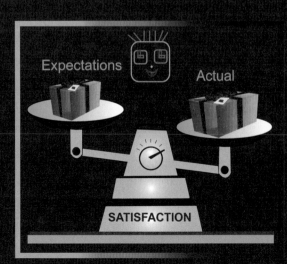

Cold Feet in a Hot Dress

haven't felt even a slight tinge of fear or doubt about marrying Chris.

I am worried about being a good wife, yes. I am worried that I'm forgetting something important that I need to do to make the wedding and reception events go smoothly, yes. I am worried that I will forget my passport as we are trying to hop the plane to Mexico, yes.

But I'm lucky because I know that all of that stuff will work itself out. I will do my best and enjoy the rest. And I'm lucky because I can tell that even in my subconscious states, marrying Chris is one of the best things I can do in my life. ... So while I've had jitters about the event, I have fortunately not had jitters about the guy. This hasn't stopped me from having cold feet about my dress, however.

I bought it last fall. Before the flowers were chosen. Before the bridesmaid and flower girl dresses were selected. Before I was able to imagine how everything would come together.

I fell for a big, foofy dress. Lots of beading. Fairly substantial train. Needs a crinoline to lie properly. That kind of dress. The dress is gorgeous. There's a reason I chose it.

Second Thoughts

Did I choose the right one? May be I should have chosen the other one.

But as everything comes together, I've realized: It doesn't work with the big picture. I think I'm breaking up with my dress. Or I'm at least going to tell it I'm thinking about seeing others.

So I took up with a second dress last night. It's sleeker, a slimmer silhouette, more metropolitan. It is more appropriate to me, to us, our combined style and the tone of the event itself.

I don't know why I feel guilt and a need to apologize to the first dress. I mean, I'm making MUCH more important commitments that day. And there's still a chance that it will work with that dress, after all. I will wake up on the morning of the wedding and choose between the two. Something about that just feels wrong, though. Perhaps I take what I wear a little too seriously. :)

Nicole M. Sikora, a consumer who wrote this entry (in May 2004) in her blog diary at http://nicole.wiw.org/archives/2004_05.html. (Reprinted with permission.)

INTRODUCTION

Everyone has heard at least one story like this. It would be nice if, after making an important decision, we could put the agonizing choice problem to rest and move on. Alas, the reality of life is different. Whether it is a wedding dress or a prom dress, a house, a car, a piece of expensive jewelry, a suit for the big interview, a choice of paint color for living room walls, or tattooing the name of your significant other on your body—every important choice decision unleashes a new train of thoughts and feelings. Ranging from doubt to gloating and from guilt to elation, these post-choice mental processes deeply influence the consumer's experience with a product and, indeed, the consumer's experience with life-as-a-consumer itself. In this chapter, we describe these processes.

We begin by describing a four-stage model of post-choice consumer experience. This experience culminates in a mental feeling consumers call satisfaction (or dissatisfaction). Simple on the surface, satisfaction is actually quite an intriguing process; we examine its nature and uncover its five fascinating facets. We also discuss the drivers of satisfaction and the role product or service performance plays in it. If the product experience is unsatisfactory, consumer complaining ensues. So, we present a model of consumer complaining—a model that explains why consumers sometimes complain and sometimes don't.

In the last section of the chapter, we revisit the entire post-choice process to identify how that process unfolds differently when the consumer is involved in the purchase decision and in the product consumption itself versus when the consumer is not involved. As the present chapter will make clear, your experience of the consumption process is worlds apart when you as a consumer care versus when you don't care. Read on.

POST-CHOICE EXPERIENCE

After the Choice Has Been Made

Let us pick up the threads from the last chapter. Like Nicole, the bride-to-be in our opening vignette, the consumer has gone through the alternative evaluation process and has identified his or her choice. In the five-step process shown in the last chapter, choice identification was not shown as a separate step. Our goal at that point was to maintain the widely respected five-step process model, along with the standard nomenclature for the last two steps of purchase and post-purchase. Our goal in the present chapter is to unravel those last two steps in greater detail.

Choice identification is the culmination of Step 3, *alternative evaluation*. Purchase and post-purchase are both post-choice processes. The fourth step in that model implies that, following choice identification, purchase ensues, inevitably and immediately. This of course was an over-simplification. The fact is that choice identification sets in motion a whole spectrum of thoughts and feelings in the consumer's mind. The focus of this chapter is on these thoughts, feelings, and action processes.

These consumer thoughts, feelings, and actions can be depicted as a four-step process: decision confirmation; experience evaluation; satisfaction or dissatisfaction; and future response, which can be exit, voice, or loyalty. Along the way, three specific actions also occur; namely, acquisition, consumption, and disposal. See Figure 12.1. This particular depiction of the post-choice processes opens up the last two steps from the previous chapter for a closer look. Decision confirmation is a *post-alternative*-evaluation and a *post-choice-* identification process that occurs just before the purchase step (which in this figure is called *acquisition*—a more general term that can include renting, leasing, or purchasing). Consumption and disposal are, obviously, post-purchase actions, and so are the processes of experience evaluation, satisfaction or dissatisfaction, and future response. All this may be a little too overwhelming at the moment, but all of these processes do occur in your everyday life, sometimes with great fanfare. So let us take a closer look.

FIGURE
12.1

A Model of Consumer Post-choice Processes

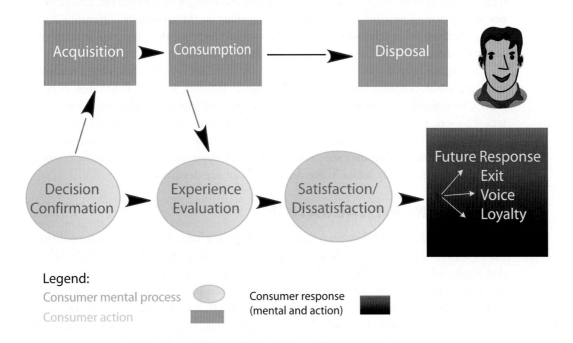

Legend:

Consumer mental process

Consumer action

Consumer response
(mental and action)

DECISION CONFIRMATION

Visualize this: After considering various cars, you settled on a 2006 Lotus Elise, a two-seater sports car from Britain, comparable to the German car Porsche Boxter 2006, and at $42,990, about $2000 cheaper than the Boxter.[1] You made a $500 deposit and want to pick up the car next week when the dealer gets it in the color you want. Now, what would you do next? Most likely you would call a friend to share the news, and you would expect your friend to congratulate you on your choice. And not just because it is polite for your friend to do so. The real reason is that you really *need* someone to praise your choice—to validate the wisdom of your decision.

After a consumer makes an important decision, he or she experiences an intense need to confirm the wisdom of that decision. On the flip side, the consumer wants to avoid disconfirmation. This step occurs immediately after the choice identification and continues through product purchase (acquisition) and its consumption. Often, following a decision and after the purchase is made, consumers experience **post-purchase cognitive dissonance**—also known as **buyer's remorse**—post-purchase doubt about the wisdom of one's choice.

After some major purchase, have you ever felt such dissonance? Or experienced some doubt? Or at least felt a need to reassure yourself that you made the right choice? If you did, do you remember how you resolved it? Most consumers reduce dissonance and confirm the soundness of their decisions by seeking further positive information about the chosen alternative and avoiding any negative information about it. Thus, they reread product literature, review the brand's positive features, and avoid competitors' advertisements. As consumers, we seek out friends to tell them about our purchase, hoping that our friends will validate our decisions by praising our choices. And if our friends begin to say negative things about our choices, and if we have set our minds to our choices, then we don't really want to hear them!

FIGHTING BUYER'S REMORSE

Marketers can put this principle to use: After the purchase (say, during product or service delivery), the salesperson can review with the customer all the features of the product or service. This review in itself should further reinforce the positive things the consumer had considered in making the choice. In addition, there might be features the consumer did not notice during product evaluation; bringing these to the consumer's attention during a post-purchase comprehensive feature review would improve the perceived attractiveness of the product.

Marketers may also communicate directly with recent buyers, conveying a reassuring message. These communications may be targeted through in-pack brochures, personal letters, or e-mails following the sale. The message may include testimonials from other recent buyers, particularly from residents in the local area, and reiteration of or additional information about the post-sale customer support available from the company. For example, a car dealership may send a letter to recent buyers, assigning a specific customer service representative by name in the dealership's service department.

EXPERIENCE EVALUATION

After the dissonance has been resolved and the wisdom of the decision is confirmed, the consumer acquires or purchases the product. Of course, there can be certain barriers that might delay or derail the actual purchase, and we covered those in the last chapter. For our present purposes, we assume that the consumer has acquired the product. We assume also that the post-purchase dissonance, if it occurred, has also been put to rest. After the acquisition, the next natural action is consumption. However, we sometimes acquire products we never end up using—such as when we acquire a product as a gift, we consider it inappropriate for our personal use, we make impulse purchases for which we later lose enthusiasm, or we acquire products in anticipation of future events or conditions (e.g., travel to a specific destination, a wedding, or a slimmer body) that never materialize. That said, for the majority of products we acquire, consumption does occur. With this next action step comes the mental process of "experience evaluation." How do you evaluate your consumption experience? Or, in fact, do you always evaluate your consumption experience?

The answer is that sometimes you do, and sometimes you don't. This depends, you guessed correctly, on your involvement with the product, and on what we call "preference finality"—the certitude (versus tentativeness) of your judgment that caused you to prefer and buy this product.

Consuming Mindlessly

In an earlier chapter, we defined enduring involvement as the interest consumers take in the consumption of the product or service on an *ongoing basis*. Of the hundreds of products and services we use in our lives, we use and consume most of them routinely or mindlessly. We simply do not have the time or the motivation to think about them at the time of each consumption. On the other hand, everybody is very enthusiastic about some products or services. In consuming these, we are conscious of the consumption experience, appraising and relishing it continually (e.g., wine drinking by wine connoisseurs). Thus, we consume low involvement products without conscious evaluation, and we consume high involvement products with full consciousness of their performance.

This high involvement comes from our enduring interest (e.g., in music CDs); it also comes from the continuing need to find good solutions to our still unsatisfied needs (e.g., persistent dandruff). In the latter case, we sometimes buy products and services on a trial basis, without deeming our preferences to be final. Consequently, we undertake the consumption of these products in an evaluative mode. This is an important concept— consuming in an **evaluative mode**—consuming with the intention of evaluating the product's performance. Think of all the products you consumed yesterday; how many of them did you consume mindlessly, without being in an evaluative mode, and how many in an evaluative mode? For most consumers, the former number far exceeds the latter. Did it for you?

Now there is a difference in how evaluation occurs when you are consuming a product in an evaluative mode versus when you are not. In the latter mode, you notice the performance only if something does not work as expected. Or, if it works exceptionally well. Thus, vivid performance difference (positive or negative) is required for consumers to notice the product performance if they are "not looking." In contrast, if they are "looking," then product performance must meet their requirements and expectations, and then some.

Free Sampling—Does It Help?

This raises an important question for marketers: Should they distribute free product samples? If consumers don't always consume new products with an evaluative mindset, does free product sampling help? The answer is, it depends. Two things determine the productivity of free product sampling. First, if free samples were targeted only to consumers who are not fully satisfied with their current product, they would actively appraise the sampled product or service. Second, free sampling is more useful when the product or service's superiority is substantial and would be conspicuous in consumption—noticeable even when the consumer is not in an evaluative mode. Of course, "me too" products can also benefit from free sampling simply by creating awareness and use-familiarity, but the benefit would not be as substantial as it is for products of noticeable superiority. If you understand this, you will save your company considerable money by not undertaking a program of free product sampling unless ___ (you fill in the blank).

SATISFACTION/DISSATISFACTION

Whether or not we actively evaluate a product or service while using it, whether we use it mindlessly or mindfully, one thing is certain. In the end, when the product has been used or consumed, we are left with a feeling. That feeling is a feeling of satisfaction. Or dissatisfaction.

Satisfaction/dissatisfaction can be defined simply as the positive or negative feeling consumers get with the outcome of product or service consumption. It is this feeling of happiness or unhappiness that sets in motion the consumer's future actions toward the brand and the company, which is the next step in our model. Measuring overall satisfaction/dissatisfaction is easy. Consumer researchers can simply ask, "How satisfied or dissatisfied are you with— (the product or service name)?" In reality, though, satisfaction is quite a mysterious process. Let us unravel its mystery.[2]

THE PSYCHOLOGY OF CONSUMER SATISFACTION

Satisfaction is the ultimate reason for all consumer behaviors. The choices consumers make in the marketplace must satisfy them, or else the whole choice decision process has been in vain, and the money has been wasted. And the problem of finding a solution to the recognized need has remained unsolved. So, just what is satisfaction? Why are consumers satisfied or dissatisfied with a product or service?

At first, the answer seems to be obvious and simple: If a product or service performs well, then the consumer will feel satisfied; if the product or service performs poorly, then the consumer will be dissatisfied. But this obvious and simple answer is deceptive. Consider a practical example: You bought a shirt at a flea market for $5, and after about five washes it began to fade around he collar. You also bought another shirt from a department store for about $40, and after five washes it too began to fade around the collar. Now, the chances are that you are likely to be much more dissatisfied with your purchase of the shirt from the department store than from the flea market. Why? It had the same performance, but it did not bring the same satisfaction. Why? This is because your expectations from the $5 flea market shirt bought for $5 are much lower than your expectations of the $40 shirt from the department store.

In this example, the root cause for satisfaction or dissatisfaction is clear: It is not the performance (in absolute terms) of a product or service that causes us satisfaction or dissatisfaction; rather, it is the product or service performance *relative* to our expectations. When performance meets or exceeds our expectations, *expectation confirmation* occurs, and the consumer feels satisfaction; when performance falls short of expectations, *expectation disconfirmation* occurs, and the consumer feels dissatisfaction. (Academic consumer researchers refer to these two conditions respectively as *positive disconfirmation* and *negative disconfirmation*—a technicality we will overlook.) This is called the expectations-confirmation-disconfirmation model of satisfaction. See Figures 12.2 and 12.3. Don't dismiss this model as mere textbook theory. Review in your mind all the instances of satisfaction and dissatisfaction you experienced, say, within the past month. Or the past year. Every time, you felt the way you did because your expectations were met or not met. Yes, this model is universal. It is true, always and inevitably.

FIGURE 12.2 THE ROLE OF EXPECTATIONS IN CONSUMER SATISFACTION

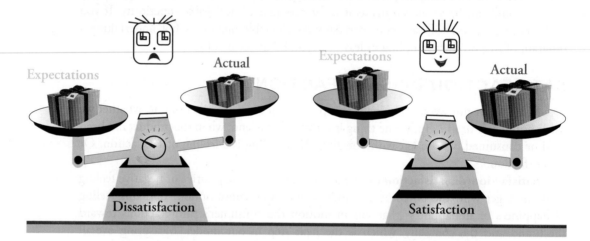

Please Stop that Advertising Hype!

Now, as a marketer, what can you learn from the model? If you want to satisfy your consumers, there are, the model tells you, only two ways to do it: (1) improve your product's performance, and (2) don't raise your customers' expectations sky high. Don't promise them the moon. There are, of course, shady salespersons and slick advertising that do just that—from miracle drugs to "bad credit, no problem" come-ons, some purveyors of commercial speech lure consumers with expectations they can't fulfill. Ultimately, the model tells us, all this does is produce utterly disenchanted consumers. So, please do your company a favor: stop all that advertising hype. It's suicidal.

Moreover, when possible, as a marketer, you should actively shape consumer expectations[3]—by realistic market communications, in advertising and personal selling and

TABLE 12.1 Measuring Satisfaction in Terms of Expectations

Hotel Guest Satisfaction			
How did we do? How was our:	Fell Below Expectations	Met Expectations	Exceeded Expectations
Room appearance	O	O	O
Room cleanliness	O	O	O
Registration speed	O	O	O
Friendliness of staff	O	O	O
Room service promptness	O	O	O

FIGURE
12.3

THE EXPECTATION-CONFIRMATION MODEL OF CONSUMER SATISFACTION-DISSATISFACTION

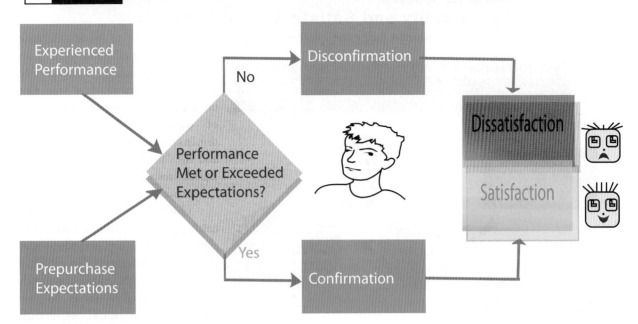

even in order-taking. We can all learn from what savvy restaurant managers do to shape customer expectations: If they are running slow, they inform customers that "today the service will be slow as we are short of employees." And notice also, how they do not over-promise. If they estimate the wait time to be 25 minutes, they inform the customer it will be 30 minutes. The customer actually gets called in 25 minutes.

To assess whether or not you (as a marketer) are on target, you can use a measure of satisfaction such as the one illustrated in Table 12.1

Consumer Satisfaction and Quality

Consumer satisfaction depends on meeting expectations. The next question is: expectations about what? What do consumers expect from a product? If we are marketing clothes, cars, colognes, detergents, or cell phones, for example, what consumer expectations should we meet? What do we build into our products to satisfy our customers? The answer: performance and quality. Consumers are satisfied if they find the product's performance and quality to be just what they expected or better.[4]

Performance is the outcome of the product's use. I use shampoo, and my oily hair is cleansed. I wear cologne and it lasts a long time. I own a cell phone, and it retains its battery life for three days unused, or for four hours of talk time, just as the company promised. These are all performances. Often, however, products have multiple performance features. Not only should my clothes not shrink, but they must also not wrinkle during use, and must not fade with washes. My cell phone must not only have long battery life, but also its memory should not get erased accidentally, it should be easy to program, and its ring tone should be pleasant and consistent.

Accordingly, consumers judge product performance by how well the product delivers the outcome on all of its expected features. Product quality is judged by two criteria: performance level and consistency. For a brand of beverage like Coca Cola, this means that it tastes good, and it does not go flat quickly (performance level). Moreover, its performance should not differ from one can to another (consistency). With mass production, branding, and standardization, consistency is not a concern for consumers in most of the advanced economies; however, in underdeveloped economies, and for cottage industries everywhere, consistency of product performance is an important concern. For pizza made by your local pizzeria (a cottage industry), for example, both its performance (taste, ingredients, etc.) and consistency from one pizza to another are aspects of quality judgments. This multidimensional quality judgment is what determines consumer satisfaction. As marketers, it is these consumer expectations of product quality that we must meet and exceed. See Figure 12.4.

Quality and Satisfaction in Services

How consumers judge the quality of a service is more difficult to specify. Because services often entail some interaction between customers and service providers (whether face to face or remote), consumer judgments of quality are based on two dimensions—namely, the "what" and the "how" of service. These are called, respectively, outcome and interaction quality. [5]

Outcome quality refers to the consequences experienced from the use of the service (e.g., in medical care, the disease is diagnosed correctly, and medication is prescribed correctly). Interaction quality refers to the pleasantness of social experience in the acquisition and use of the service—e.g., the doctor explains the diagnosis and treatment well, the nurses interact with the patient in a pleasant and caring manner, and, when you call your phone company or credit card company, you get a live customer service person who resolves your problem amicably. As a marketer of services, it is the consumer expectations of these two components of quality that you must meet and exceed. See Figure 12.5.

FIGURE 12.4 PERFORMANCE, QUALITY, AND CONSUMER SATISFACTION

PERFORMANCE OUTCOME

PERFORMANCE CONSISTENCY

PRODUCT QUALITY

SATISFACTION

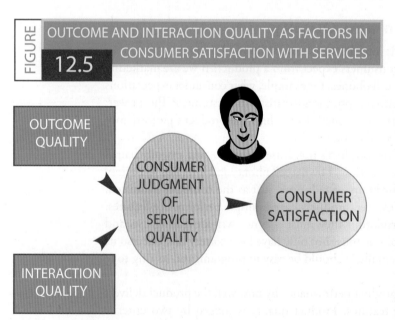

FIGURE 12.5 OUTCOME AND INTERACTION QUALITY AS FACTORS IN CONSUMER SATISFACTION WITH SERVICES

OUTCOME QUALITY

INTERACTION QUALITY

CONSUMER JUDGMENT OF SERVICE QUALITY

CONSUMER SATISFACTION

Some service marketing researchers have proposed a model of service quality called SERVQUAL. According to SERVQUAL, customers judge service quality along five dimensions as follows:[6]

Reliability—the service is performed right the first time.

Responsiveness—the service company responds to customer problems and resolves them effectively.

Assurance—the service company instills confidence in you.

Empathy—service employees empathize with, understand, and respect the consumers.

Tangibles—all tangibles that go with the service (e.g., the physical facility itself, service vehicles, employee uniforms, and even the company stationary) are neat in appearance.

If you ever get to manage a service operation, we recommend you read more about these five dimensions of service quality, in a good textbook on services management.[7]

When you call, you get a knowledgeable person within 60 seconds. **We think impatience is a virtue too.**

Call up, and in less than a minute, speak to a knowledgeable live person ready to help you. No holding for hours. No getting the runaround.

It pays to Discover®

Discovercard.com

Interaction Quality is an important component of customer satisfaction with services. Discover® Card understands this and promises a live person within 60 seconds. Photo: Courtesy of Discover Financial Services Company.

THE MANY FACES OF SATISFACTION
From Mere Satisfaction to Extreme Delight

Now that you understand the basics of consumer satisfaction, we want to tell you about its fascinating nuances. Satisfaction is, you see, merely necessary, not sufficient. Merely satisfying your customers will not win them over. Instead, you need to delight them. So, we now take you on this important journey from satisfaction to delight.

Although in overall terms, satisfaction occurs when expectations are met, it also matters how well these expectations are met. The more the performance exceeds the expectations, the higher the satisfaction. Interestingly, "high satisfaction" is not merely more of the "satisfaction" than "low satisfaction"; rather, "high satisfaction" is a qualitatively different human experience than "low satisfaction." Satisfaction has, in other words, many faces. Let us view them closely.

Consider four recent consumption experiences of a consumer we will call Monsieur Ross (after the *Friends'* famous semi-intellectual character he sometimes deems to be his alter-ego). Here, in his own words:

• I have a shirt I will refer to as Shirt 'X'. I bought it with fondness. The moment I saw it, I fell in love with it. It is dark blue (my favorite color), with a button down collar and pearl white buttons, 100% pinpoint cotton fabric that is slightly on the thick side, with a silky semi-gloss look and feel. But after two washes the collar has faded at the fold—I can't wear it any more. You can tell I am dissatisfied. What about my other shirts, you might ask? Which ones (I have several dozen of them, as do a lot of "clothes-happy" consumers)? In any case, they are all fine.

• My first cell phone was the Samsung Model # SCH 8500, bought in late 1999, when I first signed up for a wireless phone service. It was a flip-open type little gizmo, small enough to sit deep inside my shirt pocket. And it had a bunch of cool features. Then, in December 2005, I got a no-charge courtesy upgrade—so my phone is now

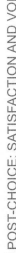

the Samsung SPH-A660 with PCS Vision Phone VI660 service. This upgraded version offers me everything my older model did and more (for one, the ring tone melodies are more enchanting). I have a choice of ring tones, and I can set it up to answer the call by merely flipping it open, and, to end the call, I would simply flip it shut. I could set the ringer to vibrate, mute the microphone, and voice-activate a call. And, yes, it is Web-enabled. My service provider is Sprint, and I haven't had any problems like call drops, or voice distortion, or billing mistakes, etc., and on a few occasions when I needed to call their customer service, I got connected quickly and someone answered my questions to my content. I have used my cell phone without any problems whatsoever.

Yes, these days, I do see some cuter phones, and maybe someday I will buy something like a T-Mobile Razr. But for now I have no desire to reopen the "phone-shopping project," and I am "settled and happy" as far as my wireless communication needs are concerned.

- In the first example above—about my Shirt 'X', when I said the others are fine, I was not thinking of one particular shirt I have in my collection. This one is a Mossimo, also in dark blue. The fabric in this one is thin, so it almost sticks to your body, and it has a chic European collar. There is something about it, the way it feels on my body and the way it looks, that I just love. Never mind that it wrinkles easily—I postpone putting it on until it is time to go out, so it would look unwrinkled at least for some time at the 'big event.' When I wear it, I feel just a bit more self-confident, a bit more spirited.

- Recently, I got a body massage at Mitchell's Salon and Day Spa. Costs $75, for one hour of full body massage. After considering and putting it off for three years, I finally gave in—actually, I had no choice, I received it as a birthday gift certificate. My masseuse, Nathan, met me at 7:05 (5 minutes past the appointment time). By the time Nathan got started, it was 7:12. I knew they would cut corners, 12 minutes were already gone, and they were not going to give me one full hour of massage after all, I was telling myself. I had been told I would really like it (thus, my expectations were quite high). Nathan began to work on my body. First legs, then hands, then shoulders, back, face, head, and so on. I was really liking it. Soon, I lost track of time. And, I had gotten enough of it—enough kneading, heavy pressing, big time muscle loosening—I really felt I had had enough (not in an "enough is enough" sense, mind you, but in a "boy, it feels great" sort of way). By now I no longer cared if Nathan gave me an entire hour. But if I thought I had had the best of it, and I did, I was in for a further surprise. The hot-towel wrap was still to come, and when it did, by itself it was worth every dollar my gift-giver had paid. And, Nathan was showing no signs of slowing down. For 15 minutes to follow still, he would find some new muscles in my body to loosen, and some to re-massage with a different technique. It was 8:10 when he finished, and we warmly shook hands, and I made a mental note to go back and ask for him again.

If you ask me whether I am satisfied with my shirt collection, my cell phone, and my massage parlor experience, my answer will be "Yes" for all but Shirt 'X.' Yes, I am satisfied with my cell phone and Sprint PCS service, and I am definitely satisfied with my blue Mossimo shirt, and with the massage parlor. But am I satisfied with them all in the same way? Certainly not. By just asking me if I am satisfied with them, you wouldn't really know the true depth of my varying satisfaction.

This autobiographical narrative from Monsieur Ross should be a beacon for marketers.

As a marketer, it pays to recognize that consumer satisfaction comes in various flavors. Let us look closer (and just to maintain flow in the narrative, we'll allow the author to assume Monsieur Ross's voice and speak for him in the first person).[8]

Dissatisfaction This is clearly a negative experience. Dissatisfaction is what I feel toward my Shirt 'X.' Dissatisfaction is not mere absence of satisfaction. Rather, it is a decidedly negative state of unhappiness.

Mere Satisfaction Satisfaction as absence of dissatisfaction At the lowest level is "mere satisfaction," defined more by an absence of any dissatisfaction, of anything negative, rather than by the presence of anything positive. Whereas my Shirt 'X' presents an example of dissatisfaction, all my other shirts (with the exception of the Mossimo shirt), which I wear in a taken-for-granted manner, are examples of an absence of dissatisfaction. I am aware of my satisfaction with them merely by not experiencing any dissatisfaction. Notice, I said, "They are just fine." Nothing more. I wear them without much thought and often without having them in my active consciousness.

Satisfaction as Contentment With my cell phone, I am more than merely satisfied. Not only do I have no dissatisfaction, but in fact I am quite content. It sits in my shirt pocket, and every once in a while, I chuckle about it: "What a nice thing it is to have in your pocket." It's not just a wireless phone per se, but this particular model, has shape, size, and features that serve me well. I am so content, in fact, that I resist the idea of upgrading it with newer incarnations. More than mere absence of dissatisfaction, it is a positive feeling of having my need fulfilled and one of life's problems solved in an admirable way. This is satisfaction as contentment.

Satisfaction as Enthusiasm Recall that with my shirt collection in general, I feel okay. But my blue Mossimo shirt—now that is something else. When it comes to how I feel about it, I can't put it in the "they are just fine" group with my other shirts. Instead, the very thought of it and certainly its use makes me feel elated. I look forward to the occasions when I will wear it. Occasionally, if there is no occasion, I wear it anyway, just to feel good. So my satisfaction with it is much more than mere satisfaction and, for that matter, more than contentment. I feel positive enthusiasm.

Satisfaction as Delight And now for my massage parlor experience. Don't you think the word "satisfaction" would actually do injustice to it? My experience with Mitchell's Salon and Day Spa was nothing short of pure delight. Delight as in what you feel when you see your old buddy after decades; delight as in when you get to buy your dream car. Delight as in when your name is called at the Oscars! Delight is an experience deluged with positive, pleasant emotions. It is the ultimate in satisfaction!

The five types of satisfaction experiences can be placed on a continuum, as shown in Figure 12.6.

FIGURE 12.6 THE SATISFACTION CONTINUUM

Dissatisfaction   Mere Satisfaction   Contentment   Enthusiasm   Delight

It deserves repeating: these five kinds of satisfaction differ not merely in their degree but also in their kind. We experience them differently. We feel activation or arousal with some (i.e., we feel energy and the desire to do something) and passivity with others. Also we feel emotional with some but not with others. Thus, our mental states differ with different kinds of satisfactions. Table 12.2 summarizes some important differences. To review them briefly, *dissatisfaction* activates us, whereas with mere *satisfaction* and *contentment* we feel passivity. With *enthusiasm* and *delight*, we feel activated again. In terms of emotion, with *dissatisfaction*, we feel negative emotion; with mere *satisfaction*, we feel no emotion. With *contentment*, *enthusiasm*, and *delight*, we feel positive emotion, in mild, moderate, and strong degrees, respectively. Thus, *mere satisfaction* is based entirely on cognitions—beliefs about how the product performed. All five states relate, of course, to expectations, but in diverse ways. *Dissatisfaction* results clearly when expectations are not met. *Mere satisfaction* is the outcome when product performance barely meets consumer expectations. *Contentment* follows when prior expectations are well met. *Enthusiasm* requires that expectations be exceeded. Finally, *delight* occurs when there is some element of positive surprise.

Surprise! Here is Your Delight!

Surprise can take two forms. First, the consumers experience suprise when the performance is markedly superior on one or more of the attributes, better than what a consumer normally expects, better in fact than what the consumer might have ever thought about or might have considered feasible. The product or service not only exceeds but in fact defies (in a positive sense) consumer expectations. When traveling by an airline, for example, we expect (and desire) the food to be reasonably tasteful rather than insipid. When we find that not only does it taste good, but it tastes great— so great in fact that we want to know the recipe and inquire if we can buy some additional food to take home— here, our expectations are exceeded and there is some degree of surprise. Furthermore, when we notice that the coffee they serve is Starbucks (as does United Airlines), we are surprised. Thus, exceed by a wide margin on an expected attribute, and you will delight the consumer.

The second source of surprise is when the product (or service) offers an attribute the consumer did not expect from that product category at all. Thus, if an airline offered a hot shower on the plane, then we would be surprised. It is surprises of this nature that produce delight.

Delighted Consumers Seek You Out

In service businesses, interaction quality is very important for customer delight.

Do consumers who experience mere satisfaction behave differently than those who are delighted? Of course, they do. Indeed, consumers' future behaviors with respect to your product differ vastly across the five levels of satisfaction. With *dissatisfaction*, consumers simply discard and discontinue using the product (as I did with my Crown Club shirt), or they use it reluctantly if they are stuck with it. With *mere satisfaction*, we use the product matter-of-factly, without reservations but also without any fanfare, so to speak (as I wear the rest of my shirts). With *contentment*, occasions to use the product are welcome (as when my cell phone rings). With *enthusiasm*, the consumer looks forward to using the product (as I do with my Mossimo blue shirt). With *delight*, consumers actively seek out or pursue the product-use occasions (as I seek other opportunities for getting a massage at Mitchell's Salon and Day Spa).

Still Looking?

Do consumers continue looking at alternative products, hoping to find better solutions, and are they open to competitors' sales pitches? That too depends on the kind of satisfaction the consumer experiences. With *dissatisfaction*, of course, they do, pursuing alternatives actively. With *mere satisfaction*, they might search for other solutions if it is convenient, and they would also be quite open to competitors' pitches. With *contentment*, consumers wouldn't want to bother searching for alternatives, as their problem is in a state of "closure." With *enthusiasm*, they would be totally closed off and unwelcoming of competitors' sales pitches. And with *delight*, they would, in fact, resist the alternatives. Thus, *mere satisfaction* does not insulate the consumer at all from the promotional trappings of competing brands. Only *enthusiasm* and *delight* do.

In fact, with *mere satisfaction*, consumer repurchase of the brand is by no means guaranteed; they are completely open to change. This openness to change progressively diminishes and repurchase likelihood progressively solidifies as we move along the continuum toward *delight*. Finally, consumer loyalty and commitment depends on the kind of satisfaction experienced. With *mere satisfaction*, it is weak at best (as with my "They are just fine" shirts); loyalty gathers strength first with *contentment* (my cell phone) and then with *enthusiasm* (my Mossimo shirt). With *delight* (the massage service at Mitchell's) consumer loyalty becomes fanatical!

Now, you have the full scoop on the not-so-simple world of satisfaction. Before you move

TABLE 12.2 — Differences Across Five Types of Satisfactions

	Dissatisfaction	Mere Satisfaction	Contentment	Enthusiasm	Delight
AROUSAL	Active	Passive	Passive	Active	Active
EMOTION	Yes, negative	None	Mild, positive	Moderate	High
EXPECTATIONS	Not met	Barely met	Well met	Exceeded	Positive Suprise
USAGE	Discontinued	Matter-of-factly	Welcome	Looked forward to	Persued
SEARCH for NEW SOLUTIONS	Yes, Defintely	Maybe	No, not really	Not at all	Definitely not
OPEN TO SWITCH/ CHANGE	Yes, pursue	Yes	No	Not at all	Definitely not
REPURCHASE	No	Maybe	Yes	Yes, definitely	Yes, at all costs
LOYALTY/ COMMITMENT	None	Weak	Moderate	Strong	Fanatic

Prepared by Author for MyCBBook

on, take a few minutes to review Table 12.2 and test it out with your own consumption experiences, recalling a past instance of each type of satisfaction. Do the table's predictions match your experience? If not, which table entries would you like to modify? In what way?

FUTURE RESPONSE: EXIT, VOICE, OR LOYALTY

Following the experience of satisfaction or dissatisfaction comes the last of the four steps in our model, *future response,* which includes exit, voice, or loyalty.

Exit As consumers, if you are dissatisfied with your experience with a brand, then there is only one thing to do. Dump the brand, and never buy it again. In other words, you would "exit" that brand. You would now consider other brands. Maybe you remember that when you were making your choice the last time, there was a brand you judged "second best." So now you might buy this brand. Or alternatively, you might want to go back to the start of the decision process, searching for information on other alternatives. Of course, this would entail engaging in the arduous process of information search, alternative evaluation, and so on, all over again. But that is a price we sometimes pay to find a satisfying product.

Voice *Voice* refers to complaining—the act of expressing one's dissatisfaction. Voice is not an alternative to exit but an additional response. After complaining, and depending on how your complaint is resolved, you might decide to give the brand or marketer another chance. Or, you might decide simply to exit. Voice can be further divided into three sub-categories: (a) the consumer complains (or occasionally expresses appreciation) to the company; (b) the consumer complains to a third party such as the Better Business Bureau or local and federal governmental agencies; and (c) the consumer complains (or praises) to friends. This last avenue is called word-of-mouth (WOM), defined as consumers' conversations with other consumers about a product or service.

The Public Chatter About Products

Voice as Word-of-Mouth Word-of-mouth by consumers is a significant factor in marketing. Positive word-of-mouth (i.e., product praise) can make a company; negative word of mouth (i.e., product criticism) can tarnish its reputation.

If there is only one thing that can be said about people, it is that they talk about their feelings and experiences. Especially if they feel having been taken advantage of. And one thing that can be said about consumers for sure is that they talk about products. Both satisfied and dissatisfied consumers talk about their experiences with products and companies. The sad fact (sad for the marketer) is that consumers spread more word-of-mouth when they are dissatisfied than when they are satisfied. Studies have shown that satisfied customers tell five other people; dissatisfied customers tell thirteen others![9]

The Internet offers a new avenue for consumers to vent their dissatisfaction publicly with a company. There are quite a few Web sites where you can post your complaint about any company. Exhibit 12.1 excerpts of one such posting we found at www.thecomplaintstaton.com (now defunct). Eager to read some more disgruntles? Try http://complaintstation.tribe.net; there you will find postings with titles like UPS Sucks, Whole Foods Sucks, and Comcast Sucks Too. Under an entry titled T-Mobile Sucks, a consumer named Lynda writes: "T-Mobile? T Mob more like it" (post dated November 6, 2005). With such public airing now made feasible by the Internet, no marketer can afford to leave dissatisfied consumers out in the cold.

CONSUMER COMPLAINING

Not for the Timid at Heart!

As a dissatisfied consumer, you might decide to complain to the company directly and give them an earful.

Imagine you are dining at Applebee's and your steak is not done well. What would you do—eat it quietly, eat the portion that looks good, or ask your waiter to take it

FIGURE 12.7 THE TWO-FACTOR MODEL OF CONSUMER COMPLAINING BEHAVIOR

Ability/Opportunity to Complain (Avenues of Complaining)

Motivation to Complain (Dissatisfaction Intensity)

CONSUMER COMPLAINING ACTION

back? No, don't tell us; instead, let us guess. Even better, let us make a scientific prediction. You see, consumer researchers have studied just such consumer behavior situations and have built a model to explain why and when consumers do or do not complain. First, recall, from Chapter 2, that all behavior or action depends on motivation, ability, and opportunity (MAO.) We recast that MAO model as a two-factor model of complaining, shown in Figure 12.7. You have read about these factors earlier in the book, so we shall spare you from a repeated explanation.

We do need to look closer into motivation, however. The motivation to complain itself depends on three factors (1) how much it hurts, (2) who is to blame, and (3) do you have the guts? Of course, scholars give these factors more technical names: *dissatisfaction, attribution,* and *personality trait* (specifically, self-confidence). Now let us apply this model to your Applebee's situation. If you feel that the steak was cooked really poorly (you feel dissatisfaction), and that serving the steak shows the cook's carelessness (attribution), then you would feel like telling your waiter; whether you would actually have the courage to tell depends on whether you have the self-confidence (personality trait). Have you sometimes noticed that when you complain, your friends squirm in their seats? Obviously, they lack self-confidence.

These three factors determine consumer motivation to complain. Whether or not that motivation materializes in the consumer act of complaining depends, as the two-factor model in Figure 12.7 shows, upon the opportunity being available to complain, i.e., how easy it is to complain. Of course, those who are strongly motivated will end up complaining even in the face of inconvenience, but more people who want to complain actually do so only if it is easy to complain. If, to complain, you have to jump through hoops, then you might just say, "Forget it."

The Art of Dodging the Whiners

Some companies love it when you say, "Forget it." Then they don't have to deal with you. So in order to keep you from complaining, they make you jump through hoops—they make you fill out long tedious forms, they do not provide a toll-free number, and they do not designate to whom you can complain. If you run a company, what other means of stopping dissatisfied consumers from complaining can you think of? The more ways you can think of, the more you push the consumer to take the exit option. The more consumers take the exit option, the fewer consumers you will have to worry about! However, if you don't want that to happen, then start thinking of all the ways you can encourage dissatisfied consumers to complain. And stop acting like you think (as many marketers do) that the consumer who complains is just a habitual whiner.

According to one research study, about 19% of dissatisfied consumers complain; of the complaining consumers, a significant majority continue to buy the product or service, compared to those who are dissatisfied but do not bother to complain. Thus, complainers care enough to complain. Non-complainers simply walk out, taking their patronage to a competitor. Believe it or not, complaining is good for your business. Consumers leaving with dissatisfaction or in disgust is bad!

An Experiment in Marketer Response to Consumer Complaints   EXHIBIT 12.2

Just to see the responsiveness of various car companies, an Advertising Age reporter wrote a complaint letter to the CEOs of 25 carmakers (both domestic and foreign). The letter read, in part:

I was a big believer in your company's advertising when I bought my car late last year.... Now, a mysterious "clucking" sound is coming from the right-front wheel. The selling dealer hasn't been able to correct it.

My warranty expires in two weeks, and I have a car I don't even know is safe to drive.... "Can you suggest how I can get my car out of this rut?"

Under the old model of transaction selling, the letter will be sent to some clerk in the consumer service department, unread in the CEO office, where a salesman would just smirk when he or she reads "My warranty expires in two weeks."

But these are the days of relationship marketing. These days, enlightened companies go the extra mile to keep the customer satisfied. Mitsubishi was one of the companies that responded early; its reply letter claimed that the chairman had actually read the letter himself. Saab, Rolls-Royce, Volkswagen, BMW, and Volvo actually looked up the "presumed" consumer's phone number in the phone book and left several messages and sent mailgrams persistently.

The reporter notes: "In general, the imports were more prompt to respond than the domestics, and they used faster means (phone, mailgrams, rather than postal mail); and seven of the 25 companies failed to respond in any form! Bad customer service? Most assuredly. Bad consumer retention practice? Absolutely."

Source: Adapted from T. Kauchak, "A Little Service, Please!" *Advertising Age* (January 21, 1991), p. S-8. (Used with permission.)

After the Complaint—Is There Justice?

What happens after the complaint? Do consumers stay with the company? Do they buy again from the company? That depends on how the company addresses the complaint. Turn a deaf ear, and your company will get even more bad word-of-mouth. Conversely, resolve the complaint, redress it to the consumer's satisfaction, and the consumer is likely to repatronize your company. Also, the consumer is unlikely to engage in negative word-of-mouth.[10]

At this point you might wonder what determines successful redress. To answer this question, you must learn a new concept called *perceived justice*. **Perceived justice** is the consumer's perception that he or she was treated fairly during the complaint resolution process.[11] This means that the offered remedy made up for the harm done by an unsatisfactory product or service.

When perceived justice seems not to have occurred—e.g., if the dry cleaner spoiled your shirt and merely refunded the dry cleaning charges, which is hardly just redress—consumer hostility increases. Turn a deaf ear to consumer complaints, and you will increase consumer hostility and unleash a stronger wave of negative word-of-mouth. Now, we will let you in on one more secret—resolve a complaint to the customer's complete satisfaction, and he or she is likely to become a stronger supporter of your company—stronger than if he or she had not even been dissatisfied in the first place! Why is that? The complaining experience gave the consumer the opportunity to learn how good your company really is. The lesson here is not that you should go about making consumers dissatisfied so they complain. Rather, the lesson is that if and when an occasional consumer becomes dissatisfied, go the extra mile to win him or her over. And, as a reward, reap a lifelong loyal supporter.[12]

DAMAGE CONTROL
The Art of Recovery

A customer who simply exits is lost forever. One who complains gives us, the marketer, a chance to recover customers. **Customer recovery** refers to the actions the company undertakes to remove the cause of dissatisfaction and to convert the dissatisfied and unhappy consumer into a satisfied and happy consumer. How does a company do it?

The dynamics of dissatisfaction and recovery are different for physical products versus services. Since mass marketed physical products are standardized, the particular unit the consumer bought is similar to all other units; dissatisfaction with that unit means the product (brand) itself does not meet the consumer's needs. Thus, dissatisfaction with a product occurs because the product failed to produce the outcomes a particular consumer expected it to produce. In such cases, the company should promptly offer to accept the merchandise back and refund the money. And the company may suggest another of its products but it should do so only if that product would fit the consumer's needs better. Even if the company has nothing better to offer, at least the prompt refund will stop the consumer from bad-mouthing the company.

In contrast, with services, the dissatisfaction often occurs because the service given to a particular consumer was of poor quality—such as a bad haircut or a poorly cooked entrée. In such cases, customer recovery requires that the company correct the mistake (i.e., re-cut the hair or cook another entrée) and sometimes not charge for the service at all (even after the correction). These consumer recovery offerings or concessions to consumers are called **make-goods**. Some guidelines for effective *make goods* are as follows:
- The make-good should be more than commensurate with consumer costs. For example, if a dry-cleaner spoiled a customer's shirt, the make-good shouldn't be merely the refund of the dry cleaning charges; rather, it should be the cost of the shirt itself.
- The make-good should be easy to obtain—the customer shouldn't have to go through hoops to obtain the make-good award (e.g., fill out lengthy forms).
- The make-good does not make an apology redundant—a mistake is a mistake, and the company should show genuine regret that the mistake occurred and offer a sincere apology. The make-good should be given cheerfully. Although the company may be spending a fortune by way of make-goods, some front-line employees who give the make-good to the

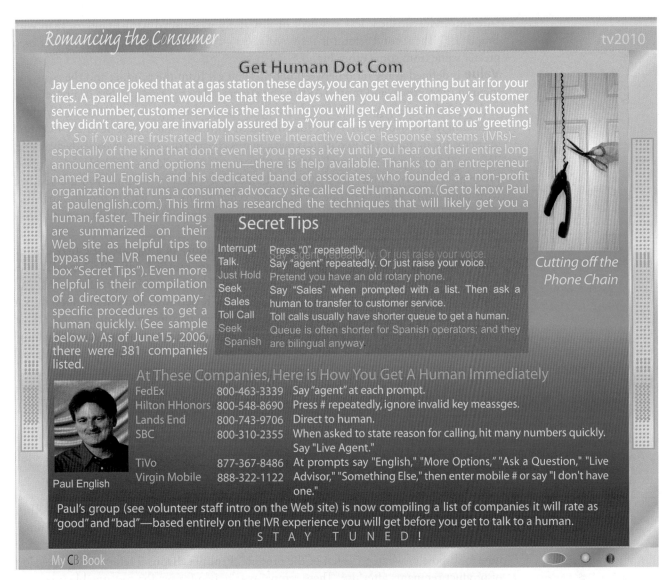

Get Human Dot Com

Jay Leno once joked that at a gas station these days, you can get everything but air for your tires. A parallel lament would be that these days when you call a company's customer service number, customer service is the last thing you will get. And just in case you thought they didn't care, you are invariably assured by a "Your call is very important to us" greeting!

So if you are frustrated by insensitive Interactive Voice Response systems (IVRs)-especially of the kind that don't even let you press a key until you hear out their entire long announcement and options menu—there is help available. Thanks to an entrepreneur named Paul English, and his dedicated band of associates, who founded a a non-profit organization that runs a consumer advocacy site called GetHuman.com. (Get to know Paul at paulenglish.com.) This firm has researched the techniques that will likely get you a human, faster. Their findings are summarized on their Web site as helpful tips to bypass the IVR menu (see box "Secret Tips"). Even more helpful is their compilation of a directory of company-specific procedures to get a human quickly. (See sample below.) As of June 15, 2006, there were 381 companies listed.

Cutting off the Phone Chain

Secret Tips

Interrupt	Press "0" repeatedly.
Talk.	Say "agent" repeatedly. Or just raise your voice.
Just Hold	Pretend you have an old rotary phone.
Seek Sales	Say "Sales" when prompted with a list. Then ask a human to transfer to customer service.
Toll Call	Toll calls usually have shorter queue to get a human.
Seek Spanish	Queue is often shorter for Spanish operators; and they are bilingual anyway.

At These Companies, Here is How You Get A Human Immediately

FedEx	800-463-3339	Say "agent" at each prompt.
Hilton HHonors	800-548-8690	Press # repeatedly, ignore invalid key meassges.
Lands End	800-743-9706	Direct to human.
SBC	800-310-2355	When asked to state reason for calling, hit many numbers quickly. Say "Live Agent."
TiVo	877-367-8486	At prompts say "English," "More Options," "Ask a Question," "Live Advisor," "Something Else," then enter mobile # or say "I don't have one."
Virgin Mobile	888-322-1122	

Paul English

Paul's group (see volunteer staff intro on the Web site) is now compiling a list of companies it will rate as "good" and "bad"—based entirely on the IVR experience you will get before you get to talk to a human.

S T A Y   T U N E D !

My CB Book

customer spoil the whole effect by responding begrudgingly to the customer complaint or by harboring the suspicion (which they convey nonverbally and inadvertently) that the consumer is concocting the story to fleece the company. A make-good offered with no apology and no cheer is not much better than not offering the make-good in the first place.

An effective customer recovery can be costly. But remember, as we already told you, research has found that a successfully recovered customer becomes even more loyal than if he or she were not dissatisfied to begin with. This means that occasional dissatisfaction among customers can be a good thing—provided you ensure that (a) they complain and (b) your recovery effort is exemplary.

LOYALTY The third response (besides exit and voice) is loyalty. Consumer loyalty means the consumer buys the same brand repeatedly and feels a psychological commitment to it. The consumer returns to buy the product again. And he or she spreads a positive word of mouth. Loyalty depends, of course, on satisfaction. However, recent consumer research has shown that, although consumers are less likely to switch brands or companies when they are satisfied than when they are not, being satisfied does not guarantee loyalty. One study showed that despite satisfaction, as many as 30% of consumers were likely to switch suppliers.[13]

There are several reasons for this. First, consumers report being satisfied with a brand, but they may also be satisfied with some other brand. The implication of this is that you (you being the marketer) should measure consumer satisfaction with your brand *relative* to your competitors' brands. This can be done easily by asking consumers a question like,

"Are you more satisfied, less satisfied, or just about as satisfied with Brand 'A' than with Brand 'L'?" The second reason is *perceived value*—consumers may expect to receive even greater value from some other brand.

Value is defined as the ratio between benefits you get from the product and the costs you incur in time, effort, and money. When consumers tell us they are satisfied or not satisfied with a product, they generally are thinking of the product's performance (i.e., benefits). Accordingly, a consumer may be equally satisfied with two brands, yet he or she may find greater value in one of the two brands because it is cheaper or more conveniently available. That is, if a competitor's brand with equal performance becomes available at a slightly lower price, the consumer may buy that brand. For example, suppose you are satisfied with your Sprint wireless phone service, but Verizon came out with a promotional deal that would knock down your monthly payment, say, by one-half. Would you still stick with Sprint?

The third and final reason is that the marginal utility of a repeated use may decline simply due to familiarity. For example, even if you are satisfied with McDonald's, does it mean you would go to McDonald's every day of the week, mornings, afternoons, and evenings? And suppose you are satisfied with Coke, CK perfume, and Puma Shoes; does it mean that next time you will not buy Dr. Pepper, Happy perfume by Clinique, and Adidas shoes? The excitement of something new or a need for variety can drive brand switching. This happens particularly for hedonic products such as jewelry and visits to recreational and entertainment places.

Because loyalty is such an important topic, we will treat it in more detail in Chapter 18. For now, let us move on to the last action in consumer behavior—product disposal.

PRODUCT DISPOSAL

The High Price of Consuming

Humans have another problem. All other species eat and drink and move on. They don't have to clean up after themselves. For humans, unfortunately, product consumption or use is not the end of consumer behavior. Following consumption, humans must decide how to dispose of whatever is left of the product. **Product disposal** refers to dispossession of product remnants after use. These remnants take two forms: for consumable products, the remnant is the container in which the product is acquired from the market, like empty cereal boxes or empty milk bottles. For durable products, the remnant is the old product that has become unusable by the consumer, like old computers, torn leather shoes, or fused light bulbs.

Disposing of these remnants is no small problem. Every time you consume something, you must make the effort to dispose of the remnants properly. Or someone else must, on your behalf (as in a restaurant). And the problem is not over as soon as you dispose of it from your house. Somebody in the community or local government must find a way to permanently get rid of it. And it is not easy. That is because it is, in sheer volume, massive. And there is not enough space on our planet to "put it all to rest," so to speak.

Useless for All?

Consider durable products first. They are durable but not immortal. The need for discarding them occurs for three reasons. First, after their expected life, they simply lose their functionality. Due to wear and tear or breakdown, they don't work anymore. Consequently, they become useless for *all*. Examples include furniture that has broken or a television with a burned out tube. In most third world countries, the appliances and other durable goods that are broken are repaired; in the western world, repair costs are often exorbitant, so consumers simply discard them. Second, the product may still be functional but no longer of use to its current owner. This happens often when the current owner/consumer's needs and/or tastes change; for example, you may outgrow your clothes, or you may simply get bored with them. Third, technology might make some products obsolete, and consumers may wish to move to newer versions. This is a common phenomenon for tech gizmos (e.g., cell phones, flat panel TVs, DVD players), keeping consumers constantly chasing ever-newer product versions.

Each situation requires a different approach to disposal. If the product has become useless merely to you, its current owner, then you can dispose of it by finding another consumer who may see value in the product. You may give it away to someone free of cost, or you may try to extract some price for it. You can find a buyer through garage sales, flea markets, on eBay, or on www.craigslist.com. Nowadays, there are some stores such as Plato's Closet (voted by readers as the best place to buy jeans in the August '05 issue of *Seventeen* magazine) that buy old clothes still in good condition and resell them to bargain-hunting, fashionable consumers (check it out in your city or in cyberspace at www.platoscloset. com). Sometimes, retailers who sell new products also offer to buy the customer's old product; this practice, called *trade in*, is very prevalent for automobiles in America, and most European countries, but is less prevalent in many Asian countries. Finally, if the durable product has lost its functionality for all, then the only thing to do is to discard it.

Then there is the waste from the consumption of everyday items, such as packages and containers (e.g., an empty bottle of cognac), and sometimes the used up product itself (e.g., newspapers, food scraps, etc.). Put together, the two types of waste create two problems: we are running out of landfills to bury the garbage, and a lot of resources from which packaging and throwaway durables are produced are being depleted. Resources like forests. And minerals, metals, and other natural materials.

Our Throwaway Society

In Western countries such as the U.S., known as throwaway societies, the volume of such throwaways can be enormous. Indeed, the U.S. leads many countries in household solid waste production: about 4.4 pounds per person per day (compared to 2 to 3 pounds per capita in Europe). This comes to 1600 pounds of trash per person per year, making up some 220 tons of waste materials every year. The majority (71%) of it consists of paper; other major waste components are metals, plastics, and glass. See Exhibit 12.3.

So, What Can You Do About the Big Waste Problem?

Now the big question is: What are you going to do about it? There are three things you can do—the "3R's of waste action": reduce, reuse, and recycle. First, you can reduce the waste. How? By buying items in packages that generate less waste. For example, buy products in bulk sizes (avoid single serving sizes) and in refillable containers. Another way to reduce waste is by using products conservatively (e.g., use both sides of the paper).

Second, reuse or help someone else reuse what is not useful to you. Instead of throwing away old furniture, appliances, and clothing, give them to someone else, sell them in garage sales, or donate them to charities. With a combination of reduce and reuse, you can contribute significantly to the sustainability of our environment. If *reduce and reuse* becomes your gig, you can find guidelines on any number of Web sites. One such guide is available on Northwestern University's Facilities Management Web page, excerpted in Exhibit 12.4. See which of these proenvironmental, reduce and reuse behaviors you would like to adopt, say, this coming year.

The third R is recycle. Do *not* throw away the packages and containers and paper products (e.g., newspaper) as garbage; instead recycle them. Reduce and reuse can make

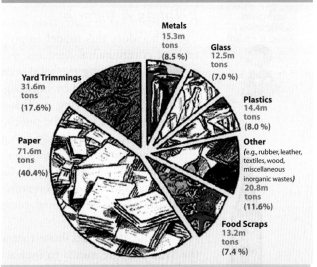

WHAT IS IN AMERICA'S TRASH   EXHIBIT 12.3

Metals
15.3m tons
(8.5 %)

Glass
12.5m tons
(7.0 %)

Yard Trimmings
31.6m tons
(17.6%)

Plastics
14.4m tons
(8.0 %)

Other
(e.g., rubber, leather, textiles, wood, miscellaneous inorganic wastes)
20.8m tons
(11.6%)

Paper
71.6m tons
(40.4%)

Food Scraps
13.2m tons
(7.4 %)

Source: General Overview of What's in America's Trash, Consumer Handbook for Reducing Solid Waste, U.S. Environmental Protection Agency, Information; posted on its Web site http://www.epa.gov/epaoswer/non-hw/reduce/catbook/what.htm (DoA: 08/10/2006).

Beverages. Don't buy straws—they're unnecessary plastic.
Condiments Squeezable plastic containers are convenient but may not be the best option, so choose glass jars for ketchup, salad dressings, peanut butter, etc. (and recycle the jars!).
Produce Buy organic produce when available—it's better for you and the environment because it's grown without pesticides, and it usually tastes better, too!
Toiletries and personal supplies Choose bar soap over liquid soap because bar soap comes with much less packaging. If you want liquid soap, bring an old container and buy it in bulk
In the kitchen To conserve water, only use a dishwasher when it is full, or wash dishes by hand in a sink full of water rather than letting the water run.
Use silverware as much as possible—if you must use plasticware, rinse and reuse it.
To conserve water, only use a dishwasher when it is full, or wash dishes by hand in a sink full of water rather than letting the water run.
In the bathroom Turn off running water when not in use—letting the water run for one minute while you brush your teeth wastes 3-5 gallons of water!
In the recreation room To save electricity, turn off stereo, TV, and VCR when not in use.
In the workplace Send electronic (e-mail) messages when possible to conserve paper.
At the cafeteria Don't take an excess of napkins—they just end up in the garbage. Even better, bring your own cloth napkin to meals!
At a party B.Y.O.C.—Bring Your Own Cup—this cuts the use of plastic or Styrofoam cups. If you forget, try and use one cup for the entire length of the party.

Source: Excerpted from the Web page of Facilities Management Unit of Northwestern University

some impact; however, it is unlikely that a substantial number of consumers in modern consumer societies will embrace these courses of action. Recycling is, however, more doable. Want to know what to recycle? Just *Google* "recycling guide." We did, and the very first entry (when accessed on November 19, 2005) was titled "The World's Shortest Comprehensive Recycling Guide," available at www.obviously.com/recycle. Check it out.

Recycling can make a big difference. The question is, will enough consumers do it. Will you? This depends on two factors: your motivation and your ability or opportunity to recycle. We call it the Two Factor Model of Recycling Action. (See Figure 12.8.)

The fundamental source of your motivation comes from whether or not you value the environment. If you are deeply concerned about the environment (and our depleting resources on the planet), then you will be motivated. But motivation alone is not enough. It should be feasible to recycle—there should be facilities in your city that enable you to recycle.

It Takes A Village

What does this model imply? It implies that everyone—marketers, public policy makers, governmental agencies, social agencies, and consumers themselves—has a role to play in combating the solid waste problem. First, the model shows that citizens can be motivated to recycle by bringing home the importance of a healthy environment and the urgency of preserving it. This can be done through informational and educational campaigns created by public policy makers and governmental and social agencies. Many such organizations are already doing their part. For instance, Waste Watch is a UK based organization promoting action on waste reduction, reuse, and recycling. In Australia, Resource NSW, an agency of the Government of New South Wales, in partnership with many social and corporate organizations, has developed a program of public education, called the Murfy educational program, with a Murfy character and related icons on recyclable products.

Second, the model shows that we have to *facilitate* recycling. Research has shown that the most effective means to increase recycling behavior is to make recycling convenient for consumers. In many cities in the U.S., local governments run the so called "curbside recycling" program: they provide a free recycling bin, and a collection truck comes by and collects them free of cost from citizens' doorsteps. These programs have shown remarkable success as a large proportion of residents in these city areas have taken to recycling.

Marketers, Too, Can Help

Marketers can also help in three specific ways: (1) reverse channel; (2) recycled content products; and (3) environmentally friendly production.

What if the manufacturers and retailers took back old products and empty containers? Some of them do, in some states and countries. This is called **reverse channel**. You can bring back empty bottles to retailers, for example, if you live in one of the U.S. states with 11 container laws (California, Connecticut, Delaware, Hawaii, Iowa, Maine, Massachusetts, Michigan, New York, Oregon, and Vermont).[14] Other than the U.S., nine other countries have the container return law (Austria, Belgium, Denmark, Finland, Germany, Netherlands, Norway, Sweden, and Switzerland).[15] The retailers charge a small deposit (e.g., usually, 5 cents a bottle) when you buy the product, and refund that money when you bring back the empty container. That is incentive enough for many consumers.

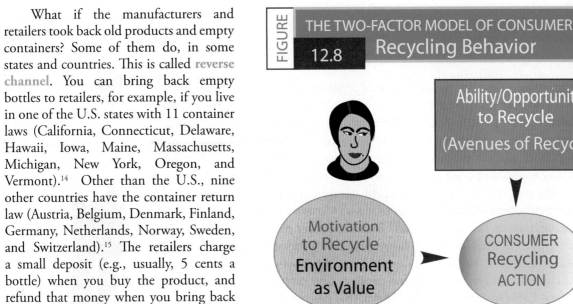

FIGURE 12.8

THE TWO-FACTOR MODEL OF CONSUMER
Recycling Behavior

Ability/Opportunity to Recycle (Avenues of Recycling)

Motivation to Recycle Environment as Value

CONSUMER Recycling ACTION

Reverse channels work for durables, too. Companies like Hewlett Packard and Dell Computers have a program for taking back your old computer and related equipment. Some of these programs have a take back fee—Hewlett Packard's fees range from $13 to $34 per item; Dell charges $15 per item. In recent years, Dell has organized a multi-city tour to collect these items without a fee.

The second way manufacturers can help save our environment is by making products from recycled raw materials. One company that uses recycled materials is Patagonia Company, which makes outdoor fleece garments. The PCR filament yarn it uses to weave its clothing contains 30-50% post-consumer feedstock—soda bottles, polyester uniforms, tents, and garments.[16] In the U.S., federal and state governments have policies to procure certain products only with high recycled content.

Third, manufacturers can ensure more environment-friendly production, and do so not just in their plants, but also upstream at their suppliers' plants. For example, Aveda, which makes its cosmetics only from natural ingredients, also ensures that the ingredients themselves were produced without harmful chemicals and with non-polluting processes.

Now, the question is, will you, as a consumer, seek out products like Aveda cosmetics to make your contribution to the environment? Governments can induce manufacturers, and they can even compel them, but the ultimate success of any such manufacturer initiative depends on consumers—if enough consumers don't seek out environment-friendly products (which may be more expensive), our consumption will continue to put at risk the sustainability of the environment for our future generations.

Disposal of Personal Possessions
Saying Goodbye is Not Easy

It is one thing to recycle product packages and other items that have lost their utility to the consumer. They are simply garbage, and disposing of them involves no emotions. But consumers come to be deeply attached to many possessions. Memories of the past are tied to them. Many consumers come to see them as an inseparable part of their life history. Accordingly, they save them as keepsakes. When circumstances force them to part with those possessions (such as moving into a smaller dwelling or to another city), they give them away to friends and relatives they can trust. And they continue to be concerned with the afterlife of these possessions, so to speak.

In 2000, an interesting project was undertaken by a Generation Xer, living in Iowa, who decided to sell everything he owned on the eBay auction site, but on one condition: the buyer had to keep him informed of the possession's life in its new home! His experiences, now documented in a book, *All My Life for Sale*, are living proof that, to many consumers, disposing of personal possessions does not come easy.

Murfy (character), glass bottle (facing page); can and bag imges (above) are part of recycling education program by NSW Government (Australia), Department of Environmental and Conservation

John Fryer

One day in 2000, a Gen Xer by the name of John Freyer decided to sell everything he owned on eBay. And that means everything, literally: all his favorite records, all his clothes and furniture, an unopened box of taco shells, half a bottle of mouthwash, his used toothbrush, and even his sideburns in a plastic bag. Consumers from all over the world bought his stuff. A bag of Porky's BBQ Skins made its way to Japan; a chair ended up in the Museum of Modern Art. The last thing he sold was the domain name itself (www.allmylifeforsale.com) to his hometown institution—The University of Iowa's Museum of Art.

Why would people buy all that stuff? Because Freyer made a project of it. He sent each buyer a brief personal history of the product and how he had purchased and used it. He also requested from the buyer regular updates on what he or she (the buyer) did with the product and pictures of the product in its new home. Later, he visited some of them. This journey began in 2001, and he later wrote a book on the entire project, called All My Life for Sale, Bloomsbury, USA (November 2002).

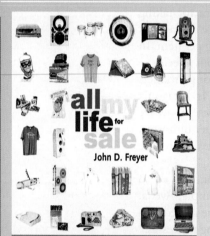

It's not the products, but the stories ...

Copyright ©2002 John D. Freyer
(Reprinted by permission of Bloomsbury)

Orange Pekoe Tea

tag # 000952
This tea tastes like Constant Comment... Another ... product that I bought based on the packaging alone. But in truth I always loved Constant Comment tea and remember having pots of Orange Pekoe Tea at my sister Marnie's farm house when I was apartment hunting in Syracuse..

There are a 10 tea bags left in this box. And each tea bag comes individually wrapped in a clean white foil wrapper with a simple Tea Cup logo on the side.. Simple Asian design..

A used answering machine tape
A musician from California bought it. He was fascinated with the idea of the spoken word" on the tape...

All images and content Courtesy of John Freyer

We are consumers and this is what we do.

CONSUMER INVOLVEMENT

How it Colors Our Post-choice Experience

"Saying goodbye is not easy" is a refrain that about sums up the experience of John Freyer, the author of *All My Life for Sale,* and his project, along with consumer opinion around the world—with one caveat: it depends on the consumer's involvement with a given possession. Indeed, involvement colors, intimately, all the post-choice processes we discussed in this chapter. In the preceding chapter, we covered the role of involvement in the three pre-choice processes. Let us complete that story here.

Involvement and Product Purchase

For low involvement products, once the evaluation is complete, and the alternative to be chosen is identified, the purchase is implemented immediately and in the same episode—e.g., at the online or offline store at which the alternative was identified. To acquire the product, typically, you don't want to drive far, and you don't want any hassle. If the item is out of stock at the store, you are more likely to buy another comparable brand (identified with a quick search or drawn from memory), rather than wait or go to another store. This is a purchase where you can afford to be lazy and allow convenience to be your guiding criterion.

In contrast, after a high involvement choice is identified, product purchase may have to wait. Since the purchase typically entails large financial outlays, some advance financial planning is called for. Often, the purchase may entail other ancillary services or products—e.g., whether to purchase an extended warranty, to order product modifications such as window-tinting on the new car, or to have a suit altered. Furthermore, sometimes the entire decision process may have to be re-opened. For example, if the preferred brand is not available or not available with the desired options (e.g., a car in red), rather than casually choosing a substitute, you are likely to re-open the alternative evaluation process. Thus, for a high involvement purchase, the product acquisition process itself can often become quite a project, with the need to coordinate several smaller decisions and multiple resources.

Involvement and Post-Purchase Consumption Experience

For low involvement products, the product fits into the ongoing consumption pattern, especially if it was a frequently consumed product. Once the purchase is made, the decision and the product are put out of mind, and the product gets consumed without conscious thought. We notice the performance only if it is substantially inferior or superior. We make a mental note never to buy the product again (for inferior products) or definitely to buy it again (for superior products).

If dissatisfied, we are unlikely to complain, writing it off instead as a one-time trial experience not to be repeated again. We may initiate some word-of-mouth communication among friends, but we are not going to talk about it with passion, either favorably or unfavorably. Finally, at the product disposal stage, for low involvement products, convenience is going to rule; we dispose of it in whatever fashion is convenient.

For high involvement products, we continue to be actively involved beyond the actual acquisition of the product. If the final choice was not a clear winner (as is often the case), cognitive dissonance is likely to afflict us. To resolve it, we are likely to continue to pay attention to product related information (including watching the ad). And even when there is no dissonance, just to reassure ourselves, we are going to be paying attention to all communications about the product. And we are going to be talking about it with friends, simply out of enthusiasm about the very acquisition of the product.

During use, we are going to be attentive. If the experience is unsatisfactory, we are likely to complain and seek redress (such as by returning or exchanging the product). And, we are likely to engage in word-of-mouth, and do so with considerable passion. If the product meets all our expectations and gives superior performance, we are likely to develop strong brand loyalty and commitment to buy the same brand again.

In terms of product disposal, for high involvement product consumption, we are likely to stretch its useful life (e.g., keep using our worn-out, favorite chair), and sometimes keep it forever as a keepsake. For high price items, the consumer seeks maximum salvage value. If we must give away the item, we often do so with concern for its afterlife (i.e., we give it to someone we know will take good care of it). In our own way, each of us writes a memorable obituary for the products we once loved but with which we must now part with. These differences are summarized in Table 12.3.

TABLE 12.3 — **Post-choice Differences Between Low & High Involvement Situations**

DECISION STEP	Low Involvement	High Involvement
Purchase	Convenience most important Decision implemented immediately Willing to substitute	Requires further planning Decisions on accessories Willing to wait Not willing to substitute
Post-Purchase	Consumed inattentively Consumed without any fanfare or rituals Less likely to complain if dissatisfied Disposal based on convenience	Consumption is mindful Possession rituals More likely to complain if dissatisfied Disposal with care and concern for after-life

Prepared by Author for MyCBBook

tv2010

MyCBBook

In the preceding chapter, we spoke of the amazing ways of the human mind.
Like how it sorts out a vast array of products in the marketplace.
Those amazing ways continue in the post-choice phases.
Following choice identification, our mind often rethinks over the chosen products,
acquires some of them, uses them, gets rid of what cannot be used, finds a home for some
it no longer needs or loves, evaluates some, experiences satisfaction (occasionally
delight) or experiences disappointment, gets angry, complains, chatters in praise or
disparage, leaves in disgust or returns looking for more, and on and on it goes on.
In these multi-layered experiences, our mind navigates, guided by
—you guessed it right—involvement.
You can understand these processes by observing up close your own post-choice
experiences. Just think back to any two low-involvement products you acquired,
consumed and disposed of most recently, and likewise, two high-involvement products.
How do the processes you experienced map against the entries in Table 12.3?

If you are like most consumers, then these must map pretty well.
If they don't, are you sure you are not highly "involved" in the post-choice
consumption experience of even trivial products?

Like you had bought some M&M candies in various colors
and then you wanted to eat them one by one to see if the
candies tasted differently based on their color!

SUMMARY

In this chapter, we unraveled consumers' post-choice processes, which are the processes set in motion following alternative evaluation and choice identification. These processes occur both as thoughts and as actions. The post-choice thought processes are captured in a four-phase model we described, comprising decision confirmation, experience evaluation, satisfaction, and future response. In parallel occur three action processes: acquisition, consumption, and disposal.

Decision confirmation sometimes takes the form of cognitive dissonance (also known as buyers' remorse), and to resolve it, consumers selectively look for positive information and look to others for praise and validation. Next, with product consumption, consumers evaluate the experience. However, the evaluation is notable only when the consumer consumes the product in an evaluative mode. The outcome of consumption is satisfaction/ dissatisfaction—which depends directly on whether or not consumer expectations are met (or exceeded). Satisfaction is not a simple consumer experience; instead, there are four forms of satisfaction, ranging from mere satisfaction to delight. There is, of course, also the exact opposite of satisfaction—dissatisfaction.

The last stage is exit, voice, or loyalty, with dissatisfied consumers either abandoning the brand or complaining. Complaining—especially complaining to the company itself—does not come easily. Our model of complaining suggests factors that explain why consumers, even though dissatisfied, may not complain—among other things, it requires a degree of self-confidence.

The last of the three action stages (following acquisition and consumption) is product disposal. Consumers essentially have three options, referred to as the 3R's of waste action—reduce, reuse, recycle. As consumers, we produce so much waste that we are running out of landfills in which to bury that waste. To overcome this alarming problem, social and public agencies urge consumers to recycle, but that urging often falls on deaf ears. Who heeds this advice is explained in a model of consumer recycling behavior. We presented this model, outlining the role of consumer psychology as well as public policy infrastructure and marketer actions.

In the final section, we re-visited the entire post-choice process from the vantage points of low involvement and high involvement consumer situations, highlighting the contrast.

3R's of Waste Action
Buyer's remorse
Cognitive dissonance
Customer loyalty
Customer recovery
Disconfirmation model

Evaluative mode
Exit
Perceived justice
Expectations
Interaction quality
Make goods

Outcome quality
Purchase-decision involvement
Product disposal
Reverse channel
Satisfaction/dissatisfaction
Value
Voice

YOUR TURN

REVIEW+Rewind

1. Name the steps consumers experience soon after they have identified their product choice. Briefly explain each.

2. Name various forms of consumer satisfaction, and briefly explain each.

3. What is the expectation disconfirmation model of consumer satisfaction? What lesson does it teach marketing managers?

4. What are the factors that motivate consumers to complain? As a marketing manager, would you want to discourage or encourage consumer complaining? Why or why not?

5. What factors determine whether or not consumers will recycle? Explain each briefly.

6. Briefly explain how consumer activity differs in each of the following stages of decision making between low and high involvement conditions:
   a. Product purchase; and
   b. Post-acquisition evaluation

THINK+Apply

1. Review the description of 'decision confirmation' in this chapter. Next, think back to two or three recent significant decisions you made as a consumer. Did you feel the need for decision confirmation, and if yes, what did you do to satisfy it?

2. Identify your own consumption experiences over the last week (or month) that you would call an example of each type of satisfaction discussed in the chapter. Briefly outline that experience and then justify why you called it that type.

3. Are you generally a complainer or a non-complainer as

a consumer? Why or why not? Are any of your friends different from you when it comes to complaining as a consumer? How are these persons different from you, as far as complaining goes

PRACTICE+Experience

1. Interview two or three consumers about their recent acts of complaining and ask them what caused them to complain and whether complaining by itself made them happy. Also ask what response they got from the company and whether that response satisfied them or not. Also explore in the interviews the sense of the justice (or injustice) they received.

2. Interview two consumers and ask them to describe consumption experiences from their own life that represent different forms of satisfaction. Then compare if for these two consumers, the source of each type of satisfaction experience is similar.

3. As a marketing manager, describe how you will motivate consumers to recycle. How does the model presented in the chapter help you plan appropriate actions.

In the Marketing Manager's Shoes

Put yourself in a marketing manager's shoes. Most concepts in the chapter have some lessons for the marketing manager; i.e., they suggest what to do differently in practice. Indeed, often these applications are implicit in our explanations of the concepts and models in the chapter. Identify at least five specific applications of the chapter's concepts, all of which should be entirely new—different from the examples cited here.

> Five faces of satisfaction—dissatisfaction, mere satisfaction, contentment, enthusiasm, delight—I like them all. Without experiencing dissatisfaction occasionally, I would not enjoy satisfaction as much.

POST-CHOICE: SATISFACTION AND VOICE

12

Some of you must have found that the models of complaining and recycling were intriguing and also of great practical use. They are. In this section, we elaborate on them further so that you can conduct some consumer research of your own.

A MODEL OF CONSUMER COMPLAINING

What does it take for a consumer to complain? We already answered this question, pointing to three factors. Beneath those three factors, however, lies a more elaborate consumer psychology. Consumer researchers have studied this elaborate psychology. If you are ready to dig more, here we cull for you their collective answers. The three factors are defined in greater detail below.

Dissatisfaction salience   Not all dissatisfaction is salient; i.e., bothersome to consumers. Generally, small gaps between performance and expectations are ignored; moreover, even substantial gaps are likely to be ignored if the product or service is trivial. Thus, the importance of the product or service and the degree of performance-expectations gap together determine dissatisfaction salience. And dissatisfaction salience in turn determines the likelihood of consumer complaining. If your shoes were not shined properly, it is one thing; if your Jeep Wrangler got repainted in the wrong color, that is quite another.

Attributions to the marketer   Making attributions means assigning blame or praise to someone or something (see Chapter 2). Suppose your pictures come back from the photo development service company faded and out of focus—is it because of the bad camera, or bad developing, or could you have forgotten to turn on the flash? It is a fact

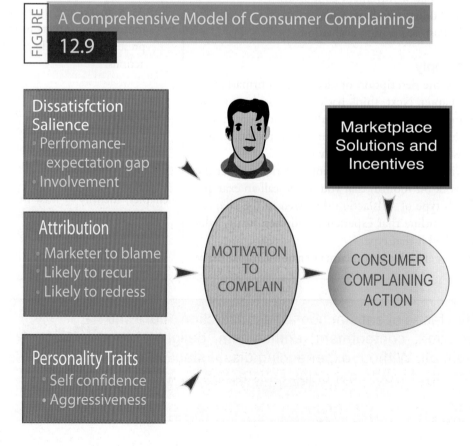

FIGURE 12.9 A Comprehensive Model of Consumer Complaining

of life that consumers make attributions about who is to blame for poor product or service performance. If consumers blame themselves or circumstances, then they are not likely to complain—after all, consumers are sensible people.

On the other hand, if they attribute failure to the marketer, then they are likely to complain. Actually, there are three attribution questions the consumer asks: (a) Is the marketer to blame? (b) Is the failure likely to be repeated? And (c) is the marketer likely to take the corrective action? Only if the answers to all three questions are affirmative is the consumer likely to complain. If consumers thought it was a one-time problem, or if they thought that redress from the marketer was unlikely, then they might consider complaining to be unnecessary or a waste of effort.

Consumer personality traits Finally, consumers' personality traits play an important role in complaining. Consumers differ in self-confidence and in their degree of aggressiveness/submissiveness. Complaining requires self-confidence, and aggressiveness drives consumers to assert themselves. These traits therefore lead consumers to complain rather than meekly accept poor marketer performance.

TABLE 12.4 Selected Measures of Factors of Consumer Complaining

Dissatisfaction Salience

SUBFACTORS: PERFROMANCE EXPECATIONS GAP and PRODUCT/SERVICE IMPORTANCE

The performance of this product/service fell:

Just a tad below   1   2   3   4   5   **Substantially below my expectations**

This product/service was:
Not much important   1   2   3   4   5   **Very important to me**

Overall, how dissatisfied were you with this product/service:

Just a tad dissatisfied 1   2   3   4   5   **Very dissatisfied**

Attribution to Marketer

SUBFACTOR: BLAME

For this experience, who do you blame and how much?

Marketer: Not at all   1   2   3   4   5   **Entirely**
Myself: Not at all   1   2   3   4   5   **Entirely**

SUBFACTOR: LIKELY TO REPEAT

Do you think that this company commits this kind of errors often or seldom:

Seldom   1   2   3   4   5   **Often**

Redress: Do you think if you complain, this firm is likely to do something for you:

Not likely   1   2   3   4   5   **Very likely**

PERSONALITY TRAITS: CONFIDENCE AND AGGRESSION

To measure personality traits of confidence and aggression, you may want to refer to some classic sources in psychology. Here, we give you some intuitive measures:

Strongly disagree   1   2   3   4   5   **Strongly agree**

I have no hesitation in standing up for my rights.
I often feel uncomfortable confronting others even if I feel I have been wronged.
I get angry when people make mistakes.
I just can't tolerate people not doing things my way.

Complaining Ease

In this particular instance: how easy or difficult was it for you to complain:

Very easy or convenient   1   2   3   4   5   **Very inconvenient**

Note: Since there is no established set of measures for these factors in the research literature, our suggestions are illustrative and open to further tailoring by you. You realize, of course, that we have not included the measures of motivation and action—a task we trust you to be by now expert at. And you would need to reverse-score some of the measures, and we leave that too for you to figure.

consumers to complain rather than meekly accept poor marketer performance.

These three factors determine consumer motivation to complain. As mentioned before, also needed is an opportunity to complain (i.e., ease of complaining). Add these two factors, along with elements of each, and you have the comprehensive model of consumer complaining behavior. See Figure 12.9.

Eager to apply this model to your company (or to any company)? To help you in that task, we give you some illustrative measures (see Table 12.4). Give this survey to a random group of consumers, ask them to identify a recent instance of dissatisfaction with a product or service, separate them into those who actually complained and those who did not, and see if their profiles on these factors are different. The model predicts it to be so, and we believe it will be so, but check it out for yourself.

What does it take for a consumer to become motivated to recycle? We already answered this question in the Two Factor Model. But each of these two factors has much more behind it. If you are ready to dig more, here, we build for you a more comprehensive model (based on the collective research of several consumer research scholars).[17]

First, what lies behind consumer motivation to recycle? Based on research literature, we can say there are four subfactors: environmental value, perceived threat, recycling instrumentality, and perceived costs/benefits. First and foremost, the consumer must value the environment; it should be important to the consumer to save the environment. Second, the environment must be seen as being threatened by depleting resources. If you value the environment but do not believe that the environment is seriously threatened, then you are not going to do anything about it. Third, the consumer should believe that his or her individual efforts at recycling will be instrumental in saving the environment. Finally, the perceived personal benefits should outweigh the costs of recycling. These benefits and costs can be both physical and psychological. Costs are incurred in terms of physical effort to sort and separate the recyclables and take them to designated recycling centers (physical) and the hassle of one more chore in one's busy life (psychological). Benefits come in the form of a cash refund received for reusable packages (physical), praise from others or avoiding disdain from others, and from a feeling of doing good for humanity (psychological). These four subfactors have to be present; if any one of these is absent, the consumer will not be motivated to recycle. See Figure 12.10.

The second main factor is the ability/opportunity for recycling. This depends on two subfactors: public policy infrastructure for recycling and marketplace solutions and incentives. As is self-evident, if a city government does not provide the necessary infrastructure in the form of recycling collection centers, then consumers will not recycle no matter how strong their motivation. And if marketers don't make products and packages recyclable, or if sorting and saving them is cumbersome, then it detracts from consumer opportunity and ability to recycle. Actually, these two subfactors also influence the fourth subfactor of motivation we discussed earlier, perceived costs and benefits. If the recycling centers are few and far between, or products packaged in recyclable packages cost more or are difficult to identify, then consumers will perceive greater costs.

The immediate precursor to action is, you will recall from Chapter 7, attitude. Yes, in order to recycle, consumers must have a favorable attitude toward recycling. The two major factors—motivation and ability/opportunity—determine that. With favorable attitudes, you would be predisposed in favor of recycling action.[18] And that completes our model.

What can you do with this model? Apart from the public policy and marketer actions we suggested earlier, that is. The most revealing use of the model is in doing applied research: you can actually profile consumers in any society on these factors and, furthermore, segment them according to their motivations and the perceived costs and benefits. You will need to measure all these factors and subfactors, and based on your reading of the book so far, it should be easy for you to construct measures of all subfactors but three—environmental value, perceived threat, and recycling instrumentality. To help you get moving on these, we give you suggested measures (Table 12.5). Now, you are ready to try it, particularly if you are a public policy agency and value the amazing insights this model can offer you on consumers in your city or state, or province.

FIGURE
12.10

A Comprehensive Model of Consumer Recycling Behavior

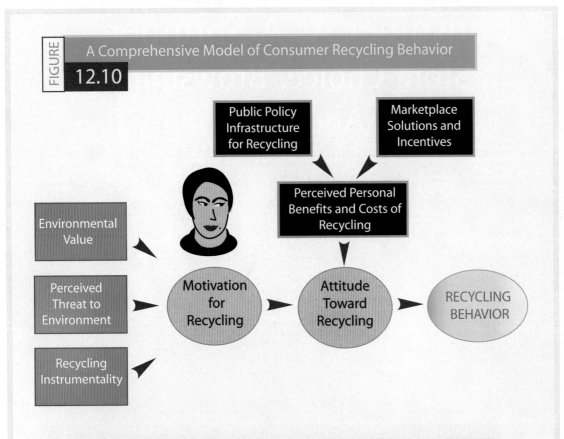

Selected Measures of Factors of Consumer Recycling

TABLE
12.5

| Strongly Disagree | 1 | 2 | 3 | 4 | 5 | Strongly Agree |

Environmental Value

	Strongly Disagree ... Strongly Agree
It is very important for humans to preserve the environment.	1 2 3 4 5
Industrial progress should not come at the cost of our environment.	1 2 3 4 5

Perceived Threat

Unless we act now, we will have destroyed our ecology.	1 2 3 4 5
There is no immediate danger of our environment being depleted.	1 2 3 4 5

Recycling Instrumentality

Recycling is hardly going to make a dent in the problem of our environment.	1 2 3 4 5
Recycling definitely helps environmental preservation.	1 2 3 4 5

Note: These measures are not tested in research. The purpose here is to illustrate the concepts and stimulate reader reflection and development of skills in translating concepts into measures.

After reading this chapter of MyCBBook, I have experienced it all—doubt, voice, satisfaction, loyalty, and yes, a bit of delight, too.

CHAPTER 13

Consumer As A Shopper
Store Choice, Browsing, And Impulsivity

My CB Book

Brides, Brides-to-Be, and Bride-Wannabes

It is four o'clock on a cold winter morning. Women from all over Boston leave on a consumer pilgrimage to a destination a few miles away. Joining them are many out-of-towners, having arrived in Boston the previous evening. The destination: Filene's Basement, an off-price clothing store and Boston landmark so famous that it attracts 15,000 to 20,000 shoppers, including many tourists, every day.

On this particular day, the store is holding its bridal gown sale, a world-famous event held every year since 1947, to clear unsold inventory and samples. Bridal gowns that are regularly priced from $800 to $9,000 are marked down today to $249 and $499 (with a few upscale designer gowns for only $699).

A consumer, Liz, at a Filene's Bridal Event in February 2005. (Source: www.lizlog.com)

The store will open at 8 a.m., but customers start lining up from 5 a.m. to get a good place in line. As soon as the doors open, the crowd instantly turns into a frenzied mob, rushing to the racks of gowns—thousands of them. Shoppers grab them by the dozen, without regard to size or style. A thousand gowns disappear in less than one minute. The shopping teams hold onto them, hoarding their inventory while the bride-to-be tries them on one by one. Rather than wait for the fitting rooms to become available, the hopefuls don't mind undressing in the aisles, "public stripping" in plain view of bystanders. They try on one and then another. The gowns they discard are quickly grabbed by others waiting and hovering around the shopping teams. The media has described this event as "a magical event, a mystery tour, a lovable, thrilling hole in the ground, as transforming and madcap as Alice's entry into Wonderland."[1]

By the end of the day, many lucky "Alices" will have walked away with the gown of their dreams. Many of them are soon-to-be-brides. But the lure of the merchandise is such that others—with no wedding plans in the near future—also come seeking and purchasing the dress of their dreams—just in case! Filene's Basement—an extraordinary shopping paradise for consumers; consumers—brides-to-be and bride-wannabes alike.

(About the bridal event, Liz writes, in her blog (February 5, 2005):

I survived the Filene's Basement Bridal Event. I admit I was actually pretty scared the night before, but it was really fun, once all the crazy mean girls put all the dresses they were hoarding back on the racks. I wasn't the girl who scored the Vera Wang for only $700 but it was an experience this die-hard Filenes devotee won't forget.

Liz tells us (personal communication) that she actually did find a gown at the event and she wore it to her wedding. Her blog canbe seen at lizlog.com.

INTRODUCTION

A Nation of Shoppers

Shopping. We are a nation of shoppers. Shopping is our pastime. Every day millions of consumers get out of their homes to hit the stores. Today, as we write this, it is Christmas Eve. This afternoon, the traffic on the road was bumper-to-bumper. Everyone seemed to be heading to the mall. Once at the mall, some were seen heading to Macy's, while others were going to Dillard's. Some teenage girls were shopping for cosmetics at Sephora, while others were shopping at the M.A.C store. Some college students were trying on clothes at Abercrombie & Fitch, while others were at the Express. Chico's was the destination for some, while New York & Company lured others. Same merchandise, more or less, but different stores. Why?

Ashley Reiley, looking cool after shopping on Michigan Avenue, Chicago.
Bring your cool self to the store and take some more cool stuff to keep you looking cool.

How do consumers choose their stores? How do *you* decide whether to go to Gap or Aeropostale for polo shirts, to Nine West or Aldo for shoes, to H&M or Urban Outfitters for Jeans? To Bebe or Charlotte Rosse for a party dress? And to Barnes & Noble or Borders for books? Do you visit the same stores every time? And what is your purpose of visiting the stores in the first place? Is it always to buy something? What other motives could there be? When you visit a store, do you buy only what you set out to buy? Do you find shopping a hassle or a pleasure? These questions are important to store managers of every ilk, whether they work for supermarkets, department stores, or haute couture boutiques. These are the questions we address in this chapter.

We begin this chapter by defining shopping itself and then documenting all the motives consumers have for shopping. No matter how much you have thought about shopping, our list is bound to include some motives that will surprise you. Once in the store, consumers browse—many don't, but just as many do. And browsing is good for the marketer. So if marketers want to increase consumer browsing in their stores, what should they do? Again, we will tell you. About browsing and then about a related habit many of us as consumers have—impulsive buying. In fact we will build an explanatory model so that you can understand your own impulsive buying behavior, and try to control it if you like. We will also reveal the answer to the ultimate question every store manager asks: how do consumers choose their stores, and what can be done to win their loyalty?

In this chapter, we ask you to wear your usual consumer hat, but we also ask you, occasionally, to wear the hat of a store manager. For now you can keep your consumer hat on.

SHOPPING MOTIVES

I Am a Shopper, But I Don't Have to Buy Anything, Do I?

It bears repeating: Shopping is our pastime. It has been for centuries. From the medieval bazaars of Morocco and Spain to the mega malls of modern times, the opportunity to look at a vast display of merchandise and bring some home has been an attraction for consumers of all nations. Each of us has known shopping for a long time. We have also indulged in it. But it is now time to define it. **Shopping** refers to all activities the consumer undertakes while in the store. This set of activities includes "walking through stores at a relaxed pace, examining merchandise, comparing products, interacting with sales staff, asking questions, trying things on, and ultimately, though not always, making purchases."[2] The store can be a bricks and mortar retailer, or, alternatively, it can be a cyberstore. In common parlance, of course, we call this activity "window shopping."

Consumers don't always make a purchase when they go shopping. In fact, they often don't have plans to buy anything. Why then, we might ask, would consumers go shopping? "Just for fun" comes to mind. To meet someone, maybe. And, maybe, for some exercise. Or just to get out of the house! What else? Actually, there are perhaps as many motives as shoppers. Consumer researchers have identified a number of these shopping motives.[3] Some of them are familiar; others have a new twist. Below is a more systematic list, and, as you read it, check off the ones that apply to you.

Browsing Browsing is the most logical motive for going shopping. **Browsing** refers to looking at merchandise without a purchase-intent. Consumers may end up buying something as a result of browsing, but they do not start out with the specific intent to acquire something. Often browsing occurs when the consumer is already in the store to buy something else and then extends the visit just to look around. Either the surrounding merchandise attracts attention, or the consumer (with a tendency to browse as a personality trait) extends the store visit to browse through the store.

Of course, the browsing activity is not always an extension of "acquisition-driven shopping." Indeed, for consumers given to browsing as a personality trait, browsing-motivated shopping trips often occur as independent, stand-alone activity. Although there is no research, a consumer's browsing activity would seem to be product and store category specific, limited to a few store types and a few product types. Thus, bookstore browsers may not browse other stores, and sports-oriented consumers may browse only or mainly sports stores.

Bargain Hunting Some consumers go shopping just looking for bargains. Although "directed search" under acquisition-driven shopping may also entail seeking the best price as a goal, many consumers look for bargains without an imminent need for the product and without a purchase-intent. Browsing is a broader activity. It can be done to discover new merchandise, or it can be done to discover a terrific bargain.

Socialization Shopping offers many an opportunity for social interaction with other people. Some hope to run into friends and acquaintances while at the mall. Many of us enjoy interacting with salespersons. Many stores hire employees who are similar in demographics and even psychographics and tastes to the intended target consumers; consumers visiting the stores ostensibly for browsing the merchandise thus have an opportunity to engage in small talk with sales staff they can relate to. Other customers in the store are also likely to be similar in their tastes and lifestyles, and shoppers looking for social interaction often strike up a conversation with fellow shoppers without concern

Sundi Brewer-Griffin, a sales consultant in Chicago, stocks up his wardrobe. The grin is genuine, reflecting a shopper's delight.

that they are strangers. Indeed, some stores even become hangouts for singles who want to meet other singles with similar tastes, such as Barnes & Noble for those wanting to meet singles with literary interests.

If you are looking for some socialization opportunities, there are two places you shouldn't shop: catalog and the Internet. These can be good channels, of course, for all other non-social motives.

Seeking Status Good store employees often attend to consumers with great politeness and courtesy. They address them with respect, and they respond to their needs for information and assistance, especially at stores that focus on high levels of customer service. Many consumers find such personal attention from store salespersons very flattering. If you want to try on a suit, for example, they will carry the suit for you to the dressing room and wait for you outside while you try it on. Thus, store visits can give consumers a sense of social status.

Self-Gratification In contrast to all other motives, this one does require making a purchase. The act of purchasing, however, is not driven as much by the utility of the product or service, but rather by the sense of rewarding oneself through spending money. You might have felt such gratification if you ever have bought something to cheer yourself up when you felt depressed, or alternatively, when you felt that you deserved a reward.

Market Learning Many find that visiting stores can be a good way to acquire information about what is new in the marketplace, as well as to learn about current trends. Some consumers have a strong interest in particular product categories, and they like to stay well-informed about these. Computer buffs want to learn about the latest software; music fans like to know about new albums; and fashion experts like to know about new styles in clothing. Market Mavens, described in Chapter 10, often visit stores to satisfy this motive. This motive is also very much at work for consumers enduringly involved in specific product categories.

Acquisition The most obvious reason to go shopping is, of course, to buy something. In this case, consumers engage in an information search directed at a specific product category. The search can be extensive or quick, depending on the risk involved, but it always begins after the consumer has formed the intent of buying a product and ends when the decision to buy has been consummated; i.e., the product has been acquired. The consumer's intent to buy may be formed in terms of the broad product category, defined either by

Two consumers who love to shop. Ashley and Alicia Assanuvat

usage (e.g., a gift for a friend's birthday, or something to perk up the room for the upcoming party) or by product class (e.g., oil to remove pregnancy stretch marks). In such cases, the purpose of shopping is to learn about various alternatives and to compare them. Or the intent may be more specific, with the name of the brand also specified (e.g., to buy a Michelin tire or a Movado watch); the consumer may still shop to get the best price.

Recreation Lastly, visiting stores can also be fun. Many stores are set up to provide sensory experiences; for example, the colorful display of clothing in specialty clothing stores such as Benetton, the rock video blasting in Hot Topic, the mellow tunes in Victoria's Secret, the strong aromas in coffee bean stores, and the fragrant air of The Body Shop. Even the hustle and bustle of people walking, chatting, and browsing—all of these can be very stimulating for the senses. Many consumers therefore visit stores for recreation when they have nothing better to do at home. In fact, some writers have argued that for many consumers, going shopping is therapeutic, a means of overcoming loneliness, boredom, or depression.[4] Technically, this motive to have fun and experience pleasure is called, you might recall from Chapter 2, a *hedonic* motive.[5]

STORE DESIGNS FOR HEDONISM

Of all the above-mentioned motives, the hedonic (or recreation) motive is a powerful motive to get consumers to visit your store even when they have no plans to buy. A major source of recreation is sensory excitement, which is produced by the environment of the store. **Store environment** refers both to the physical setting and the social stimuli within the store. If you ever get to manage a store and want to entice customers into your store, ensure that the physical environment is designed to be alluring and enchanting.

The physical environment comprise four elements: (a) design factors—the architecture, decor, furnishings, the look and feel of the place; (b) ambient factors—the sights, sounds, and smells of the place, which are in turn created by lighting, colors, music, and

Perdu, a Lingerie store in Suadi Arabia. Notice the two story high ceiling, open spaces, and feminine hues. Can anyone resist this serene and romatic ambience? The *atmospherics* in this lingerie store invite lingering!
(Coutesy: Chase Design Group; www.chasedesigngroup.com)

Perdu by night

Perdu by Day

aromas; (c) layout—the openness of the space, the ease of walking through the store, comfort facilities, etc; and (d) the merchandise variety and its order and arrangement.

What about the social environment in the store? That refers to the store's employees. Their appearance and personality make up the social setting. If you ever manage a store, make sure that your employees are neatly and modestly dressed, as well as pleasant and courteous to customers. They should also have a positive attitude about themselves and be "people persons" who truly enjoy interacting with customers. Some stores explicitly advertise that they are "Hiring happy employees!"

Other customers also are part of the social environment in the store, but you can't do much about that, except to make sure that their shopping experience is as pleasant as possible. Don't despair: the quality of merchandise and the physical ambience of the store will attract like-minded customers. It will intimidate and dissuade the type of consumers who don't fit in with your major clientele.

In any case, focus on what you can control. Mainly this means your physical setting. The design and ambience, especially, play a major role in producing sensory excitement.[6] No wonder, then, that many stores invest so heavily in design factors that contribute to the principal distinction of their brand. Indeed, recreation is a key theme of many shopping spaces, such as the Rain Forest Restaurants and the Mall of America. These are what Mica Nova, a consumer sociologist, calls *fantasy palaces*.[7]

SHOPPING ORIENTATION
What is Your Motive?

Put on your consumer hat now. How many of these motives apply to you? Generally, most people have several motives during a particular trip, and these motives may differ from one shopping trip to another. But it is also the case that, generally, and for each shopper, there are one or two motives that dominate his or her shopping pursuits. This determines a consumer's **shopping orientation**—his or her predominant motives for shopping activity. Being more or less permanent, it is like a personality trait.

Alex and Jacqueline Tsang of Hong Kong enjoy food shopping in a store.
To consumers everywhere, shopping, even routine shopping for food items, provides opportunity to "get out of the house," and the "recreation" is doubled when you also have nice company while shopping.

Broadly, this orientation can be divided into two types: task oriented and leisure oriented. The perspectives of task-oriented and leisure-oriented shoppers are quite different. **Task-oriented shoppers** focus on finding what they seek and they want to finish the shopping task efficiently. For **leisure-oriented shoppers**, in contrast, actual buying is secondary; enjoyment is primary.

If you are a task-oriented shopper, then shopping is a purely utilitarian chore for you. To finish it efficiently, you often wish to be left alone for self-paced information gathering; you seek out employees only when you need information you can't find on merchandise tags or packages. In these instances, you look to salespersons only as sources of product information, not for social chitchat. For task-oriented shoppers like you, a salesperson's product knowledge is what determines your liking for him or her.

If you are, instead, a leisure-oriented, socialization-seeking shopper, then your liking of the salesperson flows from the stylistic aspects of the salesperson's personality and the extent to which you feel you are valued by the salesperson. As a leisure-oriented shopper, you also enjoy mingling with other shoppers or simply enjoy being in the midst of other humans; you may even thrive on the hustle and bustle. In contrast, task-oriented shoppers may be bothered by the presence of other customers. They typically avoid other customers who might try to strike a conversation, and they can even feel stressed or irritated with crowds in stores and malls.

Bargain hunting can be both a leisure-oriented and a task-oriented activity. Although bargain seekers' primary goal is to obtain the best price for whatever they are buying, for many consumers, this activity does deliver other broader benefits. It can be self-fulfilling for a person who assumes the role of a "family purchase officer"—trying to provide for the family within the available budget. For some consumers, obtaining the best price can even be a life-long project, an enduring, ongoing mission, so to speak. These consumers always have this goal in mind whenever they are in the marketplace, and they are constantly browsing just for this purpose even when they don't have a specific purchase in mind. This activity intensifies when they have a purchase in mind, especially a high-ticket item, such as an appliance. Otherwise, for everyday, repeat items such as groceries, shopping is an ongoing project with "on/off" phases. In either case, successful culmination of a mini-project or a project phase gives a sense of accomplishment.

Finding a bargain gives consumers a thrill. Imagine that you have been looking for a DVD player, and after four days of searching through five physical stores and over a dozen cyber stores, you suddenly find the player you wanted at 80% off the best price you have seen so far. You might experience an adrenaline rush.

When acquisition itself is the principal goal, i.e., when the shopper is task-oriented, the consumer's shopping orientation can be further divided into four types according to the principal shopping attribute he or she seeks. These four types are:[8]

Product Quality Shopper This type of consumer seeks good product quality, buys name brands, and tends to be brand loyal. If you are a product quality shopper, you probably limit your shopping to a few stores known to carry high quality merchandise.

Economic Shopper This consumer seeks the best price possible, is deal prone, uses coupons heavily, engages in comparison shopping, and tends not to be brand or store loyal. If you are an economic shopper, you don't necessarily buy the cheapest, but you do seek the best value for your money. You tend to patronize discount stores, outlet malls, warehouse stores, and often buy in bulk or in large, economic size packages.

Convenience Shopper To this consumer, convenience is most important. Accordingly, this type of shopper buys products only when needed, and from the stores most conveniently located.

Experience Shopper This type of shopper seeks personalized attention. If you are an experience shopper, you seek stores reputed to be high on personal service. Store atmospherics are also important to you, as shopping to you must be an enjoyable activity.

Now then, what type of a shopper are you? What type is your friend? Your shopping pal should have a shopping orientation similar to yours. Otherwise, going shopping together may not be a good idea.

(Available at *www. cafepress.com*)

PLANNED, UNPLANNED, AND IMPULSE BUYING

We often visit stores without any intention to buy anything. We have other motives. Even so, we may often end up buying something. We make an unplanned purchase, or we get impulsive and buy more things. Marketers love it when consumers make unplanned purchases. How does a marketer convert a browser into a buyer? Let us understand planned versus unplanned buying.

All purchases that consumers make in a store (whether in a physical store or an Internet store) can be classified as either planned or unplanned. **Planned purchases** are those that the consumer planned to make before entering the store. **Unplanned purchases** are those that the consumer did not intend to make before entering the store. The consumer doesn't necessarily decide *not* to buy those products beforehand; rather, the consumer simply doesn't think about those products before visiting the store.

Planned purchases are, of course, self-explanatory. The consumer came with a plan to buy something and bought it. No mystery there. Unplanned purchases, on the other hand, are more interesting. So let us ponder these a bit. Unplanned purchases can be of three types:

1.   **Unplanned Restocking Purchases** These are items the shopper had not thought about buying at the time but has been using regularly. He or she buys them due to an in-store display or special deal, knowing that the item will be needed in the future.

2.   **Unplanned Evaluated, New Purchases** These are items the consumer needs, but the need for them was not recognized prior to this purchase occasion. These may either be products not already in use by the consumer (e.g., hair color), or products already in use and not in need of a replacement yet. The consumer simply decides to buy additional units to expand the collection (e.g., wardrobe, one more TV set in the house) or to get extra features in newer units (e.g., a high-definition television). The need recognition occurs in the store when the consumer sees the merchandise; however, once the need recognition occurs (i.e., the thought to buy it comes to mind), the consumer evaluates the purchase carefully.

3.   **Impulse Purchases** These are the extreme kind of unplanned purchases—items bought spontaneously and completely unpremeditated. The consumer buys in response to feeling a sudden urge to buy something. These purchases are made quickly and without an evaluation of the need.[9]

One indicator of planned buying is the consumer's use of shopping lists. According to a recent Gallup study, about 55 percent of supermarket shoppers use a shopping list. However, the use of shopping lists does not rule out unplanned buying. One reason is that the use of unplanned buying depends on how exactly an item is written out on the shopping list. A person may write only the general item type (e.g., entree), a specific product category (frozen pasta), or a specific brand (Sara Lee). Thus, there can be degrees of unplanned buying. Second, even when the product or brand is specified, consumers may deviate from the shopping list, buying a brand or product different from the one on the shopping list. Third, consumers may buy additional items not on the shopping list. For example, the same Gallup study found that an average shopping list user had planned to buy 10.5 items, on the average, but ended up buying 16.

Conversely, the absence of a list does not necessarily imply unplanned buying. Some consumers make mental rather than physical paper lists. A researcher might count these consumers among those making unplanned purchases, whereas in fact they are merely buying items on their mental lists.

Still, the use of a shopping list does signify greater use of planned purchases. A study in New Zealand found that grocery shoppers who had come to the store with a shopping list bought seven fewer items and spent $13.13 less than other shoppers who did not bring a list.[10]

An unplanned purchase can occur for several reasons. It may be a substitute for a planned item, bought either because the planned item was out of stock or because the substitute item was on sale. Alternatively, the consumer simply may have forgotten to write down the item on his or her list, but an in-store display reminded him or her to make the purchase. Or a good price deal might induce consumers to **forward buy**—buy an item for future consumption.

Whatever the reason, unplanned buying is good for marketers. The more, the merrier. To make it happen, stores try a few tricks. Some work, but some don't. To do it well, retailers need to understand what makes consumers do what they came to do: buy. Here is a brief guide.

IN-STORE FACTORS
How the Shopper Becomes the Buyer

FIGURE 13.1 Instore Factors Affecting Browsing and Unplanned Purchasing

Consumer Factors
- Familiarity with the Store
- Customer Mood

Situational Factors
- Time Pressure
- Shopping Companion

Store Factors
- Special Store Promotions
- Atmospherics

Browsing and Unplanned Purchasing

Some consumers come with an intent to buy, but they don't. Others come just to browse, and they end up buying. Why? They are already in the store, so something must happen inside the store that makes them do (or not do) what they came to do—buy. Therefore, we call them *in-store factors*. **In-store factors** refer to characteristics that surround the consumer's decision process inside the store. Notice that these factors are not limited to the characteristics of the store, i.e., what the store does or does not do. There are six factors in all: two are characteristics of the consumer; two are characteristics of the situation; and two are characteristics of the store. See Figure 13.1.

The two characteristics of the consumer are *familiarity* with the store and consumer *mood*. Generally, consumers prefer stores wherein they are familiar with merchandise display and store procedures. They like to shop where they feel in control; familiarity with the store gives them that feeling of control. This encourages **exploratory shopping**, just browsing around after collecting the planned items.

In the unfamiliar stores, on the other hand, consumers tend to be disoriented about where items are, and they must focus on finding what they need. Generally, they are not motivated to explore, unless the store has special-interest merchandise that encourages exploration. Knowledge of the store thus helps consumers expand purchases beyond pre-planned items. (Of course, if the store is totally new, and if it has interesting merchandise, the newness by itself will promote browsing.)

The second consumer factor is *mood*. In a sense, a consumer's mood is the ultimate factor that can make or break an otherwise perfect buying moment. When in a pleasant mood, the consumer tends to engage in exploratory shopping and liberal spending, and quite often, he or she purchases unplanned merchandise as a reward. An unpleasant mood, by contrast, limits the consumer's attention to the task at hand, namely to buying planned items. Consumers bring moods into the store, but moods are also created by some situational and store characteristics that we'll discuss next.

A store in Sydney only sells socks. Stores like this induce browsing.

There are two situational factors. We'll refer to them as *situational* because they occur during some store visits but not during others. One of these is related to *time*, while the other is related to the presence of a shopping *companion*.

Think about your own shopping experiences for a moment. Have you ever shopped while under a time constraint? If so, what was your shopping experience like? Chances are, you bought only what you went into the store to buy, and then you left quickly. Browsing around probably didn't occur on this particular visit. Research has found that, as you would expect, consumers who are hassled with such time pressures tend to limit their purchases only to preplanned purchase items. Moreover, the effect is compounded if the consumer is shopping while both under time pressure and in a new store about which the consumer has no prior knowledge.[11]

Companions can also influence purchases. Do you shop with a friend or family member? More than half of consumers do.[12] This factor can both promote and hinder browsing. Children accompanying parents on shopping trips, for example, might make new requests inside the store, with which parents might comply. Other companions, such as friends, might limit exploratory shopping and, consequently, could help curtail unplanned purchasing.

Finally, there are two store factors that can affect what you buy. Special store promotions, for one, play a significant role in encouraging unplanned purchases. Some consumers find special promotions and discounts simply irresistible; even when they do not need the merchandise, they often take advantage of a special deal either as a forward buy or as an impulse purchase. In fact, grand sales events that boast give-away offers and slashed prices on overstocks or clearance items bring many consumers to a retail establishment for the very first time. Who among us can resist the lure of such sales events?

The second store factor is called *atmospherics*. **Atmospherics** can be defined as the physical setting of the store. Atmospherics include lighting, colors, cleanliness and organization, scents, and, of course, background music. Atmospherics can make consumers want to linger in a store or, alternatively, to get out quickly. One study showed that when the background music's tempo is slow, consumers spend more time in the store and on an average spend more money.[13] Incidentally, *atmospherics* is one factor under a store's control that can alter a consumer's mood.[14]

CONSUMER IMPULSIVITY
When You Gotta Have It!

Has this ever happened to you? You are in a store, you see a dress, and you suddenly feel, "I gotta have it!" Don't worry, it is quite normal, and most of us occasionally feel and act in this way. Acting in in this way is called *impulse buying*. According to a national survey of American consumers, as many as 38% of respondents admitted to being impulse buyers. Many are impulse buyers only occasionally, but some do it frequently—buying on impulse every so often. They have what we call *impulsivity*—a personality trait.

Consumer impulsivity is defined as a consumer's tendency to buy and/or consume spontaneously, whenever exposed to the stimulus product. Correspondingly, **impulsive consumer behavior** refers to a specific purchase and/or consumption activity undertaken on the spur of moment.[15] It is worth repeating that *consumer impulsivity* is a personality trait, whereas impulsive consumer behavior is a specific purchase episode.

Just what does impulsive consumer behavior feel like? What is its nature? According to Consumer Researchers, it has three characteristics (see Figure 13.2):

FIGURE 13.2

PROPERTIES OF IMPULSIVE BEHAVIOR

Product Proximity ("Look at that")

Emotion-driven ("Fatal attraction")

Unreflective ("I don't wanna ")

IMPULSIVE CONSUMER BEHAVIOR "I want it." "I want it."

1. **It is unreflective** The consumer does not think it over, and does not seriously evaluate the need for the product or weigh costs versus benefits.

2. **It occurs in proximity** to the stimulus. If you see an advertisement for a wrist watch and make a mental note to buy it the next time you go to the store, then that desire and intent is not impulsive behavior because you are not exposed to the stimulus in a buying situation (and thus cannot implement spontaneous purchase or spontaneous consumption).

3. **It is emotion-driven** The spontaneous and unreflective acquisition or consumption behavior is driven by a strong emotional attraction for the product; the consumer just feels an irresistible "urge" to buy/consume it.

In other words, it is a fatal attraction.

The moment you see a product, you just get sucked in. Your mind (or perhaps your heart) says, "I want it! I want it!"

HOW CONSUMERS CHOOSE THEIR STORES
It is Not Random At All

Now we turn to that 64 million dollar question: how do consumers decide at which store to shop? Here is how it usually happens.

If you live in a fairly typical city, you most likely have the option of at least three or four general merchandise stores at which to shop and just as many supermarkets. How do consumers such as yourself choose among these store options? As every store manager will tell you, the number one factor in store choice is location. This, in fact, was also the conclusion of a survey conducted by *Consumer Reports* of about 10,000 supermarket shoppers.

But location is a relative criterion, not an absolute one. You know for yourself that you don't always go to the nearest store. Nor do most consumers, even though they want to minimize travel distance. Sometimes, they will go to a distant store if they can get better quality, selection, or price. Merchandise quality and price were the second and third

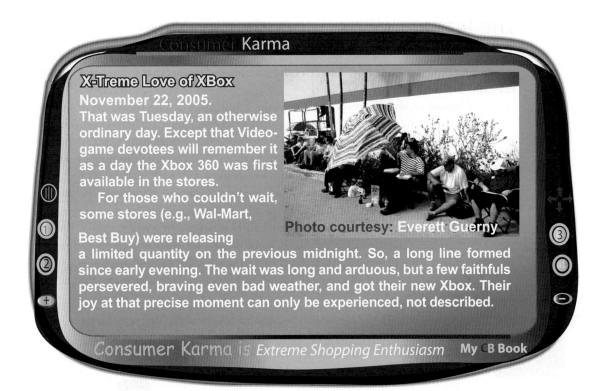

X-Treme Love of XBox

November 22, 2005.
That was Tuesday, an otherwise ordinary day. Except that Video-game devotees will remember it as a day the Xbox 360 was first available in the stores.

For those who couldn't wait, some stores (e.g., Wal-Mart, Best Buy) were releasing a limited quantity on the previous midnight. So, a long line formed since early evening. The wait was long and arduous, but a few faithfuls persevered, braving even bad weather, and got their new Xbox. Their joy at that precise moment can only be experienced, not described.

Photo courtesy: Everett Guerny

Consumer Karma is *Extreme Shopping Enthusiasm*   My B Book

criteria in the *Consumer Reports* study. In actuality, consumers do not choose a store on the basis of a single factor, or do not always value various factors in a specific priority order. Rather a dynamic *interplay* of factors influences their choice.[16]

The Osbornes Go Shopping

To understand this dynamic interplay, let us consider the supermarket shopping behavior of a family we shall call the Osborne family. The Osbornes live in a suburb of a U.S. metropolis, near two supermarkets: Kroger, two miles to the south, and Thriftway, one and a half miles to the north (both are big supermarket chains with stores in a number of U.S. cities). The nearest convenience stores are a Speedway gas station at a main-road crossing, about half a mile to the northeast, and an Ameristop at about the same distance, but slightly off the main road.

The Osbornes rarely shop at a convenience store (not counting the many trips their teenage daughter Kelly makes for her frequent refills of soda). They do patronize Speedway though, where they regularly buy gas and where they occasionally buy milk when they run out of it and it's not convenient to visit the supermarket.

They divide their main food shopping between Thriftway and Kroger, shopping more often at Kroger because it is on Mrs. Osborne's way to work and because the "double coupon" feature often lures. Some weeks, they split their major shopping between Kroger and Thriftway to take advantage of price deals at each store.

The Osbornes also shop at Meijer, a *supercenter* that sells food as well as apparel and hard goods (small appliances, electronics, and so on). Although it is farther away, the Osbornes shop there once every two to three weeks; this is usually a major shopping trip, where they typically spend substantially more than at Kroger. Finally, there is another store some 15 miles away that the Osbornes visit about once every two months—Jungle Jim's International Market—a unique, four-acre specialty store. Well known for its exotic vegetables, cheeses, wines, and foods of the world, this store was featured in *Business Week* (April 18, 2005).

The Osbornes consider the trip an excursion—a combination of shopping and the excitement of browsing exotic merchandise. If you are a foodie, Jungle Jim can be, for you, Mecca—its collection of over 950 hot sauces alone could take an entire day to browse!

THE INTERPLAY OF DECISION CRITERIA

Although no two families are alike in their food shopping (and shopping for other products), the Osborne family illustrates the interplay of factors that influence a consumer's store choice:

• Distance is an important consideration, but it is not always measured from home or in kilometers/miles; rather, it is measured by convenience, such as whether it is on the way to work and on or off the main road or main commuting route. Moreover, small differences in distances are ignored, so that a slightly more distant store may be chosen on occasion even without any other advantage.

• If two or more stores are equally convenient from the standpoint of distance, then other factors (e.g., quality, assortment, and price) influence the store choice. Moreover, if these other factors are significantly inferior at the nearest store, then too a distant, less convenient store is likely to be chosen for regular shopping. The most convenient store may continue to be chosen, however, for filler trips.

• A typical consumer does not limit food shopping to just one store. Rather, con-

FIGURE 13.3

A FLOW CHART OF CUSTOMERS' STORE CHOICE DECISION PROCESS

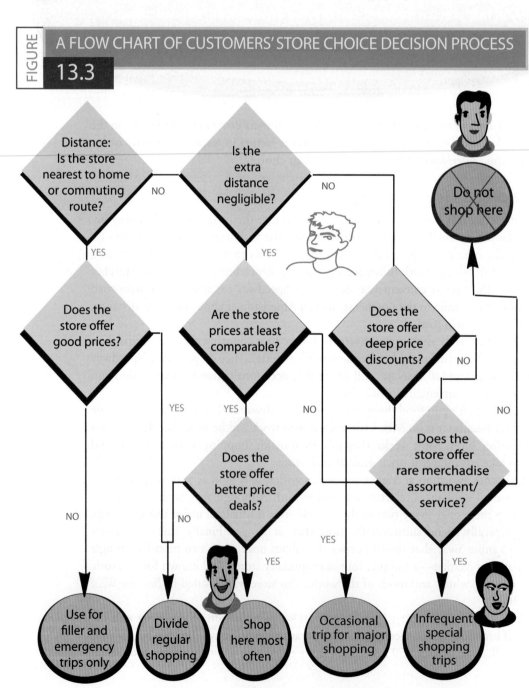

sumers have a repertoire of stores, with one store shopped most frequently and regularly. For example, an average American household makes an average of 2.2 visits per week to a supermarket. However, for a majority of households (over 80 percent), only one visit (out of 2 or 3 total visits) is made to their most preferred supermarket; at least one visit every week is made to their less preferred store—albeit for less substantive shopping. Thus, a majority of American households rely on more than one food store to meet their food needs.[17]

• If there are stores that specialize in quality, assortment, or price deals, these stores are likely to be included in the repertoire of stores (i.e., into the consideration set), even if they are not conveniently located. They will be visited despite the locational disadvantage, but only on special occasions rather than on a regular basis.

The most important point is that consumers have a repertoire (i.e., assortment) of stores at which to shop. The choice of a specific store from the repertoire is based on the exigencies of the specific situation—for example, whether it is an emergency, a major shopping trip, a filler trip, or whether one of the stores in the repertoire is running a price special, etc.[18]

As shown in the flow chart of the decision process in Figure 13.3, a store decision begins, but often does not end, with distance considerations. (The flow chart is an attempt to assemble a reasonable description of the process as inferred from a number of unrelated studies, existing marketing literature, and the author's own consumer observations and intuitive reflections.[19]) This flow chart is most applicable to food shopping. Because shopping for groceries is repetitive, a sort of pattern emerges, dividing shopping chores over periodic "fixed schedule trips" and then "filler trips" and "special trips." Now, why don't you try drawing a flow chart for your own behavior in choosing a supermarket choice?

Battle of the Stores—How They Differentiate Themselves

Since merchandise quality, assortment, and price all play important roles in helping consumers choose stores, retailers naturally try to distinguish themselves on one or more of these criteria. Supermarkets tend to offer a medium assortment of merchandise at moderate prices, levels considered acceptable by the mass market. Some supermarkets, such as Food Lion, and some supercenters, such as Meijer, feature lower prices. Warehouse stores offer a limited selection of merchandise, but at very attractive prices. Similarly, wholesale or membership clubs, such as Sam's and Costco, appeal principally to price-point sensitive consumers (to shop at these stores, you must be a member and pay an annual fee)

Specialty stores, such as Jungle Jim's in Fairfield, Ohio, or H-E-B Foods in San Antonio, Texas, focus on merchandise selection and assortment. Some supermarkets such as Harris-Teeter make fresh produce their special attraction. Such differentiation strategies work because of a process called **self-selection**—consumers self-select themselves to be the customers of the store that offers the advantage they seek.[20]

NONFOOD SHOPPING

Or When Man Does Not Live by Bread Alone

Of course, consumers buy more than food. They also buy apparel, jewelry, electronics, fragrances and cosmetics, to name a few products. This is when shopping gets interesting. For one thing, it is not repetitive, so it does not become a chore. Consumers are often excited about going shopping for these items. Besides, often these are high involvement purchases. Consequently, location takes a back seat. Merchandise quality, assortment, and price assume greater prominence. A few other factors also come into play.
Customer Service The courtesy and helpfulness of store personnel.

Wayfinding The ease of finding your way around the store. Wayfinding depends upon a store layout, in-store displays, and signage.

Atmospherics The physical ambiance of the store. Atmospherics entail the art of designing a physical space so as to create a pleasurable sensory experience for the customer. Ambiance comprises such elements as lighting, colors, background music, scents, and, overall, the cheeriness or the gloominess of the store.

Often all of these factors work in unison. By that, we mean consumers form an impression about a store based on these factors. This impression then, by and large, determines whether they visit the store or not. Even so, some factors are more important than others. Typically, factors such as merchandise quality, assortment, and price (along with location) form the first set of screening factors. The remaining three factors—service, wayfinding, and atmospherics—serve as the second tier of screening criteria. That is, when the first-tier factors are equalized, consumers are likely to then choose a store that offers one or all three of the second-tier advantages. See Figure 13.4.

FIGURE 13.4 FACTORS AFFECTING STORE CHOICE SET

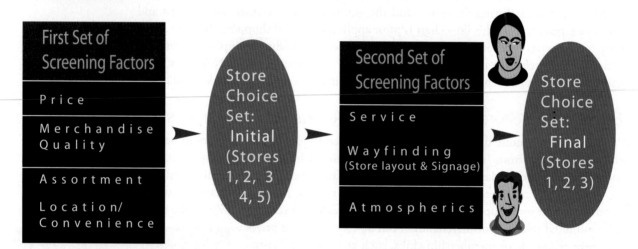

Are service, wayfinding, atmospherics, and the like not as important for food shopping, you might ask? They are, to some extent. However, these factors really play a determinant role for non-food shopping (which is not routinized).

Have we accounted for all the factors? Almost. You might notice that we did not mention advertised sales specials as a factor. This is because the advertised specials are just that—special. As such, they play a distinct role: they influence a particular *trip*. You see, the two-tier criteria depicted in Figure 13.4 determine the choice set. How do consumers select from this set of choices? They do so based on two criteria: locational convenience and advertised store specials. *Locational convenience* here refers to situation-specific-proximity. That is, wherever the consumer happens to be at the time he or she thinks about going shopping. Thus, the consumer chooses a store (out of the choice set) based on proximity. Secondly, consumers often plan shopping trips specifically around advertised specials. So out of the set of choices, consumers choose a store for a certain shopping trip based on whichever store is running the advertised specials. See Figure 13.5.

STORE IMAGE AND STORE PERSONALITY

As we said earlier, all of these factors work in unison. In the consumer's mind, they create an overall impression. Thus, all these factors come together in the concept of **store**

FIGURE
13.5
FACTORS IN STORE CHOICE FOR A PARTICULAR SHOPPING TRIP

Store 4

Store 3

Store 3

Store 2

Initial Store
Consideration Set

Locational
Convenience

Advertised
Store Specials

Store
Selected for a
Particular
Shopping Trip

image—the sum total of perceptions that consumers have about the store.

Store image is determined, first and foremost, by merchandise, service, and price factors; it is also determined by atmospherics, which drives the look and feel of the store. The clientele of a store is also an important determinant of store image, as consumers form impressions about the store from the type of customers who frequent it. Actually, the relationship between store image and clientele is mutual: store image determines the kind of clientele a store will attract, but the clientele also feeds back into store image. Finally, store image is also determined by the quality and appearance of store employees. The hip and youthful employees at Nike Town create a different image, for example, than do the more mature, warm, and folksy greeters and cashiers at Wal-Mart stores.[21]

Store displays make store image and entice shoppers.
(A store in Melbourne)

Closely related to store image is the concept of **store personality**, which refers to the characterization of a store on personality-like qualities. Many qualities that we apply to humans can also be applied to stores—such as sophisticated, modern, traditional, tacky, etc. Thus, store image is the sum total of consumer perceptions, and store personality is a subset of these—i.e., it refers to those perceptions that pertain to human-like qualities. That is, Store image = Store personality (human-like qualities) + other features of the store; i. e., non-personality-like attributes (e.g., price, merchandise variety, wayfinding, etc.).

In a pioneering study on this topic, researchers have identified five personality dimensions that capture a store's personality; these are Enthusiasm, Sophistication, Unpleasantness, Genuineness, and Solidity. A scale to measure these personality dimensions is shown in Table 13.1 below.

TABLE 13.1

Measurement of Store Personality

Enthusiasm		Sophistication		Unpleasantness		Genuineness		Solidity	
Enthusiastic	___	Chic	___	Annoying	___	Honest	___	Hardy	___
Welcoming	___	High-class	___	Irritating	___	Sincere	___	Solid	___
Lively	___	Elegant	___	Loud	___	Reliable	___	Reputable	___
Dynamic	___	Stylish	___	Superficial	___	True	___	Thriving	___

Source: Alain d'Astous and Melanie Levesque, "A Scale for Measuring Store Personality," *Psychology and Marketing*, Vol. 20/Number 6, May 2003, p. 455-469. Used with Permission.

Store image and store personality play an overarching role in how consumers choose stores. This is because, in selecting stores, consumers try to match stores with their own self-concepts. That is, they come to believe, for example, that Abercrombie & Fitch is their type of store whereas Chico's is not, or the other way around.

A survey of consumers in a major metropolitan area in Canada revealed the personality profile of selected stores in the city, presented in Table 13.2

Is the store you shop at among the stores rated in Table 13.2? No? Then, why not rate it yourself, based on your impressions? And now, let us wear a store manager's hat. As a store manager, what would you do to give your store a little bit more of each of these personality qualities? This is a question that calls for extreme creativity to identify a solution unique to each store manager. We invite you to carve out your own answer. Here is some help: Compare in your mind two stores that differ on, say, enthusiasm, and see what it is that one of them is doing that the other one is not. And then, likewise, do the same for sophistication, genuineness, solidity, and unpleasantness. Now, unpleasantness is of course, a quality you want to decrease, not increase. So what can you do to reduce it? Maybe you can make it one of your research projects.

TABLE 13.2

Personality Profile of Selected Stores in Canada

Store Name	Enthusiasm	Sophistication	Genuineness	Solidity	Unpleasantness
Wal-Mart	3.83	2.29	3.65	3.92	2.48
Sears	3.31	3.17	3.86	3.80	2.19
Zellers	3.00	2.14	3.35	3.16	2.42
La Baie	3.22	3.65	3.63	3.61	2.53
Canadian Tire	3.47	2.75	3.87	4.05	2.21
Future Shop	3.21	2.91	3.10	3.52	2.53

Source: Alain d'Astous (HEC, Montreal), personal communication.

Let us keep our store manager's hat on for a while. We now know how consumers choose their stores. And we know how to get them into our store. But getting them once is only the beginning; our real goal is, and should be, to get them to visit our store again and again. In other words, how do we make a first time visitor a loyal customer?

Let us think about Grace and Karen, two of our frequent customers. Both are in their thirties, both are single. Both shop frequently. Grace always shops at our store, Chico's. Seldom does she visit another store. Karen, on the other hand, hops from store to store on every shopping excursion. As the manager of Chico's, you obviously consider Grace a more valuable customer than Karen, because she is more loyal to your store. How can you make Karen more loyal?

For this purpose, we need to understand why consumers become store loyal. Obviously, many of the factors that influence a first time visit would also induce loyalty. But a few new factors also come into play. These factors are shown in Figure 13.6.

For the sake of exposition, it is useful to divide the determinant factors of store loyalty into two sets: the "what" factors and the "how" factors. The "what" factors refer to the products and services the consumer gets at the store. These are the factors for which consumers go to the store in the first place, and these are what they walk out with when they leaves the store. The "how" factors refer to the process entailed in a consumer's acquisition of those products and services.[22]

FIGURE 13.6 A MODEL OF CONSUMERS' STORE LOYALTY

"What" Factors
- Merchandise quality
- Assortment
- Price Value
- Store brands

CONSUMER's STORE LOYALTY

"How" Factors
- Ease of self-selection
- In-store information and assistance
- Convenience
- Problem resolution
- Personalization
- Atmospherics

THE "WHAT" FACTORS

A consumer goes into a store to acquire some mix of merchandise quality, assortment, and price value—factors we have already considered—and also one more factor, namely, availability of store brands. Although self-evident, let us make brief comments on each. Discussing these factors again in the context of store loyalty gives us an opportunity to shed light on some important nuances. Understand these nuances, and you will be richly rewarded when and if someday you get to manage your own store. So, here we go.

Merchandise Quality Merchandise quality refers to the quality of the products or services the store carries and offers. Stores differ vastly on this element, with merchandise ranging from shoddy to medium to premium quality (e.g., produce that is fresh or withered; clothing that is well tailored or carelessly sewn). The merchandise quality is generally controlled by the brand names the store decides to carry. It is immensely important, therefore, to be very careful in selecting brands to carry in your store.

Assortment A store's **assortment** is the number of different items the store carries. This includes the number of diverse product categories (e.g., appliances versus food), product varieties (e.g., in the produce section, whether or not the store carries, say, tropical fruits, exotic vegetables, and so on), the number of brands of the same product category (e.g., for photo films, Kodak, Fuji, etc.), and the size and color varieties.

Variety in Stores: Now You Want It, Now You Don't

Consumers are in two shopping modes: Either they already know exactly what they want, or they don't know and they are eager to explore and find out what is out there. In the former mode, the variety of assortment a store carries is seen as a negative store feature. In the latter mode, in contrast, the higher the perceived variety, the more the store is deemed appealing.

Source: Stephen J. Hoch, Eric T. Bradlow, and Brian Wansink, "The Variety of an Assortment," *Marketing Science*, 1999 18 (4) pp 527-546.

Although assortment will influence a consumer's patronage, the relationship is not straightforward. Consumers do not necessarily want an unlimited, vast assortment—indeed too large an assortment could create shopper confusion. Instead they want the store to carry their preferred brand. They also want the store to carry a few other related major brands. Why? Because consumers want to compare brands—both initially when their brand preference is still fluid, and later from time to time when they want to compare leading brands. For example, a regular buyer of Kodak photo film might see an advertisement for Fuji film and want to check it out in the store. If the regularly visited store does not carry Fuji film, this is likely to affect negatively the consumer's perception of the store as an adequate store option. And consumers also want availability of different sizes and colors. For example, consumers want to be able to buy, on different occasions, a Kodak film with 12, 24, or 36 exposures without having to visit another store.

In many product categories, such as clothing, cosmetics, perfumes, jewelry, music CDs, and books, consumers intrinsically desire variety. For these product categories, they value a large assortment of styles or content.

Assortment also appeals to consumer's desire for **one-stop shopping**—finding all of their requirements of related products in one place or from one source. The motivations for one-stop shopping are convenience and time savings. Stores like Meijer, Sam's, and Wal-Mart in the United States, and Food Giant and Asda's Dale's in the United Kingdom attract consumers by offering an assortment of product categories far greater than a typical supermarket (such as Kroger in the United States or Tesco or Sainsbury's in the United Kingdom) and yet at comparable prices.

Price Value Consumers seek the best possible price for the merchandise they buy. This is the appeal of deep discounters such as Costco's (United States), Kwik Save (United Kingdom), Aldo (Netherlands), Dia/Dirsa (Spain), or Netto (Denmark). However, consumers do not always, or even often, seek low-price merchandise; rather, for the quality of merchandise they desire, they seek the lowest or near lowest price. These two qualifications are important. Consumers seek low prices for acceptable quality of merchandise, not low prices in the absolute. Of course, some consumers on some occasions find very low quality acceptable, so they seek very low-price merchandise. Still, merchandise acceptability comes first; evaluation for low price comes later.

In addition—and this is a key nuance we wanted to share with you—consumers do not always bother to ensure that the price they are getting is the lowest possible; they only want to feel confident that the price is comparably low, and that if there were a lower price elsewhere, the difference would be negligible. Once again, consumers differ in their price sensitivity, so what price differences are considered insignificant or negligible will differ from consumer to consumer.

Store brands Yet another attraction for the consumer is store brands, the brands that carry a store label and are available exclusively at that store chain. Store brands add to the assortment the store presents the consumer for comparison. One of these comparisons is, of course, on price *vis-a-vis* the national brands. Since store brands are considerably lower in price, the availability of store brands becomes one avenue for consumers to maximize their price value from the store. In addition, store brands can be unique either in value or in performance or features available, by definition, only at the specific store chain. This exclusive availability is yet another way to attract consumers' loyal patronage.[23]

THE "HOW" FACTORS

Store loyalty also depends on how positive the shopping experience is in a particular store. Basically, once in the store, consumers want to get their shopping done efficiently and effectively. This requires six "how" factors: (a) ease of merchandise selection, (b) in-store information and assistance, (c) convenience, (d) problem resolution, (e) personalization, and (f) atmospherics. If you are keeping track, these factors are just a more unbundled version of the three second-tier factors shown in Figure 13.4. We break them down in this way because it is easier for us to explain how to manage them in practical terms. Here is how.

Ease of merchandise selection The ease with which a store's merchandise can be selected refers to how easily and effortlessly consumers are able to browse, inspect, and select products. This depends on several features: layout of aisles and shelf displays ('wayfinding'), shelf tags, product information cards, and signage. Merchandise should be arranged for easy access and for easy inter-brand comparisons. According to some reports, until recently, consumers complained about the tall shelves in Toys "R" Us stores; consumers, especially short and elderly consumers, found it difficult to reach the merchandise for inspection. Similarly, correct price and brand shelf tags should allow easy evaluation, and comparable size and quality brands (including store brands) should be placed side-by-side for easy comparison. Finally, items should not be out of stock.

In-store information and assistance By in-store information and assistance, we mean the availability of credible information about the merchandise; it also means availability of salesperson assistance in shopping ('service'). Merchandise selection ease provides efficiency in the self-selection of items, and most stores in the Western world are organized for self-selection. But beyond ease of self-selection, consumers sometimes need information and assistance from salespersons (for example, to see a product demonstration). If consumers find that salespersons are not easily available or they are not knowledgeable or fair and impartial in their advice, then it detracts from buying efficiency or effectiveness.

Convenience Consumers also want convenience in getting to the store and getting out of it once they have selected their merchandise. Consumers are satisfied if the store location, parking availability, and checkouts (customer service) are convenient.

Once a consumer has completed his or her product selection, nothing is more important to the consumer than to be able to checkout and go home as soon as possible. All else being equal, consumers like to patronize stores that are convenient to access and convenient to conduct the transaction (which means quick checkout).[24]

Have you noticed how some big supermarkets now have a separate entrance and independent checkout for the pharmaceutical, banking, and dairy departments? If you want to buy just a gallon of milk, you don't want to waddle your way through the labyrinthic aisles to go to the back of the store; you would rather just go to a convenience mart like Seven-Eleven or Ameristop. Hence, the separate entrance and separate checkout.

Problem resolution When they need problem resolution or a remedy for a store's mistakes or oversights, consumers want this service to be easy and hassle free. The most typical problems are the need to return or exchange merchandise (customer service). Stores that have a liberal return policy, allowing consumers to return unused merchandise within a reasonable time, or stores that will repair or replace faulty merchandise within a reasonable time, even beyond the warranty period, are likely to earn consumers' repeat patronage.

Suppose you buy a shirt and its color fades after a few washes; you would expect the store to take it back, wouldn't you? Many stores are known to accept back defective merchandise. As another example, suppose you bought a television from a store, and it had a 90-day free labor and parts warranty; suppose the TV stopped working on the 91st day. Again, you would expect the store to fix the TV free of charge since it is only one day beyond the warranty expiration. However, some stores would do it, while some, hiding behind the written policy, would not. Guess which stores would earn consumer loyalty?

True Value understands the value (to consumers) of **in-store information and assistance**.

Variety in Stores: Now You See It, Now You Don't

If people are in an analytical processing mode (wanting to examine features and detailed product information to rationally form a judgment), then organized displays appear to offer more variety; in heuristic processing mode (wanting to form a quick, global impression), consumers see random displays as having more variety.

Source: Stephen J. Hoch, Eric T. Bradlow, and Brian Wansink, "The Variety of an Assortment," *Marketing Science*, 1999 18 (4) pp 527-546.

Personalization By **personalization**, we mean positive employee behavior toward consumers. Consumers expect store employees to be pleasant and courteous in their interaction and eager to help consumers during their shopping. Stores differ greatly on this dimension. Stores that hire employees with poor interpersonal skills and low aptitude for socialization with consumers are likely to earn less loyalty from their consumers. For many consumers, personal attention from salespersons is very important, and it is expected from upscale stores like Lord & Taylor. But personalization is a matter of attitude and culture, not of pricey sophistication. Even in a supermarket, in a merely one-minute long interaction with a wandering store employee, personalization will come through. And if it looks like the employee doesn't care to help, doesn't value you as a customer, next time you might well go elsewhere.

Atmospherics Finally, a factor we have already defined before. **Atmospherics**, as you know, means the physical setting and ambiance of the store. Atmospherics influence the whole shopping experience. And the shopping experience in itself, quite apart from the products one buys at the store, can be of inherent value, and a pull toward the store.

Who buys Store Brands?

A MODEL OF STORE BRAND CHOICE

(Or Making Money on Store Brands)

Keep your store manager's hat on for just a little while more. Now that you know how to make your customers loyal, you are eager to go to work at it, so to speak. But before you rush off, it will pay off to learn about one more model—the model of who buys store brands. Store brands were, you may recall, one of the factors in winning customer loyalty. There is money to be made in store brands. There is only one snag: not everyone is lured by store brands. If you knew who was and why, you would be able to milk your store brand program for better profits. Fortunately, consumer researchers have the answer.

Two studies, one from the U.S. and the other from the U.K., have been conducted on store brand buyers. In the U.S. study, 582 shoppers were surveyed about their purchase of 28 product categories (e.g., bacon, soups, juices, frozen vegetables, paper towels, laundry detergents, etc.). The study found that consumers who bought store brands came from larger families and lower-income groups. At the same time there was no difference between the age and education levels of buyers and non-buyers of store brands. Consumers who bought store brands (compared to those who did not) saw store brands as a better "perceived value for the money" and did not see any risk in buying store brands. They were also more tolerant of ambiguity.[25]

In the U.K. study, 1000 grocery shoppers were surveyed. All consumers perceived national brands to be superior to store brands in terms of quality, packaging, consistency, and image, but store brands were perceived to be a "better value for the money." Naturally, then, consumers to whom value for the money was more important are the ones who bought store brands. These consumers were somewhat less educated, were younger, were of lower socio-economic status, and had at least one child living at home. There was one more interesting difference: store brand shoppers shopped more frequently and longer. Obviously, they were comparison shoppers who shopped often, looking for deals and taking advantage of sales.

These are the findings of the two studies as reported by their authors. Can you sort them out in terms of "who" and "why" factors? Let us help (see Figure 13.7).

In terms of "who," store brand buyers are of lower socio-economic status and from larger families. By lower socio-economic status we don't mean that all of these consumers are poor in an absolute sense. Many store brand buyers are from middle and even upper middle class backgrounds; nonetheless, store brand buyers are, *on the average*, lower in income than those who buy national brands. Next, they are also more price-sensitive and

FIGURE
13.7

A MODEL OF STORE BRAND BUYING

"Who" Factors	STORE BRAND BUYING	"Why" Factors
• Lower Socio-Economic Status • Larger Families/Families with children • Price Sensitive/Comparison Shoppers		° Motivation to save money ° Better value for money ° Quality Gap not significant

deal-prone, and therefore they engage more in comparison-shopping. These, then, are the "who" factors.

As to "why" factors, none are mentioned directly in the studies. But by now, you have learned how to "tease out" a theory behind any consumer behavior, haven't you? You know enough to be able to come up with a list of reasons why consumers would buy store brands. As you ponder their motivations, here is our list: the "why" factors are (i) motivation to save money, (ii) the perception that store brands offer better value for money (this one did come from the study directly), and (iii) the view that quality gap was not significant. This last factor may be at work either because they see these brands as fairly similar to national brands, or that the superiority, if any, of national brands is not of any material consequence to them.

Let us carry your theory-teasing skills a little further. Can you see, intuitively, some connection between the "who" and the "why" factors? As we see it, all three "who" factors provide the core motivation for buying store brands; namely, motivation to save money. Let us explain. Because of their lower economic status, consumers need to watch their spending and must buy the lowest priced items as long as the quality meets their minimum requirements. This "who" factor (lower socio-economic status) also makes these consumers seek "better value for money." A large family size means that food spending is large; consequently, a small percentage of savings can add up to large absolute savings, which also makes their effort and the time spent finding deals on store brands worth the effort.

Before you leave this section, you must note that although consumers want to save money, they still look for good quality in the core product. The packaging need not be fancy, however, and as a store brand manager you can save money on packaging and advertising. You should still strive to offer good product quality though, and your brand communications should highlight a comparable quality and better value for the money.

Marketing Implications
Milking Consumers' Impulsivity

Whereas every topic discussed in this chapter has significant action implications for marketers, consumer impulsivity has special potential. It can significantly contribute to added revenue for the store. Let us reflect on how marketers can harness and respond to consumer impulsivity.

What kinds of items do stores keep near checkout registers for people to pick up and buy impulsively? These products have four characteristics: (1) they are small ticket items—so that money does not become a major constraint; (2) they are sensory products, creating an immediate "fatal attraction" (i.e., candy, drinks, and magazines with hot models or a sensational headline on the cover); (3) these are items that do not require detailed feature evaluation, so an impulse purchase is feasible; and (4) these are items we could consume immediately—perhaps as soon as we pay for them. We are going to eat the candy, and as soon as we get to our car, we are going to flip through the pages of the magazine, postponing the driving for awhile. Thus, impulse buying is immediately going to satisfy the motive that started the process to begin with—instant gratification.

Of course, items not close to the checkout are bought on impulse as well. But here again, small-ticket items (particularly if they are on sale) are bought impulsively more than big-ticket items. We are more likely to make an impulse purchase from stores that take credit cards than those that take cash only. Too, we are likely to purchase an item on impulse if we can visualize a situation where we can use the item sooner rather than later in the distant future (e.g., if we have a social gathering to attend this weekend, we are more likely to make the impulse purchase of a dress than if we had no such event in sight).

Finally, we are more likely to make an impulse purchase when we are in a good mood in the store. If the store is uncomfortable, no assistance is available, or salespersons do not relate with us positively, then we are less likely to engage in impulse purchasing. When we are just browsing for joy, the mood and the emotion of the moment play a crucial role. The store ambience, the aesthetics, and the demeanor of salespersons can affect whether we make the purchase we never intended or leave the store without buying even though we felt the urge to buy something.[26] It is within the power of a store manager to design and create an atmosphere that encourages browsing and impulse buying. It will not make people impulse buyers, mind you. What will make people impulse buyers are those six psychological factors, as you recall. But it will make those consumer segments (who do have the six psychological factors) actually act on their impulse buying tendencies.

Romancing the Consumer tv2010

Pop-Up Retail

In November 2003, Song, a low fare, no-frills yet stylish airline opened a store in SoHo, New York. It was not just one more airline ticketing office, mind you, but rather a chic display and experience space. Consumers could buy a ticket if they needed one, of course, but, more importantly, it was designed to invite lingering, while sampling the airline's menu items, and experiencing many in-flight entertainment options. Open only from Thursdays to Sundays, the store closed down in exactly nine weeks—as had been planned from the outset!

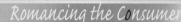

Welcome to a new concept in retailing—Pop-up Stores. The concept, so named by creative folks at an online enterprise called Trendwatching.com, has since been seen for a handful other brands. Song itself opened another eight-week long store in Boston in 2004. Other retailers who have embraced the trend include Target, J.C. Penney, Meow Mix, Comme des Garcons (a German clothing company), Levy's, and even Self, among others.

During Fall 2004, Levi's opened a store in Lower East Side, only for 4 weeks, and sold brightly colored alife Levi's for $165 a pair (limited to 501 pairs). And Self, a health and beauty magazine, opened a spa in NYC—the Self Center. Pay an entry fee of $25, and you could enjoy a relaxation area, get free makeovers, buy some organic food, and receive consultation with doctors on Botox and other facial treatments.

There is one company that operates entirely as pop up retail. Named Vacant, the company sells a range of one-off, hard to find and strictly limited edition products (clothing, shoes, home decors, gizmos) from established brands and some emerging designers. It sells and showcases them in empty space in major cities, opening the stores only for one month (past cities have included New York, Paris, Milan, Berlin, Shanghai, etc.). And, as if to add to the lure, some of the products it showcases are not for sale. And you will know of the new store opening only if you get on their mailing list, and only hours before opening.

Such spontaneity in retailing is bringing a new source of delight to some consumers.

My CB Book

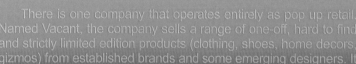

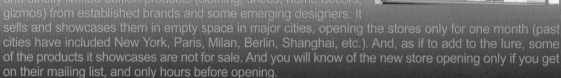

Images: ©iStockphoto.com/Olga ciob (left), ©iStockphoto.com/Marcelo Wain (top right), and ©iStockphoto.com/Andrew Hill (bottom right)

Discussion Question Why would consumers find "Pop Up stores" a source of value and delight? And what kind of consumers?

IV CHOOSER AND SHOPPER

In humankind's history of thousands of years, as recently as only a hundred or so years ago, if someone had said "I am going shopping," it would have meant only one thing: that person was going to the market to buy something. (By some accounts, John Wanamaker's Philadelphia store, opened in 1877, is considered to be the origin of the modern day department store.) In some countries, this has been the case as recently as 20 or so years ago. But in a substantial part of the world and for a majority of consumers today, this phrase has now come to mean a multi-faceted event. **Spending money and buying is a part of it, sometimes, not always. But the event full-blooms as a diversion:** it is to meet friends, to hang out with them; to do some people watching. It is also to discover new objects of desire—dresses, stilettos, colognes, books, music CDs, gadgets, body-pampering potions, and more. And it is, in general, just to soak up the atmosphere—listen to the sounds, take in the aromas, the colors, textures, and shapes of the merchandise and of the surrounding spaces we call malls.

For the moment, though, let's focus only on the act of buying. Or when consumers go shopping with the explicit goal of buying something. Even here, the consumer task, and the experience, is a complex one. Choosing a store itself is a daunting task. From a corner pony keg, to a drug store, to a supermarket, to a hyper-mart, the alternatives present un-ignorable trade-offs between store attributes, such as location, merchandise quality and assortment, the lure of promotions, wayfinding in the store, employee helpfulness and attitude, etc.

Once in the store, one can use shopping lists and stick to planned purchases; alternatively, one can browse, forward-buy to take advantage of promotions, or buy something on the spur of the moment. Each mode presents consumers gratifications, and marketers an opportunity to meet consumer needs. But not understanding the dynamics and inner workings of these modes of shopping can derail the desired outcomes.

As a consumer, you cannot go on buying thousands of products, day in and day out, and not take the time to become self-aware of these processes—the processes we described in this chapter. And as marketers, it goes without saying, you will not be able to tap into consumer strivings for their buying goals unless you understand what for consumers constitutes an efficient and effective shopping task. That is why you should make the models and processes presented in this chapter part of your marketing planning process.

Now to the other-than-buying part of shopping. For a modern day consumer, it would be difficult to imagine what life would be like without this full-bloom form of shopping. Ostensibly, the *raison d'être* of department stores, and now malls, is to enable one-stop shopping; in practice, however, their real worth springs from their ability to serve a larger societal purpose: because of their large physical space and the anonymity infeasible in mom-and-pop stores, **they serve as "public spaces"**—for people to meet, chat, mingle, watch, walk, sit, hang out, and yes, not infrequently, buy something.

Now there is no turning back. These days and going forward, consumers do and will do much of their nonessential buying only in these "fantasy marketspaces." And marketers—retail stores—had better offer these *spaces*. For two gains: successfully sell their wares; and serve a larger societal purpose at the same time, namely, make available enjoyable public spaces. **Shopping**—in its full–bloom version, is a modern day hedonism for many consumers, and a store a social venue; and serving consumer need for these, by designing stores and malls as social and hedonism venues, is indeed a lofty—commercial as well as public service—marketing endeavor.

We began the chapter with a discussion of consumer motives to go shopping. Consumers generally shop to make a purchase. Often, however, other motives also exist. These include recreation, socialization, status seeking, self-gratification (i.e., rewarding oneself by spending some money on oneself), and acquiring market information.

We next discussed three types of purchases: planned, unplanned, and impulse. Consumers do not always buy just what they planned to buy. Rather, unplanned and impulse purchases also occur. Several in-store factors play an important role in a consumer's shopping experience; they also account for whether or not unplanned and impulse purchases would occur. These factors include knowledge of the store, time pressure, special store promotions, store atmospherics, consumer mood, and whether there is a shopping companion. *Impulse buying* was defined as a spur of the moment decision, and we identified the kinds of products that are more likely to be bought as impulse purchases. We introduced browsing as a necessary activity that precedes unplanned and impulse buying, and we identified factors that promote browsing. Marketers can harness these factors to encourage browsing and, consequently, unplanned buying.

For every marketer, it is important to understand how consumers choose stores for shopping.

Consumers choose stores based on location and distance as their first criterion, but this criterion is tempered by a consideration of other factors: quality, assortment, and price. These factors lead consumers to choose a repertoire of stores at which they usually shop. We presented a flow chart model of how consumers choose this repertoire and then distribute their shopping among the stores in it.

We then presented a model of store loyalty, accounting for factors that induce consumers to become store loyal. These included "what" factors— what consumers get in the store— and "how" factors—how efficient and pleasing they find the experience of shopping. One of the "what" factors is store brands. So, next, we considered why consumers buy or do not buy store brands. Our model explains that store brand buying is more predominant among consumers who have large families, come from lower socio-economic strata, and are price sensitive. They buy store brands, motivated by a need to save money, and because they do not see product quality as significantly lower. They also see store brands as a better value for their money. Because store brands can be quite appealing in building store loyalty, store managers should understand these factors that influence consumer purchasing of store brands.

Shopping
Browsing
Store environment
Shopping orientation
Task-oriented shoppers
Leisure-oriented shoppers
Planned purchases

Unplanned purchases
Forward buy
In-store factors
Exploratory shopping
Atmospherics
Consumer impulsivity
Impulsive consumer behavior

Self-selection
Wayfinding
Store image
Store personality
Assortment
One-stop shopping

REVIEW+Rewind

1. Consumers go shopping for more reasons than to buy something. List and briefly explain various consumer motives for shopping.

2. What factors encourage consumers to browse in the store? Which of these factors are under the control of the store manager, and which ones differ from consumer to consumer?

3. What is impulse buying? Are all instances of unplanned buying also instances of impulse buying? Why or why not? What are some products and services that consumers might buy on impulse?

4. What factors determine whether a consumer will select a store or not? Are these factors different for food stores versus non-food stores? How?

5. What factors explain whether a consumer would be store loyal or not? Which of these factors are within the control of the marketer?

6. Why do some consumers buy store brands whereas others buy manufacturers' brands (which are priced higher)? Name all the reasons.

THINK+Apply

1. Why do you shop? Is your purpose purely to buy something, or are there other motives? For each of the shopping motives described in the chapter, list the kind of stores you visit with that particular motive in mind.

2. Think back to when you were choosing, for the first time in a new city (say, your new college town, city

of your first job, the city your parents just moved to, etc.), the storein which to shop for (a) groceries and (b) music CDs. Comment on the extent to which the store choice flow chart described in this chapter captures your own process of choosing a store for these two types of products.

3. Apply the model of store loyalty to yourself and discuss which "what" and "how" factors apply to your own behavior in patronizing stores for the following products: (a) clothing, (b) music, (c) coffee/tea, (d) books, (e) electronic equipment, and (f) haircuts.

4. As a store manager, you just read the model of store loyalty described in this chapter. You are excited because you believe you have found the key to making your customers loyal to your store, and so key to greater profits. Briefly outline your action plan.

5. If you were a store manager, how would you improve the chances that consumers living in your area will choose your store rather than another one across the street?

6. If you were a store manager, what would you do to encourage consumers to browse while they visit your store?

PRACTICE✚Experience

1. Interview five consumers to understand their store selection process for supermarkets. For each consumer, create a flow-chart for his or her store selection process similar to the flow chart shown in the chapter.

2. Interview a few consumers on their recent impulse purchases. For each such purchase, probe the circumstances and thought processes that led to the purchase. Does the three factor model of impulse buying hold for the consumers you interviewed? Comment briefly on why or why not.

3. (Level 2.0) Administer a survey to ten consumers to characterize their impulsive buying behavior. Administer the entire survey that measures all the components of the impulse buying model. Then do some analysis to verify if the model holds—you can verify it, for example, by dividing the consumers into two groups (low and high) on any given consumer trait (e.g., impulsivity) and then seek to understand the differences in their scores on all other concepts in the model.

In the Marketing Manager's Shoes

Put yourself in a marketing manager's shoes. Most concepts in the chapter have some lessons for the marketing manager; i.e., they suggest what to do differently in practice. Indeed, often these applications are implicit in our explanations of the concepts and models in the chapter. Identify at least five specific applications of the chapter's concepts, all of which should be entirely new—different from the examples cited here.

A photo quiz

(Courtesy: Ad agency DDB London for Harvey Nichols Store.)

This Harvey Nichols store ad conveys everything visually: the merchandise, the target consumer, and, most important, their mindset. Its one word theme—SLOTH—is a tongue-in-cheek celebration of indulgence, and an antidot to the present day's rat-race living. This brand communication (along with the merchandise the store offers) creates a unique brand identity (store image) in the consumer mind. Can you pen that image?

A MODEL OF IMPULSIVE CONSUMER BEHAVIOR

Earlier, we discussed consumer impulsivity. But that discussion was brief, leaving our desire for comprehensive knowledge unfulfilled. Now we are going to revisit that topic, this time with the intent of covering it fully. We are going to dig deeper and build a comprehensive model of impulsive consumer behavior.

Your friend Kelly is an impulsive shopper. Your coworker Julia is not. Every time Kelly goes shopping, she can't resist buying something without any prior plans. Your coworker Julia, on the other hand, wears out your patience because she is so very slow to decide if she will buy something. You have always wondered why.

By now you know that to understand a person's behavior, you must always look to motives and personality. Motives are, as we explained in Chapter 2, goals or end states that beckon you to do something. Personality produces a specific behavior as a consistent response to a situation, and by doing so, it automates that behavior (review Chapter 5). Indeed, then, Kelly is an impulsive buyer because she has certain motives and certain personality traits that produce the impulse buying behavior; in contrast, Julia does not have those motives and those personality traits.

What are those motives and personality traits, you must be curious to know? Once again, consumer researchers have come up with an answer. Although different researchers have come up with different answers, we will synthesize that research for you. Basically, two motives are responsible: the need for gratification and the need for excitement. Individuals high in need for gratification desire pleasure and seek instant gratification; individuals high in need for exploration/excitement seek to explore new things, crave new experiences, and desire excitation. We suspect that your friend Kelly is probably very high on both these motives, whereas your coworker Julia is not.

Now, these motives act as goals the consumer desires, and, driven by them, the consumer repeatedly acts to achieve them whenever there is an opportunity. Consequently, the two motives lead to two personality traits: impulsive buying personality (i.e., impulsivity) and shopping enjoyment personality.[27] Gratification leads to impulsivity, and the need for exploration/excitation produces the tendency to enjoy shopping.[28] We might clarify that while some personality traits are genetic, many personality traits are formed by a constant pursuit of motives.

While the need for gratification would inevitably produce impulsivity, the need for excitement requires channeling. By that, we mean different consumers will find their excitement in different activities, and consumers who find it in shopping have most likely "learned" it by repeated practice. Going shopping is perhaps what they choose to do every time they need some excitement.

These two motives and, driven by them, these two personality traits, make a consumer an in-store browser. These, operate, of course, with the time availability, which acts as an "enabling factor"; if you are hard pressed for time, then you do not engage in much in-store browsing. This covers the first part of our model in Figure 13.8.

At this point, it occurs to you that Megan, your sometime shopping pal, engages in a lot of in-store browsing, and yet she is not an impulse buyer. How is that? That is because in-store browsing is necessary but not sufficient for someone to become an impulsive buyer. Some other factors are required. This brings us to Part II of the model—from in-store browsing to impulse buying.

Not Every Browser Does An Impulse Buyer Make

A browsing activity, gives rise to two psychological experiences—things we feel in our head, so to speak. One, we feel a surge of emotion. We feel excited to see something, happy and joyous. It is the experience of "wow, look at that!"—the joy of sighting something that we like very much. Of course, we could be in a store where we browsed and

FIGURE
13.8
A MODEL OF CONSUMER IMPULSE PURCHASE BEHAVIOR

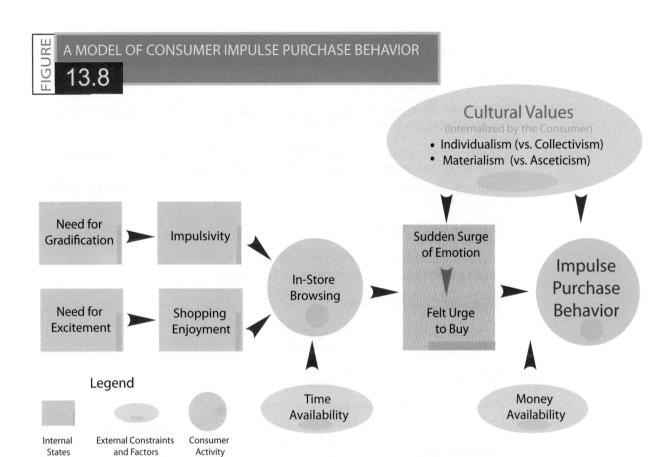

browsed and found nothing of interest; then we would feel the emotion of boredom and disappointment.

When we feel the surge of positive emotion, the sense of joy at seeing something, we also feel a sudden urge to buy. That is, we hear an inner voice say, "Buy it! Buy it!" Incidentally, it is easy to memorize this process by its rhyme: *Surge* of emotion and *urge* to buy. This is your mental experience when you browse (and see something attractive). Now, once you feel the urge to buy, you make an impulse purchase, right? Right, except for one thing. Money. Money is another enabling condition. If you don't have the money, then you have to curb your desire. If you have the money, then you are likely to let your "felt urge to buy" have a field day.

Fortunately, there is one more factor that works to protect you against yourself, so to speak. It keeps you from giving in to your urge-to-buy. It is something deeper than money—something in your culture and in your value system. You see, culture acts as a shaping force for every person's behavior. Two cultural values are particularly relevant to impulse buying: collectivism/individualism and materialism/asceticism. In collectivist cultures, such as the cultures of the East, consumers learn, within all domains of behavior, not to exercise their free will in blind pursuit of self-centered goals. In contrast, in individualist cultures of the West, consumers are expected to exercise their independence and individualism. Therefore, consumers in the individualist cultures are more likely to act uninhibited, and accordingly act on their sudden urge to buy. This role of collectivism/individualism as a cultural value was actually demonstrated in a recent consumer study across five culture/country regions: the U.S., Australia, Malaysia, Singapore, and Hong Kong.[29] Similarly, in cultures where materialism is the prevailing cultural value (compared to cultures that value asceticism), impulsive consumers are more likely to act on their felt urge to buy.

These cultural values can differ not only across countries, but also across consumers—and within the same country as well. That is, within the same country and the same culture, some consumers can be individualists; some, however, can be collectivists. Likewise,

TABLE
13.3

How to Measure Impulse Buying Factors

To prepare the survey remove all headings, and jumble up the questions. Give this survey to consumers immediately after a recent shopping trip.

Please express your opinion by writing a number (1 to 5) in front of each statement, indicating your agreement or disagreement as follows:

Strongly disagree				Strongly Agree
1	2	3	4	5

Impulsive Buying Personality

When I go shopping, I usually tend to buy things I had not intended to buy.
I am a person who often buys on the spur of the moment.

Shopping Enjoying Personality

Shopping is one of my most favorite activities.
Shopping is not a way I like to spend my leisure time.*

Browsing

On this shopping trip, I spent a lot of time "just looking around."
On this shopping trip, I was focused mostly on looking for things I had planned to buy.*

Time Availability

I was not rushed for time on this shopping trip.

Money Availability

On this shopping trip, I was on a tight budget.*
I had enough money on this shopping trip to splurge.

Emotion

On this shopping trip, I felt excited and enthusiastic about some items I saw.
I had enough money on this shopping trip to splurge.

Fell Urge to Buy

On this trip, I felt a sudden urge to buy something I happened to see.
There were a few things I wasn't looking for but when I saw them in the store, I felt like "I must have have it.

Impulse Purchases

On this shopping trip, how many items did you buy today which you had not planned to buy before entering the store.
On this shopping trip, how much money did you spend on items you bought just on the spur of the moment.

* Reverse score.

Source: Adapted in part from Sharon E. Beatty and M. Elizabeth Ferrell, "Impulse Buying: Modeling Its Precursors," *Journal of Retailing*, 74 (2) 1998, 169-191. Copyright New York University. Used with permission.Specifically, adapted items (with some word change) are: the fist item of Impulse Buying Personality, the two items of Shopping Enjoyment Personality, the two items of Browsing, one item of Time Availability, one item of Money Availability, and one item of Felt Urge to Buy.

they can differ on materialism/asceticism. Within any given country, individualist consumers (focused on self-interest and gratification) are more likely to give in to their felt desire to buy, whereas materialist consumers are more likely to act on their felt urge to buy.[30]

Now, you have the complete model (Figure 13.8). If you want to get technical about it, there should really be a lot more feedback and crisscrossing of arrows in Figure 13.8 (to

begin with, asceticism as a personal value is likely to influence and mold the gratification motive). But for our purposes, let us keep things simple the way they are in Figure 13.8. Just remember the six psychological factors that explain a consumer's impulsive buying: two motives (need for gratification and need for excitement); two personality traits (impulsivity and enjoyment of shopping); and two cultural and personal values (materialism/asceticism and individualism/collectivism).

In addition to these psychological factors, there are two material enabling factors, or conversely, constraints: time and money. Remember also, that impulsive buying is, for those who engage in it, a very emotional experience—produced, in fact, by a sudden surge of positive emotion, and resulting in emotional gratification.

Now, you understand why your friend Kelly is an impulse buyer and coworker Julia is not. And, also, why your sometime shopping pal Megan is a browser but not an impulse buyer. Let us do one better: why don't you actually test out Kelly, Julia, and Megan (and other consumers) by measuring how they stack up on all these factors? Give them a survey. Remember, you would need to measure each of the factors in Figure 13.8. For this purpose, we give you the measurement in Table 13.3. Marketers would actually use measurements like these to survey a large number of consumers and then to analyze all the factors for different consumer segments. A study or project like this can give you a first-hand experience in understanding consumer behavior.

I Love Shopping pictures are courtesy of CafePress.com

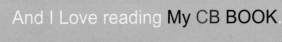

And I Love reading My CB BOOK.

Buying For More Than One:
Family, Organization, and Affinity Group Decision Making

- Family Lifecycle—Empty Nesters and Other Kinds of Families
- Husband-Wife Decision Roles—A Muddling Through Process
- Intergenerational Influence—Learning From Our Cool Moms
- The Buying Center—The VP of "No" and Other Players
- Affinity Marketing—Harnessing Social Capital

Gender role orientation
Wife's employment status
Family life-cycle stage
Time pressure
Purchase importance
Socioeconomic development of the population

It is Christmas time as we write this. Millions of parents and grandparents around the world (especially in parts of the world with a Christian majority) are buying toys for their children and grandchildren.

Let us visit one of those toy stores, located in a suburb of Manchester, England. There in the electronic toys aisle, we can see a child pestering his mom to buy him that radio-controlled car. The 9 inch by 6 inch piece of sheet metal shaped like an Indy 500 car, weighing less than half a pound, costs £60. His mother would rather buy him a Lego set. It costs only £8 British. But money is not the only issue. Mom thinks the Lego set is "good for her child." If you stick around, you will eventually see the hassled Mom at the checkout register, charging £60 on her credit card.

The same story is repeated in the clothing store, at the county fair, and in the supermarket. And, of course, there are other shopper groups— not just mother

and child—each with its own separate "screenplay." Let us visit Marks & Spencer, a large supermarket chain store in Manchester, England. There, in Aisle 3, are the Grants—Winston and Mary Beth, husband and wife. Winston is simply pushing the cart, quietly, disinterestedly, while Mary Beth is having a field day filling it up with whatever she chooses. Then, in Aisle #5 are two adolescents in their early 20s, fussing over which potato chips to buy. The young lady wants the new Frito-Lay's Tostitos Light; the young man is adamant that olestra, the new nonfat ingredient in the chips, is "not good for your body." Why is he so concerned? Is the young lady his wife? A girlfriend? Just a shopping pal? And how are they going to resolve their disagreement?

INTRODUCTION

Standing in a toy store and watching a child pester his mom to buy an expensive toy can be an interesting moment in the life of a student of consumer behavior. Is the child going to throw tantrums? Is the mom going to give in, or would she be able to persuade the child to buy another toy? And what about the Grants—in the supermarket; why is Winston so passive? Doesn't he care about how much it costs to fill that shopping cart? Is his wife Mary Beth the breadwinner in the family? Finally, what about the young couple arguing over olestra? Who is going to prevail? And how are they going to resolve their differences? You could stick around to find out.

But perhaps you should read this chapter first. It tells you about what roles husbands and wives, mothers and daughters, fathers and sons, and boyfriends and girlfriends play in influencing each other's marketplace choices. And about the various methods consumers use in order to resolve their differences over what to buy. In short, about how families and households buy. In a later section of the chapter, we will also study the buying behavior of organizations and of consumer affinity groups.

SECTION 1

BUYING BEHAVIOR OF FAMILIES

Households and Families

What is the difference between a household and a family? If you live with your parents, are you a member of a household? The answer is, "Yes." If you live with your fellow students, are you a member of a family? The answer is, "No." Here is another clue: All family members living together make a household, but not all households are families. Now for the definitions: Families are two or more persons related by blood, marriage, or adoption. Households are one or more persons living in the same dwelling unit. Thus, there can be single person household but a family requires at least two persons.

As Figure 14.1 shows, there are two types of households: family and nonfamily. Family households can further be classified into four types: (1) married couples, (2) married couples with children, (3) single parents, and (4) extended families. This last category includes grandchildren, uncles and aunts, brothers and sisters, and even cousins. Note that "extended" does not necessarily imply a larger family--two brothers living together become an extended family, as is a family of, say 20, comprising three generations related by blood or marriage. Also, family members who live apart are still a family; yet they are not a "family household."

Non-family households are of two types: (1) single person, and (2) roommates or housemates. Note that all students living in a dormitory are not a household since they do not make their purchasing decisions as a unit. Roommates and housemates, likewise, too may not make all of their purchasing decisions as a unit (e.g., clothing), but at least they make some decisions as a unit, or with consideration of the needs of all members of the unit (e.g., cleaning products or even appliances for the household as a whole).

FIGURE 14.1

TYPES of HOUSEHOLDS

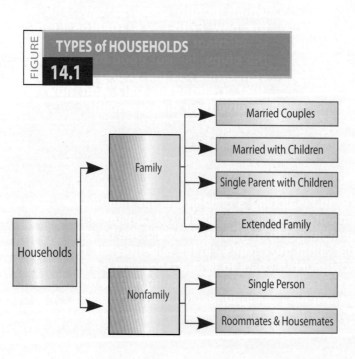

According to the U.S. Census 2000, there are now 105.5 million households; of these, 71.8 million (68 %) are family households and 33.7 million (32%) are non-family households. In the last decade, since 1990, non-family households grew faster than family households (23% versus 11% growth). Among the family households, 54.5 million are married coupled households. Among the non-family households, unmarried couple households were 5.47 million (with 4.88 million of them being opposite sex partners, and 594,391 being same sex partners). Thus, 57% of all households are couples households (married and unmarried). Among the married couples households, 46% had at least one son or daughter living with them.[1]

FAMILY LIFE CYCLE

Empty Nesters and Other Kinds of Families

If you look around your neighborhood, or the neighborhood of your parent's home, you would find that the composition of your neighbors' families is different. Your own family may consist of your parents (in their 40's) and a younger brother who is in high school. Your neighbor on the left is a young couple, in their late 20's, just married; on the right side is an elderly couple, just retired; in the house across the street is a 30-something couple with three children ages 2, 4, and 7. These various families are at different stages of family formation. How a person advances from one stage of family formation to another is called family life cycle.

Historically, marketing researchers have broken this cycle into five stages: bachelor stage, couple stage, full nest stage, empty nest stage, and survivor stage. Marketing researchers have further divided full nesters into three substages: I, II, and III. Full Nest I are families with young children under the age of six, full nest II are families with children between the ages of six and 18, and full nest III are families with grown-up children still staying at home. Similarly, empty nesters are further divided into two substages: I and II. Empty Nest I refers to an early period when children have just left home, the parent is still fully employed, and, for many, children are out of college, thus eliminating a big drain on money; empty nest II refers to the later years (usually several years after children have left home) when the parent is retired and consequently has a much reduced income.

With aging, a person advances through these stages and lives as a different type of family—starting with being a single, to becoming a young married couple without children, moving on to becoming a middle-aged married person with children, to older married couple with children who have left home, and finally to becoming an older widower. Historically, a person typically advanced through these stages in this sequence. These days, of course, a person can live his or her entire life as an unmarried person, can become a parent without being married, can divorce at any age and thus become single again, and so on. To capture these trends, marketers recognize two types of family life cycles: Traditional and Modern. The Traditional Family Life Cycle (TFLC) refers to the five-stage model where a person advances, always, in a standard sequence and unidirectionally. In the Modern Family Life Cycle (MFLC), a person can move back and forth from one stage to the other, and these movements can occur in a number of patterns, e.g., sometimes jumping two sequential stages.[2] These two family life cycle patterns are shown in Figure 14.2.

The Modern Life Cycle is Not Universal

Don't abandon the traditional life cycle yet. In marketing, it is still useful, for two reasons. First, in many countries around the world, especially in the Eastern cultures, it is still the prominent form. Second, even for more westernized cultures, the TFLC serves as a basic platform on which the diverse departures of the MFLC can be overlaid. Of course, neither TFLC nor MFLC, nor in fact any other scheme, can account for all the diverse paths different families may go through. Yet the scheme is useful for marketers to identify the changing needs of a family.

FIGURE
14.2

A MODEL OF FAMILY LIFECYCLE

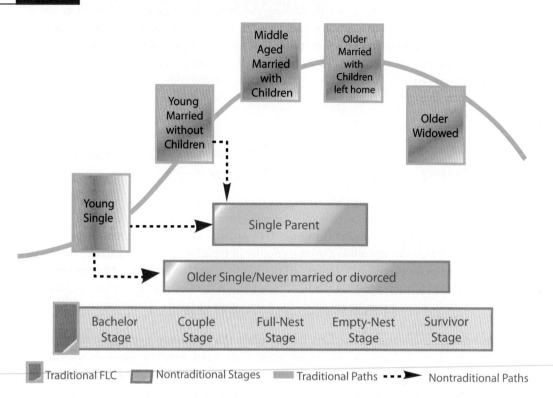

Middle Aged Married with Children

Older Married with Children left home

Young Married without Children

Older Widowed

Young Single

Single Parent

Older Single/Never married or divorced

| Bachelor Stage | Couple Stage | Full-Nest Stage | Empty-Nest Stage | Survivor Stage |

Traditional FLC   Nontraditional Stages   Traditional Paths   ◄ ►   Nontraditional Paths

Married with Children
Now, Fewer of Them

In the U.S., "married with children" is on the decline—and we are not just talking about the once popular TV show in America. The shape of the American household at large has been changing. In 1960, nearly half of the households were married couples with at least one child under the age of 18. In the Census 2000, less than one in four (23.5%) households fit this mold. That means, as a proportion of all the households, in forty years since 1960, America's "married with children" households have been reduced to half!

This trend of decline peaked during the 1970s. Why? Because baby boomers delayed getting married and/or having children. Also because older singles and empty nesters lived longer so the proportion of married couples with children became a smaller number. Now that declining trend is bottoming out. Why? For two reasons: first, because the baby boomers are no longer of the "postpone marriage and delay having a child" age. Second, the Asian and Hispanic immigrant families are on the rise and they are young and they value the traditional family pattern.[3]

MARKETING IMPLICATIONS
Is Your Brand Tuned To Family Life Cycle Changes?

Suppose you want to market your product, say, cars, to families. What kind of family would you show in your advertising? And would you make compact two person cars or large family sedans? Try selling cars, or any other product of household use, without understanding family life cycle, and the chances are your marketing efforts would prove unproductive. Indeed, it would pay to recognize the following FLC based consumer segments.

Young Married Couples Their principal "life project" is building a starter home. Thus, young married couples are a prime target market for all sorts of products needed for

Obos, a housing company
in Norway targets consumers
at differnt FLC stages.
Read text of Ads in Chapter 6.
(Photos printed by permission)

setting up a home – furniture, furnishings, small appliances, kitchen and cleaning tools and supplies. As they are generally starting out on their careers, they are likely to not have saved a lot of money. Therefore, when buying durable goods, they would be seeking the "bottom of the line," least expensive alternatives.

Full Nesters These are families with children living at home. In the early years (i.e., younger families with young children), this group is a prime target for child products (e.g., children's furniture, children's clothing, toys, etc.). They are usually strapped for time and seek time-saving products and services such as pick up and delivery of clothes for dry cleaning, easy-to-cook meal solutions, etc.

As full nesters' children grow older, consumption gets structured around the needs of adolescent children. Many of these families move up from the starter home to a larger home with individual rooms for every member of the family. Once again, they become target market for furniture, furnishings, and appliances for the new house. Families that can afford buy additional TVs and entertainment centers for adult children, additional cars, computers, etc. Dining out at fast food and affordable restaurants, visits to amusement parks, family outing to ballgames, and vacations to destinations like Disneyland become some of the frequently purchased products/services. Later, with children in college years, many full nesters are strapped for resources; as such, these families often buy bulk-sized packages of everyday household products, shop at warehouse stores, and take advantage of special sales and coupons.

Empty Nesters With children gone to live on their own, these consumers experience a sudden new-found resource: time. Consequently, they seek more leisure activities—vacations, theater, eating out, or whatever suits their tastes. By now the children are out of college and the mortgage has been paid off,; therefore, older empty nesters also become financially more secure. Many buy recreational vehicles (RVs) to travel in, and many sell off their big suburban houses and move into urban condos.

Single Parents An important departure from the traditional family life cycle comes in the form of single parents, shouldering the burden of child rearing without a spouse to share and receive support from. By the 2000 Census count, there were a total of 1.4 million single fathers and 6.8 million single mothers in the USA. Perhaps the most significant factor in this group's consumer behavior is time pressure. A single parent is always time starved and hassled. What this segment looks for most are time-saving product alternatives and services.

Christian and Martina Haag, in Hamburg, Germany—*Empty Nesters* "Free" again!

Increasingly for this segment, home-based shopping and buying is useful. For this reason, Internet shopping (including home delivery of groceries ordered on the Internet) would appeal to this segment

Singles The other important departure from the traditional family life cycle comes in the form of singles—men and women staying single well into their mature years, or divorced and not yet remarried. According to the U.S. Census 2000, there were 9.9 million single men and 14.8 million single women.

There are two areas of consumption that are markedly different for singles. One, all of their visible public consumption has to look "cool" to a potential date. Thus, clothes, jewelry, car—whatever they are buying that would be seen in public—has to impress the opposite sex (or a potential date). Second, they end up eating out a lot, rather than fix a meal at home, and when they do go grocery shopping, the foremost need is for "single-serving" size. Single person households are expected to increase by 15% by year 2010, and therefore food marketers would do well to address this "single-serving" size need of this segment of the population.[4]

THE FAMILY DECISION MAKING PROCESS

If you live with your family, invariably you buy some things as an individual and other things as a member of the family. You probably experience a different decision process when you buy something as a family member versus when you buy something as an individual. The steps remain the same as those described for individual-decision-making, namely, 1)problem recognition 2)information search 3) alternative evaluation 4) choice 5) post purchase experience. However, each step unfolds with a somewhat more dynamic and complex process. This is becasue various members of your family have different tastes and preferences; moreover, not all members have the same stakes in the decision.

If you think back to a recent purchase decision made in your family, you might recall that various members undertook various activities, en route to the final decision. Suppose that it was a family PC (personal computer) your family was considering buying. Tzvesti, your sixth-grader kid sister, first started asking for it—she was all excited about the computer they use at her school, with color graphics and all. She raved about how they could search an encyclopedia on the computer, and she wanted one at home. Your parents appreciated the educational value of a PC and decided to buy one. The task of finding out what kind of computer would be best for the family fell on your shoulders. You visited some local dealers in the college town that you live in, gathered the necessary information, and mailed it home to your parents.

Armed with that information, your mom and the junior visited some stores in your hometown. They looked at some models. Mom found an IBM clone to be a good value. Your kid sister liked a Hewlett-Packard model better. Not able to agree, they sought intervention from Dad (who had kept out of the loop so far due to his heavy travel schedule). Dad recalled reading an article in a recent issue of FamilyPC; he dug out that article and reread it. Based on his reading, he thought that Hewlett-Packard Pavilion was indeed a good buy, but that yet another model, Dell Dimension, would be even better—from the standpoint both of the graphics capability and value for the money. Mom suggested that they call you to see what you thought about this new model Dad had identified. You are in college,

FIGURE 14.3 STEPS IN FAMILY DECISION MAKING

- Post-purchase Experience
- Intrafamily Negotiation and Decision
- Alternative Evaluation
- Information Search and Sharing
- Proposal Apppproval
- Problem Recognition: Purchase Proposal

familiar with the latest in computers, and your parents value your opinion. Expect a call from them this weekend!

But right now, you are studying this book on consumer behavior, and reading about how families make decisions. You cannot help but see a pattern in the present decision your family is making and the many others that you and your family have made in the past. This pattern consists of some steps your family goes through in making major purchase decisions, and as you jot these down on your notepad, you realize how similar they look to the list of steps shown in Figure 14.3.[5]

Someone Proposes, and That Sets the Ball Rolling

The decision process begins when some member of the family recognizes a need. This much is similar to the first step in the "individual decision making" we studied in a previous chapter. What is different is that now the need recognizing member must make the proposal to other members of the family. This of course is not a formal or written proposal. Rather, it is a suggestion or request to consider a purchase. It does entail, however, that the person suggesting the purchase justify the need. In individual decision-making there is no one to justify one's need to. One may rationalize, but one is not called upon to justify to others.

Next, the proposal approval process begins. Typically, proposals for products that will serve some need of all members are readily accepted. Proposals for needs specific to the proposing member alone call for a more thorough justification. Thus if Mom suggests replacing the washer, it is a shared need. If Junior wants a videogame, or if Dad wants a treadmill, that would require more persuasion. When family members generally agree about the need, the proposal is deemed approved. Next, the tasks of information search are assigned to different members, depending on each member's area of familiarity. Alternative evaluation can be a prolonged process and different members may disagree because they differ on their evaluation criteria. The conflict ensues, and resolving it may require certain negotiations.

Following the decision and acquisition, post-purchase experience is likely to be explicit, and this is for two reasons: One, if the product is consumed jointly, members tend to express their feelings (and having to express your feelings makes you more explicit); or, two even when the product is used more by a specific member (rather than shared), other members who had participated in the decision-making may want to know how their selection was working out. The important issues in the above process are joint decisions (say, between spouses) and conflict resolution. We discuss these topics next.

A lot of consumption happens together in families
(Photo courtesy: Ian Shipley, second from right)

Throughout this process, different family members may influence the decision to varying degrees. Generally, one spouse initiates the purchase proposal, but the process becomes more of a joint process as the decision moves to advanced stages (information gathering and alternative evaluation). Of particular interest to marketers is the influence of spouses and children in this process.[6]

HUSBAND-WIFE DECISION ROLES
A Muddling Through Process

Suppose you are a salesperson in an appliance store, and a couple walks in. Who would you direct your sales pitch at? That depends on what assumptions you make about how spouses make joint decisions. Who plays an active role, and who influences

FIGURE

14.4

PATTERNS OF JOINT DECISION MAKING

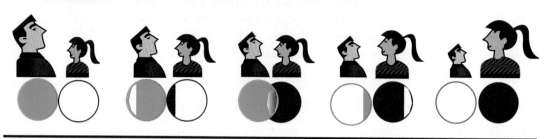

| Autonomous decision by husband | Husband dominated decision | Syncartic decision | Wife dominated decision | Autonomous decision by wife |

the decision more? To address this question, consumer researchers have identified five patterns of relative influence. These are: (1) autonomous decision by the husband only; (2) husband-dominated decision; (3) syncratic decisions (equal role by both); (4) wife-dominated decision, and (5) autonomous decision by the wife.

Autonomous decisions are decisions made independently by the decision maker. **Syncratic decisions** are decisions in which all play an equal role in making the decision (see Figure 14.4).

Which of these patterns is followed will differ from one family to another, and also across product categories. Yet, it is reasonable to expect some common prevalent patterns in any given society. In an early study of 200 U.S families, for the purchase of three products (washing machines, carpeting, television), the wife's influence was stronger for washers and carpeting, while the husband's influence was greater for televisions. The study was based on asking each spouse separately who had influenced the decision more. An interesting fact was that while mostly the spouses agreed on whose influence was more, for appliances, husbands tended to view themselves as the predominant or even solo decision makers, while wives reported more joint decision making.

JOINT DECISIONS: A GAME OF COMPROMISE AND MAKE BELIEVE — EXHIBIT 14.1

Look What CB Researchers Found

A study of 45 couples, all recent home buyers, revealed the following:
- Each person has some idea of what features the product alternative "must have." The spouses discuss these features and then agree on a common set of "must have" features.
- Spouses grant each other the right to the "optional features" provided that these features do not interfere with the utility of the product or do not raise costs.
- Spouses also grant each other certain role specialization with respect to the feature on which they consider the other person an expert. Thus, both spouses might agree that the husband is an expert on insulation, and the wife an expert on interior design.
- On these role-specialized features, spouses acknowledge the partner's relative influence. On other features, each believes he or she influenced the decision more than did the other partner.
- Spouses agree more with each other on salient objective dimensions (e.g., number of bedrooms, presence of a swimming pool, and so on) than on subjective dimensions (the interior design, the amount of insulation, and so on).
- When spouses agree on features that the product must have, this agreement on "must have" features leads them to perceive that their decision plans are similar (even when they disagree on other optional features). Contrarily, when there is disagreement on these "must have" features, spouses perceive conflict.
- Individual spouses are more satisfied with some features of the product purchased than with others, and the features with which the spouses are satisfied differ between the spouses. Each spouse feels greater satisfaction with the feature whose inclusion was influenced more by him or her.

Source: Adapted from C. Whan Park, "Joint Decisions in Home Purchasing: A Muddling-Through Process," *Journal of Consumer Research* 9 (September 1982), pp. 151-62. © *Journal of Consumer Research*. Published by The University of Chicago Press. (Used with permission.)

Joint decisions are those in which more than one decision participant makes the decision. When couples report they made joint decisions for a specific purchase, it is not easy to visualize exactly how each member participated to make it a joint decision. If you ask the couple, each spouse is likely to say he or she influenced the decision more than did the other partner!

Consumer researchers consider such answers too simplistic and believe that the interpersonal dynamics of joint decision-making is more complex. In fact, noted consumer researcher C. W. Park has termed joint decisions as a "muddling through" process. His study of 45 couples, all recent buyers of a home, revealed very interesting patterns of interpersonal dynamics among the spouses.[7] Park's findings, summarized in Exhibit 14.1, reveal that joint decision-making is often a process of compromise as well as make-believe as to one's own role in the decision.

Research on this topic shows that spousal roles and participation in decision making varies across different product or service categories. And it also varies at different stages of the decision making process. A study by marketing professors Marla R. Stafford, Gopal. K. Ganesh, and Barbara C. Garland showed that husbands played a greater role in decision making for insurance purchase, wives a much greater role in decisions about their child's school choice, and, as would be expected, vacation decisions were dominated by joint decision-making. See Table 14.1.

TABLE 14.1 Relative Roles of Spouses for Three Purchase Categories

Decision Stage		Insurance	Child's school	Vacation
Purchase Proposal	H	42	4	25
	W	20	35	22
	H + W	34	50	30
Choice	H	42	3	23
	W	15	21	27
	H + W	42	57	48
Made the Actual Purchase	H	39	2	24
	W	17	50	29
	H + W	44	41	46

Note: Percentages do not add up to 100 due to omission of roles played by other family members.
Source: Adapted from M.R. Stafford, G.K. Ganesh, and B.C. Garland, "Marital Influence in the Decision-Making Process for Services," *Journal of Services Marketing*, 10, no. 1, (1996), p.15. (Used with permission.)

FACTORS INFLUENCING INTERSPOUSAL INFLUENCE

If you observe spouses making decisions, you will notice that who influences whom varies from couple to couple. Why? Because there are several factors that influence the relative influence itself. Based on a survey of consumer research, we have identified seven such factors for you. These are: gender role orientation and role specialization, the wife's employment status, family life cycle stages, time pressure, purchase importance, consumer involvement, and socioeconomic development level of the population group (see Figure 14.5).

GENDER ROLE ORIENTATION

Gender roles orientation refers to our concepts of the specific behaviors expected of a person by virtue of that person's gender. For example, in a family, the wife may be expected to take care of food preparation and husband, of cleaning and laundry. These gender role orientations can be placed on a continuum of traditional-modern. In the traditional orientation, found in

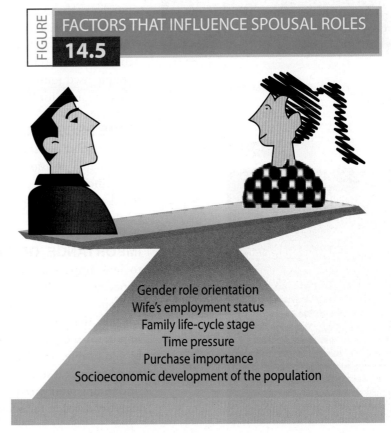

FIGURE 14.5 FACTORS THAT INFLUENCE SPOUSAL ROLES

Gender role orientation
Wife's employment status
Family life-cycle stage
Time pressure
Purchase importance
Socioeconomic development of the population

preindustrialized societies and underdeveloped and developing countries, generally wife is expected to be the homemaker and husband the breadwinner. In the modern orientation, there is more sharing of responsibilities between the two sexes.8 Therefore, modern gender role families will in general exhibit more joint decision-making, and some wife-dominated or autonomous decisions made by the wife. In contrast, in traditional role families, more decisions will be husband-dominated.

In general, even in traditional families, purchase decisions are domain-specific. In many Asian, Middle Eastern, or other third-world countries, for example, buying cooking-related raw materials and kitchen supplies is the domain of women; likewise, certain aspects of engagement and marriage ceremonies are in women's domain. Accordingly, women decide what products need to be bought and in what quantities, although men go to the market to do the actual buying. Since many staple products do not carry brand names, brand decisions are not always pertinent in these third-world countries. One of the most fascinating aspects of family decision making is the variation in gender role orientation you find across diverse countries and cultures, and how this gender role variation influences interspousal decision sharing in different population groups.

WIFE'S EMPLOYMENT STATUS The wife's employment status significantly influences gender-role orientation. In families where a wife is employed outside of the home, there is greater acceptance of her role in important family decisions. Not only does she make many decisions autonomously, but even in decisions historically the prerogative of the husband alone, the wife is often consulted. This occurs partly because the wife acquires greater recognition as a contributor to family finances. In addition, the greater exposure to the world outside of the home makes the wife more knowledgeable about a variety of products and services.

STAGE IN FAMILY LIFE CYCLE Family life cycle has also been found to influence decision making in the families. Recently married couples tend to make more joint decisions; as the marriage ages, the chores become allocated along with the purchases that accompany those chores (e.g., grocery supplies for cooking, car wax for car washing, and so on) and get to be decided autonomously. However, the age of the marriage would tend not to affect important purchases. For important purchases, if the couple used joint decision making at the early stage of marriage, they would most likely continue to do so during the later years of marriage as well.

TIME PRESSURE Families with high time pressure tend to rely less on joint decision making, since autonomous or one-member dominated decision processes are generally perceived to be more time-efficient. However, such decisions may sacrifice effectiveness; the decision may not be optimal. Furthermore, the spouse with greater time pressure is likely to delegate the buying decisions to the spouse less busy.

IMPORTANCE OF PURCHASE Purchase importance refers to how important the family perceives the product to be. The importance of the purchase may stem from the financial outlay or from the centrality of the product to the individual—that is, whether the product is an important part of one's life. The more important the purchase, the more the decision making is going to be a joint one. This is for two reasons: One reason is that multiple members have a stake in a large expense (as it would affect everyone by draining family resources). Second, the members will have to live with the decision for a long time.

CONSUMER INVOLVEMENT A related factor is that purchase importance may be different for different members of the family. That is, some members may be more involved (or interested) in a specific purchase. For example, the spouse who enjoys cooking may be more involved in kitchen tools, whereas the spouse who enjoys "fixing" things, may be more involved in buying home repair tools.

SOCIOECONOMIC DEVELOPMENT OF THE POPULATION Gender role orientations and role specializations vary from one culture and country to another. Specifically, the culture of a country is related to the stage of socioeconomic development of the population. Underdeveloped countries have a more traditional gender role orientation than do more developed countries. With development and the resulting modernization, urbanization, and concomitant increasing employment of women outside of the home, women's influence on marketplace decision-making increases.

At least three factors account for the increasing role of women in modernizing societies: First, with modernization and urbanization, families become increasingly nuclear, as young adults take up jobs in urban areas, leaving their parents and grandparents behind in their rural homes. Nuclear family forms necessitate more sharing of all household responsibilities, including procurement of goods. Second, in advanced countries, with increasing dependence by the husband on the wife's supplemental income, husbands feel obligated to consult with their working spouses on at least the major purchases. Finally, smaller family units generate a greater egalitarianism among the sexes, which leads to more participatory decision-making.

CONFLICT IN FAMILY DECISIONS

The family decision making process is often marked by conflicts among various family members. The conflicts arise due to differences in the goals of the various members. In a family vacation decision, for example, parents want to visit relatives, but the child wants to visit an amusement park. Or the husband wants a stylish, youthful car but the wife wants a large, safe car, for example. Or the other way around. Conflicts can also arise when perceptions of alternatives differ; for example, both parents and children agree it should be a fun vacation, not a family reunion; but children think that Disney World would be more fun and parents think that New York would be more fun. And, the husband thinks a convertible is more youthful and stylish while the wife thinks an SUV is more in style.[9]

Conflict Resolution

How do you and your families resolve such conflicts? Scholars have suggested four strategies: problem solving, persuasion, bargaining, and politicking (see Figure 14.6). Problem solving entails members trying to gather more information, or adding new alternatives. When motives/goals are congruent and only perceptions differ, obtaining and sharing information (i.e., problem solving) often suffices to resolve conflicts. Persuasion requires educating about the goal hierarchy; for instance, the wife might argue how a safe and large car is in the best interest of the whole family since the car is needed to transport children. Bargaining entails trading favors (the husband gets to buy a house with a den and the finished basement provided the car he buys is the one his wife prefers). When goals as well as evaluations (i.e., perceptions) are so divergent that even bargaining is infeasible, try politicking. Here, members form coalitions and subgroups within the family and by so doing simply impose their will on the minority

FIGURE 14.6 CONFLICT RESOLUTION STRATEGIES

VALUES/GOALS

	CONVERGENT	DIVERGENT
EVALUATIONS DIVERGENT	Problem Solving	Politicking/ Bargaining
CONVERGENT	No Conflict	Persuasion

EXHIBIT 14.2
HOW SPOUSES INFLUENCE EACH OTHER'S DECISIONS

Look What CB Researchers Found

In one study of married spouses' influence strategies, consumer researcher Margaret C. Nelson identified the following repertoire of influence strategies spouses used.

1. Punishments, threats, authority, and negative emotions
   - Refuse to do chores.
   - Threatens punishment.
   - Becomes angry.
   - Questions spouse's right to disagree.
2. Positive emotion and subtle manipulation
   - Puts the spouse in a receptive mood.
   - Appeals to spouse's love and affection.
   - Promises to do something nice in return.
   - Acknowledges that it would be a favor.
3. Withdrawal and egocentrism
   - Denies affection, acting cold.
   - Clams up.
   - Looks hurt, sulks.
4. Persuasion and reason
   - Uses logic.
   - Persistence in arguing and requesting compliance.
5. Miscellaneous others
   - Simply gave in.
   - I argued that I knew more.
   - Compromise; meet in the middle.
   - Plead or beg.
   - Came up with a new solution acceptable to both.

Source: Adapted from Margaret C. Nelson, "The Resolution of Conflict in Joint Purchase Decisions by Husbands and Wives: A Review and Empirical Test," in Advances in Consumer Research, Michael J Houston, ed., 15 (1988), pp. 436 -41. Reprinted with permission of the Association for Consumer Research

coalition.[10] Marketers can help household members resolve a conflict by aiding the problem-solving mode--they can provide additional information about alternatives. Such interventions are most feasible in interpersonal selling situations such as at the car dealership or with a real estate agent.

The Art of Persuasion Between the Spouses.

No matter how much harmony exists between spouses on matters of life in general, when it comes to marketplace decisions, some differences of opinions do arise. How do spouses resolve these disagreements? In fascinating ways, one study tells us. We have summarized the findings of this study in Exhibit 14.2. Read on and see if you know any couples who use any of these mutual persuasion "charms."

CHILDREN'S INFLUENCE IN FAMILY DECISION MAKING

Children—they are everywhere. And when they are not plotting pranks, they are cute. For marketers, they are also a goldmine. From fast food, to designer clothes, to video games and toys, they keep retailers' cash register's ringing. To the tune of some $30 billion a year, in U.S.A. alone. And this is only for children 12 years and under, and that too, counting only their direct purchases. They also influence the market spending by mom and dad— to the tune of over $300 billion.[11] And this influence increases with age. In one study it was found that 21 percent of mothers of five to seven-year-olds yielded to their children's requests, while 57 percent of mothers of 11 to 12-year-olds yielded to children's requests.[12] Today, the influence of children, especially the teen children, is likely to be even greater.

Children influence household buying in three ways. First, by having individualistic preferences for products paid for and bought by parents (e.g., toys). Second, children in their teen years begin to have their own money and become their own buyers of items of self-use, opening up a very valuable market to corporations selling a broad range of products and services. Third, they influence their parents' choice of products that are meant for shared consumption (e.g., family vacation or home entertainment system).[13] Exhibit 14.3 describes summary findings of a research study on children's influence.

George P. Moschis, a marketing professor at Georgia State University, is one of the leading scholars who has studied the role children play in family decision making. One of his insights is that children's influence in the family decisions depends on whether the family has a "social" or a "concept" orientation. Social-orientation families are the ones more concerned with maintaining discipline among children, whereas concept-oriented families are those that are concerned with the growth of independent thinking and individuality in children. Children from families with social orientation are less likely to make independent decisions and less likely to be involved in family decisions. Those with concept orientation are likely to have greater product knowledge, and their parents are more likely to involve them in family decision-making.[14]

Another way of classifying families is by how authority is exercised in the family. On this basis, worldwide, families can be classified into four types:[15]

1. Authoritarian families The head of the household (mother in matriarchal and

Consumer researchers Ellen Foxman, Patria Tanshuhaj, and Karin Ekstrom studied the role of adolescent children and found the following:

> Children (adolescents) had more influence for products for their own use.
> The greater the teenager's financial resources, the greater the influence he or she exercised.
> The greater the perceived knowledge, the greater the perceived influence.
> The greater the importance to the teenager of the product category, the higher the teenager influence.
> Teenager influence was higher in dual income families.
> Teenagers exercised more influence at the initiation stage than at the search and decision stage.

Mothers attributed less influence to their children than did children themselves. This discrepancy was lesser between mothers and their daughters than between mothers and their sons.

In an extension of this research, consumer researchers Sharon E. Beatty and Salil Talpade collected new data and analyzed purchases of durables (TV, stereo, phone, and furniture) made for family use versus made primarily for the use by the teenager. Some of their findings were as follows:

> Financial resources of teenagers influenced only those durable purchases that were for the teenager's own use (as opposed to family use) and only in the purchase initiation stage, not in the search and decision stages.

> Children's product knowledge was influential only in the initiation of purchase consideration and only for products intended for teenager use. For family purchases, teenager influence was significantly enhanced with product knowledge but only in the search/decision stage and only for stereos (not for the other products investigated).

> Importance of purchase to teenagers affected their influence for both for-family and for-teenager purchases, and in both initiation and search/decision stages.

> When teenagers were the major users of for-family durables, they exercised more influence (than if they were not going to be the major user) in both initiation and search/decision stages.

> Children had greater influence in dual-income families than in single-income families; however, this influence was significant only for purchases made for shared family consumption. For purchases for their own use, children had influence alike in both single and dual-income families.

Source: Adapted from Ellen R. Foxman, Patria S. Tanshuhaj, and Karin M. Ekstrom, "Family Members' Perceptions of Adolescents' Influence in Family Decision Making," *Journal of Consumer Research* 15 (March, 1989) pp. 482 -91; and "Adolescents' Influence in Family Purchase Decisions: A Socialization Perspective," *Journal of Business Research* 18 (March 1989), pp. 159 -72; Sharon E Beatty and Salil Talpade, "Adolescent Influence in Family Decision Making: A Replication with Extension," *Journal of Consumer Research*, 1994, vol. 21, #2, pages 332-41; © *Journal of Consumer Research*. Published by The University of Chicago Press. (Used with permission.) also see George E. Belch, M. A. Belch, and G. Ceresino, "Parental and Teenage Child Influences in Family Decision Making," *Journal of Business Research* 13 (1985), pp. 163 -76.

father in patriarchal societies) exercises strict authority on children, and children learn to obey their elders in all matters. Such families are found most in Asian societies. Although a culture of obedience to elders is considered to be a virtue, especially in Asian cultures, it does curb individuality among children and consequently their influence on family buying decisions.

2. Neglectful families Parents are distant from their children, who are neglected in these families because the parent(s) place more priority on their individual affairs. Single-parent families risk this behavior most, some due to time pressure, others due to undisciplined lifestyle of the single parent, which engenders being irresponsible toward one's children. Of course, not all single parents neglect their children.

3. Democratic families Every member is given equal voice. Most family matters are discussed among family members, especially those who would be affected by the decisions. Self-expression, autonomy, and mature behavior are encouraged among children. While opinions are sought from all affected members, the decision could be a joint one, or it could be exercised (or arbitrated) by the family head(s).

4. Permissive families Children are given relative independence in conducting their own affairs, especially in their adolescent years. Unlike parents in the neglectful families, however, permissive parents closely watch children's interests and exercise of freedom.

The relative prevalence of these types differs across different countries, and their proportions would change in the same country over time. Also, families could have partial tendencies of more than one type.

Children's influence would obviously differ across these four types. It would be lowest among authoritarian families. In neglectful families, children would exercise no influence on parents' purchases. For products needed for their own use, however, they are likely to exercise relative autonomy, provided they have an independent source of income. If not, their resources would be rather limited, since the neglectful parent is unlikely to support most of their requests. In democratic families, children would share influence with other members. Finally, in permissive families, children would exercise relative autonomy for products for which they are the principal or sole user.

Democratic Justice

A related concept is Democratic justice. **Democratic justice** refers to a family norm in which each family member is given a voice in family decisions. Often parents accept the norm that family members should be allowed to develop their individual identities and be treated as individual citizens of the household, with an equal voice in family matters. In the purchase of products for shared use (e.g., car, furniture, and so on), many families may consider it legitimate to give youngsters a voice. For products consumed by children exclusively (e.g., their own clothes or food) or primarily (the CD player and sound system), children are allowed to exercise their preference simply because parents grant children their democratic right to individuality.

Democratic justice can sometimes cause tensions in a family. When the offsprings' preferences become incongruent with their parents' values (e.g., getting a punk style haircut), the value incongruence can become a source of conflict. As long as the offsprings are living under the same roof, parents may resent and are likely to attempt to change their sons' and daughters' counter-value purchases.

Consumer Socialization of Children

Consider these episodes:

- A single parent is clipping coupons on a Sunday afternoon. His 10-year-old daughter is nearby, helping her dad organize them—by product categories and by date of expiration. She makes a mental note: next time she sees a coupon in the newspaper, she would clip it and place it in these sorted envelopes.
- A mother is window shopping in a department store with her eight-year-old son. Suddenly, she begins to examine gym bags. She looks at one, puts it aside noticing its high price, loudly speaking her thought (as people generally do when they are with a "shopping pal"). The son points to another. "No, I am looking for one in black only," she says. Then she looks at another. The son "scoops out" yet another black bag. The mother looks at it briefly and rejects it, saying, "It doesn't have the pocket." "It does," says the son, pointing at the zippered pocket. "No, I mean a meshed pocket (i.e., the one made of net fabric)—like this other one does," says the mother. Then the dialogue proceeds as follows:
  Son: Why is it made of a net?
  Mother: To put your wet swimming suit in it.
  Son: You can put it in the other kinds of pockets too.
  Mother: Then it won't dry off.
  Son: Why can't we dry it off at home?
  Mother: We can. But if it is left in the bag for long, the bag will smell musty.
  Son: It will?
  Mother: Yes.

How do children learn to become consumers? By this we do not mean merely how they learn to consume. Rather, we mean how they learn to shop, to value things, and to save money. How do they, in other words, become socialized to engage in marketplace exchanges? Socialized they do become, to an amazing degree. In one study, children 7 to 12 years old were found to possess strong brand preferences. And children who cannot yet read have been found to be able to recognize brand symbols, such as McDonald's arches and the Tony the Tiger mascot for Kellogg's Frosted Flakes.[16] Some observers believe that school and kindergarten children have had more experience with the marketplace than with arithmetic or writing!

Consumer socialization refers to the "acquisition of knowledge, preferences, and skills to function in the marketplace."[17] That is, consumer socialization occurs when one or more of the following are learned or acquired by children:

- Learn about various products and their role in solving their personal needs and problems.
- Knowledge about the marketplace (e.g., what is available where) and about various product features;
- Skills in judging the utility of various product features;
- Preferences among alternative brands and products;
- Skills in making "smart decisions ," such as making price and product comparisons, discounting advertising and salesperson claims, and evaluating trade-offs across options (including the option "to buy or not to buy").

Socialization can wait for a while. At this young age, children experience consumption as play and spontaneity.

That is, children learn about desirable product features, alternative products, brands, stores, and other market options, and make this information a part of their stock of marketplace knowledge. They can learn, for example, that a particular toy is available at a particular store at a particular price, or that Sony Walkman comes in an attractive, neon-colored sports model, or that "Swatch" watches are cool, since they are worn by the coolest girls seen on TV and in the mall. And, finally, children can learn the knowledge and skills to make "smart choices." They can learn to clip coupons, do comparison-shopping, and select items from mail catalogs. Delia's catalog is very popular among young teen girls, and high school kids dig catalogs from East bay and Lands' Ends, for example.

Learning and socialization are lifelong processes, continuing through a person's mature years. We focus here on childhood socialization, since that is when the first wave of socialization occurs and that is when the family has the greatest opportunity to influence the socialization process. Two factors play a role in consumer socialization of children: (a) cognitive, and (b) environmental.

Cognitive factors refer to a person's mental abilities. Very young children, for example, are unable to discriminate between a TV program and a commercial and do not understand the persuasive intent of advertisers.[18] They are also driven by immediate perceptual features of the stimuli rather than by its substantive meaning. For example, a smaller glass filled to the top is judged to contain more juice than a larger but half-filled glass.[19] Cognitive development proceeds with age, and so does children's consumer socialization.

Environmental factors refer to sources of information and influence surrounding the growing child. These sources include mass media, peers, and family. Family exercises the first and strongest influence on children's socialization.[20] As the child becomes older, peer influence grows, and the influence of family likely declines. In our experience, weakening of family influence with advancing years is less in Asian and third-world countries than in the more industrialized Western countries.

LEARNING MECHANISMS
How Children Learn to be Consumers

The socialization influence from parents to children occurs basically through the learning mechanisms described in Chapter 4: instrumental conditioning, modeling, and cognitive learning. These three mechanisms correspond to the three bases of reference-group influence (a topic covered in Chapter 10): normative, value-expressive, and informational, respectively.

Instrumental conditioning refers to learning to do those things that are rewarded. In the early years of a child, parents control most resources and inculcate values through rewarding what they consider "good" behavior. Children learn those behaviors and the underlying values that receive rewards from their parents.

The second mechanism is **modeling**. Here children look up to their parents as role models and try to internalize and adopt their values, roles, aptitudes, and so on. Thus, for example, a child who watches a father dressing up in the morning in "office clothes" is quietly making plans to wear similar clothes one day.

The third mechanism, **cognitive learning** occurs when parents become the source of information about the product. In low involvement cognitive learning, children notice the products parents are using and in later life adopt them without much thought (e.g., Crisco oil or Morton salt). This is not modeling because the product choice is not driven by a desire to be "Like them." High involvement cognitive learning occurs when parents communicate and educate about various brands or buying strategies. A mother might "educate" a daughter, for example, about what hygienic products are good, or when to use which of the several cough medicines she has in the family medicine chest.

Learning from the media can occur through cognitive and/or modeling processes. Learning from peers is predominantly via modeling. Occasionally it can be cognitive— i.e., peers can provide information. At times, peers even use instrumental conditioning, rewarding by offering approval.

Take a look at yourself, and see what kind of a consumer you have become, and reflect over how you became socialized into being the kind of consumer you are. You have no doubt picked up a lot from your peers, from the media, and from the marketplace itself. Just as likely, some of your consumer behavior is simply inherited. Yes, inherited from your parents. Let us see how.

Romancing the Consumer   tv2010

Parents Stay Free

Traveling with kids? Then you had better stay in a hotel that is kid friendly. Holiday Inn comes to mind, with its Holidome and all. Quite a few other hotels offer amenities for kids in the play and pool area inside the hotel property. Many hotel properties let kids stay free with their parents. Hilton allows, for example, children 15 years or younger to stay free, and children 10 years or younger to stay free and eat free as well.

VIPs: Moly Jones (L) and Katey Willis

But now five star properties are also turning kid friendly. Super upscale Ritz now has a program called Ritz Kids. Its goal: not only to lure affluent families with kids, but also to hook the kids themselves to the brand so when they grow up, Ritz becomes their choice.

Are you into boutique hotels—the ones that are small and artsy? There

Bambuddha Lounge at a Hotel Joie de Vivre Property

is one that takes the prize in kid-friendliness. It is California based Joie de Vivre Hospitality hotel company. Its program is called Kids Are VIPs—Parents Stay Free. When you take your family and kids for a night's or a week's stay there, it is your kids who check in. You just tag along.

The properties at Joie de Vivre provide special amenities (e.g., a lending library for games and books) and stimulating activities for kids. A dedicated concierge will customize the kids program for your kids. Kids also receive a copy of "Mommy I'm Bored"—a guide of things to do in California.

And for you, the parents, the sheer aesthetics of the hotel property will keep you relaxed, rejuvenated, and delighted for days.

My CB Book

Learning from Your Cool Mom and Dad

By inherited, we don't mean, you inherited the genes for consuming certain products. (Actually, maybe you did that too, but a discussion of genetic inheritance is beyond our scope) Rather, we mean that you "learned" certain consumptions from your parents. We have already illustrated this behavior above. But there is a new name for some of this manner of acquiring consumption behavior, Intergenerational influence (IGI).

The intergenerational influence (IGI) of family members refers to the transmission of values, attitudes, and behaviors from one generation to the other.[21] In the context of consumer behavior, IGI refers to the transfer of consumption-related values, brand perceptions, and brand choices themselves (i.e., simply adopting the brand parents had been using). In a number of studies spanning last 3 decades, adult children were found to have adopted a broad range of product choices from their parents. [22] See Exhibit 14.4.

Photo Courtesy Jamie Schworer

learning to dress like Mom–IGI at work (Jamie Schworer with daughter Katey)

The intergenerational influence (IGI) goes beyond common product choices. In a 1988 study of mothers and daughters by consumer research scholars Elizabeth S. Moore-Shay and Richard J. Lutz, for example, mothers and daughters also agreed on such choice rules (i.e., the rules-of-thumb consumers employ to make their buying more efficient) as buying items on sale, brand loyalty, relying on others for advice or information, and prepurchase planning. Furthermore, there was agreement on such statements as "there is a positive price quality relationship," "marketer-given information is useful," "advertising has positive value," and "private brands and sale merchandise are good value." Thus, children learn from parents not only which products and brands to use but also shopping strategies

Measuring IGI

When product and brand preferences are common between parents and their grown up children, we take it as an indicator of IGI. But to be sure, we need to directly measure the presence of such influence. We do so by asking consumers themselves a few questions, such as those presented in Table 14.2.

Forward and Reverse Influence

IGI can take place in both directions: forward (from parents to children) and reverse (from children to parents). Forward influence occurs because as children are growing up, they observe parents using certain products. And they "adopt" those products for use in later, independent living. The reverse influence begins to occur as children grow up. In school and on the street, children are exposed to new knowledge and to new role models. Consequently, they begin to depend less on parents as role models or for

---

INTERGENERATIONAL INFLUENCE AT WORK   EXHIBIT 14.4

Look What CB Researchers Found

Bank preference A study from the 1970s found that 93 percent of college freshmen patronize the same bank as did their parents.

Financial planning The extent to which families preplan their financial goals and then act to fulfill those goals was found to be consistent over three generations studied.

Auto insurance In one study, 32 percent of adult men had the same auto insurance agency as did their fathers.

Grocery items In a 1988 study of female college students and their mothers, 49 percent of mothers and daughters agreed on their brand preference for such products as toothpaste, facial tissues, pain reliever, and peanut butter.

In another study in 2000 of mothers and their grown up daughters (who lived on their own), soup brand choice was the same for 76% of the mother daughter pairs; for tooth paste, it was common for 43% and for facial tissue, 55%. The same sharing was much less for such products as coffee (20%), household cleaners (3%) and canned vegetables (11%).

For further reading, see Elizabeth S. Moore, William L. Wilkie, and Richard J. Lutz, "Passing the Torch: Intergenerational Influence as a Source of Brand Equity," *Journal of Marketing*, Vol. 56, April 2002, 17-37.

TABLE 14.2   A Scale to Measure IGI

To what extent have you been influenced by your parents in acquiring or not acquiring the following personal skills:

Not at all	1	2	3	4	5	Greatly

1. Planning, budgeting, saving money, etc.
2. How to choose between products and brands
3 How to assess product information
4. How to judge a brand in comparison to others.

To what extent have the following tastes and preferences of your parents influenced your own tastes and preferences as consumers:

Not at all	1	2	3	4	5	Greatly

5. Their preferences of brands and products
6. Their preferences of stores
7. Their views of advertising, sales, and other marketing practices
8. Their personal involvement or lack of it in shopping, possessing things, conspicuous consumption, simplicity, etc.

Scoring: The scores, when summated across the eight questions) could range from 8 to 40. Although national standards based on any representative study are unavailable, it is reasonable to deem consumers scoring above the middle point (3x8=24) to have been influenced more by IGI than those scoring below 24.

Source: Based on author's research, which adapted, in turn, some items from Madhubalan Viswanathan, Terry L. Childers, and Elizabeth S. Moore, "The Measurement of Intergenerational Communication and Influence on consumption: Development, Validation, and Cross-cultural comparison of the IGEN Scale, *Journal of the Academy of Marketing Science*, Summer 2000, Vol. 28, No. 3, 406-424 (Used with permission.).

guidance and begin to carve out their individual identity. In exercising their individual identity, when their preferences differ from their parent's, they begin to influence what gets bought for family consumption, such as the type of home furnishings.

Whether forward or reverse, why does this influence occur? It occurs for four reasons. Three of them you have already seen with children's socialization; a fourth mechanism of influence is especial to IGI, in particular forward IGI. It is nostalgia. More than a decade of consumption shared with one's family can leave strong emotional memories of product/brand use. Later, the grown up children simply want to relive the memorable experience they had during their childhood. One consumer in a research study expresses this emotional IGI thus:

"I like Brownberry bread.. because it has sentimental value for me. .. Before my dad remarried, we would always eat healthy food… And I would eat my vegetables and we would have Brownberry wheat bread."

(Moore, Wilkie, and Lutz, 2002, p. 28.)23

This topic is relatively new to consumer research. But it is an interesting dimension of influences on consumers' brand choices across generations, and marketers should explore this phenomenon more fully.

This brings us to the end of Section 1: Family Decision Making. One final note: Our description in this chapter of the family's consumer behavior is founded on research in North America. The feature "The Chinese Family Altar" demonstrates an example of the wide-ranging cultural variations in family life that exist across the globe. Given such cultural and international variations, we invite you, as a student of consumer behavior, to research family decision making in diverse nations and cultures.

THE BUYING BEHAVIOR OF BUSINESS CUSTOMERS

Suppose your firm makes and markets software for Internet security, something that protects a computer system from viruses and. And you have two different versions of the software, one for use by consumers at home; the other for use by corporations with hundreds of connected computers. Would you approach these two types of customers differently? Do you think the two types of customers make their purchase decisions differently? Your gut answer will be, "Yes—the business customers are perhaps much more rational than household consumers; and perhaps they use a much more systematic product evaluation process." These stereotypes are only half true; the full picture is more complex—where rational economic evaluation occurs side-by-side corporate intrigues and emotional drama.

In this section, we describe that behavior. We begin by describing key dimensions on which business buying behavior differs from individual consumer behavior. Then we discuss the components of the business buying process, including the steps in, influences on, and participants in the process. Next, we discuss how decision makers in this process resolve conflicts. Finally, we bring together all the concepts and ideas in a comprehensive model of business buying behavior.

BUSINESS VERSUS HOUSEHOLD BUYING BEHAVIOR

Business buying typically differs from individual consumer or household buying in five key ways: greater specialization of roles, more formalization of the buying process, more formal accountability for decisions, greater internal capabilities, and more complex requirements (see Table 14.3). Let us discuss these briefly

Business customers have more demanding decision criteria. Marketers need to understand the business buying process.

Greater Role Specialization In individual buying, the same person performs all the tasks needed to make a purchase—identifying a need, evaluating options, shopping, budgeting, acquisition, and consumption. In household buying, these tasks are sometimes shared by various members of the family. For organizations, they are much more formally assigned to different functionaries who specialize in those roles. For example, production department might be responsible for requisitioning a product, engineering might be assigned the role of evaluating the options, and purchasing the role of negotiating, and so on.

Formalization of the Buying Process In organizational buying, the policy and procedures are formalized. Generally, businesses have written policies and rules to guide the solicitation of proposals and price quotes, preferential treatment to a certain class of vendors (e.g., minority businesses), and the way the decisions are to be made in the buying firm. They prepare and sign detailed contracts that specify the obligations of each party. This degree of formalization is rare in family buying behavior.[24]

Accountability for Decisions Unlike household buying, business buying holds accountable those who are in charge of procurement. This results in more formal evaluation and feedback on purchase decisions. There are also internal and external audits of the buying process to ensure that the procurement follows sound business practices as well as it obtains maximum value from suppliers. For this reason, business buying encourages formal supplier ratings and scorecards as well as constant feedback and communication to its suppliers.

Comparison of Household & Business Buying

Characteristic	Household Buying	Business Buying
Specilization of Customer Roles	Combined or slightly specialized	Moderate to very specialized
Formalization of the Buying Process	Informal	Slightly formal (small businesses) to formal (large businesses)
Accountability for Decision	Usually not formally measured	Strict measures
Internal Capabilities	Weak	Weak (small businesses) to very Strong (large businesses)
Complexity of Requirements	Little Complexity	Operational & strategic complexity

MyCBBook

Internal Capabilities More often than households, business customers are capable of producing certain items in-house rather than buying them from others. This capability requires business customers to analyze the economics of the "make versus buy" options. Therefore, sellers need to be aware that customers have other options.

Complexity of Requirements Business buying entails both operational and strategic complexity. Operationally, the number of employees who participate in the buying process, often from several locations, adds complexity. Further complexity results from the need to adhere to government rules and regulations related to reciprocity of buying and selling to one another. Additionally, procurement is often a strategic function. It is often the single largest cost center to a business organization, responsible for buying both capital goods and materials.

COMPONENTS OF THE BUSINESS BUYING PROCESS

With purchasing being such a significant and complex function, organizations typically have formal procurement systems, with several components, shown in Figure 14.7 nature of the purchase, organizational characteristics, buying center, rules and procedures, and a decision process. By determining the way the components fit together in a particular business, marketers can describe the business's buying behavior.

Nature of the Purchase

Not all purchases are equal; some are more complex than others. This complexity is captured by two interrelated dimensions: buyclass and perceived risk.

BuyClass

For an individual consumer, we classified purchase needs into routine problem solving, limited problem solving, or extended problem solving. Similarly, businesses have three types of procurement needs, or buyclasses: straight rebuy, modified rebuy, and new task.

A **straight rebuy** is a product that is needed repeatedly and has been procured before. Examples include shop supplies (e.g., lubricants), worker uniforms, and office stationery. Moreover, the outcome has been satisfactory, and the total costs are low so there is no need to reopen the supplier search process. For these items, businesses often negotiate an annual purchasing agreement. Most companies now computerize procurement of straight rebuys, in a system called e-procurement. E-procurement is an Internet based buying system, with information sharing between the supplier and the buying firm. The system gives authorized suppliers access to the buying firm's inventory usage information, so that the supplier automatically supplies the required materials in required quantities at required times as needed by the production system of the buying firm.

A **modified rebuy** represents a need that is similar in broad nature to the previously fulfilled needs, but entails some changes either in design/performance specifications or in the supply environment. For example, a

FIGURE 14.7 COMPONENTS OF BUSINESS BUYING PROCESS

NATURE OF PURCHASE
• Buy Class
• Perceived Risk

ORGANIZATIONAL CHARACTERISTICS
• Size
• Purchase orientation
• Buying center

BUYING CENTER

RULES & PROCEDURES
• Minority supplier policy
• Centralized buying

DECISION PROCESS

company may have bought sheet metal before, but of a different gauge (i.e., thickness) than needed now. Or the firm wants to buy some more desktop computers; although the firm has bought these before, it wants to re-examine the latest technology available.

New task purchases pertain to those needs that are new to the organization. Given no prior history, there is considerable uncertainty about the design/performance requirements. Also, suppliers may not already be on the company list, and at any rate new suppliers may need to be added and all suppliers may have to be appraised anew.

The concept of buyclass is important because the purchase process is different across the three buyclasses (see Table 14.4). On a continuum of straight rebuy to modified rebuy to new task, the more the purchase is of the new task type, the more the buying group:

- Perceives the need for information.
- Is large.
- Is deliberative and patient.
- Is concerned with finding a good solution.
- Underplays low price and assured supply as evaluation criteria.
- Will consider new suppliers.
- Will value the influence of technical persons, relative to the influence of buying agents.[25]

PERCEIVED RISK, IMPORTANCE, AND COMPLEXITY

Each type of purchase involves a different level of perceived risk, importance, and complexity for the decision maker. Business customers use information such as the type of purchase to estimate risk, importance, and complexity. Then they adjust their decision-making strategy accordingly.

Perceived risk refers to the loss that would accrue were a wrong choice made. It has two components, namely (a) the degree of uncertainty that a choice may be wrong, and (b) the amount at stake should a wrong choice occur. Uncertainty stems from the absence of prior design/performance specifications and from lack of experience with potential suppliers. Thus, new tasks have the most uncertainty, and straight rebuys the least. Amount at stake is the financial loss or performance loss from a suboptimal choice.

The **importance of purchase** is a combination of the amount at stake and the extent to which the product plays a strategic role in the organization. A large fleet of transportation vehicles might cost more

TABLE 14.4	Buying Behavior Associated with *Buy Classes*		
BuyClass	**Description of Need**	**Buying Center Size**	**Information Search**
Straight rebuy	Item is frequently needed & has been satisfactorily bought before	Very small; ordering may even be automated	Brief or nonexistent; new suppliers rarely considered; technical expertise rarely sought
Modified rebuy	Need is broadly similr to one that has been fulfilledbefore but requires some change in specifications or the Msupply enviornment	Moderate	Some information is gathered; new suppliers may be considered; technical experts may have input into decision
New task	Need is completely new to the organization	Large	Extensive; new suppliers often considered experts usually have major input into decision

Prepared by Author for MyCBBook

than, say, a communication network; yet the latter might be viewed as a more important purchase due to its strategic role in equipping the firm for the information age.

Complexity refers to the extensiveness of effort it takes to comprehend and manage the product during its acquisition. Complexity has two dimensions: (1) the number of performance dimensions, and (2) the technical and specialist knowledge required to understand those dimensions. Thus, a single dimensional product like a chemical is simpler

FINANCE & IT
Two superpowers join forces

TOSHIBA black and white/color hybrid copiers being two opposing forces together. IT people delight
in offering their people fast and affordable black and white with the added convenience of color—all from one source.
And finance folks are attracted to the built-in color restriction codes that limit color access to a select group
while tracking monthly output. Oh, the power. *Let the Harmony Begin.com*

TOSHIBA
Don't copy. Lead.™

Can a marketer satisfy the bean counters as well as users seeking amazing product features. Toshiba here seeks to delight both.

than a multidimensional item like a personal computer (even though the risk might be greater with the purchase of a chemical than with that of a computer).

Together, the buyclass and perceived risk influence how extensive the purchase decision process will be. As perceived risk increases, more individuals will participate in the decision, who will deliberate more, consult a wide range of information sources, and experience greater conflict and role stress.[26]

Organizational Characteristics

Four organizational characteristics of the customer firm affect buying behavior: (1) size, (2) structure, (3) purchase resources, and (4) purchase orientation.

Size   First, the size of the business determines not only the customer's potential dollar volume, but also the sophistication of its buying process. Small business organizations behave more like a family in their buying behavior; large organizations, in contrast, have larger buying groups and more formalized procedures.

Business Structure   Second, a business's structure (which comprises the number of departmental units, geographical locations, and its degree of centralization) influences the buyer behavior: The more departments or geographic locations a business has, the larger the buying group and more prolonged the buying process is likely to be.

Purchase Resources   Third, **purchase resources** refer to the availability of professional buyers and product experts. Generally, large and professionally managed firms would have better resourced purchasing departments, and consequently, a more rigorous and formal vendor evaluation.

Purchase Orientation   Finally, The organization's **purchase orientation**—its purchasing philosophy—can be placed along a continuum: At the one end purchasing may be viewed simply as an administrative function that finds the most economical sources of materials needed; at the other end, it may be viewed as a strategic, managerial function expected to bring value to the organization. As a strategic function, purchasing is engaged in several key activities:

- Scrutinizing 'make versus buy' decisions.
- Continually finding better products, materials, and technology.

ValueSpace: The Magic Land for Winning Customers

You are the CEO of a Mining company, and you are digging through a difficult minefield with uneven topography. The operator on the tractor mounted with cutting blades is maneuvering through the minefield diligently, cutting here at one angle, chiseling there at another. The task is difficult, the extreme skill of the operator notwithstanding, and the trial-and-error digging is nowhere near the pace it should be. As the CEO of the mining company trying to deliver on this multi-million dollar project on time, you wish there were some way for the tractor to find the best cutting path. Like it could sense the ground's topography and automatically adjust its cutting angles. Like it could take out all the guesswork, not be so demanding of the operator skill, and cut the cutting time by half.

Take heart! There actually is. If your tractor is a CAT D11R, you can actually program it for auto-piloted optimum cutting path. CAT's Computer Aided Earthmoving System (CAES) technology actually relays the topography of the ground under the machine to a remote CAT site on a real-time basis; there, Cat engineers calculate the optimum path and beam it right back to the computer on the machine. Now, the operator can simply sit back and watch the machine do its job!

You are a small business, selling widgets to another business company. You ship your product by UPS—by Air or Ground, depending on the customer's requirement. This one particular shipment you are sending today, the customer wants it in three days. The air shipment will reach a day too soon and cost you more; the ground shipment is cheaper but will miss the deadline. So, reluctantly, you ship by air, paying more. UPS says, don't! Unless, you like spending more. "Just tell us where you want it and by when," says UPS, "and we will figure out the best mode, combining ground and air for different sectors of the journey if necessary, and save you money."

This means UPS will make less money on each shipment. So, why would UPS do it?

Andrew Sterner is a District Sales Manager in the Jacksonville Operating Division of SYSCO, the nation's number one foodservice company. He also happens to be an ex-chef. One recent month, he was helping a customer—a restaurant—organize a benefit dinner for Alzheimer's Association on the anniversary of the sinking of the Titanic. He had already secured 90 percent of the required food as donation, and he borrowed waitstaff from yet another customer (restaurant). As for finding some cooking help, he donned the apron himself and cooked a 13-course meal for 160 persons. And no ordinary meal it was—it was identical to the one served on the Titanic itself!

Caterpillar, UPS, SYSCO. Isn't it nice to be a customer of these companies?

It is. And it is because these companies are masters at creating new *ValueSpace*, the space that delivers us, their customers, unmatched value.

My C B Book

- Developing long-term sources of supply and building relationships with the suppliers.

These two ends of the continuum may be referred to as reactive and proactive buying, respectively.

The Buying Center

In most organizations, purchase decisions are handled by a formal or informal buying center—a multifunction, multilevel internal organization that is responsible for the centralized purchasing function. It comprises various individuals who play the following roles:

- **User** This is the user department that would use the product to be purchased by the organization.
- **Buyer** The buyer, alternatively called purchasing manager, purchasing executive, and so on, has the formal authority to execute the purchase contract and place a purchase order.
- **Analyzer** One who performs technical analysis of suppliers by using such tools as cost analysis, value analysis, and so on.
- **Influencer** By their expert advice, these role holders influence the evaluative criteria and supplier ratings and/or the final decision itself. Typically, these are design engineers and external consultants.
- **Gatekeepers** They regulate the flow of information from suppliers to the other members of the buying center. They permit or deny salespersons access to design

Diverse members of the ***buying center*** have diverse
concerns. Marketers need to present information customers
with different backgrounds can understand.

and user departments or to other executives. Often purchase managers, receptionists, and secretaries play this role.

- **Decider** The deciders make the final decision. This role may be played by a formal buying committee, or by the CEO, CFO, or purchasing executive alone.

    Note that buying center is a concept, not an actual group or committee name. Therefore, a salesperson selling to organizations must always try to identify all the individuals, spread throughout the organization, who might be playing the various roles of the buying center.

Rules and Procedures

Businesses generally set up elaborate policies (e.g., favor a minority supplier), rules (e.g., purchase needs must be consolidated for the entire organization), and procedures (e.g., minimum number of bids required). The degree of formalization and decision freedom varies from company to company.

Decision Process

Like individual and household buying decisions, organizational buying decisions entail a multistage process, comprising the following stages:[27]

- **Need assessment** Deciding the technical and performance specifications for the needed item.
- **Developing choice criteria** Identifying supplier selection criteria.
- **Request for proposals (RFPs)** Calling for proposals by publishing requests for quotes (RFQs) and inviting suppliers to submit bids.
- **Supplier evaluation** Rank-ordering vendors. Some negotiations may occur toward reconciling differences both on technical aspects and on price variations among various bidders or suppliers.
- **Supplier selection** Awarding the contract or placing an order.
- **Fulfillment and monitoring** Monitoring for smooth fulfillment in a timely fashion and to the satisfaction of the buyers and users.

These steps are similar to individual decision-making except that there is a lot more formal analysis as well as use of more structured procedures.

Various roles in the buying center participate more in some stages than others (see Table 14.5. Generally, users exercise more influence at the need assessment and choice criteria stages; buyers shoulder the major responsibility at the RFP, supplier search, and fulfillment stages; analyzers help most at the supplier evaluation stage; influencers, at supplier evaluation and selection stages; and decision makers, at the vender selection stages. Gatekeepers, of course, would be active throughout, depending on the inflow of information, influence, and salesperson communications, all vying for the decision makers' attention. This pattern is not universal and business-to-business marketers should identify

TABLE 14.5

VARYING INFLUENCE OF BUYING CENTER MEMBER ROLES

	User	Buyer	Decider	Analyzer	Influencer	Gatekeeper
BUYING CENTER ROLES						
Need assessment	√√		√		√	
Vendor search		√√				√√
Choice criteria	√	√		√	√√	
RFP		√√				
Supplier evaluation				√√	√√	
Selection	√	√	√√	√	√	√√
Fulfillment/monitoring	√√	√√				

√ Influence √√ Strong Influence

C.O.N.S.U.M.E.R. K.A.R.M.A.

Rock, Scissors, Paper

Back in 2005, Maspro Denkoh Corporation of Japan (an electronics firm) wanted to sell its art collection of more than $20 million (U.S.). It was choosing between the two world-leading auction houses—Christie's and Sotheby's. It decided to make its decision by an ancient Japanese game called *Rock, Scissors, Paper*.

The representatives of the two bidding firms were invited at Maspro's headquarters, seated across a table in a conference room, with their respective lawyers, and were asked to write on a piece of paper one of the three words. Christie's wrote scissors; Sotheby's wrote paper. (Yes, writing the word *paper* on paper is interesting!) Christie's won the contract. And, at a 20% commission, a chance to earn some $4 million and change at the next auction, aptly code-named S*cissors*![a]

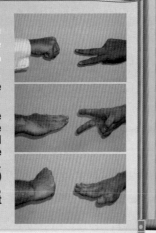

How the Game is Played

Rock, Paper, scissors is a Japanese game known in Japanese as Janken. It is a game of chance. Two teams or two players play to decide who wins (often used to decide who gets to play first or who gets a prize, etc.) Each of the two players makes with his or her hands the shape of either a rock (a clenched fist), a piece of paper (flat palm facing downward) or a pair of scissors (two fingers making a horizontal 'V'). The rule of the game is that the rock crushes the scissors, the scissors cut the paper, and the paper covers the rock. If your opponent makes a rock and you make the paper, then you win. However, if you make, instead, scissors, you lose. If you do make the scissors, you hope your opponent makes the paper. Good luck.

(Based on a report in Carol Vogel, "Rock, Paper, Payoff: Child's Play Wins Auction House As Art Sale," The New York Times, April 29, 2005.)

We are consumers and this is what we do.

and map this pattern for each business client individually.

The decision-making process is primarily driven by two psychological processes occurring in the decision makers: (1) their expectations and (2) their perceptual distortions.

Expectations One factor that sets organizational decision making apart from individual and household decision making is that the various members of the buying center tend to have a set of different expectations. Their expectations are influenced by their background and their satisfaction or dissatisfaction with past purchases.[28]

Perceptual Distortions Business customers, like individual consumers, encode incoming information selectively and in a biased manner. Expectations play a major role in selective perceptions. Thus, some buying center members might expect that only engineers are able to understand product specifications; they might then discount as unreliable any information that salespeople with non-engineering backgrounds provide. Such a premise might be entirely misguided, but the resulting perceptual distortion might cost a supplier an order.

We began this chapter with a distinction between family and nonfamily households and explained the movement of consumers from one form of family to another, due to a process of family life cycle (FLC). Next, we described family buying process as one in which different members of the family influence various stages of the decision process. Particularly, the relative influence of spouses in joint decision making was described as a "muddling-through process." The exact influence of either spouse was determined by such factors as gender roles, wife's employment status, family life cycle, time pressure, importance of purchase, and the socioeconomic development of the relevant population.

Next, children's influence in family buying decisions was described. Children influence parental choices of products and services, as well as receive influence from parents in their own marketplace preferences. The latter process is captured in the concept of consumer socialization of children. A related concept, intergenerational influence (IGI) was also discussed, where one generation influences another generation's consumption choices. This influence can occur in either direction—from parents to children or from adult children to parents. We saw that parents and their adult children share a range of common consumption of brands and products. We identified this influence due to four sources: instrumental, information or cognitive, modeling, and nostalgia.

Since family buying decisions are shared decisions with different members vying for influence and control, inevitably conflicts occur. We discussed different types of conflicts that occur, and identified four strategies of resolving these conflicts: problem solving, bargaining, persuasion, and politicking.

Business Customer Decisions

In contrast to household buying, the customer behavior of a business involves greater specialization of customer roles, a more formalized buying process, greater accountability for decisions, more sophisticated internal capabilities, and more complex requirements. The purchase processes differ for straight rebuys, modified rebuys, and new task. The procurement function itself is more complex involving multiple functions in the buying center, each with different expectations and expertise. Rather than a department or committee, it is a concept, defining the variety of roles involved in a purchase: user, buyer, analyzer, influencer, gatekeeper, and decider. A successful seller to businesses identifies the people in the organization who play each role in a particular purchase decision and addresses the needs associated with each role.

Household
Family
Nonfamily Household
Family Life Cycle
Roommate Families
Autonomous Decisions
Syncratic Decisions
Joint Decisions
Gender Role Orientation
Social Orientation Families
Concept Oriented Families
Authoritarian Families
Neglectful Families

Democratic Families
Permissive Families
Consumer Socialization
Intergenerational Influence (IGI)
Democratic Justice
Family Relationship
Buyclass
Straight Rebuy
Modified Rebuy
New Task
E-procurement
Perceived Risk

Importance of Purchase Complexity
Buying Center
Problem Solving
Persuasion
Bargaining
Politicking
Relationship Buying
e-procurement
Global Sourcing
Online Exchange
Affinity Groups
Affinity Marketing

REVIEW+Rewind

1. What is the difference between a family and a household and what is meant by family life cycle (FLC)? How does consumer behavior differ for consumers in different stages of FLC? What use can marketers make of this concept?

2. What is consumer socialization of children? What mechanisms of socialization are discussed in the chapter?

Which sources and which mechanisms of influence are likely to be at work for the following products?
   a. Toys and videogames.
   b. Music and movies
   c. Cosmetics and fashion clothing.
   d. Food items

3. How does family decision making differ from individual

decision making? Do the steps themselves differ, or the manner in which these steps are undertaken differ or both? How?

4. Briefly explain the concept of Intergenerational influence (IGI) and describe how you would measure it for consumers in your country?

5. Often, spouses play an unequal role in family purchase decisions and this role distribution differs across families; what factors does this depend on? Explain each factor briefly.

6. How does business buying behavior differ from (a) household buying behavior and (b) individual decision making? Briefly explain each point of difference.

7. What organizational characteristics affect business buying behavior and how?

8. What is the concept of a buying center and why should a salesperson understand it?

9. [Level 2.0] Define affinity group and affinity marketing. Give two examples in which consumers buy as members of an affinity group. Briefly discuss what benefits they might get by buying as members of the group.

THINK+Apply

1. Why do you shop? Is your purpose purely to buy something, or are there other motives? For each of the shopping motives described in the chapter, list the kind of stores you visit with that particular motive in mind.

2. Think back to when you were choosing for the first time in a new city (say, your new college town, city of your first job, the city your parents just moved to, etc.) the store to shop for (a) groceries, and (b) music CDs. Comment on the extent to which the store choice flow chart described in this chapter captures your own process of choosing a store for these two types of products.

3. Apply the model of store loyalty to yourself and discuss which "what" and "how" factors apply to your own behavior in patronizing stores for the following products: (a) clothing, (b) music, (c) coffee/tea, (d) books, (e) electronic equipment, and (f) haircuts.

4. As a store manager, you just read the model of store loyalty described in this chapter. You are excited because you believe you have found the key to making your customers loyal to your store, and thereby key to great profits. Briefly outline your action plan.

5. If you were a store manager, how would you improve the chances of consumers living in your area choosing your store rather than another one across the street.

6. If you were a store manager, what would you do to encourage consumers to browse while they visit your store?

PRACTICE+Experience

1. Describe the intergenerational influence you have yourself experienced in your family. Is this influence for

selected product categories (which ones?) or across the board?

2. Which stage of the family life cycle should you target (and why) as a marketer of:
   a. Vacation to Disney Land
   b. Vacation to Venice, Italy.
   c. RV
   d. One bedroom condos versus a 3 bedroom house.

3. If you are selling copy machine paper to a corporation, how would your approach be different than if you were selling, say, copiers? Would the concept of a buying center be applicable? How?

4. Interview children who are: (a) 10 years old or younger, and (b) between 11 and 17. For each of the following product categories, ask them which brands they prefer and how they came to like these brands. Probe for the sources and manner of influence.
   a. Breakfast cereal
   b. Shoes
   c. Clothing
   d. Restaurants (fast food)
   e. Cosmetics and grooming products

5. Take two countries, one from the East and the other from the Western civilization. Study the changes occurring within the family by interviewing a few families from each country. (If this is not feasible, then interview families living in your country but with origins from elsewhere). Then, discuss how marketers would need to respond to these changes within each country.

6. Interview two families who recently made a major purchase in the same product category (e.g., car, house, etc.) to understand their joint decision process. Then based on your interviews, describe what conflicts occurred and how they were resolved.

7. Choose two companies and interview their director of purchasing. The purpose of the interview is to assess whether the concept of the buying center works in that company and to identify who plays which role. Comment on how the concept differs in practice, at least at these companies, from its description in the book.

5 . Interview a sales manager or salesperson selling a product of high importance to business customers. Help him/her identify the buying center in two of his/her customer companies and understand how he or she utilizes his/her understanding of the client's buying center.[1]

In the Marketing Manager's Shoes

Put yourself in a marketing manager's shoes. Most concepts in the chapter have some lessons for the marketing manager, i.e., they suggest what to do differently in practice; indeed, often these applications are implicit in our explanations of the concepts and models in the chapter. Identify at least five specific applications of the chapter's concepts, all of which should be entirely new—different from the examples cited here.

AFFINITY CUSTOMER GROUPS

Suppose in your mail one day you find the following offers from various marketing firms:

- One letter is from your alma mater's alumni association president, introducing a Visa credit card with your alma mater's seal. The letter suggests that the Visa company will make a donation to the alumni association and that you should be proud to own a Visa with your alma mater's seal.
- Your monthly bank statement has an insert advertisement offering you a selection of merchandise (such as a watch, a small am/fm radio, or a briefcase) at a special price for cardholders only.
- Another letter, from a life insurance company, offers you a special insurance policy as a member of the American Marketing Association (AMA). The insurance company got the membership list from the AMA and claims to have designed a policy specifically for AMA members.

What do these three market offers have in common? It is that you received each because you are a member of a group. The marketer decided to take advantage of (and give you an advantage based on) your affiliation with that group. Each offer is an example of what marketers call affinity marketing.

AFFINITY MARKETING

Writers on this topic have defined affinity as "an individual's level of identification with the norms and standards of a particular reference group."29 Affinity marketing has been defined as "a strategy used by vendors of goods and services to offer special incentives to association members in return for the association's endorsement."30 A more recent definition refers to it as "a unique exchange process, in which value-expressive products and services are marketed to reference groups with cohesiveness, common interests, and/or values, usually in return for the group's endorsement."31

The second definition draws on "affinity" much more intensely than does the first one and is, for that reason, more restrictive. First, it calls for value-expressive products and services, meaning products and services that express some value held dear by the group, such as an environmentally friendly product to an environmental group, or a religious product to a religious association. Second, the definition also requires the nature of the group to be such that its members are bound by some values and common interests, such as in the case of MADD (mothers against drunk driving), or Sierra Club (an environmental group).

Many affinity programs satisfy neither of these two conditions: for example, when as a frequent-flyer club member of an airline you receive an offer of special rates for long distance calling, the market offering neither expresses any value of the group, nor are you (and other frequent-flying club members) bound to the club with any emotional, value-based or common interest based ties. Rather, the offer is no more than an instance of target marketing with the distinction that it has received the endorsement of the group of which you are a member.

TYPES OF AFFINITY GROUPS

There are five main types of affinity groups: professional, social, common-cause, demographics-based, and marketer-generated.32

PROFESSIONAL AFFINITY GROUPS

Professional affinity groups are composed of practitioners of a profession. Members join the group, usually with a membership fee, to advance their individual careers, improve their status, network with other professionals, and generally heighten their identity and visibility in the profession. The American Marketing Association is an example of a professional group with a large, worldwide membership comprising marketing managers and marketing professors.

Social Affinity Groups

Individuals with common interests (usually unrelated to school or work) may form a group. Examples of these social affinity groups include neighborhood groups, PTAs (parent-teacher associations), bridge clubs, and bowling groups. Social groups are characterized by a high degree of social bonding that comes with the members' shared interests.

Common-cause Affinity Groups

Some groups get formed to promote a socially desirable cause, such as prevention of drunk driving, promotion of certain religious values, or eradication of racial prejudice. The primary motivation for group members is the commitment to the group's mission and identification with the group's values. Examples include Christian Coalition (a religious and political group) and Green Peace (an environmental group).

Demographics-based Affinity Groups

Some other groups are formed on the basis of common demographics such as age, religion, or ethnic heritage. Their purpose is to promote interests common to the demographic group. The American Association of Retired Persons (AARP) is a prime example of age-based groups. In many communities, there are teen clubs, women's clubs, the Jewish center, or the Panhellenic group (for persons of Greek ethnicity).

MARKETER-GENERATED AFFINITY GROUPS

Finally, there are groups created by marketers themselves. These marketer-generated affinity groups include groups with special interest in a specific product-thus Harley Davidson (a U.S. manufacturer of motorcycles) has formed a Harley Owners Group (HOG). Many business firms now issue a membership card to their frequent customers, and these enrolled members then become an affinity group for other marketers.

Affinity Strength

All groups are not equal in the affinity strength-- the degree of group cohesiveness and bonding individual members feel with the group and with one another. This depends on three factors: active/passive participation, level of socialization, and value identification. Other things being equal, affinity strength is higher for groups that are more active than passive, provide opportunities for social interactions among members, and are centered around a value-based mission and strong identification among members (see Figure 14.8).

Active Versus Passive Participation

Some group memberships are based on members' active participation, while others require merely the passive enrollment of members. Examples of the former are PTA groups, the groups of volunteers for a social cause, various protest groups, and so forth. Passive enrollment groups include magazine subscribers, bank customers, or being on the mailing list of a local merchant.

Level of Socialization

Some groups' activities entail face-to-face interaction among members, while other group activities do not. For example, environmental group members may actively participate in the group's activities (e.g., promoting the cause among their work groups), but there may be few opportunities of social interaction among members. Purely social and local groups (e.g., bridge groups) score higher on this dimension than other groups.

Value Identification

The group's value identification is the extent to which members are bonded by common group values and identify strongly with the group, taking pride in their group membership. Cause-related groups score high on this dimension, but other groups can vary from low to high as well. Thus, college fraternity groups (a type of social group) elicit a much higher identification and pride from their members than, say, bingo groups. Alumni are often proud of their alma mater and feel strong identification. Similarly, many ethnic groups elicit strong identification from their members.

group members has been first approved by and endorsed by the group's management or leader. This third-party endorsement gives the offer credibility. The endorsement may be explicit (when the group leader writes the cover letter) or implicit (it is understood that the offer is issued with leadership approval).

Furthermore, the market offer to members includes an incentive that members value not as an individual benefit but as a contribution to the group's common cause or common resources. The affinity marketer typically contributes part of its profit to the group or to a cause valued by the group. For example, a credit card company may choose to contribute some money to your alumni association.

The third essential element in affinity market offerings is an enhanced benefit package for the members. The market offering is packaged to suit the needs typical of the group's members. A similar package is either unavailable in the market or more expensive; accordingly, the affinity marketer's offer is more valuable to the individual member than other available options.

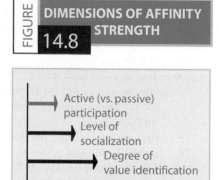

FIGURE 14.8 — DIMENSIONS OF AFFINITY STRENGTH

Active (vs. passive) participation
Level of socialization
Degree of value identification

Low ————— High
AFFINITY STRENGTH

AFFINITY GROUP BUYING MOTIVATIONS

Exchanges in affinity groups involve three parties: the affinity group organization, individual members, and the affinity marketer. For affinity buying to work, each party must benefit from the exchange. Each party receives different benefits from participating in an affinity group buying program, as summarized in Exhibit 14.6.

MARKETING PROGRAMS FOR AFFINITY GROUPS

Affinity group marketing programs are distinguished from other types of marketing by three essential elements: a third-party endorsement, a shared incentive, and an enhancement package. The market offer received by

---

BENEFITS OF AFFINITY MARKETING — EXHIBIT 14.6

A Win Win Proposition

BENEFITS TO AFFINITY GROUP ORGANIZATION
The affinity group organization benefits in a number of ways. First, clearly there is some financial incentive for the organization--typically, the marketer would offer a share of profits to the group. Second, the group receives added publicity and promotion of its own cause. Third, and finally, sometimes the affinity marketer has high social prestige, and association with such marketers gives the affinity organization a better image. For example, if AARP (American Association of Retired Persons) agrees to promote, say, Kennedy Center for the Performing Arts, the image of the AARP is enhanced.

BENEFITS TO INDIVIDUAL MEMBERS
Individual members benefit as well. First, they obtain better value from the affinity marketer's offerings, which have been customized precisely to offer better value. Second, the endorsement of the affinity group management can serve as a seal of quality for the product. Consider, for example, a parent buying a children's story on audio cassette; if a church group has sponsored it, then the parent can rest assured that there would be no risk that the cassette would contain improper material for the child. Thus, the member, in effect, shifts the risk in brand decision to the affinity organization's management. Third, the affinity-based purchase gives the member customer an implied reference group support from other members. A theater group member would feel comfortable, for example, in the knowledge that other members of the group would be buying the same product—say a ticket to a ball game! Fourth, members feel a sense of contributing to their organization by buying the affinity merchandise. Finally, if the merchandise carries the organization's logo, as it often does, members may feel proud to display that logo. For example, a Visa card with their college seal can be a source of immense satisfaction to many graduates.

BENEFITS TO THE AFFINITY MARKETER
The affinity marketer (i.e., the firm courting the affinity group) also benefits. First, it gains access to the affinity group members with a single point of contact. Second, since the affinity group members share some common interest (such as the members of a theater group share a high level of interest in literature and drama), a market offering can be customized according to that shared interest. The theater group members may be offered a CD collection of plays of interest to them. The large size of the group allows economies of scale in customization. Third, because the offering is now customized, the brand of product or service becomes differentiated from other noncustomized competitor offerings. Finally, the marketer's promotional costs are reduced as the affinity group promotes the program.

A GENERAL FRAMEWORK FOR UNDERSTANDING FAMILY DECISION MAKING

We have covered a lot of ground on family buying process. Wouldn't you like to see it all put together in a neat model and a neat diagram. Once again, several consumer researchers come to our rescue. And once again, we synthesize and adapt their models to give you an organizing framework that is comprehensive and yet easy-to-follow. See Figure 14.9. Since we have already discussed most of the variables contained in this figure, we describe the model only briefly here.

Decision Process

The linchpin of the model is the decision process, which can be either autonomous (i.e., decision made by a single family member), or joint decision making. Conflict occurrence is a significant component of the decision process. The conflict may arise either because the family members do not agree on purchase goals and criteria or because they disagree on their perceptions as to which alternatives would best meet these goals and criteria. The conflict can sometimes be intense, clouding the entire decision process. It may be manifested in angry arguments and agonizing frustration with the "irrationality of the other members." Its resolution would typically follow one of the four strategies discussed earlier: problem solving, persuasion, bargaining, or politicking.

Influences on the Decision Process

The extent to which a decision process will be autonomous or joint will depend on the nature of the purchase (e.g., degree of perceived risk), separation of the buyer/payer/user roles (who will be the principal user of the product, who is paying for it, and who actually will do the transaction)[33], individual member characteristics (e.g., wife's employment status), and family characteristics (e.g., authoritarian versus democratic families). And, of course, sources of information will influence the decision process. Different members may be exposed to different sources of information, and they will then view the alternatives differently.

FIGURE 14.9

A COMPREHENSIVE MODEL OF FAMILY DECISION MAKING

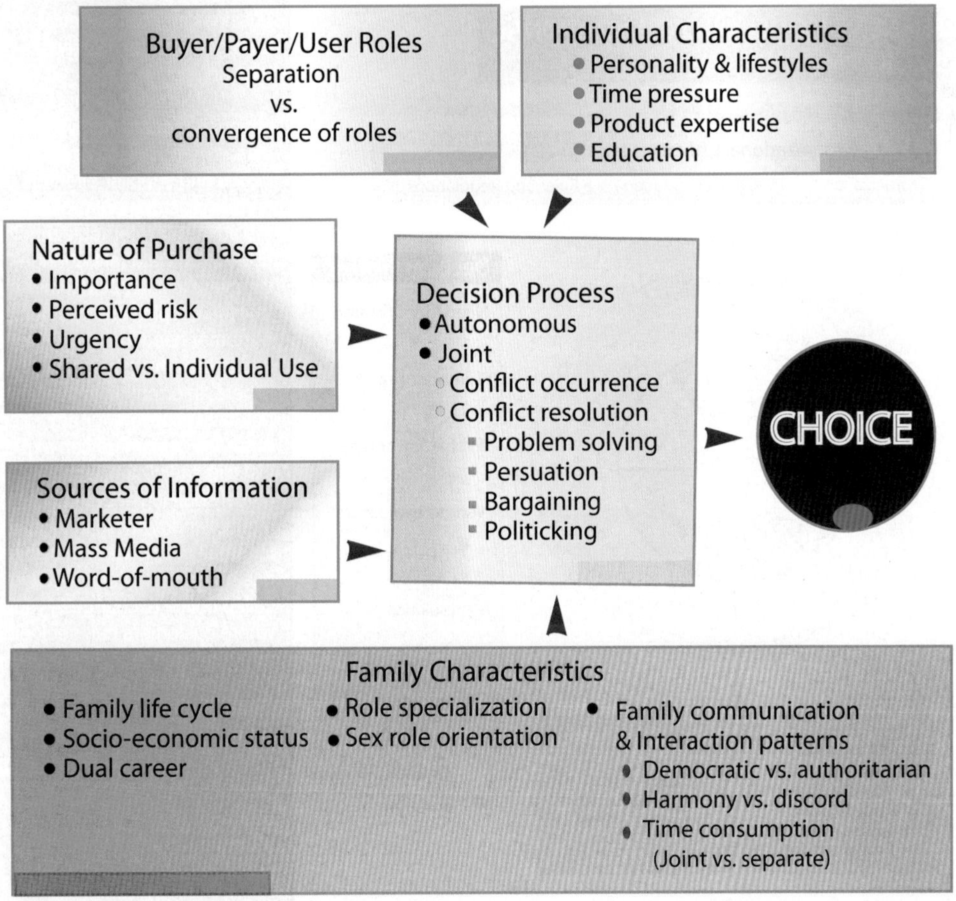

To bring together all of the ideas and concepts on business buying, we synthesize from various models available in the literature, and present a framework that is comprehensive as well as easy to follow. See Figure 14.10.

As Figure 14.10 shows, the nature of purchase and organizational characteristics (including rules and procedures) influence the structure of the buying center--whether a formal buying center exists, how many members it has, who its members are, what its charge may be, and so on. The buying center is constituted within the framework of buying policies, rules, and procedures (which are determined by the organizational characteristics), and the buying center in turn influences these by interpreting, implementing, and/or deviating from them. Decision process is influenced by the buying center as well as by the policies, rules, and procedures. Sources of information form an input at the supplier search stage of the decision process. This input is routed, of course, via the gatekeeper and is filtered through the perceptual distortion processes of the buying center members. Conflicts may occur at the supplier evaluation and selection stage, and if they do, they are resolved by one of the four methods described earlier for family buying, namely, problem solving, persuasion, bargaining, and politicking.

Macroenvironment

One factor not shown in the figure is the macroenvironment. It consists of the economic, political, legal, cultural, technological, and marketplace (i.e., suppliers and competitors). These envelop the entire buying system. For example, legal restrictions might exist against seeking foreign sources of supply. Economic uncertainty might engender shortage or surplus of certain products. The marketplace may offer no current suppliers so that a new supplier may have to be commissioned expressly, making competitive bidding irrelevant. Technology that suppliers use to offer product information (e.g., Internet) or one that buyers require (e.g., electronic ordering) might render some suppliers or buyers unsuitable for each other. And certain suppliers or supplier cultures (especially involving cross-national dealings) might mandate certain styles of negotiations (e.g., misrepresenting information) unacceptable. Thus, the entire procurement system is facilitated and constrained within the framework of the macroenvironment surrounding it.

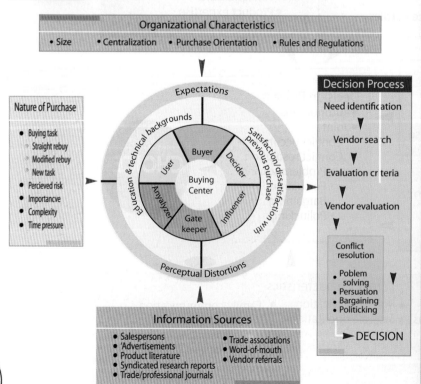

FIGURE 14.10 A COMPREHENSIVE MODEL OF ORGANIZATIONAL DECISION MAKING

Organizational Characteristics
• Size • Centralization • Purchase Orientation • Rules and Regulations

Nature of Purchase
• Buying task
  ◦ Straight rebuy
  ◦ Modified rebuy
  ◦ New task
• Percieved risk
• Importance
• Complexity
• Time pressure

Expectations
Education & technical backgrounds
Satisfaction/dissatisfaction with previous purchase
Perceptual Distortions

Buying Center
User, Buyer, Decider, Influencer, Gate keeper, Analyzer

Decision Process
Need identification
Vendor search
Evaluation criteria
Vendor evaluation

Conflict resolution
• Poblem solving
• Persuasion
• Bargaining
• Politicking

▶ DECISION

Information Sources
• Salespersons
• Advertisements
• Product literature
• Syndicated research reports
• Trade/professional journals
• Trade associations
• Word-of-mouth
• Vendor referrals

The Changing Business Buying Behavior

Business buying behavior has undergone a sea change in recent years. Three forces have driven this change:
• Supplier partnering and Relationship Buying
• Information technology
• Global sourcing

More and more business customers are now entering into supplier partnering (signing long term contracts) and firms are engaging in relationship buying and relationship selling. Relationship buying and selling refers to doing business in a collaborative mindset to bring long-term gains to each party in a mutually satisfying exchange.[34]

Information technology has also changed procurement, basically by (a) better dissemination of information about procurement needs and supplier offerings, and (b) automating certain procurement processes. Even before the advent of Internet technology, EDI systems (Electronic Data Interchange) had permitted suppliers to link to customer operations so that the supplier knew, automatically, when the customer needed the product to be shipped and in how much quantity. Now that the Internet is here, information is available instantly about potential suppliers for any specific needs, and business customers can explore the entire world just with the click of a mouse. This has made global sourcing—being able to conveniently find a supplier anywhere in the world—possible even for small businesses. Moreover, the Internet has now enabled new types of marketplaces—called online exchanges— such as auctions where customers can seek bids online and also where commodity type of products (e.g., scrap metal) can be sold and bought with minimal human effort and hence with very low procurement or selling costs.

Technology continually changes business procurement practices, and students of business customer behavior must keep a keen eye on the changing environment of business buying and selling.

HAPPY FAMILIES, CONSUMER VALUE, AND BUSINESS PRACTICES

On this last page of this chapter, we bring you a couple of thoughts and images.

First, enjoy the image of a family, photoshopped in a monent of creativity. Families are, as mentioned amply in the chapter, significant units of consumption. And a family portrait is not just a picture of family members collected in one place for a photo-op; a portait shows, as well, how "connected" and "mutually celebrating" its memebrs are. This *mutual celebration* is writ large on this photoshpped portrait, won't you agree?

Could it be that highly *connected* families will make marketplace decisions and experience joint consumption in a manner qualitatively different than families whose members share little else than a roof. This line of basic research can be intellectually rewarding. It may also yield intuitive insights on using *family connectivity* as a segmentation variable.

Second, we present a set of thoughts on the significance of value consumers seek in the marketplace (see Chapter 1) and pathways for businesses to earn customer loyalty. The thoughts are based on the themes in the cited book, composed post-hoc. As a marketer, you will find them worthy of reflection.

P.S. In case you didn't notice, all chapters end on this right side page, and rather than leave it blank, we thought it preferable to bring you this content. Read it. Enjoy it. Put in practice what you can.

Mark Mine, a professor of computer science, lives in Chapel Hill (U.S.A.) Here, in a moment of creativity, he proudly displays his family portrait.

Customer Value

It is the be-all
And the end-all
Of all business activity.

The only purpose
Of organizations.

It is the only justifiable goal
Of all reengineering,
Organizational renewal,
Entrepreneurship,
And corporate innovation.

And it is the only path
For sustained growth,
And for winning the battle
For market leadership.

—based on *ValueSpace*, 2001
www.myvaluespace.com

Customer Loyalty

How do you win it?

CRM programs, frequency
   rewards,
Corporate hospitality events ,
These are mere tools.

Customer retention
As business model,
An unwavering ethic of
Non-opportunistic behavior,
A human face on customer
Interactions,
And, most important,
A myopic obsession
With customer value innovation.

On these four pillars
Are lasting
Customer relationships founded.

—based on *ValueSpace*, 2001
www.myvaluespace.com

VALUE SPACE

Winning the **Battle** *for* **Market** *Leadership*

LESSONS FROM THE WORLD'S
MOST ADMIRED COMPANIES

BANWARI MITTAL **AND** JAGDISH SHETH

- Gender Role Identity Consumption
- Gender Differences in Gift Giving
- Metrosexuals, Retrosexuals, and Übersexuals
- Age—Why Marketers Want to Know How Old You Are
- Population Pyramids—Massive Shift in Markets
- From Boomers to Gen Y—An American Portrait

I Am A Normal Woman But Marketers Seem Not To Notice

I am satisfied with most of my body. I have always liked my face, my hair, and my upper body. I am confident in a social environment and like when other people look at me while I am walking by. Clothes are something I really enjoy because I like to get dressed up. Also, I enjoy makeup and jewelry, anything that brings out my femininity.

It is my lower body that causes me some anguish. My mood changes drastically from good to miserable whenever I go shopping in search of a pair of pants. It seems that pants only look good in sizes 2 to 4, at least when they are on mannequins. When I pick up a size 8 and hold it up side-by-side a size 4, for some reason, size 8 just doesn't hold up to size 4. Size 8 looks big, saggy and out of shape, while size 4 looks elegant, long legged, and fashionable. When I try on the size 8, the pants would fit in width, but are too long for me. What had looked so good on the mannequin in the display when I entered the store now appears so unfit on my body.

Isabell Haage battling the fitting room blues in a store (Photo: April 18, 2006)

"Do I have the wrong body?" I ask myself. I start questioning whether I am abnormal. And while I can escape being exposed to the ultra-thin models in advertising, I cannot escape the fact that most fashionable labels' clothes are designed for exactly those ultra-thin models. Why do fashion designers force average sized women into stretch jeans, which only look good when they are not "stretched" by the rather strong thighs of a normal woman? Shouldn't it be the objective of a clothing company to make its customers look good and feel happy? I don't feel happy when I want to buy pants. I feel frustrated and vulnerable. At that moment, I am nothing like the person who likes herself when looking into the mirror.

I think that most women for whom appearance is important become more depressed with their bodies after viewing very skinny models. I should perhaps not go shopping at certain stores anymore. Why do advertising and fashion magazines convey that those stores, which don't design their clothes to fit my normal body, are hip and trendy? Are the marketers supposed to cater only to skinny models? Do they not know that a majority of women are "normal" women, just like me? Or don't they know what normal women want?

INTRODUCTION

Isabell speaks for a lot of women. Her anguish is shared by "normal-sized" women everywhere. At least two marketers have heard their call, loud and clear—Nike and Unilever's Dove brand. More on them later. The point to note presently is that consumers' gender influences their product desires and preferences. Popular literature also suggests that men and women consume differently and they shop differently as well.

Men don't shop; they don't clean; they don't do household chores; they don't cry; they don't connect. Women shop; they build relationships; they feel fulfillment in home-making chores. On and on, the stereotyped gender images persist. We will study these stereotypes as well as the new roles that modern-day men and women are assuming and how it is changing their consumption and shopping patterns. Gender (actually, sex—see below) is a fixed characteristic that deeply affects our consumption behaviors. Two other unalterable characteristics are our age and our ethnic identity. Together, these three characteristics influence our consumption behaviors and differentiate one consumer from another. Marketers should be aware of these differences and their implications for marketing practice. We will discuss the first two of these individual differences in this chapter (leaving the third for the next chapter). Let's begin with gender.

GENDER

Men Are from Mars, Women Are from Venus

First, a clarification. The terms "sex" and "gender" are sometimes used interchangeably but mean different things. Sex is defined as "either of the two major forms of species who differ biologically and are typically referred to as male or female"; in contrast, "gender" refers to the roles and traits typically associated in a society with one or the other sex.[1] Thus, sex is biological; gender is sociological. We will use the word "gender" to refer to both.

Every society has men and women, roughly (though by no means exactly) in equal numbers. (In the USA, 49.1% of the population is male. In the world as a whole, there were 99 women for every 100 men in the year 2002[2].) We can observe vivid differences in their consumer behaviors, but these vary from one society to another. These differences emerge from three sources: (1) biology; (2) motivations and psychology; and (3) socialization and cultural norms.

©iStockphoto.com/Amanda Rhode

Biology creates different needs in men and women, and some of their consumption is determined by those needs. Popular literature (such as the book *Men are from Mars and Women are from Venus*) also suggests that men and women differ in their mental make up—such as women are more emotional, are more nurturing, and are more motivated to seek long-term relationships. The argument here is that men and women are "hard-wired differently."

Finally, society socializes men and women into different roles and imposes different expectations for dressing, careers, and domestic responsibilities. Without getting into the controversial issue of whether men and women are "hard-wired" differently in their psychological make up, we should note that many of the consumption and behavioral

In general, men are more focused on impersonal or individualistic goals, whereas women are more focused on achieving the goals of the groups of which they are members (e.g., family, neighborhood, coworkers, or society). Personal victory is more important to men, whereas women are more concerned with how everybody involved feels in a situation. So, masculinity is focused on achieving goals without concern for the interaction process; in contrast, femininity is focused on goals related to the interaction process itself—that the interaction be facilitated and people involved in the interaction feel good about the outcome.[5]

These traits are gender determinant. This is because, in large part, society channels our socialization according to our biological sex. Men are socialized to possess more masculinity, while women are socialized into more feminine roles. Of course, this socialization is not polarized for all people. Some men possess more feminine than masculine traits, and some women possess more masculine than feminine traits (speaking strictly in psychological terms here, please note).[6]

DIFFERENCES IN MEN AND WOMEN AS CONSUMERS

One of the popular stereotypes about men as shoppers is that they focus on buying what they went to the store to buy, and they do not look around. Now, this stereotype has been confirmed by extensive observational studies. These studies confirm that men move faster through stores, and do less browsing. "And they also shop the way they drive—never ask for directions!"[7] They like to read the product information on their own. In contrast, women like to get information by asking a store employee. In one study, at a wireless phone retailer, men were observed walking into the store, walking up to the product display, reading the product information brochures and posted details about available plans, taking a blank application and walking out to return later. Women, on the other hand, entered the store and walked directly up to the customer service counter, and had all their questions answered by a salesperson.[8] And as an example of focused shopping, men were found to take fewer items of clothing to the fitting or dressing room than did women. These differences are compared in Table 15.2.

We should note that many of the differences are relative to a time period and to particular societies. As gender roles change, marketers should be on the lookout for the changing patterns of male/female differences in consumer behavior.

Man or Woman: Who Decides?

In terms of decision-making in the household, for a long while, a stereotypical view has been that men are the principal decision makers for machine-like products—cars, kitchen and laundry appliances, lawn and garden tools, and homebuilding and repair tools; and that women are the main decision makers for products that go into everyday living and homemaking, such as groceries, kitchen and cleaning supplies, and bath and toiletry products. In home furnishing

TABLE 15.2 — Men Women Differences in Shopping

Men	Women
Finding Merchandise	
Men dont like to ask for directions in the store, but attempt to find it on their own.	Women would readily ask any available store employee, "where is ------------"?
Browsing	
Men move faster in the store and tend to not engage in much browsing. They focus on what they came to buy.	Women move at a relaxed pace and browse through merchandise even iif they came to the store with a definite purchase in mind.
Seeking Product Information	
They like to get their product information by reading merchandise tags, on pack-labels, brochures, etc.	Women like to get their information not by reading labels etc, but by asking the salesperson.
Trying Things On	
Men try out what they must. In a cllothes store, they will take only a few clothes to the dressing room, the clothes they have already decided to buy provided they will fit. Trying a product is the last stage in their purchase decision.	Whatever be the product - lipsticks, perfume, underwear---, women will try a lot of styles or variations. Trying a product is just a part of the consideration process for them, not a final stage in the decision.

Source: Compiled from *Why We Buy: The Science of Shopping*, Paco Underhill (Simon & Schuster, 1999). (Used with Permission)

This Norelco Shaver Ad appeals to men with a utilitarian benefit, of course: an unexpectedly close shave. But it also appeals to men's psyche: their love of thrill driving. And the anticipation of wherever "life takes you."

and decorating too, women are deemed to assume the primary responsibility. This conventional picture needs to be updated in two aspects: first, many products have both functional and aesthetic features, and for these products, women tend to be concerned with aesthetic features, influencing choices even for products where men take the lead. Thus, for kitchen appliances, for instance, a woman may play a more influential role in making color choices, along with such functional features as rinse clarity and cycle time.

Second, more and more men as well as women are staying single longer (either never married or divorced). Consequently, product categories that were hitherto the exclusive or predominant shopping domains of one gender are crossing over to encompass the other gender as well. Thus, men are spending more time in the kitchen, for example. According to some popular magazine writers, the way to a woman's heart is to be a good cook—and so men can be found shopping in the supermarket. Likewise, single women are becoming sole decision-makers—buying cars, appliances, and tools. Seeing this trend, Home Depot, a U.S. home improvement retailer, has positioned itself as a women-friendly store, with a considerable number of female employees available to help and advise, and special home improvement in-store classes for women

CONSUMPTION DIFFERENCES BETWEEN MEN AND WOMEN

Let us consider principal men-women differences in the three important product areas: food, clothing, and home-making,

Food Concerning food, gender differences exist in health-oriented perceptions of foods and beverages. Women tend to buy fresh vegetables more because these are healthier than canned vegetables. Diet foods and diet drinks are also more popular among women than among men. In the 25-34 age group, single men spend more of their food budget (65 percent) away from home (i.e., in buying food at restaurants) compared with women, who spend 55 percent. (See also "Why Women Go Binge Eating," Exhibit 15.1.)

Clothing In clothing, some men-women differences exist around the globe (e.g., skirts limited to women except in Scotland), but many differences are culture-based. These differences include differences in color, fabric, and style. Certain fabrics are exclusively (e.g., chiffon and satin) or predominantly (e.g., silk) employed in women's clothing. Bright, full-spectrum colors are usually used for women, whereas men are mostly clothed in white, blue, black, brown, and gray. In terms of cut and style, while both men and women have a variety of clothing to choose from to suit their own personality, women's clothing entails a wider range of styles.

While fashion and public image consciousness may be present to the same degree among men and women alike (although this too varies across cultures), the range of fashion accessories and accoutrements suitable to reflect shades of moods and personality is many times broader for women than for men in almost all cultures. Consequently, the drive to obtain a good "fit" (from a psychological standpoint) is generally much more intense among women than among men.

Furthermore, except in a few very liberated cultures, women are also more thoughtful and concerned about what they wear lest they inadvertently send, by their clothing, a wrong message to men around them. Men tend to perceive women's clothing styles as indications of the wearers' motivations and moods. Even though unjustified, this use of women's clothing as "signaling"—implicitly communicating one's attitudes and desires—is widespread in many cultures. Therefore, in office settings, there are some unwritten rules about what is correct office wear. The marketers of clothing understand these differences. Firms like Anne Klein have gone to the extent of setting up hot lines for women who may need advice about their choice in clothing for the office.

EXHIBIT 15.1

Look What CB Researchers Found...

WHY WOMEN GO BINGE EATING

Everyone occasionally eats without actually being hungry—that is, when there is no physiological need for food. We eat because we are feeling bored, alone, overwhelmed, anxious, and so on. These instances of food consumption are called emotional eating. It has generally been observed that women indulge in emotional eating much more than do men. This hypothesis has been tested in some research studies. Three studies done in Germany and Denmark found that both men and women indulge in emotional eating, but this behavior is more prevalent among women.

Why these gender differences? Suzanne C. Grunert, a marketing professor at Odense University, Denmark, has reviewed available sociological and psychological theories on the topic and has proposed the following explanation for the emotional eating behavior more prevalent among women. Grunert's model attributes this behavior to four factors:

1. Gender differences in personal values. Women more than men have hedonistic values (concepts about what is worth having) such as pleasure, fun, and enjoyment. These values lead women toward emotional eating.

2. Gender differences in personality traits- Women tend to score higher than men on such personality traits as empathy, guilt, fear, altruism, and social anxiety. Women who are experiencing negative emotions tend to resort to eating as a compensation. By giving, worrying, and so on, they feel a lack of something (e.g., self-esteem, security, and so forth), so they compensate for it by some other behavior such as eating. Compensatory eating is thus a kind of emotional eating.

3. Gender-specific roles. In most societies, women are loaded with a greater number and diversity of roles (as mothers, wives, and workers) than men. Moreover, women consider these diverse roles as more central to their self-identity (whereas men may consider only one or two of all of their roles as defining of their self-concept). Failure to fulfill all roles well causes them anxiety, which in turn causes compensatory eating. Also, situations in which new role expectations emerge while the old ones still remain may also call for some compensations through relatively easily available pleasures such as eating.

4. Body image. Society's concepts about appearance and attractiveness, applied differently across genders, also influence women's feeling of well-being and satisfaction. More preoccupied with their body weight and appearance, women go on diets more often than do men. Then, to compensate for the sacrifice they made in dieting, they indulge in periodic temporary eating binges.

This model is a rich illustration of how a multitude of factors covered in this textbook such as cultural values and norms, gender roles, and gender-specific personality traits explain a customer behavior phenomenon we frequently observe in Western societies.

This phenomenon does not occur uniformly across nations and across cultures. In developing countries, for example, we are unlikely to observe the greater prevalence of emotional eating among women than men. One reason is that a slim body is not necessarily considered more attractive in these cultures. Furthermore, eating is more of an organized activity-undertaken at specified times of the day, and as a family unit as a whole. The individual snacking, or "grazing" as it is often called, is just not the custom or habit. But even in the Western context for which the above model is proposed, Professor Grunert is careful to note that these are hypotheses, based on whatever research findings exist and that they still need verification for women consumers in a specific country.

Source: Suzanne C. Grunert, "On Gender Differences in Eating Behavior," in Janeen Arnold Costa, ed., Gender Issues and Consumer Behavior (Thousand Oaks: Sage, 1994), pp. 63-83. (Used with permission.)

Home Men-women differences in shelter preferences are also well known. In the purchase of a house, for example, men and women look for different features. Women are generally much more concerned with such functional features as the amount of closet space in bedrooms, the size and shape of the kitchen, and (if they have small children) the proximity of the house to a playground. Men, on the other hand, have historically been more concerned with such functional aspects as the construction of the house; the heating, cooling, and electrical systems; and the kind of building materials utilized.

Likewise, home decorating or redecorating choices are influenced by gender.

According to a survey done by Home Furnishings Council, in redecorating their home, husbands focus mainly on dens (where men generally gather during parties or where men retire to relax or watch sports), whereas wives focus on the living room and kitchen, where they spend a lot of time daily. Marketers should be watchful, however, for changes in gender-based preferences since many of the traditional gender roles in the United States are changing.

Consumption-at-large Men-women differences permeate many other domains of consumption. For example, one study of U.S. brides and grooms found that brides considered the wedding ceremony itself as the most important event, whereas grooms considered the reception as the key event. Thus, brides considered the wedding dress immensely significant and even sacred, requiring great planning and extensive deliberation. Also greatly significant to the bride were the choice of the church and the minister, the flowers, decorations, and the music. In contrast, grooms saw the success of the wedding more closely associated with a judicious selection of the reception hall, hearty food, and good socialization during the reception.[9]

One noteworthy issue is that men-women differences are not the same across all sections of a society. Rather they differ by certain consumer characteristics. First, the gender role differences between men and women tend to be less pronounced with education. High school-educated men and women are more likely to be divergent than college-educated men and women. This is due to a broadened perspective that comes with education. Second, with education come occupational differences—college educated men and women are more likely to have professional jobs. Consumers in professional jobs exhibit fewer men-women differences in gender roles than does the average consumer. Finally, higher-income groups (which is often accompanied with better education and occupation) are likely to show reduced men-women gender role differences.[10]

MARKETING IMPLICATIONS

Successful marketers use their knowledge about male-female preferences to meet the needs of both groups of consumers. Today, a large number of men are buying groceries, and women are buying cars. By the early 1990s, women had already become 49 percent of all new-car buyers! Today they exercise an influence on some 80 percent of all new-car sales. So carmakers are paying attention to women's needs. Chrysler Corporation has an advisory committee on the Women's Auto Market. Cars for women are designed differently. For example, the rear deck on minivans is supposed to lift easier. Also, many minivans now have integrated child seats and a purse carrier. Some car dealers have built play areas for children and diaper-changing stations in restrooms. Finally, many dealers have female salespersons, and male salespersons are learning not to disregard women who accompany their husbands for car shopping. Moreover, sales-pitches about a car's technical performance are no longer directed only to male customers.[11]

Since men's visits to a store are acquisition-focused whereas women's visits are browsing-oriented, men often make very impatient companions when they accompany a woman on shopping trips. While women are still browsing, men just hang around impatiently, and if asked for advice, they would suggest buying, just so the woman can get over with shopping and they can get out of there ASAP. It therefore behooves retailers, especially of women's apparel, to find ways to occupy men. For example, retailers could provide a lounge area with a TV turned to ESPN or some other sports program channel.

For products in which both men and women take interest, such as kitchen appliances and home furnishinga (in part, perhaps because these are high ticket items), retailers could arrange the product displays to simultaneously appeal to both the sexes. Men seek product composition information while women are more tuned to aesthetics and appearance. So, to appeal to women, products could be displayed to recreate the "product in place at home" view—e.g., appliances set in a partial kitchen and furniture in room displays, complete with flowers and other home furnishings. With Internet kiosks or portable computers, retailers could show these products in customizable settings. For men, on the other hand, point of sale displays could feature product cut-out views and information about materials and technical specifications.

One more point about men as shoppers is worth noting. Although men don't usually browse, they are not averse to buying what was not on their initial list, if it catches their attention. They are not impulsive but they are not very deliberative either. For instance, when a child accompanying his or her dad makes a request, the dad usually gives his consent. A well-known retail store researcher, Paco Underhill, has this to say about dads in the supermarket with kids in the tow:

> It is here [in the supermarket], with thousands of products all within easy reach, that you can witness the carefree abandon and restless lack of discipline for which the gender is known…. Giving him a vehicle to commandeer, even if it is just a shopping cart, only emphasizes the potential for guyness in the experience. Throw a couple of kids in with Dad and you have got a lethal combination; he is notoriously bad at saying no when there is grocery acquisitioning to be done. Part of being Daddy is being the provider, after all. It goes to the heart of a man's self-image." (p. 100).

As an aside, men make very attractive consumers on one particular shopping day: Valentine's Day. That day, men spend considerably more than women. In a recent year, the average amount for an American male consumer was $126, versus $38 by female consumers.[12]

Woman Magic in Store Design

If you are selling clothing for women, shouldn't your store design revolve around them?

Levi's Jeans for Women Shop at Macy's Harold Square, New York takes this idea to the apex.

Notice the furniture, the mannequins, the laminated glass panel behind the cashwrap. They all share an alluring feature with the target audience—womanly curves

In this masterpiece store design by San Francisco's creative design firm Morla Designs, every visual detail is designed to charm its target customer—the woman. Even the script on the carpet has, well, womanly curves—in all shapes and sizes!

Store/Fixture Design ©2006 Morla Design, Inc.

Romancing the Consumer   tv2010

My CB Book

In your role as a marketer, don't let Valentine's Day be your guide for the rest of the year. For the rest of the year, in fact, women, not men, spend more on gifts. Women, it turns out, also put more heart into gift buying year around than do men. Since women are more sensitive about relationships, we would expect them to be more engaged in gift-exchange, and research has found just that.

In research studies on gift-giving, women have shown greater awareness of the gift receiver's needs. Men, on the other hand, use certain implicit "guiding rules"—e.g., less than $20, easy to ship, convenient to buy without having to shop, etc. One overall guiding rule, for example, is, "What is the minimum expense I can get away with?" Overall, men usually consider gift-giving an obligation. In contrast, women treat gift-giving as an opportunity to bring happiness to the gift recipient, and in the others' happiness they feel happy. Although both men and women do give gifts, women are more the primary gift-givers, at least in the American culture. They are also the primary gift-recipients. Thus, while men give gifts predominantly to women (mostly in romantic relations), women give gifts to both genders and beyond romantic relations.[13]

But we do see men buying gifts all the time, you say. Yes, of course, but mostly for their romantic relationships. That, and also for important occasions (like birthdays and anniversaries) for close family members. In contrast, women buy gifts for friends, coworkers, neighbors, church group members, associates in volunteer organizations, etc. And the gifts men buy are generally flowers, perfumes, lingerie, and alcohol—mostly items for intimate relationships. Women buy, in contrast, a wider range of products for household use and as knick-knacks—kitchen tools, flower vases, small decorations, candles, etc.

Why do women buy and give more gifts? Although no conclusive research is available on the motivations for gift-giving and its prevalence among women, the following explanations can be considered:[14]

- Greater femininity and expressiveness
- Greater value on interpersonal relations
- Reciprocity
- Shopping

First, women possess more femininity traits and are more expressive (be that due to biology or sociology). As such, they like to nurture and care for others, and they like to express (rather than contain) their emotions and feelings. They find gift-giving a way to show their feelings. Buying a "little something" just to cheer up a coworker in temporary distress, for example, is not an unusual thing for many women.

Second, femininity implies putting greater value on interpersonal relations. To women, being connected with people is important and they are always endeavoring to build and solidify relations with friends and acquaintances. For example, if someone had a disagreement with a coworker, taking some homemade cookies might just be the right thing to do to repair the bruised relationship.

Third, since women receive more gifts than do men, it is natural that they also give gifts to a greater extent compared to men, just to reciprocate.

Finally, women like to shop—that is, they like to browse around, and consequently come across many items they want to buy. However, not all items they find attractive are suitable for their own use, but having found the irresistible item, they feel impelled to buy it. So, they immediately think of someone to gift and invent a gift occasion and thus satisfy their desire to buy the item. Having bought it, there is only one thing to do—gift it to someone. While just buying an item is gratifying, giving it as a gift doubles the pleasure.

> While just buying an item is gratifying, giving it as a gift doubles the pleasure.

METROSEXUALS, RETROSEXUALS, POMOSEXUALS, AND ÜBERSEXUALS

Trends in Male Branding

Metrosexuals **Metrosexuals** are urban males who have a strong aesthetic sense and spend a great deal of time and money on their appearances and lifestyles. The term was coined in 1994 by Mark Simpson, a British journalist. Popular media has since described this type of male as "a heterosexual man who is in touch with his feminine side," pointing as examples to such celebrities as Brad Pitt, George Clooney, and David Beckham.

If you have browsed (even if only occasionally) men's style magazines such as GQ, Esquire, or The Face, you might have sometimes wondered, "Who wears those dapper, fashionable clothes and extensive accessories?" Wonder no more—it is the metrosexuals. Their excessive grooming also has a new term—manscaping. **Manscaping** was a term introduced in 2004 by the American TV Show Queer Eye for the Straight Guy, and is shorthand for "landscaping" the male body by shaving, trimming, waxing, or brushing the body hair.[15] For most of the human history, men have generally not removed hair from their chests, legs, etc.; but in late 1990s, it became fashionable for some Generation Xers to shave their chests. Notably, the idea of depilating the whole male body was yet unborn until the Queer Eye celebrated this grooming ritual.

Retrosexuals The **Retrosexual** is the anti-metro—a man with a generally poor sense of style. The retrosexual is not necessarily a boor; it is just that he abhors the idea of being finicky about physical appearance. While metrosexuals would chide any male who does not pluck his eyebrows (that would definitely include retrosexuals), retrosexuals would consider metrosexuals positively, scornfully dandies. A retrosexual may also be known as a man who rejects casual sex as mindless and immoral.

The retrosexual lifestyle is most popular and socially accepted among men aged 18-24. However, the term is rarely used as a self-descriptor by such men, who tend to prefer, instead, such terms as "real man," "old school," or "masculine." In fact, they would see the term "retrosexual" as symptomatic of the very pretension they reject.

You are the male gender and you have all these *different kinds* of people as your friends. Well, how amazingly diverse your interests are. You surely live an interesting life. And reflecting that interesting life is your magazine, *Men's Journal*.

'Live the Interesting Life' Advertisement from Men's Journal
© Men's Journal LLC. All Rights Reserved. Reprinted by Permission.

GENDER AND AGE IN CONSUMER BEHAVIOR

15

441

Pomosexuals **Pomosexual** is a term that stands for *post-modern sexual*, and describes persons who do not identify with any specific classification of sexuality. Pomosexuals use this term to describe themselves, rejecting and protesting any other prevalent terms to describe sexual preferences or gender traits. Want to know who coined this term? It was "sex-positive" activist writers and editors Carol Queen and Lawrence Schimel, who popularized the term by using it as the title of an anthology of essays published in 1997. In it, they describe pomosexuality as the "erotic reality beyond the boundaries of gender, separatism, and essentialist notions of sexual orientation." Go figure that!! (Helpful hint: Google the term and read the first five entries.)

Übersexuals The word "über" has German roots and means above or superior. Thus, an ubersexual is a variant of metrosexual, a more "refined" male, who is more confident and more focused on his mind than body. The term was coined by the authors of the book, Future of Men, who describe it thus: "The future of men is not to be found in the primped and waxed boy who wowed the world with his nuanced knowledge of tweezers and exfoliating creams. Men, at the end of the day, will have to rely on their intellect and their passion, their erudition and professional success, to be acknowledged and idealised in contemporary society. Called the übersexual—a degree of greatness and perfection, an acknowledgment that this is an evolved species of man—he is so perfect as to leave little margin for error and fallacy."[16]

Perhaps, such a man—a man of such perfection and greatness—is more an utopian vision than an earthly reality. The ad agency JWT named some of the men it judged to be übersexuals: George Clooney, Ewan McGregor, Jon Stewart, Diddy, Jay-Z and Bono of the rock band U2.[17] Actually, though, George Clooney and Bono were named as metrosexuals when that term was first fashioned. Either they have now evolved into the metrosexual's more refined variety, or the new term's full meaning still needs to be fully grasped by even those in the know, let alone by men at large.

All these are nifty labels for psychographic types, and for that reason they are immensely useful. Marketers who can decipher and dissect the consumption lifestyles of these types can sight opportunity. What marketing opportunities do you see? (Source: Definitions are adapted in part from Wikipedia— a free encyclopedia that anyone can edit! ; http://en.wikipedia.org/wiki/Metrosexual)

cb

AGE

Why Marketers Want To Know How Old You Are

How old are you? Yes, we know it is impolite to ask. Still, we need to know. We are, you see, the marketer. And in a minute, you will appreciate why it is important for us to know your age.

Let us guess: Looks like you are twenty-one, right? Then you wouldn't be interested in a radio-monitored toy car, would you? Or a video of Frank Sinatra? And your dad, now in his early fifties, wouldn't be interested in a music video of Eminem or J'Lo, would he? Your age, you see, has a monumental influence on your behavior as a person and as a consumer. You see it in everyday life—people older than you generally buy different things than what you buy. Likewise, people younger than you are just not interested in many products that interest you. But being or not being interested in a toy here and a music CD there is just the tip of the proverbial iceberg. These differences go deeper: persons of different age groups differ in their abilities, resources, needs, and desires; consequently, they differ in their view of themselves and of the marketplace.

It is important for marketers to understand age-related differences for two reasons. First, since consumer behavior differs sharply across different age groups, marketers often need to fashion their products and marketing programs by age groups. Second, age is the only factor which changes (i.e., increases) simply by the passage of time; so today's 25 year olds will not stay that way tomorrow. This constant aging of consumers means that marketers must change their marketing programs as well. How?

First, we should adjust our products if we want to serve the same consumers as they age. For example, suppose we want to provide healthcare to Salma, in her 20s, and Alfred, in his 30s, for the rest of their lives. For this, we would need to adjust our healthcare resources and services as they age. To do this, we will need to know, ahead of time, what kind of healthcare will 30, 40, 50, and 60 year olds need.

Second, suppose we don't want to serve Salma and Alfred as they age; rather, we just want to serve whoever is 20-30 years old. The problem with this is that our market size will fluctuate. For example, if today there are 20 million 20-30 year olds, then 10 years from now, there could be 25 million of them or only 15 million of them—this depends largely on how many babies were born ten years ago. This will expand or shrink our market opportunity significantly. Are we ready to exploit that expansion, or cope with that shrinkage in the total number of consumers? That is why, as marketers, we need to keep track of age distribution in a population. Let us see how age distribution is changing around the world.

AGE DISTRIBUTION OF POPULATIONS
The Changing Landscape of the Market

If we want to market our products to consumers in any country, the first thing we will (or should) want to know is how many consumers there are. In 2000, the world's population was 6.057 billion. The largest population was in China (21.05%); the second largest was in India (16.65 %). The U.S. was the distant third (4.6 %). Table 15.3 shows the population of the ten largest countries. Do these numbers matter to marketers? To savvy marketers, they do. Kentucky Fried Chicken (KFC), a U.S. based fast food franchise, operates more than 900 stores in China, and earns 15% of its total profits from feeding some 20 million Chinese every day. Guess which country is next on its list? India. China and India are the most coveted consumer markets for many global brands today—Coca Cola and Pepsi, General Electric and Sony, Nestlé'

TABLE 15.3 Population of The ten Largest Countries

COUNTRY	POPULATION Millions	%
China	1,275	21.05
India	1,009	16.65
U.S.A.	283	4.60
Indonesia	212	3.50
Brazil	170	2.80
Russia	145	2.32
Pakistan	141	2.32
Bangladesh	137	2.26
Japan	127	2.09
Nigeria	114	1.88

Source: United Nation, Statistics Bureau, Ministry of Public Management, Home Affairs, Posts, and Telecommunications.

and Unilever, to cite just a few. In marketing, such is the magic of large numbers. Large numbers of consumers, that is.

Age Group Distribution Knowing the total number of consumers is, however, just the beginning. After we know the population of the world and of any specific country, the next thing we would want to know as marketers is their age distribution. As a marketer, you wouldn't market the same product to the young and the old, would you? How many children, how many adults, and how many old people, etc.,—are answers you would want to know. In the U.S., consumers 24 or younger are 35.3% of the population. Do you suppose this ratio of young consumers to total population is the same for other countries? The answer is "no." In fact, one of the most fascinating aspects of studying different countries' populations is the discovery of how the ratio of old to young people varies.

Table 15.4 gives the age distribution of selected countries for years 2005 and 2030 (projected), arranged here by the percentage of 65 years or older population as projected in 2030. Japan tops this list, with 21.0% in 2005, growing to 29.6% by 2030. India the lowest (5.3% in 2005), and the U.S. somewhere in between (19.2% in 2030). Conversely, Japan has the smallest proportion of children in its population (13.6%), and India the largest (32.1%). Guess where you would want to sell Disney cartoon movies?

Another interesting thing to note here is the projected change in these proportions over the next 25 years. Japan will still top the list in terms of the percentage of 65 years or older, but that number will grow only by about 40% (from 21.0% to 29.6%). In European countries, the proportion will rise by 40 to 60%. But in Brazil, it will nearly double; in China, it will rise by 110%; in Republic of Korea, by a whopping 150%.

Correspondingly, the proportion of other age groups will decline. Mostly by a small proportion of, say, 10 to 15%, except in three countries at the bottom of the list. In China, it will decline by approximately 20%, and in Brazil and India by 30%! Guess you will have to convert some of those Disney cartoon movies into artsy operas!

Since this is a wealth of knowledge, you must be eager to know why age distribution varies. Here is why: the total population as well as the age distribution is affected by three factors: birth rate, life expectancy, and migration. As these factors change, so does the age distribution. Most importantly, the aging of the population as seen in Table 15.4 is happening because, globally, the birth rate is declining and the life expectancy is increasing.

TABLE 15.4   Age Distribution of Population in Selected Countries

COUNTRY	2005 0-14	15-64	65 and over	2030 (Projection) 0-14	15-64	65 and over
Japan	13.6	65.3	21.0	11.3	59.2	29.6
Italy	14.0	66.0	20.0	11.9	59.0	29.1
Germany	14.3	66.9	18.8	14.0	59.5	26.6
Switzerland	16.5	67.6	16.0	14.9	58.7	26.3
France	18.2	65.2	16.6	16.1	59.6	24.2
Republic of Korea	18.6	72.0	9.4	12.7	63.9	23.4
Canada	17.6	69.3	13.1	15.6	61.1	23.3
Sweden	17.5	65.3	17.2	17.0	59.9	23.1
U.K.	17.9	66.1	16.0	17.3	61.3	21.4
Australia	19.6	67.7	12.7	17.4	62.0	20.6
U.S.A.	20.8	66.9	12.3	18.1	62.6	19.2
China	21.4	71.0	7.6	16.9	66.8	16.3
Brazil	27.9	66.0	6.1	20.9	66.6	12.5
India	32.1	62.7	5.3	22.6	68.1	9.3

* Table arranged by the 65+ population in 2030. All numbers are percentages.
Source: United Nation, Statistics Bureau, Ministry of Public Management, Home Affairs, Posts, and Telecommunications.

POPULATION PYRAMIDS

As Table 15.4 shows, the age composition of a population can change dramatically over time. This shift in population age dsitibution is captured in **population pyramids**—a layered depiction of males and females by age groups. These are shown for the U.S. in Figure 15.1.

| Figure 15.1 | Population Pyramids for U.S.A. |

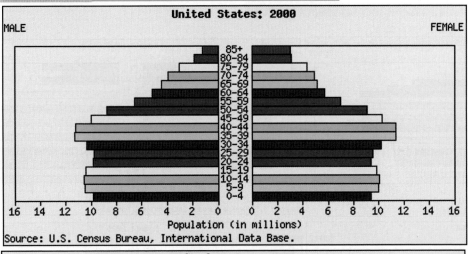

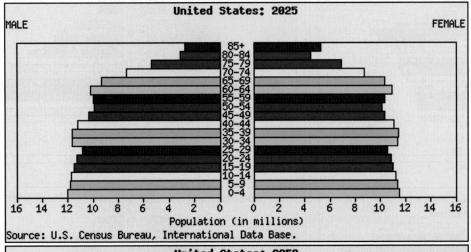

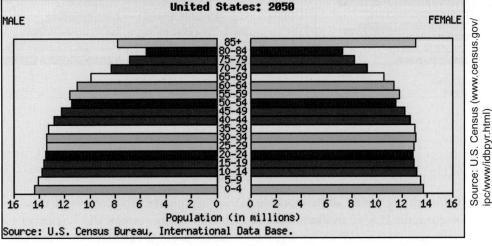

As these pyramids show, the population's aging changes the people landscape of a nation dramatically, Let us look at these pyramids for two other countries (Japan and Egypt), shown in Figure 15.2. If you are a marketer in Japan, selling clothing, music, food, cell phones, or whatever, you would realize how dramatically your product offerings and marketing communications (e.g., advertising, personal selling, etc.) will have to change over time, because of changes in the age distribution of your target customers. And, of course, the pyramid is changing in all other countries as well. (See Figure 15.2.)

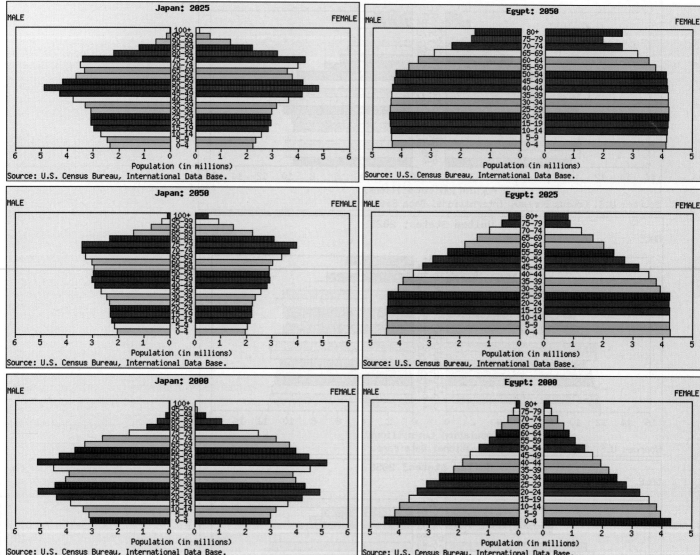

AGE BASED CONSUMER SEGMENTS

Consumer behaviors differ markedly across age groups. To understand how, we will be using the U.S. as an illustration throughout. To some extent, the differences are universal—i.e., 20 year olds everywhere tend to have some of the same mindsets and some of the same lifestyles and product tastes, which are different from the mindsets and tastes of 30 or 50 or 70 year olds, no matter where these 20, 30, 50 or 70 year olds live. Just as surely though, at least some of the differences between 20 and 30 and 50 and 70 year olds are going to be country and culture specific. To capture these differences, marketers must study diverse age groups in the countries and cultures they are serving.

Various Age Generations in North America

In many ways, a young person (say, 25 year old) fifty years ago behaved like a young person behaves today, and this young person in turn behaves today just like a 25 year old will behave 50 years from now. At the same time, there are important differences simply because that was then and this is now. Therefore, to understand consumer psychology, marketers need to divide the population not only by age but by time periods and examine a group of consumers born in a particular time period. This manner of grouping consumers is called "generations." For example, the well-known Generation X is identified not by age but by the year of its birth. Everyone born between 1964 and 1976 is a Generation Xer and will remain so no matter how old he or she becomes.

The book *Generations* identifies four age groups in the U.S. population.[18] These are: (1) The GI Generation—born from 1901 to 1924; (2) Silent Generation—born between 1925 and 1945; (3) Baby Boomers—born between 1946 to 1964; and (4) Generation X—born between 1965 to 1976. To these, we need to add two more groups: (5) Generation Y—born between 1977 to 1984; and (6) Teens and Children—born post 1987[19]. Of these, we refer to the first two generations simply as 'Seniors' and profile them under that heading in the text below (for those interested, we profile these two groups individually in a box).

Readers who are college students will probably want to read first about their own generation, Generation Y (even if you are a few years younger—born between the years 1984 and 1987, your consumer behavior most resembles that of Gen Y). But we will save it for last (almost). Let us begin with Baby Boomers, followed by their seniors, then Gen X, Gen Y, and finally, teens.

BABY BOOMERS

Seeking the Fountain of Eternal Youth

Born between 1946 and 1964, Baby Boomers number about 76 million[20]. They were dubbed Baby Boomers because in 1946 the birth rate suddenly sky-rocketed (soldiers came back from war and made, well, babies!) and subsided by 1964. Now middle-aged (42 to 60 years old, in 2006), the youngest of them are still in the parenting trap—about half of them have children under the age of 18. As a group, Baby Boomers are educated and affluent. This group contributes disproportionately to the $75,000-$200,000+ income groups. In education, the gender gap has narrowed for this group, compared with earlier generations.

About one-half of women have had some college experience, and one-fourth are college graduates. Employment rate among baby boomers is high among both the sexes. Three out of four baby-boomer men and one in every two women have full-time jobs. Unlike the preceding generations, nearly four out of five baby-boomer women are employed outside the home.[21] About 60 percent of boomer households are married couples. Among boomer households with children, about one in four is a single-parent household, mostly (9 out of 10) headed by a female. This means that time is a major constraint, and marketers who can make convenient, time-saving products and services available anytime, anywhere will be favored by this group.

Of course, baby boomers are a broad group. In the mid-1980s, this group's age ranged from 21 to 40. During these years, it was logical to distinguish between the younger boomers (21 to 30) and older boomers (31 to 40). The former group was then preoccupied with trying to find a good job and a marriage partner. Their older cohorts were living a more settled life. In the 1990s, and even more so in the new millennium, the two groups became more similar, as most had the responsibilities of parenting and home ownership. The spending patterns for most baby boomers became similar, driven by the needs and wants of their children, including the need to save for college.

One phenomenon many of the Baby Boomers are experiencing in the new millennium has resulted in their being dubbed the "Sandwich Generation"[22]—a generation sandwiched between the twin burdens of caring for their own children as well as their aging parents. This latter burden is becoming heavier due to the fact that many of the seniors are living well into 90 years of age and beyond (due to improved life expectancy), and they are becoming the responsibility of their adult children, the Baby Boomers.

©iStockphoto.com/Oleg Prikhodko

Now, at the turn of the century, the oldest of the baby boomers, say those born between 1946 and 1955, entered their empty-nest years, freed from the burdens of childrearing. This has freed them to spend both money and time more on themselves and also accelerate their investment in retirement plans. These older boomers will once again differ from their younger cohorts. Thus, baby boomers are a moving target, and marketers must learn to move along with them.[23]

The Baby Boomers are the most self-absorbed of all four generations. They have been preoccupied with career and material success. But now they have a new obsession, and it is one that cuts across both the groups (the younger and the older Baby Boomers)—it is to defy aging. Their number one concern these days is looks. Psychologically, they don't feel old, so physically, they don't want to look old. In a survey, Boomers expressed the least satisfaction about their appearance. Only 39 percent of Boomers felt happy about their appearance (compared to 53 percent among their seniors and 45% among their juniors).

The obsession with youthful looks has Baby Boomers searching for the proverbial fountain of youth. In a recent survey by the AARP (American Association of Retired Persons), half of the Boomers admitted having depressive thoughts about aging, and one in every five reported that they were doing something to resist it. That something entails a three-pronged attack: (1) exercise and dieting, (2) nutrients and chemicals—pills, creams, and gulps, (3) surgical augmentations.

1. **Exercising and Dieting** Increasingly, the Boomers are taking to exercise and diet, driven as much by a desire to look good as the desire to be healthy. About 33 million Americans go to the gym and more than half of them are over 40. Health clubs are now targeting the so-called "New Me's" and "Second Chancers,"—body conscious and divorced Boomers who want to look young again. Both gyms and spas and home exercise equipment companies are fast growing businesses

2. **Nutrients, Cosmetics, and Chemicals** The second front in the Boomer's war against aging is the use of nutrients, cosmetics, and chemicals. Nutrients work on the body internally to keep cells healthy; cosmetics and chemicals work externally to mask the signs of aging. U.S. consumers spend about $30 billion on these anti-aging products every year. Boomers are increasingly consuming health pills ranging from ginko biloba for mental alertness, glucosamine for joints, and coEnzyme Q10, which some call the miracle vitamin of the 1990s.

Anti-aging creams are also hugely popular—35% of women have used some age- defying cream such as Nivea's Visage or Nutrogena's Visibly Firm. Then, there is hair color—designed to hide the unflattering gray. Fifty three percent of Boomer women use hair color to hide their graying hair (not counting women who use it to alter their color from non-gray to other shades); among men, 6% of them use hair color and their ranks are growing.

Surgical and Medical Procedures The last and most recent front in the anti-aging war is various medical and surgical procedures to actually alter the appearance of the body and face. In 2001, over 250,000 adults underwent liposuction, and a similar number underwent eyelid surgery. About 125,000 had a facelift. Botox became the most popular surgical procedure. In 2002 alone, close to a million consumers had Botox injections (41% of them were 35 to 50), just as many had a collagen injection, about 750,000 had laser hair removal, and over a million had a chemical peel. About half of all these treatments were received by Boomers.

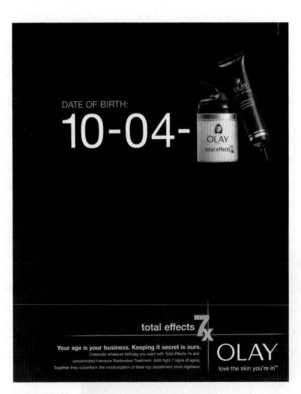

Fourth of October No Year—or rather the YEAR as you wish. Keeping Boomers forever young is Olay.
(Photo courtesy: Procter & Gamble)

It is due to their desire to continue life in "prime time" that this group has been called a "marketer's dream" by Business Week, which ran a cover story on Boomers in October 2005. Marketers are paying close attention to this booming opportunity. Christie Brinkley was a model for Covergirl brand of cosmetics during the 1970s and 80s; the company recently brought back the 51 year old superstar. Why? To appeal to Boomer women![24]

MARKETER RESPONSE

Marketers have risen to the occasion, responding to Boomers' needs for age-defying products. Exercise equipment has been modified to suit the aging boomers' physical stamina and needs; thus, low impact exercises, stationary bikes (rather than weight training), and elliptical training equipment, pilates, elastic bands, and big vinyl stability balls can be seen in sports stores and gyms nationwide. Also in vogue is yoga, which stretches the muscles, tones the body, and also relaxes and relieves stress.

Sports equipment itself is seeing a "facelift" and "liposuction" as well. For example, Wilson Sports has brought out a trimmed, lighter weight tennis racket and golf clubs. Solomon, a maker of skis, has come out with "lighter" skis, and even Nike has a line of shoes and clothing with "leaner mass" for the aging Boomer bodies.

Functional foods are now a $30 billion business. These include organic foods, soy milk, and new formulations of cereals (such as General Mills' Harmony that is enriched with antioxidants). There is even a new name for the product category: *Nutraceuticals*. These are new beverages fortified with nutrients: Acquafina Essential, Reebok Fitness Waters, and SoBe Beverages. With these cool sounding names, they are simultaneously healthy and trendy.

SENIORS

Anything but Sedated

Born before 1945, this group accounts for some 46 million Americans. Of course, it has now been some 20 years since the oldest of them entered the retirement age. In their 80's now, the older segment of this group is not very active. But don't dismiss them as sedate, depressed, indigent, or consuming only such elder care services as nursing homes and health care services. Many of them participate in regular shopping activity in national supermarkets and in the mall, and live life with good natured humor, typified by the TV Series Golden Girls' 80-something Sophia.

The youngest of the seniors are still in workforce, and only a few years away from being eligible to retire. More and more of them expect to continue to remain usefully employed (although not necessarily full-time), in part because they remain healthy and able-bodied and in part because the stock market nosedive of the Internet era (1999-2002) wiped out a significant portion of their pension and retirement funds. But even the oldest among this generation remain active, and able to provide for themselves. Their income is lowered after retirement, but they have the luxury of their house having been paid off, so their expenses are considerably less as well. Many are affluent, and indeed many support their grandchildren's education (thus lightening the burden on these grandchildren's struggling parents).

According to a recent survey done by the Georgia State University's Center for Mature Consumer Studies, 35.3 million Americans aged 65 or over had discretionary incomes of roughly twice that of debt-immersed Baby Boomers. These seniors were heavily into traveling and other leisure activities. Of course, at the other end, many were unable to provide for themselves, and are a financial burden on their adult children—the Boomers.

Seniors are also heavier consumers of leisure travel, both domestic and foreign. More than 47% own cell phones. And more than any other age groups, they are readers of the printed word, accounting for a disproportionately high readership of newspapers and magazines. They are not as attracted by fantasies or escapist appeals; rather, products must be shown to help them attain their values. With aging, consumers

Charolett Schworer, celebrating birthday, her ... well, who is counting!

process information more slowly, but they have a richer store of information to supplement the slowly acquired new information. Therefore, older consumers don't fall for advertising hyperbole. And they have more time to do comparison shopping and product research.[25]

COGNITIVE AGE

One phenomenon that marks all ages but especially the older Boomers and seniors is cognitive age. **Cognitive age** is defined as an individual's perception of how old he or she feels. It is viewing oneself as a more or less youthful person. As such, it is an integral aspect of one's self-concept.

"I am 55 but I feel like a 35!" We all know someone who has said this, or at least who acts younger thanhe or she is. At the other end of the age continuum, you might also know some teenagers who say "I am an adult now" and know someone who indeed acts like one. This is subjective age, the age a person subjectively feels he or she is. This differs from one's objective or chronological age, counting in number of years since birth. Subjective age is more formally known as "cognitive age." Typically, teenagers like to view themselves two years older than they are; the cognitive and chronological ages tend to run in parallel during the 21 to 30 years. Then consumers begin to view themselves younger than they are: by two to three years at 31 to 40 years, four to eight years at 41 to 50, and up to ten years after 50. Two caveats: these are educated guesses (as no statistical survey findings are available), and cognitive age is more of a Western World phenomenon (remember, in Eastern societies, age is revered, so consumers have no motivation to feel younger).

The important point is that it is cognitive age rather than the chronological age which determines lifestyle consumptions for Boomers and seniors.

GENERATION X

THE COMING OF AGE

After the boomers came this next group, born between 1965 and 1975. Because they represent those born during the years of low birth rate, thus busting the sharp growth of the preceding baby-boomer era, they are sometimes also called "baby busters." Because of their negation of most boomer values, they also have been dubbed *Generation X*. More than any other generation, Gen 'X' are pragmatics, not ideologues. Their image of the boomers is that of Woodstock—that they, the boomers, had a big party and didn't clean up.

The psychological makeup of Xers differs from that of Boomers. Baby Boomers, whether younger or older, came of age when the U.S. economy was sound. Therefore, Boomers have been optimistic and have had confidence in their ability to succeed. The Xers feel, on the other hand, financially less secure. They also rejected the boomers' obsession with career and making money. Instead, they sought to work just enough to get by, and for this reason, and somewhat unfairly, they got dubbed as *slackers*.

The Slacker Generation ?

©iStockphoto.com/Libby Chapman

Numbering some 45 million, the majority of them are in the workforce and also in the family formation and child rearing stage. And they want to raise their family differently than their parents did. A significant proportion of them experienced being "home alone," and many grew up in broken homes (due to divorced parents). They want to raise their children in two-parent families; therefore, dual-careers are less important to them. Many of them believe that one parent should stay home with the children. Gen X men are more involved than men from preceding generations in child rearing, and more of them are advocates of equal gender roles. With family-building, Gen Xers are realizing their financial responsibility and a majority of them (68% by a recent estimate) have already begun to save for their retirement (not far behind the 77% of Boomers today, although boomers didn't begin thinking about saving for retirement when they were as young as Gen Xers are today).

Nostalgia: A Gen Xer goofing off—and playing a mafia boss

Of course, not all Gen Xers are slackers (and they never were). Many are shaking off that moniker with upward careers.

©iStockphoto.com/Nicholas Monu

Xers' major purchases today comprise of setting up a home—appliances, furnishings, indoor games, etc. The youngest of them are starting out or have recently started a career and are first time buyers of a new car. Their partaking of music, concerts, pubs, fast food and restaurants—which filled their consumer lives of the student days—is slowing as they settle down.

Gen Y: The Most Globally Homogeneous

©iStockphoto.com/Sean Locke

The Most Globally Homogeneous

Born between 1977 and 1984, Gen Y get their name simply because they followed Gen X. Actually, there is no consensus on whom to count as Generation Y. Some authors stop counting at 1984, and some authors extend it to those born up to 1995.[26] Depending on how one counts, this group can range from 35 to 70 million. However, our profile below will focus on the group born between 1977 and 1984—this was the group that marked a departure from the previous two generations.

Like Gen X, Gen Y has disowned the Boomer values of self-absorption and materialism. But they do differ from Gen X on an important aspect. Gen X did not adopt any alternative ideology, staying uninvolved in any social issues. In contrast, Gen Y is ideological, embracing social issues such as environmentalism, animal treatment, vegetarianism, racial integration, etc. Growing up in the age of the computer (when home PCs were widespread), and coming of age in the era of the Internet, they are the most tech savvy of all generations. You can see them in constant chatter with their friends on their cell phones, on the Instant Messenger (IM), and via emails, sharing stories, music, and photos. They are the most ethnically inter-mingling, and more than any other generation, they exhibit global homogeneity. Today, youth everywhere dress alike, listen to the same music, and share the same chat rooms.

Some 35 million in number, these 22 to 29 year olds can be found mostly on college campuses, military bases, in their first jobs in corporations, in their parental homes, and, as shoppers, in stores like Express, Abercrombie & Fitch, and J. Crew. Their individual buying power is small, but collectively it is a large sum. In 2003, their combined buying power was $150 billion. The older of them have joined the workforce and now make their own money to participate fully in the marketplace. The younger of them still get some allowance from home or make some money doing odd jobs. With it, they buy clothes (e.g., T-shirts, baseball caps), shoes, athletic wear, team sport memorabilia, fast food, books, movies, cell phones and personal items…and they patronize restaurants and bars.

According to a recent report, nearly half of the never married adults aged 22 to 29 live with their parents. Many return after a brief sojourn living out of the home. They find living at home attractive because food is generally free, and the rent is either waived or subsidized, and chores are also shared. Many who live at home are motivated to save and build their bank accounts so that they can buy a car, or when they get a job, they can afford the down payment on a house. All youth, whether they live at home, on college campuses, or at military bases, differ from their boomer parents (although they are in many respects, similar to Gen X'ers.)

Their music is not rock 'n' roll or classic rock or retro; instead, it is rap, urban rhythm and blues, and industrial dance music. They will be known

Young consumers, the Gen Y, are comfortable with such situations. Indeed they enjoy them. 55DSL jeans will be comfortable (notice the demanding body postures they are upto), but more importantly, the brand here appeals to the Gen Y "psyche"—goofy fun but work hard as well.

453

most for embracing hip hop as a mainstream music style—it is they who made white rapper Eminem's 8 mile a box office hit. They wear clothing that ranges from punk to preppie, from sloppy grunge to environment-friendly eco shirts. They are dead serious about getting a job and about getting an education so they may get a job—unlike their parents (Boomers) who were sometimes in college just for the experience, or to engage in political protest and reform. Social issues have a big appeal for today's youth. Issues like the environment, drug abuse, AIDS, and discrimination arouse young people, and young adults reward those businesses that support such social causes. Another important characteristic of this group is its dislike of hype in advertising. They dislike overstatement, hypocrisy, and false pretense of status image for the advertised products. To them, a product must be advertised and sold on its utility, rather than hype. This is not to imply that Gen Yers don't buy for image, but the image is the one they give a product, and the one they perceive from their social observations and from peer groups, not the one that the advertising hypes. And they reject conspicuous consumption.

TEENAGERS

The Early Consumer Socialization

Teens are a significant consumer segment for marketers, accounting for some 30 million in 2000. The older among them earn a small amount on their own, but nearly all get some allowance from their parents. Even more important, they influence a number of purchases of the family; indeed, the more significant the purchase, the more they influence it—the car and family vacation destinations, for example. Of all the people, teenagers have the most time available to spend in the checkout lines. Not surprisingly, a large number of them do family shopping. Many live their life as latchkey children with parents working, and many parents leave a note for the older teenager (who can drive) to go to the supermarket and buy a few things. And they often accompany their parent(s) on shopping trips. More than any other generation, then, this generation is becoming socialized into being a consumer at an early age—learning the art of buying. And this is happening more for teenagers today than it happened for the teenagers of yesteryears.

©iStockphoto.com/Tadija

One of the important teen traits is that they like to look a couple of years older than they are (i.e., a 14-year-old likes to look 16). An older teen will never seek advice from, or be influenced by younger teens. As a group, teens like to hang out in the mall, and they like to go shopping. But they (the younger teenagers) are constrained by not being of the driving age yet; as such they depend on parents or older siblings to bring them to the mall.

One company recognized this "problem" as an opportunity, and started a catalog business for teen girls. The catalog was distributed in high schools, and because of the trendy clothing style and casual presentation, it became popular among them. Using their parents' credit cards, they could order the clothes they liked from home, without having to find someone to drive them to the mall. A couple of years ago, the company began experimenting with mall stores (in addition to keeping the catalog). That company is Delia's, which was acquired in early 2003 by Europe's Alloy. Another retailer, Ulta, recognized the potential of the teenagers hanging out in the mall and made special efforts to respond to their needs.

Also called millennials, because they came of age in the new millennium (i.e., those born after 1981), for families that do online shopping, teenagers are the Family Buying Officers.

Notice me. Your boyfriend is about to.
—Seen on a Torrid Tee

Consumers in the Making

In the United States, children 5 to 12 years old numbered 33 million in 2000. Even more significant than their own purchases is the amount of influence they exercise on their parents' purchase decisions. Children influence such adult decisions as where to dine out, where to

vacation, which entertainment and electronic gadgets to consider, and even which brands of household groceries to purchase.

Growing up in the age of the Internet and the wireless and multimedia entertainment, kids of the new millennium are much more sophisticated than their predecessors, and in many aspects of life, more knowledgeable than their parents. Their influence stems both from personal preference (e.g., which brands of cereals they like and insist their parents buy) and from product expertise. Older kids can offer

A product designed to please children from Pop Art Toasters

expert advice on such high-tech products as athletic shoes, video equipment, and even automobiles! One 10-year-old told in a Simmons Kids Study, "My little brother begged my dad to get a sports car. He got it."[27]

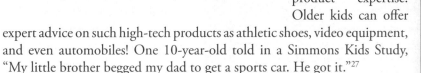

CONSUMING BY AGE

Food for the Young, Food for the Old

Yes, there really is such a thing as "food for the young" and "food for the old." You would know if you ever took a youngster to lunch or to a supermarket. For children and teenagers the main food feature has to be "fun." Supermarket aisles are filled with fun foods—foods with fun shapes, colors, flavors, and package pictures. There is Cheeto's Mystery Color Snacks (in cheesy neon orange color), green ketchup by Heinz, Magic Nestle's Wonderball, Hi-C, string cheese, spaghetti-shaped liquorices, and animal shaped candies.

For Gen X and Gen Y, convenience is most important in food buying. They want to eat on the go, so there are now supermarket foods to go, such as Go-GURT® by Yoplait® and Yoplait Express. Convenience is also important to dual career boomers, but to them, especially with advancing age, nutrition is also becoming important. The popularity of bagels owes itself to this on-the-go convenience feature. Boomers, who don't have time to sit down to eat breakfast, cannot eat cereal in their cars; but bagels they can. And supermarkets also sell pre-mixed salad bags and ready-to-go meal solutions (either to cook at home or pre-cooked and ready-to-eat). Concern

CB **F.y.i.**

When Life Begins at 50

There is a ladies' club with over one million members in some 42 countries around the globe. They meet annually in conventions, and in smaller groups frequently for an afternoon tea in town. When they go out as a group, they must wear a purple dress and a red hat. Their motto: to show how you can live with zeal after 50. Yes, they are all over fifty and proud. Check them out at www.redhatsociety.com.

My **CB Book**

about nutrition grows as consumers age, and for the aged, some medical conditions, such as diabetes, introduce dietary restrictions. For aging seniors, foods also need to be less spicy, thus compatible with their less tolerant gastrointestinal systems.

Clothes for the Young and Clothes for the Old

The intergenerational differences are even more acute for clothing. Seniors are much more concerned with performance aspects of clothing like durability and quality, and also with price. Middle-aged Boomers wear high quality brand names, valuing the classic over the trendy.

The youngsters are, in contrast, exclusively focused on the trend of the day. Popular brands of clothing and shoes such as Sketchers and Silver Tab certainly appeal to the younger consumer's desire for social image. Among teenagers and Gen Y, grunge clothing is popular, and more than to any other generation, price is most important to them, so much so that only they consider recycled clothing entirely prestigious— even the stores that buy and sell these have "cool" names--e.g., Snooty Fox and Plato's Closet.

Photo: Courtesy: Twinisles, Japan (Twinisles.com)

KNOWING THE TWO GRAND GENERATIONS

THE GI GENERATION
OVER 80 AND STILL STRONG

The G.I. generation accounted for some 17 million persons in the United States in 2000 Census (of the total 63 million ever born). Among the icons of this generation (now would have been 80 years or older) are such people as Ronald Reagan, Walt Disney, Katharine Hepburn, John F. Kennedy, Sir Winston Churchill, Walter Cronkite, and John Wayne; and among the currently living are George Herbert Walker Bush, Alan Greenspan, and Lee Iacocca. The GI generation was raised by parents determined to have "good kids," protected from urban danger and adult vices. They became America's first Boy Scouts and Girl Scouts, thus channeling their gang instinct to useful purposes. School was important for this generation, with emphasis on vocational education. Staying in school and being a "regular guy" and a team player (rather than be individualistic and stand out) were the virtues instilled in the youth.

In the late 1920s, the Great Depression tested the fervent optimism of this generation; somehow, the youth spirit stayed high. Two decades later, World War II came, and the GI generation emerged triumphant, feeling heroic and ever more optimistic. The GI Bill aided a financially secure life that the war heroes thought they deserved. A suburban house with a friendly neighborhood and comforts of new technology defined the adult GI. Among this generation, sameness rather than being different was celebrated.

Vietnam triggered an angry generation gap between the GI parents and their children, who brought crime waves, urban riots, substance abuse, eroticism—contrary to the GI generation's life mission. In politics, at work, and at home, the GI men faced opposition and rebellion from their youngsters. "Something has gone sour, in teaching and in learning," lamented a GI author George Wald.

When these GI's entered their senior years, they vowed not to grow old, tired, and defeatist, as their predecessors had; accordingly, they fought the myth of "a lonely, unhappy old person." They have worked hard to be active, energetic, happy, and hopeful senior citizens. Most live today in retirement, heavily subsidized by public funds, which they believe they have richly earned, something with which lawmakers in their children's generation don't quite agree.

THE SILENT GENERATION
THE GOLDEN YEARS

Among the first wave of the silent generation are such names as Marilyn Monroe, Clint Eastwood, Neil Armstrong, and Martin Luther King, Jr., and among the last wave, such names as Barbra Streisand, Elvis Presley, Woody Allen, and Reverend Jesse Louis Jackson, Sr.. They are Americans 61 to 80 years old (in 2006) and number approximately 44 million.

While the GI generation faced the Great Depression and World War II in their adulthood, the Silent Generation faced these crises during its youth. They believed in the success of the system rather than in individual enterprise, seeking secure careers in big corporations. One GI historian described them as "withdrawn, cautious, unimaginative, indifferent, and unadventurous," and by their own admission they were unoriginal in their clothing, manners, and lifestyles. The Silent Generation is so termed because they missed the more defining times at both ends—the first of the Silent Generation came of age just missing the war heroism, while the last of them graduated just before the early stirrings of the anti-establishment rebellion. This generation made up the bulk of the Peace Corps, and they played mainly the role of the facilitator and technocrats rather than front-runner leaders.

The Silent Generation has enjoyed a life of prosperity, and the lowest rate of any sociological evils (e.g., crime)—all with minimum initiatives. From college, they graduated with no major challenges facing their world, and with their roles as merely to fine-tune the GI wealth machine and contribute to society and the economy as managers rather than change agents. Even the civil rights protest movement led by Dr. Martin Luther King, Jr., adhered to nonviolence, appealing to GI's sense of fairness. It was left to the next generation to radicalize the dissent.

Gender and Age—the two markers of our identity, stuck to us as if "superglued."
Is there any moment in our waking life when we are not conscious of them?
We are conscious of them in buying our clothes, in partaking of our foods, in choosing
our recreation. We visit only those stores that sell the merchandise that suits our
particular gender and age, buy music CDs that echo our generation's psyche, and flock
to places—public as well as commercial—where people similar
to our age and of interest to our gender congregate.

Males and females do make different consumers. Tons of observational studies tell us
that.
To get a full skinny on that, a reading of three books will be worth every minute of your
time:
1. *Why We Buy: The Science of Shopping* by Paco Underhill (Simon & Schuster, 2000);
2. *Marketing to Women: How to Understand, Reach, and Increase Your Share of the
World's Largest Market Segment* by Martha Barletta (Kaplan Business, 2006); and
3. *The Future of Men: The Rise of the Ubersexual and What He Means for Marketing
Today* by Marian Salzman, Ira Matathia, and Ann O'Reilly (Palgrave MacMillan, 2006).
But keep in mind, these consumption differences are a moving target.
The phrase "homemaker" has long stopped being tied to a specific gender,
and the ritual of obsessive personal grooming has invaded the male specie.
Bold consumers everywhere are defying the stereotype of their gender.
Take comfort, however, in the knowledge that "putting more heart into gifts" is one thing
on which men will never catch up with women—except on the Valentine's Day, that is.

Age, our second unalterable characteristic, marks the progression of our lives.
It affects what we consume, both when we are celebrating it and when we are defying it.
Celebration and defiance consumptions offer distinct opportunities to marketers.
To harness these, keep a close watch on the psychology of the generations.
Seniors, Boomers, Gen Xers, Gen Yers, teens—they all represent unique and individually
alluring islands of opportunity.
Commune with them, grasp their mojo,
and then fashion your offerings for each age group separately.
And, for the population as a whole, keep a watch on their changing numbers.
The fortunes of whole industries can swing as today's Boomers reach their golden years
and the Millennials become tomorrow's 30-somethings. Marketers: ignore
population pyramids at grave consequences!

Photo Quiz: Here is another picture of a Pop Art Toaster.
With burn imprints like this, is the product appeal limited
to children? Which other age groups might also find the
product appealing?

(Courtesy: Pop Art Toasters)

In this chapter, we discussed two important consumer characteristics: sex and age.

We began with a discussion of the consumer behavior differences between the two sexes. These differences relate to the consumption of clothing, personal items, and emotional or mood-related products. Historically concerned with homemaking, the roles of modern day women are changing to encompass decision-making for all sorts of product categories; so are men increasingly participating in home-making chores and shopping for domestic staples. A related concept we discussed was gender roles—the social roles assigned to a person based on sex. We noted that sex roles are changing in contemporary societies, and accordingly, marketers must keep an eye on changes in redistribution of decision making between the sexes.

Age plays a significant role in defining the market size for any product and shifts in markets over time. We explored age groups as different consumer segments. Here, we enumerated the diverse categories of age groups in America: GI Generation, Silent Generation, Boomers, Generation X, Generation Y, teenagers, and children. Consumers in these age groups differ vastly in their needs and wants, desiring different products and services, both because their physical characteristics are different and because their tastes differ according to the subculture of their age groups.

Many of the age-based consumer behaviors are related not to the number of years passed since birth, but to how old a person sees him- or herself to be. This notion is captured in the concept of "cognitive age." We described the consumer behavior influences of cognitive age. In particular, we noted how this explains why consumers often don't act their age.

KEY TERMS

Gender Role Identity
Traditional Sex Role Attitude
Egalitarian Sex Role Attitude
Femininity
Masculinity
Signaling
Metrosexual
Retrosexual

Pomosexual
Ubersexual
Manscaping
Population Pyramids
GI Generation
Silent Generation
Baby Boomers
Baby Busters

Generation X
Generation 'Y'
Millennials
Cognitive Age
Health Condition
Optimism
Pessimism
Attitude toward Ageing

YOUR TURN

REVIEW✛Rewind

1. List some notable differences between men and women in terms of their consumer behaviors.
2. How are gender roles changing lately in the Western Societies and elsewhere? What should marketers do to respond to these changes?
3. Explain why a marketer should study age as a consumer characteristic.
4. What is meant by the term "population pyramids"? Why should a marketer study them?
5. Explain the differences in the psychological makeup of consumers who are:
   a. Gen X and Gen Y
   b. Seniors and Baby Boomers
6. Who are metrosexuals? How do retrosexuals, pomosexuals, and ubersexuals differ from metrosexuals?
7. Why are Boomers also called the "Sandwich Generation"? How are marketers (and public agencies) responding to the needs of Boomers in their role as "sandwich generation"?

THINK✛Apply

1. Which age group do you belong to? Does the description of consumer behavior for that age group hold true for you? To what extent? Why or why not?
2. Collect five ads targeted at seniors. Do these ads betray any stereotypes of seniors the advertisers might have held? Are seniors themselves likely to be pleased with the way people of their age group are depicted in these ads? Comment on what should marketers do to improve their advertising to seniors.
3. Would a store targeting Metrosexuals have good market opportunity? Why or why not?

PRACTICE✛Experience

1. Interview two couples similar in demographics but differing on their gender role attitudes (traditional and egalitarian). Understand and describe how their consumption roles are affected by their gender role attitudes.

2. Interview two Baby Boomers and then two Generation Xers, if possible from the same family. Focus your interview on (a) their clothes buying habits, (b) use of credit cards and importance of budgeting and savings, (c) importance of money in life. Summarize the differences and similarities you find.

3. Survey all of the marketing activities of companies marketing (a) soft drinks, (b) clothing, and (c) electronic music and communication devices, directed at Generation Y. Describe how well these marketing programs fit with the attitudes and tastes of Gen Y described in the chapter.

In the Marketing Manager's Shoes

Put yourself in a marketing manager's shoes. Most concepts in the chapter have some lessons for the marketing manager, i.e., they suggest what to do differently in practice; indeed, often these applications are implicit in our explanations of the concepts and models in the chapter. Identify at least five specific applications of the chapter's concepts, all of which should be entirely new—different from the examples cited here.

CB Level 2.0

COGNITIVE AGE AND IDENTITY CONSUMPTION

"I am 55 but I feel like a 35!" This phenomenon, you would recall, is called cognitive age—an individual's perception of how old he or she feels like. Earlier you read about it briefly. Now it will pay to read its nuances and understand its full consequences in terms of consumption behaviors.

Most of the consumer research on cognitive age has focused on the elderly. For this group, consumer researchers have tried to measure cognitive age by asking a person to rate himself or herself in terms of six related dimensions: feel-age, look-age, think-age, do-age, interest-age, and health-age.

Which age group do you view yourself as being most like:

31-40 41-50 51-60 61-70 71-80 81-90 91-100

I feel like
I think like
I look like
My activities are most like
My interests are most like
My health is most like

To compute a score, the mid-point of the decade range (e.g., 35.5, 45.5, and so on) are taken and averaged across the six items. Using this scale, researchers have measured chronological, cognitive, and desired (how old you wish you were) age in various countries. In all countries there is some bias against getting old: (a) cognitive age is lower than chronological age, and (b) the desired age is even lower than their cognitive age. However, this bias is not equally pronounced in all countries; in China it is much less, whereas in US it is much more. Moreover, the bias is much more during the middle age years than during the youth: middle age consumers really view themselves, in their abilities and interests, to be much younger than their age, and indeed desire to be even younger (by as much as 10 years):

Factors that Influence Cognitive Age

Why should one's cognitive age be different from one's chronological age? Three factors determine this: health condition, optimism/pessimism, and attitude toward aging.

Health Condition Health Condition refers to one's physical health, including ailments, physical strength, and the energy levels that one feels for everyday activities. Consumers with a sound health condition are likely to feel younger in cognitive age than others in the same chronological age group.

Optimism/Pessimism Optimism/Pessimism is a personality factor that concerns the degree to which a person is hopeful about the future and expects life opportunities for continual personal progress. Pessimistic people, in contrast to optimistic people, see their future as bleak as their present or may even expect it to worsen. Optimism is caused by one's history of successes, and pessimism by past failures and no prospects in sight to turn things around. In turn, optimism and pessimism colors one's ways of looking at the world as well as at oneself. Optimism causes one to view oneself as being in the prime of life, with a lot of life still left to live. In this way, optimism lowers chronological age.

Attitude Toward Aging The third factor influencing cognitive age is **attitude toward aging**, which refers to one's attitude toward getting old, and, indeed, attitude towards older people. This attitude stems from the society's relative treatment of their youth and the aged, as well as one's own assessment of life opportunities open to people of different age groups. Note that this assessment differs from the assessment of life opportunities discussed above as a source of optimism and pessimism, in that here the opportunities are seen as tied to age per se, not to one's own life or abilities and potential. That is, they are seen to apply to all persons of a certain age group. If a person believes that the doors of certain opportunities are shut from persons belonging to a certain age group—like no one would hire you after you are 60, or one can't find love or a spouse after 50, or one can't get an MBA degree after 45, or you won't be able to play major film-acting roles after 40, then that assessment of opportunity will influence your attitude toward aging. When these assessments of opportunity are negative, you fear aging. When you see opportunities unblocked by aging, you are more accepting, if not welcoming, of getting older.

This assessment of age-related opportunities occurs within the context of a society's treatment of the young versus old. In Western cultures, youth is valued and the elderly are considered more of a burden rather than a resource. In contrast, in Eastern cultures, age is revered and the elderly are respected and sought after both for their wisdom as well as owing to one's normative, almost sacred, duty. In families in Eastern societies, for example, adult sons and daughters take care of their elders and consider them as legitimate authoritative figures in all family decisions. In such societies, one takes pride in becoming aged, and because of the ensuing respect, actually feels they are living an accomplished and happy life. In Western societies, on the other hand, one dreads aging, and wants to put it off, psychologically speaking, as long as possible. This negative attitude toward aging, therefore, makes one act and feel like a person cognitively much younger than one's chronological age, and desire to be even younger.

Three demographic characteristics also influence cognitive age. The first, obviously, is chronological age. A person of say 60 years of chronological age does feel cognitively older than say a person of 50 years of chronological age, other things being equal. The second is income, and the third is education. Both are resources that enable a person to live a happier, more accomplished life. They affect, therefore, one's optimism/pessimism, and in fact, one's health (both mental and physical) condition as well, and thereby, they affect cognitive age.

How Cognitive Age Affects Consumer Behavior

A person's cognitive age has an immense effect on his or her actions as a consumer. These effects can be grouped into five broad categories, as shown in Figure 15.3. We discuss each in turn.

Marketplace Involvement One of the myths about the elderly is that they lose interest in the marketplace as they reach their senior years. Some do, but a majority of them, at least in the Western cultures, continue to live life to the full. Since much of everyday life depends on consumption and product acquisition, the elderly of today continue to be interested in the marketplace. Still, given two elderly persons of the same chronological age, a person with a lower cognitive age will (compared to a person of higher cognitive age) show more interest in the marketplace and also engage more in recreational shopping.

Decision-Making Another long held myth is that elderly are dogmatic and unaccepting of new ideas and new products, and become overly cautious buyers. Also, that they also tend to get overwhelmed by the plethora of marketplace information required to make product selection

FIGURE 15.3

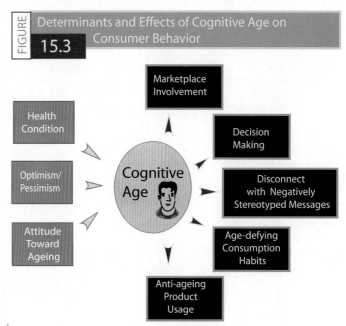

Determinants and Effects of Cognitive Age on Consumer Behavior

decisions. However, this stereotype applies mostly to chronological age. If, instead, we look at a person's cognitive age, then even older consumers who consider themselves young are much less likely to be dogmatic and much more accepting of change than their equally old counterparts who did not feel cognitively young. That is, despite their old age in chronological terms, cognitively younger consumers are not as overly cautious toward making purchase decisions for new products, and they also seek more product information.

Anti-aging Products Cognitively young consumers see themselves as younger than their age and wish to prolong their youthful looks. This explains why Baby Boomers account for the exponential growth in the consumption of anti-aging products. It is to prolong their lower cognitive age that they are attracted to such products as vitamins, organic food, age-reversing cosmetics, surgical procedures for altering body shapes and surface appearance, etc. A cognitively younger consumer is likely to consume these products much more than an average consumer of identical chronological age.

Age-defying Consumption Habits Yet another mythical image of the elderly is that they lead a sedentary life. Not true. In fact, they lead a very active life of vigor and enjoyment. Many continue to work well into their seventies or even eighties. They take vacations, trips abroad, and adventure tours. They acquire new hobbies, new sports, and so on. Marketers who understand this should market to seniors a whole range of new products, ranging from an SUV to a mountain-climbing course. Again, which elderly find these products appealing will depend on their cognitive age. The gap between cognitive age and chronological age is basically an act of "age-denial." Its incidence is the highest for the Baby Boomer age group.

Disconnect with Negatively Stereotyped Messages Remember the old commercial where a 70 year old lady falls down and says "I have fallen and I can't get up"? Today's elderly loath this kind of depiction. This stereotypical depiction of the elderly as old and helpless is at odds with toady's reality. Marketers should instead depict them as leading an active lifestyle. Again, the lower a person's cognitive age, the more he or she would feel disconnected with the ads that depict the elderly as helpless.

Ethnic and Religious Identity in Consumer Behavior

Let's Talk Hair

I am mixed w/black and white and I have really coarse hair....I keep it short cause its hard to keep clean and good looking . I've tried a lot of different products, but I need some advice on what products I should use that will give me those small sexy curls...

I want to keep my afro puffy and big , but I don´t think it looks good , it looks dry and the color isn´t dark black like when my hair is short.

I have relaxed hair and I am about to go to the Caribbean on vacation for 1 week. I am thinking of having my hair braided so that I would not have to style it every morning. However, I also plan to spend a lot of time swimming. Is braiding recommended? If so, how should I take care of my hair after swimming? If you don't recommend braiding, how should I take care of my relaxed hair after swimming?

©iStockphoto.com/Tom Marvin

©iStockphoto.com/Lise Gagne

I decided to grow out of my relaxer and wear my hair natural, ...overcoming my psychological struggle in accepting my naturally curly hair. ... The book has great tips on options for growing out of a relaxer, ... [It] is a must-read for the black woman who has even slightly considered wearing her natural hair.

Note: The four comments are from, respectively, Lightskinguy posted January 22, 2006 on Afrohair.com forum; Post dated January 23, 2006 on forum.afrohair.biz1; Lady De Q and A thread Dated 26 Dec 2005 on Afro Hair.com; and a reader review of the book *Let's Talk Hair*

INTRODUCTION

Hair. Short, long, silky, thin, thick, blonde, dark, graying, brittle, oily, kinky. No matter what shape it comes in, it is on our head and we love it. We spend anywhere from 50 to 300 hours a year on it.[5] How much time and money we spend depends in part on the type of hair we have and/or keep. That in turn depends in part on our ethnicity. And on our religious affiliations as well. Many other consumption behaviors also depend on these two characteristics. Both are also very sensitive issues—calling for a discourse with an open mind. In the marketplace, marketers ignore them at their own peril. Or harness them to serve the ethnic consumer. Let us learn more about them.

ETHNICITY

Your Bio-Cultural ID

Hello, what race are you? Yes, we know, it is impolite to ask. And politically incorrect. But you want some Sulfur8 for your braids, some apHOGEE shampoo, Afrikan Beauty Shea Butter Skin Care System, tamales, tortillas, Pan de Muerto, silk sarees, naan, basmati rice, bowls of pho and skeins of soba, hand-pulled mein and hand-pulled udon, don't you? We are marketers, and we can't offer you these products if we don't know your race. At any rate, you can't really hide your race and ethnic identity—it is writ large on your face and on your persona. Most of the time. Besides, ethnicity is a matter of pride with you, as it should be, and as it is with us. So let us talk about it.

RACE OR ETHNICITY

Which Do We Mean?

Political incorrectness is not the only problem when discussing race and ethnic issues. There is no consensus among scholars as to the definition of these terms, or the criteria on which race and ethnic distinctions should be made. Skirting this controversy, we would define these two terms as follows:

- **Race** refers to the distinction among humans based on their genes, from which stem basic differences in the subspecies of humans.
- **Ethnicity** refers to distinctions among people based on their national or cultural heritage.

Thus, race is a biological concept. It is rooted in the differences in the biological makeup of humans, and represents one of the three such distinctions that physically separate people as a group—the other two biological distinctions being age and sex. In contrast, ethnicity is a sociological concept. A respected source, *Wikipedia*, clarifies this distinction as follows:

> A race is a population of humans distinguished from other populations. … While ethnicity and race are related concepts, the concept of ethnicity is rooted in the idea of societal groups, marked especially by shared nationality, tribal affiliation, religious faith, shared language, or cultural and traditional origins and backgrounds, whereas race is rooted in the idea of biological classification of Homo sapiens to subspecies according to morphological features such as skin color or facial characteristics.[6]

There are four original race groups among humans: Caucasians, Africans, Mongolians, and Aboriginals (or Australoids). These subspecies are said to have originated in, respectively, Northern and Western Europe, Africa, Mongolia (the Chinese region), and Australia. (Some scholars believe that this last group originated in South-East Asia and later migrated to Australia. If you are contemplating the feasibility of such migration—on foot, that is—remember, the sub-continental plates have drifted apart since.) Note that race itself can be a major criterion for ethnicity, so that, for example, the term *Caucasian* can refer to both race and ethnicity. At the same time, an ethnic identity can cross more than one race, and within any one race multiple ethnic identities can exist. To illustrate, most Italians and French are Caucasians, but they are two distinct ethnic groups. In our view then, race is your bio-genetic identity; in contrast, ethnicity is your bio-cultural ID.

In the United States, the Census Bureau specifies the following four race categories: 1. White; 2. Black or African American; 3. American Indian or Alaska Native; 4. Asian, Native Hawaiian, Pacific-Islander (this last category is specified, in turn, by its 10 subcategories). The U.S. Census also asks a separate question about whether a person is Spanish/Hispanic/Latino. It is interesting to note that Hispanics are not identified as a separate race category (correctly so, since Hispanic is not a race but an ethnic identity). Yet, on the race question, many Hispanics mark themselves in the "other" category.

Another point to note is that not all Asians have the same genetic roots, and, therefore, are not the same race. Chinese, for example, are of Mongolian race, whereas Indians have either Aryan (another name for Caucasian) or Dravidian (another name for Aboriginal/Australoids) roots[7]. This may seem a jarring fact to many Westerners, but to an average resident of Thailand, Singapore, or Indonesia, for example, where these two races have vivid presence, the distinct race identities among the so called Asians is visible like daylight. To sum, then, Asian is a regional identity, not a race; as such the use of this term in U.S. Census as a race category is merely an administrative designation rather than a scientific or cultural classification. Asians tend to mark the race category because they interpret it as a geographic identity group rather than race.

RACE AND ETHNICITY IN THE AMERICAN MARKETPLACE

Los Angeles, California, is a quintessential multiethnic city. People here speak 80 plus languages and come from 100 plus cultural and ethnic backgrounds. Perhaps only in the offices of the United Nations in New York City will you find a more diverse population. In Los Angeles, at every turn of the road, you will see people who look different from you, no matter what your own race is. You will meet Filipinos, Koreans, Mexicans, Salvadorans, as well as Chinese, Ethiopians, Indians, Indonesians, Iranians, Pacific Islanders, Druze, Tamils, and Vietnamese, and, of course, infrequently, white Americans. As Marlene S. Rossman, the author of *Multicultural Marketing* observes, you can eat every night in a different ethnic restaurant without repeating the food for a year![8]

Although the ethnic potpourri is not as dramatic elsewhere, its presence is unmistakable almost anywhere in the United States, and it is on the rise. In the 1980 census, one in five persons was of nonwhite, non-European origin; in the 1990 census, this number had gone up to one in four, and it stayed that way in the 2000 census. According to the U.S. Census 2000, there are 34.65 million blacks (12.3% of population); 35.30 million Hispanics (12.5%), 10.24 million Asians (3.6%); and 2.47 million Native Americans (0.9%). By 2010, one in three American children will be minorities (see Figure 16.1).

The ever-increasing presence of immigrants and their U.S.-born offspring is altering mainstream culture and customs. Consider some popular foods in America: bagels,

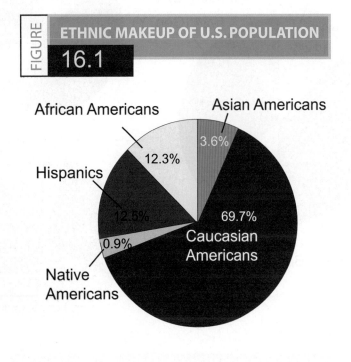

FIGURE 16.1 ETHNIC MAKEUP OF U.S. POPULATION

African Americans 12.3%
Asian Americans 3.6%
Hispanics 12.5%
Native Americans 0.9%
Caucasian Americans 69.7%

pizza, hamburgers, sushi, Szechwan chicken, burritos—all are ardently consumed by Americans of all ethnic backgrounds. Today, tortilla chips are consumed in 62% of U.S. households, and salsa outsells ketchup! Given such diversity, marketers need to understand the ethnic makeup of U.S. customers.

The marketing literature identifies four race/ethnic groups in the United States: European Americans, African-Americans, Hispanics, and Asian-Americans. The culture, values, norms, and behaviors of these four race/ethnic groups differ markedly. As noted earlier, Hispanics are not a race but an ethnic group. They can be black or white, but Hispanics tend to identify themselves as just Hispanics rather than blacks or whites. And when people speak of blacks or whites, they mean, usually, non-Hispanic blacks and non-Hispanic whites.

A PORTRAIT OF THE ETHNIC GROUPS IN U.S.

Before we discuss each of the four race/ethnic groups individually, let us briefly survey the four groups' demographic profiles. These profiles—all based on U.S. 2000 census data—are graphed in Figure 16.2 (A, B, and C).

Age In terms of age, whites have the largest proportion of the oldest population-- 14.4% are 65 years or older, compared to 8.1% among blacks, 4.9% among Hispanics, and 6.5% among Asian-Americans; at the other end of the age spectrum, the proportion of young persons (less than 25 year olds) is largest among Hispanics—48.4% compared to 42.4% among blacks, 32.3% among whites, and 35.1% among Asian-Americans. The boomer age group is the largest among whites and Asian-Americans—30.4% and 30.6%, respectively, compared to 27.7% among blacks and 23.4% among Hispanics.

FIGURE 16.2A

A DEMOGRAPHIC PORTRAIT OF ETHNIC GROUPS IN AMERICA: AGE PROFILE

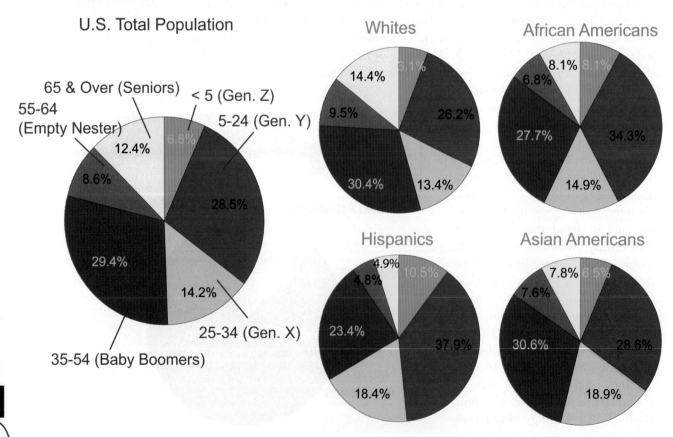

Income There are wide income disparities within each race but also across the four race/ethnic groups. The poorest are blacks, with 2 in 5 (42.9%) of them earning less than $25,000 in annual household income. Hispanics follow closely, with 1 in 3 (i.e. 36.4%) of them earning less than $25K, compared to about 1 in 4 among the remaining two races. The richest are Asian Americans with nearly 1 in 5 (21.9%) earning more than $100,000 a year, compared to 1 in 7 among whites (14.8%), and only 1 in 15 among Hispanics (7%) and blacks (5.6%).

FIGURE 16.2B — A DEMOGRAPHIC PORTRAIT OF ETHNIC GROUPS IN AMERICA: EDUCATION PROFILE

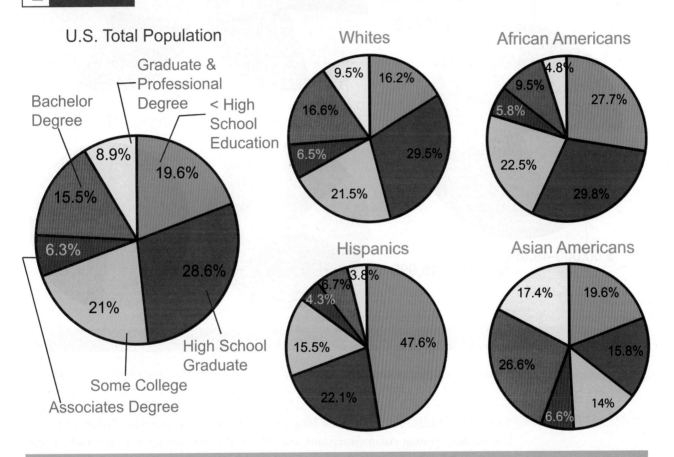

Source: Based on U.S. Census 2000.

Education The least educated group is Hispanics with nearly half of them (47.6%) with less than high school education. In comparison, among blacks, less-than-high-school educated are 1 in four (27,7%), and they are one in five among Asian Americans (19.6%) and one in six among whites (16.4%). The most educated group is Asian-Americans—44% of them have at least a bachelor's degree and 17.4% have a post-graduate degree. The next most educated group is whites with 26.1% having at least a bachelor's degree and 9.5% a post-graduate degree. The other two groups lag far behind, with only 14.3% blacks and 10.5% Hispanics having graduated from college.

Family Structure The four race/ethnic groups also differ in their family composition. More of whites and blacks live alone, each about 1 in 4, than Hispanics and Asian Americans, among whom single person households are one in six and one in five, respectively. The proportion of married couple households is the highest among Asian-Americans (61%), with whites and Hispanics closely following (54%, each); blacks have only one in three (31%) households that are married couples. The nuclear family (i.e., married couples with children) is found most among Hispanics and Asian-Americans,

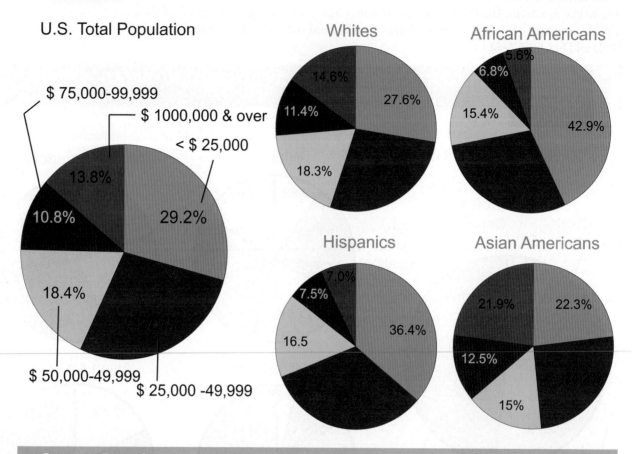

U.S. Total Population

$ 75,000-99,999

$ 1000,000 & over

< $ 25,000

13.8%

10.8%

29.2%

18.4%

$ 50,000-49,999

$ 25,000 -49,999

Whites

14.6%

27.6%

11.4%

18.3%

African Americans

5.6%

6.8%

15.4%

42.9%

Hispanics

7.0%

7.5%

16.5

36.4%

Asian Americans

21.9%

22.3%

12.5%

15%

Source: Based on U.S. Census 2000.

with about 1 in 3 (36% and 34%, respectively) such families in each group. Conversely, single mothers (with children <18yrs old) are the highest among blacks, with nearly 1 in 5 such households; next highest are Hispanics with about one in ten (12%) single mother households. Among Asian-Americans and whites this proportion is much lower—only one in 20 households are single mother households. (See Figure 16.3.)

Forewarning—Enter with an Open Mind

Profiling ethnic (and religious) groups by demographics (as in the foregoing and also below) is an easy task. This relates to objective data. But psychographic and consumption profiles are subjective and tentative. This is because research is thin on these topics, and many descriptions drawn here are based on occasional and sometimes dated studies. Some tend to confirm popular views, whereas some are revelations.

Any profile that paints an entire category of people (whether based on age, income, profession, religion, or ethnicity) has, by definition, some elements of stereotype—not necessarily false, but not applicable to every consumer by any stretch. Furthermore, some traits can be understood only by in-group members; and some only by out-group members. Not all readers may therefore interpret them in the same way. What is of interest here is to learn what the current body of knowledge—comprising systematic studies, anecdotal evidence, and conventional wisdom—says about various ethnic groups. Read these with an open mind and enjoy the colorful cultural consumption portraits various ethnic groups offer.

FIGURE 16.3
FAMILY TYPE FOR VARIOUS ETHNIC GROUPS IN U.S.A.

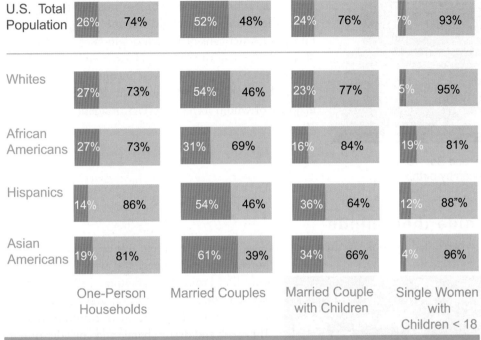

	One-Person Households	Married Couples	Married Couple with Children	Single Women with Children < 18
U.S. Total Population	26% / 74%	52% / 48%	24% / 76%	7% / 93%
Whites	27% / 73%	54% / 46%	23% / 77%	5% / 95%
African Americans	27% / 73%	31% / 69%	16% / 84%	19% / 81%
Hispanics	14% / 86%	54% / 46%	36% / 64%	12% / 88"%
Asian Americans	19% / 81%	61% / 39%	34% / 66%	4% / 96%

Source: Based on U.S. Census 2000.

CAUCASIANS (NON-HISPANIC WHITES)

Who They Are

Even though European Americans are the descendants of European immigrants themselves, it is now conventional to deem them as the mainstream population. This is because they are the largest racial group in U.S.A. It is also conventional to refer to this group simply as "whites" or "Caucasians," although neither term is exact. Hispanics could also be white, and they are counted in the U.S. census as Caucasians. A more accurate label therefore would be "non-Hispanic Caucasians."

Demographics

Let us look at their demographics first. Americans of European descent number, according to the U.S. Census 2000, about 211 million, and about 4 million of them are foreign born. Immigration from Europe boomed between 1980 and 1995, a period during which about 1.2 million Europeans migrated to the United States, in large part spurred by the breakdown of communist regimes in Eastern Europe. Although these European descendants are themselves a diverse group, representing some 15 different countries of origin, they do share some common characteristics as a group.

Because whites make up the single largest majority, accounting for 70% of the total population, their education and income distribution closely resembles the U.S. average. One in four whites has a college degree, and one in two has some college experience. One in four of lives alone. Of the other three fourths, 64% are married couples. About one in three is a member of a household with two or more persons working full-time. More than 10% are business owners, and one in four has a professional job. Forty-five

percent of them have a household income that exceeds $50,000 a year, and for one in four, it exceeds $75,000 a year, indicating the relative prosperity of this population. Of course, the prosperity of different ethnic consumers within this population varies: in general, the more recent the immigration, the poorer or less prosperous the group. Thus, the median household income is highest among European Americans of French origin ($75,000 for 40% of them), the majority of whom have been in the U.S. for more than 10 years. The lowest income is among those of Polish origin ($25,000 for about 40% of them), the majority of whom have had a U.S. residence of less than 10 years.[9]

Aron, Levin, Margi, Josh, and Ben--Caucasians by ancestry, American by birth.

Inside their minds

Next, let us look at their psychology. What is in their minds? What are their motivations and values, and what do they seek from life? From the marketplace? Caucasians are very competitive, aggressive, and explicit. They are also very direct in their communications. They seek and desire change and consider time as "money." They value youth and also materialism. Although egalitarianism is the professed ideal, class consciousness is very much alive in the mainstream culture. These cultural values and norms influence their marketplace behaviors. Market transactions tend to be impersonal, apparently rational, and efficiency-driven. Products and services are purchased with self-centered benefits in mind. These values as well as market behaviors are in sharp contrast with those of the other ethnic/race groups, as we will see.

Edmond and Teuta Cata, Caucasians and European Americans (recent immigrants from Albania)

Not all European Americans think of themselves as ethnic, but many do. Members of this latter group maintain strong ties with their homelands. These "ethnic Europeans" exhibit different marketplace behaviors from (non-Hispanic) whites in general, and from other ethnic minorities in particular.

These ethnic European Americans work longer hours than other (non-Hispanic) whites, and they spend the fruits of their labor liberally on material goods and on recreation. For example, they take cruises substantially more than an average American: compared with a 3% rate among the general population, the cruise travel rate among Americans of Swiss origin is 6%, and among those of Russian or Norwegian origin is 17%. Another conspicuous recreational activity is casino gambling, with as many as half of Germans, Italians, and Portuguese identifying themselves as "having gambled in the past year."

Conspicuous consumption is especially conspicuous among the ethnic whites. Home electronics (VCRs, stereos, etc.) are owned by more than 90% of ethnic whites, compared to about 50 to 60% among all non-Hispanic whites. Indeed, among the recent immigrants from Eastern Europe, buying American consumer goods is a symbol of having become an American. One European immigrant explained it thus: "It takes a long time to become a citizen or to be able to vote or to perfect one's English. But as soon as a person has a steady job and an income, he or she can start buying the symbols of what it is to be an American, whether it be the TV and the VCR or the designer sneakers."[10]

Caucasians—How Marketers Should Respond

To reach ethnic Europeans, that is, those Americans of European descent who still maintain ties with their homeland and its language and culture. Marketers must adapt their mainstream strategies. Cruise marketers catering to ethnic Europeans, for example, target different cruises to ethnic segments—Greeks, Italians, Eastern Europeans—and they customize food and entertainment to each group. Another strong marketing tool is the use of ethnic languages in advertisements—German, Italian, French, Russian, and so on. Ethnic whites still find their mother tongue very appealing.

Often, the product benefit or appeal needs adaptation. For instance, AT&T found that its "True Voice" campaign with Whitney Houston had no appeal for recent ethnic European immigrants. The quality of the sound (true voice) was not a value to them because they were used to having to scream into the phone in their homeland. Actually, to an immigrant from Eastern European countries, true voice often meant "the voice of Pravda," and Whitney Houston had no relevance to them either. So on Russian-language TV, AT&T instead used a Russian comic promoting its service.

Such customization is not needed for the larger group of European Americans (i.e., those other than recent immigrants). Those having lived longer in America constitute, as already mentioned, what has come to be known as the "mainstream culture." This culture, in contrast to that of African Americans, Hispanics, and Asian Americans, values individualism over the rights of the family and society. It also values a small and nuclear family, whereas the other groups value extended families.[11]

AFRICAN AMERICANS

DEMOGRAPHICS
Bridging the Economic Divide

African Americans number some 34.6 million (12.3% of the total U.S. population, per 2000 U.S. Census) and are expected to grow to some 39.57 million by 2007. (Worldwide, consumers of African origin number 1 billion.) They are concentrated in the South, mostly in major cities, with Atlanta being the major center for this subpopulation. Other major metropolitan areas with large populations of African Americans are Chicago, Los Angeles, Detroit, Washington, D.C., and New Orleans. Their median age is 25.6 years (compared with 43 years for whites), and the average household size is 3.1 (compared to 3.5 for whites). Many children live in single parent families (19% of all households are single women with children compared to only 7% in the population as a whole), and most of these are female-headed families. A large proportion is poor: the annual household income is less than $25,000 for 42.9% of African Americans, compared to only 29% of whites. In education, they lag the average population somewhat: 27.7% of them have less than a high school degree, compared to 19.6% among the average population. At the same time, many have middle and upper level incomes and are well-educated. The most notable thing about this ethnic group is that they are entrepreneurial and determined to bridge the economic divide.

Arlene Zachery poses for *MyCBBook* during her stroll on the famous Miracle Mile, Chicago (June 2006)

Values and Psychographics
Successful and Celebrating

James Hughes and Ruth Champion-Hughes (entering a restaurant)

Family and religious values are very important to African Americans. Taking care of their loved ones comes first. Middle-class African Americans display a high degree of achievement motivation, attempting to succeed financially, and they are keen to make a mark, in part to show the world what an African American can do. They are self-image conscious and like to display style. They are trendsetters and tend to define their own style. In his book, *African Americans: A Celebration of Life*, author Ronald L. Freeman writes: "Style—whether captured in an elegant hat, an eloquent phrase, a sophisticated step, or a smooth move—lies at the very heart of African American culture."

Perhaps the most indelible image that stands out in our minds, the one that epitomizes triumph of the African-American talent and success, and its celebration, is Halle Berry, receiving the Oscar at the 2002 Film awards. Basketball superhero Michael Jordan, TV show host Oprah Winfrey, U.S. Senator Barack Obama, American Express CEO Ken Chenault, and Ace filmmaker Spike Lee, among others, represent the African American pride. Two notable celebrations for this community are Black History Month (celebrated in February) and Kwanzaa (celebrated annually between December 26 and January 1).

African Americans have a strong racial awareness and ethnic pride and support marketers and stores that show respect for their ethnic pride. They feel that as a community they are discriminated against in the marketplace. A recent study (2005 Yankelovich MONITOR Multicultural Marketing Study) found that 88% of African Americans feel this way—56% noticing a security guard watching them more closely than he/she would watch other customers. Not surprisingly, more than any other ethnic group, they reported that their preference of stores depended on how the stores treated them based on their race.[12]

And How They Love Shopping!

African Americans enjoy shopping, many using it as a social occasion. Compared to the general population, African Americans spend disproportionately more on clothing, shoes, and home electronics. African American children have a greater awareness of fashion. Although all kids are fashion and brand conscious, African American kids are substantially more so. African Americans show loyalty to well-known brands, but they are also willing to try new brands. Patronage of generic and store brands is higher among middle- and upper-class African Americans than among poor African Americans. This counter-intuitive behavior may be due to a lack of awareness among the poor, or lack of access to these brands (i.e., they may be unaware of private brands, or warehouse stores that carry many private brands may not be located in poor neighborhoods.)

African Americans tend to drink regular colas (rather than diet versions) and flavored drinks such as Mountain Dew. Drinks with a lot of sugar (such as Jolt) are also popular among this group. In many product categories, African Americans tend to buy premium brands. They buy premium liquor because it is an *affordable* status symbol. Many urban youth wear gold jewelry. To them, gold is expensive but still more affordable than, say, a suburban house. While some of this conspicuous consumption is to keep up with the mainstream Joneses, it should not be assumed that all of it is to impress their white counterparts. Many middle- and upper-class African Americans spend a good deal on clothing, cars, audio equipment. They also buy other luxury products simply because doing so signifies their lifestyle, tradition, and relative affluence.

Donna Chang, a consumer posing for *MyCBBook* immediaely after receiving a professional makeup at Elon at the Tri-County Mall, Cincinnati (U.S.A.). The beaded hair Donna sports here is popular among many African Americans.

How Marketers Should Respond

Marketers have not directed much of their resources to African Americans. Until the 1980s, cosmetic companies marketed the same make-up products for whites and African Americans; then Flori Roberts introduced a new line of foundations and make-up products specially formulated for the dark skin. Likewise, for years, African American children had to make do with white dolls, white cartoons, and even white fairy tales (Goldilocks). Today, Huggy bean dolls, and Kulture Kids, smaller dolls wearing kente cloth (a fabric motif style popular in Africa), and black hero comic books are in the offing. In another exemplary case of custom-targeting African Americans, *Essence* magazine created a designer line of eyeglasses that would fit the African American consumer's style better.

Many African Americans have reported feeling that most TV and print advertisements are designed mostly for whites. In a recent study, the New York Department of Consumer Affairs studied some 2,000 plus advertisements in 10 general readership magazines (e.g., *Better Homes and Gardens*) and found that African Americans appeared in only 3.4% of the advertisements!

There are, of course, special media for African Americans that offer opportunity for marketers to target this group. Black Entertainment Television (BET) network reaches more than half of African American households. Magazines such as *Ebony, Essence, Black Enterprise, Emerge,* and *YSB* are very popular among African Americans. Some marketers and advertisers have begun to adapt their efforts for this segment. For example, the Allstate logo is a pair of hands along with the slogan, "You are in good hands with Allstate." In some advertisements, those hands are black.

J.C. Penney offers African Collection women's clothing in some 22 of its stores. These boutiques offer a wide range of African clothing and fabrics for the home, many based on kente cloth, a richly patterned fabric produced in West Africa. Kente cloth was originally worn by African royalty, woven of cotton and sometimes silk, and it was traditionally worn by men as togas and by women as dresses. Many African Americans say that kente clothing helps them appreciate the African in African American.

TeKay Designs offers ethnic clothes for African-Americans.

(www.tk-designs.com)

HISPANICS

DEMOGRAPHICS
Now the Largest Minority

With over 35.30 million in number, Hispanics overtook as the single largest minority in the U.S. Census 2000, edging out African Americans by a small margin (the latter were counted as 34.65 million). This margin is going to increase as their growth rate is the highest of all groups (12.5%). By year 2007, their number will grow to 42 million. As a group, Hispanics are the youngest of all groups in the United States, with a median age of 24 years. Their median income, counted in U.S. Census 2000, was $33,565 (compared to the U.S. average of $42,228). This largest minority will represent a huge spending power, accounting for an estimated $900 billion in the U.S. marketplace, up 300% since 1990. To target them, U.S. advertisers spent $3 billion in 2004.[13]

Presently, they are concentrated in Miami--accounting for a little more than half of the total local population (57%). In Los Angeles County, they account for a little more than

40% of the population, and in New York, about 25%. There are four major subgroups:

1. **Mexicans** Sixty-seven percent of Hispanics are of Mexican origin, and two-thirds of them are U.S. born. Most of them live in the West and Southwest. They are the youngest of all the Hispanic groups, and some have entered the country illegally, crossing the border and taking any job in the border states. Low-income Mexican Americans tend to stay in these border towns and states such as in Arizona, Texas, and California.

2. **Puerto Ricans** About 12% of U.S. Hispanics are of Puerto Rican origin. However just as many are of Puerto Rican ancestry but born in the United States. Puerto Ricans have been entitled to U.S. citizenship since 1917, when Puerto Rico became a U.S. commonwealth. Half of all immigrants from Puerto Rico have settled in New York. Many college-educated Puerto Ricans have settled in the Sunbelt States. They can move freely between the United States and Puerto Rico; however, many feel that their home is Puerto Rico. This reduces their desire for or interest in assimilation. Puerto Ricans, like other Hispanics, are warm and sociable people.

Maria Clay, born a Mexican, MBA from USA, now enjoying her Hispanic American ethnic consumer idenitity.

3. **Cuban Americans** Only 4 to 5% of U.S. Hispanics are of Cuban origin, and 72% of them were born in Cuba. A vast majority of them live in South Florida (e.g., Miami, Tampa), although a large concentration can also be found in the New Jersey area. Cuban Americans are the most affluent Hispanics, and they are also the most educated: of all Cubans above 25 years of age, 20% have completed four years of college; this compares with 6% for Mexican Americans and 10% for Puerto Rican Americans.

4. **Dominicans** Immigrants from Dominican Republic are new in the United States and were half a million in the 1990 census. Black and brown in skin color, most tend to settle near the Puerto Rican communities in the North (although a few do live in Miami and New Jersey), and yet they don't really assimilate with Puerto Ricans. They make up 40% of New York's Hispanics, and own 70% of Hispanic small businesses (predominantly supermarkets).

While these four groups broadly share a common language, cultural values, and customs, there are many important differences in tastes and activities. The style of music is different. They have different holidays and like different sports. Mexicans play soccer, whereas Cubans and Puerto Ricans play baseball. Their family size is different. Cubans tend to have smaller families than Mexicans (3.2 versus 4.4, on average).

They also differ by their region of U.S. residence. In San Francisco, about half of them are churchgoers, whereas in Phoenix and Tucson, only about one in four is. Hispanics also differ by income groups, as do all customer groups. Affluent Hispanics are more assimilated than are low-income Hispanics. Finally, they differ by the length of their residence in the United States. Recent immigrants exhibit more of their native culture and customs.

What they Value

Family and children are very important to Hispanics and take precedence over work. Religion and tradition are also respected. Hispanics are more religious than Caucasians, and a greater proportion of them are churchgoers. Play and work are interwoven; during a normal workday, they entertain social visitors or engage in extensive social conversation with business visitors. On the flip side, they tend to work late hours (especially if they have had a prolonged, fun-filled lunch hour) and make substantial business deals over food and beverage fiestas. Hispanics—both men and women—have a strong interest in appearance. Finally, Hispanics are fascinated by technology. In Miami, Florida, for instance, everywhere

Hispanics in America **Fashionable** and upbeat, enriching the American culture

except in the low-income neighborhoods, you find Hispanics nearly all carrying pagers, cell phones, and the more affluent ones, a PDA.

Building Identity in the Marketplace

Good looks and appearance being important to Hispanics, they are heavy buyers and users of cosmetics and toiletries, much more than mainstream America. Hispanics love to shop. On a typical weekend, either the whole family will go to the mall, or the women will pick up their children and go shopping with a group of friends. They prefer shopping in person rather than through catalogs or online. Hispanics also have a tendency to buy from those companies that are involved in community activities.

Hispanics tend to be more brand loyal; about half of them buy their usual brands. Many U.S. brands have made inroads in their native countries, so Hispanics continue to show loyalty to those brands. One reason is that since family is very important to them, they want to do the best for the family by buying prestige goods. Many Hispanics, of Mexican origin, in particular, don't trust putting checks in the mail because back in their homeland of Mexico, they trust neither the bank nor the post office. So they tend to pay by cash. Nationally, only one in three Hispanics has a checking account or owns a credit card (compared to more than two-thirds of all Americans).

How Marketers Should Respond

In a 2004 study, child-friendliness in a restaurant was much more important to Hispanics than to an average American (24% versus 8%).[14] Since Hispanics are family oriented, marketplaces (e.g., restaurants, stores, public vehicles, travel programs, etc.) would need to be much more child-friendly.

Since Hispanics are close knit and community oriented, word-of-mouth is very effective for them; hence, event marketing (sweepstakes, music festivals, sporting events, religious holidays) is a good tool. In media communications, it helps to use Hispanic spokespersons; one study found that members of Hispanic minority ethnic groups viewed the "same-ethnicity" spokespersons as more trustworthy.[15] In mass media, Spanish TV, and among magazines, Hispanic and Hispanic Business are important. Some marketers have adapted their products to Hispanic tastes; an example is the introduction by Dannon yogurt of guava, papaya, mango, and pineapple flavors.

One vexing question facing marketers is whether the Hispanic customers of different

Zoot Suit, a festive suit many Hispanics wear on special occasions, such as a wedding celebration. We found it, and the equally fashionable set of pants and shirt, with a hat to match, at the online store named El Pachuco Photos courtesy of Ernie Gallego of El Pachuco.

origins can be treated as a single market. The most significant common factor, from a marketing communications standpoint, is their common language, Spanish. But even here, regional nuances exist, and smart marketers ensure that their communications are free of such local or regional variations. A few years ago, Segmented Marketing Services of Winston-Salem, North Carolina, an ethnic marketing agency, prepared a magazine in Spanish called Tradiciones de Familia and distributed it free to more than 2 million Hispanics across the United States, along with free product samples from Procter and Gamble, its sole sponsor. But great care was taken to eliminate regional variations: three Hispanic editors from three different regions of origin worked on the magazine.[16]

To account for differences among Hispanic groups, Donnelley Marketing Information Services (DMIS) of Stamford, Connecticut, has identified as many as 18 segments. For example, two of those segments are "Puerto Rican high-income, younger, established homes," and "Mexican, lowest income, younger, low-mobility Hispanic neighborhoods."[17] Such microsegmentation helps local, regional, and national marketers temper national campaigns with local variations. These local adaptations can supplement a national effort, which is based on an understanding of common Hispanic cultural values: family and relationship orientation, respect for tradition and elders, religiosity, equal importance of play and work, and desire to acquire "Americanness," without losing pride in their own language and culture.

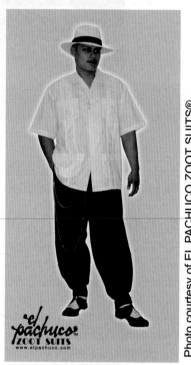

ASIAN AMERICANS

DEMOGRAPHICS
Oh, What a Potpourri!

By the U.S. Census 2000, Asian-Americans—people of Asian origin—numbered 11.7 million, representing a 60% growth since the 1990 census. By 2007, this group is estimated to grow to 14 million. The estimated growth rate between 2002 and 2007 is the highest for this group: 27% compared to 9% for Hispanics, and 11.6% for blacks. Asian-Americans' median age is 27 years, and they have the highest median household income, $53,600 in 2000 (compared with $42,200 for the U.S. population as a whole). They also have a high rate of completing college, 44%, compared to the 24% U.S. average. About half of all Asians live in California, greater New York, or Honolulu. Their share of population ranges from 65% in Honolulu, 18.8% in San Francisco, 11.4% in Los Angeles, 6.7% in New York, 5.1% in Baltimore-Washington D.C. and 4.2% in Chicago metropolitan area.[18]

Many live in acculturated neighborhoods and pricey suburbs. Asian American is merely a convenient label, since, in fact, it comprises immigrants from several countries:[19]

- Chinese Americans (23.75%)
- Filipinos (18.06%)

- Asian Indians (16.4%)
- Korean Americans (10.5%)
- Vietnamese Americans (10.95%)
- Japanese Americans (7.7%)
- Others (12.5%)

Chinese Americans Chinese Americans are about 2.43 million in number and account for over 23% of all Asian Americans. They sometimes identify themselves as either American-born Chinese (ABC), who are more educated and well-to-do and live in upscale communities and are more assimilated into the mainstream culture; or as fresh off boats Chinese (FOB), who live in downtowns and Chinatown and tend to be patriarchical, blue-collar, and conservative. They may speak one of the two major Chinese languages: Cantonese (spoken in Hong Kong) and Mandarin (spoken in Taiwan).

Filipino Americans There are about 1.85 million Filipinos in America, constituting the second largest and probably the best assimilated of all Asian Americans. Because of the 400-year long colonization by Spain, the Philippines is a Christian nation; hence, 85% of Filipino Americans are Roman Catholic. They are concentrated in San Francisco and Los Angeles, and, in lesser numbers, in Chicago, New York, New Jersey, and Connecticut.

Julian (Caucasion-American) and Kathy Fogel (Chinese-American)

Asian Indians About 1.67 million in number, immigrants from India, Pakistan, and Bangladesh are, as a group, the most educated of the entire U.S. population. A large number are professionals, and many are owners of small businesses (e.g., motels, gas stations, and convenience stores). Among recent immigrants, most came to study in polytechnical schools and in Ivy League colleges. Indian students are the most significant presence of all foreign students on college campuses, especially in doctoral programs, and lately in the Silicon Valley high-tech companies.

Korean Americans There are a little over one million Koreans in the United States, and 90% of them are foreign-born. They tend to cluster in large metro areas, mostly in New York, Los Angeles, Chicago, and Honolulu. They have the highest self-employment rate and the highest business ownership rate of any group in America. Many of them own small supermarkets and convenience stores.

Japanese Americans There are about 796,000 Japanese Americans in the United States, and more than 80% of them live on the West Coast. Close to 50,000 Japanese describe themselves as "salarymen," people who are sent by corporations to the United States on temporary assignment and have extended visas. Due to loyalty to their employers, they return to their country. Accordingly, they attempt to "stay Japanese" and believe that others have turned their backs on their homeland. However, a majority (close to 90%) are born in the United States, most have attended college, and this group's median family income is 32% above the U.S. average. Most of these U.S.-born Japanese don't even speak Japanese, and close to 50% of third-generation Japanese Americans have married whites. Many are well assimilated, breaking the stereotype and doing things the mainstream population does. Overjoyed at Kristi Yamaguchi's success in figure skating, one young Japanese-American fan commented, "We are not all math or science wizards or laundry operators or restaurant owners, but skaters, architects, writers. And more. And less. Without hyphens."[20]

Sanghoon Chang and Ju Won Suh on Michigan Avenue, Chicago (May 2006)

Vietnamese Americans Vietnamese comprise the largest number of the rest of Asian Americans, numbering more than a million. About half of them live on the West Coast (about one-third in California). Their median income is lower than that of all other Asian Americans.

VALUES
Not Mainstream at all

Kaoru (L) and Aya Hirose (Japanese-Americans sisters) pose in front of the Statue of Liberty, New York.

Confucianism has had a big influence on many Chinese. This system of beliefs (propagated by the Chinese philosopher Confucius) values hard work, long-term reciprocal relationships, respect for authority (especially, teachers and parents), harmony in all things, and discipline or delaying gratification. Accordingly, the cultural values of Chinese Americans emphasize familial relationships and obligations. Many Chinese Americans do not trust banks, preferring to borrow within their own community, and to put cash in a safe rather than in the bank.

Core Japanese-American values are hard work, loyalty to the group (work group, employer, family, community, or other groups they may join), an obligation to return favors, and respect for age and tradition. Education is also valued highly, so much so that doing well in school is considered an honor to the family or community.

Filipinos share many cultural traits with Hispanics: family values, courtship rituals, allowing enough "play" time, and so on. They are outgoing and sociable; they love having a good time and enjoy a good laugh.

Korean Americans are very hardworking—especially in the family-owned stores where the family works about 11 hours a day, six days a week. For this reason, they also tend to be tired and insulated from other communities. Like other Asians, Koreans too value family loyalty, education, and frugality, and show respect for elders. Koreans prefer Kye (a system of borrowing from individuals), rather than from banks or government. Like Chinese, they distrust banks due to bad past experience with Korean banks.

Ruel Dato-on (R), A Fillipino-American with a Japanese friend, posing for the camera, in a Japanese restaurant.

TO SMILE OR NOT TO SMILE?   *Smiling is an Ethnic Thing....*

The employee procedures manual at many fast-food restaurants such as McDonald's, Burger King, or Wendy's demands that employees "look the customer in the eye, smile, and hand over cash into customers' hands." But this procedure would not be natural in a store run by Korean Americans. In fact these actions would be considered disrespectful. In contrast, many customers consider Korean stores not friendly enough. Why? "Because they would never make eye contact with us, never smile at us, and will not place the change in our hands," report some customers.

Ask any Korean to explain this behavior, and you will discover something amazing. In the Korean culture, it is rude to look someone in the eye, it is improper or "false" to smile at someone whom you do not know socially, and it is definitely unbecoming to touch a stranger's hand!

You will find a similar lack of emotional expressiveness among Chinese or Vietnamese store owners. But don't cast your expectations in stone: with time and with increased exposure to American culture, many of these Mongolian descendent merchants are adopting more emotive postures. And you would recall from your reading of the Appendix to Chapter 9 that at least one Asian group is 180 degrees apart from this group "no smile" norm: the always generously smiling Japanese.

Smile or no smile, they respect us, and themselves, and that is what makes the ethnic potpourri a rich experience.

More than any other minorities, Koreans prefer to maintain their culture, resisting assimilation. Many Koreans see themselves as Koreans rather than as Korean Americans and may return to Korea if economic conditions are perceived to have improved. Koreans value self-reliance, extending the self to their own communities so that when they need help they tend to reach into the community rather than reach out to the mainstream population, thus causing insulation.

Sithi Assanuvat (L, Asian-American from Thailand), and Mimi Assanuvat

Among Asian Indians, one of the most remarkable traits (but not easily visible to outsiders) is a faith in the Hindu philosophy of Karma. *Karma*, a gospel from Hindu Lord Krishna, emphasizes two seemingly contradictory dictums: (1) a person is predestined to get and achieve whatever is his or her due, based upon his or her deeds in a previous life, or, otherwise, whatever the God has willed for him or her; and (2) at the same time, it is a person's duty to do his or her work diligently since that work too is willed by God. Many outsiders confuse Karma with fatalism (belief in fate), implying a lack of desire to make the effort. Traditional Indians are fatalists, but this does not imply that they shirk the effort; rather, it implies that they must make peace with whatever is the outcome of their effort (i.e., whatever is their Karma). Likewise, Asian Moslems often use the expression, "Insha Allah," which means "whatever be Allah's (God's) wish."

Yukari (Japanese-American) and Charles Infosino (Italian American) (with son, Nino)

Asian Indians value their families and many live in extended families, where adults and children care for the elderly. Many are deeply religious and like to maintain their tradition and customs. Many Asian Indian families, especially those with U.S.-born children, who act as acculturation agents for their parents, adopt modern lifestyles but at the same time preserve their customs in their activities at home and within the community, such as in dress, language, food habits, and religious rituals. They, like other Asians, are hard working; like Japanese, they are very ambitious. But unlike most other Asians, they are also content with what they manage to achieve, a trait acquired by their faith in Karma.

Most Asian-Indians migrate to USA for higher studies and then serve their adopted country in high-skilled professional jobs. They assimilate, easily, the American consumer identity while still maintianing, as do most other ethnic groups, their native culture and consumption.

The Asian-Indian-American Sharma family: Rajesh (a P&G quality assurance executive), Praveen (far right, an Insurance administrator), Ricky (far left, a Wharton School sophomore), and Rubina (a junior at Ohio State).

Four Asian Americans, soon to assume, in America, their professional roles and, just like Caucasian professionals, the consumptions that go with their new lifestyles—SUVs, Kenneth Cole clothing, and Starbucks lattes. And sure enough, they will continue to consume, unabated, Bollywood and naan & spicy curry.

(L to R) Mohit Jaiswal, Ishi Puri, Raja Kalra, and Amit Srivastave
(MBA, Class of 2006, Temple University)

Among Asians in general, humility and self-denial for the sake of the group are valued. And Asians (from some regions) don't show emotions in public.

MARKETPLACE BEHAVIOR
Most Utilitarian of Them All

The marketplace behavior of Asian Americans differs from the mainstream population as well as from other racial/ethnic minorities. Notable among these differences are these:

- Japanese Americans, both permanent immigrants and salarymen, are very sophisticated consumers, have a good deal of money to spend, and buy high-quality mainstream brands.
- Many Asian Indians are vegetarians. But even among those who are not, certain kinds of meats are prohibited; for example, Hindus will not eat beef, and Muslims will not eat pork or drink alcohol. Many Indians prefer Pizza Hut to McDonald's
- Saving face is very important to Asians. Therefore, they do not take kindly to advertisements that disparage a competitor's product. It is considered bad to make someone (e.g., a competitor) lose face.
- Koreans prefer a soft sell and face-to-face shopping. Koreans will, however, say "no" more directly than other Asians.
- In Hawaii, Chinese tend to pay cash for a car, whereas Japanese finance it.
- Looking the customer in the eye is expected in the United States, but Asian customers would view that behavior as undesirable. Similarly, in the United States, it is a practice to smile a lot at customers, but for many Asian-American customers, such as Koreans in America, this would be out of place, since smiling is done selectively in Asia, reserved for good acquaintances and friends only. Smiling at strangers is considered artificial or "false."

If you observe any Asian-American in the marketplace, there is one thing that will stand out: they are not swayed by the fad of the day, and what they seek most is utilitarian value. Every purchase is highly deliberated, and while they do comparison-shopping, big time, they are willing to spend money—since they have the money—for quality.

How Marketers Should Respond?

Language obviously is a key factor in targeting ethnic customers. Marketing communications need to be in the language that minorities are comfortable with. Most businesses in Miami offer Spanish as a menu option on their voice mail. Chemical Bank teller machines offer a Russian language option in its Brighton Beach-Brooklyn branch to cater to the

f.y.i.

You want to band-aid your wound but are bothered about how your ethnic skin makes it so conspicuous. Worry no more—an innovative marketer has heard your silent wish. Now those adhesive bandages are available in darker shades, courtesy of Omnitec Corporation. Called Band-Shades, they come in five colors: Honey, Bronze, Caramel, Cocoa, Mocha. Available online (for $3.99 per box of 30) at www.bandshades.com!

significant number of Russian immigrants living there. The New York Downtown Hospital, near Manhattan's Chinatown, serves Chinese food. And Dreyfus Corporation offers, at its San Francisco investment center, a money market prospectus in Chinese. But targeting ethnic groups goes beyond a simple language translation.

Many ethnic minority customers can't identify with the American models most advertisers predominantly use. In a recent analysis, Cover Girl was found to have shown only one minority model out of 236 ads! Beyond the use of different models, the communications should reflect the particular minorities' cultural values and marketplace norms. Since Filipinos enjoy a good laugh, humor works very well for them. Also, because of their strong community orientation, sponsorship of community events is a very effective marketing tool. For example, the Moon Festival banquet is a very special festival in the Chinese culture. And Deepawali is the Christmas-like festival for Asian Indians of Hindu origin. Many local marketers take advantage of these ethnic events and sponsor contests, prizes, and so on.

Most Asian Indians can be reached via English-language media, and since most Japanese now living in the United States are third- or fourth-generation persons, mainstream media appeal to them. However, the communication appeals need to be adapted to specific cultures of specific minorities. To Japanese Americans, don't advertise "You will stand out with this car," because Japanese Americans do not value standing out; they desire to blend in. Similarly, Chinese do not like technology much; therefore, advertising something as being "high tech" is not a good strategy for them. Asians value tradition, so the "new and improved" appeal is likely to be unattractive to them; instead, marketers should emphasize how long the company has been in business, how well established the brand is, and how long-standing its reputation is.

RACE/ETHNIC GROUPS IN E-SPACE EXHIBIT 16.3

There are marked differences between various ethnic groups in respect of their Internet use. Not everyone has a PC at home, but some ethnic groups lag behind more than others. Hispanics and African Americans lag behind, with a little less than half having a PC, compared to Asians whose PC ownership is the highest (77%). This is due in part to an income and affordability difference (Asian Americans have the highest income of all the groups). But even among Hispanics and African Americans, a large majority reported that they were planning to buy a PC soon. Different groups also use the Internet for different purposes. While e-mail is in universal use, other uses vary. Asian Americans use the Internet the most for doing research on products and topics, whereas Hispanics and African Americans use it more for entertainment and chatting with friends. More Asians shop online and, more than any other group, they also feel safe using a credit card online, whereas Hispanics feel least safe giving their credit card information online. (16% versus 21%, 31%, and 34% among African Americans, Caucasians, and Asian Americans, respectively).

Information based on "Portrait of the New America: Understanding A Multicultural Marketplace," The Market Segment Group, A Supplement to Forbes, 2002

CB **Factoid**

7.9% of the UK population is of ethnic minority origin, in London this rises to 31%; The combined disposable wealth of this group is estimated at some £32 billion.

Source: IPA Ethnic Diversity online guide. http://www.redhotcurry.com/archive/news/2003/ipa_report2003.htm

Food, Clothing, and Beyond—Consumption Differences Across Ethnic Groups

Some consumption effects of race stem from genetics, which can cause differences in biological needs—such as differences in skin color and texture and hair type. Therefore, consumers from different races need personal care items with specific performance characteristics. Beyond physiology, other differences stem from cultural differences, which in turn affect values, lifestyle, and tastes. Customs and tastes differ among different ethnic groups, for example, in food, clothing, home decoration, and leisure preferences. Food is vastly different from the main-stream population for Asian-Americans and Hispanics, and to some extent also for African-Americans. Ethnic restaurants in America come mostly from Asia, catering to Asian-American minorities, but increasingly also to the mainstream population of whites and blacks. Asian-Americans and Hispanics also cook a lot more of their meals at home, so ethnic grocery stores can be found in most major cities. According

Ethnic Skincare Market

What is the most conspicuous difference between the three major ethnic consumer groups? Skin complexion. Obviously, then, the skin care needs of ethnic consumers differ from one another. Ethnic skins differ in terms of their pigment cells, and in their sensitivity to melanin and other ingredients in cosmetics. Likewise, hair care needs differ across ethnic consumers in pronounced ways. About 75% of African American women straighten their hair, a process that causes excessive stress on hair and warrants special moisturizing and styling solutions. One recent estimate by Packaged Facts places the total ethnic spending in U.S.A. on hair care, cosmetic, and skincare products to be $1.5 billion. And marketers are waking up to this reality. Many established firms as well as new entrants are offering a bevy of ethnic cosmetics. Here is a sampler:

- In January 2005, ShoftSheen-Carson debuted Optimum Crème Haircolor, with special ingredients for moisturizing and protection against breakage, and in colors ranging from jet black to ash blonde, appealing to both Hispanic and African American consumers.[i]
- Colomer USA launched African Pride Multi-Length Texturizer—a product that helps African Americans to maintain defined curls and waves.
- Universal Colors Cosmetics bills itself as a dermatologist recommended line for ethnic women. It has adopted a four-step skin care method (in contrast to the usual and traditional "3-step, cleanse, moisturize, method") comprising deep clensing exfoliation, toning, and moisturizing.
- Carol's Daughter offers a long line of hand-made products for African American women; recently, it launched its new Mango Collection—mango body butter, cherry mango cocoa butter body soufflé, mango lip balms, etc., enhanced with vanilla, coconut, lime, blended with cocoa and shea butter.
- Inky Loves Nature bills its products as vegan/organic and uses ingredients indigenous to Africa.

Apart from these niche marketers, mass market brands such as Cover Girl and Revlon also market ethnic-targeted cosmetics. Among these big players, L'Oreal has launched a major initiative in ethnic beauty care products. In the year 2000, it established L'Oreal Institute for Ethnic Hair and Skin Research in Chicago. The Institute researches the problems peculiar to African hair as well as all types of ethnic skins, and sponsors an International Symposium on Ethnic Hair and Skin annually. In recent years, it acquired two black-centered companies, SoftSheen and Carson. But its efforts go beyond U.S. ethnic groups. It has a foothold in markets worldwide and caters to consumers of all race and ethnic origins. In China, for example, Maybelline (a L'Oreal line) is the preferred cosmetic brand for 44% of Chinese women.[b]

My CB Book

Based on: [i] **Hair care needs are different, diverse.(MERCHANDISING),** *MMR,* June, 2005; and [ii] Jennie James, "Because They're Worth It," *Time.com*, January 18, 2004; Ethnic Skin Care As consumers demand more ethnic-specific products, the market continues to expand. by Susan A. Eliya, *Happi*, October 2005 http://www.happi.com/articles/2005/10/ethnic-skin-care.php). Images: istockphoto.com.

Photo credits (from Top left, clockwise) ©iStockphoto.com/Oleg Prikhodko, ©iStockphoto.com/ Jose Antonio Nicoli Andonie, and ©iStockphoto.com/Thomas Brostrom

to a recent report, U.S. Hispanics spend $117 per week on groceries compared to the U.S. national average of $87.[21]

Similarly, clothing also differs for minorities, most notably for Asian-Americans. Although most have adopted Western clothing in offices and on the street, at home they continue to feel more comfortable in their native clothing, and they prefer lounging in loose-flowing clothing from their homeland. On festive occasions and at in-group large social gatherings, they can be seen donning festive clothing of their native origin. Many of them buy these clothes from their homeland, but there are also full-scale stores in some major cities (e.g., Chicago, New York, and Toronto) catering to their needs.

In terms of clothing, Hispanics are most assimilated into the mainstream, but they are also much more fashionable than (and not nearly as casual as) the mainstream population. Likewise, African Americans sport mainstream western clothing for the most part, particularly in the workplace, but in casual clothing they seek—much more than do most other groups—athletic clothes with images of sports teams and name brand clothing. For social occasions, a significant proportion of African Americans wear a special kind of clothing, which is still Western in overall style but unmistakably distinct in fabric, color, and specific garment design. Again, there are stores that specialize in this type of clothing.

In clothing and beyond, minorities differ in conspicuous consumption. Asian Americans tend to be frugal, and they are interested in value and quality (rather than in showing off) even when they buy luxury. Hispanics are quite conspicuous, particularly in appearance related consumption. So are many (though not all) African Americans. Some minority ethnic groups tend to seek socially prestigious consumption to compensate for their sometimes low—whether real or perceived—public image.

Money Talks

Financial resources affect consumption differently across the races. Races differ in economic conditions. This is due to historical differences in accessing opportunities, as well as race-based cultural differences in individual achievement, motivation, and belief in upward mobility. There has also been a systematic bias against certain ethnic minorities in credit approval. Both of these factors limit the buying power of some ethnic minorities. Other ethnic minorities, such as Japanese Asians or Asian Indians, are affluent (a characteristic that has a positive influence on their demand for products and services), but at the same time shun credit, thus limiting their purchases to what they can afford. In contrast, whites and blacks alike live on credit, many amassing a huge debt.

Seeking Love from Merchants

Ethnic groups also differ from the mainstream whites in their choice of merchants and salespersons. They prefer to do business with stores and firms owned or operated by persons of their own ethnic origin. This is especially the case with financial, insurance, real estate, and health care services because these services and products entail a considerable risk (and they feel greater trust with salespersons of their own ethnic background). That is why a lot of insurance, financial services, and real estate companies hire ethnic salespersons. Having said this, we must also note that many ethnic consumers are totally assimilated in the mainstream and are indifferent or even prefer mainstream salespersons. This is in part because they wish to maintain the confidentiality of their financial and medical matters, and they may suspect ethnics to gossip in their close-knit ethnic communities. Therefore, a company seeking to target minorities should employ salespersons both of ethnic and mainstream origins. (By the way, and at least for this context, Asian Americans and Hispanics consider both blacks and whites as mainstream.)

Finally, ethnic groups differ also in the kind of interaction they seek from marketers—retailers, salespersons, agents, customer service persons. In some races and ethnic cultures, friendship is limited to personal friends, and consequently, in commercial transactions, there is politeness but not personal warmth, so none is offered and none is expected. However, expectations may be different between the customer and the salesperson, if they come from different ethnic backgrounds. This causes a problem when blacks or whites visit Asian-American stores and restaurants, for example, where the level of casual warmth and personalized social interaction is often absent. Of course, many of these service providers of ethnic origin are becoming acculturated enough now to diminish this glaring gap as time goes on.

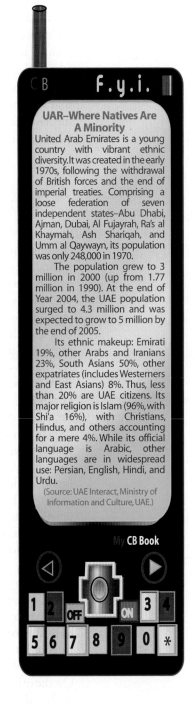

F.y.i.

UAR–Where Natives Are A Minority
United Arab Emirates is a young country with vibrant ethnic diversity. It was created in the early 1970s, following the withdrawal of British forces and the end of imperial treaties. Comprising a loose federation of seven independent states–Abu Dhabi, Ajman, Dubai, Al Fujayrah, Ra's al Khaymah, Ash Shariqah, and Umm al Qaywayn, its population was only 248,000 in 1970.

The population grew to 3 million in 2000 (up from 1.77 million in 1990). At the end of Year 2004, the UAE population surged to 4.3 million and was expected to grow to 5 million by the end of 2005.

Its ethnic makeup: Emirati 19%, other Arabs and Iranians 23%, South Asians 50%, other expatriates (includes Westerners and East Asians) 8%. Thus, less than 20% are UAE citizens. Its major religion is Islam (96%, with Shi'a 16%), with Christians, Hindus, and others accounting for a mere 4%. While its official language is Arabic, other languages are in widespread use: Persian, English, Hindi, and Urdu.

(Source: UAE Interact, Ministry of Information and Culture, UAE.)

My **CB Book**

ETHNIC IDENTITY

So far we have looked at ethnicity as an objective, an "all or none" descriptor of the consumer—a consumer is or is not Hispanic (or African American or Asian or whatever). It is not a matter of degree. But many of you might know some consumers who don't act like their ethnic type, or who don't see themselves in ethnic terms. This phenomenon is captured in the concept of ethnic identity. **Ethnic identity** refers to a person's knowledge of his or her membership in a social group and the value and emotional significance attached to that membership.[23]

Thus, it is a person's view of himself or herself as more or less ethnic, how closely he or she sees a sense of self in ethnic terms. Consumers with low ethnic identity view themselves as simply "a human person," period, rather than as "Hispanic" or "Asian." They get more assimilated in the mainstream culture. They may not necessarily abandon the consumption rituals of their ethnic groups, but they feel equally at home in the marketplace marked by mainstream culture. One characteristic of Hispanics, for example, as we learned earlier, is that Hispanics shun coupons. But what about those Hispanics who do not feel strong ethnic identity? One study found that Hispanics with weak ethnic identity tended to use coupons just as the mainstream consumers did.[24] Marketers should not assume, therefore, that all ethnics would find various marketing tools equally attractive, or that non-ethnic media would not appeal to any persons of ethnic minorities, or that they can reach all ethnic affiliation persons relying exclusively on ethnic media or ethnic salespersons.[25]

RELIGIOUS AFFILIATION

Consumers' Religious identity exercises substantial influence on consumers—their values, customs, and habits. **Religion** refers to a system of beliefs about the supernatural, spiritual world, about God, and about how humans, as God's creatures, are supposed to behave on this earth. Religious institutions indoctrinate and offer tenets by which their followers ought to live. As such, these institutions influence consumer values, both in respect to the importance and value of material possessions and the goals or benefits desired of products. As a historical example, sociologist Max Weber attributed the industrialization and rise of capitalism in Western Europe to the Protestant ethic.[26]

Major denominations (i.e., religious affiliations) in the United States are Catholics, Protestants, and Jews. Major religions of the world include Christianity, Islam, Judaism, Hinduism, Buddhism, and Confucianism. The major ideas and tenets of each are summarized in Table 16.1.

In thinking about the role of religion in consumer behavior, it is useful to distinguish between religions affiliation and religious identity. **Religious affiliation** refers to a consumer's membership, in objective terms, in a religion. In contrast, **religious identity** (or identification) is the degree of involvement and commitment in that religion as a system of belief and practice. For most consumer behaviors in the domain of religious practice and rituals, a consumer's religious identification would be more influential than mere religious affiliation.[27]

Religious affiliation affects consumer behavior principally by influencing the consumer's personality structure, that is, his or her beliefs, values, and behavioral tendencies. These personality structures, in turn, affect consumers' marketplace behaviors. For example, if you contrast the personality structures of, say, Protestants and Catholics, you would find that compared with Catholics, Protestants are more stoic, nationalistic, and ascetic individualists who believe they have control of their fate and accept delayed gratification. In contrast, Catholics are more traditional, trusting in faith that God controls their life. They believe in collectivism, rather than individualism, and family and home are priorities. On the other hand, Jews differ from both of these groups. They tend to be more innovative (rather than traditional), and they are more achievement oriented. They are also more emotional, yet more anxious, socially. These personality differences in turn affect consumer preferences for products or services.

V CONSUMERS' DIVERSITY

484

Consumer Karma

WE GOT JESUS IN A SCENT

Many consumers are buying a special candle, and smelling the scent of Jesus. The candle is branded His Essence™, and is inspired by a biblical source. The invention is the brain child of Karen Tosterud of South Dakota. She mentioned the idea to her husband Bob Tosterud, a professor of entrepreneurship at the University of South Dakota, and today the idea is a living thriving product. Bob says they got the formula from Psalm 45:8. In the Psalm, Christ returns and his garments have the scent of myrrh, aloe, and cassia. So they mixed the three ingredients in equal proportion.

The candle was first put out for sale in November 2004 and, because of a story in local paper, 768 candles sold in 24 hours. Thanks to stories in national media since then, the candles are now being sought out by customers in some 650 stores (such as Hallmark) all over USA. You can buy it also from the company's own Web site (www.hisessence.com), for $19.95. Now, they also sell a hand lotion, for $14.95 for an 8 oz. Bottle. Customers are raving about it:

"As I come and go throughout my day this fragrance is a reminder to me that God is always with me. It helps me to stay focused and reassures me of His constant presence in the busyness of life."

"I have bought and burned just about one full jar of your candle now with 3 more in my closet waiting to be used by me or given as a gift. I love the scent and when I'm not burning it I leave the lid off and still get a nice smell without it burning."

"I feel it will help bring me closer to Jesus at a time I so desperately need it. Thank you for what you do."

"I love it! The smell is amazing. It brought tears to my eyes!"

(Source: Company Web site www.hisessence.com.)

Consumer Karma is Believing   My CB Book

Marketing by Religion

Religious symbols show up in market offerings from time to time. Three popular images from Asian religions are Lord Krishna (believed to have incarnated as a mischievous, flute playing, cowherd, later delivering God's—his own, actually—WORD that became a master philosophic treatise and a primer for conducting life in the Hindu religion, *Bhagawat Gita*), Ganesha (a Hindu baby god with an elephant face), and Lord Buddha (a prince turned sage, founder of the Buddhist religion). They show up in western merchandise, not because of their religious significance but because their images are considered, well, cool!

Lord Ganesha

True Religion jeans (the second most popular brand, after Seven, according to a recent online search tracking by Yahoo) feature laughing Buddha (not to be confused with Lord Buddha, though). And then, in early 2004, Ondademar, a Columbian swimwear company, brought out a bikini with Lord Buddha images on breast and elsewhere. Victoria's Secret briefly carried it, among others, until the company withdrew it following global protests from followers of Buddha. The followers considered it profane and disrespectful; the company thought it was "a beautiful image," and later apologized for the misjudgment. (Obviously, we can't show the bikini, but you can satisfy your curiosity by *Googling* it)

Lord Buddha

The use of religious symbols in commercial merchandise can bring consumers some symbolic value, but its use must be screened by a sensitivity-check with that religion's followers.

Lord Krishna

Oh, we almost forgot about hair and religion. One particular religion prohibits hair cutting altogether—the Sikh religion; so men who follow this religion strictly grow their hair waist long and spend umpteen hours taking care of it. To cover their long hair, they also wear headgear (turbans) as do many Saudi Muslims. In the Hindu religion, a child receives his or her first hair cut amidst religious ceremonial pomp and show. Buddhist monks shave their heads, thus eliminating one more trap of the material world—tress love. And of course, they save all that money and time most other consumers spend in their devotion to their hair.

Table 16.1 provides a very general overview of the world's largest religions: Hinduism, Buddhism, Islam, Christianity, Judaism, and Confucianism.[24]

TABLE 16.1

MAJOR RELIGIONS OF THE WORLD

HINDUISM

Perhaps the oldest of all religions, Hinduism holds a strong belief in "Karma"—the idea that a person's activities determine his or her destiny in the next life and liberation of the spirit from the human body and its union with God. An important element of its belief system is the caste system, the group each person is born into; caste defines one's status. In India, the home of Hinduism, class mobility would be an inappropriate appeal for promoting products. Family is highly valued in this religion, and most Hindus live in extended families and even operate businesses as a family unit.

BUDDHISM

The Buddhist religion branched out of Hinduism in the sixth century B.C. and is found in such countries as China, Tibet, Sri Lanka, Japan, and Korea. Buddha, the Enlightened One, preached, "Blessed is he who overcomes sin and is free from passion ... and the highest blessedness comes to him who conquers vanity and selfishness." The tenet of Buddhism most relevant to customer behavior is the one about asceticism—rigorous self-denial and active self-restraint in consumption.[1] Buddhism teaches that material things cannot bring happiness.

ISLAM

Islam is the religion of the followers of the Prophet Mohammed. These followers, called Muslims, are concentrated in India, Pakistan, and the Arab nations of the Middle East. Muslims follow a detailed way of life and daily routine prescribed in the Koran, their sacred book. This routine includes prayer five times a day, a practice marketers visiting their Muslim customers should be aware of. Another noteworthy practice is fasting, especially during the lunar month of Ramadan, when Muslims must eat or drink nothing during the day. This religion holds rather traditional views on women, which may entail their seclusion and permits polygamy. Finally, Islam is a missionary religion--the faithful are supposed to uphold their religion and oppose the unbelievers.

The number of Moslems in America is estimated to be three to four million. About one in four Moslems in America is black. Moslems favor close-knit families, support religious education, and have conservative social values. Use of alcohol, dating, and sexual freedom are prohibited among traditional Moslems, although the younger generation growing up in America tends not to adhere to such strict norms of their religion.

CHRISTIANITY

Christianity comprises two main groups--Catholics and Protestants. Roman Catholicism centers around the church and its religious order. The church is supposed to mediate between God and humans. In the Catholic religion, the proper source for rules on the way to live is considered to be the Vatican. Therefore, outside knowledge not originating from the clergy is considered invalid. Consequently, Catholics are likely to be more fatalistic, traditional, and less innovative. In the United States, Catholics identify themselves with the Democratic Party.

Protestants believe that everyone has direct access to God (without the mediation of the church) and that God has intended for every person to do His work. Thus, work becomes important as a means of carrying out God's will. This work ethic, referred to as Protestant ethic, leads its followers to produce more material wealth. Protestantism does not seek to provide to its followers knowledge of the external world. It encourages them, instead, to seek scientific knowledge for that purpose. Compared to Catholics, Protestants are less authoritarian, more open to change, and have a work ethic; they consider leisure nonproductive and hence a waste of time. Politically, they may be conservative and align themselves, in the United States, with the Republican Party. Protestants believe in getting ahead by personal effort rather than by government handouts, and they strive for upward mobility.

JUDAISM

In Judaism, God is viewed as an abstract and omniscient presence; however, God is presumed to be inclined to communicate with the individual directly (as opposed to through the clergy as in the Catholic system). Judaism believes that man can only comprehend God through self-education. It also believes, similar to Protestants, that man is responsible for his own actions and for his destiny or position in life.

The Jewish personality has been described as follows:27 Compared to Protestants and Catholics, Jews are more liberal and democratic, more flexible and rationalistic, higher in achievement motivation, more enthusiastic, gregarious, and emotional, more impatient and hurried, more inclined to postpone gratification, and politically most liberal.

CONFUCIANISM

There are about 350 million adherents of Confucianism, mostly in China, Japan, Burma, and Thailand. Confucianism is a philosophy rather than a religion. It guides almost every aspect of Chinese life. Confucians urge people to strive for righteousness and improvement of one's character. Prominent Confucian values are harmony in the family, order in the state, and peace in the empire. Human duty is emphasized, and the ideal of the "superior man" rather than the divine is stressed. Man is supposed to cultivate the qualities of benevolence, propriety, wisdom, and sincerity.

Sources: Based on multiple sources: Benson Y. Landis, World Religions, New York: E.P. Dutton & Co. 1965); Undertstandong Islam in America," American Demographics, January 1994, pp 10-11.

1. Adapted from dictionary entry on www.dictionary.com.

Look What CB Researchers Found

To examine the consumer behavior differences due to people's religious affiliations, Beth Hirschman, a consumer research professor at New York University, surveyed a sample of consumers in New York City. Among her respondents were 96 Catholics, 114 Protestants, and 120 Jews. She asked them to indicate what criteria they would use to decide what to do on a weekend evening for entertainment. She also asked them to list the kind of activities they might consider doing.

Consumers' choice criteria (i.e., the considerations they use in making their choice among a set of alternatives) differed significantly across the three religious groups. Moreover, these differences were explainable by religious affiliations and the personality structure shaped by them. Specifically, among the choice criteria, price was mentioned much more by Protestants, as was also the expected enjoyment. This may result from an emphasis (found among Protestants) on capital accumulation and on using time productively. Desire for companionship and personal feeling (how "I feel about it") were other important criteria, mentioned much more by Jews than by the other two groups. This is most likely because Jews are much more sociable and emotional.

Preferred leisure activities differed significantly as well. Dinner and/or entertaining at home were mentioned much more by Catholics than the other two groups (63% of Catholics mentioned it compared to 18% of Protestants and 45% of Jews). This is an outcome of the fact that Catholics place much more emphasis on family and home. In contrast, going to a nightclub or attending a ballet was mentioned the least by Catholics, but most by Jews. The reason is that Jews are more cosmopolitan and also more hedonic (seeking sensory pleasure) in comparison to the other two groups. Visiting friends was cited the most by Jewish consumers, attesting to the gregarious, emotional, and sociable personality character their religious affiliation inculcates in them.

Reading was mentioned the most by Protestants, the second most by Jews and the least by Catholics. Note that both Protestants and Jewish religions prescribe seeking knowledge of the world from nonreligious scriptures. Also, reading is a very productive use of time, a value Protestants seek. Finally, making love was mentioned considerably more by Jews (53% compared to 3% and 13% by the other two groups). This too is explainable by religious affiliation. Both Protestant and Catholic religions consider sex as an activity whose main purpose is reproduction. In contrast, the Jewish religion recognizes sex as a legitimate hedonic (i.e., enjoyment) value!

Although this study is based on a small sample of consumers and is a bit dated, its principal arguments appear logical. At the very least, it is a powerful illustration of the pervasive influence of religion on one's personality, and, in turn, on consumption preferences.

Source: Adapted from Elizabeth C. Hirschman, "Religious Affiliations and Consumption Processes: An Initial Paradigm," in Research in Marketing, J. Sheth, ed. (Greenwich, CT: Jai Press 1983). Pp. 131-70.

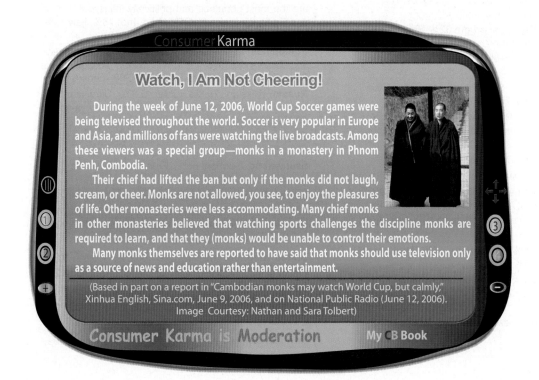

Consumer Karma

Watch, I Am Not Cheering!

During the week of June 12, 2006, World Cup Soccer games were being televised throughout the world. Soccer is very popular in Europe and Asia, and millions of fans were watching the live broadcasts. Among these viewers was a special group—monks in a monastery in Phnom Penh, Combodia.

Their chief had lifted the ban but only if the monks did not laugh, scream, or cheer. Monks are not allowed, you see, to enjoy the pleasures of life. Other monasteries were less accommodating. Many chief monks in other monasteries believed that watching sports challenges the discipline monks are required to learn, and that they (monks) would be unable to control their emotions.

Many monks themselves are reported to have said that monks should use television only as a source of news and education rather than entertainment.

(Based in part on a report in "Cambodian monks may watch World Cup, but calmly," Xinhua English, Sina.com, June 9, 2006, and on National Public Radio (June 12, 2006). Image Courtesy: Nathan and Sara Tolbert)

Consumer Karma is Moderation   **My CB Book**

Hundreds of Ethnic Groups
The Charms of Human Diversity

Because race based distinctions are easily visible (due to physiological features) and ethnic distinctions are not (especially when they are based on heritage other than race), we tend to overlook that ethnic diversity exists in every country and in ample measure. We have compiled for you a sample of ethnic group composition of selected nations of the world. (See Exhibit 16.4.) Peruse and be amazed. And the next time you get to travel to any of these countries, look for the rich cultural experience these ethnically diverse marketplaces provide.

Ethnic Diversity Around the World

Exhibit 16.4

Australia Caucasian 92%, Asian 7%, aboriginal and other 1%

The Bahamas Black 85%, white 12%, Asian and Hispanic 3%

Belgium Fleming 58%, Walloon 31%, mixed or other 11%

Brazil white 53.7%, mulatto (mixed white and black) 38.5%, black 6.2%, other (includes Japanese, Arab, Amerindian) 0.9%, unspecified 0.7% (2000 census)

Burma Burman 68%, Shan 9%, Karen 7%, Rakhine 4%, Chinese 3%, Indian 2%, Mon 2%, other 5%

Canada British Isles origin 28%, French origin 23%, other European 15%, Amerindian 2%, other, mostly Asian, African, Arab 6%, mixed background 26%

China Han Chinese 91.9%, Zhuang, Uygur, Hui, Yi, Tibetan, Miao, Manchu, Mongol, Buyi, Korean, and other nationalities 8.1%

Cuba mulatto 51%, white 37%, black 11%, Chinese 1%

Cyprus Greek 77%, Turkish 18%, other 5% (2001)
Ethiopia Oromo 40%, Amhara and Tigre 32%, Sidamo 9%, Shankella 6%, Somali 6%, Afar 4%, Gurage 2%, other 1%

India Indo-Aryan 72%, Dravidian 25%, Mongoloid and other 3% (2000)

Indonesia Javanese 45%, Sundanese 14%, Madurese 7.5%, coastal Malays 7.5%, other 26%

China Han Chinese 91.9%, Zhuang, Uygur, Hui, Yi, Tibetan, Miao, Manchu, Mongol, Buyi, Korean, and other nationalities 8.1%

Cuba mulatto 51%, white 37%, black 11%, Chinese 1%

Cyprus Greek 77%, Turkish 18%, other 5% (2001)

Ethiopia Oromo 40%, Amhara and Tigre 32%, Sidamo 9%, Shankella 6%, Somali 6%, Afar 4%, Gurage 2%, other 1%

India Indo-Aryan 72%, Dravidian 25%, Mongoloid and other 3% (2000)

Indonesia Javanese 45%, Sundanese 14%, Madurese 7.5%, coastal Malays 7.5%, other 26%

Iran Persian 51%, Azeri 24%, Gilaki and Mazandarani 8%, Kurd 7%, Arab 3%, Lur 2%, Baloch 2%, Turkmen 2%, other 1%

Israel Jewish 80.1% (Europe/America-born 32.1%, Israel-born 20.8%, Africa-born 14.6%, Asia-born 12.6%), non-Jewish 19.9% (mostly Arab) (1996 est.)

Latvia Latvian 57.7%, Russian 29.6%, Belarusian 4.1%, Ukrainian 2.7%, Polish 2.5%, Lithuanian 1.4%, other 2% (2002)

Malaysia Malay 50.4%, Chinese 23.7%, Indigenous 11%, Indian 7.1%, others 7.8% (2004 est.)

Mexico mestizo (Amerindian-Spanish) 60%, Amerindian or predominantly Amerindian 30%, white 9%, other 1%

Netherlands Dutch 83%, other 17% (of which 9% are non-Western origin mainly Turks, Moroccans, Antilleans, Surinamese, and Indonesians) (1999 est.)

New Zealand European 69.8%, Maori 7.9%, Asian 5.7%, Pacific islander 4.4%, other 0.5%, mixed 7.8%, unspecified 3.8% (2001 census)

Nigeria Nigeria, Africa's most populous country, is composed of more than 250 ethnic groups; the following are the most populous and politically influential: Hausa and Fulani 29%, Yoruba 21%, Igbo (Ibo) 18%, Ijaw 10%, Kanuri 4%, Ibibio 3.5%, Tiv 2.5%

Philippines Tagalog 28.1%, Cebuano 13.1%, Ilocano 9%, Bisaya/Binisaya 7.6%, Hiligaynon Ilonggo 7.5%, Bikol 6%, Waray 3.4%, other 25.3% (2000 census)

Russia Russian 79.8%, Tatar 3.8%, Ukrainian 2%, Bashkir 1.2%, Chuvash 1.1%, other or unspecified 12.1% (2002 census)

Singapore Chinese 76.8%, Malay 13.9%, Indian 7.9%, other 1.4% (2000 census)

Switzerland German 65%, French 18%, Italian 10%, Romansch 1%, other 6%

United Arab Emirates Emirati 19%, other Arab and Iranian 23%, South Asian 50%, other expatriates (includes Westerners and East Asians) 8% (1982) note: less than 20% are UAE citizens (1982)

United Kingdom white (English 83.6%, Scottish 8.6%, Welsh 4.9%, Northern Irish 2.9%) 92.1%, black 2%, Indian 1.8%, Pakistani 1.3%, mixed 1.2%, other 1.6% (2001 census)

Source: World Factbook 2005 (A publication of the Central Intelligence Agency, USA.)

In this chapter, we discussed two important consumer characteristics: race/ethnic identity and religious affiliation.

We began the chapter by clarifying the difference between race and ethnic identity, and profiled the four major ethnic/race groups in the United States, namely, Caucasians, Hispanics, African Americans, and Asian Americans. In the U.S., although Caucasians are a majority (comprising some 70%), minorities are growing rapidly. In the 2000 Census, Hispanics became the single largest minority ethnic group, surpassing African Americans by a small margin. Among Asian Americans, Chinese are the largest subgroup, and Japanese are the smallest. Each ethnic group differs from others in demographic as well as psychographic characteristics. Correspondingly, they differ in their consumption preferences as well.

Some of these differences are based on biological needs being different; others are produced by cultural practices and habits. Specifically, Race and ethnic backgrounds influence a consumer's needs for hair and skin-specific personal care items, taste differences in food and clothing, and in preferred interaction styles with marketers. We outlined how marketers need to respond to these ethnic differences.

Among religious affiliations, we coved all the major religions of the world: Christianity, Judaism, Hinduism, Islam, Buddhism, and Confucianism. A person's religious affiliation influences his or her consumer behavior by shaping values, beliefs, and preferences. Some products are prohibited by some religions, and many consumption rituals are tied to religious practices and customs.

Race
Ethnicity
Ethnic Identity

Religious Affiliation
Religious Identity
Hinduism

Islam
Christianity
Buddhism

Confucianism
Asceticism

REVIEW✚Rewind

1. Explain the difference between race and ethnic identity.
2. Briefly outline the comparative demographic profile of four major ethnic groups in U.S.A.
3. Briefly outline psychographic profile of four major ethnic groups in U.S.A.
4. Briefly summarize the core theme of each religion and suggest how each religion might affect consumer behavior of its followers.
5. Cite some examples of what marketers do differently (or should) when targeting different ethnic groups.

THINK✚Apply

Assume your firm was located in a college town that attracts students from all ethnic minorities in USA in large numbers. Outline some marketing ideas you would pursue if you were (a) a supermarket, (b) a movie theater, and (c) a food mall.

PRACTICE✚Experience

1. Interview eight adult female consumers, two each of Hispanic, African-American, Caucasian, and Asian-American identity about their use of cosmetics. What role do cosmetics play in their lives and how does this role differ between consumers of different ethnic identity?
2. Interview a couple of mixed ethnic identity about how the spouses shoulder and share responsibility for homemaking. Probe how they found their ethnic culture to affect the home-making expectations each

had from the other? Summarize your findings

3. Visit two online Hispanic supermarket stores. Survey the merchandise and any marketing ideas you can infer from the Web site. For comparison, also visit the Web sites of two national chains like Kroger and Safeway. Summarize the differences you notice between these two categories of stores.

Repeat the exercise with two Asian (e.g., Chinese, Indian, Korean, etc.) store Web sites.

If possible, also visit these stores in the physical world and document your observations, highlighting the differences between mainstream and ethnic stores.

At your university or college or organization, find one person who belongs to and represents each of the five major religious institutions presented in the chapter (you may include yourself if appropriate). First, ask them to think about the various routines in their daily life (e.g., food preparation, dressing, grooming, etc.). Next, ask them to describe two rituals that are based on their religion. Based on your reading of the chapter, discuss if the ritual served any function when they started and if they serve any function now

In the Marketing Manager's Shoes

Put yourself in a marketing manager's shoes. Most concepts in the chapter have some lessons for the marketing manager, i.e., they suggest what to do differently in practice; indeed, often these applications are implicit in our explanations of the concepts and models in the chapter. Identify at least five specific applications of the chapter's concepts, all of which should be entirely new—different from the examples cited here.

Income, Social Class, and Geodemographics

Three Core Markers of Consumers' Place in Society

- Money and the Consumer Mind
- Consumer Sentiment—The Spend-Save Consumer Dialog
- From Mass to Class—Pushing the Boundaries
- Geodemographics—Where You Live Says a Lot about You
- PRIZM—Not all "Hoods" Are Created Equal

©iStockphoto.com/Michelle Preast.

"We have seen poverty and we have seen affluence. And right now we are busy being **affluent consumers!**"

About 10 miles Southwest of New Delhi is a town only 10 years ago no urban person (Indian or tourist) would have even liked to visit let alone live in. But today it is the hub of modern and global malls comparable to the Mall of America and Ibn Battuta Mall in Dubai. The town is named Gurgaon and today it is a main shopping attraction for tourists and its new residents alike.

Prominent among its new residents are 20-something techies—new college graduates with jobs as programmers, software engineers, Web site designers, and of course, call center workers. Employed by some of the biggest service firms from the West (e.g., Microsoft, Convergys, SAP), who have opened sprawling call centers in this once sleepy town, these phone workers work the evening shift (that's day time in the UK and Europe) and night shift (for U.S. customers). Many of them assume American names, learn new patterns of Westernized speech, and watch American TV to catch the jargon—so they no longer look confused when called José as in "no way, 'José." They get paid well, and they are enjoying their new-found spending power.

In the afternoons, while it is 120° outside, they sit in air-conditioned cafes, sipping cappuccinos. That's after they have completed a bag full of shopping spree their older siblings could not even dream of as recently as five years ago. Speaking of dreams, so full of optimism about their future wealth they are that they dream of someday driving a Mercedes and, yes, even a Ferrari!

If you ask them—these 20-something high-wage-earning techies—about their new spending habits, they would most probably say: "We have seen poverty and we have seen affluence. And right now, we are busy being affluent consumers!"

Tanvi and Dhruv Tandon, shopping with their newfound affluence (Photo: Richa Tandon)

INTRODUCTION

Money. You have it, marketers want it. Perhaps nothing else about you is of more interest to marketers than how much money you have. The new residents of Gurgaon—the newly affluent consumers. For marketers of a range of products and services—cars, clothing, shoes, gourmet food, electronic gadgets, even books—the rising economic status of consumers like the 20-something techies of Gurgaon is a blessing.

And, of course, having money is good for you too. With it you can own the marketplace. Buy whatever you want. Without it, or without enough of it, you have to navigate carefully, assembling the necessities of life within your limited budget.

Money is also the factor that (after age, race, and gender) visibly distinguishes you in society. It's written large on your persona. In the clothes you wear, the house you live in, and the car you drive. In the restaurants you frequent, the stores you shop, and the games you play. And thihgs you accumulate.

It also determines, at least in part, your attitude toward the world and your social styles and behavior. Yes, your style, your preferences, your market choices, and your world-view, money affects them all. Money and a few other things, actually—like your education, occupation, and pedigree, for example.

Marketers are extremely interested in understanding how money, along with these other determinants, influences your behavior as a consumer in the marketplace. These determinants are captured in three related consumer descriptors: income & wealth, social class, and geodemographics. Together, these three determinants form the major *markers* of our station in life, our standing in society. They also form the subject of this chapter.

In this chapter, we will tell you about how income and wealth affect people's consumption and marketplace behavior. Some of it, you probably know already. But we will also tell you things you never knew before. Then we will describe the concept of *social class*, illuminating its distinction from income and wealth. Social class is not exactly what you think it is, and its pervasive presence in society, and, even more notably, its mighty effect on your behavior in the marketplace will surprise you! Finally, we'll look at consumer segments based on geodemographics, the cluster of neighborhoods where people of similar wealth, social class, and lifestyles live. We will introduce you to your neighbors, presenting them in a light you have never seen before. Savvy marketers already know them, neighborhood by neighborhood. Now, it is your chance to know.

INCOME AND WEALTH

First things first. Let us define income and wealth. A person's **income** is the amount of monetary earnings that person receives periodically on a more or less regular basis. This can comprise of wages and salaries, or income from one's business if self-employed. Income is of course only one component of a person's financial resources. Other components are inherited wealth, savings, and lottery winnings. A consumer's total financial resources are collectively known as "**wealth**." Your wealth is what determines whether you are poor or rich, or somewhere in between. For most consumers, though, their income is the principal or even the only determinant of their wealth. Therefore, our discussion of consumer financial resources centers on income.

INCOME AND CONSUMER SPENDING

One universal fact of life in all societies is that income is not equally distributed across population, and also that a vast majority of population earns a low income, whereas a very small percentage of people earn a very high income. This can be seen in the distribution of income in the U.S.A. See Figure 17.1.

Food, Clothing, or Videogames—What do you want to buy with your money?

How do consumers allocate their money over different product categories, such as food, clothing, transportation, etc.? Although no two families will spend their money in exactly the same way, there is, on the average, quite a consistent pattern of how income is allocated over expense categories. Based on statistical analyses of data from families with diverse income groups, economists have discovered that a nearly constant proportion is spent on various items.

Poor families spend their incomes largely on food and housing and on some basic clothing. As income increases from low to moderate levels, people tend to eat more food, and also more of the foods that are not considered staples (which are therefore more expensive). Thus, with rising income, the proportion spent on food still remains the same at first (note that although the expenditure increases in absolute terms, the proportion remains the same); subsequently, as income increases even further, the proportion spent on food declines—after all one can eat only so much!

The proportion of income spent on housing rises with income in the very low-income range, but then it remains fairly constant. Note that it remains constant as a proportion of the total income, even though in absolute terms, people tend to move into more expensive houses as their income rises. As regards clothing, automobiles, and luxury goods, expenditures on these items rise sharply with income, until a very high upper limit is reached. Finally, savings rise dramatically with income, and they never decline. These spending patterns are described by Engel's law—after the 19th century Prussian statistician Ernst Engel. According to **Engel's law,** the lower the per capita income of a nation or people, the more they tend to spend on basic necessities such as food, housing, and clothing. Consumption items other than these necessities are called discretionary products. Consumers buy these with **discretionary income**—personal income left after taxes and after the purchase of necessities. As discretionary income rises, consumers spend more on discretionary items, such as video games, vacations, art collections, or even plastic surgery.

One U.S agency that tracks how consumers allocate their income is the U.S. Department of Labor. The department conducts periodic surveys of American consumers, called the Consumer Expenditure Survey (CEX). In 2001, the department asked 15,000 randomly

FIGURE
17.1
INCOME DISTRIBUTION FOR AMERICAN CONSUMERS (2000)

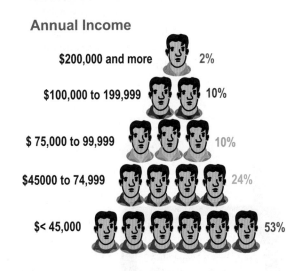

Annual Income

$200,000 and more	2%
$100,000 to 199,999	10%
$ 75,000 to 99,999	10%
$45000 to 74,999	24%
$< 45,000	53%

selected consumers to record in diaries and tell in interviews how they spent their money, down to the penny. The findings revealed some interesting patterns. Overall, the largest share of the household budget, one-third of all expenditures, goes to housing (32.4%). Next is transportation, accounting for 19.5%. Americans spend 13.6% of their budget on food, 60% of it at home. Health care, apparel, and entertainment take up approximately 5% each.

TABLE 17.1

How American Consumers Spend Their Money (2000)

	Percentage of Total Spending		
	All Households	Households in Income Groups	
		$20-30 K	$70+ K
Housing	32.4%	31.4%	30.2%
Transportation	19.5%	19.2%	17.6%
Food*	13.6%	15.1%	11.4%
Health Care	5.4%	6.8%	3.8%
Apparel	4.9%	4.7%	5.1%
Entertainment	4.9%	4.7%	5.1%
Other	10.5%	16.1%	26.4%

*Comprises 7.95% spent for food consumed at home and 5.65% away from home.
Source: Consumer Expenditure Survey, 2000, U.S. Bureau of Labor Statistics.

All other expenses (including insurance, which is the largest chunk of the remainder) take up about 10%.

These patterns change somewhat with income. See Table 17.1. Note that the income groups here are different from those described earlier in the chapter, because this is how the Bureau of Labor Statistics compiles the information. As incomes grow, American consumers spend a greater percentage of their budget on clothes, insurance, and entertainment. These expenses rise from 4.7% to 5.3% from lowest to highest income group for clothing, from 6.4% to 15.6% for insurance, and from 4.7% to 5.1% for entertainment. The share of expenditure goes down with rising income for food (from 15.1% to 11.1%), health care (from 6.8% to 3.8%), and transportation (from 19.2 to 17.6%).[2]

MONEY AND THE MIND

Money Attitudes

No, we don't mean that money itself has an attitude. But the money holder certainly does. Some money holders flaunt it; others keep it under their skin. Some see only one purpose for having money—to spend, spend, spend. Others want to see it accumulate. These diverse views show your "money attitude." **Money attitude** refers to a consumer's view of and orientation toward money—what it means to them and how they want to utilize it.[3]

For the same amount of income, consumers' money attitudes determine their spending and consumption habits. If you study people closely on how they spend their money, you will find four types:

Flaunters These are consumers who have money and want to show it. They derive pleasure in displaying their wealth, hoping to impress or arouse envy in others. They buy conspicuous items (expensive cars, luxurious clothes, diamonds, etc.) and enjoy their possessions and acquisitions more for their exhibition value than their utilitarian value.

Big-spenders These consumers are not necessarily rich; they just like to spend. Often they live beyond their means and accumulate large debt. They buy and acquire stuff not as much to impress others, but for personal enjoyment. Thus, their purchases comprise a lot of personal, inconspicuous consumption such as eating out, travel, vacationing, cosmetics, entertainment systems, and household items. They also tend to be impulse buyers.

Planners & Savers To these people, money is a means of providing for a reasonable living and assuring a secure future. They like to save and accumulate wealth for the future. They assess their purchase needs carefully, and search for value in all they buy. Unlike Big-Spenders, they are avid comparison shoppers and coupon clippers, and they invest their savings for long-term wealth accumulation.

Tightwads At the other end are *tightwads*, people who are obsessive about saving as much money as possible. They would avoid buying a thing, unless it was absolutely needed; and would seek the absolutely no-frills, barebones version at the lowest price possible. Most notably, they learn the ways of putting the things they already own to new uses or extend their useful life. There is even a journal just for this type of consumers. Check it out yourself for some tips to tightwad living at www.tightwad.com

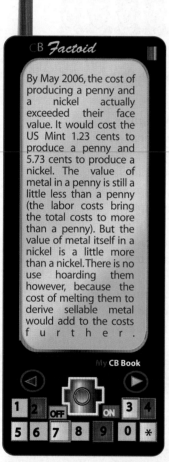

CB Factoid

By May 2006, the cost of producing a penny and a nickel actually exceeded their face value. It would cost the US Mint 1.23 cents to produce a penny and 5.73 cents to produce a nickel. The value of metal in a penny is still a little less than a penny (the labor costs bring the total costs to more than a penny). But the value of metal itself in a nickel is a little more than a nickel. There is no use hoarding them however, because the cost of melting them to derive sellable metal would add to the costs further.

My **CB Book**

Calling Tightwad Shavers!
Unbelievable prices for razor blades, eh? You can make them last two weeks instead of two shaves by drying them thoroughly. It really works! You can make them last even longer if you put some oil on the blades to protect them between shaves.

Source: www.tokyotightwad.com/stuff.html (used with permission.)

V CONSUMERS' DIVERSITY

The Joys of Being a Tightwad

I had a wee moment of joy this a.m. when I started a load of clothes. ...by experimentation I have discovered that in our machine and with our water, we can get our clothes clean using half the recommended amounts [of detergent]. And its [the better quality though more expensive detergent's] more effective formulation allows us to wash almost all our washloads on the washer's "delicate" setting, which uses less energy, is less wearing on the machine, is less wearing on the clothes themselves, etc.

Yes, I am a tightwad. I enjoy good food, nice clothes, a comfortable life. My standard of living is probably several steps above our income level, though, because I am a tightwad. I want my good food, nice clothes, etc., at a much lower cost than society in general seems to be satisfied paying, and so I make it so by various means.

...The other day, I retrieved old nails from scrap lumber discarded by my neighbor [and used them on one of my projects]...That's being a tightwad. I am not a miser, I spend freely, just always with an eye to the biggest bang for my buck. That doesn't mean "settling for" lower quality in anything that I deem a "quality of life" purchase. That's why the other day I bought a bread making machine. A bread machine, you say? What an extravagance! Well, consider just the cost of buying pizza versus making your own. In just that one example, one can save enough in a year to buy two bread machines... Besides, I bought it at a close out, for a full $40 less than the Wal Mart price.

Now, do you understand my smile when I do laundry? I get to have clean clothes, clothes that will last longer because of less stressful washings, using a less expensive (per use) cleaning agent, all the while lessening wear and tear on an expensive appliance and using less electricity to boot.
Being a tightwad is such a joy.

Trying to push the extra cream back into the tube

(Disclaimer: the hand does not belong to the blog author)

We Are Consumers And This Is What We Do   My CB Book

Source. Excerpted (and partially paraphrased by author) from a blog byDavid Needham, http://whistlinginthelight.blogspot.com/2005/01/light-comes-in-many-colors.html.

Post Script: Contrary to common, somewhat unflattering, use of the term by others (non-tightwads), the book considers both big spenders and extreme savers as consumer segments worthy of respect and study. For an interesting, worth emulating advice, read Motley Fool c olumnist Dayana Yochim's article posted July 13, 2004 titled Dueling Cheapskates."
(http://www.fool.com/news/commentary/2004/commentary04071304.)

CONSUMER SENTIMENT

A consumer's money attitude determines, as we said above, his or her spending habits. It is a relatively enduring quality of a consumer—that is, his or her money attitude does not change with the season.

A money attitude works like a personality trait. As a person, a tightwad is a tightwad, and a flaunter is a flaunter, always. But consumers also hold an attitude toward spending and that attitude is seasonal, so to speak. That is, it changes from period to period. That period depends on how you expect your economic fortunes to swing. Like how moods swing. Indeed, it is your mood—about your view of your financial wellbeing, and researchers call it consumer sentiment.

Consumer sentiment refers to a consumer's expectation about his or her financial well-being in the near future. More than the current financial circumstance, expectations about the near future determine what consumers will or will not buy. It is the economic outlook, in other words, that shapes consumer spending. This outlook can be optimistic or pessimistic, which will either spur or curb consumer spending.

The economic optimism/pessimism of consumers has been tracked since 1946 by the University of Michigan Survey Research Center. Termed **"The Index of Consumer Sentiment,"** the measure is based on monthly surveys in which a national probability sample of 500 households are asked the following questions:

1. We are interested in how people are getting along financially these days. Would you say that you (and your family living there) are better off or worse off financially

The latest number at press time for The Index of Consumer Sentiment was 84.7 (July 2006 survey), nearly identical with the 84.9 in June, but well below the 96.5 recorded in July of 2005. Current economic conditions were judged slightly less favorably, largely due to the impact of gas prices, although both current and expected economic conditions were judged much less favorably than a year ago. The Index of Consumer Expectations, a closely watched component of the Index of Leading Economic Indicators, rose slightly to 72.5 in July from 72.0 in June, but significantly below the 85.5 recorded in July of 2005. In comparison, the Current Economic Conditions Index fell to 103.5 in July, down from 105.0 in June, and was significantly below the 113.5 in June 2005.

Although the overall level of consumer confidence was unchanged in the July survey, it masked a growing divergence between the rich and the poor. "Higher prices have driven a wedge between upper and lower income households that now extends well beyond their personal financial situation," according to Richard Curtin, the Director of the University of Michigan's Survey of Consumers. Comparing households in the lower one-third of the income distribution with those in the top third, the difference in the overall measure of consumer sentiment was larger than any time since the early 1980's. "Households in the bottom third of the income distribution held significantly more negative views about their own financial prospects as well as a more negative outlook for employment and economic growth," Curtin explained. The gap between income groups is quite different than anything observed in the prior half century. In the past, the gap grew in size immediately following a recession, as upper income households were quicker to recognize and benefit from an improving economy. "The current situation is exactly the opposite as the gap is now due to lower income households voicing much less favorable economic expectations when the economy is closer to the expansion's peak," Curtin noted.

A worsening financial situation was reported twice as frequently among the bottom third compared with the top third of the income distribution, with complaints about high prices voiced nearly three times as frequently. "When asked about their financial prospects for the year ahead, half of all families in the lowest third of the income distribution expected declines in their inflation adjusted incomes, twice as frequently as among families with incomes in the top third," Curtin said.

Buying plans for homes, vehicles, and large household durable goods were all lower in the July 2006 survey than a year ago. Home buying plans posted the largest loss, falling to a fifteen year low. Although vehicle buying plans increased slightly in July due to aggressive end of model year discounts, they remain significantly below the year earlier levels.

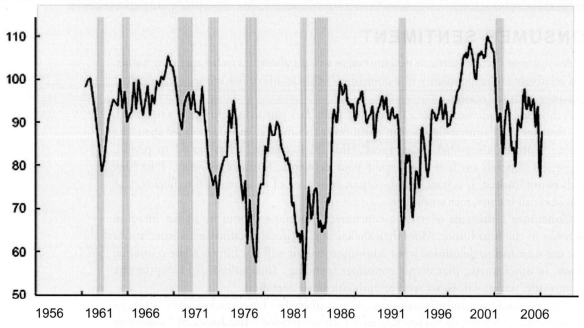

S o u r c e :
http://www.sca.isr.umich.edu/press-release.php (used with permission)
(Richard T. Curtin, Director, www.umich.edu/~umsurvey)

CONSUMERS' DIVERSITY

than you were a year ago? Why do you say so?

2. Now looking ahead, do you think that a year from now you (and your family living here) will be better off financially, or worse off, or just about the same as now?

3. Now turning to business conditions in the country as a whole do you think that during the next 12 months we'll have good times financially, or bad times, or what?

4. Looking ahead, which would you say is more likely--that in the country as a whole we'll have continuous good times during the next five years or so, or that we'll have periods of widespread unemployment, depression, or what?

5. About the big things people buy for their homes--such as furniture, a refrigerator, a stove, television, and things like that: Generally speaking, do you think now is a good or a bad time for people to buy major household items? Why do you say so?[4]

THE POOR, THE RICH, AND THE MIDDLE INCOME CONSUMERS

Every society is divided into these three broad groups, and people in every society refer to themselves and to others as "poor," "rich," or "middle income." There are other finer subdivisions, of course, but these are the divisions most commonly used in everyday conversations. We even carry in our heads some exemplars of each group, for example, that a homeless person in tatters is poor, or that a person living in a big mansion and driving a Mercedes-Benz is rich. Then, of course, there are people in between, known as *the middle class*, living in clean, comfortable, modest homes, and driving a Chevy, Oldsmobile, Honda, or Toyota.

Beyond that we actually don't know much else. People riding the metro, for example, are they poor or middle class? People shopping at Wal-Mart, what income group are they from? And theater patrons, are they rich or not? As a marketer of these and other products, you would need to know which income group your customers are from. And what is their outlook on life and on buying and consuming products. Let us look at each income group briefly.

THE POOR

Definition of Poverty If we are going to talk about poor people, then we should first define poverty. In general, **poverty** is a level of personal wealth at which a household cannot even pay for all of its basic needs, such as food, clothing, and shelter. For the U.S. population, the federal Department of Health and Human Services defines the poverty level relative to the cost of food. To do this, the department first specifies a daily market basket of foods needed to provide an adequate, nutritious diet on an "emergency" basis (i.e., when income is very low) for families of various sizes and composition. This food basket is then priced according to prevailing prices, and in turn multiplied by three because at low-income levels food represents about one-third of all expenditures. This figure defines the poverty-threshold income level. The figure used in the U.S. 2000 Census report was $18,104 for a U.S. family of four. The number of people below the poverty level was 33 million, representing 11.7 percent of the U.S. population.

THE PSYCHOLOGY OF POVERTY

What does poverty do to the poor? Fundamentally, it changes their outlook—their view of themselves and of others. Just as affluence does for the rich. More than affordability, this outlook then colors their consumption behaviors.[5] The poor see themselves as relatively deprived, powerless, cut-off from the rest of the society, and manipulated. If you peek deeper into their psyche, you are likely to find:[6]

Insecurity—The poor feel that their jobs are unstable, that their resources are inadequate to take care of sickness or other emergencies, and that police and courts exercise excessive and unfriendly vigilance against them.

Helplessness—The poor feel they lack political muscle, and because of their low-level education and limited life experiences, they are subject to the whims of others.

Fatalism—The poor feel that their own destinies are not in their hands and that chance, luck, or others control their future.

Present orientation—Since they perceive a lack of personal control of future events, the poor feel they might as well enjoy life now and let the future take care of itself.

THE MIDDLE-INCOME GROUP

Again, we should first define what middle income is. There is no single definition, of course. One conventional grouping deems income levels of less than $25,000 as low income, from $25,000 to $75,000 as middle income, and greater than $75,000 as upper income. The 2000 Census places the percentages of U.S. households in these three groups at 29.2, 46.2, and 24.6 percent respectively. Note that this approach defines the low-income group (income $25,000) more broadly (29.2 percent) than the "poverty group" identified earlier.

In Europe, average income has gone up in most European Union (EU) nations. In Belgium, France, Italy, the Netherlands, and the United Kingdom, however, the trend is toward a two-tier income distribution, where both upper- and lower-income groups are expanding but the middle-income group is shrinking. What does this mean for marketers? This two-tier pattern has resulted into a simultaneous demand for luxury products and for inexpensive products.

THE AFFLUENT

There is, of course, no universal definition of affluence either. The group with $75,000 to 99,999 can be called "near affluent," those between 100,000 to 200,000 can be called affluent, and those with incomes above $200,000 can be called superaffluents. According to US Census 2000, these three subgroups were 10.8, 11.8 and 2% of the total population, respectively.

The affluent (which amount to 24.6 percent of US households) account for some 35 percent of all wine consumption in the United States, more than 60 percent of all airline

Transportation for people of different economic means

Photo Courtesy of Paul English

travel, and 50 percent of all new-car sales. Obviously, the exquisite products advertised in such magazines as *Town and Country*, *Smithsonian*, *Architectural Digest*, *Southern Accent*, and *Worth* are consumed almost exclusively by the affluent. In third world countries, domestic servants--chauffeurs, butlers, valets--and imported cars are the status symbols for the affluent.

Different Incomes, Different Markets

Do poor, middle income, and rich consumers buy different products, and do they respond differently to marketing programs? Yes, of course they do. Most of these differences occur in the products they buy and the stores in which they shop. Most of these differences are also self-evident, so we'll describe them here only briefly.

Low-income consumers live in inner cities or factory towns and shop at discount stores such as Big Lots and at convenience stores such as Seven-Eleven and Pony Keg. They also frequent flee markets, garage sales and thrift stores. They buy on a day-to-day basis. Much of their available money is spent on food, essential clothing, and rent for the house. In these and other needed products (e.g., furniture, cooking appliances, etc.), they would buy the barebones models or versions that will just do the basic job.

The Rich are, by definition, at the other end, and accordingly they buy luxury and exclusive products and shop at high-end specialty stores that can offer them personalized service. The look and feel of the product, as well as its exclusivity, is just as important to them as its basic performance. Often price is no object, and sometimes a higher price-point is valued with an appreciation that most people can't afford to possess that particular product.

Then there is the middle majority, and it is this group that the mass-produced products of the industrialized societies are targeted at, sold in hypermarts and mega department stores, ranging from Marks & Spencer, Macy's, Kohl's, El Corte Ingles, and Takashimaya, among others. This income group seeks not only good performance and useful features in products but also good value. Thus, they are willing to pay more for a product that gives them better performance and functionality.

Why the Poor Pay More?

Now for some less self-evident quirks in the consumer behavior of the poor. Would you believe it if we were to tell you that the poor actually pay more for their purchases—more than, say, the middle income groups? The fact is they do.[7] Why? This occurs both because poor consumers do not have transportation and, even more importantly, the skills to shop for bargains and because merchants exploit their weaknesses. Also to blame is their psyche, as described earlier. Their attitudes are responsible, according to some researchers, for why they accumulate debt, do not save, and buy unwisely (without putting in the required effort to obtain a good price).[8]

Some studies have found that the poor do not follow wise purchasing strategies. That is, the poor are less likely to read newspapers (and therefore sale advertisements in newspapers), less likely to do comparison shopping, less likely to patronize low-price discount and warehouse stores and buy private or generic brands, and are more likely to accept high-interest credit. Whereas some may view these as *ir*rational behaviors, the poor might actually be quite rational, given their goals and constraints.[9]

MARKETER RESPONSE TO CONSUMERS OF DIFFERENT ECONOMIC MEANS

In light of the consumer behavior differences linked to financial resources of consumers, marketers respond by targeting different income groups. Some companies have broadened their consumer base by targeting consumers at multiple points along the economic spectrum. For example, clothing retailer Gap, Inc. sells apparel under the brands Gap, Banana Republic, and Old Navy to appeal to consumers of different economic means.

Since middle class consumption can be deemed to lie in the middle, marketer responses can be best understood by profiling it for the other two extreme groups. And again, we do not belabor the obvious differences in what marketers offer (product and store differences as described above); rather we make brief observations on how well the marketers have or have not served the two extreme income groups.

MARKETING TO THE LOW-INCOME CONSUMER

The marketer response to poor consumers has not always been admirable. A recent book, *The Low-Income Consumer: Adjusting the Balance of Exchange,* explains how low-income consumers get the short shrift at the hands of marketers.[10] One reason may be that when it comes to low-income consumers, marketers do not trust poor consumers to have enough resources to pay for the goods they want to buy, and to shop with honesty. As a result, retail stores in low-income areas tend to keep low quality merchandise and maintain extra vigilance. Sellers may also not value as much what poor consumers have to offer in exchange (e.g., food stamps, low revenue per transaction, browsing without buying), so they may offer even less variety and charge higher prices. Marketers may also act less responsibly in dealing with poor consumers, such as not caring about crowding at checkout registers meant for food-stamp-paying consumers only, not extending the same courtesy in customer service contacts as they do to their more well-to-do customers, keeping poor patients waiting longer, and so on.

Marketers may not value poor consumers as potential long-term customers. Many marketers may not realize that for some consumers, poverty may be a temporary state (e.g., students living away from their parents, a skilled worker temporarily out of job, etc.). The result is that "satisfying the consumer" may not even exist as a goal of marketers who cater to poor consumers![11]

Although individually their incomes (and therefore buying powers) are low, as a group, lower-income consumers constitute a substantial market. Business strategy guru CK Prahalad has drawn attention to the mass of consumers who are generally viewed as poor (especially the teeming millions of poor in the third world countries) who, despite their low income, collectively constitute an attractive market. Prahalad calls this untapped market a "fortune at the bottom of the pyramid." Some marketers recognize this market potential and are increasingly targeting this group with newer value-oriented strategies, or as *Business Week* states, by providing "affordable simulations of good life."[12] This is epitomized by a store called *Children's Orchard,* which sells used clothing in a non-thrift atmosphere, packaging many of the clothing items in shrink-wrap to make it look new! Today, car dealers are selling more and making more profit per car on pre-owned vehicles than on new cars. And at the used car store, they have learned to treat the consumer with the same respect they once reserved for buyers of expensive used cars.

MARKETING TO THE AFFLUENT

In contrast to the widespread ambivalence about serving the poor, most marketers are eager to target affluent consumers. Everywhere, from free market to command economies, in industrialized as well as non-industrialized nations, and in modern as well as traditional societies, there is at least a small group of affluent consumers, for whom marketers make available the finest, ferreting goods from all corners of the world. You can thus find the most exclusive designer brands in Western Europe as well as in the newly liberated Eastern European countries, in Japan as well as in Africa, in China as well as in Australia, in the United States as well as in India or Bangladesh.

In America, at least, the affluent are growing in numbers and in wealth concentration. According to an estimate by the Affluent Market Institute in Atlanta, by 2005, millionaires controlled 60 percent of the country's money.[13] Some marketers are taking note and altering their strategy. Gucci is pulling out of mid-scale Macy's and courting more upscale stores. And Saks Fifth Avenue has decided to direct its energies to its 100,000 "best customers."

Banks missed the opportunity for a while. The "new moneyed" affluent needed investment services in addition to check cashing, and commercial banks didn't provide it. So these consumers moved to investment brokerage firms such as Merrill Lynch and Fidelity, which added check services to their investment business. Now banks are fighting back. Citigroup is setting up CitiGold offices around the country and in each of its traditional branches for consumers who have $100,000 in investable assets.[14]

Target, Costco, and 99-Cents Only

Our discussion of marketer response to income-based consumer segments would not be complete without a brief glimpse of some innovative market offerings that straddle more than a single income group. Most likely Wal-Mart will qualify, as it attracts consumers from quite a broad income strata. But we want to introduce you, instead, to three stores that are rather unusual and innovative in what they offer their customers.

99 Cents Only Suppose you could get a tee shirt, a bottle of good wine, or a case of Coke, each for 99 cents only. You can. Every day. There is a store called *99 Cents Only*— and it sells everything, some 6000 items (food and beverages, health and beauty products, housewares, toys, etc.) for 99 cents each. These are not defective or second hand goods mind you; rather, they are regular products sold in other stores for as much as 5 to 10 dollars. One week in February 2006, for example, you could get an Oregon Pinot Noir wine selling everywhere else for $6 a bottle at just 99 cents! What is their secret: they buy closeout stock at rock bottom prices. There are 175 stores, mostly in Southern California, and a few in Las Vegas, Phoenix, and Texas. The stores are located in low-rent warehouse type of buildings, but they attract customers from low to middle income groups. The stores are customer friendly. Here, you won't find the usual signs like "Shirts and shoes required," or "We don't make change." Instead, the signs posted here say "We gladly make change" and "Come as you are!"[15]

Costco Would you buy diamonds from a warehouse store? Thousands of consumers do at Costco. Costco is a membership based warehouse store that sells food, clothing, electronics, and general merchandise in bulk, as well as in regular size packages. It operates 401 warehouse stores, 295 of them in 36 U.S. states, 60 in Canada, and the rest in Korea, Japan, Taiwan, the United Kingdom, and Mexico. Its main clientele is of course, lower-middle and middle income consumers, who want considerable savings on their monthly household purchases. To keep them coming back, Costco offers good-quality, high-value products at very attractive prices. And what a variety of products! Health and beauty items, furniture, home appliances, computers, books and videos, fitness equipment, tires, and pharmacy, and more. And yes, it also sells diamond jewelry, which pulls in even upper income and affluent consumers.

Target Stores Target has two faces, and even two names, and with these it targets (!), simultaneously, two distinct consumer groups: middle income consumers and upper-lower income consumers as one group and upper-middle income consumers as the second group. The first groups of consumers shops at "Tar·get" (with a hard 'g'), for staple commodity-like household products and everyday clothing. The second group of consumers, on the other hand, shop at *"Tarjay"* (an "insider-name" fondly used by some of its clientele), where artsy type upper-middle class consumers shop for its European style one-of-a-kind chair collection, kiwi scented candles, and other artsy styles of housewares. These collections come from specially commissioned world famous designers, such as Philip Starck, Isaac Mizrahi, and Michael Graves. Not all of these shoppers might know these celebrities, but just the look and feel of this unexpectedly aesthetic chic merchandise in the midst of aisles of staple commodities is unmistakable and lures the aspiring upper-middle class. (Check out http://target.com/michaelgraves/index.jhtml.)

So now you know how to classify people into the three income groups for U.S. consumers.[16] And you also know something about their psyche and outlook. You would be able to classify your own target consumer groups according to their income levels. And tailor your marketing program accordingly. However, what consumers look for in the market depends not only on their income, but also on a broader factor, *social class*. Therefore, before launching full-steam ahead into income-based consumer segmentation and targeting, it will pay to understand the concept of social class.

S O C I A L   C L A S S

Many sociologists, consumer economists, and consumer researchers consider social class, rather than income or financial resources, a more meaningful characteristic of consumers to understand and predict consumer behavior. But isn't social class the same as income? Not quite. Consider this: how much money does a priest make? And a politician—say, a member of parliament or a congressman? We don't have to know their exact income, but we do know that many small business owners, like your local car dealers, most likely make more money. Are the priest and the member-of-parliament or congressman in a lower social class than the car dealer? No, and here is why.

Social class is the relative standing of a person in society in terms of status. A person in higher social class is deemed to have a higher social status than those in the lower social class. Thus social class is a prestige hierarchy in a society.[17]

Income is an important factor in deciding a person's social class, but it is not the only determinant. Social class also depends considerably on one's education and occupation so that, despite a relatively low income, a highly educated person or someone in a more prestigious occupation could be considered to belong in a higher social class. Now, you know why a university professor or a scientist may command the same status as a sales executive earning twice as much or why a priest or a government official may in fact command more respect than a rich businessperson, at least in some societies.

Social Class—How to Get It?

What then determines a person's social class? Look around you. What determines prestige of a person in society? Money, for sure, but also your education and occupation, talent and accomplishments, and your social capital—your network of friends and personal acquaintances. These four things provide you major resources that can get you prestige. (Your health, beauty, race, age, and gender will not, not directly anyway.) Money is usually valued and given prestige everywhere, but prestige given education and occupation vary across societies.

Education is valued highly for its own sake in Eastern societies; a learned man is revered just because he is learned, no matter what his income. In Western societies, however, education is valued mostly for its instrumental outcome—that is, if it helps you earn more money or a better occupation. Likewise, certain occupations are more valued in some societies than in others. For example, teachers and professors and priests are highly respected in Eastern societies. So are engineers and doctors, and most government officials, including even a police constable. In Western societies, professions such as doctors, judges, sportsmen, and college presidents are respected, as are managers and executives, and big businessmen. A recent poll conducted by Harris Interactive revealed that the five most prestigious occupations in the USA were scientists (54%), doctors (54%), firefighters (48%), teachers (48%), and military officers (48%); and the five lowest prestige occupations were bankers (15%), journalists (14%), accountants (10%), stockbrokers (10%), and real estate agents (5%).[18]

Next, your accomplishments give you social recognition, respect, and prestige. If you are an accomplished artist, singer, poet, author, athlete, or scientist, for example, then you get social recognition, status, and prestige. Perhaps of the four sources of social prestige, this one goes farthest in getting you status. Steven King, Maya Angelou, J.K. Rowling, Luciano Pavarotti, Ravi Shankar, Kenjiro Takagakai—accomplished people like these have just as much status as the world's top billionaires, like Bill Gates and Prince Alwaleed Bin Talal Alsaud.

The fourth and final force is your **social capital**—your connections, the network of people you know.[19] People who get close to influential and powerful people also come to exercise influence of their own, and acquire status. Thus, personal advisors (even astrologers) of presidents and CEO's, personal trainers of models and star athletes, stylists, butlers, valets, and chauffeurs of kings and queens, and coworkers, subordinates, and even neighbors of politicians and other movers and shakers acquire and exercise influence among those without access to such resourceful people.

In part, of course, all four of these resources are interrelated. To get close to resourceful people, for example, one needs to have (often but not inevitably) some talent and accomplishments of one's own; education and occupation are channels to wealth, accomplishments, and personal connections. Connections feed one's career and success, and, accomplishments often produce wealth. Yet, these four resources can and do exist independently and are garnered individually. Acting in sync, they bring to the person possessing them social status, and consequently, place him or her in a social class.

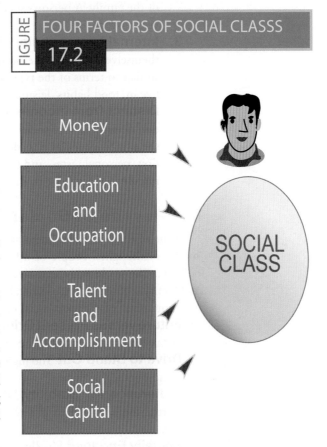

FIGURE 17.2 FOUR FACTORS OF SOCIAL CLASSS

Money

Education and Occupation

Talent and Accomplishment

Social Capital

SOCIAL CLASS

SOCIAL CLASSES
A Pervasive Phenomenon

Social classes exist everywhere. In the centrally controlled economies and polities (such as the former Soviet Union and China), social classes are based on political power, comprising the ruling classes, those close to the ruling class, and the masses. In once-traditional societies such as India, social class is based on the caste a person is born in, although these caste barriers are weakening (even breaking down) in modern India.[20] In feudal systems, classes are the landlords and the peasants; in pre-Civil War America, classes consisted of the slaves and other servants and the white European gentry. In industrializing nations, the bourgeois and the proletariat form the social classes. Democratic societies boast egalitarianism, but the class system is alive and well. Everywhere, class distinctions are almost a sociological need: People need, it would seem, a class system to distance from, belong to, and aspire to.

People everywhere identify themselves with some class, even if it is a class higher than their current objectively defined class. You will often find a person say, "That is not a class act," "That is not what people of my class do," or the like. It seems as though without a self-identification with some class, people would sense a loss of identity. At the same time, being identified with a class imposes a set of "normative" behaviors. People expect others of the same class to behave like they do--observe the class norms, so to speak. Persons belonging to the same class also share certain values, follow certain common customs and activities, and tend to acquire similar products and possessions.

Social Class Characteristics

There are certain basic truths about the very concept of social classes. Here are some important ones:

1. **Rank ordering** Social classes are ranked in terms of social prestige.
2. **Relative permanence** Social classes are relatively permanent characteristics of the family. A person's social class does not change from day-to-day or even year-to-year
3. **Internal homogeneity** Classes are homogeneous within each strata or within themselves. As such, the persons belonging to the same social class tend to be similar in terms of the types of occupations, the kinds off neighborhoods they live in, food habits, leisure activities, socializing, and so on.
4. **Distinct from income** As mentioned before, although income is an important determinant of social class, there is no one-to-one correspondence between the two. Since social class depends as much on other factors—education, occupation, personal tastes, and so on, it is not uncommon for a person of relatively middle income to be in the upper social class and vice versa.

The Psyche of Social Classes

One of the interesting ideas about social classes is that they also influence a person's "modes of thought." People of different social classes come to acquire differing ways of looking at the world and themselves, and consequently, different psychological attributes. Paul Henry, a consumer researcher, has identified the following psychological attributes on which members of different social classes are thought to differ.[21]

- **Future versus Present Orientation** Higher social classes have a future orientation versus lower social classes; the latter are more preoccupied with the presen
- **Drive to Stand Out** The higher the social class of a person, the higher the drive to stand out.
- **Preference for Stability** Higher social classes also prefer stability over change. Furthermore, they also like to avoid challenges, preferring the comfort of the easy life.
- **Socially Engaged** Finally, higher social classes are more socially engaged than their counterparts.

STATUS CRYSTALLIZATION

Have You Got It?

Are you "status crystallized"? No, it won't make you cool, rich, or high status; but it sure will give you less cause for worry. Let us explain what status crystallization means.

Because social class is made up of multiple characteristics, two persons could be placed in the same class and yet have considerably different incomes, occupations, or education. For example, John, a chemist with a Ph. D, has a much higher education but relatively lower income than an average person; Larry, a self-made small business owner, has only a high school diploma but makes much more money than an average American. Each is experiencing a lack of a discrepancy between income and education. Both would be placed, in many societies, in the upper-middle class. But the discrepancy between different dimensions (here, income and education) is likely to cause each considerable 'anxiety' in his consumption roles.

Because of higher education, John may want to live in "high culture" residential areas and consume "high culture" activities, such as the arts and theater; but, due to a restricted income, he may be unable to do so. And Larry, with high income, may want to join an exclusive country club, but because of his lack of social connections, he may not unable to do so. Or once a member, he may feel intimidated with the "high culture" attitudes of the more educated members. Such out-of-sync status, so to speak, can cause consumers considerable frustration in terms of their unfulfilled consumption wants.

When all components are in sync, status crystallization is achieved, and the consumer is likely to experience more harmony. Sociologists refer to this phenomenon as **status crystallization**—a condition when all components of social class become consistent

Societies vary in terms of status crystallization. Generally, economically stable societies have a greater degree of status crystallization. Societies undergoing rapid economic upheaval suffer a decline in status crystallization. And this economic upheaval works at both ends— economic growth and economic decline. In the "dot.com crash" in the USA in 2000- 2001, for example, many people employed in high tech industries became unemployed; consequently, they experienced a loss of status crystallization and had to cramp their lifestyles and their related consumption. At the other end, in the booming economies of China and India, where many U.S. companies are currently outsourcing such high tech jobs as software development and call center services, there is a sudden rise of a class of high-income earning persons who had for years lived a life of economic struggle. They now have money, but they still have to cultivate "the finer tastes" in consumption, so to speak. As another example, immigrant consumers often experience a lack of status crystallization: even if they acquire high education, and get into high-income occupations, they do not entirely acquire the tastes of the host countries and seldom feel fully integrated into their host societies.

Now then, are you status crystallized? You are, if your income, education, occupation, and tastes are all compatible with one another. If not, you are probably being pulled in many different directions. On the other hand, if you are status crystallized, then your mind must be at peace as far as your social class status is concerned.

UNDERPRIVILEGED AND OVERPRIVILEGED

One reason for a lack of status crystallization can be the income diversity within the same occupation and education groups. A recent M.B.A. graduate could earn, for example, anywhere from $50,000 to $150,000, depending upon his or her alma mater and employer. The median income of a recent MBA in America is about $75,000.[22] Those earning substantially below the median income feel **underprivileged**; those earning substantially above the median are **overprivileged**. Both groups have to strive to keep up the appearance of the social class defined by their education and occupation—namely, "a young executive with an MBA." The underprivileged struggle to keep up with the Joneses— buying homes, home furnishings, cars, and leisure activities that show the tastes of their fellow executives. At the other end, the overprivileged curb their desires to indulge in super-luxury for fear that they would be envied by their peers and be perceived as flaunting their disproportionate wealth. This is true for people of all occupations: engineers, doctors, businesspersons, entrepreneurs, professors, blue-collar workers, white-collar workers, etc.

What the overprivileged do is buying better things in product categories that would not be vividly conspicuous. For example, home furnishings, home appliances, better quality and prestigious brand clothing that does not look super-luxurious, higher level models of the same car (e.g., a loaded Toyota Camry or Nissan *Altima* rather than say a more basic Toyota Corolla or Nissan Maxima), or cars that are expensive but do not have the reputation of affluence (e.g., a Lexus or Acura rather than a Mercedes or Jaguar). And they would trade in their cars more often for a newer model. They would also be the first to buy new gadgets for the home that would not be conspicuous (e.g., Roomba—an automatic vacuum cleaner, or a front-loading washer-dryer, or a plasma TV, etc.).

The underprivileged, on the other hand, seek the same quality and prestige products as most people of their class, but they seek them at sale prices. Income hard-pressed professionals, for example, do not divert their clothes shopping trips to K-Mart or Wal-Mart; rather they still seek brand name clothing, but at discount stores like T.J. Maxx and Marshalls. They patronize department stores like Macy's or Bloomingdale's, but prefer to buy their clothing when on sale or at end-of-season clearance.

Indeed, the underprivileged and over privileged consumers make interesting study subjects. How these groups navigate the marketplace is interesting. The underprivileged maintain consumption tastes expected of their social class, yet they remain within the constraints of their less-than-the-median income. The over privileged spend above-the-median-incomes without flaunting their riches. Marketers must research these groups more closely so they can target them with appropriate products and marketing efforts.

SOCIAL MOBILITY

Are You Going Up or Down?

The TV show *The Apprentice*, "starring" Donald Trump, begins with several participants, all seeking only one thing–upward mobility. Both in Donald Trump's screening process, and in their everyday life.

Although a person's social class does not change year-to-year (or even less often), it is possible for a person or a family to move in and out of a social class, such as from lower to middle class or vice versa. In particular, it is possible for a person to move out of the social class of his or her birth to a higher or a lower class by acquiring the values, resources, and behaviors of the new class. Of course, some societies have strong barriers for such social class mobility, such as when jobs are restricted to certain privileged classes. When a person moves to a higher social class, it is called **upward mobility**. Contrarily, movement into a lower class is called **downward mobility**.

There are two forms of social mobility: (a) across generations, when grown-up children rise above the social class of their parents or fall below it, and (b) over-time, the same adult person moves into a different class.

A principal factor of cross-generation mobility is education; children of lower social class parents get a higher education and move into better paying jobs. All parents desire upward mobility for their children, and accordingly they invest in their education, sometimes at great sacrifice of their own comfort. In India, for example, poor and middle classes consider a private school education for their children a "must have" ticket to a better life. Accordingly, people making 1000 rupees a month ($22 US dollars) spend as much as 200 to 250 rupees ($5 US dollars) a month sending one son or daughter to a private school.[23] That is 20-25% of their salary, and it is the sacrifice they make to thrust their son or daughter up the path of upward mobility.

Another factor for upward mobility is marriage, especially for women; many of them marry into a higher social class. Sometimes, of course, adult offspring of wealthy parents may experience downward mobility because, although they make good money, living on their own they can't afford the lifestyle of their wealthy parents.

Mobility within the same generation comes mainly from shifts in one's career or in business outcomes. In societies that believe in meritocracy, a competent, hardworking, and motivated person could rise in his or her career to jump more than one class. U.S.A. is a prime example of a meritocracy society. A case in point is Jim Kelley, CEO of UPS from 1996-2001; Kelley joined UPS as a package delivery driver in New York and rose through the ranks. Likewise, another equal-opportunity country is India, the world's largest democracy. Its current president, APJ Abdul Kalam, started out as an engineer in India's Space Research Program (where he was briefly the author's direct supervisor); rising through the ranks, he became India's chief technology & scientific advisor before being elected to the highest public office in the land.

Mobility within the same generation comes mainly from shifts in one's career or in business outcomes. In societies that believe in meritocracy, like America, a competent, hardworking, and motivated person can often rise in his or her career to jump more than one class. A case in point is Jim Kelley, CEO of UPS from 1996-2001; Kelley joined UPS as a package delivery driver and rose through the ranks. Likewise, another equal-opportunity country is India, the world's largest democracy. Its current president, APJ Abdul Kalam, started out as an engineer in India's Space Research Program (where he was briefly the author's direct supervisor); rising through the ranks, he became India's Chief Technology & Scientific Advisor before being elected to the highest public office in the land.

But this cannot usually happen in tribal societies and underdeveloped countries. There, one's social class is determined by birth, period. These societies have what is called an **ascribed social class** system. In contrast, in much of the developed world, one can change social class through effort and accomplishments. These societies have an **achieved social class** system. Here, one can move up by his or her achievements, whether material (e.g., wealth) or otherwise (e.g., education, work success, political position, etc.), and of course, you can move down as well, by wasting away your life.

Your Social Class Shows

How does social class work? By work, we mean, if its supposed to get you prestige, how do people know what is your social class? They know because some of the social class ingredients are known to people around you. Such as your employment status, income, wealth, education, occupation, circle of friends (whom you know determines your influence). And then some of these factors create visible differences in you, which can be seen by others. Your education, or income, or occupation, will show, in the house you live in, the car you drive, in the way you dress, and even in your speech pattern. Actually, we make sure our social class shows. We adopt the behavior patterns—the way we talk and the way we conduct ourselves—of our social class. Some of it deliberately, by conscious cultivation; some of it we learn automatically because of the environment we grow up in and the company we keep. People generally hang out with persons of the same class, at least socially.

These adopted behaviors and resulting associations with members of our own distinct class actually make up resources, which then determine our life-chances and opportunity for success in life. In turn, such success and accomplishments reinforce a secure place in our social class. It is because of this sociology of interpersonal associations in society that social class is an inevitable fact of life in all societies and in all nations.

MEASURING SOCIAL CLASS

Social class has visible indicators, and by looking at and interacting with a person, we can often guess a person's social class. That is fine, as far as our everyday social encounters are concerned. But as a marketer, we don't have the opportunity to look at every consumer one-on-one. We ought to be able to measure it through some impersonal means. People most interested in measuring social class are sociologists (so they can then study behavioral differences across social classes), and they have come up with a few measures. Marketers have adopted them, because they are easy to use in surveys. Here we look at three of them. They get to be little technical, but they are easy to follow, and you must know them so you too may employ them in any surveys of consumers you might take. Besides, you should be eager to measure your own social class. So here they are.

Basically, what various sociologists have done is compile indexes—weighted combinations of individual components such as income, occupation, etc. Two of the currently used indexes are called Computerized Status Index (CSI) and Census Bureau's Index of Socioeconomic Status (SES). CSI uses education levels, occupation categories, income categories, and area of residence. The complete measurement is shown in Table 17.2. To compute the score, occupation is weighted double, and the education score is doubled if the respondent is not married. The total score could range from 4 to 53. Based on this score, members of a population are assigned to a social class as follows:[24] 37 to 53, Upper American; 24 to 36, Middle Class; 13 to 23, Working class, and 4 to 12, Lower American.

The U.S. Census Bureau's Index of Socioeconomic Status (SES) is based on three components: income, occupation, and education. Based on this, it recognizes four SES categories: Upper, Upper-middle, Middle, and Lower-middle. Roughly one third of the US population (34.5% and 34.1% to be exact) is placed into each of the two middle categories; the remaining one-third is roughly equally distributed into the top and the bottom groups (15.1% and 16.3% to be exact).

SOCIAL CLASSES IN AMERICA: A BRIEF PROFILE

Many sociologists have studied social classes in America. The most prominent among them, especially among consumer researchers, is Richard P. Coleman. Based on extensive analysis of population data, he has classified Americans into three broad groups (further comprising seven subgroups), shown in Figure 17.3

Let us take a closer look at the three broad groups, first in terms of their psyche and outlook, and then in terms of their consumption differences.

TABLE 17.2 — MEASUREMENT OF SOCIAL CLASS

Coleman's Method

A. Education (score separately for spouses; double the score for unmarried persons)

Grammar school	1	1 year post-high-school	4	Professional Graduate degree	7
Some High School	2	Some college	5	Masters' degree	8
High School graduate	3	Graduated College 4-year)	6	Ph.D. or higher professional degree	9

B. Occupation (double the score for married persons)

Unemployed	0	Junior managers/professionals	5
Marginal/semi-employed	1	Small business owners/professional	6
Blue collar employed	2	Middle Mangers/Professional	7
White collar/low skill employed	3	Senior Managers, Business owners	8
Technical low level skill	4	Top Executives and Business Leaders	9

C. Area of Residence

Slum Area (very run down)	1	Well-equipped, nice curbside appeal	6
Poor (inadequate) housing	2	Sumptuous houses nested on large private land	7
Barely adequate, simple, barebones housing	3	Exclusive neighborhoods with luxurious leisure	8
Adequate, well-maintained, some facilities (public areas) areas	4	Large Private Estates	9
Comfortable living housing areas	5		

D. Total Family Income

Under $10,000	1	$50,001 to $75,000	5
$10,001 to $20,000	2	$75,001 to $100,000	6
$20,001 to $35,000	3	$100,001 to $200,000	7
$35,001 to $50,000	4	$200,001 or more	8

Scoring. Add up all scores (after counting Occupation double). Scores would range from 4 to 53.

37-53:	Upper American
24-36:	Middle Class
13-23:	Working Class
4-12:	Lower American

Note 1. Occupation is counted double, as many spouses choose to not work, and dual employment would be reflected in income, in any case.

Note 2. The measurement system is improvised from Coleman's original proposal as follows: all nine categories (for education, occupation, and area of residence) are specified (the original skips a few); categories are 'described' with more descriptive (though subjective) everyday phrasing, especially for area of residence; income brackets are revised to reflect current income distribution--marking 1 and 2 as low income, 3, 4, and 5 as middle income, 6 as upper income, 7 as affluent, and 8 as super-affluents. All modifications are subjective, and readers are encouraged to refer to the original source. The distribution of population based on the suggested scheme is unknown but the score range is kept unaltered. (Don't buy it? Write to: Opinion@mycbbook.com)

Source: Adapted from Richard P. Coleman, "The Continuing Significance of Social Class in Marketing," *Journal of Consumer Research*, 10 (December 1983), 267-277. ©Journal of Consumer Research. Published by The University of Chicago Press. (Used with permission.)

LOWER AMERICANS

Typically, Lower Americans are "family folks," deriving their emotional and psychological support from family members and relatives. "Locational narrowness" marks their preference in housing, travel, sports, and news--they live close to their kin, travel nearby or to meet relatives, favor local sports heroes, and take interest mainly in local rather than national news. Illustrating the loyalties and "locational narrowness" of this class for automobiles, Coleman writes:

By the mid-1970s, ownership of an imported car had penetrated 40 percent among the upper, and 25 percent among the middle-class families but less than 10 percent among working-class families. This was three years after the gas price shock! ... gas-guzzling pick-ups and standard- and large-size cars were still in favor. Thus was the working class remaining the xenophobic heart of resistance to the foreign-car invasion and dragging its heels in accepting the idea that America should reduce the size of its automobiles; the men of this class were not yet ready to give up this macho symbol of roadway conquest.

MIDDLE AMERICANS

This class is most concerned with wanting to "do the right thing" and buying what is popular. Middle-class persons tend to emulate the lifestyles of the Upper Americans, a tendency working classes do not exhibit. This "upward gaze" makes them patronize dinner theaters and all the other trickle-down culture. Physical activities (particularly the ones in which parents can participate with their children) are becoming popular with this group.

FIGURE 17.3 — SOCIAL CLASSES IN THE UNITED STATES

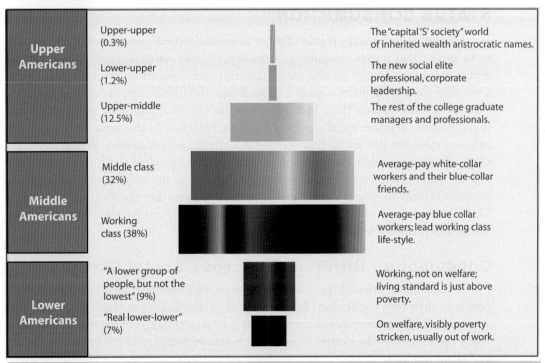

Upper Americans	Upper-upper (0.3%)	The "capital 'S' society" world of inherited wealth aristrocratic names.
	Lower-upper (1.2%)	The new social elite professional, corporate leadership.
	Upper-middle (12.5%)	The rest of the college graduate managers and professionals.
Middle Americans	Middle class (32%)	Average-pay white-collar workers and their blue-collar friends.
	Working class (38%)	Average-pay blue collar workers; lead working class life-style.
Lower Americans	"A lower group of people, but not the lowest" (9%)	Working, not on welfare; living standard is just above poverty.
	"Real lower-lower" (7%)	On welfare, visibly poverty stricken, usually out of work.

Source: Adapted from Richard P. Coleman, "The Continuing Significance of Social Class in Marketing," *Journal of Consumer Research*, 10 (December 1983), 267-277. ©Journal of Consumer Research. Published by The University of Chicago Press. (Used with permission.)

A Store in Hong Kong for a middle income consumer

Photo Courtesy: Alex Tsang

Indeed, physical activities are becoming core to middle-class life "in which possessions-pride has yielded to activities-pleasure." Of course, the middle-class struggle to uplift themselves continues, evidenced in increased enrollment from this class into local colleges and universities. "Imaged as a mental challenge and storehouse for knowledge, the home computer will do particularly well here when it reaches mass-market pricing"-- this prophecy by Coleman, made some 15 years ago, for the home computer has already come true, and can also be seen to mark a similar wide-spread, aspiration-driven acceptance and use of the Internet among this class.

UPPER AMERICANS

This class as a whole remains concerned with buying quality merchandise, favoring prestige brands, and spending with good taste. Significant numbers of upper-uppers are adopting less circumscribed ways of consumption. Two points about the Upper Americans group are noteworthy. First, a subdivision of this group has been identified and referred to by sociologist Irving Kristol as "The New Class." Consisting of media influentials (TV anchor persons, talk-show hosts, newspaper editors and journalists) and nonprofit professional (educators, government officials), the members of this subgroup tend to be anti-capitalists, and their basic thrust in ideology and consumption style has been to establish themselves above the Middle American classes.

The second point Coleman makes is that more than any other group, Upper Americans are a more heterogeneous group today: "Upper America is now a vibrant mix of many lifestyles, which might be labeled post preppie, sybaritic, counter-cultural, conventional, intellectual, political, etc. Such subdivisions are usually more important for targeting messages and goods than are the horizontal, status-flavored, class-named strata."[25]

STATUS CONSUMPTION

One key element of the psyche of social classes is the need to keep up with the Joneses, so to speak. That means, consuming according to one's status, or status consumption. **Status consumption** can be defined as acquiring and consuming products that signify a status in society. Products acquire a status image through acceptance and appreciation among the social classes. Thus, Mercedes-Benz, for example, acquires a status image that is appreciated by upper social classes; a Humvee (which is in the same price range), in contrast, connotes not social class status but a sporty, adventuresome personality style. Upper classes and middle classes are very conscious of the product and brand status when making their selections. Of course, within the same class, not every consumer is equally status conscious. To measure how status conscious you are, take the short survey in Table 17.3. Then review in your mind whether your actual purchase behavior is what your score would imply, and for which product categories.

Consumption Differences Across Social Classes

As already mentioned, people identify with and associate themselves with other people in their own social class. To be accepted in and belong to that class, consumers adopt the visible consumption of their class. It is an inevitable fact of life that almost every visible consumption—the clothes we wear, the house we live in, and the leisure we partake in—shows our class.

Correspondingly, our possession, tastes, and product choices differ markedly across social classes. In leisure, for example, lower classes prefer and engage in such sports as

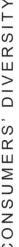

bowling, and such pastimes as boxing, fishing, watching wrestling, hunting, visiting casinos, and watching TV. Upper-class groups play golf and polo, go on cruises, attend symphonies, operas, and plays. People of middle class play team sports (e.g., volleyball), play cards, and spend a lot of time shopping and visiting friends.[26]

TABLE 17.3	Status Consumption Scale		

Express your opinion on the following statements:

	Strongly disagree	Mostly disagree	Disagree	Neutral	Agree	Mostly Agree	Strongly Agree
	1	2	3	4	5	6	7

1. I would buy a product just because it has status.   1 2 3 4 5 6 7
2. The only products that I find appealing are the ones with status.   1 2 3 4 5 6 7
3. No matter what I buy I am always conscious of its status.   1 2 3 4 5 6 7
4. Paying more for a product just because of its prestige and status is unwise.*   1 2 3 4 5 6 7
5. Maintaining my status in everything I buy is important to me   1 2 3 4 5 6 7

* Reverse score this statement, so that 1 is recoded as 7, 2 as 6, 3 as 5, 5 as 3, 6 as 2, and 7 as 1.

If you score more than 20, you are most likely status conscious in your consumption and purchases. Hope you have the money to live out your status consumption desires

Note: Composed by Author. For an alternative version, see Jacqueline K. Eastman, Ronald E. Goldsmith, & Leisa Reinecke Flynn, "Status Consumption in Consumer Behavior: Scale Development & Validation," Journal of Marketing Theory & Practice, Summer 1999, 41-51. Our item # 1 is borrowed as is, & other items are informed by but unidentical with their other items. Their other items are: I am interested in new products with status; I would pay more for a product if I had status; The status of a product is irrelevant to me; and, A product is more valuable to me if it has some snob appeal.

Prepared by Author for MyCBBook

Income or Social Class? Who Done It?

At this point, you might wonder, are all these consumption differences across social classes really differences across income groups? The answer is, "Yes" but also "No." Yes, in as much as affordability does constrain what we can afford. No, in as much as given the same prices, which style of products—furniture, home, clothing, leisure—we consume depends more on our taste rather than available money. Our tastes are molded much more by social class than by income per se. Income affects our tastes, indirectly—by first affecting, in part, our social class.[27]

Upper income consumers could afford to watch as much TV as they like, for example, but upper social class consumers actually watch less of it.

From Class to Mass— Pushing the Class Boundaries

There is a new market these days. Consider Starbucks. It sells plain coffee for $1.25 to $1.50. (You can get plain—though not identical—coffee for 75 cents in a convenience store). And then, there is a mouthful delicious menu of such coffee-latte drinks as White Chocolate Mocha, Tazo® Chai Latte, and Iced Caramel Macchiato that sell for 3 to 4 dollars. Why would consumers spend this kind of money? Simply because, these days, a considerable segment of middle-class consumers want some prestige. So they are buying an 8oz. bottle of Bath & Body Works lotion for $9, roughly three times more than a run-of-the-mill

CB FYI   Live A Little

Marketers keep a close watch on what is happening with the money consumers have. Are they making more of it, or less? Are they spending more of it or less? Saks Fifth Avenue, the luxury retailer, purveys its Prada and Yves Saint Laurent super luxury merchandise to the super-affluent. But in late 2000, it decided to extend its reach to near-affluents (i.e., those at the top of the next lower stratum). So it launched a campaign called "Live a Little." The campaign showed younger women doing playful casual things and smiling. The target consumer was still the affluent ($100,000+ income), but the campaign didn't *portray* its target consumer as snobby-rich. Rather it targeted someone with a more egalitarian outlook toward others and less assuming personality, comfortably dressed—it showed good taste rather than overbearing self-importance. "Live a little" was also an invitation to those who could afford but typically tended to not splurge.

(Based in part on Bob Francis, "Luxury for the Masses," *Brandweek*, June 25, 2001)

TABLE 17.4

Luxury Comes to Middle-Class Consumers

	Conventional Middle Income	Conventional (Old) Luxury	Mastige ("New Luxury")
Store	Sears	Neimen Marcus	Pottery Barn, William Sonoma
Autos	Pontiac, Ford	Cadillac, Rolls Royce	BMW, Mercedes
Beer	Coors, Miller	Heineken	Sam Adams
Lingerie	Maidenform	La Perla	Victoria's Secret
Personal Care	Revlon, Suave	Kohl's	Aveda
Restaurants	Burger King	Morton's	Panera bread

Source: Excerpted from Michael J. Silverstein and Neil Fiske, "Luxury for the Masses," Harvard Business Review, April 2003, p.51. Reprinted by permission of Harvard Business Review. Copyright © 2003 by the Harvard Business School Publishing Corporation; all rights reserved.

brand; an $8 lunch at Panera Bread instead of a $4 lunch at one of the burger chains; and a $28,000 BMW instead of a $20,000 Honda.[28] This class of products—a sweet spot between the conventional middle market and the conventional luxury market— is known as the *masstige* (also called 'new luxury') products. See Table 17.4 for selected products in this new class.

GEODEMOGRAPHICS

Where You Live Says a Lot about You

What is your ZIP Code? 01742? Then, you are a college graduate, earn about $75,000 a year, and are eager to learn Italian. 30132? In that case, you never finished college, have a blue collar job, make about $33,000 a year, love to read Civil War history, rarely lock your front door, and probably have a deer antler hanging on your bedroom wall. Or did you say, 94598? Okay then, you are a Generation Xer, constantly socializing on your cell phone, obsessed with recycling, and can often be found at Starbucks, sipping a latte.

How did we know? We know because of geodemographics—the art of portraying people and markets by their geographic location.

Geodemographics is the study of relationships between demographics on the one hand and geographic location on the other. The underlying premise is that people of similar demographic characteristics (age, income, occupation) tend to live in similar geographic locations. Moreover, since the natural and economic resources of a geographic location enable and constrain our activities, geographic location helps shape our lifestyles and activities. For example, if we don't live near a river, or ocean, or lake, then we won't be engaging in water sports—not frequently, anyway. If you live in a big city, your lifestyle is going to be that of a big city person; your friend, who lives in an industrial town, is going to have a different lifestyle. Thus, in a very real sense, our lifestyle and consumption is determined by where we live—i.e., by our geodemographics. And two sociologists/researchers have spent a lifetime studying these geodemographics. Let us look at their amazing findings.

NINE NATIONS OF NORTH AMERICA

First, meet Joel Garreau—a noted sociologist. Garreau traveled widely across North America, observing people and codifying their behavior and moorings. He found that the region can be divided into nine divisions. Garreau's logic was, "each nation has," (and here he refers to the nine subnations, actually) "its own list of desires ... and a distinct prism

EXHIBIT 17.2

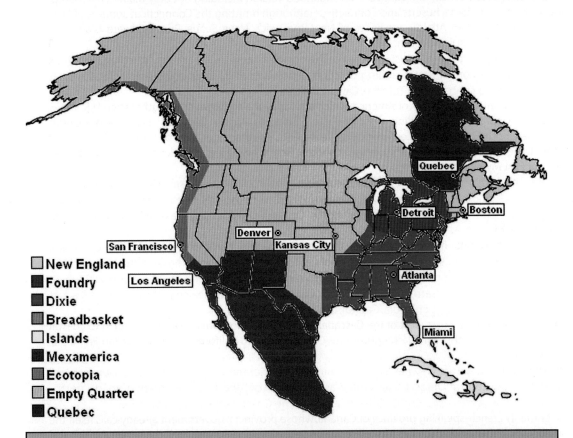

New England
Foundry
Dixie
Breadbasket
Islands
Mexamerica
Ecotopia
Empty Quarter
Quebec

Map Credit Keith Tyler, who notes: The drawing of the Nine Nation regions are based on a combination of sources, including: Descriptions at Nine Nations of North America, Maps and descriptions at Nine Nations at Harper College, and Map at Nine Nations at UND; Furthermore, Base outline map provided by WorldAtlas.com at, which includes a statement that outline maps do not need permission for use or reuse. Permission is granted to copy, distribute and/or modify this document under the terms of the GNU Free Documentation License.

through which it views the world." Thus, Garreau's nine nations differ from one another because of topography, climate, and sociocultural factors. [6] See Exhibit 17.2 for a Map and 17.3 for Summary Profile.

The undercurrent and the premise of this delineation are the value differences among different nations, so that any two cities within the same geographic region could be classified in two different "nations." Thus, San Francisco and Los Angeles, both in the pacific region, are assigned respectively to Ecotopia and MexAmerica. Ecotopians believe that "small is beautiful," contrary to the beliefs of the MexAmerica and Empty Quarters. Ecotopians share their antidevelopment view with New England, where "voluntary poverty has become rather chic." The most distinguishing feature of the Breadbasket is that people value "honest gains from hard labor," as opposed to leisure. The Islands in contrast value "fun and enjoyment" the most.

Consumer researcher Lynn R. Kahle has studied the predominant values held by people in these "nations." He used a list of nine values called *LOV* (see Chapter 5) and asked a representative sample of 2,235 Americans to choose the value most important to them. Later, he divided the sample into Garreau's nine nations, and, separately, also according to the nine U.S. Census regions. His results were twofold: (1) the nine nations do differ in the values people hold dear, and (2) similar distinctions exist across the nine Census Bureau regions. Garreau's nine nations are not any better (but not any worse)

Look What CB Researchers Found

- New England (also called New Britain or Atlantica)—an expanded version including not only Maine, New Hampshire, Vermont, Rhode Island, Massachusetts and Connecticut (although omitting the Connecticut suburbs of New York City), but also the Canadian Atlantic provinces of New Brunswick, Nova Scotia, Prince Edward Island and Newfoundland and Labrador. **Capital: Boston.**

- The Foundry—The by-then-declining industrial areas of the northeastern United States stretching from New York City to Milwaukee, Wisconsin, and including Chicago, Illinois and Philadelphia, Pennsylvania as well as industrial southern Ontario centering on Toronto. **Capital: Detroit.**

- Dixie—The traditional Confederate States of America, which are today the southern and southeastern U.S. states, centered on Atlanta, Georgia, and including most of eastern Texas to Austin. Garreau's "Dixie" also includes Kentucky, which had both Federal and Confederate governments, southern portions of Missouri, Illinois, and Indiana, and the "Little Dixie" region of southeastern Oklahoma. Finally, his "Dixie" includes most of Florida as far south as the city of Fort Myers. **Capital: Atlanta.**

- The Breadbasket—The Midwest states and part of the Prairie provinces: Iowa, Kansas, Minnesota, Nebraska, the Dakotas, most of Oklahoma, western Missouri, western Wisconsin, eastern Colorado, parts of Illinois and Indiana, and northern Texas as well as some of 'near-North' Ontario, and southern Saskatchewan and Manitoba. **Capital: Kansas City**

- The Islands—The South Florida metropolitan area, the Caribbean, and parts of Venezuela. **Capital: Miami**

- Mexamerica—The southern and Central Valley portions of California as well as southern Arizona, most of New Mexico and all of Mexico, centered on either Los Angeles or Mexico City (depending on whom you ask), which are significantly Spanish-speaking. Garreau's original book did not place all of Mexico within Mexamerica, but only Northern Mexico and the Baja peninsula. **Capital: Los Angeles**

- Ecotopia—The Pacific Northwest coast west of the Cascade Range stretching from Alaska in the north to coastal areas of British Columbia, down through Washington state, Oregon and into California just south of San Francisco. **Capital: San Francisco**

- The Empty Quarter—Most of Alaska, Nevada, Utah, Wyoming, Idaho, Montana and Colorado from Denver west, as well as the eastern portions of Oregon, California, Washington, all of Alberta and Northern Canada, northern Arizona, parts of New Mexico, and British Columbia east of the Coast Ranges. **Capital: Denver**

- Quebec—The primarily French-speaking province of Canada, whose provincial government already calls itself the National Assembly of Quebec, and which has run referenda on secession in 1980 and 1995, the latter of which the secessionists lost narrowly. **Capital: Quebec City**

Source: Joel Garreau, Nine Nations of North America, Avon Books, 1989. Also Nine Nations of North America, Wikepedia, The Free Encylopedia. http://en.wikipedia.org/wiki/Nine_Nations_of_North_America. Used under the GNU Free Documentation License (GFDL)., which in turn permits others to likewise use it.

in segmenting people by values than the Census Bureau's regions. Because the suppliers of syndicated marketing research organize information according to the Census Bureau's classification of regions and not along Garreau's nine-nation scheme, marketers can more easily use the former. The most important contribution from Garreau is that he created "literary" labels with connotative meaning for thinking about the geographical differences among consumer markets.

PRIZM

The Psychology of 90210 and Other ZIP Codes

Next, meet Michael J. Weiss, a journalist turned market researcher. Known on national talk shows as "the Demographic Detective," Weiss has traveler to every *type* of neighborhood in USA, to observe and study people and their lifestyles in those neighborhoods. Note that he did *not* travel to every neighborhood (no one could), but to every *type*. This "type" comes from a neighborhood clustering scheme devised by a company called Claritas Inc. More on that company and its monumental work later, but suffice to note presently that the company has grouped various neighborhoods in America based on their Zip Codes into the so called PRIZM clusters. At the time Weiss undertook his detective road trip, there were 62 such PRIZM clusters.

These 62 clusters grouped some 250,000 neighborhoods, based on their ZIP Codes, ZIP+4 postal codes[29], and census tracts (about 500-1000 households). All geographic units whose inhabitants have the same demographics and lifestyles are grouped together. Thus, ZIP Codes 10021 (Upper East Side, New York), 60614 (Lincoln Park, Illinois), and 90292 (Marina Del Rey, California) are placed, along with other Zip Codes, into same ZIP Code Cluster, called Urban Gold Coast.

People sharing a cluster also share a lifestyle. Why? For two reasons: first, as already mentioned, because the geography and resources and activities available in a place determine what consumers can and will do. And, second, we choose to live in the neighborhoods that fit our lifestyles. **"Birds of a feather flock together,"** as they say. Since our lifestyles influence what we buy and consume, the clustering scheme also tells the marketer what people in a given ZIP Code are likely to buy. Hence the clustering scheme is given the name PRIZM (Potential Rating Index by ZIP Code Markets).

It is these 62 *types* of neighborhoods that Weiss visited. His results have been published in a book called *The Clustered World*.[30] If you do indeed live in one of the three ZIP Codes we mentioned at the beginning of this section, you can read more about it yourself (actually, about an average inhabitant of your ZIP Code) on pages 186, 190, and 264 of that book.

For each Zip Code based cluster, the book (*The Clustered World*) describes the consumption behaviors of its residents. For illustration, we profile two clusters here: Bohemian Mix (SER 17) and Grain Belt (SER 57). Exhibits 17.4 and 17.5 depict their geographical concentration and some key facts. Let us examine these groups briefly.

Bohemian Mix You have met this group before—in Chapter 6, as an example of lifestyle profiles. Now we've got more information for you, so read on. Bohemian Mixers (SER 17) are young residents of urban hodge-podge neighborhoods; the majority (3 out of every 4) are never married or are divorced singles. They are predominantly students, artists, writers, actors, and the like. They live somewhat adventuresome, funky lives, exercising both their bodies and minds, hanging out at sidewalk cafes, public libraries, bookstores, discussion groups, health food stores, social and voluntary organizations, benefit programs, and public demonstrations and protest campaigns on social issues. "Day and Night," writes Weiss, "residents drift along the sidewalks, cruising, holding hands, and window shopping ... Many exposed limbs bear at least one tattoo." They shun domestic cars, enjoy aerobic activities like biking and Rollerblading, and buy healthy foods. They stay hip by reading such magazines as GQ, Harper's Bazaar, Rolling Stone, etc., and watching such TV shows like Nightline and Melrose Place. Because they live on apartment lined city streets, their cars are compact, and mostly import. Their open-mindedness makes the early-adopters of new products like organic pet foods and computer online services. What Bohemians value most is their uniqueness, and their rejection of the mainstream. National chains and fast food restaurants will not survive in these areas because residents resist cookie-cutter businesses so as to preserve their uniqueness. What do well instead are sidewalk cafés, art galleries and leftist bookshops. See Exhibit 17.6A.

Grain Belt In sharp contrast are Grain Belters (SER 57), who live in America's most sparsely populated rural communities and small farm towns now in economic decline. Residents are aging farmers and small-town retirees (half the residents are over 50), and they depend on nearby bigger towns for groceries,

Sean Foley, an eco-design professional, poses for author in his bohemian ensemble

©iStockphoto.com/
Greg Nicholas

gas, and entertainment. Barely solvent on farm income, they are conservative, have faith in God, support school prayers, and are believers in Providence (the purchase rate for burglar alarms is zero). Although they live in isolated villages, they believe they have plenty going for them—the primal beauty of mountains and open spaces, traffic-free streets, and communities where you know everyone by name and can count on help in times of need. They patronize domestic brands of cars, read such magazine as *Popular Mechanics, Field & Stream,* and *Guns & Ammo,* and spend leisure hours in such activities as watching rodeo, horseback riding, and fishing. See Exhibit 17.6B.

The Bohemian Mix and Grain Belt clusters are vastly different in every aspect—demographics (age, income, occupation), geographic location, life-style, values, etc. But the PRIZM clustering scheme described in Weiss's book is able to identify distinct groups among seemingly similar demographic groups. To illustrate this, let us look at Urban Achievers (SER 22). In most demographics it is similar to Bohemian Mix (except that it includes a subgroup of 65+ and excludes a subgroup of under 24). Most remarkably, the two clusters are geographic neighbors. Compare maps in Exhibits 17.4.

Urban Achievers Urban Achievers are a mix of young and old, single students and older

©iStockphoto.com/Alex Gumerov

EXHIBIT 17.4

Grain Belters: Preferences	Grain Belters: Preferences	Grain Belters: Preferences
SER 17	**SER 57**	**SER 22**
bohemian mix	grain belt	urban achievers
1.7% of U.S. households	2.0% of U.S. households	1.6% of U.S. households
Primary age groups: **under 24, 25–34**	Primary age groups: **45–54, 55–64, 65 +**	Primary age groups: **25–34, 65+**
Median household income: **$33,700**	Median household income: **$22,600**	Median household income: **$35,600**
Median home value: **$135,452**	Median home value: **$41,900**	Median home value: **$109,900**
Thumbnail Demographics	**Thumbnail Demographics**	**Thumbnail Demographics**
inner-city singles neighborhoods	married farm owners and tenants	midlevel urban couples and singles
multi-unit rental housing	single-family housing	multi-unit rental housing
ethnically mixed households	predominantly white and Hispanic households	ethnically mixed households
college graduates	grade school, high school graduates	college graduates
white-collar professionals	farming, mining, and ranching workers	professionals and managers
Politics	**Politics**	**Politics**
Predominant ideology: liberal Democrat	Predominant ideology: conservative Republican	Predominant ideology: liberal Independent
1996 presidential vote: Bill Clinton	1996 presidential vote: Bob Dole	1996 presidential vote: Ross Perot
Key issues: gay rights, legalizing marijuana, defusing racial tensions	Key issues: pro-life movement, improving the economy, reducing government size	Key issues: gay rights, defusing racial tensions, increasing military spending
Sample Neighborhoods	**Sample Neighborhoods**	**Sample Neighborhoods**
Dupont Circle, Washington, D.C. 20036	Matheson, Colorado 80830	Outer Richmond, San Francisco, California 94121
Greenwich Village, New York, New York 10014	Linneus, Missouri 64653	Hoboken, New Jersey 07030
West Los Angeles, California 90025	Long Prairie, Minnesota 56347	Reseda, California 91335
Forest Park, Illinois 60130	Ridgeland, Wisconsin 54763	Clearwater, Florida 34619
Broadway, Seattle, Washington 98102	Holly, Colorado 81047	Bitter Lake, Seattle, Washington 98133

Source: Michael J. Weiss, *The Clustered World,* Little Brown and Company 2000, p. 212-13, 222-23, 292-93, (Used with permission.)

EXHIBIT 17.5

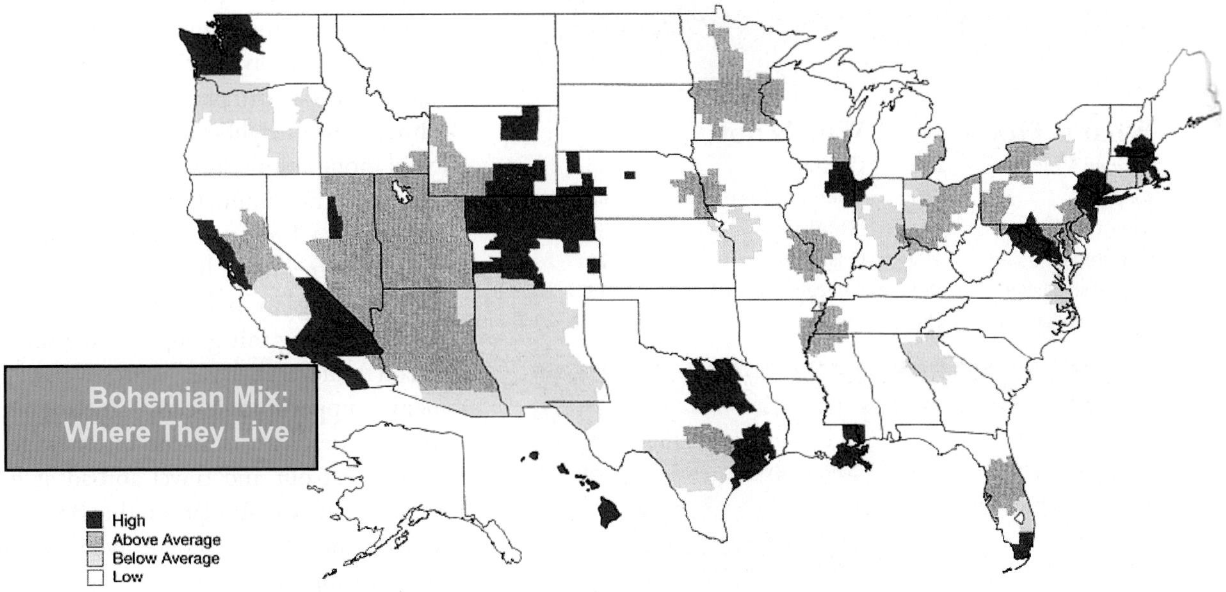

Bohemian Mix: Where They Live

- High
- Above Average
- Below Average
- Low

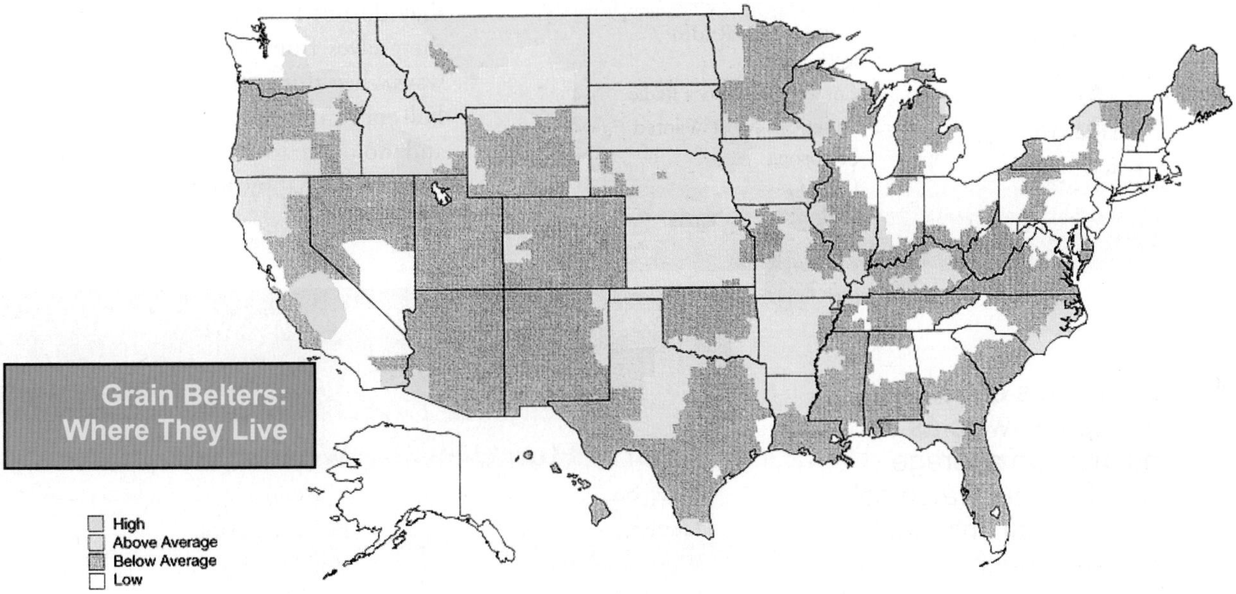

Grain Belters: Where They Live

- High
- Above Average
- Below Average
- Low

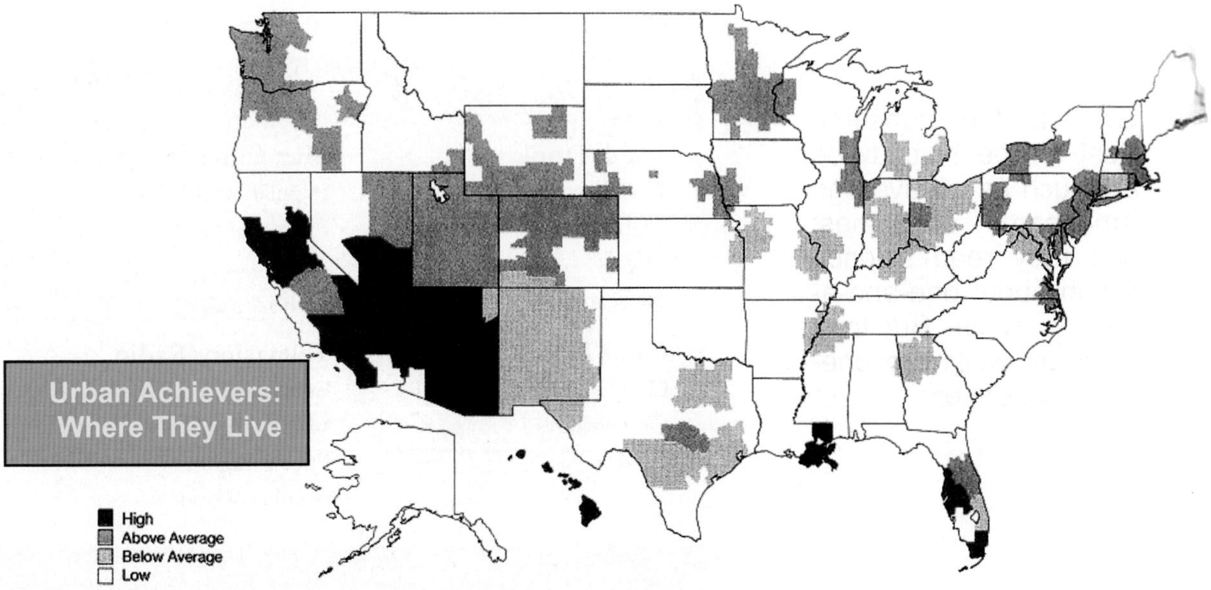

Urban Achievers: Where They Live

- High
- Above Average
- Below Average
- Low

PRODUCT PREFERENCES OF BOHEMIAN MIXERS — EXHIBIT 17.6A

Bohemian Mixers—LifeStyle Products

What is Hot		What's not	
Foreign Videos	246	Golfing	49
Jogging	236	Country Music CDs	46
Victoria's Secret'		Woodwork	30
Condoms	193	Gas grills	21
Expresso Makers	189	College Football	13
European Travel	188		

Other Products with above Average Consumption

Food/Drink		Magazines/Newspaper	
Imported Beer	201	New York	440
Gourmet Coffee bean	191	GQ	340
Imported Wine	180	Mademoiselle	292
Brown Rice	174	Rolling Stone	167
Bottled Water	146		
Pita Bread	145		

Cars/Trucks		Television/Radio	
Alfa Romeos	277	Nightline	270
Saab 900s	212	Contemporary Rock Radio	184
Land Rovers	192	America's Most Wanted	162
Honda CRXs	172	Simpsons	136

SOURCE: Michael J. Weiss, *The Clustered World*, Litle Brown, 2000, p. 212-213. (Used with Permission.)

couples, with a disproportionate number of foreigners—though not FOBs ("fresh off the boat"). They live in city centers, in upper middle class apartment buildings in multi-ethnic group neighborhoods. They seek to avoid mono-ethnic suburban communities, and they enjoy multicultural city festivities and shows. Imported food, newspapers, alternative medicine, libraries, adult classes, and listening to public radio (PBS) are popular among this group. "As consumers, Urban Achievers behave," writes Weiss, "like many upper-middle-class metropolitan sophisticates. They surf the Internet, go to movies, eat out and travel abroad at high rates." They are similar to the Bohemian Mix on their liberal progressive views and in their support of such causes as gay rights and racial issues. But unlike Bohemian Mix, they do not have any desire to distinguish themselves from the mainstream (in some ways, they think they are the mainstream). Full of optimism, they wish to achieve and hold on to the American Dream—a prosperous, happy, fulfilled life. See Exhibit 17.6C.

Bohemians eat brown rice nearly twice as much as an average American but watch college football only one-eighthas much.

Grain Belters consume Post Grape Nuts twice as much as an average American consumes; and they read science fiction about one-and-a-half as much. But their museum visits are one-fourth less likely.

PRODUCT PREFERENCES OF Grain Belters — EXHIBIT 17.6B

Grain Belt—Lifestyle Products

What is Hot		What's Not	
Motel Six	284	Museums	72
Hunting	202	Billiards/Pool	63
Woodworking	195	Builder's Square	60
Sewing	184	Weight Lifting	54
Science Fiction	158	Marshalls	13
Stamp Collection	136	Pay-per-view Movies	3

Other Products with above Average Consumption

Food/Drink		Magazines/Newspaper	
Post Grape Nuts	218	Popular Mechanics	187
Kraft Velveeta	165	Field & Stream	173
Tequila	158	Redbook	157
Mexican Food	117	Golf Digest	118

Cars/Trucks		Television/Radio	
Chevy K3500 Pickups	402	Country Music TV	199
Olsmobile 98s	176	CBS Evening News	190
Suzukis	124	Price is Right	168
		Another World	141

SOURCE: Michael J. Weiss, *The Clustered World*, Little Brown, 2000, p. 292-293. (Used with Permission.)

PRODUCT PREFERENCES OF URBAN ACHIEVERS   EXHIBIT 17.6C

Urban Achievers —LifeStyle Products

What is Hot		What's Not	
Theater	170	Golf Vacations	80
Passports	166	Victoria Secret	64
Condoms	164	Pro Football Games	62
Exercise Clubs	163	Cellular Phones	38
Gambling Casinos	142		

Other Products with above Average Consumption

Food/Drink		Magazines/Newspaper	
Brie Cheese	233	Esquire	217
Malt Liquor	207	Popular Photography	204
Taco Bell	137	Cosmopolitan	180
Bagels	120		
Kool Aid	118		

Cars/Trucks		Television/Radio	
Kias	217	News Radio	248
Nissan NX1s	172	BET	240
Toyota Corollas	150	Beverly Hills 90210	222
		NYPD Blues	157

Urban Achievers' favorite car is Kia. And they are not into golf vacations or into Victoria's Secret. There favorite TV shows: Beverly Hills 90210 and NYPD Blues!

SOURCE: Michael J. Weiss, *The Clustered World*, Litle Brown, 2000, p. 222-223. (Used with Permission.)

Product Usage Variations Across America

If lifestyles of PRIZM clusters are different, as we saw above, then it follows that the consumption of products must also vary across these clusters. And the fact is it does. *The Clustered World* contains information linking product purchase rates for hundreds of products to the PRIZM cluster profiles. Figure 17.4 shows what clusters shop at Victoria's Secret, for example. As that figure shows, Bohemian Mix, God's Country, American Dream, and Norma Ray-ville are the top four clusters, while Middleburg Managers, Urban Achievers, Gray Power, and New Beginnings are the bottom four.

What other products are consumed more by some PRIZM clusters and less by others? In Figure 17.5, we show selected products and stores and name the top two and the bottom two clusters for each. Read on and marvel at this fascinating information about product use variations. These illustrations show how useful geodemographics can be to marketing managers for segmenting and targeting their consumers for different products.

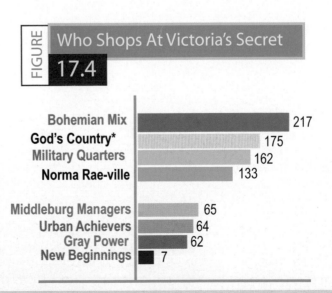

FIGURE 17.4 Who Shops At Victoria's Secret

Cluster	Index
Bohemian Mix	217
God's Country*	175
Military Quarters	162
Norma Rae-ville	133
Middleburg Managers	65
Urban Achievers	64
Gray Power	62
New Beginnings	7

Note: Average consumption is indexed at 100.
* Tied with AMERICAN DREAM
Source: Compiled by Author from: Michael J. Weiss, *The Clustered World*, 2000.

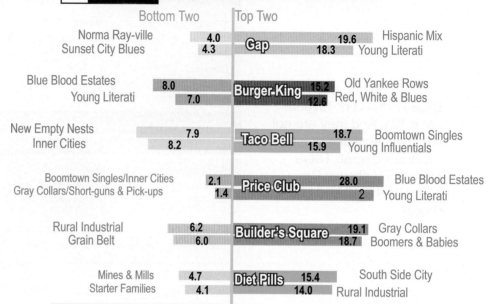

	Bottom Two		Top Two	
Norma Ray-ville	4.0	Gap	19.6	Hispanic Mix
Sunset City Blues	4.3		18.3	Young Literati
Blue Blood Estates	8.0	Burger King	15.2	Old Yankee Rows
Young Literati	7.0		12.6	Red, White & Blues
New Empty Nests	7.9	Taco Bell	18.7	Boomtown Singles
Inner Cities	8.2		15.9	Young Influentials
Boomtown Singles/Inner Cities	2.1	Price Club	28.0	Blue Blood Estates
Gray Collars/Short-guns & Pick-ups	1.4		2	Young Literati
Rural Industrial	6.2	Builder's Square	19.1	Gray Collars
Grain Belt	6.0		18.7	Boomers & Babies
Mines & Mills	4.7	Diet Pills	15.4	South Side City
Starter Families	4.1		14.0	Rural Industrial

Note: Average consumption is indexed at 100.
Source: Compiled from: Michael J. Weiss, *The Clustered World*, 2000.

V CONSUMERS' DIVERSITY

THE NEW PRIZM AND THE COMPANY BEHIND IT

The Weiss book (*The Clustered World*) provides thumbnail narratives based on ethnographic research. But the company behind the PRIZM scheme is Claritas, Inc. Founded in 1971, the company has regularly collected comprehensive information from every Zip Code in America. Churning that information through complex computer models, Claritas identified the first PRIZM segmentation scheme in 1974. Since then, the company has constantly updated the PRIZM classification system. Its current Zip Code based segmentation system is called **PRIZM® NE**, and it comprises 66 segments. The 66 segments are a rearrangement of the 62 clusters described in the Weiss book, based on the latest data. The company maintains detailed profile information on each of these segments. On the company's Web site, you can find brief profiles of those 66 PRIZM Clusters. We excerpt five of those segments below, selected arbitrarily but importantly to illustrate the diverse consumer groups in the United States. This will serve also as a befitting finale to this chapter—a grand tour of the socio-economic portrait of consumers.

Curious about which PRIZM® NE segment you belong to? The Claritas Corporation Website offers an interactive feature called You ARE WHERE YOU LIVE; you type in your Zip Code, and back comes a list of PRIZM® NE segments present in your Zip Code. Check it out at www.yawyl.claritas.com. (Web links change often, so, alternatively, just Google *You Are Where You Live*.)

FIVE PRIZM® NE CLUSTERS (An Arbitrary Selection)

02. Blue Blood Estates Blue Blood Estates is a family portrait of suburban wealth, a place of million-dollar homes and manicured lawns, high-end cars and exclusive private clubs. The nation's second-wealthiest lifestyle, it is characterized by married couples with children, college degrees, a significant percentage of Asian Americans and six-figure incomes earned by business executives, managers and professionals.

06. Winner's Circle Among the wealthy suburban lifestyles, Winner's Circle is the youngest, a collection of mostly 25- to 34-year-old couples with large families in new-money subdivisions. Surrounding their homes are the signs of upscale living: recreational parks, golf courses and upscale malls. With a median income of nearly $90,000, Winner's Circle residents are big spenders who like to travel, ski, go out to eat, shop at clothing boutiques and take in a show.

9. American Classics They may be older, lower-middle class and retired, but the residents of American Classics are still living the American Dream of home ownership. Few segments rank higher in their percentage of home owners, and that fact alone reflects a more comfortable lifestyle for these predominantly white singles and couples with deep ties to their neighborhoods.

04. Up-and-Comers Up-and-Comers is a stopover for young, midscale singles before they marry, have families and establish more deskbound lifestyles. Found in second-tier cities, these mobile, twentysomethings include a disproportionate number of recent college graduates who are into athletic activities, the latest technology and nightlife entertainment.

05. Boomtown Singles Affordable housing, abundant entry-level jobs and a thriving singles scene—all have given rise to the Boomtown Singles segment in fast-growing satellite cities. Young, single and working-class, these residents pursue active lifestyles amid sprawling apartment complexes, bars, convenience stores and Laundromats.

Source: www.Claritas.com (reprinted by permission)

Age, race, and gender are given to you by birth and you cannot alter them. They define "who you are." Income, social class, and geodemographics are, in contrast, your creation, the outcomes of the path you take in life and the choices you make. As such they define and serve as markers of "what you are." Of these three, income is the most conspicuous. You have been aware of it all your life. You know its immense utility to you as a consumer, and with enough of it, you can pick and choose from the marketplace what you dream of. But if you haven't had enough of it, you have also learned how to manage your purchases and consumption within the limits of your budget. Marketers fashion their offerings—products, prices, distribution outlets—according to income segmentation of consumers, and it is a good thing so you know where to shop and not burn a hole in your wallet.

Because in common parlance the terms are used interchangeably, it may have been news to you that income and social class are not the same thing. As you know now, they are not. Income is a part of it, sometimes and for some consumers it may be a big part, but social class is truly an index of your social standing rather than merely of your income. Your education could be a means to your income as well, but it brings you social prestige in its own right. So does your occupation, and the perceived prestige of your occupation in your society perhaps already influenced your choice of it. Lastly, your social network determines your influence and prestige. We must confess: this last factor is new to the list—proposed anew here because we see its undeniable role in life around us. Building social networks requires opportunity of access (often enabled by your education, money, and occupation), we agree, but it also takes initiative and certain wherewithal. Pay attention to this factor, cultivate it, and watch how it "upgrades" your social standing.

Social class is more consequential than you might have realized. While we all chase money because it is a tangible target, it is the intangible social class that channels our experience both as a social creature and as a consumer. Implicitly, we identify ourselves with our social class and use members of that class for social comparison. Perhaps no other variable affects more our tastes and our view of how 'noble' and 'becoming' our tastes are, or should be. This "should be" issue arises when we are being pulled in different directions by the different components of the social class (i.e., when we are not status crystallized!). The 'masstige' trend is good news, satisfying our yearning for more aesthetic and/or upscale tastes hitherto constrained by our out-of-sync income. Yet, it is fair to say that marketers and consumer researchers have not developed enough understanding of consumers' psyche under lack of status crystallization. Likewise, how consumers navigate their consumption when they find themselves in conditions of being underprivileged or overprivileged is not sufficiently understood. There is an opportunity for marketers who can understand this stage in consumers' lives. Most likely, status uncrystallized consumers, and likewise under- and overprivileged consumers warrant being treated as distinct niche segments.

Lastly, geodemographics. What can we say about it? We want to say that it is perhaps the most holistic, most insightful segmentation scheme for marking similarities and differences among consumers, but even that would be an understatement. The scheme's prowess comes from the fact that it incorporates, simultaneously, both consumers' psychographics and their demographics. Its building block is ZIP+4, and within it, believe it or not, it implicitly contains age, income, social class and other demographics (such as family lifecycle, even ethnic identity) as well as lifestyle and values and self-concepts and other ingredients of our psychological makeup. After all, our choice of the place we live in is based on all these factors.

Of course, any single identifier of segment membership (ZIP+4 is the identifier for geodemographics) that is supposed to capture a whole host of consumer characteristics is bound to have internal fission in it. For a considerable number of consumers (but hopefully not for a majority of them), all those supposed characteristics are not going to blend in. Perhaps consumers who would be misfits in the geodemographics scheme are the ones who are status non-crystallized. The basic assumption of PRIZM is that people in a neighborhood are alike, and for some consumers, this assumption is bound to be false. The lack of fit for some consumers not withstanding, **PRIZM** clusters are as good a description of neighborhoods as possible.

Indeed, we believe that if you want to know America and read a flesh-and-blood portrait of its people, you can do no better than read Michael Weiss's timeless classic, The *Clustered World*. If you want to truly understand the vibrant diversity among people— you will find that book immensely enlightening as well as deeply fascinating. We hope someday you will take the time to read it.

In this chapter, we covered three interrelated topics: income, social class, and geodemographics.

Income is a person's monetary earnings received periodically. It can comprise wages, salaries, and earnings from self-employment. It determines consumers' spending power, and influences what they buy and when. As income increases, expenditures on clothing, automobiles, and luxury goods rise sharply. These patterns of spending are captured in Engel's law. Consumers also have what we call "money attitude," defined as their orientation toward money, i.e., how they want to utilize it. Based on their money attitudes, consumers can be classified as Big-Spenders, Flaunters, Planners & Savers, and Tightwads. Along with money attitudes, consumers' expectations about their financial well-being in the near future—called 'consumer sentiments'—influence how much they will spend currently. Based on income, consumers are generally segmented into three groups, the poor, the rich, and the middle classes. Marketers usually target the three segments with different offerings.

We next discussed social class–defined as the relative standing of a consumer in society. The more prestige you have, the higher your social class. Social class comes from four factors, money, education, occupation, and social network. When these four elements are in sync, status crystallization occurs. Within each class, consumers who are on the fringe (far away from the average) are overprivileged or underprivileged—a condition that influences consumers' purchases. We described a measure of social class so, as researchers, you may measure it for your market. Social classes determine, of course, consumers' lifestyles and therefore their marketplace behaviors. We described the marketplace behaviors of each social class, and we noted how marketers are bringing prestigious products within the reach of not-so-rich consumers, a phenomenon called "masstige."

In the third and final section of the chapter, we described *geodemographics*, the art of profiling a person based on his or her place of residence. In this scheme, consumers of similar neighborhoods (counted as ZIP+4) are grouped together, resulting in 62 clusters for the entire USA. We showcased the psychographic profile of some of these clusters, demonstrating the power of geodemographics based market segmentation. Geodemographics contains within it the sum total of all of the consumer characteristics (both demographics and psychographics) that we have described in various chapters of the book. This therefore is an apt conclusion to this section of the book.

K E Y   T E R M S

Achieved social class
Ascribed social class
Consumer sentiment
Discretionary income
Downward mobility
Engel's law
Geodemographics
Income
The Index of Consumer Sentiment
Money Attitude

Overprivileged
Poverty
Prizm
Social Class
Status consumption
Status crystallization
Underprivileged
Upward mobility
Wealth

Y O U R   T U R N

REVIEW+Rewind

1. What is the difference between income and wealth? And between income/wealth and social class?
2. Why is wealth a better predictor of consumer behavior than income? And why is social class a better predictor of consumer behavior than wealth alone?
3. What is meant by "money attitude" and how does it affect consumer behavior?
4. Name and briefly describe the four segments of consumers based on their money attitudes.
5. How is poverty defined? What is the current threshold for poverty in the USA?
6. What is The Index of Consumer Sentiment? What is its utility? What questions are asked to measure this index?
7. What is meant by the term "Social Class"? Name and explain important characteristics of the concept of social class.
8. Briefly describe three social classes in America in terms of their motivations and outlook on life. Also, name some important differences between the three social classes in America in terms of food, clothing and leisure consumption.
9. What is meant by (a) status crystallization, and (b)

10. underprivileged and overprivileged? Explain briefly.
11. What is meant by "Eight Nations of the United
12. States?" Name those eight nations.
13. What is the PRIZM Scheme? What is the basis of PRIZM segmentation?
14. How does the profile of Bohemian Mix differ from those of Urban Achievers and Grain Belters?

THINK+Apply

1. "Poor generally pay more." Do you agree or disagree with this statement? Why?
2. Is status crystallization a good thing or a bad thing for consumers? What problems does it (or lack of it) cause consumers?
3. Is PRIZM a good scheme to segment the market? Why or why not?
4. As a manager, what would you do differently if you were located in a Zip Code with a predominant Bohemian Mix presence versus in a Zip Code with a predominant Urban Achievers presence, assuming you were (a) a supermarket; (b) a clothing store, and (c) a multi-brand car dealership?
5. If "masstige" trend continues, what opportunities does it offer to a marketer? What product categories (food items, clothing, cars, electronic devices, home improvement, service businesses such as banks and hospitals, and personal services such as hair salons, dry cleaning, lawn maintenance, etc.) will or will not be influenced by it? Explain your answer.

PRACTICE+Experience

1. Review the consumption patterns of three social classes described in the chapter. Which consumption pattern under each head best matches with your own consumption? Is there a discrepancy between your own consumption and consumptions of most other consumers in your social class? Explain why.
2. Visit the homes of three consumers, one from each social class, and make a note of the kind of things in the home. Summarize your observations.
3. Try to identify a consumer in each of the four segments based on "money attitudes" and interview them to understand how their consumption behavior differs for (a) food, (b) clothing, and (c) leisure activities.
4. If you live in a big city, can you identify certain broad sections of the city neighborhoods and within those, identify the PRIZM Clusters you are likely to find. Drive or walk through those sections and observe people's lifestyles and activities. Do these activities match with the PRIZM Clusters these neighborhoods belong to according to their individual ZIP Codes?

In the Marketing Manager's Shoes

Put yourself in a marketing manager's shoes. Most concepts in the chapter have some lessons for the marketing manager, i.e., they suggest what to do differently in practice; indeed, often these applications are implicit in our explanations of the concepts and models in the chapter. Identify at least five specific applications of the chapter's concepts, all of which should be entirely new– different from the examples cited here.

B *Factoid*

A $100 Laptop!

Nicholas Negroponte, formerly the director of MIT Media Laboratory, has developed a prototype of a laptop that can be prodcued at $100. He now heads a nonprofit organization he founded, One Laptop per Child (OLPC). Its goal: to make available a $100 laptop to children in developing countries. Under contract with OLPC, Taiwan's Quanta is developing a mass-manufacturable version. Soon they plan to distribute one million such laptops, limited, of course, to students. Meanwhile, independently, a high-tech firm in India, NITT, is close to developing a similar product.

CB Book

1   OFF   ON   3
5 6 7 8 9 0 *

Image: Fuse Project
(Licensed under Creative Commons)

∨ CONSUMERS' DIVERSITY

From Class to Mass
The Democratization of American Express

Once upon a time, if you were in a five star hotel and flashed your American Express Card, you were entitled to some respect. In those days, the card came only in one color, its classic green, with a centurion symbol, and cost $25 in annual fee. More importantly, it was a charge card. That is, you had to pay your entire monthly balance when you received your statement. As such it was a convenience card and was intended mostly as a travel and entertainment (T&E) card, since few retailers accepted the card (given the high fee it charged merchants). Used mostly by businessmen with generous business-expense accounts and other upper class consumers, the card's principal appeal was "exclusivity." If you had an American Express, you were somehow "exclusive." That is an image it carefully garnered, by featuring in its advertising campaign Portraits of well-known, well-heeled celebrities like Tip O'Neil (then Speaker of U.S. Congress) as cardholders.

This all changed in the eighties. The economy was turning stiff, and people were using their credit cards less for travel and entertainment, and more for buying necessities in the stores, and the American Express was not accepted in the stores! So it started courting retail stores to accept its cards, and with a lowered annual fee, and it got upper middle class consumers to sign up. And the lure changed from being prestigious (used by wealthy) to being perceived as "being prestigious" (used by the upper crust of the middle class).

That worked for a while, but by late 1980's, its competitors (MasterCard and Visa), already the cards of masses, had discovered for themselves a new source of revenue. They made more money in late fee and default charges and increased interest rate for defaulting customers than they made from discount fees collected from merchants. A good credit card customer so far was one who could and did pay the credit balances on time; suddenly, a desirable customer now was one who could not pay! And American Express was not in that market. So it did the only logical thing it could: it recruited, by lowered discount fee (although still higher than that of its competitors), the main street retailers like department stores, supermarkets, and lately, even gas stations. Its consumer recruitment campaign extended widely, even to college students and anyone who would care to sign up for its card. The transition to its "democratization" was fully complete, when toward the end of the century, it signed discount retailer, Costco to exclusively accept only American Express.

Source. Based in Part on Untitled, *Details*, December 2002, p.88, and author's research for *Valuespace* (2001).

Q1. Will a middle class consumer, who earlier was not eligible for the American Express Card, experience prestige with the now en-abled possession of the American Express card?

Q2. With the so called "democratization" of the American Express Card, will the card's old patrons feel a diminution in the prestige the possesion of the card offered them?

Q3. Do consumers differ in the extent to which they perceive a card purely as a utilitarian means of payment versus as a means of prestige as well? Will the "democratization" of the American Express Card bring them different "consumption feelings"? Explain.

Consumer Relationships with Brands: Loyalty, Romance, and Brand Tribes

- Brand Loyalty—From Behavior Scans to Mind Scans
- Brand Personality—How Products Get It
- Brand Relationships—Meet My Brand, My Alter-ego
- A Society of Consumption Communities
- Brandfests and Brand Bonding—Party Time For All Brand Lovers
- Brand Equity—Not All Brands Are Created Equal

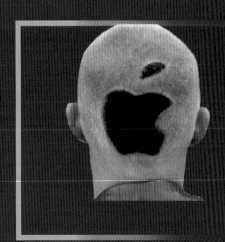

Gabriel McIntyre of www.XOLO.TV

sunny afternoon in a small town in Pennsylvania's Pocono Mountains. An outdoor wedding ceremony. A mass wedding, actually. 250 people gathered.

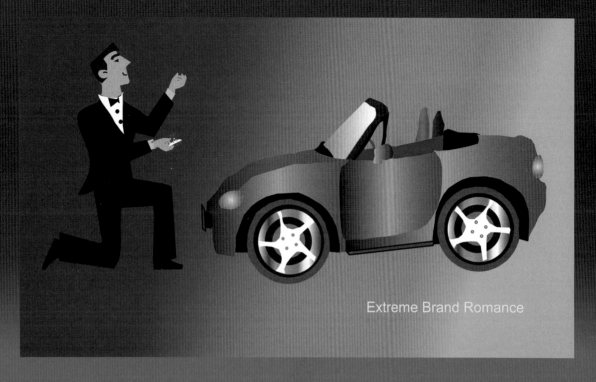

Extreme Brand Romance

Each one a bride or a groom. All love struck. All eager, all ecstatic. And then the voice of Reverend James A. Massie, Jr., an Episcopal priest, comes through the microphone. He reads a few vows, and then, with a deep breath, he utters the sentence all had gathered to hear: "By the power vested in me, I pronounce that you are... car and driver." Suddenly, 250 happy people, all married this day to their Mazda Miatas!

Reverend Massie himself is an ardent fan. Besides praying, his only other passion is driving around in his white 1996 Miata, with religious songs playing on its CD player. It is a "spiritual endeavor," says Massie of his leisurely ride. Then there is Peter Warrick, a 53 years old advertising executive in Fort Lauderdale; he owns 28 Miatas. He survived a heart attack recently, and what does he credit it to? His passion for the Miata!![1]

INTRODUCTION

he fanatic devotion some consumers show toward their Miatas is exceptional but not unique. Many consumers feel similar passion for Apple Computers, Krispie Kreme Donuts, Saturn cars, the Harley-Davidson, and of course, their iPods. Apple computer fans, for example, make an annual pilgrimage to the Macworld Expo. There, they—graphic designers, artists, musicians, techies—browse through a galaxy of Apple products and devices, and, with great enchantment, they listen to Steve Jobs, cheering his every word. And whenever a new Krispie Kreme Donut store opens up, long queues form all night long, just to taste their first bite of the legendary donut.

Other stories of fierce consumer loyalty show up in the media from time to time. The groundswell of protest at the brief withdrawal of Coca-Cola Classic was legendary. For Harley-Davidson motorcycle owners, now banded together in a group called HOG (Harley Owners Group), their attachment goes beyond the vehicle; in donning Harley paraphernalia, they have a lifestyle that is almost defined by the brand. Less visible but no less commanding of their owners' and consumers' strong loyalty are such products and services as Xbox, Nike, and Singapore Airlines, and retail stores like the upscale Saks, European haute couture Louis Vuitton, the ace purveyor of pampering potions Body Shop, and surfer haven Pacific Sun.

On the flip side of the coin, not all consumers are loyal to any one product or brand, nor is any one consumer loyal to everything he or she buys and uses. And some products and brands command almost no loyalty from their consumers—for a few cents off, consumers would just as easily buy another brand. For packaged goods, for example, U.S. consumers' loyalty to manufacturers' brands ranges from only 10 to 40 percent. The picture is no better for services. For a broad range of services, as many as half of all consumers are willing to switch their current service providers. In Europe, consumer purchases of private labels, or store brands (which is an indicator of lack of loyalty to manufacturers' brands) is remarkably high, as much as 50 to 60 percent for such supermarkets as Sanisbury's.[2]

Why such variation in consumer loyalty? Why are consumers loyal to some brands and not to others? What can marketers do to win consumers' loyalty? These questions are the subject matter of this chapter.

We begin this chapter by defining brand loyalty and describing ways to measure it. Next, we describe a model of brand loyalty that demystifies the three factors that drive it. In the final section, we take you to a higher plane—giving you glimpses of fanatic consumption and a peek inside consumption communities and brand tribes.

BRAND LOYALTY

I Have Always CHOSEN You, Haven't I?

At first, brand loyalty seems a simple idea. Ask consumers if they are brand loyal to any of the brands they use—shampoos, soft drinks, colognes, whatever. They are likely to say, yes, they have always bought the same brand of shampoo, drunk the same soda, and used the same cologne for many years. Therefore, they would say, they are brand loyal. Or, conversely, because they don't stick to the same brands, they are not brand loyal, they would tell us.

Pretty good, at least for starters. Indeed, early marketing scholars viewed brand loyalty just this way—as the consistent purchase of the same brand. Every time a consumer repurchases a product (shampoo, cologne, wine, jeans, shoes, frozen pizza, motor oil, automotive tools, computers, mail delivery service, cable, plumbing service, car insurance, or whatever), if the consumer buys the same brand of a product or service repeatedly, then that consumer can be considered a brand-loyal consumer for that product category.

Totally consistent repurchase of the same brand would show **perfect** brand loyalty. However, in practice, even brand-loyal consumers occasionally deviate from their regular brand and instead buy an alternative brand. Therefore, practical estimates of brand loyalty allow for imperfect consistency. Such imperfect but still consistent repurchase can be estimated in three ways: proportion of purchase, sequence of purchase, and probability of purchase. See Table 18.1 for details.

THE POWER OF BEHAVIOR SCANS

Measuring consistent purchasing is easy. Actually, marketing science has mastered this task. Here is how it works. When you buy a branded product, it gets scanned at the checkout register. This scan automatically records the brands you are buying. So if you are buying the same brand again and again, then the marketer knows, even without asking

TABLE 18.1 MEASURING BRAND LOYALTY BY PURCHASE HISTORY

Three Methods: Proportion, Sequence, Probability

Proportion of purchases	The number of times the most frequently purchased brand is purchased divided by the total purchases. Thus, if you buy a brand, say, eight out of ten times, then your brand loyalty is 80 percent.
Sequence of purchases	Consider two consumers, Sarah and Kristin; on the last ten purchase occasions, Sarah bought either brand A or brand B in the following sequence: AAABAAAABBB, and Kristin bought them in this sequence ABABABABABA. Both patterns reflect divided loyalty between the two brands with 60 percent loyalty toward brand A; however, Sarah's pattern shows more consistent sequence than Kristin's pattern. Accordingly, we would consider Sarah more brand loyal than Kristin.
Probability of purchase	A third way is to combine proportion and sequence measures to compute the probability of purchase based on the consumer's long-term purchase history. First, we would compute the proportion of the brand purchase (as described above). Let us say, this is 60%. Then, at any point in time, this proportion is adjusted to reflect the most recent purchase. Every time the consumer purchases a specific brand, the statistical probability of repurchasing that brand on the next occasion rises. If the consumer's most recent purchase was for our brand, we would "up the probability" to, say, 63%; if our brand has been bought twice most recently, we would raise it further to, say, 66%, and so on. This figure is merely illustrative; the exact upward or downward revision is based on statistical probability estimation.

Prepared by Author for MyCBBook

you, that you are a brand loyal consumer. Because the scanner is recording your behavior (i.e., which brand you bought), it is called a *behavior scan*. Of course, the marketer would have to know it is you at the cash register buying that item. How does the scanner machine know that? There are a few tricks to it. First, the store might give you a loyalty card that you scan every time you shop. Second, some marketing research companies such as A.C. Nielsen recruit a research panel from a national sample of consumers. These research panel members scan their membership cards every time they shop. Today, the company also runs a program called Homescan, wherein panel members are given a small hand-held scanner and asked to scan the UPC of everything they buy—groceries, medicine, clothes, shoes, electronics—when they return home from shopping.[3] Of course, when you signed up for the loyalty card or the A. C. Nielsen consumer panel membership, you gave them information about yourself. That is how, from behavior scan data, marketers can tell not only which brands command loyalty, but also what demographic groups of consumers are loyal to specific brands.

From Behavior Scan to Mind Scan

This way of defining brand loyalty—consistent repurchase of the same brand—is based on behavior, i.e., what consumers actually do, and is therefore called behavioral brand loyalty. And the ease of measuring it (by behavior scans) is wonderful. There is only one problem: It is based on what consumers DO, not what consumers THINK. For marketers, this is not good enough. Here is why.

Suppose your coworker always hangs out with you. Hangs out, that is all. You have no idea what your coworker THINKS of you. Would you feel certain your coworker is a loyal friend? Would you feel confident that if a new coworker joined your company, your current, constant buddy is not going to desert you? No? Why then should mere consistent repurchase assure marketers that a consumer is brand loyal?

The problem with behavioral brand loyalty is that it only shows that consumers repurchase the same brand, not whether they actually like the brand more than other brands. A consumer could buy the same brand merely out of habit or convenience, without thinking much about it. This kind of loyalty cannot be stable; if a competing brand offers a price deal, the consumer would perhaps readily buy the cheaper brand.

Thus, just counting the actual purchase consistency may not show true brand loyalty. Therefore, marketing scholars have argued that in measuring brand loyalty, we should also assess consumers' attitudes toward the brand. That is, we need to move beyond behavior-scans to mind-scans. We said, *mind-scan*, mind you, not brain-scan (the latter being an electro-magnetic imaging process of the brain). *Mind-scan* means probing what is in your mind, and this we can do by asking questions, as we did in Chapter 7, to measure consumer attitudes.

Only if the consumer attitude toward a brand is more favorable than it is for competing brands should the marketer consider that consumer loyal to that brand. This way of looking at brand loyalty—that is, a greater liking for the brand—is called **attitudinal brand loyalty**. This can be measured by asking consumers to rate various brands in terms of how much they like each brand or which brand they prefer the most.

Brand Loyalty as Attitude-Based Behavior

Marketing scholars who had initially proposed behavioral measures of loyalty began to later view loyalty in both behavioral and attitudinal terms. A leading consumer researcher Jacob Jacoby proposed a new definition of brand loyalty: "Brand loyalty is the biased (i.e., nonrandom) behavioral response (i.e., purchase), expressed over time, with respect to one or more alternative brands out of a set of such brands, and is a function of psychological (decision-making, evaluative) processes."[4] Another leading marketing scholar, George S. Day, currently a professor at the Wharton School, has defined brand loyalty as "consisting of repeated purchases prompted by a strong internal disposition." The phrase "internal disposition" refers to a favorable attitude. Thus, true loyalty incorporates both a behavior and an attitude.[5]

If these scholarly definitions are, well, a bit too technical for you, let us synthesize and simplify them for you. We define **brand loyalty** as *consumer commitment to a brand based on favorable attitude and preference, manifested by the consistent repurchase of the brand. Remember four key elements: consistent repurchase, favorable attitude, preference, and commitment.* That is, not only does the consumer buy the brand repeatedly, but he or she also likes the brand (holds a favorable attitude), prefers it over other brands (shows preference), and has commitment to it. Commitment means the consumer would stick around, not be lured by competing offers. In personal relations and brand relations alike, this is what commitment means, and commitment is what is required to claim loyalty.

Thus, to measure true brand loyalty, we must assess all four elements. And these can be measured by paper and pencil questions. See Table 18.2. In that table, the first three statements are meant to assess whether the consumer is loyal to any brand in a product category at all. The next six statements measure the extent to which a consumer is loyal to a specific brand. Note that these six statements capture all four elements of brand loyalty: attitude, preference, actual behavior, and commitment to repeated future behavior. Of course, you can use the same statements to measure consumer loyalty toward your competitors' brands as well.

So Should You Abandon Behavior Scans?

No, let's not go overboard. To begin with, recall what we learned about *attitudes* in an earlier chapter. Attitudes underlie and produce behavior. And, normally, attitudes and behaviors are correlated. Why would you act contrary to how you think and feel toward something? Why would you buy a brand if you did not also like and prefer it? Thus, measuring behavior implies tapping into attitudes as well—most of the time.

Yes, "most of the time," but not always. Sometimes, your consistent brand purchasing

TABLE
18.2
ILLUSTRATIVE MEASURES OF BRAND LOYALTY

Rate the following statements using this scale:

Strongly disagree				Strongly Agree
1	2	3	4	5

Existence of Loyalty (Name the product category _____)

1. In this product category, I have a favorite brand.
2. When buying——, I always buy my favorite brand no matter what.
3. If my favorite brand of—— is not available in the store, I would go to another store rather than buy a substitute brand.

Loyalty toward a Specific Brand (Name the brand _____)

4. I like this brand—— very much.
5. This brand is my favorite brand.
6. I prefer this brand to all others.
7. In the past, almost all of my purchases of this product have been this brand .
8. In the past, I have gone out of my way to buy this brand.
9. I am committed to buying this brand in the future.

Note 1. Specify the product category, such as yogurt, detergent, soft drink, jeans, athletic shoes, etc. Do not write the section headings on the survey form itself.
Note 2. Compute the average across these statements (the first three and the last six, separately). The closer the score is to '5' (meaning "strongly agree"), the stronger the brand loyalty.

behavior may not reflect your true attitude. First, you may be buying a brand simply because it is always on sale. You like it all right, but not as much as some competing brands. In fact, one of the competing brands may even be slightly higher on your attitude and preference meter, but the lure of the deal might be making you buy our brand, instead. This means if the price of the competing brand were to be reduced by a few cents, you might easily switch over. That hardly makes you brand loyal, your current consistent behavior notwithstanding.

Second, you simply might not care which brand you buy—your involvement in the brand choice in that product category could be low. You might buy our brand simply because it happens to be convenient. Tomorrow if this brand were temporarily out of stock, you would be just as happily buy a competing brand. This, too, hardly makes you brand loyal.

That is why we ask for preference and commitment. But behavior does reflect attitude, often enough. Often is not bad. So we should not abandon behavior scans. Behavior scans give us, after all, automated measures of behavior—who is buying which brands. We should continue, therefore, to use behavior scans, and then periodically supplement them with measures of attitude (including preference and commitment, of course) by surveying consumers. Indeed, this is what marketing research companies that maintain behavior scan consumer panels do (such as A.C. Nielsen Research). In effect, they have the best of both worlds. Now, you have the complete picture.

CONSUMER LOYALTY

Brands and More

The concept of loyalty that marketers have developed for brands applies equally well to use of stores, service suppliers, and other vendors. To refer to all of these targets of loyalty, we can use the general term *consumer loyalty*. Thus, **consumer loyalty** *is a consumer's commitment to a brand or a store or a supplier, based on a strongly favorable attitude and preference, and manifested in consistent repatronage.*

In a previous chapter, we described a model of store loyalty, describing factors that make a consumer loyal to a store. Did you notice how cleverly we managed to avoid giving a definition of store loyalty itself? That is because we needed all the foregoing explanation of the concept of brand loyalty. But now we are ready; in fact, the definition of store loyalty and its measurement is a straightforward adaptation of our discussion of brand loyalty.

Store loyalty is a consumer's predominant patronage of a store, based on a favorable attitude and preference. That is, the consumer shops at that store (more than at any other store for that type of merchandise) and has a more favorable attitude toward that store. Just as we measured brand loyalty, similarly we can measure a consumer's store loyalty by using a set of questions, as shown in Table 18.3. In this table, the first three statements are meant to assess whether the consumer is loyal to any store at all in a product category. The next seven statements measure the extent to which a consumer is loyal to a particular store. Note that these seven statements capture all the elements of store loyalty: attitude, preference, actual behavior, and commitment toward future behavior. Of course, you can use the same statements to measure consumer loyalty toward competing stores as well.

TABLE 18.3 — ILLUSTRATIVE MEASURES OF STORE LOYALTY

Rate the following statements using this scale:

Strongly disagree				Strongly Agree
1	2	3	4	5

Existence of Loyalty

1. For this group of products, I have my favorite store.
2. When buying this group pf products, I usually divide my shoping between 2 or 3 stores, to get the best deal.*
3. When buying this group of products, I would always go shopping to my usual store, no matter what.

Loyalty toward a Specific Store

4. I like this store very much.
5. This store is my favorite store.
6. I prefer this store to all others.
7. When buying this group of products, I always shop this store first.
8. In the past 3 months, a majority of my shopping trips have been to this store.
9. I prefer to shop at this store even if another store advertises some deal.

* Reverse-score Statement # 2.
Note. Specify the product category, such as groceries, drugstore items, clothing, shoes, etc.
Do not write the section headings on the survey form itself.
Compute the average across these statements (the first three and the last seven separately).
The closer the score is to '5' (meaning "strongly agree"), the stronger the store loyalty.

Or How to Make Julia a Believer

Measuring and knowing who is brand loyal and who is not is well and good, but now what? What do you do with that information? Let us say, you are a marketer of Swiss Mocha Chocolate Coffee Drink, and your measurements have told you that 20 percent of all consumers are loyal to Swiss Mocha Chocolate. Twenty three year old college student Britney is loyal to your brand—she has a favorable attitude toward it, prefers it, drinks it often, and is committed to it. Thirty two year old stockbroker Julia is not—no favorable attitude, no preference, no consistent use, and no commitment.

The question is, how do you make Julia, and some of the other 80 percent of consumers, who are no longer brand loyal. You would like to convert Julia into a believer, wouldn't you? You can. But to do so, you would have to understand first what makes consumers brand loyal. Consumer research literature has proposed many diverse factors, but here we synthesize them for you into a short list.

For a consumer to be brand loyal, we believe three factors should exist (see Figure 18.1):

1. Performance Excellence The product (or service) must do what it is supposed to do and do it remarkably well. Thus, the brand of shampoo must cleanse the hair well, the cell phone must not drop calls, and a pair of jeans must not fade or shrink. Honda and Saturn cars, Sony and Toshiba consumer electronics, Levi's and Ralph Lauren clothing, and Gillette and Norelco shaving systems command consumer respect because of their unfailing performance quality.

2. Self-Connection Beyond physical performance, the brand should somehow rise to make a personal connection with the consumer. The consumer must feel that the brand is cool and that it reflects him or her. This personal connection occurs because of the public persona of the brand—the brand's personality, carefully nurtured by the firm's entire marketing mix. Some brands acquire such consumer self-connection because of their adoption by other people whom the consumer considers cool and admirable. BMW and Jeep cars, Diesel, Kenneth Cole, and Boca Wear clothing, Oakley and Chanel No. 5 eyewear, and, of course iPod among MP3 players, all owe consumer loyalty to this "cool" factor.[6]

3. High Involvement Finally, consumer involvement should be high in a given product category. Not all consumers are involved in a product. For some consumers, cars are simply transportation, while others take keen interest in their cars. No matter how flawless the performance, and how cool the other product users, if I am not much involved in, say, listening to music, then I am not going to be loyal to iPod, or to any other MP3 player for that matter. Only when the activity for which I need the product occupies a significant place in my life, would I bother to notice a brand's superior performance or care about how cool it is.

All three of the above factors are necessary for developing consumer brand loyalty. What does this mean to you as a marketer? First, that if you want to develop consumer loyalty toward your brand, you should target consumers for whom the product category is of deep personal interest. To attract and keep the high involvement consumer, you will have to adopt the high ground of superior quality. And also carefully nurture its symbolic image. On the other hand, if you choose to target low involvement consumers, then price and promotion (or frequent buyer loyalty cards) would have to carry the major burden of keeping consumers coming back to you. But remember, "coming back," yes, true brand loyalty, no. "They choose it," yes; "They love it," no.

Study Figure 18.1 now and commit to memory these three factors of consumer brand loyalty. And let these always guide all your marketing plans.

FIGURE 18.1 DETERMINANTS OF CONSUMER BRAND LOYALTY

Performance Excellence
("Wow, It Works Great!")

Self-Connection
("Its Cool. Its Me")

High Involvement
"Product is Important in My Life"

CONSUMER BRAND LOYALTY
"I lOVE IT."
"I BUY IT."

FOUR FACES OF BRAND LOYALTY

Why did we say that keeping consumers coming back by using promotions is not an indicator of true brand loyalty? Because the definition of loyalty includes, you will recall, both behavior and attitude. Cross these two components, and we get four possible situations—four faces of brand loyalty, but only one of them is true brand loyalty. See Figure 18.2.

When both attitudes and behaviors are weak, no loyalty exists. Weak attitude means the consumer does not have any liking or preference for the brand. Weak behavior means purchase of the brand is sporadic (i.e., the same brand is not purchased consistently). When both are strong, (i.e., attitude is very favorable and the same brand is purchased consistently), strong loyalty exists. These two cases are cases of consistency between attitude and behavior, just as the chapter on attitudes told us.

LOYALTY NEEDS BOTH ATTITUDE AND BEHAVIOR

The remaining two cases are more interesting. They show that attitude and behavior are out of sync. One of these cases describes what happens when behavior is high but attitude is low—here, the consumer has **spurious loyalty**—loyalty that is incidental, not well-founded. The consumer buys the same brand again and again or shops at the same store regularly, but he or she feels no preferential attitude toward it. Perhaps this brand or store happens to be the only one that is affordable or convenient; given more choices, the consumer might switch to another brand. Or, perhaps the consumer perceives all the brands to be more or less the same and buys this one merely by inertia. If the other brands were to offer a price deal, the consumer might easily switch. To move this consumer into the "loyalty" quadrant, the marketer will have to strengthen the consumer's perception of the brand's *benefits*.

Finally, in the case of high attitude and low behavior, the consumer has **latent loyalty**. He or she likes the brand

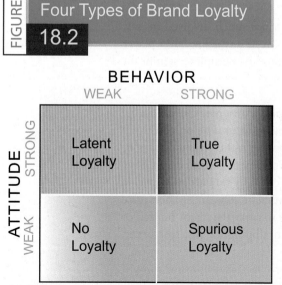

FIGURE 18.2 Four Types of Brand Loyalty

BEHAVIOR

	WEAK	STRONG
ATTITUDE STRONG	Latent Loyalty	True Loyalty
WEAK	No Loyalty	Spurious Loyalty

Source: Adapted from Alan S. Dick and Kunal Basu, "Customer Loyalty: Toward an Integrated Conceptual Framework," *Journal of the Academy of Marketing Science*, 22(2), 1994, 101. Used by permission..

but has been unable to buy it. Perhaps the price is too high or the consumer lacks access to the brand or the store. Here, the marketer needs to tap into this hidden potential market by lowering whatever barriers prevent consumers from buying their desired brand.

Once again you realize, as this model in Figure 18.2 shows, that tracking both behavior and attitude keeps your brand loyalty meter ticking—keeping you correctly informed about your consumers' loyalties.

BRAND PERSONALITY

THE SOURCE OF CONSUMERS' IDENTIFICATION WITH THE BRAND

Beyond performance, what is needed for brand loyalty is the strong ability for consumers to connect with the brand. So that consumers may identify themselves with the brand. This happens when consumers feel that the brand has the same or similar personalityto their own.

People have personalities, of course, as we saw in an earlier chapter; but do brands have personalities, too? To answer this question, let us begin with a quiz. Below is a list of qualities, or personality traits, we associate with people. Following this list is a set of brands in a few product categories (cars, soft drinks, clothing, etc.) Can you match individual brands in each product category with the following qualities?[7]

- Sincere
- Exciting
- Competent
- Sophisticated
- Rugged

Cars	Drinks	Clothes	Misc.
Mercedes	Root Beer	Gap	WSJ
Honda	Coke	Nike	Kodak
Saturn	Gatorade	Club Crown	Wall Street Journal
Rav4	Snapple	Banana Republic	Apple Computer
Blazer	Perrier	Lands' End	Campbell Soup

How did you do? Most people would assign various cars to the qualities list (in the order of A, B, C, D, and E) as Saturn, Rav4, Honda, Mercedes, and Blazer. Likewise, soft drinks as: Coke (A), Snapple (B), Gatorade (C), Perrier (D), and Root Beer (E). We'll leave clothing and other items for you to explore. As this trivia should convince you, products and brands do have personalities—that is, as consumers, we do see brands and products as possessing personalities.

If we describe ourselves and other people as having certain qualities known as personality traits, and as consumers if we use products and brands to convey the type of person we are, it makes sense that we can begin to also describe products and brands by the same human traits. Thus, just as people are cool, urbane, macho, aggressive, fun, and contemporary, so too are brands. **Brand personality** refers to the set of human qualities by which consumers describe a brand. Obviously, different consumers may see the brand differently, and thus brand personality, as seen by consumers, may vary from consumer to consumer. The question is, just what are the dimensions of brand personality?

A brand can be described by hundreds if not thousand qualities (good or bad). Many of these brand personality descriptors may be synonyms for one another (e.g., cool and trendy), and many others are closely related (e.g., prestigious and classy). Stanford University marketing professor Jennifer Aaker analyzed a battery of such descriptors that consumers use for brands and came up with a manageable set of overarching dimensions—called the *Five Brand Personality Dimensions*. You can remember these by using the acronym SECTS (if you paraphrase "rugged" as "tough"). That these dimensions are also five in number, just like the Big Five of human personality (see Chapter 5, where they were nicknamed OCEAN), is a happy coincidence. And an intuitive reading also shows a broad correspondence of individual dimensions within OCEAN and SECTS:

Conscientiousness is Competence; Agreeableness is Sincerity; Openness and Extraversion crisscross over Excitement (Excitement is more Openness but also a little Extraversion) and Sophisticated (Sophisticated is more extraverted but also a little over Openness); finally, Neuroticism's opposite, Stability, is like Ruggedness (a rugged object is stable). Remember, rather than being exact, the correspondence is intuitive, broad, and suggestive.

SECTS: The Five Dimensions of Brand Personality

Sincere—down-to-earth, family oriented, genuine, old-fashioned.
Exciting—spirited, young, up-to-date, outgoing.
Competent—accomplished, influential, high-performing.
Rugged—athletic and outdoorsy.
Sophisticated—pretentious, wealthy, condescending

TABLE 18.4 Measuring Brand Personality

Q. How well do the following words describe brand _____.

Does not describe at all					Describes very well
0	1	2	3	4	5

Sincere	Exciting	Competent	Rugged	Sophisticated
Down-to-earth	Trendy	Hard-working	Outdoorsy	Glamorous
Honest	Spirited	Successful	Western	Good-looking
Family-oriented	Up-to-date	Reliable	Masculine	Charming
Wholesome	Contemporary	Secure	Tough	Smooth
Cheerful	Imaginative	Leader	Strong	Upper class

Scoring: To score each personality dimension simply add the ratings for all the items of a dimension. The scores will range from 0 to 30. While dimension scores summarize the brand personality efficiently, individual item ratings are useful for more diagnostic understanding.

Source: Adapted from Jennifer Aaker, Dimensions of Brand Personality, *Journal of Marketing Research,* Summer 1997, Vol. 34, 347-57.
Reproduced with the permission of The American Marketing Association

100% STRENGTH
100% BEAUTY

what are you made of ?

TAGHeuer

Humans have personalities. Brand also have personalities. Brand Tag Heuer "casts" this watch in the likeness of Internationally known Chinese actress Zhang Ziyi.
(used with permission of Tag Heuer Watch Company)

MEASURING BRAND PERSONALITY

Measuring brand personality using SECTS is easy. Each dimension of SECTS is scored by using a set of six adjectives, as shown in the Table 18.4. The scores can then be profiled for any brand or a set of brands for comparison.

Brand Personality = Brand Image (NOT!)

A clarification is in order. Brand personality is not the same as brand image. What is the difference? Brand image consists of all the associations or qualities associated with a brand, which includes physical qualities (e.g., cold, runny, porous, dark, transparent, etc.) and functional qualities (e.g., sucks more dirt, zaps zits, blocks spam, autodials missed caller, etc.), in addition to human qualities; however, only human qualities count as brand personality. Thus, brand personality is a subset of brand image.

HOW BRANDS ACQUIRE PERSONALITY

How do brands acquire their personality? There are at least three sources:

1. Marketer Communications Intentionally, marketers convey to consumers certain symbolic brand images: they depict their brands in association with certain people (e.g., celebrities like Tiger Woods), person-images (e.g., the cowboy for Marlboro cigarettes), or human-like animated characters (e.g., the Pillsbury Doughboy). One recent trend in brand personality advertising is to display a brand and human model side by side, striking visual similarity—as was done in recent print ads for Tag Heuer. For want of a term, we would call it **homophyly**, which the dictionary defines as "resemblance arising out of common ancestry,"[8] but which we will here define as "resemblance arising out of love and identification."

Other marketer-managed signals also promote the intended brand personality. Indeed, all other elements of the marketing mix build a brand's personality. The brand's name, logo, price, packaging, and even the store where the brand is sold contribute to the brand's personality. The brand name Obsession gives the cologne *ruggedness,* whereas Eternity makes it sincere even though both colognes are from the same maker, Calvin Klein. Indeed, some of these elements of marketing mix are a way of giving tangible form to the intended brand personality. Visit, for example, a M.A.C. Cosmetics store, and see how young store associates are "decorated" M.A.C. style; more than anything else, these visual ambassadors personify the trendy, edgy, *exciting personality* of the brand.

2. Consumers' Social Observations In their everyday life, consumers observe who is using what products, and then assign the qualities of the brand's users to the brand. Thus, if consumers see a lot of urban youth wearing Diesel brand jeans and clothing, then Diesel will acquire, in the consumer's eye, the personality of being urban and youthful. If consumers also see these same youths (donning Diesel outfits) with conservatively well kempt hair, driving nice cars and patronizing upscale restaurants and clubs, then they would attribute to Diesel the personality of rich, yuppie, fashionable, sophisticated, urbane, and youthful (sort of like Banana Republic or Kenneth Cole brands). On the other hand, if they were to see the Diesel youth donning punk rock hairdos and tattoos, then the personality attributed to Diesel would be rebellious, unorthodox, on-the-edge and youthful (sort of like the brand personality of Hot Topic and Torrid clothing lines).

3. Cultural Gatekeepers In every culture, there are a number of public figures that influence the image of activities, ideas, and products. By adopting a product (without commercial gains from the marketer), by displaying it through personal use, by taking a position on it, by praising it or critiquing it, these cultural gatekeepers inevitably define and influence the brand image for the rest of us.

Two examples will illustrate this: Nike's Air Force One and Menolo Blahnik.

Air Force One No, we are not talking about the presidential plane. We are talking about Nike's basketball shoe designed in 1981. By itself it is so plain (a thick sole, some vent air holes on the top, and a Velcro ankle strap) that unless you knew of it already, you wouldn't give it a second look. And while it endured for two decades—thanks to an occasional lift from hip-hop celebrities—it achieved cult status in November 2001 when rapper Nelly made it the theme of his single, appropriately titled "Air Force One," which became an instant hit. Some lyrics in it include: "You couldn't get this color if you had a personal genie. I am a sneaker pro, I love Pumas and shelltoes. But can't nothin' compare to a fresh crispy white pair…" While the company (Nike) has occasionally brought out limited editions of other colors, the white-on-white, the subject of Nelly's paean, is now the most coveted shoe among hip-hop fans and pretenders alike.[9]

Manolo Blahnik The designer of this high fashion shoe is one of the most revered shoe designers of the century, but that doesn't put it on the consumer's wish list. Rather it is the roster of its famous fans—Madonna, Patti Labelle, and Winona Ryder. Of course, what really expanded its circle of admirers is its frequent appearance on the fashionable TV show *Sex and the City*.

CONSUMER RELATIONSHIPS WITH BRANDS

So, by now, you have gained an intense knowledge of consumer loyalty toward brands. You can separate consumers who would stick with your brand no matter what, from those who would ditch you in a heartbeat just to get a 25-cent promotional deal. As a brand marketer, you also know what factors enhance brand loyalty and what factors diminish it.

You have been and will continue to be offering consumers unmatchable performance. And you will manage all elements of your marketing mix to build and project the desired brand personality. You are happy already that your brand commands a good degree of loyalty from a considerable segment of your target consumers. Still, something is bugging you.

What is bugging you is that your brand is no Miata and definitely no iPod. Your brand commands its users' loyalty, but they are not nuts about it. There are no fanatics, and there is no public display of love for your brand—like the Miata owners who wed their cars in a public ceremony and the iPod bedecked consumers walking in a trance. Or like the thousands of brainy teens with a hint of nerdy looks and hundreds of funky graphic artists who flock to the nearby Apple showcase stores, to learn one more cool acrobatic move in that amazing digital music and graphics space.

In our quest to understand how consumers relate to their brands so intimately, we want to take you to an even higher plane. We want to talk about consumer-brand relationships, the consumer romance with brands, consumption communities, brand-tribes, and brandfests.

Meet My Brand—My Buddy, My Alter-ego

In a recent ad from Toshiba, the printer is shown brooding, "I do all the work of copying, and all he does [referring to a copying associate] is bring her those copies, and now he is her sushi buddy!"

This is animism at work. **Animism** refers to the belief that objects (products) possess souls, i.e., they have consciousness just like humans do. A Chrysler 300M ad declares: "The technology has changed, but the soul lives on." The fact that advertisers use this technique and that consumers accept it (acceptance here means, simply, not rejecting something as nonsensical or absurd) shows that consumers see it as something that could exist, that could happen, at least on some implicit, latent level of thought and feeling.

While the Toshiba Printer in the ad is a lonely subject of unrequited love, other products and brands are luckier. There are many products and brands that consumers notice, yearn for, adopt and incorporate into their lives, and develop special feelings toward them. Consumers develop relationships with these products and brands, just as they have relationships with people. At first, this proposition may seem absurd. You may like, adore, or even love a product or a brand, but to say that you have a relationship with it may seem a stretch to you. But as some consumer psychologists peer deeper into the consumer mind, more and more they are finding manifestations of humanlike relationships between people and their brands.

This is not to say that all people have relationships with all the products they use. Far from it. In fact, there are many products and brands that consumers possess and use without a moment's thought about them. (We call such products "low involvement" products, remember?) At the same time, for each of us, there is at least one product or brand toward which we feel a little personal, a little like it were human. We call this view of how consumers feel toward some products and brands **consumer-brand relationships**.[10]

How is it that consumers can be said to have a relationship with brands? A **relationship** is based upon a sentiment in which one feels a special sense of being connected. In a relationship, one feels that there is interdependence between two entities. Seen in this light, we as consumers do have a relationship with some of the products we consume. We depend on our cars, and our cars depend on us for proper care. If we are enduringly involved with our cars, then we also come to harbor some feeling toward it; we come to see it as having a special place in our lives. The brand becomes something more than a mere instrument for getting the job done. With the brand Jeep, for example, not the destination, but the journey itself is meaningful. This relationship occurs in several forms[11]:

1. Humanistic qualities in brands First, we bestow on some products the same qualities that humans have, and by virtue of those qualities, we then begin to see those products as almost human-like entities.

We think of soup as a nurturer, for example. Jell-O becomes a happy cheery friend, cast in Bill Cosby's image (Bill Cosby was a comedian and a TV actor who played during the 1980's and 1990's in a TV drama series called Cosby, the very likable patriarch to a family of kids ranging in age from 5 to 25 and who appealed to viewers across race, gender and social class boundaries.)Audi TT is a muscular car that packs 300 horsepower and can be thought of as a muscular, agile, robust high-speed horse. The point is not simply that we think soup is good nutritional food that nurtures; but rather that we think it is our benefactor and that it nurtures us just as our mothers did. That Jell-O is a cheery friend who would actually lift us, like a friend, out of our blues. And that Audi TT will take us places with gusto, and like the horse of the cowboy era, it will care of its master and owner, never letting us down. Since consumers think of these products as possessing specific human (or animal) qualities, they find them comforting as personal friends and companions, whose company they hope will bring the same satisfaction that other humans bring them.

Consumer researchers even have a term for this: **Anthropomorphizing** the brand—giving the brand a humanlike quality. And marketers recognize and promote this by giving brands a human-like character: Mr. Peanut, Mr. Clean, Ronald McDonald, Frisch's Big Boy, the Pillsbury Doughboy, etc.

2. Self-definition by Brand This is the mirror image of the foregoing. Instead of giving a product or brand certain humanistic qualities, consumers begin to define themselves (and others) by a product category, or by a brand. For example, as in "She is a Real Coke Girl," or "Here comes the Tommy Hilfiger Girl," or even, he is "a meat and potatoes guy." Consumers adopt the brand (product) identity—identifying themselves as possessing the essential quality of the brand (product)—like sophisticated or rugged or simple and competent. Consequently, consumers begin to view the brand as somehow related to them.

3. Surrogate Other If a possession is inherited from a loved one, or is a gift from a loved one, then a consumer comes to view that object just as he or she views that person. For example, suppose Tim received an antique clock from his grandmother whom he loved dearly; now every time he remembers his grandma, he reaches out to that clock, to connect with it—looking at it for a long while, caressing it, dusting or polishing it just one more time, even kissing it. Conversely, every time he looks at the clock, it brings back happy memories of grandma and the time spent with her. In a similar vein, we save our loved ones' letters; we also save that person's favorite perfume or cologne or even favorite flower arrangement. It is almost as if the spirit of the person lives in the brand. Thus, we develop a personal relationship with a product or brand because we see it as a repository of all the memories of the person we loved.[12]

4. Connected with Our Life Projects The fourth source of brand relationships is the role brands and products play in consumers' life projects. **Life projects** are enduring, ongoing, significant endeavors undertaken by consumers to achieve certain life goals. These goals include the social roles consumers take on (ascribed or taken voluntarily) such as father, teacher, mentor, or a committed boy-friend or girl-friend, etc. Life projects also include personal growth and self-actualization goals, such as the desire to become an accomplished musician, a renowned historian, or a crusader against environmental pollution, etc. Products and brands that help consumers fulfill these role responsibilities or accomplish personal-growth goals become the targets of consumer attachment and emotional investment. These products are then viewed as co-strivers in whatever they (the consumers) are trying to achieve in their lives. Consider an example:

Karen is reaching 40, is a divorcee, and is afraid she will end up being an unsuccessful (career-wise) unmarried person. Her current *life project* is to find a man, so she wants to look young and keep looking young, and, therefore, products that make her look young have a special place in her life. So central a role do such products play in a consumer's life project that a relationship of deep dependency develops. Says Karen:

CB Factoid

In 2005, a man named Eric James Torpy of Oklahoma City received a 30-year jail sentence. He requested his jail term be extended by 3 years. Reason: Larry Bird's jersey # is 33!! (His request was granted.)

My CB Book

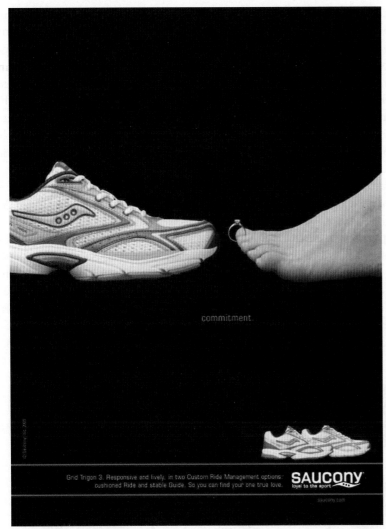

commitment.

Grid Trigon 3. Responsive and lively, in two Custom Ride Management options:
cushioned Ride and stable Guide. So you can find your one true love.

SAUCONY
loyal to the sport

saucony.com

"I use Mary Kay everything. Makeup, lipstick, moisturizer, toner. I think Mary Kay is responsible for how my skin looks now. I do, I really do. I don't think my skin would be this, so young today if I had used any other brand. ..I really can tell the difference. .. Now I depend on it; I can't live without it…. The worst is if they pull your favorite colors from the line. They did that to me with the lipstick. My favorite, absolute favorite shade. … I remember feeling, "How could they do that to me?" [13]

5. Important Role in Our Everyday Life Come to think of it, everyday life is in itself its own project. We get up, we bathe, and we groom; we have coffee and breakfast; we commute to work; we take a lunch break; we commute back home; we enjoy dinner and conversation; we watch TV; and we go to bed. This daily routine is intertwined with consumption. Some of the consumption we carry on in a taken-for-granted manner, of course, but some of it with full consciousness, at least some of the time. And consequently, we come to see a relationship between these products and brands and our life. We speak here not of deep involvement (of the type some Miata owners display toward their cars) but simply of a pleasant feeling, for example, of being served well by our faithful Saturn or Honda or Lexus.

Even objects of routine consumption, when strung together with hundreds of repeat performances, come to occupy a relished place in our consciousness. The jasmine fragrance of the bathing soap we use; the M.A.C. mascara we apply to adorn our eyelashes; the car that helps us complete our daily commute; the coffee and bagel or cereal and orange juice or milk and pancakes or tea and sushi we eat as our breakfast. All these so called "mundane consumptions" do come to define for us the "episodes" of everyday life. These episodes are not of mere consumption, abstracted from our subjective life—the life we construct and experience in our minds. Rather, their consumption is intertwined with the non-consumption life going on at the same moment. When we are commuting, we are not merely commuting, but we are also making plans for a presentation at work. When we are applying mascara, we are also admiring our physical beauty; when we are drinking beer, we are also enjoying our conversations with our drinking buddies. When we are sipping our coffee and eating our sandwiches, we are also perhaps reminiscing about the events of the previous night; or about the friends we will meet at the networking event later this evening. Invariably then, these products and brands, consumed in lockstep with non-consumption related mental activities, become an

important prop in the drama that is everyday life. (In 2005, McDonald's ran an advertising series showing just such vignettes with the theme "McGriddles and Coffee. My Time. My Thoughts.")

6. Membership in a Consumption Community Lastly, we may have a relationship with a brand through a relationship with other consumers. The brand is then seen as a way of belonging to a social group of other consumers. This last source of relationship is what makes a brand or consumption community. Consumption communities are a very potent force for creating a cult for the brand—a visible, substantial group of fanatical consumers. We peek into the lives of some of these communities in the next section, but for now, review Figure 18.3 for one look into the Six Drivers of Consumer-Brand Relationships.

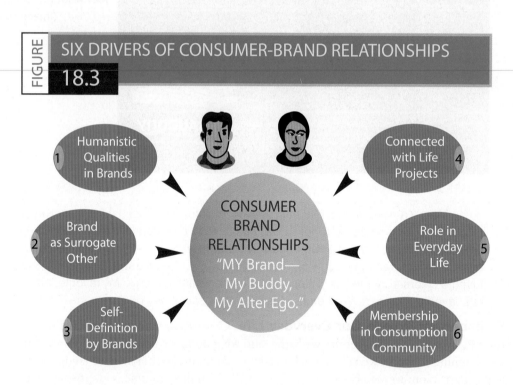

FIGURE 18.3 SIX DRIVERS OF CONSUMER-BRAND RELATIONSHIPS

1. Humanistic Qualities in Brands
2. Brand as Surrogate Other
3. Self-Definition by Brands
4. Connected with Life Projects
5. Role in Everyday Life
6. Membership in Consumption Community

CONSUMER BRAND RELATIONSHIPS "MY Brand— My Buddy, My Alter Ego."

A SOCIETY OF CONSUMPTION COMMUNITIES

Consumption communities are groups of people who share the consumption of a brand or product. Thus, Mac computer users are a consumption community, and so are all the revelers at the Dave Mathews Band concert, grunge dressers, and cross-dressers. Members of a consumption community come from a wide range of demographics. For example, a large consumption community has formed around plush toys such as Beanie Babies, and members of this community chat online. They are not all computer whiz kids; rather, they are homemakers, students, retirees, blue-collar workers, white-collar professionals, etc. In general, consumption community members are not homogeneous in demographics. Rather, it is the enthusiasm and emotion of using the brand or product that binds them.

Consumption communities play an important role in our modern societies. This is best explained by sociologist Daniel J. Boorstin:

> The modern American, then, was tied, if only by the thinnest of threads and by the most volatile, switchable loyalties, to thousands of other Americans in nearly everything he ate or drank or drove or read or used. …. Americans were increasingly held to others not by a few iron bonds but by countless gossamer webs knitting together the trivia of their lives.[14]

In the Pre-industrial Age, communities were formed on the basis of religious, political, ethnic, or geographical ties. The bonds between members were strong, members interacted frequently, and they shared many interests. But in the Post-industrial Age, these communities became much weaker, and neighborhoods are now a collection of inhabitants who often remain strangers to one another. Instead, product consumption based communities have burgeoned. There are consumption activities that occur in public spaces or in proprietary market spaces such as bowling alleys, billiard clubs, tennis clubs, health clubs, and nightclubs. Consumers identify themselves as being part of a community merely by virtue of sharing a common consumption product or service.

Consumption communities are everywhere, more than we realize. The most known is, probably, the Harley Owners Group (HOG). But there are also communities of Saturn, Miata, Citroën and Mini Cooper owners; participants in yoga classes, marathon runs, Latin dance lessons, etc.; collectors of baseball cards, Renaissance paintings, and of course, users of iPods (visit www.iPodlounge.com), among others.

What Makes Consumption Communities Tick?

Scholars have identified four elements or properties that make a community tick—by that we mean function: (a) geographical proximity; (b) temporal convergence; (c) high or low context; and (d) consciousness of the kind.[15] (See Figure 18.4) Some communities score low on these, others score high. The higher the score, the more cohesive that community is and the stronger the identification with the community.

To understand what these four elements mean, consider students in an online course. What kind of a community are they? These students can download lessons posted on the Web, submit assignments, ask questions, send emails, and post messages or topic-specific opinions on message boards. However, this community, if one can call it a community at all, scores low on all four criteria. First, the students taking this course are geographically dispersed. Second, they engage in "product consumption" at different, uncoordinated times, so there is high temporal separation.

Third, they don't interact face to face, which makes it a

FIGURE 18.4

FOUR ESSENTIAL ELEMENTS OF CONSUMPTION COMMUNITIES

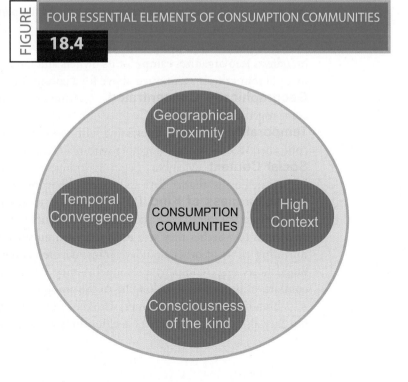

"low context" interaction. High context interactions are those where it is necessary to be familiar with the speaker's context (background, culture, and style) to understand what is being communicated. Emotionally charged communications are high context because words go beyond their literal meaning, and often the communication is nonverbal. Therefore, high context interactions often require face-to-face meetings or at least voice-based communications (i.e., phone conversations). Until voice and video based two-way communications become widely used over the Internet, communications between students and professors in an online course will remain low context, thus preventing the formation of a strong consumption community.

Finally, in the online course, there are no group activities, and if there is any collaboration among students, it is in small groups rather than with the class as a whole. Indeed, as a group, these students don't consider themselves as part of any community—this last characteristic is called **consciousness of kind**; i.e., the consumers have to become aware of others of their kind and recognize other consumers as part of their common group. This clearly is lacking in online student groups. As a result, online course participants do not make a strong "consumption community."[16]

Now that you understand the four elements, can you assess other communities on these four characteristics and rate them on whether they are weak or strong communities. Most likely HOG will qualify as a strong community. What else? Will Friendster.com? Members of myspace.com?

There are two kinds of consumption communities: product or activity, and brand. The first kind is built around consumers sharing a common product category. Examples are bikers, golfers, net surfers, roller-bladers, country music fans, and punk rockers. The second type is built around consumers sharing a specific brand; examples are Harley, Apple, Jeep, and Xbox.

One approach to building a strong brand-based consumption community is to organize brandfests.

BRANDFESTS

Party Time for All Brand Lovers

Brandfests are events that bring consumers together in geo-temporally concentrated events and entail coordinated activities and brand happenings. Since here all four elements come together, brandfests are an excellent way to build a brand community. The Saturn owners who came to Spring Hill, Tennessee one recent summer were participating in a brandfest. Jeep organizes camps for its owners and fans, called Jeep Meet. Brandfests must meet all four criteria mentioned above for a consumption community to exist.

Geographically Concentrated Consumers from geographically dispersed areas come together in one location.

Temporality Members (interacting with the brand, with the marketer, and with other consumers) are all brought together within a compact timeframe.

Social Context Members begin as strangers but develop close acquaintances, even lasting friendships that endure and continue beyond the confines of the event.

Consciousness of Kind The very decision to attend and join a brandfest raises the consciousness of there being a community of brand users. Many do arrive with trepidation, anxious as to whether they will fit in, but—in no small part due to the socialization and nurturing effort of other brand veterans, devotees, advocates, and evangelists, as well as brand hosts (e.g., company personnel)—they slowly ease into a state of psychological comfort, of being seen as belonging to the group.

Brandfests connect consumers with the rest of the community of consumers, of course, but they also deepen consumers' relationships with the brand and with the company.

BRANDFESTS AND BRAND BONDING

Brandfests are a great way to bond with your brand. You already like the one specific unit of that brand that you own. Now suddenly, you are face to face with the company behind the brand; you tour the plant, see the product being "born," and you talk to the designers and makers of the brand, who are proud of their creation. The hosting role the company plays inevitably endears the company to you.[17]

You go behind the scenes and see the full life of the brand—in flesh and blood, so to speak. Through product demos and product use and maintenance lectures and seminars, you also learn about the hidden features of the brand. And, you see newer brand concepts in the works, thus feeding your excitement about what is yet to come.

Equally important, you see an incredibly large group of other brand users—you realize in no uncertain terms (if you didn't already know) that there is really a community out there, totally fanatic and evangelic about the brand. And, most of all, you have fun (music, food, conversations, new friends). Can anything beat this kind of event in building consumer bonds with the brand?

In the context of a Jeep Meet, a relationship with a product means that consumers become more involved in an off-road jeep qua vehicle—e. g., "Earlier I was not into off-road trips, now I will be, using my off-road vehicle," as one brandfest attendee reported. Brand involvement also deepens as illustrated by a quote from another brandfest attendee: "Toward the brand Jeep, I feel more affectionate, so I'll buy other things that are Jeep related."

CONSUMPTION TRIBES

Because these groups of consumers show tribe-like behavior while consuming specific products, they are also called consumption tribes. **Consumption tribes** are consumption communities that consume a product in a public place, in some ritualistic setting. A tribe differs from an isolated consumer who may be deeply involved in a specific product, such as a consumer who might only wear Nike clothing, or one who loves her Saab, or has a huge collection of Elvis music and paraphernalia. Conversely, **tribal consumption** is consumption of brands and products that is public and where there is some participation in planned events of the community.

All consumption can be marked along two dimensions: consumption venue (which can be either public/ group or private/individual) and consumption event (which can be either everyday or organized). If all of your consumption of a product is at a private place such as your home and/or when you are alone, then your consumption is individual, not tribal, no matter how passionate your consumption of that product. Likewise, if the consumption is an everyday usage event and no more, then also it is individualized consumption. Only when at least some of the consumption occurs through participation in an organized public

Tribe members are happy to spot each other. (Photo courtesy: nathan tolbert)

event does it become a tribal consumption. Products consumed in tribal communities can also be consumed in private and individually, but the more the product is used in public and group consumption events at specially planned gatherings, the more it becomes an object of tribal consumption.

The intensity of tribal consumption is characterized by four dimensions:

- **Institutionalization** Whether or not there is a formal organization or institution consumers can join.
- **Community Events** Whether or not special large gatherings are organized as public consumption events.
- **Accessorization** The extent to which the consumer uses the product by itself versus whether the customers accessorizes the product (e.g., placing decals on the car) or accessorizes himself/herself (i.e., using the product with other related products; such as a Harley jacket, Harley clothing, Harley credit card, key chains, etc).
- **Consumption Rituals** Are there certain consumption rituals to be followed for proper consumption? For example, the game of football follows certain rituals.

Thus, the higher it rates on each of these four dimensions, the more intense is the tribal nature of the consumption. (See Figure 18.5.) To understand these qualities of tribal consumption, let us visit one such tribe—the French Roller Skaters (see box on adjacent pages).

One more point: The consumption community need not be a singular entity; often it includes more than one subgroup. For example, among the Harley motorcycle riders, there are the hard core Hell's Angels, with the bad boy/bad girl image, and the adventuresome biker who just likes the identity of being a biker. Among roller skaters, there are fitness skaters, and there are urban youth stunt skaters.

The most important feature of the consumption community is that it gives the consumer a sense of identity and belonging to some larger group. Such community linkage is especially important in modern societies where big cities are dubbed "lonely spaces" for an average consumer, and he or she desperately needs something to hang on to—something with which to identify.

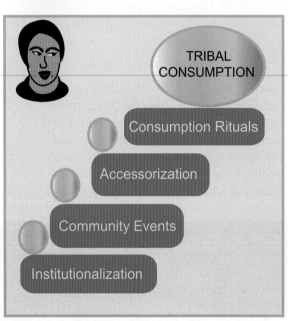

FIGURE 18.5 FOUR STEPS TO TRIBAL CONSUMPTION

TRIBAL CONSUMPTION

Consumption Rituals

Accessorization

Community Events

Institutionalization

FOUR ROLES IN CONSUMPTION COMMUNITIES

French professors Bernard Cova and Veronique Cova have researched this topic, identifying four roles of individuals with respect to any tribe: Practitioners, Participants, Devotees, and Sympathizers or Spectators (see Figure 18.6). *Practitioners* are those who have adopted the use of the product on an everyday basis; *Participants* are those who attend especial gatherings; *Devotees* join the club or organization; and *Sympathizers* or *Spectators* do not belong to any formal organization of the consumption community, do not participate in gatherings, and do not use the product on an everyday basis. They could either be curious spectators, or sympathizers of the consumption participants. The next time you run into one such community, interview a few members and try to place them into one of these four groups.

How to research consumption tribes

Suppose you wanted to do some firsthand consumer research on one of these tribes. How would you do it? Here is a quick guide:

1. **Secondary research** Find and read everything published about a particular consumption community—newspaper and magazine stories; TV and radio news and special reports; books; e-zines; personal Web pages; and discussion groups, forums, and chat rooms.

2. **Observation** Simply observe the users of the product as consumers use it in public places. For example, if we are interested in roller-blades, then we should observe who uses them (young or old, males or females or both, and from what socio-economic classes), where they use them (in skating rinks, on city sidewalks, in the suburban cul-de-sacs, on school grounds, etc.), on what occasions (weekends, nights, days, evenings, summer, all year long, holidays, etc.), for what purpose (fun, commute, competitive games, etc.), with whom (alone, with a pal, with a group of friends, coworkers, etc.), in what mind-set (it is fun, "have to do it," efficient means of commuting, it is cool, goes with lifestyle, etc.), and with what other accoutrements (casual clothing, special clothing, accessories, etc.).

3. **Direct questioning** Directly question a representative group of consumers who are members of the consumption communities. This can take the form of focus group discussions, one-on-one interviews, or more structured surveys. Here, we can ask consumers directly about their purpose and mindset in consumption, what their self-perceptions are as a consumer of that product, whether they differentiate themselves from other subgroups of their consumption communities, and how they think outsiders perceive their community.

4. **Participant observation** The final phase and the ultimate method for learning to understand a consumption tribe deeply is participant observation; become a member of the tribe by consuming the product yourself, attending consumption community events, and mingling freely with community members. This method offers insight in two ways: (a) by experiencing the consumption firsthand and then reflecting on that experience; and (b) by knowing and analyzing the inner thoughts and subjective experiences of other consumers—as revealed by these other consumers, in their words and in their deeds.

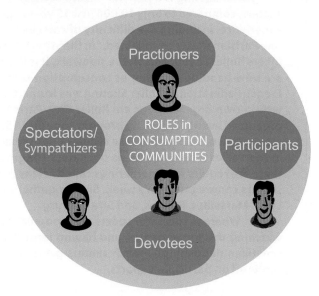

FIGURE 18.6 FOUR CONSUMER ROLES IN CONSUMPTION COMMUNITIES

Practioners

Spectators/ Sympathizers

ROLES in CONSUMPTION COMMUNITIES

Participants

Devotees

CONSUMPTION COMMUNITIES AS MARKETING OPPORTUNITY

Consumption communities provide both a special target group of consumers and a special avenue for promoting the product. That is, the community becomes both the target customer segment and the channel. Here is how marketers can utilize this opportunity[18]:

1. **Organize community events** Community members are always looking for opportunities for public consumption and for other pretexts of coming together. So for roller skaters, for example, a company could organize a big roller skating event. Brandfests are a prime example. Furthermore, a company could organize and sponsor an unrelated event (albeit an event that is of interest to members),

French Roller Skaters as a Consumption Community

Roller skating is a popular leisure activity in France. Today there are over 2 million French skaters, compared to only 10,000 just 15 years ago. French roller in-line skaters share a common experience, including the difficulty of carrying on the consumption and use of the product. As one Parisian skater complained, "In the street, cars blast their horns at you; in the bike lanes, the bikers holler at you; and on the sidewalk, it is the pedestrian who screams at you." These skaters are now banding together as consumption communities. In 1990, an organization called The French Federation of Roller Skating was formed, with 28,000 card-carrying members. Two other well-known organizations are Roller City, Paris Roller, and Roller et Coquillages. In one recent organized event, Roller City brought together 15,000 skaters who skated through Paris.

And of course there are regular unorganized gatherings such as those at Plage du Prado in Marseilles where hundreds of skaters congregate daily. In Paris around 10 pm on Fridays, there are regular local gatherings called Friday Night Fever. At Place d'Itilie, about 3000 to 5000 skaters congregate every week. Similar gatherings also occur on Friday evenings in Bordeaux, Lyon, Marseilles, Rennes, and Strausbourg.

Whereas spectator sports are a popular activity for consumption communities, such as watching the soccer games, and having large private parties on Superbowl evenings (a North American happening), French skaters present a good example of a consumption community centered on participant sports.

Source: Information based on Bernard Cova and Veronique Cova, "Tribal Aspects of Postmodern Consumption Research: The Case of French in-line roller Skaters," Journal of Consumer Behavior, 2000, Vol. 1, 1, 67-76.

such as a theatrical performance earmarked exclusively for the members of a brand community.

2. **Design and market accessories** Since community members like to accessorize their products, smart marketers should create accessories and market them. The best source for ideas is to see what consumers have already improvised on their own or to think about anything else that would be functional. For example, a specially designed oversized water or drink bottle with a special logo might appeal to roller-bladers, especially if sold along with color coordinated outfits.

Often community members use special paraphernalia (e.g., outfits) along with the primary products associated with their core consumption. Marketers of these accessories could add branding appeal for these paraphernalia by licensing the brand name. For example, they might add a designer name like Calvin Klein or a celebrity name like Tiger Woods.

3. **Product extensions** These products expand the market and the communities—create easier to use products that would appeal to the timid or not so bold or not so skilled whereas more high performance product versions would appeal to diehards.

Keep one point in mind: If there are sub-communities, as there usually are, then the marketer should conduct the marketing program so as not to annoy one sub-community just to please one another. This is a particular challenge for Harley Davidson, whose consumption communities and individual consumers are very divergent in their tastes and lifestyles. The best option is to use a campaign vague enough so that each sub-community may interpret it favorably.

These Brands I live for, I die for

You no doubt have heard about Apple/Mac fans. Many of them even sport a tattoo of Apple/Mac. But here is one that takes the cake—an Apple haircut. The head belongs to Gabriel McIntyre, a well-known presence at technology and new media conferences. He lives in Holland where he runs a company called Whisper Media, and lately also XOLO.TV. He was happy we spotted him. Check him out at www.XOLO.TV.

Now, This next story will look concocted so let us state it for the record. It happened unsolicited. Kimberly Bruce, a business senior, happened to comment in class: "If I were on death row and had to select my last meal it would be Dewey's Pizza. It is the perfect pizza. When someone in this situation selects the last meal they will ever eat, they pick their absolute favorite food. For me, that is Dewey's Pizza."

From Pizzas to computers, consumer loyalty runs wild. It is a tribute to marketers who painstakingly maintain the brand's inherent and extraordinary value for its target consumers; just as important, it is a joyous tale of how brand attachment enriches our lives as consumers.

Consumer Karma is **Extreme Brand Love**   My CB Book

LOVE/HATE BRAND SCORES

Just for fun, I started typing in "I hate (brand)" in Google to see what comes up. I then got curious about the findings for "I love (brand)." Here's the love/hate score for a random selection of brands. While I was at it, I did a " buzz index"—calculated as the total number of comments (positive or negative) for a brand as a ratio of the average number of comments for the 12 brands. And McDonalds is the big loser on the Love/Hate score. No surprise. (And yes, this is the random stuff I do when I'm procrastinating.)—Jennifer Rice, Brand Mantra, Inc. (www.brandmantra.com)

Brand	Hate	Love	L/H Score	Buzz Index
Apple	696	16100	23.1	159.2
Google	1170	22900	19.6	233.2
Linux	3860	34000	8.8	358.8
Target	438	4950	11.3	51.1
Ikea	469	3350	7.1	36.2
Yahoo	2800	2950	1.1	54.4
McDonalds	3540	2730	0.8	59.4
Starbucks	861	878	1.0	16.5
Dell	2410	2240	0.9	44.1
Microsoft	16600	5990	0.4	214.1
Comcast	1800	318	0.2	20.1
Wal-Mart	4850	534	0.1	51

Courtesy: Jennifer Rice, Brand Mantra, Inc. (www.brandmantra.com)

Coolness is a nebulous concept, hard to define, even harder to dissect. Brands earn this label, sometimes, based on performance excellence or a new feature—e.g., cars equipped with a system that would auto-correct their steering if they stray out of their lane; sometimes, an innovation that solves a previously unrealized problem, e.g., Post-It Notes. But a new factor is design. The aesthetics and sensory appeal of the product, achieved through artistic design, can instantly make a product look and feel cool. The most well known case is of course the Apple iMac and now the iPod. But this tool is taken to new heights when the design is deployed to achieve both aesthetic and sensory pleasure as well as functional performance enhancement. Case in point: Bang and Olufsen's home electronics products. Its BeoCom2 phone is *sculpted* out of a single piece of aluminum and its ring tone scored by a composer so its voice is clearer and ring tone distinct.

Ironic that a phone would leave you speechless.

Interesting things happen when a sculptor and composer collaborate over a phone. The BeoCom 2 is formed from a single piece of aluminum with an original ring tone scored to set it apart. The result is a phone that enhances communication, especially nonverbal. Find your nearest Bang & Olufsen store at www.bang-olufsen.com or call 888 625 3421.

The remarkable BeoCom 2

BANG & OLUFSEN B&O

Watch TV for hours. Then turn it on.

So much pleasure is gained from viewing the aluminum framed plasma screen and matching sound system that its beauty almost renders the 'on' button irrelevant. It makes watching TV as enjoyable as watching what's on it. Find your nearest Bang & Olufsen store at www.bang-olufsen.com or call 888-625-3421.

The all-powerful BeoVision 5 & BeoLab 5

BANG & OLUFSEN B&O

Its BeoVision 5 TV monitor works in sync with BeoLab5 sound system, both cast in aluminum enhance the look and feel of consumers' living spaces. The design pleases the senses when the product is being used, but also when it is not. Indeed, its ad images are cool too. The BeoCom 2 ad proclaims, "Ironic, that a phone would leave you speechless." Its TV ad says, "its beauty almost renders the 'on' button irrelevant. The consumer—albeit a certain kind of consumer—finds these designs cool. You could almost hear him or her echo the brand's message: "Ironic that my phone leaves me speechless," and "I watch TV for hours and then I turn it on." Can you think of a better scenario for consumer-brand connections?

So now you know also that our consumer on the cover was raving about just this TV and this phone.

Brandfest: Jeep® Jamboree

For Fans of Jeep and to build and nurture a brand community, Jeep (the company) organizes Camp Jeep and Jeep Jamboree. What is a Jeep Jamboree? Read about it, straight form the Website of Jeep Jamboree USA.

WHAT'S A JEEP® JAMBOREE?

It's a full two-day, family-oriented four-wheel-drive adventure that's probably unlike anything you've ever experienced. Jeep® Jamborees cater to every level of expertise so they're fun for everyone — from novice to veteran and everyone in between. Any Jeep vehicle with a 4-LO transfer case can participate: that includes everything from showroom stock all the way up to highly modified rigs. Experienced guides help navigate you through scenic switchbacks and some of the most challenging off-highway situations you never thought your Jeep vehicle was capable of. And, perhaps best of all, you'll be meeting and making new friends every day.

The event schedule includes:

- Orientation on proper four-wheeling technique
- Jeep vehicles inspected for trail capability
- Trail Ride along the trail, crossing streams, negotiating boulders, and conquering steep grades—all under the watchful eyes of veteran Jeep Jamboree guides.

There are hundreds of Jamborees, organized for Jeep owners by a dozen or so organizations. For example, Jeepers Jamboree organized one on July 27-30 called the 54th Annual Jeepers Jamboree. in the Rubicon Trail in Californai. The 45-mile trail is considered the "Granddaddy" of all 10-mile trails, and includes the Devil's Post Pile made up of thousands of tons of boulders and passes Spider and Buck Island Lakes. Over the last 53 years, some 90,000 people in some 35,000 vehicles have enjoyed the brandfest adventures.

Writes one recent participant:
I survived the 4WD Hardware Meet and Greet. And, despite the rain, hail, and mud, I had a hell of a good time. ….the atmosphere and the people were just so fun — it was like a non-stop party all weekend. Check out the one coming near you soon.

Source: http://www.jeep.com/jeep_life/events/jamborees ; and http://www.jeepersjamboree.com/
Photos Courtesy: 4Wheel Drive Hardware, LLC (www.4wd.com)

We conclude this chapter with an interesting tidbit on brands. Speaking of brands, would you know which brand of jeans is the hottest? The answer: Seven Jeans. Close runner up: True Religion. Rock & Republic (which, incidently, rocks the body of our ace consumer on the cover) is #14; Levi's is #7 and Gap is #29. The ranking is based on the average number of Yahoo members searching for brands of jeans on any given day; these ratings are for Oct 29, 2006.

Based on a report by By Molly McCall
http://buzz.yahoo.com/buzzlog/47708/30-pairs-of-the-hottest-jeans
(October 29, 2006)

To consumers, a brand is many things. It is a name to refer to the specific version of a product they want. It is short hand, also, for all the qualities the physical thing contains, and all the benefits its use will deliver. It is assurance that the brand will do what the brand says it will. It is a badge for its user, reflecting for the consumer a certain kind of persona. It is the target of consumption, consumed by the consumer.
But it is also the *subject* of consumption, with the consumer being the target— the brand consumes the consumer!

Consumers are fanatic about some brands. They depend on some brands, and, in turn, the brand depends on them. By constantly thinking about them and by repeatedly consuming them, we become attached to them, yearning for their company, whenever pertinent. We connect to them as if they were people, like friends, trusting and trustworthy. And through them, we connect to other people. In consumption communities and at consumption events called *brandfests,* a new form of public discourse built around the brand. We celebrate brands, and in so doing, we celebrate our life itself as consumers.

With such rich potpourri of brand *mantra,* it is hard to overstate the import of understanding the role brands play in consumers' lives.
This chapter has been our foray into the world of brand consumption.
Explore it as a consumer and relish your current brand relationships even more.
Explore it as a marketer and strategize how you can offer greater brand value to your target consumers.

SUMMARY

We began this chapter with a description of brand loyalty. We defined behavioral brand loyalty as consistent purchase of the same brand, and attitudinal brand loyalty as high liking for the brand. Combining these two concepts, brand loyalty is the consistent repurchase of the same brand based on favorable attitude toward and preference for it. We then presented a model of brand loyalty, which is based on three factors: performance, self-connection, and consumer involvement.

In the final section, we presented a fascinating topic: How do consumption communities get formed, and what role do they play in modern-day life? These communities have tribe-like rituals and norms for product usage, and members accessorize their use of products. Companies can foster brand communities through organizing brandfests, which serve to create and foster relationships between consumers and brands and the companies that stand behind those brands.

KEY TERMS

Behavioral Brand Loyalty
Attitudinal Brand Loyalty
Brand Loyalty
Store Loyalty
Spurious Loyalty
Latent Loyalty
Brand Personality
Homophyly
Consumer Brand Relationship

Animism
Anthropomorphizing
Life projects
Consumption Communities
Consumption Tribes
Tribal Consumption
Brand Tribes
Brandfests

REVIEW➕Rewind

1. What are values and what role do they play in 1. How would you define brand loyalty? If a consumer repeatedly buys the same brand, can we call him or her brand loyal? Why or why not?

2. What is behavior scan, and what is its utility to marketers? How well does it help marketers in assessing consumer brand loyalty?

3. Explain the three factors in the simple model of brand loyalty. Using this model, how would you build brand loyalty for high and low involvement consumers?

4. Explain the four faces of brand loyalty. Give an example of each.

5. List and explain the dimensions of brand personality. How do marketers create brand personality?

6. Can consumers have relationships with brands? Why do these relationships get formed?

7. What are the four defining characteristics of brand communities? Do brandfests satisfy these conditions? Why or why not?

8. What are consumption tribes? What are the four dimensions that determine the intensity of tribal consumption?

9. How can marketers (a) research and (b) utilize the concept of tribal consumption?

THINK➕Apply

1. Identify any five brands to which you are loyal. Discuss why you are loyal to those brands, using the explanation offered in this chapter.

2. Assume you are a marketing manager for (choose one): (a) a music CD store; (b) a book store; (c) a clothing store; (d) a brand of cola; or (e) a brand of hair color. You want to know what proportion of your customers are brand (store-) loyal and why or why not. Prepare a questionnaire for a consumer research project to address this issue.

3. Assume you have completed the above-mentioned survey. Based on the ideas presented in the chapter, what sort of reasons do you expect to find for consumers being loyal or not loyal to the brand or store for the product category you have chosen? Next, as a marketing manager, prepare a plan of action to increase loyalty among the currently non-loyal consumers. Identify separate actions for each of the possible factors.

4. For which of the following products would a marketer be able to create tribe-like brand consumption communities: (a) electric shaver, (b) beer, (c) videogames, (d) Yoga, (e) shopping at Target, and (f) shopping at Wild Oats (see www.wildoats.com). Why or why not? Describe how.

PRACTICE➕Experience

1. The chapter describes five segments of consumers based on their loyalty. Interview five consumers and identify to which segment each of them belongs, if any.

2. Spend some time as a participant observer in a consumption community. Describe and comment on how those communities compare with the textbook descriptions in the chapter.

3. Put together a survey to measure (a) involvement, (b) brand loyalty, and (c) brand personality. Interview ten consumers, asking them to describe their preferred brands of (a) a pair of jeans, (b) cars, (c) laptops, and (d) cell phones. Obtain these descriptions as open-ended answers (take notes). Next, have them fill out the survey for each product category. Analyze your data. For example, are brand loyalty scores higher for high involvement consumers? Are brand personality scores remarkable only for high involvement consumers? Do consumers' open-ended descriptions correlate their scores on the questionnaires?

In the Marketing Manager's Shoes

Most concepts in the chapter have some lessons for the marketing manager, i.e., they suggest what to do differently in practice; indeed, often these applications are implicit in our explanations of the concepts and models in the chapter. Identify at least five specific applications of the chapter's concepts, all of which should be entirely new—different from the examples cited here.

CONSUMER RELATIONSHIPS WITH BRANDS

18

Or How All Brands Are Not Created Equal

You have studied brand loyalty. Now, meet a closely related concept—brand equity. In a sense, it is the mirror image of brand loyalty. Brand loyalty is the consumer's commitment to a brand. Brand equity is the brand's power to attract the patronage and commitment of its customers.

Assume for a moment that one day a three-star hotel property removes all signs that identify it by name. You are given a tour of the hotel and then asked how much you would consider a reasonable price for a night's stay at the hotel. Suppose you said $70. Next, assume that you are also invited by Marriott Hotel Corporation to tour one of their new properties, a three-star hotel almost identical to the first one, and asked how much you would pay for a night stay there. Would your answer be $60, $70, $90, or what?

It turns out that just such a study was actually done. A few years ago, when Marriott Hotels built a new chain of mid-priced inns, they tested two alternative names for the property: Fairfield Inn and Fairfield Inn by Marriott. The results: Survey respondents who saw the property under the second name estimated a reasonable price that was 35% more than that estimated by the other group of respondents who were shown the same property but under the first name (i.e., Fairfield Inn). That is the power of the brand name! This power of the brand name is referred to as "brand equity." [19]

Brand equity may be defined as "the enhancement in the perceived utility and desirability that a brand name confers on a product." Brand equity comes from the value of that brand to the consumer compared to other brands. It is the overall superiority of a product carrying that brand name over similar products carrying other brand names.

Brand equity reflects the greater confidence that consumers place in the brand than they do in the competing brands. This confidence then translates into consumer preference for the brand, brand loyalty, and even a willingness to pay a premium price for the brand. For example, a study by McKinsey & Company and Intelliquest Inc. found that consumers tend to buy brands with low brand equity like Packard Bell only at a discounted price compared to those of such brands as Dell or IBM. The resulting market share and profit potential translate into financial gains, so much so that the brand-owning company's net worth is raised. For example, when Cadbury-Schweppes bought the Hires and Crush brands of soft drink from Procter & Gamble, it paid a total price of $220 million; of this amount, 90 percent is said to be associated with the brand equity itself.

What is the difference between brand loyalty and brand equity? As we mentioned earlier, brand loyalty is a characteristic of the consumer—Tom is brand loyal to Coke and Nicole is not; Jennifer is not brand loyal to Nike but Julia is. This tells us about the brand loyalty of Tom and Nicole toward Coke and the brand loyalty of Jennifer and Julia toward Nike. But it does not tell us anything about the brand equity of Coke and Nike. There will always be some people who would not like or be loyal even to the best brand. So, what makes a brand powerful is how consumers perceive the brand and how many consumers perceive it that way. Brand equity comes, in other words, from the sum total of perceptions of desirable qualities of the brand, accumulated across all of that product category's target consumers.

VI CONSUMERS IN THE NEW MILLENNIUM

FIGURE 18.7 SOURCES OF BRAND EQUITY

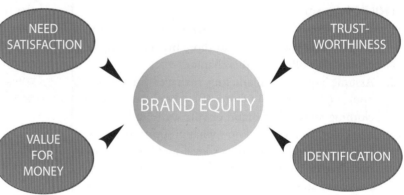

NEED SATISFACTION — TRUST-WORTHINESS — BRAND EQUITY — VALUE FOR MONEY — IDENTIFICATION

Do You Know My Name?

What do these perceptions include? First and foremost, target consumers have to be aware of the brand name. If very few people know of a brand's name, then that brand has no equity. On the other hand, a lot of people could be aware of it, but if they don't think much of it, then too it has no equity. Thus, brand name awareness is a necessary condition, but it does not entirely make up brand equity. What makes up brand equity is the kind of **brand associations**—what consumers think the brand is, does, or stands for. Brand associations include both tangible and intangible qualities, such as, for example, that Harmon Kardon keeps acoustic fidelity; that W Hotels offer artistic living spaces; that Levi's Manufacturing Co. supports diversity in the workplace; that Tommy Hilfiger clothing is trendy; or that Mercedes is the subtle statement of success. Associations like these are the basis of all value perceptions about the brand. These associations are at the heart of brand equity.

Where do these perceptions or associations come from? They come from two sources: (1) the consumer's personal use of the brand, and (2) from a long history of brand communications and the image projected in these communications.[20] Indeed, therefore, brand usage is not even necessary, and the consumer could base his or her brand perceptions entirely on exposure to brand communications.

Now, although brand equity is a characteristic of the brand, not of the individual, that characteristic matters only as perceived by consumers. Basically, to assess a brand's equity among a target group of consumers, we would want to know what value these consumers see in the brand. What is this value? And what are its sources?

TABLE 18.5 Illustrative Measures of Components of Brand Equity

State your opinion on the following statements by rating them 1 through 5, where

Strongly disagree				Strongly Agree
1	2	3	4	5

Need Satisfaction value

N1. This brand meets my needs very well.
N2. From this brand of———, I can expect superior performance
N3. The quality of this brand is superior.

Value for the Money

V1 This brand is well-priced
V2 Considering what I would pay for this brand, I will get much more than my money's worth.
V3. In view of the quality of this brand, its price makes it a great bargain.

Trustworthiness

T1 I consider the company and people who stand behind this brand to be very trustworthy
T2 This company seems to be very caring of its consumers' interests.
T3 I can trust this company not to take advantage of consumers like me.

Identification

I1. I feel a personal connection with the brand.
I2. This brand of——— fits my personality well.
I3. I very much like the values and principles of the company behind this brand.
I4. If this brand is discontinued, I would miss it very much.

Note: To compute the score on each source, simply take the average on that source for all three question, and also average it across all target consumers. The score would range from 1 to 5. To compute an overall score, compute an average across all four sources. The higher the score, the greater the brand equity for that brand.

Source: Adapted and modified by author from Walfried Lassar, Banwari Mittal, and Arun Sharma, "Measuring Consumer-Based Brand Equity," Journal of Consumer Marketing 12, no. 4, (1995), pp. 11-19; and Charles Bonghee Yoo and Neveen Donthu, "Developing and Validating a Multidimensional Consumer-based Brand Equity Scale," Journal of Business Research, April 2001, vol. 52, Issue 1, 1-14.

Brand Equity as Value Delivered by the Brand

A brand's perceived value is the sum total of physical and psychological benefits the consumer receives from the brand. This perceived value comes from four sources.[21] (See Figure 18.7.)

1. **Need Satisfaction** Value comes from the brand's potential to satisfy the consumer's needs—the purpose for which the consumer seeks the brand to begin with. The better the brand satisfies those needs, the greater the perceived brand value; in turn, the more the consumer will value and desire that brand.

2. **Value for the Money** Value comes from the brand's perceived utility relative to its costs, based on a comparison of what is received with what is given up.

3. **Trustworthiness** Brand value encompasses the consumer's trust—the trust in the brand's commitment to quality and to its customers; that the brand will maintain its strengths, and that it will not compromise its quality or otherwise take advantage of consumers. An example of a trust-failure is the press story a few years ago about Sears automotive shops doing unneeded repairs on cars; this story diminished consumer trust and, in turn, Sears lost some of its brand equity.

4. **Identification** The degree to which consumers identify themselves with the brand, or feel some attachment to it. In effect, consumers would say that it is their brand; it is the kind of brand they would be happy to be associated with. Often, identification occurs because the brand is

associated with things, persons, ideas, or symbols we find engaging. In particular, celebrities and role models are often used to develop identification. But even more potent drivers of identification are the firm's social policies such as environmentalism, kindness to animals, etc. Benetton has long employed shocking images of social issues (e.g., AIDS research, racial harmony); it hopes to generate bonds of identification among its core consumers in whom such images strike an emotional chord. Identification suffers when the brand marketer adopts some policy that goes against the value system of its consumers.[22]

By now, you have probably developed a reflex: The moment we discuss a concept and build a model around it, you want to measure it. That is good. Indeed, understanding consumer behavior means being able to measure it. So, in Table 18.5, we give you a scale to measure each of the four components.

Your brand's equity will be high when it scores well on all four components. As a manager, you can identify which components are weak, and work to improve those aspects of the brand. Thus, measurement of these components will also help you, the manager, map your brand vis-à-vis your competitors' brands. You will then be able to take action to improve the deficient component.[23] We will leave it to your creativity to figure out what exactly you would do to bolster and enrich each component. We suggest only that whatever you do, you also assess whether it is working by measuring it again, say, a year later.

A COMPREHENSIVE MODEL OF CONSUMER BRAND LOYALTY

You found the three-factor model of brand loyalty useful, didn't you? Actually, it was a simplified account. If you want to dig deeper—and you should want to if you really want to outsmart your competitors in winning consumer loyalty—then we build for you a more comprehensive model.

In this model, we represent all factors that determine consumer loyalty in terms of positive and negative forces (good and evil, if you will). Positive forces or factors induce brand loyalty; negative forces work against it. The degree of brand loyalty is, according to research, the net outcome of these positive and negative forces. See Figure 18.8.

CONTRIBUTORS TO BRAND LOYALTY

First, there are the positive factors. Basically, these are what produce satisfaction from the current brand. These are divided into (a) product factors, and (b) consumer factors. Product factors are subdivided into (i) performance-fit, and (ii) psychological bonding. These two subfactors are the same as the first two factors of the simpler three factor model presented earlier; their slightly modified names capture a more elaborate meaning and reality. Let us discuss each.

PERCEIVED PERFORMANCE FIT

Basically, consumers like brands that meet their needs and wants well. If they have a positive usage experience, consumers want to seek that rewarding experience again

Indeed, positive product performance is the first requisite for any brand loyalty to even begin to occur. Consumers want their brands to perform—to do well whatever they are supposed to do. Thus, a Norelco Razor must give a close shave—really, really close. Nike shoes must really support and catapult our feet. And a Garnier Fructis XXL Volume Gel should turn our Spock-flat hair (remember the Vulcan Star Fleet officer on *Star Trek*?) into an Orlando Bloom head, every morning.

In addition to the overall quality of product performance, brands also differ on their specific performance dimensions. For example, some shampoos give hair body, and some eliminate dandruff. Some are meant to deep cleanse and leave no residue, others are meant to give thickness to thin hair. This is because consumers with different hair types (thin, thick, oily, dry, etc.) have different hair cleansing needs. Thus, performance is judged not only on the overall quality but also on the degree of fit between the consumer's specific performance requirements and the brand's performance capability. Brands targeted to specific consumer segments are more likely to fit particular needs better than those mass-marketed to the public at large. That is why consumer loyalty is generally higher in niche markets than in to mass markets.

Psychological Bonding

Although the performance-fit produces satisfaction and in turn causes a fair degree of loyalty, strong loyalty also requires psychological bonding. **Psychological bonding** can be defined as the connection consumers feel toward the brand. This occurs when somehow consumers feel a sense of personal-connection with the brand. Somehow they identify with the brand, feeling that the brand reflects them and the type of people they are, or that the brand is somehow a necessary part of their lives.

Psychological bonding comes from the symbolic and emotional value of the brand. Brands come to acquire certain social images through marketing communications and/or when buyers directly observe who is buying what brands. Such associations are particularly inevitable and indeed quite strong for conspicuous products such as clothing, cars, and even places of leisure and recreation. It is very fashionable to wear designer clothing with specific brand names, drive the car that reflects one's personality, or belong to a country club befitting one's social status. Brands that reflect social self-concept—the kind of person you like to be seen as—become a part of your identity—your "extended self."

The extended self-connectivity also results from other aspects of a brand's persona—the things the brand stands for in larger society; i.e., the societal values the brand espouses. Companies that espouse desirable societal values are referred to as **socially conscious businesses**. Companies show their societal values by participating in certain programs and practices. Let us tell you about three of them: cause marketing, value-based business practices, and community support.

Cause marketing In cause marketing, companies sponsor and support some social causes such as an AIDS awareness program or a "feed the hungry" program.

Value-based business practice Value-based business practice is the adoption of some socially desirable value as a corporate value, which then guides everything that the company does. This can be a program of hiring people a certain disadvantaged class of people (e.g., people on welfare), taking extra care of employees, adopting pro-environmental practices such as use of recyclable packaging, or avoiding cruelty to animals. The Body Shop, for example, shuns animal testing of its products,

and, for this reason, many consumers love to identify with the company.

Note that this differs from cause marketing in that in cause marketing the support and nurture of the social cause does not affect the internal organizational and business practices themselves; in value-based business practice, it does.

Community support In community support, companies sponsor certain community events, such as an ethnic food festival, Black History Month, or even local high school football teams. Some companies even offer financial help such as giving minority scholarships.

The first two types of programs create psychological bonding by connecting with consumers at the level of life's important values—the big causes and societal goals that are important to consumers. The third type creates affinity—the consumer notices that the marketer understands and values the culture and sentiments of his or her community.

The "extended self" phenomenon was vividly demonstrated by the classic case of old Coke's brief withdrawal from the marketplace which resulted in a groundswell of public protests from the brand's loyal fans who believed that the brand's absence had created a void in their personal lives! The Miata and Apple stories presented at the beginning of this chapter also illustrate cases of strong psychological bonding, where consumers are able to identify with and attach themselves to these products and to the companies and people who stand behind them.

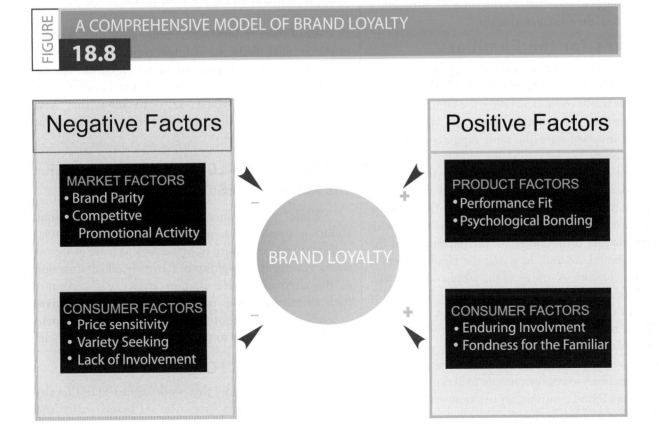

FIGURE **18.8** A COMPREHENSIVE MODEL OF BRAND LOYALTY

This thing, *psychological bonding*, is mighty powerful, mind you. As a marketer, after you have ensured high performance-fit in your brand, try creating psychological bonding. Capture the consumer's heart by engaging his or her emotions. And capture the consumer's soul by espousing causes, higher values, he or she holds dear.

CONSUMER FACTORS: ENDURING INVOLVEMENT AND FAMILIARITY

Involvement

Not all consumers are involved in a product. For some consumers, cars are simply transportation. Others take keen interest in their cars. As discussed in Chapter 2, this quality of ongoing interest in a product is called enduring involvement. Enduring involvement creates brand loyalty for two reasons: first, a desire to obtain as close a fit between the product and the benefits one seeks in a product—specific performance, social image, and identity benefits. Once the consumer finds a product that offers these desired benefits, he or she wants to not forego these same benefits in the future.

Second, enduring involvement also creates personal connections or psychological bonding. Enduring involvement means ongoing interest in the product. This ongoing interest means that the consumer becomes attached to the brand. Once this attachment develops, the consumer wants to stay with the brand. If you have an ongoing interest in your car, for example, then you would be using your car with enthusiasm and derive pleasure from that brand of car, thus etching the brand name in your mind as a source of pleasurable experience. Consequently, you would seek the same brand again.[24]

Fondness for the Familiar

The second consumer factor driving brand loyalty is what we call "fondness for the familiar." This refers to the fact that many consumers prefer the familiar and the tested. Consider this example: There are two Chinese restaurants in town; have the same reputation for their identical cuisines. You have tried one and liked it. You may want to explore the other, or you may want to stay with the familiar. Many consumers prefer to stay with the familiar. This desire to stay with the familiar comes from diverse sources. First, familiarity brings certainty; by staying with the brand already used, one avoids the uncertainty of the alternative brand. Second, in seeing the familiar, there is some extra comfort—warmth of the familiar, if you will. This is because the familiar is a slice of our lives, and it brings back the happy memory of the past experience.

Third, there is the happy state of "problem closure." Let us explain. You might recall that one view of the consumer we discussed in Chapter 1 was that the consumer is a problem solver—seeking solutions to life's problems. So once we have found a satisfactory solution to a particular problem, that problem is closed and we can put it behind us. There is a natural satisfaction that comes from having found closure to the problem, and there is no desire, indeed there may be an aversion, to reopening the search for new problem solutions. We receive so many pitches everyday from insurance agencies, mortgage companies, and wireless services, all promising better rates, but we don't want to look at their offers because we would then be opening up the whole insurance or mortgage or wireless service problem again.

There is a fourth source of this fondness with the familiar; namely, habit and a long history of brand usage. As consumers, we acquire some of our preferences for brands simply through repeated use. And for some products, we even become biologically conditioned— i.e., our bodies begin to crave the same experience. For example, initially we may not like Mexican or Chinese food, but upon repeated consumption, we may not only learn to like it but, in fact, to crave it. Likewise, we crave certain brands of wine, food items (e.g., Kentucky Fried Chicken's chicken wings), perfumes and colognes, music styles, or even artists. Notice, for example, how, by simply living in Nashville, Tennessee (reputed to be the country music capital of the world), many consumers become country music fans. This acquired taste is the reason why many brands try to catch consumers young.

Furthermore, if consumers, as children in their parents homes saw a brand being used, they are likely to view this long history of use by parents as testimony to the brand's goodness. Intergenerational influence by family members, a topic we discussed in Chapter 14, is an important driver of acquired brand loyalty for some products and for some consumers.

All of these factors—uncertainty avoidance, warmth of the familiar, desire to maintain problem closure, and habit and history are grouped under "fondness for the familiar." Consumers vary on this factor and to that extent their brand loyalty would vary—the more they have fondness for the familiar, the more they are likely to be brand loyal.

FORCES AGAINST LOYALTY: ATTRACTION OF THE ALTERNATIVES

While performance fit, psychological bonding, enduring involvement, and fondness for the familiar engender and contribute to brand loyalty, a set of factors works against it. This group of factors is called attraction of the alternatives; that is, how attractive a consumer finds alternative brands to be. **Attraction of alternatives** depends on factors relating to the market environment and factors pertaining to the consumer himself or herself.

MARKET FACTORS

Two market factors that work against brand loyalty by making alternatives attractive are brand parity and competitive promotional activity. **Brand parity** refers to how similar and mutually substitutable the brands are. The more alike the brands in a product category are, the less motivation there is for a consumer to stick with a particular brand. Of course, the parity matters, not in its absolute form, but rather it is perceived by the consumer. If the consumer perceives that the brands lack parity, that perception is what matters.

Competitive promotional activity refers to the special price deals available on competing brands. These price deals provide the motivation to switch from a favorite brand to a featured brand. Generally, such switching is limited to comparable brands, say the brand the consumer might have perceived to be a close second or a close third to his or her first preference. In many product categories, consumers are quite open to switching brands in return for a reasonable amount of savings. Of course consumer response to promotional activity depends on the consumers' price sensitivity.

CONSUMER FACTORS AGAINST LOYALTY

Also working against brand loyalty are consumer factors, and there are three of them: price sensitivity, variety seeking, and lack of involvement.

Price Sensitivity Consumers differ in their price sensitivity. Some consumers check the prices even on small items and notice even small price differences. Others are generally unaware of price variations across brands and, if aware, do not value small savings enough to switch brands. A number of marketing studies have found that consumers' price sensitivity is negatively related to brand loyalty and positively to coupon use.[25] Of course, not all consumers are equally price sensitive. Accordingly, they differ in their brand loyalty behavior and in their response to competitors' promotional activities.[26]

Variety Seeking Some consumers like to seek variety in their experience; they get bored with the same product or life experience. Other consumers find one solution and see no need to look at alternatives. The variety-seeking consumer may switch from one brand to another, not because he or she is dissatisfied with the first brand's performance and other values, but rather simply for the sake of change and variety. The more variety seeking a consumer is, the less loyal he or she is likely to be.

Lack of Involvement Lack of involvement is the last of the three consumer factors. Lack of involvement is not simply the absence of enduring involvement. Rather it is an absence of any reason, whatsoever, to deliberate over the brand choice. It comes from an absence of enduring involvement plus a lack of any perceived risk inherent in the purchase decision. It is, in other words, a lack of purchase decision involvement. Thus, even a consumer who is not enduringly involved at all in cars will most likely experience a high degree of purchase decision involvement because of a high degree of perceived risk. But for many staple products like gas, paper towels, light bulbs, milk and frozen meats, some consumers may be totally indifferent about their brand choices. For these consumers, involvement is totally lacking at the time of brand selection, and, therefore, they are likely not to show any brand loyalty.

The best defense for marketers to fight such consumer indifference is to raise the level of involvement in consumers. This is done by breaking out of the parity barrier—i.e., raise their brand above parity by having some superior features that offer a better set of benefits to consumers.

If you now think back to the Miata and its loyal owners, to Macintosh and its loyal users, and to The Body Shop and its frequent patrons, you will find this model at work. What is immediately apparent is that breaking through the brand parity barrier, these iconic brands stand alone and distinguished, carefully garnering the identity and the experience dear to their fans.

DEEP INVOLVEMENT
Extreme Interest in Things

(We repeat this subtopic from Chapter 2 because it relates to brand loyalty intimately.)

One special case of enduring involvement is **deep involvement**—defined as a consumer's *extreme interest* in a product or activity on an ongoing basis. Often it borders on product fanaticism. Devotees like Gabriel McIntyre have a haircut styled like the Apple logo. One consumer in Sydney had the brand name 'Apple' tattooed on his forehead. The phenomenon of deep involvement is important to study because it is a window on a consumer's key motivations and emotions. People are fanatic about things they deeply care about. They use them for enjoyment, to derive life satisfactions, and even to define their identity for themselves. What are you deeply involved in? Cars? Sports? Art? Gizmos? Cooking? Shoes? If you are, then you know how a significant part of your consumer behavior—contemplating, searching, browsing, buying, collecting, caring, nurturing, and relishing—is dedicated to the object of your deep involvement. You also know first hand, then, how your deep involvement is, for you, a constant source of motivation—perhaps even a reason to live!

Deep involvement produces deep brand loyalty. And deep personal relationships with the brand and with objects that carry that brand name. The wedding ceremony in Pennsylvania's Pocono Mountains a few years ago where 250 consumers married their Miatas is a rare happening, but it is a telling proof that the idea of "relationships" consumers feel with and for some brands is REAL and ALIVE.

CHAPTER 19

Consumer Behavior In e-Marketplace

- Internet Consumer Universe
- Online Shoppers—Seeking Freedom and Control
- e-Satisfaction—Pre-and Post-Purchase Factors
- Internet in the Life of Teens
- Cyberspace and the Pursuit of Faith
- Google, Dude/Dudess, Google!

Stress

that's why I **blue**fly.com

It Is Important To Believe In It

From September 1999 through the end of September 25, 2000, I will be doing ALL OF MY RETAIL SHOPPING ONLINE and I will NOT enter a traditional bricks-and-mortar retail establishment

—Professor Bruce Weinberg, Bentley College, 1998.

Bruce Weinberg is a professor of marketing at Bentley College, and, arguably, one of the most celebrated netizens of cyberspace.

The year was 1998. He was a professor of marketing at Boston University and was denied tenure.[1] Consequently, he spent the next year as a visiting professor at Northwestern University where he met two individuals who influenced him deeply. Professor Mohan Sawney, a much celebrated author on e-commerce, and Professor Sid Levy, a sociologist and a scion in qualitative consumer research. In the company of these two luminaries, he finally found the answer to a self-searching question he had begun to ask himself a year earlier: "What is my thing? What do I love? What do I know that can be mine?" The answer he found: "A pioneering experiential explorer of life in cyberspace.

Professor Bruce Weinberg simulates, at author's request, his Intenet surfing moments of 1998.

For one whole year after that day, Professor Weinberg bought everything online. Everything except milk and gasoline, that is. And not just for himself but also for his wife and new twin babies that arrived that year as well. At first, it was a hard life. Setting up accounts online and finding merchandise seemed like a never-ending chore. Soon though, everything got under control. He would order merchandise and then wait for the parcels to arrive. He recorded in his diary that waiting for parcels became a new source of excitement in his life.

Professor Weinberg would often talk about his experience as if he had gone through a religious conversion. "It is important to believe in it," he said. For him it was a "leap of faith." So total was his conversion that, when speaking of online shoppers, he would use the pronoun "we," and, when speaking of offline shoppers, he would say "they"; and he would call offline shopping environments "the 'dirt' world."

While on the Internet, Professor Weinberg was clearly "in the flow." He moved easily from site to site in search of information and deals. He was frequently up late, until 3 am, surfing around. He was of a consumer obsessed and addicted. When he concluded his experiment, he was not quite himself. Said his wife, Amy: "when he stopped, he got depressed and withdrawn. Something important was ending."

1 Tenure—confirmation of a more or less long-term employment at universities—based on high standards of accomplishments both in scholarship and teaching. Tenure decisions often entail close judgment calls; many professors denied tenure at one university catch up on their accomplishments and prove their merit at another comparable university, and Professor Weinberg did just that, now an accomplished professor at the prestigious Bentley College.

Source: Bruce D. Weinberg (2001), "Research In Exploring The Online Consumer Experience," in Advances in Consumer Research Volume 28, eds. Mary C. Gilly and Joan Meyers-Levy, Valdosta, GA : Association for Consumer Research, Pages: 227-232. Reprinted with permission of the Association for Consumer Research. Further reading: http://www.internetshopping247.com/

INTRODUCTION

While only a few among us can claim to be as devoted to the Internet for our consumption needs as Professor Bruce Weinberg once was, most of us have had at least some familiarity and experience with the Internet. Of course, around the world, not everyone has access to the Internet, and of those who use the Internet, not everyone uses it for shopping. While online retail revenues are on a sharp rise to a whopping $50 billion, they still represent only 5% of total retail sales. To tap the full potential of online marketing, as marketers, we need to understand why consumers shop or do not shop on the Internet. The goal of this chapter is to understand the motivations and experiences of online shoppers.

We begin the chapter by describing the Internet Consumer Universe: how many consumers are online worldwide and for what purposes? Next, we recognize a principal distinction between two types of online consumers: goal-oriented shoppers and experiential browsers. We examine the motives of each group, and explore the features of Internet shopping that satisfy these motives. Following this, we present a model of e-satisfaction, highlighting the attributes and behaviors of online vendors that produce it. We then describe segments among online shoppers.

In the last section, we take our exploration beyond the domain of shopping. We draw a portrait of the enriching role the Internet plays in the social life of teenagers and in the spiritual life of faith seekers. We chose these two dramatically divergent segments to drive a point home: The portraits we present beckon marketers of commercial as well as noncommercial firms to find creative uses of the Web to bring their customers great value.

INTERNET CONSUMER UNIVERSE

Globally, 580 million consumers have access to the Internet via a home PC; of these 168 million are in the USA alone. The next four countries are Germany (35.6m), UK (29.0m), Italy (22.7m), and Spain (17.0m).

The penetration of Internet varies across nations. In the USA, 71% of the adult population has Internet access. Western European countries together average 50 % penetration. Eastern European countries lag far behind, averaging about 17%. In recent years, there has been a steady growth in the number of users. During 2002, the global Internet population grew by 4% in 11 major Internet markets. In Spain it grew by 22%. Among the Internet users, Spain also has the highest usage of Instant Messenger (49%) and Chat Rooms (44%).

Consumers without Access via a Home PC can access the Internet via PC at work, at commercial Internet kiosks, and at public libraries, and many do. In Europe, for example, Internet cafes (with multiple Internet access machines) can be found in cities everywhere, and in developing countries, both government-run and individual mom-and-pop owned kiosks serve millions of consumers. Thus, the number of Internet users is more than those with access to PC at home. Access is different from active use. Active internetr users are trapped by Nielson//netRatings in 10 selected countries. See table 19.1.

TABLE 19.1 ACTIVE HOME INTERNET USERS IN SELECTED COUNTRIES

Country	Internet Users
U.S.	144.35 m
Japan	43.51 m
Germany	32.98 m
U.K.	24.28 m
France	17.68 m
Italy	16.45 m
Brazil	13.39 m
Spain	11.27 m
Australia	10.56 m
Switzerland	3,71 m

Excerpted from ClickZ Stats, Active Home WebUSe by Country, July 2006. www.clickz.com.

Demographic Profile of Internet Users

The adoption of the Internet has not been even across various demographic groups. Overall, among US consumers, men have adopted the Internet slightly more. Younger consumers are more on the Internet than older consumers. Hispanics lead where as African Americans lag Caucasians somewhat. Internet use increases, as expected, with income, education, and urban (rather than rural) residence. See Table 19.2.

Time Spent on the Internet and TV

Not only is the Internet use highest in the US, the extent of use by individual consumers is also much greater in the US than other countries. For example, US Internet users log on 30 times a month from home and twice that many times from work, visiting a total of some 150 domains. On an average they spend about a 100 hours a month (roughly 3/4th of this at work) on the Internet, about 8 to 10 times the amount consumers in the U.K and Australia spend. See Table 19.3.

According to a Pew Internet Project survey done in Nov-Dec 2000, little more than half of all Internet users go online on any given day, and a majority (nearly 90%) of them do so to check their email; in turn about half of them (or one-fourth of all Internet users) go online everyday to browse for fun and just as many use it to get the News.

For a significant number of consumers, the time spent on the Internet comes at the expense of time spent on other media, particularly TV. And this time shift grows as the experience of using the Internet rises. On an average, Internet users watched nearly 5 ½ hours less television per week compared to Internet nonusers. Among those with six or more years of experience online, 38.2% reported spending <u>less</u> time watching TV. See Table 19.4.

How Consumers See the Internet?
Internet as a Huge Information Reservoir

All consumers familiar with the Internet are aware of its principal property: it is a huge reservoir of information. Accordingly, consumers have come to expect the Internet to be a source of information about commercial as well as non-commercial agencies. As many as 65% of all Americans expect government agencies to have a Web site; 63% expect all commercial companies to provide product information over the Internet; 67% expect the Internet to provide healthcare information; and 69% expect Internet to contain news. Obviously, this percentage is much higher for Internet users than for nonusers (about 80% versus 40%).

The Internet in fact meets these expectations. Of the consumes who go online looking for news, 87% say they either "always" or "mostly" do find the news; 85% of those looking for commercial information say they always or mostly do find that information; likewise, 76% of health information seekers and 71% of government agency information seekers mostly or always find that information online. One prominent use of the Internet is to learn about new cities. Forty million Americans, one third of all Internet users, have used the Internet for finding information about a place to live. On an average, three millions Americans go online everyday looking for information about a new place to live.[2]

Even though most consumers recognize the Internet as a resource for information, not every one finds it easy to search information online. Some factors make it a helpful medium, while others act as barriers. See Table 19.5.

TABLE 19.2 Demographics of Internet Users

Seventy-three percent of American adults now use the Internet (As of April 2006).

SEX	
Total Adults	73%
Women	71%
Men	74%

AGE	
18-29	88%
30-49	84%
50-64	71%
65+	32%

RACE/ETHNICITY	
Whites	73%
African Americans	61%
Hispanics	76%

COMMUNITY TYPE	
Urban	75%
Suburban	75%
Rural	63%

HOUSEHOLD INCOME	
Less than $30,000/yr	53%
$30,000- $50,000/yr	80%
$ 50,000- $75,000/yr	86%
More than $75,000	91%

EDUCATIONAL ATTAINMENT	
Less than high-school	40%
High school	64%
Some college	84%
College +	91%

Source: Demographics of Internet Users, Pew Internet. http://www.pewinternet.org/trends.asp (Used with permission)

TABLE 19.3 Average Internet Usage in USA, UK, & Australia

	USA	UK	Australia
Number of sessions/ visits per month	97	22	23
Number of sessions/ visits per month	151	56	50
Time spent per month (in hours)	100.4	11.45	12.85

The data are for home plus work combined.
For USA consumers, Home and Work breakdown is 30 and 67 session/visits per month, 52 and 99 domains visited per month, and 24.2 and 76.2 hours per month.
Source: Nielsen//Net Ratings, April 2003, *Cyberatlas.com*

TABLE 19.4

Impact of Internet Usage on TV Viewing

Q. How Has Internet Use Changed Your TV Viewing? Do you Spend:			
	Less Time	Same	More Time
New Users (< 1 year)	15.7%	69.7%	14.6%
Very Experienced Users (6 + years)	38.2%	60.3%	1.5%

Source: Pew Internet.

TABLE 19.5

FACTORS FOR AND AGAINST CONSUMER INFORMATION SEARCH ON THE INTERNET

HELPFUL FACTORS

- **Data Warehouse** The Internet is a vast storage medium. It is a huge warehouse of information where one can access merchants worldwide.
- **Accessible Anytime, Anywhere** This information is accessible anywhere—anywhere the consumer has access to an Internet device (e.g., a PC, a web-enabled cell phone, etc). Moreover, the Internet information warehouse is always open, 24 hours a day, seven days a week.
- **Searchability** The ability for consumers to search for information quickly. Just by typing a keyword, the consumer can get information from multiple vendors all at once (in contrast to the physical world, where the consumer has to contact multiple vendors individually).
- **Reorganization of Information** The ability to manipulate, organize, and store information easily. The information on the Internet can also be configured and organized easily by the consumer in any format; for example, you can sort a list of brands and vendors by price (ascending or descending order), by make and model, by features, by location, and so on. Moreover, you can also store this re-configured information instantly on a file (by bookmarking the page, for example), for perusing later.

BARRIERS

- **Lack of Access to Computer and the Internet** Not everybody has access to a computer, the Internet, and a high-speed connection.
- **Lack of Internet Literacy** Many consumers' use of the Internet is limited to emails; they do not have the necessary Internet literacy to search efficiently.
- **Massive, Undifferentiated Information** Many search engines present a huge number of information documents. For example, on google.com (a popular search engine) if you type "online business degree," in .23 seconds, the number of entries that show up is 4,430,000! Now, you have to click on them individually only to find that most of them are poorly selected and have low relevance.
- **Information Overload** Even when information is selected by using shopbots and the displayed database is all relevant, it is still large in size, totaling to some 20 to 50 brands;
- **Impersonalness** The information comes in low-context. By "low-context" we mean that there is no human element in communication, no nonverbal gestures, and no referent opinion. Thus, the Internet is good for objective information, but if you wanted some nonverbal and symbolic information, the Internet is not the place to look.

Prepared by Author for MyCBBook

ONLINE SHOPPING

It is one thing to search for general information on the Internet. It is quite another to shop online. In 2002, US consumers spent $45.5 billion on online shopping. In 2003, this figure was expected to climb up to 58 billion dollars. Some 97 million U.S. consumers were estimated to have shopped online during 2003. By 2007, some 142 million U.S. consumers are expected to shop online, and spend about $105 billion. Although large, it still amounts to only 5% of total retail sales, so the potential for online consumer spending is substantial. To understand this potential, let us see what consumers are buying online, and what they are not buying.

PRODUCTS CONSUMERS BUY ONLINE

Would you buy your wedding dress online? What about your engagement ring? A pet bird? A tire for your car? A new painting by an unknown artist? A vacation home? A designer brand Italian leather sofa from an Italian merchant? Exotic fruit from a merchant in Hawaii? Milk? Bread? Beer?

At first, your answer is likely to be a "no" for each of these. The correct answer should be "it depends." You could buy your wedding dress online, for example, if you have first searched and identified a similar dress in a brick & mortar (b&m) store. The same with the engagement ring, provided, of course, that the online merchant has a good reputation. The pet bird and the Italian sofa? Yes, if the vendor can certify their pedigree and authenticity. The same goes for exotic fruit. Tires? Yes, if you don't need them immediately. And you could buy milk, bread, and beer from the Web site of a local vendor who can make the same day home delivery. You would recall that for one full year, Professor Bruce Weinberg of Bentley College did just that. Other than gas and a few services (haircut, laundry, medical, etc), he bought everything online. Including the baby clothes, baby furniture, and baby food for his newborn twin sons. Of course, an average consumer is not as Net savvy. Most consumers who buy online buy some products online but not others. Here is what consumers buy or do not buy online and under what conditions:

Digital Products Digital products are products that exist in or can be transformed into digital form, such as computer software, music, pictures, video, and information material such as manuals, brochures, books, educational lessons, etc. Since these products can be transported digitally, they are available for downloading immediately.

Branded Products with Established Preference Lands' End clothing, Calvin Klein Cologne, Folgers Coffee, and any number of other products, which we have already tried and formed preferences for—we are willing to buy them online, especially if we want to avoid physical shopping.

Technical Products from Trusted Vendors Thousands of consumers buy Dell PCs everyday, online, sight unseen. Also, they buy other Internet devices, printers, cables, and computer components (memory, sound cards, etc). These are products that are specified by technical attributes, and, therefore, there is nothing to inspect in person. Consequently, and as long as they can trust the vendor, consumers feel no hesitation buying these products online.

Products Not Needed Immediately If our tire busted and we needed a new one immediately, then we could not afford to wait for it to arrive in the mail. But if products are not needed immediately, and if they are branded (e.g., Goodyear Tire, or Tommy Hilfiger Cologne), and are standard in size, colors, etc. (e.g., fits feet size 10-13), then consumers would not hesitate buying them online.

Products Generally Not Bought Online

New Experiential Products **Experiential products** are those that you need to try or actually use in order to enjoy them and judge their value or utility to you. New cologne— you have to smell it; a new make or model of car, you have to test drive it; you want to buy a dress, you have to try it on, even if it is a known brand. Since these experiential products cannot be tried or experienced in virtual space, consumers need to shop and buy them in brick-and-mortar stores.

Small Ticket, Bulky Items If the product costs say three dollars and shipping and handling (S&H) costs four dollars, you are not going to buy it online. Unless, of course, if multiple items could be combined so that the cumulative value makes total shipping costs a small proportion.

Perishables Milk, bread, and other groceries are not bought online, unless the online vendor has a local distribution center and can deliver frequently.[3]

that's why I **blue**fly.com

One characteristic of products is "high touch"—products that require touch and feel, and consequently cannot be judged or bought in virtual space. Dress material, designs for home furnishing, cologne, jewelry, accessories—these are all products that call for "high touch" shopping, possible only in brick & mortar stores.

Online Shopping Behavior

To describe online shopping, we must first briefly review some concepts of shopping in general, recapitulating important ideas from preceding chapters.

Shopping does not mean buying. Shopping means visiting stores. Consumers visit stores, sometimes for buying, but sometimes just for browsing. Browsing may culminate into a purchase, but, regardless, the process of browsing itself is seen by many consumers as enjoyable. Indeed, consumers browse, and continue to browse, only as long as they are deriving enjoyment. Once, the enjoyment stops, they stop browsing and leave the store. When the principal reason for shopping is enjoyment-seeking, it is called a hedonic motivation. On the other hand, when shopping (i.e. visiting the store) is driven by intent to buy something, that drive is called a utilitarian motive. In utilitarian shopping, the process of examining and evaluating the merchandise may be tedious, but it continues until the goal is accomplished, i.e., the right product or brand is identified. That is why, utilitarian shopping is also called task-oriented or goal-directed shopping.[4]

These two motives apply equally to brick-and-mortar stores and online stores. Consumers could visit online stores either for the hedonic experience or for the utilitarian purpose of making a purchase. However, a majority of consumers visit online stores for utilitarian rather than hedonic motives. That is, a majority of them are "buyers" rather than "browsers." In a recent survey, 71% of online consumers reported that their most recent online purchase had been planned, whereas 29% said they had been browsing when they made their most recent online purchase.[5]

What is important to online buyers versus browsers? Do they seek different features on the Web site? Do they have different needs, expectations, and reasons for preferring online stores over bricks & mortar stores? Do they seek and receive different experiences from their online shopping? What, in other words, is the psychology of online buyers versus online browsers? We address these questions below.

How the Web Enables Efficient and Effective Shopping
➢ Convenience
➢ Access to a wider assortment
➢ Comprehensive product information
➢ Easy product comparisons
➢ Best prices
➢ Stored shopping history

Goal Oriented Online Shoppers

Goal oriented online shoppers go on the Internet with a purchase goal in mind. They want to buy something. The question is, instead of going to a mall or a physical store, why do they like to go shopping online? Their reasons (or motivations) are two: (1) Efficient and Effective Purchasing; and (2) Freedom and Control.[6]

EFFICIENT AND EFFECTIVE PURCHASING

The primary motive of goal-oriented shoppers to go online is to make the required purchase more efficiently as well as more effectively than they consider possible offline. This efficiency and effectiveness comes from certain enabling features of online stores, namely: (a) convenience, (b) access to a wider assortment, (c) comprehensive product information, (d) easy product comparisons, (e) best prices, and (f) memorized shopping history.

Convenience Sure, consumers could go to the mall; but that would mean driving to the mall, finding parking, walking up to the store, finding the merchandise, dealing with the sales clerk, carting the merchandise to the car, loading it, and then driving back home and unloading it. Online stores remove all this hassle. This convenience can be a strong motive, particularly for time-starved consumers. Moreover, consumers can shop online anytime, and from anywhere (wherever they have access to Internet).

Access to a Wider Assortment However, convenience can only go so for. Beyond convenience, consumers want to find what they want. Can they find it on the Internet? Indeed, much more than bricks and mortar stores, online stores display a much wider assortment. For example, if you are looking for shoes, at Footsmart.com, you can find 19 types of men's shoes; 74 types of women's shoes, 25 varieties of walking shoes, 22 varieties of slippers and 16 types of therapeutic shoes! Not only do online stores carry a wider assortment, but you can also find an online store for a rare item of merchandise. Suppose you wanted to buy a pair of retro-western women's boots; where would you go? Whom would you ask? The chances are, you wouldn't know. But on the Internet, we typed "Retro women's boots," and back came a list of stores; we clicked on the first name on the list (Caboots.Zoovy.com), and the next page proved a feast for our eyes. See Exhibit 19.1.

Comprehensive Product Information Consumers who shop online also seek and find comprehensive product information. For example, the US Cellular Web site (www.USCC.com) gives information on the cell phone model Motorola RAZR (V3c). It is often difficult, in physical stores, to find knowledgeable salespersons who can match this level of product information.

Easy Product Comparisons Moreover, on the Web, it is possible to compare competing products or brands side-by-side. For example, online store www.bizrate.com offers side by side comparison across alternatives. In the physical world, the two product brochures are unlikely to list the features in the same order, thus making comparisons cumbersome.

Best Price The Internet is also a haven for price-based comparison-shoppers. This is not only because we have access to stores worldwide, but also because there are shopping agents (e.g. mysimon.com, pricescan.com) which search the entire e-space and assemble the requested product in a list with ascending price order. For example, on Pricescan.com, we searched for Coby TF-DVD7100 7 inch Portable DVD Player and found 11 vendors, with prices ranging from $107 to $189 (on August 25, 2006). See Exhibit 19.2.

Memorized Shopping History Finally, the best thing about the Web is that an online store can record and save information from your previous visits. Thus, if you register with a site, and give it your address and payment information once, you don't have to give that information again. On your next visit, it even brings up on the screen products you might have searched before. At the Lands' End store, for example, you can create your own model

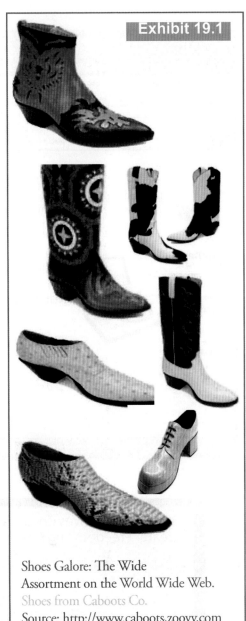

Exhibit 19.1

Shoes Galore: The Wide Assortment on the World Wide Web.
Shoes from Caboots Co.
Source: http://www.caboots.zoovy.com
(Used with permission)

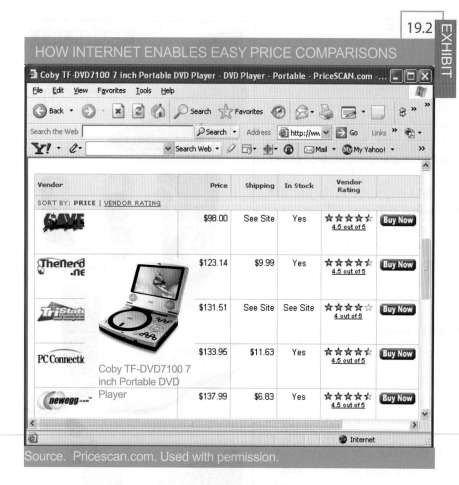

Source. Pricescan.com. Used with permission.

(a visual model to your size), and store it. Not only does this tool enable you to check how a particular clothing item will look on you, but you can also retrieve this model every time you visit the store.

Thus, it is easy to see how online shopping makes searching, selecting and acquiring products more efficient (saving time, effort, and money), and also more effective (better product selection).

GREATER FREEDOM & CONTROL

The second motive for goal-driven shoppers to shop online is that they feel more freedom and greater control when they shop online. They feel that they are free to do whatever they like, that they are not being pushed around and they are in control of their shopping. This sense of freedom and control comes from six features of online shopping, discussed next.

Shop Anytime, Anywhere First, you are not tied down to the hours the physical stores are open. On the Internet, the stores are open 24 hours. Besides, you can shop from anywhere, as long as you have access to the Internet—and nowadays even mobile wireless phones provide Web access. Furthermore, when shopping online, you, the consumer, do not need to be groomed, dressed, and presentable. Imagine what that kind of freedom can mean to you.

No Pressure from Salespersons On the Internet, there is no salesperson to shadow you, and no salesperson to intimidate you. For example, some men and old women might feel awkward entering Victoria's Secret (the physical store). But on the Web, there is no such fear.

No Obligation to Buy In physical stores, if a salesperson spends time with us, we sometimes feel obligated to buy something. Online shoppers feel free from such perceived normative pressures.

Control What Information to See Online store visitors also feel they have control over what information to see. For example, if you go to the Jeep Web site (www.Jeep.com), and if you click on Grand Cherokee, you get the option to view the exterior or interior, learn about 4WD capability, or take a virtual tour which allows you to scan every square inch of the vehicle and learn about hidden features.

Multi-trip Purchase Because the effort to visit online stores is low, as an online visitor you don't have to conclude your purchase in a single trip. You can leave the store any time,

VI CONSUMERS IN THE NEW MILLENNIUM

568

and return to it later, by "book-marking" the page (i.e., by saving the Web page). Many Web sites "remember" the products you viewed, and they save your shopping carts from previous trips.

Order-tracking Online shoppers also feel that they have greater control over their orders. Once you place an order, you typically receive an e-mail confirmation. Subsequently, you can track the order simply by going to the Web site and typing your tracking number.

It is important to note that while these features make online shopping desirable, by enabling freedom and control, not every consumer views these as sources of freedom and control. Indeed, for a majority of consumers, when it comes to shopping, there is nothing like the real store.

MOTIVES OF EXPERIENTIAL BROWSERS

Experiential browsers are consumers whose principal and overall motive for going to the Web sites of online stores is, of course, fun and excitement. Just as visitors to an amusement park go there and ride the rides for fun and enjoyment, so do many consumers go online to find enjoyment. Such consumers are called Web surfers.

There are four potential sources of fun and enjoyment on the Web. That is, within the overall motive of fun and enjoyment, there are four more specific motives that online surfers seek: (1) to explore favorite topics or products; (2) treasure hunt; (3) game-like exchanges; and (4) multi-media sensation.

1. Explore favorite topics or products If you are a sports fan, you watch ESPN on TV and read Sports Illustrated, and you enjoy them. And you enjoy browsing sports paraphernalia in sports stores. Now, the Internet is one more medium for you to extend your love of sports and experience the joy of sports in some new ways. For example, on ESPN.com, not only can you read all the sports stories (which you could also read in a sports magazine), but you also can visit the photo gallery (something you cannot do with a magazine); you can chat, if you like, with other sports fans; and you can express your opinion about current issues. For example, if you visited ESPN Web site recently, you could have answered this opinion question: How did Michael Jordan's two seasons with the Wizards impact his legacy: (a) Enhanced it; (b) Diminished it; or (c) Nothing changed. And you could also click on "Sony Store" icon on that Web site and buy a flat-screen TV, a laptop, a digital camera, or a PDA.

Sources of Enjoyment for Web Surfers
- Exploring favorite topics or products
- Treasure hunt
- Game-like exchanges
- Multi-media sensation

Browsers go on the Internet to explore and gain deeper knowledge about their pet topics or products in which they are deeply involved. If you are interested in, say, exotic cars, you type in "exotic cars" in the search field of google.com (which is a search engine) and, instantly, a list of sites shows up. Click on one (WWW.fantasycars.com), and you can spend some enjoyable time looking at such exotic cars as Josse, Marcos, Isdera, Vector, and Stola, for example.

Thus, consumers who are enduringly involved in a topic go online to have fun—exploring and learning about their favorite topic. The Internet enables this due to two features it has. First, it has search engines, which (after you type in a keyword such as "exotic cars") cull together a visual library of hundreds of sites for you to explore. Second, there are topic-specific sites, such as ESPN.com which offer a wealth of information, with easy to search and explore features.

2. Treasure hunt The second motive of browsers is treasure hunting—finding something unusual. This something can be a product or a special deal. For example, suppose you were surfing ESPN.go.com, and you clicked on "People and Chat." The Web page that appears next features an ad. For e-kiss. Yes, you can send someone a personalized animated card featuring audio-video of a kiss in motion. Now, you did not know that, did you? And you realize that not only is this an unusual product, but that such a product is, in fact, not even feasible in brick & mortar stores. What a delightful treasure find!

How the Web Enables
Treasure Hunts
➢ Search engines as virtual scavengers
➢ Targeted pop up ads
➢ Opt-in e-mails
➢ E-Bay and other auction Sites

Another kind of treasure find is a price deal or a bargain. Bargain hunting is a strong motive for browsers, both online and offline. However, only the Internet brings bargains home to the browsers without the prolonged process of physically roaming from store aisle to store aisle. And consumers just love the "thrill of a bargain."[7]

The Internet has at least four features that enable treasure hunting. First, there are search engines and shopping bots (like mysimon.com), which act as virtual scavengers, scoping out the entire e-space. These shopping bots are primarily useful to the goal-oriented shoppers, but, often, during net-surfing, these sites present whatever they find anyway, and some of these finds can be rare either as a product or in price. Then, there are targeted pop-up ads, which display ads relevant to the topic the consumer is browsing. Third, browsers often register at sites to receive interesting offers, and then receive opt-in-e-mails (e-mails that consumers opt to receive). Finally, there are sites such as eBay which are like warehouses both for unusual and usual products, often at bargain basement prices. These four features of the Internet offer ample opportunities for consumers to find some unexpected treasures. Consumers who know this, therefore, make browsing part of their leisure activity.

3. Game-like Exchange In brick and mortar stores, you like an item, pay a fixed price, and take the item home. This exchange itself is nothing special. Occasionally, when you happen to visit a flee market or a car or Estate auction, then you get to bargain and bid, and this, especially the bidding process, can be quite a game. Some consumers go to these auctions regularly, and even become addicted, feeling the adrenalin as they wait to see if someone ups the bid they just made. Now, on the Internet, you can go to an auction every day. eBay.com is the most famous of them, and here not only can you buy something, but you can also sell your stuff, new or used. The Internet has enabled at least two new exchange platforms for price negotiation: auction and price bidding. They are not entirely new, of course. For example, when we buy a house, we make an offer. But the Internet has brought these platforms to a wide range of products. So, on priceline.com, for example, you can bid your price for airlines and hotels, and just wait for a reply. If you don't have to be some place on a fixed day or time, then this game of bidding and waiting can itself be exciting. On the auction site eBay, you can even see the bidding history—who bid, when, and how much. Many consumers enjoy such game-like exchange modes available on the Internet.

4. Multi-media Sensation The fourth source of enjoyment, and the motive for online browsing, is the multi-media sensation of the Web. If you go to the BMW Web site (www. BMWfilms.com), for example, you can watch four short films (duration: 8 minutes 40 seconds, each). Likewise, if you go to the Levi's Web site (US.Levi.com), the home page opens on a close up shot of the back pocket of Levi's Type I Jeans, a close up shot so close that you can see every stitch and the yarn of the dark blue denim; you can also see an intriguing picture of a denim clad model— the view alters between different shots. Inside ("inside" for a Web site means the deeper layers of the Web site), there is more feast, including five games. One of these games features a section of a jean with rivets; your challenge is to connect all the rivets by clicking on them in the order they appear. There are 21 of them, and they appear at random locations. I tried it five times and each time failed after only three connects (18 rivets still left) and some 50 seconds into the game. But you, the reader, with possibly thousands of hours playing videogames, might find it a breeze. More to the point, participation in such game-like activity built around a product feature can be fun; and it can also "rivet" you to the product.

These four elements, then, are the sources of enjoyment and motivations for online browsers. Table 19.6 summarizes the goals, experiences, and the Internet's enabling features for the two types of Online Shoppers.

TABLE 19.6 Goals & Experiences of Goal-oriented Versus Experiential Online Shoppers: Selected Excerpts

Goal-Oriented Shopper	Experiential Shopper
Goals and Mindset	**Goals and Mindset**
You know exactly what you want [online], you order it and go away.	Online shopping is a fun and exciting way to shop.
Show me what I want fast, and get me on my way.	I constantly browse [online]. That is what I do in my spare time.
I don't think any body goes online to have an enjoyable experience.	I am software guy, and its always interesting to see what the latest program will do, so I visit all kinds of software companies [online].
What they experience	**What they experience**
In a store, a salesperson spends time with me and I feel obligated to buy. No such pressure online*.	It makes me sound like a cheese ball, but I like the chancy-ness of auctions.
You can even shop naked.	Promos seem to beckon me.
The single most satisfying aspect of online shopping is] the freedom to shop when and where I want. So easy and convenient.	Online has made me into a collector.
	I have developed friendships with [fellow E-bay users] and they all communicate with me. They are all over the U.S. and it's something, and I feel like a family.
How Web stores offer that experience	**How Web stores offer that experience**
The online is the world's store in your face.	I find wonderful deals. Online coupons have made my Christmas Shopping almost a game. What a wonderful deals.
I know that I have the full information at hand online. At a store, I only know what the clerk knows, I don't know the Clerk.	I like reviews at Amazon.com, you read about what people like and dislike, and it is kind of like an online community.
If you have a real person involved, the transaction might go wrong.	" A good site will surprise you with stuff you had no idea existed."

Source: Mary Wolfinbarger and Mary C Gilly, " Shopping online for Freedom, Control, and Fun," *California Management Review* 2001,vol. 43, no-2, 34-55. Copyright ©2001, by the Regents of the University of California. Reprinted from the *California Management Review*, By permission of The Regents.

FLOW ONLINE

No matter which particular source of enjoyment is at work on a Web site, the essential quality of online browsing enjoyment comes from what has been termed flow. **Flow** refers to a situation where the consumer gets immersed in site navigation, losing a sense of time. Flow is correlated to the fun that surfers feel in Web site surfing, in the use of Web sites for leisure and recreational purposes, and the amount of time spent surfing. Flow comprises several elements: (1) challenging task; (2) focused attention; (3) loss of self-consciousness; (4) perceived control over the stimulus; (5) clear task demands; (6) unambiguous feedback; and (7) intrinsic enjoyment.[8]:

Outcomes of flow include: (1) increased sense of control, (2) prolonged participation, (3) liking for the Web site, (4) a fun experience, and (5) purchase and revisit intentions[9] To help consumers experience a state of flow, Web sites should offer:

- A balance between the task challenge and consumer skills
- Unambiguous demands on the consumer—a sense of knowing what one is

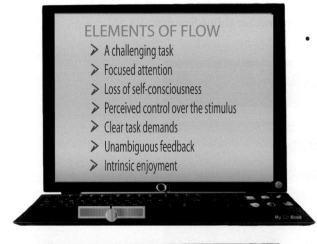

ELEMENTS OF FLOW
➢ A challenging task
➢ Focused attention
➢ Loss of self-consciousness
➢ Perceived control over the stimulus
➢ Clear task demands
➢ Unambiguous feedback
➢ Intrinsic enjoyment

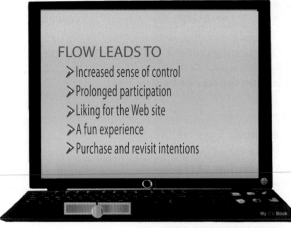

FLOW LEADS TO
➢ Increased sense of control
➢ Prolonged participation
➢ Liking for the Web site
➢ A fun experience
➢ Purchase and revisit intentions

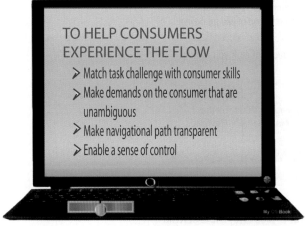

TO HELP CONSUMERS
EXPERIENCE THE FLOW
➢ Match task challenge with consumer skills
➢ Make demands on the consumer that are unambiguous
➢ Make navigational path transparent
➢ Enable a sense of control

supposed to do. This is also called "Inherent Transparency" of a site navigation path.[10]

- A sense of perceived control--minimal pop up ads, no need to register before further browsing, not too many links to click or too many screening questions, etc.

But before you get carried away with online selling, it is only fair to point out that not everyone is "click happy," and some would rather seek these same enjoyments in brick and mortar stores.

MARKETING IMPLICATIONS

Now that you know why online shoppers shop online, what would you do if you are a Web merchant? Clearly, since you know that three out of four online shoppers are goal-oriented, you need to provide, first and foremost, features that are important to them. So, as an online retailer, you must feature the widest assortment of products possible. If you sell Italian sofas, for example, then carry a virtually unlimited collection of sofas; at the same time, organize your inventory in easy-to-scan categories. Make detailed information available, but organize it under sub-headings that consumers may choose to view. Make possible side-by-side comparisons between two or more alternative brands. Give consumers the option to see products listed in rank order by price, by make, and by other relevant features. Finally, make your company's Web site remember the history of browsing by visitors who have registered, and you should definitely offer the option to save the shopping cart.

In addition, to cater to experiential browsers, you need to make your Web sites fun to navigate. Again, if you sell Italian leather sofas, you might feature some interesting facts about leather, and, maybe give a behind-the-scenes look at the making of the sofas. If you sell golf clubs, make the site a golfing information site rather than merely a golf-merchandise selling site; however, you must organize the site such that the goal-oriented shoppers can see the "golf-clubs" button clearly on the home page, so they are not hindered by information intended for experiential browsers.

To satisfy the "treasure hunt" motive of browsers, feature some rare merchandise, and also feature one or two items at a "terrific bargain." You may also feature one or two items available for auction, or at least feature some product/activity related contests of skill or chance like the game of rivets at the Levi's Web site. Finally, any animation and sensory features will go a long way in fulfilling the sensation-seeking motive of the browsers. It can be as simple as the virtual tour offered by the Jeep site, which also allows viewers to change the outdoor scenery surrounding the Jeep model being viewed. The leather sofa retailer could feature an animation where the consumer is able to change colors on any sofa to see how it will look in that color, place the sofa in various style rooms (e.g., contemporary, classic, etc.), or even show some snippets of a person living in the room furnished with the chosen sofa. In e-space, the possibilities of building audio-visual motion sensations around your product are virtually limitless. At the very least, the Web pages must be aesthetically pleasant to look at.

Satisfaction With Online Sellers

We discussed satisfaction with bricks and mortar stores in Chapter 13. The factors that lead to customer satisfaction with bricks and mortar stores also apply to online stores, but, in addition, a few new factors become relevant.[11] These factors pertain to pre-purchase and post purchase stages. Pre-purchase factors are (1) ease of navigation through the Web site, (2) quality of product information, (3) shopping cart and order ease, and (4) privacy and trust features. See Figure 19.1.

FIGURE 19.1 Factors of Consumer e-Satisfaction

Pre-Purchase Factors
- Ease of Navigation through the web site
- Quality of Product Information
- Shopping Cart and Order Ease
- Privacy and Trust Features

Post-Purchase Factors
- Keeping Informed
- Quality of Order Fulfillment
- Problem Resolution
- Multi-channel Customer Support

CONSUMER E-SATISFACTION

PRE-PURCHASE FACTORS

Site navigation can be confusing (if buttons are not easy to locate or not labeled well) and tedious (requiring too many mouse clicks), or the Web site can be visually clear, well organized, and a breeze to get through (only a few mouse clicks lead to the desired information). To be satisfied, consumers must find site navigation easy. But the Web site must go beyond easy navigation: It should provide quality information, the second factor on our list. This is because easy navigation means only that it gets you "there"(i.e., to the correct page) efficiently; but once you get there, the question is, what do you find on that page? Is the information comprehensive or sketchy, and is it easy to understand and process?. For example, is the information about various models and alternatives described in the same format, and is it possible to sort out various alternatives by price, features, makes, etc.? Thus, the quality of product information matters to consumer satisfaction.

The third factor for satisfaction is the ease and reasonableness of item selection and ordering procedures. For example, sometimes you may want to complete your shopping in more than one session; to enable this, the Web site should have the feature of saving your shopping cart. Also, shipping and handling costs should be reasonable, clear, and available before you place the item in the shopping cart (it can be very frustrating to spend the time to place 10 selections in the cart, click "shopping completed" or "proceed to checkout" (or whatever label they use) and then discover that shipping and handling costs are exorbitant.

Fourth, since you are going to be giving your credit card information to the online seller, you would want to know that the site offers secure transactions and that privacy policies are clearly stated and reassuring.

POST–PURCHASE FACTORS

Okay, you have placed the online order, and so far you are satisfied. But your dealings with the online retailer are not concluded yet. What happens between the time you place the online order and when you actually receive and use the product is also important. There are four features of online retailers post-order behavior that can cause you satisfaction or dissatisfaction. See Figure 19.1.

Keeping the Consumer Informed First, after you place the order, you like to be kept informed about the status of the order. Good online retailers such as Amazon.com send you an e-mail soon after you place the online order, confirming the details of your order. The company then sends another e-mail when the order is shipped. Moreover, many Web sites enable "order-tracking," so that you can go online and track the progress of your order any time. Consumers like this feature as it satisfies their need to stay informed about the status of their order.

Order Fulfillment After placing the online order, you hope and expect the merchandise to arrive on time and you expect it to be exactly what you ordered. If you order a sweatshirt of size "large" in blue, and then you open the package and find a size "medium" and in red, you are not going to be happy. And you also expect it to arrive on time, as promised. Timing is even more important for time-sensitive orders. For example, if you ordered flowers to be delivered to your Mom on her birthday, it is no use if the flowers are delivered a day late. Thus, the quality of order fulfillment is crucial for online consumer satisfaction.

Problem Resolution A mistake in order fulfillment is bad enough, but if getting that mistake corrected requires you to jump through hoops, then that is only going to aggravate you even more, causing grave dissatisfaction. The Web site should feature clear

SATISFYING ONLINE SHOPPERS EXHIBIT 19.3

Look What CB Researchers Found ...

In a recent survey of Internet shoppers, members of an NFO panel were surveyed by sending them an online survey via email. A total of 2108 panel members (prescreened to ensure that they had shopped online) were mailed the survey; 1007 members returned the survey.

The results showed that convenience was the most important driver of satisfaction; closely following it were site design and financial security. Product information (its quality and adequacy) also played some role. However, the product offerings (the variety and number of product offerings) played a less significant role in consumer satisfaction

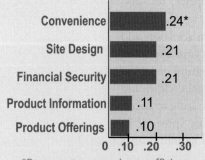

*Represents regression coefficients. A higher value implies greater importance of the factor. Thus, convenience, site design, and finacial security are twice as important as product information and product offerings.

Measuring Components of e-Retail Experience

Q1. Compared to bricks & mortar retail stores, how would you rate Internet storefront on the following aspects:

(Much worse than 1 2 3 4 5 6 7 Much better than)

A. Convenience
- Ease of browsing — 1 2 3 4 5 6 7
- Total shopping time — 1 2 3 4 5 6 7
- Convenience — 1 2 3 4 5 6 7

B. Merchandise--Product offerings
- Number of product offerings — 1 2 3 4 5 6 7
- Variety of product offerings — 1 2 3 4 5 6 7

C. Product Information
- Quality of information — 1 2 3 4 5 6 7
- Adequacy of information — 1 2 3 4 5 6 7

D. Financial Security
- Financial security of the transaction 1 2 3 4 5 6 7

Q2. Rate the site design for Internet storefronts
(Scale: 1 Poor – 5 Excellent)
- Presenting uncluttered screen — 1 2 3 4 5
- Providing easy to follow search paths — 1 2 3 4 5
- Presenting information fast — 1 2 3 4 5

Q3. Overall, how do you feel about your Internet shopping experience

Very displeased — 1 2 3 4 5 6 7 — Very pleased

Very dissatisfied — 1 2 3 4 5 6 7 — Very satisfied

Source: Excerpted from David M. Szymanski and Richard T. Hise, "e-Satisfaction: An Initial Validation," *Journal of Retailing*, Vol. 76(3) 2000, 309-322. © The New York University. Used with permission.

instructions on what to do if you have any problem with your order. If you need to make a change after placing the order (say, you want to change that blue sweatshirt to gray), you should be able to do it online. And, you should definitely be able to return the wrong merchandise, and be able to do so with ease and without incurring any costs. In a recent survey of online consumers, as many as 67 % of online shoppers desired that a retailer's agent pick up the product returns, and nearly 35% considered this a "must have" feature.[12]

Multi-channel Customer Support As a consumer, sometimes you just want to speak to a live person to explain your need or problem. Does an online retailer offer this option? Good online retailers offer consumers the option of contacting customer service through multiple channels. On the FTD.com Web site (an online flower retailer), for example, if you click on customer service, it offers you three options: a toll free phone number (1-800-send-FTD), an e-mail option, and a postal mail address. In the same survey of online shoppers we cited earlier, 95% of consumers said that online retailers should have "toll free telephone access for customer service."

Consumer Liking for Web Sites

The factors in consumer satisfaction with online vendors are broader than for their liking for Web sites in general. When consumers visit a Web site for reasons other than buying, what other features are important? The information content continues to be an important dimension, of course, but a few other features become influential. These are: personalization, communities, graphics style and multimedia sensory experience, and cultural congruency.

Personalization **Personalization** on the Web can be defined as giving users the information they seek without their asking for it. Web sites track consumers' online click stream and analyze these data to identify consumer tastes and preferences—what kind of things the consumer searches for. The next time you visit that Web site, it automatically presents that information. A prime example is Amazon.com's personalization: When you visit that site from your computer, it automatically flags books and titles likely to be of interest to you (assuming, of course, that you are accessing the site via the same computer as before). Of course, companies should be careful since there is a fine line between helpful personalization and personal intrusion.

Communities Next, many consumers like a Web site based on communities it features. Microsoft, for example, has a community site for users to chat. Users post their questions and comments; another consumer answers their question. Many users like to answer other users' questions and they like to read comments others have posted.

Graphics and multi-sensory features Third, graphics and multi-sensory features play a role. For many users, graphics can slow down the surfing experience and can otherwise interfere with their surfing goals, particularly for task-oriented consumers. On the other hand, well-designed graphics and multi-sensory (i.e., audio visual) features can enhance the experience, particularly for fun-seeking surfers.

Cultural Congruency Cultural congruency refers to how similar the culture depicted in the Web site is to the audience's culture.

Imagine two Web sites for the same product (say, cameras) by the same company: one is in Spanish and the other in English. Both sites feature the same product and both use a celebrity as a spokesperson and show some people having a good time together, captured by a few snap shots. The English site featured roommates at a Thanksgiving dinner enjoying a turkey; the Spanish site showed a family having dinner on the day of the Feast of the Three Kings (a Spanish celebration) and eating paella (a Spanish traditional meal). As for the celebrity, the English language site features Helen Hunt while the Spanish language site features Penelope Cruz.

Which site do you think consumers would like more? In a research study, non-Hispanic Americans liked the English Web site better, while Hispanics liked the Spanish Web site better. It was not just because of the language. Other elements of Web sites that were culturally congruent also played a big role. Think global; act local.[13]

How Consumers Perceive Online Shopping

Consumers know that every purchase they make entails some risk. Many consumers perceive these risks to be greater in the online channel. A recent study examined four type of risks consumers perceived in online shopping: financial risk (defined in the study as the risk of credit card information being misused), performance risk (defined as the difficulty of judging quality), psychological risk (defined as one's personal information not being kept private), and time/inconvenience risk (online purchase might turn out to be more time taking or more hassle-some). The study compared three groups of consumers: browsers, light online shoppers, and heavy online shoppers. Its findings were exactly what we would intuitively expect: browsers perceived these risks the most, heavy shoppers the least, and light shoppers were in the middle. See Figure 19.2. That is, even among consumers who did go online searching for products, these perceived risks prevented them from going beyond browsing and completing the purchase transaction online.[14]

Consumers' risk perceptions are attenuated by two factors: prior experience and risk aversion personality. Consumers who have shopped online before are the ones most likely to shop again. This is because their prior experience turned out to be positive and risk-free. For example, in one study with survey data from more than a million respondents of an ebizrate.com survey (after a consumer makes a purchase on a site, ebizrate.com presents a banner ad asking them to complete a survey of the site—ebizrate.com administers this survey on more than 2,000 e-retailer sites), it was found that consumers who were buying online for the first time ordered on an average 1.8 items per order. In contrast, moderate buyers (those who had bought 4 to 5 times from a given merchant) ordered 2.4 items, and heavy online buyers (those who had ordered 11-20 times from the merchant) ordered 3 items per order on an average.[15] Another national survey showed that consumers who had made an online purchase in the past three months were more (80%) likely to make another purchase in the subsequent three months. That degree of likelihood plummets to about 20% if no prior purchase had been made.[16] Familiarity breeds reduced risk perception and, consequently, comfort.

The second factor is the consumer's own **risk-averseness**. Some consumers are more risk averse (i.e., they like to avoid risks) than others. In one research study, risk aversion, as a personality trait, was a strong predictor of whether consumers would shop online or not. Those who shopped online frequently were much less risk-averse (i.e., more risk taking) than those who shopped online occasionally or not at all. On a scale of 1 to 6 where "1" meant risk taking and "6" meant risk averse, the former group scored 1.33 (risk taking) compared to the latter group's average score of approximately 3.5.[17]

Consumers are more inclined, naturally, to buy low risk products online, such as CDs, printer ink cartridges, and blank cassettes. They are less likely to buy high-ticket items and risky products such as electronics, jewelry and watches, and colognes. Of course, this risk is mitigated, even for expensive items, by two factors. The first factor is longevity

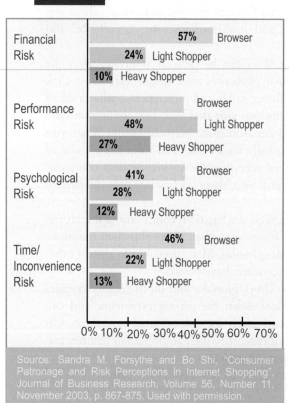

FIGURE 19.2

PERCEIVED RISKS OF ONLINE SHOPPING AMONG BROWSERS, LIGHT SHOPPERS, And HEAVY SHOPPERS

Source: Sandra M. Forsythe and Bo Shi, "Consumer Patronage and Risk Perceptions in Internet Shopping", Journal of Business Research, Volume 56, Number 11, November 2003, p. 867-875. Used with permission.

VI CONSUMERS IN THE NEW MILLENNIUM

and prevalence of an online channel for that product category. If consumers know that a particular product category is usually sold online, then they accept online to be an established and, therefore, a relatively risk-free channel. Thus, high priced computers and printers are bought online, but consumers are hesitant to buy watches or jewelry, simply because of the former product group's longevity and prevalence in online selling.

The second factor is if the retailer name or brand name (or both) are well-known and reputed, then consumers perceive less risk and are willing to buy online. In one study, if the retailer was an established retailer, consumers expressed greater likelihood of buying a product even if the brand name itself was new. Likewise, the purchase of an established brand was seen less risky than a new brand, and this was so even when the online retailer was not an established retailer.[18]

Another study explored the online retailer features that consumers desired in greater detail. The study, done by Indiana University marketing professor Raymond R. Burke, asked consumers to indicate which features they considered "must have" and which features the online storefronts (i.e., Web sites) "should have."[19] Selected data from this study is presented in Table 19.7.

Almost all consumers (more than 90%) want price information. But a significant number also want such features as product warranty information, product and feature comparisons, and expert quality ratings on products. About one in four saw these figures as "must have," while more than 50% thought Web sites "should have" these features.

What was perhaps most revealing in this study is the value customers see in integrating the off line retailers with online presence. Many customers want to browse product information on the Web but buy the item in real stores. Or they want to order online but then pick it up at the local store. Likewise, they want to buy online but be able to return a wrong purchase to the physical store.

TABLE 19.7	Online Retailer Website Features Consumers Consider Important—The Must Have & Should Have Features	
Store Features	**Must Have (%)**	**Should Have (%)**
Product Information		
Online Product Prices	93	98
Product specifications, usage instructions & warranty information	57	82
Comparison of product prices across online stores	28	67
Comparison or products across brands	20	60
Expert ratings of product quality	20	57
Payment, Fulfillment, Customer Service		
Email order confirmation	73	94
Secure payment system	69	84
Online shipment tracking	56	87
Retailer's agent picks up returns	35	67
Pay retailer when merchandise is returned	25	57
Shopping Aids		
Website saves prior purchase records	29	68
Website save shipping and billing information for one click ordering	22	57
Clicks & Mortar Integration		
Product prices & promotions in nearby stores	64	92
Product returns to nearby retail stores	34	73
Product pick up at retail stores	24	60

Source: Excerpted from Raymond R. Burke, "Technology and the Customer Interface: What Consumers Want in the Physical and Virtual Store," *Journal of the Academy of Marketing Science*, Fall 2002, 30(4), 411-432. (Used with permission.)

The lesson of this story is that pure online stores—stores without a brick and mortar counterpart—are less likely to appeal to some consumers. And those companies that have both brick and mortar and online stores need to integrate the two channels rather than run them as independent operations. These retailers should give consumers the ability to choose whichever channel they like for individual steps and components of the transaction.

To Which Segment Do You Belong?

A. SEGMENTS AMONG ONLINE SHOPPERS

Shopping Lovers (11.1%)

As its name implies, the segment loves to shop online and accounts for the highest level of purchases among online consumers. Consumers in this segment have an average age of 44, and average household income $60,200. About 36 percent are college graduates.

The primary home computer in this segment is in use 26.6 hours per week, with 16.2 hours online use. Shopping Lovers agree with the statements, "I like browsing on the Internet," and. "I search for lowest price in everything." As Table 19.12 shows they find Internet shopping fun and hassle free.

Adventuresome Explorers (8.9%)

This segment has an average age of 45.8 and average household income of $61,500. About 35 percent are college graduates. People in this segment are versatile and prolific in their online use. They are higher than other segments in the use of their computer for checking or sending e-mail messages; in looking at financial information (stocks, trends); reading on-line news or magazines; visiting Internet sites related to [their] hobbies; visiting sites looking for tickets or reservations; looking for job opportunities; finding and viewing photographs, clipart, or images; searching for or download software; chatting on-line; and in visiting message news-groups. Online shopping is fun for these people; it is just one more adventure for them to explore.

Suspicious Learners (9.7%)

This segment has an average age of 49.6 and an average household income of $58,300. About 42 percent are college graduates. The primary home computer in these households is in use for 21.5 hours per week, of which 13 hours is online. Their compute literacy is low. Their online use is primarily to play games; visit sites looking for tickets or reservations; chat online; look for job opportunities; and to find and view photographs, clipart, or images.

People in this segment are just learning how to use the Internet. They are frustrated by it, struggling to complete tasks. They strongly agree with the statements, "I want to see things in person before I buy," and "It's hard to judge merchandise quality on Internet."

Business Users (12.5%)

This segment has an average age of 47.5, and average household income of $64,000. This segment has 88 percent college graduates. Business Users are more likely than any segment use their online access to conduct business-related work. They are less likely than any segment to chat online or to go online to play games. Business Users are not troubled by any of the issues that so many would-be shoppers struggle with—fear of online credit card theft, lack of trust of Internet retailers, or lack of knowledge about the Internet.

B. THE ONLINE NON-SHOPPER SEGMENTS

Fearful Browsers (10.6%)

This segment has an average age of 44 and average household income of $63,700. About 43 percent are college graduates. The primary home computer in this household is in use 23.8 hours per week, of which 14.8 hours is online. Even though this segment does not purchase online, its people do like to visit online vendor sites. When online, they most often visit auction sites, other retail sites looking for merchandise, sites offering tickets or reservations, and Internet sites related to their hobbies.

This segment consists of lookers, not buyers. Along with other non-shoppers, this segment is fearful of several online risks: having their credit card number stolen, shipping charges, and wishing they could see products in person before they buy.

Shopping Avoiders (15.6%)

With an average age of 56, this is the oldest group. Average household income is for people $61,700, and 70 percent are college graduates. People in this segment like to use the Internet to look at financial information (stocks, trends); check or send e-mail messages; read on-line news or magazines; play games; and to conduct business-related work. But they abhor shopping online, holding values which are inconsistent with Internet shopping. For example, they want to see things in person before buying, find it a hassle to return merchandise bought on-line, and don't want to give credit card number to an online Web site.

Technology Muddlers. (19.5%)

This segment has an average age of 49.3, and an average household income of $54,400. About 62 percent are college graduates. People in this segment use the computer the least of any segment, and are the least computer-literate. Their favorite uses for the Internet are to look for job opportunities; chat on-line; play games; visit message news-groups; and conduct business-related work. Just like the preceding segment, they also have strong hesitation to give their credit card number to a Web site, and want to see merchandise in person.

Fun Seekers (12%)

This segment has an average age of 49.3, and an average household income of $48,100. About 25 percent are college graduates.

The primary home computer in this household is in use for 30.6 hours per week, of which 21.5 hours is online. Among the eight segments, this is the highest in computer use. Members of this segment look to the Internet for its entertainment value. They like to use the Internet to play games; chat on-line; find & view photographs, clipart, or images; search for or download software; and visit Internet sites related to [their] hobbies. But they do not like using it for shopping, fearing privacy concern and feeling uncomfortable buying anything without seeing it in person.

Note: Segment sizes (in percent) are proportion of all online consumers. Of these, online shoppers make up 42.2%)

Source: William R. Swinyard and Scott M. Smith, "Why People (Don't) Shop Online: A Lifestyle Study of the Internet Consumer," *Psychology & Marketing*, June/July 2003. (Used with permission).

The Consumer Internet Barometer

Because consumer trust and satisfaction is important to e-businesses, it is paramount to measure and track it. One measure does just that. It is called the Consumer Internet Barometer. Based on a quarterly survey of 10,000 households, the Consumer Internet Barometer is produced jointly by The Conference Board and the Taylor Nelson Sofres Plc (TNS). For Q1 2006, the Barometer showed that 67.4% of surveyed adults used the Internet. But only 45.3% were satisfied, and 25.0 trusted the Web sites they used. Check out the current readings at http://www.conference-board.org.

SEGMENTS AMONG ONLINE SHOPPERS

Not all consumers shop online for the same reason. Some prefer to shop online because of convenience. Others go online because they believe they get a better assortment. Those who are price-sensitive and do comparison-shopping even in the bricks & mortar stores probably go online in search of better prices. A recent research study identified four segments among online shoppers, and likewise four segments among non-shoppers. Their perception profile is presented in Exhibit 19.4.

INTERNET BEYOND SHOPPING

INTERNET IN THE LIFE OF TEENS

"I multi-task every single second I am online. At this very moment, I am watching TV, checking my email every two minutes, reading a newsgroup about who shot JFK, burning some music to a CD and writing this message."
— A 17-year-old boy[20]

"The Internet is the telephone, television, game console, and radio wrapped up in one for most teenagers and that means it has become a major 'player' in many American families. Teens go online to chat with their friends, kill boredom, see the wider world, and follow the latest trends. Many enjoy doing all those things at the same time during their online sessions. Multitasking is their way of life. And the emotional hallmark of that life is enthusiasm for the new ways the Internet lets them connect with friends, expand their social networks, explore their identities, and learn new things."[21]

"Among the many striking things about teens' use of the Internet is the way they have adapted instant messaging technologies to their own purposes. The majority of teenagers have embraced instant messaging in a way that adults have not, and many use it as the main way to conduct most mundane as well as the most emotionally fraught and important conversations of their daily lives. They have invented a new hieroglyphics of emoticons [text-based sequence of characters that depict human emotions, such as a tearful eye] to add context and meaning to their messages and a growing list of abbreviations to help them speed their way through multiple, simultaneous online conversations."[22]

According to a survey by Pew Internet Organization in late 2000, 45% of all American children under the age of 18 go online. Of those, between 12 and 17, 73% go online; of those 11 or younger, 29% go online. Children who go online come disproportionately from higher income and more educated families. Forty two percent of all online teens go online everyday (in comparison, 59% of all online U.S. adults go online everyday). While one-third go online only a couple of times a week, a considerable number are heavy users and go online everyday. Among the heavy and enthusiastic users, most go online everyday to check email. The next highest level activity is the use of Instant Messaging (89%). Listening to music, downloading music, and researching products (without buying) is the next set of activities (70-74%); about 60% visit a chat room; and 39% have bought something online.

Research has shown that the use of Internet helps teenagers further their friendship ties. Teens who already have many friends in the physical world use the Internet to email and IM to them, and thus strengthen their pre-existing bonds. Those with few pre-existing friendships use the Internet to find new friends.[23]

While social communications (emails and IM) and recreational activities (playing online games, downloading music, listening to music online, etc.,) dominate teenagers' use of the Internet, they also use it considerably to find out what is "cool" and to do online shopping. More than half (54%) of teenagers say that they use the Internet to find out what is cool in fashion and music. About 66% of online teens have used the Internet to research products they were considering buying. And about half of the latter group (31%) has actually shopped online. In part, this gap between online browsing and shopping is due to lack of credit card availability to teens. It is also because some consumers (teens and adults alike) prefer to buy items from a physical store even though they might research them online.

Internet Mavens

Increasingly, teens are getting exposed to marketplace information through the Internet. And many teens are a source of information even for products their parents want to buy. Parents who know that their teen children are more adept at using the Internet tend to ask their teen son or daughter to search for the product on the Internet.

In fact, teens who may not have been particularly interested in the broad marketplace information, or news from their physical world (things broader than their narrow personal interests), or may not have had time to acquire much marketplace information, might now develop a new-found interest both in news and marketplace information simply because they get exposed to it while surfing the Net. This group of teenagers may be termed **Internet Mavens**. In an earlier chapter, we defined market mavens as consumers who possess market information about a cross-section of products and are generally more knowledgeable (than the general population) about what is available in the market and what is new there; they serve as a source of market information to others. Analogously, an Internet Maven is a consumer who is more knowledgeable than the average consumer about the e-marketplace, and about product information available on the Internet.

In one study, it was found that teens who used the Internet heavily and for diverse purposes (work, school, entertainment) were more likely (than other teens who used the Internet less) to be perceived (by both themselves and their parents) to be Internet Mavens. Furthermore these Internet maven teens influenced their parents' decisions on the choice of a family vacation destination.[24] To what other product categories this influence will extend, and whether it will extend to product categories parents want to buy for themselves, has not been researched. But it is logical to expect that Internet savvy teens will exercise considerable influence as a source of information on their family's choice of a wide range of products, especially new technology products for use in homes.

CYBERSPACE AND THE PURSUIT OF FAITH

The Internet has also become a way for consumers to obtain life satisfaction that the practice of their faith and religion brings them. According to a 2001 survey of some 2,247 American adults, about 28 million Americans have surfed a religious Web site. A majority (91%) of these religious adults are Christians, which reflects their proportion (77%) in the U.S. population. Yet, among the religion-seeking surfers, minority religions are equally well represented. Twenty five percent of all U.S. Internet users have obtained religious or spiritual information at one time or another. Every day, more than three million consumers log on to a religious web site. This is more than the number of U.S. consumers who have gambled online, done online banking, traded stocks online, or used online dating services.[25]

Finding Religion Online

Religious surfers engage in a variety of activities online. Two out of three go online to look for information about their faith. A little more than one in three of them have downloaded religious music, e-mailed a request for a prayer, given spiritual guidance to someone, and/or bought a religious item online. About one in four have downloaded sermons, obtained ideas for ways to celebrate religious holidays, and sought spiritual guidance via email. About 14% have gone online to find a new church, and one in ten have participated in religious chat rooms. About 4% have participated in online worship, 3% have taken an online religion course, and 3% have used a faith-oriented matchmaking service. Perhaps the most noteworthy fact about online religious surfers is that they are very open-minded about other religions, eager to learn about them: 50% of them went online to look for information about another faith. See Table 19.8.

Internet Religion Does Not Make Churches Irrelevant

The Internet brings religion closer to members of congregations as well as non-members. For non-members, the Internet serves as a more convenient and psychologically comforting avenue. Not connected to or socialized into any offline congregation, they find it easier to relate to other "virtual" worshippers, and they also find the precise religious activities of the offline congregation they're seeking. The Pew Internet Reports puts it well.

The most enthusiastic beneficiaries of the Internet are those who do not belong to a congregation of worshippers. Non-members as a whole are less likely to describe themselves as having a "somewhat' or "very" strong commitment to their faith (81% Vs 99%) but they are by no means less interested in the state of their souls. The Internet appears to provide for them many of the benefits of a congregation. Non-members are almost twice as likely as members to find it easier to meet people of their faith online than offline. They are also more likely to rely on the Internet than on offline resources for reference materials, faith-oriented conversations, prayer resources, worship, speaking with clergy, and finding volunteer opportunities.[26]

As regards to the members of congregations, 83% of congregations who participated in a study reported that their Web sites had helped the spiritual life of their congregation. Whereas non-members do outpace members in perceiving the Internet as an easier source of many religious activities, members also find that the Internet is quite helpful in finding these activities online. See Table 19.9.

TABLE 19.9 Online Benefits Perceived by Congregation Members & Non-Members

The Percent who say it is easier online than offline	Non Members	Members
To access reference materials	77%	62%
To learn about volunteer activities	31%	14%
To meet people of the same faith	28%	15%
To participate in faith-oriented conversation	18%	9%
To speak with clergy	15%	6%

Source: Pew Internet & American Life Project Religion Surfer Survey, in Elena Larsen, p.20. www.perinternet.org. (Used iwth permission.)

The Pew Internet reports summarizes it thus:

By creating better ties within a pre-existing community, by creating a Web presence, and by facilitating discussions that can be difficult to hold in other settings, congregations tightened bonds within their groups, re-established connection with former members, and in some cases, expanded mission on a global scale.[27]

―――――――― O ――――――――

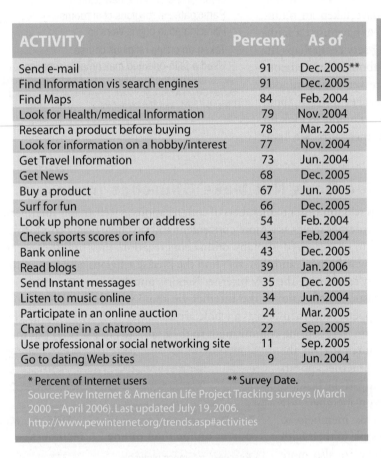

ACTIVITY	Percent	As of
Send e-mail	91	Dec. 2005**
Find Information vis search engines	91	Dec. 2005
Find Maps	84	Feb. 2004
Look for Health/medical Information	79	Nov. 2004
Research a product before buying	78	Mar. 2005
Look for information on a hobby/interest	77	Nov. 2004
Get Travel Information	73	Jun. 2004
Get News	68	Dec. 2005
Buy a product	67	Jun. 2005
Surf for fun	66	Dec. 2005
Look up phone number or address	54	Feb. 2004
Check sports scores or info	43	Feb. 2004
Bank online	43	Dec. 2005
Read blogs	39	Jan. 2006
Send Instant messages	35	Dec. 2005
Listen to music online	34	Jun. 2004
Participate in an online auction	24	Mar. 2005
Chat online in a chatroom	22	Sep. 2005
Use professional or social networking site	11	Sep. 2005
Go to dating Web sites	9	Jun. 2004

CONSUMER ACTIVITIES ON THE INTERNET

TABLE 19.10

* Percent of Internet users   ** Survey Date.
Source: Pew Internet & American Life Project Tracking surveys (March 2000 – April 2006). Last updated July 19, 2006.
http://www.pewinternet.org/trends.asp#activities

KEY TERMS

Goal-oriented Online Shoppers
Experiential Browsers
Digital Products
Experiential products
High touch products
Book-mark

Web surfers
Treasure hunt
Emoticons
Low-context information
Internet Maven
Flow

Cognitive Lock-in
Switching Costs
Immediacy bias
Web site Stickiness

VI CONSUMERS IN THE NEW MILLENNIUM

The Internet. What will life be without it? Its use is growing everyday, both in population penetration and range of online activity. The latest stats on online activity are shown in Table 19.10; use it as a baseline and monitor it periodically—for example at the end of the course, or year or quarter, using the Pew Internet site the table footnotes. That in itself can be a fascinating and informative exercise.

Since you are reading this book, you are the kind who depends on the Internet for information. For your class projects or for your work projects. And, of course, you surf the net for entertainment and for product information. You already buy at least a few products on the net. The Internet is transforming the way consumers shop. It has empowered consumers vis-a-vis marketers. And savvy marketers are removing the few barriers that consumers have historically experienced. Such as the difficulty of returning the merchandise—by integrating online and physical stores—thus, you can buy online and return the merchandise in the neighborhood physical store. And new tools to visualize the merchandise, and sometimes, customize it. The ranks of Internet users is bound to grow, around the world.

Want to experience a state of *flow?*
Transport yourself to the Web site www.youtube.com. You can have hours of entertaining video journey. If your goal is more task-oriented information search, then Google or Yahoo or MSN or any number of other search portals will serve you well. This book has depended a lot on Google. For the information we printed; and also for the information we did not—you see, knowing that you could always search the Web for anything, we felt less the need to answer every potential "What is that" question.
Hint, hint: Google, dude/dudess, google!

SUMMARY

We began this chapter by describing the Internet consumer universe—the number of people using the Internet worldwide (580 million) and in major countries. Among U.S. consumers, male and female users are roughly equal; Internet usage is higher among Hispanics and lower among African-Americans than Caucasians. It is also the highest among the 18-29 age group, and lowest amongst the 65+ age group. The most common use of the Internet is for e-mail. A majority of consumers consider the Internet as a legitimate and expected source of information both for government and commercial information, and indeed, they find that their expectations are fairly well met.

Next, we discussed the two broad groups of consumers who go online: goal-oriented searchers and experiential Internet surfers. The goals and motives of each group are different. Goal-oriented shoppers seek efficiency in purchasing and a sense of freedom and control. Certain features of the Web in general, and individual Web sites, in particular satisfy these goals. On the other hand, experiential browsers go online seeking enjoyment, and here, too, certain other features of the Web become relevant. These features were discussed.

Finally, we covered two facets of online consumer behavior that go beyond shopping. One, we described the behavior of teenagers. Most Internet savvy of all age groups, teenage consumers spend considerable time on the Web, enjoying its linking and communication benefits to enhance their social life. Second, we examined the utilization of the Internet for practicing one's faith. The Internet can enhance the religious experience of both those who belong to a congregation and those who do not. These serve as illustrations of how marketers (of commercial and non-commercial enterprises alike) can harness the Internet to bring more benefits to onsumers.

REVIEW✛Rewind

1. How would you describe the Internet Consumer Universe? Roughly, what proportion of consumers worldwide are Internet users, and which countries are at the forefront?
2. Describe major segments of Internet consumers and briefly describe their Internet surfing behavior.
3. Describe the major differences between the goals, motivations, and experiences of goal-oriented shoppers versus experiential browsers.
4. Describe factors that determine whether or not an online shopper will be satisfied with the online shopping experience.
5. Which type of products are most appropriate for buying online? Which type are least appropriate? Why?

THINK✛Apply

1. Reflect on your own recent online shopping experience. Then assess to what extent each of the goals of goal-oriented shoppers described in the chapter were true in your experience.
2. If you wanted to target each of the four types of segments described in the chapter for (a) clothing and (b) electronic appliances, discuss for each product line how your Web design and online marketing would be different for each segment.
3. How can churches use the Internet to improve the value they offer their members?

PRACTICE✛Experience

1. Visit the Web sites of two competing vendors of the same product, and rate each Web site on the attributes that online goal-oriented shoppers seek. Now, repeat this exercise from the perspective of experiential browsers.
2. Interview three consumers about their most recent online shopping experiences. Ask each of them to describe one instance where they were satisfied, and one instance where they were not. Then ask for reasons for their satisfaction or dissatisfaction. Summarize your findings and comment on the extent to which the reasons discussed in the chapter were or were not verified in these consumer experiences.
3. Conduct an in-depth interview of five consumers, trying to assess their online shopping behavior pattern. Then determine which of the segments described in the chapter best fits them. [Note: Do not tell them or ask them about the segments or segment-specific behaviors. Instead it is your job to figure it out.]. Justify your answers. Then, think about what you would do differently (in respect to Web design and other marketing efforts) to reach and appeal to each type of these consumers.

In the Marketing Manager's Shoes

Put yourself in a marketing manager's shoes. Most concepts in the chapter have some lessons for the marketing manager, i.e., they suggest what to do differently in practice; indeed, often these applications are implicit in our explanations of the concepts and models in the chapter. Identify at least five specific applications of the chapter's concepts, all of which should be entirely new—different from the examples cited here.

that's why I bluefly.com

A Photo Quiz

Study the ads by Bluefly.com. We believe they capture the experience of many shoppers and the relief these shoppers find switching to online shopping.

Do the reasons given here (*Why I Bluefly*) represent the situations consumers typically face? What kind of consumers? Goal-oriented shoppers or explorers? And, for what kind of products and shopping tasks?

What kind of consumers will find these ads appealing? Will the ads convert non-online shoppers to online shoppers? Why or why not?

(Sorry, the adjacent ad text is not legible, but its theme is similar to the ad below.)

(Ads courtesy of Bluefly.com)

Crisis.
I need a little black dress.
Not just *any* little black dress.
The little black dress.
Okay, I admit.
I have a closet full of
little black dresses.
Just not *the* little black dress.

You know what I mean?

that's why I...

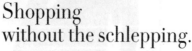

CB LEVEL 2.0

COMPARISON SHOPPING ON THE INTERNET

An important question is this: Do consumers engage in more comparison shopping or less in cyberspace? We know that in the physical marketplace, consumers undertake very limited information search, often limited to one or two stores and one or two brands. But because the costs of information search are very low in cyberspace (as the various online stores are just a mouse click away), we would expect the online consumer to engage in extensive information search. However, research has found that consumers searching for products and shopping online actually do very limited information search. In one study based on panel data from 10,000 consumers, it was found that on an average consumers visited, only 1.2 CD sites, 1.1 book sites, and 1.8 travel sites. Why? There are three factors that explain why consumers do limited search online: switching costs, cognitive lock-in, and immediacy bias.

Switching costs   *Switching Costs* are costs in time and effort that consumers have to incur in searching a new store or a new Web site and shopping from there. When you take your insurance business to another insurance company for example, you have to fill out an application, and also understand new company's

offerings and terms and conditions. Even if the terms and price of new company turn out to be better, there is the effort of opening a new account. Likewise on the Web, many sites require you to register before browsing, and at any rate you have to fill in your credit card and address information while purchasing the product or service from that company. This switching cost encourages consumers, both in the offline and online marketplaces, to stick with one's current suppliers.[28]

Cognitive lock-in The second factor refers to a mental predisposition to visit the site with which one has had prior experience. The consumer becomes naturally biased in favor of visiting the sites previously visited and navigated, and develops a disinclination (if not resistance) to visit other sites. Of course, the prior experience has to have been a positive one; if the Web site of the vendor from whom the consumer bought or attempted to buy last time proved cumbersome to navigate, then the consumer is likely to explore a new site, but even here the consumer's exploration is likely to be limited to one or two new sites. Some experts have tried to explain cognitive lock-in as "user skills" or habit; the consumer develops the skill to use a site and perceives himself or herself to be skilled in navigating that site and unskilled in navigating alternative sites. Not that this thought of being "unskilled" is explicit; rather the task of visiting a new site is deemed to entail having to learn how to navigate that site (i.e., how to find the relevant linkages to the required information). Generally the switching costs are greater in the bricks and mortar market due to the cost of physical travel to a new store and/or having to talk to a new service provider. Yet, consumer loyalty is greater online than offline. This has been called "site stickiness," a site's ability to get the consumer to not leave the site and/or to come back to the same site in the future. The reason for this goes beyond switching costs. It is because of cognitive lock-in.[29]

Immediacy bias One great benefit of the Internet is that you don't have to wait for the physical store to open. Thanks to the 24/7 network news channels, consumers now expect the news immediately. This desire for immediate outcome is called *immediacy bias*. The Internet satisfies this consumer motive as far as consumer desire for immediate information is concerned. But the same bias also becomes a liability in relation to information search. The immediacy bias produces a tendency to grab what one can instantly and run (rather than dig some more in the hope of finding a better deal). In other words, the immediacy bias has produced an inertia against browsing additional sites. Consequently, even though consumers might suspect that a search of a new Web site (or visit to a new store) might help them find a better deal, and once found, that better deal would be available for all future occasions, they tend not to undertake the search of alternative Web sites. Indeed, research has found that consumers stick to the same site with which they have had prior experience,

WHY THE INTERNET IS NOT A FRICTIONLESS MARKET?

Cognitive lock-in also explains, why online marketers don't have to go for the lowest price strategy? Because going from one store to the other is very easy, being only a mouse click away, experts thought the online market was frictionless; i.e., navigation across sites encountered no friction. And therefore, the frictionless market would work as an equalizer across competitors who would be forced to offer their comparable merchandise at the same price. In reality, the prices are different across sites and the online markets turned out to be anything but frictionless. Cognitive lock-in explains why the Internet is not a frictionless marketplace. As more and more companies opened their online storefronts, making more and more products available for online shopping, the experts had initially predicted that prices for products would decrease and that they would also level off across merchants. The

logic was that because the costs of searching the alterative vendors were very low for consumers (because one mouse click was all it would take to visit a new Web store), consumers would engage in more comparison shopping. Contrary to this initial expectation, however, research found that few consumers generally visit more than one site (and fewer visit more than two). And this is the case even for commodity-like products (i.e., products where there are no feature differences) for which the price should be the only basis of comparison. Since consumers do not search multiple sites, cyber vendors are indeed able to keep their prices at levels they consider appropriate rather than routinely match competitors' prices.[30]

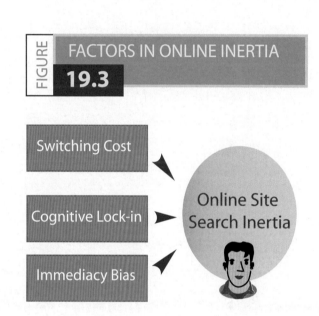

FIGURE 19.3 FACTORS IN ONLINE INERTIA

Review for Level 2.0

Q1. Explain in your own words the concepts of (a) Cognitive lock-in, (b) Switching Costs, (c) Immediacy bias, and (d) Flow. What is their relevance to consumer behavior and why should a market know about them.

Q2. Interview five consumers to understand what causes them to switch around Web sites versus sticking to one or two of them for specific topics or product categories. Do you find evidence of such factors as cognitive lock-in, perceived switching costs (specify what these costs for these consumers are), immediacy bias, and flow? Illustrate your findings.

Marketers, Public Policy, And Consumer Conscience

Who Is Watching Whom

- Questionable Marketing Practices
- Ills of Advertising—Over-commercialism
- Big Brother Watching—Protecting the Consumer
- Consumer Conscience—Wanting to Gain Without Paying
- Obseity—The Curse of Over Consumption
- Every Culture Is Fat Culture

The Bitter Joy Of Winning A Million Dollar Lottery That You Did Not Even Play

ttnetion: Sir/Madam,

We happily announce to you the draw of the LOTTERY UK INTERNATIONAL, Online Program held on 14-Jan-2006. Your email and address attached to reference Number: 208,ZK,11,663/ UK with Ticket Number: 99/bnk/533. which subsequently won you one of the Jackpot cash prizes.

You have therefore been approved to claim a total sum of £3,200,000.00 (Three Million Two Hundred Thousand Great Britain Pounds) in cash credited to file L/UK/010/71/2/33 ...To file for your claim, please contact our claims director via contact information below;...
Congratulation once again from me, and entire members of staff of the LOTTERY UK INTERNATIONAL and it is our hope that you participate in any of our international programs in the nearest future.

Too good to be true. But the greed gets the better of some of us. To the delight of scam artists.

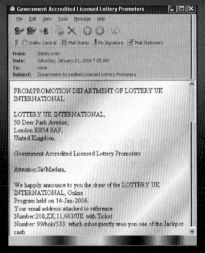

Thank you.
Yours faithfully,
CHRISTY IVAN,
PROMOTION DEPARTMENT,
LOTTERY UK INTERNATIONAL,
50 Deer Park Avenue,
London EH54 8AF,
United Kingdom.
email: ivanchristy@
lotteryukinternational.com

PLEASE NOTE: YOU ARE TO KEEP ALL LOTTERY INFORMATIONS FROM PUBLIC AS WE WILL NOT ENTERTAIN CASES OF MULTIPLE CLAIMS PROCESSING OR COMPROMISE THE PRIVACY AND SECURITY OF ALL OUR WINNER.THIS IS IN LINE WITH THE DATA PROTECTION ACT OF THE LOTTERY UK INTERNATIONAL

INTRODUCTION

his email, received by author, is part of a scam called 419 Schemes, so named after the Nigerian law under which such schemes are prosecuted. The scamming companies operate out of Nigeria (with affiliate divisions using a UK address). Lottery winning notices are just one of the many ploys these companies use. Other ploys include a letter from some imposter posing as a helpless heir to a large fund (or on his/ her behalf, from someone posing as an attorney). The recipient is promised a portion of the fund (typically 15%) for providing help in getting that fund deposited in a new account to be opened by the recipient. If you receive one such letter and respond, after a series of correspondence you would be asked to deposit some advance fee (thousands of dollars) to obtain the release of the funds from local authorities!

The deception is orchestrated with elaborate props. If you ask for proof, for example, they will send you a *Certificate of Winning*, official documentation indicating the funds, photos of the deceased rich uncle, a notarized passport with photo—the whole works, all fake, of course. Out of greed for the windfall income, once you part with your hard-earned money, the company simply disappears!

If you want to know more about these schemes, there are a number of Web sites (all designed to protect you from crooks bringing you those schemes): http://www.joewein. de/sw/419scam.htm; www.419eater.com; and www.419.bittenus.com. The last one is specially fascinating: here, Miss Yog, the Web site's owner, actively corresponds with the scammers (under several fake identities), seemingly falling for their traps. She is scamming the scammers, in other words. All the power to her. Meanwhile, many consumers are no doubt falling victims to these frauds.

Whereas marketing is a worthy activity that brings consumers admirable value, some marketers no doubt exploit the consumer. This chapter examines the unethical practices of such opportunisitc marketers.

————o————

INTRODUCTION

Marketers give us products, we consume them. They charge us money, and, as consumers, we are happy to pay it. We derive the benefits we seek from those products, and marketers get financial rewards in return. This exchange relationship is mutually beneficial. But as is true of all relationships, these marketer-consumer relationships also have to rest on mutual trust. Unfortunately, that trust is sometimes broken—from both sides. Some marketers occasionally engage in opportunistic practices that make them exorbitant sums of money but at the cost of consumer wellbeing. Many of these practices positively harm the consumer; others detract from benefits the consumer was promised. In this chapter, we examine these practices.

First, we examine marketer practices that harm the consumer interest. Next we describe how governments and public policy protect the consumer against marketer malpractices. Third and last, we examine consumers' own behaviors that are self-destructive. Ranging from addiction to crime, these constitute what some call "the dark side of consumer behavior."

QUESTIONABLE MARKETING PRACTICES

Marketing practices that potentially cause harm to consumer interests can be grouped into four categories:

1. Selling unsafe products
2. Unfair Pricing
3. Misinformation and deception
4. Intrusion and Over-commercialism

1. SELLING UNSAFE PRODUCTS

All products have the potential of being unsafe—even seemingly safe products. The milk we drink could upset our stomach, the clothes we wear could give us skin irritation, the electric bulb could ignite fire, and our cell phones could permeate our brains with some unfriendly, IQ—depleting electromagnetic waves. We depend on marketers to ensure that the products they put out in the market are safe. In most of the developed world, governments ensure that they are. But if you were visiting a foreign country, and if you are not familiar with that country's legal framework for product safety, you cannot assume that the products sold there are safe. At every step of everyday consumption, you would have to assess product safety.

In USA, a number of government agencies monitor product safety. The Consumer Product Safety Commission (CPSC) monitors the safety of a variety of products including toys, furniture, tools, electronics, and various household items. The Food & Drug Administration (FDA) monitors both the safety and the efficacy of drugs, food, and medical devices. The National Highway & Traffic Safety Association (NHTSA) monitors automobile safety. And the Environmental Protection Agency (EPA) is responsible for the safety of pesticides, chemicals, and other products that would impact the environment.[1] Policing by government agencies can, however, never eliminate unsafe products completely. A recent study by Consumer Reports magazine found that dozens of unsafe products do manage to find their way onto retail shelves. And many items banned in U.S.A. end up finding their way into foreign markets. In U.S.A., the injuries and property damage caused by unsafe products costs some $700 billion annually.[2] What is required is a desire on the part of marketers to ensure product safety.

Sometimes, products that are potentially unsafe enter the marketplace without the marketer's awareness of their being unsafe—such as when milk gets contaminated or when third party suppliers accidentally use a restricted ingredient (e.g., peanuts in a product labeled peanut-free). Conscientious marketers cooperate with government in withdrawing such products from market as soon as they are detected. See Exhibit 20.1: Unsafe Product Recalls: When Marketers Cooperate.

Of real concern are instances when a marketer knowingly allows unsafe products to be sold just to make money. Some critics point to the marketing of Vioxx as a case-in-point. Read the story and decide for yourself. See Exhibit 20.2: Marketing of Unsafe Products: Did Vioxx Play Fair?

RECALLING UNSAFE PRODUCTS   Exhibit 20.1

WHEN MARKETERS COOPERATE

January 16, 2006. Hurley International of Costa Mesa, California recalled 300 Boy's Windbreaker Jacket with Drawstring. The jackets have a drawstring through the hood, posing a strangulation hazard to children. In February 1996, the CPSC had issued guidelines to help protect children from strangling or getting entangled on the neck and waist drawstrings of upper garments such as jackets and sweatshirts.

January 13, 2006. Target Stores voluntarily agreed to recall about 860,000 sets of holiday lights (UL number E254698 or E182192) because of fire hazard.

January 4, 2006. Trader Joe's Company Recalled Gourmet Chocolate Fudge Original (8 oz. original) code BB 07/01/06 LOT 008. The reason: the product may have contained walnuts that are not declared on the label—walnuts are an allergen. "You can find the code on the back of the package marked on a small white sticker next to the nutritional label; People who have an allergy or severe sensitivity to walnuts run the risk of serious or life-threatening allergic reactions if they consume this product," said a company press release.

December 16, 2005. CPSC, in voluntary cooperation with Dell Corporation, announced the recall of some 22,000 batteries installed in the company's Latitude and Inspiron Notebook computers. The batteries tended to overheat; three such incidents were reported.

Stephanie Moore, "Lemon Laws," Consumers Affairs web site http://www.consumeraffairs.com/lemon_law/ (DoA: September 10, 2006).

2. UNFAIR PRICING

Nobody wants to pay more. But consumers don't resent a price just because it is high; rather, they resent it when they believe it is unjustified—when they suspect that the marketer is indulging in **price gouging**—a practice wherein the seller hikes up the price just to take advantage of some short-term shortage or emergency circumstances. In the State of Florida, where Hurricane Katrina took a heavy toll on people, during the year 2005, the government received 3464 written price-gouging complaints.[3] Whether or not marketers are engaging in price gouging to this extent—although some of them clearly are, what is important is the public's perception. These complaints show consumer perception of price unfairness.

According to research,[4] consumers infer price unfairness on the basis of three judgments:

i. The price of a comparable alternative or of the same product in normal circumstances;
ii. The price offered to another buyer; and
iii. Whether the seller is responsible for the price spike.

Based on the first judgment—price of the comparable option—consumers perceive a price to be unfair when:

i. The price is substantially more than their "internal reference price"—a price they expected the item to cost them;
ii. They see that an environmental event or a specific situation has increased the demand but should not have affected the cost of production of the item (e.g., a snow shovel priced more today after a snow storm than yesterday).

Based on the second judgment—price offered to other persons—consumers perceive the price to be unfair when they suspect that other consumers in similar circumstances paid less. The worst case is when a consumer is discriminated blatantly on an individual basis (e.g., persons of certain demographics are quoted a higher price, just to discourage them). But this can also happen in subtle ways when, for example, a service company does not inform all customers of the rebate program currently in effect. However, consumers tend not to resent price concessions offered to less resourced persons (e.g., senior citizens) or persons whose presence in the same servicescape is deemed desirable (e.g., no cover charge for women).

Based on the third judgment—attribution to sellers—consumers perceive a price to be unfair when they believe the marketer is motivated to make exuberant profits. For example, if a marketer were to raise the price of a theater ticket when only a few tickets remain, or a car dealer tells you that the $500 rebate is available for cars in all colors except

---

SELLING UNSAFE PRODUCTS
Exhibit 20.2

DID VIOXX PLAY FARE?

Vioxx is an arthritis and pain drug made popular through aggressive marketing by pharmaceutical giant Merck & Co. Introduced in 1999, its worldwide sales reached $2 billion in 2003. More than 2 million people around the world were estimated to be taking the drug.

The company announced a recall on September 30, 2004. According to the FDA, studies demonstrated that Vioxx is associated with a higher rate of heart attacks and stroke. During the five-year period of its availability, it might have already led to some 27,000 heart attacks and deaths caused by sudden cardiac arrests. Some blame the company for marketing the drug despite some knowledge of its dangers. In fact, in September 2001, the FDA had issued a warning letter to the company. In that letter, the FDA charged that its advertising contained "false, lacking in fair balance, or otherwise misleading" claims "in violation of the Federal Food, Drugs and Cosmetic Act and applicable regulations."

Specifically, the FDA had determined that Merck "engaged in a promotional campaign for Vioxx that minimizes the potentially serious cardiovascular findings that were observed in the Vioxx Gastrointestinal Outcomes Research

(VIGOR)." VIGOR was an independent study entailing a 13-month, placebo-controlled, double-blind trial with 8076 patients in some 300 centers in 22 countries.

Some blamed the FDA for not acting more decisively on the study's findings to stop the drug marketer. Others blame the company for underplaying or disputing the validity of early studies such as VIGOR. Merck was forced to withdraw the medicine only after the evidence of its severe side effects mounted.

On the flip side, Merck's market offering, as long as it remained available, served as the source of much relished relief from otherwise debilitating arthritis pain. The competing drugs Celebrex and Bextra were also amicable remedy for some, but they did not work for all and caused gastric distress in many patients. So, when Vioxx hit the market in 1999, doctors and patients were elated. Over time, many received a lot of relief from pain, and became devotees of Vioxx. Willing to take the increased risk of adverse effects, they wish that their wonder drug could have still stayed. ■

Discussion Q. Did Merck act appropriately in continuing to market the drug? Could it have taken a different course of action? What is right or wrong for marketers in a case like this one?

Sources: Information based on: Virginia Anderson, "Patients look beyond Vioxx for arthritis pain relief," The Atlanta Journal-Constitution, 12/06/04; James M. Scheiman, "Outcomes Studies of the Gastrointestinal Safety of Cyclooxygenase-2 Inhibitors," Cleveland Clinic Journal of Medicine, Volume 69, Supplement 1, SI 40-46. Another study examined the records of 1.39 million Kaiser Permanente patients, including 26,748 treated with Vioxx. The study found that high doses of Vioxx tripled risks of heart attacks and sudden cardiac death. Reported on www.vioxxwarning.com.

red—the color you want.

In addition, consumers tend to perceive price unfairness when:

    i.   The product in question is a necessity rather than a luxury (e.g., gasoline than a car).

    ii. A fee is charged for minor non-compliance with business procedures; e.g., you missed the noon deadline by 2 minutes for returning your rented video; you paid your credit card companies $35 instead of $35.15, and you got charged $15 fee!

What can marketers do to combat price unfairness perceptions? First, they have to ask themselves whether their goal and business ethic is to make exorbitant profits and be opportunistic or, instead, to be fair

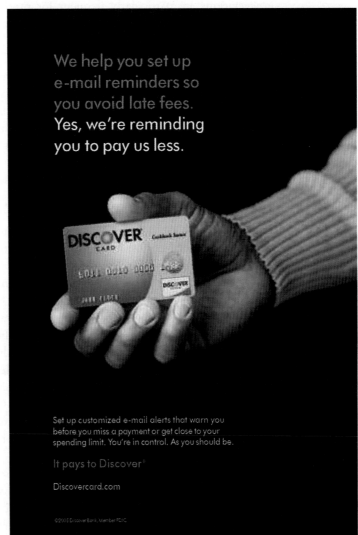

We help you set up
e-mail reminders so
you avoid late fees.
**Yes, we're reminding
you to pay us less.**

Set up customized e-mail alerts that warn you
before you miss a payment or get close to your
spending limit. You're in control. As you should be.

It pays to Discover

Discovercard.com

©2008 Discover Bank, Member FDIC

Discover® Card helps consumers keep track of deadlines. This is of immense value to consumers who feel the pain of paying a late fee. Photo: Courtesy of Discover Financial Services LLC

in deed as well as in word. If it be the former, then the issue of improving consumer perception of unfairness is irrelevant. If their goal is to be fair and the price spike is not their doing, then following actions can help:

    i.   Educate consumers about the value of the item, and about how the item is superior to products consumers might have mistakenly assumed to be comparable alternatives;

    ii. Make their costs and effort transparent (e.g., the quality of materials used, the level of skills needed, etc.);

    iii. Explain the extent of control or latitude (or a lack of it) they have at their command in the value-chain;

    iv. Make information about price deals available openly and to everyone;

v. Ensure that price differentials offered to different customer groups seem logical to all customers (e.g., dynamic pricing practices by airlines).

vi. Not be a stickler on business procedural compliance, allowing instead for small human failures.

vii. Help consumers keep track of deadlines.

3. MISINFORMATION AND DECEPTION

When consumers buy a product, they buy it believing what the marketers say the product will do. Marketers do not always tell the whole truth about a product, hide the demerits of the product, or make exaggerated claims about product benefits. Such exaggerations are particularly frequent for product categories that promise miracles—rapid weight loss, memory enhancement drugs, hair regrowth formulas, training programs promising jobs and careers, etc. A historic case in point:

In 1982, Microalgae International Sales Corp. (MISCORP) marketed spirulina products, claiming that they were effective for weight control and had therapeutic value against diabetes, anemia, liver disease, and ulcers. These claims are bunkum. The FDA has concluded that there is no evidence that spirulina (or phenylalanine) is effective as an appetite suppressant. The FDA has also noted that the company's "65% protein" claim is meaningless because, taken according to their label, spirulina products provide only negligible amounts of protein.[5]

Most established and brand name health insurance companies do business honestly. Many mail order agencies, however, are not as honest, hiding substantive details in complicated policy documents; or they blatantly stretch the truth. In September 2005, Financial Services Authority (FSA), a UK governmental agency, in its review of 25 policies that offer cover for critical insurance, found that some policy documents (a) used scare tactics by citing misleading data—e.g., that there were 100,000 cases of cancer every year, but the policy did not provide insurance for all those types of cancer; (b) hiding exclusions in small print; and (c) deliberately using language likely to mislead—for example, it asked, "What will you do if you are unable to work because of an illness?" This statement gives the impression that it is an income protection policy, which, of course, it is not.[6]

Sometimes, consumer deception occurs inadvertently. Cell phone services represent such a situation. Cell phone service companies refer to their plans as nationwide coverage; it means only that the service areas include locations from all parts of the country, not that service is available in all locations of the country. Consumers assume, of course, that they can call anywhere in USA. Furthermore, consumers can't always keep track of when they are entering a *roaming* area (which costs a higher rate) and sometimes the call switches to "roaming" even in the midst of a conversation.

In the U.S., most factual product claims (e.g., "reduces wrinkles," or "contains less fat") are regulated by governmental agencies, a point we will cover in more detail in the next section.

Of greater harm are the so called "Ponzi schemes," which promise consumers enormous rewards either for buying a product or for joining some promotional scheme of the company. The Nigerian 419 Scams are an example. The other example is various multi-level marketing programs, also known as *pyramid schemes*. Typically, these schemes reward you (more accurately, promise to reward you) for recruiting others to sell products, and you get a portion of the commission on what they sell, and on what those they in turn recruit sell, and so on. In these pyramid schemes, only a few at the top get rich; others lose their shirt—some give up their day jobs hoping to make more money in this new "occupation"—a hope that ends in bitter disappointment.

Many State governments publish a list of prevalent consumer frauds. A short excerpt from one such list appears in Exhibit 20.3. Some unscrupulous groups come up with elaborate ploys to trap you into a fraud. Read about one such scheme—a staged auto accident—in Exhibit 20.4.

When Sellers Abandon Conscience

.While the majority of businesses deal honestly and fairly with the public, there is a small minority who, through the promotion of unfair schemes, prey upon the public under the cloak of legitimate business. There are somewhere between 800 and 1,000 of the more prevalent frauds and schemes which are being practiced at any one time with hundreds of variations on the basic con games. In every scheme there is both a perpetrator and a victim. Every consumer is a potential victim. Below are some more prevalent consumer frauds.

BAIT AND SWITCH FRAUDS A company advertises a product at an exceptionally low price. When you go to buy it, the salesperson tells you that the advertised product is sold out. Or you might be told, "You really don't want the cheap merchandise." The salesperson will then try to sell you a similar but more expensive product. Bait and switch is illegal. However, there must be sufficient evidence against a business before legal action can be taken.

EARN-AT-HOME SCHEMES A company promises high profits for making products such as costume jewelry, artificial flowers, pillows, or toys. The company will require some money before explaining the scheme or make you buy some starter kit. It will also promises to buy the finished products. But later on, the company would reject the finished product as not up to its standards. Or the company is simply not to be found.

MEDICAL MIRACLE CURE FRAUDS These frauds are prevalent among elderly people, especially those who suffer from arthritis. Remember, there are no miracle patent medicines that can do

anything for people that a reputable doctor's care can not do.

TRADE AND CORRESPONDENCE SCHOOL FRAUDS These fraud entail exploiting a consumer's belief in education as a key to better and higher paying jobs and general self improvement. Tuition is usually high, schools are seldom accredited, and the training jobs may be no easier to get after training because the training does not meet company standards or the field may be overcrowded with applicants.

DEATH VULTURE FRAUDS This category is possibly one of the lowest forms of all con games. They visit close members of a bereaved family and attempt to collect sums of money for items which they maintain were purchased by the deceased before his death.

Lotteries A person offers to sell a winning lottery ticket or a "law firm" says someone has left you a winning lottery ticket, but you must send money so a computer can verify your identity. The "winning" ticket may be counterfeit or not exist. Be suspicious—do NOT buy a ticket from an individual, and do NOT send money!

CONTEST SCAMS These are fake contest notices stating that one has won a "free" prize, and in order to redeem any prize the victim should send "x" number of dollars.

DOOR-TO-DOOR HOME REPAIR These involve someone coming to the door and offering home repair work quickly at what seems like a reasonable cost. But, they suddenly "discover" that it will cost much more that the original estimate. Always get references and several estimates before allowing anyone to make repairs.

Source: SOUTH CAROLINA DEPARTMENT OF CONSUMER AFFAIRS http://www.scconsumer.gov/publications/frauds_schemes.htm

4. INTRUSION AND OVER-COMMERCIALISM

The Ills of Advertising

The fourth, and last in our list, problem with marketing is its attribute of intrusion and over-commercialism. First, consider intrusion. Marketers typically interrupt us when we are not looking to buy anything, and we are either busy with productive work or are enjoying life's everyday pleasures. Telemarketers call us anytime they will, even at our diner hours. E-mails show up in our email servers from merchants we never sought and whose merchandise has no relevance to us or even is demeaning to our dignity. Commercial messages show up on our PCs in the form of banner ads and pop ups and on our mobile phone screens when we are in the midst of typing in our short-message-text (SMS). And of course, all those commercial breaks on network TV annoyingly interrupt our entertainment.

> Advertising must tell the truth and not mislead consumers. In addition, claims must be substantiated.

Advertising is a double-edged sword, actually. On one hand, it provides consumers information about all the products and brand choices available in the marketplace. On the other, by interrupting TV and radio programs, and by constant repetition, it becomes annoying. These are gains and losses for the consumer as an individual. Then there are some societal benefits and harms. The principal societal benefit is that it keeps the economic system moving, particularly the system that depends on the economies of large-scale production and distribution. Its societal harms are three: (i) materialism, (ii) value-corruption, and (iii) falsity/no sense.[7]

Materialism Materialism is a set of consumer beliefs that sees the acquisition and consumption of more and more products and services as the route to life's satisfaction and happiness. And advertising spreads materialism, social critics argue, by

Total Eclipse of The Consumer Conscience

Consider this scenario: You're stuck in heavy traffic on a busy highway. Another car cuts off the driver in front of you, forcing him to slam on the brakes. You try to stop, but there's no time ... and you rear-end the guy in front of you.

An everyday accident? Not this time. Turns out you've been had by a well-organized criminal ring that staged the entire thing.

This particular scam is called the "swoop and squat." (The first car "swoops" in while the second car "squats" in front of you.) After the "accident," everyone in the car you rear-ended—usually crammed full of passengers—will file bogus injury claims with your insurance company. Each will complain of whiplash or other soft-tissue injuries—things difficult for doctors to confirm. They may even go to crooked physical therapists, chiropractors, lawyers, or auto repair technicians to further exaggerate their claims.

We're talking big money here. Staged accidents cost the insurance industry about $20 billion a year. Those losses get passed on to all of us in the form of higher insurance rates—an average of $100-$300 extra per car per year.

How can you protect yourself?

If you're in an accident, call the police immediately.

Report accident claims to your insurance company. Don't settle on site with cash.

Be careful with your personal information, mindful of identity theft.

If you can, photograph the car and passengers and write down names, addresses, and phone numbers.

Use medical, car repair, and legal professionals you know and trust.

Don't tail gate ... drive safely.

What are we doing to protect you from these schemes? Plenty. Like Operation Soft Tissue, where a Chicago agent posed as a corrupt lawyer and caught hundreds of these con artists and crooks red-handed. We've investigated more than 90 staged accident fraud cases over the past decade. With more to come!

Source: "How to Protect Yourself from Common Fraud Schemes," A CAUTIONARY TALE, Staged Auto Accident Fraud: Don't Let it Happen to You (2/18/05) http://www.fbi.gov/page2/feb05/stagedauto021805.htm

---

parading an endless array of goods in an enticing way.

Value-corruption Social critics accuse advertising of corrupting our values. In addition to materialism, it promotes self-centeredness and greed (the slogan "you can have it all"), insensitive competitiveness (Nike's briefly used slogan, "You don't win a silver; you lose a gold."!), disrespect for tradition, etc. Some would argue, for example, that a 1995 campaign for Calvin Klein brand of clothing depicting scantily clad pictures of children promoted sexuality in young children; worse, among adults it promoted, critics argue, pedophilia! Some social critics charge that advertising promotes stereotypes about sexes (genders), race and ethnicity ("two wongs won't make a white"[8]), the elderly ("I have fallen and I can't get up"[9]), etc.

Falsity/no sense Some of the advertising is misleading. But at a more

WHAT IS WRONG WITH SEX IN ADVERTISING?   B Good to Know

In the world of advertising, only young and beautiful people have sex. Advertising constantly confuses authentic sexuality with narcissism. Identical models parade alone through the commercials, caressing their own soft skin, stroking and hugging their bodies, shaking their long silky manes, sensually bathing and applying powders and lotions and then admiring themselves at length in the mirror. They are sexy because of the products they use. The jeans, the perfume, the car are sexy in and of themselves. The point is not to arouse desire for the person, but to arouse desire for the product. Things become lovers and lovers become things. Although the sexual sell, overt and subliminal, is at a fever pitch in most advertising, depictions of sex as an important and potentially profound human activity are notably absent. Couples in advertisements rarely look at each other. Sex in advertising and the media is often criticized from a puritanical perspective. But sex in advertising has far more to do with trivializing sex than promoting it, with narcissism than with promiscuity, with consuming than with connecting. The problem is not that it is sinful, but that it is synthetic and cynical.

—Jean Kilbourne, "What else does sex sell?" *International Journal of Advertising*, 2005, 24 (1), 119-122.

benign level, much of it fills our airwaves with ad-speak that is trite and trivial, confusing, and plain silly. It has the effect of making commonplace the telling of half-truths and other self-serving silliness, and justifying cynicism.

PUBLIC POLICY AND ITS ROLE IN CONSUMER PROTECTION

Governments at the federal, state, and local levels enact various laws that influence both business behavior and consumer behavior. These laws establish public policy that influences consumer behavior in four ways: (a) by constraining choices, (b) by mandating certain products and services, (c) by setting up facilitative infrastructures, and (d) by protecting the consumer in his or her purchases.

A. CONSTRAINING CHOICES

No matter where on earth you live, you can pretty much consume what you wish. Unless it is harmful to you; or to those around you. Thus, you cannot imbibe alcohol unless you are 18; you cannot drive without a license; and you may not litter our highways and city roads. You may not park your car anywhere you like, may not use mail services to send combustive materials, and may not drive a car not inspected for emissions. You cannot allow the grass in your front yard to grow uncut; cannot dispose off pollutant liquids (e.g., used motor oil) in public sewage, and you may not fill gasoline in unauthorized containers. You may not use cell phones during a flight, may not carry firearms in public transportation vehicles, and may not smoke in enclosed public facilities. And you must wear clothes in public places.

Government constrains choices in two ways: one by imposing controls directly on the consumer, and second, imposing control on businesses who make products available to consumers. As examples of the former, government bans driving while under the influence of alcohol, the use of steroids and other drugs, smoking, highway littering, etc. As an example of the latter, government bans use of certain products in the manufacture of products (e.g., asbestos in building materials).

Government regulations monitor **negligent consumer behavior.** Negligent behavior puts a person or others at risk and imposes heavy costs on society or otherwise deteriorates its quality of life in the long run.

Many government regulations are intended to protect other consumers from the consumption of individuals. In August 2004, British government imposed, for example, a fireworks restriction—firecrackers were banned between 11pm and 7am. The goal: residents can now sleep undisturbed.[11] China already had a similar ban. However, the

> Advertising appeals are based on value premises, which, it is alleged, do more to reinforce the seven deadly sins (greed, lust, gluttony, envy, sloth, pride, and anger) than to promote the seven virtues (prudence, temperance, justice, fortitude, faith, hope, and charity).
>
> —Richard W. Pollay
> Curator of the History of Advertising Archives at the University of British Columbia (*Journal of Marketing*, 1993, 57, 3, 99-114.)

B Good to Know

Slim Hopes: Advertising and the Obsession with Thinness

In this video, Jean Kilbourne offers an in-depth analysis of how female bodies are depicted in advertising imagery and the devastating effects of that imagery on women's health. Addressing the relationship between these images and the obsession of girls and women with dieting and thinness, Slim Hopes offers a new way to think about life-threatening eating disorders such as anorexia and bulimia, and it provides a well-documented critical perspective on the social impact of advertising. Using over 150 magazine and television ads, this illustrated lecture is divided into seven sections for easy classroom viewing and discussion: Impossible Beauty, Waifs and Thinness, Constructed Bodies, Food and Sex, Food and Control, The Weight-Loss Industry, and Freeing Imaginations. Distributed by the Media Education
http://www.jeankilbourne.com/video.html

Chinese government recently lifted the ban for the Lunar New Year's Day and loosened its restrictions, now limiting only to the hours of midnight and 7 am during the following 14 days. The 12-year old ban was lifted because the Chinese tradition required that the Lunar New Year be celebrated with fireworks. This tradition is based on the Chinese belief that the sounds of firecrackers will scare away a monster called "nian" and are, therefore, a symbol of good luck.[12]

Governments also control what products may be consumed in public places, for example, by prohibiting smoking, drinking, and gambling in public buildings. In recent times, smoking was banned on airplanes, even on transcontinental or trans-Atlantic flights. In Hongkong and Singapore, restrictions are very severe for those who are caught transporting drugs. In fact, the death penalty is used as a deterrent for such activities. On a less severe note, Singapore has used government control to affect the use of credit by its people. The monetary authority of Singapore, Singapore's central bank, has clamped down on consumer credit because it feared that Singaporeans were finding it too easy to borrow money. Citizens were using the credit to finance consumption instead of fixed investments, so the restrictions were applied to car loans and unsecured personal loans for lower- and middle-income earners.

B. MANDATING CHOICES

Governments not only forbid some choices, they mandate others. **Compliance** refers to the government mandate for consumers to obey defined rules and regulations with respect to purchase, payment, and, more importantly, product usage, including disposal. To obtain customer compliance with these mandates, governments pass laws and issue regulations with penalties for failure to comply. For example, in the United States, the federal and state governments require the use of certain products, such as motorcycle helmets by riders and seat belts by drivers and passengers of automobiles.[13] In Australia, even passengers are given tickets if they are not wearing their seatbelts. Small children must always be restrained in child-seats.

Many consumer choices are regulated indirectly and in ways invisible to consumers—by mandating manufacturers to make products with certain construction and/or ingredients. If you want to build a house, for example, your builder will not use any materials that are not approved and the builder will follow strict safety codes in respect of electric wiring, gas pipes, water lines, etc. Car manufacturers have to build-in a set of safety requirements. Two examples illustrate how governments serve consumer wellbeing through mandates on businesses.

In U.S.A., if you eat a bowl of cereal, you will also be giving your body a good vitamin—specifically vitamin 'B' in the form of folic acid. Folic acid is a crucial vitamin that your body needs for cell replication and growth. Its deficiency leads to anemia and starves rapidly growing tissue of essential elements. In 1996, FDA began to require that all enriched flour, rice, pasta, and other grain products such as cereals contain 140 mcg of folic acid per 100 grams. Although pregnant women need to take as much as 400 mcg of folic acid a day

Why We Need Iodized Salt

☐B Good to Know

Iodine deficiency disorders (IDD) jeopardize children's mental health—often their very lives. These disorders start before birth. Serious iodine deficiency during pregnancy may result in stillbirths, abortions and congenital abnormalities such as cretinism, a grave, irreversible form of mental retardation that affects people living in iodine-deficient areas of Africa and Asia. However, of far greater global and economic significance is IDD's less visible, yet more pervasive, level of mental impairment that lowers intellectual prowess at home, at school and at work. (Source: http://www.who.int/nut/idd.htm (DoA: June 12, 2006)

So now you know why salt comes in two forms: iodized and uniodized. However, which salt you need depends on whether you live in an iodine-deficient area. Read more at www.saltinstitute.org.

(since the fetus has special needs of its growing tissues), for most of us, this government mandate quietly takes care of our tissue growth needs.[14]

For our second example, we travel across the globe to the world's largest democracy—India. Consumers in India cannot buy non-iodized salt—its sale was banned by a regulation passed in October 2005 by the Indian Ministry of Health and Family Welfare. Why? Because a World Health Organization (WHO) study has identified Iodine deficiency to be the world's leading cause of preventable mental retardation. The Indian government has determined that no State in the country was free from iodine deficiency. By mandating that all salt sold in India be iodized, the government has taken a crucial step in advancing consumer wellbeing.[15]

C. FACILITATIVE INFRASTRUCTURE

The third mechanism by which government policy shapes customer behavior is the development of infrastructure. Governments can influence customer behavior by establishing incentives and infrastructures to encourage certain customer behaviors. One example is the electric vehicle initiative in California. Another example is the program to encourage bicycling as a means of commuting. The U.S. government's 1990 Clean Air Act and 1991 Intermodal Surface Transportation Efficiency Act (ISTEA) give local communities a mandate to build bicycling into their transit plans. The clean air act specifies air quality standards and requires metropolitan areas to develop methods of maintaining air quality, including the encouragement of bicycling for commuting purposes. The ISTEA requires states and local governments to develop plans that would encourage the use of nonmotorized transportation. The federal government earmarked billions of dollars to back up this mandate. Local governments have utilized these funds for building biker's lanes on public roadways within the city limits, and bikers everywhere are enjoying these facilities as well as helping our environment.

D. PROTECTING THE CONSUMER FROM MARKETERS

Finally, governments can and do play a very intense role in enacting and enforcing laws to protect consumers from marketers and marketing practices. In effect, all elements of the marketing mix (product, promotion, price, and place) are covered in various laws meant to protect the customer. Such role and laws vary greatly by country and by eh from of government, of course. We illustrate the role of government with U.S. as a case in point.

In 1914, the U.S. Congress established the Federal Trade Commission (FTC) as a body of specialists with the power to investigate and enforce laws that require businesses to engage in fair business practices. The scope of what is or is not a fair business practice has been constantly evolving. That scope, and consumer protection, received a shot in the arm with the passage the **Consumer Bill of Rights**. These rights, set forth by President John F. Kennedy, and then passed into law are:
1. The right to safety
2. The right to be informed
3. The right to be heard
4. The right to choose

To implement these rights, the U.S. Government has established several agencies (see a brief list in Exhibit 20.5). And U.S. Congress has passed many additional laws designed to protect the consumer from being misled by businesses (see list of selected laws in Exhibit 20.6). Various laws include Truth in Lending, Truth in Advertising, Truth in Packaging, Truth in Leasing, and so on. Other laws monitor or prohibit certain product

Protecting the Consumer

Federal Drug Administration The FDA was set up under the 1905 Food and Drug Act. Its goal is to protect consumers from unsafe food and drug products.

Federal Trade Commission The FTC was set up in 1914. Its purpose is to prevent unfair trade practices and anticompetitive practices. It also regulates deceptive advertising.

The National Highway Traffic Safety Administration The NHTSA was created in 1970; this agency's charge is to regulate the safety performance of motor vehicles and establish fuel economy standards for new vehicles.

Consumer Product Safety Commission The CPSC was established in 1972 under the Consumer Product Safety Act. The agency is responsible for investigating the causes of product-related accidents and taking corrective actions. These corrective actions may include product recalls, banning unsafe products, ordering refunds, and mandating correct labeling and safety instructions (such as those found on electric appliances).

Environmental Protection Agency The EPA was established in 1970 to create a national policy to protect the environment.

Source: www.FTC.gov

features or certain product formulations judged to be physically harmful to a customer. A case in point is a 1996 law banning mini-blinds coated with certain harmful materials. See Box: *Your Blinds Are Safe and Here is Why.*[16]

One of the FTC's most important duties is to oversee all advertising and ensure that no company engages in deceptive advertising. (See Exhibit 20.7) The FTC defines **deceptive advertising** as that which "has the capacity to deceive a measurable segment of the public." A classic example of the regulation of deceptive advertising is the case of Listerine. Warner-Lambert, the manufacturers of Listerine, claimed in its advertising from 1921 to 1975 that Listerine would prevent or lessen common colds and sore throats. In 1975, the FTC determined that the claim was misleading and ordered **corrective advertising** (advertising whose message includes a correction of a previous deception). Accordingly, the company was required to insert the following disclaimer in its future advertising: "while Listerine will not prevent colds or sore throats or lessen their severity, ..." [this was followed by whatever new selling appeal it wanted to employ, such as countering bad breath.]

The FTC requires that companies substantiate any claims made in an advertisement by documenting all verifiable benefits in company files. A **verifiable benefit** is one that can be verified by independent laboratory tests, such as whether a brand cleans clothes whiter than a competitor's brand, or whether a shampoo will prevent hair thinning. The stipulation is that the company must have clinical tests of the product's performance on file before making such advertising claims. A case involving Firestone illustrates this point. In the 1970s, Firestone advertised that a tire it manufactured would stop 25 percent quicker on ice than the competing brands. The FTC questioned this advertising because Firestone did not have test data on file already.

B Good to Know

Your Blinds Are Safe and Here is Why...

A study by the U.S. Consumer Product Safety Commission had found that the matte-finish models of inexpensive imported mini-blinds were treated with lead stabilizers to make the blinds more durable. However, sunlight and heat can cause the plastic to deteriorate, releasing lead dust, which is harmful to young children if they ingest it by touching or licking the slats. The response from retailers was mixed: Home Depot and Lowe's stores stopped selling the blinds; Hechinger and Wal-Mart posted warnings and announced they would phase out the old blinds as new unleaded versions came in. Most stores offered refunds or exchanges. Ultimately, the Consumer Product Safety Commission banned the blinds from being imported. However, the greater safety comes at a price—an increase of 15 percent for the new unleaded versions.

Why did we choose a dull topic of blinds, you might ask. After all blinds are the last thing on our minds.

Precisely, our point. Thanks to benevolent government regulations. Without them, we will have to keep thousands of similarly "boring" products on our minds. Now You know!

Public policy regulations enable us to enjoy carefree consumption. So get up, get out, and vote, the next time a lawmaker is being elected. Thank you.

Advertising to Children

The FTC also plays a very important role in protecting children from unfair advertising practices. Because younger children (under age seven) in general cannot differentiate between a commercial and a program, and many older children do not

Exhibit 20.6

SELECTED U.S. CONSUMER PROTECTION LAWS

Protecting by Laws

National Traffic and Safety Act Established in 1958, this act sets safety standards for automobiles and tires.

Automobile Information Disclosure Act Established in 1958, this act prohibits automobile dealers from changing the factory price of new cars

Fair Packaging and Labeling Act Established in 1966, this act regulates the packaging and labeling of consumer goods by requiring manufacturers to identify the amount and type of contents contained within it.s.

Child Protection Act This act was established in 1967 and requires that every cigarette package state: "Warning: The Surgeon General Has Determined That Cigarette Smoking Is Dangerous to Your Health.".".

Consumer Product Safety Act Established in 1972, this act set up safety standards for consumer products and outlined penalties for companies that did not follow them.

Toy Safety Act Established in 1984, this act makes it possible for the government to immediately recall dangerous toys.

The Nutrition Labeling and Education Act This was created in 1990 to guide consumers in choosing processed foods and products with dietary supplements. The bill enables the FDA to give approval to those products with beneficial health effects and to stop those that make false claims.

Telemarketing and Consumer Fraud and Abuse Prevention Act Passed in 1994, this act alters the way in which credit repair companies operate. These companies will not be able to remove accurate information that tells the truth about a consumer's bad credit history. Furthermore, this act stipulates that these companies cannot encourage consumers to change their identities with new addresses and social security numbers.

comprehend the persuasive intent of commercials, special regulations apply to children's advertising.

In Addition, Better Business Bureau (BBB), a non-governmental organization, monitors advertising practices of businesses. To monitor children's advertising, it has a special unit called Children's Advertising Review Unit. (CARU). CARU has issued special guidelines for children's advertising (See Exhibit 20.8). It behooves all marketers to understand the spirit and logic of those guidelines and follow them, as many well-intending businesses do.

The FTC is also authorized to monitor manufacturers' adherence to warranty promises and consumer redress for failed warranties. Most businesses themselves try to reduce a customer's perceived risk by offering warranties and written satisfaction guarantees. But

FTC Regulations on Advertising

Exhibit 20.7

Protecting by Laws

The Federal Trade Commission Act allows the FTC to act in the interest of all consumers to prevent deceptive and unfair acts or practices. In interpreting Section 5 of the Act, the Commission has determined that a representation, omission or practice is deceptive if it is likely to:

1. Mislead consumers, and
2. Affect consumers' behavior or decisions about the product or service.

In addition, an act or practice is unfair if the injury it causes, or is likely to cause, is:

a. substantial
b. not outweighed by other benefits and
c. not reasonably avoidable.

The FTC Act prohibits unfair or deceptive advertising in any medium. That is, advertising must tell the truth and not mislead consumers. A claim can be misleading if relevant information is left out or if the claim implies something that's not true. For example, a lease advertisement for an automobile that promotes "$0 Down" may be misleading if significant and undisclosed charges are due at lease signing.

In addition, claims must be substantiated, especially when they concern health, safety, or performance. The type of evidence may depend on the product, the claims, and what experts believe necessary. If your ad specifies a certain level of support for a claim - "tests show X" - you must have at least that level of support.

the reason these warranties and guarantees are effective and helpful to customers is that the government enforces business compliance with them. In the area of pricing, unit pricing and price disclosure laws reduce opportunities for price gouging and deceptive pricing practices. Consider some of protections you are receiving because of FTC regulations:

- Companies may promise to ship the merchandise by certain time, but what is the guarantee that they will? FTC ensures that. Internet shopping is also covered and any promises by an online vendor (e.g., delivery over the holidays) are governed by the FTC.
- Your clothes have labels with fiber content information and care instructions; has it occurred to you what would happen if you were allergic to some fibers and if the label was wrong? You needn't worry about it because the U.S. Government ensures that the label is accurate.
- If a product makes the claim that it is environmentally safe or eco-friendly, can you believe it? You can.
- If it says it is made in USA, can you trust it? Yes, because the FTC ensures it be true.
- You pay by credit card and the merchant alters the amount; what would you do? You will pay only the amount you spent—the Fair Credit Billing Act protects you!

In addition, various state governments have created laws and corresponding agencies to protect consumers against business's possible wrongdoing. For example, in New York State, a law termed a "**lemon law**" protects a car buyer against being sold a substandard car. If the car breaks down or fails to perform as expected within 90 days of the purchase, the car dealer is required to make good on the purchase and to pay punitive damages to the customer. This allows the customer to buy products in a relatively risk-free market environment. Similarly, there are "cool off" laws that give a customer 72 hours to return a product without penalty.

CARU Guidelines for Advertisers   Exhibit 20.8

Self-Regulation at Work

1. Advertisers should always take into account the level of knowledge, sophistication and maturity of the audience to which their message is primarily directed. Younger children have a limited capacity for evaluating the credibility of information they receive. They also may lack the ability to understand the nature of the personal information they disclose on the Internet. Advertisers, therefore, have a special responsibility to protect children from their own susceptibilities.

2. Realizing that children are imaginative and that make-believe play constitutes an important part of the growing up process, advertisers should exercise care not to exploit unfairly the imaginative quality of children. Unreasonable expectations of product quality or performance should not be stimulated either directly or indirectly by advertising.

3. Products and content which are inappropriate for children should not be advertised or promoted directly to children.

4. Recognizing that advertising may play an important part in educating the child, advertisers should communicate information in a truthful and accurate manner and in language understandable to young children with full recognition that the child may learn practices from advertising which can affect his or her health and well-being.

5. Advertisers are urged to capitalize on the potential of advertising to influence behavior by developing advertising that, wherever possible, addresses itself to positive and beneficial social behavior, such as friendship, kindness, honesty, justice, generosity and respect for others.

6. Care should be taken to incorporate minority and other groups in advertisements in order to present positive and pro-social roles and role models wherever possible. Social stereotyping and appeals to prejudice should be avoided.

7. Although many influences affect a child's personal and social development, it remains the prime responsibility of the parents to provide guidance for children. Advertisers should contribute to this parent-child relationship in a constructive manner.

* CARU stands for Children's Advertising Review Unit, a division of Better Business Bureau, a non-governmental, industry self-regulatory agency.

Source: www.caru.org/guidelines

POTECTING CONSUMER PRIVACY

Privacy has always been important to consumers; now in the age of transactions at a distance (where you don't know the merchant) it is becoming a major concern. There are three domains of privacy as a consumer: (a) our purchases; (b) our personal information; and (c) our financial information. We buy things all the time and what we buy is known to the seller. But we don't want the seller to reveal it to others. Second, sellers also have our personal information (name, address, age, income, etc.) and we don't want sellers making that information public. And finally, we want our credit information (credit history, credit card numbers, etc.) to not be revealed to people or agencies who might misuse it.

Fortunately, US laws protect consumers against such misuse. The law, governed by FTC, is called the *Financial Privacy Rule* (FPR). The rule requires financial institutions to give their customers privacy notices that explain the financial institution's information collection and sharing practices. In turn, consumers have the right to limit some sharing of their information. Also, financial institutions and other companies that receive personal financial information from a financial institution may be limited in their ability to use that information.[17]

If you've ever applied for a charge account, personal loan, insurance, or job, there's a file about you. This file contains information on where you work and live, how you pay your bills and whether you've been sued, arrested, or have filed for bankruptcy. Companies that gather and sell this information are called Consumer Reporting Agencies (CRAs). CRAs may sell information about you to creditors, employers, insurers, and other businesses in the form of a consumer report.

If this credit report is inaccurate, you might not be able to obtain the loan for you car or house, etc. You are protected against such risks by the Fair Credit Reporting Act (FCRA). This law, enforced by the Federal Trade Commission, promotes accuracy in consumer credit reports and is meant to ensure the privacy of the information in them.

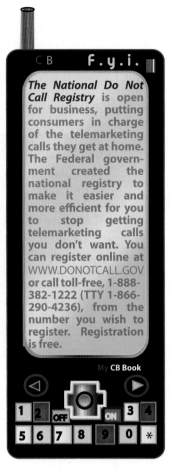

CB **F.y.i.**

The National Do Not Call Registry is open for business, putting consumers in charge of the telemarketing calls they get at home. The Federal government created the national registry to make it easier and more efficient for you to stop getting telemarketing calls you don't want. You can register online at WWW.DONOTCALL.GOV or call toll-free, 1-888-382-1222 (TTY 1-866-290-4236), from the number you wish to register. Registration is free.

My **CB Book**

COPPA—The Children's Online Privacy Protection Act

Exhibit 20.9

Because Children Are Vulnerable

The primary goal of the Children's Online Privacy Protection Act (COPPA) Rule is to give parents control over what information is collected from their children online and how such information may be used.

The Rule applies to Operators of commercial Web sites and online services that collect personal information from children under.

The Rule requires operators to:

1. Post a privacy policy on the homepage of the Web site and link to the privacy policy on every page where personal information is collected.
2. Provide notice about the site's information collection practices to parents and obtain verifiable parental consent before collecting personal information from children.
3. Give parents a choice as to whether their child's personal information will be disclosed to third parties.
4. Provide parents access to their child's personal information and the opportunity to delete the child's personal information and opt-out of future collection or use of the information.
5. Not condition a child's participation in a game, contest or other activity on the child's disclosing more personal information than is reasonably necessary to participate in that activity.
6. Maintain the confidentiality, security and integrity of personal information collected from children.

Source: http://www.ftc.gov/bcp/conline/pubs/buspubs/coppa.htm and www.coppa.org/comply.htm

Cyber Privacy

Surfing the Net can be fun and educational. Email is a great way to stay in touch with family and friends, Chat groups and discussion groups allow you to communicate with people with similar interests. Most people are aware of the Internet's benefits, but not everyone is aware of how the Internet can threaten personal privacy and the steps you can take to protect your privacy in cyberspace. There are some simple steps you can take to safeguard your own privacy, and you do have certain protections under the privacy laws of the land.

Children are especially vulnerable to cyber-privacy infringement. There is a risk that they would easily give out personal information to strangers (on commercial sites or social networks such as chat rooms, and some unscrupulous merchant or online person could exploit that information. To protect children from such risks, US government has enacted a law called Children's Online Privacy Protection Act (COPPA), in effect since April 2000. You can read about it in Exhibit 20.9.

PIPEDA—The PRIVACY LAW IN CANADA

In Canada, the relevant law is the Personal Information Protection and Electronic Documents Act (PIPEDA). The Act applies to personal information collected, used or disclosed in the course of commercial activities, whether in the "real" world or on the Internet The Act specifies what information a Web site can collect from you, and how, and also how it may or may not use that information. The Act also gives you the right to gain access to and correct information a Web site has about you.

Source: http://www.privcom.gc.ca/fs-fi/02_05_d_13_e.asp
Office of the Privacy Commisionae of Canada web site (DoA 2/2/2006).

CONSUMER CONSCIENCE

Marketers' misdemeanors—such as the 411 Schemes, deceptive advertising, and price gouging—become widely known because of the publicity they receive. But often consumers too indulge in marketplace behaviors that are unethical. The basic concept of ethic is "don't do unto others what you wouldn't want others do to you." But an even more simple guide rule to remain ethical can be this: don't do anything you wouldn't want the concerned marketer to know about. Basically, all kinds of consumer frauds are acts that violate ethics. These include stealing from a store, reporting false information about yourself (e.g., misreporting your age to qualify for a transaction—Yes, fake ID to claim "21 and over" status is included!), making false claims on loss recovery under warranties and property insurance.

Table 20.1 presents a list of common unethical practices and the findings of a study in six countries. According to the study, UK consumers engage in some of these practices the most. Before you jump to conclude that UK consumers are the most unethical, it is worth noting that the sample sizes are small and non-representative of the population as a whole. Still the findings give some reason for reflection.[18]

Beyond general ethics (or the lack of them), consumers also indulge in practices which are harmful to them or to others in society. Here we discuss three such consumer behaviors: (a) compulsive consumption; (b) shoplifting; (c) and obesity.

THE CURSE OF COMPULSIVE BUYING

Compulsive buying and compulsive consumption seem to stem from the personality trait of neuroticism. We all know people who are compulsive buyers, always shopping, always buying stuff, some of which they may never use, or stuff they already have more of than they can use, and buying it even if they can barely afford it or even when they are short on money. They are compulsive buyers. **Compulsive buying** can be defined as a chronic tendency to purchase products far in excess of both a person's needs and resources.

Although some compulsive buying is harmless, when done in excess, it becomes positively harmful. The example of a benign compulsive buyer is someone who is always buying things whenever they are on sale, accumulating them for future use. Such a compulsive buyer is benign because he or she limits the purchases to items he or she does need and is generally very deliberative as to the "value" of the purchase, buying it only if the item represents a good bargain or a rare find; the compulsiveness resides in constantly looking for opportunistic merchandise. The less benign kind is the one in which the buying is rampant without evaluation of future need and without regard for available means. Such people often accumulate huge debts and a large stock of unused products. For them, the act of buying becomes a thrill in itself.

TABLE 20.1

Selected Unethical Consumer Practices

	Overall	Rank[a]	UK	Brunei	H. K.	France	USA	Austria
Questionable Consumer Behaviors:								
Drinking a can of soda in a supermarket without buying it.	1.8	1	2.2	1.2	1.4	1.7	1.3	2.9
Using long distance phone access code that does not belong to you.	1.8	2	2.2	1.5	1.3	1.6	1.2	3.0
Reporting a lost item as stolen to an insurance company to collect the money.	2.3	4	2.5	1.7	2.0	2.1	1.3	3.9
Changing price tags on merchandise in a store.	1.9	3	2.1	1.3	1.5	1.8	1.3	3.4
Using the work telephone to make private calls.	2.4	7	3.2	1.9	2.6	2.5	1.8	2.2
Not saying anything when the waitress miscalculates the bill in your favor.	2.3	6	3.2	1.6	2.4	2.5	1.8	2.2
Getting too much change and not saying anything.	2.7	8	3.2	2.4	3.4	2.5	2.2	2.5
Taking towels from hotels and blankets from aircraft as souvenirs.	3.1	11	3.6	3.2	3.6	3.0	3.0	2.3
Renting one double bedroom hotel room for more than two people.	2.3	6	3.1	2.2	2.5	2.2	2.0	1.8
Taking advantage of free trail period.	3.0	9	3.6	3.0	3.4	3.6	3.2	1.6
Cutting in when there is a long line.	3.1	10	3.7	3.3	2.8	3.8	3.4	1.5

a. Note. Overall ranking ascends from less favorable (1) to more favorable (5) responses

Source. Emin Babakus, T. Bettina Cornwell, Vince Mitchell, and Bodo Schlegelmilch, "Reactions to unethical Consumer Behavior across Six countries," *Journal of Consumer Marketing*, 21(4), 2004, 254-263. Reproduced with permission. Courtesy Emerald Publishing Group.

It is this "negative" behavior that detracts from individual welfare and thus deserves study. Consumer researchers have described this negative compulsive behavior as "chronic, repetitive purchasing that becomes a primary response to negative events or feelings."[19] This description implies that compulsive buying is a compensatory response to cope with some stressful or depressing event.

Compulsive buyers have been found to differ from other consumers in a number of respects. Compared with others, compulsive buyers have a lower self-esteem, are more depressed, show a greater tendency to fantasize, experience greater "emotional lift" at the time of purchase, experience remorse in the post-purchase phase; and accumulate a much higher debt. Moreover, research has found that compulsive buying is motivated less by a desire to possess things, and more as a means of maintaining self-esteem.[20]

COMPULSIVE CONSUMPTION

Compulsive consumption comes in various forms: alcoholism, eating disorders, compulsive gambling, compulsive exercising, compulsive videogaming or Internet surfing, and compulsive sexuality.[21] Beyond purchasing, some consumers are compulsive users of products and services. Whereas compulsive buying occurs for a broad range of products (i.e., consumers buy things in general, often regardless of their need), compulsive consumption is limited to one or two related product or service categories (e.g., compulsive eating, drinking, or gambling). **Compulsive consumption** can be defined as an uncontrolled and obsessive consumption of a product or service frequently and in excessive amounts, likely to ultimately cause harm to the consumer or others. Here is how one consumer described her compulsive consumption behavior:

When I was using drugs, they were the focal point of my whole life. They were all I thought about. Every two hours I would think, "How can I do my drugs? ... They were what I allocated my time to first, my money to first...."
—A research respondent in consumer researcher Elizabeth Hirschman's study.[22]

In the consumer research literature, three characteristics of compulsive consumption have been reported. Compulsive consumers experience a drive or urge to engage in a behavior, deny harmful consequences, and face repeated failure in attempts to control that behavior.[23]

In a broader sense, compulsive buying is a form of compulsive consumption, just like compulsive gambling—time and money are wasted in both but psychological thrill is gained. All compulsive behaviors are clinically called **impulse control disorder**—failure to control our impulse to do something. University of Minnesota professor Ron Faber and University of Illinois professor Tom O'Guinn have studied compulsive behaviors (specifically, compulsive buying) extensively and have advanced a **three-factor theory of compulsive buying**.[24] Those three factors are biological, psychological, and sociological.

Biological Factors Biologically, two subfactors are responsible: genetics and brain chemical deficiency. Some of the compulsive behavior is hereditary— sons of alcoholics have been found, for example, to be at a higher risk of becoming alcoholics even when separated from the parent. And a neurotransmitter called serotonin (whose deficiency causes depression) has been found to lead to compulsive behaviors.

Psychological Factors Psychologically, childhood experience of inadequacy and rejection, continuing in adult years as chronic self-esteem void, cause compulsive buying and other compulsive consumption behaviors. Incidents that produce self-esteem loss (e.g., a rebuke by the boss at work) have been found to lead the consumer to go shopping or engage in yet another episode of binge eating or gambling or whatever. In particular, compulsive shopping serves for many as a means of earning some short-term self-esteem, (e.g., when attended to by a salesperson, or the feeling of being able to do whatever one wants, feeling powerful by spending money or using a charge card, etc.).

Sociological Factors Finally, sociologically, our culture and social values and norms determine whether the biological and psychological factors would find their outlet in compulsive buying or some other impulse control disorder. If gambling is outlawed and unavailable, for example, then the individual will simply not become a gambler. If unfettered access to shopping or credit is unavailable, then the individual will not become a compulsive shopper. Sometimes, cultures dilute the seriousness of a disorder or even suggest shopping as a cure for a 'negative situation'–as in the bumper sticker in USA: "When the going gets tough, the tough go shopping"; such social nod further feeds the compulsive shopping frenzy.

While the sociological factors are difficult to alter—except credit availability regulation, the individual consumer can act on the other two factors: chemical deficiency and self-esteem. Both medical consultation and psychological counseling can do the suffering consumer some good.

To score yourself on compulsive buying, take the test in Exhibit 20.10.

<table>
<tr><td colspan="6">MEASUREMENT OF COMPULSIVE BUYING</td><td>Exhibit 20.10</td></tr>
</table>

Are You a Compulsive Buyer?

Consumer researchers Ronald J. Faber and Thomas C. O'Guinn have developed the following measurement scale to score customers on compulsive buying. If you want to score yourself, answer the questions, and then apply the formula given at the bottom of that table.

1. Please indicate how much you agree or disagree with each of the statements below. Place an X on the line that best indicates how you feel about each statement.

	STRONGLY AGREE	SOMEWHAT AGREE	NEITHER AGREE NOR DISAGREE	SOMEWHAT DISAGREE	STRONGLY DISAGREE
	(1)	(2)	(3)	(4)	(5)
a. If I have any money left at the end of the pay period, I just have to spend it.					

2. Please indicate how often you have done each of the following things by placing an X on the appropriate line.

	VERY OFTEN	OFTEN	SOME-TIMES	RARELY	NEVER
	(1)	(2)	(3)	(4)	(5)
a. Felt others would be horrified if they knew of my spending habits.					
b. Bought things even though I couldn't afford them.	___	___	___		
c. Write a check when I knew I didn't have enough money in the bank to cover it.	___	___	___		
d. Bought myself something in order to make myself feel better.	___	___	___	___	___
e. Felt anxious or nervous on days I didn't go shopping.	___	___	___	___	___
f. Made only the minimum payments on my credit cards.	___	___	___	___	___

To score yourself, enter your responses into the scoring equation and calculate the total:

$$\text{Scoring equation} = -9.69 + (Q1a \times .33) + (Q2a \times .34) + (Q2b \times .50) + (Q2c \times .47)$$
$$+ (Q2d \times .33) + (Q2e \times .38) + (Q2f \times .31).$$

If your final score is less than or equal to −1.34, you are classified as a compulsive buyer. If you score this low, you may want to reflect on your motivations and resolve to identify strategies to overcome this psychographic aspect of yourself.

Source: Ronald J. Faber and Thomas C O'Guinn, "A Clinical Screener for Compulsive Buying," *Journal of Consumer Research*, 19, December 1992, pp.459-69. Copyright © 1992 Journal of Consumer Research, The University of Chicago Press, Used with permission.

THE MENACE OF SHOPLIFTING

Shoplifting is a crime. Yet it happens. In U.S.A., about 400 million times a year. American retailers lose about $10 billions worth of merchandise every year due to shoplifting.[25] And it is not limited to prankster teenagers, professional thieves, or the starving, utterly helpless, destitute, with no option left. It is done by "regular" people and at least occasionally, even by the affluents, as the case of Academy Award-nominated actress, Winona Ryder attests.[26]

Why do consumers engage in it? If you ask someone who has shoplifted, they would probably tell you they forgot to pay for it; or that they didn't have the money but wanted the product? Or even that because the store makes a lot of money. Whatever be their expressed reasons, one thing is sure: no one ever expected to get caught. But that is, at best , the most circumstantial factor that led the consumer to shoplift on that particular

FIGURE 20.1 · A MODEL OF CONSUMER SHOPLIFTING BEHAVIOR

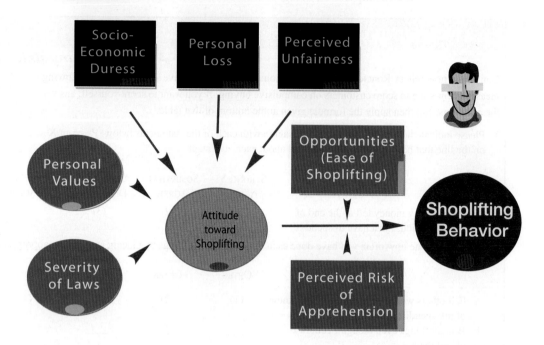

occasion; the real reason lies deeper—inside the person. To capture both types of factors—those that lie deep inside the person and those that lie outside—in one's circumstances or environment, we build a model of shoplifting.

The fundamental reason for, and the source of, shoplifting is consumers' personal value system—their sense of right or wrong. If a person's personal value were that stealing is sin, then he or she would never even harbor the thought. He or she would abhor the very idea of stealing—in other words, he or she would be predisposed against stealing. Thus, consumers' attitude toward or against stealing (or shoplifting) is driven basically by their moral values. However, consumers also are aware of how severe the law against stealing is, and these laws vary across societies. In some societies, stealing is punished by cutting off a thief's limbs; accordingly, in these societies, even a person with otherwise no moral qualms about stealing would over time purge any thoughts of stealing. Values and severity of laws are thus two permanent or enduring factors that explain consumers' enduring attitudes toward stealing.

These enduring attitudes become more or less intense depending on three personal circumstances. First, consumers' current personal duress (financial difficulty) makes buying the needed item infeasible, and they begin to consider stealing as an option. Second, if they have recently suffered a personal loss (e.g., divorce, death of a relative), this loss makes them irrational and impaired to evaluate the right from wrong. Third, if they feel that they have been treated unfairly—by life, by other people, and especially by the retailer, then they abandon any qualms about stealing. Thus, these three personal circumstances also influence consumers' attitude at the current stage of their life.

Attitudes lead to behavior, as you read in Chapter 7. Accordingly, consumers' attitude toward stealing should, when they are pro-stealing, lead to stealing behavior. They do—except in two circumstances. First, if there is an opportunity to steal. If items are in locked showcases, no one can steal them. Second, if the apprehension to get caught is high, then people will not steal them. That is why security cameras in stores are the best deterrent.

In Figure 20.1, we show consumer factors (those for which the consumer is responsible) in ovals. We show circumstantial factors in rectangles—personal circumstances above the 'values-attitude-behavior' axis, and environmental factors below that axis (both with some degree of color differential as well). This environmental versus personal grouping of factors

CONSUMER K.A.R.M.A.
Faucet Part Number 90716

On December 18, 2005, a consumer we will call Roberto bought two plumbing parts for Moen faucets—a dome for shower faucet cost ($70) and a ring valve for kitchen faucet (cost $13), with a total invoice (after tax) of $87.88. On December 21, he called the store to say he would be returning the parts. "Why," asked the store manager. "One of them is the wrong part—I need ring valve part #93456; and the other, I don't need." "How come you don't need it." "Because I fixed the old part." "Well, we will see when you get here."

Apprehensive and prepared to fight, Roberto came back the next day and was pleasantly surprised when the manager accepted back the merchandise promptly and with courtesy, gave him the correct part, and debited the account. Then this exchange took place:

Kevin: You get back $89.10.

Roberto: You are returning me more than what I paid?

Kevin: Yes, that is what my computer shows. Maybe the price of the part you are returning has gone up.

Roberto: And what about this part I bought, are you not charging for that?

Kevin: I did.

Roberto left the store, still puzzled. Five minutes later, he called the store from his cell phone.

"Hi, I am still nearby your store, and before driving away, I wanted to make sure you did charge me for the part I just bought.

Kevin: "Yes, we did. You are okay. Take care now."

When Roberto narrated this incident in his CB class, a fellow student asked, "Why did you call the merchant?" "Because," said Roberto, "I believe that if you pocket something you did not earn, God will punish you in some fashion. Like you will lose your wallet or something!"

(Based on a true story contributed by a consumer. The store's name is Noel's at the corner of Walnut and 12th in Cincinnati, Ohio)

Consumer Karma is Reciprocal Fairness

can be a useful guide for a society to curb shoplifting. We will leave you to ponder that.

OBESITY—THE HIDDEN EPIDEMIC
Every fourth person on earth is too fat

Of all the nations, America is the land of the obese. Fully 120 million or 65% of adults are overweight; about 25% are obese, up from 20% in 1997.27 As many as 300,000 Americans die every year due to obesity.[28]

Obesity is determined by Body Mass Index (BMI). To calculate it, divide your weight in kilograms by the square of your height in meters. If your BMI is <25, congratulations. If, for one of your friends, this number comes to 25 or more but less than 30, then he or she is "overweight." If this number comes to 30 or more, your friend is obese. Furthermore, if the number is over 40, that person is "morbidly obese," at serious health risk.[29]

Around the world, about 300 million people are obese. Obesity is now classified as a growing *epidemic*. According to a UK's Department of Health estimate, among children aged 2-15, as many as 25% were overweight (22% among boys and 27% among girls); and 5.5% of boys and 7.2% of girls were found to be obese (up from less than 1% in 1975). Worldwide, a report places about 155 million (one in ten) children to be overweight; about 45 million of them (About 3%) are obese.[30]

Although USA is a leading country in overweight, it is not at the top of the list. That dubious distinction belongs to the Western Pacific Islands of Naura and Tonga; according to a recent WHO report, nine out of every 10 adults in those Island nations are overweight.

More than 75% of women over the age of 30 are overweight in countries as diverse as Barbados, Egypt, Mexico, South Africa, Turkey and United States; over 75% men are overweight in such countries as Argentina, Germany, Greece, Kuwait, New Zealand, and UK.

In general, there are three factors responsible for obesity: genetics and ethnicity, sedantary lifestyle, and dietary habits. (See Figure 20.2.)

Genetics and Ethnicity For some consumers, their genetics make their metabolism work in a manner that there is no fat build up; others are not as blessed. Likewise, some ethnic groups are more susceptible to fat build up. But we can control the influence of this factor by monitoring the other two culprits.

Sedentary Lifestyle If our lifestyle is sedentary and we do not exercise enough, then we are bound to gain weight.

Dietary Habits Finally, our diets are perhaps the most to blame—not only does an average person not consume the five foods of the so-called food pyramid, but our diets are positively unhealthy. Americans drink an equivalent of 55 gallons of soda a year (up from 20 gallons in 1970).[31]

At least two of these factors are entirely within consumers' power to control. Even the much maligned fast food chains now have a broader menu with many healthy items. McDonald's now offers, on its Web site, opportunity to see exactly what you are getting—how many calories, fat, protein, carbs, sodium, etc. For example, a McMeal consisting of a hamburger, small French fries with ketchup will give you 500 total calories, with 20 grams of fat, 30 milligrams of cholesterol, 1040 milligrams of sodium, 66 grams of carbs, and 15 grams of protein. Substitute the burger by Chicken McNuggets (4 pieces) and the calorie count goes down by 40 (though fat remains almost unchanged).

Want even lower calories? You can get a bacon ranch salad with grilled chicken for mere 260 calories; add Newman's Own® Low Fat Balsamic Vinaigrette for mere 40 more calories. You can check out various other health food combinations; the helpful nutrition calculator will tell you—what you choose is of course entirely up to you.

It is a myth that we have to sacrifice the pleasures of our taste buds to lose those extra pounds. Healthy food can be very tasteful and you can indulge in every imaginable food, albeit with some changes in the frequency of trips to the fast food places. And it is easy to cultivate some natural exercise habits that can in fact become pleasurable: park your car a little farther and walk and smell the air; shun the elevator and race up the stairs with a colleague; at parties and in clubs, stand rather than sit. That is all.

To fully appreciate these ideas, read a national bestseller, French Women Don't Get Fat: The Secret of Eating For Pleasure (Hardcover) by Mireille Guiliano (Knopf, 2004). And, take a tour of the Mayo

FIGURE 20.2 THREE FACTORS CAUSING OBESITY

Genetics and Ethnicity

Sedantary Lifestyles

Dietary Habits

CONSUMER OBESITY

Despite standing all day long, this Indian Police-man is out of shape; perhaps dietery habits are to blame.

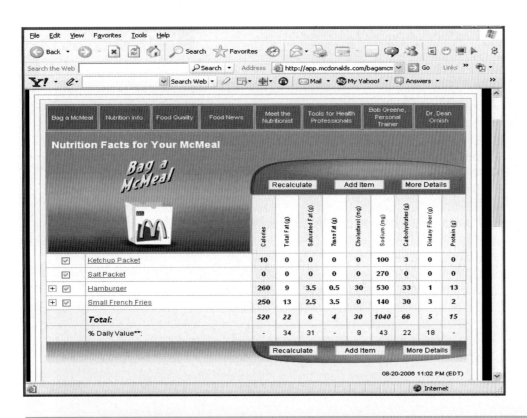

What's Your Brand's Ethical Score?
Helping Consumers Consume Ethically

ethiscore.org
the online ethical shopping guide

Ok, so you are interested in buying products that are produced by companies that follow ethical business practices. The problem is, you don't know which companies qualify, in what manner, and for which products. Don't you wish there were a source to guide you though all this? Well, now there is.

An organization based in the UK has dedicated itself to this very mission: The Ethical Consumer Research Association (ECRA), a non-profit worker's cooperative founded in 1988 to "provide information on the companies behind the brands and to promote the ethical use of consumer power." Its subsidiary Ethical Consumer Information Systems Ltd. has developed a rating system for companies and products both adaptable to changing ethical norms and wholly transparent to users for critical review. It publishes that data on a dedicated Web site, www.ethiscore.org.

The database contains ratings of some 30,000 companies, evaluated on five criteria:

1. Environment (Environmental Reporting, Nuclear Power, Climate Change, Pollution & Toxics, Habitats & Resources)
2. People (Human Rights, Workers' Rights, Supply Chain Policy, Irresponsible Marketing, Armaments)
3. Animals (Animal Testing, Factory Farming, Other Animal Rights)
4. Politics (Political Activity, Boycott Call, Genetic Engineering, Anti-Social Finance, Company Ethos)
5. Product Sustainability (Organic, Fair Trade, Positive Environmental Features, Other Sustainability)

Want to buy an MP3 Player? The highest scoring brands are Archos, mobiBLU, Pure PocketDAB Radio, and Rio (all scoring 12 out of 20); the lowest, Hitachi MP3 player. The iconic iPod is in the comfortable middle (score 9). Craving for chocolate bars? The highest scoring brand is Plamil chocolate (score 15 out of 20); the lowest, Galaxy Chocolate (score 3.5); Lindt receives a comfortable 10.5. Click on the company name and you will get the detailed break down in the five categories.

visit
www.corporatecritic.org
for in-depth
company
research
ec is

For consumers eager to consume with a conscience—in terms of our planet's ecology and our collective societal ethos—such wealth of information is invaluable. It is an incentive as well for companies to reassess their business practices and strive forward toward a higher ethical standard in the production of goods.

(Source. Ethiscore.org)

My CB Book

PUBLIC POLICY AND CONSUMER CONSCIENCE

20

Marketers bring us good products, mostly. Or at least products consumers desire. Occasionally, they sneak in products they know are harmful to consumers, which consumers wouldn't buy or consume if they knew the truth. Fortunately, such greed-driven consumer-harming marketing practices are far and few. Most marketers understand the brand-damaging consequences of deceit marketing, and some are held in check by our governments.

Either way, our consumer life in most of the civilized world is infinitely worry-free because of a climate of responsible marketing and our public policy watchdog. Imagine buying bottled water in a distant underdeveloped village—how would you know that the seller did not fill it from the backyard well, contaminated with all sorts of bacteria. And that is just the beginning. We can never, as consumers, thank our benevolent laws and our vigilant government agencies on the one hand, and our mostly conscientious, self-enlightened marketers on the other, for creating a climate of consumer trust.

Sure, there are some unscrupulous marketers, but they are the proverbial exceptions that prove the rule. More notably, they are, after all, people, and people everywhere are driven supremely by self-interest. As consumers, aren't we all? But even in our moments of high greed, it is a very small number who indulge in shoplifting—a dark practice.

Materialism, vanity, fast food—it is too easy to blame marketers for these consumer gratifications. Yes, marketers advance them, but no more than our culture does in general—and definitely no more than consumers want, desire, and wish. It is not the gift or curse of modern marketing, and it is not limited to Westernized nations.

Take India, for example: there, fast food is everywhere. Every block has a shop making fresh samosas and kachoris, and sugar-syrup-dripping gulabjamuns. In restaurants and in homes, flat dough breads are deep-fried, and vegetable curries float in sumptuous quantity of oils. (Ah, believe us, it is heavenly to partake of those dishes!) Fast food is partially a misnomer, as is junk food. The correct term should be fat food. Some fat food is fast, while some is junk; however, not all fast food is fat. A lot of fat food is even produced through laborious, creative cuisine. Every nation on earth is a fat food nation, and every culture is a fat food culture. It has always been this way, and it will always remain as such. Fortunately, in each culture and in every nation, fat food exists side by side the enclaves of bountiful nutritious salubrious edibles both in nature and human made.

The responsibility is clear: It takes three to tango—the conscientious marketer, the vigilant public policy, and the self-monitoring consumer. As we said before, you can eat healthy; the marketplace offers plenty of choices. And do remember the part about leading an active life. Stand rather than sit, and walk rather than stand. Run rather than walk, and, may we even suggest, dance rather than merely hang out.

Life is wonderful!

KEY TERMS

Price Gouging
Negligent Consumer Behavior
Compliance
Consumer Bill of Rights

Deceptive Advertising
Corrective Advertising
Verifiable Benefit
Lemon Law

Cyber Privacy
Compulsive Buying
Compulsive Consumption
Impulse Control Disorder

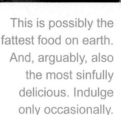

Indian fat food (from left, Clockwise) A friend in author's kitchen deep-fries flat bread, *batura*. A friend in India makes *jalebees*; plate of *jalebees* (*suger syrup dripped*); *samosas* (spicy snack), and *laddoos* (another syrup soaked snack food).

This is possibly the fattest food on earth. And, arguably, also the most sinfully delicious. Indulge only occasionally.

SUMMARY

In this chapter, we covered three broad topic areas: questionable marketing practices, government regulation of marketing practices, and consumers' ethical behaviors. Among questionable marketing practices, we discussed (a) selling unsafe products, (b) unfair pricing, (c) misinformation and deception, and (d) intrusion and over-communication.

Product safety is closely monitored by the U.S. government's Consumer Product Safety Commission, and most marketers ensure that products they sell are safe. Conscientious marketers voluntarily recall products if and when they are discovered to be unsafe. Unfair pricing is a practice where the seller charges a price to take advantage of a situation, a practice also called price gouging. Consumers suspect price gouging when the price is too high to be justified by possible costs, when it exceeds their "reference price," and when they see sellers exploiting a temporary situation. They also perceive unfair pricing if the price charged to them is disproportionately higher than the price usually charged to comparable other customers.

Misinformation and deception in advertising and selling takes the form of product benefit claims that are untrue or exaggerated. Deception in advertising and in selling messages is regulated by U.S. Government's Federal Trade Commission.

The fourth practice, and last in our list, is intrusion and over-communication. By nature, advertising intrudes on our activity of the moment, and when repeated frequently (over-communication), it becomes irritating. Commercial messages also are criticized as a cause of materialism and corrupted values (instant gratification, obsession with one's body, etc.), a concern especially for advertising directed at children.

Next, we discussed the role of government in protecting the consumer. By regulation and laws, it mandates many of consumers' choices (e.g., wearing a helmet) and constrains others (can't smoke in public buildings, etc.). It also facilitates desirable consumption by making infrastructure facilities available (e.g., a bikers' path on city streets). Finally, and most importantly, through its various agencies and laws, U.S. Federal Government, and then State Governments as well, monitor many marketer practices, guaranteeing four basic rights to consumers: the right to safety, the right to be informed, the right to be heard, and the right to choose.

Of special concern are children as targets of commercial messages. In addition to government agencies, a self-regulatory organization called Children's Advertising Review Unit (CARU) of the Better Business Bureau (BBB) closely monitors advertising directed at children. Children are also protected online by a law enacted in April 2000, called Children's Online Privacy Protection Act (COPPA).

In the third and last section, we discussed consumer's own behavior—unethical or self-damaging. We discussed compulsive buying as a chronic tendency to purchase products as a primary response to negative events or feelings. Compulsive buying, and compulsive consumption in general, is an impulse control disorder and we discussed the three factors thought to cause it, namely, biological, psychological, and sociological.

Next we discussed the consumer evil of shoplifting and presented a model depicting all of its causal factors. It is caused, we learned, primarily by one's personal value system, aided by opportunity in the external environment. Lastly, we discussed obesity as an alarming and rising consumption consequence. Responsible for it are biological and ethnic makeup, sedentary lifestyle, and diet habits. Increasingly, marketers are offering consumers a choice of healthier menus.

PUBLIC POLICY AND CONSUMER CONSCIENCE

REVIEW+Rewind

1. List the four marketing practices discussed in the chapter that could be harmful to consumers. Explain each briefly.
2. What factors lead consumers to infer the incidence of price gouging?
3. What could marketers do to avoid consumer wrongly suspecting that they (the marketers) are engaging in price gouging?
4. Name the four approaches by which the government influences consumer behavior, and give an example of each.
5. Name some agencies involved in consumer protection. Then name some regulations or laws for the same purpose.
6. What four rights Did President Kennedy's Consumer Bill of Rights give consumers?
7. How does FTC define deceptive advertising? And what is meant by "corrective advertising?"
8. Mention any five guidelines that COPPA has proposed.
9. List any five unethical consumer behaviors.
10. Explain the three factors in the three-factor theory of compulsive buying.
11. Draw the model of consumer shoplifting.
12. What factors lead to consumer obesity? Which of these factors is the consumer (versus the marketer) responsible for?

THINK+Apply

1. Is consumer deception always to be blamed on the marketer? Is consumer also to blame? Why or why not?
2. Why do some thinkers consider advertising a bad thing? Do the issues in those criticisms bother a typical consumer? Why or why not?
3. List any three negligent consumer behaviors. Then propose an action plan to reduce their incidence. Think of actions for each party: public policy, the marketer, and the consumer him/herself.
4. List any five unethical consumer behaviors you are aware of from your everyday life. Next suggest what could be done to motivate the consumer away from these behaviors.
5. What would be your advice to consumers to avoid becoming a victim to marketer fraud like the Nigerian 419 Scheme?
6. Review the model of consumer shop-lifting. Then write a memo for the management of a mall on possible actions to reduce shop lifting in their malls.

PRACTICE+Experience

1. Interview a few consumers about their personal experiences with price gouging. Next ask them, for each specific instance, what made them conclude that the vendor (or marketer) was price-gouging rather than that the price was high due to factors beyond any marketer's control.
2. Interview a few consumers to ask what sort of behaviors would they consider unethical on the part of consumers. Ask them if they personally know of any incidents of unethical consumer behaviors. Then ask them why in their opinion some consumers engage in these behaviors. Summarize your findings.
3. Interview a few consumers about their concerns about the growing obesity problem? Next obtain their views about the extent to which the consumer versus fast food chains and food marketers, in general, are responsible. Ask them if they are aware of nutrition information now available on Web sites of individual fast food chains and in the restaurants, and if they use it and why or why not? Ask them why consumers in general may not use such information? Summarize your findings.

In the Marketing Manager's Shoes

Put yourself in a marketing manager's shoes. Most concepts in the chapter have some lessons for the marketing manager, i.e., they suggest what to do differently in practice; indeed, often these applications are implicit in our explanations of the concepts and models in the chapter. Identify at least five specific applications of the chapter's concepts, all of which should be entirely new–different from the examples cited here.

RESPONSIBLE MARKETING, RESPONSIBLE CONSUMPTION

As an example of responsible and conscientious marketing, consider the cup in which Starbucks serves you your latte.

Those cups you get at Starbucks have something special about them. They now have a 10% recyclable content. You are hardly impressed ("only 10%, duh!") until you realize that even this small but significant gain came after an eight-year effort. Among other things, FDA needed to approve the recyclable content, since the cup would touch both the beverage and our lips directly. And the company needed to ensure the content was approvable and harmless and, furthermore, that the cup will have the requisite physical strength to hold hot coffee. And do it "alone"—after all, little does it help the environment if we are to double up the cups, as we often do, because we fear a single cup will not hold the beverage or because the cup becomes too hot to hold in hand.

The use of a post-consumer recyclable paper is a first in the beverage industry. For this seemingly trite but in fact very significant accomplishment, the company last year received a Recognition Award from the National Recycling Coalition (NRC). The new cup will mean the company will reduce its consumption of tree fiber by five million tons annually. The company also offers customers 10 cents as discount if they use their own mug. In 2004 (the latest year for which this information was available), customers obtained their coffee this way 15 million times, saving some 655,000 pounds of paper waste.

If you don't have a commuter mug, you can buy a cool one at a Starbucks store. The idea of using your own mug is easy to practice. Hopefully, more and more consumers will adopt the idea. Will you be one of them?

(Information based on a report on NRC press release dated October 13, 2005 (www.nrc-recycle.org)

Consumer Experience In The New Millennium:

The Esoteric, The Enchanted, And The Emergent— Insights, Foresights, And The Marketer Response

- Objects of Desire—Deep Meaning in Consumption
- Eight Trends in Consumer Space—From Revenge of the Boomers to New Forms of Social Relations
- Deep Consumer Profiling—Putting Humpty Dumpty Together
- The 5P's of Marketing—Now, With This Book Under Your Belt, Craft Them Again
- Co-Creating Consumption Value— Marketing's Honorable Mission

American Cool, Japanese Cool—
The New Face of the Global Consumer

On Sunday mornings, teenagers crowd the sidewalks of Tokyo's Shibuya district until they spill over the curbs and into the streets. They start at Hachiko Square, under a video monitor that takes up the entire face of a glass and steel high-rise, and spread out, 30 or 40 wide in the crosswalks. They mill around displays stacked with new sneakers—Nike and New Balance from the United States, Puma and Adidas from Europe via New York. They gather in a small music store that specializes in the American vinyl records played in Tokyo's popular soul bars—Grandmaster Flash, Curtis Mayfield, Parliament. They spend 370 yen (roughly $3) at Starbucks for a tall iced latte, which tastes just as it does in Washington, D.C., and is just as overpriced. Like any global metropolis, Tokyo serves up a substantial dose of American culture, particularly to its youth. Sometimes, like Starbucks or Nikes, it is authentic. Sometimes, like a "Harbard University" sweatshirt or a potato salad pizza, it is not. But cultural accuracy is not the point. More important than authentic American origin is the whiff of American cool.

Japanese youth in Shibuya on a recent Sunday morning pose for the camera

A few blocks from the Starbucks in Hachiko Square you will find Mandarake, a shop that sells used manga and anime (Japanese comic books and animation, respectively). There is no storefront here, just a maw of an entrance carved cavelike out of fake rock and flight after flight of stairs down to the basement-level shop. There, comic books and videotapes are stacked to the ceiling, alongside the toys and collectibles they inspired. The real esoterica are under glass, rare Godzilla and Ultraman action figures selling for hundreds of dollars each.

Mandarake's reach is global. New stores opened in Los Angeles in 1999 and in Bologna in 2001. The buxom, gun-toting pixies, cute monsters, and transforming robots that fill Mandarake in Shibuya show up in America. They are in MTV graphics, street fashions, bars and dance clubs, and even museums. Last year, the Getty Center in Los Angeles debuted a blockbuster show on Japan's "Super Flat" movement—young Japanese art inspired by the two-dimensional look of commercial cartoons.

Sometimes, like an Issey Miyake gown, the Japan that travels is authentic. Sometimes, like cream cheese, salmon sushi, and some knock-off of the Japanese super flat art, it is not. But cultural accuracy is not the point. What matters is the whiff of Japanese cool.

Source: Excerpted from Douglas McGray, "Japan's Gross National Cool," *Foreign Policy*, May 2002. (Used with permission.)

INTRODUCTION

The American consumer. The Japanese consumer. On the face of it, no two people could be more different. No two cultures could be more different. No two objects of consumption, in style and substance, could be more different. In housing, food, clothing, and popular art, Japan's traditional and mainstream consumption differs vastly from that of America.6 Yet, there is a curious presence of each nation's indigenous consumption on the other's soil.

There, host countries' consumers embrace it and assimilate it into their own lives—not all of them, of course, but a significant number of them do. Consumption objects differ vastly—not just across nations and cultures but even within any given nation and culture. What they share in common is "meaning." Beyond their physical form and utilitarian outcomes, it is meaning that they share, and it is also meaning that sets them apart. It is, after all, not goods per se but the meaning of these goods that consumers consume.

The "consumption of meaning" comes into full focus when the goods being consumed are intangible—such as art and memories and body tattoos. How consumers consume the meaning of these symbolic goods and what life satisfactions they derive from such consumption is an apt topic for this concluding chapter.

In 20 chapters long and short, we have covered the ins and outs of consumer behavior. We have defined and described almost all of the concepts and principles of consumer behavior; woven them into theories and models that explain how consumers think, feel, and act in the marketplace; and illustrated their applications for the benefit of consumers themselves as well as marketers. Now, in this chapter, we want to take you on an excursion, visiting enclaves of esoteric and enchanted consumption. Each of us has one, which somehow is unique and intense and has deep personal meaning to us—like body-piercing. Here, we select nine of them, and get inside the skin of the consumer (and we mean it not just for body-piercing) to understand the psychodynamics of that experience.

We divide this chapter into three sections. In Section 1, we explore the consumer experience of esoteric consumption. In the second section, we survey current and emerging trends in consumer behavior in the new millennium. In the third and final section, we describe how knowledge and understanding of consumer behavior should fashion the marketing manager's "response" to the consumer. Through this excursion and forward-gazing, we bring our exploration of consumer behavior to its logical fruition—to grasp the quintessential value of diverse domains of consumption, and to "plot" how we should, as marketers, become co-creators of consumption value for consumers.

OBJECTS OF DESIRE:
DEEP MEANING IN CONSUMPTION

What does your car mean to you? And your pair-of-jeans? Do your sunglasses have a special meaning for you? Do you have a special attachment to your cell phone? Your i-Pod? And, would you feel sad giving away your old high school football outfit? To explore the symbolic meaning of goods, we have selected nine unique and significant consumption entities, here simply called "consumption potpourri." This is a rich cornucopia of the culture of consumption itself, so let us immerse and experience it.

1. APPROPRIATION OF PRODUCTS
"How I Anoint What I Buy"

The clothes you wear, the car you drive, the mobile phones you use—these products are produced by the thousands and bought by millions of other consumers. How is it, then, that you come to consider your car as your own, separate from other identical units

CONSUMPTION POTPOURRI: IN SEARCH OF MEANING OF CONSUMPTION

PRODUCT APPROPRIATION "How I Anoint What I Buy"	**AUTHENTICITY CONSUMPTION** Bringing Glorious Past to Present Life	**GIFT EXCHANGE AS CONSUMPTION** "I Will Love You if You Love Me."
BODY ADORNMENT CONSUMPTION "My Body is a Scrapbook"	**MEDIA FICTION CONSUMPTION** "Dear Producer: Don't Forget I Am the Arcmchair Director"	**PARTICIPANT SPORTS CONSUMPTION** "Life is a Game. Game is Life."
TECHNOLOGY CONSUMPTION EXPERIENCE "Gizmos: I love them, I hate them."	**THE WIRELESS CONSUMER** "I am not really here; but 'here' is nowhere."	**VIRTUAL LIVING** "Finally, I am My Dream-self."

of the same brand; you come to view your jeans as something special and unlike any others; and you come to like your own mobile phone so much that if you were to lose it, replacing it by another exactly identical unit wouldn't be the same thing? When you bought it—the car, the pair of jeans, the cell phone—it was one of the countless many; but after you acquired it, something happened to it; you did something to it, so it somehow became different, unique, and special to you. What you did is called **appropriation**—the process of making something one's own. Although consumers never call it so, they are always attempting to appropriate their acquisitions—the products they acquire as gifts or as purchases, at least the important ones. When objects are appropriated, they somehow become special, and as such they become sources of extra satisfaction. Let us see how this process of appropriation works.[1]

Basically, this entails investing ourselves in the product and somehow separating and distancing the product from its original existence as a mass produced unit. This process consists of five rituals: selection, acquisition, exchange, possession, and usage. Of these, we have covered possession and exchange rituals (Chapter 9). Selection, acquisition, and usage rituals are new in this chapter and unique to appropriation.

Selection Ritual This is the process the consumer undertakes to identify and select the desired object. The fact that the consumer selected it from so many other products makes that brand or object more salient to the consumer. The more time the consumer spends in selecting the product, the more he/she sees himself/herself invested in it. Somehow the very process of selection puts the self into the product and distinguishes the specific object from others (notwithstanding similarity in a physical sense).

Thus, products whose selection entails much personal investment of time will become more appropriated. In particular, when we choose a specific product after rejecting several others (like that apothecary coffee table from Pottery Barn), then by contrast to those

...cts we rejected, we feel an affinity toward those selected. Moreover, in ...rocess of selection, if we judged them also by how well they reflect our ...nalities, then we will experience that much more the affinity and personal ...g toward the chosen product.

...xchange Ritual An exchange ritual is an event surrounding the ...sition of a product as a gift from someone. A product received as a gift ...mes unique because of the memory of the gift-giver. Occasionally, we ...uy products as self-gifts, and in these instances, the memory of the cause ...ebration serves to distinguish the product in our minds as something ...l.

Acquisition Ritual Many consumers follow certain acquisition rituals; for instance, they will take their best friends when they go to take possession of a new car, or wear special clothing to get a diamond or the like, and they will consult an astrologer to decide exactly when to buy an engagement ring. In many ethnic cultures, certain days are considered more auspicious for acquiring a significant new product like a car or a house or a domestic animal. Many ethnic groups also perform certain religious rituals, such as worshiping in the name of the newer possession or anointing the object itself.

Possession Ritual Often consumers try to modify a product before they take possession of it—for example, by retrofitting or customizing a new car, or by remodeling a house. When we acquire previously owned objects (e.g., a house, car, clothing, etc.), often we attempt to transform or alter them, in part to exorcise the ghost of the previous owner, so to speak. For example, we change the paint or window treatments on a house, get new wheel covers on the car, wash clothes we buy from a thrift store, and so on. Through these rituals and transformations, we appropriate all objects we consider significant in our lives.

Usage Ritual Finally, we appropriate some objects simply by using them; somehow, they seem to mold themselves to our individual bodies and idiosyncratic behaviors. As I drive my car, I feel it is getting used to the way I drive so it is now mine and special. Likewise, as I break in my shoes, or wear my jeans, I see them progressively fitting better and better over time (in part because they become softer with washing). I also personalize a product through some modifications in its use—for example by downloading certain software, configuring the desktop, and changing the wallpaper, I appropriate my computer. It is no longer just any computer; rather it is *my* computer. By selecting the ringer tones for my cell phone, I make a mass produced phone unique, special, and *my* own.

Sometimes, we perform these rituals as second nature; sometiems, with great fanfare (drving out a new car to show it off). Regardless, such rituals result into products being annointed, and such annointment both begins and nurtures our attachment to the products we acquire and own. That is why, our products become very especial to us.

2. CONSUMING AUTHENTICITY
"Bringing Glorious Past into Present Life"

Authentic (adj)—Conforming to fact and therefore worthy of trust, reliance, or belief; Having a claimed and verifiable origin or authorship; not counterfeit or copied.[2] Here, in the context of consumer products, we will define **authenticity** as the genuineness of an object in its likeness as it existed at a time in history.

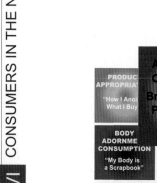

Authenticity is an important source of value and life satisfaction for consumers. Although consumers differ in the extent to which they seek authentic experience, most consumers do enjoy authentic experience at least occasionally in their lives. Who among us has not paused at Dick Clark's American Band Stand or Planet Hollywood to look at a dress originally owned by Marilyn Monroe? Original? Well, almost!

Some consumers seek authenticity as an occasional experience.

Others want to incorporate it into their everyday lives. Likewise, some are deeply attached to a particular domain of interest; others are curious but not deeply attached. Thus, the Elvis Presley museum in Memphis attracts thousands of visitors every week; some come for the first and only time, and they enjoy viewing all the Elvis artifacts. Later in their lives, they will occasionally remember this experience with fond memory, but beyond that they will go about their lives without thinking of Elvis. Others will wrap themselves in the Elvis experience—visiting the Memphis museum frequently, having several Elvis items (replicas) in their homes, listening to Elvis music, reading his biographies, and frequently talking about him with friends and even strangers.

Authenticity in objects comes in two forms: original and replica. In the original form, the object is believed to have actually existed in a specific time period and to have been used in a specific circumstance. Thus, an "original" Marilyn Monroe dress is indeed the one that was actually worn by Ms. Monroe. In contrast, in a replica, authenticity is judged by how similar the object is to the original real object—e.g., the dress on display is not the one actually worn by Ms. Monroe, but the dress she actually wore looked exactly like this one.[3]

Consumer enjoyment and satisfaction from the experience of authenticity also comes in two forms: exploration and connection.[4] For consumers who are not enduringly involved in the domain of the authentic experience, viewing an authentic object or witnessing a replica of an authentic historical event is simply an **exploration**, an act of getting to learn and know about that object or event. These consumers feel the joy of simply seeing the object or place from times past; it satisfies their curiosity and gives them the satisfaction of knowing a slice of the past more directly, more intimately. The second group of consumers—those who are enduringly involved in the specific domain—feel the experience as a much more personal event. Viewing an authentic object or being in an authentic place gives them the sense of **being connected** with the past, somehow being part of that era. It is for them a fantasy world come true.

Exploration-oriented consumers are quite satisfied with the replica form of authenticity. *Connection-seeking consumers* seek out, in contrast, the authenticity in its original form; they are unlikely to experience the same joy by viewing or experiencing a replica—they want the "real thing." Moreover, connection-seeking consumers will not stop at simply viewing the authentic exhibit; rather they will want to bring back with them a substantial part of the authentic exhibit (in replica form, of course)—tangible objects with which they can then surround themselves in everyday life.

3. GIFT-EXCHANGE AS CONSUMER BEHAVIOR
"I Will Love You if You Love Me"

Gift exchange—perhaps no other custom among humans is so pregnant simultaneously with economic as well as social meaning. In every culture and nation, people of virtually all ages and economic means expend considerable time, money, and thought in buying gift items. For several weeks preceding Christmas day, for example, in most of the Western world, consumers are on a mission and adventure, combing stores of all stripes, trying to find suitable gifts for as many as 20 to 30 persons. For some, it is a period of economic hardship, scraping together enough money to buy a gift for everyone on their lists. And this economic burden is joined by considerable social risk as each gift must fit the recipient's expectations and still be within the buyer's budget. One wrong move, and it could jeopardize the relationship with the intended gift recipient. Therefore, let us understand the consumer psychology of gift exchange.

A **gift** is defined as a tangible or intangible product voluntarily given by one person to another, through some ritual presentation and embodying some symbolic representation of the giver's sentiments for the recipient.[5]

CULTURAL MEANING OF GIFT EXCHANGE

The very idea of gift-exchange (regardless of the specific gift occasion or the gift item) is embedded in culture. Every society imposes certain obligations about gift-giving. In fact, we all have three obligations: an obligation to give, an obligation to receive; and an obligation to reciprocate. All gifts have some symbolic meaning. Basically, a gift-giver expresses empathy—saying in effect that "I share in your life, in your joy, in your celebration; I am happy because you are happy." Not giving a gift when expected communicates that the expected giver does not wish to maintain a relationship with the assumed recipient. Conversely, the recipient has the obligation to receive. Not accepting a gift would imply that the targeted recipient does not accept either the relationship itself or the specific sentiment the gift conveys. Third, reciprocation is a core norm between gift-exchange partners. **Reciprocation** means returning the favor in like manner. Once accepted, the recipient is expected to reciprocate at some future time. Non-reciprocation will convey a desire not to maintain the relationship.[8]

There is one exception to the norm of reciprocity. Generally speaking, reciprocity is expected among status equals (i.e., people of equal status) but not from status subordinates

---

PSYCHOLOGY OF GIFT-GIVING

EXHIBIT 21.1

HOW CB SCHOLARS LOOK AT GIFTS

Although there are literally hundreds of occasions for gift-exchange, and thousands of possible gift items, they can all be characterized along following dimensions.

- Structured versus emergent
- Anticipated versus Surprise
- Ritualistic versus Expressive
- Altruistic versus Agonistic
- Utilitarian versus aesthetic

First, gift occasions can be structured or emergent. Structured occasions are standard occasions that occur repeatedly on the same predetermined days. Christmas and Valentine's Day are examples of structured occasions for an entire population of consumers, and birthdays, and anniversaries are standard for individual consumers. Emergent occasions are those that are not predetermined and do not repeat in a regular pattern. Examples are baby shower, weddings, hospitalization, etc.

Second, gifts are either anticipated or a surprise. Most gifts are expected by their recipients; the occasion demands it; social norms nearly mandate it. Occasionally, however, consumers indulge in gift-giving just to show extra caring for the recipient, as a pleasant surprise.

Third, and related to the above characteristic, is the concept of ritualistic gift. Ritualistic gifts are given simply because it is a ritual, the occasion demands it. There are no personal feelings on the part of gift giver. Weddings, baby showers, birthdays of close relatives, Christmas, promotion of a close colleague, farewell party, etc., are all examples of ritualistic gifts. Positively expressive gifts on the other hand are given to people one has special feelings for. These may be given on ritualistic occasions, but they go beyond mere obligation. Positively expressive gifts, as opposed to merely ritualistic gifts, are chosen with consideration of receiver's needs (often unexpressed) or preferences and one goes beyond the call of duty, in expense as well as in involvement in finding the gift.[1]

Fourth, gifts differ in their "self-serving" content. Altruistic gifts are those given largely for the recipient's benefit, with no consideration of immediate personal gain. In contrast, agonistic gifts are intended to gain an immediate personal advantage. Most business gifts tend to be of this type.

Finally, gifts can be utilitarian--products the gift recipient can use for his or her currently felt needs--e.g., a small appliance, kitchen utensils, or an airline ticket. Alternatively, gifts can be aesthetic or symbolic--items whose principal value is not material but sentimental or intangible—e.g., jewelry, pictures, artwork, etc. Of course many products when given as gifts are a mix--utilitarian but at the same time also symbolic----e.g., a monogrammed shirt, a picture frame, or intimate apparel.[2]

1 for further reading, see Mary Ann Mcgrath and John Sherry, "giving voice to the gift: the use of projective techniques to recover lost meanings," *j. of consumer psychology*, 2 (2), 1993, 171-191.

2 this section is based on diverse literature: John Sherry (1983, "Gift giving in anthropological perspective," *J. of Consumer Research*, vol. 10, (sept), 157-167; Mary Wolfinbarger (1990), "Motivations and symbolism in gift-giving behavior," in Advances in Consumer Research volume 17, eds. Marvin e. Goldberg and Gerald Gorn and Richard W. Pollay, pages: 699-706; Cele Otnes, Julie A Ruth, Constance C. Milbourne (1994), "The pleasure and pain of being close: men's mixed feelings about participation in valentine's day gift exchange," in *Advances in Consumer Research*, Vol. 21, eds. Chris t. Allen and Deborah Roedder John, 159-164.

(e.g., personal assistants, valets, servants, mailpersons, etc.); to these recipients, the gift generally conveys appreciation for the services rendered. Occasionally, status superiors may also not reciprocate (or not reciprocate with the same personal touch), signifying that the gift is viewed as a token of gratitude from the gift-giver for their patronage or tutelage. Every gift serves three functions:

1. Social Integration The gift integrates the giver into the social group. By giving the gift, the giver in effect says to the recipients, "I want to integrate myself into your group, in your society. I want to be seen as part of it."

2. Social Distance Reduction By giving a gift, the gift-giver gets closer to the recipient. It is a means of building a relationship with the desired person or increasing the distance (by not giving the gift) from those who are less desired. We fashion our gifts accordingly, being generous or incorporating a personal touch for the former group or people, and barely meeting the obligatory expectation in the latter case. When properly used, gifts serve as social lubrication.

3. Tangible Expressions of Relationships Not only do gifts build relationships (i.e., reduce social distance), but they also specify the nature of relationship. Gifts exchanged by family members are different than those exchanged by coworkers, which in turn are different from gifts between lovers.

Cultural Meaning

Beyond these general functions, specific gifts are means of conveying one's identity or status. Gift givers consider gifts a reflection of their own identities and status as well as the status of the intended recipient. Certain characteristics of gifts convey status and identity. These characteristics are market price, brand name reputation, and uniqueness. (See Figure 21.1.) Other characteristics convey expressiveness. **Expressiveness** refers to the extent to which the gift is accompanied by the giver's sentiment. Purely utilitarian gifts (e.g., coffee mugs) are low in expressiveness. Non-utilitarian gifts (e.g. flowers) are high in sentiment. Often, utilitarian gifts possess expressive qualities because of the prestige of the brand name, such as Godiva chocolates.

In purely obligatory gift situations, often the recipient tries to "signal" what items he or she is expecting or can use. Sometimes this signaling is explicit, as in a bridal registry. Many cultures do not allow such explicit signaling. For example, in Eastern cultures, the concept of a bridal registry does not exist, and it would be considered rude to indicate what one wants as a wedding gift—although, as in everything else, even here, the city dwellers are adopting some modified version of the concept.

When the gift recipient is not forthcoming with any such indication, the gift giver may try to "read" the intended recipient's wishes or needs, especially if he or she feels sentimental toward the latter and is consequently motivated to delight the gift recipient. The more correctly the giver is able to read these wishes and fashion the gift accordingly, the more expressive and sentimental the gift becomes. Some gifts are acquired or produced with personal labor and skills; other givers transform the gift item with some personal touch. The more the giver invests personal effort in finding the gift or in producing or modifying the gift, and correspondingly, the farther the giver removes the gift from the realm of a marketable (or market-available), mass-produced commodity, the greater the expressiveness of the gift.

Whereas the gift-item is in itself a vehicle for communicating sentiment (or the absence of it), often the expression of it is made explicit by an accompanying inscription. It ranges from the minimal and matter-of-fact to the deeply personalized, reflecting, correspondingly, the inner sentiments of the giver.

Because gifts have cultural meaning, the selection of a gift is a serious consumer task, filled with great social risks. The social risk stems from the following potential errors:

a. Status Incongruent The gift item may be perceived inappropriate to the status of the giver and/or the receiver

   b. Disproportionate The gift might violate the norm of reciprocity—unequal to the gift previously received by the present giver

   c. Impersonal The gift might be considered less personal or more personal than desired.

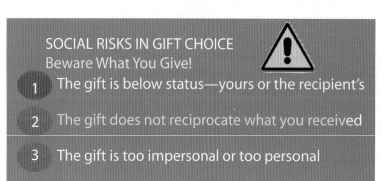

SOCIAL RISKS IN GIFT CHOICE
Beware What You Give!

1 The gift is below status—yours or the recipient's

2 The gift does not reciprocate what you received

3 The gift is too impersonal or too personal

When relationships are in the formative stage, the risk is one of over-reaching rather than under-reaching; the exchange parties must start with relatively impersonal gifts and progress in small steps to more personal gifts—constantly reading with each exchange episode the recipient's acknowledgement and acceptance of the giver's sentiments.

Such is the fascinating world of gift exchange and the all too important role gifts play in our lives.

4. CONSUMPTION OF BODY ADORNMENTS
"My Body Is a Scrapbook."

All humans are motivated to look good. That goal leads to three forms of consumption: (1) regular grooming rituals such as applying makeup; (2) permanently altering the body mass, such as through liposuction and by pumping iron; and (3) making relatively permanent marks on the body, such as piercings and tattoos. All three forms of consumption have the same underlying motives, although some motives are more prominent in one form than another. We explore these in the context of tattoos.[9]

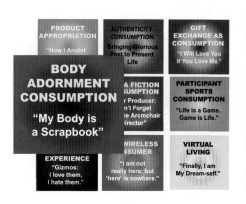

Tattooing has its roots in ancient history when tribal societies engraved their bodies with symbols of animals, gods, and elements of nature. In modern times, and in the West, the revival or Renaissance of tattooing began in the late 1950s with the influence of artists like Lyle Tuttle, who founded the Tattoo Museum and Hall of Fame in San Francisco. The academic and commercial art worlds began taking notice of tattooing as an art form; gallery showings of tattoos as an art form increased, creating general awareness among consumers. Furthermore, this "art culture" positioning of tattooing attracted both better artists and a better clientele—not merely those who were on the fringe of society. At one time, only rough bikers, rebels, and sailors got tattoos, but now middle class consumers, college students, sports heroes, and media celebrities have all taken to getting tattoos.

Although no current statistics are available, according to a 1990 survey by American Households (unpublished) of 10,000 random households, 3% of the respondents had a

CONSUMER MOTIVATIONS FOR GETTING TATTOOS

1. **Aesthetic Beauty** Aesthetic value as art and decoration of the body.
2. **Magic/Mystery** Belief in the power of certain symbols to bring good luck or to protect oneself from evil.
3. **Affiliation** Desire to affiliate with certain people, groups, or institutions.
4. **Alienation** Desire to alienate oneself from the mainstream society.
5. **Self-Esteem** Renders tangible the feeling of one's control over one's body.
6. **Identity Construction** Construction, reconstruction and definition of self-identity.

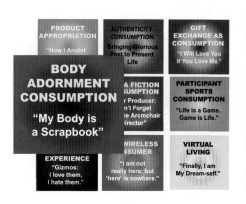

tattoo.[10] A source puts this number in 1996 at 12 to 20 million Americans.[11] Tattooing costs money. Even a small, basic, one-color tattoo costs about a $100; a tattoo by a renowned artist large enough to cover the entire back can cost about $5,000. The decision to get a tattoo is a two-part decision: the consumer has to select a symbol and decide where on the body it will be applied. There are three broad categories of tattoos:

1. "Vow" tattoos Tattoos that signify a relationship to someone or something (e.g. a girl friend's name) or a commitment to someone.
2. Group affiliation tattoos Tattoos depicting a gang or sports team symbols.
3. Symbolic tattoos Tattoos of birth signs, symbols signifying some self-association like occupation, hobbies, etc.

In terms of body site, men generally tend to get them on arms; women choose from a greater range of locations: in addition to arms, they use ankles, thighs, back, lower back, hips, etc.

In general, consumer motivations for getting tattoos can be summed up in six ctegories shown in the box.

Males tend to view tattoos primarily as symbols of self-concept or self-control. In contrast, women view them primarily as a beauty aid and decoration, although self-identity is as strong a motive for them as for men. When aesthetic beauty is the principal motive, designs are chosen not because they symbolize anything about the consumer but because they are beautiful art works and because consumers think they look good on the body. Many consumers choose astrological or religious symbols both because of their beliefs in the power of supernatural beings and also to show their identities as religious persons. Many consumers choose tattoos depicting their favorite stars, sports team names, significant others, and romantic interests, and for these consumers the primary motivation is group affiliation. For Latinos, for example, tattoos on the hand often signify ethnic pride and group affiliation—the most common symbols popular among Latinos are Christian religious symbols (e.g., angels, crosses, devils, fairies).[12]

Alienation is perhaps the motive that comes closest to the historic motives of the majority of tattoo consumers—those on the fringe of society. They adopted tattooing simply as a means of rebelling against the mainstream, a sort of "in your face gesture." Consumers of this ilk are the ones who go heavy—getting multiple tattoos and covering large areas of the body.

Self-esteem comes from feeling a sense of freedom to get whatever tattoo one wants and to put it on one's body. As one tattooee (a 30-something female who recently had been divorced) said, "My body is NOW mine, so I can do whatever I like with it." This ability to alter one's body becomes a powerful symbol of self-definition.

Finally, the most potent motivation is identity construction and identity display. A body is really a writing surface on which consumers want to write, for the whole world to see, their identities and the kind of people they are. For many consumers, tattoos become a collection and the body a vehicle for displaying collections. One consumer, who had gotten tattoos from 35 different artists, described his body as a "scrapbook" symbolizing his life history. Consumers who see tattoos as a means of identity construction and identity display have to deliberate a lot in choosing their tattoos—a misstep could permanently engrave the wrong identity on their bodies. Tattoo artists play an important role—they have to understand the consumer's motives and understand the kind of identity to which the consumer aspires. As one tattoo artist says: "The tattoo is already inside the consumer; all we do is bring it out for every one to see."

The tattoo is already inside the consumer…

Erin Williams, a college sophomore, sports a tattoo of a Chinese symbol for family harmony and THE names of her children. She believes that the symbol captures her devotion to her family.

5. CONSUMPTION OF MEDIA FICTION
"Dear Producer: Don't Forget I Am the Armchair Director."

Today television reaches all corners of the world, including the remote villages of third-world countries. Most consumers are exposed to at least some TV on a regular basis. Whereas some of this TV viewing is to get news and information, much of it is for entertainment. Millions of consumers around the world become regular viewers of specific program series such as *The Apprentice*, *Survivor*, *Friends*, or *The Real World*. Not only do they watch these, but they then spend considerable time discussing the episodes with friends and family and often thinking about them. They become enduringly involved. This enduring consumption of TV episodes becomes a significant source of life satisfaction for many consumers, who manifest a fan-like devotion to the show. What is the nature of this consumption experience? What is the source of satisfaction here?

Consumer researchers have identified three components of this consumption experience: (1) meaning negotiation, (2) belief consumption, and (3) consuming the artifacts. **Meaning negotiation** refers to seeing meaning in the episode, understanding the episode and accepting it as logical and plausible. If a show or a movie has events that do not seem logical, then we typically do not like the show; we reject it as silly or implausible. Sometimes we are not sure we have understood the meaning, so to validate our view, we discuss the event or episode with others, and through their agreement or correction, we come to establish the meaning or validate our own opinion.

Belief consumption refers to believing in the core values and concepts underlying the show. The popular TV show *Will and Grace*, for example, is based on the theme of people living an alternative lifestyle; in watching the show regularly, we in effect accept the legitimacy (and normality) of that lifestyle. Finally, by consuming the artifacts—the accoutrements that accompany the show—consumers bring the show more squarely into their lives. Let us illustrate these three "benefits" with *The X-Files*.

X-Philes Consumption Community[13]

X-Philes are fans of the daring TV show that premiered on September 10, 1993, on the American TV network Fox Channel. Its grand finale was a 2-hour long show that aired on May 19, 2002, ending a 9-year blockbuster run. The show featured two FBI agents, Fox Mulder and Dana Scully, with each episode oriented toward solving a crime case. What was unusual about the show is that it juxtaposed truth and fiction drawn from popular conspiracy theories and also belief in supernatural powers. The show's creator, Chris Carter, once stated that the show was based on three maxims: "Trust No One," "I Want to Believe," and "The Truth is Out There." More than 14 million viewers, typically young, urban, educated consumers, tuned in every week. A small but significant proportion of this group are *X-Philes*, the show's ardent fans who not only watched the show but also spent hours in chat rooms, attended fan conventions, and bought and sported show-related merchandise.

Embracing the show's driving maxims, the fans themselves seemed to be driven by analogous supra-beliefs: "I Want to Believe," "The Meaning is Out There," and "Trust This One." This is how these supra-beliefs translated into consumption behaviors.

Negotiating Aesthetic Consumption Standards Media events that are consumed are always evaluated against some unwritten aesthetic standards (for example that "the story should be internally consistent"); if the media product (e.g., a TV show or a movie) falls short of this standard, the consumer views the consumption as not enjoyable. This judgment-making is itself a consumption experience. Fans typically communicate about what they found substandard and what was above par in meeting the unwritten aesthetic standard. For example, one chat room participant wrote:

"What is up with these killer kitties? A cat cannot kill a human! Even if it is possessed

by some spiritual dude."

Another fan initially interpreted the feral cats shown in one episode as a nonphysical manifestation. However, after an explanation from another X-phile member, she altered her interpretation:

"Ok, I have thought better of it. … The feral cats were probably real… I just assumed they were illusions because they vanished at the end of the episode. Could be… doesn't have to be. I'll go with it."

This is what we mean by *meaning negotiation* being a part of consumption experience —and it is both a challenge and source of consumption satisfaction.

This meaning negotiation (not just understanding the logic of a show, but also that the understood meaning meets a shared aesthetic standard) is why most consumers discuss and opine about any media event they consume. Thus, consumption occurs at two times: once when consumers are watching the show, and second when consumers are discussing it (to validate their perception of its meaning).

Consuming Beliefs About Mysterious Experiences X-Philes also shared their real-world encounters with mysterious things. One fan posted: "A couple of nights ago, I saw these two bright lights just hanging in the sky…" And another one wrote: "People think these UFOs are just Hollywood fantasies. It is not true! Don't be a fool. Be a believer!"

X-philes thus consume their beliefs in mysterious objects first while viewing the show and later validate them through assertive sharing with others like them who also want to believe in these mysteries.

Consuming the Artifacts There is a poster behind Mulder's desk that says "I want to Believe." A fan wanted to know where he could buy one. Possessing this poster and other merchandise is yet another way for fans to connect to the show, to bring the shows' mysterious themes into their own lives. On the X-Net there is considerable buying and selling of such merchandise and exchange among the members. Now, first the possession of artifacts is in itself a way of bringing the show into one's life in a tangible way, but using exchange as a mechanism to acquire them brings consumers into interaction with other community members, and this in turn is a means of social adhesion and community building.

6. CONSUMPTION OF PARTICIPANT SPORTS
"Life is Game. Game is Life"

For many consumers, participation in sports starts in early childhood. Sometimes interest on sports runs in the family. More often, it starts with participation on a school team. Often neighborhoods and work groups organize teams to play their favorite sports. In the Indian Peninsula, such teams are widespread among high school and college students, specially for playing cricket, a popular game there. In much of Europe, it is soccer; in North America, it is baseball or softball. Many begin to participate in sports only in their adult years, at which point participants often take up such games as tennis and golf.

It goes without saying that the principal motivation for participating in a sport is enjoyment. But what are some other motives? For many consumers, the more specific motives and sources of satisfaction are these: (a) exercise and fitness; (b) a sense of accomplishment; (c) social affiliation; and (d) excitement and exhilaration.

The exercise and fitness benefits of sports participation are obvious. When this benefit is the principal goal, consumers choose the sport that fits the level of activity they desire; for instance, tennis for more vigor and softball or golf for less vigor (although each game itself can be played with varying degrees of intensity). A sense of accomplishment comes from achieving certain skills and proficiency in playing

Consumption of participant sports; begins early in life.

©iStockphoto.com/Jason Lugo

the game. Social affiliation is a primary motivation for many, particularly in league sports. Finally, excitement comes from each individual play in the game. For example, each double play or touchdown scored creates a rush of adrenalin that provides instant gratification.

Participation in sports entails considerable market exchange. This occurs in three forms: (a) facility fees, (b) purchase or rental of equipment and paraphernalia, and (c) concomitant consumption. Facility fees are paid for the playground or club membership. Sports equipment and uniforms can be a considerable expense for many. And, finally, participation in a game is, for many consumers, part of a whole event that culminates in dining out or drinking with friends. On each such occasion, consumers can spend a lot or a little, depending both on their involvement and the affordability of the sport. These extremes are illustrated by two consumers we interviewed recently.

- Dave, 44, has been playing softball for 25 years. He owns 4 bats, a bat bag, cleats, batting gloves, several balls, a knee brace, and an ankle brace; cost, approximately $1050. In contrast, Andy, 37, who has been playing softball for 10 years, owns 2 gloves, a hat bag, and 2 pairs of cleats, at a total cost of approx. $120. Dave also reported spending about $400 a year on his kids for food and candy while they watch him play. And he spends about $200 a year on beer on the days he plays softball.

Selected Excerpts from Consumers Who Play Sports:

- Softball–Keeps me active but doesn't overwork me. (M, 44).

The joys of controlling the ball.

©iStockphoto.com/Galina Barskaya

- What do I enjoy the most about the game (softball)? It is the preciseness of batting; being able to control the ball and place hits where you want. Then, being able to read the ball, know how it is going to go. (M, 42, married, 4 kids).
- Other activities I associate with playing the game are drinking, being out in the sun, a lot of kidding around, and parties. (M,23, single)
- My reason for playing the game? Memories with friends; exercise; develop athletic skills; sun; relieve stress; T-shirts from winning leagues (F, 21)
- Why play softball? I can drink beer and play at single the same time (M, 37, divorced with no kids)
- Volleyball—I started playing it in my country (SriLanka) when I was 11. It is now a passion. I love being on the court, feeling the emotion, enjoy the level of competition, and always want to do more. (F, 21, student)
- I like adventure sports—white water rafting, hiking, rock-climbing, boogey boarding. I like them all, because of the rush of personal experience and the knowledge of knowing [sic] anything can be done. (F, 26, grew up in Sri Lanka, now in U.S.A.).[14]

7. TECHNOLOGY CONSUMPTION EXPERIENCE

"Gizmos: I love them, I hate them"

Elaine is talking to her friend (Jill) on her cell phone while out on the street. George and Jerry are with her. George and Jerry express surprise that she used her time on the street to call Jill. Elaine asks, "What is wrong with that?" Thereupon followed this disapproving rhetorical questioning from Jerry and George acting as a team (paraphrased): "Elaine, are you not telling Jill she is not important enough for you to make time for her while you are home?" "Just fit her into your schedule as a side activity while you can do something else? That way you are not wasting your time, eh?"

Yes, this is a scene from Seinfeld, a popular TV show in the United States, starring comedian Jerry Seinfeld—a show aptly dubbed "a show about nothing." As viewers around the world (the show is seen in many foreign countries) know, Jerry and George were speaking tongue-in-cheek in an effort just to create self-doubt in Elaine (they succeeded, briefly). Although Elaine quickly saw it as a lame and silly argument (and got irked), it did illustrate a fundamental dilemma consumers face in using technology. Technology in consumers' lives is a "mixed blessing." This "mixed blessing" nature of technology is referred to as a *paradox*. Consumer researchers David Glen Mick and Susan Fournier have identified eight paradoxes of technology, discussed below.

Control/Chaos Caller ID service gives you control of whether or not to take the call. But it also gives your friends a reason to suspect that you are screening out their calls.

Freedom/Enslavement A cell phone gives you freedom not to be tied to a place if you are expecting a call; at the same time, you now have to take it everywhere, and you feel so helpless on days you forget to take it with you. Also because people can reach you no matter where you are, you feel enslaved.

New/Obsolete You are fascinated by the newness of a model of car or phone etc., but also saddened at the thought that it too will soon be obsolete.

Competence/Incompetence Technology makes you feel more competent, more able. For example, using publishing software, you can now publish professional quality resumes, invitation cards, and reports, and you can automatically spell-check the document. At the same time, the same software can be daunting to learn or can suddenly produce errors from which you wouldn't know how to recover. And you can suddenly feel technology-illiterate and thus experience a new level of incompetence.

Efficiency/Inefficiency Using the Internet to gather information and even shop can be efficient. At the same time, sometimes you can spend hours surfing the net or getting an online merchant to answer your questions or resolve problems.

Fulfills/Creates Needs Having an e-mail account is great—so you can now send messages to friends and acquaintances. But suddenly, you start receiving junk mail, so now you need software to block unwanted emails (although many email services such as AOL now provide this utility to its subscribers).

Assimilation/Isolation Big screen TV becomes an excuse for having a Superbowl party so you can have friends and feel socially connected; at the same time, the TV becomes the focal point of the occasion, replacing social conversations.

Engagement/Disengagement Creating a Powerpoint presentation can be a fascinating, all-absorbing creative task with opportunities for customization. On the other hand, in the presentation, the form takes over the substance, and there is less opportunity to establish an emotional connection with the audience—the kind that an erudite speaker speaking directly without any technological aid can make.

Consumer Experience of Paradoxes

How does a consumer experience these paradoxes? What mental and psychological reactions does the experience of these paradoxes create? And how do consumers manage that experience? Researchers Mick and Fournier have outlined a model, shown in Figure 21.1.

As shown in the model, consumers feel the paradox as a conflict or ambivalence; for example, I know that the computer will raise my competence but also that I will have to understand the manual. The anticipation of this paradox, and in fact actually experiencing the paradox (I have already bought the computer and am enjoying many of its benefits but am also now struggling through the manual) produces conflict or ambivalence among consumers. Next, this conflict or ambivalence produces anxiety and stress—anxiety about how to avoid the negative side of technology while embracing the positive side. This

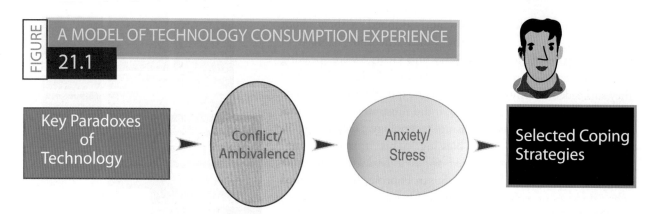

anxiety and stress can lead consumers to adopt many coping strategies. Mick and Fournier have identified a set of these, presented in Exhibit 21.2.

Some examples of these coping strategies are provided by the following excerpts from some consumer interviews:[16]

"[Prior to my purchase] I first borrowed it (a camcorder) from my brother-in-law so I would know what I was getting into."

"It is a brand new machine and I certainly would not go with them if they didn't have the money back guarantee."

"The dishwasher—it takes us three days to fill it; and while the dish washer is being filled, we may run out of unused dishes; so my husband and I now simply don't use it; we just wash the dishes right away."

"I will simply not get into preparing the powerpoint myself; I will always let my secretary handle it."

"When I am doing gourmet cooking, I simply don't use the microwave. Microwave is okay for fixing regular meal; but for gourmet cooking, microwave is out; it is a rule I follow."

"We just decided to unplug the TV for a year."

"We put the answering machine in a corner not visible easily from rest of the room area, so we wouldn't be tempted to retrieve the messages continually."

8. THE WIRELESS CONSUMER

"I am not really here; but 'here' is nowhere."

Wireless phones. They are everywhere these days. Their availability to the masses was presaged by a TV commercial a few years ago. In that TV ad, a teenager in the backseat of

---

CONSUMER STARTEGIES FOR COPING WITH TECHNOLOGY   EXHIBIT 21.2

LooK What CB Researchers Found

Consumers have been found to cope with technology by

- Avoiding or Delaying Technology Adoption **Ignore and not adopt new technology;**
- Adopting with Enough Safeguards **Borrow and try out someone else's product; seek extended warranties.**
- Avoiding or Abandoning Usage **Avoid using the technological product after buying and owning it.**
- Adopting with Dedicated Effort **Taking the time to learn and master the technology so as to not experience incompetence in using it.**

a car taps her window to catch the attention of a tycoon in a stretch limo in the adjacent lane. She asks, "Excuse me, do you have a cell phone?" Annoyed, the wealthy old tycoon answers, "Of course I do," to which the young girl cheerily chirps, "So do I. So do I!"

Today, nearly every consumer in the western world carries a cell phone, and most in the developing nations have access to one. Whereas men and women are equally represented in the wireless world, men tend to use wireless communication more often than women (8.3 calls per day versus 5.5 by women), in part because men use their phones for work as well (three times more often than do women).[17] Until only a few years ago, the principal reason and use of cell phones was for work and business. Today, its dominant use is for personal and social communications, especially among the masses. Its principal defining feature—mobility—has given a new sense of freedom and control to consumers. No longer are they tied down to a place. They can connect any time, anywhere, to anyone whose cell phone number they know. Also, as Web access via cell phones becomes more widespread, consumers will access any information anytime anywhere.

The latest development in wireless phones is, of course, the incorporation of a digital photography feature. You simply point the "eye" of the combined device toward someone or something, and you capture the image instantly. This digital image can then be downloaded onto your PC. If your cell phone is also equipped with a wireless Internet application, you can then email that picture instantly to a friend.

Ethnographic studies[18] in Europe, the United States, and Latin America have revealed that cell phones have brought several changes in consumer lives, as described below.

Increased Personalness A cell phone is not shared with others. It is with the consumer always, as a constant personal companion. Consumers give their cell phone numbers only to their selected friends (and coworkers). So calls received on the cell phone are somehow more important, more personal. Teenagers, who had to put up with a parental ear snooping on their conversations, finally feel a new sense of privacy.

Emotional Security Because consumers can call their friends and family anytime, they believe they have instant access to social support in their hour of need. Many parents buy their teenage children cell phones so they can keep tabs on their whereabouts, and of course, teenagers constantly are able to connect with their friends at will; in fact they are chattering with their friends all the time. Loneliness is now a thing of the past. In surveys, teenagers report that because of cell phones, they have expanded their circle of friends and casual acquaintances.

The Blurring of the Private and the Public Because we are accessible to friends, family, coworkers, and bosses all the time, the distinctions between work time and non-work time, between being at home and being at work, and between private and public has blurred. Increasingly, consumers have lost their hesitation about carrying on personal conversations in public places, and, conversely, business related conversations in social company.

The camera feature now available on many wireless phones raises fresh concerns about privacy. Anybody can take anyone's picture, and without his or her knowledge.

Spontaneity Cell phones have also given consumers a greater degree of spontaneity. When they are late for a meeting—social or business—they feel no regret, simply because they can just call the other party to advise them of the delay. In turn, there is less pressure to be punctual. Moreover, now there is less planning and more tentativeness in setting up a time and place for a meeting, often leaving these details to the last minute. This tentative scheduling allows consumers to micro-manage their time and squeeze the maximum utility and pleasure, so to speak, out of whatever they are doing at the current moment. This spontaneity is a new source of perceived freedom.

Marketers' Alert: A Mixed Opportunity

For marketers, cell phones enable anytime, anywhere access to consumers. This phenomenon opens a floodgate of new opportunity. Imagine you are in a supermarket, passing by the cereal aisle, and suddenly your phone rings, announcing a coupon for a brand of cereal available for you to download on the phone. This place-based communication has given rise to a new term in marketing practice—**contextual marketing**—the practice of sending consumers messages pertinent to the purchase and consumption situation of the moment. Obviously, this has the danger of being seen by the consumer as a grave intrusion upon privacy, and marketers have to be cautious in using this application. One barrier of course is that the consumer has to pay for the received call, but even more importantly, such an unsolicited context-based marketing message can create an emotional backlash against the company.

But consumers can use their cell phones to order a product anytime, anywhere, and can also use them to make payments, using their digital wallets. This means that vendors of impulse-purchase products (e.g., street hawkers, event-based vendors, etc.) will have to be Internet ready (including possessing the ability to accept digital payments) if they are to avail themselves of this opportunity to do business.

The ideal utilization of this new marketing channel is one that gives consumers what they want, and this would mean piggybacking marketing messages onto services offering those applications that consumers seek on their cell phones. Two such applications are already on the horizon. First, consumers wish to stay connected to people and events pertaining to their areas of interest. Thus, teenagers want to know, for example, about music events; most consumers want to be in the know, on a real time basis, about sports; and some consumers want to have up-to-date information about financial markets. And, they want to communicate information in these areas to their friends. Marketers can build interest-based information Websites (accessible on wireless phones) and communities for which consumers would voluntarily register.

Second, marketers can integrate their messages with two existing features of cell phones—ring tones and "wallpaper." Marketers can create wallpapers that incorporate their logos or brief text messages, which consumers can then download. Likewise, commercial jingles can be re-formulated as ring tones. Of course, consumers will seek and accept these only if the wallpaper design and tones are intrinsically "cool." A company called Zingy (Zingy.com) offers precisely this service and represents a creative example of how marketers can exploit this new channel in a way which, rather than intruding on consumers' privacy, offers them something they welcome.

Third, the picture camera ability of wireless phones can also change shopping. A consumer in a store can simply point and shoot a picture of the merchandise and then email it to someone and seek advice. Marketers should be on the lookout for opportunities to observe and understand how this "virtual shopping pal" phenomenon affects consumer behavior in the store.

9. VIRTUAL IDENTITY

"Finally, I am my-dream-self."

In the physical world, we have an identity we can't alter. We have to be what we are.

The virtual world has liberated us. We no longer need to be hampered by our identity in the physical world.

Millions of consumers are enjoying this newfound freedom.

With a simple click of the mouse, millions of consumers are getting connected with one another. Increasingly, consumers are living in a virtual world. Consumers, young and old, spend considerable time online. Checking out information, reading stories, playing online games, chatting with people of similar

The Utterly Fantastic Consumption Experience in Second Life!

There is a world in cyberspace that is at once so surreal and yet so very lifelike. It is called Second Life. We introduced you to it briefly in Chapter 1, courtesy of Bon Milano. Now, here is the full skinny on it.

First, a prefatory note. Don't dismiss Second Life as mere virtual reality. Or a mere online multiplayer game (like World of Warcraft). Or a mere leisure pastime for techies or geeks or Myspace teens. Part online multiplayer game, part social networking, part LEGO building skills, part graphic design (a la Adobe Illustrator and Photoshop), part entrepreneurship, part innovation, Second Life is nothing like we have ever seen or imagined before. And not only will you experience all these facets here, you will actually create them!

Let's start at the beginning. You simply sign up for free at www.secondlife.com, download the software, and install the program.

Happy Island in SecondLife

Immediately after launching the program, you are asked to create your online persona. And then you are free to roam the world!

You can create objects (Lego style) from simple 3D shapes (cars, motorbikes, designer clothing— whatever you wish). You can get some land, and then you can build a house on it. At the time of writing (July 29, 2006, at 14:00 hours GMT), there were 357,775 "residents." Many of them are celebrities in their First Life on planet earth.

You will have plenty to do here. There are live musical performances. Two radio stations broadcast live. Warner Brothers is making a movie there, shot entirely in digital space using bytes, not physical cameras. MTV is holding a virtual fashion show featuring the Avatars. An author is autographing his latest book. And two Avatars are getting married in the local church.

Even more fascinating, and of great import for our purposes, is the fact that Second Life is a marketplace! There are restaurants in which you can dine; libraries in which you can check out books; and stores where you can buy surfboards, bikes, and even clothes. Yes, American Apparel actually has a store there, selling virtual clothing. You can hang out at a bar or club, or be invited to a private party. You can post your pictures there (courtesy of

Happy Island Residents Roam the Island

Flickr). You buy land and anything else, and you can sell what you make or buy. All using Linden dollars, which you can exchange for actual earthly currency (current exchange rate: about Linden $300 to one US dollar).

One more thing. All of those objects are created not by the company that invented this "in-world," but by residents like yourself. The site offers you tools and invites you to build the 3D objects you desire. Residents have built entire cities and shopping areas. Check out Mai Tai Beach Club, complete with virtual sun bathers, and The Midnight City, a funky shopping district.

Most of all, build your avatar to your fanciest dreams. This is the über-consumption world of the future. And the future is already here!

Resident Bon Milano surfing the island

interests. From Myspace to Facebook, and from YouTube to Flickr, consumers are placing their autobiographies online, for the whole world to see. These autobiographies—called *my profile* in e-space, comprising pictures, films, stories, likes/dislikes, etc., are sometimes real and true; sometimes, they are made up; reflecting the identity consumers wish they had. From email reading, to IM, to chatrooms, to Web surfing, count the number of hours we are spending online, and we will realize that a considerable part to our lives, we are living online.

Now, the business organizations are joining the online community networks. Type up Flocabulary in Google, for example, and one of the early entries is on MySpace. Yes, Flocabulary is on MySpace. As are umpteen other businesses. And why not? After all businesses must go where consumer are. This means more and more consumers are going to find, online, stuff of interest.

Web surfing as a spectator (browsing content already there) is one thing. But the Internet also offers many opportunities to become an active participant, creating online content. Now SecondLife takes this feature to a new level. You can construct for yourself a new identity, complete with physical metamorphosis to personality overhaul. We need not elaborate. After all, you will be Googling soon, isn't it?

II Foresights:

EIGHT TRENDS IN CONSUMER SPACE

What will the future of consumer behavior be like, say over the next decade? What will change and in what manner? Forecasting the future is always risky business, yet not to form an educated expectation can be even more risky by leaving us unprepared to face the future. In this section, we survey the broad environment of consumption, describe the social and cultural milieu, and project eight upcoming trends in consumer behavior.

The Revenge of the Boomers

Let Power Be to Women

Greater Diversity

Telecommuting

The Global Consumer

New Forms of Social Relations

The Technology Suffused Consumption

Experiential Marketing

1. THE REVENGE OF THE BOOMERS

Baby boomers (those born in America between 1946 and 1964) are up in arms. They are 78 million in number, and 38 million of them will be in the age range of 55-64 over the next decade. Call them self-centered, materialistic, dreamers, anything. Just don't call them old. They don't see themselves that way, and they definitely don't want to look their age. Yes, they are up in arms, fiercely battling aging looks. Hair coloring, anti-wrinkle creams, Botox, lipo-suction, they will take them all. Whatever it takes. And they will have the money to afford it all. After all, unlike their predecessor cohorts, they are vibrant and active, and they don't plan to retire anytime soon.

Elsewhere, especially in the cultures of the East, aging and aged looks actually bring more respect, so the pursuit of age-reversal is going to be much more subdued. But growing ranks of 70, 80, and 90-somethings, specially in Japan, are buoyed by rising longevity and will create unprecedented levels of demand in health and elder care, as well as for innovations in medicine.

2. LET POWER BE TO WOMEN

Women are not going to abandon the apron anytime soon, but the days when a woman's place was, by definition, in the home are long over—at least in much of the Western world. Women now outnumber men among college students (54%),[19] and a recent report

shows that academic achievement scores are higher for girls than for boys.[20] In most of the industrialized world, women aged 25-34 outnumber men in possessing at least a college degree.[21]

With degrees under their belts and an 8-10 year longevity advantage over men, women's life-time earning capacities will be substantially improved. Already, 30% of working-women in the United States earn more than their husbands.[22] A significant number of men, especially those who worked in high tech industries have been laid off, whereas their spouses took up or continued working in their jobs in the growing service industries (healthcare, retail, etc.). And men are quickly becoming adept at raising the kids and completing domestic chores, thereby earning the appellation "Mr. Mom."

©iStockphoto.com/Amanda Rohde

The contemporary woman, in industrialized and third world countries alike, is surely and rapidly moving toward an egalitarian role in corporate, government, and household affairs. Increasingly, then, marketers will have to treat women as having equal importance in decision making about all major purchases.Conversely, even to market household consumables, they will also have to include men in their target audiences.

3. GREATER DIVERSITY

As we move toward the end of the first decade of the new millennium, there will be greater population diversity, certainly in the U.S., but also in Europe, especially in those countries with growing service economies (e.g. Switzerland). In the United State, the largest growth will be in the Hispanic population, which is expected to grow 35% by 2010 (rising from the current 35 million to 47 million). Also, the number of immigrants from the newly liberated countries of the Eastern Europe (e.g. Poland) will increase, and the current inflow of international students into the nation's universities (who later become permanent U.S. residents and join the work force) will continue. There will also be growing diversity in lifestyles and a public recognition of it.

With all this "mixing" of ethnicities and lifestyles, there will be greater cosmopolitanism (a population open-minded enough to change and to accepting differences among people) peacefully co-existing with population enclaves still steeped in ethnocentric conservatism. At any rate, and undeniably, marketing will have to adjust to acknowledge and embrace this diversity. In the language, culture, people, and consumption of products depicted both in the media at large and in advertising in particular, smart marketers will promote their products and services both to the new niches of non-majority groups, as well as via mass-market campaigns that embrace people of all sorts. As an example of the former (new niches of the non-majority population), in addition to such channels as BET (Black Entertainment Television) and Telemundo, the International Cable Channel now features programs in the Japanese, Chinese, Hindi, French, and German languages. As an example of the latter (i.e., incorporating diverse consumers into a single general marketing campaign), TCM (Turner Classic Movies) recently experimented with a new programming idea: every Thursday, it showed eight hours of movie entertainment from the famed Bollywood (Bombay's Hollywood).

4. TELECOMMUTING

Telecommuting—the practice of working at a distance from a formal place of employment—will grow. The basic motivation for telecommuting for individuals comes from the need to play multiple roles simultaneously, most notably raising children and working. And this role is being thrust increasingly onto men (i.e., the "Mr. Mom" phenomenon). Also, if a company moves, the employee with a preference for the current location may not want to. Besides, the desire to be free to be wherever, whenever, is a basic human motivation. For corporations, the motivation for telecommuting comes from the fact that real estate in business districts, particularly in major metropolitan areas, is very expensive, and it pays to let employees work from home. Corporations also find it cost effective to outsource many operations to free-lance skilled designers, artists, engineers, consultants, etc., who work from their homes.

Enabling this trend is technology. With network computer technology, it is now possible for any employee to gain access to any of a company's databases and information, so employees can work from home, or from the road; millions of salespersons already do. Moreover, a supervisor in a central location can "emulate" the screen on a distant employee's computer both to monitor as well as to support the employee's work. Furthermore, video conferencing, Web-based broadcasting of audio-visual presentations (dubbed "webinars"), and other related technologies will reduce the need for central location-based corporate meetings. Thirdly, the new advances in wireless communication are giving everyone the capacity to communicate with anyone anytime.

What will be the impact of telecommuting on consumer behavior? Well, employees are consumers too. Telecommuters dress more casually (so the market for business suits will be down and casual clothing up), more likely fix lunch at home (hence, the demand for easy-to-fix, supermarket-based "meal solutions," e.g., pre-cut salad in bags) and will order more delivered food. Because of isolation from coworkers, telecommuters will also look increasingly for participation opportunities in local professional and social organizations, and marketers who organize such networking activities will need to be responsive to this need.

5. THE GLOBAL CONSUMER

The marketplace will increasingly become global. By this we mean that products and styles with origins in diverse regions and cultures of the world, both far and near, will become available in every region and every nation of the world. Historically, and for the most part, culture has migrated from the West to the East; in contrast, the future will see an all-directional cross-pollination. Fashions of the West will be available in the East, and the West in turn will borrow heavily from the East. These imported products and styles will be available (and desired by consumers) both in original, historical forms as well as in adaptations (e.g., kimonos as loungers and kimono-style Western dresses in the West; pure McDonald style burgers and local pita-bread based adaptations in the Middle East). This cross-pollination will be most noted in fashion clothing, furnishings, food, and music; moreover it will be most apparent among the youth of all nationalities.

Such globalization will not mean homogenization, however. Far from it. Indeed, consumers in each country as a whole will continue to retain their national cultures, both in values and attitudes and in overt consumption styles and substance (e.g., a majority of Indians, even a 100 years from now, will believe in extended family living and will continue to wear *saree* and *kurta* on special occasions and eat *chapaati* as their everyday food). Nor will the population of consumers within any nation look homogeneously globalized. Rather multiple cultures of consumption will be present simultaneously, such that slowly but surely more and more imported cultures of consumption will exist side by side with the indigenous ones.

This cultural diffusion will present a challenge and opportunity to marketers. They will have to be quick-footed, scan the globe for transferable material culture, test-market new ideas and prototypes, and bring the cross-cultural potpourri to market at the right time to the right consumers.

6. NEW FORMS OF SOCIAL RELATIONS

There will be a continuing decline in conventional sources of social advice and support—kith and kin, life-long friends, and strong local community will lose their reach and influence over individuals. Not only has there been a trend away from extended families, but there is also a decisive trend away from the conventional family type. And it is in the nature of modern contemporary living that life-long friendships and integration into a local community are hard to form and maintain. This is due to increased urban mobility; it is also due to a task-oriented, utilitarian mindset about relationships that most people growing up in contemporary modern societies acquire. In such a setting, there is a void—and an unfulfilled need for having someone to share one's emotions with, to turn for advice to, and to generally feel connected. What will fill this void?

Look for the emergence of a new industry—let us call it the **Industry of Social Relations**. Increasingly, consumers will turn to commercialized sources of social support. Already, dating services are burgeoning, the latest quirk on it being "speed dating"—in a musical-chairs style, eligible singles meet prospective partners for 3 minutes each to identify an initial match. A professional organization is experimenting with a similar practice for speed networking.[23] As another example, a number of parents—frazzled moms and dads—are turning to so called "Parent-Coaches"—self styled professionals who advise parents (by phone or via email) what to do to rein-in a cranky child.[24] Marketing opportunities exist for organizing this industry. Opportunities exist for market-based personal conversation partners—and we don't mean the 1-900-phonelines. Rather, we mean human-to-human, wholesome, personal conversations, with someone willing to lend an empathetic ear. Love doctors in the mall, if you will.

GLOBAL CONSUMPTION CULTURE IN ACTION

Scenes from ethnic life in USA: (Top L to R, clockwise) Indu and Ashwin Madan (a bank administrator and a medical devices scientist, respectively) relax in their ethnic loungewear. TeKay Designs decks these two African-Americans in ethniic wedding ensemble. Aya Hirose, author's student, gets ready for a formal evening in a kimono.

Speaking of global consumer, guess where this picture was taken? Melbourne, Australia, Spring 2004.

7. TECHNOLOGY-SUFFUSED CONSUMPTION

Digital and wireless technologies have revolutionized our lives. Only a decade ago, you would not have believed us if we had told you that there would be cell phones with built in digital cameras so that you could take the picture anywhere and then instantly email it to your mom or just download it to your website, without actually being connected to a PC. Now that device is already so yesterday, and that is just the beginning.

In a different domain, now there are cars in the making that will sense a potential collision with an object or a person in its path and stop automatically. With Tivo or Replay, consumers can watch any TV program anytime, untethered by the programming schedule. And, now there is computerized clothing. Small computer chips and digital circuits are built into clothing. You will wear them just like your regular clothes, and they will unobtrusively monitor your pulse rate and other biological functions and automatically send information to your doctor. Or they will call 911 if need be.

Then, there is the wired household. Imagine this: your refrigerator and your pantry are fitted with small computers. They automatically sense when your milk carton or your box of cereal is about to run out and needs replenishing, and they will reorder the pre-specified quantity from pre-specified vendors (don't worry, you will have control to intervene if necessary). Virtual shopping will be even more advanced, both online and offline. You and your mom (who lives on the other coast or continent) will be able to shop together. Already, you can do it on the Lands' End Web site. In the future, you could be shopping in a physical store and be able to beam to your mom a real size real time view of clothing you are trying on.

Technology will bring new convenience to physical store shopping. Shoppers will be able to make payments (at increasing number of retail stores) using "digital cash" via their wireless phones. And they will be able to scan the merchandise on a hand held wireless mouse-like device throughout the mall, deposit the device (actually called a "frog") at a central Kiosk (called a "pond"), and leave—after which someone will assemble all the merchandise from various stores and deliver it to their homes, or the list could be posted on a consumer's Website as a "wish-list" for gifts.

Courtesy: NTTDoCoMo (Photography by John Swannell, 2005)

You and Your Car in the Future

Meet Toyota PM. For this concluding chapter, we can think of only a few stories that fit the Romancing the Consumer moniker and are also futuristic, and Toyota PM is a leading contender. Toyota PM—Toyota's Personal Mobility and Communication vehicle. It is a driver-only concept car unveiled at the 2003 Tokyo Motor Show.

The single-person cockpit has no side doors; rather you enter from the front (the windshield hatch lifts up). And actually you don't enter it; you just stand on the ground, turn around, and lower yourself into the seat. Then the seat slides back into the body of the car, and the windshield snaps back into place.

The vehicle body can assume three positions: upright for you to get in and out; a middle position for city driving, where its shorter length helps you maneuver through the narrow urban spaces; and a more horizontal posture for an aerodynamic shape for high-speed, highway driving. All this happening automatically.

There is no hood. In fact, there is no engine. Rather, an in conspicuously placed electric motor powers the vehicle. There is no key. To start the PM, you push a button, as you would on your laptop. There is no steering wheel either. Instead, a couple of joysticks take up the tasks of accelerating and controlling the vehicle's direction. And each wheel is independent of the others so that the left and right wheels can turn in opposite directions. Imagine how this can help you steer the vehicle around tight corners.

My CB Book

8. EXPERIENTIAL MARKETING

Marketing scholars have always maintained that consumers don't buy products; rather they buy product benefits. And the experience of consuming them. Now, smart marketers are taking note. There is a new form of car rental—in metropolitan areas like New York and Washington, D.C., for example. Consumers arrive by the Metro (subway); pick up a car; go around town, do their shopping, or whatever; return the car; hop on the metro; and go home. They don't have to hassle with the maintenance and ownership of the car.

Reality shows are on the rise. They are a hit because they are an excellent source of vicariously lived life experiences. Many of course are juvenile in taste, appropriate to the youth they target. An untapped market opportunity exists, however, for a mature audience equivalent. Many videogames are hit because they allow consumers to experience life vicariously, with interactivity to boot, like *Sim City*.

Stores like The Body Shop and restaurants like Rainforest are a hit because of the sensory experiences they offer. Many consumers love electronic pets because they come as close to giving consumers the experience as possible, but without the hassle of taking care of the pet. For example, a robotic pooch called *I-Cybie* not only barks and wiggles but also walks and does tricks like pushups and headstands. Now, a human robot is also available—called *Robosapien*, and made by Wow Wee International. (Check it out at Woowee.com.) The robot can do household chores plus entertain you by dancing and talking back to you. In other domains, consumers are increasingly trying out yoga, adventure camps, and other exotic leisure activities. Marketers who can offer these and other experiential products will have ample opportunities to advance their fortunes.

The Revenge of the Boomers

Let Power Be to Women

Greater Diversity

Telecommuting

The Global Consumer

New Forms of Social Relations

The Technology Suffused Consumption

Experiential Marketing

This is amazing stuff in a transportation vehicle. But wait—the PM is more than a vehicle. It is actually an integrated transportation and communication device. The instrumentation panel keeps you informed of your coordinates and offers a full entertainment guide. That instrument panel is not in the dashboard. In fact, it is not physical at all. It is, rather, a holographic display, a virtual interface, hanging in mid-air, and it receives your commands by sensing the position of your fingertips.

More importantly, it communicates with other PMs in the area. It will communicate your coordinates to them and theirs to you, and it will share other vehicle information. You can surrender the control of your vehicle to another PM nearby, if you like. So, for example, a group of PMs can move as a platoon, piloted by the leading vehicle in the front (with some controls left to you). It is a one-person vehicle, but don't confuse it with a "lonely person's vehicle." It is designed, instead, to be in full communion with other PMers.

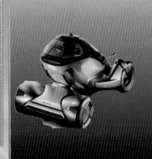

When communicating with other fellow PMs, you will notice your vehicle changing colors. The door tips, headlamps, side and rear panels, and rear wheels light up in different colors to signal the activity inside your vehicle and to communicate different emotions!

This is of course a concept car. But stay tuned. Personal transportation and communication devices delivering romance such as this, on the cover of this book as well as in the world of Toyota, are just around the corner. Welcome to the future consumption world!
Source: Toyota.com News Room. Also reports, based on Toyota News releases, on Howsuffworks.com and Gizmag.com.

My CB Book

III. CONSUMER INSIGHTS AND MARKETER RESPONSE

Now that we understand consumer behavior, the inevitable question is, how can we put all this knowledge to use to serve the consumer better? As a customer oriented marketer, we know already that we serve our business interests best by satisfying the consumer. The understanding of consumer behavior—how consumers think, feel, and act—should enable us to fashion a marketing program that is in accord with our target consumers' modes of thinking, feeling, and acting. To satisfy them, marketing programs must respond well to their motivations and needs. In this section, we develop some key ideas for a consumer-behavior informed and responsive marketing program.

Basically, from a consumer behavior standpoint, there are three parts of a marketing planning project: (a) segmentation and target identification, (b) deep consumer profiling, and (c) responsive offering presentation. See Figure 21.3. First, since no marketer can satisfy and serve all consumers, we must recognize salient differences among consumers and identify the consumer segments we can serve best (through segmentation and targeting). Next, we should research, understand, and describe detailed consumer behaviors of the chosen groups (through deep consumer profiling). Finally, we must create offerings (e.g., products or services, pricing, and associated messages) that respond well to our target consumers' world-view (the concept of responsive offering presentation). Let us look at each.

SEGMENTATION AND TARGET IDENTIFICATION

Some differences between consumers are obvious; for example, age, sex, race, income, education, social class, and geographic location. Collectively known as demographics, these form the first basis for segmenting consumers, and we outlined various demographic

FIGURE
21.3

THREE STEPS TO MARKETING RIGHT

segments throughout this book. The next set of characteristics pertains to psychographics, and in Chapter 6, we covered some well-known psychographics-based segmentation schemes such as VALS™. Geodemographics, while anchored in residential locations, actually incorporate a heavy component of psychographics. Many research companies offer other, country-specific psychographic segmentation schemes, and, as a marketer, you should avail yourself of these and choose the one that seems most appropriate. Beyond these established ways of segmenting the market, virtually any of the other consumer characteristics discussed in the book can be used to segment your market: values, motives, perceptions, attitudes, loyalty, and involvement, among others.

Take values. These segment consumers who are materialistic versus those who are not; pro-lifers versus pro-choicers; environmentalists; consumers who value animal rights; and nationalists versus globalists. All these can be useful segments. In terms of motivation, consumers could differ on where they fall on Maslow's hierarchy, for example. Product specific motivations could also differ. For example, some consumers might buy a motorcycle as a more economic means of transportation than a car; others might buy one to experience outdoor adventure and the thrill of the ride; and still others might want one as a badge of a particular lifestyle. Consumers with different perceptions about your product class or brand may need to be classified as different segments (e.g., those who see SUVs as devilish vehicles versus those who see them, naturally, as very utilitarian vehicles). Likewise, consumers may be classified as those with low involvement versus high involvement; those who are brand (or store) loyal versus those who are not; knowledgeable versus consumers who are unfamiliar with a product; those who have recognized a problem versus those who have not; avid information seekers versus information minimizers; technophiles versus technophobes; net-surfers versus non-surfers; those who love to shop versus those who dread shopping; and so on.

These and many other concepts covered throughout the book are all useful bases of segmenting your market. A contemplation of all these bases may appear to be an arduous task, but identifying the right consumer segment to serve is a singularly important responsibility in marketing planning. Admittedly, segmentation is less important if your product is one that can be mass-marketed. On the other hand, if you want to identify a niche market or an emergent market, contemplating and evaluating all of these consumer differences can be a very fruitful exercise. The benefit of reading this book is that you are now aware of a comprehensive list of variables on which to segment your target consumers.

DEEP CONSUMER PROFILING

Once you have identified your target market segment you must now prepare a comprehensive, deep profile of this segment. By *comprehensive deep profile*, we mean a description of as many of the consumer concepts as possible, as covered in this book. For example, suppose your target segment is college seniors from upper middle-class families in metropolitan areas with a cosmopolitan but change-resistant outlook. Now, for this segment, describe everything: their values, motivations (e.g., achievement or ego-needs), their lifestyles, and their activities and interests. For example, what kind of music do they like? Are they into fine arts, fine wine, dining, sports, or community volunteering? What is their culture, their ethnic identification, and their self-concept? What is their life theme, and what are some of their current life projects? Also, describe their perceptions about the marketplace, your product category, your brand and competitor brands. Is this product category one of high or low involvement to them? How knowledgeable are they about this product category and about your brand? In what way do they see the product as related to their life themes? What are their reference groups? And which reference groups do they consider relevant and seek influence from when selecting a brand from your product category? What specific product benefits are they seeking? What are their evaluation criteria? Which brands are in their evoked and consideration sets? What is their attitude toward your brand on all three of the attitude components (know, feel, do)? Are they comparison shoppers, impulse buyers, coupon clippers? Etc.

To prepare such a profile, you will need to do in-depth consumer research. Initially, qualitative research using focus groups and in depth interviews may be used. These may be followed by large-scale quantitative studies. If your product typically engages hedonic, social, and identity (rather than exclusively utilitarian) product values, then you may also want to deploy creative research methods such as visual collage construction or ethnographic studies (see Appendix 1). In essence, you are preparing a dossier on your target consumers. Such in-depth profiling might in turn reveal important sub-segments, and you must, naturally, recognize them and profile them individually. You may also revisit your decision to target or not target a specific segment or sub-segment in the first place.

Actually, *targetting* might be a misguided term, its use in marketing for more than four decades notwithstanding. A better term would be *frame-forming* (note: "frame-forming," not "framing"). Targetting implies that consumers are the target (as in a bull's eye). What marketers need to do instead is to *form* (or adjust) their *frame of view*, to bring the consumer into the frame so they (marketers) could then keep the consumer in focus. Mere semantics? Actually, no. Labels do reflect our implicit view of a phenomenon, and in turn they guide (and misguide) our actions themselves.

©iStockphoto.com/Amanda Rohde

©iStockphoto.com/Mikhail Laverenov

Targetting **vs.** Frame-forming
Lables do reflect our mindsets!

RESPONSIVE OFFERING PRESENTATION

The third and final step is *responsive offering presentation*. By "offering," we mean the product or service with all its associated entities—its branding, packaging, assortment, warranties, price, distribution channels, and advertising messages. The so-called "augmented" product, that is. This offering must be responsive to all of the elements of the deep profiles you will have prepared—responsive to how consumers think, feel, and act. Essentially, this entails planning the 5P's of marketing—four of which are classic, and the fifth a recent realization. Let us briefly discuss each.

Product The principal instrument of creating consumer satisfaction is the product. For established consumer needs, product design should create configurations that best meet the needs of your target consumers. In a car, for example, do your target consumers want fuel economy or high performance, style or comfort? What amenities do they want? Many needs are latent, but placing yourself in consumers' proverbial shoes and making keen observations can suggest products for hitherto unmet needs—this is how teeth whitening strips or Torrid stores for plus-sized teenage girls were conceived. Observing consumers' changing lifestyles can also uncover needs for new services such as speed-dating.

Pricing Several characteristics in the psychological makeup of your target consumers should inform your pricing decisions. Price should obviously be set at a level your target consumers can afford, based on their income. Beyond that, a product's desired image (e.g., economy or prestige) affects pricing. Consumers' reference price and price-quality associations also dictate pricing levels. If the target segment is price-sensitive and given to comparison-shopping, then the prices would have to be set at market competitive levels. The more the product is bought for reasons beyond the utilitarian, the less price-sensitive the consumer is. Likewise, the more the product plays a role in consumers' life-themes, the less price-sensitive the consumer is. Less price sensitivity means consumers are willing to pay more for intangible dimensions of the product or service, such as the prestige of the brand.

Place Marketers have a choice of a wide array of retail stores and distribution channels. By classical conditioning, the image of the store rubs off on the product and brand, and conversely the brand's image rubs off on the store. That is why Target Stores Company has commissioned renowned artist Philippe Starck to create signature merchandise exclusively for itself, and Sears/K-Mart Stores carry the Martha Stewart brand. The reciprocal conditioning between product image and store image occurs primarily for products with social and ego-identity value components (e.g., clothing, accessories), but not noticeably for primarily utilitarian products (e.g., appliances). Stores themselves carve out their personae through atmospherics, making them more or less inviting for browsers. In making place decisions, marketers also need to decide if they should sell their products on the Web—either exclusively, or in addition to bricks-and-mortar stores. Likewise, bricks-and-mortar stores need to decide if they should have a storefront on the Web as well. This would depend in large part on whether or not your target market is Net-savvy.

Promotions Promotions, as you know, consist of personal selling, publicity, sales promotions and advertising. In personal selling, one of the most significant factors is whether the consumer looks to the salesperson as an informational and expertise referent or, alternatively, as an identificational referent. Furthermore, the salesperson's product knowledge should dovetail with customers' own product knowledge levels and should complement their need for more information. Sales promotions are a valuable tool for *attracting* deal seeking consumers, but their periodicity and predictability should be managed so as not to create an enduring expectation in the consumer's mind. *Publicity* is non-advocate (i.e., independent of marketer) communication either in the mass media (e.g., a newspaper article on the brand) or through person-to-person word-of-mouth. Since dissatisfied consumers talk (and they talk more than do satisfied consumers), it is imperative for marketers to resolve dissatisfied consumer experiences; for example, through effective service recovery. Beyond that, advertising in newsworthy ways itself creates publicity. For example, CBS's Egg-writing—laser-inscribed program promo short text, such as CSI: Crack the Case on CBS; or a TV commercial by Honda wherein a very voice-talented choir simulates, using only their mouths, the aural and sensory experience of driving a Honda Civic.

Advertising (or, more broadly speaking, marketing communications) is also where consumer behavior concepts most intimately influence marketing practice. Different media reach different consumers, defined both in terms of demographics

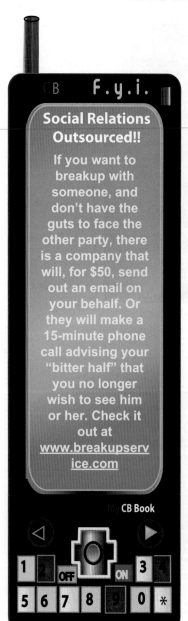

CB **f.y.i.**

Social Relations Outsourced!!

If you want to breakup with someone, and don't have the guts to face the other party, there is a company that will, for $50, send out an email on your behalf. Or they will make a 15-minute phone call advising your "bitter half" that you no longer wish to see him or her. Check it out at www.breakupserv ice.com

CB Book

and psychographics (e.g., *Self* magazine for image-focused teenage girls, and *Men's Health* magazine for fitness-obsessed adult men). Within the ad itself, the persons shown using the product should be similar to the target consumers in both demographics and lifestyle. Brand advertising should even capture the desired mood and attitude of the prospective consumer. Celebrities must be carefully chosen to serve as a type of referent (namely, informational or identificational) that your target segment is seeking. The specific appeal itself must be determined through a careful consideration of the total consumer profile. It has to be congruent with the consumer's culture (e.g., individualistic or collective), address the consumer's motives, help bolster his or her self-concept, be an instrument of identity projection, and create the kind of brand relationship the target consumer seeks. If the consumer has misconceptions, then the firm should set out to correct those misperceptions. If the consumer has no brand knowledge, then the marketer should focus on imparting that knowledge. If consumer cognitions about the brand are adequately and truthfully formed already, then advertising should move to creating emotions and feelings, by attaching some element of feeling to the product (see Chapter 7, *Romancing the Consumer: Rational Brands Go Emo!*).

Advertising should be fashioned also according to the diverse levels of consumer involvement—more visual with banner copy for low involvement consumers, and detailed product story for high involvement consumers. Marketers should also harness the enthusiasm and interest of highly involved consumers to build brand communities by organizing brandfest events (as does Jeep, among others).

Personalization Personalization refers to how a business organization treats an individual consumer—as a number, or as a person. This is the "how" dimension of business transactions. It is most pertinent to consumer-marketer interface, the interaction between the consumer and the marketer. Whether that interaction be face to face or via telecommunications, consumer initiated or marketer initiated, pre-purchase or post purchase, it should be functional (meets consumers' needs), efficient (minimizes consumer inconvenience and costs), and socially rewarding (the consumer feels respected and valued as a person). Functionality, efficiency, and social reward are judged, of course, from the consumer's point of view, not marketers'. Interactive Voice Response (IVR) systems might be efficient from the marketer's point-of-view, but if they force the consumer into a mile-long nested menu, then, from the consumers' point of view, they are a negative value. (See *Valuespace*, McGraw-Hill, 2001; www.myvaluespace.com.)

Once connected with a live human (see www.gethuman.com. described in Chapter 12), the challenge is even greater—the live human should be, well, human. She/he should have good listening skills, be knowledgeable about the product, and genuinely enjoy people.

Everything in the book about consumers will help a marketer shoulder this role responsibility. Consumers experience approach-avoid conflict; they make attributions (e.g., "why this salesperson is recommending this option"); they make quick inferences and form distorted perceptions; they need mnemonics to remember market information; they need recognition cues rather than having to recall unaided; they sometimes enter the marketplace trying to form evaluation criteria ("don't push them toward a quick decision"); they enjoy browsing; to get information, women approach the salesperson quickly; men like to discover it on their own; rather than being persuaded, consumers persuade themselves. And so on. The utility of re-reading these behaviors of consumers in the book to managing the interface with consumers can never be overemphasized. Ultimately, the purpose of the interface, the interaction, is not to merely go through the routine, or to see that the system runs efficiently, or to play the standard script, but, instead, to satisfy the consumer. Consumer—the curious, engaged, distracted, bored, hassled, anxious, confident, risk-averse, venturesome, task focused, playful and spontaneous, self-doubting, motivated, unmotivated, feeling low involvement, enduringly involved, angry, delighted, frugal, indulgent, living out his/her self-concept, and visiting upon us, the marketer, seeking products to advance his or her current life projects.

As a marketing manager, and now armed with all of this knowledge
about the consumer, how do you feel?
Do you feel some kind of Mel Gibson-esque power (as in *What Women Want*)
to read the consumer mind and manipulate it to your advantage?
Are you gloating because you now know exactly how to classically condition the consumer
mind, engineer consumer attitudes, exploit consumers' reference groups,
and mastermind their decision processes?
That is certainly one perspective. But, as you should recall from Chapter 1,
to seek to manipulate and maneuver the consumer mind is the old-fashioned, selling-
oriented view of marketing. The new customer-oriented view is that the purpose of
marketing is to create and present an offering that will meet consumer needs
and create genuine value for the consumer.

In this view, consumer knowledge empowers the marketer, not to manipulate,
but to respond to consumers' strivings and wishes; to their modes of thinking
and modes of feeling; and to their common values and personal preferences.

In this view, consumers are deemed to accept classical conditioning when the brand is paired
with the symbols they want the brand to have; they embrace the brand's intended intangible
social image if it conforms to their idea of what is currently cool. It is they who choose
(beforehand and independent of marketing) what reference groups, what social icons, what
cultural divas they will want to adore and worship. And it is they
(consumers) who want to use one particular decision heuristic rather than another.
What marketers can do is, simply but importantly,

R E S P O N D.

In this latter perspective, marketers place themselves on the side of consumers. Together,
they try to create solutions to consumer problems, create offerings that deliver one or more
of the values consumers are always seeking—the values we captured (in Chapter 1) in the
acronym **USER**—utilitarian, social, ego/identity, and recreational. It is this partnership for
which the study of consumer behavior in this book has, we hope, prepared you, both in terms
of skills and knowledge and in terms of perspective and your world-view.

This bears repeating. Marketing is not about what organizations do to consumers. It is not
about outsmarting the consumer. And it is certainly not about masterminding their thoughts,
feelings, and actions in the service of your company's, your product's,
and your brand's necessarily self-serving missions.

Marketing is, rather, about casting your company, your product, your brand
in their (consumers') image. It is about making yourself and your brand offerings more
endearing to consumers. It is about creating products and services, and crafting the
symbolic images to accompany, that bring them (consumers) real value—both tangible and
intangible, material as well as fantastic, for their physical as well as their social and
psychological worlds.
The only legitimate mission of marketing is, or should be, to create real value for the
consumer. Understanding consumer behavior helps us grasp the quintessential value of
consumption and to understand how we should, as marketers, fulfill marketing's
ultimate purpose: to become co-creators of the consumption value,
and thereby, happiness, humans seek.

In this chapter, our goal was to make excursions into some unique domains of consumption—things consumers consume and activities consumers undertake fervently—with a hobby-like zeal. From a potentially larger list, we chose nine. Two of them come from the world of entertainment (media fiction and sports); two come from technology (technology per se and wireless communication); two from the domain of niche consumption (body adornment and authenticity); two from the domain of the ubiquitous yet non-mundane consumer behavior (gift exchange and appropriation); and one—the most nascent and most pregnant with possibilities—is about the über virtual identity consumption.

In each of these excursions, we learned something that is, well, quite esoteric—gained insights that are rare. We never would have known, but do now, that in media consumption, for example, we are engaged in the quite complex process of meaning negotiation, and that, in media watching, it is our own beliefs that we are consuming. Reciprocity norms govern gift exchange as a socio-cultural consumer practice. We seek authenticity, sometimes as exploration but sometimes as connectivity. Technology is a mixed blessing and consumers have to learn both to harness and to cope with it. Wireless communications empower us with anytime anywhere communicability but also enslaves us always to be accessible. We also dissected how consumers anoint important things they buy, making them their own, and in their minds, unique, even though they were mass-produced by a firm. The details of the nine consumption domains are too varied and too rich to summarize here and must be read in the body of this chapter.

Next, projecting into the next 10 years or so, we identified eight trends: (1) the revenge of boomers, (2) growing power of women, (3) greater ethnic diversity, (4) telecommuting and working from home; (5) globalization of consumption, (6) new forms of social relations, (7) technology suffused consumption, and (8) experiential marketing. Each of these trends offers opportunities and challenges to marketers.

In the third and last section, we described a three-step process for a firm to use to make its marketing more consumer-behavior-knowledge informed: target market identification, deep consumer profiling, and responsive offering presentation. These steps require judicious utilization of all the concepts and principles discussed in this book. Thus, we bring our learning to fruition. And, thus we bring our grand reading of this book to *commencement*!

Appropriation
Authenticity
Meaning Negotiation
Belief Consumption
Gift
Altruistic gifts
Agonistic gifts

Reciprocation
Ritualistic gifts
Expressive gifts
Contextual marketing
Meaning negotiation
Belief consumption
Industry of Social Relations

Paradox
Telecommuting
Frame-forming
Deep Consumer Profiling
Personalization
Responsive Offering Presentation

REVIEW✚Rewind

1. What do the following terms mean: (a) appropriation, (b) agonistic and altruistic gifts, (c) egalitarian sex role attitudes, and (d) contextual marketing.

2. Explain the different motivations of exploration versus connection-oriented consumers seeking authenticity.

3. Explain the three functions gifts serve for consumers.

4. Briefly describe the six motivations of consumers who get tattoos.

5. Explain the three components of the experience of watching a TV series for consumers who are enduringly involved in specific TV shows.

6. List eight paradoxes of technology that consumers experience.

7. Name eight trends in the consumer marketplace mentioned in the chapter, and explain each briefly.

8. One of the trends in consumer behavior discussed in the chapter is "new forms of social relations." Explain how social relations will change in the future and what opportunities it will present for marketers.

9. What is meant by experiential consumption, and what challenge and opportunity will it bring marketers?

10. Briefly explain the three-step process described in the chapter that will permit marketers to apply this book.

THE ESOTERIC, THE ENCHANTED, THE EMERGENT

21

647

THINK+Apply

1. Think of the next three separate occasions for giving a gift to three persons with whom you have different relationships. After reading this chapter, think about how the concepts presented here will apply to these gift decisions. Briefly summarize your thoughts.

2. Reflect on your own behavior of watching your favorite TV episodes. For each, list the beliefs you "consume." Also think about the discussions you might have had recently with others on some recent episodes. In these conversations, identify the instances, if any, of "meaning negotiation" and why such "meaning negotiation" was important to you.

3. List all the paradoxes of technology consumption. Illustrate each of these from your own experience with any new technologies.

PRACTICE+Experience

1. Interview three consumers on their favorite TV shows. In the interviews, probe for the extent to which these consumers engage in belief consumption, meaning negotiation, and artifacts acquisition. Summarize your findings.

2. Interview each of three consumers about two of their favorite possessions. Ask them what rituals they have performed on each possession and how these rituals have affected what these possessions mean to them.

(Note: do not use the words "rituals," "possessions," or "meaning of possession," etc., in your questions; instead use everyday language in the interview, but frame your answers using these concepts.)

3. Interview two consumers, one with heavy tattoos and one with a lot of body piercing. Explore their motivations and the satisfactions they derive from these examples of consumption.

4. Interview three consumers on their use of wireless phones. Summarize which of the paradoxes listed in the chapter these consumers have experienced and also what strategies they have used to cope with these paradoxes. (Note: do not use the words "paradox," "coping," 'strategies,' etc., in your questioning; instead use everyday language in the interview, but frame your answers using these concepts.)

In the Marketing Manager's Shoes

Put yourself in a marketing manager's shoes. Most concepts in the chapter have some lessons for the marketing manager; i.e., they suggest what to do differently in practice. Indeed, often these applications are implicit in our explanations of the concepts and models in the chapter. Identify at least five specific applications of the chapter's concepts, all of which should be entirely new—different from the examples cited here. (Remember, "manager" here includes public policy.)

Accessory Nerve—the future of personal communications (see story on facing page) (photo courtesy CuteCircuit)

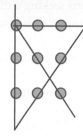

Think outside the box

Welcome to the World of Future Consumption

Before we conclude *The Chapters*, we bring you some news on future consumption possibilities.

First, the future consumer is going to be Internet savvy, and this so even in third world countries. Foretelling this are not just the *MySpace* generation teens, but also some innovative projects designed to bridge the "big divide" between the "have" and "have not" nations. One such project: *Hole in The Wall.* You already read about the $100 laptop project (Chapter 17). Even more fascinating is a project by India's NITT's Cognitive Research Team, called *Hole in The Wall* Project. The company's office complex sits in the middle of a slum near New Delhi, separated by a wall. One day, NITT's chairman, Sugata Mitra, got an idea. He cut a hole in the wall, put a computer screen there facing the slum side, turned the Internet on, and watched quietly. Within hours, kids from the slum neighborhood were learning to surf the net on their own. So he formulated a plan to put Internet computer kiosks in poor neighborhoods in Delhi. Now the project has been embraced by the government and is expanding to other states. And children who don't even go to school are learning a wealth of information. Assuming 200 children learn from each Kiosk over the next five years—the project's current term, there will be, among the very poor in India, 100 million otherwise unschooled but computer-literate children.

Second, technology-suffused consumption is going make waves. The doorways that opened automatically on the Enterprise Ship will someday be abundantly in use, for example. Already, Tanaka of Japan is offering a door that opens not only automatically as you approach it but also to your exact silhouette—you see, the slates slide out individually to allow your body, but no more. This can help isolate a room from outside elements (hot or cold air, dirt, insects, bacteria, etc.), maximize privacy, and make possible more aesthetic doorways.

Then, wearable technology is making big strides. This is taking two directions: (a) technological functions woven into clothing, such as cell phones, viewing screens, body condition/health monitors, etc., and (b) experiential clothing—clothing that enables hedonic and sensational wearing experience. First consider the functions woven into clothing. One such product is accessory nerve.

Accessory Nerve is a sleeve-like textile device that you wear on your sleeve. Its embedded technology connects to your mobile phones (via Bluetooth). When you receive a phone call, the phone won't ring; instead the sleeve will form a pleat pattern, each pattern distinct for a pre-programmed caller. That way you will know who is calling. If you are in a meeting, you simply flatten the pleats, and the caller will get a text message saying, "I'll call you back later." *The Accessory Nerve* allows users to exchange information and greetings in a subtle and intimate way. The device is in prototype development at CuteCircuit. (See picture on facing page).

Among experiential clothing, you already read about the Hug Shirt (Chapter 1). The same company (Cute Circuit) is experimenting with other ideas. Among them:

Kinetic Dress. The dress follows closely the body of the wearer. When seated and alone, it is black; then as the wearer moves and interacts with others, blue luminescent embroidery patters begin to appear. It even creates a halo around the wearer.

Mystique. This dress follows closely the mood of the wearer, depending on the context. In the beginning, as soon as you wear it, let us say in the morning, it is a short, knee length pale gray. Later as the day dawns, it begins to lengthen and show strands of red. By evening, it is a full-length totally red dress.

Consumers in all countries are going to get more exposure to cultures of the world. Barring some countries whose politics and policies will keep them isolated, the future consumer is going to become more and more global.

In transportation, well, just read *Romancing the Consumer* in this chapter. And speaking of wearable technology, did you notice, on the male mannequin on the cover, a viewing screen woven into the jeans?!

Getting back to experiential technology (we just can't leave you without inviting you to experience this sometime), an intriguing product in development is Embedded Theater (ET). ET allows you

Kinetic dress—the outer skirt develops blue circles as the wearer interacts with other people.
(photo courtesy CuteCircuit)

to experience your surroundings (say, a street scene) in a new way: the objects and persons in your vicinity begin to speak to you, or you hear imaginary conversations as if they are coming from people you are seeing on the street at the moment.

You wear a headset with sensors and a belt with embedded wireless network capabilities. Then, as you move through a city, the system receives audio files that are dynamically adjusted in volume to create a "tridimensional audioscape" depending on the direction or objects you are looking at. The system understands your location in the environment, and the sensor understands the direction that you are looking. It then creates a fictional audio landscape, in three-dimensions, that corresponds exactly to real world objects and locations. For example, as you walk to the right of a statue, you may hear the statue whispering in your left ear; turning to look at the statue, the sound is now in front of you. Or you could hear a conversation in the street between two people that took place three hundred years ago. The path you take and the places you explore will actively affect the course of the narrative, so that you experience your environment like never before.

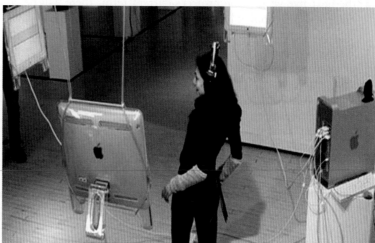

**Embedded Theater
(www.cutecircuit.com)**
(photo courtesy CuteCircuit)

It is in the human psyche that consumers will forever seek novel experiences. For such experiences, art, science, and technology provide core innovations, but marketers must give direction as to their usability and consumer value. Marketers must constantly innovate, in the lab and in the store, "offerings" that produce such experiences. Offerings that will at once serve consumer interests as well as those of our society at large (e.g., sustainable consumption—see CB fyi on this page). This *is* marketers' challenge and privilege.

Welcome **to the** fascinating **world of** future **consumption!!**

Section Editor: Arch G. Woodside

PART VII

CONSUMERS JUST WANNA HAVE FANTASIES, FEELINGS, AND FUN!!

Morris B. Holbrook, Columbia University

As any reputable dictionary informs us with only a moment's consultation, the word "consumer" is a noun—that is, a person, place, or thing. When asked which of these designations applies to the typical consumer, members of my classes always tend to vote with near-unanimity for "person" as the obviously correct description. I, of course, agree wholeheartedly. Yet this recognition turns out to be an elusive truth that needs rediscovering repeatedly during the historical development of consumer-behavior theory, as the consensus of opinion wanders from one corner of the triangle (place) to another (person); from there to yet another (thing); and finally back again (person).

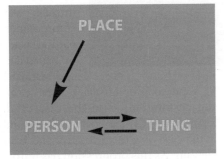

Is the Consumer A Place, A Thing or A Person?

Arguably, the earliest systematic consumer researchers were the macroeconomists of the 1930s who, responding to the Depression and reflecting the influence of the great economist John Maynard Keynes, worried about the aggregate level of consumer spending—a perspective that still manifests itself today in such phenomena as our ingrained preoccupation with the Consumer Confidence Index and other symptoms of dollars waiting to be spent on consumption. From this viewpoint, the consumer is a place—that is, a marketplace—where dollars are exchanged for goods or services in ways that boost the gross domestic product or other measures of national welfare. And hooray for the multiplier effect!

Unfortunately, this macroscopic focus tells us very little about the fine-grained behavior that flies underneath the radar of the large-scale economic system and says nothing about how marketing managers of particular brands can win the hearts of their target consumers. And so it happened that, during the post-War 1940s and 1950s, the pendulum swung in the direction of recognizing that the consumer is actually a person—that is, human or (in the words of Friedrich Nietzsche) all-too-human. Specifically,

> The Consumer is a rather wondrously complex human being deserving of our careful study and endless fascination.

a type of study referred to as Motivation Research or MR came into vogue as a way of applying insights from psychoanalysis to the understanding of consumer behavior at the individual level. This refreshingly microscopic approach—championed by clinical psychologists such as Ernest Dichter who had fled Europe and come to the USA during the difficult times surrounding WWII—applied the methods of psychotherapy to the investigation of consumer motivations. Toward this end, MR followed the Freudian model—which assumed that forbidden urges from the Id were repressed in the service of the Super-Ego but escaped in the form of surrogate responses that disguised the illicit unconscious desires in ways acceptable to the Ego (dreams, slips of the tongue, jokes, phobias, neurotic symptoms, artistic masterpieces, and so

> Asking an all-too-human consumer why she bought a new hat would produce nothing but a meaningless rationalization.

forth). Asking an all-too-human consumer why she has bought a new hat would produce nothing but a meaningless rationalization ("It matches my new grey suit"), whereas the true reason has been repressed and therefore remains unconscious, waiting to be discovered via the methods of psychotherapy ("I am a narcissist, and shopping for the hat gave me an excuse to stand in front of the mirror and admire myself for an hour and a half").

Then, during the 1960s, MR—which had the merit of recognizing consumers as human beings—succumbed to highly publicized attacks by (1) social scientists who regarded its clinical methods as invalid and therefore as unlikely to produce useful results and (2) social critics who labeled its effects unethical because of its alleged tendency to manipulate innocent consumers as unwitting victims. (Ironically, nobody noticed that the combination of Points 1 and 2 was self-contradictory.) In its stead, a new approach based on the premise of scientific modeling began to gain ascendancy during the 1960s. Under the sway of Nobel Laureate Herbert Simon, marketing researchers came to view the consumer as a decision maker who processes information to make brand choices in a manner undeniably similar to the kind of information-processing task performed by a computer. Specifically, in this view, the consumer became a thing—a calculating machine—that added up the features, attributes, or benefits (FABs) of a brand (perhaps adjusting these by suitable multiplicative importance or desirability weights) in order to construct a brand-preference hierarchy as a manifestation of rational economic utility. Even while the more enlightened modelers admitted that various simplifying rules led to certain kinds of cognitive shortcuts (otherwise known as "heuristics"), this decision-oriented view of consumers as computer-like machines (things) came to dominate the discourse on consumer behavior during the 1970s and, indeed, continues to shape the thinking of marketing researchers to the present day..

But, moving into the 1980s and beyond, an increasing number of marketing researchers rediscovered the nature of the consumer as a flesh-and-blood human creature — that is, a person (consumer) rather than a place (market) or thing (computer).

Increasingly, consumers were viewed less as robotlike calculating machines (things) whose brand choices lead to buying behavior in the form of purchasing outcomes and more as living humans (persons) who daydream about various pleasures, respond emotionally to consumption-related events, and use products or brands as parts of their playful leisure activities.

Expounding on this emerging view, Beth Hirschman (then a marketing professor at NYU, now at Rutgers) and I wrote an essay on the human consumer (Holbrook and Hirschman 1982) in which we explored various aspects of the *consumption experience* under the headings of what we might call the *Three Fs*—namely, Fantasies, Feelings, and Fun (for further historical background, please see Holbrook 1995). Briefly, *fantasies* include all those conscious and unconscious aspects of thought that reflect how we subjectively experience the world of consumption—starting with conventional notions about our beliefs concerning features-attributes-and-benefits or FABs, of course, but also including the rich tapestry of daydreams, nighttime dreams, altered states of consciousness, and unconscious associations that lie below the surface: I believe that Crest toothpaste will fight cavities; but, in my dreams, I imagine that it will make me a handsome stud with gleaming white teeth that will appeal powerfully to beautiful women everywhere. Meanwhile, *feelings* encompass the full spectrum of emotional responses that arise in a consumption experience—beginning with traditional concerns for the unidimensional aspects of a liking-versus-disliking reaction, a positive-versus-negative affect, or a pro-versus-con attitude, but also including the full panoply of relevant emotions such as joy, sorrow, love, hate, fear, anger, disgust, envy, guilt, surprise, and so forth: I prefer Crest to Colgate on an affective scale of favorability or preference, but I also feel a deeply loving and joyful fondness for the dentist who recommended Crest and thereby spared me from the fear, guilt, and sorrow of filling cavities resulting from my use of the wrong brand. Finally, *fun* refers to those aspects of playful leisure activities that are pursued for their own sakes as ends in themselves—ranging from ordinary sports (tennis) or games (chess) to more exotic pastimes such as bizarre hobbies (collecting old shoelaces), unusual avocations (playing the vibraphone with wooden spoons), or unique skills (stereographic photography).

In the intervening years—through the work of Russ Belk, Melanie Wallendorf, John Sherry, Craig Thompson, Doug Holt, Stephen Gould, Stephen Brown, and many others too numerous to mention (for whose omission, I hereby apologize)—this view of the consumption experience has crept into our repertoire of accepted ways to understand the consumer (Holbrook 1995, 1999) and, indeed, has recently flourished in various managerial selfhelp books such as the one published by Pine and Gilmore

Fantasies include all those conscious and unconscious thoughts that reflect how we subjectively experience the world of consumption

Feelings encompass the full spectrum of emotional responses that arise in a consumption experience.

Fun refers to those aspects of playful leisure activities that are pursued for their own sakes as ends in themselves

(1999) and entitled *The Experience Economy*. Especially among managers and practitioners, this book has inspired an evangelical fervor in celebration of the mandate for businesses to transform themselves into experience providers. Thus, Pine and Gilmore argue that "experiences represent an existing but previously unarticulated *genre of economic output*" (p. ix). They propose that the provision of experiences achieves the sort of brand differentiation that can rescue a firm from the dangers of commoditization (p. x). In this spirit, Pine and Gilmore offer the manager "tools to begin staging compelling experiences" (p. xii).

Developing this train of thought, Pine and Gilmore (1999) view the course of economic history as progressing through various stages: (1) commodities (fungible and natural, as in the case of potatoes or bananas); (2) goods (tangible and standardized, as in the case of hand soap or Model-T Fords); (3) services (intangible and customized, as in the case of dry cleaning or auto repairs); and (4) experiences (memorable and personal, as in the case of a meal at a five-star restaurant or a cruise to Hawaii). As this progression has unfolded, the seller/buyer relationship has evolved from trader/market (commodities) to manufacturer/user (goods) to provider/client (services) to stager/guest (experiences).

So, today, we are all guests at the festivals produced by those who stage consumption experiences. Some master purveyors of experiences at this latter phase of development include Disney, Starbucks, Harley-Davidson, or Nike—all gifted at reaping the rewards of mounting memorable experiences. But notice that this phenomenon is far from new. Ever since the time of Adam and Eve in the Garden of Eden, we have been irresistibly tempted by the attractions of forbidden fruit and have longed for a delicious taste of that secret-revealing, knowledge-providing, experience-enriching apple.

Pine and Gilmore (1999) argue that—rather than reflecting mere entertainment—the rich and memorable experiences of the types they advocate involve different degrees

	PASSIVE	ACTIVE
ABSORBED	Entertainment	Education
IMMERSED	Esthetics	Escapism

of passive-active participation and absorbed-immersed engagement. These combine to produce four distinct realms of experience. Indeed, Pine and Gilmore support the commercial potential for offerings that cater to all four of these experiential realms:

The sweet spot for any compelling experience—incorporating entertainment, educational, escapist, and esthetic elements into otherwise generic space—is similarly a mnemonic place, a tool aiding in the creation of memories, distinct from the normally uneventful world of goods and services. (p. 43).

So, armed with the Pine-Gilmore four-way categorization scheme, let us consider the experiential merits of a trip to Benihana of Tokyo—which bills itself as promising "an experience at every table." First, we enjoy the entertaining spectacle of the chef ostentatiously flipping food in the air and dramatically hacking away at it with a sharp cleaver that he wields with circus-like applause-inspiring precision. Second, as educational fallout, we learn about a type of cuisine that we have perhaps never encountered during our culturally-deprived childhood in Hometown USA. Third, we appreciate and savor the deeply-satisfying esthetic subtleties of this hedonically-rich culinary presentation. Fourth, we escape imaginatively to another world—a world of Asian adventure and Oriental mystery. Put it all together, while struggling to repress the thought that we've had better-tasting steak at Denny's, and we've got the promised "experience at every table"—a combination of fantasies-feelings-&-fun that adds up to an overall gestalt-like feast for the eyes (bright red meat), ears (sizzling steak), nostrils (beefy aroma), fingers (chopsticks, please), and palette (tangy sauces, yum).

> Thus, as consumers, we have come to expect something more than just meat-and-potatoes on a plate. Even very choice meat and very delicious potatoes no longer suffice. Rather, we want a Three-Fs Fiesta—a delectable extravaganza of gastronomic entertainment. Extend this basic concept to every corner of our economy, pushing it as far as it will go (better yet, as Pine and Gilmore recommend, charging admission), and you've got a whole new ballgame—a whole new way of charming otherwise reluctant consumers into parting with their hard-earned cash.

As specific illustrations, Pine and Gilmore suggest various ways of jazzing up the experiential aspects of our offering to accomplish what—speaking of Benihana and recalling the old days of sales-oriented marketing—we used to refer to as "selling the sizzle instead of the steak." Thus, we might play on special themes, as at the Forum Shops in Las Vegas with their cleverly-staged scenes and statues meant to evoke the atmosphere of Ancient Rome. Or we might appeal to nostalgia, as when the Hard Rock Café assaults our senses with the sights-and-sounds of a bygone rock-'n'-roll era. Or we might strive for a fully multisensory experience, as when Barnes & Noble designs its coffee bars to provide a rich offering of sights, sounds, smells, tastes, and—O, Yes—books to smudge with our sticky fingers. Speaking of books, readers of this text will find a pertinent example of experiential enhancement based on the case of Singapore Airlines and their "branded scent"—yes, a patented smell, a unique aroma—as featured in the box insert from Chapter 3 on Perception. This aromatic triumph reflects the essence of what Beth and I meant when we talked about the hedonic nature of multisensory experience (Hirschman and Holbrook 1982).

Bernd Schmitt (1999), my colleague at Columbia University, takes this idea of engaging the five senses a step closer to implementation via branding and marketing communications. I'll review Bernd's framework briefly before adding a few observations on how students of consumer behavior and managers who strive to build brands to satisfy the wishes of the experiencing consumer might work toward their realization. Schmitt rightly argues that positioning a brand as no more than a package of functional features-attributes-and-benefits or utilitarian FABs misses the boat. Demonstrably, the brand is much more than the sum total of the FABs emphasized by the computer-like decision-oriented view of the consumer. Indeed, Schmitt (1999) finds the FAB fixation "ugly" because it neglects "the very essence of a brand as a rich source of sensory, affective, and cognitive associations that result in memorable and rewarding brand experiences" (p. 21). From this perspective, contemporary consumers take FABs for granted and seek much more powerful kinds of experiential rewards:

> Today, customers take functional features and benefits, product quality, and a positive brand image as a given. What they want is products, communications, and marketing campaigns that dazzle their senses, touch their hearts, and stimulate their minds.... They want products, communications, and marketing campaigns to deliver an experience (p. 22)

I say, Amen. However, some might argue—the importance of Schmitt's insights notwithstanding—that this is exactly what consumers have *always* wanted and *always will* want (Holbrook 2000). That is, as members of the human species, consumers do now and always did value consumption experiences. In relinquishing the more extreme assumptions of the decision-oriented focus on brand choices in buying behavior, it is *we*—that is, we marketing thinkers and *not* the consumers themselves—who have changed. Thus, the experiential view is *radical*—not in the sense of being weird or bizarre—but rather in the sense of reviving the *roots* of our thinking about consumer behavior. Today, as before, consumers sensuously savor their food. They daydream about their spring vacations in Bermuda. They feel happy at musical comedies and sad when their team loses the World Series. They play checkers or canasta for fun and derive esthetic pleasure from a Bach cantata or a Yeats poem. As always—in attracting consumers—the race is to the swift. And—in marketing, as elsewhere—there is nothing new under the sun.

> Thus, the experiential view is radical—not in the sense of being weird or bizarre—but rather in the sense of reviving the roots of our thinking about consumer behavior.

Schmitt (1999) breaks the underlying process of experiential consumption into five aspects that he calls—as reflected in his subtitle—"Sense," "Feel," "Think," "Act," and "Relate." He proposes these five facets as the Strategic Experiential Modules on which a company can build its marketing efforts. In his view, these efforts should be designed to help the consumer sense (e.g., Richart luxury chocolates with their mouth-watering appeal to the taste buds); feel (Campbell's soup as a heart-warming evocation of a mother's love); think (the claim that Apple computers provide an intelligent alternative to the monopolistic excesses of an IBM/Microsoft PC); act (the call to action represented by Nike's "Just Do It" campaign); and relate (the reassuringly virile sonority of the engine on a Harley-Davidson motorcycle).

If you are now wondering how this five-facet conceptualization differs from the Three-Fs scheme that we mentioned earlier, the answer is: Very little. Specifically, in our scheme based on the Three Fs—fantasies, feelings, and fun—Beth and I followed the traditional Cognition-Affect-Behavior (CAB) framework and, for that reason, collapsed two of Schmitt's types into one and omitted the last of the five. Thus, in our conceptualization, Fantasies include all aspects of experientially-oriented Cognitions (Schmitt's "sense" and "think"). Feelings emphasize manifold components of consumption-related Affect (Schmitt's "feel"). And Fun refers to various play- or leisure-oriented aspects of Behavior (Schmitt's "act").

Combining all this into a perspective that has begun to gain currency, entertainment is the label that best encapsulates a meaningful prescription for capitalizing on the appeal of the consumption experience. As noted by various commentators such as Michael Wolf (1999) in his book on *The Entertainment Economy,* success in business no longer hinges on (say) good accounting practices or production efficiency. Increasingly, the firm must "create an experience ... inform and amuse ... build a destination": "Consumers are looking for the E-factor in every product ... that's E as in Entertainment" (p. 27).

Put differently, in the spirit of the Three Fs, we all search incessantly for fun ways to spend our most scarce or even vanishing resource—namely, time—planning its allocation in something like the manner in which a TV network slots its daily programming. Wolf (1999) calls this the "new mentalité" wherein "we see our lives in the same kind of grid in which we see television schedules" (p. 40). Choosing between eating and sleeping, reading and writing, tennis and golf, or homework and partying starts to resemble a choice between The View (weekdays at 11:00 am, the ABC network, Channel 7) and The Price Is Right (same time, different station, CBS, Channel 2). Either way, it's all about entertainment. Thus, much of Wolf's book consists of juicy examples drawn from companies and industries in which the "E-factor" has come to the fore. These include latte-enhanced browsing at Borders or Barnes & Noble; nostalgic reincarnations of rock-'n'-roll at the Hard Rock Café or the silver screen at Planet Hollywood; hotels as shopping extravaganzas in Las Vegas; fast food as a family fiesta at McDonald's with its festive Disney-related movie merchandising and super-sized brightly-colored playpens and, always, fries with that; travel on luxury flights aboard Singapore Airlines; retail environments that resemble theme parks (Mall of America) or the theater (Bloomingdale's) or a sports event (Niketown); fashion as an instantiation of the Hip-Hop lifestyle (Tommy

> "Consumers are looking for the E-factor in every product ... that's E as in Entertainment"

Hilfiger) or a manifestation of WASPish clubbiness (Ralph Lauren); cyberwheeling and internetdealing on the World Wide Web via E-trade; and, of course, all sorts of delightful activities bordering on consumer misbehavior such as gambling at Foxwoods or pornography on Pay-Per-View or voyeuristic opportunities via various dedicated sites that feature strategically-placed 24/7 Webcams.

In short, everywhere we look—from books to crooks—we find the E-factor at work … or... at play. In this connection, a possibly apocryphal story has been told about William Dillard—founder of the tried-and-true, everywhere-you-look, but not-overly-adventurous Dillard's Department Store chain. Apparently, back when Bloomingdale's was suffering from some financial difficulties, someone asked Mr. Dillard if he had considered acquiring the troubled company. Reportedly, Dillard replied, "O, no. I'm in the retailing business. Bloomingdale's is in the entertainment business." Subsequently—in department stores, as elsewhere—the latter orientation has won the day. The E-factor rules.

Along these lines, in celebration of shopping as a form of entertainment, we often encounter happy evocations of the shopping experience with its tendency to rival the fun often associated with a theme park. Indeed, this orientation permeates the marketing episteme of today so thoroughly that—like fish in water—we may have ceased to notice its pervasiveness. Embracing this ethos, television news programs now strive for infotainment—a polite term for dumbing down the content to provide a maximum taste of visceral excitement and a minimum dose of thoughtful content. Similar logic spills over into academic institutions as edutainment with its treatment of learning as a candy-coated pill—up to and including the present essay, I must confess. Best of all, when these threads are combined—as in shopping for educational toys—we can have fun and enter the themed environment while hoping that some sort of edutainment rubs off on our kids ... all at the same time.

> In celebration of shopping as a form of entertainment, we often encounter happy evocations of the shopping experience with its tendency to rival the fun often associated with a theme park. Indeed, this orientation permeates the marketing episteme of today so thoroughly that—like fish in water—we may have ceased to notice its pervasiveness.

A comparable E-spirit has extended to everything from day spas that "pamper your body and heal your soul" to air travel. After enduring the indignities of negotiating the militarized checkpoints at Kennedy Airport en route to Tampa, we wearily board our plane and encounter a paradoxically cheerful invitation to enjoy the "JetBlue Experience." As this high-flying company expresses that thought on its Website, "the 'JetBlue Experience' has become the phrase defining our goal of outstanding Customer care.... this phrase developed from the unique and unexpected level of care we provide in every aspect of our operation." (Notice that here the word "Customer" is capitalized—like "God"—presumably out of respect or deference bordering on sycophancy or adulation.) Or, speaking of airlines, consider the heroic style in which Richard Branson transformed his company into a multifaceted experience machine:

> There's Virgin Atlantic, the world's most hedonistic airline. There's Virgin Net ... Virgin Hotels ... Virgin Cola—perfect for washing down popcorn bought at the concession in one of the chain of Virgin Cinemas ... Virgin Brides ... for that most fun of nights ... Virgin Rail ... Virgin Megastores—where everything you can buy has to do with enhancing the fun in life and a visit to the store is itself an entertainment experience (Wolf 1999, p. 137).

So strong is this push toward constant entertainment in all areas of human existence that consumers have become increasingly impatient and restless when faced with anything less. Fail to amuse them for even a moment, and you will lose their attention forever. Thus, natural-born surfers—habituated to fingering the mouse clicker or pawing the remote control—will be lost to the zipping-and-zapping impulse unless they are strongly lured by appealing emotional responses. Advertising messages stand no chance of attracting viewers or readers unless they pack an experiential wallop. Worse yet, the members of Generation Y—who have played with computers since infancy and who therefore have very itchy trigger fingers when clicking-or-switching with a mouse or a channel changer—will increasingly dominate the viewing habits of the population. Their dwindling attention spans plus their ingrained pointing-and-clicking inclinations will dictate the need for an even higher level of the E-factor in GenY-directed advertising campaigns. In this climate, one wonders if any sort of sustained commercial message that demands anything more than the most minimal eye blink of attention might become a thing of the past. As innumerable commentators have noted, a dawning Age of Product Placements appears inevitable. Increasingly, consumers will need to be tricked into noticing our merchandise.

Reflecting this temper of the times, advertsing draws increasingly on experinetial themes as a way of wooing viewers and readers. A by-no-means exhaustive sampling of recent examples that have caught my eye is presented in Table 1, roughly in decreasing order of seeming plausibility.
Overall, for consumers and marketers alike, the pursuit of experiences provides an epicurean dimension of consumption that extends beyond mere materialism. Rather than focusing only on our possessions—the stuff we own—we have, with the gentle guidance of marketers, begun to channel our desires and urges toward the existential moment of consumption in which we experience the fantasies, feelings, and fun that seem—if we don't think too carefully about it—to make life worthwhile. That such all-too-human pleasures—however tempting and enjoyable—can be evanescent or illusory appears all-too-obvious. As with other consumption-based orientations (materialism, asceticism, stoicism, tribalism, hedonism, connoisseurship, gastronomy, oenophilia), this New Epicureanism risks the danger of running against the grain of human dignity. Possibly we threaten the human potential for discerning creativity or refined judgment. Perhaps we succumb to ru-

TABLE 1.0 — EXPERIENTIAL THEMES IN ADVERTISING

Those who buy their clothes at Ralph Lauren on Madison Avenue at 72nd Street will enjoy "The Ultimate Experience"

Motorists with a yen for adventure can pursue "The Land Rover Experience"

Jablum from Jamaica promises "The Coffee Experience Beyond Compare"

Your personal wine service, Geerlings & Wade, delivers "The Vineyard Experience"

When cruising the Caribbean, the Holland America Line's new ms Noordam provides "A classic cruise experience"

Prospective visitors to Paradise Island in the Bahamas will find that the Atlantis Hotel presents "An Exceptional Offer For An Experience Like No Other"

Travelers with a flair for the dramatic are invited to "Live Your Myth in Greece ... Starring You ... Amazing Sights, Diverse Experiences"

Gamblers with a thirst for casinos come to the Mohegan Sun for "a legendary getaway experience"

In a scenic but remote and chilly corner of Northeastern Pennsylvania, you can "Enjoy the Honesdale Experience!"

Patrons of the theater in New York are drawn to the Broadway production of John Patrick Shanley's Doubt by the claim that it offers "an experience to last you a lifetime"

Those who prefer Broadway musicals will gravitate toward "Live Music ... Experience It!"

Marine-friendly tourists at St. Armands Circle in Sarasota can buy ocean-related artistic gifts as part of the "Wyland Galleries Experience"

Web browsers at www.dollgallery.com, www.go4allsports.com, or www.shophop.com can enjoy "The Ultimate Collector's Experience," "The Premium Sports Shopping Experience," or "The Online Shopping Experience"

Vicks VapoRub lets you "experience the feeling of free breathing"

Flushable Moist Wipes from Charmin help you "experience the fresher feeling"

Clairol's Herbal Essence urges you to "Experience the intensity"

Those still seeking an intense experience can suck Tic Tacs, which offer "entertainment for your mouth"

Old folks in need of a home for themselves or a loved one are "Invited to Experience ... The Esplanade Senior Residences"

Potential donors to the Red Cross can "Experience the feeling of making a difference"

Meanwhile, "At first International Bank of Israel, you experience the traditional Private Banking of the renowned World Wide Safra Banking Group"

Or, for those who would like to understand the historical background of the language that many Americans speak, the Teaching Company urges you to "Experience the Power and Beauty of English"

And even your cat can "Experience the very latest of the very best from Fancy Feast"

inously addictive shopping habits, to impulse-control disorders that end in credit-card abuse, or to obsessive compulsions that lead toward something as meaningless as a closet full of expensive never-worn shoes or a shelf loaded with costly periodicals still in their wrappers. Maybe we max out our own selfish interests at the expense of irreparable damage to society or to the ecosystem. Figuratively, it could be that—as inveterate seekers of personally satisfying consumption experiences—we all emit massive billows of poisonous second-hand smoke.

Though concerned, I do not wish to make ethical prescriptions concerning such trends and developments, but only to describe a widespread phenomenon that appears to have seized the day. Toward that end and in conclusion, I shall offer a table that contrasts the experiential view (on the right) with the decision-oriented view (on the left) that it complements as part of any well-balanced attempt to understand the consumer as an integrated whole. (See Table 2A and 2B.) In this, I envision the two complementary perspectives as something like the left and right sides of the brain. The left is linear, logical, and verbal. The right is holistic, impressionistic, and visual. To achieve integrated functioning, we need an integration of the two. Analogously, an understanding of consumption in depth requires that we reconcile, synthesize, or fuse the decision-oriented and experiential views into one well-rounded and deeply profound conception of the consumer—who, to end on an answer to the question with which we began, is not a place and is not a thing but is instead a rather wondrously complex human being deserving of our careful study and endless fascination.

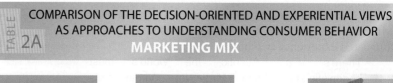

TABLE 2A

COMPARISON OF THE DECISION-ORIENTED AND EXPERIENTIAL VIEWS AS APPROACHES TO UNDERSTANDING CONSUMER BEHAVIOR

MARKETING MIX

Decision-oriented View	THEME	Experiential View
Tangible offerings (goods) with objective FABs. Examples: gasoline, toothpaste, light bulbs	Product (Characteristics)	Intangible offerings (services) with subjective meanings Examples: TV programs, rock concerts, museums
Cost measured in money Example: ticket for a movie priced at $10.00	Price (Cost)	Cost measured in time Example: duration of movie calculated in minutes
Informational advertising Example: Unique Selling Proposition as reason for purchase ("M&Ms melt in your mouth, not in your hand")	Promotion (Communication)	Transformational advertising Example: Michael Jordan, Nike, the "swoosh," awesome image ("Just do it.")
Retailer viewed as purchase facilitator Examples: K.mart or corner grocery	Place (Channels)	Retailer viewed as source of shopping experience Examples: Mall of America or Bloomingdale's

TABLE 2B

COMPARISON OF THE DECISION-ORIENTED AND EXPERIENTIAL VIEWS AS APPROACHES TO UNDERSTANDING CONSUMER BEHAVIOR

THE CABS MODEL

Decision-Oriented View	THEME	Experiential View
Beliefs Example: perceptual map of department stores on two dimensions, traditional/innovative & expensive/inexpensive	Cognition	Fantasies Example: daydreams about an exciting consumption experience ("Dreams Do Come True ....Maidenform")
Preference Example: like/dislike, favorable/unfavorable, pro/con, good/bad, or positive/negative response to headache remedy	Affect	Feelings Example: emotions such as joy, sorrow, love, hate, fear, anger, surprise, disgust, jealousy, or envy over the victory of a political candidate
Purchase Example: check-out line for the cash register at Wal-mart	Behavior	Fun Example: riding the roller coaster or cruising the food court at the Mall of America
Instrumental Learning Example: habit formation, repeat buying, or brand loyalty due to reinforcement via positive rewards to the rational, utilitarian problem solver	Satisfaction	Classical Conditioning Example: favorable or positive associations, pleasurable image, hedonic appeals, or an enjoyable "flow" due to symbolic meanings linked to product usage

REFERENCES

Hirschman, Elizabeth C., and Morris B. Holbrook. 1982. Hedonic consumption: Emerging concepts, methods and propositions. Journal of Marketing 46 (Summer): 92-101.

Holbrook, Morris B. 1995. Consumer research: Introspective essays on the study of consumption. Thousand Oaks, CA: Sage Publications.

Holbrook, Morris B. 1999. Introduction to consumer value. In Consumer value: A framework for analysis and research, ed. Morris B. Holbrook, 1-28. London, UK: Routledge.

Holbrook, Morris B. 2000. The millennial consumer in the texts of our times: Experience and entertainment. Journal of Macromarketing 20 (December): 178-192.

Holbrook, Morris B., and Elizabeth C. Hirschman. 1982. The experiential aspects of consumption: Consumer fantasies, feelings, and fun. Journal of Consumer Research 9 (September): 132-140.

Pine, B. Joseph, II, and James H. Gilmore. 1999. The experience economy: Work is theatre & every business a stage. Boston, MA: Harvard Business School Press.

Schmitt, Bernd H. 1999. Experiential marketing: How to get customers to sense, feel, think, act, and relate to your company and brands. New York, NY: The Free Press.

Wolf, Michael J. 1999. The entertainment economy: How mega-media forces are transforming our lives. New York, NY: Random House.

Dear Xperiencing Consumer: Please Make Yourself Xtra Comfortable

A Crash Course on Becoming a Model Consumer in Our Xperience Economy

by Sharon Beatty, University of Alabama

Consumer: Do you know how to serve me my Xperience?
Marketer: Do you know what it takes to be served a great Xperience?

Dear Consumer:

Welcome to our consumption Xperience world. This world is full of opportunities for varied experience. For starters, there is the mall, with a range of merchandise and physical ambience. Then there are the restaurants, bowling alley, ballpark, theater, museums, and discotheque. You can dine here on sushi, steak, or pasta. You can visit art galleries or take in a musical. You can dance at the World Bar, or lounge in the BEDS club. You can take a few tango lessons or join a yoga class. And if you up to it, you can reserve a seat on a future commercial flight to the moon!

We are ready to serve you the Xperience you deserve. We have been through a marketing school and a school of consumer behavior. That is where we learned what it takes for a consumer to experience a great encounter (more on that later) and what it takes for a marketer to provide it. We'll share this knowledge with you. Knowledge of what we have to do as marketers; and what you do as a consumer matters too! With shared understanding, you'll be ready to squeeze the maximum out of your visit to the Xperience City. Ready? Let's go!

Welcome to the World Of Consumption!

Photo Courtesy: Sharon Beatty

WHAT IS AN EXPERIENCE?

Simply put, Experience is the process of consuming a product or service and the intrinsic pleasure (or displeasure) we derive from it. Thus, when we go to a restaurant, we consume food, and its outcome is a full belly. That is consumption. But we seek more. We seek an experience—going into a fun-filled, exciting setting, being welcomed by a personable host or hostess, getting a neat table, checking out the activity and people all around us, being greeted and treated by a friendly waitperson, antici-

pating some great, fun food that will please our pallets. All of this is independent of the fact that we just need food to fill our hungry belly. And we hope that each of these components of our visit will be a source of pleasure for us. This is what we seek. If you think about it: more and more of our consumption is "experiences." Some business writers have aptly called it the "Experience Economy"—we have moved from commodities to goods to services and now to experiences.[1] We are in the experience economy of our times.

Let's think about an example. Recently I went out to eat with a friend. We met at a nice upscale restaurant in town. I hadn't been there for a while and I was impressed that they had done some remodeling and the whole place was nice and roomier. We selected a quieter table by the window. Our waiter was Kevin, a new employee, but he was personable and attentive and seemed to do everything right.

I knew the menu so I didn't even look at it in ordering. My wine and food were quite good—although the piece of fish was very small (I didn't want to complain—because after all it was pretty tasty). My evaluation of the whole experience was very positive—although I felt that it was too expensive for what I got, especially given the small portion of fish I received. However, I feel positively towards this restaurant based on my continuing experiences with it over the years and I will certainly go back many times. Overall, we walked away satisfied (no longer hungry) and we had had a pleasant evening.

There isn't anything unusual about this experience and I only use it to illustrate a point. Consumer behavior is just real, everyday life. Actually the example above is full of consumer behavior concepts that you've read in this book. Can you find them all? Also in this scenario we could play the "what if" game and ask what could have gone wrong? For example, perhaps:

- My friend didn't show up and I had to eat alone;
- The restaurant was still in the process of remodeling and was in disarray;
- The restaurant was too busy and we had to wait 20 minutes for a table;
- The waiter took a long time to attend to us, seemingly ignoring us at first and the service was slow throughout;
- I had had car trouble earlier in the day and ate the whole meal concerned about whether I was going to need major car repairs or not.
- The people around us were noisy and obnoxious.

These are just a few of the things that could have occurred to impact the overall experience we had at the restaurant. Which of these things do the restaurants have control over and which do you have control over?

In this chapter, we want to know more about this world of our everyday consumption experiences and how we react to them. Let's see if we can classify them better, dissect them better, and therefore, know them better.

THE EXPERIENCE CYCLE

The experience cycle begins with an encounter—the consumption experience episode itself. Then we react to that episode. And the ultimate outcome is the relationship we form (or do not form) with the experience provider—that is, the marketer. That relationship feeds back

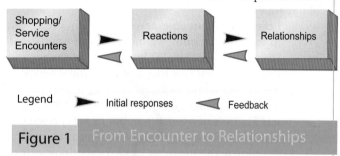

Figure 1 From Encounter to Relationships

into future encounters. (See Figure 1.) Let us begin with encounters.

THE EXPERIENCE ENCOUNTER

The encounter is where it all happens. When we interact with an individual in a service environment or retail setting, we call this a service encounter. Service encounters have been referred to as "moments of truth."[2] Jan Carlson, president of Scandinavian Airlines (SAS) at the time, used this term to refer to all the interactions customers have with employees—often only lasting seconds. Carlson turned SAS around by focusing on getting these moments right.

Obviously, these are moments in which we decide are we happy, are we having fun, do we wish we were somewhere else, are we getting good value…and the answers to these questions pretty much need to be positive for us to consider using this firm again and recommending it to others. This is the service provider's chance to either wow us or infuriate us!

THE ENCOUNTER DIMENSIONS

These encounters come in various shapes; they vary along certain dimensions (see Figure 2). Your encounters could be with a person or persons (the doctor or the salesperson) or with a machine (e.g., ATM machine or the Internet). Often we have a series of encounters, perhaps with multiple persons and/or machines, and often in multiple settings (e.g., during a three-day hotel stay). They could range from a short duration of a few minutes (e.g., getting our ice cream at Coldstone) to extended duration (e.g., a river rafting adventure). They could be inherently positive (a night out) or negative (a visit to the dentist) or

could just be neutral (getting money from an ATM machine). You may be shopping or eating out with a friend or you may be flying somewhere by yourself, surrounded by strangers. And, finally, it may be in your hometown or it may be across the world somewhere. All these dimensions influence our experience, as we shall see.

Your Place or Ours?

While so far we have been speaking of consumption in our place, our mall, our restaurant, our theater, let us not forget your home. Actually a good number of your experiences occur inside your home. And you know the anatomy of the experience is impacted a lot by whether it occurs at our place or yours.

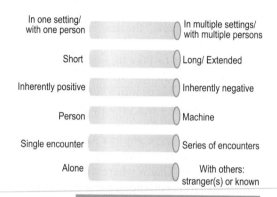

Figure 2 Encounter Dimensions

Service Provider/Store Environment

This is the environment created by the service provider (e.g., a doctor's office) or retail firm (e.g., a shoe store) or chosen by the service provider (the river and route chosen by the riverboat cruise ship). We generally go to the setting rather than the setting coming to us (e.g., visiting a beauty salon).

These environments are called servicescapes. The physical servicescapes include the real estate (the buildings, the comfort of seating in an airplane, etc.) as well as the inside atmospherics (e.g., the lighting, the music, the colors, etc.); the social servicescape includes the presence or absence of people (employees and other consumers) and their behaviors. These servicescapes encourage approach behaviors, or alternatively, avoidance behaviors. Pleasant atmospherics invite us to linger on. Crowds sometimes stress some of us, but for some contexts, and for some of us, they enhance our experience such as at a ballgame. Other customers could be too talkative or too loud for your taste or too aloof, and this affects your consumption experience, something over which we as marketers have no control.[3]

Home Environment

Home may be your most comfortable environment. It's where you go back to every night. It's where you live with people, hopefully that you like (!). Your home is where we (service providers) come to offer you our services—e.g., to clean your carpets, to repair your refrigerator, or to show you samples of flooring for your kitchen floor. If you want your home remodeled, we are going to be there for a long time, perhaps, from your point of view, too long. And many services, you purchase them from your home, perhaps in your loungewear, surfing a Website or phoning in your pizza order. And finally, you consume products and services at home—e.g., eating our Pizza, watching TV, listening to your wedding planner's ideas. The quality of these at-home experiences depends, in part, on your home servicescape, which marketers have no control of, and you alone are in the driver's seat.

REACTIONS

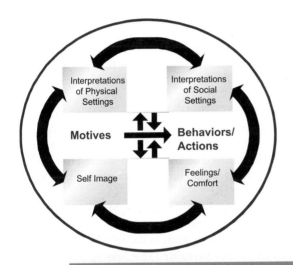

| Figure 3 | What's Involved in the Encounter? |

So How Do You Really Experience These Encounters?

Given a variety of these encounter environments, naturally, your reactions to them are also varied and your experience, to put it simply, far from straightforward. As you spend time in these environments, a lot of thoughts and feelings are churning in your head. These processes are depicted in Figure 3. Let's discuss these components.

Motives To begin with, you enter a service environment with specific motives. You visit a store, for example, not just to buy something but for social, adventure, role, gratification, hedonic, and exploration motives as well. In one study, consumers talked about the thrill and stimulation they received during the shopping experience: "It gets me all excited! So it's kind of like exploring, only in a shopper's world…It's an adventure for me."[4] As consumers, you are looking for more than just the right product—that would be too easy! As retailers, we have heard your voice—now some of us provide you such experiences as rock-climbing walls in shoe stores, and "singles nights" in grocery stores. Some other recent examples include:

- Wal-Mart hosted a live Garth Brooks

concert telecast in its electronics department nationwide;
- At Gibson Showcase customers watch as guitars are hand made;
- At the Toys R Us Times Square store you can ride the 60 feet high Ferris wheel or wander by the occasionally roaring, huge T-Rex, on your way to the overwhelming Candy Land or even to "Barbieland."
- At The American Girl store in Chicago, girls can bring their dolls into the Doll Hair Salon, where their doll can receive a whole new look.
- And when you've had too much excitement and want to relax, in some locations you can purchase a sleep chamber for as little as $.70/minute and take a short nap. Mall of America, which is in the Minneapolis-St. Paul area, now offers Power Nap Sleep Centers. Each Dream Suite has its own themed setting, featuring sleep aids such as bubbling fountains to allow for a peaceful but somewhat expensive sleep.[7]

Behaviors/Actions Motives drive our actions/behaviors. We may be engaged in shopping from a shopping list (in a grocery store), making a planned purchase (buying an airline ticket on the internet), browsing around to see what is new and fun (looking in gift stores while traveling), or engaged in some activity (such as playing tennis at our club). Our browsing and searching may lead to a purchase—which could be planned or impulse. And, we may win or lose our tennis match and feel good or bad about the event.

Interpretations Of course, what matters is not so much the servicescape per se, but rather our interpretations of it. Different consumers interpret the same environment differently. You might be the type who prefers a quite table at a restaurant and may find a hustle and bustle-type environment disconcerting; your companion, in contrast, might find this busy environment very entertaining. You might see the social distance maintained by your waiter as respectful while you friend might see it as aloofness.

As a consumer, you are always evaluating the service environment by your own criteria, asking questions such as: Is the environment one you wish to approach or avoid? Is it inviting? Is it intimidating? In fact, it is these interpretations of the physical and social aspects that cause you to feel like you belong or don't belong.

Self-Image Interpretations occur in the context of your self-image. If service providers seem to treat you badly, you might ask is it something about them or me? As consumers, you make attributions about why you are being treated the way you are being treated—you try to understand "the why" of the treatment you are receiving. You might look around and ask do you fit in? Are you similar to others? You might even ask, "Do I need to be here and do I want to be here?"

The fit between the service environment and self-identity is very important. Some writers have advanced the concept of place identity—consumer perceptions that the place fits with their own self-image. When we feel comfortable in a setting, we begin to identify with that place and with the people working there or visiting there.

We may develop an attachment to that place and even an intense bond. That then becomes the place we like to hang out at. Remember Cheers? More recently, Central Perk Coffee Shop? The popular hang out of Chandler, Ross, Joey, Monica, Rachel, and Phoebe. Sometimes these places are called "third places," places where everyone knows everyone and customers are friends with each other and the owner and employees. [5]

It has been suggested that place identity may be more important for certain groups than for others (e.g., minorities or elderly citizens). Questions of fit may involve the employee(s) and their behaviors, verbal or non-verbal. A Hispanic consumer reported: "In small shops they (employees) follow me around. They think I'm going to take something."[6] Or a potential patron may be concerned that she won't be compatible with the other patrons in the setting. A customer said this, "I get a sense of how a restaurant will feel by the vehicles in the parking lot. If I see a lot of pickups in those places, then I don't go in."[7]

Feelings/Comfort The fourth component in Figure 3 is feelings/comfort. From our interpretations of the social and physical environment, we experience a certain level of comfort or discomfort and decide whether to remain in or exit from the environment. Actually, comfort seeking is universal. It is different from seeking pleasure. Often it simply involves not being in discomfort or pain. One researcher called it a negative good, i.e., freedom from pain. Its importance to our everyday existence is illustrated in the following quote: "Twenty-four hours a day, seven days a week, awake or asleep, every individual on our planet, without exception, is constantly trying to increase his or her comfort level."[8]

One source of comfort or discomfort is other patrons—are they like you or very different from you. For example, restaurants, hotels, bars, and apartments struggle with these issues all the time. In our college town, some bars allow 18-20 year olds in and some do not. Some 21 or over patrons are turned off by the presence of the younger students, while some don't care. But how does a bar control its clientele?

And…what about those Problem Customers?
In the PBS series Airlines, Southwest Airlines employees had to deal not only with the problems customers had (e.g., forgetting their medication), but also with problem customers (customers showing strong signs of intoxication even before boarding). Obviously, many industries and companies must have policies related to how to handle problem customers or problems customers have so as to minimally affect other customers' experiences. For example, what happens when, in a 3-day cruise, your room is next to a crying infant? What

Other customers in the servicescape are a part of your service experience.

should the attendants do? What should you do?

More dramatically, there is a growing problem with customers who may engage in dysfunctional, deviant or destructive behaviors ranging from simply boycotting a company and grudge-holding (which are fairly passive activities) to retaliation against the firm or the employee, which is described as aggressive behavior aimed at getting even.

This might include vandalism, trashing, personal attacks, stealing, and creating losses for the company. There are even occasionally extreme cases of customer violence, such as the enraged customer who speared the back of the head of a flight attendant with her stiletto shoe when her flight was delayed.[9]

Service providers train their employees to handle a myriad of customer issues and problems. In fact, employees take on various roles, such as the legislator (where certain behaviors are not permitted, e.g., going on the plane too intoxicated) or the Santa Claus (recognizing or rewarding customer behaviors, for example, thanking a customer who looks after a child traveling alone).[10] See list in Table 1. But employees are human too. So it is natural that they sometimes can't take the abuse!

Now…what about those customers you came in with?
Your shopping companions influence your experience? For example, teens may shop with their moms or with their friends mostly. Perhaps the environment is designed for teens—loud cool music and flashing lights. So, how will mom feel in that environment? How do teens choose who to shop with or where to shop, and how does the choice of their companions influence their shopping?

What about a couple or a family shopping? How do couples or friends shop together differently than alone? Do they argue? Can they find bliss in the same store? More and more malls have decided to become lifestyle malls to appeal more to families and couples, recognizing that these individuals may be in malls together to both shop and to enjoy their time together

One of the ways they are trying to keep all parties interested and involved in the mall is through the development of new mall concepts, like the lifestyle mall and hybrid center.

Lifestyle malls Open-air plazas with street shopping, restaurants, entertainment, urban residences and services, aimed at affluent consumers and feel like villages…but are

TABLE 1 SOME ROLES OF SERVICE EMPLOYEES

ROLES	DESCRIPTION	EXAMPLE
Legislator	Write rules for customers to behave.	Be here when called or lose your place.
Police Officer	Enforce rules.	Bouncer in a club.
Match Maker	Group customers in a way so they are compatible with other guests.	Don't seat a family with children next to a romantic couple.
Santa Claus	Watch and reward good behavior.	On a flight, you exchanged your seat to accommodate a fellow customer's special needs, so you get a small box of candy.
Cheer Leader	To build communality among customers; To place customers in a cheerful mood.	Make a witty comment after demonstrating flight safety procedures.

Source: based on Charles A. Pranter and Charles L. Martin, "Compatibility Management: Roles in Service Performers," *Journal of Services Marketing*, 5 (Spring 1991): 43-53.

privately owned space. These "malls" are hot—growing at twice the rate of traditional malls, with approximately 130 in the U.S. today. [11]

Hybrid centers Combination of lifestyle and power centers (specialty centers). Sixteen of the 37 new major mall projects opening in 04 and 05 were hybrids. They have: Proper restaurants, theatres, furniture, groceries, big box stores—less emphasis on the department store anchor but they require lots of space

Example: General Growth's Jordan Creek, Des Moines, 200 acres, 2 level shopping district with retailers, such as Ann Taylor, along with the largest movie complex in the state, a village district with specialty and big-box retailers, such as Costco, a lake district, with 3.5-acre lake with bike trails and waterfront dining on a boardwalk.[12]

When things go wrong…

Sometimes, of course, your service experience fails to meet your expectations. As a result you may feel dissatisfied. If you do, you should complain. More and more service providers are realizing that your complaining is good for them. Companies need to hear those complaints so that they can improve, and employees need to be trained to encourage dissatisfied customers to complain.

But sometimes you get really angry with a service provider. Anger is actually a different emotion than dissatisfaction. While dissatisfaction may occur when something unpleasant occurs or when some goal is not fulfilled, anger involves strong feelings directed at someone or something and often includes feelings of being overwhelmed by the emotion and wanting to take some responding action. Thus, it appears that dissatisfaction can sometimes produce anger (depending on a number of factors such as who is to blame, could it have been avoided, was it perceived to be unfair, etc.), which then can produce complaint behaviors or other negative responses. However, researchers have also discovered that anger is more likely to produce complaining if customers have developed coping

strategies oriented to standing up for their rights. One researcher calls this "seeking redress propensity." Again, this suggests the importance of customers being encouraged to complain and feeling that the complaint will be effective—that is someone will actually do something to remedy the problem! [13]

A Ph. D student of mine, Carrie, talked about a situation in which she and I found the need to complain in a restaurant in Rome. She said:
I'm not typically a complainer, but recently I learned that complaining can be helpful but also somewhat embarrassing! I was with my professor in a restaurant in Rome when we were served some terrible pizzas. While I said "let's just eat them"; she said "no way" and proceeded to refuse to eat or pay for them. The waiter immediately asked us to get up and go with him to talk to the manager, where he proceeded to explain the situation to her. Then, the manager in broken English said accusingly, "A Pizza is a pizza!" but did allow us to leave after paying only for our drinks and we went to a restaurant down the street and had some great pizza. We wondered what the customers nearby, who had not yet received their food, must have thought about this!

Also firms recognize that it is hard for employees to react positively when customers are angry so employees need to work extra hard at developing a positive posture towards the customers even though the customers are angry and acting badly. For example, service providers do a much better job dealing with anxious customers than they do with angry customers. This is due to the highly contagious nature of anger—it is hard not to react to anger with more anger. But service providers still do a poor job with anxious customers, with only one out of three customers receiving supportive responses from employees. Thus, complaint training programs, as mentioned earlier, should be focused on understanding and responding to consumer emotions. As one researcher suggested, complaint-handling representatives need to first "fix" the customer, then they can attempt to fix the problem.[14]

When things go right...

What do we really want from a service experience? Perhaps to be entertained, our tasks accomplished with minimum pain, or maybe even having a sense of comfort or satisfaction with what we did doesn't seem out of line. Often we want to be wowed or delighted—to receive a pleasant surprise. When these things happen then we might say that we were "delighted" with the service experience.[15] Delight is thought to occur primarily when we are surprised by the service performance or performer. The employee or company gives you something you weren't expecting or goes out of their way to treat their customer in a special way. Can you think of a situation where a service provider has done this for you?

These positive emotions are translated into feelings of goodwill towards specific employees and the firm. We acknowledge how happy we are and we tell our friends. Perhaps we also tell the service employee how pleased we are and then, of course, that makes their day and they become even better service providers for us as well as others in the future. So as we are delighted with the extra special service we get, we vow our loyalty to that firm. As one of our research consumers told us, a retail salesperson loaned her a pair of her own earrings to wear with an outfit she had just purchased. She said she was so delighted that she became "locked" into a relationship with the salesperson.[16]

RELATIONSHIPS

When you experience satisfaction with a service provider repeatedly, you tend to develop a relationship with that employee and/or the firm. Often we have multiple encounters with the same person(s) or firm day after day or even year after year. For example, I've had the same lawn care provider for seventeen years, the same attorney for ten years, the same hairdresser for two years, and I have a long-standing relationship with various restaurants and retailers in town or around the country for years. Thus, these ongoing encounters with firms and service employees may be characterized as relationships similar to the ones you might have with your friends. In fact, sometimes your service provider becomes a close friend!

WHY DO WE HAVE RELATIONSHIPS?

Relationships are built basically on positive reactions such as satisfaction, trust and/or comfort. Figure 4 shows these factors.

Relationships built on Positive Reactions

In order for you to develop and stay in a relationship with a marketer, your benefits need to outweigh your costs. These benefits come in three forms: [17]

1. Special treatment benefits—the special way you are treated because you have that relationship (maybe your favorite bartender has your drink poured before you even ask for it).

2. Confidence benefits—the faith you have in your service provider and the service they deliver.

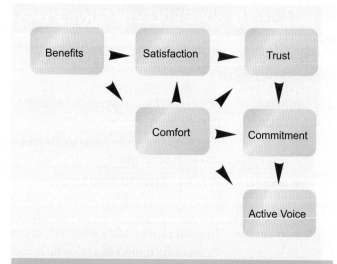

Source: Adapted from Deborah F. Spake, Sharon E Beatty, Beverly K Brockman, and Tammy Neal Crutchfield, " Consumer Comfort in Service Relationships: Measurement and Importance", *Journal of Service Research* 5 (4, 2003), pp. 316-332.

Figure 4 Relationships Built on Positive Reactions

3. Social benefits—the friendships that develop and the social interaction and conversations that occur (your massage therapist may also be your source of local news or you may love listening to your bartender's newest jokes).

Relationships are not equally important to all customers. Some people are simply more social and seek out relationships to fulfill their social needs; others may have relationships because they fulfill functional needs (for example one retail customer had this to say about her long-time relationship with a retail salesperson: "I don't have time to keep up with the trends and to mix and match things. Joan does this for me. The social part of the relationship is not important to me."[18]), while still others may be seeking both social and functional benefits. Further, sometimes due to the perceived risk or the importance of the service to the individual, developing a relationship becomes more important to them.[19] For example, Bonnie, an African-American professor, said this about her relationship with her hairdresser:

> My hairdresser is like a member of my family. Getting my hair done is expensive and it takes hours so I have to be comfortable personally and professionally with the person taking care of my hair. Getting your hair done is like therapy—a lot more than gray comes out at the wash bowl.

Next, comfort is an important factor in the growth of relationships. We talked about comfort earlier. It might be best described as when you get home after a long day and you put on your favorite sweats and slippers, grab a cold beer, and sit in your favorite chair to watch television or read a newspaper. You are just totally relaxed and not worried about anything. Well, consumers tell us that's how they feel in a relationship with the right service provider. For example, in discussing her pharmacist, Sue told us: "I feel safe there. I would never question that it wouldn't be done right."[20]

Thus, receiving benefits and feeling comfort influence relationship development. You can also think about the satisfaction issues—satisfaction with the outcome ("Wow—my hair looks great!"), or satisfaction with the process, ("Wow—the hairdresser was so nice!"). Generally as part of this process, at least when we feel the relationship is voluntary and positive, we develop a sense of trust of the service providers and a sense of commitment to them. That is, we think our hairdresser is doing a great job and isn't going to make any grave mistakes, so we develop a sense of loyalty to that person or firm. Scholars refer to a combination of these three factors—satisfaction, trust, and commitment—as relationship quality.[21] Finally, our willingness to complain to the firm and express our opinion, especially if we don't like something, is referred to as active voice, and is more likely to occur in relationships that we care about and wish to perpetuate.[22]

Relationships built mostly on switching barriers

Of course, not all relationships are peachy. Sometimes, we stay in relationships, both in social circles and in the marketplace, not because we want to but because we have to. This "have to" factor generally takes the form of switching barriers, i.e., it is not convenient or cost-free to switch our supplier. Such relationships are based more on convenience, or some type of obligation, inability to switch or even just inertia. We illustrate this in Figure 5. We may not be all that happy with our bank—but it may be inconvenient or a hassle to switch and frankly in the scheme of things it just isn't that important to us. So we often stay with service firm or employees based on what we call switching barriers or switching costs (things that make it difficult for us to switch). Further, we may stay because we think that basically all banks are the same (no reasonable alternatives to switch to) or because we feel we have to—maybe we have some kind of contract (like with our cell phone company) or we feel locked in for some reason (our accountant has all of our records), or due to a sense of duty (e.g., this is the attorney our family has always used).[23]

WHEN AND WHY DO RELATIONSHIPS END?

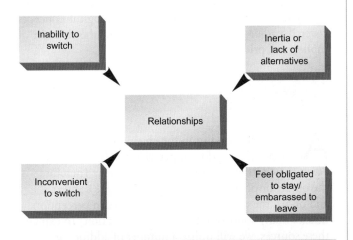

Inability to switch → Relationships ← Inertia or lack of alternatives

Inconvenient to switch → Relationships ← Feel obligated to stay/ embarrassed to leave

Figure 5 Relationships Built on Switching Barriers

Relationships have life cycles and don't last indefinitely. Service providers move or close their business; customers move, no longer need the service, or decide to try something or someone new (out of boredom or in a search for variety). It may be hard to leave for many reasons but it is often inevitable to think about the relationship dissolving.

Sometimes it seems quite difficult to break away from our current service providers. If we don't have to confront them and can just go quietly in the night, then it may be easier; but confronting someone to tell them we are abandoning them is difficult—for example, it may be difficult to tell your cleaning lady (who is doing a poor job) that her services are no longer required—so you might lie and say you just can't afford her anymore. When I left my hairdresser of seventeen years, I just decided not to return; I found someone else I liked much better. But I felt so bad about it—it was like breaking up with a friend. Actually I've seen that hairdresser a few times in the grocery store but I always sneak away before she can see me because I'm still embarrassed about leaving her![24]

> Ms. Cohen called in to cancel her dry-cleaning service—it had been ruining her husband's shirts—but the driver must have not gotten her message and showed up at her house to pick up the dirty clothes. When he saw a bag of laundry on the porch for the new dry-cleaner she'd hired, he rang the doorbell. "I panicked," says Ms. Cohen. "I ran upstairs to hide."
>
> After a few minutes, she realized she was being silly and finally opened the door. "Was it something I did?" the driver asked. She mumbled that it had nothing to do with him or his company. She now likens the experience to dumping a boyfriend. "You have to say, 'It's not really you, it's me.'"

While many of the reasons for dissolving our relationships are beyond our control, as service providers, we should make sure that we don't violate your trust. We have to understand that major infractions may lead to feelings of betrayal and anger, causing you to sever the relationship.[25]

CONCLUSION

So here we are, at the end of your journey through your service Xperience.

In this chapter we have focused on customers and their many service experiences. We talked about your shopping and service encounters, how you react to them as a consumer, and how and why these encounters progress into becoming relationships with service providers, and how these relationships offer you benefits and comfort in particular and hopefully, great Xperiences, as well!

Well, I guess you are now ready for your adventure into the Xperience world. So get comfortable and then go

(Endnotes on page 679)

PSYCHOLOGY MEETS ECONOMICS:

Why Consumers Can't Count Their Money Correctly

Priya Raghubir, Haas School of Business, University of California at Berkeley

Consumers feel happier if they discover that the complimentary ticket they received was priced at $200 rather than $100. They see greater value in two 10% discounts than in a single 20% discount. And they buy a $200 appliance placed next to a $220 model but not when it is placed next to a $180 model. Economics calls these consumer behaviors "irrational." Psychology considers them "normal." This chapter illuminates why.

The "Irrational" Consumer Goes to Market

Barbara and Jenny, two friends, both traveled on frequent flyer miles from San Francisco to New York over Spring break. During the flight, Barbara found out that the person sitting next to her, had paid $475 for his ticket; Jenny found out that the person in the seat next to her had paid $936. Later, when they told each other about this, Barbara felt sad: "I am always unlucky. I saved only a half of what you saved"!

Vicky had always wanted a pashmina scarf. In her local store they sold for US$99. When she went to India she found the same scarves selling for 500 Rupees each (approximately US $9.99). She was delighted and bought herself a pale pink scarf. She took pleasure in knowing that she spent only $10. Her friend, Christie, on her trip to India went to an upscale store where the prices were displayed in U.S. dollar currency. There, she found the scarves selling for $19.99 and bought three of them. Back home, Vicky was kicking herself for not having bought more scarves; Christie, on the other hand, could barely contain her joy.

Geeta and Rita, two friends in college, always hung out together. When they went out shopping or clubbing, they would always buy each other coffee, beer, or lunch, in turn—ignoring small price differences between what each bought for the other. Once, they went on a vacation together to Europe. There, suddenly, they started accounting for every penny they paid for each other's meal or drink, ensuring that in the end, they evened out. Back in the USA, they resumed their old pattern! [a]

Barbara, Vicky, and Geeta. Three perfectly rational consumers. Just like you and me. Yet, their behavior in the above episodes is, from an economics point-of-view, totally irrational. A free plane seat is a free plane seat, period. So why should it matter (to Barbara) how much a fare paying passenger paid for it? The price of a scarf marked in rupees was, when converted in dollars before buying it, still only $9.99, so why did it not seem (to Vicky) a deal enough to buy more than one unit of the highly desired scarves. And, the fellow vacationer (Rita) is the same friend, so why should the joint consumption, and paying for it in turn, change (for Geeta) from one of mutual friendly favors to bean counting?

It is clear that economic theory fails to explain these and many other everyday behaviors of consumers. In this chapter we draw on current and classical psychological theories of consumer behavior to understand how consumers think, feel, and act in the marketplace when they are deciding whether or not to pay, and how much to pay, for a product or service. Our main point is that both the prices on products and the money that consumer have are valued *subjectively*. That is, $10, say, as a price or as a sum of money a consumer owns means something different depending on who the individual is, how the price is presented, how the money is owned, and the shopping context facing the consumer.

What is money? Does money in another shape, size, color, or form feel different? Is it spent differently? Saved differently? Recalled differently? Stored differently? Allocated differently to different expense categories?

What are prices? Does a price communicated using another set of words or numbers or currency feel more or less expensive? Does the sequence in which a price is seen before or after other prices, or before or after information about the product or service it is related to, affect how attractive or unattractive it appears? Does the visual placement and size of price information matter in terms of how prices are processed, integrated and recalled?

The anecdotes above suggest that the answer to all these questions is a resounding, unequivocal "Yes!" We invoke psychological rules to understand and explain how consumers feel, think, and act when they are making economic transactions. These rules draw on psychological concepts covered earlier in the book, as applied to the domain of money and prices.

PERCEPTION

As you understood from the chapter on perception (Chapter 3), we do not perceive an object or its price, *objectively*. Rather, we perceive it *subjectively*. Therefore, the object or price perceived depends on the context and on us, the perceiver. This subjectivity in perception utilizes many sources of bias in our perception. To explain these sources, we will utilize a number of additional consumer episodes, described in the Box titled PSYCH

VII SPECIAL TOPICS

PSYCH RULES !

■ Bob and Jay liked going out Friday night for a beer at the beach. They would happily pay $5 for a pint at the hotel bar which had a balcony facing the ocean, but hated paying the same price for the same beer at the beachside kiosk that was right on the beach!

■ Tully loved spa treatments. However, she restricted herself to one every few months. She had always wanted to buy the full day $575 treatment at her favorite spa, but had been holding off on it. When her husband, Sandy, bought her that spa treatment for her birthday, she was overjoyed. The interesting thing is that Sandy does not work for a salary, and used the joint account he shares with Tully to buy her birthday gift. The next year, though, the price of the spa treatment went up to $675, and Sandy did not buy it again for Tully!

■ Allan was planning a trip to Vegas. He was going to be staying with friends, and wanted to get the cheapest flight possible. He narrowed his options down to two flights that cost the same: one with a free hotel night stay over but a less convenient departure time; and the other with a slightly better departure time, but no additional free hotel. Despite the less convenient times, and a friend's apartment being available to stay, Allan took the first offer!

■ Lisa's mother used a special "age-defying" cream that Lisa would buy for her for Mother's Day. But she would always wait for the brand to offer a "free gift," which comprised a set of six items like a lipstick, etc. The thing was that Lisa (and her mother) rarely used any of the products they received in the free gift hamper, but Lisa still liked to wait for the sale before making her purchase and always inspected her free gift packet carefully! On one occasion, she had got a free full sized lipstick that was in a color she never wore. While the brand made a number of other lipsticks in her preferred shades, she hesitated buying them at full price after that.

■ Michael and Ben, two students of economics, both liked to shop on price. But while Michael was more satisfied the more he had paid for a pair of shoes, Ben was happier when he had purchased it on sale. Ben was particularly happy when he saw that the "regular price" advertised against the sale price he had paid was higher than what Michael had paid for his shoes!

■ Ed and Tom, dormmates, friends, and competitors in college, both started a similar job after graduating. Ed got the job in his college town. Tom got a job in a big city where, as both Ed and Tom knew, the cost of living was higher by at least 20% than in their college town. When Ed saw his offer of $60,000 p.a., he was delighted about making a "real" salary. However, when his dormmate, Tom, told him he was being paid $65,000, Ed's euphoria evaporated!

Okay, now it is your turn. Got any similar stories of your own? (Write them down here):

....

What about a similar story of a friend or a family member (Name your friend or family member and write the story)

....

- A free ticket evaluated against a full price ticket of $936 will seem to be a much greater benefit to the consumer than the same ticket valued against a full price ticket of $475.
- An annual salary of $60K seems high when evaluated against a student stipend; but when evaluated against a friend's salary of $65K, it appears to be low. This is despite the fact that in real terms (adjusting for cost of living) the lower salary in a lower-cost city will buy more.
- A sale price evaluated against a regular price will seem a better value than the sale price just on its own.
- A $5 pint of beer will appear to be more affordable when purchased from an expensive hotel than from a cheap beachside kiosk.

So, you see, change the reference points, and perceptions change!

How Reference Points are Formed

You might now ask, where do these reference points come from? Consumers acquire these reference points in many different ways.[c] They can be based on:

- One's past experience (as in the example of Ed assessing his salary against his student stipend, or Sandy not buying the spa treatment at a higher price).
- One's knowledge of what others pay (as in the example of Jenny feeling that her frequent flyer purchase was a better deal).
- One's knowledge of what other vendors or stores offer for the same price (as in the case of Allan's being tempted to choose the less convenient flight time to get the offer with a free hotel room that he would not use).
- Consumers' beliefs as to what is *fair* (as in the case of Bob and Jay feeling ripped off by the beachside kiosk charging the same price for a beer as the adjacent hotel, since they know that the kiosk's costs of operation are much lower than the hotel's operational costs).
- Consumer expectations of what the product would be available for eventually (as in the case of Lisa waiting for the sale to buy her mother's gift, or the case of Jay waiting for a sale).

The useful thing to know for students of consumer psychology is that many of these reference points come from marketers.[d] The manner in which a consumer perceives your price is determined to a large extent by how you communicate the price. See box, "How Marketers Create Reference Points."

The interesting thing is that consumers actually view the same amount spent for the same product as a "gain" when they pay less than their reference point; and they view it as a "loss" when they pay more than their reference

---

RULES. Read them now, and pause for a minute to contemplate whether you would have acted differently. Done? Okay, here we go.

REFERENCE POINTS

One of the most influential ideas in how people perceive money and prices is the idea that their values are not an absolute, but are based on a "reference point"[b] against which they are evaluated. To illustrate this in terms of the vignettes in the box:

point. No matter how natural it seems to you, economics calls this behavior "irrational." Psychology explains why it is but natural for us to perceive and react this way!

Why Is My Loss More Than Your Gain?

Here is another interesting phenomenon. To most consumers, the joy of a five dollar "gain" is less than the felt pain of a five dollar "loss!" How come? The law of asymmetry, technically called prospect theory, explains it.[e]

Prospect Theory suggests that the perceived disutility (that is, "pain") of a loss is greater than the perceived utility (that is, "joy") of a gain of the same amount. Here is how it translates into everyday consumer decisions:

When a price is perceived as a gain (i.e., the price is lower than one expected to pay), consumers are more likely to think it is a better price, feel better about it, and are more likely to act toward purchasing it. On the other hand, when a price is perceived as a loss (i.e., the price is a "sticker shock," higher than what one thought it would be), then consumers are not only less likely to act on it, but the size of the effect is even greater. To explain, if a price perceived as a "gain" of $5 will make a consumer buy ten more units of a product (say, from 25 that s/he would have bought to 35), then the same price perceived as a $5 loss will make the same consumer reduce his/her purchase quantity by more than 10 units (say, from 25 units s/he would have bought to less than 15, say 10 or 12). Said differently, consumers feel the pain associated with a price increase more sharply than they feel the joy associated with a price decrease. They react more strongly to a negative change than they do to a positive change. In other words, they punish to a greater extent than they reward a company for giving them a (painful) loss rather than giving them a (joyful) gain.

MARKETING IMPLICATIONS

Marketers can put Prospect Theory to good use.[f] Here is how:

1. TWO SMALLER GIFTS ARE BETTER THAN ONE LARGE GIFT: That is, rather than offering a single gift, i.e., a single lump sum "gain," offer the same amount in two or more separate rewards. The value the consumer will assign to two separate rewards, A and B, will be higher than the value they will assign to the rewards C (where C = A+B). In the example of Lisa's gift purchase for her mother, the set of free gifts provided by many cosmetic companies, rather than a single gift that is of equivalent value, seems of greater value to Lisa, and makes her happy with her purchase. Likewise, two coupons for 10% discount each would be valued more by consumers than a single 20% discount coupon.

2. TWO SEQUENTIAL DISCOUNTS: Suppose that a store offers a discount of 10% and then an additional discount of 10% on the new discounted price; that would seem a better value to the consumer than a single 20% discount. Note that this point is different than the fact that a total discount split into two equal parts is better than a single discount of the same value. To understand the difference, let us do some simple math. Suppose the price of an item is $100. A 10% discount means, its discounted price is $90. Now, an additional, sequential discount of 10% on the discounted price would be $9, so the final discounted price would be $81, one dollar more than what the final price would have been with a straight 20% discount or two simultaneous 10% discounts. Yet, most consumers would feel that two 10% discounts, even when applied sequentially, offer a better value!

3. BUNDLING THE PRICE: If two items are priced at $50 and $25, then it is better to bundle them and sell them at $75. Why? You see, to a consumer a price is a "loss." And having to incur a loss twice is more painful than incurring a loss once. (This is the mirror opposite of "gaining two rewards is more pleasurable than gaining one of same total value.") By the same logic, if a credit card company has to impose a late fee of, say, $25 and a returned check fee of $29, then it is better to bundle them into a single invoice for $54. The $54 fees can still be itemized, but knowing of them (and paying them) in a single transaction is better than knowing of them at two separate points in time.

4. DEDUCT TAX AT SOURCE: Prospect theory would also imply that if consumers have to pay tax on their income after receiving the income, it will hurt them more than paying tax at the time of receiving the income, i.e., receiving a net income. You now know why it is painful for restaurant waiters who receive a bulk of their income without any tax withheld at source to declare the whole amount of their income in tax filings. Luckily, sales tax is deducted at source, and it is just as well with consumers.

5. CHARGE MORE NOW, REBATE IT LATER (SILVER LINING): A final implication of prospect theory is that when there is a large loss (e.g., as in the case of a high price that a consumer needs to pay) with a small gain (e.g., a discount), then separating the gain (e.g., in the form of a cash back offer or money back) would lead to greater utility than netting the gain

> To consumers, the joy of a five dollar "gain" is less than the pain of a five dollar "loss!"

> **How Marketers Create Reference Price Points**
> ■ Manufacturer suggested retail price (MSRP) ....
> ■ Past or regular price information. Was $ .... Now $ .....
> ■ Competitors' Price _____ Our price _____

> Option 'A' Buy this item for $100 now, then receive $20 cash back.
> Option 'B' Buy it now for a discounted price of $80.
> "I will take Option 'A'. I want my cash back."

VII SPECIAL TOPICS

out from the cost (as the benefit of receiving the gain is greater than the reduction in the disutility due to a lower price). To illustrate: Suppose an item costs $100, and the seller is prepared to sell it for $80. Then, rather than giving an instant cash discount of $20, it is better to charge the full price and then let the consumer receive $20 in a cash rebate. This is because the pain of paying $100 is a little more than the pain of paying $80, but the joy of getting $20 back more than makes up for this small increase in the initial pain. Yes, for the consumer, the pain of paying $80 now is *higher* than the pain of paying $100 now net of the pleasure of $20 cash rebate received later.

REFERENCE POINTS AS ATTRACTION & COMPROMISE

Two applications of reference points are especially useful to marketers of multiple options in a product line.[g] These include a store that carries an assortment, or a company that offers 3 or more product versions in the same product category but at different price points. This is how it works.

The Attraction Effect: Suppose a travel agent offers two packages to Las Vegas: Package 'A': air plus three nights in a four star hotel, priced at $299; Package 'B': air plus two nights in the same four star hotel, priced at $199. Now, suppose, the travel agent adds a third option, Option 'C': air plus two nights in a *three* star hotel, also priced at $199. What do you think would happen? Believe it or not, the sales of Option 'B' will receive a boost. This is because, to consumers, with Option 'C' as a reference, Option 'B' suddenly looks more attractive!

The Compromise Effect: Next, consider an option in a product line that is high quality and high priced (say, business class airfares), and a second option that is relatively lower priced and of relatively lower quality (say, economy class). If the company now introduces a third option that is priced still higher but is also of higher quality (e.g., first class seats), what do you think will happen now? The sales of the middle-priced option (e.g., business class seats) will increase! This is because, to the consumer, the business class fare now seems a good compromise option.

Unintended Reference Points: While attraction and compromise effects of reference points can be used by marketers to manage consumer perceptions of the price of their products, some other reference points created by marketers have unintended effects. Understanding these can help us avoid them.

a. Prevent Sale Price from Becoming a Reference Point A sale price works by inducing a consumer to buy because the consumer uses the regular price as a reference point. But when the item is often on promotion, the reverse happens: the consumer begins to use the sale price as a reference point, and, consequently, never buys on regular price. [h] Remedy: avoid frequent promotions. And offer them at irregular intervals.[i]

b. Make Comparisons Difficult Rather than offering the regular item on sale, create a somewhat different version of the same item for sale. Make a different package—different in color, size, etc. For example, if the regular item is 50 grams of a candy bar for 50 cent, offer a 40 gram bar for 30 cents, only during the promotion period. Or bundle two bars together and offer them for, 80 cents. Or a limited time bundle with premium. The point is that the difference in the promotional version should be beyond the just noticeable difference described in Weber's law (see Chapter 3 for a refresher).

c. Follow Weber's law—make the difference as vivid as possible. If you are a pizzeria for example, you could offer pizzas in three non-comparable forms: single servings as a triangular slice, those in an individual pie as a circle, and those in a large party pack as squares, making it more difficult for consumers to compare the sizes and prices across the three offerings.[j]

Extending this principle further, if you want consumers not to be able to use your competitors' price as a reference point, then differentiate your brand sufficiently from your competitors' brands. If differentiation in the core product itself is infeasible, at least differentiate it on superficial features such as package size and shape. Of course, follow the opposite strategy—make your brand look as similar as possible—when your price is advantageous.

MONEY ILLUSIONS

Reference points are one source of biased perception. The second source is what we will call *money illusions.* This takes three forms: (1) Visual appearance biases. (2) number reading biases, and (3) face value biases.

(1) Visual Appearance Bias—Bigger Is Better.
In our everyday life, we are exposed to money in certain shapes and sizes, and we get used to those shapes and sizes, valuing them more. And we inherently value larger numbers, larger sizes and larger shapes more. This inherent bias leads us to value money according to its form rather than its actual value. As a consequence, here is how our money illusions work.

a. Gift certificates or checks may be viewed as worth less than an equivalent amount in cash.

b. Payments by a credit card may be perceived to be less painful than the equivalent amount paid by cash. Buying food and paying five dollars on your cafeteria debit card is less painful than paying cash; what is more, it is less painful than paying even by a credit card.[k]

c. Coins may be valued less than notes and may be more likely to be spent.

d. Amounts of a larger denomination are valued more and therefore may be less likely to be spent. That is, if you have a $50 bill, you may be less likely to buy anything than if you have, say, only a $10 bill.

e. Notes (that are representative of higher denominations) are likely to be valued more than coins, leading to consumers spending coins more readily than bills. That is why many restaurants bring back "change" in coins and small notes, as they are more likely to be left as tips.

f. Monetary forms that are more colorful and less serious are likely to be spent more readily.[l]

g. Larger coins may be valued more than smaller coins (even when the latter are of higher value), especially by young children.[m]

(2) NUMBER READING BIASES.

Left to right processing: Despite the fact that when we learned arithmetic as kids we were taught to add and subtract numbers from right to left, as adults we appear to process prices from left to right. This leads to the well-known effect of "99 cent pricing." Consumers are likely to ignore the numbers on the right (typically the cents in low value purchases), and focus on the left most numeral to assess price. This implies that a price of $3.99 is perceived to be cheaper than a price of $4.00. This also suggests that when discounts are offered they should be across the whole number. For example, if a product priced at $425 is to be discounted, it will be more effective to discount it to $399 than to discount it to $400. By the same token, offering a discount of $10 is more effective than offering a discount of $9.99.

(3) FACE VALUE BIASES.

Face value biases occur in that the face value of a price or currency influences us more immediately than the implicit real value.[n] This effect is most vivid in foreign currencies.[o]

A price of 200 units in a foreign currency feels much more than a price of, say, 120 units in our own currency, even if in monetary value the latter might be of much higher than the former. Now you know why Vicky could not bring herself to buy more than one 500 Rupees pashmina scarf; and why, once back in US, re-connected with the dollar currency, she regretted not having spent Rs.1000 or Rs.1500 buying those scarves.

Euro effects: The face value effect in currencies has grave impact for the Euro currency. In 1999, the General Council of the European Central Bank set the conversion rates for the Euro for 12 countries that went on the Euro standard: Belgium, Germany, Greece, Spain, France, Ireland, Italy, Luxembourg, the Netherlands, Austria, Portugal and Finland. In all of these countries, except Ireland, the nominal prices of goods were lower in Euros than they were in the prior local currency. By the end of February, 2002, all 12 countries had discontinued the use of the local currency. Several studies have shown that consumers in these countries perceive the Euro priced goods to be cheaper than the same goods priced equivalently but in the former, familiar currencies.[p] Several merchants, such as duty free shops and multinational retailers, list their product prices in multiple currencies, and they are wise for it.

PRICE As A SIGNAL

Why is it that consumers sometimes are happy paying a higher price; and, sometimes, unenthusiastic about buying a product at a reduced price? This is because they use price as a signal, to infer other things. Here is how signaling works:

Price as a Signal for Quality Often consumers don't have the expertise to judge a product's quality. In such cases, they use the product's price as a signal of quality.[q] That is why they are happier buying a more expensive item. Recall that Michael was happy even though he paid a lot for his shoes. (Other attributes consumers use to infer a product's quality are warranties, country of origin, and brand name.)

From an economics point-of-view, consumers should be less willing to pay a higher price. However, from a psychological point of view, if consumers use high prices as a signal of high quality, then, consumer should be more willing to buy a high priced product.

Conversely, consumers may use a lower price as a signal of low quality. If the promotion is steep, this too may backfire. If a product's regular price is, say, $1, and it is promoted at 50 cents, then consumers would infer that the product must cost less than 50 cents to make. At such a low cost, it may not be worth even 50 cents. So they would then never buy the product at its regular price, and may not even buy it at deeply discounted promotional prices.

The Emotional Side of Price

After reading through the rest of this book, it should come as little surprise to you that price also has an emotional side. That is, consumers experience some emotions when they pay a particular price rather than another.

a. Excitement of Sweepstakes Consider the excitement of taking part in a sweepstake. Even though the economic value of a sweepstake may be mere pennies, the possibility, however small, that a person could win one big prize, adds feelings of excitement to the purchase. Therefore, promotions that are more exciting are better at generating sales than the regular "percentage off" or "dollar off" promotions that merely represent a reduction in the economic price that a consumer has to pay.

Another area where excitement can play a large role is that of auctions. In an auction, the excitement fuelled by winning a bid may lead consumers to over-pay (compared to the economic utility of that deal). The fact of winning leads to extra utility.

b. Feelings of self-worth Making an expensive purchase can make consumers freshly aware or cognizant that they can afford it and are therefore worth it. This is another reason why Michael may be happier paying a full price even if he knew that he can probably find a lower price elsewhere.

c. Feelings of smartness On the other hand, finding a deal and paying a lower price may help the consumer feel that he/she is smart.[s] This is the reason why Ben was happy with his purchase of shoes at the discounted price. The different ways in which Michael and Ben relate to prices is based on their individual differences: one appears to be insecure about his self-worth and needs the purchases he makes to reassure himself; the other appears, in contrast, to be less than secure about his smarts or feels guilty about buying himself indulgences, and, consequently, uses his purchases to reassure himself that they are good value.

d. Feelings of guilt In the domain of self-gifts, consumers often feel guilty about rewarding themselves with hedonic pleasures. This is one of the reasons that they would prefer to get something as a gift from another person, rather than buying it for themselves, as in the case of Tully who loved her gift of a spa treatment when she received it as a gift. Even though the funds would come from the same joint account, she would not allow herself to buy it for herself.

e. Feelings of Embarrassment Frequently consumers may forego the satisfaction of positive emotions in order to avoid negative emotions, such as embarrassment, anxiety or uncertainty. Despite the fact that coupons are widely used, consumers may still feel embarrassed about using one at a checkout counter when there is a large line behind them; or at a dinner for Valentine's day; or for a gift for a special person. This is because they don't want to look cheap to others, and to the extent that the use of a coupon or promotion suggests that they are money-conscious, they may wish to avoid this impression by not using it.

Memory Games with Price

How much did I pay for that puppy in the window?

One of the reference points for price is the price in one's mind already. Actually, "in memory," we should say, since that is where all prior information is stored. Our memory often plays games when it comes to our recall of price.

One thing about memory is, as you read in Chapter 4, that there is a lot of information in it, and all of it is not equally easy to retrieve. Depending upon the situation, our memory recalls things selectively.

1. Low levels of price recall One of the most amazing findings was based on a field study where researchers asked consumers who had just placed an item in their shopping basket how much they had paid for it.[t] They found that as many as half of the consumers did not recall the price of the item minutes after they had placed it into their basket, even when they had purchased it on the basis of it being on deal or having a low price. Thus, there is evidence that price does not enter into the equation in the traditional manner that economists would argue that it does. Instead, consumers encode a price in broad categories such as a "good" price, or a "low" price, or a "bargain" or a "steal" or a "rip-off." They make their decisions on the information coded this way rather than on the actual price of the product. As a consequence then, what is needed for a promotion to induce consumer purchase is that the promotional discount be just sufficient so as to be coded as a "good deal," and no more. Keeping this insight in mind, managers should not give away too much money in promotions, but rather should find the level worthy of the "it's a good deal" coding.

2. Biases in the recall of money Recent work in consumer psychology has shown that consumers have strong biases in their recall of how much money they have. The larger the denomination of a monetary instrument, the more accurate they are, but as the number of each note or coin increases, they underestimate the amount that they are carrying.

3. Biases in the recall of spending Can you recall how much you spent last month on your credit card bill? Or how much you spent on your last vacation? The fact is that these are difficult tasks as they are made up of identifying individual transactions and then aggregating them. People can forget not only the fact of the transaction, but the amount of it. They are more likely to forget transactions that are infrequent, and those that happened a while ago, as compared to those that happened recently or frequently, or those that happen on a regular basis. Further, they are more likely to forget transactions that are small in value as compared to those that are large in value. Finally, they are more likely to forget transactions associated with a lower pain of paying. Given this, credit card bills may be extremely difficult to recall, as each transaction was less painful than the same transaction made in cash. This could be one of the reasons why people overspend on their credit cards, as they lose track of their expenses.[u]

4. Biases in the recall of prices Finally, consumers are more likely to recall prices that stood out—these are likely to be the less expensive prices than they had searched for. Thus, prices of products on promotion may be better recalled overall than their regular prices.[v]

To Summarize, memory biases in how people recall information can also lead to departures from traditional economic theory.

THE IRRATIONAL CONSUMER—NOT THAT IRRATIONAL AFTER ALL

Now, let us return to the anecdotes with which we started the chapter and those in the box:

- Jenny has reason to feel happier than Barbara with her frequent flyer purchase as her reference price was $936 (the price the person sitting next to her paid), rather than the $475 that Barb must have compared her free seat to.

- Michael and Ben differ from each other in terms of their deal proneness and their need to use price as a signal for quality. While Ben does not use price as a signal of quality, Michael does. As such, Ben gets greater happiness from getting a good deal, while Michael gets it from paying full price.

- Geeta and Rita began to start accounting for their purchases while traveling as they were dealing in foreign currencies and they could not get used to thinking in those currencies in a short time. They probably wished to control their spending, knowing that they may be making errors by over- or underspending, as they were unfamiliar with the foreign currency.

- Vicky, by the same token used the face price (which was Rs. 500) to not buy more pashmina scarves. It is possible that had their price been marked in dollars, at barely $ $9.99 she would have bought a lot more.

- Tom was happier than Ed because his nominal salary was higher than that of Ed's. This is explained by the money illusion phenomenon, along with reference point effects. Whether the reference point is a point in the past (a student stipend, or past price) or another point at the same time (a friend's salary, or a competitor's price), it will determine whether or not a salary is evaluated as a good one.

- Sandy and Tully are both rational. Tully enjoyed her spa treatment gift because she did not have to experience the negative feeling of guilt when she got the treatment as a gift from her husband. If she had bought it herself, her enjoyment may have been diminished because she may have felt guilty about spoiling herself. Sandy knew this.

- Bob and Jay hated paying $5 for the beer at a beachside kiosk because they knew that the kiosk owner had lower costs of operation than the hotel bar. Consequently, they may have coded the price at the kiosk as a "rip-off."

- Allan believed the free-hotel offer to Las Vegas was a better offer for exactly the same reason. He did not wish to reward a company that was overcharging him, and would have rather gone through the inconvenience of worse flight times, as it had the benefit of punishing a company that he believed was not offering him the best deal that they could afford.

- Finally, Lisa always waited for the "free gift" sale because she had begun to expect this promotional pattern and had got habituated to getting more for her money. She refused to buy the lipstick she had received for free once, as she assumed it was a cheap brand of lipstick since it had been given away for free.

SUMMARY

The way consumers think, act and feel in the marketplace is a function of psychological factors that go beyond our traditional understanding of economics. By accepting that consumer perceptions may be based on reference points and the effort they put into a decision, the fact that consumers use price as a signal of quality, that they use their feelings to make decision, and the fact that they do not use all the information at their disposal (either memory based, or available in their context) but use only a subset of it, which is then integrated in a manner that allows them to make a decision that is "good enough" rather than the best decision that they could make, one can get at a better understanding of why consumers react to prices the way they do. And that understanding can help marketers understand how to set and communicate prices so as to be in sync with the consumer's ways of encoding them.[w]

Endnotes

a These anecdotes are based on various papers referenced at the end of this chapter.

b Kahneman, Daniel and Amos Tversky (1979). Prospect theory: An analysis

of decision under risk. *Econometrica, 47,* 263-291.

c Raghubir, Priya, J. Jeffrey Inman, and Hans Grande (2004), "The Three Faces of Price Promotions: Economic, Informative and Affective," *California Management Review,* 46 (4), Summer, 1-19.

d Winer, Russell S. (1988), "Behavioral Perspectives on Pricing: Buyers' Subjective Perceptions of Price Revisited," in Timothy M. Devinney, ed., *Issues in Pricing: Theory and Research,* Lexington, MA: Lexington Books, 35-57

e Kahneman, Daniel and Amos Tversky (1979). Prospect theory: An analysis of decision under risk. *Econometrica, 47,* 263-291.

f Thaler, Richard. H. (1985). "Mental accounting and consumer choice," *Marketing Science,* 4 (3), 199-214.

g Simonson, Itamar (1989). Choice based on reasons: The case of attraction and compromise effects. *J. of Consumer Research,* 16, 158-172.

h Winer, Russell S. (1986), "A Reference Price Model of Brand Choice for Frequently Purchased Products," *J. of Consumer Research,* 13 (Sep), 250 - 256.

i Krishna, Aradhna (1991), "Effect of Dealing Patterns on Consumer Perceptions of Deal Frequency and Willingness to Pay," *J. of Marketing Research,* 28 (4) (November), pp 441-51

j Robert E. Krider, Priya Raghubir, and Aradhna Krishna (2001), "Pizzas: π or Square? Psychophysical Biases in Area Comparisons," *Marketing Science,* 20(4), Fall, 405-425.

k Prelec, Drazen and Duncan Simester (2001), "Always Leave Home Without It: A Further Investigation of the Credit-Card Effect on Willingness to Pay," *Marketing Letters,* 12 (February), 5-12.

l Bruce, Vicki, David Gilmore, Lynn Mason, and Pamela Mayhew (1983). "Factors Affecting the Perceived Value of Coins," *J. of Economic Psychology,* 4 (December), 335-347.

m Kirkland, John and David Flanagan (1979). "Long-term Memory and the Value-Size Hypothesis," *Perceptual & Motor Skills,* 48 (June), 1149-1150.

n Shafir, Eldar, Peter Diamond, P., and Amos Tversky (1997). Money Illusion. *Quarterly J. of Economics,* 112, 341-374.

o Raghubir, Priya, and Joydeep Srivastava (2002), "Effect of Face Value on Monetary Valuation in Foreign Currencies," *J. of Consumer Research,* 29(3), December, 335-347.

p Desmet, Pierre (2002). A study of the potential effects of the conversion to euro. *J. of Product and Brand Management,* 11(3), 134-146.

q Raghubir, Priya, and Kim P. Corfman, (1999), "When do Price Promotions Affect Brand Evaluations?" *J. of Marketing Research,* Vol. XXXVI (May), 211-222.

r Chandon, Pierre, Brian Wansink, and Gilles Laurent (2000), "A Benefit Congruency Framework of Sales Promotion Effectiveness," *J. of Marketing,* 64 (Oct), 65-81

s Schindler, Robert M. (1992), "A Coupon is More Than a Low Price: Evidence From a Shopping-Simulation Study," *Psychology and Marketing,* 9 (Nov/Dec), 431-451

t Dickson, Peter R., and Alan G. Sawyer (1990), "The Price Knowledge and Search of Supermarket Shoppers," *J. of Marketing,* 54 (July), 42-53.

u Srivastava, Joydeep, and Priya Raghubir (2002), "Debiasing Using Decomposition: The Case of Memory-Based Credit Card Expense Estimates," *J. of Consumer Psychology,* 12(3), 253-264.

v Krishna, Aradhna and Gita V. Johar (1996), "Consumer Perception of Deals: Biasing Effects of Varying Deal Prices," *J. of Experimental Psychology: Applied,* 2 (3), 187-206

CONSUMERS IN SEARCH of PROPER PLEASURE
How Brand Stories Help Consumers Enact Dramas in Their Lives
Arch G. Woodside, Boston College, USA

Consumers are hard-wired to tell stories of their consumption. Through storytelling, consumers interpret, make sense of, and relive their original consumption experience itself. Such re-experiencing through storytelling, Aristotle calls "proper pleasure." Residing in our unconscious and behind these stories is an archetype—the hero of the story if you will. While brand communications often tell brand stories of their own, few rise to the level of successfully incorporating the archetypes specific consumers are trying to achieve—archetypes such as the hero, the anti-hero, the rebel, or the change master, for example.

We illustrate the role of such archetypes in brand communications though a brand consumption story about Versace and the archetype some consumers might well experience—namely, the siren, the seductress in a Versace coat. This story is vivid proof that archetypes are real, and it is an invitation to brand managers to become familiar with the repertoire of various archetypes, or else miss an opportunity to bring consumers "proper pleasure" they (the consumers) are seeking.

"So Where the Bloody Hell Are You?"

Thus asks the tag line in a new TV commercial campaign for Australian Tourism. The commercial shows vignettes uniquely available for experiencing in Australia:

- The first scene shows a young male drinking a beer in a remote outback pub; he says, "We've bought you a beer" and turns to face the bartender
- In the second scene a yellow sea plane lands in the Great Barrier Reef; a snorkeller swims towards the plane as the pilot sits on the float to tell us, "Your taxi's waiting."
- In the third scene an Aboriginal dance troupe goes through its moves; a young woman says, "And we've been rehearsing for over 40,000 years."
- The final scene shows the Sydney Opera House with dozens of moored sail boats and the tag line in the skyline.

This tag line, and the commercial in which it embeds, was not invented in thin air. Rather, the Australian Tourism Board had done extensive consumer research—at a cost of $5 million (AUD), using focus groups, for six months to learn what people thought about Australia. "What we found from a massive research campaign is that people like Australia not so much for Australia but for Australians," says Tom McFarlane, M&C Saatchi's regional creative director in Sydney. He settled on the "bloody hell" tagline after considering and tossing out dozens of others. "What I think this captures is the real Australia and who we really are—an easy-going, welcoming nation," Mr. McFarlane says, "And people like that."[a]

This Australia advertising and brand experience case study implies more than just an advertising message. The tagline represents the "gist" of a story that the viewer/listener of the TV commercial is supposed to learn and enjoy about the brand—Australia. You will meet easy-going welcoming people and will experience (more than only see) breath-taking sights during your Australian visit. The story promises personal transformation, self-improvement and self-mastery—fulfilling the iconic myth of the *change master.*

Change master is one of the many iconic myths we live, and as consumers we live them through brands. In this essay, we will tell you exactly how it happens. How consumers build stories around brands they consume? How these stories bring them "proper pleasure"? How the telling and listening of stories helps them become, even if only momentarily, mythical "heroes," and other mythical icons? How brand communications help, or can help, consumers experience their "proper pleasure," achievable through the realization of aspired mythical icons?

Brand Communications: Lecture or Drama

Writers on advertising have classified all approaches used in brand communications, especially in broadcast media, into two types: (a) lectures, and (b) dramas.[b] In the lecture format, a spokesperson faces the camera and presents the brand benefits (or a voice over voices them off camera). In the drama format, in contrast, there is no spokesperson; rather consumers are shown using the brand in a consumption episode. These episodes are sometimes everyday use situations, but often they are built around entertaining melodrama. Lectures are particularly effective in covering many points in a message quickly, although, being "lectures," they can be unengaging for the viewer. Dramas are, in contrast, particularly effective in drawing in the reader or viewer to vicariously feel the emotional experiences of the brand user.

A third form is a variation of the drama format, namely,

vignettes. The vignette approach includes brief, often un-related, scenes from the same or multiple sources and the scenes tell a story about a brand; or someone assuming the role of the narrator narrates the scenes. Vignettes combine the desirable features of both lectures and dramas: cover a lot of topics quickly while suggesting brief user experiences of the brand. Each scene features its own narrator—thus making the vignette a disjointed narrative. What this disjointed narrative does is tell brand stories (in the plural).[c] The Australian ad is a prominent example.

Brand Stories and the Consumer Experience of Mythical Icons

Brand stories narrated in commercials through vignette formats help consumers internalize and experience mythical icons. Just what are mythical icons and how they relate to consumers' brand experiences? To explain this, we will need to employ five technical terms: myth, icons, archetypes, mythical icon, and gist.

A myth is an ancient story, or a popular current belief, involving a hero or representing an ideal act (e.g., the myth of Santa Claus). An archetype is an original model or thing after which subsequent versions are built (e.g., the original movie Dracula which then becomes "the archetype" or the model for the sequel). Thus, if a business executive inspires and steers innovative product designs in his or her firm, we could say his or her archetype is, say, Steve Jobs. It can also stand for a representation of a quality or property (e.g., hero, loyalist, altruism). Simply speaking then, an archetype is "a model" (of a person or a quality) in our minds that we use to emulate or try to personify. An icon is an enduring symbol of something that is widely admired. McDonald's arch is an icon of modern day fast food culture. A mythical icon is a symbol from mythical stories. A gist is a summary of a story usually in a word or sentence of a story, that stands as shorthand for the entire story.

The gist of the story captures the core brand or consumption experience. Rebel without a Cause is both the title of a movie as well as the gist of a story. This story represents a stage in life when teenagers seek independence from parental authority and control. The plot structure in the movie illustrates one th atric prodution of the story. Each of our arguments with our parents as teenagers reflects a scene and our own personal "production" of the rebellion story. Becoming a rebel is attempting to enact one archetypal myth.

In brand communications, story telling is a powerful means of building brands. This power is because consumers themselves experience and live with brands inside the stories. Such lived experiences have two layers: first, the situations and settings in which the original consumption occurs itself is a drama or a story, unfolding naturally. Second, consumers narrate it later, and thus relive that drama, and, thereby, relive the original product consumption experience itself.

According to psychologist Carl Jung, each of us has a

GLOSSARY OF TERMS

Myth. A traditional, typically ancient story dealing with supernatural beings, ancestors, or heroes that serves as a fundamental type.
A popular belief or story that has become associated with a person, institution, or occurrence, especially one considered to illustrate a cultural ideal.

Icon. An important and enduring symbol; One who is the object of great attention and devotion; an idol.

Archetype. An original model or type after which other similar things are patterned; a prototype: For example "'Frankenstein'... 'Dracula'... 'Dr. Jekyll and Mr. Hyde'... the archetypes that have influenced all subsequent horror stories" (New York Times).
In Jungian psychology, an inherited pattern of thought or symbolic imagery derived from the past collective experience and present in the individual unconscious.

Protagonist. The main character in a drama or other literary work

Antagonist. The principal character in opposition to the protagonist or hero of a narrative or drama.

Gist. A summary of a story usually in a word or sentence of a story.

mythical icon in our unconscious mind that we want to implement.[d] We may be a 16-year old regular teenager or a 40-year old dad of two or a college student, and that is how we think of ourselves most of the time. But existing often unconsciously in our psyche there is another image of ourselves—this image is sometimes an alter ego—different from our regular visible image, such as "accountant by day, cowboy by night"; or alternatively, it may be the extension of our regular self stretched out to its outer limits—a slightly altruistic person by day, Robinson Cruiso by night; or merely a shopper ostensibly, but a warrior deep within, or a soccer mom in casual appearance but Supermom inwardly. Humans live and relive these myth icons of self by reflective thoughts and by fantasizing about them, and by constructing these fantasies around our everyday chores and everyday consumptions. We build them also by narrating the stories to ourselves and to others, and in these narrations we sometimes stretch, extrapolate, embellish, dramatize, and give heroic qualities to everyday consumption experiences. Brands help consumers play out such myths. But by telling them first in drama-based ads, or in vignette-based narratives, brands also help us experience the stories vicariously.

> **Accountant by day, cowboy by night!**

Jung on Myths and Icons

While all archetypes exist in all of our psyches, each of us tends to enact a lmited set of them in our lives—we tend to form scripts unconsciulsy based in part on early personal experiences and the associations of these experiences with specific archetypes. Scripts here refer to unconscious life-plans each of us attempts to enact. Humans attempt to neither enact one archetype nor act out one script every day; yet, one or two particular archetypes are especially relevant to each of us. Over decades as well as due to unique major events in our lives, both archetypes and scripts may undergo dramatic transformations. For example, the teenage rebel and fan of heavy metal music becomes the mother of four children and singer of bedtime lullabies.

How Consumers Experience Brand Stories

Myths have heroes. Likewise, all stories have a protagonist—the main character in the story. Often, they also have an antagonist—the character who blocks the mission of the protagonist. Eventually, the protagonist wins. This is recognized, in popular parlance, as the triumph of the hero over the villain.

Consumers both live the myth stories and then they tell them. They live these stories in that, modeling after the archetype in the myths, they try to enact the product drama, i.e., the drama surrounding the product's use, in a manner that will make them the protagonist in the related myth story. Living the stories enables consumers to achieve archetype outcomes: become Mr. Evil—an anti-hero—by dawning a WWII helmet and a black leather jacket, and riding a Harley-Davidson motorcycle on a Saturday afternoon, even though this consumer might be an accountant five-days a week.

Next, after living the story during brand consumption, consumers try to tell the stories of their consumption. Let us closely consider four questions:

(1) Why do consumers tell stories?
(2) How do the stories consumers tell illustrate underlying myth icons?
(3) What are the components of a good story?
(4) What should brand managers do to help consumers tell stories?

Q1. Why Consumers Tell Stories?
Humans (consumers) tell stories:

- To make sense as to what is happening and what has happened
- To experience the inherent pleasure in telling and hearing stories, &
- To enrich the psyche by fulfilling unconsciously, and possibly consciously, original patterns or prototypes in the human mind—archetypal primary forms.

First, telling stories helps the storyteller make sense of what s/he saw and/or did. "How do I know what I think

until I hear what I say?" By telling others what happened, humans help themselves make sense of their own experiences. Telling others also serves as a "member check"—seeing if others provide similar or very different interpretations of the events and outcomes of the story told. Member check is a method of validating one's experience by sharing it with others who will then confirm, or, alternatively, present a different view of the same experience. Example: a consumer sees a movie and then talks about how he or she felt; then, when the listener echoes similar sentiments, the first consumer's experience is validated. He or she then feels assured that he or she "understood" the film and experienced it the right way. Remember, then, that the first purpose of story telling is validating one's own brand experience.

Second, stoires are inherently pleasurable. Consumers' reports of journeys to, in, and out of a destination provide "proper pleasure."[f] Proper pleasure is a term introduced by Aristotle, and its full meaning is deep and its scope vast; For the purpose of this essay, let's keep this simple guiding meaning in mind: proper pleasure is the pleasure humans experience in telling stories. (And vicariously, they experience it in listening to or watching those stories.)

Third, while some stories consumers tell are simple accounts of mundane events (e.g., on my way to office, I picked up a bouquet of flowers), many are quick narratives with a mythical icon or an archetype in the background. That is, consciously or unconsciously, we build and narrate those stories with an archetype as the model. These stories always involve journeys to a physical and/or emotional place by a protagonist—with obstacles, help, setbacks, and triumph experiences constituting the plot structures unfolding in these journeys. We experience proper pleasure either as the protagonist in the story or vicariously living the story from hearing or watching the story told. Thus, and thirdly, stories help us experience archetypal primary forms, i.e., help us play out in our minds being a rebel or a Supermom, for example.

Q2. How do the stories consumers tell illustrate underlying myth icons?

Psychologist Roger Shank proposes that people think mainly in terms of stories (rather than concepts). "They understand the world in terms of stories that they ave

> Jung believed that icons are primary forms of the collective unconscious, covering a range of basic elements of the human psyche, for example, *evil*, *mother*, *heroes*, *sirens*, *power brokers*, *happiness* (Jung, 1995). He believed also that myth icons or archtypes are not something learned or acquired—rather, they are with us from birth and they are as natural and embedded in us as our own DNA. A number of influential thinkers, most notably Joesph Campbell and Bruno Bettelhein, assert that mythology, folklore, and fairytales provide the most natural expressions of archetypes in society.

already understood. New events or problems are understood by references to old, previously understood stories and explained to others by the use of stories."[g]

Substantial research literature provides a strong justification for storytelling theory in consumer psychology as well as for creating and testing the impact of storytelling in marketing contexts. This literature has confirmed that consumers often include products and brands in reporting their own lived experiences.[h] They frequently assign roles, actions, and relationships to brands in the stories they tell themselves and to others; brands in these stories are depicted as enablers of archetype myths.[i] For example, drinking Mountain Dew enables the slacker myth;[j] a **slacker** is a person rebelling against the dominant life themes of work and family—someone seeking to hang out and experience fun with friends at the expense of productive work.

Q3. What are the components of a good story?

Classical drama provides a definition of a "good" (McKee, 2003)[k] or memorable story. Classical drama is a story that includes several incidents increasing in excitement and suspense preceded by conditions/settings that initiate the unconscious/conscious identification of one or more goals. Actions by a protagonist and possibly by additional actors result in an outcome. Along the way, some temporary world blocks surface (e.g., an antagonist preventing the protagonist from achieving the main goal) and some personal blocks may also hold up progress (e.g., the protagonist lacks the skill to perform an act necessary to reach the goal). These blocks and the struggle against them serve to increase the emotion and involvement in a story. When the protagonist achieves the final goal, the viewer feels an emotional peak.

Figure 1 depicts the emotional experience in the story. This experience has five stages: prequel, act1, act2, act3, and act4. The prequel is simply the common ground between the teller and listener. For example, a consumer story about her Halloween costume assumes the listener is familiar with the custom of Halloween. The four subsequent stages are the ones through which the actual story telling unfolds. The experience in these four stages is, respectively, of balance, imbalance, resolution, and sense making & storytelling.

The mountain-shape graph line shows the emotional roller coaster the consumer experiences (technically called the Evaluative slope). Note that this is the emotional state of the consumer narrating the story; and it is also the emotional state experienced by the listener or viewer. Yes, storytelling and listening is a pleasure for both the storyteller (original consumer) and the story listener (who now enjoys the "original" consumption vicariously).[l]

The evaluative slope is at its least emotional level in the prequel stage. The prequel stage is, as stated earlier, the often-unstated background information of the ordinary world of the protagonist occurring before the beginning of the story. Act 1 includes a call to adventure[m]—the narrating consumer unconsciously or consciously sees her/himself in changing circumstances, such as an opportunity to buy or experience a new brand. Act 2 is some event or dilemma that occurs for the protagonist that results in a state of psychological imbalance[n]—such as the Jewish couple recognizing their desire consciously to buy a German car and their automatic retrievals from their unconscious minds denying permission to do so.

The protagonist experiences the highest emotional state in Act 3 whereby the protagonist seizes the opportunity, buys the brand, and/or experiences using the brand and witnessing the outcome or receiving the benefit. Act 4 includes sense making by the protagonist and telling the story of what happened that includes buying and/or using the brand. Act 4 can sometimes occur on separate occasions, over weeks, months, years, and even decades of storytelling (e.g., telling grandchildren about the wedding day and honeymoon trip one experienced 50 years ago). The increasing emotional slope in Figure 1 represents the positive change in anxiety, tension, excitement, and/or joy as the story unfolds. The rapid decrease in emotional slope occurring betweens Acts 3 and 4 represents a catharsis—an experience or feeling of spiritual release brought about by an intense emotional experience.

This figure provides, thus, a summary of storytelling theory relevant for understanding consumers' own interpretations of their lived experiences—interpretations that they use so as to make sense of what happened as the product drama had first unfolded in their lives. It is also an account of how consumers enjoy proper pleasure over-and-over again in retelling stories to themselves, family members, and friends.

The Role of Archetypes in Consumer Stories

At this point you might be wondering, in describing the story telling process, we did not use the words "archetypes," "mythical icons" etc. This is because we were describing the process of storytelling, not the content of

FIGURE 1   CONSUMER STORYTELLING THEORY

Emotion

Evaluative slope

Prequel   Act 1   Act 2   Act 3   Act 4
          (Balance)   (Imbalance) (Resolution) (Sensemaking & Storytelling)

Acts through Time (Seconds, Minutes, Hours, Days, Weeks, Months, Decades)

stories. We do so now.

The brand stories that consumers live and tell are built around archetypes. Recall that archetypes are original prototypes (or "models") based on which subsequent similar "products" are built. Well then, consumers do not build brand consumption stories in vacuum; rather, they always have some image of an ideal person or an ideal consumption setting they are trying to replicate. These images are stored in their memory from popular culture, or from their own past experience.

These images are the archetypes. These images are also placed there, sometimes, by brand marketers. A number of brands in our culture have icons. How? By telling good stories— stories that are anchored in archetypes that individual consumers find appealing. Let us take a tour of 12 of them. (See Table 1 and Table 2)

Q4. What should brand managers do to help consumers tell stories?

If you are a brand manager, you cannot but be eager to apply the concept of archetype in building your brand story. The foregoing account of 12 archetypes in brand stories has energized you. You now want to build an archetype-based brand story.

TABLE 1	ARCHETYPES, STORY GIST, & BRAND EXAMPLES

Archetype	Story Gist	Brand Examples
ULTIMATE STRENGTH	When an obstacle is there, it must be overcome, strength must be proven in use.	Timex— "It takes a licking and keeps ticking.
THE SIREN	Power of attraction, linked with the possibility of destruction	Allure by Chanel; Envy by Gucci
THE HERO	Fortitude, courage, and victory; a journey and transformation	Michael Jordan and Nike shoes; Joe DiMaggio and Mr. Coffee; Power Puff Girls; Forrest Gump
THE ANTI-HERO	Universal message of destruction and attraction of evil; the bad dude	Heavy metal icons; Howard Stern; Jerry Springer; Oakland Raiders; Che Guevara; Harley-Davidson
THE CREATOR	Creative inspiration and the potency of imagination; originality; authentic	Coca Cola—the real thing; Walt Disney; Kleenex
THE CHANGE MASTER	Transformation, self-improvement and self-mastery	Curves—workout stores for women;Gillette's Mach 2 Razor; Porsche 911
THE POWER BROKER	Authority, influence and domination—the world's leading -….; the best …; number one	CNN; E.F. Hutton; Bill Gates; Microsoft
THE WISE OLD MAN	Experience, advice and heritage; staying the test of time	Levi's; Obi-Wan kenobi
THE LOYALIST	Trust, loyalty and reassurance	Coca Cola and "Mean" Joe Green with boy of 12 TV commercial; *I Love Lucy*; *Friends* TV sitcom
THE MOTHER OF GOODNESS	Purity, nourishment and motherly warmth	Just Juice; Ivory Soap; Tropicana Orange Juice; Aunt Jemima; Fairy Godmother; Witch of the East; Snow White
THE LITTLE TRICKSTER	Humor, non-conformity and the element of surprise	Dennis the Menace; Bart Simpson; *Pee-Wee's Big Adventure*; *SpongeBob SquarePants*
THE ENIGMA	Mystery, suspense and uncertainty	Zorro; Abercrombie and Fitch; Star Trek

Source: developed in part from several chapters in Weretime (2002).

The question is which archetype and how? To address that question, let us understand how the brand stories consumers adopt come to be. Figure 2 depicts the processes surrounding the construction of archetypal brand stories. Substeps 1-6 describing this process include the following points:

1. Each consumer has certain archetypes he or she aspires to accomplish. For instance, some consumers may wish to enact in their life the archetype of the Supermom, and others of a siren.

2. Only certain archetypes are relevant to a given product category and to a given brand. For example, the archetype of siren is unlikely to be relevant to a brand of washing machine but the archetype of the Supermom might well be.

3. The brand stories that brand managers build, which may or may not based on any archetype.

4. The brand stories consumers construct for some brands, basing those stories in aspired archetypes. Consumer may construct stories of their own, or adopt stories told by brand managers.

5. Brand managers attempting to build archetype-based brand stories tap into the pool of archetypes. That archetype may or may not be the one the consumer finds relevant or aspires to.

FIGURE 2	HOW BRANDS BUILD ARCHETYPAL STORIES

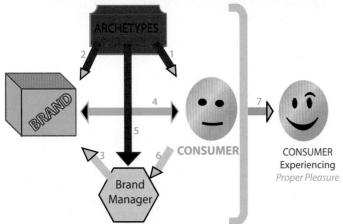

1. Core archetypes the consumer aspires to achieve.
2. The Archetype most fitting for the brand.
3. The brand stories that brand managers build.
4. The brand stories consumers build, accept, and relish. This link reflects consumer-brand relationship.
5. The archetype the brand manager taps to build brand stories
6. Brand manager researches consumer brand stories.
7. Consumer tells (or listens to) the archetype-based brand story.

6. Brand manager researches the consumer so as to identify proper archetype.
7. The consumer tells the desired brand story and derives proper pleasure.

Note that not all products lend themselves to archetype-based myth consumption for all consumers. And consumers don't construct such stories for all products. But just as likely, they intuitively "sight" opportunities in some brands to play out their aspiring archetypes. And then they play an archetype out, first imagining the archetype as they use the brand, and then later when narrating the brand consumption story. They may not be aware of the archetype or may not know it by that name (of course they don't know the concept of archetype itself) and may be living it out at the level of subconscious; in that case the story they tell may have the archetype in an implicit not explicit form. This is best illustrated in the Versace brand story from a consumer (see below). Brand managers may tap an archetype from a pool at random (not recommended) and then build a brand story around it. Consumers will not accept such a story, of course. But when consumers accept the archetype in the brand story brand managers tell, they

are able to live out and tell better stories.

This is because the brand story provides the plot and the narrative. But just because a brand tells a story, consumer don't have to accept it. It is imperative therefore that the brand stories brand managers build be based on the ar-

TABLE 2	**From the Mother of Goodness to the Siren—Archetypal Stories in Brand Communication**

Ultimate Strength A brand personifying ultimate strength considers an obstacle as a challenge that must be overcome. (Believing that a nonhuman brand, e.g., a car, beverage, or a watch, can overcome an obstacle is an example of anthropomorphism—the attribution of a human form, human characteristics, or human behavior to nonhuman things; see Chapter 18). TV commercial demonstrations of Timex watches successfully completing torture tests—being strapped to the bottom front end of powerboat moving at 50 mph and still ticking afterwards fit the ultimate strength profile. The unstated implication is that the consumer wearing a Timex possesses such ultimate strength to overcome obstacles that she or he may confront.

The Siren A brand personifying the attributes of a siren enables its consumer to become irresistibly attractive. The name and commercial displays of Allure by Chanel is an example of one marketer's attempt to tap into this archetype. Sea nymphs luring sailors onto rocks is an early description of a siren—note the inherent danger of doom to the person responding to a siren's call. Successfully adopting a siren stance is, for the consumer, an inherently, unconsciously, dangerous act, and it helps overcome boredom. Thus, wearing Allure—becoming a siren by proxy—adds spice to a relationship or situation.

The Hero A hero is somebody who commits an act of remarkable bravery or shows great courage, strength of character, or another admirable quality. Michael Jordan, Tiger Woods, Joe DiMaggio, the Power Puff Girls, and Forrest Gump are examples of real-life and fictional heroes (you have to have a sister or daughter who is six years old to know about the Power Puff Girls). The consumer presents her/himself to her/himself as a hero by adopting brands worn/advocated by well-known heroes. Perhaps the most known example of a brand helping consumers enact this archetype is Nike.

The Anti-Hero "Yeah, I'm bad!" captures the essence of the anti-hero. Silver and black clothing personifies the anti-hero stance—witness the bad boys of the NFL, the Oakland Raiders. "Anti-Hero" and " Alien" are brand names of skateboards designed to enable users to enact this archetype. "Anti-Hero Scumbag T-shirts" are also available to wear while riding your Anti-Hero skateboard. Take a look at http://www.skatewarehouse.com/TSANTIHERO.html.

The Creator Originality, being authentic, and bringing something new into existence are attributes of a creator. Associating with a creator is inherently appealing because alternatives imply imitations of the original—fake, knockoffs, cheap, poor quality, bad. The message by Coca Cola—"It's the real thing"—reflects both the primal attributes of the creator and the implied fakery by the brand's competitors.

The Change Master The change master possesses and displays the ability to transform her/himself into something better—an improved position of the prior condition or stance. Curves is a franchise of workout gyms for women that enables them to become change masters because Curves projects itself as a change master.

The Powerbroker Being the supreme authority, possessing dominant influence, represents the powerbroker. The following story illustrates a brand's application of the powerbroker archetype.
There's a famous TV advertisement from about 20 years ago for brokerage firm E.F. Hutton. In the ad, a group of people sit at a crowded, noisy restaurant or something, and one stuffy guy says to another stuffy guy, "My broker is E.F. Hutton, and E.F. Hutton says ... " and the whole crowd of mostly stuffy guys falls silent, listening. The tag line: "When E.F. Hutton talks, people listen." (http://www.thestreet.com/basics/gettingstarted/999737.html)
The fact that many Americans over 50 can fill in the blank when asked ("When ___ talks, people listen") illustrates the power of archetype storytelling applications to building brand awareness and preference.

The Wise Old Man Being experienced and offering reliable, tested, high performance are attributes of the wise old man. Levi's invented jeans during the California gold rush of 1849, and the brand often presents itself as having the attributes of the wise old man.

The Loyalist Trust, loyalty, and reassurance are marks of the loyalist. All sport fan clothing displays of the loyalist archetype. Illustrations of the loyalist include the following behaviors:
·Wearing the apple brand's icon as a tattoo;
·Screaming, "We are Penn State!"
·A NFL football player identifying his alma mater as, "The Ohio State University!"
·Wearing a Wisconsin cheese head hat;
·Displaying the Nike swoosh on hats, jerseys, and jackets.

The Mother of Goodness Purity, nourishment, and motherly warmth define the mother-of-goodness archetype. The brand, Just Juice, reflects purity—no water or other filler additives is the promise inherent in the name. "Soup is good food," is the famous Campbell's Soup tag line that personifies the mother-of-goodness.

The Little Trickster Humor, non-conformity, and the element of surprise are attributes central to the little trickster. Being a little trickster offers release, liberation, and fun—overcomes conscience and super ego controls. The little trickster is the child's version of the anti-hero. A child's love of Sponge Bob Square Pants morphs into a teen's love of James Dean's movies with the rebel archetype. Dennis-the-Menace line of clothing and wigs permits the wearer to enact tricks on nearby neighborhood adults unwittingly assigned the role of Mr. Wilson—a child's production of scripts illustrative of the little trickster. (See http://www.a2zkids.co.uk/products/costumes/books_nursery_rhymes_and_fairytales/dennis_the_menace.html#)

The Enigma Displays of angst, mystery, and uncertainty typify the enigma. Attributes captured perfectly in the facial expressions and physical posturing of models shown at Abercrombie and Fitch's website. Check it out for yourself: http://www.abercrombie.com/anf/lifestyles/html/homepage.html. Such displays reflect the anti-hero and the siren archetype as well—causing a widespread negative reaction by some consumers and commentators (e.g., for one such review, see http://www.americandecency.org/abercrombie.html).

chetype consumers harbor in relation to a specific product category.

To achieve this, what is required is that brand manageres research these potential archetypes. To research archetypes consumers hold, a program of ethnocentric research is required. Ethnocentric research studies consumers in their everyday, natural settings. The researchers observe the consumer using the product, conduct qualitative interviews, and drop in on the marketplace conversations. And in the age of the Internet uppon us, participate in chat rooms and forums, and peruse and reflect on brand/consumption related blogs. The goal is to listen to the consumer narrating the brand stories with all the melodrama built in.

A Versace Coat and the Siren:
A Fascinating Brand Story based on Archetype

Now, let us tell you one of the most fascinating consumer stories we have heard and read. This one comes from a blog (Web log) and is about a British woman, Pollee, buying and using a Versace coat. In the story, Pollee buys a Versace coat, wears it sans knickers (no underpants), and transforms herself into a siren. Read the story in the box.

Note in the story that Pollee also buys lingerie at Rigby & Pellar (a retail store) and she decides to pull "into a garage to use the loo [bathroom]." She decides to surprise her "man of the moment" [live-in boyfriend] by removing her dress and knickers in the loo to wear only her coat and lingerie (likely a slip and stockings) home to "my man." She is stopped by two police officers for using a cell phone while driving (illegal in Britain) and the officers ask her why she was wearing a coat on such a warm (August) evening. "Quick as a flash I told them I was going to a fancy dress vicars and tarts party." Such parties are an English tradition and require guests to arrive dressed as a vicar or as a prostitute.

This story expresses characteristics of the Versace coat assisting in a courtship relationship and participating directly in a secret affair. Courtships refer to an interim relationship state possibly on the road to a committed partnership contract. In Pollee's account, the man of the moment morphs into "my man" with no hindrances apparent to a possible committed relationship. Versace is a co-conspirator with Pollee in a secret affair when she wears the coat without knickers—a highly emotive, private bonding that leads to a risky exposure to police officers. In the story's ending in the blog, Pollee includes a happy face symbol (;)) in suggesting that her secret affair drama with Versace leads to her achieving her goal for the evening—a warm embrace with her boyfriend and the happy face follows this development. The opening segments of the story in the blog include a hint of a brief imbalanced relationship among Pollee, fur coats, and design shops. Pollee twice mentions that she "wouldn't

| EXHIBIT 1 | POLLEE'S STORY |

" I am a Siren and I wear Versace"

Pollee, a British woman, writes a story about her purchase and consumption of a Versace coat.

Out on shopping one day, she had just bought new lingerie from a store and then at a second hand ladies wear shop in Beauchamp Place (London) she found her prized purchase: a beautiful cream colored cashmere coat—Versace at a price of 150 pounds (price of new, £1,000). Here is how she described her treasure find:

> The feel of the cashmere was sooo soft and it was lined with a beautiful silver embossed lining that felt beautiful against the skin and epitomised luxury all the way. The fit of the coat was wonderful and I felt like I was one of those film stars sweeping into the room wearing the most wonderful outfit.

She started her journey home and she called to check if her "man of the moment" was at home. He was. Pleased, she stopped to pick up some food and then while using the restroom, on a whim she thought of surprising her man by showing off her purchases (lingerie and the coat) by donning them. She did, and on a further whim, she decided to not redress her shirt and skirt ("no knickers," so to speak).

As luck would have it, cops pulled her over since they caught her using the cell phone while driving. They asked her to get out of the car.

"I got out of the car...trying the hardest not to reveal what was (or wasn't) underneath my coat." Writes Pollee. Here, Pollee remembers to note: "Versace did not let me down. The coat, all encompassing, only using two of the buttons provided kept my chastity covered. This coat has quality and after several dry cleanings because of the colour still looks as good as new!"

The cops were asking Pollee why she was wearing a coat when it was so hot. Pollee's answer and the rest of her blog, you had better read it in the original:

> "Quick as a flash I told them I was going to a fancy dress vicars and tarts party. [Refers to a party where the theme requires guests to arrive dressed up as either a vicar or a prostitute. It is a very English tradition.]
>
> 'Let's have a look' said the youngest one, who was the one if I had a choice I would have accepted a drink from! I pulled up my coat to show the top of a leg and told them that was all they were getting! They laughed and we all went our separate ways.....thank goodness.
>
> Five or six minutes later I arrived at my mans house, 'nice coat' he said as I wafted in like a film star…
>
> As I tried to kiss him he shifted me out of the way as the football was on. I resorted to standing in front of the TV and slowly unbuttoning my two buttons......luckily he ..... ;-)

> --Pollee (posted 24 August 2001)

Source: Pollee's blog can be read in full at http://www.dooyoo.co.uk/fashion/versace/

wear fur." But her addition, "I'm inconsistent," indicates both an imbalanced state as well as her achieving balance by having learned to live with a little inconsistency. The imbalance is likely resolved in the subsequent Acts, by her assumption of the siren role, which gives her the pretext to break free from all the norms of her "everyday self"—i.e., the self when she is not playing the siren.

Pollee's story includes several touch points matching the Versace siren myth of enabling a woman to intoxicate men with her overt eroticism. Note that Pollee's attempting to kiss her man results in his shifting out of the way to continue to watch football on the TV. Only by "slowly unbuttoning the two buttons [of my Versace]" does she achieve the desired intoxicating effect—her ultimate goal for the evening intended in the story.[o]

For You, the Brand Marketer, the Wisdom of Consumer Stories

If you are a brand manager, you have probably already "sighted" the amazing opportunity this storytelling consumer action, and our theoretical analysis, offers. Here let's briefly summarize it for you. Crafting an archetype-based story—wherein a brand is a supporting actor—enables a consumer to achieve conscious and/or unconscious goals. Such storytelling helps build very favorable consumer-brand relationships (e.g., committed partnerships, best friendship, flings, or a secret affair, see Fournier 1998)[p]. The storytelling analysis in this chapter includes self-oriented thinking by the storyteller with near-conversational interactions with the primary brands appearing in the stories (e.g., Pollee's, "Versace did not let me down."). Consequently, learning—not only thinking about—what buyers and users say to the brand and what the brand says first provides valuable clues for designing highly effective marketing and advertising strategies.

Narrative reports and drama enactments are more likely to encourage vicarious participation while lecture forms of advertising tend to evoke argumentative forms of thinking.[q] Given that learning via storytelling is more memorable and retrievable than lecture-based learning,[r] learning the stories consumers tell in natural settings represents a useful grounding for crafting naturalistic stories or fantasies that are acceptable and enjoyable to the intended audience.

Consumer storytelling research provides evidence as to how and why brands become icons in the informants' own words. Informant reported enactments of the iconic roles played by brands likely include symbols and expressions that match with imprinted unconsciously driving myths that affect the informants' behavior—the originating core myths may be uncovered via word searches using blog search engines (e.g., Technorati, Feester, or Blogdigger). Consequently, becoming aware of the consumer enactments of imprinted myths via brand icons provides direction for story genre and consumer-brand relationships (e.g., the Fairy godmother myth is one plotline worthy of producing alternative enactments to encourage one segment of travelers to visit Paris; showing alternative scenes of a protagonist wearing a Versace coat sans knickers is a story gist useful for rejuvenating romance in a tired relationship).

Summary

While commercials-in-lecture formats quickly become irretrievable (to say nothing of irritable), consumers are hardwired to attend to, tell, and retrieve stories. Consumers are driven to tell stories to others to achieve deeper understanding—bring to consciousness relationships their consumption of brands and products have to archetypes. Archetypes are "prototypes" of characters (e.g., superman, supermom, vixen) and qualities (e.g., altruism, seduction, etc.) consumers dream about and try to implement and achieve.

It is through consumption stories consumers tell others that they understand and validate their consumption experience—"How do I know what I think until I hear what I have to say?" Classical drama storytelling enables consumers to achieve Aristotle's "proper pleasure" (i.e., the pleasure of experiencing the consumption experience by interpreting the original experience) and to experience one or more specific archetype primary forms.

Lecture-format in commercials is a good option to communicate a brand's features and benefits. However, in many product categories, consumers buy brands more than for the features and the benefits that these brands offer—they buy and consume them to enact archetype experiences. Classical dramas as a format in advertising include but go beyond showing features and benefits to connect consumers to archetypal outcomes. The brand stories in these dramas should therefore invoke and connect with the archetypes.

Conclusion

A substantial proportion of consumption experiences are "realized" by consumers through the telling of stories to themselves and to others—stories built around the brand's use. Brand communications also sometimes tell such stories, but, in order to be effective, they should resonate with what consumers are trying to achieve through brand consumption. To achieve such resonation, brand managers should listen to stories consumers tell.

This requires ethnographic studies, but weeks and months of ethnographic data entailing consumer stories will be of no avail without knowledge of archetypes. Existing unconsciously behind these stories are archetypes—the hero in the story if you will. To identify the specific archetype in a story, the managers must become familiar with the repertoire of archetypes and the kinds of myths and stories associated with them. Our description of twelve of such archetypes along with current marketing examples is a demonstration of the living, vivid reality that archetypes are in current brand dramas. Our essay is thus also an invitation to brand managers to study archetypes and harness their potential in their brand communications.

Endnotes

a See Stanley, B. (2006). Australian tourism ministry swears by its new ad. The Wall Street J. Asia, March 10, 1-2.2006 for further details about the Australian advertising campaign; for a review see David McLeod's report at David McLeod's report at http://www.duncans.tv/?p=270. 2006 for further details about the Australian advertising campaign; for a review see David McLeod's report at http://www.duncans.tv/?p=270.

b Chebat, J.C., Vercollier, S.D., & Gelinas-Chebat, C. (2003). Drama advertisements: Moderating effects of self-relevance on the relations among empathy, information processing, and attitudes. Psychological Reports, 92, 997-104.

c See Escales, J. E. (1998). Advertising narratives; what are they and how do they work? In B. Stern (Ed.), Representing Consumers: Voices, Views, and Visions (pp.267-289). New York: Routledge Press; Adaval, R., & Wyer R.S. (1998). The role of narratives in consumer information processing. J. of Consumer Psychology, 3, 207-245.

d Jung, C.G. (1959). The archetypes and the collective unconscious. Princeton, NJ: Princeton University Press.

e See the work by Eric Berne (1964/1996) for a full development of scripts as unconscious life-plans: Berne, E. (1964/1996). Games People Play : The basic handbook of transactional analysis. New York: Ballentine.

f Aristotle, 360 BC; Hiltunen, A. (2002). Aristotle in Hollywood. Bristol: Intellect Books.

g See Schank, R.C. (1990). Tell me a story: A new look at real and artificial memory. Cambridge, U.K.: Cambridge University Press, p. 219.

h See Arnould, E.J. & Wallendorf M. (1994). Market-orientated ethnography: Interpretation building and marketing strategy formulation. J. of Marketing Research, 31, 484 -503. ; Hirschman Hirschman, E. (1986). Humanistic inquiry in marketing research: Philosophy, method, and criteria. J. of Marketing Research, 23, 237-250. Hirschman, E. (2000a). Consumers' use of intertextuality and archetypes. Advances in Consumer Research, 27, 57-63. Hirschman, E. (2000b). Heroes, monsters, and messiahs. New York: Andrews McMeel.; Kozinets, 2002; Moore, 1985; Woodside & Chabet, 2001); also see Stern, B. (1994). Classical and vignette television advertising dramas: Structural models, formal analysis, and consumer effects. Journal of Consumer Research, 20, 601-615.

i Fournier, S. (1998). Consumers and their brands: Developing relationship theory in consumer research. J. of Consumer Research, 24, 343-374.

j See Holt, D.B. (2003). What becomes an Icon Most? Harvard Business Review, 3, 43-49.

k McKee, R. (2003). Storytelling That Moves People - A conversation with screenwriting coach, Robert McKee. Harvard Business Review, 6, 51-55.

l See Gergen K. J. & Gergen M. M. (1988). Narrative and the self as relationship. Advances in Experimental Social Psychology, 21, 17-56; Delgadillo, Y. & Escalas, J.E. (2004). Narrative word of mouth communication: Exploring memory and attitude effects of consumer storytelling. Advances in Consumer Research, 31, 186-92.

m See Volger, C. (1998). The writer's journey: Mythic structure for writers (2nd edition). Studio One, CA: Michael Wise Productions.

n See Woodside, A.G., & Chebat, J.-C. (2001). Updating Heider's balance theory in consumer behavior. Psychology & Marketing, 18, 475-496.

o For additional interpretations of Pollee's story, See Woodside, A.G., Sood, S. (2007), "Advancing consumer storytelling research," Psychology & Marketing, forthcoming.

p Fournier, S. (1998). Consumers and their brands: Developing relationship theory in consumer research. J. of Consumer Research, 24, 343-374.

q See Boller, G.W. (1990). The vicissitudes of product experience: 'Songs of our consuming selves.' Advances in Consumer Research, 17, 621-626; Boller, G.W., Babakus, E., & Olson, J.C. (1989). Viewer empathy in response to drama ads: Development of the VEDA scale. Unpublished working paper number 402-489. Memphis State University: Fogleman College of Business and Economics; Booth, W.C. (1961). The Rhetoric of Fiction. Chicago: University of Chicago Press.

r See Bruner, J. (1990). Acts of meaning. Cambridge, MA: Harvard Business School Press, 1990; Schank, R.C. (1990). Tell me a story: A new look at real and artificial memory. Cambridge, U.K.: Cambridge University Press.s Wertime, K. (2002). Building Brands & Believers. Singapore: Wiley (Asia).

Endnotes (for Beatty's article...)

[1] Pine, B. Joseph II and James H. Gilmore, The Experience Economy, Boston, Mass.: Harvard Business School Press, 1999.

[2] Carlson, Jan, Moments of Truth, NY: Harper Collins Publisher, 1989.

[3] Bitner, Mary Jo, "Servicescapes: The Impact of Physical Surroundings on Customers and Employees," J. of Marketing 56 (April 1992), pp. 57-71. Baker, Julie, Druv Grewal, and A. Parasuraman, "The Influence of Store Environment on Quality Interferences and Store Image,"J. of the Academy of Marketing Science 22 (4,1994), pp. 328-339; Beatty, Sharon E., Morris Mayer, James E. Coleman, Kristy Ellis Reynolds, and Jungki Lee, "Customer-Sales Associate Retail Relationships," J. of Retailing 72 (3, 1996), pp. 223-247; Tombs, A. and Janet R. McColl-Kennedy, "Social Servicescape Conceptual Model," Marketing Theory 3 (4, 2003), pp. 447-475.

[4] Arnold, Mark J. and Kristy E. Reynolds, "Hedonic Shopping Motivations," J. of Retailing 79 (2, 2003), (2), pp. 77-96. (p.93).

[5] Rosenbaum, Mark and Detra Montoya, "Exploring How Ethnic Consumers Assess Their Place Identity," presented at Royal Bank Research Seminar, Montreal, Sept. 2005.; Altman, I. and S.M. Low, Place Attachment, NY: Plenum, 1992; Proshanksy, H., "The City and Self-Identity," Environment and Behavior 10 (2, 1978), pp. 147-169; Proshansky, H., A. K. Fabian, and R. Kaminoff, "Place Identity: Physical World Socialization of the Self," Environmental Psychology 3 (1, 1983), pp. 57-83.

[6] Rosenbaum, Mark and Detra Montoya, Ibid, p. 11.

[7] Ibid, p. 9.

[8] Scitovsky, Tibor, The Joyless Economy: The Psychology of Human Satisfaction. Rev. ed. NY: Oxford University Press, 1999; Slater, Keith, Human Comfort, Springfield, Il: Charles C. Thomas, 1985, p.3.

[9] Harris, Lloyd C. and Kate L. Reynolds, "The Consequences of Dysfunctional Customer Behavior," J. of Service Research 6 (2, 2003), pp. 144-161; Huefner, Jonathan C. and H. Keith Hunt, "Consumer Retaliation as a Response to Dissatisfaction," J. of Consumer Satisfaction, Dissatisfaction and Complaining Behavior 13 (2000), pp. 61-82; Nelms, Douglas, "Passenger Violence," Air Transport World 35 (3, 1998), pp. 34-43.

[10] See Charles A. Pranter and Charles L. Martin, "Compatibility Management: Roles in Service Performance,"Journal of Services Marketing, 5 (Spring 1991), 43-53.

[11] Bhatnagar, Parija, "Not a Mall, It's a Lifestyle Center," http://money.cnn.com, 11/28/2005.

[12] Hirschfeld, Bob, "Mixing It Up," Retail Traffic (Feb. 2005).

[13] Bougie, Roger, Rik Pieters, and Marcel Zeelenberg, "Angry Customers Don't Come Back,They Get Back: The Experience and Behavioral Implications of Anger and Dissatisfaction in Services," J. of the Academy of Marketing Science 31 (4, 2003), pp. 377-393; Chebat, Jean-Charles, Moshe Davidow, and Isabelle Codjovi, "Silent Voices: Why Some Dissatisfied Consumers Fail to Complain," J. of Service Research 7 (4, 2005), pp. 328-342; Richins, Marsha, "An Analysis of Consumer Interaction Styles in the Marketplace," J. of Consumer Research 10 (June, 1983), pp. 73-82.

[14] Menon, Kalyani and Laurette Dube, "Service Provider Responses to Anxious and Angry Customers: Different Challenges, Different Payouts," J. of Retailing 80 (2004), pp. 339-347; Whitely, Richard, "Fix the Customer First," Sales and Marketing Management 146 (August, 1994) pp. 49-50.

[15] Rust, Roland T. and Richard L. Oliver, "Should We Delight the Customer?" J. of the Academy of Marketing Science 28 (1, 2000), pp. 86-94.

[16] Beatty, Sharon E. et al. Ibid.

[17] Based on Beatty, Sharon E. et al. Ibid; Gwinner, Kevin P., Dwayne D. Gremler, and Mary Jo Bitner, "Relational Benefits in Services Industries: The Customer's Perspective," J. of the Academy of Marketing Science 26 (2, 1998), pp. 101-114; Kristy E. Reynolds and Sharon E. Beatty, "A Relationship Customer Typology," J. of Retailing 75 (4, 1999), pp. 509-523.

[18] Beatty, Sharon E. et al., Ibid, p. 232.

[19] Spake, Deborah and Sharon E. Beatty (2001), "The Importance of Consumer Comfort: Some Initial Assessment," AMS Marketing Congress, Cardiff, Wales, July (p. 31)

[20] Spake, Deborah F., Sharon E. Beatty, Beverly K. Brockman, Tammy Neal Crutchfield, "Consumer Comfort in Service Relationships: Measurement and Importance," J. of Service Research 5 (4, 2003), pp. 316-332.

[21] Holloway, Betsy B., The Role of Switching Barriers in the Online Service Recovery Process, Ph. D. Dissertation, University of Alabama, 2003.

[22] Spake, Deborah F. et al. Ibid, p. 320.

[23] Jones, Michael A., David Mothersbaugh, and Sharon E. Beatty, "Switching Barriers and Customer Retention in Services," J. of Retailing 76 (2, 2000), pp. 259-274.

[24] Zaslow, Jeff, "Breaking Up With Your Manicurist: The Challenge of Awkward Dismissals," Wall Street J. (June 10, 2004), D1.

[25] Based on Priluck, Randi, "Relationship Marketing Can Mitigate Product and Service Failures," J. of Services Marketing 17 (1, 2003), pp. 37-52; Betsy B. Holloway, Ibid; Huff, Lenard, "An Evolutionary Model of the Development, Decline and Restoration of Trust," working paper.

CASES
FROM ADIDAS
TO ZIP CARS

Comprehensive CASE

THE REAL TRUTH ABOUT BEAUTY
Brand Dove Asks Women When They Feel Beautiful

Imagine a Car like this one: The front end of the car is very low, lower than most other cars. The rear window is very steep and extends all the way to the edge of the trunk lid. And the fenders are curved convex and (thanks to the extended front and rear wind shields) they are visible from the driver's position. For the first time, you can see all four corners of your car's outside. And see the roads better.

There is no hood. Only a garage mechanic can get to the engine by lifting the front end of the chassis. There is no cap for the gas tank. Rather you just push the nozzle into the pressure-lid covered gas intake. And there is a wind-shield washer fluid filler outside (remember, you can't lift the hood), next to the gas tank intake, and it too is similarly capless. The two doors of the coupe are gull-wing to allow very easy entry and exit. And the car can run on flat tires for a while.

You are puzzled and then it hits you: This car is dedicated to minimizing any demands on the driver. What car is this and how did they ever dream these things? Here is the skinny on it.

The car is a Volvo, not actually available yet, but in the works. A few years ago, Volvo put together a women-only product design team. The teams focus-grouped hundreds of women drivers, and brainstormed among themselves, brining "gender empathy" to the project. Project name: Your Concept Car (YCC)—a car designed by women for women.

How else is the car different? Let us count the ways.

- The gear shifter is in the steering wheel, and the brake is invisible—it is electronic.
- The space released by the relocated gear box is now expended on an oversized storage center console, with three compartments, of varying sizes: a small one for keys and coins and cell phone; the second, larger one, for purse, umbrella, etc.; and the third holds your laptop.
- There is a cooler and also a wastebasket.
- Individual chair car seats in the back fold up and slide back (more cargo space!).
- The engine cuts off at stoplights and comes back to life with a tap at the accelerator.
- There is parallel parking assist.
- It has "ergo vision." When you buy your car, your body is scanned at the dealership and the information is stored in your car's digital key. Insert it in the center console, and, voila, your

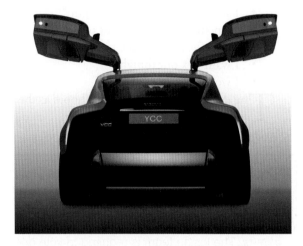

seat, steering wheel, pedals, head restraint, and seatbelts adjust automatically.
- And those seats, they come equipped with detachable pads with changeable fabric coverings. So also the carpets.

In short, this feels more like your living room than a car. And those sleek, feminine contours in the bodyline— what woman can resist these? Can you?

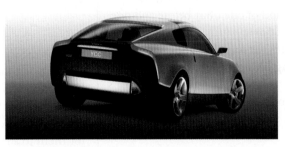

DISCUSSION QUESTIONS

1. Will the car appeal to women? How likely will they want to buy this car compared to other cars they might be considering?
2. Will all women want this car? Who will buy and who will not, and what factors will separate these two groups?
3. The all-women-design-team—is it really necessary to identify "what women want"?
4. Will this car also appeal to men? Why or why not? Which features will appeal and which ones will be unappealing, or, worse, unwanted?
5. How would you set up a research study (or studies) to investigate these questions?

Source. Volvo Web site (used iwith permission).
Additional sources: Edmunds.com; Howstuff works.com.

- "I sure hope Lex is gone tonight."
- "Hopefully Lex will be out tonight."
- "I hope Lex goes home tonight!"
- "I want Lex out tonight."
- "I would like to see Lex go."

The cyber chat was abuzz with hopes as the hour for the TV broadcast later that evening for Episode 12 of *Survivor* was approaching.

> **The Plot** Participants are organized into two teams and the teams are taken to some remote locations away from civilization. Each team is responsible for finding food, shelter, water, etc. The teams also contest in some survival games. The losing team is required to vote one of their members out. As the teams dwindle, they are combined into one and further trimming continues till only two players remain. The winner is then chosen by a vote from the rest of the players (who were eliminated in the previous episodes).

This CBS show was watched every week by some 28 million consumers. And many viewers did more than watch. During the week, they brooded over the events of the past episodes and forecasted what the next episode will, or rather should, bring. Many of them shared their thoughts, fears, and hopes in chatrooms, which were hosted by CBS. Two marketing professors decided to study this chatter. Professors Vassilis Dalakas and Jeff Langenderfer collected the postings, sampling various chatrooms during the period of one hour before and one hour after each episode of *Survivor III*, and analyzed the text of the postings. What they found is an eye-opener:

1. Viewers formed strong liking and disliking for characters:

Some postings after Episode #5:

"I detest Lindsey."

"I hate Brandon!"

"Silas, u suck….all muscles and no brain"

"Don't get me started on Lindsey, that horrible witch!"

2. So much so that they created user names indicating love or hate feelings:

Lindseysucks, Loser_Linda, Ethan2win, Ethansucks, Ethan_Lover, Lexsucks, Lexisthebest

3. Viewers Rooted for their heroes, of course:

"Ethan has been a good guy; he should win." And "I wanted Kim to win. She was working so hard."

4. But they rooted against those they disliked even more passionately:

" I sure hope Lex is gone tonight."

" I'd rather see Tom win than Lex and I don't like Tom ..

but I despise Lex even more."

"If big Tom" doesn't win, I'll boycott the next show."

5. Viewers felt satisfaction when their heroes won but they felt delight when their "villains" suffered:

"The right person won…Finally a survivor who deserved it."

Tell him [Silas] I did a happy dance when he got the boot."

"Almost cried with joy when Brandon was voted out!"

That viewers come to love some characters and hate others is as expected. That they would want their heroes to win and villains to lose is also expected. Finally, we would expect viewers to be happy when their heroes win, but that they would also be joyed when their villains lose is interesting even if not surprising. This much the postings revealed.

But the real intrigue is in an insight Professors Dalakas and Langenderfer offer: When a player whom the viewer hated and expected to be eliminated in a particular epi-

> **FYI** In the first season of Big Brother, another reality TV series, viewers were able to vote off the "houseguests" at the show. As a result, all of the "villains" were eliminated by the fans right away. The contestants who were left were all liked by the audience, and the audience interest in the show nose-dived. In subsequent seasons, the elimination procedure was changed, and dislikable characters were retained longer. Audience interest remained strong till the end.

sode was not eliminated, the viewer interest and anticipation for the next episode increased!

But then (and this is our quandary, not researchers'): Do consumers themselves have this self-realization that while they are wishing for their villains to be ousted or suffer in the next episode, they should really be wishing for them to survive the next episode?

[Source: Excerpted from Vassilis Dalakas and Jeff Langenderfer, "Consumer Satisfaction with Television Viewing: Insight for the Entertainment Industry," unpublished manuscript.]

DISCUSSION QUESTIONS

1. Do you agree or disagree that this is how it really happens: that most consumers really experience greater emotional pleasure if their villains are not voted out.

2. Why do viewers come to like some characters and hate others? Shouldn't they like those who provide them greater emotional experience? Does it have to do with their self-concepts? How so?

3.   From this it would follow that program directors should keep the intensely disliked characters "alive" till the last moment!! They should, it follows, even "manage" the outcome—i.e., rather than let the team players eliminate a player people hate, they should maneuver to keep that player until the last episode. Should they do it and what are the ethics of this, if any?

4.   As a show's consumer researcher, how would you assess when the optimal point of hatred is reached so that program directors don't "engineer" the villains' retention beyond that point?

CASE 3   Don't Wear Your Stockings! Spray Them

Say goodbye to all those runs in your stockings. And in Hot Summer, no more need to suffer the confining fabric garment on your legs. Instead of wearing stockings made of fabric, now all you do is hold a can and spray on the stockings directly on your legs. The can sprays silk powder and the powder coating makes it look like you are wearing a pantyhose.

This innovative product was introduced in Japan, in February 2003, by C.C. Medico CO. Ltd of Japan. Japanese women had bought about 1 million cans in that year itself. And they continue buy the product with enthusiasm.

The sprayed-on stockings last a day. Don't worry, they won't wash away in rain—they are waterproof. Of course, you can wash them off with soap and a loofah.

A SouthWest Flight Attendant who tried it on a flight had this to say,

" I haven't sweated it off. It hasn't rubbed off on my clothes or on the seat."

Said another: "I would rather wear this than a hose; it makes my skin more smooth."*

You can buy it at beauty.com (search Air stocking). It comes in three colors: Terra-cotta, natural, and bronze. Alas, for the fish-net look, you will have to stay with the real thing. But in Air Stockings, you get to show your pedicured toes.

Check them out on www.airstockings.com

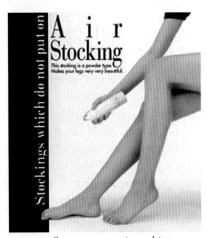

Source: www.airstocking.com

DISCUSSION QUESTIONS

1.   The product has yet to gain popularity in USA and other European and Asian countries. Why might its adoption by consumers be slower outside of Japan?
2.   Why will women find this product appealing? Or, why not? Describe the mindset of the prospective consumer.
3.   Draw a means-end chain for this product.

* From the company's web site.)

(Source; Based on a report in CBS On You Side, April 29, 2004 and on information at www.airstockings.com.)

Suppose you didn't have to own a car. And yet, you could get a car to drive whenever, wherever you wanted it. With all the hassle, not to mention the costs, of maintenance, repair, insurance and parking, that is something you may have occasionally dreamed of. Well, that dream is now a reality.

A company named Zipcar has made it possible. Founded in 2000, the company offers cars for hourly or daily driving in selected locations in cities like San Francisco, Minneapolis, Boston, New York City, Chapel Hill (North Carolina), and Washington, D.C. Here is how it works:

- Apply online for a membership and you will receive a Zipcard.By using a phone or online, reserve your car.
- Walk to the car, and just hold your Zipcard to the windshield. The doors will unlock.
- Drive away.
- At the end of your trip, simply bring the car back to the same spot.

And the cars you will get are new models of cool cars like BMW, Volvo, Mini Cooper, Prius Hybrid, etc. With a fleet of 1500 cars and growing, you are bound to get a car you will like, including a pick up if you need one. In most locations, you will need to walk only a block or two (which may actually do you some good, compared to your current door-to-door driving routine). Check out the locations and rates, for Georgetown, for example. You can find similar maps, for other locations, on its friendly Web site.

The company's Web site also cites these environmental benefits.

ENVIRONMENTAL BENEFITS
- Fewer Cars: Forth per cent of Zipcar members decide against owning a car. Each Zipcar replaces about 20 privately owned vehicles.
- Drive Less: Car usage of individuals is reduced by as much as 50%.
- Newer Cars: Older cars are replaced with newer cars that are safer and more environmental friendly.

TOTAL COST OF OWNERSHIP—YOUR CAR

How much do you pay per month for your:

Car payment (including depreciation) $287
Finance charges $62　　Insurance $75
Gas $23　　　　License, registration, taxes $ 46
Maintenance $71　　Parking $175　Other $ .00

Total $839 per mont, $10068 per year.　Vs

Zipcar cost (based on 10 trips a month of 2 hour average duration)= $2400 per year* ($6000 for 25 trips a month)
(* Based on $10 per hour rate)

DC--Georgetown			
Can Name	Where It Lives	Price (/hr)	Price (daily)
S40 Savannah	20th/H St NW	$10.75	$72
xB Benedict	20th/H St NW	$8.75	$62
Element Elsa	33rd/Water St NW - On Street	$10.75	$72
Tacoma Pickup Tonya	Foggy Bottom/GWU Metro	$10.75	$72
Escape Elliott	Foggy Bottom/GWU Metro	$10.75	$72
Matrix Mammoth	Foggy Bottom/GWU Metro	$8.75	$62
V50 Velma	Georgetown Central	$10.75	$72
xA Africa	Georgetown Central	$8.75	$62
3 Menudo	Georgetown Central	$8.75	$62
xA Alexis	Ritz-Carlton Hotel at 1155 23rd St NW	$8.75	$62
Matrix Martian	Ritz-Carlton Hotel at 1155 23rd St NW	$8.75	$62
MINI Megalon	Ritz-Carlton Hotel at 1155 23rd St NW	$10.75	$72
Matrix Mordecai	Wisconsin Av/O St NW (CVS)	$8.75	$62

Note. Prices include gas, insurance, and XM Satellite Radio.

- Green Spaces: Fewer parking spaces are required.
  - Urban Congestion: Fewer cars on the road means less congestion, saving everyone time and thus improving nation's productivity.

Proudly, it displays a banner that pronounces:

Imagine a nation with a million fewer cars on the road—we do.

The company also offers a program for Universities for on campus access to Zipcars. Some 20 universities have joined the program including Harvard, MIT, American University, Tufts, Princeton, and Columbia.

Look out, one maybe coming soon to your neighborhood.

DISCUSSION QUESTIONS

1. As a consumer, would you want Zipcar to come to your neighborhood? Why or why not?
2. As a consumer research specialist, would you recommend to Zipcar they come to your neighborhood? What factors make a region/neighborhood an ideal site for a car share service like Zipcar?
3. What demographic and psychographic characteristics (motivations, values, outlook, and lifestyles) make a consumer an ideal candidate for becoming a Zipcar member?
4. Should your University or company sign up with Zipcar? Why or why not?

CASE 5 "Don't Breathe.... Buy Our Diesels"

Don't Breathe. Don't Think. Share Your Bath Water. But Buy our Diesels.

Is this anyway to sell Clothing?

Here is one market research report proclaiming:
- 294 days in planning
- 16, 497 hours of collating
- 348 bits of clip art
- 27 vague conclusions reached.

One of those conclusions is Result #08. It is a psychographic analysis of the ways in which individuals put their hands in their pockets. Put one thumb in your back pocket, and you are a "passive type"; both thumbs in the two back pockets would make you a "shy type"; one thumb in front pocket makes you a "confident type" and put both thumbs in your two front pockets, and you are definitely an "aggressive type."

The truth is that there was no research to uncover this or any of the other 26 results the company has posted on its Web site. These are just tongue-in-cheek spoofs on market research. From a company called DIESEL.

It is not that the company doesn't believe in market research; it just doesn't believe in anything that is conventional, expected, normal. Another of its ad campaigns features scenes of street protests with young 20 somethings carrying posters that read such off-the-wall slogans as "Share your bath water," "Legalize the 4-day Weekend," and "World Needs more love letters."

Finally, its Web site features a guide for being "young forever"—with some 20 illustrated pages showing models born in 1880s but frozen in time with their fresh youthful adolescent looks, and such irreverent tips as "Don't Breathe," "Don't have Sex," and "Don't think." The one with "Don't Breathe" has a quote from Mario Derion, born 1891 (Yes, 1891, and still looking 20) that reads: "I limit my breathing to just a few times a day. It helps me stay as beautiful as a century ago. After living so long, I may smell and what do I care. I look absolutely breathtaking."

Is this anyway to sell clothing?

If the proof of pudding is in eating it, the answer is a resounding "Yes." This Italian maker of blue jeans and related fashion merchandise has seen its sales boom, doubled from some 300 million in 1998 to more than 600 million in recent years. It has more than 200 stores in major cities spanning the globe from Miami to Berlin., and expanding exponentially. It churns out about 1500 new designs every six months, more than half in denim, made to look soft and worn. Its edgy designs include such items as a man's pants with racing stripes and Hindu lettering. Its appeal is international, but mention that to Diesel owner Renzo Rosso, and he would correct you promptly: "I want to mask that we are multinational. Individuality is the sex appeal of the brand."

Sex appeal? Maybe that is why even Karl Lagerfesld, the famous high fashion designer himself, sports Diesel clothing. And its Research Result #29 shows: 18% of Diesel fans are plain "bored," 14% lazy, and 25% are "horny." While the company shows these psychographic profiles as tongue-in-cheek spoof, they do underscore the point that the brand appeals to persons of certain psychographic profile. What the company won't reveal, of course, is just what the true psychographics of its fans are.

DISCUSSION QUESTIONS

Visit the company's web site www.Diesel.com and explore the brand and its communications. Based on this exploration,
(a) Draw a psychographic profile of its target customers.
(b) Describe the brand's image/brand personality.

Source: Based on information on the company's Web site (www.Diesel.com) and Gail Edmondson, "Diesel is Smokin'" Time, February 10, 2003, p.64.

CASE 6

Going to the Ball Game?
Take Your Psychographics With You

Astudent group was given a project with this objective: To identify the psychographic profile of sporting event season ticket holders.

The student group proceeded as follows. They listed 10 psychographic factors that they believed would differentiate season ticket holders from non-holders. Of these, they chose five they expected to be most differentiating. They also named, as directed to do, two factors that they expected *not* to differentiate the two groups.

Next, they wrote five AIO statements to measure each factor, making sure that the items tapped, separately, an activity, an interest, and an opinion; they tried to include as well some negatively worded items. For each factor, then, they selected the three items they thought best measured the factor.

Next, they removed the factor names and jumbled all 21 statements. And they placed a 5-point scale: 1-Deos not describe me at all, 5-Describes me very well. Adding some questions on demographics completed the questionnaire.

Their task was to find a convenient sample of 10 season ticket holders and ten non-season ticket holders. With permission from the manager, they surveyed customers at an Applebee restaurant. With 20 surveys completed, they entered the data in an Excel sheet and computed the mean score on each statement for each of the two groups separately. Their findings are summarized in Table 1.

Psychographic Profiles of Sporting Events Season Ticket Holders and Non-holders.   **TABLE 1**

(Scale: 1-Does not describe me at all, 5-Describes me very well.)

FACTOR	Season Ticket Holders	Non-Holders of Season Tickets.
SENSATION SEEKING		
I crave excitement.	3.8	3.0
I enjoy the outdoors.	4.4	4.2
It is important to experience life to the fullest by trying new things.	3.6	3.2
COMPETITIVENESS		
I only play to win.	4.2	2.8
I don't think it is important to win a game as long as you are having fun.*	2.8	1.8
I would not enjoy a situation in which there is a winner and a loser.*	4.0	3.0
SOCIAL DRINKER		
I only drink on the weekends.	4.0	2.6
I think going to bars is a waste of money.*	4.2	3.4
I would rather go to a bar than stay at home.	3.4	2.6
EXTROVERTED		
Having a positive attitude is important to me.	3.4	4.8
I would rather spend time with others than by myself.	4.4	3.2
I go out with my family/friends every weekend.	4.6	3.6
NEWS JUNKIE		
I never watch the news.*	2.8	2.0
I would like to know what's going on in the rest of the world.	3.2	4.2
The local news does not provide enough information.	3.2	2.8
SUPERSTITIOUS		
I do not have an umbrella open indoors.	3.2	3.6
I do not believe in lucky numbers.*	2.6	3.4
I would like to visit a psychic.	2.0	2.8
INTERNET SAVVY		
I would feel comfortable buying on the Internet.	4.0	3.4
I believe a computer without the Internet is worthless.	3.4	2.8
I do research on new products online	2.4	2.4

Now they were eager to examine the tabulated results and write a verbal profile of the season ticket holders. They were aware that the sample was not representative and their findings could be entirely off base. But they were to assume that the data represented a large random sample. They hoped the findings would at least enable them to answer the central question: Do season ticket holders differ, in their psychographics, from non-holders?

They are keeping their report a secret. Can you piece together your own report? And while you are at it, you can't help critiquing their effort. Sure, go ahead; that too will be immensely useful.

*In the table, items marked asterisk are reverse-coded so that each score actually shows pro-factor average. To illustrate, "I think going to bars is a waste of money" means the opposite of "social drinkers." To make it a pro-factor item, a rating of '1' was recoded as '5', of '2 as '4', '4' as '2', and '5' as '1'. Holders score 4.2, more than the score of non-holders, 3.4, thus implying that holders are more of a social drinker than non-holders.

CASE 7 NASCAR—Balancing Your Attitude

Two Consumer Researchers (Professors Vassilis Dalakas and Aron Levin) surveyed 220 NASCAR fans attending a race. In the survey, respondents were asked to name their favorite driver and then they rated themselves on how much they identified with the named driver (a questionnaire called Sports Spectator Identification Scale (SPIS) was used for this rating). Survey respondents were also asked to indicate their least favorite driver and to name the companies that sponsored the driver. Next, their attitudes toward 11 NASCAR drivers and attitudes toward brands and companies who sponsor them were measured.

On the ten–point scale that the SPIS uses, respondents scored 7.66 for Dale Earnhardt, Jr., 7.39 for Jeff Gordon, 6.87 for Mark Martin, 8.34 for Tony Stewart, and 7.66 for Dale Jarrett. Note that these are ratings not across all respondents but only across all those who named a specific driver as their favorite.

Was the sponsoring company liked more by the sponsored drivers' fans than by an average race visitor? Their findings are summarized in the table below.

TABLE Atttude Toward A Company/Brand

Company/Brand	Average Attitude Among All Visitors	Average Attitude Among Fans of Sponsered Driver	Average Attitude Among Visitors Who Chose This driver as Their Least Favorite	Correlation (Sponsor versus Driver Atttiude)*
Budweiser (Dale Earnhardt, Jr.)	8.49	9.39 (61**)	5.20 (5)	.370
UPS (Dale Jarett)	7.80	9.50 (10)	6.50 (2)	.412
Home Depot (Tony Stewart)	7.53	9.54 (13)	6.67 (18)	.397
GM Goodwrench (Kevin Harwick)	7.48	9.14 (7)	4.64 (11)	.535
Dupont (Jeff Gordon)	6.50	9.42 (36)	3.87 (52)	.681
Viagra (Mark Martin)	5.97	7.62 (13)	1.0 (2)	.170
Miller Lite (Rust Wallace)	5.96	6.0 (4)	3.60 (14)	.289
Coors Light (Sterling Marlin)	5.82	5.67 (3)	3.08 (12)	.228

Note. Attitudes measured on a 0-10 point scale.

* Corelation between Attitude toward the brand/company and attitude toward the sponsoring driver. The scores can range from -1.0 to +1.0 with a larger number signifying a higher correlation.

** Numbers in parentheses are number of respondents.

Source: Excerpted from Vassilis Dalakas and Aron Levin, "The Balance Theory Domino: How Sponships May Elicit Negative Consumer Attitudes,"

* In reading the table, small respondent numbers, say, less than five, are not meaningful to draw any inferences from.

As the marketing manager of one of the companies that participates in NASCAR sponsorship, you wonder what lessons these findings hold for you? Failure to draw those lessons can cost you a big fortune.

DISCUSSION QUESTIONS

1. Are the findings in Table 1 consistent with Heider's Balance Theory (Chapter 8)? Explain your answer.

2. Do all brands benefit from sponsorships? Which companies are benefiting more or less? If you were a marketing manager of a company, and if you decided to stop NASCAR sponsorships, for which company would the loss be the least and for which ones the most?

3. Why are the correlations so different across companies?

What do these wide- ranging correlations show for specific companies?

4. Since all drivers will have both their fans as well as dislikers, how would you, as a marketer, choose the driver to sponsor?

5. Suppose some drivers became available and if you were (a) Coors Light or (b) the company behind Viagra, would you sign up that driver (dumping your current driver) and which driver will you sign? Why or why not?

Source: Vassilis Dalakas and Aron Levin, "The Balance Theory Domino: How Sponsorships May Elicit Negative Consumer Attitudes," Advances in Consumer Research, Volume 32, 2005, p. 91-97. (Reprinted bt permission)

CASE 8   A Festival of Love
Courtesy of Your Government!

Call of a Nation: The *Romancing Singapore* Campaign

There is a dinner party in progress. Guests are 30 eligible unmarried men and women, strangers to one another. A few months later, there will be a mass wedding, and then a few weeks later, tango parties. The food will include generous portions of ginger and pumpkin broth, oysters, and chocolate torte—items chosen for their reported aphrodisiac value. Who is paying the bill? The Government of Singapore and its partners in the government's *Romancing Singapore* campaign.

Started in February 2003, the campaign is an unprecedented and bold government move to socially engineer, among Singaporeans, well, ROMANCE! Romance within marriage, that is, and expressly designed to make babies. Faced with a declining birth rate and shrinking population, the government considers it a matter of national priority. And it is incentivizing love-making as a patriotic duty.

For marketers, this is a one-of-a-kind business opportunity. Some 80 businesses have partnered with government on its *Romancing Singapore* campaign. Its Web site promotes specially branded Eau de Parfum and Chocolate Truffle cake called Aphrodisiac!

An entertainment entrepreneur, famous in Singapore as Dr. Love, has, in conjunction with the Singapore government, launched a TV show called "Dr. Love's Super Baby-Making Show." Nine couples will participate, and the couple having the baby first will be the winner of the $100,000 (USD).

Dr. Love has started another business, Meggpower. The company calls itself "A bio-communication" company and purports to sell a "wireless hormonal monitoring service." It will text-message or email a subscriber when she is due to ovulate. Based on its monitoring of the members' hormonal cycle, the company will also recommend totally customized diets to enhance conception.

Want some beach reading this Summer? Pick up a copy of "When Boy Meets Girl. The Chemistry Guide." Want to learn some creative tips on dating? Pick up a copy of "Dare to Date." Both are free! They are published by the Singapore government.

Incidently, the *Romancing Singapore* campaign is not a one shot campaign. Rather, it is an ongoing celebration. The idea is to keep the issue in continuous awareness of people.

Some readers might wonder why love making—a behavior that comes naturally to most humans—needs to be promoted at all? The answer is three fold: first, it is love making within a marriage; second, it is love-making undertaken to procreate. And the third reason has to do with the value system and life themes of Singaporeans.

Singapore is an achievers' society. Everyone, especially the educated Chinese, is driven to work hard and obtain success. These educated Chinese—the native people—just don't have the time for leisure and forming a family. *Romance Singapore* is therefore a lifestyle and value priority altering mission. Its goal is nothing less than to shape your world-view and your life-theme. It is to make you respect and embrace leisure and family life. It is not merely hedonic and personal; it is, rather, a patriotic duty. If you are a citizen of Singapore, your nation is calling you. So get some romance. Make babies. Will You?

(See Discussion Questions, next page.)

(Sources: RomancingSingapore.com.sg; Wow-her.com.sg; Loveclinic.com.

DISCUSSION QUESTIONS

1. Is the persuasion the Singapore government is attempting a low or a high involvement context for the consumer? Which model of attitude is applicable, and to what extent is the government utilizing the guidelines suggested by various models of attitude? Specifically, which route to attitude change is the government trying to pursue?

2. Is the target market a single homogeneous group? What segments might be useful to recognize?

3. In terms of people's reasons for not getting married and not making babies, what factors might be responsible? How might the campaign work (or fail to work) depending on the specific factor?

4. What other new components to the program would you suggest, speaking from a consumer behavior point-of-view?

5. Does the government's sponsorship of such programs raise any ethical issues? Discuss.

CASE 9   Selling Victoria's Secret in Saudi Arabia

When you see women in Saudi Arabia, all in long black wrapper dresses, you would not guess that, underneath, many of them wear fancy, colorful underwear. So these women in Saudi Arabia would seem to be a natural target market for Victoria's Secret. Except one big snag: Saudi culture does not permit open display of lingerie in a store.

Buying underwear is a nightmare for Saudi women. Since women salespersons are not allowed to sell in public places, stores that sell lingerie employ only male salespersons, and women customers must ask male salespersons for help in assessing their bra sizes. Once the bra size is determined, the salesperson would speak it out loud and an assistant would dig out the merchandise from hidden shelves. The whole experience of having to discuss their bodies with male salesmen is so embarrassing, that many women would just guess their bra size; as a result, a majority of Saudi women are reported to be wearing the wrong size bras.

It is against this background, that Lingerie Purdue, a Western style lingerie store opened on the first day of Ramadan in November 2001 on Tahlia Street in Jeddah, Saudi Arabia. How, Al-Mashat, the store's owner did it is a lesson in creative trans-cultural marketing—marketing that respects a host culture's mores and yet creates a trans-cultural experience for the consumer.

The task of designing the store was assigned to Los Angeles based Chase Design. Chase chose the name Purdue, French for lost. Saudi Arabic women fascinated

with France and France is the country they most associate with lingerie. It also captures the experience of a woman who enters the store and can happily feel lost in the two story store that features translucent glass and has mysterious ambiance.

Lingerie Perdu Store in Suadi Arabia
Design: Chase Design Group, Los Angeles, U.S.A.

Because of the Wahhabi principles of Islam practiced in Saudi Arabia, stores can't show female body parts or pictures of women wearing lingerie. So what Chase Design did was to use language and poetry in a rich sensual way. First, it created a custom alphabet, altering English characters to look more like Arabic letters and vice versa. This bilingual wordmark appeared more sensual; and it bridged the visual gap between the English and Arabic letters. Then, it selected poetry and words that evoke the experience of wearing lingerie.

In the middle of the store, a large banner hangs from the ceiling to the floor, with these poetic words inscribed in English: Wrap this beautiful robe of words around you and dream. Also hanging are many other long banners with words like "passion," "love," "dreams" etc., inscribed both in English and Arabic. These words also appear on signage, display cases, and even shopping bags.

Because of Saudi laws, Purdue does not have any fe-male employees. Lifelike mannequins are not allowed so Purdue features abstract, fabric wrapped shapes. And, stores can't have mirrors in the dressing rooms. So, one day local religious police (called mutawa) came in and took down the mirrors in the store's fitting rooms. But mirrors or no mirrors, Saudi women are enjoying this new experience of shopping lingerie—Victoria Secret style. Minus of course the images of Tyra Banks.

Source: Logolounge.com and information provided by Chase Design Group.

 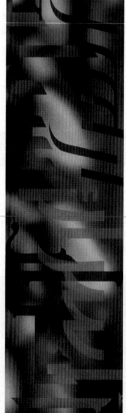

Banners that hang from high ceilings and create the feminine ambience in the store Lingerie Perdu Store in Suadi Arabia Design: Chase Design Group, Los Angeles, U.S.A.

DISCUSSION QUESTIONS

1. Culture in Saudi Arabia seems to promote among women extreme modesty (where they should not flaunt their bodies); yet, many women there are as eager to acquire and consume the fashionable clothing and luxurious lingerie from western countries. What role does culture play in consumer desires—does it encourage or curb consumption?

2. Is it important for a marketer, especially a designer of physical market-space (i.e., a store) to be fully aware of the culture of its customers? How did Chase Design Group, a U.S. firm, meet this challenge?

3. What lessons can we learn from this story about culture and marketing?

CHANGING FACES

Cosmetic surgery is
a notion I entertain
regularly amid the
voices of caution that
punctuate my peace.

"Why not grow old like everyone else,"
snarls my son.
"If it will make you happy, dear"
smirks mom.

What do they know?
Do they have the skin of Cochise?
Do they view the world beneath billowing lids?
Do they dread passing reflective surfaces?

The knife is my magic wand,
a Maginot Line keeping
time on the other side.
I'll have no second thoughts,
I'll have no second thoughts

A poem by Shay Sayre, see story on facing page

(A Personal Narrative by Shay Sayre)

California Girl

I am 49 and a single mother of two. My employment takes me to Southern California. Southern California—where appearance is the established medium of exchange. I live near the beach so I am constantly exposed to youth, fitness and beauty. Weather encourages abbreviated dresses, necessitates fitness, and requires youthfulness. … A 1996 national survey by American Society for Plastic and Reconstructive Surgery showed that of the 87,000 breast augmentations reported nationally, 25% were in California. You see celebrities all the time. In this capital of "hedonic consumption," who can be oblivious to appearance?

Media—the Hyperreal Persuaders

My cohorts in the media were film stars Marilyn Jones and Liz who all were preoccupied with snagging men, and television's Jeanie and Samantha (Biwitched) whose sole preoccupations were looking good for the men they loved. During this age of "commercialized feminism," women were encouraged to emulate fabricated perfection depicted by advertising's Ivory complexions, Breck-girl hair, and Coke bottle figures.

Likewise, today's media continue to provide a visual plethora of visual justifications for the good looks. Television commercials imply that everyone colors gray hair. Magazine ads depict men conquering baldness with hair transplants, and women enjoying new popularity with silicon implants; Cosmetic advertisements boast complexions instantly transformed by tanning creams. Video and film personalities are ageless reminders of the power of surgical restoration. All around, I see synchronized endorsements of manufactured body images.

Friends are Having a Ball

Daily activity furnishes the creative moments in which the matrices of my identity are transformed to a new actuality. There are friends who drop names of surgeons, suggest anti-aging treatments, and recall their own transformative experiences. Among friends, silver-haired Irene hosts a tea party in a white, low cut cotton frock that proudly reveals her implant acquisitions; Elisabeth hugs her beau-de-jour, a man twenty years younger who is obviously infatuated by her purchased-youth-enhancements; Bali Bill is surrounded by saronged female companions who are probably unaware of his hair transplant; Linda sports tight pants proudly purchased to fit her newly liposucked thighs; and Grecian Formula improved Ray kisses a twenty-something fiancée at his retirement celebration.

Mirror Tells Me the Truth

Once my mirror reveals signs of the aging process, I began to consider dealing with the sun-baked skin that could push me way out of the socially acceptable envelope. Group snapshots {of friends at parties] are cruel reminders that I lack the cosmetic advancements implemented by most of my friends.

Blood is Thickest

My family members pull in different directions. Mother doesn't count because she loves me whatever. But my sister, a surgical nurse herself, is a devout advocate of surgical solutions to nature's mistakes. Beverly has subjected many parts of her body to the knives of various care givers: Navy surgeons for breast implants during a husband's military career; a surgeon-employer for a face and brow lift; a physician friend for liposuction. All procedures are free of charge, but none are free from payment—implants break; nerve damage inhibits facial movement; cellulite comes back in a less desirable location than the one from which it is removed. Photographs are the only remaining evidence of a pre-surgery sister.

Daughter Aubyn believes that nature should be allowed to take its course, and son Ryan contends that "outward is as inward does." Purists be damned, I think. If they are against it, then it must be a good idea. After all, what do offspring understand about the ageing process.

Money and Affordability

Even in the capital of hedonism, the cost of cosmetic surgery is substantial. One can expect to pay in the neighborhood of $10,000 for a basic face lift. I am faced with a pending costly repair to my residence devastated by termites, and then there is the uncertainty of potential unemployment. But considering the alternative—aging and reclusion—I rationalize the expense as an investment in myself. A gift to me.

When the physician is chosen, the date is set and the cash paid, my surgery is a fait accompli. I write a poem to commemorate the occasion: *Changing Faces* (see facing page)

Shay Sayre is a professor of consumer behavior at California State University at Fullerton.
Source: Excerpted from Shay Sayre, "Facelift Forensics: A Personal Narrative of Cosmetic Surgery," *Advances in Consumer Research*, 1999, Vol. 26, 178-83. (Used by permission of the Association for Consumer Research)

DISCUSSION QUESTIONS

1. Identify various influences (both in terms of sources and nature of influence) on this consumer's decision to get a face lift surgery.
2. Could you visualize a consumer facing the same influences and yet choosing to not get the face lift; if this consumer (let us call her Rita) too were to write a self-narrative on her decision considerations, what would that narrative read like? Write a sample narrative.
3. Explain influences on Rita's decision process not to get the cosmetic surgery.

By Stephanie Riesing

One of my most memorable experiences as a consumer occurred only about three months ago. In January of 2006 I purchased a brand new 2006 Mazda 3. I considered many things when deciding what car to buy, what features to get on it, and what color to get. The first thing that I had to decide was what kind of car that I wanted to buy. Many things went along with this, such as price, reliability, and looks. I wanted something that was in my price range, that looked good, and also

that had been known to last for a long time. One afternoon my boyfriend and I drove to different car lots in our area just to glance around. When that day was done I had narrowed my choices down based on looks and price because these were the things I could see from driving around. My choices were the Corolla, Mazda 3, Ion, and Civic. Over the next couple of days I read consumer reports on these cars, I talked to people about their experiences, and I surfed the Internet reading a lot about these cars. Finally, I decided that I wanted to go back to the Mazda dealership. Honestly, even though I did extensive research I really just liked the way the Mazda 3 looked the best. And although I was trying to keep my options open I knew in the back of my mind that was the car

I wanted. When it came to features I knew I wanted a five speed and four doors, the rest could be negotiated. I was pleasantly surprised to find out that the Mazda 3 gets 35 miles to the gallon expressway and averages 33 miles per gallon. With gas prices soaring the way they are this was a huge added bonus in my mind. There were certain features that I knew going in that I could live without. When it came to power windows and locks, I could do without. Although I would like to have them on my car, keeping the overall cost down was more important to me. Finally after looking at about 35 Mazda 3's, going from the cargo net to the interior color, I had narrowed it down to two cars, one was red and one was black. This is the decision that I agonized over. I went home and printed out a picture of each car and carried them with me for two days constantly looking at them. Finally, I went back to the lot and had the salesman pull the cars side by side so I could compare them in person. I think I must have walked circles around the cars at least twenty times comparing every inch. Finally, I decided the black color made the car resemble a Cavalier and the red one just looked sharp and speedy so I went with the velocity red with metallic in it. When actually purchasing my car I had a sense of nervousness and excitement mixed together. I was about to own a beautiful brand new car but I felt like I was signing my life away. It was a lot of money but it was worth it. I am delighted with it. I would buy the car all over again.

(Stephanie Riesling is a 20-something senior and a resident of Northern Kentucky.)

DISCUSSION QUESTIONS

1. Review various concepts in Chapter 11 (Consumer Decision Making) and see which of the methods, procedures, and decision rules did this consumer apply?

Is this a typical experience of consumers buying a car? How might this experience differ across consumers.

Look at Honda Element. Overall a boxy rectangle. With an almost vertical hatchback. The Color trim is noticeable maroon with black trim. Inside, the seats come off. The carpets are all rubber. You can hose them out.

Scion is even more boxy (the full height back is entirely vertical). XB comes with customizable entertainment console—you can place Sirius Satellite and XM radio.

The cars were designed to appeal to youth, Gen 'Y'—the group of seven million Americans born between 1977 to 1995.

In concept tests, indeed Gen 'Y' liked them. (Somewhere, when the older ones among us were asleep, the square look seems to have become hip.] What appealed to Gen 'Y' the most in the car is how roomy it was. It was, in fact, a dorm room on wheels. So they can carry half of their belongings if they like. And driving the car was just an extension of lounging in their dorm room. With entertainment and all.

This all seems sensible. There is only one problem. The Gen Y is not driving it. Instead, it is their parents—boomers or even seniors driving them. The targeted age of Element, Scion, Matrix was each between 27 and 20. Actual age: 42 to 45. This is the story for car after car. Dodge Neon is 39 instead of the anticipated 23; Pontiac Vibe 48 compared to targeted 30 years.[1]

The snag; the cars, designed to be inexpensive, still cost a hefty $18 to 22 K. And few Gen Y have that kind of money. What are they buying instead: 4 to 10 years older models of Civics, Corollas, Jeeps, Ford Escorts, etc. Or family hand-downs as their parents replace their own cars with new ones.

One option might be to strip down the model even more to bring down the price to say $12,000. But this strategy has its own risks. For starters, the car may be left bereft of any thing desirable at all. (Remember Echo?). Second, they will embrace the brand only as a stop gap, yearning to graduate to better brands as soon as they can afford. So a scaled down skeleton brand will be a poor strategy to lure youngsters into becoming customers for life.

That older people like the Hondas and Scions seems a puzzle only at first. Come to think of it: room on wheels, movable seats, easy to hose, aren't all these features inherently appealing to older people as well. And the vertical body structure means easy to get in and out—something even more valuable to seniors. Oh, the square boxy look, didn't someone say, among the new generation, it is hip to be square?!

Incidentally, Toyota name means too mainstream, so just as GM did years ago with Saturn, the company set up Scion as a separate division. Now the company has come up with a more mainstream yet sleek design, in tC (see Chapter 1) which appeals to youth, but for 20-somethings, it is pricey. So the search for a car as sleek as a tC and as "cool" as Element or the vertical back Scion and still within a youth's budget is on.

DISCUSSION QUESTIONS

Q1. Why would a car appeal designed for Gen 'Y' appeal to more mature consumers?

Q2. Are the sources of value from a car like the Element or the Scion same for the two group of consumers—20-somethings and forty-somethings? How might they differ? Would each group consider the car "cool" and in the same way?

Q3. If a group other than originally intended adopts a product/brand, will this then discourage the originally intended group to move away from the product/brand? Would the brand develop a stereotype that may then limit its appeal to some groups?

Q4. Does the Element and Scion story mean age is not a good segmentation basis? Discuss.

1 A report by CNW Marketing Research. For a more fact-filled report, see "The Car is for Kids, but Gramps is Driving," NY Times (www.nytimes.com/2005/07/03/automobiles/03AUTO.html?); also: 50-plus Marketing (www.20plus30.com/50plusmarketing/archive/2005_09_01_archive.html).

Jean's Life Story

Jean is 59 years old and lives with Henry, her husband of 40 years, in a middle-class suburb of a northeastern city not 10 miles from the town in which both she and he were born. While Henry will soon retire, Jean still works-- 60 hours and six days a week-- tending a small neighborhood bar in her blue-collar hometown.

Jean grew up in the house her Italian grandfather built. It is the house her brother, his wife, and two of their three grown children now occupy. The house is a symbol of all Jean believes in: it is at once family, independence, and hard work.

Jean "didn't grow up with very much," both in the way of money or family support. The illegitimate child of a father she would never know, Jean was somewhat an outsider in her own home. Many aunts and uncles were against her remaining in the family at all. Jean soon discovered that superior performance of household tasks offered a surefire mechanism through which she could fit in with her family and garner their support. To this day, Jean wants desperately to be affirmed by society in the roles she values most: mother and wife. Accomplishment as a cook and housekeeper remain a major source of happiness, pride, and satisfaction in Jean's life.

> What do I do everyday? I cook. I clean. My white clothes are white. You can pick up a sheet of mine that is 10 years old and people think they are brand new. I iron them...... Everybody always says what a beautiful house I have. That makes me feel good.

With no more then a high school education, Jean discovered the value of diligence and hard work. She lives by one of her mother's credos: "You want, you work, you get." As Italian wife and mother, she loves to make Spaghetti sauce:

> My mother always used to make the sauce too. All Italians do. When you make sauce, it's like your trademark. (My youngest brother) Johnny always says that he can tell people by the sauce that they make. Everybody loves my sauce. My brother Frankie says I make the best sauce he ever had, and he is a gourmet.

> When I make the sauce, it takes all day. I let it cook on the stove for 8 hours. I have a really big pot. Stainless steel from Revere Ware. 12 quarts. I blend the Pastene tomatoes in the blender. Whole tomatoes. And I add a little can of the Hunts special sauce. Then I fry up the sausage in a frying pan with the Bertolli olive oil and a little bit of onion, pepper. Pastene tomatoes, I always buy those, they are the best. They make the best sauce. You can tell the difference... I buy the best vinegar. Progresso..

> Bounty paper towels, they are the best...Maytag, they say that is the best...Frigidaire makes the best fridge...Krups makes the best coffee....Electrolux is the best vacuum. It's expensive, yeah, but...

> I always used the Bon Ami but then I noticed that it started scratching the sink.... I tried the Comet and that really is better.

After 40 years of shopping, cooking, and cleaning, Jean has become somewhat of an expert consumer (" You ask me how I know it is good tomatoes? I've been making the sauce for 40 years and you ask me how I know?")

Karen's Life Story

Karen is a recently divorced 39-year-old single Mom, raising two girls aged 8 and 12 while working full-time as an office manager. Karen's demographics in large part speak to her current life situation: money is tight and Karen is busy. Her day starts at 5:00 A.M. to give her time for exercise while still getting the kids off to school and herself to work before the 8:00 check-in. Afternoons are crazy, with Karen running the kids back and forth to dance classes, music lessons, and Girl Scouts. In her "spare time," Karen is trying to fix up the new apartment she just rented, meet new friends, and decide on a car to replace her broken-down Ford.

> What's my life like? A blur. A rush. A rush from the minute I get up in the morning. I go from one thing to another all day long..... I have clothes over there to fold and put away, and the food shopping is still out. The kids have homework to do. You wanna help?

Karen has the added project of negotiating a prominent midlife crisis. She experiences a sense of disparity between what she has attained and what she "really wants." A powerful sense tells her that the 40-year mark is a last chance opportunity for pursuing significant paths of change. Another strong voice tells her to focus, instead, on raising her children in this new single-parent world.

> Should I go back to school and get the degree I never finished? Should I move out of this town and go somewhere else? I dunno. The kids...

> Wherever am I going to find a man, where? I never thought that I would be the one left alone after the divorce. Never, I am turning 40, and there aren't that many available men that age in general left anymore, let alone good ones, and God forbid they live in this small town. Wherever am I going to find a man?

One of the few areas of life satisfaction for Karen is that she has managed to maintain a youthful appearance. She adheres closely to a regular exercise routine ("I run three miles every day at 5:30, no matter what) and a highly scripted personal care regimen.

People always tell me that I do not look my age. I mean, I work hard not to, so that's good.

Speaking of the products and brands she buys, Karen says:

I don't really know what all I buy. I am thinking about it, and it seems I don't buy many brands.... I don't spend a lot of time at the store. I don't really remember when all I started using that (brand). I guess it just really didn't, it just really does not matter to me that much. A lot of things are just here because I never tried anything else and I just use that brand out of habit. It works. It gets me through.

I always buy Comet...I hate Ajax.... At work I use Gateway [Computer]. I don't really care that it is a Gateway, but we only had the choice between an Apple and the Gateway and I am definitely not an Apple person..... I buy Success Rice. Success Rice is the only one in the kind of rice that I want. Ready in five minutes. The others take twenty-five.

Mop and Glo? That was my ex-husband Jim. I never really did like that...Palmolive? That was Jim... The Dove started with him...Mayonnaise? I just bought the brand Jim told me....Cereals? I just buy what is demanded of me.

But when it came to cosmetics, Karen spoke excitedly:

I use Mary Kay everything. Makeup, lipstick, moisturizer, toner. I think Mary Kay is responsible for how my skin looks now. I do, I really do. I do not think that my skin would be this, so young today if I had used any other brand. I mean, I do see it. I really can tell the difference. I can't live without it now...

Karen also embraces Reebok, the brand of running shoe she dons each morning at 5:30 A.M.

I started running again when umm, right after I decided to leave Jim. I used to run in college when I was training for tennis tournaments. I was quite good at distance running. So, I picked it back up. I wear Reebok running shoes. Me and my Reeboks. They are beat up by now. Want to see them? Like a favorite pair of jeans, you know? You go through so much together.

And Karen drinks Coke Classic, not a diet soft drink:

I think I am one of the last people that still drinks Coke. Everyone I know wants a Diet Coke all the time. It's always diet something. Everyone knows I drink regular Coke. Because I sort of make a statement when I don't drink Diet that I don't do what everybody else does, that I don't really care about the extra calories that much, that I can afford it. Sorta like, "so there!"

DISCUSSION QUESTIONS

1. Describe the main life themes of Jean and Karen and how products play a role in these life projects.
2. Who is more involved in consumption (across the board) and why?
3. Is either of them using products to construct self-identity? Who? Which products? How?
4. Jean has strong opinions on a range of products (whereas Karen has opinions only on a few products). How would you explain the role having an opinion plays in consumer's life theme and/or self-identity?

(Source: Excerpted from Susan Fournier, "Consumers and their Brands: Developing Relationship Theory in Consumer Research," *Journal of Consumer Research*, Vol. 24, March 1998, 343-373. ©Journal of Consumer research, University of Chicago Press.)

CASE 14 — Reader's Digest Gets Psychic

What do you get when you combine turkey burgers and mayonnaise with a few "Quotable Quotes" and a little "Humor in Uniform?"* Distinctive and discrete research on critical market segments that illustrate the unique relationship readers have with the legendary magazine title. That's what Reader's Digest Research Manager Joseph Pilla found when he analyzed his book's readership using LifeMatrix, the psychographic-marketing tool launched in December 2002 by MRI and RoperASW. "Increasingly, Request for Proposals (RFPs) are looking for information that tells them more about their target consumers than basic readership, demographics, or commonly used psychographic data," says Pilla.

To learn about the behaviors, lifestyles, values and needs of consumers common to Reader's Digest and to packaged goods advertisers, Reader's Digest researchers prepared a presentation using the combined power of MRI media and product data in conjunction with Roper ASW's LifeMatrix segments. LifeMatrix includes ten segments that group consumers according to lifestyle, values, and life stage (see Chapter 6).

"The analysis yielded data that was spectacular in that it provided information about our audience that we had not previously known," says Pilla. He adds, "MRI/LifeMatrix tells us, for example, how many hours readers spend commuting, and gives us a recount of time spent with children and spouses, adding depth to the data." Consider the Priority Parents segment, a group of full-time working parents: their families define them, and their leisure activities revolve mainly around their children. "When we found out things such as what type of activity is popular among this target, why they engage in this activity and if they participate alone or with company, we gain knowledge that brings us beyond numbers in terms of understanding the day to day lives of our readers and our clients' targets."

He also reflected "as a researcher, this project allowed me to absorb what our readers are really like. MRI/LifeMatrix enables us to marry the segments with the values and with the demographics, in the context of our editorial."

-------------------------------.

*Two popular features in Reader's Digest
Source: THE SOURCE, Fall 2003, Newsletter, MediaMark Research, inc.

Core Findings Reader's Digest discovered that their readers could be grouped into four core LifeMatrix groups, segments in which packaged goods advertisers would be eager to increase customers: Priority Parents, Renaissance Women, Dynamic Duos and Free Birds. The unique behaviors, motivations, and values results of each segment showed a strong propensity to buy certain products. For example, Reader's Digest's audience includes 6.3 million Priority Parents who are the consumers most likely to be the best customers for instant flavored coffee (185 index) and packaged lunch products (176 index), among others. On the other hand, Reader's Digest's 5.2 million Renaissance Women are natural customers for veggie burgers (189 index) and light salad dressing (167 index).

DISCUSSION QUESTIONS

1. Why is it not sufficient to profile consumer segments by demographic? What additional insights, if any, result from psychographic studies?

2. How can understanding the psychographics of its readers help Readers' Digest? After all, that some of its readers consumed instant flavored coffee more than average, for example, could be found out without psychographics?

3. Will psychographics help other magazines, or other marketers, in general? Why or why not?

| **TABLE 1** | **(FOR CASE 15, SEE FACING PAGE)** |

. STATEMENTS USED TO MEASURE ETHICAL STANDARDS

- Changing price tags on merchandise in a retail store.
- Drinking a can of soda in a supermarket without paying for it.
- Giving misleading price information to a clerk for an unpriced item.
- Using a long distance access code that does not belong to you.
- Reporting a lost item as "stolen" to an insurance company in order to collect the money.
- Returning damaged merchandise when the damage is your own fault.
- Not saying anything when the server miscalculates the bill in your favor.
- Getting too much change and not saying anything.
- Taping or burning a CD instead of buying it.
- Moving into a new residence, finding that the cable TV is still hooked up, and using it rather than signing up and paying for it.
- Using an expired coupon for merchandise.
- Lying about a child's age in order to get a lower price.
- Stretching the truth on an income tax return.
- Using a coupon for merchandise you did not buy.
- Taping a movie off the TV.
- Returning merchandise after trying it and not liking it.
- Using computer software games that you did not buy.

The artists are rich, the record labels are filthy rich, and copyright laws have not been extended to the Internet and I am on a college budget.

Thus wrote a college student who had frequently downloaded many songs from the Internet. The student was one of 22 participants in a study by marketing professors Aron M. Levine, Mary Conway Dato-on, and Kenneth Rhee. The three professors were interested in uncovering consumers' reasons, or rather justifications, for engaging in free and unauthorized music downloading from Web sites such as Napster. This was not a vain question, mind you, since consumers could download music, for example, because they were unconscious that such a practice could be illegal or unethical, or alternatively, because they saw little chance of being caught. The range of responses they obtained revealed both the reasons and then more; their responses can be organized in following categories (categories are ours, not respondents'):

1. No Real Harm to Companies or Artists
2. No Norms Are Violated
3. CDs are too Expensive
4. Napster is Actually Doing Them Good
5. Companies and Artists are Too Rich Already

There were, of course, a few respondents who did recognize harm to companies and artists.

The three marketing professors followed up their qualitative study with a quantitative study, surveying 210 student respondents by a questionnaire. Included in the questionnaire was a scale to measure respondents' attitude toward unethical behavior in general (designed by two other marketing professors, Scott Vitell and Jim Muncy, see Table 1). Respondents answer on a five-point Likert scale: 1—"strongly believe it is wrong" to 5—"strongly believe it is not wrong." Also included in the survey were, of course, measures of the extent to which respondents engaged in music-downloading and the degree of their agreement with some statements about music downloading—statements derived from the earlier qualitative study.

The Ethical attitude scale had four factors:

1. Willful wrongdoing: such as drinking soda in the store without paying for it, and changing price tags.
2. No Harm, No foul: such as taping a movie, returning merchandise bought elsewhere, etc.
3. Deceptive Practices: such as lying about a child's age, using expired coupon, stretching truth on taxes, etc.
4. Passive Benefiting: Server miscalculates, cashier returns too much change, etc.

Summarized in Table 2 are findings on how the downloaders (63% of all respondents) and non-downloaders (37%) scored on these ethical attitude dimensions and on beliefs about downloading practices.

One noteworthy finding was that music downloaders actually purchased more CDs on an average! Now explain that!

TABLE 2

ATTITUDES AND BEHAVIORS OF MUSIC DOWNLOADERS

	Downloaders	Non-Downloaders
ETHICAL ATTITUDE		
1. Willful Wrongdoing	1.52	1.22
2. No Harm, No Foul	4.12	3.47
3. Willful Wrongdoing	2.63	2.14
4. Willful Wrongdoing	2.57	2.02
BELIEFS about DOWNLOADING		
1. Harms companies	2.87	3.41
2. Harms artists	2.83	3.39
3. Companies make excess profits	4.16	3.89
4. CDs contain few good songs	4.06	3.57
Does Downloading Affect CD Buying		
No. of CDs in Collection	3.33	2.64
No. of CDs Purchased during Past 6 Months	2.41	2.11

Levin, Aron, Mary Conway Dato-on, and Ken Rhee. (2004) "Money For Nothing and Hits For Free: The Ethics of Downloading Music from Peer-to-Peer Web Sites." *Journal of Marketing Theory & Practice* 12 (1): 48-60. Used with permission.

DISCUSSION QUESTIONS

1. Which of the practices in the Ethical Attitude Scale do you yourself consider unethical? Discuss why.

2. Does the practice of free music downloading influence consumer's CD purchasing? Does this practice harm the artists or recording companies?

3. The availability of music online (whether free or at a fee) is here to stay; it is a sign of the times, i.e., The Internet Age. How should recording companies and artists adapt to this new reality?

Tweens are a group to be reckoned with. They're complex, demanding, and difficult to understand. They're a challenging group for marketers but vitally important to get to know.

Today's tweens (9-14 year-olds) are more affluent than those of any previous generation, and there are more of them. They're more vocal and powerful. Not only do they have their own pocket money, but they also wield influence beyond their spending power.

Millward Brown's research for the book *BRAND-child* found that in more than half of tweens' households (58%), parents ask their kids' advice when it comes to buying high ticket items like cars, or the tweens actually tell their parents what they should buy (see charts below).

In India, 71% of tweens claim to influence cars bought by their parents. In America the corresponding figure is 63% and over half of 9-14 years-olds in Brazil, China, Japan and Germany also believe that they affect this purchase. Motor manufacturers such as Ford, Honda, VW and Vauxhall have all recently developed marketing activity acknowledging the role of the child in brand choice.

Additionally, today's tweens are tomorrow's adult consumers. On estimate, the average US tween will have an uninflated per capita income of $2m (£1.07m) throughout their life. How they spend this income will partly be driven by the brand associations formed at a young age.

Kids and brands

Mental associations, shortcuts and loyalties to brands begin to form at a very early age. And many habits formed as tweens can persist long into adulthood. As early as six months of age, babies are beginning to form mental images of corporate logos and mascots. At the age of three, before they can read and write, one out of five US children is making specific requests for brand-name products.

The research shows that overall brand loyalty increases sharply from the age of 10, and peaks around the age of 30 (see graph on page 55). There is a pattern of strengthening bonds with brands that starts and grows throughout the tween years.

However, on average tweens are 40% less loyal to brands than adults. Furthermore, among kids, around half of all brands change their 'typology' (a measure of overall brand equity) every two years, highlighting an extremely rapid migration of attitudes.

But why this promiscuity? Children are programmed to want to explore and experience, and this is just as true of brands as it is of other things. Tweens are less brand loyal simply because they have had less experience and involvement with brands. But this is not the only reason.

The news and promotions bombarded at kids in an attempt to drive sales and build loyalty often does little to build strong brand foundations. Most mothers have been browbeaten into buying a particular

How tweens influence household purchases (%)

- My parents ask me for my advice
- I tell my parents what I think they should buy
- I do not have an opinion
- **I have my opinion but I don't discuss it**
- Other

14 2 30
26 28

Source: Millward Brown 2002

Tweens claiming to influence car buying parents (%)

India	71
America	63
China	59
Brazil	59
Japan	53
Germany	51
Spain	40

Kids bonding to car brands (%)

	Germany	Spain	Brazil
New MINI	13	8	15
Ford Focus/Ka	0	15	3
VW Golf	12	8	6
New Beetle	12	9	7

Source: Millward Brown 2002

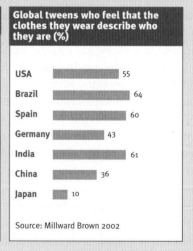

Global tweens who feel that the clothes they wear describe who they are (%)

USA	55
Brazil	64
Spain	60
Germany	43
India	61
China	36
Japan	10

Source: Millward Brown 2002

brand strategy february 2005

DISCUSSION QUESTIONS

1. Tweens influence family purchases of important products such as a car. What is the nature of this influence (normative, informational, identificational)? Why would parents give in to influence from their teen children?

2. Does this finding imply that marketers should direct their brand communications for all family consumption products to tweens as well as adult family members?

3. Consider the finding that brand loyalty among tweens is 40% less than adults. Is this likely to be true for all products? Which of the three reasons cited in the study will become less influential as tweens grow up.

4. What role might the concept of involvement play in (a) tweens' influence on family purchases, and (b) tweens' brand loyalty?

5. Discuss each of the Tips for Marketers.

product which comes with a free gift or promotion, only to find the product itself being ignored. Such promotions rarely generate loyalty, although they may drive short-term sales. And with more promotional activity around, it's easy for tweens to jump from one brand to another.

Tween tribes

On average, eight in 10 of today's urban tweens need to feel part of a group, and what the group says, goes. The lowest agreement score on 'It is important to me to feel part of a group' was seen in Germany (71%), and the highest in Brazil (89%). In China 81% agree that it's important to feel part of a group. Half of all girls and around four in 10 boys believe that 'the clothes they wear describe who they are'.

Peer pressure drives how tweens behave and what brands they buy. Tweens want to belong, so it's no surprise that brands play such a big role in helping them do this. And kids beneath the tween threshold feel their own pressure. In a phenomenon known as 'fish streaming', younger children look up to tweens and aspire to use their brands. Brand tracking work showed that children with older siblings were more likely to pick up on PlayStation on its initial release. Those without older siblings took around a year longer to reach the same level of brand exposure.

As kids move from tween to teen, peer pressure diminishes. But tweens have a strong emotional need to fit in and feel secure, and this is one of the major contributors to both strong and weak brand loyalty among this group.

David Chantrey is group account director at Millward Brown. Millward Brown has conducted BRANDZ research for WPP and interviewed over 2,000 urban tweens worldwide for Martin Lindstrom's book BRANDchild.

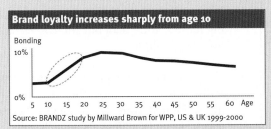

Brand loyalty increases sharply from age 10

Source: BRANDZ study by Millward Brown for WPP, US & UK 1999-2000

Children aged 6-8 who favoured Playstation initially

	No older siblings	With older siblings
1999	45%	57%
2000	57%	64%

Source: Millward Brown, 1999/2000

Tweens who feel peer pressure to buy certain products

Age:	12-13	14-15	16-18
Yes:	54%	30%	17%

Source: The Center for a New American Dream, 2002 Youth Survey

Tips for marketers

● **Whether you're marketing kids' brands or grown-up brands, consider tweens as a potential target:** Establish how many tweens know your brand and what they think of it. Understand the role tweens play in purchase decisions in your category. If you decide to include tweens as a target, consider how you'll manage the brand relationship from child to adult.

● **Make ethics your number one priority when marketing to tweens:** Never forget that tweens are still children and the ethical responsibility that comes with this. Products need to be safe, and as marketers you need to be honest, keep your word, and earn the trust of both tweens and their parents.

● **Make sure brands work around how tweens live, not around traditional business hours:** Once they reach the age of eight or nine, today's kids are a 24/7 generation and expect 24/7 brands and instant gratification.

● **Make sure your concept has potential to keep evolving over time:** Today's tweens thrive on upgrades – product evolution now needs to happen over weeks and months, not years. However, there must be a sense of consistency that ties subsequent evolutions together – know exactly what your brand stands for and remain true to it.

● **Build peer-to-peer marketing programmes around community leaders and put tweens at the centre:** Belonging to a group is crucial in tween life. Tweens look up to their leaders and inspire each other. Peer-to-peer marketing will play an increasingly important role in creating successful tween brands, and the most successful will use viral marketing tools to enable tweens to market for them.

● **Think and act mobile:** You will increasingly need to be where your target is, which won't be in front of the TV. TV ads may well be used to inspire, but interactive channels will increasingly do the informing.

● **Be flexible and patient with your own lack of understanding of how the tween world operates:** Tweens hate to be sold to but love to be respected. They want to be listened to, heard and understood. Marketers should spend time with them; listen to them; talk to them; discover what they dream about. The future of a brand rests in their hands.

Courtesy: David Chantrey and Brand Strategy magazine (www.brandstrategy.co.uk)

If you walk casually in Greenwich (New York, City), you will pass right by it. It's a clothing store, owned by Abercrombie and Fitch (A&F), with the name of the store so inconspicuous that you won't notice it. The store front, with no display windows, looks more like a house than a store. The name of the store: Ruehl # 925!

Once inside, you will find none of the mega size steamy posters of bare-chested, models that decorate the parent company's stores. Instead you will get a wide range of clothes, a bit more fashionable and a bit more expensive.

Abercrombie and Fitch (A&F) is implementing a life-stage need identification concept. It knows that most of its current customers are college students; when they graduate and enter the job market, they take their patronage, at least for part of their casual wardrobe, elsewhere, such as to stores like Banana Republic or Polo. Now to lure them, the company has embarked a new store concept, where it features casual clothing, still bearing the same urban casual look, of course, but somewhat upgraded in quality, and correspondingly in price. Its media advertising and in store poster displays are also subdued as far as overt sexiness is concerned. And the new stores are designed more like a vintage apartment with soft lighting that invites lingering and lounging.

In part it resembles Hollister, the A&F's other brand extension a few years ago. Hollister, you might know, similarly has no visible store front or nameplate, but looks and feels more like an apartment than a store. Walk inside and at the entrance you will find chair and cocktail tables, littered with book and magazines. Merchandise aisles are dimly lighted and are set in meandering lanes so the whole walk thru the store feels more like a walk through a Homorama house. If you buy something, you will have to find the cash register which is set in the center of the store and looks more like a DJ booth in a clubby lounge—yes, with living-room style sofa seating in the foreground. And as you browse through the merchandise, you can watch on giant screens scenes from the surfing haven beach of California's …beach, so as to experience the lifestyle of .

While Hollister appeals to a high school teenage segment a few years younger than a typical still in college

A&F customer, Ruehl is designed to capture a just-graduated, new career person. And like Hollister, Ruehl also sells items beyond the expected including; vintage books, art, newspapers, magazines ad CDs.

What's with the name of the new store chain, Ruehl No. 925! Nine-to-Five, get it?.

And Ruehl is a created family name of an imaginary German immigrant. The story on company's Web site goes:

> "A German immigrant moved to the United States circa 1850 and opened a fine leather goods shop that stayed in his family for generations. His great grandson, 100 years later, decided to enter the apparel business, focusing on denim and inspired by screen idol James Dean."

Ruehl # 925 sells, you see, not just merchandise, but, rather, it tells you a story. It wants you to feel as if, in shopping there and wearing its merchandise, you are living a story. The question is whether that story is the one you want to live.

DISCUSSION QUESTIONS

1. Will the store appeal to recent college graduates who are now seeking amore mature, career centered merchandise, and would otherwise go to stores like Banana Republic and Kenneth Cole?

2. How well does the store meet the challenge of looking more mature than but still connected to the A&F image? Should it?

3. "Consumers seeking career wardrobe just want good, stylish career clothing. They are not there for the dimly lighted store atmosphere. They are in other words, more in a "find-the-merchandise, goal-oriented" mode, not in a leisurely browsing mode." Do you agree or disagree, and do you believe the store ambience will hinder or help attract the target group and sell them the merchandise.

4. Design a research study to identify consumer segments to whom the store will appeal? What mindset will make this segment an ideal prospect for the store?

The Joy of *Lacing Up* Without A Shoe

In early 2005, you could logon to adiidas.com Web site, enter the code given in the ad shown here, and redeem a free lace for the shoe. Even without and BEFORE buying the shoe. The reason, as the copy in the attached ad explains: The A3 cushioning in the shoe has an extended life; consequently, the lace might need replacing before the show will "*ever* need replacing"!

View and enjoy the ad. Then contemplate it and answer the Discussion Questions.

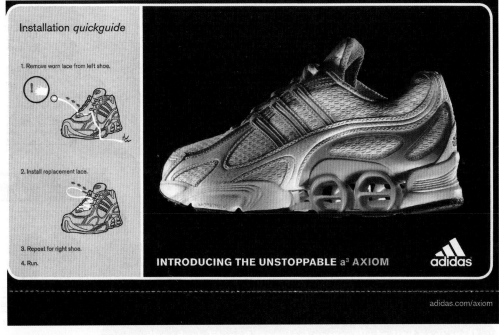

Images: Courttesy: Adidas Company

DISCUSSION QUESTIONS

1. To Whom will the ad appeal? To whom will it not appeal? Why? (Describe these two groups of consumers in demographic and psychographic terms.

2. Will the ad work differently for (a) consumers with low vs. high involvement in the product category? (b) consumers with or without prior brand attitudes, (c) consumers who are knowledgeable versus not knowledgeable about the product category?

3. Does the ad activate a particular decision model (Chapter 1), such as Lexicographic? How, with respect to which attribute?

4. Will consumer actually go to the Web site and redeem the free lace? Will some consumers request the lace and never end up buying the shoe?

5. Finally, what long term brand building do the ads like this enable or do not enable, and how?

FROM ADIDAS TO ZIP CARS

17-18

Comprehensive CASE
THE REAL TRUTH ABOUT BEAUTY
Brand Dove Asks Women When They Feel Beautiful

Marketers spend millions of dollars (or euros or yens) every year, helping women achieve beauty. They assume that women are chasing beauty and they believe their brands help them achieve it. But just what is beauty and what do women feel about it? This question has never been researched. Until now. In 2004, UK based Unilever's Dove brand commissioned a study, pioneering in conception and vision, vast in scope, and an eye-opener in its findings. Below are some key findings:

FINDINGS CAPSULE

Feeling Positive

90% of American women consider their looks average or above average.

Claiming "Looks," Not Beauty

36% say their looks are above average; in contrast, only 18% say their "beauty" is above average.

Redefining Beauty

75% of women agree that beauty does not come from a woman's looks, but from her spirit and life.

Owning Beauty

79% of women wish a woman could be considered beautiful even if she is not "physically perfect."

Relationship Over Beauty

Women consistently rated relationship as most important and beauty as least important.

Feel beautiful when:

- they feel loved (70%)
- husband/significant other:
  - » Looks at them admiringly (68%)
  - » Does something special for them (65%)
  - » Goes out with them for a special occasion (64%

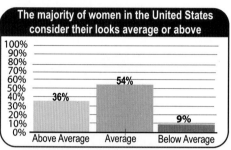

The majority of women in the United States consider their looks average or above

Above Average 36% — Average 54% — Below Average 9%

The Downing Street Group, LLC

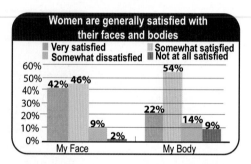

Women are generally satisfied with their faces and bodies

Very satisfied / Somewhat satisfied / Somewhat dissatisfied / Not at all satisfied

My Face: 42%, 46%, 9%, 2% — My Body: 22%, 54%, 14%, 9%

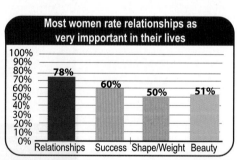

Most women rate relationships as very important in their lives

Relationships 78% — Success 60% — Shape/Weight 50% — Beauty 51%

The Downing Street Group, LLC   Rate as "Very Important" in Top 3 in 1-10 scale

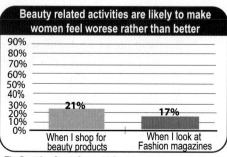

Beauty related activities are likely to make women feel worese rather than better

When I shop for beauty products 21% — When I look at Fashion magazines 17%

The Downing Street Group, LLC   Makes Me Feel Much More Beautiful 1-10 Scale Top 3

The study produced a wealth of information, covering such issues as women's self-perceptions of their looks, their opinions on media's depiction of beauty, and how they experience their self-esteem. Study these findings in the charts that follow.

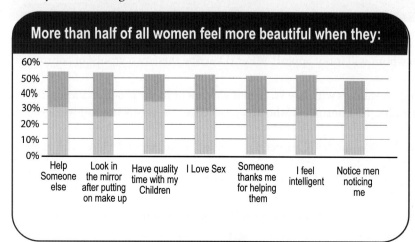

More than half of all women feel more beautiful when they:

Help Someone else — Look in the mirror after putting on make up — Have quality time with my Children — I Love Sex — Someone thanks me for helping them — I feel intelligent — Notice men noticing me

Self-descriptors for One's Looks

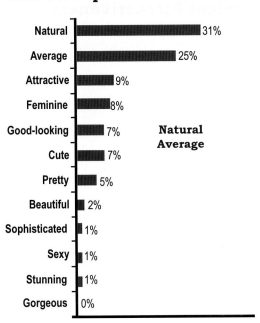

Natural	31%
Average	25%
Attractive	9%
Feminine	8%
Good-looking	7%
Cute	7%
Pretty	5%
Beautiful	2%
Sophisticated	1%
Sexy	1%
Stunning	1%
Gorgeous	0%

Natural Average

U.S. Study
A national projectable phone survey of 1600 women, along with a qualitative research component encompassing in-depth interviews, ethnographic studies, and a variety of projective techniques.

Global Study
3000 women, aged 18-64, in some ten countries.

Satisfaction
beauty - physical attractiveness - face - body

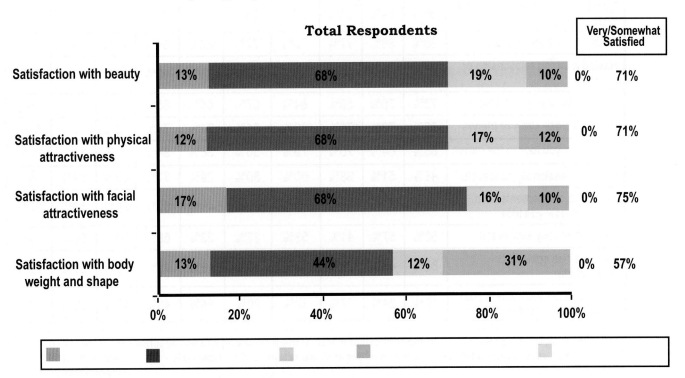

Total Respondents

Very/Somewhat Satisfied

Satisfaction with beauty	13%	68%	19%	10%	0%	71%
Satisfaction with physical attractiveness	12%	68%	17%	12%	0%	71%
Satisfaction with facial attractiveness	17%	68%	16%	10%	0%	75%
Satisfaction with body weight and shape	13%	44%	12%	31%	0%	57%

0%   20%   40%   60%   80%   100%

C2 - How satisfied would you say you are with your own beauty?
C3 - How satisfied would you say you are with your own physical attractiveness?
C41 - Now thinking about your face, how satisfied would you say you are with your facial attractiveness?
E1 - How satisfied would you say you are with your current body weight and shape?

Popular Portrayals of Bauty/Physical Attractiveness
Total Respondents

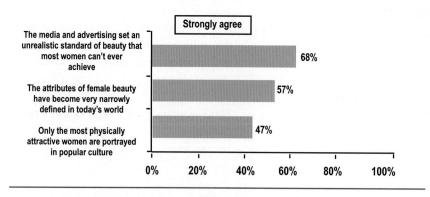

	Strongly agree
The media and advertising set an unrealistic standard of beauty that most women can't ever achieve	68%
The attributes of female beauty have become very narrowly defined in today's world	57%
Only the most physically attractive women are portrayed in popular culture	47%

D6, D2, D1 - Now, I am going to read you a list of statements, and I'd like you to tell me to what extent you agree or disagree with each. Please use a 10 -point scale where 1 means you "Completely disagree" and 10 means you "Completely agree."

Top 3 boxes of 10 pt. scale.
Strongly agree

IMPORTANCE IN MAKING "YOU" FEEL BEAUTIFUL

	USA	CAN	GBR	ITA	FRA	NLD	PRT	BRA	ARG	JPN
Being loved	91%	89%	91%	91%	82%	84%	92%	94%	93%	70%
Doing something you really love to do	86%	84%	83%	88%	80%	91%	91%	96%	96%	68%
Taking good care of yourself	86%	86%	77%	79%	72%	80%	84%	97%	84%	78%
Having a strong relationship or marriage	82%	68%	82%	86%	82%	78%	90%	91%	89%	56%
Being in good physical shape	75%	76%	69%	84%	87%	65%	85%	85%	79%	46%
Having a close circle of friends	65%	78%	76%	68%	64%	74%	78%	78%	76%	51%
Liking how you look in the mirror	65%	64%	70%	79%	56%	36%	84%	94%	81%	31%
Being professionally successful	48%	51%	38%	60%	60%	29%	77%	83%	69%	36%
Receiving compliments from others on how you look	35%	43%	55%	52%	50%	46%	62%	80%	59%	39%
Being financially successful	50%	57%	41%	53%	37%	23%	68%	76%	56%	45%
Having a rich spiritual or religious life	68%	43%	23%	49%	19%	18%	46%	79%	56%	72%
Looking better than others you know (co-workers/friends)	19%	24%	27%	37%	26%	14%	43%	48%	38%	22%

C26 - C 36 - Now, thinking about yourself, how important is each of them in making you feel beautiful? Please use a 10 point-point scale where 1 means it is "Not at all important" and 10 means it is "Extremely important."

Top 3 box of 10 pt. scale
Ranked on total respondents

Perceptions about beauty
Total Respondents

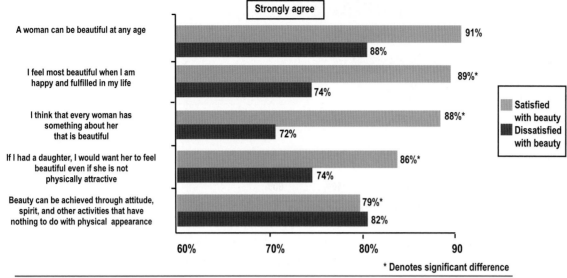

| Strongly agree |

A woman can be beautiful at any age — 91% / 88%

I feel most beautiful when I am happy and fulfilled in my life — 89%* / 74%

I think that every woman has something about her that is beautiful — 88%* / 72%

If I had a daughter, I would want her to feel beautiful even if she is not physically attractive — 86%* / 74%

Beauty can be achieved through attitude, spirit, and other activities that have nothing to do with physical appearance — 79%* / 82%

Satisfied with beauty
Dissatisfied with beauty

60% 70% 80% 90

* Denotes significant difference

C2-C42, C61-C63, C56 - How satisfied would you say you are with your own beauty ? Now, I am going to read you a list of statements, and I'd like you to tell me to what extent you agree or disagree with each. Please use a 10-point scale where 1 means you "Completely disagree" and 10 means you "Completely agree".

Top 3 box of 10 pt. scale
Satisfaction top 2 box
Dissatisfaction bottom 2 box
Ranked on total respondents

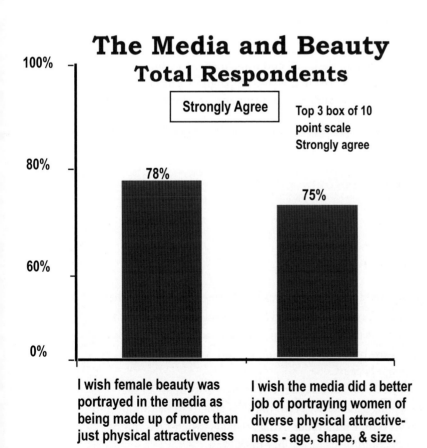

The Media and Beauty
Total Respondents

| Strongly Agree |

Top 3 box of 10 point scale
Strongly agree

78% — I wish female beauty was portrayed in the media as being made up of more than just physical attractiveness

75% — I wish the media did a better job of portraying women of diverse physical attractiveness - age, shape, & size.

D3 & D4 - Now I am going to read you a list of statements and I'd like you to tell me to what exent you agree or disagree with each. Please use a 10-point scale where 1 means you "Completely disagree" and 10 means you "Completely "agree."

Better Ways to Depict Women in the Media
Total Respondents - Top Two Choices

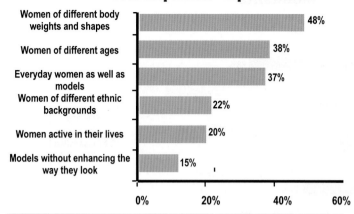

Women of different body weights and shapes	48%
Women of different ages	38%
Everyday women as well as models	37%
Women of different ethnic backgrounds	22%
Women active in their lives	20%
Models without enhancing the way they look	15%

D8 - I am going to read you a list of things regarding the media. Please tell me in which two of the following ways, if any you must think the media could be doing a better job of depicting women in the media and advertising.

Commenting on this trail-blazing study, Naomi Wolf, well-known author, feminist and social critic, wrote:

It appears that American women have deconstructed the beauty myth.
When I first wrote about the oppressive power of prevailing norms of "the physical ideal" in 1991, very few women felt comfortable challenging them. It was taken for granted.. that the ideal was tall, young, thin, blond, Caucasian, and large-breasted…

[Now, this report shows] a majority of women have worked out a beauty philosophy that is inclusive, not exclusive, related to their inner lives, not their weight on a scale or the number of lines in their faces, and, most importantly, psychologically empowers them as attractive women on their own terms.

Based on the study, Unilever's Dove brand designed and implemented a communication campaign titled Campaign for Real Beauty. See it at www.campaignforrealbeauty.com. A few images from that campaign, which also appeared in print ads, are shown here.

Hometown: Landover, Maryland
Occupation: Manicurist
Favorite food: Anything with curry
Favorite color: Red
Favorite movie: Old classic sappy love stories
Beautiful time:
I felt absolutely beautiful on my wedding day. That was one moment in my life when I was the queen of the night. It was a special day when everything was about me. I felt like I was floating on a cloud. Throughout the day, everyone was surrounding me with loving comments and reminding me of how beautiful I looked.
You're excited about this campaign because…
I absolutely love what it represents. I love the thought of being a part of an ad that would potentially touch many young girls to tell them that it is alright to be unique and everyone is beautiful in their own skin. I remember being at an age when I felt out of shape and wondering if one day I could be beautiful in others eyes.

Gina Crisanti

Hometown: Fort Worth, Texas
Occupation: Barista at Argo Tea Café
Favorite food: Artichokes
Favorite color: Red
Favorite movie: You Can Count on Me
Favorite curves: The small of my back, because it's so nice and subtle compared to some of my other curves.
Interests:
I love being out in the sun, exploring the city, playing catch, rollerblading, jogging, yoga, shopping, hanging out at the lake, and, of course, spending time with friends and family.
Surprising fact:
I've never seen Star Wars or The Matrix.
Beautiful time:
In general, I feel beautiful when I keep a positive attitude, take responsibility for what is within my control and leave the rest up to life.
You're excited about this campaign because…
It encourages the viewer to let go of society's narrow, fantastical idea of beauty, and embrace beautiful reality.

DISCUSSION QUESTIONS

1. What does the Dove Report show about women's self-concept and the role beauty plays in it?

2. Would the Dove campaign appeal to women? More than an ad that, say, presents beautiful models of the type the media has been criticized for depicting as "the beauty ideal"? Support your answer with findings from the study (or despite the findings)

3. The import and significance of the study, and of the Dove campaign based on it, reaches far beyond—by presenting a new vision about beauty, the campaign is an invitation to society at large to break free of the false beauty ideal. Comment on this statement and also outline some ideas as to how a marketer or a social agency might bring this message to societies at large.

RESEARCHING CONSUMER BEHAVIOR

Dear Consumer: May We Hang Out with You for a While?

Laskerville—a code-named small town outside Chicago. The town has a population of 8,000 to 10,000, not counting three or four visitors who slip in and out of town. You can see them in the market square, in local bars, at car dealerships, even at the funerals. It is they who have given the town this code name, and the townspeople don't even know it.

They are researchers from the Chicago-based Foote, Cone & Belding (FCB) advertising agency, whose founder's name was Albert Lasker. Since 1989, the researchers would cast away their business suits and don jeans and boots. To mingle with the villagers. To chat with them casually. About whatever interests them—the villagers. Trying to get a fix on what turns the wheels in small-town U.S.A.

Laskerville, you see, was chosen because it is typical of small towns across the nation. And a lot of advertisers want to sell to very common folks in these very common towns. What better way to find out about their attitudes, lifestyles, concerns, and mores, than to observe them firsthand in their natural habitat.

INTRODUCTION

You don't have to live in Laskerville to know about consumer research. In one form or the other, we have all experienced it first hand. If you visit a restaurant, on the table there, you might find a comment card, requesting your opinion on your experience during the visit. If you are in a mall, someone might approach you with a request to answer a few questions. Sometimes when your phone rings, there is a marketing researcher on the line, wondering what you think of the detergent you are currently using, whether you have an opinion on the upcoming election, what your future computer needs might be, or how you spend a typical weekend.

These are not idle questions someone decided to ask to kill some free time on a Friday afternoon. These are questions, instead, designed to understand you as a consumer—what products you buy, how you buy them, and what your experience is with them. These questions determine whether the consumer type that you represent would be a prospect for a company's product or service, what kind of specific product or service design changes might appeal to you and to the kind of consumers you represent, and how that product or service may be offered to you. Researching consumer behavior is critical for marketing success.

Lest you shudder at the thought of someone watching you in the supermarket, remember a supermarket is a public space and surveillance cameras are watching you in retail stores all the time anyway. More importantly, all consumer research, if done properly and ethically, aims to bring more value to you, the consumer. As marketers, we can learn a lot by simply observing shoppers quietly; and by hanging out with consumers. Actually, there are a number of other methods of researching the consumer, each with its own charms and challenges. In this chapter, we describe them all—the various methods of researching the consumer.

Two Types of Consumer Information: Qualitative and Quantitative

Consider these two questions:

Q1. Why do you like Rain Forest restaurants? Is it because of their: 1. Food quality; 2. Menu variety; 3. Atmosphere; 4. Value price; 5. Other

Q2. How do you feel when you dine at a Rain Forest Restaurant? Describe your experience and feelings during your first visit there?

These two questions are meant to obtain two different types of information, respectively called quantitative and qualitative. Quantitative information is information collected in a form that can be easily coded into numerical value. Qualitative information is information that is collected and presented in the consumer's own words and cannot be easily coded into numerical value. The quantitative questions contain pre-specified responses for consumers to choose and mark; qualitative questions leave the response totally unspecified, thus offering the consumer an opportunity to give the answer in his or her own words.

An important question is, when should we use qualitative versus quantitative research? The answer lies in a simple but unique difference in the way we form the question, In Q1 on Rain Forest restaurant, notice that we are providing the list of possible answers; in Q2, in contrast, we are leaving it for consumers to provide the answer. Why? It is because, in Question 1, we assume we already know the range of possible reasons for consumers to like or dislike Rain Forest restaurants, and we just want to find out which of the possible reasons are true for how many consumers. In contrast, Q2 implies that we don't know the possible answers, or are not sure what sort of reasons might exist for people to visit Rain Forest Restaurants. Moreover, quantitative research method lets us know only the cut and dry reasons for consumer behavior; in instances where we believe that the underlying reasons for a specific consumer behavior are, instead, some deep felt human experiences, then we resort to qualitative research.

Thus, the principal reason we choose to employ qualitative research is that we do not want to restrict the consumer to limit his or her answers to pre-assigned response categories; instead the consumer is free to use his or her own words, and describe his or her experience and reasons with all its intricacies and mystique, if you will. As researchers, when we use qualitative research methods, we are looking to "discover" consumers' personal experiences we do not know about, and we are looking to understand their consumption values, motives, attitudes, opinions, perceptions, preferences, experiences, actions, and future intentions. As you can see, this type of research—qualitative research—can be quite rewarding, even fun. Let us see how it is done.

QUALITATIVE RESEARCH

There are six principal methods of qualitative research: focus groups, directed interview, motivation research, observation, participant observation, and interpretive research. Let us describe each below.

Focus Groups

With **focus groups**, a small group of consumers is assembled in a room, and a moderator steers the group discussion along certain questions of interest to the marketer. The group members can range in number from 6 to 15 and are generally chosen by **convenience sampling** (a method in which respondents are recruited based on convenient availability) but are prescreened to represent the target market. The moderator is a trained marketing research professional, and he or she generally uses a discussion guideline (a list of issues to probe). A good moderator endeavors to avoid biasing the opinions expressed by the group members. He or she also tries to ensure that no one member dominates the discussion, that all group members get a chance to have their say, and that the discussion stays focused on the topic at hand. The discussion room is generally a specially equipped room, with a one-way mirror on one of its walls. Behind the mirror, client companies' executives sit and watch the group session. Also, the focus group is generally audio and/or video recorded for later review and analysis of data. Focus groups are often used in consumer research, principally to explore various facets of consumers' worldview about the topic at hand.

Since focus groups are not a statistical sample of the target population, the findings of focus group research are not projectable to the entire population of target consumers. Rather, focus groups offer a window into the consumer's mind, bringing to surface things the marketer may not have known about the consumer and his or her view of the product. What the marketer discovers through focus group (and other qualitative research methods) he/she can then use to design specific questions for a subsequent large-scale quantitative research study. Thus, the principal utility of focus group research is to "explore" the consumer behavior about which marketers didn't know much to begin with. In this role, focus groups have several applications:

- Generating ideas for product improvements or new products. We can learn of the problems consumers currently face in using the product, or of how the product can be made more convenient in use.
- Understanding consumer's hopes and fears about a new product innovation, such as the liquid condom discussed above; this understanding can then help the marketer in designing a communication campaign that would respond to these hopes and fears.
- Understanding consumer perceptions of competing brands. A firm can display its own brand (keeping the sponsor's identity unrevealed) and competing brands and engage the consumer group in comparing these.
- Testing new concepts. New product concepts, packaging prototypes, new brand names, and certainly, advertising photo boards or finished commercials can all be presented to focus group members for their feedback.

Directed Interview

If you are up at 11:30 at night and you are watching Tonight Show with Jay Leno, you are seeing directed interview in action; except that Leno is interested merely in helping the celebrity guest put on display some aspect of his or her life that would interest the audience, not in learning anything about the guest as a consumer. But Jay Leno does have a broad interview guide—a set of topics to broach with his guests. In consumer research, we do the same. We interview a sample of consumers one on one on a topic area. This method is called directed interview.

Directed interview (also called in-depth interview or simply depth interview) is a method of learning about consumers' views and activities in a particular topic area by asking mostly pre-conceived questions in a conversational format. By pre-conceived questions, we mean that the main topic areas to cover and the sort of questions to ask have been thought out in advance. These are written down in what is known as an "interview guide." The interview guide is broad in three respects: first, the interviewer does not have to read the questions exactly; rather he or she should phrase the questions conversationally. Second, the guide contains not only the topic areas and loose phrasing of questions, but also directions for probing. Third, the interviewer is expected to exercise discretion both to skip a question (for example, if it has been already covered by the respondent's answer to another question) and to probe whenever necessary (for example when a response is too brief) even if the guide does not specifically ask for it.

Of course, the guide contains no predetermined answers (remember, it is qualitative research). The interviewer (who is generally trained in this free-flowing interview method) uses the 'guide' to ask initial questions and then follows up with new questions formed on the spot based on the consumer's answers. The interviewer records consumers' answers verbatim, either manually by writing them down or by a mechanical recording device such as an audio or video recorder. All survey respondents are asked the same broad set of questions although of course the specific follow up questions differ.

MOTIVATION RESEARCH

Motivation research (MR) is research directed at discovering the reasons (i.e., motives) for a person's behavior—reasons the consumer is either unaware of or is unwilling to admit in direct questioning. In consumer behavior, motivation research is conducted to find out the conscious or subconscious reasons that motivate people to buy or not to buy a particular product, or to engage or not engage in other marketplace behavior (e.g., browsing, shop lifting, fanatic love for a product, etc.). Motivation research uses a number of techniques—all disguised and no-structured—disguised in that the consumer is not able to figure out that the researcher is trying to find out his or her (the consumer's) deep motives; non-structured in that the answers are not pre-structured for the respondent to choose from; rather, the consumer is encouraged to say whatever comes to mind.

Observation

In our everyday life, we learn a lot by observing people. We learn about what people do and how they do what they do. If people learn about people by watching people, why couldn't marketers learn about consumers by watching consumers? This simple art of observing people has been the stock in trade for anthropologists who study culture. With varying degrees, it has also been one of the methods in consumer research for as long as consumer research has existed. But now it is being revived with new vigor. One consumer researcher, Paco Underhill, has spent a lifetime on it. His firm, Envirosell, has placed video cameras and human observers in shopping malls and stores around the world, observing some fifty thousand shoppers a year. An excerpt form his research findings, reported in a book titled *Why We Buy*, reveals the power of observation.

> *We did a supermarket study for a dog food manufacturer. We staked out the pet food aisle and observed consumers picking up the food ration of their dogs. We noticed something interesting: dog food ('main course', if you will) was being bought by adults and while adults were placing the dog food in the cart, children were picking dog treats (e.g., flavored biscuits). Seldom did adults themselves picked these treats. However, they readily accommodated their children's pleas for dog treats. Perhaps children loved their dogs more; or perhaps they just found feeding Fido those doggie cookies loads of fun.*

(Adapted from Paco Underhill, Why We Buy: The Science of Shopping, Simon and Schuster, 1999 (P. 18).

The marketing implications are clear. While dog food should be advertised to adults, dog treats should be advertised to children; and in the store, they should be placed on a lower shelf where children can reach them.

Now, then, some basic principles about observations.

Observation is a method of discovering some information about consumers by simply recording what they do without intruding. Thus, we do not ask them any questions directly (as we do in directed interviews); in fact, we don't even let them be aware that they are being followed or observed. We do not intrude or bother them or interfere with whatever they are doing; rather we record their activity in as natural a form as it occurs. The consumer activity can be recorded by the human eye (i.e., observed by a person) or it can be recorded by mechanical devices such as a video recorders. We can even time their pace by using a stopwatch.

This method has several features worth noting. First, we observe consumers naturally—"in situ," so to speak; we are thus uncovering what consumers do, not what they say they do. Thus, the observed behavior is more close to truth. Second, and this is a limitation of observation as a method—we can only observe the behavior, not consumer attitudes and perceptions. Thus, we know how consumers act but not why they act the way they do. We cannot learn, for example, which product features they like and which they dislike, and we certainly cannot learn of their deep seated motives for buying or not buying or using or not using a product. Third, while the method is simple to implement in the data collection phase (all we do is place some recorders and some human observers in strategic locations), it requires both patience and skill in data interpretation. A typical observation study would produce at least a hundred hours of tape (some may produce as many as a thousand hours of tape), and a group of researchers has to view them, some portions more than once, patiently; furthermore, the researcher viewing the video has to have the knack of "seeing" something of insight in a forest of data.

Participant Observation

Suppose you want to understand a French family's food consumption behavior—what kind of food do they eat, when and how, with what kinds of rituals, do they eat certain foods with certain beverages, at certain times? How often do they entertain, and what food do they serve on these occasions? Etc, etc., The best way to find that out is to live with a French family as a house guest for a week or so. This is participant observation at work.

Participant observation takes the observation method one step further. We are no longer simply observing quietly, unobtrusively; rather we are observing and living everyday life with them. **Participant observation** is a method of research where the researcher observes consumers in their natural setting, living life in their midst as they do. He or she arranges to spend time with a consumer or consumers in their natural setting and simply goes about doing daily chores, participating in life as it unfolds. Often the consumers being researched do not know that the researcher is an outsider and is observing them.

The Laskerville project, described at the beginning of this chapter, is a prime example of this research method.

This method enables a first hand look at consumer's behavior and offers a deep understanding, perhaps more than any other method can. It is also extremely time consuming and requires a skilled and trained observer, who must earn the trust of the host family or host community.

Interpretative Research

Interpretative research is a class of qualitative research methods where a researcher obtains a thick slice of consumer behavior data and interprets them for meaning. The researcher usually has training and special skills in data collection and meaning analysis and bases his or her interpretation based on an extensive understanding of the social and cultural characteristics of that setting. These types of studies are also called ethnographic studies. The term ethnographic means taking the cultural perspective of the population being studied. Thus, the behavior of specific consumers is interpreted from the vantage point of the consumers themselves. The question the researcher asks is What meaning does a particular consumer behavior have for the consumer him- or herself? How does it make sense within the context of the culture that the consumer group shares?[7]

Interpretive research is also called post-modern research. The focus of the post-modern research is on understanding the meaning of a product or consumption experience in a consumer's life. The purpose here is not limited to the buying decision, but rather it covers the consumer's lifestyle, his or her well-being, satisfaction, and so on and the role that material objects and worldly activities play in his or her life.[8] The research methods themselves are not new, but they are being used with new rigor and enthusiasm, and more importantly, the perspective is new. It is called post-modern because after some half a century of widespread use of quantitative survey research and use of sophisticated statistical techniques, the attention is turning back to qualitative data, and a goal to capture, rather than the black and white, cut and dry quantifiable information, the "touchy feely" stuff. To capture consumers' emotions, raw feelings, intimate experiences, and subjective feelings. To uncover deep seated motives, aspirations, hopes, and emotions.

The methods include extended field research, consumer narratives and creative expressions. The Laskerville project described at the beginning of the chapter, is an example. **Field research** entails spending extended time in the field, observing consumers but not necessarily living there to become one of them. The researcher may retain his or her identity as an outsider. (Thus, participant observation is one type of field research where the researcher camouflages his or her identity and becomes one of the consumers.) For an example, see Odysee Project (Exhibit). **Consumer narratives** is a method where consumers are encouraged to write long narratives (or maintain a J.) about their experience as a consumer in a particular domain, such as using make up or buying clothes, or getting cosmetic surgery.

Finally, **creative expression** (our name for this group of techniques) is a method wherein consumers are encouraged to express their feelings in creative ways such as by drawing, by acting out, or by finding suitable pictures. A noteworthy example is ZMET (see box).

Advantages And Disadvantages Of Subjective, Interpretative Research

The advantages of interpretive research are manifold. First, the researcher is able to encounter consumers and consumption activities in their natural settings, thus eliminating the artificialness of surveys, focus-group rooms, or laboratory settings. Also, a thicker slice of everyday activity is sampled—for example, one observes a consumer for one hour or one day or one week as necessary rather than for a few minutes. The researcher observes firsthand the consumer activity, rather than inquire about it of respondents. Even when the consumer is interviewed, the researcher's own observations supplement the consumer's answers. Besides, the questioning is much more open ended and qualitative rather than close ended and quantified. Because of the extended mutual exposure between the researcher and the consumer, a greater trust is built, which then leads to consumer answers being more sincere. Finally, the consumer activity being analyzed and questioned is much more immediate and physically present. For example, a researcher who observes certain possessions in a consumer's house can actually point to them rather than ask the question in the abstract.

This method also has some shortcomings. It requires highly skilled and well trained researchers who are less preoccupied with recording but more oriented to constantly interpreting what they are observing. It is obviously very time consuming and very expensive. In addition, the interpretation of data is too subjective, despite following certain analytic procedures. Finally, the methods are good at generating hypotheses, but not at confirming hypotheses or suggesting generalizable principles. Overall, they can uncover some rare insights on the consumer, which can then be confirmed by quantitative methods described below.

C B F . Y . I . CREATIVE EXPRESSIONS

McCann Ericsson, an advertising agency, asked housewives to draw pictures of how they felt when they saw cockroaches. The study was sponsored by the marketer of Combat roach killer. The product, a poison, was in trays designed to kill cockroaches that fell in it. But women were not buying it. The creative expression drawings revealed the deep-seated reason: some women saw their husbands (who would sneak in at night) as cockroaches and wanted to have the pleasure of spraying the cockroaches and *watch them squirm to death!*

QUANTITATIVE RESEARCH

Have you read a film review lately? That is qualitative information. Now, have you seen a beauty contest (like Miss America Pageant)? Or, the Olympic games? Remember, how judges give a numerical scores to each contestant. That is a quantitative measure. In quantitative research, the consumer responses themselves need not be numerical (although we often ask them to circle some numbers); the main characteristic of quantitative research is that we offer the consumer a set of predetermined responses to choose from; we are later able to easily code this information into numbers by simply assigning a different number to each response category. Thus, gender information can be easily coded as male=1 and female=2; or the converse. So can a 'Yes' and 'No' answer, or an 'agree'/'disagree' answer.

Quantitative research can use either of two broad methods: survey and experiment.

SURVEY

Survey is a method where consumers are asked a question and requested to mark one of the pre-specified response categories. The researcher may read (on the phone or in face-to-face settings) a series of predetermined questions, one at a time, and records the consumer's answers. Alternatively, in a self-administered questionnaire (sent by mail or given in person), respondents can write in the answer themselves.

Basically, the method is useful to elicit consumers' beliefs, opinions, attitudes, perceptions, and so on. It has several advantages and disadvantages. Advantages are quick data collection in a relatively short time, and ability to reach consumers in widespread geographic locations. The disadvantage is that consumers will give the answers they consider safe to give. Thus, they will not give information they consider personal. Also, consumers do not like to appear ignorant and will therefore make up an answer even if they have never before thought about the topic. When the topic might be one in which consumer motivations might be hidden or where consumers may hesitate to candidly share their opinion, qualitative disguised techniques discussed before are more appropriate.

Surveys typically use pre-specified numerical scales for answer categories, so we discuss this method as a quantitative technique. However, surveys can be used just as well for eliciting respondent answers verbatim (i.e., in their own words). In many cases, questionnaires contain a few questions that seek open-ended verbatim responses, even though the majority of the questions seek numerical responses.

With the advent of the Internet, online surveys are becoming quite common. You might be surfing the Net and suddenly an ad pops up, inviting you to fill in a survey (usually some incentive is offered such as free coupons or entry into a sweepstakes. The big advantage of online surveys is of course the cost savings as the consumer enters the responses directly into the computer thus avoiding the need for someone to later enter the information. An example of an online survey is presented in below..

EXPERIMENT

One limitation of survey methods is that questionnaires are limited to assessing consumer opinions and thoughts that exist in the consumer mind. Often we are interest in finding out how consumers will respond to some potential market offering or communication. Moreover, it measures what respondents say they will do, not what they will actually do. An experiment overcomes this shortcoming. An **experiment** is a method in which the researcher places respondents in a situation that does not normally occur and then observes or records their response.

A prime example of experimental research in marketing is test marketing. **Test marketing** is a method of testing a marketing mix on a limited market as a precursor to deciding whether to implement that mix in the entire market. Suppose, for example, that you wanted to launch a new product. Rather than launch it in the entire nation (and incur huge losses in case the product does not sell), you could launch it in two cities and observe consumer response. Or let us say that you simply wanted

THE CONSUMER BEHAVIOR ODYSSEY PROJECT Exhibit A.1

Ethnography Research

The Consumer Behavior Odyssey was a qualitative research project involving personal visits by an interdisciplinary team of academic consumer researchers to a variety of consumer sites. The project was undertaken in summer 1986 by a group of leading consumer researchers (trained in such disciplines as sociology, psychology, anthropology, consumer behavior, and marketing research) who traveled in a recreational vehicle (RV) from coast-to-coast on a journey of discovery, so to speak. The data collection methods consisted of taped interviews, still photos, on-site recording of diaries, and day-end writing of reflections in personal J.s. Researchers visited department stores and garage sales, county fairs and tourist resorts, opera performances and rock concerts, and picnics and weddings (i.e., virtually any "consumption site" that came their way). The objective was to observe in a nonintrusive way the acquisition, consumption, and disposition of products and services wherever these occurred.9

Motorized versus Nonmotorized Mobile Homes

In one of their projects, The Odyssey researchers visited and observed the owners and renters of motorized and nonmotorized mobile homes. They found notable differences in the "consumption experience" of mobile home living by these two groups. Nonmotorized mobile homeowners seemed to view their mobile units as much more of a "home" than did the owners of motorized mobile homes. The former parked their units more permanently, shared community activities with others in the RV park, and externally personalized (e.g., named their units by their last names) and beautified their mobile units. The latter, in contrast, did not engage in any joint activities with their "neighbors," were preoccupied more with traveling and reaching their destinations than with relaxing in one spot in their units, and did not attempt any personalization in the external appearance of their mobile units.

This consumer perspective could not have been discovered by the more conventional quantitative methods. It can be helpful to marketers of mobile homes, travel accessories, and travel destinations to identify these two different groups of consumers.

Read more on this at: Russell W. Belk, Melanie Wallendorf, and John F. Sherry, "The Sacred and the Profane in Consumer Behavior, Theodicy on the Odyssey," J. of Consumer Research, June 1989, 16, 1-38. Russell W. Belk, "The Role of the Odyssey in Consumer Behavior and in Consumer Research," in Advances in Consumer Research, ed. by Paul Anderson & Melanie Wallendorf, 1987, vol. XIV, p. 357-361, Provo, UT: Association for Consumer Research. Russell W. Belk, John F. Sherry, and Melanie Wallendorf, "A Naturalistic Inquiry into Buyer and Seller Behavior at a Swap Meet," J. of Consumer Research, March 1988, Vol 14, 449-470. Harold H. Kassarjian, "How We Spent Our Summer Vacation: A Preliminary Report on the 1986 Consumer Behavior Odyssey," Advances in Consumer Research 14, pp. 376-77.

to test the relative appeal of two types of packages, or two different price levels, or two different advertisements or any combination of these. You could select two matching cities (i.e., cities similar in their demographic profiles) and place one package, price, or advertisement (called a stimulus) in one city and the second stimulus in the second city, and observe which elicits a more favorable consumer response. These are called **field experiments**, because they are conducted in natural marketplace settings and often consumers are unaware of their being in an experimental research.

A second variety of experiment is called Laboratory experiment or lab experiment for short. In lab experiment, consumers are invited in the research laboratory and then presented with a stimulus. Consumers are aware that they are participating in some research, but the research purpose is typically camouflaged.[11] For example, suppose you want to find out what consumer perceptions of taste of a new type of candy would be if the candy is presented under one brand name versus another and when it is priced low versus when it is priced high (say, 99cents versus $1.25 for a bar). To find this out, we invite, say 500 consumers to our lab and at random assign them to one of the four lab rooms. Consumers in each lab room are offered a candy bar, asked to try it and then rate the candy on a number of features such as quality, taste, price reasonableness, and even such image dimensions such as luxurious, rewarding, sophistication, etc. The candy bar remains the same, only the price and brand names are different. Consumer ratings for each of the four group reveal which brand name and price combination appeals to consumers the most.

SIMULATION

Simulation is a special form of quantitative, experimental method, in which researchers create real-world conditions in a laboratory to study the behavior of consumers. By observing their behavior in this laboratory setting, marketers are able to forecast how they (the consumers) would behave in the real marketplace. Just as astronauts use a flight simulator to train for the real flight, so too marketers simulate the marketing mix (i.e., create the market mix on a smaller scale in the laboratory) before investing money on the full-fledged marketing program.

Pretest market lab simulation is a specific procedure for testing new-product concepts and prototypes. In a typical procedure, consumers representative of the target market are recruited by mall interception and invited to view a TV program and look at some product samples.

They are also shown a 15-minute program segment, a pretaped TV program with one change: One of the commercials has been substituted by the test commercial. After viewing the program, the consumers are surveyed on the perceptions and persuasive impact of the commercial. Next, they are given some shopping money (say, $3.00) and are requested to examine the mock up store display that contains the new test brand as well as other brands. Consumer purchases are recorded and later consumers are called to obtain their reactions to the test product. The data can then be analyzed by statistical models to predict the performance of the new product in the real world. For details about an actual simulation model, see the Window on Practice box.

MEASUREMENT SCALES

No matter which quantitative method we use, to measure consumer responses, we must use some numerical scales. We describe a few of these scales below.

Ranking scales ask consumers to simply rank order various items, as shown below.

Please rank the following attributes of wireless phone service in terms of their importance to you, assigning 1 to most important and five to least important.

Attribute	Rank
Voice quality	———
Speed of connection	———
Signal clarity	———
Signal availability	———
Reach (area covered)	———

Semantic differential scales ask consumers to rate a product or brand or an ad etc., on a pair of opposite adjectives, as shown below.

Sprint Wireless phone service is:

Poor	1 2 3 4 5	Excellent
Economical	1 2 3 4 5	Uneconomical
Low quality	1 2 3 4 5	High quality

My opinion of Sprint Wireless phone service is:

Favorable	1 2 3 4 5	Unfavorable
Negative	1 2 3 4 5	Positive
I dislike	1 2 3 4 5	Like it very much

Another scale is Likert scale which requests a numerical rating, but asks respondents about the degree to which they agree or disagree with statements:

Please express your opinion on the following questions about seatbelts, by circling an appropriate number.

1. Strongly Disagree   2. Disagree   3. Feel Neutral   4. Agree
5. Strongly Agree

Seatbelts prevent injuries.

1   2   3   4   5

Seatbelts are inconvenient.

1   2   3   4   5

Seatbelts can trap you in case of an accident.

1   2   3   4   5

Measurement scales can also be pictorial, rather than numerical. Such a scale is particularly useful for less literate respondents, or respondents who speak a different language. When the research purpose is to measure the emotions the respondent experiences, pictures of various facial expressions can be used.[13] Pictorial scales are also especially useful for researching children as consumers.

The Internet and Virtual Reality: New Tools of Consumer Research

Imagine a focus-group discussion without the discussants really present in the same room. This is focus group online. The discussion groups communicate on the Internet via discussion forums moderated by a host, in real time. The participants are recruited in advance and asked to log on to their PCs at a prespecified time. Everybody, including the moderator, is ready to communicate online. Everything else is the same as in the conventional focus groups. The only difference is that the participants can be continents apart.

The advantages of online focus groups compared to its conventional counterpart are time savings, costs savings, and ability to bring together consumers or users from around the world. An added feature of this medium of discussion is that new product concepts can be presented via computer graphics so that they are more realistic than conventional paper-and-pencil concept descriptions. (Of course, this feature of computer graphics can be utilized also in face-to-face discussion groups.) Its disadvantages are lack of face-to-face interpersonal dynamic, and reliance on "verbalizable responses," thus making emotional responses more difficult to surmise.[16]

Online focus groups constitute an interesting use of information technology. However, as is true with any new application of a technology, consumer researchers should be aware of some still-unanswered questions about this method. Is an online focus-group moderator able to establish rapport with and communicate trust to the discussion group members? In comparison to face-to-face focus groups, do online respondents assume that they are being exposed to a large number of online users, or do they assume anonymity because no one can identify them? Finally, does such anonymity bring forth more candid or less candid responses? As experience with the method grows, these questions will get answered.

VIRTUAL REALITY TECHNIQUES IN CONSUMER RESEARCH

An even more advanced use of technology is virtual reality simulations. Virtual reality (VR) refers to interactive, computer-generated 3D immersive displays of images and sound. The VR equipment consists of a stereoscopic head-mounted display, body suit, and glove to provide tactile and sensory input. With virtual reality, test environments can be simulated to be indistinguishable from their real (physical) versions.

To show how this technique is utilized, let us describe

two of its typical applications: virtual shopping and virtual test marketing.

VIRTUAL SHOPPING

Using computer technology, a store aisle can be simulated on the computer. Sitting in front of a video game type of screen, consumers can walk through the aisle, look at a shelf display, examine a product, read the label, request additional information, learn if a coupon is available, put the item back on the shelf, or place it in a cart (depicted by a visual icon), and so forth, all with the click of a mouse. The computer displays whatever information the consumer wants, and in turn keeps a record of consumer activity. Thus, it is a useful tool to study consumers' information-seeking behavior, as well as

at the car display, walk around it, talk to salesmen, read press reports, ask other consumers, and so on. After this simulation, they were asked to drive a conventional car with the engine replaced by an electric engine. Following the real-world test drive, they returned to their computers to answer questions on their attitudes and preferences. The proprietary name of this technique is the Information Acceleration, designed by MIT professor Glen Urban and his colleagues.

Advantages Of Virtual Reality Techniques

Virtual-shopping research has several advantages over other methods. Compared to conventional focus-group and concept-test research, and also conventional store simulation

---

A Virtual-Reality Consumer Research Project   B   F.Y.I.

VIRTUAL STIMULI, REAL SUBJECTS

A snack manufacturer wanted to find out if its line of snacks included items that consumers perceived as close substitutes. If two or more items were perceived as substitutes, then the firm could trim the line without reducing sales (but reducing the costs). On the flip side, the firm wanted to know what snack products of the competition were perceived to be substitutes of the firm's own products. If there was a competitor's snack product against which the firm's product was briefly compared but then rejected as not being a good substitute, this would suggest a gap in the firm's own product line. The firm could fill this hole by bringing out a new product.

To answer these questions, the firm employed a virtual-shopping experiment. Four hundred consumers were recruited from six shopping malls across the United States. They were invited to the local simulation lab repeatedly to buy snack products from a virtual vending machine—vending machine on the computer screen. Since they were invited for repeated shopping trips, it was possible to fi rst study their preferences and then custom-design the vending machine inventory to force a reconsideration of their choices. For example, in a subsequent shopping trip, the vending machine display was manipulated to show the item of a particular consumer's preference as being "out of stock." The consumer was thus forced to consider substitutes (although he or she was free to buy or not buy a substitute). This enabled the researcher to study consumer perceptions of what was a close substitute of their favorite brand versus what was not.

This method had three advantages: First, it was much less costly to set up vending machine displays on the computer screens than would have been the case with the physically real displays. Second, the "out-of-stock" manipulation could be custom designed for each consumer based on the knowledge of what his or her current preference was. Finally, the consumer perception and preference data could be collected unobtrusively.

Read more: Raymond R. Burke, "Virtual Shopping," *ORMS Today*, 22, no. 4 (August 1995), pp. 28-34.

---

consumer responses to alternative shelf displays. A version of this system, called Visionary Shopper, has been tested in the United Kingdom. It will cost a fifth of the conventional simulated test-marketing approaches.

VIRTUAL TEST MARKETING

In an actual VR test marketing project, the goal was to evaluate demand for electric cars. Respondents were placed in front of a multimedia display. The screen flashed newspaper stories from an imagined future time. This was done to move respondents forward in time. Respondents then interacted with the program and a laser disk full of an array of verbal, pictorial, text, and video material. Respondents could look

tests, the virtual-shopping method is able to simulate the real-world shopping environment much more realistically. In the virtual-shopping experiment, the consumer is exposed to very realistic shelf displays, complete with the clutter of competing brands; even the hustle-bustle and the sight and sound of other shoppers can be simulated. Another advantage is that the computer is able to record much more detailed data about the shopper behavior. These data include the amount of time the shopper took to examine the product and make the decision, the content of information he or she sought and examined, the sequence in which the information was examined, the sequence in which brands were examined and products chosen, and so forth.[18]

CB Level 2.0

In this section, we discuss two advanced methods of consumer research: information processing research and mechanical measures.

INFORMATION PROCESSING RESEARCH

Information-processing research studies what information consumers are looking for, looking at, paying attention to, considering, and using to make decisions. Ultimately, we hope to discover what information led consumers to choose certain brands or products and services.

A number of procedures are available for conducting such research. We can quietly observe consumers, keeping an eye on the information they are acquiring and evaluating; or we could ask them to share with us their information acquisition and processing behavior. All these procedures have, as a group, certain merits and demerits. The merit is that as consumer researchers, we come closer to understanding what goes on inside the mind of the consumer. It tells us what effect certain information has on the final decision. The disadvantage is that it is very time consuming, but it can offer valuable insight on consumer decisions. Overall, the insights we obtain serve as guidance on how to present product information to consumers. Let us discuss two principal procedures briefly, Information boards, and protocols. Note that these methods are really a hybrid of quantitative and qualitative methods – Information boards more quantitative and protocols more qualitative; however in their precision in data recording and/or interpretation, they are akin to quantitative methods.

Information Boards

An **information board** is a table of information with brand names in the rows and attribute names in the columns. Cells contain the information about the extent to which the brand specified in the corresponding row contains the attribute specified in the corresponding column. Initially, all the cell entries are covered; the consumer participating in the research study is asked to make a brand decision by uncovering the cells in whatever order he or she desires, and as many or as few cells as he or she feels necessary to come to a decision. Some brand names may be hypothetical (often designated by letters of the alphabet (e.g., brand K), or one of the brands may be the sponsor's brand. As the consumer uncovers the cells, the sequence of this uncovering is recorded.

Later, the researcher analyzes consumers' sequence of "information acquisition." Based on the sequence, the researcher draws inferences about the evaluative criteria consumers use in appraising alternative brands and the comparison process they employ in making their choice.

This kind of research helps a marketer understand which product features are important to consumers, and which features should be emphasized in marketing communications. It is possible, for example, that the very last attribute uncovered on the information board was the one on which the marketer's brand was edged out by a competitor's brand, even though the former was superior on all the preceding attributes. The marketer now has the choice of either improving this last-considered feature in his or her brand, or educate the consumer about his or her brand's considerable superiority on all the features taken as a group.

An information board can be a simple card or wooden board with pegs on the cells for hanging information cards. More often, it is an electronic information board created and displayed on a computer. The research participant simply clicks on the desired cell to reveal the information. The computer automatically records the sequence of uncovering the information cells.

Protocols

Information boards indicate to the consumer researcher only what information the consumer "acquired," not what information was "processed," much less how it was processed. For example, after uncovering a cell in the information board study, the consumer may simply decide to discard that information from further consideration, but the researcher has no way of knowing this.

The "protocol" method, in contrast, allows a peep into the consumer's mental processing. In the **protocol**

C . F . Y . I .　　**SEARCH MONITOR**

One menu-driven microcomputer-based program for information search experiments is called Search Monitor. Devised by consumer researcher Marrie Brucks (marketing professor at University of Arizona), Search Monitor enables the consumer to obtain information on various alternatives by offering a battery of such questions as:

Q. What type of . . does brand . . have?
Q. What price is brand . . in store . . ?
Q. Does brand . . have a . . ?

The consumer chooses a question from the list and fills in the blanks with the desired brand, store, and feature name. Then the answer appears on the screen. In some applications, the researcher can build in delays in response times in order to make the respondent realize that information search will consume time just as it does in the real world. The program permits the researcher to design the question menu, key in the answers according to the product and brands being studied, and vary the waiting times before the answer will appear on the screen.

Read more: Merrie Brucks, "Search Monitor: An Approach for Computer-Controlled Experiments Involving Consumer Information Search," J. of Consumer Research 15 (June 1988), 117-21.

method, the consumer is asked to speak his or her thoughts out loud. For example, a consumer making a selection in a supermarket aisle would be asked to say what information he or she is looking at, thinking of, deciding about. The researcher who is accompanying the consumer and recording the respondent's spoken thoughts would periodically prompt the respondent with questions like "Now what are you thinking?"; "Why did you just look at that?"; "Why did you put that brand down?"; or "Why did you finally select that?" These consumer thoughts, spoken aloud and recorded, are called protocols. The protocols are later analyzed to gain insight into consumers' decision-making process.

There are two types of protocols: concurrent and retrospective. **Concurrent protocols** are the consumer thoughts recorded at the time of decision making, such as in the supermarket aisle when the consumer is actually making a brand selection. Concurrent protocols can also be combined with data from information boards so that we gain information on both consumers' information acquisition and processing.

Retrospective protocols are consumers' reports on the decision process for a decision they made in the recent past. For example, a researcher might contact recent car buyers and ask them to describe the process of information search and alternative evaluation they went through in making their car purchase. The researcher would begin by asking such questions as "When did you begin thinking of buying a car?"; "What cars did you consider in the very beginning?"; "Then what did you consider about these cars, and how did you narrow down the field?" In effect, the consumer is remembering and "reconstructing" the decision process. Obviously, the less time elapsed since the decision was made, and/or the more significant the decision, the more accurate would be the protocols.

An obvious criticism of concurrent protocols is that they might interfere with the actual information processing; that is, if the consumer didn't have to verbalize his or her thoughts, his or her information processing may have been different. Researchers have found, however, that after a few initial minutes of performing the required "speak out" task, respondents return to their normal way of making shopping decisions.

MECHANICAL MEASURES

The research methods we have discussed in this chapter so far all use verbal responses—the answers consumers tell us. And this is true whether they tell us using quantitative scales or free-flowing prose. However, many of the responses actually also occur in the physical body – in the eyes, on the skin, and in the brain—they occur as physical activity (change in temperature, pressure, or electric current, etc.) Mechanical measures are intended to measure these bodily responses to marketing stimuli. These are briefly discussed below.

One device to capture consumers' information processing is an eye camera. The camera records the pupil movement as the consumer looks through a piece of information. This method can be used to study consumer's information acquisition while reading or viewing an advertisement, looking at aisle displays and examining package information on products in a supermarket, or participating in an experiment such as an information board.

The researcher uses data gathered by the eye camera to identify the information at which the consumer gazed longest. Such data help the researcher pinpoint the selective appeal and use of information by the consumer.

GSR

Galvanic skin response (GSR) measures the amount of skin resistance to electric current between two electrodes. When a consumer reacts to any stimuli, her or his sweat glands are activated; this, in turn, reduces the skin resistance. Thus, GSR activity indicates consumer response to a stimulus, such as an item of information (e.g., price) or an emotional storyline in an advertisement.

Brain Activity

When consumers process any information or react to any marketing stimulus, electric impulses are generated in the brain. These impulses can be measured by sensors attached to the skull, which generate electroencephalographic (EEG) measures.

One of the brain activities measured in this way is called alpha activity. Alpha activity inversely measures the degree of the brain's attentiveness. When we are sleeping, resting, or otherwise inactive, the alpha activity is high; when we are paying attention to a commercial, the alpha activity is low. During the viewing of different ads, viewers' alpha activity levels would vary, and accordingly they will serve as indicators of the ad's ability to attract and hold viewer attention.

Measuring Involvement

We conclude this note with a scale of involvement (see Table A-1, next page)

SUMMARY

Methods of researching consumer behavior are either qualitative or quantitative. Qualitative methods include focus groups, directed interview, motivation research, observation (Simple and Participant), and interpretative research. Quantitative methods entail surveys or experiments. Surveys find out what consumers think, know, or feel already. Experiments, in contrast, present some new stimuli and seek consumer reactions to these stimuli. Some major topics researched by quantitative methods are consumer attitudes, image or self-concept measurement.

Although these methods differ in their technique as well as goals, the common purpose is to help marketers understand the consumer—to get inside consumers' minds, to know what concerns them, what they like and dislike, how they perceive various marketing stimuli, how they respond to them, and why they respond that way.

TABLE A-1

MEASURES OF CONSUMER INVOLVEMENT

Consumer involvement is, perhaps, one of the most important concepts in consumer behavior. It influences every thing. consumer does or does not do (See Chapter 11, and 12). Therefore, we provide selected ways of measuring this concept.

ENDURING INVOLVEMENT

Strongly disagree   Strongly Agree
    1   2   3   4   5

- Cars offer me relaxation and fun.
- Driving my car is one of the most enjoyable and satisfying things I do.
- I enjoy discussing cars with friends.
- I get bored when other people talk about cars.*
- Sometimes I get too wrapped up in my car.
- I don't pay much attention to car advertisements.
- Cars are nothing more than appliances.
- I generally feel sentimental attachment to the cars I own.
- I use this product to define and express the "I" and "Me" in myself.
- When I am with friends, I often end up talking about cars.

(Adapted from: Peter Bloch, "Involvement with a Product Class," *Advances in Consumer Research* 8, 61-65.)

INVOLVEMENT AS IMPORTANCE OF A PRODUCT

To me, this product (nmae the product) is:

Unimportant	1 2 3 4 5	Important
Insignificant	1 2 3 4 5	Significant
Not relevant	1 2 3 4 5	Relevant
Unexciting	1 2 3 4 5	Exciting
Uninteresting	1 2 3 4 5	Fascinating
Means nothing to me	1 2 3 4 5	Means a lot to me

(Based on Zaichkowski, J. Measuring the Involvement Construct," *J. of Consumer Research*, Dec. 1985, 12, 341-352.

INVOLVEMENT IN YOUR PARTICULAR SPECIFIC BRAND/PRODUCT POSSESSION

Strongly disagree 1 2 3 4 5 Strongly agree

1. I feel emotionally attached to my ___.
2. My ___ holds a special place in my life.
3. My ___ is central to my identity—my sense of who I am.
4. If I lose my ___, I would feel as if a part of me was missing.
5. I take good care of my ___.
6. I trust my ___.

(In part adapted from Kimberly J. Dodson, "Peak Experiences and Mountain biking: Incorporating the Bikes in the Extended Self," *Advances in Consumer Research*, 1996.)

PURCHASE DECISION INVOLVEMENT

1. In selecting __, I would not care at all (1)/I would care a great deal (7), as to which one I buy.
   Would not care at all   Care a great deal
        1 2 3 4 5 6 7
2. In making your selection of this product, would you be not at all concerned (1) or very concerned (7) about the outcome of your choice?
   Not at all concerned   Very concerned
        1 2 3 4 5 6 7
3. How important would it be for you to make the right choice of this product?
   Not at all important   Very important
        1 2 3 4 5 6 7

(Based on Banwari Mittal, "Measuring Purchase Decision Involvement," *Psy. & Marketing*, 6, 147-162, 1989.)

CHAPTER 1

1 This and all similar quotes are, unless otherwise specified, from author's research files. Some consumer statements are slightly modified for economy of space, but the original sentiment is preserved. Where only first names are given, names are disguised.

2 Banwari Mittal and Jagdish N. Sheth, ValueSpace: Winning the Battle for Market Leadership," New York, NY: McGraw-Hill, 2001.

3 For further reading see, Jillian C. Sweeney and Geoffrey N. Soutar, "Consumer Perceived Value: The Development of a Multiple Item Scale," *Journal of Retailing*, 77, 2001, 203-220; Barry J. Babin, William R. Darden, and Mitch Griffin, "Work and/or Fun: Measuring Hedonic and Utilitarian Shopping Value," *Journal of Consumer Research*, 1994, 20 (March), 644-656; Rajeev Batra and Olli T. Ahtola, "Measuring the Hedonic and Utilitarian Sources of Consumer Attitude," *Marketing Letters*, 2(2), 159-170;

4 Source: http://inventors.about.com/library/inventors/blansweringmachines.htm

5 Source: www.testmark.com/develop/tml_callerid_cnt.html

6 Charming Shoppes Corporate Web site.

7 Ibid.

8 Lane Bryant Announces American Idol Finalist, Kimberley Locke, as New Spokeswoman for Designer Jeans Collection, Company Press release June 29, 2005.

9 Theodore Levitt, Marketing Myopia, *Harvard Business Review*, July-August 1960.

10 Peter F. Drucker, *Management: Tasks, Responsibilities Practices* (New York: Harper & Row, 1973).

11 These definitions are adapted from various sources: http://www.asanet.org/public/what.html http://encarta.msn.com/encnet/features/dictionary/DictionaryResults.aspx?search=anthropology Encarta® World English Dictionary [North American Edition] © & (P)2003 Microsoft Corporation. All rights reserved. Developed for Microsoft by Bloomsbury Publishing PLC.

12 See, story on the Website of Advertising Educational Foundation, posted March 29, 2004: http://www.aef.com/06/news/data/2004/2539

13 A brand of diet aid.

CHAPTER 2

1. Penned by author based on a report on ABCNews.com, "Looking like a celebrity: Plastic Surgery at the Frontlines of Glamour,: April 10, 2002; http://abcnews.go.com/Health/print?id=132633 (DoA: October 16, 2005).

2. Ibid. Name (Julie L.) disguised in the current narrative.

3. For a foundational discussion of motivation, see John W. Atkinson, *An Introduction to Motivation* (New York, NY: D. Van Nostrand Company, 1964); Edward J. Murray, *Motivation and Emotion* (Englewood Cliffs, NJ: Prentice Hall, 1964).

4. For an illuminating review of various needs, see Janice Hanna, "A Typology of Consumer Needs," *Research in Marketing* 3, J. N. Sheth, ed. (Greenwich, CT: JAI Press, 1980), 83-104.

5. Abraham H. Maslow, "A Theory of Human Motivation," *Psychological Review* 50 (July 1943), 370-96; also, Abraham H. Maslow, *Motivation and Personality* (New York: Harper & Row, 1970).

6. Maslow, *Motivation and Personality*, 1987, 3rd ed., HarperCollins, p. 22.

7. I owe this example to Jagdish N. Sheth, personal communication.

8. No, these are not self-referencing examples.

9. D. MacInnis, C. Moorman, and B. Jaworski, "Enhancing and Measuring Consumers' Motivation, Opportunity, and Ability to Process Brand Information from Brands," *J. of Marketing*, Oct. 1991, 32-53.

10. For an application to consumer Internet Behavior, see Zheng Zhou, Yeqing Bao, "Users' Attitude toward Web Advertising: Effects of Internet Motivation and Internet Ability," *Advances in Cons. Res.*, 29, (2002), 71- 78.

11. For one recent academic study, see J. A. Ruth, "Promoting a Brand's

Emotional Benefits," *J. of Cons. Psych.*, 11, 2, 2001, 99-113.

12. As for motivation, so too for emotions; our treatment is necessarily oversimplified due to space limitations. For fuller discussion, see P. T. Young, *Motivation and Emotion* (New York: John Wiley and Sons, 1961); E. J. Murray, *Motivation and Emotion* (Englewood Cliffs, NJ: Prentice Hall, 1964); and George Mandler, *Mind and Body* (New York: Norton, 1984); C. E. Izard, *Human Emotions* (New York: Platinum, 1977), and for a marketing application, see R.R. Bagozzi, M. Gopinath, P. U. Nyer, "The role of emotions in marketing," *J. of the Acad. of Marketing Science*, 1999, 27(2), 184-206.

13. See Robert Plutchik, "A Language for the Emotions," *Psychology Today*, 1980, 13(9), 68-78; R. Plutchik, "Emotions: A General Psychoevolutionary Theory," in K.R. Scherer & P. Ekman (Eds.), *Approaches to Emotion*, Hillsdale, NJ: Erlbaum.

14. See Marsha L. Richins "Measuring Emotions in the Consumption Experience," *J. of Cons. Res.*, 1997, 24 (Sept.),127-146.

15. Based on Morris B Holbrook and Maryl P. Gardner, "Illustrating a Dynamic Model of the Mood-Updating Process in Consumer Behavior," *Psychology & Marketing*, Mar2000, 17(3), 165-194; also see, Gordon C. Bruner, "Music, mood and marketing," *J. of Marketing*, 1990, 54(4), 94-104.

16. For further reading, see J. Russell, "A Circumplex Model of Affect," J. of Personality and Social Psychology, 1980, 39, 1161-1178; and Morris B. Holbrook and Meryl P. Gardner, "Illustrating a Dynamic Model of Mood Updating Process in Consumer Behavior," *Psychology and Marketing*, March 2000, 17(3), 165-194. Also see, Rajeev Batra and Douglas M. Stayman, "The Role of Mood in Advertising Effectiveness," *J. of Cons. Res.* 17,2 (Sept. 1990), 203-14.

17. For a classic review of Mood effects in marketing, see Merryl P. Gardner, "Mood State and Consumer Behavior: A Critical Review," J. of Cons. Res., 1985, 12, 281-300; Harri T.Luomala and Martti Laaksonen, "Contributions from mood research," *Psychology and Marketing*, 2000, 17 (3), 195-233; J. B. Cohen and C. S. Areni "Affect and consumer behavior," *Handbook of consumer behavior*, 1991, 188-240; R. A. Westbrook and R. L. Oliver, "The dimensionality of consumption emotion patterns and consumer satisfaction," *J. of Cons. Res.*, 1997, 18, June, 84-91.

18. For some research on the effects of negative moods, see Sarah Maxwell and Arthur Kover, "Negative Affect: The Dark Side of Retailing," *J. of Bus. Res.*, 56(7), 2003, 553-559; Barry J. Babin and William R. Darden, "Good and Bad Shopping Vibes: Spending and Patronage Satisfaction," *J. of Bus. Res.*, 1996, 35, 201-6.

19. See, Morris Holbrook and Elizabeth Hirschman, "The Experiential Aspects of Consumption: Consumer Fantasies, Feelings, and Fun," *J. of Cons. Res.* 9 (Sept. 1982), 132-40; Elizabeth Hirschman and Morris Holbrook, "Hedonic Consumption: Emerging Concepts, Methods, and Prepositions," *J. of Marketing* 46 (Summer 1982), 92-101.

20. For academic research on hedonic motives, see Meera P. Venkatraman and Deborah J. MacInnis, "The Epistemic and Sensory Exploratory Behaviors of Hedonic and Cognitive Consumers," in *Advances in Cons. Res.* 12, E. C. Hirschman and M. B. Holbrook, eds. 1988,102-7.

21. Russell Belk, Güliz Ger, and Søren Askegaard, "The Fire of Desire: A Multisited Inquiry into Consumer Passion," *J. of Cons. Res.*, 2003, December, 30, 328-51; also, Russell Belk, Güliz Ger, and Søren Askegaard, "Consumer Desire in Three Cultures: Results from Projective Research," *Advances in Cons. Res.*, 24, 1997, 24-28.

22. Quote borrowed from Belk, Ger, and Askegaard, 1997 (Ibid), p. 26.

23. There is a rich body of academic research literature on the topic of involvement, including: Peter Bloch, "Involvement beyond the purchase process: conceptual issues and empirical investigation," *Advances in Cons. Research*, 1982 Vol. 9, 413-417; Marsha L. Richins, Peter H. Bloch, Edward F. McQuarrie, "How Enduring and Situational Involvement Combine to Create Involvement Response," *J. of Cons. Psych.*, 1992, 1,143-153; Y. Evrard and P. Aurier, "Identification and validation of the components of the

person-object relationship," *J. of Bus. Res.*, 1996, 37, 127-134; J.L. Zaichkowsky, "Measuring the Involvement Construct," *J. of Cons. Res.*, 1985, 12, 341-352; J.N. Kapferer and G. Laurent, "Consumer Involvement Profile: A New Practical Approach to Consumer Involvement," *J. of Advertising Research*; 1986, 25(5), 48-59. Mark B. Traylor, "Product Involvement and Brand Commitment," *J. of Advertising Research*; 1981, 21, 51-56; B. Mittal and M.S. Lee, "A causal model of consumer involvement," *J. of Economic Psychology*, 1989, 10, 363-389; J. C. Andrews, S.S. Durvasula, and S. H. Akhter, "A framework for conceptualizing and measuring the involvement construct in advertising research," *J. of Advertising*, 1990, 19, 27-31.

24. Wayne Weiten, *Psychology: Themes and Variations* (Belmont, CA: Wadsworth, 1989), 596.

25. See, Harold H. Kelley, "Attribution Theory in Social Psychology," *Nebraska Symposium on Motivation,* 15 (1967), 191-241; Harold H. Kelley, "The Process of Causal Attribution," *American Psychologist* 28 (1973), 107-128, and for Cons. Res. on attribution, see Valarie S. Folks, "Recent Attribution Research in Consumer Behavior: A Review and New Directions," *J. of Consumer Research.*, 1988, 14,548-565; W. Sue and M.J. Tippins, "Consumer Attributions of Product Failure to Channel Members and Self: The Impact of Situational Cues," in T.K. Srull (ed.), Advances in Cons. Res., 25, 139-145, Provo, UT: Association for Cons. Res.; B. Weiner, "Attributional Thoughts about Consumer Behavior," *J. of Cons. Res.*, 2000, 27, 382-387. Also see, D. Forlani and Orville C. Walker, Jr., "Valenced Attributions and Risk in New Product Decisions: How Why Indicates What's Next," Psychology & Marketing, 2003, 20(5), 395-432. R. D. Mizerski, L.L. Golden, and J.B. Kernan, "The Attribution Process in Consumer Decision Making," *J. of Cons. Res.*, 1979, 6, 123-140.

CHAPTER 3

1 Bond traders: Ross Diamond on how product placement thrives in the world of 007. (Advertising). New Statesman, Nov 25, 2002, by Ross Diamond

2 Paul D. Bolls, Darrel D. Muehling and Kak Yoon, "The effects of television commercial pacing on viewers' attention and memory," *J. of Marketing Communications*, Mar2003, 9(1),17-28.

3 See Rik Pieters and Michel Wedel, "AttentionCapture and Transfer in Advertising : Brand, Pictorial, and Text size effects," *J. of Marketing*, 2004, 68, 36-50.

4 See Stuart Henderson Britt, "How Weber's Law Can Be Allied to Marketing," Business Horizons, February 1975, 21-29.

5 Stuart Rogers, "How a Publicity Blitz Created The Myth of Subliminal Advertising," Public Rel. Quarterly, Winter92/93, 37(4), 12-17.

6 See J. A. Bargh, M. Chen, and L. Burrows, "Automaticity and Social Behavior: Direct Effects of Trait Construct and Stereotype Activation," *J. of Personality & Social Psychology,* 1996, 71, 230-44.

7 See for a review of these psychological processes, J.A. Bargh, S. Chaiken, P. Raymond, and C. Hymes (1996), "The Generality of Automatic Attitude Activation Effect," *Journal of Personality and Social Psychology*, 62, 893-912.

8 For further reading, see Timothy E. Moore, "Subliminal Advertising: What You See IS What You Get," *J. of Marketing*, 46, 1982, 38-47.

9 For academic research on 'mere exposure', see William E. Baker "When Can Affective Conditioning and Mere Exposure Directly Influence Brand Choice," *J. of Advertising*, 1999, 28, 21-46; and Chris Janiszewski, "Preattentive Mere Exposure Effects," *J. of Consumer Research*, 1993, 20, 376-393.

10 Koffka, K. (1935). Principles of Gestalt Psychology. New York: Harcourt, Brace & World.

11 For a recent consumer research study on closure, see David C. Houghton and Rajdeep Grewal, "Please, Let's Get An Answer – Any Answer: Need for Consumer Cognitive Closure," Psychology & Marketing, Nov. 2000, 17, 11, 911-934.

12 See Abhijit Biswas and Edward A. Blair, "Contextual Effects of Reference Prices in Retail Advertising," *J. of Marketing,* 55 (July 1991), 1-12; Robert Jacobson and Carl Obermiller, "The Formation of Reference Price," Advances in Consumer Research 16 (1989), 234-40; Joel E. Urbany, William O. Bearden, and Dan C. Weilbaker, "The Effects of Plausible and Exaggerated Reference prices on

Consumer Perceptions and Price Search," *J. of Consumer Research*, 15 (June 1988), 95-110.

13 For studies on how consumers use price itself as a surrogate indicator of product quality, see, See Valarie A. Zeithaml, "Consumer Perceptions of Price, Quality, and Value: A Means-End Model and Synthesis of Evidence," *J. of Marketing* 52 (July 1988): 2-22. Also see Steven M. Shugan, "Price Quality Relationships," in Thomas C. Kinnear, ed., Adv. in Cons Res 11 (Association for Consumer Research, 1983), 627-32; and C. Obermiller and John J. Wheatley, "Price Effects on Choice and Perceptions under Varying Conditions of Experience, Information, and Beliefs in Quality Differences," in Thomas C. Kinnear, ed., Adv. in Cons Res 11 (Association for Consumer Research 1983), 453-58.

14 For a recent summary of research findings on this topic, see, Narasimhan Srinivasan and Subhash C. Jain, (2003) "Country of Origin Effect: Synthesis and Future Direction," (book chapter), Handbook of Research in International Marketing, (ed.) Subhash C. Jain , Edward Elgar, MA, 458-476. Some of the notable research studies on this topic are Jyh-shen Chiou, "The Impact of Country of Origin on Pretrial and Posttrial Product Evaluations: The Moderating Effect of Consumer Expertise," Psychology & Marketing, 2003, 20, 10, 935-954; W. Li and R. S. Wyer, Jr. "The Role of Country of Origin in Product Evaluations: Informational and Standard-of-Comparison Effects," *J. of Consumer Psychology* 3, no. 2 (1994), 187-212; Sung-Tai Hong and R. S. Wyer, Jr., "Effects of Country of Origin and Product-Attribute Information on Product Evaluation: An Information Processing Perspective," *J. of Cons. Research*, 16, 2 (September 1989), 175-87; Chih-Kang Wang and Charles W. Lamb, Jr., "Foreign Environmental Factors Influencing American Consumers' Predispositions Toward European Products," *J. of the Academy of Marketing Science* 8 (Fall 1980), 345-56; D. Tse and G. J. Gorn, "An Experiment on the Salience of Country-of-Origin in the Era of Global Brands," International Marketing Review 9 (1992), . 57-76. W. K. Li, K. B. Monroe, and D. Chan, "The Effects of Country of Origin, Brand, and Price Information: A Cognitive-Affective Model of Buying Intentions," Adv. in Consumer Research 21 (1994), 449-57. J. K. Johansson, "Determinants and Effects of the Use of "Made in Labels," International Marketing Review 6 (1989), 47-58. Murray A. Young, Paul L. Sauer, and H. Rao Unnava, "Country-of-Origin Issues," in S. H. Hassan and R. D. Blackwell, Global Marketing: Perspectives and Cases (Fort Worth, TX: Dryden Press, 1994), 196-210; Sevgin A. Eroglu and Karen A. Machleit, "Effects of Individual and Product-Specific Variables on Utilizing Country-of-Origin as a Product Quality Cue," International Marketing Review, 6, 1998, 27-41; G. Erickson, J. K. Johansson, and P. Chao, "Image Variables in Multiattribute Product Evaluations: Country-of-Origin Effects," *J. of Consumer Research* 11, 1984, 694-99. C. M. Han, "Country Image: Halo or Summary Construct," *J. of Marketing Research* 16, 1989, 222-29; S. Lohr, "Made in Japan or Not: That Is the Question," New York Times 3, no. 1 (April, 1988), cited in L. D. Dahringer and H. Muhlbacher, International Marketing: A Global Perspective (Reading, MA: Addison-Wesley, 1991), p. 354; Giana M. Eckhardt, "Local Branding in a Foreign Product Category in an Emerging Market," *J. of International Marketing*, 2005,13(4), 57-79.

15 For research on the role of odors in retailing, see Jean-Charles Chebat and Richard Michon, "Impact of Ambient Odors on Mall Shoppers' Emotions Cognitions, and Spending: A Test of Competitive Causal Theories," *J. of Business Research*, July 2003, 56(7), 529-540.

16 Barry J. Babin, David M. Hardesty, and Tracy A. Suter, "Color and Shopping Intentions: The Intervening Effect of Price Fairness and Perceived Affect," *J. of Business Research*, July 2003, 56(7), 541-552.

CHAPTER 4

1 Reported in http://www.usatoday.com/tech techreviews/2001/12/31/devil-design-examples.htm

2 RadioShack doesn't sell it anymore; actually, the device is discontinued.

3 For a fuller description of the Pavlov experiments, see Leland C. Swenson, Theories of Learning: Traditional Perspectives/Contemporary Developments (Belmont, CA: Wadsworth Publishing Company, 1980), pp. 13-30.

4   For academic research on classical conditioning, see, See Gerald Gorn, "The Effects of Music in Advertising on Choice Behavior: A Classical Conditioning Approach," Journal of Marketing (Winter 1982), pp. 94-101; Ronald E. Milliman, "Using Background Music to Affect Behavior of Supermarket Shoppers," *Journal of Marketing* (Summer 1982), pp. 86-91; Richard A. Feinberg, "Credit Cards as Spending Facilitating Stimuli: A Conditioning Interpretation," *Journal of Consumer Research* (December 1986), pp. 348-56.

5   A foundational discussion of modeling can be found in Neal E. Miller and John Dollard, Social Learning and Imitation (New Haven, CT: Yale University Press, 1941).

6   For recent research on this topic see, S.A. Hawkins, S. Hoch, and Myers-Levy, "Low Involvement Learning," *Journal of Consumer Psychology*, 11, 31, 2001, 1-11.

7   George A. Miller, "The Magic Number Seven, Plus or Minus Two: Some Limits on Our Capacity for Processing Information," Psychological review 63 (March 1956), pp. 81-97.

8   For research on effects of repetition on memory, see Douglas M. Stayman and Rajeev Batra, "Encoding and Retrieval of Ad Affect in Memory," J. of Mark Research, 1991, 28, 232-240; H. R. Unnava and Robert E. Burnkrant, "Effects of Repeating Varied Ad Executions on Brand Name Memory," J. of Mark Res, 1991, 28, 406-417.

9   For consumer research based on this concept, see William E. Baker , Does Brand Name Imprinting in Memory Increase Brand Information Retention?, *Psych & Mark*, 2003, 20 (12), 1119-1135.

10 One of the recall cues can be brand names suggestiveness; see, Kevin L. Keller, Susan E. Heckler,and Michale Houston, "The effects of Brand Name Suggestiveness on Advertising Recall," *Journal of Marketing*, 1998, 62, 48-57; and S. Holden and M. Vanheule, "Know the Name, Forget the Exposure: Brand Familiarity versus Memory of Exposure Context," *Psychology & Marketing*, 1999, 16, 479-496.

11 . For original exposition of this theory, see, R. Anderson, "A Spreading Activation Theory of Memory," *Journal of Verbal Learning and Verbal Behavior*, 1983, 22, 261-295.

12 For further reading see E. Hirschman and M. Wallendorf, "Some Implications of Variety Seeking for Advertising and Advertisers," *Journal of Advertising* 9, (1980), pp. 17-25; W. D. Hoyer and N .M. Ridgway, "Variety Seeking as an Explanation for Exploratory Purchase Behavior: A Theoretical Model," Advances in Consumer Research 11 (1984), pp. 114-99; L. McAlister and E. A. Pessemier, "Variety-Seeking Behavior: An Interdisciplinary Review, *Journal of Consumer Research* 9 (December 1982), pp. 311-22.

13 For foundational treatment of this topic, see E. M. Rogers, "New Product Adoption and Diffusion," in R. Ferber, ed., Selected Aspects of Consumer Behavior, NSF Government Printing Office, 1977, pp. 223-38, Everett M. Rogers, *Diffusion of Innovations*, 3rd ed. (New York: Free Press, 1983), p. 281-84. Also see P. Ellen, W O. Bearden, and S. Sharma, "Resistance to Technological Innovations: An Examination of the Role of Self-Efficacy and performance Satisfaction," *J. of the Academy of Marketing Science* 19, no. 4, (Fall 1991), pp. 297-307; S. Ram and Jagdish N. Sheth, "Hurdling the Barriers to Technological Innovation," *R&D Strategist*, 1990, 4-14.

14 For a classic treatment of nostalgia, see F. Davis, Yearning for Yesterday: A Sociology of Nostalgia, New York, The Free Press.

15 Based on author's reflections.

16 For recent studies on consumer nostalgia, see Robert M. Schindler and Morris H. Holbrook, "Nostalgia for Early Experiences as a Determinant of Consumer Preferences," *Psychology & Marketing*, 2003, 20, 4, 275-302.

17 Stauth, Georg, and Bryan S. Turner. "Nostalgia, Postmodernism and the Critique of Mass Culture." Theory, Culture and Society 5.2-3 (1988): 509-26.

18 Personal interview as reported in ValueSpace—Winning the Battle for Market Leadership, Banwari Mittal and Jagdish N. Sheth, McGraw Hill, 2001, p. 202.

19 For a scholarly study, see S. Brown, R.V. Kozinets, and J.F. Sherry, Jr. "Teaching Old Brands New Tricks: Retro Branding And The Revival Of Brand Meaning," *J. of Marketing*, 2003, 67, 19-33.

20 Lesley Speed, Together in Electric Dreams: Films Revisiting 1980s Youth. *Journal of Popular Film and Television*, Spring, 2000.

CHAPTER 5

1. See Milton Rokeach, *The Nature of Human Values* (New York: Free Press, 1973); David E. Vinson, Jerome E. Scott, and Lawrence Lamont, "The Role of Personal Values in Marketing and Consumer Behavior," *J. of Marketing* 41 (April 1977), 44–50.

2. The list is protected as intellectual property by Consulting Psychology Press. The examples given here are based on intuition and are merely to serve as illustrations that logically exemplify the two types of values, without implying whether these items in fact belong in the Rokeach list. Interested readers can find a list in Rokeach, ibid; moreover, a simple Google search will bring up hundreds of Web pages listing the values in their entirety, as it did at least as of May 1, 2006.

3. The nine LOV values were developed by the Survey Research Center at the University of Michigan, as reported in Lynn Kahle R. (ed.), *Social Values and Social Change: Adaptation to Life in America*, New York, Praeger, 1983. An exposition of these values for marketing can be found in subsequent research studies: Lynn R. Kahle, Sharon E. Beatty, and Pamela Homer, "Alternative Measurement Approaches to Consumer Values: The List of Values (LOV) and Values and Life Style (VALS)," *J. of Consumer Research* 13 (December 1986), pp. 405–409; Sharon Beatty, Lynn R. Kahle, Pamela Homer, and Shekhar Misra, "Alternative Measurement Approaches to Consumer Values: The List of Values and the Rokeach Value Survey," *Psychology & Marketing* 2 (Fall 1985), 181–200.

4. Kahle, Beatty, and Homer, 1986, Ibid.

5. For further reading, see "Value-System Segmentation: Exploring the Meaning of LOV," *Kamakura*, Wagner A. and Novak, Thomas P.. *J. of Consumer Research*, Jun 92, 19(1), 119-132.

6. Rajeev Batra, Pamela M. Homer, and Lynn R. Kahle, "Values, Susceptibility to Normative Influence, and Attribute Importance Weights," *J. of Consumer Psychology*, 2001, 11(2), 115-128.

7. Irene Tilikidou and Antonia Delistavrou,, "Utilisation of Selected Demographics and Psychographics in Understanding Recycling Behaviour," Greener Management International, Summer2001, 34, 75-94.

8. Thomas J Reynolds and Jonathan Gardner, Laddering Theory, Method, Analysis, and Interpretation," *J. of Advertising Research*, 28 (January–February 1988), pp. 11–31; also see Thomas J. Reynolds and Alyce Byrd Craddock, "The Application of the MECCAs Model to the Development and Assessment of Advertising Strategy: A Case Study," *J. of Advertising Research* (April/May 1988), pp. 43–54. And for some recent suggestions in research method, see Arch G. Woodside, "Advancing Means-End Chains by Incorporating Heider's Balance Theory and Fournier's Consumer Brand Relationship Typology," *Psychology & Marketing*, Vol. 21, #4, April 2004, 279-294. Also see Gillian Sullivan Mort and Trista Rose, "The effect of product type on value linkages in the means-end chain: Implications for theory and method," *J. of Consumer Behaviour*, Mar2004, Vol. 3 Issue 3, 221-35; and Simon Manyiwa and Ian Crawford, "Determining linkages between consumer choices in a social context and the consumer's values: A means--end approach, " *J. of Consumer Behaviour*, Sep2002, 2(1), 54-71.

9. For research on compulsivity as a personality influence, see George Balabanis , "The relationship between lottery ticket and scratch-card buying behaviour, personality and other compulsive behaviours," *J. of Consumer Behaviour*, Sep2002, 2(1), 7-23.

10. Actually, there are other important theories: among them Humanistic Theories – which view a person's development as a function of his or her view of the world learning from environment as well as pursuit of self-actualization goals, and Social Cognition Theories which see a person's personality as a result of a person's cognition of our own beliefs, values, abilities and of environmental constraints and factors (such as oppression and our value system that makes us view that oppression as unjust can develop us into a rebel and freedom fighter personality.). These theories are not covered here, although many ideas related to them would be covered elsewhere—for example, Maslow's hierarchy of motives which has its roots in Humanistic theory, and many personal ability factors such as locus of control, self-efficacy and self-monitoring which have their basis in Social Cognition Theories.

11. See Freud, S. (1923). *The Ego and the Id*. New York: W.W. Norton & Company

12. For a more formal definition and treatment of personality and trait theory, see Ernest Hilgard, Richard Atkinson, and Rita Atkinson, *Introduction to Psychology*, 6th ed. (New York: Harcourt Brace Jovanovich, Inc., 1975); and Walter Mischel, "On the Future of Personality Measurement," *American Psychologist*, 32 (April 1977), p. 2.

13. For other views and further reading on personality, see Paul J. Albanese *The Personality Continuum and Consumer Behavior* (Quorum Books, 2002) and Albanese, "The Personality, Consumer Behavior, and Marketing Research: A New Theoretical and Empirical Approach," *Research in Consumer Behavior*, vol. 4, (1990), pp. 1-50. Add Albanese (1990) on p. 18. Also see, Morris B. Holbrook, "The Psychoanalytic Interpretation of the Consumer Behavior: I Am an Animal," (1988), *Research in Consumer Behavior*, vol. 3, 149-178, and Morris B. Holbrook, Consumer Research: Introspective Essays on the Study of Consumption (Sage, 1995).

14. R.B. Cattell, H.W. Eber, and M.M. Tatsuoka, Handbook for the Sixteen Personality Factor Questionnaire (Champaign, IL: Institute for Personality and Ability Testing, 1970).

15. For a different, equally rigorous view, see John C. Mowen, *The 3-M Model of Motivation and Personality* (Kluwer, 2000). For further reading, see John, O. P. (1990). The "Big Five" factor taxonomy: Dimensions of personality in the natural language and in questionnaires. In L. A. Pervin (Ed.), *Handbook of personality: Theory and research* (pp. 66-100). New York: Guilford; McAdams, D. P. (1992), "The five-factor model in personality: A critical appraisal," *Journal of Personality*, 60, 329-361.

16. This Acronym appears in Rod Plotnik, *Introduction to Psychology*, Sixth edition, Wadsworth, 2002. p.463.

17. Elizabeth C. Hirschman and Barbara B. Stern, "Do Consumer's Genes Influence Their Behavior: Findings on Novelty Seeking and Compulsive Consumption," ACR, XXVIII, Mary C. Gilly and Joan Myers-Levy (eds), 2001, 28, 403-410.

18. J.C. Loehlin, *Genes and Environment in Personality Development*, Newbury Park, CA, Sage, 1992.

19. *Cambridge Advanced Learner's Dictionary* © Cambridge University Press 2003.

20. For a closely related definition, see http://en.wikipedia.org/wiki/Vanity.

21. Richard G. Netemeyer, Scot Burton, and Donald R. Lichtenstein. "Trait Aspects Of Vanity: Measurement and Relevance to Consumer Behavior," *J. of Consumer Research*, 21, March 1995, 612-625.

22. Robert H. Frank, Luxury Fever: Why Money Fails to Satisfy in an Era of Excess, Princeton University Press, 2000.

23. Harold H. Kassarjian, "Personality and Consumer Behavior: A Review," *J. of Marketing Research*, Vol. 8 (November 1971), pp. 409–418. Also see Paul J. Albanese, "The Personality, Consumer Behavior, an Marketing Research: A New Theoretical and Empirical Approach," *Research in Consumer Behavior*, vol. 4, (1990), pp. 1-50.

24. For a state-of-the-art review of self-theory in the context of people's work life, see Robert A. Snyder and Ronald R. Williams, "Self-Theory: An Integrative Theory of Work Motivation," *J. of Occupational Psychology* 55 (1982), pp. 257–67. For more current treatment of this theory, see Paul J. Albanese *The Personality Continuum and Consumer Behavior* (Quorum Books, 2002), 113-114.

25. For discussions of self-concept, see M. Joseph Sirgy, "Self-Concept in Consumer Behavior: A Critical Review," *J. of Consumer Research* (December 1982), pp. 287–300; also, Harold H. Kassarjian, "Personality and Consumer Behavior: A Review," *J. of Marketing Research*, Vol. 8 (November 1971), pp. 409–418. M. Joseph Sirgy, "Using Self-congruity and Ideal Congruity to Predict Purchase Motivation," *J. of Business Research*, Vol. 13 (June 1985), pp. 195–206. Warren S. Martin and Joseph Bellizzi, "An Analysis of Congruence Relationship between Self Images and Product Images," *J. of the Academy of Marketing Science*, December 1982, 473–488.

26. Beyond brand choice, many of our leisure activities also are influenced by self-concept; for recent research on this topic, see Peggy Sue Loroz, "Golden Age Gambling: Psychological Benefits and Self-Concept Dynamics in Aging Consumers' Consumption Experiences,"

Psychology & Marketing, Vol. 21(5), May 2004, 323-349.

27. Adapted from Author's working paper of the same title, 2004.

28. Yi-Fu Tuan, Space and Place:The Perspective of Experience, Minneapolis, MN: University of Minnesota Press (1978)

29. William James, The Principles of Psychology 1, 1890, New York, Henry Holt, Quoted in Russell W. Belk, "Possessions and the Extended Self", *J. of Consumer Research* 15, (1988), pp. 139

30. Russell W. Belk, (1988), pp. 151
    Also see, Susan Schultz Kleine, Robert E. Kleine III, and Chris T. Allen, "How Is a Possession "Me" or "Not Me"? Characterizing Types and an Antecedent of Material Possession Attachment," *J. of Consumer Research*, Vol. 22, December 1995, 327-343.

31. This finding about preferences of leisure travel destinations was validated in a study, Morris B. Holbrook and T. J. Olney, "Romanticism and Wanderlust," *Psychology & Marketing*, May 1995, 207-22.

32. Adapted from Author's working paper of the same title, 2004.

33. Russell W. Belk, "Possessions and the Extended Self", *J. of Consumer Research* 15, (1988), pp. 140

CHAPTER 6

1 Adapted from William D. Wells and Douglas J. Tigert," Activities, Interests, and Opinions," *Journal of Advertising Research* 11 (August 1971), p. 35.

2 Adapted from The Clustered World: How We Live, What We Buy, And What It All Means About Who We Are (Little, Brown And Company) by Michael J. Weiss

3 Adapted from Author's working paper, 2004.

4 "Focus Sponsors Area: One Festival," Ford Motor Company Press Release, April 23, 2001.

5 Hilary Cassidy, "Saucony Laces Up for Lifestyle Effort," *Brandweek*, Feb 5, 2001.

6 Elizabeth Goodgold, "Talking shop: wonder what makes shoppers tick? 5 retail superstars reveal how to please customers and, more important, how to keep them coming back for more." *Entrepreneur*, Sept, 2003.

7 Rebecca Piirto, "Global Psychographics," American Demographics 12, no. 12 (December 1990) p. 8.

8 Russell W. Belk, "Materialism: Trait Aspects of Living in the Material World," *J. of Consumer Research* 12 (December 1985), pp. 265—80.

9 Marsha L. Richins and Scott Dawson, "A Consumer Values Orientation and Its Measurement: Scale Development and Validation," *J. of Consumer Research*, 19, 3 (December 1992), p. 385.

10 For academic research on this topic, see Margaret Craig-Lees and Constance Hill, "Understanding Voluntary Simplifiers," *Psychology & Marketing*, 2002(Feb), 19(2), 187-210; Diedre Shaw and Terry Newholm, "Voluntary Simplicity and the Ethics of Consumption," Psychology & Marketing, 2002(Feb), 19(2), 167-186; and Steven Zavestoski, "The Social-Psychological Bases of Anticonsumption Attitudes," *Psychology & Marketing*, 2002(Feb), 19(2), 149-165.

11 Stephen Zavestoski, "The Social-Psychological Bases of Anti-consumption Attitudes." *Psychology & Marketing*, 2002, 19(2), Feb, 149-169.

12 http://en.wikipedia.org/wiki/Buy_Nothing_Day

13 From BND Japan Web site.

14 From BND Japan Web site.

15 http://www.ddh.nl/pipermail/bnd-list/2002/000078.html

16 Leah Paulos, "Why Men Fear These Women," *Marie Claire*, September 2002, p.188.

CHAPTER 7

1 Gordon W. Allport, "Attitudes," in C.A. Murchinson, ed., *A Handbook of Social Psychology* (Worcester, MA: Clark University Press, 1935), pp. 798-844.

2 See story in Julia Boorstin, "For God's Sake," *Fortune*, November 24, 2003, p. 62.

3 http://www.amazon.com/exec/obidos/ASIN/0718003586/qid=1076246817/sr=2-1/ref=sr_2_1/102-6265492-3163367#product-details

4   For recent research, see Sharon E. Beatty and Lynn R. Kahle, "Alternative Hierarchies of the Attitude-Behavior Relationships: The Impact of Brand Commitment and Habit," *J. of the Academy of Marketing Science*, 1988, 16, 1-10. "The Integrated Information Response Model," Finn, David W.. *J. of Advertising*, 1984, 13(1), 24-33. "Web Commercials and Advertising Hierarchy-of-Effects," Bruner II, Gordon C.; Kumar, Anand. *J. of Advertising Research,* Jan-Apr2000, 40 (1 & 2), 35-43; "Point of View: Does Advertising Cause a "Hierarchy of Effects"?" Weilbacher, William M.. *J. of Advertising Research*, Nov/Dec2001, Vol. 41 Issue 6, p19-26,

5   For research on how the hierarchy works for Web sites, see Gordon Bruner, and Anand Kumar, "Web Commercials and Advertising Hierarchy of Effects," *J. of Advertising Research*, January 2000, 35-43; and J.S. Stevenson, Gordon Bruner, and Anand Kumar, "Web page Background and Viewer Attitudes," *J. of Advertising Research*, January 2000, 29-34.

6   Daniel Katz, "The Functional Approach to the Study of Attitudes," *Public Opinion Quarterly*, 1960, Summer, 24, 163-204. Also see, Sharon Shavitt, "The Role of Attitude Objects in Attitude Functions," *J. of Experimental Social Psychology*, 1990, 26, 124-48. Also see R. Grewal, R. Mehta, and F.R. Kardes, "The Role of Social Identity Function of Attitudes in Consumer Innovativeness and Opinion Leadership, *J. of Economic Psychology*, 21, 2000, 233-52.

7   For further reading, see "Why We Evaluate: Functions of Attitudes," Gregory R. Maio and James M. Olson (eds.), Lawrence Erlbaum Associates (November, 1999).

8   For research studies, see "Attitude functions in consumer research: comparing value-attitude relations individualist and collectivist cultures," Gregory, Gary D.; Munch, James M.; Peterson, Mark. *J. of Business Research*, Nov2002, 55(11), 933-942. "Attitude Functions in Advertising: The Interactive Role of Products and Self-Monitoring," Shavitt, Sharon; Lowrey, Tina M.; Han, Sang-Pil. *J. of Consumer Psychology*, 1992, 1(4), 337-65. "A reconceptualization of the functional approach to attitudes." Lutz, Richard J., Research in Marketing, 1981, 5, 165-70.

9   The acronym TORA existed in prior writings; TOVA and TOTA are proposed by author to help reader "encoding."

10   Martin Fishbein, "An Investigation of the Relationships between Beliefs about an Object and the Attitude toward that Object," *Human Relations*, 1983, 16, 233-40. For some applied research using this theory, see Richard P. Bagozzi, Hans Baumgartner, and Youjae Yu, "Coupon Usage and the Theory of Reasoned Action," in Rebecca Holman and Michael R. Solomon, eds. Advances in Consumer Research, 1991, 18, 24-27; and Terence A. Shimp and Alican Cavas, "The Theory of Reasoned Action Applied to Coupon Usage," *J. of Consumer Research*, 1984, 11, 795-809.

11   For recent research studies using the Fishbein model, see "Consumer attitude toward US versus domestic apparel in Taiwan,"Wang, Yun; Heitmeyer, Jeanne. *International J. of Consumer Studies*, Jan2006, 30(1), 64-74; "Investigating Consumer Responsiveness to Service Contract Attributes: A Choice Experimental Approach," Oppewal, Harmen; Grant, David J.I.. *Advances in Consumer Research*, 2002, 29(1), 133-138. "Modeling Personal and Normative Influences on Behavior," Miniard, Paul W.; Cohen, Joel B., *J. of Consumer Research*, Sep83, 10(2), 169-71. "An Experimental Investigation of Causal Relations Among Cognitions, Affect, and Behavioral Intention," Lutz, Richard J., *J. of Consumer Research*, Mar77, 3(4), 197-209; Kulwant Singh, Siew Meng Leong, Chin Tiong Tan, and Kwei Cheong Wong, "A Theory of reasoned Action Perspective of Voting Behavior: Model and Empirical test," *Psychology & Marketing*, 12, No. 1, January 1995, 37-51.

12   For an application of this idea to personal selling, see Arun Sharma, and Michael Levy, "Salespeople's Affect Toward Customers: Why Should It Be Important for Retailers," *J. of Business Research*, July 2003, 56(7), 523-528.

13   See, D.S. Kempf, "Attitude Formation from Product Trial," *Psychology & Marketing*, January 1999, 35-50; and also Michel Laroche, Frank Pons, Nadia Zgolli, Marie-Cecile Cervellon, and Chankon Kim, "A Model of Consumer response to Two Retail Sales Promotion Techniques," *J. of Business Research*, July 2003, 56(7), 513-522.

14   The theory, more properly called a Theory of Trying is owed to marketing professors Richard P. Bagozzi and Paul R. Warshaw: "Trying to Consume," *J. of Cons. Res.*, 17 (September 1990), 127-40.

15   For recent studies, see "The Theory of Trying and Goal-Directed Behavior: The Effect of Moving Up the Hierarchy of Goals," Bay, Darlene; Daniel, Harold. *Psych. & Marketing*, Aug2003,20(8), 669-684.

CHAPTER 8

1   Source: http://www.spain-info.com/Culture/bullrunning.htm (DoA: December 11, 2005.)

2   Source: http://www.runningofthenudes.com/index.asp   (DoA: December 11, 2005.)

3   Source: http://furisdead.com/feat-jcrewvictory.asp   (DoA: December 12, 2005).

4   For a State-of-the-art review, see Meyers-Levy, Joan and Prashant Malaviya, "Consumers' Processing of Persuasive Advertisements: An Integrative Framework of Persuasion Theories," *J. of Marketing*, 1999, 63, Special Issue, 45-60.

5   Richard Vaughn, "How Advertising Works: A Planning Model," *J. of Advertising Research*, 1980, 20(5), 27-33; Brian T. Ratchford, "New Insights About The FCB Grid," *J. of Advertising Research*, Aug/Sep1987, 27(4), 24-38.

6   This theory was proposed by Richard E. Petty, John T. Cacioppo, and David Schumann, "Central and Peripheral Routes to Advertising Effectiveness: The Moderating Role of Involvement," *J. of Cons. Res.*, 1983, 10, 135-46. Recent research on this topic includes, J. Craig Andrews and Terence A Shimp, "Effects of Involvement, Argument Strength, and Source Characteristics on Central and Peripheral Processing in Advertising," *Psychology and Marketing*, 1990, Fall, 7, 195-214.

7   Also see Peter W. Reed and Michael T. Ewing. "How Advertising Works: Alternative Situational and Attitudinal Explanations," *Marketing Theory*, Mar 2004, 4(1/2), 91-112.

8   Petty, R.E., and Cacioppo, John T. (1986), "The Elaboration Likelihood Model of Persuasion", *Advances in Experimental Social Psychology*, ed. L. Berkowitz, 19, Orlando, FL: Academic Press, 123-205.

9   For recent research, see "Self-Schema Matching and Attitude Change: Situational and Dispositional Determinants of Message Elaboration," Wheeler, S. Christian; Petty, Richard E., Bizer, George Y., *J. of Consumer Res.*, Mar2005, 31(4), 787-797.

10   For a scholarly treatment, see Joel B. Cohen, Joel B. and Americus Reed II (2004), "Multiple Attitudes as Guides to Behavior," Working Paper, Marketing Department, Warrington College of Business, University of Florida, Gainesville, FL.

11   For research on this topic, see Richard J Lutz, "Changing Brand Attitude through Modification of Cognitive Structure," *J. of Consumer Research,* 1975, 1, 49-59.

12   Fritz Heider, "Attitudes and Cognitive Organization," *J. of Psychology,* 21, 1946, 107-12; also, Robert Zajonc "The Concepts of Balance, Congruity, and Dissonance," in *Attitude Change,* P. Suedfeld, ed. Chicago, Ill: Aldine, Atherton, Inc. 1971.

13   See Kelly, H. H. (1973), "The Process of Causal Attribution," *American Psychologist,* 28 (February), 107-28.

14   Settle, Robert B., and Golden, Linda L. (1974), "Attribution Theory and Advertiser Credibility," *J. of Marketing Research,* 11, 181-185; Richard W. Mizerski, Linda L Golden, and Jerome B. Kernan, "The Attribution Process in Consumer Decision Making," *J. of Consumer Research*, Sep1979, 6(2), 23-40.

15   Bem, D. J. (1972) Self-perception theory, In L. Berkowitz (ed), *Advances in Experimental Social Psychology*, (Vol. 6. pp. 1-62), New York: Academic Press.

16   For various academic studies, see Alice M. Tybout, "The Relative Effectiveness of Three Behavioral Influence Strategies as Supplements to Persuasion in a Marketing Context," *J. of Marketing Research,* 1978, 15 (May), 229-42. Freedman, J. L. and S. Frazer (1966), "Compliance Without Pressure: The Foot-in-the-Door Technique," *J. of Personality and Social Psychology,* 4 (October), 195-202. Cialdini, R. B.,J. E. Vincent, S. K. Lewis, J. Catalan, D. Wheeler, and B. L. Darby (1975), "Reciprocal Concessions Procedure for Inducing Compliance: The Door-in-the-Face *Technique," J. of Personality and Social Psychology,*31 (February), 206-15. P. H. Reingen, "On Inducing Compliance With

Requests," *J. of Consumer Research,* 1978, 5 (Sept.), 96-102.

17 See Francis Buttle, "What Do People Do With Advertising?" *International J. of Advertising,* 1991, 10(2), 95-110.

18 See "Effects of Absurdity In Advertising: The Moderating Role of Product Category Attitude and the Mediating Role of Cognitive Responses," Leopoldo Arias-Bolzmann, Goutam Chakraborty, and John C. Mowen, *J. of Advertising,* Spring 2000, 29(1), 35-50; "A cross-cultural comparison of cognitive responses, beliefs, and attitudes toward advertising in general in two Asian countries," Durvasula, Srinivas; Lysonski, Steven, Subhash C. Mehta, *J. of Marketing Management,* Winter 1999, 9(3), 48-59; Amitava Chattopadhyay, Darren W. Dahl, Robin J.B. Ritchie, Kimary N. Shahin, "Hearing Voices: The Impact of Announcer Speech Characteristics on Consumer Response to Broadcast Advertising," *J. of Consumer Psychology,* 2003, 13(3), 198-204; Alice M. Tybout, Brian Sternthal, and Bobby J. Calder, "A two-stage theory of information processing in persuasion: an integrative view of cognitive response and self-perception theory," *Advances in Cons. Res.,* 1978, 5(1), 721-723; Self-Validation of Cognitive Responses to Advertisements, Briñol, Pablo; Petty, Richard E.; Tormala, Zakary L., *J. of Consumer Research.,* 2004, 30(4), 559-573.

19 This insight is owed to a classic paper, Herbert E. Krugman, "The Impact of Television Advertising: Learning without Involvement," *Public Opinion Quarterly,* 1965 Fall, 349-356.

20 For research literature on this topic, see Scott B. Mackenzie and Richard J Lutz, and George E. Belch, "The Role of Attitude toward the Ad as a Mediator of Advertising Effectiveness: A Test of Competing Explanations," *J. of Marketing Res.,* 1986, 23, 130-43; Scot Burton and Donald R. Lichtenstein, "The Effect of Ad Claims and Ad Context on Attitude toward the Advertisement," *J. of Advertising,* 1988, 17, 1, 3-11; and Meryl P. Gardner, "Does Attitude toward the Ad Affect Brand Attitude Under A Brand Evaluation Set?" *J. of Marketing Research.,* 1985, 22, 192-98.

21 Also see Jennifer L. Aaker and P. Williams, "Empathy versus pride: The influence of emotional appeals across cultures," *J. of Cons. Res.,* 1998, 25, 241-261; Karen A. Machleit and R. D. Wilson, "Emotional Feelings And Attitude Toward The Advertisement: The Roles Of Brand Familiarity And Repetition," *J. of Advertising,* 1988, 17(3), 27-35.

22 On public attitudes toward advertising, see Sharon Shavitt, Pamela Lowrey, and James Haefner, "Public Attitudes Toward Advertising: More Favorable Than You Might Think," *J. of Advertising. Research.,* 1998 Issue July, 7-22.

23 For comprehensive understanding, see James Price Dillard and Jason W. Anderson, "The Role of Fear in Persuasion," *Psych. & Marketing,* 2004, 21(11), 909-926; Tony L. Henthorne, Michael S. LaTour, and Rajan Nataraajan, "Fear Appeals in Print Advertising: An Analysis of Arousal, and Ad Response," *J. of Advertising,* 1993 (Summer), 59-69; Omar Shehryar and Hunt, David M Hunt, "A Terror Management Perspective on the Persuasiveness of Fear Appeals," *J. of Consumer Psychology,* 2005, 15(4), 275-287; Damien Arthur and Pascale Quester, "Who's Afraid of That Ad? Applying Segmentation to the Protection Motivation Model," *Psych. & Marketing,* 2004, 21(9), 671-696; Lucy Cochrane and P. Quester, "Fear in Advertising: The Influence of Consumers' Product Involvement and Culture," *J. of International Consumer Marketing,* 2005, Vol. 17 Issue 2/3, p7-32; John C. Mowen and Eric G. Harris and Sterling A. Bone, "Personality Traits and Fear Response to Print Advertisements: Theory and an Empirical Study," *Psychology & Marketing,* 2004, 21 (11) 927-943.

24 For research studies, see Stephen M. Smith and Curtis P Haugtvedt "Understanding Responses to Sex Appeals in Advertising: An Individual Difference Approach," *Advances in Cons. Res.,* 1995, 22 (1), 735-739; Michael S. LaTour and Tony L. Henthorne, "Ethical Judgments of Sexual Appeals in Print Advertising," *J. of Advertising,* 1994 (Fall) 81-90; Stephen J. Gould, "Sexuality and Ethics in Advertising: A Research Agenda and Policy Guideline Perspective," *J. of Advertising,* 1994, 23(1), 73-80; Ming-Hui Huang, "Romantic Love and Sex: Their Relationship and Impacts on Ad Attitudes," *Psych. & Marketing,* 2004, 21(1), 53-73.

25 See Michael S. LaTour, "Female nudity in print advertising: An analysis of gender differences in arousal and ad response," *Psych. & Marketing,* 1990, 7)1), 65-81.

26 See Golden, Linda L., and Alpert, Mark I. (1987), "Comparative

Analysis of the Relative Effectiveness of One-and Two-Sided Communication for Contrasting Products," *J. of Advertising,* 16,18-25; Hastak, Manoj, and Park, Jong-Won (1990), "Mediators of Message Sidedness Effects on Cognitive Structure for Involved and Uninvolved Audience," *Advances in Consumer Research,* 17, 329-336; Crowley, Ayn E., and Wayne D. Hoyer, (1994), "An Integrative Framework for Understanding Two-sided Persuasion," *J. of Consumer Research,* 20, 561-574. Etgar, Michael, and Goodwin, Stephen A (1982), "One-Sided versus Two-Sided Comparative Message Appeals for New Brand Introduction," *J. of Consumer Research,* 8, 460-465; Hastak, Manoj, and Park, Jong-Won (1990), "Mediators of Message Sidedness Effects on Cognitive Structure for Involved and Uninvolved Audience," *Advances in Cons. Res.,* 17, 329-336; Michael A. Kamins, and Henry Assael, "Two-sided versus One-sided Appeals: A Cognitive Perspective on Argumentation, Source Derogation, and the Effect of Disconfirming Trial on Belief Change," *J. of Marketing Research,* 1987, 24, 29-39; Kamins, Michael A., Brand, Meribeth J., Hoeke, Stuart A., and Moe, John C. (1998), "Two-Sided Versus One-Sided Celebrity Endorsements: The Impact on Advertising Effectiveness and Credibility," *J. of Advertising,* 18, 4-10; Belch, George E. (1981), "An Examination of Comparative and Non comparative Television Commercials: The Effect of Claim Variation and Repetition on Cognitive Response and Message Acceptance," *J. of Mark Res.,* 18, 222-249.

27 See Sawyer, Alan G. (1973), "The effects of Repetition of Reputational and Supportive Advertising Appeals," *J. of Mark Res.,* 10, 22-23.

28 See McGuire, William J. (1961), "The Effectiveness of Supportive and Reputational Defenses in Immunizing and Restoring Beliefs Against Persuasion," *Sociometry,* 24, 184-197; "The Application of Attitude Immunization Techniques in Marketing," Stewart W. Either, *J. of Marketing Research,* 1971, 8(February), 56-61.

29 For academic research, see S. Putrevu and Kenneth R. Lord, "Comparative and noncomparative advertising: attitudinal effects under cognitive and affective involvement conditions," *J. of Advertising,* 1994, 23 (June), 77-91; Kawpong Polyorat and Dana L. Alden, "Self-construal and need-for-cognition effects on brand attitudes and purchase intentions in response to comparative advertising in Thailand and the United States," *J. of Advertising,* 2005, 34 (1), 37-48; "Attitude toward a Comparative Advertisement: The Role of an Endorser." Raju, Sekar, Rajagopal, Priyali, Unnava, H. Rao. *Advances in Cons. Res.,* 2002, 29(1), 480-481.

30 William R. Swinyard (1981), "The Interaction between Comparative Advertising and Copy Variation," *J. of Mark Res.,* 18,175-186.

31 For further academic studies on this topic, see G. Belch, "An examination of comparative and noncomparative television commercials: The effects of claim variation and repetition on cognitive response and message acceptance," *J. of Marketing Research,* 1981,18, 333-349; "A cross-country investigation of recall and attitude toward comparative advertising," Donthu, N., J. of Advertising; 1998, 27(2), 111-122; M. Etgar "One-sided versus two-sided comparative message appeals for new brand introductions," *J. of Consumer Research,* 1982, 8, 460-465; "Comparative Advertising Effectiveness: The Role of Involvement and Source Credibility," Gotlieb, Jerry B. and Sarel, Dan *J. of Advertising,* 1991, 20(1), 38-45; "Comparative versus Noncomparative Advertising: A Meta-Analysis," Grewal, Dhruv; Kavanoor, Sukumar; Fern, Edward F.; Costley, Carolyn; Barnes, James, *J. of Marketing,* 1997, 61(4), 1-15; "The Effects of Information Processing Modes on Consumers' Reactions to Comparative Advertising," Thompson, Debora Viana and Hamitton, Rebecca W., Advances in Consumer Research, 2005, 32, 560-560; "Comparative Advertising Effectiveness: A Cross-Cultural Study," Shao, Alan T., Bao, Yeqing Gray, Elizabeth. *J. of Current Issues & Research in Advertising,* Fall 2004, 26(2), 67-80; Modelling consumer response to differing levels of comparative advertising, Del Barrio-García, Salvador; Luque-Martínez, Teodoro. *European J. of Marketing,* 2003, 37 (1/2), 256-274.

32 For research study, see "Source Credibility and Attitude Certainty: A Metacognitive Analysis of Resistance to Persuasion," Tormala, Zakary L., Petty, Richard E.. *J. of Cons. Psychology,* 2004,14(4), 427-442. "Prepurchase Attribute Verifiability, Source Credibility, and Persuasion," Jain, Shailendra Pratap; Posavac, Steven S., *J. of Cons. Psychology,* 2001, 11(3), 169-180; Grewal, Dhruv, Gotlieb, Jerry, and

Marmorstein, Howard, "The moderating effects of message framing and source credibility on the price-perceived risk," J. of Consumer Research, June 94, 21(1), 145-54.

33 See Michael A. Kamins, "An investigation into the 'match-up' hypothesis in celebrity advertising: When beauty may be only skin deep," *J. of Advertising*, 1990, 19(1) 4-13. Stephen K. Koernig and Albert L. Page, "What If Your Dentist Looked Like Tom Cruise? Applying the Match-Up Hypothesis to a Service Encounter," *Psychology & Marketing*, 2002, 19(1), 91-110. Brian D Till and Michael Busler, "The Match-Up Hypothesis: Physical Attractiveness, Expertise, and the Role of Fit on Brand Attitude, Purchase Intent and Brand Beliefs," *J. of Advertising*, 2000, 29(3), 1-13.

34 For an academic framework, see Robert Cialdini and Noah Goldstein, "Social Influence: Compliance and Conformity," *J. Annual Review of Psychology*, 2004, 55(Feb.), 591-621.

35 For a State-of-the-Art scholarly work on this topic, see Robert B. Cialdini, "The Science of Persuasion," *Scientific American*, Jan 2004 Special Edition, 14(1), 70-77.

Chapter 9

1 For a classical description, see Robin M. Williams , 1970, *American Society: A Sociological Perspective*, 3rd ed. New York, Knopf. But note, that treatment is quite dated; the present author has culled only those values that are deemed relevant today and re-profiled them to reflect current embodiment of those values.

2 Paraphrased by author based on such source literatures as Robin M. Williams, *American Society: A Sociological Interpretation*, NY, Knopf, 1960; C.M. Seah, *Asian Values and Modernization*, 1997, Singapore, Singapore University Press; William Theodore de Bary, *Asian Values and Human Rights: A Confucian Communitarian Perspective*, Harvard University Press, 2000; William K. Cummings, "Asian values, education and development," *Compare: A Journal of Comparative Education*, 1996, Vol. 26, Issue 3, 287-95.

3 Geert Hofstede, *Cultural Consequences: International Differences in Work-Related Value* (Beverly Hills, CA: Sage,1980); Geert Hofstede and Michael H. Bond, "Hofstede's Culture Dimensions: An Independent Validation Using Rokeach's Value Survey," *Journal of Cross-Cultural Psychology*, 15 (December 1984), pp. 417-33. Hofstede G. *Culture and Organizations: Software of the Mind*, London: Mc Graw-Hill, 1991.

4 See for example, Han Sang-Pil, Shavitt S. Persuasion and Culture: Advertising Appeals in Individualistic and Collectivistic Societies. *Journal of Experimental Social Psychology 1994*; 30 (July): 8-18; Tse DK., Belk RW, Zhou N. "Becoming a Consumer Society: A Longitudinal and Cross-cultural Content Analysis of Print Ads from Hong Kong, The People's republic of China, and Taiwan," *Journal of Consumer Research* 1989; Vol. 15, (March): 457-472; Pollay RW. Measuring the Cultural Values Manifest in Advertising. In *Current Issues and Research in Advertising*, James H. Leigh and Claude R. Martin (eds), Ann Arbor: MI: University of Michigan Press, 1983. pp 72-92.

5 Edward T. Hall, *Beyond Culture*, Garden City, NJ: Doubleday, 1976.

6 Fons Trompenaars & Charles M. Hampden-Turner, *Building Cross-cultural Competence: How to Create Wealth from Conflicting Values*. Yale University Press, November 2000; also see, Trompennars F. *Riding the Waves of Culture. Understanding Diversity in Global Business*, New York: Professional Publishing, 1994.

7 Although it is not a value but a behavioral characteristic (the way people communicate – explicitly or not), for tactical efficiency, we incorporate it under universal "value" dimensions.

8 Adapted from http://www.japanesekimono.com/kimono_patterns. htm

9 Compiled by author from various sources including: *Signature Bride Magazine*, Spring 1998 issue as cited in **http://www. africanweddingguide.com/history/lobola.html**; and **Sudheer Birodkar,** "Dowry, Sati and Child Marriage"sudheerbirodkar@yahoo. com sudheerbirodkar@yahoo.com

10 For further reading, see Don Slater, *Consumer Culture and Modernity*, Polity Press, 1997; D.A. Briley, M.W. Morris, and I. Simpson, "Reasons as Carriers of Culture," *J. of Consumer Research*, Sept. 2000, 157-77.

11 Further reading: D.A. Ricks, *Big Business Blunders*, Homewood, Illinois, Dow Jones-Irwin, 1983.

12 D.A. Ricks, *Big Business Blunders*, Homewood Illinois, Dow Jones-Irwin, 1983.

13 For another view of color meanings, see http://universalfacts.blogspot. com/2005/12/meaning-of-colors-color-symbolism.html (Accessed November 12, 2005).

14 Several academic studies of cultural themes in advertising across different countries are worth reading; these include Caillat, Zahna., and Barbara Mueller. (1996), "The Influence of Culture on American and British Advertising: An Exploratory Comparison of Beer Advertising," *Journal of advertising Research*, 36 (3), 79 – 87; Cho B, Kwon U, Gentry JW, Jun S, Kropp F. Cultural Values Reflected in Theme and Execution: A Comparative Study of U.S. and Korean Television Commercials. *Journal of Advertising* 1999; 28 (4), 59-73; Cutler, Bob. D., and Raj Shekhar G. Javalgi. (1992), "A Cross-Cultural Analysis of Visual Components of Print Advertising: The United States and European Community, *Journal of Advertising Research*, 32 (Jan/Feb), 71- 80; Mueller, B. (1987), "Reflections of Culture: An Analysis of Japanese and American Advertising Appeals," *Journal of Advertising Research*, (June/July), 51-59; Mueller, B. (1992) 'Standardization vs. Specialization: An Examination of Westernization in Japanese Advertising', *Journal of Advertising Research*, 32 (1), 15-24; Cheng H, Schweitzer JC. Cultural Values Reflected in Chinese and U.S Television Commercials. *Journal of Advertising Research* 1996; May/June: 27-45; Albers-Miller ND, Gelb BD. Business Advertising Appeals as Mirror of Cultural Dimensions: A Study of Eleven Countries. *Journal of Advertising* 1996; 25 (Winter): 57-70.

15 The ad appeared in Business Week, February 3, 2003, p. 95.

16 For recent research on ethnocentrism, see Magne Supphelen and Terri L. Rittenburg, "Consumer Ethnocentrism When Foreign Products Are Better," *Psychology & Marketing*, 2001(September), 18(9), 907-28. de Ruyter, K. van Birgelen, and M. Wetzels, "Consumer ethnocentrism in International Services Marketing," *International Business Review*, 1998, 7, 185-202.

17 Edward T. Hall, *Beyond Culture*, Garden City, NJ: Doubleday, 1976.

18 Fuat Firat and Alladi Venkatesh, "Postmodernity: The Age of Marketing" *International Journal of Research in Marketing*, Vol. 10, 1993, pp. 227-249 (Quotation on p. 245).

19 Russell W. Belk, "Hyperreality and Globalization: Culture in the Age of Ronald McDonald," *Journal of International Consumer Marketing* 8 (March/April 1995), pp. 23-37.

20 Also see, Mooij, De M. (1998) *Global Marketing and Advertising. Understanding Cultural Paradox*. Sage Publications: California; and Gannon MJ Associates (1994). *Understanding Global Cultures*. Sage Publications.

CHAPTER 10

1 This particular run happened on July 28, 2003.

2 Guidelines on the San Francisco Club's Web site.

3 The term was coined by sociologist Herbert H. Hyman in "The Psychology of Status," Archives of Psychology, 38, 1942, No. 269.

4 Francis S. Bourne, "Group Influence in Marketing and Public Relations," in *Some Applications of Behavioral Research,* eds. R. Likert and S.P. Hayes (Basil, Switzerland: UNESCO, 1957).

5 William O. Bearden and Michael J. Etzel, "Reference Group Influence on Product and Brand Purchase Decisions," *J. of Consumer Research* 9, (1982), pp. 183-94.

6 See C. Whan Park and V. Parker Lessig, "Students and Housewives: Differences in Susceptibility to Reference Group Influence,ö *J. of Consumer Research* 4, no. 2 (1977), pp. 102-110. and Robert E. Burnkrant and Alain Cousineau, "Informational and Normative Social Influence in Buyer Behavior," *J. of Consumer Research* 2 (December 1975), pp. 206-215.

7 The concept was proposed by marketing professor Bill Bearden and colleagues; see *William O. Bearden and* Randall L. Rose "Attention to Social Comparison Information: An Individual Difference Factor Affecting Consumer Conformity," *J. of Consumer Research*, March 1990, Vol. 16 Issue 4, p461-71; *William O. Bearden,* Richard G. Netemeyer, and Jesse E. Teel, "Measurement of Consumer Susceptibility to Interpersonal Influence," *J. of Consumer Research*, March 1989, Vol. 15

Issue 4, 473-81.

8 For a non-U.S. study using this concept, see Byoungho Jin and Byungsook Hong , "Consumer Susceptibility to Salesperson Influence in Korean Department Stores," *J. of International Consumer Marketing*, 2004, 17(1), 33-53.

9 Banwari Mittal, 2005, 2006.

10 Reported in Newsweek, June 1992, p. 41.

11 These terms are used in Robert K. Merton, "Patterns of Influence," in Paul F. Lazersfeld and Frank N. Stanton (eds.), Communications Research, New York: Harper and Brothers, 1949, pp. 180-219.

12 Ed Keller and Jon Berry, The Influentials, Free Press, 2003.

13

14 For further reading, see, Everett M. Rogers, "New Product Adoption and Diffusion," in R. Ferber, ed., Selected Aspects of Consumer Behavior, Washington, D.C.: NSF Government Printing Office, 1977, pp. 223-38; Everett M. Rogers, *Diffusion of Innovations*, 3rd ed. (New York: Free Press, 1983), p. 281-84; Frank M. Bass, "A New Product Growth Model for Consumer Durables," Management Science, 15 (January 1969), 215-27.

15 Paul Lazarsfeld, B. Berelson, and H. Gaudet (1948). *The People's Choice*. New York: Columbia University Press. Also see, Katz, Elihu (1973). The two-step flow of communication: an up-to-date report of an hypothesis. In Enis and Cox(eds.), *Marketing Classics*, p175-193.

16 Alissa Quart, "Ol' College Pry," Business2.0, April, 2001, 68-70.

17 Reported in Deidre Breakenridge, *Cyberbranding: Brand Building in the Digital Economy*, Prentice Hall, 2001, p. 140.

CHAPTER 11

1 M. Joseph Sirgy, "A Social Cognition Model of Consumer Problem Recognition," *J. of the Academy of Marketing Science*, Vol. 15, Winter 1987, p. 53-61.

2 "New IRC Study Shows Safety Overwhelming Concern of Auto Consumers," 9 December 1999, http://www.ircweb.org

3 Cheryl Burke Jarvis, "An Exploratory Investigation of Consumers' Evaluations of External Information Sources," in Joseph W. Alba and J. Wesley Hutchinson (eds.), *Advances in Consumer Research*, Vol. XXV, p. 446-452, Provo, Utah: Association for Consumer Research, 1998.

4 See Shelley Chaiken, (1980) for a technical discussion of the terms heuristic versus systematic; and Furse, Punj, and Stewart (1984) for discussion of their use by consumers in one study; Shelly Chaiken, "Heuristic versus Systematic Information Processing and the Use of Source versus Message Cues in Persuasion," *J. of Personality and Social Psychology* 39 (November 1980), pp. 752-66; David H. Furse, Girish N. Punj, and David W. Stewart, "A Typology of Individual Search Strategies among Purchasers of New Automobiles," *J. of Consumer Research* 10, no. 4 (March 1984), pp. 417-31.

5 C. Whan Park and V. Parker Lessig, "Familiarity and Its Impact on Consumer Decision Biases and Heuristics," *J. of Consumer Research* 8 (September 1981), pp. 223-30; James R. Bettman and C. W. Park, "Effects of Prior Knowledge and Experience and Phase of Choice Process on Consumer Decision Processes: A Protocol Analysis," *J. of Consumer Research* 7 (December 1980), pp. 234-48.

6 Narasimhan Srinivasan and Brian T. Ratchford, "An Empirical Test of a Model of External Search for Automobiles," *J. of Consumer Research* 18 (September 1991), pp. 233-42; also see Rajan Sambandam and Kenneth R. Lord, "Switching Behavior in Automobile Markets: A Consideration-Sets Model," *J. of the Academy of Marketing Science* 23, no. 1 (1995), pp. 57-65.

7 Banwari Mittal, "An Integrated Framework for Relating Diverse Consumer Characteristics to Supermarket Coupon Redemption," *J. of Marketing Research*, 1996. Also see, Aviv Shoham and Maja Makovec Brencic, "Value, Price Consciousness, and Consumption Frugality: An Empirical Study, *Journal of International Consumer Marketing*, Vol. 17, Issue 1, 2004.

8 Peter L. Wright, "The Harassed Decision Maker: Time Pressure, Distractions, and the Use of Evidence," *J. of Applied Psychology* 59 (October), pp. 555-61; C. Whan Park, Easwar Iyer, and Daniel C. Smith, "The Effects of Situational Factors on In-Store Grocery Shopping Behavior: The Role of Store Environment and Time Available for Shopping," *J. of Consumer Research* 15 (March 1989), pp.

4222-33.

9 For a fuller discussion of these and other models, see James R. Bettman, An Information Processing Theory of Consumer Choice (Reading, MA: Addison-Wesley, 1979), pp. 173-228.

10 See Hillel J. Einhorn (1970), "Use of Nonlinear, Noncompensatory Models in Decision Making," Psychological Bulletin 73, pp. 221-30.

11 Amos Tversky, "Elimination by Aspects: A Theory of Choice," Psychological Review 79 (July 1972), pp. 281-99.

12 For research literature on some of these ideas, see [MEMO type Park et al, 2000 FIND IT IN SOME SOURCE; Hamilton.. the piece on p. 156, *Advances in Consumer Research*, 29.

13 For further understanding, see Susan M. Broniarczyk and Joseph W. Alba, "The Role of Consumer Intuitions in Inference Making," *J. of Consumer Research*, 21 (December), 1994, pp. 393-407.

14 Herbert A. Simon, Models of Man (New York: John Wiley & Sons, 1957); also see, Peter L. Wright, "Consumer Choice Strategies: Simplifying versus Optimizing," *J. of Marketing Research* 11 (1975), pp. 60-67.

15 Banwari Mittal, "The Role of Affective Choice Mode in the Consumer Purchase of Expressive Products," *J. of Economic Psychology* 9 (1988), pp. 499-524.

16 See, James R. Bettman and Michael A. Zins, "Constructive Processes in Consumer Choice," *J. of Consumer Research* 4 (September 1977), pp. 75-85; James R. Bettman and C. Whan Park, "Effects of Prior Knowledge and Experience and Phase of Choice Process on Consumer Decision Processes: A Protocol Analysis," *J. of Consumer Research* 7 (December 1980), pp. 234-48; Denis A. Lussier and Richard W. Olshavsky, "Task Complexity and Contingent Processing in Brand Choice," *J. of Consumer Research* 6 (1979), pp. 154-65.

17 Based on a survey by NPD Group, as reported in USA Toady online edition, dated 10-3-2005.

18 See Peter L. Wright, "Consumer Judgment Strategies: Beyond the Compensatory Assumption," in M. Venkatesan, ed., Proceedings of the Third Annual Conference (Chicago: Association for Consumer Research, (1972), pp. 316-24.

CHAPTER 12

1 Prices for the base models of both makes, per Edmunds.com accessed on March 30, 2006.

2 For a comprehensive treatment and definitive research-based work on Consumer Satisfaction, see Richard L. Oliver, Satisfaction: A Behavioral Perspective on the Consumer, 1997, New York: McGraw Hill.

3 Jagdish N. Sheth and Banwari Mittal, "A Framework for Managing Consumer Expectations," *J. of Market-Focused Management,* (1996), 1, 137-158.

4 For academic studies on consumer satisfaction, see Sivadas, E. and Famie, L. Baker-Prewitt (2000), "An examination of the relationship between service quality, customer satisfaction, and store loyalty", International J. of Retail& Distribution Management, 28, 2, 73-82. Barnes, J. G. (1997), "Closeness, strength, and satisfaction examining the nature of relationships between providers of financial services and their retail customers", *Psychology and Marketing*, Vol. 14, No. 8, pp. 765-90; Jones, T. O. and Sasser, W. E. (1995), " Why satisfied customers defect", Harvard Business Review, November- December, pp. 88-99.

5 In academic literature, these are called technical and functional quality, respectively. See, Christian Gronroos "A Service-Oriented Approach to the Marketing of Services," European *J. of Marketing;* 1978, 8 (12), 588-602.

6 SERVQUAL's architects are renowned Services Marketign scholars Professors Zeithaml, Berry, and Parasuraman; see SERVQUAL: A Multiple-Item Scale for Measuring Consumer Perceptions of Service Quality, By: A. *Parasuraman*, Valarie A. *Zeithaml*, Leonard L. *Berry*, *J. of Retailing*, Spring 1988, 64 (1), 12-40; also see R. Johnson, M. Tsiros, and R.A. Lancioni, "Measuring service quality: a systems approach," *J. of Services Marketing*, 1999, 9 (5), 6-19.

7 For book length treatment on the topic, see Services Marketing, Valarie Zeithaml, Mary Jo Bitner, and Dwayne D. Gremler, McGraw-Hill?Irwin, NY: New York, 2002; and Principles of

Service Marketing and Management (2nd Edition) (Paperback), Christopher H Lovelock, and Lauren Wright, Prentice Hall, 2001.

8 A seminal treatise on consumer satisfaction can be found in Richard L. Oliver, Satisfaction: A Behavioral Perspective on the Consumer, New York, NY: McGraw Hill, 1997. Our discussion here borrows and adapts heavily from his ideas.

9 Reported in William H. Davidow and Bro Uttal, Total Customer Service: The Ultimate Weapon, Perennial (HarperCollins), 1990.

10 On the role of a salesperson in complaint resolution, see Stephen W. Clopton, James E. Stoddard, and Jennifer W. Clay, "Salesperson characteristics affecting consumer complaint responses," *J. of Consumer Behaviour*, Nov 2001, 1(2), 124-39.

11 C. Goodwin and I. Ross, "Salient Dimensions of Perceived Fairness in Resolution of Service Complaints," *J. of Satisfaction, Dissatisfaction, and Complaining Behavior* 2 (1989), pp. 87-92.

12 Further reading on customer complaining and post complaining experience, see Jeffery G. Blodgett, Donna J. Hill, S. Tax, Stephen, "The Effects of Distributive, Procedural, and Interactional Justice on Postcomplaint Behavior," *J. of Retailing*, 1997, 73(Summer), 185-210; M.C. Gilly and B.D. Gelb, Post-purchase consumer processes and the complaining consumer,'' *J. of Consumer Research*; 1982, 9(4), 323-28; R.S. Spreng, G. Harrell, and R.D. Mackoy, Service Recovery: Impact on Satisfaction and Intentions, *J. of Services Marketing*, 1995, 9(1), 15-21; S. A. Taylor and T. L. Baker, "An assessment of the relationship between service quality and customer satisfaction in the formation of consumers' purchase intentions,: *J. of Retailing*, 1994, 70(2), 163-78.

13 See Bradley T. Gale, Managing Customer Value, Free Press, 1994.

14 Sources: http://www.bottlebill.org/geography/usa.htm

15 Source: http://www.bottlebill.org/geography/worldwide.htm

16 See http://www.patagonia.com/enviro/pcr/shtml?src+ls

17 See, Carmen Tanner and Sybille Wölfing Kast (2003), "Promoting sustainable consumption: Determinants of green purchases by Swiss consumers," Psychology and Marketing, 20(10), 883 – 902; McCarty, J.A., and L.J. Shrum, 'The Recycling of Solid Wastes: Personal Values, Value Orientations and Attitudes about Recycling as Antecedents of Recycling Behaviour', *J. of Business Research*, 1994, 30, 53-62.; Anita L. Jackson and Janeen E. Olsen "An Investigation of Determinants of Recycling Consumer Behavior," *Advances in Consumer Research*, 1993, 20(1), 481-487; Seema Bhate, "An examination of the relative roles played by consumer behaviour settings and levels of involvement in determining environmental behaviour," *J. of Retailing & Consumer Services*, Nov 2005, 12(6), 419-429; Cleveland, Mark; Kalamas, Maria; Laroche, Michel, "Shades of green: linking environmental locus of control and pro-environmental behaviors," *J. of Consumer Marketing*, 2005, 22(4), 198-212; "Beyond the intention-behaviour mythology: An integrated model of recycling," Janette Davies and Gordon R Foxall. Marketing Theory, Mar 2002, 2(1), 29-113; and "The Recycling Cycle: An Empirical Examination of Consumer Waste Recycling and Recycling Shopping Behaviors," Biswas, Abhijit; Licata, Jane W.; McKee, Daryl; Pullig, Chris; Daughtridge, Christopher. *J. of Public Policy & Marketing*, Spring 2000, 19(1), 93-105.

18 For further academic research on the role of consumers' environmental value, see Linda R. Stanley, Karen M. Lasonde. And John Weiss, "The Relationship Between Environmental Issue Involvement And Environmentally-Conscious Behavior: An Exploratory Study," *Advances in Consumer Research*, Volume 23, 1996, 183-188.

CHAPTER 13

1 Penned by author based on several reports: "Bridal Wave Sweeps Store," Chicago Tribune, November 8, 1994. Patrick Collins, "Charge of the White Brigade," Sunday Standard Times, January 15, 1995, 87, 4, E1-E2, New Bedford, Massachusetts. Susan Davis, "No Blushing Brides in Filene's Frenzied Mob," Westwood Suburban World, May 25, 1995, n.p. Although dated, the image of shoppers seen here rings as true today as ever.

2 Paco Underhill, Why We Buy, Simon and Schuster, New York, NY, 1999, p. 98

3 For some research literature on this topic, see Edward M. Tauber, "Why Do People Shop?" J. of Marketing, 36 (october), 1972, 47-8. Danny Bellenger and Pradeep K. Korgaonkar, "Profiling the Recreational

Shopper," J. of Retailing, 56, 3, 1980, 77-92; and Barry J. Babin, William R. Darden, and Mitch Griffin, "Work and/or Fun: Measuring Hedonic and Utilitarian Shopping Value," *J. of Consumer. Research.*, 20 (March 1994), 644-56; Robert A. Westbrook and William C. Black, "A Motivation-Based Shopper Typology," *J. of Retailing*, 61, 1985, Spring, 78-103

4 See Peter N. Bloch, Nancy M. Ridgway, and Scott A. Dawson, "Shopping Mall as a Consumer Habitat," *J. of Retailing* 70, no. 1 (1994), 23-42.

5 See "Work and/or Fun: Measuring Hedonic and Utilitarian Shopping Value, Babin, B. J.; Darden, W. R.; Griffin, M. J. of Cons. Res., 1994, 20, 644-656; "Profiling the recreational shopper," D. Bellenger and Pradeep Korgaonkar, J. of Retailing; 1980, 53, 29-38.

6 Kirk L. Wakefield and Julie Baker, "Excitement at the Mall: Determinants and Effects on Shopping Response," *J. of Retailing*, 74(4), 1998, 515-539.

7 Mica Nava (Editor) and Alan O'Shea (Editor), <u>Modern Times: Reflections on a Century of English Modernity</u>, Routledge,1996.

8 Based on prior studies including Edward M. Taylor, "Why do people shop," *J. of Marketing*, 36 (October 1972), 46-59; Robert A. Westbrook and William C. Blake, "A Motivation-based Shopper Typology," *J. of Retailing*, Vol. 61, Spring,1985, 78-103; and Joseph P. Guiltinan and Kent B. Monroe, "Identifying and Analyzing Consumer Shopping Strategies," Advances in Cons. Res., Vol. 7, ed., Jerry Olsen, 1980, 745-748.

9 Rook, "The Buying Impulse," *J. of Consumer Research* (September 1987), 189-99.

10 Thomas and Gardland, "Supermarket Shopping Lists," International *J. of Retail and Distribution Management* 21, no. 2 (1993), 8-14.

11 See, C. Whan Park, Easwer S. Iyer, and Daniel C. Smith, "The Effects of Situational Factors on In-Store Grocery Behavior: The Role of Store Environment and Time Available for Shopping," *J. of Consumer Research*. 15 (March 1989), 422-33.

12 Quoted in Kahn and McAlister, p.123.

13 Ronald E. Milliman, "Using Background Music to Affect the Behavior of Supermarket Shoppers," *J. of Marketing* 46, no. 3 (1982), 86-91.

14 For further reading on the effect of store atmospherics on consumer shopping behavior, see Robert J. Donovan, John R. Rossiter, Gilian Marcoolyn, and Andrew Nesdale, "Store Atmosphere and Purchasing Behavior," *J. of Retailing*, 70 (3), 283-94, 1994; E. Sherman and A. Mathur, "Store environment and consumer purchase behaviour: mediating role of consumer emotions," *Psych. & Marketing*, 1997, 14(4), 361-378

15 Adapted from Dennis W. Rook, and R.J. Fisher "Normative Influences on Impulsive Buying, *J. of Consumer. Research.*, 1995, 22, 296-304. And Dennis Rook, The Buying Impulse, *J. of Consumer. Research.*, 1987, 14(Sept), 189-199.

16 An excellent reader on American consumers' supermarket shopping behavior-a source that has richly informed our own description here is by Barbara E. Kahn and Leigh McAlister, Grocery Revolution: The New Focus on the Consumer (Reading, MA: Addison-Wesley, 1996). Also see, Fiona M. Davies, Mark M.H. Goode, Luiz A. Moutinho, and Emmanuel Ogbonna, "Critical Factors in Consumer Supermarket Shopping Behaviour: A Neural Network Approach," *J. of Consumer Behaviour*, 1, 1, 35-49.

17 Ibid., p. 96.

18 For academic research on store patronage, see Mark D. Uncles and Kathy A. Hammond, "Grocery Store Patronage", *International Review of Retail, Distribution and Consumer. Research.*, 5, 3, (July), 1995, 287-302.

19 For further reading, see Dennis W. Rook, "The Buying Impulse," *J. of Consumer. Research.* (September 1987), 189-99; Easwer S. Iyer, "Unplanned Purchasing: Knowledge of Shopping Environment and Time Pressure," *J. of Retailing* 65 (Spring 1989), 40-57.

20 Art Thomas and Ron Gardland, "Supermarket Shopping Lists," International J. of Retail and Distrib. Management 21, 2 (1993), 8-14; Also see Susan Spiggle, "Grocery Shopping Lists: What Do Consumers Write?" in Melanie Wallendorf and Paul F. Anderson eds., Advances in Cons. Res. 14, (Provo, UT: Association for Consumer Research., 1987), 241-45.

21 See Jay D. Lindquist, "Meaning of Image," *J. of Retailing*, Vol. 50 (Winter 1974-75), 31.

22 For academic studies on store loyalty, see Joseph D. Brown, "Determinants of Loyalty to Grocery Store Type," *J. of Food Products Marketing*, 2004, Vol. 10, 3, 1-11; Sawmong, Sudaporn; Omar, Ogenyi. "The Store Loyalty of the UK's Retail Consumers," *J. of American Academy of Business*, Cambridge, Sep2004, Vol. 5, 1/2, p503-509; Michel Laroche, Frank Pons, Nadia Zgolli, Marie-Cécile Cervellon and Chankon Kim, **"A model of consumer response to two retail sales promotion techniques,"** *J. of Bussiness Resesrch.*, 56,, 7, July 2003, 513-522; Francis Piron, "Effects of Service and Communication Initiatives on Retail Grocery Consumers' Loyalty," Singapore Management Review, 2001 2nd Half, 23, 2, 45-61; Laura A. Williams and Alvin C.Burns, "Factors Affecting Children's Store Loyalty: An Empirical Examination Of Two Store Types," *J. of Applied Bussiness. Research.*, Winter2001, 17, 1, 61-82. Cristy E. Reynolds and Arnold, Mark J. Arnold "Customer Loyalty to the Salesperson and the Store: Examining Relationship Customers in an Upscale Retail Context," *J. of Personal Selling & Sales Management*, Spring2000, 20, 2, 89-98. Alan S. Dick and Kenneth R. Lord, "The Impact of Membership Fees on Consumer Attitude and Choice," *Psychology & Marketing*, Jan98, 15, 1, 41-58; Niren Sirohi, Edward W. McLaughlin, and Dick R. Wittink, "A Model of Consumer Perceptions and Store Loyalty Intentions for a Supermarket Retailer," *J. of Retailing*, Summer 1998, 74, 2, 223-45; Bloemer, Josee; de Ruyter, Ko "On the relationship between store image, store satisfaction and store loyalty," Euro *J. of Marketing*, 1998, 32, 5/6, 397-413.

23 For academic studies, see Sudhir Kale and Debabrata Talukdar, "Does Store Brand Patronage Improve Store Patronage?" Review of Industrial Organization, Mar2004, 24, 2, 143-160; André Bonfrer and Pradeep K. Chintagunta, "Store Brands: Who Buys Them and What Happens to Retail Prices When They Are Introduced," Review of Industrial Organization, Mar 2004, 24, 2, 195-218; De Wuif, Kristof; Odekerken-Schröder, Gaby; Goedertier, Frank; Van Ossel, Gino, "Consumer perceptions of store brands versus national brands," *J. of Consumer Marketing.*, 2005, 22, 4, 223-232.

24 For a comprehensive essay on the role of convenience, see Leonard Berry, Kathleen Seiders, and Dhruv Grewal, "Understanding Service Convenience," *J. of Marketing*, July 2002, 1-17.

25 Source: Paul S. Richardson, Arun K. Jain, and Alan Dick, "Household Store Brand Proneness: A Framework," *J. of Retailing* 72, 2, 1996, 159-85; Ogenyi Ejye Omar, "Grocery Purchase Behavior for National and Own-Label-Brands," Service Indus. J. (January 1996), 16, 1, 58-66.

26 Julie Baker, A Parasuraman, Dhruv Grewal, and Glenn B. Voss, "The Influence of Multiple Store Environment Cues on Perceived Merchandise Value and Patronage Intentions," *J. of Marketing*, 2002, April, 66(2), 120-41. Kirk L. Wakefield and Julie Baker, "Excitement at the Mall: Determinants and Effects on Shopping Response," *J. of Retailing*, 1998, 74(4), 515-539.

27 Motives act as goals whose achievement is scripted—by which we mean there is an automatic action code built into our minds, built through repeated action, so that anytime we see an opportunity for gratification, we impulsively reach for it, for example.

28 Suresh Ramanathan and Baba Shiv, "Getting to the Heart of the Consumer: The Role of Emotions and Cognitions (or lack thereof) in Consumer Decision Making," Advances in Consumer Research., eds. Mary Gilly and Joan Myers-Levy, 2001, 28, 49-50.

29 Jacqueline J. Kacen and Julie Anne Lee, "The Influence of Culture on Consumer Impulsive Buying Behavior," *J. of Consumer Psychology.*, 2002, 12(2). 163-176.

30 For further reading, see Sharon E. Beatty and M. Elizabeth Ferrell, "Impulse Buying: Modeling Its Precursors," *J. of Retailing*, 1998, 74(2), 169-191. Also see Peter Weinberg and Gottwald Wolfgang, "Impulsive Consumer Buying as a Result of Emotions," *J. of Bussiness Research.*, 10, 1982, Mar, 43-57.

CHAPTER 14

1 U.S. Census 2000.

2 For literature on this topic, see Mary C. Gilly and Ben M. Ennis, "Recycling the Family Lifecycle," in Advances in Consumer Research, vol. 9, Andrew M. Mitchell (eds.) 1982 (Association for Consumer Research).

3 William H Frey, "Married with Children," American Demographics, March 2003, p. 17-21. Also, U.S. Census 2000.

4 U.S. Census 2000.

5 The present model is author's adaptation and modification. For a review of models in prior literature, see Jagdish N. Sheth, "Models of Buyer Behavior: Conceptual, Quantitative, and Empirical," in A Theory of Family Buying Decisions, (New York: Harper & Row), pp. 17 -33.

6 Ibid.; Harry L. Davis, "Decision Making within the Household," Journal of Consumer Research 2 (March 1976), pp. 241 -60.

7 C. Whan Park, "Joint Decisions in Home Purchasing: A Muddling-Through Process," *J. of Consumer Research* 9 (September 1982), pp. 151 -61.

8 Dennis L. Rosen and Donald H. Granbois, "Determinants of Role Structure in Family Financial Management," *J. of Consumer Research* 10 (September 1983), pp. 253 -58; Charles Schaninger and Chris T. Allen, "Wife's Occupational Status as a Consumer Behavior Construct," *Journal of Consumer Research* 8 (September 1981), pp. 189 -96; Mary Lou Roberts and Lawrence H. Wortzel, "Role Transferral in the Household: A Conceptual Model and Partial Test," *Advances in Consumer Research* 9, (1982), pp. 261 -66.

9 An interesting conceptual framework with a description of group decision-making processes in conflict situations is found in Kim P. Corfman and Donald R. Lehmann, "Models of Cooperative Group Decision-Making and Relative Influence: An Experimental Investigation of Family Purchase Decisions." *J. of Consumer Research* 14 (June 1987), pp. 1 -13, also see Rosann L. Spiro, "Persuasion in Family Decision making," *J. of Consumer Research* 10 (March 1983), pp. 393 -402; and Daniel Seymour and Greg Lessne, "Spousal Conflict Arousal: Scale Development," *J. of Consumer Research* 11 (December 1984), pp. 810 -21.

10 James G. March and Herbert A. Simon, Organizations (New York: Wiley, 1958).

11 Sheila Long O'Mara, "Kids a Powerful Market Force,"

12 George P. Moschis, "The Role of Family Communication in Consumer Socialization of Children and Adolescence," *J. of Consumer Research*, 11, (1985), pp. 898-913.

13 Pierre Filiatrault and J. R. Ritchie, Ibid.

14 George P. Moschis, "The Role of Family Communication in Consumer Socialization of Children and Adolescence," *J. of Consumer Research*, 11, (1985), pp. 898-913.

15 Adapted from Conway Lackman and John M. Lanasa, "Family Decision Making: An Overview and Assessment," *Psychology and Marketing* 12 no 2 (March -April 1993), pp. 81 -93; and from Les Carlson and Sanford Grossbart, "Parental Style and Consumer Socialization of Children," *J. of Consumer Research* 15, no. 1 (June 1988), pp. 77 -94.

16 Moschis and Moore 1982, Bahn 1986, and James U. McNeal, "The Littlest Shoppers," American Demographics, Vol. 14, No. 2 (February 1992), pp. 48 -53.

17 Moschis and Churchill, 1978, Ibid.

18 Carole M. Macklin, "Do Children Understand TV Ads?" *J. of Advertising Research*, 23, (1983), no. 1 pp. 63 -70.

19 See Jean Piaget, The Child's Conception of the World (New York: Harcourt Brace, 1928).

20 Moschis and Moore; Scott Ward and Daniel Wackman, "Children's Purchase Influence Attempts and Parental Yielding," *J. of Marketing Research* 9 (August 1972), pp. 316 -19; G. W. Peterson and B. C. Rollins, "Parent Child Socialization," in M. B. Sussman and S. K. Steinmetz, eds. Handbook of Marriage and Family (New York: Plenum Press), pp. 471 -507; Jan Møller Jensen, "Children's Purchase Requests and Parental Responses: Results from an Exploratory Study in Denmark," in Flemming Hansen, European Advances in Consumer Behavior, Vol. 2 (Provo, UT: Association for Consumer Research, 1995), pp. 61 -68. Sanford Grossbart, Les Carlson, and Ann Walsh, "Consumer Socialization Motive for Shopping with Children," AMA

Educator's Proceedings (1988); Bonnie B. Reece, Sevgin Eroglu, and Nora J. Rifon, "Parents Teaching Children to Shop: How, What, and Who?" AMA Educators' Proceedings (1988) pp. 274 -78; Les Carlson and Sanford Grossbart, "Parental Style and Consumer Socialization of Children," *J. of Consumer Research* 15 (1988), pp. 77 -94.

21 For an exhaustive annotated review of the literature in this area, see Reshma H. Shah, "Toward a Theory of Intergenerational Influence: A Framework for Assessing the Differential Impact of Varying Sources of Influence on the Preferences and Consumption Values of Adult Children," Unpublished working paper, University of Pittsburgh, 1992. Also see Reshma H. Shah and Banwari Mittal, "The Role of Intergenerational Influence in Consumer Choice: Toward an Exploratory Theory," eds. Merrie Brucks and Debbie MacInnis, *Advances in Consumer Research* (Provo, UT: Association for Consumer Research, 1997), pp. 55-60; Ruby Roy Dholkia, "Intergenerational Differences in Consumer Behavior: Some Evidence from a Developing Country," *J. of Business Research* 12, no. 1 (1984), pp. 19-34; Patricia Sorce, Philip R. Tyler, and Lynette Loomis, "Inter-generational Influence on Consumer Decision Making," *Advances in Consumer Research* 16 (1989), pp. 271-75.

22 Collectively from these sources: Elizabeth S. Moore-Shay and R. J. Lutz, "Intergenerational Influences in the Formation of Consumer Attitudes and Beliefs about the Marketplace: Mothers and Daughters," Advances in Consumer Research, M. Houston, ed., 15 (Ann Arbor, MI: Association for Consumer Research 1988), pp. 461 -67; J. Fry, D. C. Shaw, C. H. von Lanzenauer, and C. R. Dipchard, "Consumer Loyalty to Banks: A Longitudinal Study," *J. of Business* 46, pp. 517 -25; Hill, 1970; L. G. Woodson, T. L. Childers and P. R. Winn, "Intergenerational Influences in the Purchase of Auto Insurance," in W. Locander, ed., Marketing Looking Outward: Business Proceedings, (Chicago: American Marketing Association, 1976, pp. 43 -49. Elizabeth S. Moore, William L. Wilkie, and Richard J. Lutz, "Passing the Torch: Intergenerational Influence as a Source of Brand Equity," *J. of Marketing*, Vol. 56, April 2002, 17-37.

23 Elizabeth S. Moore, William L. Wilkie, and Richard J. Lutz, "Passing the Torch: Intergenerational Influence as a Source of Brand Equity," *J. of Marketing*, Vol. 56, April 2002, p.28.

24 Philip Kotler, Marketing Management: Analysis, Planning, Implementation, and Control (Englewood Cliffs, NJ: Prentice-Hall, 1991), p. 247.

25 Based on research by Erin Anderson, Wujin Chu, and Barton Weitz, "Industrial Purchasing: An Empirical Exploration of the Buyclass Framework," Journal of Marketing 51 (July 1987), pp. 71-86.

26 Wesley J. Johnston and Jeffrey E. Lewin, "Organizational Buying Behavior: Toward an Integrative Framework," *J. of Business Research*, 1996, 35 (January), pp. 1-15.

27 See, Niren Vyas and Arch G. Woodside, "An Inductive Model of Industrial Supplier Choice Process," *J. of Marketing* 48 (Winter 1984), pp. 30-45.

28 For a fuller discussion, see Jagdish N. Sheth, "A Model of Industrial Buyer Behavior," *J. of Marketing*, 37 (October 1973), pp. 50-56.

29 See Bart Macchiette and Abhijit Roy, "Affinity Marketing: What Is It and How Dos It Work?" *J. of Services Marketing* 6, no. 3 Summer 1992, pp. 47-57.

30 Bart and Roy, Ibid

31 Bart and Roy, Ibid

32 For a complete discussion of the five major sources of affinity marketing, see Bart Macchiette and Abhijit Roy, "Affinity Marketing: What Is It and How Dos It Work?" *J. of Services Marketing* 6, no. 3 Summer 1992, pp. 47-57

33 We borrow the concept of buyer, payer, and user roles from Jagdish Sheth (personal discussion) and as reported in Jagdish Sheth and Banwari Mittal, Customer Behavior: A Managerial Perspective, Thomson, 2004.

34 For further reading on relationship buying, see; Jagdish N. Sheth and Atul Parvatiyar, "Relationship Marketing in Consumer Markets: Antecedents and Consequences," *J. of the Academy of Marketing Science* 23, no.4 (Fall 1995), pp. 25-71; James C. Anderson, Hakan Hakansson, and Lars Johanson, "Dyadic Business Relationships within a Business Network Context," Journal of Marketing 58 (October 1994), pp 1-15; Ingmar Bjorkman and Soren Kock, "Social Relationships and Business

Networks: The Case of Western Companies in China," International Business Review 4, no. 4 (1995), pp. 519-35; Banwari Mittal, "Trust and Relationship Quality: A Conceptual Excursion," in Atul Parvatiyar and Jagdish N. Sheth (eds.), The Contemporary Knowledge of Relationship Marketing (Atlanta, GA: Emory University, Center for Relationship Marketing, 1996), pp 230-240; Neeli Bendapudi and Leonard Berry, "Customers' Motivations for Relationships with Service Providers," *J. of Retailing* 73, no. 1 (1997), pp. 15-37; Michael R. Leenders and David L. Blenkhorn, Reverse Marketing: The New Buyer-Supplier Relationship (Free Press, 1996), pp. 164-170.

Chapter 15

1 See entry in www.dictionary.com.

2 Populaiton Referenc World.

3 Sandra Gill, Jean Stockard, Miriam Johnson, and Suzanne Williams, "Measuring Gender Differences: The Expressive Dimension and Critique of Androgyny Scales," Sex Roles 17, (1987), pp. 375-400 p.380; Sandra L. Bem, "Gender Schema Theory: A Cognitive Account of Sex Typing," Psychological Review 88, (1981), pp. 354-364; Steve Craig, "Men, Masculinities and the Media," London: Sage, (1992); Cathy Goodwin, Kelly L. Smith and Susan Spiggle, "Gift Giving: Consumer Motivation and the Gift Purchase Process," *Advances in Consumer Research*. 17, eds. Rebecca H. Holman and M.R.Solomon, Provo, UT: Association for Consumer Research, (1990), pp.690-698; Cele Otnes, Tina M. Lowrey and Young Chan Kim, "Gift Selection for Easy and Difficult Recipients: Social Roles Interpretation," *J. of Consumer Research* 20, (1993), pp. 229-244; Cele Otnes and Mary Ann McGrath, "Ritual Socialization and the Children's Birthday Party: The Early Emergence of Gender Difference," *Journal of Ritual Studies* 8, (1994), pp. 73-93; Cele Otnes, J.A. Ruth and C.C.Milbourne, "The Pleasure and Pain of Being Close: Men's Mixed Feelings About Participating in Valentine's Day Gift Exchange," *Advances in Consumer Research*. 21, eds. Chris T. Allen and Deborah Roedder John, Provo, UT: Association for Consumer Research, (1994), pp. 159-164; Mary Ann McGrath, "Gender Differences in Gift Exchanges: New Directions From Projections," *Psychology and Marketing* 12, (1995), pp. 371-393; Eileen Fischer and Stephen J. Arnold, " Sex, Gender Identity, Gender Role Attitudes, and Consumer Behavior," *Psychology & Marketing* 11, (1994), pp. 163-182.

4 A pioneer in Gender role identity research is noted psychologist and Sandra L. Bem; her theory is documented in her 1993 book, The lenses of gender: Transforming the debate on sexual inequality. New Haven, CT: Yale University Press. Further suggested readings on the topic include Sandra L. Bem, "The Measurement of Psychological Androgyny," *Journal of Consulting and Clinical Psychology*, 42, (1974), pp. 155-162; Sandra L. Bem, "Theory and Measurement of androgyny: A Reply to the Pedhazur-Tetenbaum and Locksley-Colten Critiques," *Journal of Personality and Social Psychology*, 37, (1979), pp/ 1047-1054; Barbara B. Stern, Benny Berek and Stephan J. Gould, "Sexual Identity Scale: A New Self-Assessment Measure," Sex Roles, 17, (1987), pp. 503-519.

5 See Stern et al, ibid.

6 See Stern, Berek, and Gould, Ibid.

7 Paco Underhill, Why We Buy, Simon and Schuster, 1999, 102

8 Paco Underhill, Why We Buy, Simon and Schuster, 1999.

9 Tina M. Lowrey and Cele Otnes, "Construction of a Meaningful Wedding: Differences in the Priorities of Brides and Grooms," in Gender Issues and Consumer Behavior, Janeen Arnold Costa, ed., (Thousand Oaks: CA: Sage, 1994), pp. 164-83.

10 For further reading, see Bernd H. Schmitt, France Leclerc, and Laurette Dub-Rioux, "Sex Typing and Consumer Behavior: A Test of Gender Schema Theory," *J. of Consumer Research*. 15 (June 1988), 122-28; Barbara B. Stern, "Sex Role, Self-Concept Measures and Marketing: A Research Note," *Psychology & Marketing* 5 (Spring 1988), 85; Janeen Arnold Costa, ed., Gender Issues and Consumer Behavior (Thousand Oaks: Sage, 1994).

11 Adapted from Frieda Curtindale, "Car Dealers Give the Lady Some Respect," American Demographics 14 no. 9 (September 1992), p. 25.

12 Further reading: TO Buy Love."

13 Authors' formulation based on diverse literature readers are encouraged to read firsthand: "Gender Differences in Gift Exchanges: New

Directions from Projections," *McGrath*, Mary Ann. *Psychology & Marketing*, Aug 95, 12 (5), 371-393; "The Pleasure and Pain of Being Close: Men's Mixed Feelings About Participation in Valentine's Day Gift Exchange," Cele Otnes, Julie A. Ruth, and Constance C. Milbourne, Advances in Cons. Res. , 21, 1994, 159-164. Also Barbara B. Stern, Ibid.

14 Based on several sources including Kay M. Palan, Charles S. Areni, Pamela Kiecker (2001), Gender Role Incongruency And Memorable Gift Exchange Experiences, in *Advances in Consumer Research* Volume 28, eds. Mary C. Gilly and Joan Meyers-Levy, Valdosta, GA: *Association for Consumer Research*, Pages: 51-57. Cele Otnes, Julie A. Ruth, Constance C. Milbourne (1994), The Pleasure And Pain Of Being Close: Men's Mixed Feelings About Participation In Valentine's Day Gift Exchange, in *Advances in Consumer Research* Volume 21, eds. Chris T. Allen and Deborah Roedder John, Provo, UT : *Association for Consumer Research*, Pages: 159-164; Sherry, John, Jr. (19833, "Gift Giving in Anthropological Perspective," *J. of Consumer Research*, Vol. 10, (Sept), 157-167. Mary Finley Wolfinbarger (1990), Motivations And Symbolism In Gift-Giving Behavior, in *Advances in Consumer Research* Volume 17, eds. Marvin E. Goldberg and Gerald Gorn and Richard W. Pollay, Provo, UT : *Association for Consumer Research*, Pages: 699-706.

15 Wikipedia.

16 Wikipedia contributors, "Übersexual," Wikipedia, The Free Encyclopedia, http://en.wikipedia.org/w/index.php?title=%C3%9Cbersexual&oldid=49716925 (accessed May 9, 2006).

17 Wikipedia contributors, "Übersexual," Wikipedia, The Free Encyclopedia, http://en.wikipedia.org/w/index.php?title=%C3%9Cbersexual&oldid=49716925 (accessed May 9, 2006).

18 William Strauss and Neil Howe, Generations: The History of America's Future, 1584-2069 (New York: William Morrow & Company, 1991).

19 This leaves a gap of 2 years (1985-1987) between Gen 'Y' and Teen groups; for all practical purposes, their traits might be deemed to be similar to Gen 'Y'.

20 Based on U.S. Census 2000.

21 Cherryl Russell, "On the Baby-Boom Bandwagon," American Demographics 13, no. 5 (May 1991), pp. 24-31.

22 Laura Koss-Feder, "Providing For Parents"--The "sandwich generation" looks for new solutions, Time, March 17, 2003.

23 Ibid.

24 Louise Lee, "5, p. 100.

25 "Older Consumers 21-22.

26 http://en.wikipedia.org/wiki/Generation Y

27 Children as Consumers," American Demographics, September 1990, pp. 36-39, p. 10.

CHAPTER 16

1 http://forum.afrohair.biz/forum/viewtopic.php?t=14

2 http://forum.afrohair.biz/forum/viewtopic.php?t=15

3 http://forum.afrohair.biz/forum/viewtopic.php?t=19

4 By Pamela Ferrell (Cornrows and Company, 1996) Excerpted with stylistic adaptation from a reader review of the book on the book's Web site.

5 Author's estimate based on an (assumed) average ranging from 10 minutes a day to 6 hours a week.

6 http://en.wikipedia.org/wiki/Human_race

7 There is no consensus on this issue and opinions among scholars differ vastly.

8 This section is informed by a number of prior works of other authors. Important among these are: Marlene L. Rossman, Multicultural Marketing: Selling to a Diverse America (New York: AMACOM, 1994).

9 This 1994-1995 survey was done by Paul Sladkus International, Inc. (PSI), a New York-based multicultural advertising and marketing firm. The survey results are reported in American Demographics, March 1997 issue.

10 Portions of this section are based on a report published in American Demographics, March 1997. See Shelly Reese, "When Whites Aren't a Mass Market," American Demographics, March 1997, p. 51-54.

11 See "How to Sell across Cultures," American Demographics, March 1994, p. 56-57.

12 Reported in Business Wire, July 7, 2005, "Market Research Study Finds Race Matters When African Americans Shop."

13 Adweek.com, June 13, 2005, "Study: Gaps in Hispanic Consumer Behavior," reporting on a study by Havas' Euro RSCG.

14 Study done by ADVO, Inc. reported in Hispanicad.com, dated October 31, 2005.

15 Rohit Deshpande and Douglas M. Stayman, "A tale of two cities: Distinctiveness theory and advertising effectiveness," *J. of Marketing Research*, February 1994, Vol. 31 Issue 1, 57-64.

16 Patricia Braus, "What Does Hispanic Mean," American Demographics 15, no. 6 (June 1993), pp. 46-51.

17 Ibid.

18 Reported in Asian-Nation.org (citing U.S. Census 2000).

19 Source: Computed by author based on U.S. Census data.

20 Quoted in Marlene Rossman, Multicultural Marketing: Selling to a Diverse America.

21 See Matthew Heller, **"A big slice of home: Mexican retailer Gigante bets on large stores to attract higher-spending U.S. Hispanics," Latin Trade**, April, 2004.

22 Note that these are 2001 data as reported in "Portrait of the New America: Understanding A Multicultural Marketplace," The Market Segment Group, A Supplement to Forbes, 2002.

23 Based on Phinney, J.C., "The Multigroup *Ethnic Identity* Measure: A New Scale for Use with Diverse Groups." *J. of Adolescent Research*, 7, 2 (1992) 156-76.

24 Naveen Donthu, and J. Cherian, "Hispanic Coupon Usage: The Impact of Strong and Weak *Ethnic* Identification," *Psychology and Marketing* 9, 6, 1992. 501-10.

25 Further readings: Rohit Deshpande, Wayne Hoyer, and Navin Donthu. "The intensity of *ethnic* affiliation: a study of the sociology of hispanic consumption," *Journal of Consumer Research* 13, 2, 1986, 214-20. Eun-Ju Lee; Ann Fairhurst, Susan Dillard, "Usefulness of Ethnicity in International Consumer Marketing," *Journal of International Consumer Marketing*, 2002, Vol. 14 Issue 4, 25-49; Osei Appiah, *Ethnic identification on adolescents' evaluations of advertisements, J. of Advertising Research*, Sep/Oct, 2001, Vol. 41, Issue 5, 184-99. Rohit Deshpande and Douglas Stayman. "A tale of two cities: distinctiveness theory and advertising effectiveness," *J. of Marketing Research* 31, 4 (1994): 57–64; Eithel M. Simpson, Thelma Snuggs, Tim Christiansen, and Kelli E. Simples, "Race, homophily, and purchase intentions and the black consumer," *Psychology & Marketing*, October, 2000, vol. 17 issue 10, 877-889; Jerome D. Williams, and Kimberly Dillon Grantham, "Racial and ethnic identity in the marketplace: an examination of nonverbal and peripheral cues," *Advances in Consumer Research*, 1999, vol. 26 issue 1, p451-454; Michel Laroche, Chung Koo Kim; Madeleine Clarke, "The effects of ethnicity factors on consumer deal interests: an empirical study of French- and English-Canadians," *J. of Marketing Theory & Practice*, Winter 1997, vol. 5 issue 1, 100-113.

26 Priscilla Barbara, "Consumer Behavior and Born Again Christianity," Research in Consumer Behavior, 2, 1987, 193-222.

27 See, Metin M. Cosgel and Lanse Minkler, "Religious Identity and Consumption," Review of Social Economy, September 2004, Vol. 62 Issue 3, 339-350; Andrew Lindridge, "Religiosity and the Construction of a Cultural-Consumption Identity," *J. of Consumer Marketing*, 2005, Vol. 22 Issue 3, 142-151.

28 Adapted from dictionary entry on www.dictionary.com.

29 http://www.mideasti.org/countries/countries.php?name=uae (accessed November 11, 2005)

30 (UAE Interact – Official Web site of the Ministry of Information and Culture in the UAE, accessed November 11, 2005).

31 Hair care needs are different, diverse.(MERCHANDISING), MMR, June, 2005.

32 Jennie James, "Because They're Worth It," Time.com, January 18, 2004; Ethnic Skin Care As consumers demand more ethnic-specific products, the market continues to expand. By Susan A. Eliya, Happi, October 2005 http://www.happi.com/articles/2005/10/ethnic-skin-care.php).

1. Lately the press has been bursting with accounts of this new class in India. See, for example, Fareed Zakaria, India Rising, Newsweek, March 6, 2006 (http://www.msnbc.msn.com/id/11571348/site/newsweek/); Michael Schuman, "Hey, Big Spenders—India's young are becoming world-class consumers, and multinationals are taking note," Time, Asia, September 1, 2003, 162(8); Brier Dudley, "Microsoft's call-center business in India gets an American accent," Seattle Times, August 16, 2004.

2. Adapted from Michael J. Weiss, Inconspicuous Consumption, American Demographics, April 2002, 31-39 (Table on p. 36).

3. For literature on this topic, see James A. Roberts And Eli Jones, " Money Attitudes, Credit Card Use, and Compulsive Buying among American College students," *J. of Consumer Affairs,* Winter 2001, 35(2), 213-241; Alice Hanley, Mari S. Wilhelm, "Compulsive buying: An exploration into self-esteem and money attitudes," *J. of Economic Psychology*, Mar 1992, 13(1), 5-19. Melvin Prince, "Self-concept, money beliefs and values," *J. of Economic Psychology,* 1993, 14, 1,161-173; Mark Oleson, "Exploring the relationship between money attitudes and Maslow's hierarchy of needs," International *J. of Consumer Studies,* 2004, Vol. 28 Issue 1, 83-92; James A. Roberts and Cesar J. Sepulveda, "Money Attitudes and Compulsive Buying: An Exploratory Investigation of the Emerging Consumer," *J. of International Consumer Marketing*, 1999, 11, 4, 53-74; Diane M. Masuo and Mahendra Reddy, "Comparison of students 'money attitudes': a cross-cultural sampling of selected U.S. and Japan universities," *European Advances in Consumer Research*, Volume 3, 1998, 185-191. For as study on how money attitudes affect consumers' investing behavior, see Steven Michael Burgess, Nick Battersby, Leonard Gephardt, and AntonySteven, "Money Attitudes and Innovative Consumer Behavior: Hedge Funds in South Africa," Advances in Consumer Research, 32, 2005, 315-323.

4. Richard T. Curtin, "Indicators of Consumer Behavior: The University of Michigan Survey of Consumers," Public Opinion Quarterly 46 (1982), 340–52. Also see, E. James Jennings and Paul McGrath, "The Influence of Consumer Sentiment on the Sales of Durables," *J. of Business Forecasting*, 13 (Fall 1994) 17–20.

5. Further readings: Kath Hamilton and Miriam Catterall, "Toward a Better Understanding of the Low Income Consumer," *Advances in Consumer. Reseqrch.*, 2005, 32, 627-632; Ronald Paul Hill, "Stalking the Poverty Consumer: A Retrospective Examination of Modern Ethical Dilemmas," *J. of Business Ethics,* 2002 Part 1, 37(2), 209-219.

6. For seminal work on this topic , see Alan R. Andreasen, The Disadvantaged Consumer (New York: Free Press, 1975).

7. This is based on a 1963 study by Sociologist David Caplovitz, The Poor Pay More (New York: Free Press, 1967).

8. See Alan R. Andreasen, The Disadvantaged Consumer (New York: Free Press, 1975); David Caplovitz, Ibid; David Hamilton, The Consumer in Our Economy (New York: Free Press, 1962); and Judith Bell and Bonnie Maria Burlin, "In Urban Areas: Many of the Poor Still Pay More for Food," *J. of Public Policy & Marketing*, 1993, 12, Fall, 260-270.

9. Insightful essays on the psychology of the poor include: Ronald Paul Hill and Debra Lynn Stephens, "Impoverished Consumers and Consumer Behavior: The Case of AFDC Mothers," *J. of Macromarketing*, 1997 17, Fall, 32-48; Ronald Paul Hill, "Stalking the Poverty Consumer: A Retrospective Examination of Modern Ethical Dilemmas," *J. of Business Ethics*, May2002 Part 1, 37, 2, 209-219; Hill, "Surviving in a Material World: Evidence from Ethnographic Consumer Research on People in Poverty;" *J. of Contemporary Ethnography*; 2001 Vol. 30 Issue 4, p364-391; Kath Hamilton and Miriam Catterall, "Toward a Better Understanding of the Low Income Consumer," *Advances in Consumer Research*, Volume 32, 2005, 627-632.

10. Linda F. Alwitt and Thomas D. Donley, "The Low-Income Consumer: Adjusting the Balance of Exchange," (Thousand Oaks, CA: Sage Publications, 1996).

11. E.J. Boyer and A. Ford (1992), "Black-owned Businesses Pay a Heavy Price," *Los Angeles Times,* May 8, pp. A1, A5.

12. Story based on a long report titled "Two-Tier Marketing," *Business Week,* March 17, 1997, p. 82.

13. As reported in Jeff Gates, *The Ownership Solution: Toward a Shared Capitalism for the 21s Century*, Reading, MA: Addison-Wesley, 1998, p.6

14. Noted in "The State of the Banking Industry," *SOBI*, KPMG Report, April 1 through June 30, 2004.

15. Brendan Coffey, "Every Penny Counts," Forbes, 09.30.02.

16. If your market is another country, you will need to find out the definition of diverse income levels in that country and its population distribution, which you can find in local government publications.

17. See Warner, W. Lloyd (1949) Social Class in America, Science Research Associates, Inc.

18. Del Jones, "Are you proud of your job?" USA TODAY, May 24, 2005.

19. Social capital is one of the three resources (along with cultural and economic) Sociologist Pierre Bourdieu, Pierre Bourdieu, *Distinction: A Social Critique of the Judgment of Taste*, Cambridge, UK: Cambridge University Press, 1984.

20. Among Hindus, social classes are, from the highest to the lowest, are the Brahmin (the priest and learned), the Kshatriya (the ruler, prince, and warrior class), the Vaishyas (or the trader class), and the Shudras, the untouchable class--although these caste barriers are weakening (even breaking down) in modern India.

21. Paul Henry, "Modes of Thought that Vary Systematically with Both Social Class and Age," *Psychology & Marketing*, May 2000, 17(5), 421-440.

22. According to a survey by *Business week*, reported in Businessweek Online issue of October 2, 2005.

23. In India, continuing a custom from the British Raj era, private schools (i.e., non-government schools) are called "public schools"!

24. Source: Richard P. Coleman, "The Continuing Significance of Social Class to Marketing," *J. of Consumer Research*, December 1983, p.277.

25. Coleman, "The Continuing Significance of Social Class to Marketing." *J. of Consumer Research,* 10 (Dec. 1983), 265-80.

26. See Martineau, Pierre (1958), "Social Classes and Spending Behavior," *J. of Marketing*, 23, 121-30. Rainwater, Lee (1960) *And the Poor Get Children*, 1960, Quadrangle Books. Also see, Levy, Sidney J. (1966), "Social Class and Consumer Behavior," in *On Knowing the Consumer*, ed. Joseph W. Newman, New York: John Wiley & Sons.

27. For academic research on social class, see Rajesh Kanwar and Notis Pagiavlas, "When Are Higher Social Class Consumers More And Less Brand Loyal Than Lower Social Class Consumers? The Role Of Mediating Variables," *Advances in Consumer Research*, Volume 19, 1992, 589-595; Scott Dawson, Bruce Stern and Tom Gillpatrick, "An Empirical Update And Extension Of Patronage Behaviors Across The Social Class Hierarchy," *Advances in Consumer Research*, Volume 17, 1990, 833-838; James E. Fisher, "Social Class And Consumer Behavior: The Relevance Of Class And Status," *Advances in Consumer Research*, Volume 14, 1987, 492-496; Scott Dawson and Melanie Wallendorf, "Associational Involvement: An Intervening Concept Between Social Class And Patronage Behavior," *Advances in Consumer Research*, 12, 1985, 586-591; Terence A. Shimp and J. Thomas Yokum, "Extensions Of The Basic Social Class Model Employed In Consumer Research," *Advances in Consumer Research*, Volume 8, 1981, 702-707; Robert B. Settle, Pamela L. Alreck, Michael Belch, "Social Class Determinants of Leisure Activity," *Advances in Consumer Research*, 6, 1979, 139-145; Rich, Stuart U., and Jain, Subhash C., "Social Class as Predictor of Shopping Behavior," *J. of Marketing Research*, 1968, 5, 41-49; Myers, James H., and Mount, John F. (1973), "More on Social Classes Vs. Income As Correlates of Buying Behavior," *J. of Marketing*, 37, 71-73; Jain, Arun K. (1975), "A Method for Investigating and Representing an Implicit Theory of Social Class," *J. of Consumer Research*, 2, 53-59; and Kernan, Jerome B. (1977), "Retrospective Comment on Martineau's "Social Classes and Spending Behavior," in *Classics in Consumer Behavior*, ed. Louis E. Boone, Tulsa, OK: The Petroleum Publishing Co.

28. Adapted from Michael J. Silverstein and Neil Fiske, "Luxury for the Masses," Harvard Business Review, April 2003, 48-59.

29. "A ZIP+4 code uses the basic 5-digit ZIP plus an additional 4-digits

to identify a geographic segment within the 5-digit delivery area, such as a city block, a group of apartments, an individual high-volume receiver of mail, or any other unit that could use an extra identifier to aid in efficient mail sorting and delivery." Wikipedia.org (DoA: January 5, 2006).

30. Michael J. Weiss, *The Clustered World*, 2000, New York, Little Brown and Company.

CHAPTER 18

1 From a Blog by Nicole Sikora.

2 Reported in John A. Quelch and David Harding, "Brand versus Private Labels: Fighting to Win," Harvard Business Review, January-February 1996, 99-109. For classical literature on brand loyalty, where these measures are developed, see R. M. Cunningham, "Measurement of Brand Loyalty," The Marketing Revolution, Proceedings of the Thirty-Seventh Conference of the American Marketing Association, Chicago: American Marketing Association, 1956, 39-45.

3 Louise Witt, "Inside Intent," American Demographics, March 1, 2004., 26(2), 34-39.

4 Jacob Jacoby and Robert W. Chestnut, Brand Loyalty Measurement and Management (New York: John Wiley & Sons, 1978), p. 2.

5 See Alan S. Dick and Kunal Basu, "Consumer Loyalty: Toward an Integrated Conceptual Framework," *J. of the Academy of Marketing Science* 22, no. 2 (1994), p. 101.

6 For additional reading, see C.B. Bhattacharya and S. Sen, "Consumer-Company Identification: A Framework For Understanding Consumers' Relationships With Companies," *J. of Marketing*, 2003, 67(2), 76-88, and Understanding the Bond of Identification: An Investigation of its Correlates Among Art Museum Members," Bhattacharya, C.B., Hayagreeva Rao, and Mary Ann Glynn, *J. of Marketing*, 1995, 59(Oct.), 46-57.

7 Adapted from Building Strong Brands, David Aaker, Free Press, 1995.

8 www.dictionary.com (DoA: November 28, 2005)

9 Adapted from Maureen Tracik, "Why This Season's Hot Sneaker Is Nowhere to Be Found," Wall Street J., December 10, 2002, B1.

10 The concept of brand-relationships is fully developed in (and adapted here from) Susan Fournier, "Consumers and Their Brands: Developing Relationship Theory in Consumer Research," *J. of Consumer Research*, 24, March 1998, 343-373. Also see, Jagdish N. Sheth and Atul Parvatiyar, "Relationship Marketing in Consumer Markets: Antecedents and Consequences," *J. of Academy of Marketing Sciences* 23, No. 4 (Fall 1995), 255-71.

11 I owe my understanding of these idea to eclectic scholars and sources (however, I alone am responsible for this particular formulation): Susan Fournier, "Consumers and their Brands: Developing Relationship Theory in Consumer Research," *J. of Consumer Research*, 24, 1998, 343-373; Terrence Shimp and Thomas Madden, "Consumer-Object Relations: A Conceptual Framework Based Analogously on Sternberg's Triangular Theory of Love," *Advances in Consumer Research*, 15, ed. M. Houston, Provo, UT: *Association for Consumer Research*, (1988), pp. 163-168; Craig Thomson, "Caring Customers: Gendered Consumption Meanings and the Juggling Lifestyle," *J. of Consumer Research*, 22, (March 1996), 388-407; William B. Locander and Howard R. Pollio, "Putting Consumer Experience Back into Consumer Research: The Philosophy and Method of Existential-Phenomenology," *J. of Consumer Research*, 16, (September 1989), 133-146.

12 Mary Ann McGrath and John Sherry, "Giving Voice to the Gift: The Use of Projective Techniques to Recover Lost Meanings," *J. of Consumer Psychology*, 2 (2), 1993, 171-191.

13 A consumer interviewed by Harvard Researcher Susan Fournier, reported in Susan Fournier, "Consumers and their Brands: Developing Relationship Theory in Consumer Research," *J. of Consumer Research*, 24, March 1998, 343-373.

14 Daniel J. Boorstin, 1974, The Americans: The Democratic Experience, New York, Vintage, 148.

15 Albert M. Muniz and Thomas C. O'Guinn, "Brand Community," *J. of Consumer Research*, 2001, 27(March), 412-32. Also see, John W. Schouten and James H. McAlexander, "Subcultures of Consumption: An Ethnography of the New Bikers," *J. of Consumer Research*, 1995, 22(June), 43-61; and also Muniz, Albert M., Jr.; Schau, Hope Jensen,

"Religiosity in the Abandoned Apple Newton Brand Community," *J. of Consumer Research*, 2005 , 31(4), 737-747.

16 Further reading: Rene Algesheimer, Utpal M. Dholkia, and Andreas Herrman, "The Social Influence of Brand Community: Evidence from European Car Clubs, " *J. of Marketing*, 2005, 69 (July), 19-34.

17 For a role of brandfest in building brand equity, see "Brand-fests: Servicescapes for the Cultivation of Brand Equity," McAlexander, James H.; Schouten, John W., Servicescapes: The Concept of Place in Contemporary Markets, 1998, 377-401..

18 This formulation is intuitive, independent of a more scholarly view that interested readers would find rewarding in "Building Brand Community," McAlexander, James H., Schouten, John W., and Koening, Harold F. *J. of Marketing*, 2002, 66(1), 38-54.

19 David A. Aaker, Managing Brand Equity (New York: The Free Press, 1991).

20 See Kevin L. Keller, "Conceptualizing, Measuring, and Managing Consumer-Based Brand Equity," *J. of Marketing* 57 (January 1993), 1-22.

21 See an earlier version of this model in Walfried Lassar, Banwari Mittal, and Arun Sharma, "Measuring Consumer-Based Brand Equity," *J. of Consumer Marketing* 12, no. 4, (1995), 11-19. Also, Charles Bonghee Yoo and Neveen Donthu, "Developing and Validating a Multidimensional Consumer-based Brand Equity Scale," *J. of Business Research*, April 2001, 52, 1, 1-14.

22 For further reading on 'bonds of identification,' see C.B. Bhattacharya, Hayagreeva Rao, and Mary Ann Glynn, "Understanding the Bond of Identification: An Investigation of Its Correlates Among Art Museum Members," *J. of Marketing*, Oct. 1995, 59(4), 46-57.

23 For further reading, see Kevin L. Keller, Wagner A. Kamakura and G.J. Russell, "Measuring Consumer Perceptions of Brand Quality with Scanner Data: Implications for Brand Equity," Report Number 91-122 (Cambridge, MA: Marketing Science Institute). Pierre Francois and Douglas MacLachlan, "Ecological Validation of Alternative Consumer-Based Brand Strength Measures," International *J. of Research in Marketing* 12 (1995) p. 322; R. Kenneth Teas and Terry H. Grapentine, "Demystifying Brand Equity," Marketing Research 8, no. 2, (Summer 1996), 25-29.

24 See Sharon Beatty and Lynn Kahle, "The Involvement-Commitment Model: Theory and Implications," *J. of Business Research*, 6 (30), 149-168. Also, Utpal M. Dholkia, "An Investigation of Some Determinants of Brand Commitment," Advances in Consumer Research, Vol. 24, eds., Marrie Brucks and Deborah J. MacInnis, 1997, 381-386.

25 See Banwari Mittal, "An Integrated Framework for Relating Diverse Consumer Characteristics to Supermarket Coupon Redemption," *J. of Marketing Research*, 31, Nov. 1994, 533-544; David R. Fortin, "Clipping Coupons in Cyberspace: A Proposed Model of Behavior for Deal-Prone Consumers," *Psychology & Marketing*, June 2000, 17(6), 515-534.

26 A recent study showed that luring banking consumers by incentives takes away from consumer loyalty to banks; see Paul M. Dholakia, "The Hazards of Hounding," Harvard Business Review, 2005, 83(10), 20-24.

CHAPTER 19

1 Tenure—confirmation of a more or less long term employment at universities—based on high standards of accomplishments both in scholarship and teaching. The decisions often entails close judgment calls; many professors denied tenure at one university catch up on their accomplishments and prove their merit at another comparable university, and Professor Weinberg did just that, now an accomplished professor at the prestigious Bentley College.

2 John B. Horrigan and Lee Rainie, Pew Internet and American Life Project, "Counting on the Internet," December 29, 2002, Found at http://www.pewinternet.org/reports/toc.asp?Report=80 (as of June 7, 2003).

3 For further reading, see Peterson, R. A., Balasubramanian, S., & Bronnenberg, B. J. (1997). Exploring the implications of the Internet for consumer marketing. *J. of the Academy of Marketing Science*, 25 (Fall), 329-48; Phau, I., & Poon, S. (2000). Factors influencing the types of products and services purchased over the Internet. Internet Research: Electronic Networking Applications and Policy, 10 (2), 102-113; and

Tulay Girard, Ronnie Silverblatt, and Pradeep Korgaonkar, "Influence of Product Class on Preference for Shopping on the Internet," JCMC 8(1) October 2002.

4 In writing this section, I benefited from several papers, specifically: Sung-Joon Yoon, "The Antecedents and Consequences of Trust in Online Purchase Decision," *J. of Interactive Marketing*, 16, 2, (2002), 2-17. Mary Wolfinbarger and Mary C. Gilly, ".comQ: Dimensionalizing, Measuring, and Predicting Quality of the E-tail Experience," Marketing Science Institute Report No. 02-100, (2002) Srini S. Srinivasan, Rolph Anderson, Kishore Ponnavolu, "Customer Loyalty in e-commerce: An Exploration of its Antecedents and Consequences," *J. of Retailing*, 78, (2002), 41-50. Mary Wolfinbarger and Mary C. Gilly, "Shopping Online for Freedom, Control, and Fun," *California Management Review*, Vol. 43, no. 2, (Winter 2001). Mary Wolfinbarger and Mary C. Gilly, "A Comparision of Consumer Experiences with Online and Offline Shopping," *Consumption, Markets and Culture*, Vol. 4(2), (2000), pp. 187-205. Gautam Chakraborthy, Vishal Lala, David Warren, "An Empirical Investigation of Antecedents of B2B Web sites' Effectiveness," *J. of Interactive Marketing*, Vol. 16, No. 4, (Autumn 2002), pp. 51-72. David M. Szymanski, Richard T. Hise, "e-Satisfaction: An Initial Examination," *J. of Retailing*, Vol 76 (3), (2000), pp. 309-322. Carol Kaufmann-Scarborough, Jay D. Lindquist, "E-Shopping in a Multiple Channel Environment," *J. of Consumer Marketing*, Vol 19, No. 4, (2002), pp. 333-350. Chung-Hoon Park and Young-Gul Kim, "Identifying Key Factors Affecting Consumer Purchase Behavior in an Online Shopping Context," International *J. of Retail & Distribution Management*, 31, No. 1, (2003), pp. 16-29. Andrew G. Parsons, "Non-functional Motives for Online Shoppers: Why We Click," J. of Consumer Marketing, Vol. 19, No. 5, (2002), pp. 380-392. Ruby Roy Dholakia and Outi Uusitalo, " Switching to Electronic Stores: Consumer Characteristics and the Perception of Shopping Benefits," International *J. of Retail & Distribution Management*, 30, 10, (2002), 459-469.

5 Mary Wolfinbarger and Mary C. Gilly, "Shopping Online for Freedom, Control, and Fun," California Management Review, 43, 2 Winter 2001, 34-55

6 Wolfinbarger and Gilly, ibid.

7 Schindler, et al ibid.

8 Mihalyi Csikszentmihalyi, Beyond Boredom and Anxiety: Experiencing Flow in Work and Play, San Francisco: Jossey-Bass, 2000.

9 Thoams Novak, Donna Hoffman, and Yiu-Fai Yung, "Measuring the Customer Experience in Online Environments: A Structural Modeling Approach, " *Marketing Science*, 2000, 19 (1) 22-42.

10 Novak and Hoffman (Ibid) call this "unambiguous demand"

11 See David M. Szymanski, Richard T. Hise, "e-Satisfaction: An Initial Examination," J. of Retailing, Vol 76 (3), (2000), pp. 309-322; also Evanschitzkya, Heiner; Iyer, Gopalkrishnan R.; Hessea, Josef; Ahlerta, Dieter , E-satisfaction: a re-examination," *J. of Retailing*, Fall2004, 80, 3, 239-247,

12 Raymond Corey, ibid.

13 David Luna, Laura A. Peracchio, and Maria D. de Juan, "Cross-Cultural and Cognitive Aspects of Web Site Navigation," *J. of the Acad. of Marketing Science*, 2002, 30(4), 397-410.

14 Sandra M. Forsythe and Bo Shi, "Consumer Patronage and Risk Perceptions in Internet Shopping," *J. of Business Research*, 56, 11, November 2003, 867-875.

15 David J. Reibstein, "What Attracts Customers to Online Stores, and What Keeps Them Coming Back," *J. of the Academy of Marketing Science,* Fall 2002, 30, 4, 465-473.

16 Conference Board Report, April 03. 2003 Press Release "Consumers Continue Flocking to the Internet."

17 "Khai Sheang Lee and Soo Jiuan Tan," E-Retailing versus Physical Retailing: A Theoretical Model and Empirical Test of Consumer Choice," *J. of Business Research*, 56, 11, Nov. 2003, 876-885.

18 Khai Sheang Lee and Soo Jiuan Tan, Ibid.

19 Raymond R. Burke, "Technology and the Customer Interface: What Consumers Want in the Physical and Virtual Store," *J. of the Academy of Marketing Science*, Fall 2002, 30, 4, 411-432.

20 Amanda Lenhart, Lee Rainie, Oliver Lewis, "Teenage life online: The rise of the instant-message generation and the Internet's impact on friendships and family relationships," http://www.pewinternet.org,

21 Source:Pew Internet & American Life ProjectTeenage life online: The rise of the instant-message generation and the Internet's impact on friendships and family relationships, JUNE 20, 2001

22 Amanda Lenhart et al, Ibid, pp.10

23 Elisheva Gross, Jaana juvonen, Shelly L-Gable, "Internet Use and well being in adolescence," UCLA 2001

24 Michael Belch, Kathleen A Krentler, and Laura A. Flurry, "Teen Internet Mavens: Influence in Family Decision Making," *J. of Bussiness Research.*, Forthcoming.

25 Most of this information is excerpted from a richly documented report, Elena Larsen, "Cyber Faith: How American Pursue Religion Online," December 23, 2001, Pew Internet & American Life Project, available at www. PewInternet.org

26 Elena Larsen, Ibid, p.20.

27 Elena Larsen, Ibid, p.21.

28 See "Measuring Switching Costs and Their Determinants in Internet-Enabled Businesses," Pei-yu Chen and Lorin M. Hitt, Working Paper, Wharton School, University of Pennsylvania, 2001.

29 Further reading: Murray, K. B., & Häubl, G. (2007). Explaining cognitive lock-in: The role of skill-based habits of use in consumer choice. *J. of Consumer Research*, Forthcoming.

30 Further reading, "Frictionless Commerce? A Comparison of Internet and Conventional Retailers," Erik Brynjolfsson and Michael Smith, Management Science, April 2000, 46(4), 563-585.

Chapter 20

1 A source of succinct information on consumer protection under law is provided at http://www.recalledproduct.com/ with many useful links.

2 Caroline E. Mayer "Unsafe Products Reaching Retail Shelves, Consumer Reports Says," *Washington Post*, Tuesday, October 5, 2004; Page E01.

3 Florida State Government Press Release, dated 12-30-2005, "Bronson Announces Price Gouging Included in Top Ten List of Complaints in 2005."

4 See Lan Zia and Kent B. Monroe, and Jennifer L. Cox, "The Price is Unfair! A Conceptual Framework of Price Fairness Perceptions" *J. of Marketing*, 2004, 68(October), 1-15; and Margaret C. Campbell, "Perceptions of Price Unfairness: Antecedents and Consequences," *J. of Marketing Research*, 1999, 36(May), 187-99.

5 www.quackwatch.org/01QuackeryRelatedTopics/algae.html (DoA: January 20, 2006).

6 Nicky Burridge, "Consumers 'Misled' Over Critical Illness Cover," The Press Association Limited, September 2, 2005.

7 See Rick Pollay and B. Mittal, "Here's the Beef: Factors, Determinants, and Segments in Consumer Criticism of Advertising," *J. of Marketing*, 1993, 57(3), 99-114.

8 A slogan Abercrombie and Fitch used once in the past on its tee-shirts.

9 A tagline in a TV Commercail for Life Alert, a medical service, in 1980s.

10 In Pollay and Mittal, ibid.

11 See report http://news.bbc.co.uk/cbbcnews/hi/uk/newsid_3540000/3540914.stm (DoA: 1/12/2006)

12 For further reading, see http://www.chinadaily.com.cn/english/doc/2005-09/10/content_476636.htm (DoA: 1/12/2006)

13 Ward's Auto World, "NTSB: Enforce Seatbelt Laws, Airbag Injuries Will Decline" 32, no. 10 (October 1996), p. 10.

14 For further information, see http://www.newstarget.com/000976.html (DoA 12/15/2005)

15 Based on a report by RxPGnews, see http://www.rxpgnews.com/medicalnews/healthcare/india/article_2694.shtml (DoA 12/15/2005)

16 Anna Mulringe, et al., "Window Blinds That Can Poison Kids," *U.S. News & World Report* 121, no. 2 (July 8, 1996), p. 76.

17 http://www.ftc.gov/privacy/ privacyinitiatives/financial_rule.html

18 Also see Van Kenhove P., De Wulf K., and Steenhaut S. 2003. The relationship between consumers' unethical behavior and customer loyalty in a retail environment. *J. of Business Ethics*. 44 (4) : 261 -278.

19 Thomas C. O'Guinn and Ronald J. Faber, "Compulsive Buying: A Phenomenological Exploration," *J. of Consumer Research* 16 (September 1989), pp. 147–57.

20 Ibid.

21 For a fascinating theoretical understanding of compulsive consumption, see Elizabeth C. Hirschman, "The Consciousness of Addiction: Toward a General Theory of Compulsive Consumption," *J. of Consumer Research* 19 (September 1992), pp. 155–79

22 Hirschman, Ibid.

23 See Faber and O'Guinn; also Dennis W. Rook, "The Buying Impulse," Journal of Consumer Research (September, 14, 1987) pp. 189–199; and Dennis W. Rook and Steven J. Hoch, "Consuming Impulses," Advances in Consumer Research 12, E.C. Hirschman and M.B. Holbrook, eds. (Provo, UT: Association for Consumer Research), pp. 23–27

24 Faber and O'Guinn themselves do not call it a Three-Factor Theory, and I owe my understanding of the three factors to Ron Faber, "Money Changes Everything – Compulsive Buying from a Biopsychosocial Perspective," *American Behavioral Scientist*, 1992, 35(6), 809-819.

25 Chris E. McGoey, "Shoplifting Facts: Retail Theft of Merchandise," www.crimedoctors.com/shoplifting.html (DoA: 1/16/2006)

26 On December 12, 2001, Winona Ryder, was caught by security surveillance cameras, shoplifting in a Saks Fifth Avenue store in Beverly Hills some 5000 dollars worth of merchandise—as reported in www.courttv.com, "Winona Scissorhands? Actress goes on trial for shoplifting designer duds," updated on October 31, 2002 (DOA: 1/14/2006)

27 Source: National health Interview Surveys 1997-2005.

28 Reported in BBC News, Matthew Davis, "US Slowly Wakes Up to Obesity Crisis," 19 December 2005; www.news.bbc.co.uk

29 Based on a WHO report, see http://www.who.int/nut/documents/obesity_executive_summary.pdf

30 International Obesity Taskforce Report (www.iotf.org/childhoodobesity.asp)

31 A Tuft University Report; see http://president.tufts.edu/ontherecord/issue.php?num=31

32 News "Mayo Clinic Creates 'Office of the Future'" Wednesday, May 25, 2005. Mayoclinic.org (http://www.mayoclinic.org/news2005-rst/2836.html); "Mayo Clinic Developing a Treadmill Workstation," June 13, 2005, Consumeraffairs.com (http://www.consumeraffairs.com/news04/2005/mayo_treadmill.html)

Chapter 21

1 For further reading: Per Ostergaard, James A. Fitchett, and Christian Jantzen, "On Appropriation and Singularisation: Two Consumption Processes," *Advances in Consumer Research*, Vol. 26, 0. 405-408.

2 Dictionary.com.

3 Technically, these two forms of authenticity are called 'indexicality' and 'iconicity'. Kent Grayson and Radan Martinec, "Fact or Fiction? The "Authentic" Homes of Shakespeare and Sherlock Holmes," *Advances in Consumer Research*, 2002(29), 44; Gary Bamossy and Vrije Universiteit, " Truth or Myth? Commercializing the "Authentic" Vincent Van Gogh," *Advances in Consumer Research*, 29, 2002, 44-45; Caroline Lego, Natalie wood, Michael R. Soloman, Darach Turley, Martin O' Neill and Basil Englis, "Real or Replica? Deciphering Authenticity in Irish Pubs," *Advances in Consumer Research*, 29, 2002, 45.

4 Author

5 Based on Sherry, John, Jr. (19833, "Gift Giving in Anthropological Perspective," *J. of Consumer Research*, Vol. 10, (Sept), 157-167.

6 For further reading, see Mary Ann McGrath and John Sherry, "Giving Voice to the Gift: The Use of Projective Techniques to Recover Lost Meanings," *J. of Consumer Psychology*, 2 (2), 1993, 171-191.

7 This section is based on diverse literature: Sherry, John, Jr. (19833, "Gift Giving In Anthropological Perspective," *J. Of Consumer Research*, Vol. 10, (Sept), 157-167; Mary Finley Wolfinbarger (1990), "Motivations And Symbolism In Gift-Giving Behavior," *In Advances In Consumer Research* Volume 17, Eds. Marvin E. Goldberg And Gerald Gorn And Richard W. Pollay, Provo, Ut : *Association For Consumer Research*, Pages: 699-706; Cele Otnes, Julie A. Ruth, Constance C. Milbourne (1994), The Pleasure And Pain Of Being Close: Men's Mixed Feelings About Participation In Valentine's Day Gift Exchange, *In Advances In Consumer Research* Volume 21, Eds. Chris T. Allen And Deborah Roedder John, Provo, UT : *Association For Consumer Research*, Pages: 159-164.

8 Sherry, Ibid.

9 Source: Anne M. Velliquette, Jeff B. Murray, And Elizabeth H. Creyer, "The Tattoo Renaissance: An Ethnographic Account of Symbolic Consumer Behavior," in Joseph W. Alba and J. Wesley Hutchinson (eds.), *Advances in Consumer Research*, XXV, 1998, 461-467; Joel Watson, "Why Did You Put That There?: Gender, Materialism, and Tattoo Consumption," in Joseph W. Alba and J. Wesley Hutchinson (eds.), Advances in Consumer Research, XXV, 1998, 453-460.

10 Whitney T. Tope, "State and Territorial Regulation of Tattooing in the United States," *J. of the American Academy of Dermatology*, 1995, 32, 791-799.

11 Melissa Blouin, "Tattoo You: Health Experts Worry About Artful Trend," Northwest Arkansas Times, Sunday, July 14, 1996, C4.

12 Allan Govenar, "The Variable Context of Chicano Tattooing," in Marks of Civilization, ed., Arnold Rubin, Los Angeles, CA: Museum of Cultural History, 209-218.

13 Based on Robert V. Kozinets, "'I Want to Believe': A Netnography of the X-Philes' Subculture of Consumption" Advances in Consumer Research, Vol. 24, eds. M. Brucks and D. MacInnis, p. 470-475.

14 From Author's research files.

15 This section is based largely on David Glen Mick and Susan Fournier, "Paradoxes of Technology: Consumer Cognizance, Emotions, and Coping Strategies," *J. of Consumer Research*, 1998, 25, September 1998, 123-143 (Table on p. 126)

16 Adapted and paraphrased from consumer interviews reported by researchers Mick and Fournier (1998), Ibid.

17 Adapted from Hassan Fattah, "America Untethered,"American Demographics, March 2003, 35-39.

18 See as an example Risto J. Moisio (2003), "Negative Consequences Of Mobile Phone Consumption: Everyday Irritations, Anxieties And Ambiguities In The Experiences Of Finnish Mobile Phone Consumers," in Advances in Consumer Research Volume 30, eds. Punam Anand Keller and Dennis W. Rook, Valdosta, GA : Association for Consumer Research, Pages: 340-345

19 Peter Francese, "Top Trends for 2003", American Demographics, January 2003, 48-51

20 Michelle Conlin, "The New Gender Gap," Business Week, May 26, 2003, 75-82

21 Ibid, p.77.

Ann L McGill. (2000) "Counterfactual Reasoning in Causal Judgment: Implications for Marketing," *Psychology & Marketing*, 17, 323-343.

22 Newsweek, May 12, 2003, Peg Tyre and Daniel McGinn, "She Works, He Doesn't", 45 –52.

23 Eileen P Gunn, "Business Contacts A-Go-Go," Business 2.0, June 2003, 134-135.

24 Barbara Carton, "Need a Game Plan for a Cranky Kid? Call a 'Parent Coach', *The Wall Street Journal*, May 22, 2003, pp. A1, A7.

APPENDIX 1

[1] See Fortune, November 22, 1993; Carrie Goerne, "Researchers Go Undercover to Learn about 'Laskerville,'" Marketing News, May 11, 1992, p. 11; Andrew Stern, "But Will It Play in Laskerville? Ad Guys Peek in on Anytown, USA," The Record, April 23, 1991, p. C01; Andrew Stern, "Advertisers Peek in on 'Anytown' in Search of Consumer Tastes," The Reuter Business Report, April 22, 1991.

[2] Edward F. McQuarrie, Consumer Visits: Building a Better Market Focus (Newbury Park, CA: Sage, 1993).

[3] Gary McWilliams, "A Notebook That Puts Users Ahead of Gimmicks," Business Week, September 27, 1993, p. 92.

[4] For an example of how Japanese use consumer visits as a research tool, see Johnny K. Johansson and Ikujiro Nonaka, "Market Research the Japanese Way," Harvard Business Review, May/June 1987, pp. 16-19.

[5] Thomas J. Reynolds and Jonathan Gutman, "Laddering Theory, Method, Analysis, and Interpretation," J. of Advertising Research 28, no. 1 (February/March 1988), pp. 11-31.

[6] See Gerald Zaltman and Robin A. Higie, "Seeing the Voice of the Consumer: The Zaltman Metaphor Elicitation Technique," Report Number 93-114, September 1993, Cambridge, MA: Marketing Science Institute; Gerald Zaltman and Robin Higie Coulter, "Seeing

the Voice of the Consumer: Metaphor-Based Advertising Research," J. of Advertising Research, July/August 1995, 35-49.

[7] For further readings see Bobby J. Calder and Alice M. Tybout, "Interpretive Qualitative, and Traditional Scientific Empirical Consumer Behavior Research," in E. C. Hirschman, Interpretive Consumer Research, 1989, pp. 199-208. Provo, UT: Assoc. for Cons. Res.

[8] E. C. Hirschman and Morris B. Holbrook, Postmodern Consumer Research: The Study of Consumption as Text, (Newbury Park, CA: Sage, 1992).

[9] Russell W. Belk, Melanie Wallendorf, and John F. Sherry, "The Sacred and the Profane in Consumer Behavior, Theodicy on the Odyssey," J. of Consumer Research, June 1989, 16, 1-38. Russell W. Belk, "The Role of the Odyssey in Consumer Behavior and in Consumer Research," in Advances in Consumer Research, ed. by Paul Anderson & Melanie Wallendorf, 1987, vol. XIV, p. 357-361, Provo, UT: Association for Consumer Research. Russell W. Belk, John F. Sherry, and Melanie Wallendorf, "A Naturalistic Inquiry into Buyer and Seller Behavior at a Swap Meet," J. of Consumer Research, March 1988, Vol 14, 449-470. Harold H. Kassarjian, "How We Spent Our Summer Vacation: A Preliminary Report on the 1986 Consumer Behavior Odyssey," Advances in Consumer Research 14, pp. 376-77.

[10] Robert F. Kelley, "Culture as Commodity: The Marketing of Cultural Objects and Cultural Experiences," Advances in Consumer Research 14, pp. 347-51.

[11] For further discussion, see Naresh K. Malhotra, Marketing Research: An Applied Orientation (Upper Saddle River, NJ: Prentice Hall, 1996); David Aaker, V. Kumar, and George S. Day, Marketing Research (New York: John Wiley & Sons, 1995).

[12] Raymond Burke, Barbara E. Kahn, Leonard M. Lodish, and Bari A. Harlam, "Comparing Dynamic Consumer Decision Processes and Real and Computer-Simulated Environments," Report # 91-116, June (Cambridge, MA: Marketing Science Institute, 1991).

[13] See G. A. Churchill, Marketing Research: Methodological Foundations 6th ed. (Fort Worth, TX: Dryden, 1994).

[14] Merrie Brucks, "Search Monitor: An Approach for Computer-Controlled Experiments Involving Consumer Information Search," J. of Consumer Research 15 (June 1988), 117-21.

[15] For more detailed coverage of this topic, see David W. Stewart and Michael A. Kamins, Secondary Research: Information Sources and Methods (Newbury Park, CA: Sage, 1993).

[16] Margaret R. Roller, "Virtual Research Exists, but How Real Is It?" Marketing News (January 15, 1996), p. 13.

[17] For further reading, see Philip J. Rosenberger III, and Leslie de Chernatony, "Virtual Reality in NPD Research," J. of the Market Research Society, Vol. 37, No. 4, 345-354. Burke, Raymond R. (1995), "Virtual Shopping," OR/MS Today, August, 1995, pp. 28-34.

[18] For further reading, see "Virtual Shopping," Raymond R. Burke, ORMS Today, 22(4), August, 1995, pp. 28-34.

A

Acculturation	Learning a new culture.
Achieved social system	When one can change social class through effort and accomplishments.
Active audience theory	Holds that consumers are actively processing the information in the ad, and that it is they who are persuading themselves.
Actual self	Who a person currently is.
Adoption of an innovation	Consumer acceptance of an innovation for continued use.
Advocate sources	Sources that have a vested point-of-view to advocate or promote.
Affective choice mode (ACM)	A choice decision making mode wherein *affect* or liking for the brand ensues based not on attribute information, but based on judgments about how the product will reflect the person.
Agonistic gifts	Gifts are intended to gain an immediate personal advantage.
Agreeableness	Being friendly, sympathetic, warm, kind, and good-natured.
AIDA	Sequence of four stages, or four mental states, that an adopter goes through: awareness, interest, desire, and action.
AIO inventory	AIO stands for "activities, interests, and opinion," and it comprises a set of statements to which respondents indicate their agreement or disagreement on a numerical scale.
Altruistic	Gifts are those given largely for the recipient's benefit, with no consideration of immediate personal gain.
An innovation	A product or an idea that is new to the consumer.
Animism	The belief that objects (products) possess souls, i.e., they have consciousness just like humans do.
Anthropolgy	The study of humankind in its habitat.
Anthropomorphizing	Giving the brand a humanlike quality
Approach motivation	The desire to attain a goal object.
Approach-approach conflict	Choosing between two desirable options
Approach-avoid conflict	When we find an object desirable as well as undesirable.
Appropriation	The process of making something one's own.
Arousal seeking	the drive to maintain our stimulation at an optimal level.
Arts	Represent a society's appreciation of the aesthetic experience as well as the society's values, obsessions, and life-conditions.
Asceticism	The tenet of Buddhism which teaches rigorous self-denial and active self-restraint in consumption.
Ascribed or assigned group	Is one in which membership is automatic—you don't have a choice.
Ascribed social system	When one's social class is determined by birth.
Aspirational group	When a person is not already a member of the group (real or symbolic) but desires and expects to become a member.
Assimilation	Occurs when a stimulus is perceived to belong to a category.
Associated network	A network of various concepts organized and stored in memory.
Assortment	A store's assortment is the number of different items the store carries.
Atmospherics	The physical setting of the store (includes lighting, colors, cleanliness and organization, scents, and background music).
Attention	Allocation of mental processing capacity.
Attitude hierarchy	Refers to the sequence in which the three attitude components occur.

Attitudes	Learned predispositions to respond to an object in a consistently favorable or unfavorable way.
Attitudinal brand loyalty	Consistent brand preferences reflected in favorable liking for the brand
Attraction of the alternatives	How attractive a consumer finds alternative brands to be
Attribution	The process of assigning causes—i.e., figuring out why something happened.
Attribution motivation	The motivation to assign causes
Attribution Theory	Theory that consumers always assign causes to events.
Authentication	Realizing that one is what one truly is.
Authenticity	The genuineness of an object in its likeness as it existed at a time in history.
Authoritarian families	Families where the head of the household (mother in matriarchal and father in patriarchal family societies) exercises strict authority on children, and children learn to obey their elders in all matters.
Autonomous decisions	Are decisions made independently by the decision maker.
Autonomy	The desire to feel free to do whatever one wants.
Avoidance motivation	the desire to protect oneself from an negative object, such as a bee sting or a stale or unhygienic burger.
Avoid-avoid conflict	Choosing between two options that are equally undesirable.
Awareness set	Comprises all the brands you are aware of as a consumer.

B

Baby Boomers	Americans bron between 1946 and 1964.
Baby Busters	Americans who were born between 1965 and 1975
Behavioral brand loyalty	Consistent repurchase of the same brand
Behavioral compatibility	Means consumers won't need to alter their behavioral routines.
Belief consumption in media	Believing in the core values and concepts underlying the show.
Beliefs	Expectations about what something is or is not or what something will or will not do.
Big-spenders	Consumers who like to spend without necessarily being rich.
Biogenic needs	Are conditions of discomfort stemming from our biology as humans.
Bottom-up customization	A process wherein consumers build a product starting from the basic version.
Brand associations	What consumers think the brand is, does, or stands for.
Brand belief	A thought about a specific property or quality of the brand.
Brand equity	The enhancement in the perceived utility and desirability that a brand name confers on a product
Brand image	Consists of all the associations or qualities associated with a brand, including physical, functional, and human.
Brand loyalty	Consumer commitment to a brand based on favorable attitude and preference, manifested by the consistent repurchase of the brand
Brand personality	The set of human qualities by which consumers describe a brand.
Brandfests	Events that bring consumers together in geo-temporally concentrated events and entail coordinated activities and brand happenings.
Browsing	Looking at merchandise without a purchase-intent.
Buddhism	A religion found in such countries as China, Tibet, Sri Lanka, Japan, and Korea, with its principal teaching being that material things cannot bring happiness.

Buzz marketing	The rapid-spreading of product news through word-of-mouth.
	Companies sponsor and support some social causes

C

Cause marketing	
Central route	When a consumer processes the message with attention.
Character	the behavior of a person, at test particularly in the face of tempting opportunities for opposite behaviors.
Choice group	A group that a person voluntarily decides to join.
Christianity	A system of religion centered around the church and its religious order.
Chunking	The combination of bits into a new unit.
Classical conditioning	A process of learning by an extension of a pre-existing response from one stimulus onto another stimulus through exposure to the two stimuli simultaneously.
Closure principle	Suggests that consumers have a natural tendency to complete a partial stimulus, supplying the missing information from memory (assuming of course that they are already familiar with the complete stimulus).
Cognitive Age	Also known as subjective age, is defined as an individual's perception of how old he or she feels.
Cognitive factors	Refers to a person's mental abilities.
Cognitive learning	Refers to learning by acquiring new information from written or oral communication.
Cognitive responses	The thoughts generated in the mind upon exposure to a message.
Cognitive style	Consumer mindset about the task of processing information.
Collectivism	Individuals are expected to show consideration for the well-being of their family, group, or organization.
Communicability	Refers to the extent to which an innovation is socially visible or is otherwise easy to communicate about in social groups.
Community support	Companies sponsor certain community events, such as an ethnic food festival, Black History Month, or even local high school football teams.
Comparative advertising	The advertised brand compares itself to competing products or brands.
Compensatory model	The consumer arrives at a choice by considering all of the attributes of a product or service and mentally trading off the alternative's perceived weakness on one or more attributes for its perceived strength on other attributes.
Competitive promotional activity	The special price deals available on competing brands
Compliance	Government mandate for consumers to obey defined rules and regulations with respect to purchase, payment, and, more importantly, product usage, including disposal.
Compulsive buying	A chronic tendency to purchase products far in excess of both a person's needs and resources.
Compulsive consumption	An uncontrolled and obsessive consumption of a product or service frequently and in excessive amounts, likely to ultimately cause harm to the consumer or others.
Concept	A name or label given to any object or quality of an object, person, situation, or an idea.
Concept-oriented families	Are those that are concerned with the growth of independent thinking and individuality in children.
Conditional stimulus	A stimulus to which the consumer either does not have a response or has a pre-existing response that needs modification, so a new response needs to be conditioned.

Confucianism	Confucianism is a philosophy, rather than a religion, that guides almost every aspect of Chinese life.
Conjuctive model	The consumer uses certain minimum cutoffs on all salient attributes.
Conscientiousness	Being organized, determined, responsible, and dependable.
Consideration set	Brands which a consumer will consider buying.
Consumer	Anyone engaged in the acquisition and use of products and services available in the marketplace.
Consumer behaviour	The mental and physical activities undertaken by consumers to acquire and consume products so as to fulfill their needs and wants.
Consumer Bill of Rights	Rights granted by U.S. Congress to every consumer: 1.The right to safety 2.The right to be informed. 3.The right to be heard. 4.The right to choose.
Consumer impulsivity	A consumer's tendency to buy and/or consume spontaneously, whenever exposed to the stimulus product.
Consumer loyalty	A consumer's commitment to a brand or a store or a supplier, based on a strong favorable attitude and preference, and manifested in consistent repatronage
Consumer problem	Any state of felt deprivation
Consumer sentiment	Refers to a consumer's expectation about his or her financial well-being in the near future
Consumer socialization	Refers to the acquisition of knowledge, preferences, and skills to function in the marketplace.
Consumer-brand relationships	How consumers feel toward some products and brands
Consuming the artifacts	The accoutrements that accompany the show—consumers bring the show more squarely into their lives.
Consumption	Any and all usage of products whether or not the products are actually "consumed" away, i.e., depleted.
Consumption communities	Groups of people who share the consumption of a brand or product.
Consumption constellation	A group of products that are consumed together in a typical consumption setting.
Consumption enmeshed self-identity	The extent to which a person defines his or her identity by consumption.
Consumption tribes	Consumption communities that consume a product in a public place, in some ritualistic setting.
Context	The setting or surrounding in which a stimulus is situated.
Contextual marketing	The practice of sending consumers messages pertinent to the purchase and consumption situation of the moment.
Contrast	A stimulus' distinct difference from its environment or background.
Corrective advertising	Advertising whose message includes a correction of a previous deception
Cultural categories	The division of the world's objects and qualities into groups with given names, e.g., masculine or feminine, upper class or lower class, intellectual or peasant, nerd or jock, modern or traditional, sophisticated or simpleton.
Cultural congruency	Refers to how similar the culture depicted in the Web site is to the audience's culture.
Cultural Gatekeepers	People who, through their position and reputation, exercise influence and promote certain cultural meanings.
Cultural Practises	Supra-logical behaviors that are rooted in the traditions and history of a cultural group.

Cultural symbolism	The meaning that any characteristic or entity comes to have in particular cultures.
Cultural Values	The values a society as a whole embraces.
Culture	Everything humans learn from and share with members of a society
Customer recovery	The actions the company undertakes to remove the cause of dissatisfaction and to convert the dissatisfied and unhappy consumer into a satisfied and happy consumer.
Customs	Ways of doing something.
Cyber-buzz	Buzz through the Internet channel.

D

Deceptive advertising	Advertising that has the capacity to deceive a measurable segment of the public.
Deep involvement	A consumer's extreme interest in a product or activity on an ongoing basis.
Defense mechanisms	Psychological processes we employ to protect our ego.
Deficit hypothesis	The idea that consumers with low prior expertise would seek more information to overcome their knowledge deficit.
Democratic families	Every member is given equal voice. Most family matters are discussed among family members, especially those who would be affected by the decisions.
Democratic justice	Refers to a family norm in which each family member is given a voice in family decisions.
Diffusion process	The spreading of an innovation's acceptance and use through a population.
Digital Products	Are products that exist in or can be transformed into digital form, such as computer software, music, pictures, video, and information material such as manuals, brochures, books, educational lessons, etc
Discretionry income	Personl income left after taxes and after purchasase of necessities.
Disjunctive model	A judgment model in which the consumer is willing to make trade-offs between aspects of choice alternatives.
Divestment rituals	Activities we perform before discarding or parting with a product.
Door in the face	The marketer makes a large request that is sure to be refused; subsequently, after the consumer declines the first request, the marketer then makes a much smaller request, which is what s/he wanted of the consumer in the first place.
Downward mobility	Movement into a lower class.
Drive	A force or energy that impels us to act.

E

Early adopters	The first group of consumers who deliberate rather than rush, but are independent in their thinking and are quick to evaluate and reach a decision on an innovation.
Early majority	A large group of consumers who are very deliberate, and adopt an innovation if they do not see much risk in it.
Economics	The study of goods—how they are produced, distributed, and consumed.
E-fluentials	A subgroup of Influentials—the persons who are net-savvy and influence other people both offline and online.
Egalitarian sex role attitudes	The view that men and women are both equal and must share equally in all tasks. In this view, women are as entitled to and capable of pursuing a career as men are.
Ego needs	The need to feel good about ourselves and to have self-esteem.

Ego/identity value	Comes from our need to construct and nurture our identity or self-concept, our sense of ego, our idea of who we are.
Ego-defense	Defending our ego against others' attacks on it.
Elaboration	The active processing of information in conjunction with other information already in the memory so as to identify meaning in the new information.
Elaboration likelihood model	The higher the consumer involvement, the higher the likelihood that the consumer would elaborate on the message.
Elements of Culture	Values; Norms; Rituals; Customs; Myths; Knowledge, Science and Technology; Laws; Arts; and Material Culture
Elimination by aspects	A decision-making model similar to the lexicographic model, but with one important difference. The consumer rates the attributes in the order of importance; and, in addition, s/he defines minimum required values
Elimination stage	Consumers narrow down the set of alternatives for closer comparisons, eliminating those not judged suitable.
Emergent occasions	Those that are not predetermined and do not repeat in a regular pattern.
Emoticons	Text-based sequence of characters that depict human emotions, such as a tearful eye
Emotional hierarchy	The sequeence in which we feel first, then act, and think last
Emotions	A sudden surge of feelings.
Enculturation	Learning one's culture.
Enduring involvement	The degree of interest a consumer feels in a product or service on an ongoing basis.
Engel's law	According to Engel's law, the lower the per capita income of a nation or people, the more they tend to spend on basic necessities such as food, housing, and clothing.
Envionmental factors	Refers to sources of information and influences surrounding the growing child.
Episodic knowledge	Knowledge that consists of description of events.
Ethnic Identity	Refers to a person's knowledge of his or her membership in a social group and the value and emotional significance attached to that membership.
Ethnicity	Refers to the distinctions among people based on their national or cultural heritage.
Ethnocentrism	The belief in the superiority of one's own culture over all others.
Evaluation criteria	Standards against which consumers evaluate a product.
Evaluative mode	Consuming with the intention of evaluating the product performance.
Evoked set	Subset of the brands in the awareness set
Exchange	An interchange between two parties where each receives from the other something of more value and gives up something of less value.
Experiential browsers/ web surfer	Are consumers whose principal and overall motive for going to the Web sites of online stores is fun and excitement.
Experiential products	Products that we need to try or actually use in order to enjoy them and judge their value or utility to you.
Expertise	Possession of knowledge about a topic, or product—especially knowledge that is not yet common knowledge.
Exploratory shopping	Refers to browsing around after collecting the planned items.
Expressive gift	The extent to which the gift is accompanied by the giver's sentiment.
Extended problem solving	Where search is extensive and deliberation prolonged.

Extended problems	Purchase tasks for products never purchased before, or made long ago, or where risks of wrong choice are high.
Extended self	Comprises all the external entities and objects that we consider, with pride, part of ourselves.
External reference price	the price the marketer uses to anchor a price advantage (e.g., "compare at___").
External stimuli	Sources of information you see outside—in the marketplace and on the street.
Extraversion	Being outgoing, persuasive, and displaying leadership roles
Extrinsic reward	External to the product, e.g., coupons, sweepstakes, rebates,

F

Families	Are two or more persons related by blood, marriage, or adoption.
Family life cycle	How a person advances from one stage to another is called a family life cycle.
Fantasy consumption	Vicarious consumption, consumption by imagining things and situations.
Fashion System	A society's collective ideas (or conventional wisdom) about what is in fashion and what is out of it.
Feminity	Refers to the personality traits of compassion, sensitivity, and politeness. Persons with these traits tend to value interpersonal relations over self-centered gains.
Flaunters	These are consumers who have money and want to show it. They derive pleasure in displaying their wealth, hoping to impress or arouse envy in others. They buy conspicuous items (expensive cars, luxurious clothes, diamonds, etc.) and enjoy their possessions and acquisitions more for their exhibition value than their utilitarian value.
Flow	Refers to a situation where the consumer gets immersed in the site navigation, losing a sense of time.
Foot in the door	A marketer makes a small request to which the consumer cannot (or usually won't) refuse; subsequently, the marketer makes a larger request.
Formal group	Membership is granted by a formal admission into the group.
Forward buy	Buying an item for future consumption.
Framing	The context in which information is presented.
Framing-effect	The bias in the interpretation of the information due to its framing or context.
Functional theory of attitude	Katz's theorythat people hold certain attitudes (or come to acquire those attitudes) because these attitudes serve one or more of the following four functions: utilitarian, value expressive, ego-defense, and knowledge.

G

Gender role orientation	Refers to our concepts of the specific behaviors expected of a person by virtue of that person's gender.
Generation X	Are those that are born between 1965 to 1976.
Generation Y	Are those that are born between 1997 to 1984.
Geodemographics	Is the study of relationships between demographics on the one hand and geographic location on the other.
GI Generation	Are those that are born between 1901 to 1924.
Gift	A tangible or intangible product voluntarily given by one person to another, through some ritual presentation and embodying some symbolic representation of the giver's sentiments for the recipient

Goal object	Something in the world the acquisition or attainment of which will bring us happiness—by reducing our current discomfort or tension.
Goal oriented online shoppers	Shoppers who go on the Internet with a purchase goal in mind.
Group	Two or more persons sharing a common purpose.

H

Health Condition	Refers to one's physical health, including ailments, physical strength, and energy levels that one feels for everyday activities.
Hedonic consumption	The use of products/services for the sake of intrinsic enjoyment.
Hedonic motives	Consumer need and desire to obtain pleasure.
Heider's balance theory	Maintains that in any relationship between three entities, a state of unbalance cannot be sustained, and it will be resolved by altering one of the relationships.
Heuristic search	Ad hoc acquisition of information to reach intuitive judgments.
Heuristics	Quick rules of thumb and shortcuts used to make decisions.
High involvement learning	A mode o flearning when the product is very important to us as consumers and a lot is at stake.
High touch	Products that require touch and feel, and consequently cannot be judged or bought in virtual space.
High-Context Culture	Culture where to understand something, you need to know the context. Behind everything, there are layers of meaning not immediately apparent.

Hinduism	A system of religious beliefs founded in India
Homophyly	Resemblance arising out of love and identification
Household	A household is one or more persons living in the same quarters.

I

Ideal self	The person we would like to become
Identificational influence	Occurs when a consumer emulates the behavior of another person.
Image congruity theory	We like to associate ourselves with objects (things, activities, and people) that have an image that is congruent with our own image of ourselves.
Immediacy bias	Desire for immediate outcome
Impulse control disorder	Failure to control our impulse to do something.
Impulsive consumer behavior	Refers to a specific purchase and/or consumption activity undertaken on the spur of the moment.
Income	The amount of monetary earnings that person receives periodically on a more or less regular basis.
Independent sources	Those not controlled by marketers and also not known to us personally.
Individualism	The idea that individuals are responsible for their own success, which is achieved through individual ability.
Inept set	Brands in the evoked set that are considered unfit for your needs.
Inference making	The consumer act of assuming the missing information to make a judgment about a product.
Informal group	A group that has few explicit rules about member behavior, e.g. family
Information processing mode (IPM).	In this mode, "the consumer is thought to acquire information about brand attributes, form evaluative criteria, judge the levels of these attributes in various brands, and combine these attribute-levels for overall brand evaluation."

Informational influence	Occurs when a consumer is influenced by the product information someone provides.
Infromation overload	A condition in which the information being presented is too much to process for you as a consumer.
Innate needs	Needs we are born with.
Innovativeness	Being predisposed to embrace new products, ideas, and behaviors.
Insight	The ability to see the hidden nature of a solution.
Institutions	Permanent groups or entities with a pervasive and universal presence in a society, such as schools, religions, and family.
In-store factors	Characteristics that surround the consumer's decision process inside the store.
Instrumental learning	A process where one learns to act in a certain way that is rewarding.
Instrumental values	The means, paths, or behavioral standards by which we pursue those goals (e.g., honesty, altruism, etc.)
Instrumentality	Refers to valuing things and people merely for their utility.
Interaction quality	The pleasantness of social experience in the acquisition and use of the service.
Intergenerational Influence	Refers to the transmission of values, attitudes, and behaviors from one generation to the other.
Internal reference price	Price we believe to be the right price.
Internal stimuli	Perceived states of discomfort arising from something inside you.
Internet Maven	A consumer who is more knowledgeable than the average consumer about the e-marketplace, and about product information available on the Internet.
Intrinsic reward	The reward built into the product itself
Involuntary attention	Attention that is forced on the consumer.
Involvement	the degree of interest a consumer finds in a product or service or object or activity.
Islam	The religion of the followers of the Prophet Mohammed.

J

Joint decisions	Are those in which more than one decision participant made the decision.
Judgement models	Also called "decision models" and "choice rules," are procedures and rules consumers use to consider various product attributes to arrive at their product choice.
Just noticeable difference (j.n.b)	The magnitude of change necessary for the change to be noticed.

K

Key informant method	Ask prominent people in a community to name a few persons they consider able to influence others' opinion on a given topic.
Knowledge	The basis of beliefs on which we base actions.
Knowledge function	The ability of an object to serve our need for knowledge and certainty.

L

Laddering	A procedure to map a consumer's view of how a product's use ultimately fulfills his or her higher level values.
Laggards	Consumers who are most hesitant to adopt anything new and who try to resist or postpone adopting the new product or new behavior.

Late majority	Consumers who are very skeptical of anything new, are extremely risk-averse, and resist adopting unless an innovation has been proven useful and safe.
Latent loyalty	When the consumer likes the brand but has been unable to buy it.
Laws	Norms with legal consequences.
Learned needs	Needs that are acquired in the process of growing up and living.
Learning	Acquiring a response to a stimulus.
Learning hierarchy	A sequence of learning wherein cognitions come first, affect next, and action last.
Lemon law	Protects a car buyer against being sold a substandard car.
Lexicographic model	A choice making rule wherein the consumer rank orders product attributes in terms of importance.
Life projects	Enduring, ongoing, significant endeavors undertaken by consumers to achieve certain life goals.
Lifestyle	Our pattern of living
Limited problem solving	The consumer invests some limited amount of time and energy in searching and evaluating alternative solutions.
Limited problems	Nontrivial, but risks are moderate, and the product or service is not overly complex or technical in terms of its features.
Long-term memory	The part of the brain where information we do not currently need is stored away.
Low involvement learning	The learning method when product is relevant but not much is at stake, such as a low priced item of routine use.
Low-context	Meaning that there is no human element in communication, no nonverbal gestures, and no referent opinion.
Low-Context Culture	Culture where to understand the meaning of something, you don't have to look at the context; the thing in itself is self-explanatory; also people are explicit in their communication.

M

Make-goods	recovery offerings or concessions to dissatisfied consumers
Manscaping	Was a term introduced in 2004 by the American TV show Queer Eye for the Straight Guy, and is shorthand for "andscaping" the male body by shaving, trimming, waxing, or brushing the body hair.
Market mavens	Individuals who are generally knowledgeable about the marketplace happenings and possess information about a range of products, prices, distribution outlets, and even special promotions in effect at the time.
Marketer	An individual or an organization with an organizational goal that offers products and services in exchange for the consumer's money or (occasionally) other resources.
Marketer sources	Those that come from the marketer of the product or service.
Marketer System	All the agents involved in bringing the product to the market.
Masculinity	Personality traits of independencfe, competiveness, assertiveness.
Maslow's hierachy of needs	Psychologist Maslow's theory about the order in which humans experience needs.
Match-up hypothesis	The celebrity chosen for promoting a brand should have an image similar to the brand's image (or desired image).
Material Culture	All man-made objects in a society that represent the degree of affluence and progress of a society in contrast to the life lived entirely in and with nature.
Materialism	The extent to which one considers possessing and consuming more and more products as a sign of success and a means of happiness.

Meaning negotiation in media shows	Seeing meaning in the episode, understanding the episode and accepting it as logical and plausible.
Means-end chains	Pathways connecting product attributes to ultimate consumer goals or values.
Membership groups	Those in which an individual claiming to be a member is so recognized by the head or leader and/or key group members, even when the membership is informal.
Memorabilia	Products designed to capture the authenticity of a person, place, or event from a historic period.
Memory	Information storage area of the mind and its stored contents.
Mental activities	Acts of the mind, and they relate to what we think, feel, and know about products.
Metrosexuals	Urban males who have a strong aesthetic sense and spend a great deal of time and money on their appearances and lifestyles.
Modeling	A process whereby learning occurs by observing others
Money attitude	Consumer's view of and orientation toward money—what it means to them and how they want to utilize it.
Moods	Emotions felts less intensely.
Motivation	The human drive to attain a goal object.
Motivation research	A method directed at discovering the reasons (i.e., motives) for a person's behavior–reasons the consumer is either unaware of or is unwilling to admit in direct questioning.
Multiattribute models of attitude	Suggests that overall attitude is based on the component beliefs about the object, weighted by the evaluation of those beliefs.
Myths	Tales and stories handed down from history without known origins and with no test of truth.

N

Need	A discomforting human condition.
Need for cognition	Our discomfort with ignorance, our need for information, our need for understanding the world around us, and our need for knowledge.
Neglectful families	Parents are distant from their children, who are neglected in these families because the parent(s) place more priority on their individual affairs.
Negligent consumer behavior	Consumption that puts a person or others at risk and imposes heavy costs on society or otherwise deteriorates its quality of life in the long run.
Neuroticism	Being emotionally unstable, nervous, and anxious.
Nonmarketer sources	Sources of information that are independent of the marketer's control.
Non-profit organization	A firm that offers products and services either free of cost or at a nominal charge insufficient to cover costs or make any profit.
Normative influence	Occurs when a consumer's decision or action is based on his or her desire to conform to the expectations of someone else.
Norms	Unwritten rules of behavior
Nostalgia	A longing for the things and lifestyles of the past.

O

OCEAN	Openness; Conscientiousness; Extraversion; Agreeableness; Neuroticism
Odd pricing	A practice wherein prices are set just below the next round number.
One-stop shopping	Finding all of the consumer's requirements of related products in one place or from one source.

Openness	Being curious, insightful, imaginative, original, and open to new experiences and diversity.
Opinion leadership	The giving of information and advice, leading to the acceptance of the advocated position by the recipient of the opinion.
Opportunity recognition	Problem recognition aroused by an external, solution stimulus.
Optimism	Is a personality factor that concerns the degree to which a person is hopeful about the future and expects life opportunities for continual personal progress.
Outcome quality	The consequences experienced from the use of the service.
Overprivileged	Those earning substantially above the median income of their group.

P

Paradox	When reality is contrary to the intuitive expectation.
Particularism	Valuing the individuality of each situation
Passive audience theory	The view of the cosnumer procesing the message that consumers' minds sit there, like couch potatoes, passively, and absorb whatever is thrown at them.
Peer-to-peer marketing	A special case of buzz marketing where the goal is not just to spread the word but to get the target audiences to act on the word which comes from their peers.
Perceived justice	The consumer's perception that he or she was treated fairly during the complaint resolution process.
Perceived risk	The degree of loss (i.e., amount at stake) in the event that a wrong choice is made.
Perception	The process by which the human mind becomes aware of and interprets a stimulus.
Perceptual distortion	Information being encoded non-objectively, resulting in the consumer seeing it as being different from reality.
Perceptual maps	Visual depictions of consumer perceptions of alternative brands of a product category in multi-dimensional grids.
Perceptual or Differential threshold	The minimum level or magnitude at which a stimulus begins to be sensed.
Peripheral route	The processing of a message superficially.
Permissive families	Children are given relative independence in conducting their own affairs, especially in their adolescent years.
Personal sources	Family members, friends, and other acquaintances with past experience with and/or greater knowledge of the product category.
Personality	A person's psychological makeup that engenders characteristic responses to the environment in which he or she lives.
Personalization	Refers to a business organization treating a consumer as a person rather than a number.
Pessimism	Tendency to see the future as bleak.
Physical activities	Acts of the human body, and they relate to what we physically do to acquire and consume products.
Picture matching method	Consumers who have just been shown a test advertisement are shown a set of faces with differing expressions and are asked to mark the face that comes closest to how they themselves felt when they viewed the ad.
Planned purchases	Purchases that the consumer planned to buy before entering the store.
Pomosexual	Is a term that stands for *post-modern sexual*, and describes persons who do not identify with any specific classification of sexuality.

Population Pyramid	A bar graph which displays the age and sex distribution of a population.
Posession Rituals	Set of activities we perform to transform or modify products obtained from the marketplace.
Positively expressive gifts	Gifts are given to people for whom one has special feelings
Post-purchase cognitive dissonance	Also known as "buyer's remorse"—post-purchase doubt about the wisdom of one's choice.
Poverty	The level of personal wealth at which a household cannot even pay for all of its basic needs, such as food, clothing, and shelter.
Power Distance	The extent to which the less powerful members of the society accept the authority of those with greater power.
Price gouging	A practice wherein the seller hikes up the price just to take advantage of some short-term shortage or emergency circumstances.
Primary group	Groups with whom a person interacts frequently (not necessarily face-to-face) and considers their opinion or norms important to follow.
Problem recognition	The consumer's realization of the gap between his/her current state and the desired state.
Problem solving	Actively processing information to reach certain judgments that wil conclude the issue.
Problem stimulus	One in which the problem itself is the source of information, such as the sight of dirty laundry or the printer's empty ink cartridge.
Product	Any physical or nonphysical product or service that offers some benefit to the consumer, including a place, a person, or an idea offered for exchange.
Product disposal	Dispossessing product remnants after use.
Product placement	Strategy of embedding a product within the media program content
Psychogenic needs	Needs that stem not from our bodies, but from our mental makeup—the way we think about ourselves and about the world.
Psychographics	The sum total of values, self-concepts, personality and lifestyles.
Psychological bonding	The connection consumers feel toward the brand.
Psychology	The study of the human mind and mental processes that influence a person's behavior.
Psychology of price perception	How consumers psychologically perceive prices.
Purchase decision involvement	The degree of concern you experience about making the right choice.
Purposive behavior	When energy is expended to attain some goal object.

Q

Quality cue	Any information used for making inferences about the quality of the product or service.

R

Race	Refers to the distinction among humans based on their genes, from which stem basic differences in the subspecies of humans.
Recall	Becoming conscious of some information residing in LTM without current encounter with it externally.
Reciprocation	Returning the favor in like manner.
Recognition	Refers to identifying a stimulus as having been encountered before.
Recognition sset	Brand names the consumer recognizes as being familiar.
Recreation/Hedonic value	Comes from objects and activities when they recreate our moods and regenerate our mental ability—removing our fatigue and boredom, stimulating the senses, and rejuvenating our minds.

Reference groups	Persons, groups, and institutions one uses as points of reference.
Reference price	The price consumers expect to pay.
Referent	Any person, group, or institution that serves as a point of reference
Relationship	A sentiment where one feels a special sense of being connected.
Relative advantage	How much better the innovation is compared to the current product that it would substitute.
Religion	A system of beliefs about the supernatural, spiritual world, about God, and about how humans, as God's creatures, are supposed to behave on this earth.
Religious Affiliation	Membership, in objective terms, in a religion.
Religious Identity	The degree of involvement and commitment in that religion as a system of belief and practice.
Repetition	The incidence of an occurrence more than once.
Resource	Something we own or possess that people value.
Retro products	Products that are designed to capture significant stylistic aspects of some old, once popular but since retired product.
Retrosexual	A man with a generally poor sense of style.
Reverse channel	When the manufacturers and retailers take back old products and empty containers.
Risk Averseness	Preference for avoiding risks.
Ritualistic gifts	Gifts are given simply because it is a ritual, the occasion demands it
Rituals	A set of activities done in a fixed sequence and repeated periodically.
Rote memorization	Rehearsing the information until it gets firmly lodged in our long-term memory.
Routine problem solving	Generally, no new information is considered and consumers usually solve these problems by simply repeating their previous choices.
Routine problems	Are those that, as a consumer, you have solved many times in the past.

S

Sacred	An intangible entity that is other-worldly.
Safety and security need	The need to be protected from danger.
Satisfaction/ dissatisfaction	The positive or negative feeling consumers get with the outcome of product or service consumption.
Satisficing	A consumer's (or a decision maker's) acceptance of an alternative that he or she finds satisfying, acknowledging that there might be a better alternative.
Search strategy	The pattern of information acquisition that consumers utilize to solve their decision problems.
Secondary group	Groups marked by infrequent contacts, and norms of the group are considered less binding or obligatory.
Selection stage	The decision making stage in which an alternative is selected out of several.
Self-actualization	The need to realize one's true potential.
Self-concept	A person's conception of himself or herself.
Self-designation method of identifying opinion leaders	A survey method where the respondent rate or designatie themsleves on a quality..
Self-efficacy	Viewing oneself as effective, in control.
Self-esteem	Holding oneself as valued.
Self-Perception Theory	Bem's theory that we infer our attitude from our own behavior.

Self-selection	Consumers self-select themselves to be customers of the store or consumers of the product or brand that offers the advantage they seek.
Semantic knowledge	Consists of information about objects and their properties.
Semantic memories	Memories for objects and their properties.
Sensation	An event wherein a stimulus comes within the reach of one or more of our five senses: seeing, hearing, smelling, touching, and tasting.
Sensory memeory	The ability of our senses to keep information alive briefly.
Shopping	All activities the consumer undertakes while in the store, physical or virtual. This set of activities includes "walking through the stores at a relaxed pace, examining merchandise, comparing products, interacting with sale staff, asking questions, trying things on, and ultimately, though not always making purchases.
Shopping orientation	A consumer's predominant motive for shopping activitiy.
Short-term memory	The part of the brain where information is being held and being processed currently.
Signaling	Implicitly communicating one's attitudes and desires.
Silent Generation	Those born between 1925 to 1945.
Situational involvement	The degree of interest a consumer takes in a specific situation or on a specific occasion.
Social archetype groups	Categories of persons sharing a lifestyle, such as bohemians, literati, jocks, bookworms, cowboys, etc.
Social capital	the network of friends and professional connections that can be of help in our hour of need.
Social capital	Your social connections, the network of people you know.
Social Class	The relative standing of a person in society in terms of status; a prestige hierarchy in a society
Social self-concept	The way others see us.
Social value	A products ability to enable us to manage our social worlds (as opposed to the physical world).
Socially conscious businesses	Companies that espouse desirable societal values.
Social-oriented families	Families that are more concerned with maintaining discipline and harmony among family members.
Sociology	the study of social systems—groups, organizations, and societies.
Solution stimulus	The information emanating from a solution itself.
Source	Any person or organization that is conveying the message or stands behind the message.
Source attractiveness	The quality of making an emotional connection with the viewer.
Source credibility	Refers to how credible (believable or trustable) the source is judged to be by the target audience.
Source independence	Separation of the source from the company that would benefit from the message.
Source similarity	How similar to themselves consumers see the spokesperson to be.
Spurious loyalty	Loyalty that is incidental, not well-founded
Status consumption	Acquiring and consuming products that signify a status in society.
Status crystallization	A condition when all components of one's social class become consistent.
Stereotype	A perception we come to form about a whole category of things or people.
Stimulus	Any object or event in the external environment.
Stimulus discrimination	A process wherein a consumer perceives two stimuli as different so that the response learned for one stimulus is not repeated for the other.

Stimulus generalization	A process wherein a consumer extends a learned response for one stimulus to other similar stimuli.
Store enviornment	Refers both to the physical setting and the social stimuli within the store.
Store image	The sum total of perceptions that consumers have about a store.
Store loyalty	A consumer's predominant patronage of a store, based on a favorable attitude and preference
Store personality	Characterization of a store on personality-like qualities such as sophisticated, modern, traditional, tacky, etc.
Structured occasions	Standard occasions that occur repeatedly on the same predetermined times or days.
Subjective norm	What others expect us to do (i.e., normative expectations).
Subliminal perception	the perception of a stimulus without being aware of it.
Subliminal stimuli	Stimuli of which one is not conscious.
Susceptibility to Interpersonal Influence (SIPI)	Consumer motivation to follow other people's expectations and advice.
Symbolic	Items whose principal value is not material but sentimental or intangible
Symbolic groups	Groups Have no provision or procedure for granting membership.
Syncratic decisions	Are decisions in which all parties play an equal role in decision making.
Systematic information search	An organized pattern of seeking information, directed at answering specific questions.

T

Task-oriented shoppers	Shoppers who focus on finding what they came to seek and want to finish the shopping task efficiently.
Telecommuting	The practice of working at a distance from a formal place of employment.
Terminal values	The goals we seek in life (e.g., freedom, wealth, salvation, etc.)
The theory of reasoned action	Attitude toward an object is based on the consequences the object has, weighed by the desirability or undesirability of these consequences.
Thematic apperception test	A form of story completion task based on a series of ambiguous pictures shown to the consumer.
Three-factor theory of compulsive buying	Biological, psychological, and sociological determinants.
Tightwads	People who are obsessive about saving as much money as possible.
Top-down customization	A process wherein consumers build a product starting from the loaded version.
Traditional sex role attitude	The view that a woman's place is in the home and man's place is out of the home, working and earning a living.
Treasure hunting	Finding something unusual and unexpected.
Trialability	The extent to which it is possible to try out the innovation on a smaller scale.
Tribal consumption	Consumption of brands and products that is public and there is some participation in planned events of the community.
Trustworthiness	Perceived benevolence and dependability of the opinion giver.
Two-sided messages	Present both the merits and demerits of a product, brand, or issue.
Two-step flow of communication theory	suggests that communication from mass media reaches the masses in two-steps—first from mass media to opinion leaders and then from opinion leaders to the masses.

U

Übersexual The word "über" has German roots and means above or superior. Thus, an ubersexual is a variant of metrosexual, a more "refined" male, who is more confident and more focused on his mind than body.

Uncertainty Avoidance The extent to which people in a society feel threatened by ambiguous situations and want to avoid them.

Unconditioned stimulus A stimulus to which the consumer already has a pre-existing response.

Underprivileged Those earning substantially below the median income of their own income group.

Uniqueness seeking A personality trait wherein a person seeks to be unique, different from others.

Universalism Belief in the universal application of the same rule

Unplanned purchases Purchases the consumer did not intend to buy before entering the store.

Upward mobility When a person moves to a higher social class

Utilitarian The concrete (not symbolic) outcomes of a product or activity,

Utilitarian value The set of tangible outcomes of a product usage (or an activity).

V

Value The sum total of net benefits we receive from an activity or an exchange.

The ratio of benefits from the product versus the costs the consumer incurs in time, effort, and money.

Value compatibility Consistency with consumers' deeply held values.

Value-based business practice The adoption of some socially desirable value as a corporate value, which then guides everything the company does.

Values Desired end-states of life and preferred paths to achieving them.

Values A society's ideas as to what in life is worthy of pursuit and how those pursuits should be conducted.

Vanity Excessive pride in one's appearance and accomplishments.

Verifiable benefit Benefits that can be verified by independent laboratory tests.

Viral marketing Seeking the spread of product acceptance from one consumer to another in an exponential fashion.

Vividness A stimulus' brightness and distinctness.

Voice Complaining or praising someone or something—the act of expressing one's dissatisfaction or satisfaction

Voluntary attention Attention given by choice—the consumer chooses to pay attention.

Voluntary simplicity Acquiring a belief system that too much consumption is undesirable, and, accordingly, living life with fewer products and services.

W

Want A desire for a specific object or product.

Wayfinding The ease of finding your way around the store.

Wealth A consumer's total financial resources.

Weber's law The larger the base quantity, the larger the magnitude of change needed for the change to be noticed.

Weblogs Journals or logs people keep on their personal Web sites.

Word-of-Mouth The consumers' conversations with other consumers about a product or service.

Z

Zapping Consumers avoiding commercials by switching channels.

Zipping Consumers avoiding the commercial by fast-forwarding while watching a prerecorded program

SUBJECT INDEX

heuristics, 315
hierarchy
    attitude, 188
    emotional, 188
    learning, 188
    low-involvement, 189
    rational, 186
Hinduism, 486
Hispanics, 473
    demographics, 473
    what they value, 474
    building identity, 475

I
id, 132
ideal self, 143
identity,
    virtual, 632
ignorance paradox, 318
image
    congruity, 144
impulse purchase,
income, 492
    income groups, 797
Index of Consumer Sentiment, 495
individualism,
    vs. collectivism, 240
inference making, 324
influence
    identificational, 279
    informational, 278
    normative, 279
information,
    processing modes, 335
    processing strategies, 313
    information processing mode (IPM), 335
    search, 309
    sources, 311
innovation, 113
    adoption of, 112
    characteristics of, 114
innovativeness, 138
innovators, 291
instrumental conditioning, 97
intergenerational influence (IGI), 413
interpretative research, A-4
involvement, 42
    enduring, 53
    measures of A-11
    purchase decision, 53
    situational, 53

J
Japan
 aging of population in, 444

joint decisions, 404
Judaism, 486
just noticeable difference (j.n.d.), 74

K
Knowledge
    episodic, 109
    semantic, 109
knowledge function of attitudes 193

L
laddering, 131
learning, 94
    cognitive, 99
    instrumental, 97
    models of, 95
Lemon Law, 602
lexicographic choice model, 321
life-stage, 308
lifestyle, 158
limited problem solving, 316
List of Value (LOV), 127
low-involvement attitude hierarchy, 189
loyalty,
    brand. See brand loyalty, 530
    store, 383

M
MAO model, 44
Market,
    Frictionless, 587
    Mavens, 278
Marketer, 12
marketer sources,
    information, 312
marketing,
    concept, 21
    contextual, 632
    experiential, 640
market mavens, 278
Maslow's hierarchy of needs, 37
Mason Haire Technique, 42
Match-up hypothesis, 226
materialism, 129
mavens, market, 278
    Internet, 580
means-end chain, 130, 131
Memory, 103
    Short term, 104
    Sensory, 103
    Long term, 103
mental activities, 9
modeling, 98
modified rebuy, 416. 417
Mnemonics, 106

THE "BIG FIVE" OF MY OWN*

Five wisdom bits have sustained and energized my journey through this book.

1. If Aristotle Ran General Motors It's impossible to read Tom Morris' interpretation of Aristotle and not feel rejuvenated about one's work. In *If Aristotle Ran General Motors*, Morris answers the 64 million dollar question: What is the meaning of life? The meaning of life, says Morris, is CREATION—the thing or outcome we produce as we work. To make that outcome the very best one is capable of, that is the purpose and meaning of life. Writing this book, I have experienced the Aristotelian meaning first hand, finding both inspiration and fulfillment. For more than a decade (five years, more focused), this book has been my *Karma*.

2. Great Minds Discuss Ideas *Small minds discuss people. Average minds discuss events.* This quote, attributed to Eleanor Roosevelt, has reassured me a thousand times of the power of ideas. While people- and event discussions will continue to offer us comic relief, the world moves, ultimately, by the power of ideas. By bodies of knowledge. Knowledge that is created, recreated, shaped and disseminated. In this great enterprise of our times, *MY B Book* is presented as a modest contribution. Because, ultimately, the inherent worth of ideas prevails—above people and over events.

3. Kanter's Law of Success *"Every project in the middle seems a failure,"* says Harvard professor Rosabeth Moss Kanter, author of *Confidence: How Winning Streaks and Losing Streaks Begin and End.* Although I never quite encountered that specific middle moment, I came close, often. Kanter's Law helped me glide over.

4. Let's At Least Be Interesting During my graduate days, Jerry Zaltman (then at my Alma Mater, Pitt, retired recently from Harvard) penned and circulated a paper titled "Let's At Least Be Interesting." His paper, to the extent I recall, was a call to academics to not make scholarly papers boring. I, in total awe of the utterly fascinating writings of Belk, Holbrook, Holt, Pollay, and Sherry, among others (here counting only

the academics), have tried to cultivate an "interesting" style myself, sometimes to the utter dismay of some reviewers, but, also to one most rewarding outcome, when, several years ago and out of the blue, Arch made contact to tell me (to humor me, I am sure) that of my writings he was a fan.

The goal of writing to "be interesting" was particularly important to this book project. If you have come this far, you know of course that the book is more than mere interesting writing. It is also a retelling of a body of knowledge, and, in so doing, sometimes altering its original form as well as content, and not infrequently, creating some anew. "New Theory" in what is primarily a textbook? I have heard some ask, and then immediately respond with another rhetorical question: to the first-time reader, unfamiliar with the CB body of knowledge (or unfamiliar in this depth), aren't ALL theories new?

The book has turned out to be a mix of the old and the new, the established and the venturing, the gravitas and the playful, the professorial and the usability-biased, and a mix of science and literature that the calm, curious, and innovation-embracing minds will find rewarding. From opposite mindsets, though, I fancy, and then fear, the sobriquet (borrowing from *Freakonomics* subtitle) of a rogue CB author.

5. Find Your Voice Find your voice. And then help someone else find his/hers. (Stephen R. Covey, The 8th Habit: From Effectiveness to Greatness.)

"Finding" is what I had been doing for more than a decade; Covey helped me (like thousand others) put it in words. Making it a tangible goal.

It is worth asking, though, which is more fulfilling: finding your voice, or helping someone else find his/hers? Not all are blessed to find it—some never had this 'voice' wisdom dawn on them; others never knew what their voice was. And many lack one or more of the requisite five resources (money, time, physical energy, knowledge/skills, and social capital/network, see Chapter 1).

Some who have found their voice never graduate to the next level—thus, missing the joy of helping others find theirs. (And the joy of morphing from a muffler to a booster is even more surreal.) I have been fortunate to have as benefactors more than some six-dozen people, who have, during this book project and over my professional life as well, served to boost my voice. **This book is one embodiment of my voice.** Dear voice finders and voice supporters—old friends and those who may now gather: For making the book possible and now for reading it in (almost) its entirety, as well as for sharing your opinions, please accept my gratitude.

ban mittal

---

*Maslow models humans by five core categories of needs (Chapter 2). Personality psychologists portray a person by five personality supra-traits (Chapter 5). There are five universal cultural value dimensions (Chapter 9). Academic marketing literature profiles brand personality also by five dimensions. And the famous P's of marketing are (or should be) also five (for the fifth 'P', see Chapter 21, and also *Valuespace*, 2001, www.myvaluespace.com).

Banwari ('Ban') Mittal holds an MBA from IIMA and a Ph. D. in marketing from the University of Pittsburgh. A professor of marketing, Ban has taught at SUNY, Buffalo, the University of Miami, Northern Kentucky University (current affiliation), and University of New South Wales (Sydney, Australia).

His research has been published in such journals as *Journal of Marketing*, *Psychology & Marketing*, *Journal of Consumer Behaviour*, *Journal of Retailing*, and *Marketing Theory*. He has previously coauthored two books: *ValueSpace* (McGraw-Hill 2001, www.myvaluespace.com) and *Customer Behavior* (Dryden Press, 1998, and Thomson Learning, 2002), both with Emory's Jag Sheth. The present book, arguably his proudest, is a digest of his understanding of Consumer Behavior, sixth-sensed through a decade of research, teaching, and contemplating consumer behavior.

When not working, which is seldom since he considers even TV viewing and Halloween parties work—observing consumption culture—he indulges in Yoga and in playing Jay Leno to any audience of one or more he can get attention from. (bm@mycbbook.com) (www.myvaluespace.com)

(Ban's *Second Life* Avatar appears in Chapter 1 and another picture in Chapter 9.)

Priya Raghubir is an Associate Professor at the Haas School of Business, University of California at Berkeley where she teaches Marketing Research, Consumer Behavior, and Marketing Strategy. She received her Ph.D. in Marketing from New York University in 1994. An MBA from the Indian Institute of Management, Ahmedabad, India (1985), her undergraduate degree is in Economics from St. Stephen's College, Delhi University, India (1983). Her pre-Ph.D. experience included the financial industry in Hong Kong (with Jardine Fleming and Citibank) and India (with Citibank) for 5 years. She taught at the Hong Kong University of Science and Technology in Hong Kong from 1994-1997.

Priya's research interests are in the areas of survey methods as well as psychological aspects of price promotions, visual information processing, and the subjective value of money. She has published widely in such journals as the *Journal of Marketing Research*, *Journal of Consumer Research*, *Organizational Behavior and Human Decision Processes*, *Journal of Consumer Psychology*, *Marketing Science*, *California Management Review*, *Memory and Cognition*, *Journal of Retailing*, *Personality and Social Psychology Bulletin*, *Public Opinion Quarterly*, *Journal of Applied Social Psychology*, *Psychology and Marketing*, and *Marketing Letters*. Priya has made some 100+ academic as well as executive education presentations in India, China, and the U.S. (priya@mycbbook.com)

Sharon Beatty received her B.S. from the University of Central Florida, her M.B.A. from the University of Colorado, and her Ph.D. from the University of Oregon in 1980. She focuses her research on shopping and services issues. She has been at the University of Alabama for twenty years and has been doctoral coordinator during all those years. She has published over fifty journal articles, in such journals as *Journal of Marketing Research*, *Journal of Consumer Research*, *Journal of Retailing*, *Journal of Service Research*, and *Journal of Advertising*. She is on the editorial boards of six journals, such as the *Journal of the Academy of Marketing Science*, *Journal of Retailing*, and *Journal of Business Research*. She is a past member of the Board of Governors for the Academy of Marketing Science and of the American Marketing Association's Academic Council.

In 1998, Sharon was named a Distinguished Fellow by the Academy of Marketing Science, and in 2001, she was chosen to be a Distinguished Scholar by the Society for Marketing Advances. (Sharon@mycbbook.com)

Morris B. Holbrook is the W. T. Dillard Professor of Marketing in the Graduate School of Business at Columbia University, New York, NY, 10027, USA. Holbrook graduated from Harvard College with a BA degree in English (1965) and received his MBA (1967) and PhD (1975) degrees in Marketing from Columbia University. Since 1975, he has taught courses at the Columbia Business School in such areas as Marketing Strategy, Sales Management, Research Methods, Consumer Behavior, and Commercial Communication in the Culture of Consumption. His research has covered a wide variety of topics in marketing and consumer behavior with a special focus on issues related to communication in general and to aesthetics, semiotics, hermeneutics, art, entertainment, music, motion pictures, nostalgia, and stereography in particular. Recent books include The Semiotics of Consumption: Interpreting Symbolic Consumer Behavior in Popular Culture and Works of Art (with Elizabeth C. Hirschman, Mouton de Gruyter, 1993); Consumer Research: Introspective Essays on the Study of Consumption (Sage, 1995); and Consumer Value: A Framework for Analysis and Research (edited, Routledge, 1999).

Morris pursues such hobbies as playing the piano, attending jazz and classical concerts, going to movies and the theater, collecting musical recordings, taking stereographic photos, and being kind to cats.

(Morris@mycbbook.com)

Arch Woodside is Professor of Marketing, Boston College. He is a Fellow of the Royal Society of Canada, Society for Marketing Advances, American Psychological Association, and the American Psychological Society. He is the author of Market-Driven Thinking (Butterworth-Heinemann, 2005).

Arch is the Editor-in-Chief of the Journal of Business Research (published by Elsevier, twelve issues per annual volume). He is the Editor of Managing Product Innovation (2005) and Designing Winning Products (2000), both published by JAI Press, an Imprint of Elsevier. He is a Fellow of the International Academy of Tourism Research. He co-founded the Advertising and Consumer Psychology Symposium held annually by the Society of Consumer Psychology. He has served as a Visiting Professor of Marketing at the University of Warwick, University of Hawaii—Monoa Valley, University of Hawaii—Hilo, University of Innsbruck; International Management Center, Budapest, Helsinki School of Economics and Business Administration, Swedish School of Economics—Helsinki, University of Osijeck, Croatia, Hernstein Institute—Vienna, University of Prince Edward Island, University of Auckland, and University of Christchurch, Canterbury. Currently he serves as Honorary Professor of Marketing at the University of New South Wales, Sydney.

Arch's management consultancy work is in the areas of marketing and customer thinking, advertising effectiveness, marketing strategy performance auditing, customer and patient satisfaction program design, customer acceptance of alternative new product designs, and tourism marketing strategy and tourism behavior. (Arch@mycbbook.com)

Arch also served as Editor for the *Special Topics* section